THE BUSINESS OF
TOURISM

PEARSON
Education

We work with leading authors to develop the strongest educational materials in business studies and geography, bringing cutting-edge thinking and best learning practice to a global market.

Under a range of well-known imprints, including Financial Times Prentice Hall, we craft high-quality print and electronic publications that help readers to understand and apply their content, whether studying or at work.

To find out more about the complete range of our publishing, please visit us on the World Wide Web at: **www.pearsoned.co.uk**

Eighth edition

THE BUSINESS OF
TOURISM

J. Christopher Holloway

with Claire Humphreys
and Rob Davidson

FT Prentice Hall
FINANCIAL TIMES

An imprint of **Pearson Education**
Harlow, England • London • New York • Boston • San Francisco • Toronto • Sydney • Singapore • Hong Kong
Tokyo • Seoul • Taipei • New Delhi • Cape Town • Madrid • Mexico City • Amsterdam • Munich • Paris • Milan

Pearson Education Limited
Edinburgh Gate
Harlow
Essex CM20 2JE
England

and Associated Companies throughout the world

Visit us on the World Wide Web at:
www.pearsoned.co.uk

First published 1983
Eighth edition 2009

ISBN: 978-0-273-71710-2

British Library Cataloguing-in-Publication Data
A catalogue record for this book is available from the British Library

Library of Congress Cataloguing-in-Publication Data
Holloway, J. Christopher.
   The business of tourism / J. Christopher Holloway, with Claire Humphreys and
Rob Davidson. – 8th ed.
      p. cm.
   Includes bibliographical references and index.
   ISBN 978-0-273-71710-2 (pbk. : alk. paper)   1. Tourism.   2. Tourism–Marketing.
I. Humphreys, Claire.   II. Davidson, Rob.   III. Title.
   G155.A1H647 2009
   910.68–dc22

                                                          2009000482

10   9   8   7   6   5   4   3   2
13   12   11   10

Typeset in 9.5/12pt Giovanni Book by 35
Printed and bound by Rotolito Lombarda, Italy

The publisher's policy is to use paper manufactured from sustainable forests.

Contents

Part 4 Case studies   645

Supporting resources
Visit **www.pearsoned.co.uk/holloway** to find valuable online resources

For instructors
- Testbank of question material
- A full updated Instructors Manual, including sample answers, useful Websites and discussion
- PowerPoint slides which are downloadable and available to use for teaching.

For more information please contact your local Pearson Education sales representative or visit **www.pearsoned.co.uk/holloway**

Preface to the eighth edition

It is with great pleasure that I introduce, with this edition, two new co-authors who have assisted significantly in the preparation of this substantially revised text. Claire Humphreys and Rob Davidson lecture at the University of Westminster and both have had extensive experience working in tourism, both in the public and private sectors. They are committed to the long-term future of this text, the longest running in the UK and now in its 26th year. Over its lifetime, apart from the regularly updated English version, it has also appeared in numerous foreign languages, notably including Russian, Chinese and Spanish. In recognition of its widespread influence, the new edition also moves for the first time to full-colour presentation.

The contents represent a substantial rewrite of the previous edition. Although the tried and tested structure of previous editions has largely been retained with only minor adjustments, some new features have been introduced. Discussion questions have been expanded on and task rather than assignment questions set, to allow teachers to use these ideas as a basis for drawing up assignments or examination questions at a variety of different ability levels. A new visitor management chapter is an expanded version of the previous section devoted to design and management, while for the first time this edition also carries a chapter devoted exclusively to business tourism. In addition, the proportion of case studies and examples drawn from countries outside of the UK has increased to reflect a greater internationalization of this edition. Material from the previous edition devoted to the future of the industry is now integrated within each chapter, offering specific expectations and predictions relating to future prospects for each travel and tourism sector in the coming years. The increasingly global nature of the industry and the critical importance of the part played by information technology in moulding and changing the character of the industry is given full coverage throughout the text, which is rounded off with a set of new case studies of international relevance, relating to material appearing in the body of the text.

While the contents of the previous edition were formed by the impact of terrorism, the present edition is overshadowed by two new factors: the increased volatility of oil prices and growing concern about climate change, both of which pose a threat to the long-term health of the industry far exceeding that of terrorism. As we go to press, no one could forecast what the price of oil is likely to be in the coming years, whether or not new forms of energy will emerge that will allow leisure travel to remain a choice for the masses and if the remarkable and renowned resilience of the industry can adapt and cope, even with a crisis of this magnitude. Certainly, the industry will change and most sectors will learn to adapt to a very different world of travel from that with which we have become familiar since the origins of mass tourism in the 1950s/1960s.

Chris Holloway

List of abbreviations

AA	Automobile Association
AAA	American Automobile Association
ABTA	Association of British Travel Agents
ABTAC	Association of British Travel Agents' Certificate
ACD	Automatic Call Distribution
ACE	Association of Conference Executives
ACTE	Association of Corporate Travel Executives
ADS	Approved Destination Status
AIC	Airbus Integrated Company
AIEST	Alliance Internationale d'Experts Scientifiques de Tourisme
AIT	Air inclusive tour
AITO	Association of Independent Tour Operators
ALVA	Association of Leading Visitor Attractions
APEX	Advance purchase excursion fare
APT	Advanced Passenger Train
ARTAC	Association of Retail Travel Agents' Consortia
ASEAN	Association of South East Asian Nations
ASTA	American Society of Travel Agents
ATB	Automated Ticketing and Boarding Pass
ATC	air traffic control
ATOC	Association of Train Operating Companies
ATOL	Air Travel Organizer's Licence
ATTF	Air Travel Trust Fund
ATTT	Association of Tourism Teachers and Trainers (formerly Association of Teachers of Tourism, ATT)
AUC	Air Transport Users' Council
AVE	*Alta Velocidad Espagnola* (Spanish high-speed train)
B2B	business to business
B2C	business to consumer
BA	British Airways
BAA	British Airports Authority (organization that operates airports, now privatized, formerly publicly owned)
BABA	book a bed ahead
B&B	bed-and-breakfast accommodation
BACD	British Association of Conference Destinations (formerly British Association of Conference Towns, BACT)
BCG	Boston Consulting Group
BEA	British European Airways (later merged with BOAC to form British Airways)
BHA	British Hospitality Association
BH&HPA	British Holiday and Home Parks Association
BHTS	British Home Tourism Survey
BITOA	British Incoming Tour Operators' Association (now renamed UKInbound)
BITS	Bureau International de Tourisme Sociale
BNTS	British National Travel Survey
BOAC	British Overseas Airways Corporation, later merged with BEA to form British Airways
BRA	British Resorts Association
BTA	British Tourist Authority (now VisitBritain)
BTI	Business Travel International
BW	British Waterways
CAA	Civil Aviation Authority
CAB	Civil Aeronautics Board (USA)
CBI	Confederation of British Industry
CECTA	Central European Countries Travel Association
CGLI	City and Guilds of London Institute
CIM	Chartered Institute of Marketing
CIMTIG	Chartered Institute of Marketing Travel Industry Group
CIT	Chartered Institute of Transport
CLIA	Cruise Lines International Association

COTAC	Certificate of Travel Agency Competence
COTAM	Certificate of Travel Agency Management
COTICC	Certificate of Tourist Information Centre Competence
COTOP	Certificate of Tour Operating Practice
CPT	Confederation of Passenger Transport
CRN	Countryside Recreation Network
CRS	computer reservations system
CTC	certified travel counsellor
CTT	Council for Travel and Tourism
DCMS	Department for Culture, Media and Sport
DEFRA	Department for Environment, Food and Rural Affairs
DMO	Destination Management Organization
DTI	Department of Trade and Industry
EADS	European Aeronautic Defence and Space Company
EC	European Commission
EIA	environmental impact assessment
ETB	English Tourist Board (later, the English Tourism Council)
ETC	(1) English Tourism Council (now integrated with VisitBritain) (2) European Travel Commission
EU	European Union
FFP	frequent flyer programme
FIT	fully inclusive tour
FTO	Federation of Tour Operators
GBTA	Guild of Business Travel Agents
GDP	gross domestic product
GDS	global distribution system
GISC	General Insurance Standards Council
GIT	group inclusive tour-basing fare
GNE	global new entrant
GNP	gross national product
HCIMA	Hotel and Catering International Management Association (now Institute of Hospitality)
Htf	Hospitality Training Foundation
IAE	International Aero Engines
IATA	International Air Transport Association
IBTA	International Business Travel Association
ICAO	International Civil Aviation Organization
IFAPA	International Foundation of Airline Passenger Associations
IFTO	International Federation of Tour Operators
II	Interval International
IIT	independent inclusive tour
ILG	International Leisure Group
IPS	International Passenger Survey
ISIC	International Standard Industrial Classification
ISP	Internet service provider (a company providing Internet access for commercial payment)
IT	(1) inclusive tour (2) information technology
ITM	Institute of Travel Management
ITS	International Tourist Services
ITT	Institute of Travel and Tourism
ITX	inclusive tour-basing excursion fare
IUOTO	International Union of Official Tourist Organizations (now United Nations World Tourism Organization, **UNWTO**)
IVR	interactive voice response
LAI	Local Area Initiative (formerly Tourism Development Action Plan, **TDAP**)
LCLF	low cost low fare
LDC	lesser-developed countries
LTU	Lufttransport-Unternehmen
MIA	Meetings Industry Association
MICE	meetings incentives conferences and events
MMC	Monopolies and Mergers Commission (now Competition Commission)
MOMA	Museum of Modern Art, New York
MTAA	Multiple Travel Agents' Association
MTOW	maximum take-off weight
NAITA	National Association of Independent Travel Agents (later Advantage, now part of Triton)
NBC	National Bus Company
NCVQ	National Council for Vocational Qualifications
NGO	non-governmental organization
NITB	Northern Ireland Tourist Board
NPTA	National Passenger Traffic Association
NTB	(1) National Tourist Board (2) former National Training Board of **ABTA**

NTO	National Tourist Organization
NUR	Neckermann und Reisen
NVQ	National Vocational Qualifications
OECD	Organisation for Economic Co-operation and Development
ONS	Office for National Statistics
PATA	Pacific Area Travel Association
P&O	Peninsular and Oriental Steam Navigation Company
PNR	passenger name record
PSA	Passenger Shipping Association
RAC	Royal Automobile Club
RCI	Resort Condominiums International
RDAs	Regional Development Agencies
RFF	Reseau Ferré de France (French equivalent of Britain's Network Rail, responsible for operating the national rail track)
RTB	Regional Tourist Board
RV	recreational vehicle
SARS	severe acute respiratory syndrome
SAS	Scandinavian Airlines System
SIC	Standard Industrial Classification
SME	small- to medium-sized enterprise
SNAT	Societé Nouvelle d'Armement Transmanche
SNCF	Societé National de Chemins de Fer
SOLAS	Safety of Life at Sea, International Convention for the
SPR	size to passenger ratio
SSSI	Site of Special Scientific Interest
STB	Scottish Tourist Board (now VisitScotland)
STOL	short take-off and landing
TAC	Travel Agents' Council
TDAP	Tourism Development Action Plan
TGV	Train à Grande Vitesse
TIC	Tourist Information Centre

TIM	Tourism Income Multiplier
TIP	Tourist Information Point
TIQ	Tourism Intelligence Quarterly
TOC	Tour Operators' Council
TOMS	Tour Operators' Margin Scheme
TOP	Thomson Open-line Programme (Thomson Holidays' computer reservations system)
TOSG	Tour Operators' Study Group (now Federation of Tour Operators, **FTO**)
TRIPS	Tourism Resource Information Processing System
TSA	Tourism Satellite Account
TTC	Travel Training Company
TTENTO	Travel, Tourism and Events National Training Organization
TUI	Touristik Union International
UATP	Universal Air Travel Plan
UBR	uniform business rate
UKTS	United Kingdom Tourism Survey
UN	United Nations
UNESCO	United Nations Educational, Scientific and Cultural Organization
UNWTO	United Nations World Tourism Organization
VAT	value added tax
VFR	visiting friends and relatives
VTOL	vertical take-off and landing
WISE	wing-in-surface effect
WPC	wave-piercing catamaran
WTB	Wales Tourist Board
WTO	World Tourism Organization (now **UNWTO**)
WTTC	World Travel and Tourism Council
WWW	World Wide Web
YHA	Youth Hostels Association

Acknowledgements

The publisher would like to thank the following for their kind permission to reproduce their photographs:

41 Alamy Images: Barry Lewis (Figure 2.3). **350 Alamy Images:** Iain Masterton (Figure 13.1). **404 Alamy Images:** Craig Ellenwood (Figure 14.1a). **450 Alamy Images:** Peter Titmuss (Figure 15.1). **452 Alamy Images:** Directphoto.org (Figure 15.2)

We are grateful to the following for permission to reproduce copyright material:

Figures
Figure 14.5 from Carnival Corporation and Carnival plc consolidated Form 10-Q for the quarterly period ended May 31, 2006, Carnival Cruise Lines, http://www.carnival.com, Figure 14.5 Carnival Corporation and Carnival plc consolidated financial results at May 31, 2006

Tables
Table 4.2 from CACI, 2002, http://www.caci.co.uk, CACI Limited; Table 5.6 from WTTC, 2008, World key facts at a glance http://www.wttc.org/eng/Home/, World Travel & Tourism Council, Source: World Travel & Tourism Council (WTTC); Table 9.1 adapted from Top 150 City Destinations: London leads the way, http://www.euromonitor.com/Top_150_City_Destinations_London_Leads_the_Way, Source: Euromonitor International; Table 18.1 from UNWTO, Tourism Highlights, 2007, http://www.unwto.org/index.php, World Tourism Organization, Copyright UNWTO, 9284400209; Table 19.3 adapted from Annual Report, 2006, http://www.tcf.org.au, Travel Compensation Fund

Text
Example on page 240 from The de la Warr Pavilion, Bexhill-on-Sea C20, *Journal of the Twentieth Century Society*, Winter (2007/8), C20, Magazine of the Twentieth Century Society, Winter 2005/6; Example on page 621 adapted from Annual Report and Travel Compensation Fund, 2008, 2007, http://www.tcf.org.au, Travel Compensation Fund

The Financial Times
Example on page 305 from Business travel agents, *Financial Times* 4 September 2006 (Bray, R.)

In some instances we have been unable to trace the owners of copyright material, and we would appreciate any information that would enable us to do so.

List of reviewers

- Dr Gang Li, School of Management, University of Surrey
- Richard Bentley, Southampton Business School, Southampton Solent University
- Brandon Grimes, Head of Tourism, University of Hertfordshire
- Rod Gilbert, Birmingham College of Food, Tourism and Creative Studies
- Dr Constantia Anastasiadou, School of Marketing and Tourism, Napier University Business School
- Ruth Taylor, School of Management, Curtin University of Technology, Australia

Part 1

Defining and analysing tourism and its impacts

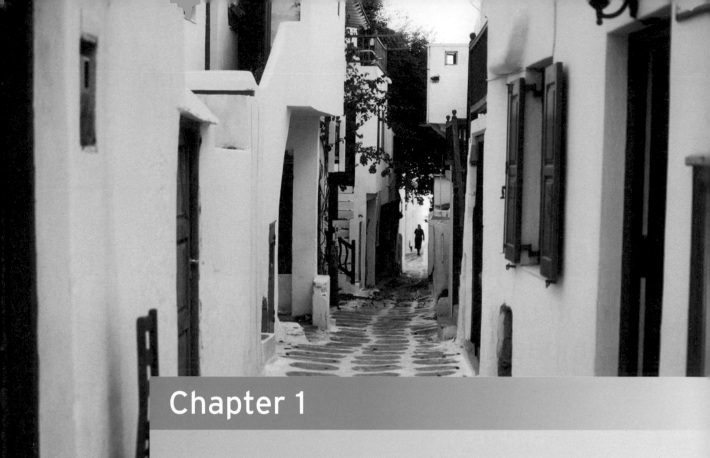

Chapter 1

An introduction to tourism

Learning outcomes

After studying this chapter, you should be able to:

- recognize why tourism is an important area of study

- define what is meant by tourism – both conceptually and technically – and distinguish it from travel, leisure and recreation

- identify the composition and major characteristics of tourism products

- outline the various forms of tourist destination and their appeal

- explain why destinations are subject to changing fortunes.

Why study tourism?

The world is a book, and those who do not travel read only a page.
St Augustine of Hippo, philosopher and theologian (AD 354–430)

This book will introduce you to a fascinating industry, tourism. Through its various chapters, you will learn about the factors that have led up to making this the world's fastest-growing business and then examine what that business entails. You will look at the nature of tourism, its appeal, its phenomenal growth over the past half century, the resulting impact on both developed and developing societies and, above all, its steady process of **institutionalization** – that is to say, the manner in which tourism has become commercialized and organized since its inception, but more especially over the past half-century. It will also be about travel, but only those forms of travel specifically undertaken within the framework of a defined tourism journey.

The tourism business deals with the organization of journeys away from home and the way in which tourists are welcomed and catered for in the destination countries. Those who plan to work in this industry will be responsible for ensuring that the outcome of such journeys, whether domestic or international in scope, is the maximizing of satisfaction in the tourist experience.

Formal study of tourism is a relatively recent development, the result of which has been that the tourism business has sometimes lacked the degree of professionalism we have come to expect of other industries. Indeed, in many destination countries it remains the case that much of the industry is in the hands of amateurs – sometimes inspired amateurs whose warmth and enthusiasm is enough to ensure that their visitors are adequately satisfied, but amateurs nonetheless. However, a warm climate, friendly natives and a few iconic attractions are no longer enough in themselves to guarantee a successful tourism industry – least of all within the principal destination countries of the developed world, which now find themselves in an increasingly competitive environment in the battle to attract global tourists.

In itself, this unwillingness to develop a more professional approach to delivering the tourism product and building careers in the industry is a surprise, given that, for many developing nations, tourism was, even in the early twentieth century, if not the key industry, then certainly among the leading industries in their economies. This attitude is still more surprising in the developed world, given the early importance of international and domestic tourism in countries such as the USA, Spain, France, Switzerland and Great Britain.

It was the expansion of tourism in the 1960s and 1970s that finally led to the recognition that the study of tourism was something to be taken seriously. Up to that point, the educational focus had been on training for what were perceived to be low-level craft skills that could be learned principally by working alongside experienced employees, to watch how they did the job and emulate them. This would be typical of the way in which hotel and catering workers, travel agents, tour operator resort representatives, visitor attractions employees and airline ground handling staff would be expected to learn their jobs. Not surprisingly, in many cases this merely helped to perpetuate outdated modes of work, not to say errors in practice. In due course, those who performed best in these skills would be promoted to management roles – once again with no formal training – and expected to pick up their management skills as they went along. Gradually, it became recognized that this was not the ideal way to amass all knowledge and skills and a more formal process of learning, based on a theoretical body of knowledge and its practical application, would lead to improved professionalism in the industry. From basic-level craft skills, courses emerged in the 1970s, 1980s and 1990s at diploma, degree and, ultimately, postgraduate levels to train and educate the workers and managers of the future, as well as equip them with the necessary knowledge and skills to cope at all levels with the rapid changes that were to occur in the tourism industry in the closing years of the last century.

Recognition of the need for formal training is one thing. Determining the body of knowledge that should be appropriate for someone planning to spend a lifetime career in the industry is something else. Tourism is a complex, multidisciplinary subject, requiring knowledge of not only business and management but also such diverse disciplines as law, town and country planning, geography, sociology and anthropology. There is as yet no common agreement among academics, or between academics and practitioners, as to what should form the **core curriculum** of a tourism programme and, in many countries, practitioners still make clear their preference for courses delivering practical skills over more academic content. The difficulty the tourism industry faces is that trainers will deliver only the knowledge required by employees who will be taking up work in a specific tourism sector, while a career in that industry today is likely to require frequent transfers between the different sectors – and, initially, an overview of how each of these operates. Any formal programme of tourism education must take these needs into account and prepare students for a life in the industry as a whole. Due to the multidisciplinary nature of tourism, however, courses offered in this subject in colleges and universities around the world differ substantially in content – some choosing to deliver what is essentially a business and management programme tuned to the specific needs of the industry, others focusing on issues such as sustainable tourism or public-sector planning for tourism, where the input may be built around urban and regional planning programmes. Still others may choose to deliver courses where the focus is on understanding tourists, drawing on the disciplines of psychology, sociology and anthropology. A well-rounded student of tourism is going to require some knowledge of all of these disciplines and it is to be hoped that, given time, common agreement can be reached globally between academics and across the industry on what best mix of these disciplines would form the ideal curriculum for a career in tourism.

Defining tourism

A good starting point for any textbook that sets out to examine the tourism business is to try to define what is meant by the terms 'tourist' and 'tourism' before going on to look at the many different forms that tourism can take. While an understanding of the term's meaning is essential, in fact, the task of defining it is very difficult. It is relatively easy to agree on technical definitions of particular categories of 'tourism' or 'tourist', but the wider concept is ill defined.

First, it is important to recognize that tourism is just one form of activity undertaken during a period of *leisure*. Leisure is defined as 'free time' or 'time at one's disposal'[1] and therefore can be taken to embrace any activity apart from work and obligatory duties. Leisure can entail active engagement in play or recreation or else more passive pastimes such as watching television or even sleeping. Sports activities, games, hobbies, pastimes – and tourism – are all forms of recreation and discretionary uses of our leisure time.

We can go on to say that, self-evidently, the tourist is one who engages in tourism. Tourism, as one element of leisure, involves the movement of a person or persons away from their normal place of residence: a process that usually incurs some expenditure, although this is not *necessarily* the case. Someone cycling or hiking in the countryside on a camping weekend in which they carry their own food may make no economic contribution to the area in which they travel, but can nonetheless be counted as a tourist. Many other examples could be cited in which expenditure by the tourist is minimal. We can say, then, that tourism is one aspect of leisure that usually, but not invariably, incurs some expenditure of income and that, further, money spent has been earned within the area of normal residency, rather than at the destination.

The term 'tourism' is further refined as the movement of people away from their *normal* place of residence. Here we find our first problem. Should shoppers travelling short distances of several kilometres be considered tourists? Is it the *purpose* or the *distance* that is the determining factor? Just how far must people travel before they can be counted as tourists for the purpose of official records? What about that growing band of people travelling regularly between their first and second homes, sometimes spending equal time at each?

Clearly, any definition must be specific. In the United States, in 1973, the National Resources Review Commission established that a domestic tourist would be 'one who travels at least 50 miles (one way)'. That was confirmed by the US Census Bureau, which defined tourism 11 years later as a round trip of at least 100 miles. However, the Canadian government defines it as a journey of at least 25 miles from the boundaries of the tourist's home community, while the English Tourism Council proposed a measure of not less than 20 miles and 3 hours' journey time away from home for a visit to constitute a leisure trip, so consistency has by no means yet been achieved.

Early attempts at defining tourism

One of the first attempts at defining tourism was that of Professors Hunziker and Krapf of Berne University in 1942. They held that tourism should be defined as 'the sum of the phenomena and relationships arising from the travel and stay of non-residents, in so far as they do not lead to permanent residence and are not connected to any earning activity'. This definition helps to distinguish tourism from migration, but it makes the assumption that both *travel* and *stay* are necessary for tourism, thus precluding day tours. It would also appear to exclude business travel, which is connected with earnings, even if that income is not earned in the destination country. Moreover, distinguishing between business and leisure tourism is, in many cases, extremely difficult as most business trips will combine elements of leisure activity.

Earlier still, in 1937, the League of Nations had recommended adopting the definition of a 'tourist' as one who travels for a period of at least 24 hours in a country other than that in which he or she usually resides. This was held to include persons travelling for pleasure, domestic reasons or health, those travelling to meetings or otherwise on business and those visiting a country on a cruise vessel (even if for less than 24 hours). The principal weakness in this definition is that it ignores the movements of domestic tourists.

Later, the United Nations' Conference on International Travel and Tourism, held in 1963, considered recommendations put forward by the International Union of Official Travel Organizations (later the United Nations World Tourism Organization) and agreed to use the term 'visitor' to describe 'any person visiting a country other than that in which he has his usual place of residence, for any reason other than following an occupation remunerated from within the country visited'. This definition was to cover two classes of visitor:

1. tourists, who were classified as temporary visitors staying at least 24 hours, whose purpose could be categorized as leisure (whether for recreation, health, sport, holiday, study or religion) or business, family, mission or meeting
2. excursionists, who were classed as temporary visitors staying less than 24 hours, including cruise travellers but excluding travellers in transit.

Towards an agreed definition

Once again, these definitions fail to take into account the domestic tourist. The inclusion of the word 'study' above is an interesting one as it is often excluded in later definitions, as are longer courses of education.

A working party for the proposed Institute of Tourism in Britain (which later became the Tourism Society) attempted to clarify the issue and reported, in 1976:

> Tourism is the temporary short-term movement of people to destinations outside the places where they normally live and work, and activities during their stay at these destinations; it includes movement for all purposes, as well as day visits or excursions.

This broader definition was reformulated slightly, without losing any of its simplicity, at the International Conference on Leisure-Recreation-Tourism, organized by the AIEST and the Tourism Society in Cardiff, Wales, in 1981:

> Tourism may be defined in terms of particular activities selected by choice and undertaken outside the home environment. Tourism may or may not involve overnight stay away from home.

Finally, the following definition devised by the then WTO was endorsed by the UN's, Statistical Commission in 1993 following an International Government Conference held in Ottawa, Canada, in 1991:

> Tourism comprises the activities of persons travelling to and staying in places outside their usual environment for not more than one consecutive year for leisure, business or other purposes.

These definitions have been quoted here at length because they reveal how broadly the concept of tourism must be defined in order to embrace all forms of the phenomenon and how exceptions can be found for even the most narrowly focused definitions. Indeed, the final definition could be criticized on the grounds that, unless the activities are more clearly specified, it could be applied equally to someone involved in burglary! With this definition, we are offered guidance on neither the activities undertaken nor distance to be travelled. In fact, with the growth of timeshare and second home owners, who, in some cases, spend considerable periods of time away from their main homes, it could be argued that a tourist is no longer necessarily 'outside the home environment'. It is also increasingly recognized that defining tourists in terms of the distances they have travelled from their homes is unhelpful as locals can be viewed as 'tourists' within their own territory if they are engaged in tourist-type activities and, certainly, their economic contribution to the tourism industry in the area is as important as that of the more traditionally defined tourist.

Figure 1.1 illustrates the guidelines produced by the UNWTO (then, the WTO) to classify travellers for statistical purposes. Some loopholes in the definitions remain, however. Even attempts to classify tourists as those travelling for purposes unconnected with employment can be misleading if one looks at the social consequences of tourism. Ruth Pape[2] has drawn attention to the case of nurses in the United States who, after qualifying, gravitate to California for their first jobs as employment is easy to find and they can thus enjoy the benefits of the sunshine and leisure pursuits for which the state is famous. They may spend a year or more in this job before moving on, but the point is that they have been motivated to come to that area not because of the work itself, but because of the area's tourist attractions. Frequently, too, students of tourism, after completing their course, return to work in the areas in which they undertook work placements during their studies, having found the location (and, often, the job) sufficiently attractive to merit spending more time there. People increasingly buy homes in areas where they can enjoy walking, skiing or other leisure activities, so that tourism is literally on their doorsteps, yet this growing group of 'resident tourists' is not taken into consideration for statistical purposes. Indeed, the division between work and leisure is further blurred today by the development of e-mail and websites that offer immediate access from wherever a worker happens to be spending time. This has led many to buy second homes in the countryside, where work may be engaged in between bouts of leisure and relaxation. Internet cafés and laptop computers allow workers to keep in touch with their business while away from home, further blurring the distinction between travel for work and travel for leisure. Many examples

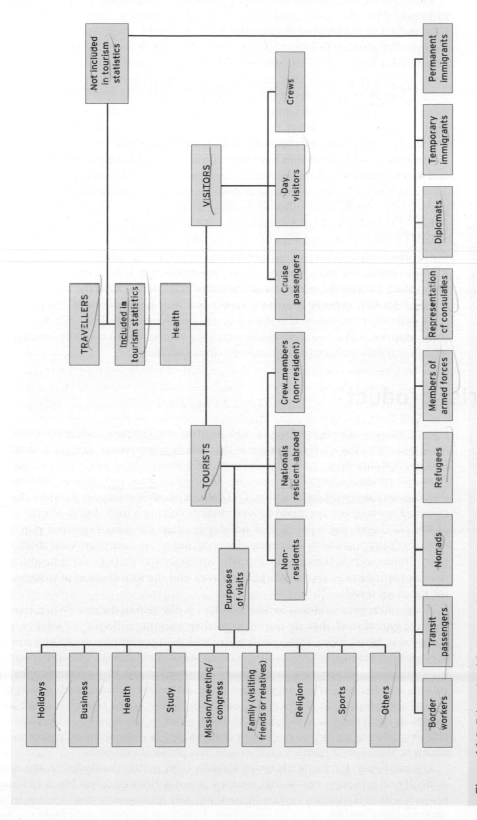

Figure 1.1 Defining a tourist.
(Courtesy of the UN World Tourism Organization.)

could also be given of young people working their way around the world (the contemporary equivalent of the Grand Tour?) or workers seeking summer jobs in seaside resorts.

Finally, we must consider the case of pensioners who choose to retire abroad in order to benefit from the lower costs of living in other countries. Many Northern Europeans have moved to Mediterranean countries after retirement, while Americans, similarly, seek warmth and gravitate to Mexico; they may still retain their homes in their country of origin, but spend a large part of the year abroad. Canadians and Americans living in northern states are known as 'snowbirds' because of their migrant behaviour, coming down in their mobile homes and caravans to the sunshine states of the US south west during the winter months to escape the harsh winters of the north. Once again, the motivation for all of these people is not simply to lower their costs of living but also to enjoy an improved climate and the facilities that attract tourists to the same destinations.

Up to this point, definitions have been discussed in terms of their academic importance and for the purposes of statistical measurement. We need to recognize that the terms are used much more loosely within the industry itself, with a distinction being made between travel and tourism. If we think of **tourism as a system**[3] embracing a generating region (where the market for tourism develops), a destination region or regions (places and areas visited by the tourist) and a transit zone (where some form of transport is used to move the tourist from, and back to, the generating region and between any destinations visited), it is becoming common practice among practitioners to refer to the second of these as comprising the *tourism industry*, with the other two referred to as the *travel industry*.

Conceptually, defining tourism precisely is a near-impossible task. To produce a technical definition for statistical purposes is less problematic. As long as it is clear what the data comprise, and one compares like with like, whether inter-regionally or internationally, we can leave the conceptual discussion to the academics.

The tourist product

Having attempted to define 'tourist' and 'tourism', we can now look at the tourist product itself. The first characteristic to note is that this is a **service** rather than a tangible good. The intangibility poses particular difficulties for those whose job it is to market tourism. A tourist product cannot, for example, be inspected by prospective purchasers before they buy, as can a washing machine, DVD player or other consumer durable. The purchase of a package tour is a speculative investment, involving a high degree of trust on the part of the purchaser, the more so as a holiday is often the most expensive purchase made each year (although, with increasing affluence, many consumers are now able to purchase two or more such holidays annually). The necessary element of trust is heightened by the development of sales via the World Wide Web and the introduction of ticketless booking for much air travel.

It has often been said that 'selling holidays is like selling dreams'. When tourists buy a package tour abroad, they are buying more than a simple collection of services, such as an airline seat, hotel room, three meals a day and the opportunity to sit on a sunny beach; they are also buying the temporary use of a strange environment, incorporating what may be, for them, novel geographical features – old world towns, tropical landscapes – plus the culture and heritage of the region and other intangible benefits, such as service, atmosphere and hospitality. The planning and anticipation of the holiday may be as much a part of its enjoyment as is the trip itself. Then, recalling the experience later and reviewing videos or photos are further extensions of the experience. These are all part of the product, which is, therefore, a psychological as well as a physical experience.

The challenge for the marketer of tourism is to match the dream to the reality. The difficulty of achieving this is that tourism is not a homogeneous but a **heterogeneous** product – that is, it tends to vary in standard and quality over time and under different circumstances, unlike, say, a television set. A package tour or even a flight on an aircraft cannot be consistently uniform: a bumpy flight, or a long technical flight delay, can change an enjoyable experience into a nightmare, while a holiday at the seaside can be ruined by a prolonged rainy spell.

Because a tour comprises a compendium of different products, an added difficulty in maintaining standards is that each element of the product should be broadly similar in quality. A good room and fine service at a hotel may be spoilt by poor food or the flight may mar an otherwise enjoyable hotel stay. An element of chance is always present in the purchase of any service and, where the purchase must *precede* the actual consumption of the product, as with tourism, the risk for the consumer is increased.

The introduction of **dynamic packaging**, which is rapidly changing the traditional package tour, is beginning to obfuscate this analysis. Dynamic packaging is the process by which travel agents, or other retailers of travel, themselves put together flights, accommodation and other elements of travel and sell the resulting package of components to consumers. Of course, tourists can today put their own packages together through Internet suppliers, but, if they choose to do so, uncertainty about the uniformity of the product is heightened. Even when packages are tailor-made by the travel agent or other retailer in a similar manner, the lack of a single tour operator or supplier to oversee the final package threatens to undermine the concept of a 'standard quality' product. Moreover, reinforcing the nature of this uncertainty, a package put together by the tourist does not meet the definition of a legal package holiday and is therefore exempted from protective guarantees, meaning that the tourist may lose out in the event of the financial collapse of one or more of the companies they have booked with.

Another characteristic of tourism is that it cannot be brought to the consumer. Rather, the consumer must be brought to the product. In the short term, at least, the supply of this product is fixed – the number of hotel bedrooms available at a particular destination cannot be varied to meet the changing demands of holidaymakers during the season, for example. Similarly, the unsold hotel room or aircraft seat cannot be stored for later sale, as is the case with tangible products, but is lost forever – hence the great efforts that must be made by those in the industry to fill empty seats or rooms by last-minute discounting or other techniques. If market demand changes, as it does frequently in the business of tourism, the supply will take time to adapt. A hotel is built to last for many years and must remain profitable over that period. These are all problems unique to tourism and call for considerable marketing ingenuity on the part of those in the business.

The nature of tourism

Now that we have made an attempt to define what is meant by tourism, let us look at this topic systematically. It is useful to examine the characteristics of a tour in terms of the following five broad categories.

The motivation for a trip

Motivation identifies, first, the purpose of a visit. Purposes themselves fall into three distinct categories:

- holidays (including visits to friends and relatives, known as VFR travel)
- business (including meetings, conferences and so on)
- other (including study, religious pilgrimages, sport, health and so on).

It is important to be aware of the underlying purpose behind the tourist's travels, because each of these categories will reveal a different set of characteristics. Let us consider, for example, how business travel differs from leisure travel. The business traveller will have little discretion in choice of destination or the timing of the trip. In general, destinations will bear little similarity to the destinations of the leisure traveller, as enjoyment of the attractions and facilities do not form part of the purpose of the trip (even if those that exist may be enjoyed as an adjunct to it). Business trips frequently have to be arranged at short notice and for specific and brief periods of time – often only a day, even where substantial journey time is involved. For these reasons, business travellers need the convenience of frequent, regular transport, efficient service and good facilities (in terms of accommodation and catering) at the destination. Because their company will usually be paying for all the travel arrangements, business travellers will be less concerned about the cost of travel than they would if they were paying for it themselves. Higher prices are not likely seriously to deter travel, nor will lower prices encourage more frequent travel. We can say, therefore, that business travel is relatively **price inelastic**. Holiday travel, however, is highly **price elastic** – lower prices for holidays to a particular destination will tend to lead to an increase in the aggregate number of travellers, as tourists find the holiday more affordable, while others may be encouraged by the lower prices to switch their planned destination. Leisure travellers will be prepared to delay their travel or will book well in advance of their travel dates if this means that they can substantially reduce their costs.

While these generalities continue to hold, we must also recognize the fact that growing disposable income among the populations of the developed world is having the effect of reducing price elasticity for many holidaymakers as upmarket winter sports holidays, cruises, special interest and long-haul travel attract a greater percentage of the mass market travellers (especially the growing numbers taking second and third holidays every year). For these travellers, service is becoming more important than price. At the same time, narrowing profits in the business world are driving up elasticity among business travellers. In the latter case, the growth of the low-cost air carriers has made discounted air travel so attractive by comparison with fares on the established carriers (particularly first and business class) that low-cost airlines now claim a large proportion of their passengers are people travelling on business.

Beyond price, we must also identify other reasons for a specific type of holiday or resort being chosen. Different people will look for different qualities in the same destination. A particular ski resort, for example, may be selected because of its excellent slopes and sporting facilities, its healthy mountain air or the social life it offers to skiers and non-skiers alike.

The characteristics of a trip

These define what kind of visit is made and to where. First, one can differentiate between **domestic** tourism and **international** tourism. The former refers to travel taken exclusively within the national boundaries of the traveller's home country. The decision to take one's holidays within the borders of one's own country is an important one economically as it will have an impact on the balance of payments and reduce the outflow of money from that country. Many governments therefore encourage residents to holiday in their own countries in order to aid the economy.

Next, what kind of destination is being chosen? Will travel be to a seaside resort, mountain resort, country town, health spa or major city? Is it to be a single-centre visit, a multi-centre one (involving a stopover at two or more places) or a longitudinal tour that will involve extensive travel with brief overnight stays along the route? If a cruise is to be taken, statisticians have to decide whether or not to count this as international travel if the vessel visits foreign ports and, if so, whether to count each country visited as a separate visit to a foreign country or include only the main port visited. Does a one-night stopover in Miami before boarding a cruise vessel bound for the Caribbean count as a separate visit to the USA for the European or Asian visitor?

Next, what length of time is being spent on the trip? A visit that does not involve an overnight stay is known, as we saw earlier, as an excursion or is frequently referred to as a 'day trip'. The expenditure of day trippers is generally less than that of overnight visitors and statistical data on these forms of tourism are often collected separately. A visitor who stops at least one night at a destination is termed a 'tourist', but can, of course, make day trips to other destinations which could even involve an international trip. For instance, a visitor staying in Rhodes may take a trip for the day by boat to the Turkish mainland; another in Corfu can go on an excursion to the nearby coastal resorts of Albania. For the purposes of Turkey's and Albania's records, that visitor will be recorded as an excursionist. Domestic American tourists travelling through New England often make a brief visit to the Canadian side of the Niagara Falls and, hence, are excursionists as far as the Canadian tourism authorities are concerned.

Finally, in order to maintain accurate records, some maximum length of time must be established beyond which the visitor can no longer be looked on as a tourist. There are different approaches here – some using a low figure of three months, others six months and, in some cases, a full year is viewed as the maximum period.

Modes of tour organization

This further refines the form that the travel takes. A tour may be **independent** or **packaged**. A package tour, for which the official term is 'inclusive tour' (IT), is an arrangement in which transport and accommodation are purchased by the tourist at an all-inclusive price. The price of individual elements of the tour cannot normally be determined by the purchaser. The tour operator putting together the package will buy transport and accommodation in advance, generally at a lower price because each of the products is being bought in bulk, and the tours are then sold individually to holidaymakers, either directly or through travel agents. Agents and operators can also package independent inclusive tours by taking advantage of special net fares and building the package around the specific needs of the client.

As explained earlier in this chapter, 'dynamic package' is the term used to describe holidays that are put together as tailor-made programmes, whether by the operator, the retailer or even by the holidaymakers themselves. This form of holiday package is rapidly changing the standard inclusive tour, although it is not thought that this will lead to the demise of the traditional package. Rather, operators are adjusting their products to make them more flexible by means of tailor-made alterations to duration and other arrangements.

The composition of the tour

This consists of the elements comprising the visit. All tourism involves travel away from one's usual place of residence, as we have seen, and, in the case of 'tourists' – as opposed to 'excursionists' – it will include accommodation. So, we must here identify the form of travel – air, sea, road or rail – that is to be used. If air transport is involved, will this be by charter aircraft or scheduled flight? If there is to be an overnight stay, will this be in a hotel, guesthouse, campsite or self-catering accommodation? How will the passenger travel between airport and hotel – by coach, taxi or airport limousine? A package tour will normally comprise transport and accommodation, often with transfers to and from the accommodation included, but, in some cases, additional services will be provided in the programme, such as car hire at the destination, excursions by coach or theatre entertainment. The inclusion of some form of comprehensive insurance is now demanded by most companies and is sold automatically with the tour, unless individual tourists can confirm that they are covered by alternative travel insurance.

The characteristics of the tourist

Analysis of tourism must include analysis of the tourist. We have already distinguished between the holidaymaker and the business traveller. We can also identify the tourist in terms of nationality, social class, sex, age and lifestyle. What life stage are they in? What type of personality do they have?

Such information is valuable not only for the purpose of record-keeping; it will also help to shed light on the reasons why people travel, why they select certain destinations and how patterns of travel differ between different groups of people. Research is now focusing much more intently on personality and lifestyle as characteristics which determine the choice of holidays, rather than looking simply at social class and occupation. The more that is known about such details, the more effectively can those in the industry produce the products that will meet the needs of their customers, and develop the appropriate strategies to bring those products to their attention.

The tourist destination

We can now examine the tourist destination itself. The nature of destinations will be explored in Chapter 9, but at this point in the book an initial understanding of what attracts tourists to different destinations will be helpful. A **destination** can be a particular resort or town, a region within a country, the whole of a country or even a larger area of the globe. For example, a package tour may embrace visits to three separate countries in Latin America that have quite distinct attractions – say, an initial visit to Peru to see the cultural life of the Peruvian Indians and the ruins at Macchu Pichu, followed by a flight to Buenos Aires, Argentina, for a typical capital city experience of shopping and nightlife, returning home via Cancún, Mexico, where a few days' recuperation are enjoyed at a beach resort.

This 'pick and mix' approach to the varieties of destination and their relative attractions is becoming increasingly common, with the earlier concept of being expected to choose between a beach holiday, cultural holiday, short break city tour or some other uniform package arrangement no longer holding true. Cruise companies have come to recognize this and now commonly market fortnight combination holidays, consisting of several days of cruising, preceded or followed by a few days at a beach resort close to the port of embarkation.

In the case of cruises, for many tourists, the 'destination' is the ship itself, and its actual ports of call may be secondary to the experience of life on board. Indeed, it is by no means unusual for regular cruise passengers to fail to disembark at ports of call, preferring to enjoy the company of the cruise staff and entertainment on board while the ship is in port.

In other examples, the destination and accommodation are inseparable – as in the case of a resort hotel that provides a range of leisure facilities on site. In such cases, it may be the tourist's objective to visit the hotel purely and simply because of the facilities that hotel provides and the entire stay will be enjoyed without venturing beyond the precincts of the hotel grounds. This is a characteristic that is commonly found among certain long-established resort hotels in the USA, but an example more familiar to UK holidaymakers would be the Sandals all-inclusive resorts in the Caribbean.

All destinations share certain characteristics. Their success in attracting tourists will depend on the quality of three essential benefits that they offer them: **attractions, amenities** (or facilities) and **accessibility** (or ease with which they can travel to the destination). At this point we will do no more than outline the variety of destinations attractive to tourists, before considering their attractions, amenities and accessibility.

Varieties of destinations

Destinations are of two kinds – either 'natural' or 'constructed'. Most are 'managed' to some extent, whether they are natural or constructed. National parks, for example, are left in their natural state of beauty as far as possible, but nevertheless have to be managed, in terms of the provision of access, parking facilities, accommodation (such as caravan and campsites), litter bins and so on.

Broadly, we can categorize destinations by delineating them according to geographical features, under the following three headings.

- **Seaside tourism** This will include seaside resorts, natural beaches, boating holidays along coasts, coastal footpaths and so on.
- **Rural tourism** This will include the most common category of lakes and mountains, but also countryside touring, 'agritourism' such as farm holidays, visits to vineyards, gardens, visits and stays at villages or rural retreats, river and canal holidays, wildlife parks and national parks.
- **Urban tourism** This will include visits to cities and towns.

Health resorts, including spas (which are important to the tourist industries of many countries), may be based in rural, seaside or urban areas. Adventure holidays and active holidays, such as winter sports, are commonly associated with rural sites, but if one thinks of the appeal of towns such as St Moritz in Switzerland, Aspen in Colorado or Jackson Hole, Wyoming, in the United States, which developed primarily to attract winter sports enthusiasts, it must be recognized that pigeonholing all forms of tourism as being one or other of only these three types of destination is inappropriate.

All destinations can suffer from overuse and, for the most popular, this is a growing problem. The difficulties created by too great a demand and the need for careful management of city centres, beaches and natural countryside are subjects that are discussed in Chapters 6 and 7.

Attractions, amenities and accessibility

All destinations require adequate attractions, amenities and accessibility if they are to appeal to large numbers of tourists. In this section, we will look at these issues.

The more attractions a destination can offer, the easier it becomes to market that destination to the tourist. Listing and analysing attractions is no easy matter, especially when one recognizes that what appeals to one tourist may actually deter another.

In looking at the destinations mentioned above, it will become clear that many of the attractions of a destination depend on its physical features: the beauty of mountains, the fresh air of a seaside resort and the qualities of a particular beach, the historical architecture, shopping and entertainment opportunities and 'atmosphere' of a great city. To these can be added numerous purpose-built attractions to increase the pulling power of the destination. For example, Blackpool maintains its lead among the seaside resorts in Britain by investing in indoor entertainments, a conference centre and other features that appeal to a cross-section of tourists. Key cities and capitals build new museums, art galleries or exhibition centres (the impressive contemporary designs of which play an increasingly important part in attracting the urban tourist – see Figure 1.2), while former stately homes or castles are transformed by development into focal points for visits by tourists and day trippers alike.

Sometimes, the constructed attraction becomes a destination in its own right, as is the case with theme parks such as the Disney complexes in Anaheim (California), Orlando (Florida), near Paris, France, and in the Far East. Similarly, the success of many spa towns on the Continent rests on their ability to combine constructed attractions such as casinos with the assumed medical benefits of the natural springs, while the popular ski resorts must provide adequate ski runs, ski lifts and après-ski entertainment to complement their combinations of suitable weather and mountain slopes.

The operation of managed visitor attractions is dealt with in Chapters 10 and 16. At this point, therefore, it is sufficient to highlight certain distinctions between attractions.

Figure 1.2 Contemporary design appeals to the cultural tourist. The Neue Nationalgalerie in Berlin, Germany, designed by Mies van der Rohe.
(Photo by Chris Holloway.)

First, attractions may be either *site* or *event* attractions. Site attractions are permanent by nature, while event attractions are temporary and often mounted in order to increase the number of tourists to a particular destination. Some events have a short timescale, such as an air display by the famed Red Devils' close formation flyers, as part of a one-day event; others may last for many days (the Edinburgh Festival, for example) or even months (for instance, the Floriade Garden Festival in Holland). Some events occur at regular intervals – yearly, biennially (the outdoor sculpture exhibition at Quenington in the Cotswolds, England, is such an event), four-yearly (the Olympic Games) or even less frequently (the Oberammergau Passion Play in Germany and the Floriade Festival mentioned above occur only once every ten years), while other festivals are organized on an ad hoc basis and may, indeed, be one-off events. A destination that may otherwise have little to commend it to the tourist can, in this way, succeed in drawing tourists by mounting a unique exhibition, while a site destination can extend its season by mounting an off-season event, such as a festival of arts.

Second, destinations and their attractions can be either *nodal* or *linear* in character. A nodal destination is one in which the attractions of the area are closely grouped geographically. Seaside resorts and cities are examples of typical nodal attractions, making them ideal for packaging by tour operators. This has led to the concept of 'honey pot' tourism development, in which planners concentrate the development of tourism in a specific locality. Whistler in Canada is an example of a purpose-built nodal tourism resort, built largely to satisfy the growing needs of winter sports enthusiasts. With its extensive range of accommodation, attractions and amenities, it now draws high-spend tourists throughout the year from all over the world. Linear tourism, however, is where the attraction is spread over a wide geographical area, without any specific focus (see Figure 1.3). Examples include the Shenandoah Valley region in the United States, the Highlands of

Figure 1.3 Britain's countryside and landscape has enormous appeal for both domestic and overseas visitors. Tarr Steps, in Exmoor National Park, Somerset (probably of medieval construction but originating some 3000 years ago), are a popular linear tourism attraction. *(Photo by Chris Holloway.)*

Scotland or the so-called 'romantische Strasse' (romantic trail) through central Germany – all ideal for touring holidays, rather than just 'stay put' holidays. Motels or bed-and-breakfast accommodation spring up in such areas to serve the needs of the transient tourist, who may spend only one or two nights at a particular destination. Cruising is another form of linear tourism, currently enjoying growing popularity as it enables tourists to see a multitude of different sites conveniently and with minimal disruption.

It is important to remember that much of the attraction of a destination is intangible and greatly depends on its image, as perceived by the potential tourist. India may be seen by one group of travellers as exotic and appealing, while others will reject it as a destination because of its poverty or its unfamiliar culture. Images of a destination, whether favourable or unfavourable, tend to be built up over a long period of time and, once established, are difficult to change. Britain, for instance, is still seen by many as a fog-engulfed, rain-battered island with friendly but rather reserved inhabitants – an image reinforced in old Hollywood films and still frequently stereotyped in foreign media. Overcoming such stereotyping is an important task for a country's national tourist board.

Amenities are those essential services that cater to the needs of the tourist. These include accommodation and food, local transport, information centres and the necessary infrastructure to support tourism – roads, public utility services and parking facilities. Naturally, such amenities will vary according to the nature of the destination itself: it would clearly be inappropriate to provide an extensive infrastructure in an area of great scenic beauty, such as a national park, and those planning to visit such a destination will recognize that the availability of hotels and restaurants must inevitably be limited. Such sites are likely to attract the camper and those seeking only limited amenities – indeed, this will be part of the attraction for them (see Figure 1.4).

Figure 1.4 The managed wilderness. Attractive look-out points have been constructed within the Darling National Wildlife Refuge on Sanibel Island, Florida, an otherwise pristine natural environment. Note the ramp provided for disabled access.
(Photo by Chris Holloway.)

It should also be recognized that, on occasion, the amenity itself may be the attraction, as was discussed earlier, in the case of a resort hotel offering a comprehensive range of in situ attractions. Similarly, a destination such as France, which is famed for its regional foods, will encourage tourists whose motive in travelling may be largely to enjoy their meals. In this case, the amenity is its own attraction.

Finally, a destination must be accessible if it is to facilitate visits from tourists. While the more intrepid travellers may be willing to put themselves to great inconvenience in order to see some of the more exotic places in the world, most tourists will not be attracted to a destination unless it is relatively easy to reach. This means, in the case of international travel, having a good airport nearby, regular and convenient air transport to the region at an affordable price and good local connections to the destination itself (or, at very least, good car hire facilities). Cruise ships will be attracted by well-presented deep water ports with moorings available at reasonable cost to the shipping line and situated at a convenient distance from major attractions in the area. Cities such as Helsinki, Stockholm and Tallinn have the great advantage of providing deep water moorings close to the very heart of the capital, allowing passengers to disembark and walk into the centre of the city. Warnemünde is a popular port for cruise visitors to visit Germany as Berlin is a comfortable day's excursion by fast motorway from the coast, whereas Vilnius, capital of Lithuania, cannot attract cruise ships precisely because it is situated too far inland for the excursion market. Other travellers will be drawn by good access roads or rail services and coach links.

On the other hand, if access becomes too easy, this may result in too great a demand and resultant congestion, making the destination less attractive to the tourist. The building of motorways in Britain opened up the Lake District and the West Country to millions of motorists, many of whom now find themselves within a two-hour drive of their destination. This has led to severe congestion due to large numbers of weekend day trippers and summer holidaymakers during the peak tourist months.

It should be noted that the *perception* of accessibility on the part of the traveller is often as important as a destination's *actual* accessibility. In particular, the introduction of low-cost airlines operating from the UK to less familiar destinations on the Continent has led many people in Britain to perceive Mediterranean destinations as being more accessible than Cornwall or the Scottish Highlands in terms of both cost and travelling time. Such perceptions will undoubtedly affect decisionmaking when tourists are making their travel plans.

Notes

1. *Concise Oxford English Dictionary*, Oxford University Press.
2. R. Pape (1964) Touristry: a type of occupational mobility', *Social Problems*, 11 (4), pp. 327–36.
3. The concept, suggested by Neil Leiper, is discussed more fully in C. Cooper et al., (2005) *Tourism Principles and Practice* (3rd edn), Prentice Hall.

Questions and discussion points

1. What have been your own experiences as a customer of tourism services – enthusiastic amateurism or trained professionalism? Which did you prefer? Will good training ensure more even performance? Discuss the benefits of formal training in a college or university versus the 'apprenticeship' schemes that have often been preferred by practitioners in the industry.
2. The curriculum for learning about tourism varies greatly from one institution to another and between countries. What core subjects within your own curriculum do you feel could be dispensed with and what others would you like to see introduced? Should vocational skills be an essential ingredient of all tourism programmes, regardless of level?
3. Intangibility is a characteristic of the tourism product, requiring the tourist to trust the supplier. What other services can you think of that also cannot be inspected before purchase and how are customers reassured about their suitability?
4. Discuss the chief factors that either encourage us to travel or hinder our plans to do so and, in the case of the latter, suggest ways in which resistance could be overcome.
5. The image projected of the UK in promotions abroad is often a dated one, with its emphasis on Beefeaters and similar outdated features of British heritage. Some argue that Britain should be projecting a more modern, dynamic image. Would a change of direction attract more tourists? Would it undermine existing tourism?

Tasks

1. Analyse the attractions, amenities and accessibility of any area familiar to you that currently fails to attract tourists. Determine the reasons for this and examine ways in which a tourist market might be built for the area.
2. Although efforts have been made to tighten up legislation to protect the tourist, a number of loopholes still exist. Research the legal situation in your country and indicate how legislation could be improved to reduce the risks incurred in (a) domestic tourism and (b) international tourism, both incoming and outbound.

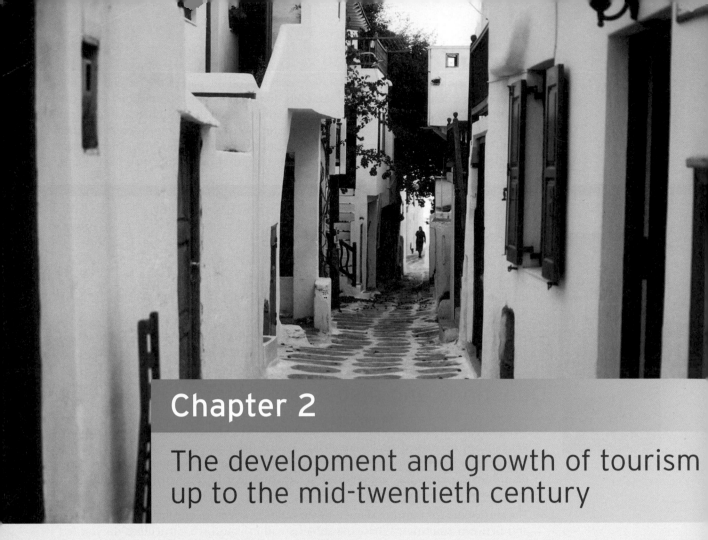

Chapter 2

The development and growth of tourism up to the mid-twentieth century

Learning outcomes

After studying this chapter, you should be able to:

- explain the historical changes that have affected the growth and development of the tourism industry from its earliest days

- understand the relationship between technological innovation and tourism development

- explain why particular forms of travel and destinations were chosen by the early tourists

- identify and distinguish between enabling conditions and motivating factors affecting tourism demand.

Introduction: the early years

> Hadnakhte, scribe of the treasury, came to make an excursion and amuse himself on the west of Memphis, together with his brother, Panahkti, scribe of the vizier.

Inscription on an Egyptian pyramid, dated to 1244 BC, quoted in Lionel Casson, *Travel in the Ancient World*, George Allen & Unwin 1974, p. 32

A study of the history of tourism is a worthwhile occupation for any student of the tourism business, not only as a matter of academic interest but also because there are lessons to be learned that are as applicable today as in the past. One thing we learn from history is that the business of tourism, from its earliest days some 3000 years ago, shares many of the characteristics of the business as we know it today. Many of the facilities and amenities demanded by modern tourists were provided – albeit in a more basic form – all the way back then: not just accommodation and transport but also catering services, guides and souvenir shops.

The earliest forms of travel can be traced at least as far back as the Babylonian and Egyptian empires, some three millennia BC, but these originated for business purposes rather than leisure. People travelled largely out of obligation, for reasons of government administration, trade or military purposes. However, there is also evidence of significant movements of religious tourists to the sites of sacred festivals, from very early on. Leisure travel took a little longer to develop. It is traceable to as far back as c. 1500 BC, when the Egyptians began to travel to visit their pyramids, partly for reasons of religion but largely out of curiosity or for pleasure.[1] Most travel, however, entailed very little pleasure and was viewed as a stressful necessity by travellers. Indeed, the origin of the word 'travel' is to be found in its earlier form of *travail* – literally, a painful and laborious effort.

Even earlier than this, around 1900 BC, we find the first extant example of Western travel literature – the classic *Epic of Gilgamesh*. In it, the eponymous hero king is obliged to travel as both a challenge and an educational experience – perhaps the first example of what became known much later as the Grand Tour.[2]

While some limited travel along the coasts and rivers of those ancient empires must have occurred even earlier than these dates, travel was greatly facilitated when shipwrights first designed vessels capable of travelling safely and relatively comfortably over open water some time after 3000 BC.[3] These would primarily have been used to carry freight, but would also have been capable of carrying a limited number of passengers. One of the earliest recorded journeys for the purposes of tourism was that of Queen Hatshepsut, from Egypt to the land of Punt (now Somalia) in around 1490 BC.[4] In landlocked areas, transport was, at the time, limited to donkey riding pending the introduction – probably by the Sumerians at first – of solid-wheeled wagons drawn by oxen or onagers (a type of wild ass), also from around 3000 BC.

In the first millennium BC, the world was to change dramatically, as new empires grew, fought and died. Most forms of transport around this time (such as the chariot) were first developed for military purposes, but this soon led to the use of horse-drawn wagons to convey goods and people. Horse riding also appeared, at first, in military guise, as warriors from Asia swept down from the Steppes. From about 500 BC, however, it was adopted by the Western nations, first in the form of cavalry, but, later, as a more peaceful form of transport.

A museum of 'historic antiquities' was opened to the public in the sixth century BC in Babylon, while, as we have noted, the Egyptians held many religious festivals, attracting not only the devout but also many coming to see the famous buildings and works of art in the cities. To provide for these throngs during the festivals, services of all kinds sprang up: street vendors of food and drink, guides, hawkers of souvenirs, touts and prostitutes. Some early tourists took to vandalizing buildings with graffiti to record their visit – Egyptian graffiti dating back to 2000 BC have been found.

From about the same date, and notably from the third century BC, Greek tourists travelled to visit the sites of healing gods. Because the independent city states of ancient Greece had no central authority to order the construction of roads, most of these tourists travelled by water and, as most freight also travelled in this fashion, the seaports prospered. The Greeks, too, enjoyed their religious festivals, which, in time, became increasingly orientated towards the pursuit of pleasure and, in particular, sport. Already by the fifth century BC Athens had become an important destination for travellers visiting major sights such as the Parthenon and so inns – often adjuncts of the temples – were established in major towns and seaports to provide for the travellers' needs. Innkeepers of this period were known to be difficult and unfriendly and the facilities they provided very basic: a pallet to sleep on, but no heating, no windows and no toilet facilities. Courtesans 'trained in the art of music, dance, conversation and making love' were the principal entertainment offered.

Early guides and guidebooks

Around 500 BC, some travellers took to recording their observations. Aristedes, for example, made reference to the appalling conditions of the highways in Asia Minor in his *Sacred Discourses*. We have the writings of Herodotus, however, who lived between c. 484 and 424 BC, to thank for much of what we know of travel around this period. A noted historian and early traveller who can be accurately described as one of the world's first significant travel writers, he recorded extensively, and with some cynicism, the tall stories recounted to him by the travel guides of the day. It appears that these guides varied greatly in the quality and accuracy of the information they provided. The role of guides was divided between those whose task was to shepherd the tourists around the sites (the *periegetai*) and others who were to provide information for their charges (the *exegetai*). Liberties with the truth included the story that the great pyramids at Giza extended downwards into the Earth to the same extent as their height and the perfection of the dazzling white marble used in the greatest statues was such that viewers risked damaging their eyesight unless they averted their gaze. The philosopher Plutarch wrote to complain, a century before the birth of Christ, that guides insisted on talking too much about the inscriptions and epitaphs found at the sites, choosing to ignore the entreaties of the visitors to cut this short.

Guidebooks, too, made their appearance as early as the fourth century BC, covering destinations such as Athens, Sparta and Troy. Pausanias, a Greek travel writer, produced a noted 'Description of Greece' between AD 160 and 180 that, in its critical evaluation of facilities and destinations, acted as a model for later writers. Advertisements, in the form of signs directing visitors to wayside inns, are also known to have existed from this period.

It was under the Roman Empire, however, that international travel first became important. With no foreign borders between England and Syria, and with the seas safe from piracy owing to the Roman patrols, conditions favouring travel had at last arrived. Roman coinage was acceptable everywhere and Latin was the common language of the day. Romans travelled to Sicily, Greece, Rhodes, Troy, Egypt and, from the third century AD, the Holy Land. The Romans, too, introduced their guidebooks (*itineraria*), listing hostels with symbols to identify quality in a manner reminiscent of the present-day Michelin guides. The Roman poet Horace published an anti-travel ode following his travel experiences from Rome to Brindisi in 38–37 BC.

It is interesting to note, too, the growth of travel bureaucracy from the earliest stages of travel. Reference to passport-type documents can be traced to at least as far back as 1500BC and there are biblical references to 'letters' allowing passage for travellers relating to the period around 450 BC.[5] Later, exit permits were required to leave by many seaports and a charge was made for this service. The Roman *tractorium* is an early example of a passport-type document, issued during the reign of Augustus Caesar. Souvenirs acquired abroad were subject to an import duty and a customs declaration had to be completed.

The Roman Empire, too, suffered its share of 'cowboy operators', both at home and abroad. Among the souvenirs offered to Roman travellers were forgeries of Greek statues, especially works bearing the signature of Greece's most famous sculptor, Praxiteles. Popular souvenirs of the day included engraved glass vials, while professional stonecutters offered their services to inscribe graffiti on tourist sites. Roman writers of the day complained that Athens was becoming a 'city of shysters', bent on swindling the foreign tourist.

Domestic tourism flourished within the Roman Empire's heartland. Second homes were built by the wealthy within easy travelling distance of Rome – they were occupied particularly during the springtime social season. The most fashionable resorts were to be found around the Bay of Naples and there is evidence of early market segmentation for these destinations. Naples itself attracted the retired and intellectuals, Cumae became a high fashion resort, while Puteoli attracted the more staid tourist and Baiae, which was both a spa town and a seaside resort, attracted the downmarket tourist, becoming noted for its rowdiness, drunkenness and all-night singing. As the Roman philosopher Seneca put it, 'Why must I look at drunks staggering along the shore, or noisy boating parties?'

The distribution of administrators and the military during the days of the Roman Empire led to Romans making trips abroad to visit friends and relatives, establishing a precedent for the VFR movements of the present day. The rapid improvement in communications resulting from the Roman conquests aided the growth of travel. First-class roads, coupled with staging inns (precursors of the modern motels), led to comparatively safe, fast and convenient travel that was unsurpassed until modern times. There is even relatively recently found evidence that leisure cruises were taken by super-rich Romans. a 150-foot cruise ship, designed to provide luxurious travel along the coastal waters of the Mediterranean, was discovered by divers off the Sicilian coast in 2000. The ship was fitted with bedroom suites and even passenger lounges for social interaction.

Travel in the Middle Ages

Following the collapse of the Roman Empire and the onset of the so-called Dark Ages, travel became more dangerous, difficult and considerably less attractive – more synonymous with the concept of *travail*. The result was that most pleasure travel was undertaken close to home, although this does not mean that international travel was unknown. Adventurers sought fame and fortune through travel, merchants travelled extensively to seek new trade opportunities, strolling players and minstrels made their living by performing as they travelled (the most famous of these must be Blondel, a native of Picardy and friend of King Richard I, the Lionheart, whom he is reputed to have accompanied during the latter's crusade to the Holy Land). However, all these forms of travel would be identified either as business travel or travel from a sense of obligation or duty. In order for people to travel for pleasure, the conditions that favour travel must be in place.

Nonetheless, closer to home, holidays played an important role in the life of the public. The word 'holiday' has its origin in the old English *haligdaeg*, or 'holy day', and as we saw in the last chapter, from earliest times, religion provided the framework within which leisure time was spent. For most people, this implied a break from work rather than movement from one place to another. The village 'wakes' of the Middle Ages, held on the eve of patronal festivals, provide an example of such 'religious relaxation'. Such public holidays were, in fact, quite numerous – far more so than today; up until as recently as 1830, there were as many as 33 saints' days in the holiday calendar, which dispels the myth of peasants being engaged almost constantly in hard manual labour. For the pious, intent on fulfilling a religious duty, pilgrimages would be undertaken to places of worship, notably including Canterbury, York, Durham and, by the thirteenth century, Walsingham Priory in Norfolk. Chaucer's tales of one pilgrimage to Canterbury provide evidence that there was a pleasurable side to this travel, too.

Religious travel was not limited to the home country at this time. Once political stability was achieved on the Continent and in Britain following the Norman invasion of Britain in 1066, pilgrimages to important sacred sites abroad became increasingly commonplace. Among the most notable were Santiago de Compostela (where the ever-increasing flow of pilgrim tourists led to the creation of relatively sophisticated travel facilities along the pilgrim route by the fifteenth century), Rome and the Holy Land itself. Visits to the latter countries were generally routed via Venice, which itself became a wealthy and important stopover point and a trading centre for the pilgrims. In twelfth-century Rome, a marketing-orientated pope of the day encouraged the sale of badges bearing images of Saints Peter and Paul, iconic souvenirs of their visit.[6]

The focus on Western travellers has tended to mean that the development of travel elsewhere in the world has been ignored. Religious travel, to Mecca, birthplace of Mohammed, became important in the Middle East following the death of its founder in 632 and the rise of Islam. Yet Arab travel was by no means restricted to religious journeys.

Among many travellers, the name of Ibn Battuta (1165–1240)[7] stands out. A spiritual philosopher, he undertook journeys comparable to those of Marco Polo, travelling over 70,000 miles in 25 years, visiting Russia, India, Manchuria and China, as well as nearer countries in North Africa and the Middle East. His travelogue, the *Rihla* (its full title may be translated as 'A Gift to the Observers concerning the Curiosities of the Cities and the Marvels encountered in Travels') examined not only the social and cultural history of Islam but also the politics, immigration and gender relations within the countries he visited.

Developments in road transport in the seventeenth to early nineteenth centuries

Before the sixteenth century, those who sought to travel had three modes for doing so: they could walk (many who were too poor to afford any other form of transport walked, regardless of the distance involved), ride a horse or be carried, either on a litter (carried by servants – an option restricted largely to the aristocracy) or on a carrier's wagon. This horse-drawn vehicle was slow and appallingly uncomfortable, as it had no springs. The roads of the time were poorly surfaced, potholed and, in winter, deeply rutted by the wagon wheels that churned the road into a sea of mud, making the journey an endurance test for passengers.

Toll roads were in evidence as early as 1267, but tollgates on turnpike roads became common from around 1663, adding to the cost of long-distance journeys. Any journey was also unsafe. Footpads and highwaymen abounded on the major routes, posing an ever-present threat to wayfarers. Apart from royalty and the court circle, who were always well guarded, only a handful of wealthy citizens, such as those with 'country seats' (second homes in the country) travelled for pleasure until well into the eighteenth century.

The development of the sprung coach was a huge advance for those who were obliged to travel. The construction of these coaches, in which the body of the coach was 'sprung' by being suspended from primitive leather straps, encouraged travel by offering a greater measure of comfort. The later introduction of metal, leaf-spring suspension further improved comfort. The invention in its most primitive form is traced to the Hungarian town of Kocs in the fifteenth century (from which the word 'coach' originates).

By the mid-1600s, coaches were operating regularly in Britain, with records of a daily service operating between London and Oxford. The concept of the stagecoach, for which teams of horses would be used and changed at regular points along the route, greatly aided mobility. These appeared in England as early as the seventeenth century and were in use widely throughout Continental Europe by the middle of the eighteenth century (Austria, for example, introduced its first services in 1749). In the eighteenth century, the introduction of turnpike roads, which provided improved surfaces, for which tolls would be charged, enabled stagecoaches carrying between 8 and 14 passengers to cover upwards of 40 miles a day during the summer. However, this still meant that a journey from London to Bath would take some 3 days, while the 400 miles to Edinburgh took fully 10 days.

Stagecoaches greatly aided the development of the North American colonies, with a service between Boston and New York introduced in 1772, and other routes serving Providence (Rhode Island), Philadelphia and Baltimore. However, mail coaches, which were to provide additional passenger accommodation, were not to make an appearance until the 1780s in Europe and the USA.

For those who could afford private transport, a wide variety of coaches came into service in the eighteenth and nineteenth centuries, including phaetons, landaus, barouches, broughams and cartouches.

Travel of some distance requires accommodation. At this time, such accommodation was basic. Inns sprang up to serve the needs of overnight guests and provide fresh horses, while lodgings or 'chambers' were available for rent to visitors when they arrived at their destinations.

Around 1815, the discovery of tarmacadam revolutionized the road systems of Europe and North America. For the first time, a hard surface less subject to pitting and ruts enabled rapid increases to be made in the average speed of coach services. Charabancs (public coaches drawn by teams of horses, with rows of transverse seats facing forwards) have been identified as far back as 1832. The name (which was derived from the French *char à bancs*, seated carriage) was later applied to the first motor coaches used for leisure travel in the early twentieth century. By the 1820s, the horse drawn omnibus was a common sight in London and Paris, greatly improving local city transport. Mail coaches were now covering the distance between London and Bath in $12^1/_2$ hours, and the London to Brighton run was reduced to a little over 5 hours.

The Grand Tour

From the early seventeenth century, a new form of tourism developed as a direct outcome of the freedom and quest for learning heralded by the Renaissance. Under the reign of Elizabeth I, young men seeking positions at court were encouraged to travel to the Continent to finish their education. This practice was soon adopted by others high in the social circle and it eventually became customary for the education of a gentleman to be completed by a 'Grand Tour' (a term in use as early as 1670) of the major cultural centres of Europe, accompanied by a tutor and often lasting three years or more. Travel for reasons of education was encouraged by the fact that, under Elizabeth I, a special licence had to be obtained from the Crown in order to travel abroad, though universities had the privilege of granting licences themselves for the purpose of scholarship. The publication in 1749 of a guidebook by Dr Thomas Nugent entitled *The Grand Tour* gave a further boost to this educational travelling and some of the more intrepid ventured as far afield as Egypt. While ostensibly educational, as with the spas, the appeal soon became social and so pleasure-seeking young men of leisure travelled predominantly to France and Italy to enjoy the rival cultures and social life of cities such as Paris, Venice and Florence. By the end of the eighteenth century, the custom had become institutionalized for the gentry.

As a result, European centres were opened up to the British traveller. Aix-en-Provence, Montpellier and Avignon became notable bases, especially for those using the Provence region as a staging post for travel to Italy. When pleasure travel followed in the nineteenth century, eventually to displace educational tours as the motive for Continental visits, this was to lead to the development of the Riviera as a principal destination for British tourists, aided by the introduction of regular steamboat services across the Channel from 1821 onwards. However, the advent of the Napoleonic wars early in the nineteenth century inhibited travel within Europe for some 30 years. By the time of Napoleon's defeat, the British had taken a greater interest in touring their own country.

Example

The rise of Nice as a popular tourist destination

Nice was seen initially as an unpleasant stopover point for those undertaking the Grand Tour. It was poor, had few facilities for the visitor and the roads along the Mediterranean coast were appalling. It was convenient geographically, however, and so, gradually, the number of English visitors grew.

By the end of the eighteenth century, a small colony of English invalids would winter in the town. The reputation of the town soon spread. Between 1860 and 1914, Nice was one of the fastest-growing European cities and entertainments proliferated, including shooting and roller skating.

Gradually, adjacent villages along the Côte d'Azur began to benefit from the prosperity of Nice. Not only the English, but wealthy Russians, too, were choosing to spend their winters in a more temperate climate. By the early twentieth century, however, newer resorts, such as Antibes and Cannes, had begun to entice visitors away from the town and its importance as a tourist base declined.

Authorization to travel

Travel outside the boundaries of one's country had often been subject to restrictions, as we have seen from constraints imposed by the state under the Roman Empire and even earlier authorities. In fact, at various times, some states have even imposed limitations on travel between towns and regions within their own territory. In eighteenth-century France, for example, internal passports were needed to travel between towns, while, prior to the War of Independence in America (1776–1781), similar internal passports were required to move between states.

The first use of the term 'passport' in law in Britain is thought to have occurred in 1548.[8] Such passports hark back directly to the medieval *testimoniale* – a letter from an ecclesiastical superior given to a pilgrim to avoid the latter's possible arrest on charges of vagrancy. Later, papers of authority to travel were more widely issued by the state, particularly during periods of warfare with neighbouring European countries.

Prior to the eighteenth century, few people travelled any great distance and those who did so were generally involved with affairs of state. Monarchs were suspicious of intrigues and alliances with foreign states and vetted such travel carefully, issuing letters of authority to members of court, ostensibly to facilitate travel but equally to ensure that they were familiar with the movements of their subjects. In Britain, it was the prerogative of the monarch to control any movements of their subjects overseas and so, throughout the sixteenth and seventeenth centuries, applications had to be made for a 'licence to pass beyond the seas'. Such 'licences' became more frequent in the eighteenth and nineteenth centuries, but were prohibitively expensive for all but the wealthy as, in 1830, a British passport had cost £2/7/6 (or around £2.37 in today's decimal currency, equivalent to around £166 today), then a high weekly level of pay. Demand was to cut this figure to just 2/- (or 10 pence) by 1858 – still equivalent to a day's pay for many.

Nevertheless, from the late eighteenth century on, demand for travel was growing, to a point where it became impossible to issue passports in the traditional way by the mid-nineteenth century. In Britain, it had been the practice for the Foreign Secretary to issue all passports, based on his personal knowledge of the applicant, but this was clearly no longer practical.

The Alien Bill (1792) – introduced in Britain at a time when the government was becoming concerned about who was coming to Britain (in the lead-up to war with France) – required foreigners entering Britain to be in possession of passports from 1793 onwards and to register on arrival – the first modern form of immigration control. This restriction was not lifted until 1826. Curiously, however, around this period, countries such as France and Belgium appeared willing to issue passports to non-citizens, including Britons. Lloyd[9] recounts the story of the poet Robert Browning eloping with Elizabeth Barrett Browning in 1846 travelling on a French passport.

By the mid-nineteenth century, many European countries began to abandon most passport requirements other than in times of war. This paralleled policy in the United States, which made no requirement for passports except during the Civil War (following the War of Independence, individual states, as well as the Department of Foreign Affairs, had been permitted to issue passports for foreign travel). Regulations were introduced in 1846 in the UK for the movement of merchants and diplomats, but those travelling purely for leisure were no longer obliged to carry formal documentation (although immigration controls were reintroduced in Britain by the Aliens Act of 1905).

Once a nation deems travel documents no longer necessary for its citizens, it becomes difficult to reimpose such a requirement. When Belgium sought to oblige visitors to present passports for inspection in 1882, there was widespread indignation in the British press. World War I was to change all this. New passports, accompanied by a photograph of the bearer, were widely introduced and the League of Nations standardized their design in 1921. Britain made passports compulsory in 1916, although by 1924 Belgium was again allowing Britons to travel on no passport excursions to the Continent.

Other political hindrances to travel

Many other essentially political factors will affect the movement of tourists between countries. A critical one is the political relationship between the generating and destination countries. All through history, the European nations have been at war with one another and clearly the desire to travel in the territories of a recent or former enemy will be limited, just as willingness to visit those of former allies will be enhanced. At times of tension, border controls will inhibit travel and some nationalities may be excluded, while, at the very least, visas or other documentary requirements may be imposed on less friendly nations. It has also been common, particularly in recent history, for countries to refuse entry to visitors who have travelled to or through a nation with which the destination country is in conflict or which it does not recognize (a number of Middle East countries refuse entry to visitors with an Israeli stamp in their passport, for example).

Decisions concerning the value of a currency relative to others, even where economically motivated, are nonetheless political. Such decisions directly affect the buying power of tourists travelling abroad and will either discourage travel or switch travellers to destinations where exchange rates are more favourable. Of course, the use of common currencies in different countries facilitates travel. As we have seen, under the Roman Empire the universal acceptance of Roman coinage greatly encouraged travel, by contrast with the vast range of currencies to be found, even within individual countries, in the Middle Ages. Fynes Moryson, an academic who travelled extensively on the Continent, was to write in 1589 that he found over 20 different coinages in Germany, 5 in the Low Countries and as many as 8 in Switzerland. Moneychangers cheated visitors as a matter of course and were sometimes difficult to find. The adoption of the euro as a common currency throughout most of the 25 countries within the European Union – the first such common currency since the days of the Roman Empire – has been a motivating factor in generating inter-European tourism. It also has its downside, however, as we shall see in the next chapter.

Further political hindrance occurs in the form of taxation, which has affected travel from the very earliest periods of tourism history. The opportunity to enhance a nation's coffers at the expense of the foreign tourist was also widely recognized in the Middle Ages. Indeed, the first spa tax is known to have been introduced in Bad Pyrmont, Saxony, as early as 1413. History also reveals how tourists react to high taxation, switching to other destinations where costs are lower, so measures to tax tourists are always subject to economic sensitivity.

The development of the spas

Spas were already well established during the time of the Roman Empire, but their popularity, based on the supposed medical benefits of the waters, had lapsed in subsequent centuries. They were never entirely out of favour, however. The sick continued to visit Bath throughout the Middle Ages. Renewed interest in the therapeutic qualities of mineral waters can be traced to the influence of the Renaissance in Britain and other European centres.

In 1562, Dr William Turner published a book drawing attention to the curative powers of the waters at Bath and on the Continent. Bath itself, along with the spa at Buxton, had been showing a return to popularity among those 'seeking the cure' and the effect of Dr Turner's book was to establish the credibility of the resorts' claims.

In 1626, Elizabeth Farrow drew attention to the qualities of the mineral springs at Chalybeate in Scarborough, which became the first of a number of new spa resorts. In the same year, Dr Edmund Deane wrote his *Spadacrene Anglica*, which praised what he claimed were 'the strongest sulphur springs in Great Britain' at Harrogate. This rapidly led to the popularity of the town as a spa resort – a role it continues to enjoy today.

Soon, an astonishing number of other spa resorts sprang up, sometimes in unlikely places. Streatham in south London, for instance, became briefly fashionable following the discovery of mineral springs there in 1659. Between 1560 and 1815, at one time or another as many as 175 different spas were operating in England, although only 3 of these – at Bath, Buxton and Hotwells in Bristol – actually incorporated thermal springs in their cures. By 1815, 7 of the spas had purpose-built theatres to provide entertainment.

'Taking the cure' rapidly developed social status and the resorts changed in character as pleasure rather than health became the motivation for visits. Bath in particular became a major centre for social life for high society during the eighteenth and early nineteenth centuries, aided by visits from the monarchs of the day. Under the guidance of Beau Nash at the beginning of the eighteenth century, it soon became a centre of high fashion, deliberately setting out to create a select and exclusive image. The commercial possibilities opened up by the concentration of these wealthy visitors were not overlooked and facilities to entertain or otherwise cater for these visitors proliferated, changing the spas into what we would today term holiday resorts rather than watering places. The building of the Pump Rooms as a focal point within Bath was a key development, leading to the town's success as a resort, while Harrogate, similarly, benefited from the construction of its own Pump Room in 1841–1842.

Eventually, in the early nineteenth century, the common tendency of resorts to go 'downmarket' in the course of their lifecycle led to a changing clientele, with the landed gentry being replaced by wealthy merchants and the professional class. By the end of the eighteenth century, the heyday of the English spas was already over, although they were to have a far longer lifecycle on the Continent (see Figure 2.1).

The popularity of the spas on the Continent may be ascribed to the belief in their efficacy by the general public, supported by members of the medical profession, to the extent that public funding was, and still is in some cases, provided by the state for those needing treatment. The town of Spa in Belgium gave its name to the concept of a centre

Figure 2.1 The Continental spa: the casino at Spa, Belgium.
(Photo by Chris Holloway.)

for the treatment of illness through taking, or bathing in, the mineral waters (or later, by the application to the body of mud or other substances with perceived healing qualities). Spas rapidly became popular in Germany (town names with the appendage 'Bad' or 'Baden' all owe their origins to their spas), Italy (resorts with the title of 'terme' also originated as spas) and middle European countries such as Hungary and Czechoslovakia.

There are interesting parallels between the decline of the English spas and of the English seaside resorts 150 or so years later. The spa towns were seen as attractive places in which to live and residents gradually supplanted visitors. Those residents tended to be older and their demands for more passive and traditional entertainment, with a preference for entertaining at home rather than seeking commercial entertainment, hastened the spas' economic decline. However, it was the rise of the seaside resorts that did much to undermine the success of the inland spas, just as later it would be the rise of the Mediterranean resorts which would lead to the decline of the British and other more northerly seaside resorts.

The rise of the seaside resort

Until the Renaissance, bathing in the sea found little favour in Britain. Although not entirely unknown before then, such bathing as did occur was undertaken unclothed and this behaviour conflicted with the mores of the day. Only when the sea became associated with certain health benefits did bathing gain popularity.

The association of sea water with health did not find acceptance until the early years of the eighteenth century and, initially, the objective was to drink it rather than bathe in it. It is perhaps to be expected that health theorists would eventually recognize that the minerals to be found in spa waters were also present in abundance in sea water.

By the early eighteenth century, small fishing resorts around the English coast were beginning to attract visitors seeking 'the cure', both by drinking sea water and by immersing themselves in it. Not surprisingly, Scarborough, as the only traditional spa bordering the sea, was one of the first to exploit this facility for the medical benefits it was believed to offer and both this town and Brighton were attracting regular visitors by the 1730s. However, it was Dr Richard Russell's noted medical treatise 'A dissertation on the use of sea water in the diseases of the glands, particularly the scurvy, jaundice, king's evil, leprosy, and the glandular consumption', published in 1752 (two years earlier in Latin), which is credited with popularizing the custom of sea bathing more widely. Soon Blackpool, Southend and other English seaside resorts were wooing bathers to their shores (see Figure 2.2). Blackpool, in fact, had attracted some categories of sea bather well before its growth as a resort. Workers in the area are known to have travelled there by cart in order to wash off the accumulation of dirt resulting from their jobs. The heyday of these 'Padjamers', as they were known, was in the century between 1750 and 1850.

The growing popularity of taking the cure, which resulted from the wealth generated by the expansion of trade and industry in Britain at the time, meant that the inland spas could no longer cater satisfactorily for the influx of visitors they were attracting. By contrast, the new seaside resorts offered almost boundless opportunity for expansion. Moral doubts about exposing one's body in the sea were overcome by the invention of the bathing machine and the resorts prospered.

Undoubtedly, the demand for seaside cures could have been even greater in the early years if fast, cheap transport had been developed to cater for this need. In the mid-eighteenth century, however, it still took two days to travel from London to Brighton and the cost was well beyond the reach of the average worker, at the equivalent of six weeks' pay. Accommodation provision, too, grew only slowly, outpaced by demand, but all this was to change in the early nineteenth century.

First, the introduction of steamboat services reduced the cost and time of travel from London to the resorts near the Thames Estuary. In 1815, a service began operating between London and Gravesend and, five years later, to Margate. The popularity of these services

Figure 2.2 An English beach scene in 1810, painted by English caricaturist James Gillray.

was such that other pleasure boat services were quickly introduced to more distant resorts (the first commercial service between Scotland and Ireland was established in 1819). This development required the construction of piers to provide landing stages for the vessels. The functional purpose of the seaside pier was soon overtaken by its attraction as a social meeting point and a place to take the sea air.

It was the introduction of steamboat services also linking Britain and Continental Europe, however, that posed the first threat to the British seaside resorts. Brighton established a ferry link with Dieppe as early as 1761 and later this was followed by links between Shoreham and Newhaven and France. It has been estimated that by the 1820s some 150,000 visitors a year were travelling from Britain to mainland Europe, many for the purposes of visiting coastal resorts.

At first, from about 1780 onwards, travel was concentrated along the Riviera, between the mouth of the Var and the Gulf of Spezia. The Italian resorts benefited from direct steamer services from London and Liverpool to Genoa. Before the advent of the railways, stagecoaches or hired carriages took three weeks to travel from London to Rome, but direct steamboats to Italy were to reduce this by half. Soon, French resorts were attracting British visitors along the north coast between Boulogne and Cherbourg. The British visitors insisted on facilities that met their particular needs, including churches of their favourite denominations and British shops, chemists, physicians and newspapers. The more successful French resorts quickly provided these. From 1880 onwards, the Train Bleu offered wealthy British visitors elegant sleeping accommodation from Paris to the Riviera, popularizing not only summer but also winter holidays to escape the cold of the British climate.

Seaside resorts were also finding favour with the nobility and wealthy of other countries by this time. Aristocratic Russians travelled to the Crimea, the Baltic and the South of France for their holidays, while wealthy Americans on the Eastern seaboard frequented the first resorts developed along the New Jersey, New York and New England coastlines, with the most wealthy of them building second homes in the nineteenth century along the Rhode Island shores.

Conditions favouring the expansion of travel in the nineteenth century

From this brief history of travel from earliest times to the nineteenth century, we can see that a number of factors have been at work in encouraging travel. We can divide these into two categories: factors that make travel possible (*enabling* factors) and those that persuade people to travel (*motivating* factors).

In order for travel to be possible at all, people must have adequate time and money to undertake it. Throughout most of history, however, and until very recently, both of these have been the prerogative of a very few members of society. Leisure time for the masses was very limited. Workers laboured from morning to night, six days a week, and were encouraged to treat Sundays (and the not infrequent Saints' days) as days of rest and worship. Pay was barely adequate to sustain a family and buy the basic necessities of life. The idea of paid holidays was not even considered until the twentieth century.

Equally important, the development of pleasure travel depends on the provision of suitable travel facilities. The growth of travel and transport are interdependent: travellers require transport that is priced within their budget and is fast, safe, comfortable and convenient. As we have seen, none of these criteria was being met until the latter half of the eighteenth century, but, from the early nineteenth century onwards, rapid improvements in technology led to transport that was both fast and moderately priced.

The development of transport during the nineteenth century will be examined in greater detail shortly. Suffice it to say here that good transport must be complemented by adequate accommodation at the traveller's destination. The traditional places to stay for travellers in the Middle Ages were the monasteries, but these were dissolved in Britain during the reign of Henry VIII and the resulting hiatus acted as a further deterrent to travel for everyone apart from those planning to stay with friends or relatives. The gradual improvement in lodgings that accompanied the introduction of the mail coaches and stagecoaches went some way to correcting this shortcoming. The general inadequacy of facilities away from the major centres of population, though, meant that towns such as London, Exeter and York, with their abundant social life and entertainment as a magnet, were to become the first centres to attract large numbers of visitors for leisure purposes.

Other constraints awaited those prepared to ignore these drawbacks to travel. In cities, public health standards were low, so travellers risked disease – a risk compounded in the case of foreign travel. Exchange facilities for foreign travel were unreliable, rates of exchange were inconsistent and travellers risked being cheated, so they tended to carry large amounts of money with them, making them prey to highwaymen. Foreign currencies were, in any event, chaotic, as noted earlier. In the sixteenth century, for instance, Germany, with its multiplicity of small states, had no fewer than 20 coinages, as well as the Reich's Dollar, while there were similar multiple coinages in other European countries. Before unification, Italy, a popular venue for the cultural tourist, boasted 16 different coinages. As we have also seen, travel documents of some kind were generally necessary, too, and, at times, not easy to come by. Political suspicion frequently meant long delays in obtaining permission to travel.

Removing these constraints encourages growth in travel. The real motivation for travel must be intrinsic, however – the desire to travel for its own sake, to get away from one's everyday surroundings and become acquainted with other places, cultures and people. It was the rapid urbanization of the population in Great Britain that provided the impetus for travel in the nineteenth century.

The industrial revolution had led to massive migration of the population away from the villages and countryside and into the industrial cities, where work was plentiful and better paid. This migration was to have two important side-effects on the workers themselves. First, workers became conscious of the beauty and attractions of their former rural surroundings for the first time. Cities were dark, polluted and treeless. Formerly, workers had little appreciation of their environment – living in the midst of the natural beauty of the countryside, they accepted it without question. Now, they longed to escape from the cities in what little free time they had – a characteristic still evident among twenty-first-century citydwellers, too. Second, the type of work available in the cities was both physically and psychologically stressful. The comparatively leisurely pace of life in the countryside was replaced by monotonous factory work, so any escape from its routine and pace was welcome.

The expansion of the British economy that took place as a result of the increased productivity created by the industrial revolution led to growth in real purchasing power for every worker, while worldwide demand for British goods created a huge business travel market. Increased wealth stimulated rapid growth in the population at this time, too.

In short, Britain at the beginning of the nineteenth century stood poised on the threshold of a considerable escalation in the demand for travel. The introduction of modern transport systems at this point in history was to translate this demand into reality.

The age of steam

The railways

Two technological developments in the early part of the nineteenth century were to have a profound effect on transport and the growth in travel generally. The first of these was the advent of the railway.

The first passenger railway was built in England, between Stockton and Darlington, in 1825. It was to herald a major programme of railway construction throughout the world and a huge shift in the ability to travel. We have noted the problems of travelling by road that existed up to that point and, although travel by canal had become possible by 1760, it was too slow a mode to attract travellers as it was used essentially for the carriage of freight. As a means of transport for all purposes, canals were to suffer a rapid decline after 1825, when railways made travel at 13 mph possible for the first time – which was also at least 3 miles an hour faster than the fastest mail coaches.

Invicta, the first steam-driven passenger train (based on the design of Stephenson's *Rocket*), made the first passenger journey between Whitstable Bay and Canterbury on 3 May, 1830, carrying day trippers. In the decade that followed the construction of a rail link between Liverpool and Manchester in the same year, trunk routes sprang up between the major centres of population and industry in Britain, on mainland Europe and throughout the world. In the USA, for example, passenger services on the east coast were being built from the 1820s and, by 1869, a transcontinental link was in place. One of the last great rail routes – the Trans-Siberian – opened in 1903, connecting Moscow with Vladivostok and Port Arthur (now Lüshun).

In the UK, after their initial function to serve the needs of commerce, new routes emerged linking these centres to popular coastal resorts such as Brighton, for the first time bringing these within reach of the mass of those travelling for pleasure. On the whole, however, the railway companies appeared to be slow to recognize the opportunities for travel for pleasure offered by the development of rail services, concentrating instead on providing for the needs of business travellers. Certainly, in the 1840s, the growth of regular passenger traffic was enough to occupy them: between 1842 and 1847, the annual number of passengers travelling by train rose from 23 million to 51 million.

Competition between the railway companies was initially based on service rather than price, although from the earliest days of the railways a new market developed for short day trips. Before long, however, entrepreneurs began to stimulate rail travel by organizing excursions for the public at special fares. In some cases, these took place on regular train services, but, in others, special trains were chartered in order to take travellers to their destinations, setting a precedent for the charter services by air that were to become so significant a feature of tour operating a century later. As an indication of the speed with which these opportunities were put in place, within 12 days of the rail line to Scarborough being opened in 1845, an excursion train from Wakefield was laid on to carry a thousand passengers to the seaside.

Thomas Cook, contrary to popular opinion, was not, in fact, the first entrepreneur to organize tours for the public. Sir Rowland Hill, who became chairman of the Brighton Railway Company, is sometimes credited with this innovation (others have suggested that the first package tour can, in fact, be traced to a group of tourists taken from Wadebridge to Bodmin to witness a public hanging!) and there were certainly excursion trains in operation by 1840. All the same, Cook was to have by far the greatest impact on the early travel industry. In 1841, as secretary of the South Midland Temperance Association, he organized an excursion for his members from Leicester to Loughborough, at a fare of 1 shilling (the equivalent of 5 pence) return. The success of this venture – 570 took part – encouraged him to arrange similar excursions using chartered trains and, by 1845, he was organizing these trips on a fully commercial basis.

The result of these and similar ventures by other entrepreneurs led to a substantial number of pleasure-bound travellers to the seaside. In 1844, it is recorded that almost 15,000 passengers travelled from London to Brighton on the three Easter holidays alone, while hundreds of thousands travelled to other resorts to escape the smoke and grime of the cities. The enormous growth in this type of traffic can be appreciated when it is revealed that, by 1862, Brighton received 132,000 visitors on Easter Monday alone.

Supported by a more sympathetic attitude to pleasure travel by public authorities such as the Board of Trade, the railway companies themselves were actively promoting these excursions by the 1850s, while at the same time introducing a range of discounted fares for day trips, weekend trips and longer journeys. By 1855, Cook had extended his field of operations to mainland Europe, organizing the first 'inclusive tours' to the Paris Exhibition of that year. This followed the success of his excursions to the Great Exhibition in London in 1851, which in all had welcomed a total of three million visitors.

Cook was a man of vision in the world of travel. The success of his operations was due to the care he took in organizing his programmes to minimize problems. He had close contacts with hotels, shipping companies and railways throughout the world, ensuring that he obtained the best possible service as well as cheap prices for the services he provided. By escorting his clients throughout their journeys abroad, he took the worry out of travel for the first-time traveller. He also made the administration of travel easier by introducing the hotel voucher in 1867, which allowed tourists to prepay for their hotel accommodation and produce evidence to the hotels that this had been done. In 1874, he also introduced the 'circular note', the precursor to today's traveller's cheque – a promissory note that could be exchanged abroad for local currency. This greatly helped to overcome the problems arising from the many different coinages in use in Europe. The latter was not a totally new concept – a certain Robert Herries set up the London Banking Exchange Company in 1772 in order to issue similar documents – but it was Cook (and, later, in North America, American Express, which introduced the first traveller's cheque in 1891) who popularized these ideas, making travel far more tolerable for the Victorian traveller.

The coincidental invention of photography in the mid-nineteenth century further stimulated overseas travel for reasons of prestige. For the first time, visitors abroad could be photographed against a background of the great historical sites of Europe, to the envy of their friends.

The expansion of the railways was accompanied by a simultaneous decline in the stagecoaches. Some survived by providing feeder services to the nearest railway stations, but overall road traffic shrank and, with it, the demand for the staging inns. These offered very different services from those expected of a hotel and, while the concept of the 'modern hotel' can be traced back as far as 1764, it was the railways, from around 1840 onwards, that were to drive the development of hotels as we know them today. Inns situated in resorts were quick to adapt to meet the needs of the new railway travellers, but the supply of accommodation in centres served by the railways was totally inadequate to meeting the burgeoning demand of this new market.

A period of hotel construction began, in which the railway companies themselves were leaders, establishing the great railway terminus hotels that came to play such a significant role in the hotel industry over the next hundred years. The high capital investment called for by this development led to the formation of the first hotel chains and corporations.

Social changes in the Victorian era all encouraged travel. The new-found interest in sea bathing meant that the expanding rail network favoured the developing resorts, accelerating their growth. At the same time, Victorian society placed great emphasis on the role of the family as a social unit, leading to the type of family holidays for which the seaside was so well suited. The foundations of traditional seaside entertainment were soon laid – German bands, 'nigger minstrels' and pierrots, Punch and Judy shows, barrel organs, donkey rides and the seaside pier all became essential components.

Resorts began to develop different social images, partly as a result of their geographical location: those nearer London or other major centres of population developed a substantial market of day trippers, while others deliberately aimed for a more exclusive clientele. These latter generally tended to be situated further afield, but, in some cases, their exclusivity arose from the desire of prominent residents to resist the encroachment of the railways for as long as possible. Bournemouth, for example, held out against the extension of the railway from Poole until 1870. Some areas of early promise as holiday resorts were quickly destroyed by the growth of industry – Swansea and Hartlepool, for example, and Southampton, where beaches gave way to the development of docks.

Health continued to play a role in the choice of holiday destinations, but the emphasis gradually switched from the benefits of sea bathing to those of sea air. Climate became a feature of the resorts' promotion. Sunshine hours were emphasized or the bracing qualities of the Scarborough air, while the pines at Bournemouth were reputed to help those suffering from lung complaints. Seaside resorts on the Continent also gained in popularity and began to develop their own social images – Scheveningen near the Hague, Ostend, Biarritz and Deauville offering the same magic for British holidaymakers as the Mediterranean resorts were to provide a century later. Some overseas resorts flourished as a result of a reaction to middle-class morality in Victorian England – Monte Carlo, with its notorious gambling casino, being a case in point.

The desire to escape from one's everyday environment was as symptomatic of nineteenth-century life as it was to become in the middle of the twentieth century. Of course, destinations on the Continent were to attract only the relatively well off and the railways produced services to cater for these high-spend tourists. Trains such as the Blue Train, which entered service between Paris and the Côte d'Azur and Rome in 1883, and the Orient Express of the same year, operating from Paris to the Black Sea, provided unsurpassed levels of luxury for rail travellers on the Continent.

Long-distance rail services became possible with the introduction of sleeping cars, invented in the USA by George Pullman and Ben Field in 1865 and introduced into Europe by the French Wagon-Lit company in 1869. These luxury carriages were first introduced into Britain on the London to Glasgow route in 1873 and were operating on the London to Brighton run by 1881. The first restaurant car arrived in 1879, on the London to Leeds route.

Other forms of holidaymaking – opened up by the advent of the railways on the Continent – arose from the impact of the Romantic Movement of mid-Victorian England. Even limited rail charters were introduced for travel to Germany, Italy, the French Riviera and Spain. The Rhine and the French Riviera in particular benefited from their new-found romantic appeal, while the invigorating mountain air of Switzerland, combining the promise of better health with opportunities for strenuous outdoor activities, was already drawing tourists from Britain by the 1840s. Mountaineering became a popular pastime for the British in the 1860s and was later spurred on by the introduction in Switzerland of skiing.

The origins of skiing are lost in antiquity, but using skis as a sport is credited to a certain Bjorland Blom, Sheriff of Telemark in Norway, in the 1660s. By the beginning of the 1890s, a number of individual British visitors to that country had transported the sport to Switzerland, while Mathias Zdardsky, similarly, brought skis to his native Austria in 1890. Sir Henry Lunn, the British travel entrepreneur, is credited with the commercialization of winter ski holidays in Switzerland, having organized packages to Chamonix before the end of the nineteenth century.

The railways made their own contributions to these developments, but, above all, they encouraged the desire to travel by removing the hazards of foreign travel that had formerly existed for travellers journeying by road.

Early tourism in North America

Just as tourism was growing within Europe during the nineteenth century, parallel patterns of tourism were developing across the Atlantic, too. At first, in the early part of the century, a few seaside resorts grew up to cater for tourists from the major North American conurbations within the 13 states. Fashionable resorts developed at Newport, Rhode Island, Cape May and Atlantic City in New Jersey and along the Massachusetts coast, while more popular resorts closer to New York City, such as those on the coast of New Jersey and Long Island, catered to the needs of the masses, who could reach these on day trips. Spa resorts were also developing at this time, with Saratoga Springs in upstate New York becoming particularly popular. Others, in resorts such as French Lick, Indiana, White Sulphur Springs in West Virginia (popular with early US presidents), Hot Springs, Arkansas, and Glenwood Springs, Colorado, prospered and they still owe some economic dependence to their attraction as tourist resorts today.

Interest in rugged landscapes, especially mountain tourism, ran parallel with this development in Europe, with travellers visiting the mountainous regions of eastern USA by the 1820s. The Americans were quick to adopt the newly invented steam railways, with the Baltimore and Ohio Railroad formed as early as 1830. The Pacific Railroad Act (1862) gave the green light to a cross-continental rail service, completed in 1869, that served both business and leisure needs. The less adventurous visited the mountain ranges across New England. The Catskill Mountains, in upstate New York, were popular, an especial draw being the accommodation at the Mountain House, which flourished from 1824 until the 1930s (an early example of accommodation and destination being inseparable).

A short time later, Niagara Falls became the travellers' target, soon to be popularized by improved accessibility, with the development of paved roads and railways. Canadian tourism, meanwhile, was developing to cater to the needs of expanding populations in and around Toronto and Montreal, with visits to the St Lawrence Seaway, Niagara Falls and the Maine coast soon becoming popular. The absence of any border formalities between Canada and the USA, and the common language (at least for the large part of Canada), facilitated the movement of tourists between the countries, giving holidaymakers the comforting sense of reassurance with the familiar while 'travelling abroad' – a characteristic that continues to enhance travel in North America to this day.

Steamships

Just as the technological developments of the early nineteenth century led to the development of railways on land, so steam was also harnessed at sea, to drive new generations of ships. Here, necessity was the mother of invention. Increasing trade worldwide, especially with North America, required Britain to develop faster, more reliable forms of communication by sea with the rest of the world. Although, as we have seen, ferry services were operating as early as 1761 between Brighton and Dieppe, the first regular commercial cross-Channel steamship service was introduced in 1821, on the Dover–Calais route. The railway companies were quick to recognize the importance of their links with these cross-Channel ferry operators and, by 1862, they had gained the right to own and operate steamships themselves. Soon after, control over the ferry companies was in the hands of the railways, which rapidly expanded cross-Channel services.

Deep sea services were introduced on routes to North America and the Far East, with the paddle-wheel steamer *Savannah* being the first to operate across the Atlantic, sailing between Savannah and Liverpool in 1819 and using steam as an auxiliary to sails. The Peninsular and Oriental Steam Navigation Company (later P&O) is credited with the first regular long-distance steamship service, beginning operations to India and the Far East in 1838. This company was soon followed by the Cunard Steamship Company, which, with a lucrative mail contract, began regular services to the North American continent in 1840. Britain, by being the first to establish regular deep sea services of this kind, came to dominate the world's shipping in the second half of the century, although it was soon to be challenged by other leading industrial nations on the popular North American route. This prestigious and highly profitable route prospered not only from mail contracts but also from the huge demand from passengers and freight as trade with the North American continent expanded. Later, the passenger trade would be boosted by the flow of emigrants from Europe (especially Ireland) and a smaller but significant number of American visitors to Europe. Thomas Cook played his part in stimulating the package tour market to North America, taking the first group of tourists in 1866. In 1872, he went on to organize the first round-the-world tour, taking 12 clients for 220 days at a cost of some £200 – more than the average annual salary at the time.

The Suez Canal, opened in 1869, stimulated demand for P&O's services to India and beyond, as Britain's Empire looked eastwards. The global growth of shipping led, in the latter part of the century, to the formation of shipping conferences, which developed cartel-like agreements on fares and conditions applicable to the carriage of traffic. The aim of these agreements was to ensure year-round profitability in an unstable and seasonal market, but the result was to stifle competition on the basis of price and eventually led to excess profits that were to be enjoyed by the shipping companies until the advent of airline competition in the mid-twentieth century.

Other late nineteenth-century developments

As the Victorian era drew to a close, other social changes came into play. Continued enthusiasm for the healthy outdoor life coincided with the invention of the first modern bicycle in 1866 (derived from the earlier and far more clumsy velocipede of 1818). A London Bicycle Club was established in 1875 and, three years later, the formation of a national Cyclists' Touring Club did much to promote the enjoyment of cycling holidays. This movement not only paved the way for later interest in outdoor activities on holiday but also may well have stimulated the appeal of the suntan as a status symbol of health and wealth, in marked contrast to the earlier association in Victorian minds of a fair complexion with gentility and breeding. The bicycle offered, for the first time, the opportunity for mobile rather than centred holidays and gave a foretaste of the popularity of motoring holidays in the early years of the following century.

Political stability in the final years of the nineteenth century and opening years of the twentieth also allowed the expansion of travel. Significantly, no conflicts occurred on the European Continent between 1871 and 1914 – one of the longest stretches of peacetime in history – and a Europe at peace was becoming an attractive place to visit, both for Europeans and tourists from further afield, such as the United States.

As tourism grew in the later years of the century, so the organizers of travel became established institutions. Thomas Cook and Sir Henry Lunn (who founded Cooperative Educational Tours in 1893, and whose name was retained until very recently in the company Lunn Poly, now renamed Thomson by its TUI owner) are two of the best-known names of the period, but many other well-known companies also became established at this time. Dean and Dawson appeared in 1871, the Polytechnic Touring Association (the other half of the Lunn Poly name) in the following year and Frames Tours in 1881. In the United States, American Express (founded by, among others, Henry Wells and William Fargo of Wells Fargo fame) initiated money orders and travellers' cheques, although the company did not become involved in making holiday arrangements until early in the twentieth century.

Mention has already been made of the impact of photography on nineteenth-century travel. As the century drew to a close, the vogue for photography was accompanied by the cult of the guidebook. No British tourist venturing abroad would neglect to take a guidebook and a huge variety of these soon became available on the market. Many were superficial and inaccurate, but the most popular and enduring published were those of John Murray, whose 'Handbooks' appeared from 1837 onwards, and Karl Baedeker, who introduced his first guidebook (to the Rhine) in 1839. By the end of the century, Baedeker had become firmly established as the leading publisher of guidebooks in Europe.

The years 1900–1950 and the origins of mass tourism

In the opening years of the twentieth century, travel continued to expand, encouraged by the gradually increasing wealth, curiosity (inspired, to some extent, by the introduction in Britain of compulsory education under the Education Act 1870), outgoing attitudes of the post-Victorian population and steady improvement in transport. Travellers were much safer from disease and physical attack, mainland Europe was relatively stable politically and documentation for British travellers uncomplicated as, since 1860, passports had generally not been required for travel to any European country. The popularity of the French Riviera resorts as places for wealthier British visitors to spend the winter is evidenced by the fact that, immediately before World War I (1914–1918), some 50,000 UK tourists are estimated to have been wintering on the coast.

Disastrous though it was, the Great War proved to be only a brief hiatus in the expansion of travel, although, as we have seen, it led to the widespread introduction of passports for nationals of many countries. The prosperity that soon returned to Europe in the 1920s, coupled with large-scale migration, meant unsurpassed demand for travel across the Atlantic, as well as within Europe. The first-hand experience of foreign countries by combatants during the war aroused, for the first time, a sense of curiosity about foreign travel generally among the less well-off sectors of the community. These sectors were also influenced by the new forms of mass communication that developed after the war – the cinema, radio and, ultimately, television, all of which educated the population and encouraged an interest in seeing more of the world.

Forms of travel also began to change radically after the war. The railways went into a period of steady decline following the introduction of the motor car. Motorized public road transport and improved roads led to the era of the charabanc – at first, adapted from army surplus lorries and equipped with benches to provide a rudimentary form of coach. These vehicles achieved immense popularity in the 1920s for outings to the seaside, but their poor safety record soon resulted in licensing regulations being brought in to govern road transport. For those who could afford superior public transportation, more luxurious coaches also made an appearance. The coach company Motorways offered Pullman coaches – generally accommodating 15 people in comfortable armchairs with tables, buffet bars and toilets. These coaches operated to many parts of Europe and North Africa, were used on safaris in East and Central Africa and even provided a twice weekly service between London and Nice, taking a relaxing five to six days to make the trip.

It was the freedom of independent travel offered by the private motor car, however, that contributed most to the decline of the railways' monopoly on holiday transport. The extensive use of the motor car for holidaying has its origins in the United States, where, in 1908, Henry Ford introduced his popular Model T at a price that brought the motor car within reach of the masses. By the 1920s, private motoring was a popular pastime for the middle classes in the United States and, soon, camping and caravanning followed. Caravans (or trailers in American terminology) arrived by the 1930s, with over 100,000 owners taking them on holiday in the first year of that decade.[10] Equally, by the 1930s private motoring had arrived on a large scale in Britain and the threat to domestic rail services was clear, although Continental rail services survived and prospered until challenged by the coming of the airlines.

In an effort to stem the decline, domestic rail services in Britain were first rationalized in 1923 into four major companies – the London, Midland and Scottish Railway (LMS), London and North Eastern Railway (LNER), Great Western Railway (GWR) and Southern Railway (SR) – and later nationalized following World War II, remaining under public control until again privatized in the mid-1990s.

While long voyages by sea were popular as means of leisure travel, the concept of cruising caught on only slowly. Among early examples of ship voyages treated essentially as a cruise, the Matson Line services between the US West Coast and Hawaii were to open up those islands to tourism. The Royal Hawaiian Hotel – built to accommodate visitors in the 1920s to those then exotic islands – was one of the first to offer what we today know as 'all-inclusive' holidays, although hotels along the French Riviera and in Switzerland were to follow suit. Hawaii was to remain an upmarket destination until mass package tours arrived with air services in the 1950s.

The era of the Great Depression

The 1930s are generally thought of as a period when the economic collapse in the Western world was similarly accompanied by the collapse of the international tourist market. While it is true that travel was severely curtailed, the Depression hit Europe rather later than the USA and, in the early 1930s, there remained a substantial market for those with sufficient wealth to travel. In Britain, however, government-imposed limits on foreign exchange for travel abroad proved a severe constraint.

The ever-resilient travel industry reacted with typical enterprise. The formation of the Creative Tourist Agents' Conference (CTAC) in the early 1930s brought together the leading travel agents (who were by this time also tour operators), including Thomas Cook, Dean and Dawson, Hickie Borman and Grant, Frames, Sir Henry Lunn, Pickfords, Wayfarers' Touring Agency, the Workers' Travel Association and the Polytechnic Touring Association (PTA). These formed what amounted to a cartel to hold down and fix prices for foreign excursions. The PTA was instrumental in persuading the Continental railways to discount their fares for bulk purchases – a move the railways had always resisted in the past. Soon, special rail charters were being organized to Germany, Italy, the Riviera and Spain and, by 1938, the PTA was operating its own regular train charters to Switzerland – then one of the most popular destinations on the Continent. This agency also packaged one of the first air charters, approaching Imperial Airways (which was in financial difficulties) in the opening years of the decade to charter a Heracles to carry 24 passengers from Croydon airport to Basle, Switzerland and Paris.[11] By 1932, the company was carrying nearly 1000 passengers by air to the Continent, mainly then as a means of avoiding foreign currency payments to rail and bus companies abroad, and the following year it organized a 14-day air cruise to 7 European capitals. Doubtless these air charters would have been continued, but the partial recovery of Imperial Airways' financial situation led the carrier to withdraw charter privileges, ending these first entrepreneurial modern package tours and making the point that tour operators of the future would have to avoid dependence on suppliers over whom they had no control – a lesson the first large-scale operators were quick to learn.

Cruising remained a popular holiday for those who could afford it. The formation of the Soviet Union after World War I had led the country to build up a strong fleet of cruise vessels. These carried some 5000 tourists from Britain to Russia in 1932, curious to learn about the country and its new political system. By 1938, it has been claimed that as many as one million holidaymakers were cruising on 139 cruise ships.[12]

The growth of the airline industry

The arrival of the airline industry signalled the beginning of the end – not only for long-distance rail services but also, more decisively, for the great steamship companies. British shipping lines had been under increasing threat from foreign competition throughout the 1920s, with French, German and US liners challenging British supremacy on the North Atlantic routes particularly.

The first commercial air routes were initiated – by Air Transport & Travel, the forerunner of British Airways – as early as 1919, from Hounslow airport, London, to Paris. In the same year, a regular service was introduced in Germany between Berlin, Leipzig and Weimar. The infant air services were expensive (nearly £16 for the London–Paris service, equivalent to several weeks' average earnings) and uncertain (passengers were warned that forced landings and delays could occur). Consequently, initial growth in air services was limited to short-haul flights, over land. It was to be many years before air services achieved the reliability and low price that would make them competitive with world shipping routes.

In America, Pan American Airways was formed in 1927, introducing transatlantic air services in the 1930s, initially using flying boats (long-haul services were delayed due to the inability to fly higher than 4000 feet). In addition to its expense, however, the aircraft proved unreliable and uncomfortable by modern standards, so long-distance journeys necessitated frequent stopovers.

In the early years, commercial aviation was more important for its mail-carrying potential than for the carriage of passengers. Only with the technological breakthroughs in aircraft design achieved during and after World War II did air services prove a viable alternative to shipping for intercontinental travel. As for air package holidays, although the PTA reintroduced limited air charters in 1947, the holiday market would have to wait until the 1950s before this form of transport came into its own.

The arrival of the holiday camp

Among the major tourism developments of the 1930s, the creation of the holiday camp deserves a special mention. Aimed at the growing low-income market for holidays, the camps set new standards of comfort, offering 24-hour entertainment at an all-inclusive price. They were efficiently operated, with the added benefit of childminding services – a huge bonus for young couples on holiday with their children. This was in marked contrast to the lack of planned activities and the often surly service offered by the traditional seaside boarding houses of the day.

The origin of these camps goes back to early experiments by organizations in Britain such as the Co-operative Holidays Association, Workers' Travel Association and Holiday Fellowship (although some summer camps for boys, such as those offered by the Young Man's Holiday Camp run by Joseph Cunningham on the Isle of Man, have been dated to as early as 1887). In the USA, summer camps for children were already a strong institution by the early twentieth century. The popularity and widespread acceptance of holiday camps by the adult public, however, have commonly been ascribed to the efforts and promotional flair of Billy (later Sir Billy) Butlin. Supposedly, Butlin, who built his first camp at Skegness in 1936, met a group of disconsolate holidaymakers huddled in a bus shelter to avoid the rain on a wet summer afternoon (although it is thought he was also influenced by a visit to Trusville Holiday Village in Mablethorpe, Lincolnshire, which had been opened and operated successfully by Albert Henshaw since 1924). Butlin determined to build a camp with all-weather facilities, for an all-in price. The instant success of the concept led to a spate of similar camps being built by Butlin (see Figure 2.3) and other entrepreneurs such as Harry Warner and Fred Pontin in the pre-war and early post-war years. On the Continent, pre-war Germany had introduced the concept of the highly organized and often militaristic health and recreation camp that enabled many to enjoy holidays who would otherwise have been unable to afford them.

In France, the 'villages de vacance' arose from similar political and social influences. The success of this concept of all-in entertainment was later to be copied by hotels (we noted earlier that the all-inclusive hotel with its own leisure complex had originated in the United States even earlier; between the two World Wars (and into the 1960s), Grossingers resort hotel in the Catskills flourished as a popular all-inclusive destination in its own right, targeting principally the New York Jewish market).

Interest in outdoor holidays and healthy recreation was also stimulated by the Youth Hostels Association in 1929 (the French equivalent opened in the same year), which provided budget accommodation for young people away from home.

Figure 2.3 The holiday camp era. Butlin's camp at Skegness.
(Courtesy of Barry Lewis/Alamy.)

The popular movement to the seaside

In spite of the rising appeal of holidays abroad for those who could afford them, mass tourism between the wars and in the early post-World War II era remained largely domestic. This period saw the seaside holiday become firmly established as the traditional annual holiday destination for the mass of the British public. Suntans were, for the first time, seen as a status symbol, allied to health and time for leisure. Blackpool, Scarborough, Southend and Brighton consolidated their positions as leading resorts, while numerous newer resorts – Bournemouth, Broadstairs, Clacton, Skegness, Colwyn Bay – grew rapidly in terms of both visitors and residential population. Until the Great Depression of the 1930s, hotels and guesthouses proliferated in these resorts. The tradition of the family holiday, taken annually over two weeks in the summer, became firmly established in Britain at this time.

The growing threat of competition from the European mainland was already apparent, for those who chose to take note of it. From the 1920s onwards, the Mediterranean Riviera had begun to attract a summer, as well as a winter, market from the UK, while the resorts of northern France were seen as cheaper and began to offer competition for the popular south coast resorts of Brighton, Hove, Folkestone and Eastbourne. These nearby French resorts, however, were seen primarily as places for short summer holidays rather than the longer winter stays that had been popular with a wealthy British clientele in the nineteenth century.

The growth of public-sector involvement

It was in this period that Britain experienced the first stirrings of government interest in the tourism business. Britain was well behind other European countries in this respect. Switzerland, for example, had long recognized the importance of its inbound tourism and was actively involved in both promoting tourism overseas and gathering statistics on its visitors.

The British Travel and Holidays Association was established by the government in 1929, but, with the theme 'travel for peace', its role was seen as essentially promotional and its impact on the industry was relatively light, until a change in status some 40 years later. By the outbreak of World War II in 1939, the British government had at least recognized the potential contribution tourism could make to the country's balance of payments. Equally, it had recognized the importance of holidays to the health and efficiency of the nation's workforce. The French government had already introduced holidays with pay in 1936 and the publication of the Amulree Report in 1938 led to the first Holidays with Pay Act for Britain in the same year. This encouraged voluntary agreements on paid holidays and generated the idea of a two-week paid holiday for all workers. Although this ambition was not fulfilled until several years after the end of World War II, by the outbreak of war some 11 million of the 19 million workforce were entitled to paid holidays – a key factor in generating mass travel.

In this chapter we have seen how social and, in particular, technological change had begun to make mass travel feasible. In Chapter 3 we will see how contemporary mass tourism developed with further advances in technology and, above all, improved standards of living throughout the developed world.

Notes

1. Casson, L. (1974) *Travel in the Ancient World*, George Allen & Unwin, p. 32.
2. Leed, E. J. (1991) *The Mind of the Traveller: From Gilgamesh to global tourism*, Basic Books.
3. Casson, 1974, p. 21.
4. McIntosh, R. W. and Goeldner, C. R. (1984) *Tourism Principles, Practices, Philosophies* (4th edn), Wiley.
5. Lloyd, M. (2003) *The Passport: The history of man's most travelled document*, Sutton Publishing.
6. 'Footbinding protest badge', *The Times*, 4 August 2004.
7. Dunn, Ross E. (1986) *The Adventures of Ibn Battuta, a Muslin Traveller of the Fourteenth Century*, University of California Press.
8. Lloyd, 2003, p. 25.
9. Lloyd, 2003, p. 10.
10. Löfgren, O. (1999) *On Holiday: A history of vacationing*, University of California Press, p. 37.
11. Studd, R. G. (1950) *The Holiday Story*, Percival Marshall, pp. 145, 196/7.
12. Studd, 1950, p. 146.

Further reading

Brodie, A., Sargent, A. and Winterby, G., (2005) *Seaside Holidays in the Past*, English Heritage.

Burke, T. (1942) *Travel in England: From pilgrim and packhorse to light car and plane*, Batsford.

Feifer, M. (1985) *Going Places: The ways of the tourist from Imperial Rome to the present day*, Macmillan.

Hern, A. (1967) *The Seaside Holiday: The history of the English seaside resort*, Cresset Press.

Perrottet, T. (2003) *Route 66 AD: Pagan holiday on the trail of ancient roman tourists*, Random House.

Pimlott, J. A. R. (1947) *The Englishman's Holiday: A social history*, Harvester Press.

Swinglehurst, E. (1982) *Cook's Tours: The story of popular travel*, Blandford Press.

Ward, C. and Hardy, D. (1986) *Goodnight Campers! The history of the British holiday camp*, Mansell Publishing.

Websites

Seaside History (the history of the British seaside holiday)   **www.seasidehistory.co.uk**

Questions and discussion points

1. Discuss the ways in which pleasure travel developed from earlier forms of travel for other purposes, both historically and more recently. What patterns of similarity do you find?

2. Why do you think innkeepers in early Greece were noted as 'difficult and unfriendly'? Could the reasons for this be related to those for similar weaknesses in hospitality that have been noted in more recent times?

3. Compare and contrast the influence of the euro on international travel today with currencies in use during (a) Roman times and (b) the sixteenth century.

4. Explain the factors that encouraged the growth of tourism under the Roman Empire. To what extent do these factors still account for tourism growth?

5. The importance of religious tourism in earlier history accounts for the rise in wealth of many European towns and cities. To what extent is this comparable with the wealth of some cities today? Which places in particular have benefited from religious tourism and how have they exploited their opportunities?

6. Could the current growth in resort crime, casual violence in society, the threat of global terrorism and sky high oil prices lead to another 'dark age' for tourism similar to that following the collapse of the Roman Empire?

Tasks

1. Select and read any text by one of the great pre-twentieth-century explorer/travellers and examine the similarities and differences in the experiences they encountered in tourism then and now. As a result, give your views on whether you consider tourism today more or less rewarding than in earlier times.

2. Write a brief article comparing information given by guides in the days of the Greeks and Romans and that given today. Listen to guides taking walking tours in an area known to you and determine whether they still give inaccurate information or 'too much information', as they had been accused of doing in earlier history. What steps have now been taken in your country to ensure that guides take their informational role more responsibly?

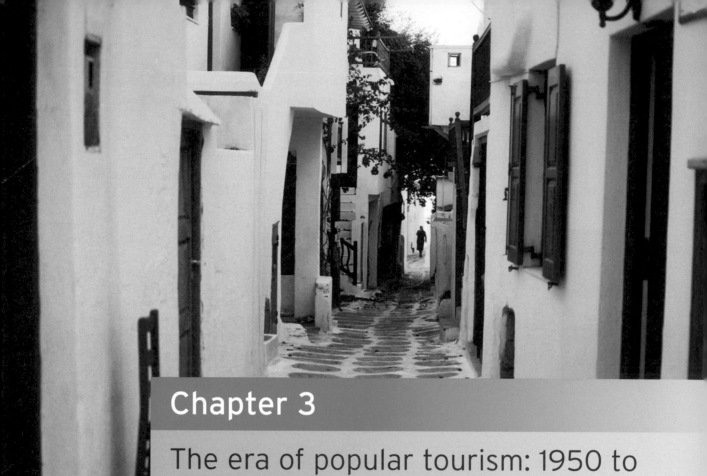

Chapter 3

The era of popular tourism: 1950 to the twenty-first century

Learning outcomes

After studying this chapter, you should be able to:

● describe the factors giving rise to mass tourism after 1950

● explain the origins and development of the package holiday

● understand the significance of rapid change in political, social and economic circumstances giving rise to the current uncertainties facing the tourism industry.

Tourism since World War II

Those who wish to see Spain while it is worth seeing must go soon.

Reverend Henry Christmas, *The Shores and Islands of the Mediterranean. Including a Visit to the Seven Churches of Asia* (1851), quoted in Löfgren, pp. 184–5

In the aftermath of World War II, the long and deprived years led to an increased desire to travel to foreign destinations, although the ability to do so was limited for many – restricted by both political barriers and inadequate finance. In Britain, as in other lands in Europe, there were also strict limits on the availability of foreign currency – a major barrier to cross-border travel. Nevertheless, the war had given rise to a curiosity among many British travellers to witness the sites of battles such as those fought on the Normandy beaches and at St Nazaire, while North Americans and Japanese alike felt similarly drawn to sites of conflict in the Pacific, such as Iwo Jima and Guadalcanal – although it was to take some 40 years or more before interest in these historic military battle sites was to approach the level of those of World War I. Interest was also limited to the sites on the western front in Europe – the horrors of warfare on the eastern front were such that neither side showed much inclination to visit the former battlefields, many of which were, in any case, banned to visitors until after the fall of the Soviet government. The extensive theatre of war had introduced the many combatants to not only new countries but also new continents, generating new friendships and an interest in diverse cultures. Another outcome of the war, which was radically to change the travel business, was the advance in aircraft technology that was soon to lead to a viable commercial aviation industry for the first time. With the ending of the war in 1945, the first commercial transatlantic flight took place between New York and Bournemouth, calling at Boston, Gander and Shannon. That flight, operated by American Overseas Airlines using a Douglas DC4, served to point the way ahead, although the cost and the time involved – a result of the frequent stops required – ensured that long-haul flights would not become popular until the advent of the jet age.

The surplus of aircraft in the immediate post-war years, a benevolent political attitude towards the growth of private-sector airlines and the appearance on the scene of air travel entrepreneurs such as Harold Bamberg (of Eagle Airways) and Freddie Laker (of Laker Airways) aided the rapid expansion of air travel after the war. More significantly for the potential market, however, aircraft had become more comfortable, safer, faster and, in spite of relatively high prices in the early 1950s, steadily cheaper by comparison with other forms of transport. The war had seen many new airports built in Europe to serve the military and these were later adapted for civilian use. This was to prove particularly valuable in opening up islands in the Mediterranean that were formerly inaccessible or time-consuming to reach by sea.

Commercial jet services began with the ill-fated Comet aircraft in the early 1950s (withdrawn from service after crashes resulting from metal fatigue), but advances in piston engine technology were already beginning to impact on price. With the introduction of the commercially successful Boeing 707 jet in 1958, the age of air travel for the masses had arrived, hastening the demise of the great ocean liners.

The number of passengers crossing the Atlantic by air exceeded those by sea for the first time in 1957 and, although the liners continued to operate across the Atlantic for a further decade, their increasingly uncompetitive costs, high fares (saddled by conference agreements on routes across the Atlantic and Pacific that banned discounting) and the length of the journey time resulted in declining load factors from one year to the next. The new jets, with average speeds of 800 to 1000 kph, compared with older propeller-driven aircraft travelling at a mere 400 kph, meant that an air traveller could reach a far more distant destination within a given time (the key New York to London route fell from 18 hours in 1949 to just 7 hours in 1969) than had been possible before. This was particularly valuable for business journeys where time was crucial.

The early 1970s saw the arrival of the first supersonic passenger aircraft, the Anglo-French Concorde. Never truly a commercial success (the governments wrote off the huge development costs), it nevertheless proved popular with business travellers and the wealthy. Travelling from London or Paris to New York in three and a half hours, it allowed businesspeople for the first time to complete their business on the other side of the Atlantic and return home without incurring a hotel stopover. The limited range and carrying capacity (just over 100 passengers) of the aircraft, and restrictions regarding sonic booms over land, acted as severe constraints on operable routes. The fatal crash near Paris of a chartered Concorde in 2000 sealed the aircraft's fate, leading to its withdrawal from service. It is thought unlikely that any further supersonic aircraft development will take place within the next 20 years (although the possibility of private supersonic jets arriving rather sooner than this is discussed in Chapter 13).

The development of the package tour

Inclusive tours by coach soon regained their former appeal after the war. The Italian Riviera was popular at first – French resorts proving too expensive – and resorts such as Rimini became affordable for the North European middle market. The inclusive tour by air – or 'package tour' as it has become known – was soon to follow.

Cheap packages by air depend on the ability of tour operators to charter aircraft for their clientele and buy hotel beds in bulk, driving down costs and allowing prices to be cut. Initially, the UK government's transport policy had restricted air charters to the movement of troops, but, as official policy became more lenient, the private operators sought to develop new forms of charter traffic. Package holidays were the outcome, as the smaller air carriers and entrepreneurs learned to cooperate.

In the late 1950s, the larger airlines began to purchase the new jets, allowing smaller companies to buy the stock of second-hand propeller-driven aircraft coming on to the market, which were then put into service for charter operations. For the first time, holiday tourists could be transported to Mediterranean destinations faster than, and almost as cheaply as, trains and coaches. These new charter services soon proved highly profitable. Meanwhile, across the Atlantic, the first stirrings of an air package holiday industry emerged as regional operators began chartering aircraft from so-called 'supplemental' carriers on routes between major cities in the USA and Canada and the Caribbean Islands.

Although there are instances of charter flights as early as the 1920s (Thomas Cook, for example, had organized an escorted charter, believed to be the first, to take fans from New York to Chicago in 1927 to see the Dempsey–Tunney heavyweight title fight) and the National Union of Students is known to have been organizing charter flights for its members as early as 1949, Vladimir Raitz is generally credited with founding the mass inclusive tour business using air charters as we know it today. In 1950, under the Horizon Holidays banner, he organized an experimental package holiday trip using a charter flight to Corsica. By chartering the aircraft and filling every seat instead of committing himself to a block of seats on scheduled air services, he was able to reduce significantly the unit cost of his air transport and, hence, the overall price to his customers. He carried only 300 passengers in the first year, but repeated the experiment the following year and was soon operating profitably. Other budding tour operators, both in Britain and on the Continent, were soon copying his ideas (Club Méditerranée being among the best-known of the early entrepreneurs) and, by the early 1960s, the package holiday to the Mediterranean had become an established product for the mass holiday market.

The Spanish coastline and the Balearic Islands were the first to benefit from the new influx of mass tourism from Britain, Germany and the Scandinavian countries, carried by the workhorse Douglas DC-3 aircraft. First, the Costa del Sol, then other coasts along the eastern seaboard, the islands of Majorca, Ibiza and, finally by the 1970s, the Canaries became, in turn, the destinations of choice for millions.

By 1960, Spain was already welcoming 6 million tourists every year and this was to grow to 30 million by 1975. Italy, Greece and other Mediterranean coastal regions all benefited from the 'rush to the sun'. Greece in particular, although slower to develop than Spain, provided a cheaper alternative as prices in the latter country rose. Only 50,000 visited in 1951, but a decade later this had grown to 500,000 and, by 1981, Greece was vying with Spain, welcoming 5,500,000.

The Nordic countries were also soon setting up their own package holiday arrangements to the Mediterranean and began to compete with Britain and their southern counterparts for accommodation along the Mediterranean coast. In Denmark, Pastor Eilif Krogager conducted a group of package tourists by coach to Spain in 1950, using the name of his village, Tjaereborg, as the company name. In 1962, Tjaereborg Travel moved into the air charter market with the formation of Sterling Airways, which soon became Western Europe's largest privately owned charter airline of the period.

In Britain, post-war difficulties in the economy forced the government to impose ever tighter controls on foreign exchange. For a brief interval in 1947, a travel ban was imposed, during which no foreign currency allowance was made. Although the ban was lifted in early 1948, severe currency restrictions remained into the late 1960s, at which point the foreign currency (V-form) allowance for travel abroad was limited to £50 per person (for business travellers, additional funds, under T-form regulations, were granted). There was, however, a silver lining to this particular cloud: it encouraged people to take package holidays rather than travel independently, so the industry continued to flourish. Also, as air transport costs were payable in sterling and as only the foreign currency element of the tour – the *net* costs of accommodation and transfers – had to be paid out of the allowance, the benefits of dealing with an operator became clear. The limits were relaxed from 1970 onwards and, with further liberalization of air transport regulations

Figure 3.1 The mass market beach holiday. Grömitz is a popular German resort in Mecklenburg Bay, North Germany.
(Photo by Chris Holloway.)

Figure 3.2 The linear tour. An example of the 'milk run' around Britain.

and longer paid holidays, which encouraged a growing number of tourists to take a second holiday abroad each year, a new winter holiday market emerged in the 1970s. With a more even spread of package holidays throughout the year, operators found that they were able to reduce their unit costs still further, so package holiday prices continued to fall, boosting off-season demand. Britain was not alone within Europe in imposing currency restrictions during these early post-war years. Indeed, exchange controls were not totally abolished in France until as recently as 1990.

A further technological breakthrough in air transport occurred in 1970, when the first wide-bodied jets (Boeing 747s), capable of carrying over 400 passengers, appeared in service. The unit cost per seat fell sharply and the result was an increased supply of seats at potentially cheaper fares. This innovation meant that, once again, the aviation industry had to unload cheaply a number of obsolescent, although completely air-worthy, smaller aircraft and these were quickly pressed into service for charter operations.

The innovation coincided with a steady increase in demand by North American visitors to Europe for basic tours of Britain and the Continent, hitting as many 'high spots' as possible in a 10- to 14-day visit. This gave rise to the concept of the 'milk run' – a popular route that would embrace the top attractions in one or more countries in a limited time-scale for the first-time visitor (see Figure 3.2). Similar short 'taster' tours around Western Europe, visiting the key cities, provided an introduction to long-haul travel for millions of Americans.

The movement to the sun

By the 1960s, it was clear that the future of mass market leisure travel was to be a north–south movement, from the cool and variable climates of North America and northern

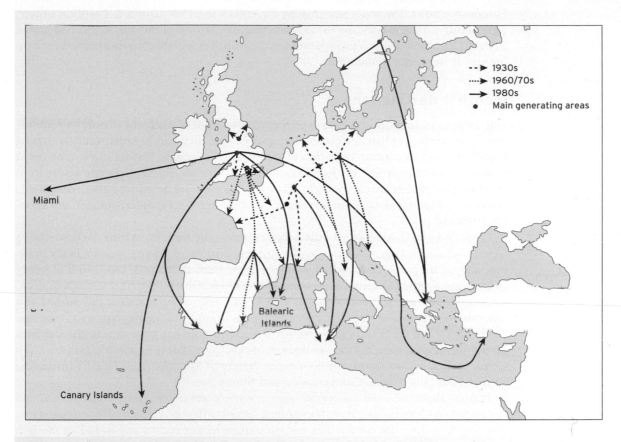

Figure 3.3 Changes in destination trends for mass market holidays, 1930s to 1980s.

Europe, where the mass of relatively well-off people lived, to the sunshine and warmth of the temperate to tropical lands in the southern part of the northern hemisphere (see Figure 3.3). These southern countries were also, for the most part, less well developed economically and so offered low-cost opportunities for the formation of a tourism industry. The new breed of tourism entrepreneurs involved with packaging tours recognized this trend very early on. Major hotel chains, too, were quick to seize the opportunities for growth in these countries and those such as Sheraton and Hyatt in the USA quickly expanded into Mexico and the Caribbean, as well as into Florida and Hawaii – the states offering the most attractive climates for tourism development. Hawaii in particular proved popular as an 'overseas' destination, following its incorporation into the USA (from 100,000 visitors in 1955, the flow of tourists increased to 2 million in 1970 and 6.5 million by 1990).

In Europe, British and German tour operators such as Thomson and TUI developed bulk inclusive tours to the Mediterranean and North Africa and, due to increasing volume, were able to charter jumbo jets for the first time, bringing prices still lower. As transport costs fell, operators were also able to attract a mass market for long-haul travel on chartered jumbo jets. Florida – boosted particularly by the attractions of the Walt Disney World Resort and Miami Beach – has become almost as popular a destination for Europeans as the major Mediterranean destinations.

By the end of the twentieth century, the expert packaging of these tours had been extended to many other types of destinations. Initially, tours to cultural and heritage sites, city breaks to major cities like London, Paris, Rome, Brussels and Amsterdam and river cruises on the Rhine or Danube were being efficiently packaged and sold to the northern

European market. The result was that, by the end of the 1960s, some 2.5 million Britons were taking packaged holidays abroad each year. By the end of the 1980s, this had grown to over 11 million, with over 70 per cent of the British population having been abroad on holiday at least once in their lives.

Identikit destinations

One important result of the growth of the mass tourism market was that those responsible for marketing tourist destinations recognized that they had to satisfy tourists sharing broadly similar aspirations, regardless of their country of origin. The destinations accepted that, apart from geographical location, there was little to differentiate one resort from another and consumers' needs were centred on good climate and beaches, reasonable standards of food and accommodation, good opportunities for entertainment and shopping and low prices.

Consumers themselves cared little which country they were in, as long as these criteria were fulfilled. The larger the mass market, the less distinctive destinations are likely to be, especially if they are small and have only recently been developed. One can find newly built 'marina'-type resorts with yachting, basins, hotel/apartment/villa accommodation, similar restaurants, cafés and shops, as well as golf, tennis, water sports, folk singers and barbecue nights in any one of a dozen countries around the Mediterranean, Caribbean, North Africa and the South Pacific. Vernacular architecture has given way to the standard monobloc development typical of all beach resorts from Miami Beach to Australia's Gold Coast, by way of Benidorm and the faceless resorts of Romania and Bulgaria (including the optimistically named 'Golden Sands' and 'Sunny Beach').

This is also true even where business travellers attending conferences abroad are concerned. A convention centre, for example, is today likely to be a multi-purpose venue containing facilities for conferences and committee/lecture rooms and including modern single or twin-bedded hotel rooms with private facilities, restaurants with banqueting rooms, bars, exhibition space, a leisure centre with pool, indoor and outdoor sports facilities and good scheduled transport links. The location may be Birmingham, Barcelona or Brisbane, but, once inside their hotel or conference centre, delegates may not even notice where they are. Indeed, one can find ubiquitous furniture of identical design (such as faux Regency chairs spray-painted in gold) in conference centres and hotels throughout the world.

The term **identikit destination** will be used to define and identify this form of resort. Each has emerged following comprehensive market research among various generating markets to find products with guaranteed mass demand. They may be contrasted with the piecemeal development of resorts two or three generations ago, the attractions at which may have been developed with very different aims and markets in mind. This is not to say that all identikit destinations are chasing identical markets. Many may be 'downmarket' in their attractiveness – that is, they may offer cheap tourism to a large number of people with the image of great popularity – while others may offer a more upmarket, but nonetheless uniform, image, offering the perception of higher quality and, thus, more expensive services to fewer visitors. In the former category we may think of Benidorm, Magaluf, Benitses in the Mediterranean, Miami Beach in Florida (see Figure 3.4) or Seefeld in Austria, while in the latter category we may think of Tahiti, Fiji, Malindi in Kenya or Barbados. Many identikit destinations have been developed through the activities of multinational tour companies, such as the all-inclusive resorts run by Sandals in the Caribbean, France's Club Méditerranée, Germany's Robinson Club or the United States' Sheraton Hotel chain. Within their establishments, the mass tourist will find a comforting degree of uniformity.

Mass tourism has therefore demanded, and been supplied with, products designed specifically for its needs, as revealed through the process of market research. Such products

Figure 3.4 Miami Beach typifies the popular North American identikit mass holiday destination. High-rise blocks now tower over the few remaining traditional motels in Florida. *(Photo by Chris Holloway.)*

are *user-orientated* as opposed to *resource-orientated* (based on the resources available at a destination).

Many of these identikit destinations, however, are now finding themselves at a disadvantage as the world tourism market becomes more sophisticated. Research by the former English Tourism Council revealed that one of the weaknesses of many English seaside resorts has been their failure to project a unique image. Those that have succeeded – notably Blackpool and a handful of other major or minor resorts – have done so through a combination of significant investment and differentiation from other, often similar, resorts. Those resorts unable to make the investment needed to change their image are faced with the prospect of decline or have to appeal to newer, generally lower-spend markets. The later years of the last century found several of the formerly popular Mediterranean resorts attracting new tourists from the central European countries to replace the gradual decline in numbers of Western European visitors. One saving grace for those identikit destinations that developed around the core of an established town has been the ability to retain and improve the original 'old town', which is now promoted as a core attraction in its own right.

Private motoring and holidays

After a slow post-war recovery, the standard of living rose steadily in the 1950s and after. Many people could contemplate buying their first car, even if it was second-hand. For the first time, the holiday masses had the freedom to take to the roads with their families in their own private cars and, in Britain, the popular routes between London and the resorts on the south coast were soon clogged, in those pre-motorway days, with weekend traffic.

The flexibility that the car offered could not be matched by public transport services and both bus and rail lost the holiday traveller. In 1950, some two out of every three holidaymakers took the train for their holidays in Britain; this fell to one in seven by 1970. In this period, private car ownership in Britain rose from 2 million to over 11 million vehicles and, by the end of the 1980s, it had risen to some 20 million.

This trend led, in turn, to a growth in camping and caravanning holidays. Ownership of private caravans stood at nearly 800,000 by the end of the 1980s (excluding static caravans in parks), while 13 million holidaymakers in the UK took their holidays in a caravan. This development was a cause for some concern, however, as the benefits to a region of private caravan tourism are considerably less than most other forms of tourism (owners can bring most of their own food with them and do not require accommodation). Also, caravans tend to clog the holiday routes in summer. Both mobile and static caravans on site are perceived as something of an eyesore, too.

The switch to private transport led to new forms of accommodation that catered for this form of travel. Britain saw the development of its first motels, modelled on the American pattern, which are the contemporary version of the staging inn for coach passengers.

The construction of a new network of motorways and other road improvements made the journeys to more distant resorts manageable for those in centres of population and, in some cases, changed both the nature of the market served and the image of the resort itself.

The ever resourceful tour operators met the private car threat to package holidays by devising more flexible packages, such as fly–drive holidays, with the provision of a hire car at the airport on arrival. Hotels, too, spurred on by the need to fill their rooms off-peak, devised their own programmes of short-stay holidays, tailored to the needs of the private motorist.

Another effect was that the demand for car rental *abroad* rose sharply, too, as the overseas holidaymaker was emboldened to move away from the hotel ghettos, so car rental businesses in popular areas profited accordingly.

The shipping business in the post-war period

By contrast with other elements of the travel business, passenger shipping companies, hit by rising prices and competition from the airlines, were struggling to survive. Forced to abandon their traditional liner routes by the 1960s, some attempted to adapt their vessels for cruising. In this, they were far from successful as vessels purpose-built for long-distance, fast, deep sea voyages are not ideally suited to cruising, either economically or from the standpoint of customer demand. Many were incapable of anchoring alongside docks in the shallower waters of popular cruise destinations such as the Caribbean islands.

Companies that failed to embark on a programme of new construction, either due to lack of resources or foresight, soon ceased trading. Others, such as the Cunard Line, were taken over by conglomerates outside the travel or transport industries. American cruise lines, beset by high labour costs and strong unions, virtually ceased to exist.

Many new purpose-built cruise liners, however, of Greek, Norwegian and, later, Russian registry, soon appeared on the market to fill the gaps left by the declining maritime powers. These vessels, despite their registry, were based primarily in Caribbean or Mediterranean waters.

British shipping was not entirely devoid of innovations at this time. Cunard initiated the fly–cruise concept in the 1960s, with vessels based at Gibraltar and Naples and passengers flying out to join their cruise in chartered aircraft.

The rapid escalation of fuel and other costs during the 1970s threatened the whole future of deep sea shipping, but, although declared dead by the pundits, this sector refused to lie down. Gradual stabilization of oil prices and control of labour costs (largely by recruiting from developing countries) enabled the cruise business to stage a comeback in the 1980s and 1990s, led by entrepreneurial shipping lines like Carnival Cruise Line, the American operator that set out to put the fun back into cruising. More informality, to appeal to more youthful family markets, helped to turn the business round, so that, by the end of the twentieth century, cruising had again become a major growth sector. Carnival absorbed many of the traditional carriers, including British companies Cunard and P&O, and had the financial backing necessary to make substantial investment in new vessels.

By contrast with the cruise business, ferry services achieved quite exceptional levels of growth between the 1950s and the end of the century. This largely resulted from the increased demand from private motorists to take their cars abroad, influencing particularly routes between Scandinavian countries and Germany, and between Britain and Continental Europe. This growth in demand was also better spread across the seasons, enabling vessels to remain in service throughout the year with respectable load factors (although freight demand substantially boosted weak passenger revenue in the winter period). Regular sailings, with fast turnarounds in port, encouraged bookings and costs were kept down by offering much more restricted levels of service than would be expected on long-distance routes. Hovercraft and jetfoil services were introduced across the Channel, although their success was limited by technical problems and being unable to sail in severe weather. Reliable, fast ferry services did not appear until the advent of the catamarans in the 1990s.

The growing importance of business travel

The growth in world trade in these decades saw a steady expansion in business travel, individually and in the conference and incentive travel fields, although recession in the latter part of the century caused cutbacks in business travel as sharp as those in leisure travel. As economic power shifted between countries, so emerging nations provided new patterns of tourism generation. In the 1970s, Japan and the oil-rich nations of the Middle East led the growth, while in the 1980s, countries such as Korea and Malaysia expanded both inbound and outbound business tourism dramatically. The acceptance of eight Eastern European nations (together with Malta and Cyprus) into the EU in May 2004 led to new growth areas in the movement of tourists during the first decade of the century, plus the rise of a new, free-spending elite within the Russian community and adjacent countries has resulted in those nationalities being among the fastest-growing sector in international tourism, albeit from a low base. Meanwhile, uncertainty in the Western world – particularly the fall and slow recovery of the stock market since the events of September 2001, followed by a deepening recession and escalating oil prices – has continued to limit the recovery of business and leisure travel well into the twenty-first century.

Nevertheless, business travel of all kinds remains of immense importance to the tourism industry, not least because the per capita revenue from the business traveller greatly exceeds that of the leisure traveller. Motivational factors involving business travel are discussed in the next chapter and the nature of business travel is explored more fully in Chapter 11, but it should be stressed here that business travel often complements leisure travel, spreading the effects of tourism more evenly in the economy. A major factor is that business travellers are not generally travelling to areas that are favoured by leisure travellers (other than in the very particular case of the conference market). Businesspeople have to go to locations where they are to conduct business, which generally means city centres, and often those cities have little to attract the leisure tourist. Travel also takes place all year round, with little peaking, and the demand for hotels occurs between Mondays and Fridays, encouraging the more attractively situated hotels to target the leisure market on weekends. Often, spouses will travel to accompany the business traveller, so their leisure needs will have to be taken into consideration, too. Thus, in practice, it becomes difficult to distinguish between business and leisure tourism.

Although business travel is less price-elastic than leisure travel, as was noted earlier, efforts to cut costs in the world of business today are ensuring business travellers no longer spend as freely as they did formerly. Fewer business travellers now travel first class or business class on airlines (many are making use of the new budget airlines to minimize costs) than before, less expensive hotels are booked and there is even a trend to travel on weekends to reduce prices. Companies are buying many more tourism products, particularly air tickets, through the Internet, where they can shop around for the cheapest tickets. These changes are not seen as short-term trends and, in future, any distinction between the two major tourist markets is likely to become less apparent.

Conference and incentive travel business

Conferences and formal meetings have become very important to the tourism industry, both nationally and internationally, with continued growth between the 1960s and the end of the century. The British conference market alone is responsible for the organization of some 700,000 individual conferences each year, the very large majority lasting just one or two days. As most of them are held in hotels, this market is vital to the accommodation sector. Low-cost carriers, having broken the traditional carriers' imposition of conditions requiring a weekend stopover to gain low fares, changed business protocol and began to win a share of those important markets.

Major conferences, such as that of the American Bar Association, which accounts for up to 25,000 delegates each year travelling all over the world (the 2000 conference was held in London), impact on all sectors of the industry, from hotels to the destination itself, which benefits from expenditure in shops, theatres, nightclubs and other centres of amusement. To serve the needs of the largest conferences, international conference centres seating up to 5000 or more delegates have been built in major cities such as London and Berlin, but the number of conferences of this size is inevitably limited, so the competition to attract them is intense.

The logistics of organizing these and other major events are generally in the hands of professional events organizers, most of whom in Britain belong to the Association of Conference Executives (ACE). As international conferences generally have English as the common language (although simultaneous translations are always available where necessary), countries such as Britain and the USA greatly benefit from this market.

Exhibitions also account for another form of business travel. Major international exhibitions can be traced to at least as far back as the Great Exhibition, held at Crystal Palace in London in 1851, and world fairs have become common events in major cities around the globe as a means of attracting visitors and publicizing a nation's culture and products. Many national events are now organized on an annual basis, some requiring little more than a field and marquees or other temporary structures – the Royal Bath & West agricultural show being one example of a major outdoor attraction, held annually in the UK's West Country. As such events have grown and become more professionally organized, so have they, too, become an important element in the business of tourism.

The all-inclusive holiday

Mention has already been made of the trend for *all-inclusive* holidays. As the term indicates, such a holiday includes everything – food, alcoholic drinks, water sports and other entertainment at the hotel. The attractions of this form of tourism are obvious – it is seen by tourists as offering better value, because they can pay up front for the holiday, know what their budget will be well in advance and be unconcerned about changes in the value of foreign currency or the need to take large sums of money abroad. For more timid foreign travellers or those who are concerned about being badgered by local souvenir sellers and 'beach salesmen', there is the added reassurance that they do not even have to leave the hotel complex to enjoy their holidays.

Critics argue that the growth of all-inclusive holidays has implications for the local economy, as local bars, shopkeepers and others no longer stand to benefit from visitors to the same extent as before. At the same time, greater profits can leak back overseas when the all-inclusive holiday sites are foreign-owned. In this sense, one may question whether or not all-inclusive tourism can be judged sustainable. Operators themselves, however, would refute this, arguing that, by keeping tourists in 'ghettos', they are in fact helping to reduce the negative impact of tourism on locals.

In its modern form, this type of tourism originated in the Caribbean and upmarket tour operators such as Sandals have promoted these programmes very successfully to the US and European markets. The concept later moved downmarket, however, and became popular in the more traditional European resorts, such as those of the Balearic Islands. Further expansion is seen as a direct threat to the livelihoods of many in the traditional coastal resorts.

Mass market tourism in its maturity

Mass market tourism to southern European resorts can be said to have entered a period of maturity by the 1980s. Although still showing steady growth, expansion was not on the scale found between the 1950s and 1970s. Short-haul travel was changing geographically, with tourists seeking new resorts and experiences. Portugal, having an Atlantic rather than a Mediterranean coast, wisely kept an upmarket image for its developments in the Algarve, while the Canaries, being within the crucial four hours' flying time from northern European airports, were the closest destinations to offer guaranteed warm winter sunshine and prospered from their year-round appeal. Other rather more exotic destinations attracted the upmarket winter holidaymaker. Tunisia, Morocco, Egypt and Israel pitched for the medium-haul beach markets. As prices rose in the traditional resorts, tourists moved on to cheaper, and less developed, destinations still close at hand. Turkey – seen as cheap, uncontested and mildly exotic – boomed in the 1980s, proving an attractive alternative to Greece. The then Yugoslavian Adriatic Coast provided charming architecture and cultural attractions in its seaside resorts, although good sandy beaches were missing. Malta had always had an appeal with the more conservative British tourist, but Crete and Cyprus began to attract larger numbers (especially following the war in Lebanon). Spain woke up to the despoliation of its resorts and made efforts to upgrade them, especially on the island of Majorca and in popular coastal towns such as Torremolinos.

By the end of the century, it was becoming clear that seaside tourism was moving in a new direction. Visitors were no longer willing simply to lie on a beach; they sought activities and adventure. For the young, this meant action, from sports to bungee jumping and discos. Taking over popular resorts on Ibiza and in Greece, they encouraged the family holiday market to move on. For the older tourist, it meant more excursions inland to cultural sites and attractive villages.

The long-haul market was changing, too. Attempts to sell some long-haul destinations as if they were merely extensions of the Mediterranean sunshine holidays failed to take into account the misunderstandings that could occur between hosts and guests, first in the Gambia, then in the Dominican Republic. Cruising, dormant for so long, suddenly found a new lease of life. Long-haul beach holidays in Kenya and Thailand, marketed at costs competitive with those in Europe, attracted Western tourists.

The American and northern European markets were joined by a rising flow of tourists from other parts of the world. The Asian market has become a leading source of business for the travel industry – in the West as well as throughout Australasia. The flow of Japanese tourists to Australia is noteworthy. Travel times to Australia are shorter than those to Europe and, equally importantly, because the travel is largely within the same longitude, there is no time change or jet lag to face. With typically only eight days of holiday, avoidance of jet lag becomes an attractive bonus for the Japanese market and makes Australia doubly attractive. Absence of jet lag is also helping to accelerate tourism to South Africa from the European nations, although uncertainty over crime and the country's political future remains.

Destinations in the Pacific began to attract Europeans in significant numbers, just as they have long attracted the Japanese and Australian markets. A large proportion of these visitors, however, were using the Pacific islands as stopover points for a night or two rather than a holiday base. The impact of technology can be seen when, for the first time, aircraft became capable of flying direct between the west coast of the USA and Australia with the introduction of the Boeing 747-400SP aircraft. Tahiti, slightly off the direct route between these continents and long established as an attractive stopover point but expensive for longer holidays, immediately suffered a sharp decline in visitors as the airlines concentrated their promotion efforts on direct non-stop services between Los Angeles and Sydney or Auckland.

The influence of information technology

The development of technology that can manage the reservation information held by tour operators, airlines and hotels has had a significant influence on the operations of such companies. Computer systems that can hold and process large amounts of data have become a key business tool for many tourism companies.

The 1970s saw the introduction of computer reservation systems (CRS) by airlines. Such systems provided them with the capability of tracking seat pricing and availability on their ever-expanding routes and schedules. By the 1980s, those systems were being installed in travel agencies, too, as the airlines realized that the agents could enter the data for the bookings, thus making them more productive for the airline. The most prominent CRSs (now known as global distribution systems (GDSs) used within the airline distribution systems) are Amadeus, Sabre, Galileo and Worldspan (the latter two merging in 2007), while regional systems also exist (such as Axess, based in Japan, and Abacus, which serves the Asia Pacific region). Often, however, the regional GDSs have links with the 'big four' GDSs. The 1990s saw the introduction and rapid growth of the Internet, allowing business to customer (B2C) systems to be developed alongside business to business (B2B) systems provided by GDS. This was coupled with the development of mass produced personal computers.

The affordability of computers and the penetration of the Internet, including the availability of broadband access, have ensured that more customers than ever before can now search for information about holiday destinations, compare travel companies (and user reviews) as well as reserve travel products online. The growth of online booking was partially fuelled by the budget airlines offering cheaper rates for online reservations, but was also encouraged by customers seeing this method of booking their travel as more convenient. The numbers of people booking their travel online has often been suggested as a threat to travel agents, but, while in some countries the high street travel agents may have declined, online travel agencies are prospering.

Furthermore, experienced travellers are prepared to book separate elements of their travel online, either direct with providers or though an intermediary, often using price comparison websites to explore the range of products open to them. Coupled with the expectation that they can book their travel online, many customers also expect short response times. They expect to have an accurate picture of the availability of their chosen product and that they will receive almost immediate confirmation of their booking, usually via e-mail. E-mail correspondence – to address questions either prior to or post booking – must therefore be dealt with quickly, usually within hours, as customers are rarely prepared to wait days for a response.

The introduction of the Internet has also led to adaptations being made to business practices. As the budget airlines encouraged booking online, customers became more comfortable with the idea of making their own reservations, which significantly impacted on the chain of distribution. Some scheduled airlines saw opportunities to sell seats direct to the customer, in the process becoming less reliant on travel agents (and, consequently, reducing levels of commission payments). More recently, travel agents have fought back, trying to make themselves indispensible to customers by offering a specialized service, creating holidays from separately selected elements, rather than offering standard packages. A further development has been the introduction of online travel intermediaries, who act as a convenient outlet for last-minute sales.

Database and Web technology has now developed to a point where companies can tailor the information they provide to customers, adjusting the Web page content according to the customer profile (determined overtly or covertly through methods such as tracking sites visited or prior bookings). Such adaptability can enhance sales by more closely matching customer needs to relevant product offers. This can also help to develop customer loyalty to particular websites.

Search engines can be an important factor for both travel companies and holiday destinations. While there are several search engines that people use to track down information, customers rarely move beyond the first few pages of results. Therefore, achieving a high ranking for key search terms can be important in ensuring that customers reach their website.

Destinations use advanced technology that allows them to offer customers detailed information about the locality, as well as providing an accommodation reservation system. Such destination management systems can help to provide a coherent link between the many small companies operating at a destination, as well as feeding information to other websites, thus further extending the marketing reach for the destination.

Back office systems have also been enhanced by the affordability of computer systems, allowing travel businesses to develop databases of customer records, which are used to enhance their marketing activities, as well as financial accounts systems and sales records. The convenience of storing customer details and sales data means that business decisions can be made that are based on analysis of this information – especially useful if there are plans to invest in activities such as new marketing campaigns.

Finally, we need to consider the impact of both wi-fi and mobile technology. Wi-fi technology has allowed many travel businesses to provide customers with convenient access to the Internet. In the past, businesses such as hotels would have charged customers to use Internet systems as they had to invest in installing network cables throughout the building. The minimal costs of installing wi-fi systems, however, as well as the wider availability of wi-fi zones in coffee shops, airports and other areas, has led to customers expecting access to the Internet as standard (and often for minimal or no charge).

Mobile technology is also increasing access to the Internet, as more phones are WAP-enabled and as the cost of accessing websites is seen to be more affordable. This allows customers to access the Web while on the move. Furthermore, the development of text messaging now allows travel companies to send booking confirmations or travel updates to a customer's mobile phone. This area of technology holds perhaps the greatest potential for changing the way travel companies interact with their customers.

Further reading

Bray, R. and Raitz, V. (2001) *Flight to the Sun: The story of the holiday revolution*, Continuum.

Brodie, A., Sargent, A. and Winterby, G. (2005) *Seaside Holidays in the Past*, English Heritage.

Franco, V. (1972) *Club Méditerranée*, Shepheard-Walwyn.

Grant, G. (1996) *Waikiki Yesteryear*, Mutual Publishing.

Löfgren, O. (1999) *On Holiday: A history of vacationing*, University of California Press.

Questions and discussion points

1. In 1984, McIntosh and Goeldner, in their classic text *Tourism Principles, Practices, Philosophies*, made a number of predictions about the future of the travel business by 2009, among which were the following:

   - red tape problems in travel would be largely eliminated
   - fast and comfortable room-to-room service would be available
   - all data of interest, and all reservations, would be made by instantaneous home video
   - consistent travel planning by weather, weeks ahead; resorts would enjoy a controlled environment
   - tourist pollution would recede as a controversial issue, largely controlled by local option and improved management
   - real-time pictures would be available from point-of-destination agencies
   - tourism and leisure would stabilize, but options would be growing, with diverse specialized tourism; extensive worldwide travel, with some space travel available
   - a typical working week would be no longer than 20 hours
   - business travel would be partly or largely superseded by new telecommunications
   - third-generation supersonic aircraft would be in operation, with many various and big jets, guided surface transport with rail services operating between 200 and 400 mph and cars with auto control operating at 100 to 200 mph.

   Now that this milestone has been reached, consider the extent to which these predictions have been fulfilled. Are those currently unfulfilled likely to come to pass within the next few years? What reasons would you give for the failure of the authors to accurately predict events at the end of the first decade of the twenty-first century?

2. The first package tours were to Corsica, a destination that has failed to fulfil its early potential and now caters largely for independent tourists or modest numbers of package holidaymakers. Suggest possible reasons for Corsica's failure to develop as a major resort destination in the manner of, for example, the Balearic Islands.

3. Offer possible explanations for the resurgence of cruising in the 1980s and the reasons for its limited appeal in the preceding decades. What lessons are to be learned from the failure of shipping managers to adapt their products to the needs of the time?

4. Critically evaluate the potential benefits and drawbacks of the popular 'taster' tours that have introduced so many North Americans to Europe.

5. With the present free currency market in Europe, it is no longer possible for a European government to restrict foreign travel as a means of aiding the balance of payments. What other steps can a government take to improve the tourism balance?

Tasks

1. Using the example of any all-inclusive holiday resort or destination known to you, draw up plans to ensure that the tourism you are attracting can be made more sustainable, both environmentally and socioculturally.

2. Prepare a talk on where you think the travel industry is going in the face of changing economic circumstances. What sectors of the industry will benefit and which will face serious challenge over the next few years? Identifying any one sector, examine how companies operating in it can best respond to the challenges faced by a faltering economy.

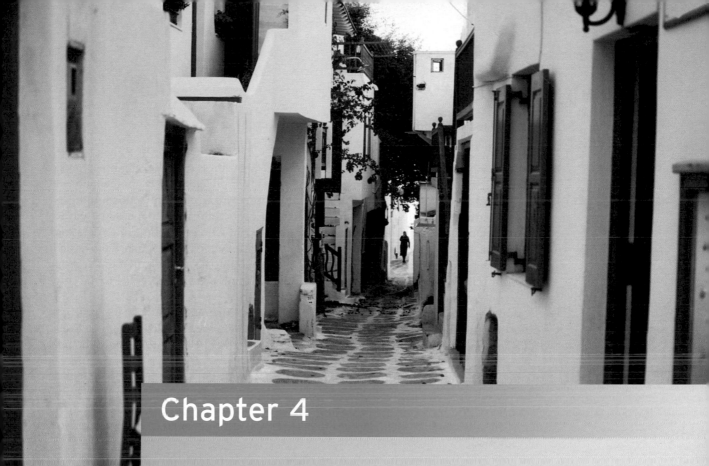

Chapter 4

The demand for tourism

Learning outcomes

After studying this chapter, you should be able to:

- distinguish between motivating and facilitating factors

- understand the nature of the psychological and sociological demands for tourism

- recognize how the product influences consumer demand

- be aware of some common theories of consumer behaviour, such as decisionmaking and risk avoidance

- be aware of the factors influencing demand and how demand is changing in the twenty-first century.

Introduction

> Of all noxious animals, the most noxious is a tourist.

Reverend Francis Kilvert, *Kilvert's Diary: 1870–1879*

An understanding of why people buy the holidays or business trips they do, how they go about selecting their holidays, why one company is given preference over another and why tourists choose to travel when they do is vital to those who work in the tourism industry. Yet, curiously, we still know relatively little about tourist **motivation** and, although we gather numerous statistics that reveal a great deal about who goes where, the *reasons* for those choices are not well understood. This is not entirely the result of a lack of research because many large companies do commission research into the behaviour of their clients, but, as this is 'inhouse' research and the information it reveals is confidential to the company concerned, it seldom becomes public knowledge.

Motivation and purpose are closely related and, earlier in this book, the principal purposes for which tourists travel were identified. These were classified into three broad categories: business travel, leisure travel and miscellaneous travel, which would include, inter alia, travel for one's health and religious travel. However, simply labelling tourists in this way only helps us to understand their *general* motivations for travelling – it tells us little about their specific motivation or the needs and wants that underpin it and how those needs and wants are met and satisfied. It is the purpose of this chapter to explain the terms and the complex interrelationship between the factors that go to shape the choices of trips made by tourists of all kinds.

The tourist's needs and wants

If we ask prospective tourists why they want to travel to a particular destination, they will offer a variety of reasons, such as 'It's somewhere that I've always wanted to visit' or 'Some friends recommended it very highly' or 'It's always good weather at that time of the year and the beaches are wonderful. We've been going there regularly for the past few years'. Interesting as these views may be, they actually throw very little light on the real motivations of the tourists concerned because they have not helped to identify their *needs* and *wants*.

People often talk about their 'needing' a holiday, just as they might say they need a new carpet, a new dress or a better lawnmower. Are they, in fact, expressing a need or a want? 'Need' suggests that the products we are asking for are necessities for our daily life, but this is clearly seldom the case with these products. We are merely expressing a desire for more goods and services, a symptom of the consumer-orientated society in which we live.

Occasionally, a holiday (or at least a break from routine) can become a genuine need, as is the case with those in highly stressful occupations where a breakdown can occur if there is no relief from that stress. Families and individuals suffering from severe deprivation may also need a holiday, as is shown by the work of charitable organizations such as the Family Holiday Association.

Let us start by examining what it is we mean by a need.

People have certain physiological needs and satisfying them is essential to their survival: they need to eat, drink, sleep, keep warm and reproduce – all needs that are also essential to the survival of the human race. Beyond those needs, we also have psychological needs that are important for our well-being, such as the need to love and be loved, for friendship and to value ourselves as human beings and have others value and respect us. Many people believe that we also have inherently within us the need to master our environment and understand the nature of the society in which we live. Abraham Maslow conveniently grouped these needs into a hierarchy (see Figure 4.1), suggesting that the more fundamental needs have to be satisfied before we seek to satisfy the higher-level ones.

Example

Wants versus needs

A London hotel undertook research in 2004 to find out the specific requirements of its clientele of various nationalities. Some of these wants proved to be quite detailed. German tourists preferred mixer taps rather than individual hot and cold taps in their bathrooms; Americans wanted fixed-head, not hand-held, showers. Italian guests asked for menus that would be available around the clock, including pizza, while Japanese visitors were pleased if they could be given tabi (socks) with their bathrobes. All of these things are desirable for the individuals concerned, but it would be unlikely that tourists expressing these preferences would refrain from travel if they were unavailable.

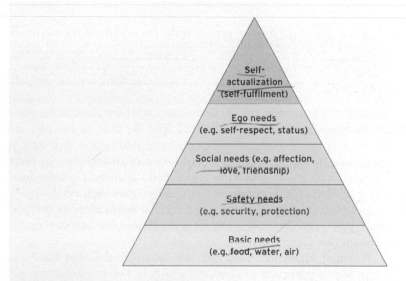

Figure 4.1 Maslow's hierarchy of needs.
(From A. Maslow, Motivation and Personality, 1987. Reprinted by permission of Pearson Education, Inc.)

The difficulty with exploring these needs is that many people may actually be quite unaware of their needs or how to go about satisfying them. Others will be reluctant to reveal their real needs. For example, few people would be willing openly to admit that they travel to a particular destination to impress their neighbours, although their desire for status within the neighbourhood may well be a factor in their choice of holiday and destination.

Some of our needs are innate – that is, they are based on factors inherited by us at birth. These include biological and instinctive needs such as eating and drinking. However, we also inherit genetic traits from our parents that are reflected in certain needs and wants. Other needs and wants arise out of the environment in which we are raised and are therefore learned, or, socially engineered. The early death of parents or their lack of overt affection being shown towards us may cause us to have stronger needs for bonding and friendship with others, for example. As we come to know more about genomes, following

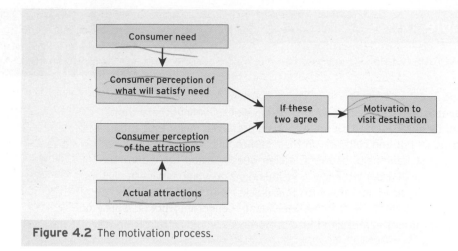

Figure 4.2 The motivation process.

the discovery of the human genetic code, DNA, early in the twenty-first century, so we are coming to appreciate that our genetic differences are, in fact, very slight, indicating that most of our needs and wants are conditioned by our environment.

Travel may be one of several means of satisfying a need and, although needs are felt by us, we do not necessarily express them and we may not recognize how travel actually satisfies our particular needs. Consequently, if we re-examine the answers given earlier to questions asking why we travel, it may be that, in the case where respondents are confirming the desire to return to the same destination year after year, they are actually expressing the desire to satisfy a need for safety and security, by returning to the tried and tested. The means by which this is achieved – namely, a holiday in a resort well known to them – reflects the respondents' 'want' rather than their need.

The process of translating a need into the motivation to visit a specific destination or undertake a specific activity is quite complex and can best be demonstrated by means of a diagram (see Figure 4.2).

Potential consumers must not only recognize that they have a need, but also understand how a particular product will satisfy it. Every consumer is different and what one consumer sees as the ideal solution to the need another will reject. A holiday in Benidorm that Mr A thinks will be something akin to paradise would be for Mr B an endurance test; he might prefer a walk in the Pennines for a week, which Mr A would find a tortuous experience. It is important that we all recognize each person's perception of a holiday, like any other product, is affected by experiences and attitudes. Only if the perception of the need and the attraction match will a consumer be motivated to buy the product. The job of the skilled travel agent is to subtly question clients in order to learn about their interests and desires and find the products to match them. Those selling more expensive holidays may need to convince their clients that the experience on offer is worth paying the difference over and above what they had expected for an ordinary holiday.

General and specific motivation

We have established that motivation arises out of the felt wants or needs of the individual. We can now go on to explain that motivation is expressed in two distinct forms. These are known as **specific motivation** and **general motivation**.

General motivation is aimed at achieving a broad objective, such as getting away from the routine and stress of the workplace in order to enjoy different surroundings and a healthy environment. Here, health and relief from stress are the broad motives reflecting the needs discussed above. If the tourist decides to take a holiday in the Swiss Alps, to take walks in fresh mountain air and enjoy varied scenery, good food and total relaxation, these are all specific objectives, reflecting the means by which their needs will be met. Marketing professionals sometimes refer to these two forms of motivation as 'push' factors and 'pull' factors – that is, the tourist is being pushed into a holiday by the need to get away from their everyday environment, but other factors may be at work to pull, or encourage, them to travel to a specific destination. For this reason, marketing staff realize that they will have to undertake their promotion at two distinct levels, persuading the consumer of the need to take a holiday and also to show those consumers that the particular holiday or destination the organization is promoting will best satisfy that need.

If we look at the varied forms of leisure tourism that have become a part of our lives in the past few years, we will quickly see that certain types of holiday have become popular because they best meet common, and basic, needs. The 'sun, sea and sand' holiday that caters to the mass market is essentially a passive form of leisure entailing nothing more stressful than a relaxing time on the beach, enjoyment of the perceived healthy benefits of sunshine and saltwater bathing, good food and reasonably priced alcohol (another relaxant). The tendency among certain groups of tourists abroad to drink too much and misbehave generally is, again, a reflection of need, even if the result is one that we have come to deplore because of its impact on others. Such tourists seek to escape from the constraints of their usual environment and enjoy an opportunity to 'let their hair down', perhaps in a more tolerant environment than they would find in their own home country.

Those travelling on their own might also seek opportunities to meet other people or even find romance (thus meeting the need to belong and other social needs).

In the case of families, parents can simultaneously satisfy their own needs while also providing a healthy and enjoyable time for their children on the beach. Parents may also be given the chance to get away and be on their own while their children are being cared for by skilled childminders.

What is provided, therefore, is a **bundle of benefits** and the more a particular package holiday, or a particular destination, can be shown to provide the range of benefits sought, the more attractive that holiday will appear to the tourist compared with other holidays on offer. The bundle will be made up of benefits that are designed to cater to both general and specific needs and wants.

Today, there is a growing demand for holidays that offer more strenuous activities than are to be found in the traditional 'three S' holidays, such as trekking, mountaineering or yachting (see Figure 4.3). These appeal to those whose basic needs for relaxation have already been satisfied (they may have desk-bound jobs that involve mental, rather than physical, strain) and they are now seeking something more challenging. Strenuous activities provide opportunities for people to test their physical abilities and, while this may involve no more than a search for health by other means, there may also be a search for competence – another need identified by Maslow. Because such holidays are purchased by like-minded people, often in small groups, they can also help to meet other ego and social needs.

The growing confidence and physical fitness of many tourists (and not just the young!) has put 'extreme sports' on the agenda of many holiday companies. Formerly limited to winter sports such as skiing and snowboarding and summer white water rafting, adventure holidays now embrace off-piste skiing, snowboarding, windsurfing, BMX biking, paragliding, heli-skiing, kitesurfing, kitebuggying, landboarding and base jumping (leaping off tall buildings with parachutes – seldom available as a legal activity!) – the range of activities increasing each year.

Figure 4.3 The need for adventure and the desire to 'get away from it all' may have inspired these climbers to reach the top of Mount Snowdon, North Wales.
(Photo by Chris Holloway.)

Example

Extreme sports

Destinations that offer the appropriate topography for extreme sports and have developed organized programmes to support them, include:

- the coast of Kauai, Hawaii (cliffside kayaking)
- Bolivia and Morzine in the French Alps (downhill cycling)
- Shaggy Ridge Mountains, Papua, New Guinea (jungle hacking)
- Yucatan, Mexico (underwater cave diving)
- Utah Canyonlands, USA, and the Himalayas (trekking).

It must also be recognized that many tourists are constantly seeking novelty and different experiences. However satisfied they might be with one holiday, they will be unlikely to return to the same destination. Instead, they will be forever seeking something more challenging, more exciting, more remote. This is, in part, an explanation for the growing demand for long-haul holidays. For other people, such increasingly exotic tourist trips satisfy the search for status.

Example

The shock of the new

My holiday wanderlust (which, fortunately, my husband shares) is by no means a symptom of dissatisfaction. It's not as if we are restlessly searching for somewhere better than the year before. In fact, some of the places we've visited over the past couple of decades are close to perfection . . . for us, it is their very novelty which makes them so appealing.

Mary Ann Sieghart, writing in *The Times*, 12 August 2004.

The author of the quote given in the Example was reacting to news of research that revealed almost 50 per cent of Italian tourists choose to return to the same hotel at the same destination for their annual holidays over a period of at least 10 years.

The need for self-actualization can be met in a number of ways. At its simplest, the desire to 'commune with nature' is a common to many tourists and can be achieved through scenic trips by coach, fly–drive packages in which routes are identified and stopping-off points recommended for their scenic beauty, cycling tours or hiking holidays. Each of these forms of holiday will find its own market in terms of the degree of rural authenticity sought, but all, to some extent, meet the needs of the market as a whole.

Alternatively, the quest for knowledge can be met by tours such as those offered to cultural centres in Europe, often accompanied by experts in a particular field (see Figure 4.4). Self-actualization can be aided through packages offering painting or other artistic 'do it yourself' holidays. Some tourists seek more meaningful experiences through contact with foreign residents, where they can come to understand the local cultures. This process can be facilitated through careful packaging of programmes arranged by organizers, who build

Figure 4.4 The drive for self-actualization will have led these culture enthusiasts to trek to Nobel prize-winning novelist Thomas Mann's isolated house on the dune-lined coast of Lithuania. *(Photo by Chris Holloway.)*

up suitable contacts among local residents at the destination. Local guides, too, can act as 'culture brokers', overcoming language barriers or helping to explain local culture to inquisitive tourists, while at the same time reassuring more nervous travellers.

As people come to travel more and as they become more sophisticated or better educated, so their higher-level needs will predominate in their motivation to go on a particular holiday. Companies in the business of tourism must always recognize this and take it into account when planning new programmes or new attractions for tourists.

Segmenting the tourism market

So far in this chapter we have looked at the individual factors that give rise to our various needs and wants. In the tourism industry, those responsible for marketing destinations or holidays will be concerned with both individual and **aggregate**, or total, demand for a holiday or destination. For this purpose, it is convenient to categorize and segment demand according to four distinct sets of variables – namely, geographic, demographic, psychographic and behavioural. These categories are examined in more detail in a companion book to this text,[1] but will be briefly summarized here.

Geographic variables are determined according to the areas in which consumers live. These can be broadly defined by continent (North America, Latin America, Asia, Africa, for example), country (such as Britain, France, Japan, Australia) or according to region, either broadly (for instance, Nordic, Mediterranean, Baltic States, US mid-western States) or more narrowly (say, the Tyrol, Alsace-Lorraine, North Rhine-Westphalia, UK Home Counties). It is appropriate to divide areas in this way only where it is clear that the resident populations' buying or behaviour patterns reflect commonalities and differ from those of other areas in ways that are significant to the industry.

The most obvious point to make here is that chosen travel destinations will be the outcome of factors such as distance, convenience and how much it costs to reach the destination. For example, Europeans will find it more convenient, and probably cheaper, to holiday in the Mediterranean, North Americans in the Caribbean, Australians in Pacific islands such as Fiji and Bali. Differing climates in the generating countries will also result in other variations in the kinds of travel demand.

Demographic variables include such characteristics as age, gender, family composition, stage in lifecycle, income, occupation, education and ethnic origin. The type of holiday chosen is likely to differ greatly between 20–30-year-olds and 50–60-year-olds, to take one example. *Changing* patterns will also interest marketers – declining populations, increasing numbers of elderly consumers, greater numbers of individuals living alone and taking holidays alone or increases in disposable income among some age groups – all these factors will affect the ways in which holidays are marketed.

Significant factors influencing demand in the British market in recent years have been the rise in wealth among older sectors of the public, as their parents – the first generation to have become property owners on a major scale – died, leaving significant inheritances to their offspring. This, and the general rise in living standards, fuelled demand for second homes in both Britain and abroad, changing leisure patterns and encouraging the growth of low-cost airlines to service the market's needs.

Demographic distinctions are among the most easily researched variables and, consequently, provide readily available data. Market differentiation by occupation is one of the commonest ways in which consumers are categorized – not least because it offers the prospect of a ready indication of relative disposable incomes. Occupation also remains a principal criterion for identifying social class.

The best-known socio-economic segmentation in Britain was introduced after World War II and is still widely used in market research exercises, including those conducted under the aegis of the National Readership Surveys (NRS). Using this tool, the consumer

- A   Higher managerial, administrative or professional
- B   Middle managerial, administrative or professional
- C1   Supervisory or clerical, junior managerial
- C2   Skilled manual workers
- D   Semi- and unskilled manual workers
- E   Those at lowest levels of subsistence

Figure 4.5 Social classification by employment, previous version.

Example

The rising demand for holidays among older consumers

The increasing size of the ageing population in the developed countries is of particular interest to those marketing tourism as holidaymakers within this group now form a growing proportion of the total market. In Britain, the over-50s now take eight or nine holidays or short breaks a year, compared with just one or two in 1957. The length of time enjoyed in retirement by UK-resident males has risen from 7.6 years to 15 years over this same period, while female retirement has risen from 13.9 years to 22 years. As a result, pensioners are worth over £3 billion per annum to the UK travel industry.[2]

market is broken down into six categories on the basis of the occupation of the head of household (see Figure 4.5).

The ABC1 grouping – still in common use in the media – has been of key interest to the travel industry, which has identified this segment as major travellers, having both leisure and the funds to purchase high-end holidays. Of these groups, around 16 per cent of the UK population are younger consumers, without families, and a further 13 per cent have children under 16; 12 per cent are 'empty nesters' in the so-called 'third age', while a further 9 per cent are retired. This attempt to distinguish between market segments on the grounds of social class arising from occupation, however, is open to the criticism of being increasingly anachronistic as society becomes more egalitarian. Indeed patterns of purchasing or behaviour are now less clearly determined by social class, although the categories may well offer some indication of the *ability* to purchase, on the grounds of income. Also, the proportion of those travelling on holiday each year is, as one would expect, far higher among the higher income brackets than among the lower. In an era where plumbers and electricians may earn up to twice as much as university lecturers, however, new forms of guidance are necessary to meet the needs of the market researchers.

Various attempts have been made in recent years to overcome this stigmatic characterization by occupation. A new system of social classification was introduced in Britain in 2001 (see Table 4.1). However, the new classification leaves some 29 per cent unaccounted for, including the long-term unemployed, students and those never employed. It also perpetuates the belief that behaviour can be ascribed largely to occupation, which, given the changes taking place in twenty-first-century society, can be a misleading fallacy.

Nevertheless, categorizing demand for a company's products by social class can be of some value in helping to determine advertising spend and the media to be employed. Similarly, breaking down demand by age group is also helpful – even vital if the aim is, say, to develop holidays that particularly appeal to young people.

Market research in recent years has been transformed by the efforts of researchers to bring together both geography and demography, through a process of pinpoint **geo-demographic** analysis. This is based on combining census data and postcodes to reveal that fine-tuning

Table 4.1 Social classification by employment, new version.

Class	% of UK population	Occupations	Examples include
1	8	large employers, higher managerial and professional	doctors, clergy
2	19	lower managerial and professional	writers, artists
3	9	intermediate managerial and professional	medical, legal secretaries
4	7	small employers and own account workers	hotel, restaurant managers
5	7	lower supervisory and technical	plumbers, mechanics
6	12	semi-routine occupations	sales assistants, chefs
7	9	routine occupations	waiters, couriers

by region can produce a picture of spend and behaviour that will be common to a large proportion of the population of that region. Among the best known of such systems is ACORN (A Classification of Residential Neighbourhoods), operated by CACI Limited, which takes into account such factors as age, income, lifestyle and family structure (see Table 4.2). However, even with the sophistication and refinement of this approach, this will not be sufficient to explain all of the variation in choice between different tourist products, and for this we must look to consumer psychographics for further enlightenment.

Psychographic variables are those that allow us to note the impact of aspirational and lifestyle characteristics on consumer behaviour, and the ACORN model outlined in Table 4.2 goes some way towards incorporating these into its classification of consumers. Beyond simple demographic distinctions, as buyers, we are heavily influenced by those

Table 4.2 Social classification by neighbourhood.

Aspiration	Composition	% of population
A Thriving	Wealthy achievers, based in suburbs	15
	Affluent greys	2.1
	Prosperous pensioners	2.6
B Expanding	Affluent executives, family areas	4.1
	Well-off workers, family areas	8.0
C Rising	Affluent urbanites	2.5
	Prosperous professionals, metropolitan	2.3
	Better-off executives, inner cities	3.8
D Settling	Comfortable middle-agers, mature In homeowning areas	13.6
	Skilled workers in homeowning areas	10.7
E Aspiring	New homeowners, mature communities	9.6
	White-collar workers, better-off multi-ethnic areas	4.0
F Striving	Older residents in less prosperous areas	3.6
	Council estates, better-off homes	10.8
	Council estates in areas of high unemployment	2.8
	Council estates in areas of greatest hardship	2.3
	Multi-ethnic low-income areas	2.0

Source: CACI Limited, 2002.

immediately surrounding us (our so-called **peer groups**), as well as those we most admire and wish to emulate (our **reference groups**). In the former case, while we may develop choices favoured by our parents and teachers in early life, as we become more independent, we prefer to emulate the behaviour of our immediate friends, fellow students, colleagues at work or others with whom we come into regular close contact. In the latter case, the influence of celebrities is becoming paramount, as the holiday choices and behaviour of pop idols, cinema and TV 'personalities' and those in the media and modelling worlds come increasingly to influence buying patterns, particularly those of younger consumers.

In short, the ways in which significant others live and spend their leisure hours exerts a strong influence on holiday consumerism among all classes of client. Some niche cruise companies have marketed themselves for many years on the basis that their passengers will mingle with the great and the good, and the Caribbean island of Mustique successfully promoted itself as an exclusive hideaway for the rich, largely because Princess Margaret had been a frequent visitor.

As members of society, we tend to follow the norms and values reflected in that society. We all like to feel that we are making our own decisions about products, but do not always realize how other people's tastes influence our own and what pressures there are on us to conform. When we claim that we are buying to 'please ourselves', what exactly is this 'self' that we are pleasing? We are, in fact, composed of many 'selves'. There is the self that we see ourselves as, often highly subjectively; the ideal self, how we would like to be; there is the self as we believe others see us and the self as we are actually seen by others. Yet, none of these can be construed as our real self – if, indeed, a real self can be said to exist outside of the way we interact with others. Readers will be aware that they put on different 'fronts' and act out different roles according to the company in which they find themselves, whether family, best friend, lover, employer. Do any of these relationships truly reflect our real self?

The importance attached to this theory of self, from the perspective of this text, is the way in which it affects those things that we buy and with which we surround ourselves. This means that, in the case of holidays, we will not always buy the kind of holiday we think we would most enjoy or even the one we feel we could best afford, but, instead, we might buy the holiday we feel will give us status with our friends and neighbours or reflect the kind of holiday we feel that 'persons in our position' should take. Advertisers will frequently use this knowledge to promote a destination as being suited to a particular kind of tourist and will perhaps go further, using as a model in their advertisements some well-known TV personality or film star who reflects the 'typical tourist at the destination', with whom we can then mentally associate ourselves.

In the same way, status becomes an important feature of business travel as business travellers are aware that they are representing their companies to business associates and must therefore create a favourable impression. As their companies usually accept this view and pay their bills, this is one of the reasons business travel generates more income per capita than does leisure travel.

Finally, **behavioural variables** allow us to segment markets according to their usage of the products. This is a much simpler concept and facts about consumer purchasing can be ascertained quite readily through market research. The frequency with which we purchase a product, the quantities we buy, where we choose to buy (from a travel agent or direct, using company websites, for example) and the sources from which we obtain information about products are of great interest to marketers, who, armed with this knowledge, will be able to shape their strategies more effectively in order to influence purchases. A key element in this is to know which benefits a consumer is looking for when they purchase a product. The motives for buying a lakes and mountains holiday, for example, can vary substantially. Some may be seeking solitude and scenic beauty, perhaps to recover from stress or to enjoy a painting or photography holiday; some will seek the social interaction of small hiking groups or evening chats in the bar of their hotel with like-minded guests; others will be looking for more active pastimes, such as waterskiing or mountaineering.

Only when the organization arranging the holiday knows which elements of the product appeal to their customers can a sale effectively take place.

Consumer processes

If all consumers responded in the same way to given stimuli, the lives of marketing managers would become much easier. Unfortunately it has to be recognized that, while research continues to shed more light on our complex behaviour, the triggers that lead to it are still poorly understood. We can make some generalizations, however, based on research to date that can assist our understanding of consumer processes and, in particular, those of decisionmaking. Marketing theorists have developed a number of models to explain these processes. Perhaps the best-known, as well as the simplest, model is known as AIDA (see Figure 4.6).

This model recognizes that marketing aims to move the consumer from a stage of unawareness – of either the product (such as a specific destination or resort) or the particular brand (such as an individual package tour company or a hotel) – through a number of stages, to a point where the consumer is persuaded to buy a particular product and brand. The first step in this process is to move the consumer from unawareness to awareness. This entails an understanding of the way in which the consumer learns about new products.

Anyone thinking about how they came to learn about a particular destination they have visited quickly recognizes how difficult it is to pinpoint all the influences – many of which they may not even be consciously aware of. Every day, consumers are faced with hundreds of new pieces of knowledge, including information about new products. If we are to retain any of this information, the first task of marketing is to ensure that we perceive it – that is, become conscious of it.

Perception is an important part of the learning process. It involves the selection and interpretation of the information that is presented to us. As we cannot possibly absorb all the messages with which we are faced each day, many are consciously or unconsciously 'screened out' from our memories. If we are favourably predisposed towards a particular product or message, there is clearly a greater likelihood that we will absorb information about it. So, for example, if your best friend has just returned from a holiday in the Cayman Islands and has enthusiastically talked to you about the trip, that may stimulate your interest. If you then spot a feature on the Cayman Islands on television, that may further arouse our interest, even if, up to the point when our friend mentioned the place, you had never even heard of it. If what you see in the television programme reinforces the image of the destination that you gained from your friend, you might be encouraged to seek further information on the destination, perhaps by searching the Web or contacting the tourist office representing the destination. At any point in this process, you might be put off by what you find – for instance, if you perceive the destination as being too far away, too expensive or too inaccessible for the length of time you are contemplating going away, you may search no further. If, however, the search process leads you to form a positive image of the destination, you may start mentally comparing it with others towards which you are favourably disposed.

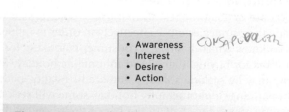

Figure 4.6 The AIDA model.

The process of making choices involves constant comparison, weighing up one destination against others, estimating the benefits and the drawbacks of each as a potential holiday destination. As this process goes on, three things are happening.

Image

First, we develop an **image** of the destination in question. That image may be a totally inaccurate one, if the information sources we use are uninformed or deliberately seek to distort the information they provide. We may then find that we become confused about the image itself. For example, in the early 1990s, the British media was full of exaggerated reports of muggings of tourists in the Miami area, while the destination itself continued to try to disseminate a positive image and the tour operators' brochures concentrated on selling the positive benefits of Miami with little reference to any potential dangers faced by tourists.

Images are built around the unique attributes that a destination can claim. The more these help to distinguish it from other similar destinations, the greater the attraction for the tourist. Those destinations that offer truly unique products, such as the Grand Canyon in the USA, the Great Wall of China or the pyramids in Egypt, have an inbuilt advantage, although, in time, the attraction of such destinations may be such that it becomes necessary to 'de-market' the site to avoid it becoming overly popular. In the early 1990s, the Egyptian Tourist Office also faced the problem of negative publicity, associated with attacks made on tourists by Islamic fundamentalists soon after a large influx of Western tourists, many of whom failed to conform to the norms of behaviour expected in an Islamic country. A major objective of tourist offices in developing countries is that of generating a long-term positive image of the destination in their advertising, to give it a competitive edge over its competitors.

Example

Stereotyping destination images

Destinations are frequently stereotyped, often saddled with outdated images that, nevertheless, remain effective forms of communication with potential visitors. Such images are still reinforced by the media as a form of shorthand for describing countries. Thus, the image of Britain for many foreigners remains that of bowler hats, red buses, black taxis, beefeaters and the Beatles; Africa is 'dark and mysterious', with associations of drum music and bare-breasted dancers more appropriate to 1930s Hollywood movies. The Caribbean is 'friendly and welcoming', with swaying palm trees and white beaches (often apparently devoid of humanity), while Japan offers a landscape of immaculate gardens, simpering geishas and cherry blossom. While such images may have been appropriate when first building the image of a country, today they insult the intelligence of the sophisticated traveller. Even the travel trade, however, persists in retaining these images – witness the dances, food and national costumes seldom encountered in real life, yet still on show at trade fairs such as the World Travel Market.

By contrast with those destinations offering unique attractions, many traditional seaside resorts, both in Britain and increasingly elsewhere, suffer from having very little to distinguish them from their competitors. The concept of the identikit destination as the popular choice for tourists is becoming outdated and simply offering good beaches, pleasant hotels and well-cooked food in an attractive climate is no longer enough in itself. In some way, an image must be *induced* by the tourist office to distance the resort from others. Then, for example, if changes in exchange rates or inflation rates work against the destination, it may still be seen as having sufficient 'added value' to attract and retain a loyal market.

Attitude

Second, we develop an **attitude** towards the destination. Several theorists suggest that an individual's lifestyle in general can best be measured by looking at their activities (or attitudes), interests and opinions – the so-called A–I–O model.

Attitude is a mix of our emotional feelings about the destination and our rational evaluation of its merits, both of which together will determine whether or not we consider it a possible venue for a holiday. It should be stressed at this point, however, that, while we may have a negative image of the destination, we may still retain a positive attitude towards going there because we have an interest in seeing some of its attractions or learning about its culture. This was often the case with travel to the Communist Bloc countries before the collapse of their political systems at the end of the 1980s and, similarly, notwithstanding the increasing strains in the early twenty-first century on relationships between Western nations and countries with large Islamic populations, interest in their tourist sites and cultures remains high. In fact, media coverage of some previously little known countries will have helped to expand curiosity about those countries and not purely on the grounds of 'dark tourism' (see Chapter 10).

Risk

Third, there is the issue of risk to consider when planning to take a trip.

All holidays involve some element of risk, whether in the form of illness, bad weather, being unable to get what we want if we delay booking, being uncertain about the product until we see it at first hand, its representing value for money. We ask ourselves what risks we would run if we went there, if there is a high likelihood of their occurrence, if the risks are avoidable and how significant the consequences would be.

Some tourists, of course, relish a degree of risk, as this gives an edge of excitement to the holiday, so the presence of risk is not in itself a barrier to tourism. Others, however, are risk averse and will studiously avoid risk wherever possible. Clearly, the significance of the risk will be a key factor. So, there will be much less concern about the risk of poor weather than there will be about the risk of crime. The risk averse will book early, may choose to return to the same resort and hotel they have visited in the past, knowing its reliability, book a package tour, rather than travel independently.

The American Hilton and Holiday Inn chain hotels have been eminently successful throughout the world by offering some certainty about standards in countries where Americans could feel at risk regarding 'foreign' food, poor plumbing or other inadequacies of a tour that are preventable if there is good forward planning. Travel businesses such as cruise lines, which offer a product with a reassuring lack of risk, can – and do – make this an important theme in their promotional campaigns.

Risk is also a factor in the methods chosen by customers to book their holidays. There is evidence that much of the continuing reluctance shown by some tourists to seek information and make bookings through Internet providers can be attributed, in part, to the lack of face-to-face contact with a trusted – and, hopefully, expert – travel agent and, in part, to the suspicion that information received through the Internet will be biased in favour of the information provider.

The extent to which risk is a product of personality is an issue that has been addressed by a number of tourism researchers, most notably Stanley Plog.[3] Essentially, Plog attempted to determine the relationship between introvert and extrovert personalities and holiday choice and his theories have been widely published in tourism texts (see Figure 4.7).

Plog's theory attempted to classify the population of the United States by distinguishing between those judged to be **allocentrics** – those seeking variety, self-confident, outgoing and experimental – and **psychocentrics** – those who tend to be more concerned with themselves and the small problems of life. The latter are often anxious and inclined to seek security. The theory would suggest that psychocentrics would be more inclined to return to resorts with which they are familiar, stay closer to home and use a package holiday for

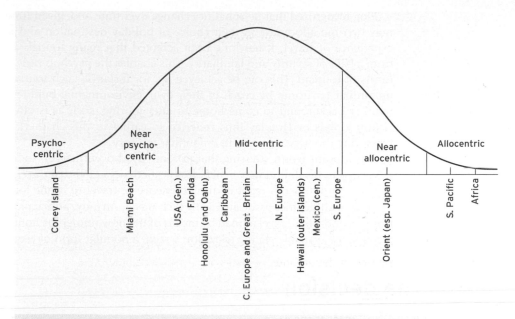

Figure 4.7 Personality and travel destination choices: the allocentric–psychocentric scale.

their travel arrangements. Allocentrics, by contrast, would be disposed to seek new experiences, in more exotic destinations, travelling independently.

Of course, these are polarized examples and, in practice, most holidaymakers are likely to fall somewhere between the extremes – **mid-centrics**.

Those tending towards the psychocentric were found by Plog to be more commonly from lower-income groups, but it is also the case that these groups are more constrained financially as to the kinds of holidays they can afford to take. Whether or not Plog's findings are similarly applicable to European markets is by no means certain.

Example

Tourism to the Balearics

Unpublished research conducted during the 1980s found that British tourists visiting the Balearic Islands for the first time were, in many cases, those who had tended to spend their holidays previously in UK domestic resorts. Although by that date Majorca was well established as a popular venue for many British tourists, it was also becoming seen by others as a safe place to enjoy a first holiday abroad. It was observed that the psychocentrics who were holidaying there tended to spend their time at or close to their hotels, venturing further afield only on organized excursions. They also restricted their eating to the hotel restaurant, where they would order only familiar food.

Overcoming initial timidity, these tourists would return, often to the same hotel, for holidays in subsequent years. After two or three such visits, they became bolder, seeking alternative hotels and even hiring cars to tour lesser-known regions of the island (although it took a while for them to adjust to driving on the right). They chose to widen their choice of eating places, too, and began to experiment with their diet by selecting typically Spanish recipes.

Source: Chris Holloway, unpublished research, 1981–1983.

Plog recognized that personalities change over time and, given time, the psychocentric may become allocentric in their choice of holiday destination and activity as they gain experience of travel. It has long been accepted that many tourists actually seek novelty from a base of security and familiarity. This enables the psychocentric to enjoy more exotic forms of tourism. This can be achieved by, for instance, such tourists travelling through unfamiliar territories by coach in their own 'environmental bubble'. The provision of a familiar background to come home to after touring, such as is offered to Americans at Hilton Hotels or Holiday Inns (referred to earlier in this chapter), is a clear means of reassuring the nervous while in unfamiliar territory.

It is a point worth stressing that extreme pyschocentrics (or, indeed, those unable to travel due to disability) may benefit from experiences of virtual travel. Increasingly sophisticated computers can replicate the experience of travel to exotic locations with none of the risk or difficulties associated with such travel. Already, armchair travellers can benefit from second-hand travel abroad by means of the now numerous holiday programmes and travelogues available via the television screen, a popular form of escapism.

Making the decision

The process of sorting through the various holidays on offer and determining which is the best for you is inevitably complex and individual personality traits will determine how the eventual decision is made. Some people undertake a process of **extensive problem solving**, in which information is sought about a wide range of products, each of which is evaluated and compared with similar products.

Other consumers will not have the patience to explore a wide variety of choices, so will deliberately restrict their options, with the aim of **satisficing** rather than trying to guarantee that they buy the best possible product. This is known as **limited problem solving** and has the benefit of saving time.

Many consumers engage in **routinized response behaviour**, in which choices change relatively little over time. This is a common pattern among brand-loyal consumers, for example. Also some holidaymakers who have been content with a particular company or destination in the past may opt for the same experience again.

Finally, some consumers will buy on **impulse**. While this is more typical of products costing little, it is by no means unknown among holiday purchasers and is, in fact, a pattern of behaviour that is becoming increasingly prevalent – to the dismay of the operators, who then have less scope for forward planning and reduced opportunities to gain from investing deposits in the short term. Impulse purchasing is a valuable trait, though, where 'distressed stock' needs to be cleared at short notice and can be stimulated by late availability offers particularly.

Fashion and taste

Many tourism enterprises – and, above all, destinations – suffer from the effects of changing consumer tastes as fashion changes and 'opinion leaders' find new activities to pursue, new resorts to champion. It is difficult to define exactly what it is that causes a particular resort to lose its popularity with the public, although, clearly, if the resources it offers are allowed to deteriorate, the market will soon drift away to seek better value for money elsewhere.

Sometimes, however, it is no more than shifts in fashion that cause numbers of tourists to fall off. This is most likely to be the case where the site was deemed a fashionable attraction in the first place. This happened, for example, to Bath after its outstanding success as a resort in the eighteenth century and the celebrity culture of the late twentieth and early twenty-first centuries has reinforced this trend. Resorts in the Mediterranean, such as St Tropez (fashionable from the 1960s and 1970s onwards after film star Brigitte Bardot chose to reside there) and the Costa Smeralda in Sardinia (developed by the Aga Khan and attracting a number of well-known Hollywood stars) became popular venues for the star-struck. Similarly, increasing wealth in this century, compounded by the availability of relatively cheap flights, have tended to mean that the celebrity resorts are further afield. In the Caribbean, Barbados – in particular the Sandy Lane Hotel – attracts many celebrities and others who seek to bask in their light. Travel journalists make a point in their articles of identifying celebrities who have been spotted holidaying at certain resorts, further boosting demand.

It remains the case, however, that all products, including tourism, will experience a life-cycle of growth, maturity, saturation and eventual decline if no action is taken to arrest it (see Figure 4.8). Generally, this will entail some form of innovation or other investment helping to revitalize the product.

In the earlier historical chapters we looked at some of the ways in which tourism has changed over time due to changes in consumer behaviour. Fashion, of course, is one element critical to this process. In recent years, however, there has also been a swing towards improving health and well-being, affecting the types of holiday and activities chosen. As a direct consequence, most large hotel chains now incorporate a health centre as an element in their facilities.

Physical fitness already plays a larger role in our lives than in the past and is directly responsible for the growth in activity holidays. Tour operators have learned to cater for this changing demand pattern. Greater concern about what we eat has led to better-quality food, better preparation, better hygiene and cuisine that caters for increasingly segmented tastes, from veganism and vegetarianism to low glycemic index and fat-free diets. Similarly, the growing interest in personal development and creativity and the desire to lead a full, rich life promises well for those planning special interest and activity holidays of all kinds, especially the arts.

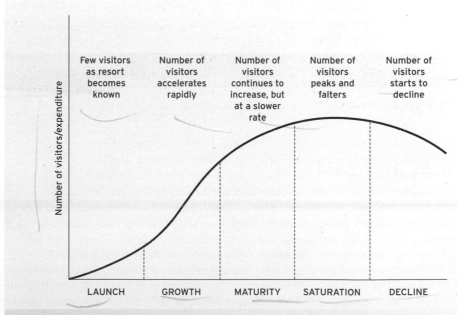

Figure 4.8 The lifecycle of a resort.

Holidays and skin cancer

Awareness of how to be healthier, of course, includes greater concern about the danger of developing skin cancer as a result of exposure to the sun, which has been well documented.[4]

In 2005, the UK recorded 8025 new cases of malignant melanomas, the commonest skin cancer, resulting from sudden and intensive exposure to the sun and, typically, resulting from concentrated periods of sunbathing. This represents an increase of 43 per cent on figures from the previous decade. Of those afflicted, over 1800 died. Cases of carcinoma – a cancer that develops through more gradual exposure to sunlight (and particularly UVB radiation) over a much longer period of time – occurs far more frequently (around 65,000 cases annually in the UK, resulting in around 500 deaths), although, if treated in its early stages, this will seldom prove fatal. Carcinomas affect many employees in the travel industry, due to their frequent exposure to the sun while at work (consider, for instance, the jobs of resort representative, lifeguard, ski instructor or coach driver).

In Australia, where love of the sun is inbuilt in the culture, the number of new cases of skin cancer diagnosed each year ran into the hundreds of thousands, of which around 1000 proved fatal. As a result, the authorities there launched a nationwide, and highly effective, campaign to reduce cancer by encouraging sunlovers to cover up and use sunscreen.

As the depletion of the ozone layer heightens risk, so tourists will be forced to reconsider the attraction of the beach holiday – at least, in the form in which it has been offered up to the present. The fashionability of suntans may well disappear. This is, after all, a twentieth-century phenomenon. Up until the early part of this century, tans were disparaged by the middle classes as they were indicative of those who worked outside – that is, 'the labouring classes'.

Despite the widespread media coverage of skin cancer in Great Britain, however, it is proving difficult to change long-standing attitudes and it is recognized that younger people will be slow to absorb this lesson! This is an issue that will be dealt with in depth in Chapter 6.

Example

Bavarian barmaids

In 2005, the media gave widespread coverage to an EU proposal that would require barmaids who serve tankards of beer outdoors (particularly at the popular beer festivals) wearing traditional Bavarian costume to cover up their bare shoulders and décolletage to avoid potential skin damage from the sun. Employers were warned that they could face compensation claims if barmaids were to suffer illness resulting from such exposure.

In the event, the European Parliament voted instead to allow individual EU states to determine whether or not employers should be required to protect their outdoor workers from solar radiation. The EU does, however, now require member states to impose legislation to protect their populations from both UBA and UVB radiation and is seeking to ban the use of sunbeds (an increasingly common cause of skin cancer) by those under 18 years of age.

The motivations of business travellers

What we have examined in this chapter applies mainly to the leisure traveller. Those travelling on business often have different criteria that need to be considered.

We noted earlier that business travellers are, in general, less price-sensitive and more concerned with status than leisure travellers. They are motivated principally by the need to complete their travel and business dealings as efficiently and effectively as possible within a given time-frame – this reflects their companies motivation for their trip. They will, however, also have personal agendas that they take into account. Through the eyes of their companies, then, they will be giving consideration to issues such as speed of transport and how convenient it is for getting them to their destinations, the punctuality and reliability of the carriers and the frequency of flights so that they can leave at a time to suit their appointments and return as soon as their business has been completed. Decisions about their travel are often made at very short notice, so arrangements may have to be made at any time. They need the flexibility to be able to change their reservations at minimal notice and are prepared to pay a premium for this privilege. The arrival of the low-cost airlines, however, has persuaded many to stick with a booking as large savings can be achieved in this way, even for a flight within Europe.

Travel needs to be arranged on weekdays rather than weekends – most businesspeople like to spend their weekends with their families. Above all, businesspeople will require that those they deal with   agents, carriers, travel managers – have great, in-depth knowledge of travel products. It is known that many business travellers will undertake their own searches online for information, frequently competing with their own travel managers for data on prices and flights, in the belief that their own research ability is superior to that of the travel experts.

Personal motivation enters the scene when the business traveller is taking a spouse or partner with them and when leisure activities are to be included as an adjunct to the business trip. A businessperson may also be interested in travelling with a specific carrier in order to take advantage of frequent flyer schemes that allow them to take a leisure trip with the airline when they have accumulated sufficient miles. This may entail travelling on what is neither the cheapest nor the most direct route.

Factors such as these can cause friction between travellers and their companies as the decision regarding whether or not to travel, how and when, may not rest with the travellers themselves but, rather, with senior members of their companies, who may be more concerned with ensuring that the company receives value for money than comfort or status.

It was believed that when videoconferencing facilities were introduced a few years ago, this would herald the decline of business travel. In fact, the reverse has occurred – traditional meetings continue, while conferences and trade shows are continuing to expand.

Motivators and facilitators

Up to now, we have dealt with the factors that motivate tourists to take holidays. In order to take a holiday, however, the tourist requires both time and money. These factors do not motivate in themselves, but they make it possible for prospective tourists to indulge in their desires. For this reason, they are known as **facilitators**.

Facilitators play a major role in relation to the specific objectives of the tourist. Cost is a major factor in facilitating the purchase of travel, but, equally, an increase in disposable income offers the tourist the opportunity to enjoy a wider choice of destinations. Better accessibility of the destination, or more favourable exchange rates against the local currency, easier entry without political barriers and friendly locals speaking the language of the tourist all act as facilitators as well as motivating them to choose a particular destination over others.

A growing characteristic within wealthier countries in this new century is the presence of 'cash rich, time poor' consumers who are prepared to sacrifice money to save time. The implications of this phenomenon are significant for the industry. Those who can offer the easiest and fastest communication opportunities, prices and booking facilities, coupled with reliability and good service, can gain access to a wealthy, rapidly expanding market. Whether this race will be won by the direct selling organizations using websites and call centres or retailers using new sales techniques (such as experienced travel counsellors prepared to call on customers at times convenient to them and in their own homes, including evenings and weekends) remains to be seen.

Factors influencing changes in tourist demand

It is fitting to complete this chapter by recognizing that patterns of demand in tourism are affected by two distinct sets of factors. First, we have factors that cannot be predetermined or forecast but which influence changes, sometimes with very little advance warning. The second set of factors includes cultural, social and technological changes developing in society, many of which can be forecast and for which there is time to adapt tourism products to meet new needs and expectations.

In the first category, we must include changes influenced by economic or political circumstances, climate and natural or artificial disasters. Economic influences will be examined more thoroughly in the following chapter, but here it is salutary to look at just some of the factors that have impacted on demand for foreign tourism so severely in recent years.

Undoubtedly, the outbreak of war has been the single greatest threat to foreign travel for the past half century. Millions of tourists visited the former Yugoslavia every year during the 1980s, but this market virtually disappeared in the 1990s when civil wars broke out. The Vietnam War and its aftermath killed off much tourism to South-East Asia in the 1960s and 1970s, while the various wars in the Middle East curtailed travel there, if for a shorter time. Civil war and ethnic strife have long inhibited the development of tourism in many African countries.

More recently, it has been the threat of terrorist attacks, actual or perceived, that has inhibited global travel – both Western fear of travel to Muslim countries and a general fear of travel to cities threatened by Islamic extremists. Terrorism has been a factor with which the tourism industry has had to cope for at least the past 25 years and, if we summarize the terrorist attacks that have occurred since 2002 and resulted in deaths following the attack on the Twin Towers in New York, which accounted for 2973 dead (excluding the 19 hijackers), we can see that, of 15 countries listed, 10 of them are important for tourism (see Table 4.3). These figures ignore attacks by Chechen separatists in Russia and countries actively engaged in warfare.

The escalation in the number of attacks, together with the near-certainty of officials that further attacks will take place, especially in the USA and UK, has led to long-term uncertainty about growth prospects for global travel. The ongoing wars in Iraq and Afghanistan, coupled with concern over relations in 2008 between Russia and Georgia, are further destabilizing the desire to travel, although it has to be said that some countries, such as the USA, are far more averse to risktaking in travel abroad than are others, such as the UK and Germany.

No less serious for global travel has been the threat posed by the rising impact of disease on a worldwide scale. The emergence of more virulent and vaccine-resistant forms of malaria in Africa and Asia has discouraged tourists from visiting those areas. Countries in Asia suffered the extra blow of a serious outbreak of severe acute respiratory syndrome (SARS) early in 2003, which led to the cancellation of many flights and tourist movements. Indeed, travel to China virtually ceased, apart from its adjacent neighbours, for a period of

Table 4.3 Terrorist attacks resulting in fatalities, 2002–2006.

Year	Site	Death toll
2002	Yemen	1
2002	Tunisia	21
2002	Bali	202
2002	Kenya	13
2002	Pakistan	12
2003	Morocco	33
2003	Djakarta, Indonesia	12
2003	Saudi Arabia (three attacks)	26 + 17 + 22
2003	Turkey (two attacks)	25 + 27
2004	Saudi Arabia (two attacks)	7 + 5
2004	Madrid, Spain	191
2004	Egypt	34
2004	Indonesia	9
2005	Indonesia	20
2005	Qatar	1
2005	London, UK	52
2005	Jordan	60
2005	Egypt (two attacks)	3 + 88
2006	Egypt	24

some six months. During this time, Britain was also severely hit by outbreaks of disease. First, there was the discovery of BSE in British herds, which, although with only limited ability to cross the species to humans, scared away many potential visitors. Subsequently there was an outbreak of foot and mouth disease, which, while far less dangerous to human beings, received massive negative publicity in the form of scare stories in the foreign press (to some extent the result of inept and draconian control measures in the UK that were perceived as actively discouraging tourists from visiting rural areas). More recently, China and Vietnam have been hit by outbreaks of virulent Asian bird flu, which has the potential to cross the species and create a pandemic among humans. Britain, along with other European countries, has also had to contend with its own outbreaks of bird flu, together with the first cases of blue tongue disease in cattle. Any such outbreaks threaten tourism in the countryside.

Finally, one must include the issue of climate change, which is contributing to natural disasters affecting tourist destinations globally. Areas already prone to heavy rainfall or hurricanes have witnessed conditions that have been catastrophic for locals and tourists alike, crowned by the disasters of the tsunami in the Far East at the end of 2004 and the impact of Hurricane Katrina on New Orleans and the US Gulf Coast in 2005. Less calamitously, several low-lying areas of England suffered deluges in the heavy rains of 2007, with more widespread flooding being only narrowly avoided.

The future pattern of tourist demand

Few of these events were predictable in advance. The lesson for the industry has been that, wherever possible, companies must be prepared for rapidly changing circumstances, often at very short notice. They need to build up an organization and products that are flexible and adaptable so that they can cope with change. The lessons for governments have been that the tourism industry is often vital to the economy and recovery should be supported with public funds if small firms are to remain viable.

Some low-lying countries, such as islands in the Pacific, are already having to come to terms with the fact that their nascent tourism industries are doomed by rising sea levels, with the costs of safeguarding their coastlines too great to be practicable. Other developing countries, such as the Maldives, which have invested heavily in tourism in response to the boom in long-haul travel and the demand for active water-based adventure holidays, face the threats posed by global warming with trepidation.

In terms of demand for foreign travel, undoubtedly such events compound fears of foreign travel generally and those most averse to risktaking – our psychocentrics – are likely to choose to spend their holidays nearer to home or at the very least in countries viewed as being safer. Such a trend may even be welcomed by environmentalists, eager to see a fall in the demand for long-haul air travel, but this is to ignore the economic consequences for the destination countries concerned, several of which have no ready alternative means of generating foreign income and investment.

Social change is easier to predict, as are long-term trends in travel patterns. All too often, however, the industry has been slow to respond to these indicators. We know, for example, that only one family in four in the UK now conforms to the stereotypical pattern of two parents and two children and increasing numbers of people are living alone or bringing up children as single parents, yet such 'untypical' families are often not welcomed by operators as their pricing structures weigh unfairly against such tourists. Similarly, with increasing life expectancy, the rise in divorce and fall in marriage rates, there are now some seven million single-person households in Britain, yet high additional charges for single tourists in package tours remain the norm and the demand for single accommodation is often difficult to meet.

Other notable changes in British society include an increase in spending power of working women and the earlier maturation of children, leading to a demand for more adult holidays. Children now exert much more influence in the making of travel decisions and are tending to travel more with friends than in the traditional family group.

Perhaps most notable has been the impact of a growing market of senior citizens who are active, have high levels of spending power and are looking for new experiences in their travels (for those who dismiss the senior market as unadventurous, it's worth bearing in mind that Dennis Tito, the world's first space traveller, was over 60 when he took his space flight in 2001). The over-50s today account for one-third of all the disposable income in the UK. While the total population of Britain is expected to fall in the medium term, it is estimated that there will be a 31 per cent increase in the over-55s by 2020, with many of them taking early retirement to spend the inheritances arising from the sale of their parents' properties on long-haul and cruise holidays.

By 2017, there will be more people aged over 65 in Britain than those under 16, and 25 per cent of the population will be over 65 by 2050 (against 15 per cent in 2007). Projections by the Cass Business School[5] anticipate that men born in 1985 can expect to live to at least 91, possibly as long as 97. Even the lower figure is six years more than the projections by the British Office of National Statistics. It has been estimated that this will lead to senior citizens enjoying an additional five million holidays a year by 2020 – many of these far more active than the erstwhile 'sitting on the beach with a knotted handkerchief on the head' stereotype so popular with the media.

Another fast-growing market is the lesbian, gay, bisexual and transgender (LGBT), now commonly referred to as the 'pink market'. Members of this group in the UK typically take one domestic and two foreign holidays each year. They earn more – and spend more – than the average traveller. They particularly enjoy travelling to destinations where their sexual orientation is unquestioned, such as Montreal, Bangkok and the Sydney Mardi Gras festival.

Example

Catering for the pink pound

The UK's first call centre aimed at the LGBT market opened in 2004. Outlet 4 Travel, a member of the Freedom Travel Group, planned to include travel to destinations other than the obvious ones, inspired by dedicated gay agencies in the USA. The agency claims, 'Most gay men and women have to spend a lot of time looking on the Internet to book a holiday, unless they want to go to the usual places. They have to put it together themselves, which often works out more expensive'.

Source: *The Observer* travel news, 29 August 2004.

This market has already been successfully tapped in the USA, where travel propensity is high: 91 per cent take annual holidays (54 per cent overseas) compared with a national average of only 64 per cent (9 per cent overseas).

Travellers of all kinds are now both sophisticated and demanding, often being more familiar with world travel destinations and attractions than those selling the products. This produces a new kind of challenge to the industry to provide a professional level of service that it is still a long way from achieving.

There are many other clear social trends in the industry in the opening years of the twenty-first century that suppliers and agents must learn to cater to. Greater choice in consumer purchasing of all kinds is leading to demand for more flexible packages of differing durations. Many will require tailor-made approaches to packaging and companies are establishing divisions specifically for this purpose. This has led to the phenomenon of **dynamic packaging**, where agents and operators put together individual elements of the package, usually by searching websites. This process, however, is labour-intensive and requires great product knowledge.

Example

The changing market for independent travel

Independent travellers to Spain from the UK overtook those travelling on package holidays for the first time in 2004 and the gap between the two has continued to increase in the succeeding years, rising to 59 per cent in 2006. The change is accounted for in part by the growth of older travellers to Spanish destinations, while the number of younger travellers is falling. Travellers are increasingly well off and are selecting two-centre holidays instead of the traditional single-centre resort.

Earlier, reference was made to the way in which the mass demand for passive beach holidays has given way to demand for more active holidays of all kinds, even from those in the upper age brackets. Special interest holidays now cater for the widening range of hobbies of a leisure-orientated society. Adventure holidays, both domestic and foreign, are now packaged by operators to appeal to a range of markets.

In the latter years of the last century, tour operators attempted to gain market share by cutting prices and making budget offers that often fell below the quality levels anticipated by consumers. Selling on price rather than quality became the keynote for the industry. Consumers were encouraged to buy on price and seek out the cheapest. Inevitably, the rising numbers of complaints forced companies to reconsider value for money and quality assurance, although deep discounting remains the bugbear of the industry, for both traditional package tours and the cruise market.

In the format of package tours, we find demand moving in two distinct directions. On the one hand, self-catering has become increasingly popular, partly as a cost-saving exercise but equally as a means of overcoming the constraints imposed by package holidays in general and the accommodation sector in particular. Set meals at set times gave way to 'eat what you please, where you please, when you please'. In reply, the package tour industry provided the product to meet this need: the French gîte holidays became popular and across Southern Europe self-catering villas and apartments flourished, while in the UK demand moved from resort hotels and guesthouses to self-catering flats. Hundreds of thousands of Britons invested in timeshare properties in order to own their own 'place in the sun' or increasingly found their own accommodation abroad, while the operators provided 'seat only' packages on charter aircraft to cater for their transport needs.

Perhaps the most significant development has been the increase in second home ownership. Accurate statistics on this trend are difficult to find (doubtless in part because many UK residents are unwilling to keep the UK tax authorities advised of their owning homes abroad), but the most recent government figures claim some 177,000 English households owned homes abroad in 2004, while some 229,000 residents owned second homes within the UK. Other sources, however, put levels of UK property ownership abroad far higher, with some estimates suggesting that as many as 500,000 Britons own properties in France alone. This has fuelled the growth of the low-cost airlines from and to regional airports on the Continent. These figures do not include the large number of British citizens who no longer count the UK as their principal place of residence. Around 1 in 12 Britons – some 5.5 million – live abroad and 385,000 British residents left the UK in the 12 months to July 2007 (more than half of whom were native Britons). A decision to live abroad does not indicate a willingness to cut off all connections with the mother country, so these changes in country of residence in themselves generate subsequent high levels of tourism mobility in both directions. One can only speculate at this point on the likely impact of higher aviation fuel prices on demand in this market, as budget airlines, frequently used by second home owners, increase ticket prices and cut back services.

The other side of the coin is reflected in the growth in demand for all-inclusive holidays, which we looked at earlier in this chapter. This particular type of holiday is likely to experience continuing demand, both for short- and long-haul destinations.

The market for short-break holidays of between one and three nights has also expanded rapidly, becoming frequently an addition to the principal holiday. The British tourism industry has benefited as many of these breaks are taken within the UK, helping to make up for the decline in traditional two-week summer holidays at the seaside. The choice of short-break destinations abroad has also widened, with the traditional destinations of Paris, Amsterdam, Brussels, Barcelona and Rome being joined by Budapest, Prague, Kraców, Reykjavik, Carcassonne, Graz, Kaunas, Trieste and even New York.

Long-haul traffic has enjoyed a steady rise as disposable incomes were matched by ever-reducing air fares, especially across the Atlantic. Holidays to the USA boomed, especially to Florida. Many Britons now own second homes there, not only along the coast but also within easy driving distance of Orlando, where the popular Disney World theme park attracts millions eager to rent self-catering accommodation during their stay. Once again, this market is threatened by substantial rises in ticket prices (some British Airways long-haul flights were carrying fuel surcharges in excess of £200 per passenger as this text went to press), although in general the market is far more price-inelastic than that for budget carriers.

All this is not to say that the traditional sun, sea and sand holiday is in terminal decline, but those still loyal to this form of holiday are seeking more activities, including cultural visits inland from the popular resorts of Spain and Greece. Nor are these traditional holidaymakers content merely to seek out the familiar beaches of the Mediterranean – many are now travelling as far afield as Pattaya Beach and Phuket in Thailand, Goa in India and Mombasa in Kenya to enjoy their beaches in more exotic surroundings.

The traditional 'law of tourism harmony' – every aspect of the tour being of broadly similar standards and quality – has given way to a 'pick and mix' approach, in which savings may be effected in one area in order to indulge oneself in another. Tourists may decide, for example, to choose cheap B&B accommodation while eating out at expensive restaurants; others are booking cheap flights on low-cost airlines and luxury hotels at their destinations, on the grounds that the flight lasts a mere couple of hours, while they intend to stay several days in the hotel, so standards there are more important.

Example

Mixed status leisure

Raymond Blanc's famed restaurant in Oxfordshire, Le Manoir au Quat' Saisons, is notably luxurious – and expensive – as is the accommodation in the associated hotel. An alternative 'package' has become available, however. Rival accommodation in the form of a small campsite near the restaurant is now catering for those prepared to pay for the meal   among the most expensive in Britain – but not an overnight stay in the hotel.

By contrast, the term 'Hilton Hippies' has been used to describe those who may want to engage in rough activities such as mountainbiking by day, but look for luxury in their overnight accommodation. A further example is offered in Chapter 15 of a French tour operator combining travel by hired moped with top-class accommodation and food. These are further examples of the more flexible approach to holidays that the travel industry is learning to cater for.

In most developed countries, those in work are forecast to enjoy increased disposable incomes and a higher propensity to travel abroad. On the other hand, there will continue to be a relatively high number of unemployed in the population, most of whom will be unable to take holidays of any kind. In the past, those with spouses who have not wished to travel abroad have tended not to do so themselves, but lifestyle changes could mean that an increasing number of happily married couples will choose to holiday separately, each 'doing their own thing'.

Those charged with the task of marketing to tourists must be fully familiar with these and other patterns of tourist behaviour and any trends that might suggest these are changing. Some such changes will be generated by tourists themselves, others will come about as a result of changes taking place in the business environment and in society as a whole. What must be recognized is that the pace of change in the world of tourism is constantly accelerating, requiring entrepreneurs to react faster than they have needed to do in the past. Of equal importance is the requirement for the industry to recognize that protection of the environment and the indigenous populations in the destination countries must also be taken into account. Companies will also have to ensure that any new initiatives do not depart from the obligation to ensure products are sustainable. The days of 'slash and burn' exploitative tourism are over.

Notes

1. Holloway, J. C. (2004) *Marketing for Tourism* (4th edn), Prentice Hall.
2. Study by Help The Aged/Intune, 2007.
3. Plog, S. (1972) 'Why destination areas rise and fall in popularity', paper presented to the Southern Chapter of the Travel Research Association.
4. See, for example, Mighall, R. (2008) *Sunshine: One man's search for happiness*, John Murray.
5. Reported in *The Times*, 26 November 2007.

Further reading

Carey, S. (2003) 'Why it just got a little bit harder to see the world', *Wall Street Journal*, 20 November, p. 1.

Krippendorf, J. (1984) *The Holiday Makers: Understanding the impact of leisure and travel*, Heinemann.

Ross, G. (1994) *The Psychology of Tourism*, Hospitality Press.

Ryan, C. (1991) *Recreational Tourism: A social science perspective*, Routledge.

Questions and discussion points

1. Given the increasing emphasis on serving the individual needs of the tourist, is it still possible to segment markets today? How can providers offer an unlimited supply of alternative opportunities?

2. Do travel agents have the necessary skills to understand their customers' needs and match these to products? Is such an ability based on education, training, experience, native intelligence or some combination of all these?

3. Discuss the pull of adventure holidays incorporating increasingly dangerous sports such as white water rafting, paragliding or even base jumping versus the natural desire to avoid excessive risk. Is age the dominant factor in this dichotomy? Where do you and your colleagues place themselves on this continuum? Why?

4. Suggest examples of the ways in which our current concern for healthy living is influencing patterns in holidaytaking.

5. Identify some destinations that currently suffer from a negative image with tourists and suggest ways in which these can influence certain markets to visit them.

Tasks

1. Undertake a programme of research among your peers to determine their attitudes to sunbathing. Find out the extent of their existing knowledge of the relationship between sunbathing and skin cancer and whether or not that knowledge is influencing behaviour. Suggest some approaches that might be taken to reduce the growing numbers of young tourists affected by skin cancer.

2. Complete a report that explores the extent to which suppliers of tourism products are catering to the growing numbers of solo holidaymakers. Examine a cross-section of tour brochures, hotel websites and so on to see how single travellers are affected by discriminatory pricing in particular.

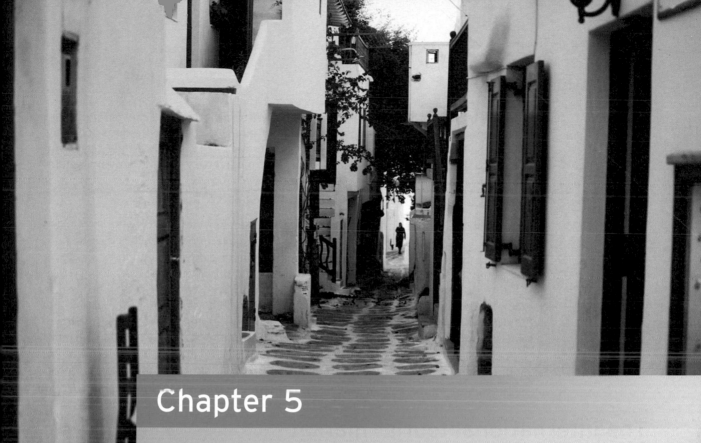

Chapter 5

The economic impacts of tourism

Learning outcomes

After studying this chapter, you should be able to:

- identify the economic benefits of tourism for a nation, both nationally and regionally

- be aware of the negative economic effects of tourism for destinations

- understand how tourism is measured statistically

- recognize the limitations of statistical measurement.

Introduction

> Global tourism is an $8 trillion industry. Over the past 20 years, developing countries have harnessed the rapid expansion of global tourism to promote economic growth. Through good planning, the tourism industry can powerfully transform communities, reducing poverty, protecting biodiversity, and improving gender equality, healthcare, education, and local governance.
>
> USAID, Global Development Alliance newsletter, March/April 2008

Tourism as an economic activity is important for the many countries that try to obtain a share of this $8 trillion. While it can bring in wealth and economic benefits, there are also some negative consequences for those nations and their regions. For both these reasons, it is important to understand the economic impacts of tourism.

This is a complex topic that can only be touched on in this text. Those who wish to examine the subject in depth are referred to texts designed for this purpose, such as Bull (1995). The aim of this chapter, therefore, is primarily to explore the economic impacts of tourism resulting from national and international tourist flows and the ways in which this is measured and recorded. In later chapters, the economics of the firm, the industry and its various sectors will be examined. First, however, we will look at the movement of tourists internationally and some of the economic factors influencing those flows.

The international tourist market

Tourism is probably the single most important industry in the world. According to the World Travel and Tourism Council (WTTC, 2008/2009), the global tourism industry would account for 3.4 per cent of global GDP in 2008, while the broader impacts (including the indirect effects on the economy as a result of tourism) would mean that it could be expected to account for 9.9 per cent of global GDP. Furthermore, it was estimated that the travel and tourism industry worldwide would provide 238.3 million jobs, representing 8.4 per cent of total employment.[1] According to the most recent estimate by the UNWTO,[2] 903 million international trips were taken in 2007, which represented an increase of more than 6 per cent on the previous year. The UNWTO also notes that provisional worldwide tourism receipts for 2007 suggest an increase of US$114 billion over the previous year, with a total of US$856 billion (see Table 5.1).

The rapid increase in international travel during the early post-war years – exceeding 10 per cent per annum from 1950 to 1960 – could not be permanently sustained, of course, as it reflected the pent-up demand that had built up in the war years and the slow economic recovery after the war. It is worth noting, however, that, apart from the odd hiccup, from 1970 to the 1990s, annual growth ran above 4 per cent, even in the early 1990s when there was a global recession. The WTTC has estimated that the annual growth between 2004 and 2008 averages at 4 per cent, with the tourism industry estimated as contributing US$5890 billion to global GDP in 2008. The good news for the tourism industry, therefore, is that, although the rate of increase in arrivals in some recent years has faltered – scarcely surprising, given the many turbulent world events since September 2001 – the long-term trend continues to be an upward one.

Domestic tourism

It is important to note that the data above relates to international travel and the figures do not include the vast number of people taking trips within their own countries. Often, in fact, much higher levels of domestic tourism take place. Here, Americans lead the field, with over 3.1 billion domestic trips in 2006, compared to 66 million international outbound

Table 5.1 A profile of international tourist arrivals and receipts, 1950–2007.

Year	Arrivals (m)	Receipts (US $bn)
1950	25.3	2.1
1960	69.3	6.9
1970	165.8	17.9
1980	278.2	106.5
1990	445.8	272.9
1995	544.9	410.8
2000	685.5	476.4
2001	683.8	464.4
2002	702.8	482.3
2003	689.8	524.2
2004	764.4	633.0
2005	803.4	676.5
2006	847.3	742.0
2007 (P)	903.2	855.9

Note: Excludes international fares. (P) = provisional.
Source: UNWTO, *Yearbook of Tourism Statistics*, UNWTO.

Table 5.2 A comparison of domestic trips with international tourist arrivals (2006).

Country	Domestic trips (m)	International arrivals (m)	Ratio of domestic trips to international arrivals
India	445.7	4.3	103.2
USA	3079.5	52.5	58.7
Japan	341.3	7.1	47.8
Indonesia	225.7	5.1	44.3
Brazil	225.0	6.2	36.2
Selected other countries			
China	1196.2	53.5	22.4
Australia	71.5	5.5	13.1
Germany	209.3	23.6	8.9
UK	125.8	31.2	4.0
Austria	9.8	20.0	0.5

Source: Based on Euromonitor, 2008.

trips. India, however, is the fastest-growing market for domestic tourism, with predictions of more than 1 billion domestic trips taking place by 2011. For many countries, domestic trips far exceed the level of arrivals from international tourists[3] (see Table 5.2). It is important to consider, however, that the spending of international tourists may be higher than that of domestic tourists.

Trends in international travel

As controls over the freedom of movement of populations in many countries are gradually lifted, many are seeking the opportunity to travel outside their own borders for the first time,

Table 5.3 Leading tourism-generating countries, 2006 (based on provisional tourism expenditure).

Position	Country	Expenditure (US$ billion)
1	Germany	74.8
2	USA	72.0
3	UK	63.1
4	France	32.2
5	Japan	26.9
6	China	24.3
7	Italy	23.1
8	Canada	20.5
9	Russian Federation	18.8
10	South Korea	18.2

Source: UNWTO, *Yearbook of Tourism Statistics*, UNWTO 2007.

not least residents of China, now the sixth biggest generator of overseas tourist expenditure. The UNWTO therefore continues to take an optimistic view of the long term, estimating that international tourism trips will continue to increase for the foreseeable future.

International tourism is generated, for the most part, within the nations of Europe, North America and Japan – the result of low prices, frequent flights and large, relatively wealthy populations (see Table 5.3). Japan in particular has been growing strongly as a tourism-generating country in recent years, due to its wealth and a growing willingness on the part of its population to take holidays. Traditionally, the Japanese work ethic militated against their taking all the holidays to which they are entitled, but with government encouragement and changes in attitude to work and loyalty to their firms, the Japanese have taken to travelling abroad in greater numbers and for longer periods of time. As a result, Japan is now fifth among the top ten generating countries which together are responsible for well over half the total expenditure on foreign travel.

It is interesting to note the dominance of the top three countries, which far exceed the spending levels of the rest in this list. While the half-dozen countries currently in fourth to ninth places have held positions in the top ten for several years, a new entry to this list is South Korea, which has edged out the Netherlands. The growth in the South Korean market can be attributed to a strengthening economy, which has helped to stimulate a strong business travel market. Furthermore, alongside economic growth, increased leisure time and continued enthusiasm for study abroad have fuelled expenditure on international travel. As the Chinese gain greater freedom of movement, there are expectations that its market will become more important for many destinations. With almost 40 million departures in 2006 (107,000 of whom came to Britain), predictions are that, given existing conditions, the number of Chinese travelling will have doubled by 2011.[4]

Looking at the flow of international tourism over the long term, one can conclude that the tourism business is surprisingly resilient. Whatever short-term problems emerge – acts of terrorism, medical emergencies such as SARS and bird flu, the 2004 Asian tsunami and flooding in places such as New Orleans following Hurricane Katrina in 2005 and in areas of the UK in the summer of 2007 – tourists eventually return in ever greater numbers.

Tourist destinations

While Western Europe continues to dominate, Eastern Europe has seen a growth in popularity, as expansion of the European Union and changes in the Schengen Agreement have made travel in this area easier. Also, China has experienced a rapid rise in popularity,

Table 5.4 Leading tourism-receiving countries, 2006 (based on provisional international tourist arrivals in millions) and their tourism receipts

Position	Country	Arrivals (millions)	Receipts (US$ billion)	Per capita receipts (US$)
1	France	79.1	42.9	542.35
2	Spain	58.5	51.1	873.50
3	USA	51.1	85.7	1677.10
4	China	49.6	33.9	683.47
5	Italy	41.1	38.1	927.01
6	UK	30.7	33.7	1097.72
7	Germany	23.6	32.8	1389.83
8	Mexico	21.4	12.2	570.09
9	Austria	20.3	16.7	822.66
10	Russian Federation	20.2	7.0	34.67

Source: UNWTO, 'Tourism highlights', UNWTO, 2007.

and some researchers suggested that in the period 2006/7 it surpassed the USA to become the third most visited nation, with over 53 million visitors.[5]

Simply looking at receipts, though, will not give a sound picture of the value of tourism to an economy. It is important to consider how many tourists make up the total receipts (see Table 5.4). The countries with the highest per capita receipts are generally those where prices are highest and include countries such as Sweden, Denmark and Japan. In economic terms, the financial value of tourism to a country may be more important than the number of tourists it receives. It is vital, therefore, that the average spends of tourists from different countries are assessed, which may be influenced by the average length of time tourists from a particular country stay in a country and their average daily spend.

It is also important to take account of factors likely to lead to the growth or decline of tourism from each country. The potential for growth is high for those living in Eastern Europe, whose income, for the most part, is rising strongly since the fall of communism. The entry of several of these countries into the EU in 2004 has already boosted tourism in both directions within Europe.

The potential of Japan remains high also, as only a small proportion of its population currently travels abroad and those who do are relatively free spenders. This is partly accounted for by their high spend on shopping and souvenirs for friends and relatives.

In spite of the high revenues generated from Americans travelling abroad, only a small minority of the population actually possess a passport as most American tourists tend to travel to adjacent countries that, until recently, did not require them to carry passports. Also, because of the size and diversity of their own landscape, many are content to take holidays within their own country.

So the *propensity* to take holidays abroad is another important characteristic to take into account. The propensity to take foreign holidays varies considerably within Europe, too. It is high among the Scandinavians – no doubt this is due in part to the long winters and lack of sunshine – while only a quarter of Italians share this desire for foreign travel. Italians are surprisingly unadventurous in their travelling, with nearly half of those travelling on holiday being content to return to the same resort, and even the same hotel, every year for a decade. The French, too, prefer to travel within their own country, often to second homes in the countryside, rather than venture abroad. Although Britons have a reputation for travelling abroad, a third of the population takes no holidays at all during the year (but not necessarily the same third every year).

We should also recognize that, while tourism expenditure in aggregate will be highest for wealthy countries having large populations, the high levels of disposable income among the populations of smaller nations with a significant proportion of wealthy residents, such as Switzerland or Luxembourg, will tend to lead to higher levels of participation in international tourism. Where international borders are close to places of residence – as is the case with Switzerland and Luxembourg – this will significantly increase the propensity to travel abroad.

Propensity to travel

To help understand the travel habits of particular nations, it is possible to calculate the **travel propensity** – that is, the percentage of the population taking trips. This can be considered in two dimensions – the **net travel propensity** and the **gross travel propensity**.

Net travel propensity reflects the percentage of the population that has travelled for at least one trip (though many will have taken more). As some of the population will not have taken a trip at all, the net travel propensity will be less than 100 per cent.

Gross travel propensity reflects the total number of trips taken in relation to the total population. In areas, such as Western Europe, where the local population may take several trips, the gross travel propensity may exceed 100 per cent (as those who have been on multiple trips counterbalance those who have not travelled at all).

Example

UK travel propensity

In the case of net travel propensity, it is estimated that, 'In any given year more than a third of the UK population still does not take a holiday at all'.[6]

The gross travel propensity of the British to take a holiday – that is, the ratio of trips taken out of the total population – is high (see Table 5.5). The total number of trips is 195.79 million and, for a population of 60.59 million, this provides a gross travel propensity of 323 per cent. The propensity for international travel is lower at 115 per cent.

Table 5.5 Trips taken by the UK population, 2006.

Population (million)	Domestic trips (million)	International trips (million)
60.59	126.29	69.5

Source: Social Trends, 38, 2008, Office of National Statistics, 'United Kingdom Tourism Survey 2008', VisitBritain, VisitScotland, VisitWales and the Northern Ireland Tourist Board.

Other factors affecting the economic value of tourism

While there are many factors that motivate people to travel abroad, a major one is likely to be the relative cost compared with their income. Since greater demand also leads to lower prices, with transport and accommodation costs falling for each additional person booked, there is a direct relationship between cost, price and demand (see Figure 5.1). This helps to explain the vicious price wars in the travel industry, designed to capture market share and increase numbers, which have been so much a feature of competition in the travel industry over the past twenty years.

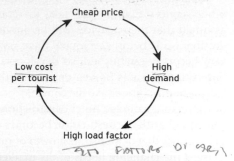

Figure 5.1 The relationship between cost, price and demand.

The continued popularity of the no frills airlines has seen an increased range of routes being offered, opening up low-cost travel to places in Eastern Europe as well as islands such as Malta. This trend is likely to continue, unless sharply curtailed by rising fuel prices or the imposition of fuel taxes to offset pollution.

Other factors to take into account include attitudes to the use of leisure time. In the USA, some 30 per cent of the workforce take less than half the holiday time to which they are entitled – and this is in a country where the average paid holiday is still only two to three weeks compared with the four to five weeks now standard throughout Europe. The Japanese, as we have seen, seldom take their full entitlement. With average holidays of 17 days, they typically take only 9.5 days. Even in the UK, roughly a quarter of the working population fails to take its full entitlement.

The value of economic data

Gathering data on tourists is a vital task for the government of a country as it is vital to its own national tourist office and the providers of tourism services. Governments need to know the contribution that tourism makes to the economy in terms of income, employment, investment and the balance of payments. Concern about regional development requires that these statistics be sufficiently refined to allow them to be broken down by region. Governments will also wish to compare their tourism performance with that of other countries, as well as to establish how well they are doing regarding attracting tourists to the country over a period of time.

Tourism organizations, whether in the public or the private sector, need such data to enable them to forecast what will happen in the future. This means identifying trends in the market, patterns of growth and changing demand for destinations, facilities or types of holiday.

On the basis of this knowledge, future planning can be undertaken. The public sector will make recommendations and decisions regarding the **infrastructure** and **superstructure** needed to support growth. Infrastructure will include, for example, the building of new airports and seaport terminals or the expansion of existing ones, the provision of new or improved roads to growing destinations and the improvement of other services, such as public utilities, including water and electricity, that will be needed to cope with the expected expansion of tourism. Some of these plans may take many years to implement. For example, the discussions surrounding the building of a fifth terminal at London's Heathrow airport took place over more than a decade, far longer than the time taken to actually construct the terminal itself. Furthermore, congestion at London airports has encouraged carriers to switch air traffic to alternative airports. Schiphol in the Netherlands is one such airport that has actively promoted itself as an alternative to Heathrow, using the hub-and-spoke system, given that it offers services to around a dozen UK airports.

Superstructure comprises the tourist amenities needed – hotels, restaurants, shops and other services that tourists take for granted when they visit. It cannot necessarily be assumed that these services will be provided by developers in the private sector. If a new destination is being developed, there will be a degree of risk involved while the destination becomes established, so developers may be reluctant to invest in such projects as hotels until there is proven demand at the destination. Governments or local authorities can themselves undertake the construction of hotels, as often occurs in developing countries, or they can encourage hotel construction by underwriting costs or providing subsidies of some kind until the destination becomes established. Similarly, private companies can use the statistics that demonstrate growth or market change, extending or adapting their products to meet the changing needs of the marketplace.

To show how this information can be used, let us take the example of a destination such as London, which attracts a high volume of overseas visitors. The flow of those visitors will be affected by a great many different factors. For example, if tourists can purchase more pounds sterling for their own currency or air fares to the destination have fallen or a major event, such as an international sports event – the Olympics – is being organized – all these factors will encourage tourists to visit the city.

Negative factors also have an effect. Terrorist activity in the capital (as in July 2005) affected decisions to come to Britain, while other global events – war in Iraq and SARS in 2003, avian flu in 2004/2005 – all influence travel plans. US tourists are particularly sensitive to the threat of terrorism and will revert to holidaying at home if they sense that the risk of foreign travel is increasing. Negative first impressions, such as air pollution in the city, extensive littering, a decaying and overcrowded public transport system, even large numbers of homeless people on the streets, can all affect tourism adversely, tourists deciding to go elsewhere or recommending to their friends that they do so.

Example

The influence of exchange rates – a UK example

Recessions may hit countries to different extents, so that, in one year, the forecast might be for a reduced number of tourists from the USA, but a growth in the number from Japan.

In the third quarter of 2000, the pound fell sharply against the dollar, while remaining relatively strong against European currencies. This encouraged Americans to travel to Britain and the British to visit the Continent, while tourists from countries such as Germany and France were dissuaded from coming to Britain and, similarly, fewer Britons visited the USA. In 2004/2005, however, the dollar weakened against both sterling and the euro, increasing travel from Britain and the Continent to the USA (and, incidentally, further heightening the demand for second homes in Florida for the British). In 2007/2008, the dollar again weakened against the pound (at times reaching a rate of US$2 for £1). However, 2008 also saw sterling weaken by about 20 per cent on the euro, making Europe a more expensive proposition for British travellers, and, by the autumn of that year, against a background of threatening recession, sterling was falling fast against both the dollar and the euro.

This uncertainty about currency movements makes forward planning difficult, adding another element of risk to product pricing, although this can be offset to some extent by the forward purchasing of foreign currencies. If Britain does eventually join the euro, one benefit will be that it will help to stabilize their travel business with Europe. It will also allow British travellers to share with their counterparts in other EU countries the benefits of using a single currency across several countries, leading to a substantial saving on foreign exchange when calculating the costs of a holiday abroad. Such savings are less likely to be welcomed by those in the industry who provide foreign exchange facilities, however!

Companies and tourist offices will have to take all of these factors into account when drawing up their promotional campaigns – and may need to consider employing staff with the appropriate language skills to deal with any new incoming markets. On the basis of the forecasts made, organizations must decide where they will advertise, to whom and with what theme.

International tourism depends on more than merely the economic behaviour of tourists, however. As we noted in the previous chapter, it is also influenced by motivators arising from the tourists' efforts to meet their psychological or sociological needs.

The economic impacts of tourism

This chapter examines the economic effects of tourism and how these are measured. As in other industries, tourism affects the economy of those areas – whether regions, countries or continents – where it takes place. These are known as tourist **destinations**, or **receiving areas**, and many become dependent on an inflow of tourism to sustain their economy. This is especially true of developing countries, some of which are largely or almost totally dependent on tourism.

The areas from which the tourists come to visit these destinations are known as **generating areas** and, of course, as the tourists are taking their money with them to spend in other places, this represents a net loss of revenue for the generating area and a gain for the receiving area. We can say that incoming tourist spend is an **export**, while outgoing tourist spend is an **import** (as the tourist is buying services from overseas).

The flow of tourists between generating and receiving areas can be measured in four distinct ways. We must examine the effect on **income**, **employment**, the area's **balance of payments** and **investment and development**. Let us look at each of these in turn.

Income

Income is generated from pay and salaries, interest, rent and profits. In a labour-intensive industry such as tourism, the greatest proportion is likely to be derived from pay and salaries for those working in jobs either directly serving the needs of tourists or benefiting

Example

The Côte d'Azur

This resort area by the French Mediterranean sea satisfies most of the above criteria for generating a great deal of income, attracting not only many overseas visitors for a fairly long season (even through the winter some tourists will be attracted to the milder climate) but also bringing in many domestic tourists from other areas of France.

A number of upmarket resorts in the area, such as Nice, Cannes, Antibes, St Tropez and Juan les Pins, provide a good range of relatively expensive hotels. There are also expensive shops and restaurants, casinos, nightclubs and discos where the high-spend tourists can be relieved of their money, thus providing income for local businesses. There are opportunities for water-based activities, such as yachting or fishing, with marinas to attract the wealthy motor yacht owners. There are also numerous attractions nearby that bring in the day excursionists by coach or car. Finally, the area is also well served with conference and exhibition halls, which attract high-spend business tourists. All these services are labour-intensive and, thus, invaluable for providing local employment.

indirectly from the tourists' expenditure. Income will be greater in those areas that generate large numbers of tourists, where visitors tend to stay for longer periods, where the destination attracts an upmarket or more free-spending clientele and where there are many opportunities to spend.

It is essential to recognize that, while income may be greatest where levels of pay are high and there is relatively little unemployment in the area, tourism may in fact be of greater importance in those areas where there are few other opportunities for employment. Thus, tourism is the main income generator for one-third of the developing nations,[7] but is also a major income generator in the Western world. In Britain, to take one example, tourism is of prime importance in areas where there is little manufacturing industry, such as in the Scottish Highlands, western Wales and Cornwall. While tourism jobs are often seen as low-paid and seasonal, many are neither seasonal nor temporary. As to low-paid jobs, one must take into account that, without tourism, many workers would have no source of income at all, given that tourism often takes place in areas where there is little alternative work, forcing workers to move away from the area.

Income is also generated from interest, rent and profits of tourism businesses. These could include, for example, the interest paid on loans to an airline in order to buy aircraft or rent paid to a landowner for a car park or campsite near the sea. We must also count taxation on tourism activities, such as sales tax (for example, VAT), room taxes on hotel bills, duty and taxation on petrol used by tourists and other direct forms of taxation that countries may choose to levy on tourists to raise additional public income. In Austria, to give one example, there is a *Kurtaxe*, which is imposed on accommodation to raise money for the local authority. Equally, most countries levy a departure tax on all passengers travelling by air, while in the USA airline taxes are levied on both departing and arriving travellers.

Example

Tourist taxes

The Czech Republic was admitted to the EU in 2004. As a direct result, it raised VAT on restaurant meals from 5 per cent to 19 per cent; VAT on hotel accommodation also increased to the same level in the following year. The industry has argued against common VAT policies in the EU, on the grounds that it would tend to discourage international tourists, but it provides governments with a substantial tax bonus.

In 2008, the Australian government announced an increase in departure tax, expected to raise nearly half a billion dollars. The local tourism industry highlighted its concern that the tourists were being treated by government as a source of extra income, at a time when a strong Australian dollar was already impacting on the industry negatively.

In Canada, the introduction of an air travellers' security charge in 2002 increased the tax revenue earned by the government – in 2006, more than CAN$19 billion was raised. Over half of this came from taxes on products, while just under a quarter of the revenue came from taxes on income (from employment and business profits): 'Government tourism revenue rose at an annual average rate of 4.5 per cent during this period, while spending by tourists increased at an average rate of 3.8 per cent.'[8]

The sum of all incomes in a country is called the **national income** and the importance of tourism to a country's economy can be measured by looking at the proportion of national income that is created by tourism. The National Tourism Administration of the People's Republic of China forecast that, by 2020, tourism income would exceed US$439 billion, accounting for about 11 per cent of GDP.[9] Some regions of the world, particularly the Caribbean countries, are heavily dependent on the income from tourism (see Table 5.6). Some might see this as an unhealthy overdependence on one rather volatile industry.

Table 5.6 Contribution of travel and tourism to GNP, 2006.

Country	Percentage
Antigua and Barbuda	76.5
Anguilla	69.6
Aruba	69.3
Bahamas	50.8
Barbados	40.7
St Lucia	41.6

Source: WTTC, 'World key facts at a glance', WTTC, 2008.

Attempts at measuring the impact of tourism are always difficult because it is not easy to distinguish the spend by tourists from the spend by others, in restaurants or shops, for example. In resorts, even such businesses as laundromats – which we would not normally associate with the tourism industry – might be highly dependent on the tourist spend where, for instance, a large number of visitors are camping, caravanning or in self-catering facilities.

Furthermore, tourism's contribution to the income of an area is enhanced by a phenomenon known as the **tourism income multiplier**. This arises because money spent by tourists in the area will be re-spent by recipients, augmenting the total.

Tourism multiplier

The multiplier is the factor by which tourist spend is increased in this process of respending. This is easiest to demonstrate by way of the following fictitious example.

Example

The tourism income multiplier

A number of tourists visit Highjinks on Sea, spending £1000 in hotels and other facilities there. This amount is received as income by the hoteliers and owners of the facilities, who, after paying their taxes and saving some of the income, spend the rest. Some of what they spend goes on buying items imported into the area, but the rest goes to shopkeepers, suppliers and other producers inside the area. These people, in turn, pay their taxes, save some money and spend the rest.

From the £1000 of tourist spend, let us assume that the average rate of taxation is 20 per cent and that people are saving on average 10 per cent of their gross income, so are left to spend 70 per cent on goods and services (for this example, this would be £700). Let us further assume that, of this £700, the tourist has spent £200 on goods and services imported from other areas, while the remaining £500 is spent on locally produced goods and services, which is money that is retained within the local community. The original £1000 spent by the tourists will then circulate in the local community as shown in Figure 5.2, in the category 'First circulation', the arrows shown in black.

Of the £500 spent within the community, some will go to tourism businesses, that, in turn, will make payments to their local suppliers for such items as food. The shopkeepers or restaurateurs then pay their employees, who, in turn, shop in other shops locally, although some of what they purchase will have been brought into the region from outside.

This second circulation (The arrows shown in red) highlights the further spend by the recipients, including taxation (again at 20 per cent), savings (10 per cent) and leakages due to the purchase of imports.

Once again, the income received by employees and local businesses will circulate through the economy (third circulation, the arrows shown in blue) and so the cycle goes on, with a declining level of expenditure at each level of circulation.

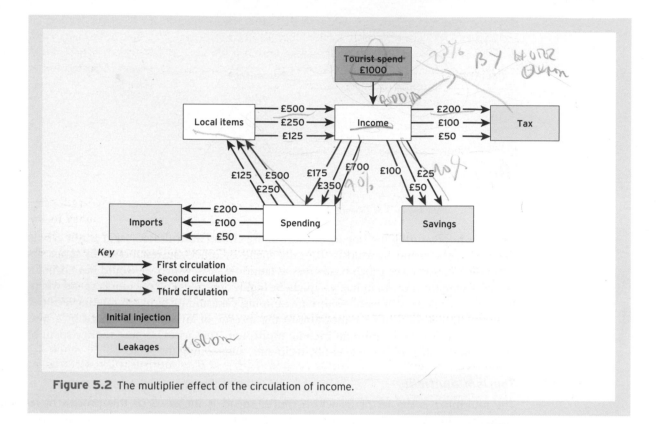

Figure 5.2 The multiplier effect of the circulation of income.

The money spent directly by tourists is considered to be the **direct income** received by a destination. This spend goes to tourism businesses, which provide tourists with the goods and services they require for their holiday (for example, accommodation, meals, guided tours). These tourism businesses will then spend some of this earned income obtaining goods and services from their suppliers, which allows them to fulfil their obligations to the tourists. For example, a tourism business providing guided tours may have to pay entry fees to an attraction or the salary for a guide. This secondary spend of income is termed **indirect income**. At this stage, some spend – such as residents spending their pay on food in a local supermarket or a visit to the cinema – may occur. Such spend is known as **induced income**, available as a result of direct or indirect tourist expenditure.

Example

The effect of leakages on the tourism income multiplier

Each time the money is circulated in this way, some will be lost to the area. For example, taxes paid are transmitted outside the area, some savings, similarly, may be removed from the area and some of the spend has gone on paying for goods imported into the area from other regions of the country or even abroad.

Expenditures that mean money is lost to other areas are known as **leakages** from the system. Leakages in this sense can therefore be regional or national, the latter being a loss of revenue to the country as a whole.

So far, how much income has been created? From Figure 5.2, we can calculate this by considering the money entering the field marked 'income'; it is £1,000 + £500 + £250 + £125 + . . . A progression is developing and, by adding up all the figures (until the circulations become so small that the additional income is negligible) or by using the appropriate mathematical formula, we will find that the total sum is £2000. The original injection of £1000 by tourists visiting the area has multiplied by a factor of 2 to produce an income of £2000.

It is possible to forecast the value of the multiplier if one knows the proportion of leakages in the local economy. In the example above, tax was 20/100ths of the original income, savings were 10/100ths of income and imports were 20/100ths of income. Total leakages, therefore, amounted to 50/100ths, or half the original income. The multiplier can be found by applying the formula:

$$\text{Multiplier} = \frac{1}{\text{Proportion of leakages}}$$

In the example given, the multiplier was 1/0.5, or, 2.

Leakages

So, in an economy with a high proportion of leakages – such as high tax rates (although we must remember that the government may choose to reinvest this tax money in the local economy, so much of it may not be lost for all time) or where many of the goods demanded by consumers are imported – the tourism income multiplier may be quite low and then the economy will not benefit greatly from tourism. Local hotels may also be foreign-owned, so profits achieved are then transmitted to the hotel chain's head office and lost to the area. This might be true of other tourist facilities in the area and even local ground-handling agents or coach operators may be owned by companies based elsewhere, leading to further losses in the multiplier effect.

If, alternatively, many firms are in the hands of locals and leakages of these kinds are minimized, the multiplier effect may be quite high and then tourism will contribute far more than the amount originally spent by the tourists themselves.

The principal reasons for leakages include:

- cost of imported goods, especially food and drink
- foreign exchange costs of imports for the development of tourist facilities
- remittance of profits abroad
- remittance of pay to expatriates
- management fees or royalties for franchises
- payments to overseas carriers and travel companies
- costs of overseas promotion
- additional expenditure on imports resulting from the earnings of those benefiting from tourism.

Example

National tourism income multiplier

Many studies have been undertaken of the tourism income multiplier in different areas, ranging from individual resorts, such as Eastbourne and Edinburgh in the UK, to entire countries, such as Barbados and Fiji. In most cases, the multiplier has varied between 1 and 2.5 (estimates have put it at about 1.7 for Britain as a whole and around 1.2–1.5 for individual towns and regions in the UK), although, in the case of some destinations in the developing world that depend heavily on outside investment and must import much of the food and other commodities demanded by tourists, the figure may be well below 1. The figure for Barbados, for instance, has been estimated at 0.60. Leakages in Western developed nations are generally estimated at around 10 per cent of tourism income, while in developing economies with strong tourism dependency, such as Fiji, the Cook Islands, Mauritius and the Virgin Islands, estimates suggest that imports consume between 36 and 56 per cent of gross tourism receipts.

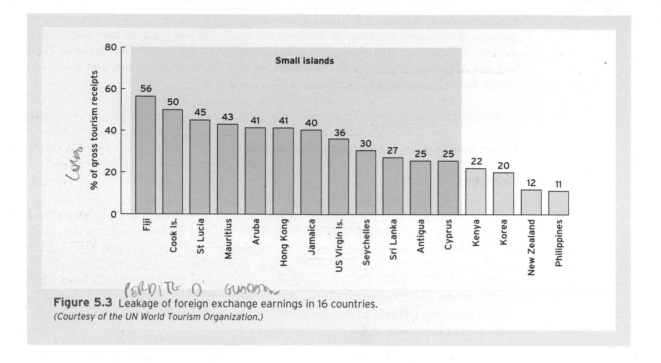

Figure 5.3 Leakage of foreign exchange earnings in 16 countries.
(Courtesy of the UN World Tourism Organization.)

Employment

The WTTC anticipates that employment in tourism will rise from 238.3 million jobs in 2008, accounting for 8.4 per cent of total employment, to more than 296 million jobs by 2018.[10] The industry's importance to many economies as a generator of employment is therefore clear.

As noted, several of the leading tourist destinations in the world are developing countries and, in some tourism-dependent economies such as the Caribbean, as many as 25 per cent of all jobs are associated with the industry. Estimates suggest that some three million tourism jobs will be created in the ten nations that joined the European Union in 2004, most of which are expected to be in Poland and Hungary.

Jobs are created in travel agencies, tour operators and other intermediaries who supply tourist services in both the generating and destination areas. Transport companies such as airlines also employ staff to serve tourists in both areas, but the bulk of employment is in the destination country. The jobs range from hotel managers to deckchair attendants, from excursion-booking clerks to cleaners employed in the stately homes that are open to the public or maintenance staff who keep the rides going at leisure centres or theme parks in the resort.

Many of these jobs are seasonal or part-time, so tourism's contribution to full-time employment is considerably less than the total employment figures may suggest. While this is a criticism of the industry in economic terms – and one that has resulted in large sums of money being spent in an effort to lengthen the tourist season in many resorts – it is important to realize that these jobs are often being created in areas where there is little alternative employment. It is also worth making the point that many of the jobs attract those who wish to work seasonally, such as students seeking jobs as resort representatives during the summer or householders who wish to open their house for summer periods only as bed-and-breakfast establishments.

For countries that are major receiving destinations or enjoy a strong domestic demand for tourism, employment figures will be far higher. On balance, tourism as a form of employment is economically beneficial, although efforts must be made to create more full-time jobs in the industry. The extent to which tourism benefits employment can be seen when it is appreciated that, given the figure quoted earlier, roughly 1 job in 12 in the world is directly ascribed to tourism. Tourism is considered by many to be the largest industry in the world and it is believed to be growing the fastest.

Just as tourism is globally important, so it is important for regions within an economy. The multiplier that affects income in a region affects employment in the same way. If tourists stay at a destination, jobs are directly created by the tourism industry there. Those workers and their families resident in the neighbourhood must also buy goods and services locally, their families require education and need medical care. This, in turn, gives rise to jobs in shops, schools and hospitals to serve their needs. The value of the employment multiplier is likely to be broadly similar to that of the tourism income multiplier, assuming that jobs with average rates of pay are created.

Recent developments in technology however, are threatening labour opportunities in tourism. For example, computer reservation systems (CRS) are rapidly replacing manual reservation systems and, as a result, many booking clerk jobs in large companies such as airlines, tour operators and hotel chains are disappearing. Similarly, the trend towards online bookings via the Internet threatens jobs in travel agencies and suppliers. Call centres are replacing branch shops and, increasingly, these are set up abroad, in countries with low levels of pay, such as India. Fortunately for the future of the industry, at the 'sharp end' – where the tourist seeks a high level of personal service at the destination – the nature of the tourist experience should ensure that technology cannot replace many jobs (although, as discussed in Chapter 18, even the key job of resort representative has been sharply curtailed in recent years). The success of tourism in a country however, will, in part, be dependent on an adequate supply of skilled labour with the right motivation towards employment in the industry and appropriate training.

Example

Tourism employment in Britain

Employment in the tourism industry in Britain is often considered to have a poor image. Turnover of labour is high (attributable to relatively poor pay and working conditions compared with many other fields of business). Training, while it has improved considerably over recent years, still lags behind that of many other countries. Also, attitudes towards working in a 'service industry', where many people in Britain still equate service with servility, make recruitment of good staff difficult. Furthermore, as many as nine out of ten tourism jobs are in small- to medium-size enterprises (SMEs), with turnover lower than £40 million. The European Commission defines these as micro enterprises if employees number fewer than 11, small if between 11 and 50, and medium-sized if between 51 and 250. Firms at the lower end of this scale tend to have fewer qualified staff, fewer training facilities and poorer management, as well as paying less, thus making careers in tourism less attractive to high-flyers and impacting on their ability to compete with other organizations.

Balance of payments

In a national context, tourism may have a major influence on a country's balance of payments. International tourists are buying tourist services in another country and those payments are noted in a country's accounts as 'invisibles'. A British resident going on holiday to Spain will be making an invisible payment to that country, which is a debit on Britain's balance of payments account and a credit to Spain's balance of payments.

Similarly, the money spent by an American visitor to Britain is credited to Britain's balance of payments, becoming an invisible receipt for Britain, while it is debited as a payment against the American balance of payments. It is important to remember at this point that, as mentioned earlier, the outflow of British money in the form of spending abroad by British residents counts as an *import*, while the inflow of foreign holidaymakers' money spent in Britain counts as an *export*.

The total value of receipts minus the total payments made during the year represents a country's **balance of payments on the tourism account**. This is part of the country's entire invisible balance, which will include other services such as banking, insurance and transport. This latter item is, of course, also important for tourism. If an American visitor to Britain decides to travel on a British airline, then a contribution is made to Britain's invisible receipts, while the fare of a Briton going on holiday to Spain flying with Iberia Airlines is credited to Spain and represents a payment on the British balance of payments account. Of course, with the demise of national airlines and the growth of global integration, it may no longer be the case that the leading airlines will in the future be so clearly identified with their country of origin and, if the majority shareholding is abroad, ultimately the profits, if not the earnings, will find their way to other countries in the form of leakages.

Some countries, particularly developing countries, cannot afford to have a negative balance of payments as this is a drain on their financial resources and, in such a case, they may be forced to impose restrictions either on the movement of their own residents or the amount of money that they may take abroad with them. Some countries may suffer severe deficiencies in their tourism balance of payments, which can be sometimes offset by manufacturing exports. Germany and Japan have in the past been examples of countries heavily in deficit on the tourism balance of payments, but which have nevertheless enjoyed a surplus overall through the sale of goods overseas. With both countries now finding it increasingly difficult to compete against low-pay economies in the industrial sector, they are now seeking to boost their own inbound tourism to compensate for this net outflow on the tourism account. By contrast, Spain and Italy both enjoy a strong surplus on their tourism balance of payments as they are popular receiving countries with fewer residents going abroad for their own holidays.

Example

Tourism balance of payments for the UK

Throughout the 1970s, Britain enjoyed a surplus on its tourism balance of payments, reaching a peak during 1977, the year of the Queen's Silver Jubilee. Since then, however, spending by British tourists travelling abroad has increased faster than receipts the country has gained from overseas tourists, with the result that, as we have seen, there has been a net, and steadily increasing, deficit since 1986 (see Figure 5.4).

For a country such as Britain, which has experienced a steady decline in terms of trade (amount of our goods sold abroad, compared with the amounts of goods that we import), it is important to try to redress the balance by a better showing on our invisible exports. As can be seen, however, tourism is not producing a net gain for Britain, which is a concern. The government has attempted to resolve this deficit by encouraging more visitors to come to Britain via the marketing efforts of the national tourist boards or more Britons to take domestic holidays. However, the lure of the sun is a strong magnet for British tourists, so the tourist boards may find it easier to attract the overseas tourist to Britain.

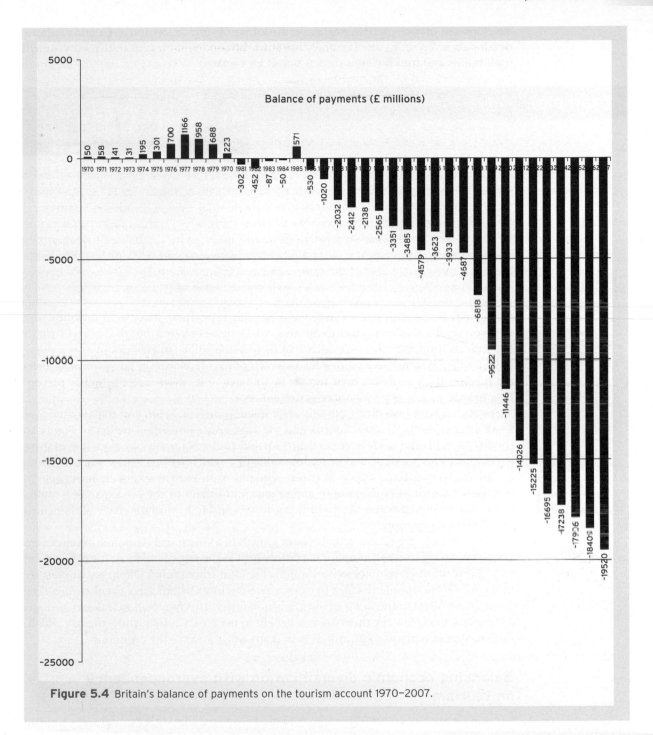

Figure 5.4 Britain's balance of payments on the tourism account 1970–2007.

Investment and development

One factor helping to determine the success or otherwise of tourism in a region is the level of investment, whether private or public, in the industry. Unfortunately, tourism – indeed, leisure generally – are seen by private investors as high-risk investments. Banks are reluctant to lend money for tourism projects and developers are not very willing to take investment risks. This often means that tourism cannot take off until the public sector is prepared to 'kick-start' the economy – that is, invest risk capital in order to encourage the development of tourism. This might take the form of grants or low-interest loans to private developers or, in some more centrally operated economies, it may mean that government itself builds and runs facilities such as hotels for tourists.

Example

Developing Disney resorts

A good example of this 'partnership' between the public and private sectors is the development of the Disney resort site near Paris, involving investment of many hundreds of millions of dollars. The French government, in order to ensure that the Disney Corporation built in France rather than in competing European countries, provided subsidies to attract the company to the site near Paris, which was eventually selected.

The development of the Hong Kong Disneyland resort was also supported by subsidies. Early reports suggested that Disney was seeking US$3 billion in concessions.[11] An agreement to provide land and financial subsidies by the Hong Kong government led to this theme park being opened in 2005.

Investment is something of a chicken and egg situation. There may be an unwillingness to invest until a flow of tourists to the area can be demonstrated, but the area will attract few tourists until they can see evidence of there being sufficient facilities to attract them. Once tourism is shown to be successful, however, private developers or government agencies are often willing to invest even further in the area – in short, success breeds success. Economists refer to this as the **accelerator concept**.

Areas that have benefited from this phenomenon include Spain and the Mexican East Coast in the 1960s, Hawaii, Tunisia and the Languedoc-Roussillon region of France in the 1970s and Turkey and Greece in the 1980s and 1990s. Naturally, the attraction of these regions to tourists will also attract other industries, which will recognize the benefits to be gained from a large inflow of consumers and a pleasant working environment for staff. Resorts such as Bournemouth and Brighton in Britain or the fast-expanding resorts of Florida in the USA and the Gold Coast in Queensland, Australia, have all benefited from this phenomenon.

Unfortunately, the relationship between growth in tourism and economic development is uneven, owing to other complicating factors such as the rate of inflation, the ability of an area to diversify and attitudes to work among the local labour force. Often, key workers are brought in from outside the area in cases where the local labour force is either unwilling or unable to adapt to the needs of the tourism industry. This may lead to leakages as pay is repatriated, thus reducing the economic benefit to the area. Consequently, the risk attending investment remains high, as it does in many other areas of the economy.

Balancing economic diversification with overdependency on tourism

For some countries or even regions, such as rural areas or declining industrial areas, tourism may offer an opportunity to diversify the economy, increasing the variety of empowerment opportunities available for the local population. In addition to this, any downturn in one particular sector may be offset by an increase or stability in other sectors.

An example of this is the city of Bradford in the UK, which sought to encourage tourism to the city when it suffered a decline in the textile and engineering industries – the traditional mainstays of its economy. An initiative by the local government in the mid-1980s saw the introduction of initiatives and funding to encourage tourism to the city. By the turn of the millennium, the number of hotel bednights sold annually in the city had quadrupled, to over 370,000.[12]

In some rural areas, tourism is being amalgamated with farming businesses to provide additional income as well as new products for an area. Farm tourism, or **agritourism** (discussed at greater length in Chapter 9), is just one form of rural tourism that can help to bring income and jobs to remote areas.

Such a reliance on attracting visitors must be placed in context, however. While tourism has been used as a catalyst for expanding economies, perhaps in less developed countries or regions, a concern raised is that over-reliance on this one sector can bring difficulties. A significant downturn in the tourist demand, perhaps through no fault of the destination, or a recession in the home market, may reduce tourist numbers, leaving the destination economically vulnerable. For destinations where tourism is an important component of the economy, attracting tourists from many different source regions as well as different market segments may help to spread the risk. This will not guard against problems experienced in the local tourism area, however. An example of this was seen when foot and mouth disease effectively closed many rural areas of England for most of 2001. While cities across England could still be visited, estimates suggested that this had cost the tourism industry more than £3.3 billion.[13]

While tourism is valuable to many economies, often, as noted, acting as a catalyst for attracting inward investment, the pressures it places on the economy should also be acknowledged and it should not be relied on to the exclusion of other opportunities.

Inflationary pressures

While tourism can bring money into a tourism destination, creating job opportunities and wealth, the demand for resources (including land and labour) can push the cost of those resources higher as that very demand creates an imbalance in terms of supply. As prices of those resources rise, it can create an inflationary effect – employees seek higher levels of pay in order to be able to afford the higher costs of accessing land or property, food and entertainment and so on. Ultimately, some of the local population may be unable to afford the increased costs and become excluded from accessing their own community's resources.

Example

Is tourism to blame for inflation in Argentina?

Following devaluation of the peso in 2002, Argentina experienced growth in international tourist numbers as the depressed value of the local currency helped to make Argentina a more affordable destination than previously. By 2006, visitor numbers had increased by more than 120 per cent. This increase in demand was beneficial for the country as it provided employment, brought in foreign money and encouraged inward investment. It was estimated that more than $3.61 billion was spent by foreign tourists in 2005, amounting to 7 per cent of GDP.

Alongside this apparent success, however, was a concern – inflation. The increased demand led to price rises for products such as hotel rooms. Furthermore, the pressure on supply meant that there was a scarcity of rooms and prices went up – both of which effectively crowded out the domestic market. Furthermore, tourism businesses themselves were having to deal with the higher levels of pay demanded by their employees, as inflationary pressure eroded the purchasing power of their pesos. The outcome of this growth in tourism was a major inflationary headache for the government.

Source: Michael Casey, 'Argentina finds new inflation culprit in tourism sector', *Dow Jones International News*, 8 February 2006.

The opportunity cost of tourism

Further to the key economic impact discussed above, it is necessary also to consider that, by developing tourism, many resources (such as land, labour and capital investment) are used to support the industry, thus making them unavailable for other industries. This is termed the **opportunity cost**.

Crompton proposes that 'Opportunity costs are the benefits that would be forthcoming if the public resources committed to a tourism project were (1) redirected to other public services or (2) retained by the taxpayer.'[14] This principle acknowledges the lost opportunities as a result of using such resources for tourism development and those costs should be set against the benefits received.

A further area of opportunity cost to be considered is that of taxation. When governments tax residents, in order to be able to invest in tourism projects, they reduce the spending capability of the local population, which can impact on the multiplier effect of induced or indirect expenditure. Thus, any positive effect of the tourism project may need to be set against the negative impact on residents' spending.

Statistical measurement of tourism

Gathering data on tourism is a vital task for the government of a country. Governments need to know the contribution that tourism makes to the economy in terms of income, employment, balance of payments and investment. Sufficiently detailed figures must be available in order to know how they have affected regional as well as national economies. Governments will wish to examine trends over time, not only within the country, but also in comparison with the performance of other, competing countries. National tourist offices will use this information to forecast growth, plan for tourism in their areas and as a guide for their promotional campaigns.

Information must be both **quantitative** and **qualitative** in nature – that is, data should be provided about not only the numbers and composition of tourists but also their nature and purpose. For example, national statistics on tourism should include:

- the number of international visitors (arrivals) as well as the number of domestic tourists
- how these are distributed over the months of the year
- the countries generating the international tourists and the regions generating the domestic tourists
- the growth, year on year, of those tourists
- their spend – in absolute terms and how they distribute it between accommodation, transport, shopping, catering and so on.
- their mode of travel – that is, what form of transport they use, whether they are travelling independently or on an inclusive tour
- the duration of their visit
- the types of accommodation they use
- the purposes of their visit – whether leisure, business, VFR
- demographic profiles – age, group composition, social class
- sociographic profiles – personality, lifestyle, interests and activities
- what these tourists seek and the extent to which they are satisfied with what they find.

This is a great deal of information and relates to both inbound and domestic tourism. Data must also be gathered for outbound tourism – residents travelling abroad. Thus, the task of collecting tourism data is daunting, but it is vital that governments undertake it and, as far as is possible, the data collected are based on commonly defined criteria, so that meaningful comparisons can be made between countries.

If the collection of data allows the nation to know what trends are developing over time, what patterns of growth are taking place and how tastes and preferences are changing over time, this information will enable governments to determine where to site roads and airports, where to plan for expansion in local government plans and in what countries to increase or decrease the spend on advertising (as well as how to redirect the themes of advertisements when it is found that new types of tourists are being reached).

The private sector will benefit from this information, too, when deciding whether or not and where to invest in hotels or tourist attractions and the forms those facilities should take. Furthermore, the industry requires an understanding of the propensity to take holidays – that is, the proportion of the population choosing to take a holiday each year and, in particular, a holiday abroad or more than one holiday a year – and how that propensity is affected by a growth in disposable income.

Public-sector planners must be aware of the multiplier effect, which will call for sophisticated research techniques if the figures produced are to be accurate.

We will examine the two most commonly used measurements of tourism – international and national surveys.

International surveys

Statistics of Intra-European and transatlantic tourist flows were collected even before World War II. The systematic collection of tourism data on a global scale, however, can be dated back to the early post-war years. The methods of measurement used have been gradually refined and improved in recent years, particularly in those developed countries that have seen tourism expand rapidly.

Example

The British International Passenger Survey (IPS)

In Britain, information on travel in to and out of the country is obtained in a variety of ways. Until the early 1960s, most basic data on incoming tourism were obtained from Home Office immigration statistics, but, as the purpose of gathering such data was to control immigration rather than to measure tourism, the data had major weaknesses, including a failure to distinguish the purpose of travel – obviously a key statistic when surveying tourists. The government, therefore, decided to introduce a regular survey of visitors entering and leaving the country.

The International Passenger Survey (IPS) has enabled data to be collected on tourists since 1964. It is undertaken by the Office of National Statistics for the Department for Culture, Media and Sport and the national tourist boards and over a quarter of a million international travellers are interviewed annually. Records are made of the number of visitors, purpose of their visit, geographical region visited, their expenditure, mode of travel, transport used and duration of stay. The information is based on their country of residence, so, for example, the large number of British visitors living in America and travelling to visit friends and relatives in Britain each year would be counted as American visitors. This information is published quarterly and compounded annually in the government's *Business Monitor* series (MQ6, *Overseas Travel and Tourism*).

The IPS is a random sample of all visitors travelling in to or out of the UK via the major seaports and airports and the Channel Tunnel, stratified by port of arrival or departure, time of day and mode of transport used.

Global tourism statistics – covering traffic flows, expenditure and trends over time – are collated annually by the UNWTO and the Organization for Economic Cooperation and Development (OECD). The figures are published in the UNWTO's *World Tourism Statistics Annual Report* and *Compendium of Tourism Statistics*, and in the OECD's annual *Tourism Policy and International Tourism*. These statistics are not always strictly comparable, however, as data-gathering methods vary and differences in the definitions of terms remain.

Other surveys are undertaken to provide additional data on the volume of tourists and their expenditure, although reductions in resources have led to cutbacks in the collection of data by the public-sector bodies, so supplementary information is now largely collected by private organizations. For example, IPK International undertakes more than half a million interviews each year, asking populations of more than 50 countries about their travel behaviour. The results of these interviews are published in the *World Travel Monitor* and *European Travel Monitor*. They also provide businesses with extracts of data, on request, ensuring that they can access the most relevant data for their needs. It should be mentioned that full reports as well as data extracts are often quite expensive to purchase.

National surveys

The need for data on domestic tourism is important for both national and regional governments. With this in mind, many governments invest in surveys that can provide details of the travel habits of residents. For example, in Britain, as in other countries in Europe, surveys are regularly carried out on tourism flows within the country. The most important of these is the 'United Kingdom Tourism Survey' (UKTS) on behalf of VisitBritain, VisitScotland, VisitWales and the Northern Ireland Tourist Board.

This survey was originally carried out using monthly telephone interviews, but, since 2005, over 2000 adults are now questioned face-to-face on a weekly basis. Information is collected on the volume and value of all trips involving at least one overnight stay, including

Example

Occupancy surveys for accommodation in Spain

Following an EU directive requiring the collection of tourism data, the Spanish Institute of Statistics introduced the Hotel Occupancy Survey in 1996. This survey examines the number of overnight stays and levels of occupancy of hotel establishments.

In addition, other forms of accommodation are also surveyed in order to understand more about this sector of the industry. They include:

- the Tourist Accommodation Occupancy Survey, which covers tourist apartments
- the Campsite Occupancy Survey, which provides data on tourist stays at campsites
- the Rural Tourist Accommodation Occupancy Survey, which covers establishments registered as rural tourist accommodation.

The data are reported on both a national and regional basis.

These surveys complement the expenditure, national and inbound surveys (FRONTUR and EGATUR) also undertaken by the Ministry of Industry, Tourism and Trade.

Source: Instituto Nacional de Estadíctica, Hotel Occupancy Survey, available online at: **www.ine.es/inebmenu/ mnu_hosteleria.en.htm**

the purpose of the trip, accommodation and transport used, activities engaged in, the method of booking and demographic details of respondents.

In the UK, information on day visitors is less widely available. A Leisure Day Visits Survey is carried out biennially in England (and a similar survey is completed in Scotland, but not currently in Wales or Northern Ireland). This survey collects data on the volume and value of leisure visits to rural areas as well as cities and towns across the country, including seaside resorts.

National tourist boards often provide the funding for surveys that provide data on tourism in their area. For example, in the UK, the national tourist boards collect information on hotel occupancy in each of their own regions.

Techniques and problems regarding measurement of tourism

From the descriptions of the methods for gathering tourist statistics outlined above, it can be seen that most research employs quantitative methods in order to provide descriptive information about issues such as when and where tourists travel, where they come from, how long they stay and how much they spend. In some cases, this information is available in considerable levels of detail. For instance, expenditure can be broken down into sectors (shopping, food, accommodation) and data on visits can be identified by tourism region within the country. Although the data collected are not above criticism, by and large there is a sufficient body of information on which to base decisions.

The demand for qualitative research

Research dealing with why people travel is far more limited, however. This situation is beginning to change, though, as organizations become more concerned with understanding the behaviour of tourists – how they choose their destinations, what they do when they arrive and why, what satisfies them, their purchasing patterns (preferences to book directly rather than through an agent or to book early rather than close to departure time).

None of these factors is easily addressed by the use of structured questionnaires – a more qualitative approach to research is needed. This can involve lengthy interviews in the home or in panels, or groups, of up to eight consumers who will talk about their behaviour under the guidance of a skilled interviewer. Some information is best obtained by observation rather than questioning. For example, watching how customers visiting a travel agency choose their brochures from the racks.

All these types of research are expensive, and time-consuming to administer. What is more, unlike quantitative methods, they cannot be subjected to tests of statistical probability in order to 'prove' the accuracy of the findings, no matter how carefully and scientifically the information is collected. Many organizations are therefore reluctant to commission research involving qualitative methods, although a growing number of research experts now recognize that they may produce richer and more complete data than the more common survey. After all, the information provided by the use of questionnaires will only be as accurate as the honesty of the answers, but it is particularly difficult to know if respondents are answering questionnaires honestly or giving sufficient thought to the questions. This problem is compounded where mailed questionnaires are used.

Some criticisms of quantitative methods

Asking questions of passengers arriving at a destination is, in reality, an *intention* survey rather than an accurate picture of what those passengers actually end up doing while in the country. Equally, surveys carried out on departing travellers require good levels of recall, so some answers will be, at best, guesswork, especially where the aim is to assess the expenditure that the tourist has incurred.

The categories or definitions used may vary by survey. For instance, the travel survey for Finnish residents limits the sample to adults aged between 15 and 74, which may effectively ignore the unique travel habits of the increasingly significant senior citizen (or grey) market. Age is not the only definitional difficulty. One of the issues that occurs when comparing data for different countries as reported by the UNWTO is that some countries may count international tourists by country of residence, while other countries use nationality (determined either by passport or based on immigration forms completed on arrival).

Even if common definitions are used, direct comparisons may be misleading. For example, an international journey may require an American resident to make a trip of several hundred kilometres or cross a stretch of water, which will usually mean forward planning, while a resident of Continental Europe may live within a couple of kilometres of an international border and think nothing of crossing it regularly to go shopping or for a meal out. In some cases, it is even difficult to think of border crossings as international. The Schengen Agreement, for example, eradicated border controls between several of the EU countries, with the result that monitoring visitors has become much harder. Another issue is that some countries still use hotel records to estimate the number of visitors – a system known to be notoriously inadequate because visitors travelling from one hotel to another are counted twice, while those visiting friends and relatives will be omitted entirely from the count.

While international standards for methods of data collection and definitions of terms have become widely accepted, particularly among the developed countries, small variations continue to make genuine comparison difficult, not only between countries but also within a country over a period of time. Above all, if specific types of tourist activity are being examined, as part of a larger sample of general tourists, limits of confidence may fall sharply. Some survey data in the past have produced results that are accurate only to within 20 per cent either way, owing to the small number of respondents in the particular category being examined.

Accurate measures of tourist expenditure are equally difficult to make. Shopping surveys have problems distinguishing between residents and tourists, and tourists frequently under- or overestimate their expenditure. Above all, much of the real tourist expenditure is not recorded at all, especially in developing countries, because it is not taken into account. This includes secondary spend by recipients of tourist monies and even direct spend by tourists in shops and other outlets. In countries where cash, rather than credit cards, is still the normal means of payment and bargaining normal for even the smallest of items, calculating spending patterns reliably is particularly difficult.

Tourism satellite accounts

In an effort to provide more accurate assessment, the UNWTO has introduced the concept of the **tourism satellite account (TSA)**. This technique attempts to include all such indirect expenditures and their resultant contribution to GDP, employment and capital investment. The technique was approved as an international standard by the United Nations Statistical Commission in 2000. It created a set of standardized procedures that aim to ensure that all countries are operating similar systems and, thus, the resulting data are comparable across nations.[15]

The creation of a TSA provides information regarding the economic importance of tourism for a national economy, as well as providing details of both the employment created by tourism and the tax revenues earned as a direct result of tourism activity. Such information can assist with planning tourism resources and may encourage greater awareness of the tourism industry and further investment in the industry.

The implementation of TSAs, however, is fraught with difficulties. It is not only expensive and time-consuming to employ, but accepts all tourism expenditure as beneficial, disregarding the question of sustainability. Neither can the results revealed in one country or region necessarily be transposed to another as each situation is unique and there is no magic formula that will allow estimates of statistical measures to be obtained without full-scale research within the area.

Example

Tourism satellite accounts for New Zealand

Since the end of the last century, the statistics office for New Zealand has worked towards the regular collection of data to provide an account of the value of tourism to its economy. The first account was provided in 1995 and these are now published annually. The reports provide details specifically on the following:

- total tourism expenditure, incuding separate figures for international and domestic tourism
- direct contribution of tourism to GDP
- indirect value of tourism
- employment in tourism, including figures for part-time employment.

Tourism satellite accounts, 2006

Tourism expenditure	NZ$ (million)	
International	8,325	
Domestic	10,264	
GDP	**NZ$ (million)**	**Contribution to GDP (%)**
Direct contribution	6,931	4.8
Indirect contribution	5,898	4.1
Tourism employment	**Persons**	**Tourism employment as percentage of total employment**
Full-time (including working proprietors)	80,600	
Part-time (including working proprietors)	55,900	
Total employment (FTE)	108,600	5.9%
Indirect employment (FTE)	74,500	4.0%

FTE = Full-time equivalent employment
Source: Statistics New Zealand, 'Tourism satellite accounts, 2006'.

Providing such details allows the tourism industry as well as government to understand its value and importance. It also allows comparisons to be made with other years, which can provide insight into changes within the industry. The full report provides a convenient source of additional data on tourism, including expenditure in different sectors of the industry, such as accommodation, air travel and so on.

Future issues

The issue of sustainability is a critical one when discussing the economic impacts of tourism. It can be argued that often far too much concern is given to measuring the economic impacts of tourism on a region at the expense of considering the social or environmental impacts. The industry's sole concern with growth in annual trends may conceal the very real danger that the number of tourists visiting a region will eventually exceed the number the region can comfortably contain. Statistics on the ratio of tourists to residents, for example, or the number of tourists per square kilometre would provide some guidance on the degree of congestion experienced by the region. The social impacts of tourism are also outcomes of many other variables, however, and statistical measurement is still a comparatively recent art that will require continual refinement in the future for the purposes of both economic and social planning. Furthermore, as awareness of the need to protect the environment grows, and media attention encourages greener travel, the need to balance economic development with environmental protection will become more significant for destinations globally.

As new destinations develop their tourism potential, greater understanding of the tourism industry will encourage destinations to maximize the potential to be gained. This will require efforts to maximize the multiplier effect, especially by reducing the leakages. This may include implementing legislation to restrict or control foreign ownership of tourism businesses or the repatriation of profits or pay to foreign employees. Managing the benefits may also include ensuring that the economic benefits of tourism are filtered down to the community rather than an elite few. Balancing the need to attract investment in order to develop the destination with the need to control their own future may be a difficult dilemma for many upcoming destinations.

Computerization has made storage, manipulation of data and, via the Internet, access to data more convenient for businesses interested in the tourism industry. As a consequence, data on many areas of the tourism industry can be used to support planning and development decisions. It needs to be recognized, however, that conflicting data may exist as different survey methodologies can all impact the accuracy of the results. Ultimately, greater information cautiously used can ensure that informed decisions lead to greater levels of business success.

Notes

1. WTTC (2008) 'Progress and priorities 2008/2009' WTTC.
2. UNWTO (2008) 'Tourism highlights', UNWTO.
3. Euromonitor (2008) 'Tourism flows domestic: world', and 'Tourist flows inbound: world', Euromonitor, 10 April.
4. Euromonitor (2008) 'Tourism flows outbound: world', Euromonitor, 22 April.
5. Euromonitor.
6. Policy Research Bureau (2005) 'Briefing paper for policy makers and service providers', Family Holiday Association.
7. Department for International Development *Developments*, Department for International Development 27, 3/2004.
8. 'Tourism tax revenues rise in 2006', Canadian Press 10 September 2007.
9. WTTC (2006) 'China, China Hong Kong and SAR and China Macau SAR: The impact of travel and tourism on jobs and the economy', WTTC p. 46.
10. WTTC (2008) 'Progress and priorities 2008/9', WTTC, p. 6.
11. Stewart, A. (1999) 'Lawmakers raise theme park doubts', *South China Morning Post*, 17 June.
12. Hope, C. A. and Klemm, M. S. (2001) 'Tourism in difficult areas revisited: the case of Bradford', *Tourism Management*, 22 (6).

13. 'Foot-and-mouth has cost English tourism 3.3 billion pounds, government says', Associated Press, 30 October 2001.

14. Crompton, John L. (2006) 'Economic impact studies: instruments for political shenanigans', *Journal of Travel Research*, 45 (1), p. 75.

15. UNWTO, 'Basic concepts of the tourism satellite account (TSA)', UNWTO, available online at: **www.unwto.org/statistics/tsa/project/concepts.pdf**

Further reading

Bull, A. (1995) *The Economics of Travel and Tourism* (2nd edn), Longman.

Lennon, J. (ed.) (2003) *Tourism Statistics: International perspectives and current issues*, Continuum.

OECD, *Tourism Policy and International Tourism in OECD Member Countries* (annual).

Sinclair, M. T. and Stabler, M. (1997) *The Economics of Tourism*, Routledge.

Tribe, J. (1999) *The Economics of Leisure and Tourism* (2nd edn), Butterworth-Heinemann.

UNWTO, *Compendium of Tourism Statistics* (annual).

UNWTO, *Yearbook of Tourism Statistics* (annual).

UNWTO, *World Tourism Barometer* (monthly).

Veal, A. J. (1997) *Research Methods for Leisure and Tourism: A practical guide* (2nd edn) Longman.

Websites

Organisation for Economic Co-operation and Development (OECD)   **www.oecd.org**

UN World Tourism Organization (UNWTO)   **www.unwto.org**

World Travel and Tourism Council   **www.wttc.org**

Questions and discussion points

1. The UK has a significant deficit in its tourism balance of payments. To narrow the gap between receipts and expenditure, it is necessary to encourage a reduction in spend by residents abroad or an increase in spending by international visitors or residents domestically. How might the UK government achieve each of these changes? Do you think some changes may be harder to achieve than others?

2. A weak exchange rate can make a destination appear cheaper for tourists. Discuss whether this is an important factor influencing a family's decision over where to take a holiday or not.

3. Outbound data for tourists often do not correspond with arrivals data. For example, the number of outbound tourists from Australia visiting the UK reported by the Australian Bureau of Statistics does not match the number of arrivals from Australia reported by the UK Office of National Statistics. Discuss the reasons for there being a difference between these two figures.

Tasks

1. Drawing on specific examples to support your report, explain the main reasons for gathering statistics on international tourism and discuss some of the problems that are encountered in gathering and analysing such data.

2. For a country of your choice, gather statistics on outbound and domestic tourism. Using these data, calculate the gross travel propensity. What does this figure tell you about the travel habits of your selected country? How useful is that information for a tour operator selling holidays to that market?

3. Developing countries often focus on promoting tourism to their region in order to gain from the positive economic benefits of visitors. However, it has often been suggested that rich countries are better able to profit from tourism than poor ones. Explain why this may be the case and discuss the actions that a developing country may take to maximize the benefits of developing tourism.

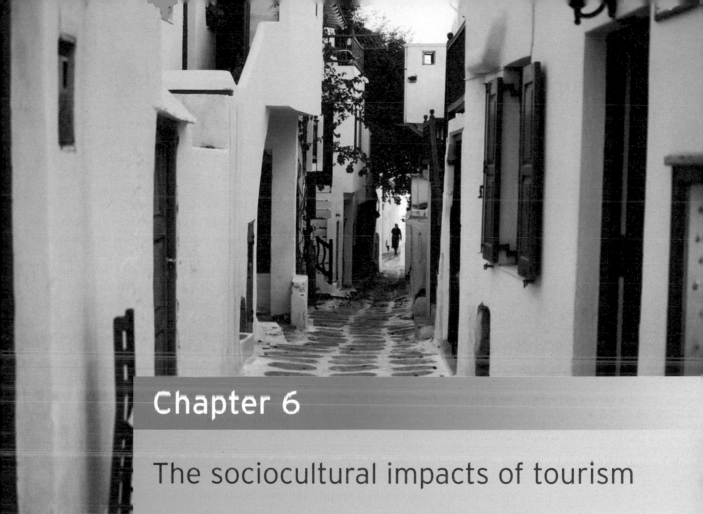

Chapter 6

The sociocultural impacts of tourism

Learning outcomes

After studying this chapter, you should be able to:

- understand the various ways in which tourism can impact on the populations of both destination and generating countries

- identify and evaluate different approaches to finding solutions to those problems

- understand the concept, and importance, of sustainable tourism in a sociocultural context

- recognize the need for adequate planning and cooperation between the private and public sectors as means of overcoming problems.

Introduction

> It is hard to say the positive impact travelling has can ever outweigh the damage done by simply travelling to the destination. Balancing all the positives and nega-tives, I'm not convinced there is such a thing as a 'responsible' or 'ethical' holiday.
>
> Mark Ellingham, founder of *Rough Guides*, interviewed in 2007

Up to this point, it has been generally accepted that tourism is, for the most part and with relatively few exceptions, beneficial to both generating and destination countries. Environ-mentalists, however, are less sure that this is the case and many are arguing for a decline – or, at very least, a stabilization – in the volume of global travel as an essential measure to save the planet. In this chapter, we will look at a different and, in many ways, darker side of the tourism business – its impact (other than in purely economic terms) on those who participate in tourism and the residents of countries subject to tourist flows. This will mean looking at both sociocultural issues affecting hosts and tourists and the impact of tourism on the individual tourist's health – quite an important issue as there is growing concern about the effects of the sun on tourists and workers in the tourist industry, the global spread of AIDS and increasing impact of tropical and sexual diseases on ever more adventurous mass tourists.

As we saw in the previous chapter, tourism can be a potent force for economic good, creating employment and wealth. Equally, it can be argued that tourism provides a basis for widening our understanding of other societies, developing and maintaining links, reducing tensions and even avoiding conflicts. Indeed, in the first half of the twentieth century, tourism was seen, and actively promoted by the authorities in many countries, as a force for good.

While the interplay between tourists and their hosts was seen initially as a means of stabilizing relations between nations, it readily became apparent that foreign visitors with a curiosity about other cultures could, through their enthusiasm, ensure the survival of those very cultural attractions that might otherwise have withered away for lack of support. This book contains numerous examples of the ways in which incoming tourism has benefited the culture and traditions of a particular country or region. In Britain, for example, many great buildings – particularly those serving the needs of eighteenth- and nineteenth-century industry – would have been lost had it not been possible to convert those same factories, mills and warehouses into living and working museums for tourists. With the increasing secularization of Western societies, arguably it is also tourists who will eventu-ally ensure that our great cathedrals survive as the costs of maintaining these buildings for dwindling numbers of worshippers can no longer be borne by the ecclesiastical author-ities alone. Similarly, whole inner-city and dockland areas have been restored and developed to make them attractive as tourist sites. Even a city such as London would be a poorer place without tourists. Around 40 per cent of West End theatre tickets are bought by tourists and undoubtedly the cornucopia of theatres available to Londoners (together with residents of New York and other great cultural cities) owes much to patronage by visitors. In London, as with other major cities, tourists' use of public transport enables residents to enjoy a better and cheaper service than would otherwise be possible. In rural areas and small seaside resorts, too, many heritage attractions, such as local museums, art galleries and provincial theatres, would be forced to close without tourist support, impoverishing the lives of local residents. Country crafts, pubs, even the restoration of traditional pastimes (such as morris dancing in England), all owe their survival, in part, to the presence of tourists.

The rapid growth of tourism during the twentieth century produced problems, however, as well as opportunities on a vast scale for both developed and developing countries. Authorities in these countries came to realize that unrestrained and unplanned tourist development could easily aggravate problems to the point where tourists would no longer

Figure 6.1 Intense demand to view the interiors of famous buildings can lead to congestion, reducing the value of the experience, unless numbers are controlled. Visitors to the Royal Palace at Aranjuez, Spain.
(Photo by Chris Holloway.)

wish to visit the destination – and residents would no longer wish to receive them. This is, therefore, not just an environmental issue: a point can be reached where residents feel swamped by the sheer numbers of tourists at peak periods of the year, resulting in disenchantment and, eventually, alienation, with the risk of growing numbers of altercations taking place between residents and visitors. In short, without adequate planning, tourists may well destroy what they come to see (see Figure 6.1). The problem accelerates as long-haul travel to previously unaffected destinations increases.

Legislation and guidance protecting the tourist destination

Awareness of the need for planning is the first step in attempting to control the worst effects of mass tourism. However, in the early stages of such awareness, authorities failed to make the distinction between cultural and environmental impacts, with concern for sustainability initially concentrating largely on environmental issues. The origins of sustainable tourism legislation to cover both cultural *and* environmental impacts will therefore be examined at this point, while specifically environmental issues will be examined in the next chapter.

Broad awareness of the problems that tourism creates can be traced back to at least the 1960s, but it was another 20 years before they began to be addressed, with legislation introduced to dampen their impact. Influential voices made themselves heard, calling for a new tourism, variously described as 'sustainable tourism', 'eco-tourism', 'green tourism', 'soft tourism' and, eventually, 'responsible tourism'. Proponents of sustainability have

SOSTENIBILITA

argued that **responsible tourism** should be defined as underpinning a properly thought out management strategy, with collaboration between the private and public sectors to prevent irreparable damage to the environment before it is too late.

One of the early expressions of concern was manifested when the then World Tourism Organization (WTO) and the United Nations Environment Programme issued a joint declaration in 1982 calling for the rational management of tourism to protect, enhance and improve the environment. In the following year, they suggested employing zoning strategies to concentrate tourists in those regions that could best absorb them and disperse them where environments were viewed as being too fragile to sustain mass tourism.

It is important to recognize that not all tourists are seeking the same forms of tourism, just as the terms used above to describe the new tourism are not necessarily synonymous. Eco-tourism in its early days was described by the environmentalist Hector Ceballos-Lascurain as, 'that tourism that involves traveling to relatively undisturbed natural areas with the specific object of studying, admiring and enjoying the scenery and its wild plants and animals, as well as any existing cultural aspects (both past and present) found in these areas. Ecotourism implies a scientific, esthetic or philosophical approach'.[1] This is clearly not a description of the activities of the vast masses of tourists who go on holiday each year. Nor does the definition specifically embrace sustainability. It is appropriate to argue that all forms of tourism should be 'sustainable' and not destroy the destination to which the tourist is attracted. Perhaps a better definition is that offered by the International Ecotourism Society itself: 'Ecotourism is responsible travel to natural areas that conserves the environment and improves the well-being of local people'.[2] This definition makes it clear that responsible tourism includes responsibility to both the environment and the indigenous populations.

Tourism must be environmentally compatible, as the World Travel and Tourism Council proposed in its ten-point guidelines (see Figure 6.2). It will be noted that only two of the ten points refer specifically to issues that can be defined as sociocultural.

1. Identify and minimize product and operational environmental problems, paying particular attention to new projects.
2. Pay due regard to environmental concerns in design, planning, construction and implementation.
3. Be sensitive to conservation of environmentally protected or threatened areas, species or scenic aesthetics, achieving landscape enhancement where possible.
4. Practise energy conservation, reduce and recycle waste, practise freshwater management and control sewage disposal.
5. Control and diminish air emissions and pollutants.
6. Monitor, control and reduce noise levels.
7. Control, reduce and eliminate environmentally unfriendly products, such as asbestos, CFCs, pesticides and toxic, corrosive, infectious, explosive or flammable material.
8. Respect and support historic or religious objects and sites.
9. Exercise due regard for the interests of local populations, including their history, traditions and culture and future development.
10. Consider environmental issues as a key factor in the overall development of travel and tourism destinations.

Figure 6.2 Guidelines for sustainable tourism.
(Courtesy of the World Travel and Tourism Council.)

By comparison, the following ten-point set of principles established by Tourism Concern[3] in 1992 appears to achieve a more equal balance between sociocultural and environmental elements:

1. using resources sustainably
2. reducing overconsumption and waste
3. maintaining diversity
4. integrating tourism into planning
5. supporting local economies
6. involving local economies
7. consulting stakeholders and the public
8. training staff
9. marketing tourism responsibly
10. undertaking research.

The issue of sustainability was boosted by the concern expressed by the United Nations General Assembly in the mid-1980s, which established a commission to look in depth at the planet's people and resources and make recommendations on ways to achieve long-term sustainable development. The Brundtland Commission presented its report – *Our Common Future*[4] – in 1987, adopting the definition of sustainable development as, 'Development that meets the needs of the present without compromising the ability of future generations to meet their own needs'.

The influence of this report soon led to the UN organizing a major international conference on the topic. The Conference on Environment and Development (the so-called **Earth Summit**) was held at Rio de Janeiro in 1992. Although tourism neither appeared as an issue in the original Brundtland Report, nor was included in the agenda of the Rio meeting, the industry's planning and development have been heavily influenced by the recommendations emerging from these two sources, most notably by the conference's Agenda 21 – a guide for local government action to reconcile development and sustainability regarding the environment.

The year 1992 was a momentous one for sustainability. The hospitality industry launched its International Hotel Environment Initiative (IHEI), designed to reduce the impact of staying visitors on the environment, while, in the same year, the UK-based pressure group Tourism Concern set out its own guidelines (listed above) and began actively to lobby the private sector to take more account of the need for sustainable planning. This volunteer-aided organization has been a leader in drawing the UK industry's attention to the issue of sustainability. It was first perceived as an irrelevant and esoteric subject, but is now taken more seriously by those responsible for planning and marketing.

By the start of the twenty-first century, the concept had become familiar, both within the industry and among the travelling public. The United Nations Environmental Programme (UNEP) introduced its Initiative for Sustainable Tourism, which was aimed at tour operators and adopted, in 2000. This was followed by a UN declaration to designate 2002 as the International Year of Ecotourism (IYE). A World Summit on Sustainable Development was held in Johannesburg, also in 2002, and, for the first time, it took into account the importance of sustainability in the tourism industry. A world eco-tourism summit held in Quebec in the same year, however, appears to have had relatively little impact. Nonetheless, 2002 proved to be the year when the industry in Britain began to take an active interest. As a direct result of the Johannesburg summit, the British Foreign Office introduced a Sustainable Tourism Initiative, to which over 40 companies (including the leading four tour operators) subscribed. The result was the formation of the Travel Foundation, which is strongly supported by both commercial and environmental organizations and industry bodies, such as the Association of British Travel Agents (ABTA),

Association of Independent Tour Operators (AITO) and the Federation of Tour Operators (FTO). The Foundation's stated aims are to change the practice of tourism to ensure that it makes a greater contribution to the welfare of the environment and populations of tourist destinations.

Other organizations with links to industry, such as the UNWTO and the World Travel and Tourism Council (WTTC), have added their support for the principles of sustainable development, which aim to minimize damage to the environment, wildlife and local indigenous populations. These organizations have particularly recommended the use of local building materials for tourist sites, recycling of waste and water and recruitment of locals for jobs within tourism. Together with the Earth Council, the two bodies also published a report – *Agenda 21 for the Travel and Tourism Industry: Towards environmentally sustainable development*[5] – encouraging the industry to take the lead in preserving the environment in the areas they develop.

Example

The Travel Foundation

Two of the Travel Foundation's early activities to support sustainable tourism both centred on sociocultural issues.

In Cyprus, tour operators were encouraged to develop small group tours to the interior of the island, to comparatively unspoilt villages, allowing the villagers to benefit both commercially and socially from interaction with tourists. The organization supported tours by Support Abandoned Villages and their Environments (SAVE) that were designed to encourage exploration away from the coastal resorts. Aiming to show visitors a true picture of Cypriot rural life, the tours have encouraged shops and other tourist facilities to open and labour forces to seek jobs in their villages rather than migrating to the coast.

In the Gambia, traders found it difficult to sell direct to customers, who resented being hassled on the beaches to buy what were often viewed as inferior products. The Foundation helped local traders to sell their products direct to tourists by overseeing quality control and compiling a directory of local businesses that met the improved standards. In 2002, the Gambia introduced a tax on all visitors arriving at Banjul Airport to raise revenue for tourism advertising and environmental improvements.

While joint action of this kind is invaluable, many businesses – particularly the smaller, independent companies, which were quick to recognize the value of selling the concept of sustainable tourism to their sophisticated markets – introduced their own policies to support sustainability. The Association of Independent Tour Operators (AITO) has shown great enthusiasm for its members to embrace responsible tourism, offering a series of guidelines, including:

- protection of the environment – flora, fauna, landscapes
- respect for local cultures – traditions, religions and the built heritage
- economic and social benefits for local communities
- conservation of natural resources, from the office to the destination
- minimizing pollution caused by noise, waste disposal and congestion.

The organization awards from one to three gold stars to member companies in recognition of their efforts to ensure that tours are planned and operated responsibly. One star is awarded for the appointment of a responsible tourism manager, acceptance of the AITO guidelines and advice to customers in published information; another star is awarded for specific action in undertaking an environmental review and developing a company policy towards responsible tourism and a third star is given to companies engaged in specific initiatives at destinations.

One specialist long-haul operator and member of AITO that has had notable success in this field has been Journey Latin America, which has been awarded two stars by AITO.

Example

Journey Latin America

In the Andes, JLA has worked with reputable local agents to protect porters and the environment on the Inca Trail.

In 2003, the company ran a clean-up campaign in the Cordillera Blanca, Northern Peru (where, as yet, there is little legislation to protect the environment). The company has stated its intention to help protect the integrity of indigenous populations, particularly those in the Amazon basin where adventure holidays are offered. They have also cooperated with Climate Care to offset the effect of carbon dioxide emissions in the flights that transport their staff travelling on business.

The sociocultural effects of tourism

With this overview of legislation and directives encouraging a more sustainable approach to tourism development, we can go on to examine the specific cultural and social impacts on a host country that result from the influx of large numbers of people, often sharing different value systems and away from the constraints of their own environment. In the following chapter we will address the issue of environmental impacts.

The sociocultural impact of mass tourism is most noticeable in less developed countries, but is by no means restricted to them as tourism has contributed to an increase in crime and other social problems in such diverse centres as New York and London, Hawaii and Miami, Florence and Corfu.

Any influx of tourists, however few, will make some impact on a region, but the extent of that impact is dependent on not just numbers but also the kinds of tourists the region attracts. Those who generally go on package holidays are less likely to adapt to the local cultures and will seek amenities and standards found in their home countries, while independent travellers or backpackers will adapt more readily to an alien environment. This has been exemplified in a model devised by Valene Smith (see Table 6.1).

Table 6.1 Levels of adaptation of tourists to local norms.

Types of tourists	Numbers of tourists	Adaptation to local norms
Explorer	Very limited.	Adapts fully.
Elite	Rarely seen.	Adapts fully.
Off-beat	Uncommon, but seen.	Adapts well.
Unusual	Occasional.	Adapts somewhat.
Incipient mass	Steady flow.	Seeks Western amenities.
Mass	Continuous influx.	Expects Western amenities.
Charter	Massive arrivals.	Demands Western amenities.

Source: Valene Smith, *Hosts and Guests*, Blackwell, 1992.

According to Smith's model, explorers – tourists whose main interest is to meet and understand people from different cultures and backgrounds – will fully accept and acclimatize to the foreign culture. Such travellers generally travel independently and blend in as much as possible. As increasingly remote areas of the world are 'packaged' for wealthy tourists, however, and as ever larger numbers of tourists travel further afield to find relaxation or adventure, they bring with them their own value systems, often expecting or demanding the lifestyle and facilities to which they are accustomed in their own countries.

At its simplest and most direct, the flow of comparatively wealthy tourists to a region may attract petty criminals, as evidenced by increases in thefts or muggings – a problem that has become serious in some areas of the Mediterranean, Florida, Latin America, the Caribbean and Russia. For example, as tourism expands in Central and Eastern Europe, taxi drivers in those countries have been found to overcharge gullible tourists, in some cases by manipulating their meters. Tourists may also be seen as easy prey when making purchases in shops or from street vendors. This has become a noted problem in London, where street vendors have overcharged tourists for items such as ice-cream. A familiar anecdote in Continental European nations is that the pricing policy of shop goods in resort regions falls into three bands: the cheapest price is available to locals, a slightly higher price is demanded from visitors with sound knowledge of the local language and the highest price is applied to visitors with little or no knowledge of the language (some argue that a fourth tier is applicable for gullible Americans!)

Example

Venice

Venice represents a good example of the final stage in Doxey's irridex model (see Table 6.2 later in this chapter). For many years, this heritage city has attracted tourists in numbers far in excess of what it can cater for comfortably. In 2006, some 540 cruise vessels called at the port, while as many as 60,000 visitors make day trips to Venice during the peak months of the year. One result has been that tourists are exploited financially and, as a consequence, tend to spend less for fear of being cheated. Recorded examples (leading to official complaints) in 2006 include a couple paying the equivalent of £348 for a meal in St Marks Square, while another was charged £140 for a 10-minute private charter launch transfer. Privately hired water taxis will still charge up to £56 for transfers, against a vaporetto (water bus) fare of £4.20. The price to locals, however, for the same journey by vaporetto is only 70 pence. Such discriminatory pricing policies are a source of concern for the European Commission.

Anecdotally, it is claimed that there are three distinct pricing policies in force in Venice: one for Italians, one for visitors who make a bit of an effort to speak the language and one for visitors who are 'off-hand and rude'. This can double the price of a capucccino in the local cafés. In their defence, Venice's officials have claimed that the 60,000 local residents are completely overwhelmed by the 20 million visitors who come to the city annually.

Source: 'Premium price Venice', *The Sunday Times*, 12 August 2007.

Where gambling is a cornerstone of tourism growth, prostitution and organized crime often follow. Indeed, concerns about the proposed unlimited expansion of Las Vegas-style mega-casinos in British cities led to the UK government abandoning plans for their introduction. Certain countries that have more relaxed laws on sexual behaviour than those in the West attract tourists who are in search of sexual encounters, with their governments often turning a blind eye to crimes such as organized child abuse. In some countries – for example,

Germany and Japan – tour operators specialize in organizing sex package tours to destinations such as the Philippines and Thailand. This public promotion of commercial sex, especially where it involves sex with minors, has come under increasing criticism in the Western world from organizations such as the World Council of Churches and Tourism Concern. Britain, following the example of other Western countries, has passed legislation to enable paedophiles to be prosecuted in their home countries for offences committed abroad.

There are a number of less direct, and perhaps less visible, effects on tourist localities, including the phenomenon known as 'relative deprivation'. The comparative wealth of tourists may be resented or envied by the locals, particularly where the influx is seen by the latter as a form of neo-colonialism, as in the Caribbean or some African countries. Locals can experience dissatisfaction with their own standards of living or way of life and seek to emulate those of the tourists. In some cases, the effect of this is superficial, as in the adoption of the tourists' dress or fashions, but in others the desire to emulate the tourists can threaten deep-seated traditions in the community, as well as leading to aspirations that are impossible to achieve.

Job opportunities and the higher levels of pay that workers in the tourist industry earn will attract workers from agricultural and rural communities who, freed from the restrictions of their families and home environments, may abandon their traditional values. This can result in an increase in promiscuity and the breakdown of marriages.

There can be a problem regarding interactions between hosts and tourists in that any relationships which develop are usually fleeting and superficial, often conducted for commercial ends. A report by UNESCO[8] in 1976 identified four characteristics of host–guest relations in tourism:

- relationships are transitory and superficial
- they are undertaken under constraints of time and space, with visitors compacting sights into as limited amount of time as possible
- there is a lack of spontaneity in relationships – meetings tend to be prearranged to fit tour schedules, and involve mainly financial transactions
- relationships are unequal and unbalanced, due to disparities in the wealth and status of the participants.

Most tourists visiting a new country for the first time, who may be spending no more than a week there and do not expect to return, will be eager to condense their experiences, which tends to make them brief and superficial. Add to this an initial fear of contact with locals, and tourists' comparative isolation – hotels often being dispersed, away from centres of local activity – and opportunities for any meaningful relationship become very limited. Few relationships are spontaneous; contact is generally with locals who work within the tourism industry or else it is mediated by couriers. Language may form an impenetrable barrier to genuine local contact and this limitation can lead to mutual misunderstandings. The relationship is further unbalanced by the status of the visitors, not only in terms of wealth but the fact that the tourists are on holiday while the locals are likely to be at work, often being paid to serve the needs of the tourists.

Sometimes, locals are exploited as 'tourist objects'. In picturesque localities such as villages, local residents can be annoyed by coachloads of tourists descending on the village to peer through their windows or swamp local bars and pubs in order to 'get a flavour' of the local life.

Exploitation of this kind can result in both sides seeing any contact in purely commercial terms. In Kenya's Masai Mara region, the Masai tribespeople extract payment for photographs, either of themselves or of a 'real' (but purpose-built) village (see Figure 6.3). Charging for photographs has become the norm in many parts of the world. In exchange, feeling themselves exploited, tourists feel that it becomes acceptable to steal the towels from their hotel, so the host–guest relationship has changed to one of supplier and customer.

Example

Exploiting the Padaung

A more extreme example of human exploitation is to be found in Thailand, where, on the border with Myanmar (Burma), refugee Padaung tribeswomen have been forced into 'human zoos' as objects of curiosity for tourists. These refugees are known as 'long-neck' or 'giraffe' women due to the brass rings worn around their necks and, although overseas tour operators have refused to deal with this trade, during the high season, around 150 tourists daily pay local operators to visit their camps.

While outcries in the world's press have helped to release some of these women from virtual slavery, in other cases Thailand has rejected their applications for exit visas under the UNHCR resettlement scheme because of their economic value to the villages and, at the same time, the refugees are not given opportunities to take up Thai citizenship. They are paid £24 a month (if wearing rings), but receive payment only during the high season, having to depend on food aid at other times. Another encampment is planned at Sattahip, near the popular resort of Pattaya Beach, to expand on this form of tourism.

Source: 'Padaung refugees trapped by tourism', *Tourism in Focus*, Spring 2008, p. 6.

Figure 6.3 Turning the tables: a Masai photographs visitors in Kenya.
(Photo by Chris Holloway.)

Photography itself is a sensitive issue for many. Tourists from the West expect to be permitted to take what may often be intrusive photographs at will, yet seldom feel it necessary to seek permission from their subjects (see Figure 6.4). In some less developed countries it is viewed as offensive to take any pictures of people (one of the authors witnessed a tribesman on horseback in Uzbekistan deliberately turn his horse's backside to the camera, much to the bemusement of the would-be photographer), while in others

Figure 6.4 Tourists visit Khayelitsha shanty town near Cape Town, South Africa.
(Photo by Chris Holloway.)

care must be exercised to avoid taking photographs of landscapes that include military or quasi-military installations. Some British planespotters were arrested, prosecuted and jailed for just such an activity at a Greek airport and released only after the intercession of the British Government – planespotting is an unknown, not to say eccentric, activity in Greece. Similarly, birdwatchers have been arrested in some countries when using binoculars close to militarily sensitive areas.

In these situations, the role of the courier or representative as a 'culture broker' becomes vital. These members of the industry enjoy local knowledge (and are often from the local community), help to avoid misunderstandings, interpret the local culture for visitors and explain what is appropriate and inappropriate behaviour for the guests. Interpretation plays an important role in sustainable tourism and the guide as interpreter of local customs provides one of the most effective means of communication.

The breakdown in host–guest relationships can be largely ascribed to the volume of visitors. Doxey (1975)[7] developed an 'Irridex' model of the relationship between the growth of tourism and community stress (see Table 6.2). In the early stages of tourism development, the locals are euphoric, pleased to see investment and improved job prospects for local people. The comparatively small numbers and the fact that most tourists will belong to the 'explorer' category and accept the norms and values of the hosts, mean that tourists are welcomed and even cultivated as 'friends'. As locals become used to the benefits they receive from tourism and aware of the problems that tourism generates as it grows, so they come to accept it and their meetings with tourists become more commonplace and commercial. Further growth leads to a general feeling among locals that tourists are an irritant rather than a benefit, as they note how tourism is changing their community and their cultural norms. In the final stages, locals show open antagonism towards the steady stream of visitors, many of whom will have the attitude that locals are there to meet the tourists' needs, and insist on Western standards.

Table 6.2 Irridex model of stress relative to tourism development.

Stages	Characteristics	Symptoms
Stage 1	Euphoria	Visitors welcomed, little formal development.
Stage 2	Apathy	Visitors taken for granted, contacts become commercial.
Stage 3	Irritation	Locals concerned about tourism, efforts made to improve infrastructure.
Stage 4	Antagonism	Open hostility from locals, attempts to limit damage and tourism flows.

Source: G. V. Doxey, 'A causation theory of visitor–resident irritants: methodology and research inferences', *Proceedings of the Travel Research Association Sixth Annual Conference*, San Diego, 1975.

Naturally, this is a simplified model of the fairly complex relationships that actually develop between tourists and locals. Other factors that must be taken into account are the length of time tourists stay in the community (those staying longer will fit in better and be seen as making a more effective contribution to the local economy) and the cultural gap between locals and tourists (domestic tourists, sharing the values of the locals, will be less resented than those who have no understanding).

Examples abound of the antagonism engendered between locals and tourists, even within Britain. An attitude change among locals can be detected by changes in the vocabulary of tourism. For example, in some parts of England, derogatory terms such as 'grockles' or 'emmets' are in use and locals may carry bumper stickers on their cars that read, 'I'm not a tourist, I live here'. More open hostility can be detected in the city of Bath, where hoses have been turned on open-top tourbuses where guides use megaphones to provide a commentary.

Breaking cultural taboos can produce a backlash; for example, Alassio banned bikinis in the streets, and in the Alto Adige region of the Italian Dolomites in 1993 a local movement erupted spontaneously to prevent the spread of topless bathing in the lakes, although other residents expressed their concern that the publicity accorded this might dissuade some tourists from visiting the area! In Greece, what has become known as the 'Shirley Valentine factor' (after the title of the film dealing with the issue of British women escaping a humdrum life at home to find romance in Greece) has led to a reaction from women in Corfu and Crete, who resent the attention Greek men pay to foreign females and feel that Greek women are now undervalued. It is also true to say, however, that some Greek women have welcomed the increasing liberation from male dominance that tourism has brought.

Example

Ignorance of local cultural tradition

Following the crash of a Pakistani Airlines plane over Nepal in 1992, it was reported that British Embassy officials were appalled by the public display of the bodies for relatives of the English victims, which they described as a 'grotesque peepshow'. In Nepal, however, viewing the remains of the dead is an important part of the act of grieving, so the Nepalese were merely extending this courtesy to the foreign mourners.

A lack of understanding of local cultural traditions is common where those traditions appear to be contrary to what we view as tasteful and appropriate. British tourists in Tokyo may be surprised to see signs outside some nightspots declaring 'Japanese only here', reflecting a nineteenth-century imperialist tradition that has long died out in the Western world.

The hosts' impacts on tourists

While a considerable amount of research has now been undertaken into the effects of tourists on locals, rather less is available to tell us how locals, in turn, influence the tourists. What we do know, though, is that we can ascribe our widening acceptance of foreign food, drink and fashions in Britain to the influence, in part, of overseas travel. The quality of foreign food, service, transport and hotel facilities has encouraged us to become more demanding in the provision of these things in Britain.

The research that is available (Gullahorn and Gullahorn, 1963)[8] suggests that tourists go through three stages when adapting to the local culture of their holiday environment. In the first stage, the tourists are excited by the environment and the novelty of the situation; later, a second stage is reached in which the tourists become disillusioned with and more critical of the environment as they become accustomed to the situation. Finally, in what may be a slow process, they learn to adapt to the new setting and, in doing so, may experience 're entry crisis', where it becomes difficult to adapt again to their home environment when they return.

Other studies have examined the extent to which pre travel attitudes affect adaptability and whether travel broadens understanding or reinforces stereotypes (see, for example, Sutton 1967[9]). The evidence suggests that a self-fulfilling prophecy is at work here – that, if we travel with the expectation of positive experiences, we will experience them. Much more work is needed, however, to explore the relationship between the tourist and the host from the tourist's perspective.

Finally, the phenomenon of second homes abroad is due in large part to the increase in travel, which has led to greater awareness of, and desire for, residences in attractive resorts on the Continent, and around the Mediterranean in particular. One survey (drawing on statistics provided by the office of the Deputy Prime Minister) revealed that 229,186 English households owned second homes outside of the UK in 2004, while other sources have put the figure even higher, suggesting that the total for UK second home ownership in France alone may be as high as half a million. Where expatriates are willing to learn the language and blend in with the culture, little conflict emerges, but where large groups of British (or other nationals) buy homes within a small region and begin to seek products and forms of entertainment with which they are familiar in their own country, this can transform the indigenous culture and undermine traditional lifestyles. Many of these homes are bought with the intention of renting, largely to nationals of the same country as the owners, which reinforces both the cultural gap and transitional nature of the interactions between locals and tourists.

Of course, the problems arising from second home ownership are not restricted to homes purchased abroad. In Britain, there has been resentment between locals and 'incomers' from other parts of the country, which is compounded where regional rivalries already exist. This has happened where second homes have been purchased in attractive areas of Wales by English incomers as it has driven up house prices and owners may intend to rent out their properties only to tourists. Where these homes are occupied infrequently, this leads to resentment by shopkeepers and others who fail to benefit. If it is not an all year round destination, this can soon result in an apparently 'dead' village in the off-season where a high percentage of the homes are owned by outsiders. In some regions, such as South Hams, Devon, prices have been driven up to a point where houses can no longer be purchased by locals. In the popular coastal resort of Salcombe, 45 per cent of homes are said to be owned by outsiders – the highest percentage in the country after Central London.

Staged authenticity

Given the constraints of time and place, tourists demand **instant culture** – an opportunity to sample, even if superficially, the 'foreignness' of the destination. This gives rise to what Dean MacCannell (1989)[10] has referred to as **staged authenticity**, in which a search by tourists for authentic experiences of another culture leads to locals of that culture either providing those experiences or staging them to appear as realistic as possible (see Figures 6.5a and b). In this way, culture is in danger of becoming commercialized and trivialized, as when 'authentic' folk dances are staged for the package tourists as a form of cabaret in hotels or traditional tribal dances are arranged, often in an artificially shortened form, as performances for groups of tourists. Such trivialization is not unknown in Britain, with pastiche 'mediaeval banquets', town criers and ceremonies reminiscent of earlier times. One proposal was made that the traditional ceremony of Changing the Guard should be mounted more frequently each day, in order to give tourists more opportunities to view it. Similarly, a suggestion was made (and considered seriously by the authorities) that Stonehenge be replicated in fibreglass near the actual site, to give the tourist an 'authentic' experience of seeing the stones more closely than is now possible.

Tourists will seek out local restaurants not frequented by other tourists in order to enjoy the 'authentic' cuisine and environment of the locals, but the very fact of their discovering such restaurants makes them tourist attractions and, ultimately, the 'tourist traps' that tourists are looking to avoid. Meantime, the locals move on to find somewhere else to eat.

The downgrading of the traditional hospitality towards tourists in Hawaii is exemplified by the artificial welcome to which they are subjected on their arrival at the islands. Traditionally, welcoming natives would place a lei of flowers around the neck of each tourist, but, over time, the cost of this courtesy and the huge volume of tourists has led to the lei

Figure 6.5(a) Staging the authentic: the reconstruction of a Neolithic lake village on the shores of Lake Constance, Germany.
(Photo by Chris Holloway.)

Figure 6.5(b) Waxwork figures depict local life in the Neolithic age.
(Photo by Chris Holloway.)

being replaced by a plastic garland, reinforcing the impression of a commercial transaction, which this has now become.

Tourists seek local artefacts as souvenirs or investments. In cases where genuine works are purchased, this can lead to the loss of cultural treasures from the country. Many countries now impose strict bans on exports of such items for this reason. Tourists, however, are often satisfied with purchasing what they believe to be authentic examples of local art, which has led to the mass production of poorly crafted works (sometimes referred to as **airport art**), such as are common among African nations and the Pacific islands. An effect of this is that it encourages the freezing of art styles in pseudo-traditional forms, as in the case of the apparently 'mediaeval' painted wooden religious statuary produced in Oberammergau and other villages in southern Germany. In turn, artists and craftspeople are subtly encouraged to change their traditional styles, making their works in the colours that are found to be most attractive to the tourists or reducing the sizes of their works to make them more readily transportable.

It is perhaps too easy to take a purist stance in criticizing these developments. One must also point to the evident benefits that tourism has brought to the cultures of many tourist destinations. Indeed, in many cases it has helped to regenerate an awareness and pride in local culture and traditions. But for the advent of tourism, many of those traditions would have died out long ago. It is facile to ascribe cultural decline directly to the impact of tourism – it is as likely to be the result of mass communication and technological development.

As Western (and specifically American) culture is the dominant influence around the world, it will inevitably undermine other cultures, particularly those of the developing world. It is equally clear, however, that tourism from the Western nations travelling to such nations has led to a revival of interest in tribal customs in those countries. It is not just in developing countries that this is the case – the revival of morris dancing in English communities is a direct result of the impact of tourism. Traditional local cuisines in Britain, too, have been regenerated, with the support of the national tourist boards with 'taste of England', 'taste of Wales' and 'taste of Scotland' schemes – a concept regenerated in promotions undertaken by VisitBritain since 2004, emphasizing once again the originality and quality of regional dishes in Britain. Dying local arts and crafts have been revived through cottage industries in rural areas that have benefited economically from the impact of tourism.

Example

Staging authenticity: the pastiche building

One notable example of staging authenticity is to be found in the planned construction, between 2009 and 2011, of an entire pastiche French village – Domaine Haut-Gardegan. The village is to be built by ski resort developer Intrawest, close to St Emilion. It will resemble classical early French mountain villages, but the only authentic buildings in the new village will be a ruined castle and stables, with a twelfth-century church on the outskirts.

A twist to staging authentic buildings is to first destroy them, then reconstruct them somewhere else. Former Beatle Ringo Starr's home is expected to be taken down to make way for redevelopment, then rebuilt brick by brick within the new Museum of Liverpool.

Cultural transgressions

Although not exclusively a British problem, other patterns of behaviour among a small but significant minority of Britons while abroad have made such tourists unwelcome in several leading resorts on the Continent. Freed from the normal restraints of their every-day surroundings, many young tourists have been attracted to resorts promising unlimited cheap alcohol, 24-hour entertainment and readily available sex, either with fellow tourists or locals. Some of the less responsible tour operators have promoted these resorts to niche markets of youngsters, driving away the family market. This, in turn, has fuelled the growth of bars and discos offering popular music of the day, while resort reps for the operators organized bar crawls, earning high commissions from favoured bars.

The popularity of the resorts quickly led to their becoming overwhelmed by ill-behaved visitors, soon commonly referred to as 'lager louts'. Bar and street brawls, open drunkenness and impolite behaviour quickly led to conflicts with locals, not infrequently resulting in visitors being hospitalized. One after another, resorts such as Benitses and Kavos on Corfu, Ibiza in the Balearics and Faliraki on Rhodes found their more traditional markets drying up. Efforts to change the image of the destinations were often taken too late. As local authorities intervened, imposing curfews, licensing bar crawls by groups, employing undercover police and even attempting to quarantine noisy groups within zones, the revellers simply moved on to other resorts, threatening their decline in turn.

This 'slash and burn' approach to tourism is not easily resolved, although the tour operators responsible for some of the worst excesses have sobered up as a consequence of the bad media publicity they received and modified their packages and promotions. The problem for the destinations – of how to regain public trust and to reposition their product – is less easily solved.

Where cultural differences are tied to religion, conflicts become greater. Some Islamic countries in the Middle East, such as the United Arab Emirates, have actively pursued policies to attract Western tourists, but expect them to respect local mores. Dubai, one of the Emirates States, is among those that initially turned a blind eye towards inappropriate beachwear or consumption of alcohol by visitors, but flagrant breaches of behaviour reduced levels of tolerance and led to a tightening up of control, notably in the case of two British tourists accused in 2008 of having sex on the beach and insulting the policeman who sought to arrest them.

The exploitation of indigenous populations

Perhaps the most serious accusation that can be made against tourism is the manner in which both members of the industry and destination authorities alike have exploited indigenous populations in their desire to develop tourism in ways that would maximize their own interests. There are countless examples of such exploitation, involving child labour, sexual exploitation and the wholesale removal of locals from their tribal lands to permit the development of tourism. There are several recent examples, too. The Masai tribespeople have been removed from their Ngorongoro crater hunting lands in Tanzania in order to allow tourists free movement to photograph wildlife. Botswana has evicted Gana and Gwi bushmen from their land in the central Kalahari game reserve to open the area to tourism. International opprobrium followed the removal and forced labour of Burmese people to enhance tourist projects in Myanmar.

Tourism Concern and other groups such as Tourism Watch in Germany have been particularly active in recent years in drawing attention to the exploitation of porters engaged in trekking and mountaineering tours in several countries. Publicity about their plight led to the formation of an International Porter Protection Group to oversee conditions on Mount Kilimanjaro, Tanzania (where porters were frequently obliged to carry loads of up to 60 kg for low pay, dressed in inadequate protective clothing: around 20 guides and porters die in their jobs each year), in the Himalayas and on the Inca Trail in Peru, where official guidelines are designed to ensure that packs do not exceed 20 kg and are weighed by government officials.

Sexual exploitation, especially of minors, has also been a cause of considerable concern in several developing countries and pressure groups such as End Child Prostitution, Pornography and Trafficking (ECPAT) and the World Council of Churches have encouraged the implementation of legislation to protect minors and prosecute offenders within their own countries for offences committed abroad. Britain reacted in 1997 with the passing of the Sex Offenders Act (UK), including a section that, for the first time, allowed such prosecutions to take place, although the difficulty of gathering evidence in developing countries has hindered the implementation of the Act.

Managing the social impacts of tourism

Sustainable tourism – in terms of the social impacts of tourism on indigenous populations – needs to be managed in two ways. First, it is important that good relations are established between locals and guests, so that guests are welcomed to the region or country and social interactions benefit both parties.

There are different approaches to ensuring this and the choice is essentially between two diametrically opposed management methods. Responsible officials can attempt to integrate guests into the local community and control the overall number of visitors so that the local population does not become swamped by tourists. This is really only practical where demand for the destination is limited to comparatively small numbers and the market attracted shows empathy for, and sensitivity towards, local culture. Thus, specialist tourism will allow for this solution to be adopted, but mass tourism will not.

Alternatively, officials can aim to concentrate the visitors in particular districts (sometimes referred to as tourist 'ghettos', often some distance away from residential neighbourhoods) so that any damage is limited to the few locals who will have contact with those guests, usually in the form of commercial transactions. In this way, most locals and visitors will not come into direct contact with each other, though this may also reduce the economic benefit of tourism to the local community. One solution of this kind is the integrated resort complex offering all-inclusive packages. Such resorts are becoming increasingly common at long-haul destinations – examples being found in Cancún, Mexico, Nusa Dua in Bali, Indonesia, Puerto Plata in the Dominican Republic and the Langkawi development in Malaysia. All-inclusive resorts can also be operated sustainably if locals are employed in skilled as well as less-skilled jobs at the site and much of what is consumed at the resort is produced in the surrounding area.

Government policies to attract large numbers of tourists have given way to policies designed to attract particular tourist markets. While this has, in most cases, meant trying to attract wealthy, high-spend visitors, it has sometimes led to a move to encourage visits by those who will have the least impact on local populations – that is, those who will integrate well and accept local customs rather than seek to impose their own standards on locals. Some have gone further, however. The local authority at Alassio, Italy, took rather extreme action in 1994 in an effort to discourage day trippers and sacopelisti (sleeping baggers) who slept on the beaches and brought little income into the town. It asked the railways to provide fewer trains to the resort on weekends. Tourists were also to be accosted and asked to show that they were carrying at least 50,000 lira as spending money. Such approaches are isolated, however, and, for the most part, destination authorities have recognized that their obligation is to grow tourism, while ensuring that, as far as possible, whatever impact tourists have on local populations should be beneficial to the locals.

Bringing economic benefits to locals

One other issue is the need to ensure that locals are involved in all stages of the development of tourism at a destination. This means that the onus is on developers and authorities to consult with locals at all levels during the process of development, encourage their participation and ensure that indigenous populations benefit economically from incoming tourism, by the provision of employment at all levels and ownership of facilities. All these activities, however, require a measure of sophistication among the local population, the provision of essential education and training, as well as assistance in raising finance for investment in local tourist businesses. The solution cannot be achieved merely by putting businesses into the hands of local residents. To illustrate this, the example can be given of a tour operating company in Arnhem Land, Australia, that was originally managed by foreign nationals, but was eventually handed over to local Aboriginal administration. While the new Aboriginal owners were fully capable of handling the operational aspects of the programme, they had little knowledge of, and no contacts with, the overseas markets

Example

Blue Lagoon Cruises

Blue Lagoon Cruises operates in the Yasawa Islands north west of Fiji. The company makes direct and indirect contributions of some £165,000 annually to the islands, whether visited or not. Locals are employed and care is taken to minimize the impact of tourists on the islands during visits.

Expansion plans include calling at some of the more northerly, seldom visited islands, such as Rabi and Kioa, where locals have notable basketry skills and the economy can be boosted by craft sales. Funds earned will be channelled into community halls, water tanks and the construction of sea walls against erosion.

Figure 6.6a Daweb children entertain visitors at a school in Maltahoehe, central Namibia. Donations go to fund their education.
(Photo by Chris Holloway.)

Figure 6.6b A resident of Khayelitsha, South Africa, makes flowers from metal cans to sell to visitors.
(Photo by Chris Holloway.)

they existed to serve and, in consequence, found it difficult to attract new business. Other, more recent, schemes, however, have been handled more successfully. One simple example is the innovation of employing local Bedouin tribesmen to act as escorts for groups of trekkers across the Sinai Peninsula. Similarly, a sustainable village project in Gomorszolos, Hungary, involves tours of small groups (a maximum of 12 people) staying in locally owned hotels, using local guides, and with local conservation projects being undertaken that are partly funded by the income generated by the tours.

The impacts of travel on tourists' health

An impact is a two-way process and we have examined both positive and negative effects of tourism in this chapter. It is notable how the lifestyles of many tourists have changed as a result of their experiences of travelling abroad. They often have more adventurous tastes in food, consume more wine at the expense of beers and hard spirits, have a wider appreciation of foreign cultural activities, even a greater willingness to master the elements of a foreign language (a real breakthrough for the British!) These are just some of the things that tourists bring back with them to enrich their lives in their home countries. Unfortunately, other things they bring back with them can be less welcome.

As noted in Chapter 4, severe sunburn is among the commonest of the ailments afflicting tourists from the generating countries – the result of a desire to maximize exposure to the sun during the brief period spent abroad on holiday. While sunburn is by no means uncommon among tourists visiting the seaside in northern communities, the increased intensity of the sun's rays nearer the equator, coupled with higher consumption of alcohol abroad, leading to carelessness in taking measures to protect against burns on fair skin, has resulted in rather more than the pain and nausea that accompany a bad case of sunburn.

The propensity to develop skin cancer has been enhanced as the world's protective ozone layer has been reduced by atmospheric pollution. It has been estimated that 160,000 new cases of malignant melanoma occur annually, many resulting from over-exposure to the sun. The long-term effect of such exposure to the sun is a substantial rise in skin cancers, anything up to 20 years or more after the sunburn occurred. Although the danger has been recognized for some years and governments have mounted campaigns to draw attention to the problem, many tourists either remain ignorant of it or choose to ignore it in their desire to cultivate an attractive tan (research indicates that over 70 per cent of young people between the ages of 16 and 24 in Britain still want to get a tan while on holiday). The United States experiences over a million new incidences of skin cancer (both melanomas and carcinomas) annually and the problem has also been well publicized in Britain, where some 40,000 cases occur each year. By the early twenty-first century, the incidence among British males was increasing at a rate of 4.2 per cent per annum, with mortality increasing at 2.9 per cent. In Australia, however (where in Queensland as many as one in three of the population is affected), the 'slip, slap, slop' campaign (slip on a T-shirt, slap on a hat, slop on suncream) has been far more effective in educating a country of sunlovers, resulting in a sharp decline in the number of all forms of skin cancer in that country.

Skin cancer is of two varieties. The commoner carcinoma occurs as a result of *long-term* exposure outdoors. It is therefore common among people such as construction workers and farmers who spend long hours each day in the sun, but there is also a danger to employees in the tourism industry such as bus and coach drivers, lifeguards or resort representatives, all of whom spend long hours exposed to the sun in their daily work. A melanoma results from *short but intensive* exposure to the sun, such as is commonly experienced by tourists on holiday. The danger of a malignant melanoma is greatest for fair-complexioned tourists, especially those from Anglo-Saxon races such as Britons,

Germans and Scandinavians – young children are particularly at risk – although the effects of such exposure may take many years to develop into cancer. There were over 8000 cases of malignant melanoma in Britain in 2005, following a rise in incidence of almost a quarter during the period 1995–2000.

The problem with the sun's rays is that tourists going on holiday, whether to beaches at home or abroad, remain largely unaware of their danger. There are, in fact, two forms of ultraviolet light rays, known as UVA and UVB. The former (which are also those to which people are exposed when using sunbeds) have longer wavelengths and affect the skin throughout the day whenever it is exposed to light, even during cloudy periods. These rays have long-term effects on the skin, creating wrinkles and liver spots, and can also lead to the development of carcinomas. There is doubt as to whether or not most SPF (sun protection factor) creams offer adequate protection from these rays.

UVB rays are shorter in wavelength but stronger, far more damaging than UVA rays, and at their most dangerous when the sun is at its height, between the hours of 11 a.m. and 3 p.m. While SPF creams prevent the skin burning, it is now believed that they have little effect on reducing the incidence of long-term skin cancer unless sunblock creams are used.

Attitudes towards getting a suntan are expected to change only gradually over the next few years, with many tourists still choosing to visit seaside resorts for their perceived health and relaxation benefits. The media, with the support of health experts, are encouraging tourists to change their behaviour patterns while at the seaside, by applying high-factor suncreams or, better still, sunblocks, while sunbathing, reapplying these frequently if entering the water to swim, ensuring young children are well covered and generally reducing outdoor activities when the sun is at its most intense. Seaside resorts are coming to recognize that, if they are to survive, they must construct more indoor facilities and offer their visitors better protection from the sun (such as parasols, now commonly found on Caribbean beaches) while on the beach.

Exposure to contaminated food results in other common holiday ailments, ranging from simple upset stomachs to hepatitis and dysentery. The incidence of these kinds of illnesses are increasing as holidaymakers become more adventurous, visiting areas of the world where poor hygiene and inadequate supervision are widespread and taking more risks when sampling the local food.

Tropical diseases are, similarly, becoming more commonplace, with malaria leading the field – several deaths occurring each year among British tourists, many of whom disregard even the most basic recommended precautions. Some forms of malaria are becoming highly resistant to standard prescription drugs, although recent research offers hope of a vaccine within a generation.

Outbreaks of SARS have also severely impacted on recent tourist movements, especially to popular Asian countries, while the global spread of HIV/AIDS, especially but by no means restricted to African and Asian destinations, coupled with lax sexual mores among many travellers, compound the health threats for tourists.

The solution to most of these problems lies in better education, of both hosts and guests, with the onus being on the travel industry to get the message across to their customers through brochures, websites and on-the-spot resort representatives.

Politicocultural impacts

Where significant economic benefits are likely to follow from influxes of tourists, tourism can be a force for good politically. This is exemplified by the 2008 Olympics, held in the Republic of China, where the government felt obliged, during the period in which the Games were in progress, to relax – if only marginally and temporarily – some of its authoritarian controls and display a more democratic face to the world. It is almost inevitable that large numbers of tourists visiting a country over extended periods of time will eventually influence the political culture of that country, often for the good.

Controversy inevitably surrounds the question of whether or not tourists should be encouraged to visit more extreme regimes – Myanmar (Burma) being a case in point. The argument *favouring* visits is that interactions between hosts and guests, however closely controlled, will be of some benefit to locals, culturally as well as economically, while the contrary view is taken by those who believe that tourist revenues flowing into authoritarian coffers benefit and reinforce the regime.

A presently more critical political issue confronting the global tourism industry, however, is the growth in terrorism, which threatens to undermine both travel and understanding between nations. As we saw in Chapter 4, attacks directed against Westerners, especially in Islamic countries, can lead to a dramatic reduction in the flow of tourists to those countries, some of whose economies (Egypt and Bali, for example) are heavily dependent on tourism. Local civil wars in some popular areas of the globe inhibit tourism. Kathmandu in Nepal, for example, saw a sharp decline in tourist arrivals following the rise of Maoist revolutionaries in the country, but, with a more stable government in place following the deposition of the monarch, it can be anticipated that tourists will begin to flow to the area again.

The British foreign office frequently has been accused of ambivalence in the guidance given to tourists, while the industry itself – and travel insurance companies – are obliged to follow their governments' directives in determining whether or not holidays should be withdrawn following attacks. The authorities in the leading generating countries are seldom consistent in tackling these issues and tourists themselves tend to vary in their reactions. American tourists, for instance, show greater reluctance to travel to countries where there is a perceived threat, however remote, while European travellers appear more resilient. Indeed, following the events of 9/11 2001, Americans have been slow to travel abroad again, even to relatively safe countries, which has slowed the global expansion of tourism considerably.

Notes

1. Definition given at forum 'Conservation of the Americas', Indianapolis, 18–20 November 1987.

2. **www.ecoturism.org**

3. Eber, S. (1992) *Beyond the Green Horizon: Principles of sustainable tourism*, Tourism Concern/WWF.

4. Brundtland Commission (1987) *The Brundtland Report: World Commission on Environment and Development: Our common future*, OUP.

5. UN Conference on the Environment and Development, Rio de Janeiro, 1992.

6. UNESCO (1976) 'The effects of tourism on socio-cultural values', *Annuals of Tourism Research*, 4, pp. 74–105.

7. Doxey, G. V. (1975) 'A causation theory of visitor–resident irritants: methodology and research inferences', *Proceedings of the Travel Research Association Sixth Annual Conference*, San Diego.

8. Gullahorn, J. E. and Gullahorn, J. T. (1963) 'An extension of the U-curve hypothesis', *Journal of Social Sciences*, 19, pp. 33–47.

9. Sutton, W. A. (1967) 'Travel and understanding: notes on the social structure of touring', *International Journal of Comparative Sociology*, 8 (2).

10. MacCannell, D. (1989) *The Tourist: A new theory of the leisure class* (2nd edn), Schocken Books.

Website

International Porter Protection Group   **www.ippg.net**

Questions and discussion points

1.   'This is the agony of holidaying in developing countries. Some say you are bringing welcome cash into the economy, others that you are exploiting the impoverished locals'.

> Stephen Merchant, on a visit to Cambodia and Vietnam,
> 'An Englishman abroad', *The Observer*, 8 June 2008

Do you believe that the economic benefits of tourism to developing countries outweigh the drawbacks? If not, and given that international tourism is unstoppable and growing, how best can the situation be improved? What are your views on visiting countries with authoritarian regimes?

2.   Compare and contrast the points made in Figure 6.2 and Tourism Concern's 10-point set of principles on page 177. In your opinion, which better satisfies the requirements of sustainability for tourism industry guidance and why? Are there any issues that you would like to see added to the list?

3.   UNESCO's 1976 report cited in this chapter identified four characteristics of host–guest relationships. How closely does this model fit your own experiences of meeting locals abroad? Are the characteristics more pronounced where the guest is from the developed world and the host from a developing country?

4.   Is the Irridex model described in the chapter modified or reinforced depending on the level of tourist spend in a destination, do you think?

5.   How far does authenticity matter when cultural activities are laid on for incoming tourists? Are some inauthenticities more significant than others? And does concern for authenticity depend upon the level of educational background and/or cultural awareness of the visitor?

Tasks

1. The tourism industry has been accused of paying only lip-service to the concept of sustainability, ignoring its implementation due to the high cost involved, and, in times of recession, it is sustainable measures that are the first to be cut back. Collect evidence to refute these allegations and defend the industry in a short report.

2. List the good and bad points of tourist integration at destinations versus the establishment of tourism ghettos and, in a written summary, give your own opinion on which is the better way forward for cultural sustainability.

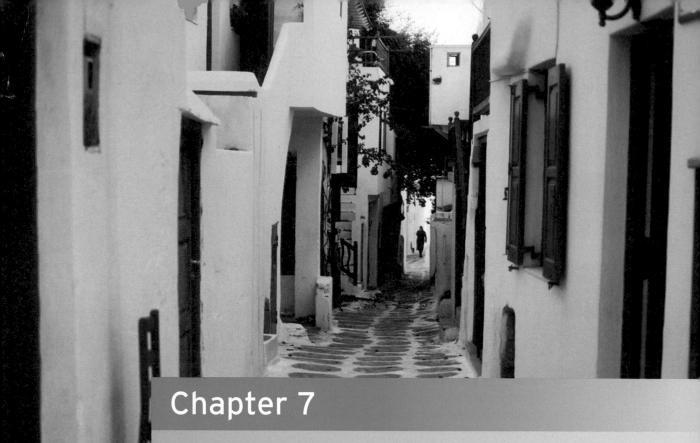

Chapter 7

The environmental impacts of tourism

Learning outcomes

After studying this chapter, you should be able to:

- understand the various ways in which tourism can impact on the environment

- identify and evaluate different approaches to finding solutions to these problems

- understand the importance of sustainable tourism as it relates to the environment

- recognize how appropriate planning and cooperation between the private and public sectors can help to ensure sustainability.

Introduction

Half our operators are bankrupt. What reward is there for being more environmentally friendly?

Noel Josephides, MD Sunvil Holidays, quoted in *Tourism*, 119, Winter 2004

In Chapter 6, we explored the different ways in which tourism can impact on people, both travellers and residents in the destination countries. In this chapter, we go on to look at tourism's impacts on the environment in which they travel. While the obvious focus will be on how tourism affects the environment at popular tourist destinations, we need to be aware at the same time that the rise in global tourism has environmental impacts that go far beyond those destinations alone. In fact, it is no exaggeration to say that tourism is a major contributor to the despoliation of the environment, notably as a result of transport's contribution to pollution, whether by air, sea or on land.

As tourism expands, so new destinations are put at risk; and twenty-first-century tourists are tending to seek out ever more remote areas of the globe.

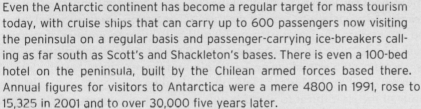

Example

Antarctica

Even the Antarctic continent has become a regular target for mass tourism today, with cruise ships that can carry up to 600 passengers now visiting the peninsula on a regular basis and passenger-carrying ice-breakers calling as far south as Scott's and Shackleton's bases. There is even a 100-bed hotel on the peninsula, built by the Chilean armed forces based there. Annual figures for visitors to Antarctica were a mere 4800 in 1991, rose to 15,325 in 2001 and to over 30,000 five years later.

Package tourists can now enjoy visits to this least-explored continent that, in addition to penguin watching, can include anything from travel by snowmobile to 'adventure flights' to the South Pole itself.

The popularity of the huge penguin colonies has meant that some of the colonies are receiving as many as three visits every day, impacting on the birds' behaviour and breeding patterns. One unexpected result of this influx has been the large number of birds contracting diseases found in chickens, thought to be the result of food carelessly discarded by visiting tourists.

Such ill-effects have led to members of the International Association of Antarctic Tour Operators adopting a voluntary code of practice to minimize the impacts of visitors, including limiting the numbers of passengers put ashore at any one time to 100 and restricting how close they may approach the penguin colonies. The difficulty, however, is in policing the rulings.

In other ecologically sensitive regions, such as the Galapagos Islands, Costa Rica and Belize, the development of tourism is also controlled and efforts are made to ensure that all visitors respect the natural environment. The pressures of demand are difficult to resist, however, where the economic benefits to less-developed countries are significant. While in 1974 the authorities set an original target of 12,000 visits to the Galapagos (later revised to 40,000), visitors now number close to 100,000, and the ceiling has been to all intents and purposes abolished. The authorities have now agreed to allow 12 visits a year by cruise ships carrying up to 500 passengers, far exceeding the previous limit of 100 – although all visitors are escorted and restricted to just 8 per cent of the total land mass.

The environmental effects of tourism

Transport pollution

Large-scale tourist movement requires the use of mass transportation, particularly by air, and, while aircraft are now twice as fuel-efficient as they were three decades ago, air travel has quadrupled in that time. In 1970, airline passengers travelled some 350 billion air passenger miles (APMs; this figure, of course, includes all forms of passengers, not merely tourists); by 2000, APMs had increased to 1500 billion and forecasts are for this to double by 2015 and triple by 2050 (given the rapid expansion of the low-cost carriers, these figures may prove conservative). While exceptional increases in oil prices may have some impact on these forecasts, nevertheless, marked increases in the number of flights over the next two decades are beyond doubt.

Apart from emissions of nitrous oxides (unfortunately, the introduction of quieter, more fuel-efficient and cleaner jet engines has the side-effect of increasing those emissions), these aircraft currently pump some 600 million tons of carbon dioxide into the upper atmosphere each year. According to the Intergovernmental Panel on Climate Change, this accounts for at least 3.5 per cent of all greenhouse gases. Again, this will rise to 15 per cent by 2050, on present estimates.

One EU study in 2004 claimed that air travel was responsible for 9 per cent of all global warming. In Britain alone, according to a Government Aviation White Paper in 2003, the number of people flying in to and out of the UK would rise from 180 million to over 500 million in 2030, while an environmental audit committee estimated that aviation would have become responsible for two-thirds of all the UK's greenhouse gas emissions by 2050. These figures also do not take into account the costs of congestion, leading to stacking over airports and the resultant fuel waste – a problem that is likely to grow as air corridors become more crowded. The rapid expansion of the low-cost airlines, operating on short-haul routes, accounts for a sizeable increase in pollution figures, given that one-fifth of a short-haul aircraft's fuel load is burnt in take-off and landing.

Yet, in spite of the clear threat to world health, aviation fuel remains largely untaxed. Fuel taxation was ruled out at the 1944 Chicago Convention in order to boost the post-war airline industry and even VAT has not yet been applied to airline tickets, in spite of protests from the environmentalists. Aviation is specifically exempted from the Kyoto Protocol on climate change.

There are growing calls for a carbon tax on fuel, which it is thought would help lead to airlines converting from high carbon kerosene to low carbon liquid methane and, ultimately, the development of carbon-free liquid hydrogen fuels – a move likely to be hastened by the current growing fear of world oil shortages. Any such tax, however, to be truly effective, would have to be applied globally and would encounter strong resistance from the airlines and authorities in countries such as the USA that are heavily dependent on low-price air travel. Alternatively, carbon trading agreements could be extended to airlines, requiring them to either reduce emissions or purchase expensive permits (fees for which would have to be recovered through higher ticket prices). Regionally, taxes have been mooted (in Britain, a government Green Paper, 'The future of aviation' (2000) accepted the principle that polluters should pay and the Royal Commission on Environmental Pollution proposed a green tax on air tickets in 2002), but not implemented.

Other forms of tourism transport make their own contributions to pollution. Up to 300 passenger ships now ply world cruise routes, carrying in excess of 15 million passengers each year. The US-based Ocean Conservancy estimates that, apart from the daily fuel burn, each ship generates some 30,000 gallons of sewage and 7 tons of rubbish each day – not all of it properly disposed of. Indeed, several leading cruise companies have been prosecuted in recent years for pollution of the seas and rigging instruments to deceive inspections. Water-borne vessels of all kinds, whether on the high seas or on inland rivers,

Example

Taxing to offset carbon dioxide damage[1]

Climate Care estimates that each passenger flying to Mauritius is responsible for releasing 2.7 tonnes of carbon dioxide into the atmosphere. Flyers on this route are to be advised by a computer 'aviation calendar' how much pollution their flight is causing.

The organization has also estimated the cost of offsetting carbon dioxide damage on short-haul and longer flights. This would call for payment per passenger travelling from London on return flights of the following sums:

- £5 to Lisbon, Portugal
- £16 to Los Angeles, USA
- £31 to Sydney, Australia.

lakes and canals, by cleaning out their tanks or dumping waste overboard, significantly contribute to water pollution, which, in turn, impacts on aquatic wildlife. Even without such illicit dumping, the sheer number of cruise vessels plying popular waterways such as the Caribbean poses a threat through leakages and congestion at key ports. Bermuda is among a number of islands that now impose restrictions on the number of cruise ship visits permitted each year.

Example

Alaskan cruises

Alaskans, once overjoyed at the arrival of tourist ships, have become angered by the rapidly increasing numbers of cruise ships visiting the state, fearing contamination of their waters. Also, the large number of vessels being routed to the area to engage in whale-watching is having the effect of driving these mammals away from the Alaskan shores.

The state's Department of Environmental Conservation now levies a charge on all cruise vessels to pay for the clean-up of pollution.

Inland waterways are, if anything, even more fragile and endangered than coastal waters as a result of excessive use by water-borne leisure transport, whether private or public. Apart from the danger of pollution caused by fuel or oil leaks in rivers, lakes and canals, unless strict speed limits are enforced, riverbanks may be damaged or undermined by the wash from passing boats, causing soil erosion and endangering wildlife. The popularity of the Norfolk Broads in Britain among boaters has led to overuse of these waterways during the past 50 years, with resultant damage to banks.

Finally, account must also be taken of the impact of the many millions of motorists using private and hire cars for their holidays and short breaks. While congestion is the more visible problem arising from the expansion in the numbers of vehicles at popular tourism destinations, pollution resulting from the concentration of exhaust gases in both city and rural tourist destinations can seriously affect the health of tourists and residents alike. The uncontrolled expansion of private vehicles in key tourist cities such as Bangkok

Example

Venice

Venice, with its network of canals, receives up to seven million visitors every year. Most are transported by water during their stay and gondola trips (see Figure 7.1) are an expensive but popular form of excursion.

The city is slowly sinking and its paved areas are subject to frequent flooding. As public transport on the canals is largely motorized, the wash from these vessels is contributing to undermining the foundations of many historic buildings. The Italian government thus gave Venice the power to limit motorized transport, introduce speed limits and tolls on tourist boats and establish 'blue zones' where transport is limited to gondolas and rowing boats.

Figure 7.1 Gondolas on the congested canals, Venice, Italy.
(Photo by Chris Holloway.)

can so adversely affect the visitor experience that it threatens to discourage visitors from either travelling there or staying in the city.

A significant proportion of the petrol purchased all over the world is for leisure purposes, whether for touring or day trips, and, in some regions, the exhaust fumes from these vehicles, when added to those from local traffic, can damage the clean air that is the prime attraction for tourists. This is particularly true of mountainous destinations, where not only touristic appeal but also even plant and animal life can be adversely affected.

Example

Mountain resorts

Some popular mountain resorts, such as Zermatt in Switzerland, have banned non-residential private vehicles from the town, requiring tourists to use park and ride services or rack-and-pinion railways into the resort. The latter provide a picturesque additional attraction to visitor staying there.

The popularity of off-roading with sports utility vehicles (SUVs) is also damaging to the environment in sensitive areas of the world. This sport is popular among American tourists and some wilderness areas are now under threat, particularly in Utah. Moab (scene of Butch Cassidy's adventures) has attracted significant numbers of such vehicles, as have sand dunes in several parts of the world, where these vehicles can destroy sparse scrubland and erode the landscape.

Noise pollution by transport

All motorized forms of road, sea and air transport can intrude on the calm of a resort by raising noise levels, whether in rural surroundings or in residential areas, and this, too, must be considered a form of pollution.

Aircraft taking off and landing at busy airports severely disturb local residents and tourists alike. Authorities have long recognized the problem of air traffic noise and action has been taken to reduce it. For example, aircraft are grouped under three classes, known as chapters, according to the noise levels they emit. Under government regulations, especially in the United States, the more recently introduced Chapter 3 aircraft, such as the Airbus, are 85 per cent less noisy than were Chapter 1 aircraft and are, consequently, allowed greater freedom to operate. The problem is compounded for night flights, where restrictions are often in force to reduce the problem. While effective lobbying in the UK has largely restricted the problem to Luton and Stansted Airports, in India all airports are still obliged to accept jumbo aircraft throughout the night.

Noise from water-borne vessels is most notable along coasts and in tranquil rural areas where boats using their motors can disturb the peace of the night when travelling along rivers and canals. New water-borne vehicles such as jet bikes and water bikes, often used offshore at popular beach resorts, are particularly noisy and this (coupled with possible danger to life) has been a factor in attempts to reduce their use offshore at popular Mediterranean resorts.

Pollution at tourist destinations

The physical pollution of popular destinations poses a growing threat for global tourism. Perhaps the most widespread example is seen in coastal resorts, where beach and offshore water contamination is both visible and, in some cases, can be life-threatening to bathers. In this respect, British coastal resorts have in the past fared badly by comparison with their European neighbours, although recent years have witnessed marked improvements, following clean-up drives within the EU. Nevertheless, some popular bathing areas in Britain remain seriously contaminated by raw sewage or other pollutants.

Beaches in Britain are monitored in several ways. Key certification is in the hands of Environmental Campaigns (ENCAMS), which runs the Keep Britain Tidy campaign, awarding yellow and blue flags to beaches and bathing water satisfying certain minimal criteria, including water purity and freedom from litter and other pollutants on the beaches themselves. More criteria are applied to beaches qualifying as resorts rather than rural, but both require the beaches to meet at least the mandatory standards of bathing water applied in the EU. ENCAMS also administers, within Britain, the more stringent Blue Flag campaign on behalf of the international body Foundation for Environmental Education (FEE), which monitors beaches in some 40 countries in Europe, South Africa and the Caribbean. In 2003, 332 beaches in Britain were awarded yellow and blue flag status (compared with only 92 in 1992, the first year of monitoring), while 105 achieved European Blue Flag standard. By 2005, however, 98 per cent of beaches were passing the more stringent tests, with just 13 of the 562 failing. Nevertheless, a handful of UK tourist beaches, including such popular resorts as Blackpool, have consistently over the years failed to meet minimum standards. Perhaps it is as well that only some 7 per cent of those spending time on beaches in the UK actually have any intention of bathing!

Environmental 'pollution' is as much aesthetic as physical. An area of scenic beauty attracts greater numbers of tourists, so more and more of the natural landscape is lost to development, the countryside retreating before the growth of hotels and other amenities that spring up to cater for the tourists' needs. The eventual result is that the site is no longer seen as 'scenic' and the tourists move on to find somewhere more tranquil as well as beautiful. Similarly, without careful control, stately homes that try to meet the needs of visitors provide an ever-expanding range of facilities, such as larger car parks, cafés, shops, directional signposts and toilet facilities, all of which detract from the appeal of the main attraction. Extreme examples of despoliation of the scenery by signposting are readily found in the United States where, with fewer controls than are exercised in Britain, both countryside and towns can be destroyed by directional signs and advertising hoardings (however, some might argue that, at night, the forest of illuminated signs in towns such as Reno and Las Vegas is very much part of the attraction of the resort). There are fears that a relaxation of regulations in Britain could lead to a similar explosion of countryside signage.

Noise pollution is a common problem relating to contemporary life and not merely in towns. At the Treetops Hotel in Kenya's Masai Mara National Park, animals visiting the adjacent waterhole at night are driven from the site by the careless loud talk or laughter of a minority of the visitors waiting to see them. In the seaside resorts of the Mediterranean, building construction in fast-developing resorts can be both visibly and audibly offensive, especially during hours of darkness. The peace of the night is also frequently destroyed by late-night disco bars catering to younger tourists. In some such resorts, the authorities have perceived the danger of negative publicity driving away the family market and authorized the police to undertake night patrols to combat excessive noise. One such example is Magaluf in Majorca, where police act against pubs or nightclubs registering noise levels higher than 65 decibels.

Another aesthetic form of visual pollution is illustrated by the frequent insensitivity in the design of tourist buildings. Lack of planning control is often to blame, as developers prefer to build cheaply, resulting in high-rise concrete hotels lacking character and out of keeping with the surrounding architecture.

Many British towns are also losing their local character, as builders have chosen to build in ubiquitous (but cheap) London brick rather than the materials available locally (although planning authorities have adopted stricter measures in recent years to control this practice). In seaside resorts around the world, too, the concrete skyscraper hotel has become the norm and from Waikiki in Hawaii to Benidorm in Spain, tourists are confronted with a conformity of architecture that owes nothing to the culture or traditions of the country in which it is found.

Some far-seeing authorities have recognized the potential for this kind of damage and brought in controls to limit it. In some cases this has led to an insistence that hotels be built using local materials or conform to the vernacular architecture – that is, styles indigenous to the region. Others require that buildings not exceed a certain height. For example, Tunisia requires that new hotel developments in tourist resorts should be no higher than the normal height of the palm trees that will surround them. Mauritius has imposed constraints on both the architectural style and the materials employed in hotel building. While some critics have questioned the rather 'staged' results, with thatched cottages vaguely resembling African kraals, no one doubts the appeal these accommodation units have for tourists. Such legislation clearly must apply to all buildings, not just those for tourism.

Example

Lanzarote

On Lanzarote, in the Canary Islands, all housing, apartments and hotels are required to conform to rigorous building regulations imposed by the Department of Tourism on the Island. These control not only the style of the buildings but also the colours in which doors and windows may be painted – only white, blue or green paintwork is permitted.

Sometimes, planning controls have the effect of restricting innovation in architecture, leaving developers to play it safe by falling back on pastiche or bland designs, attractive only to the most conservative visitor. The attempt to protect local building styles and materials can sometimes have unexpected results, as in Ireland. The traditional corrugated roofs have now become such a familiar feature of the landscape that it has been designated a vernacular building material.

Sometimes, the problem of scale can relate to buildings far smaller than hotels, but it is no less significant. During the early 1990s, two historic properties were under threat owing to plans to either build or expand visitors' centres adjacent to the site. The Haworth Parsonage, once the home of the Brontë sisters on the Yorkshire Moors, was threatened with a massive expansion of the visitors' centre, which would have greatly exceeded the size of the original house. The project resulted in an outcry from the public and a rethinking of the plans. Similarly, trustees of the birthplace of Sir Edward Elgar, in the Malvern Hills, submitted plans for a new visitors' centre adjacent to, and much larger than, the composer's original cottage. This, too, led to a public outcry in the media. In this case, though, construction went ahead, with a visitor centre resembling, according to one architectural critic, a Tesco supermarket. The problem of providing sufficient room to accommodate all the visitors – some 10,000 a year – at such a small site is a common one and there is no easy – or at least cheap – solution. One plan proposed at Haworth was to conceal the new visitor centre underground, which, although an ideal solution, proved to be too costly for the available funds.

Other common forms of visual pollution by tourists include littering, particularly in areas around picnic sites, and graffiti on buildings. It is a curious fact that even those tourists who come from large cities, where they are so used to seeing litter that they become unconscious of it, immediately become sensitive to litter at a tourist destination.

Resorts that have made the effort to improve their image in recent years tend to start by undertaking a drive against both rubbish in the streets and graffiti on buildings. An important point here is that litter bins should be not only readily available but also attractively designed. Unfortunately, at many sites, both in Britain and elsewhere, the fear of terrorist bombs or vandalism has caused rubbish bins to be sealed or removed, making rubbish disposal more difficult for tourists.

In environmentally sensitive areas of the world, such as wilderness regions, littering becomes a critical issue because these areas are too far from any public services that could resolve the problem, so the onus is on tourists themselves to safeguard the environment by taking their rubbish with them. This is a very real issue in the Himalayas, now that trekking has become more popular in the region. Many trekkers and organized trekking parties are failing to carry out their litter or dig latrines to hide human waste, with the result that some valleys have become littered with unsightly rubbish, much of which fails to decompose at the high altitudes there. Environmentalists and enlightened tour operators are encouraging visitors to ensure that their rubbish is either burned or carried out (although local villagers often make use of tins, bags or bottles left behind) and human waste is buried. The authorities are being encouraged to build more permanent composting toilets in frequented areas, using the twin vault principle – each vault being used in alternate years to allow waste to decompose. Nutrients from composted waste can then be used to encourage rapid growth of willow trees, providing a much-needed source of timber for local villagers.

Graffiti has become a common problem in the Western world, with thoughtless tourists desecrating ancient monuments with spray-painted, scratched and even chiselled messages. This, of course, is no new development: the Romans were chiselling their names on Greek monuments two thousand years ago. The sheer scale of modern tourism, however, has forced authorities to take action. In extreme cases, this had led to denial of access, as in the case of Stonehenge, where visitors are no longer permitted to walk among the stones themselves, but must be content to view them from a distance.

Problems of congestion and erosion

Perhaps the most self-evident problem created by mass tourism is that of congestion. In the previous chapter, we considered some of the social implications of overcrowding for tourists and, in this chapter, we will be equally concerned with the effects of overcrowding, in particular on the natural environment.

Congestion is a complex problem because it exists at both a *psychological* and a *physical* level. The latter is more easily measured – in terms of the capacity of an area to absorb tourists. Car parks, streets, beaches, ski slopes, cathedrals and similar features all have a finite limit to the numbers of tourists that they can accommodate at any given time. Theoretically, this is also true of entire regions and countries, although attempts to define the tourist capacity of a city or country have seldom been attempted. Most national tourist offices continue to develop policies aimed at creating an ever-expanding influx of tourists year-on-year without considering the ability of the areas to absorb those numbers, although efforts are made to divert these influxes to off-peak periods or to less crowded areas of the country. At the urban level, a few cities under extreme pressure, such as Florence and Venice, have taken more positive action, as will be seen later in this chapter.

It is also necessary to understand the psychological capacity of a site – that is, the degree of congestion that tourists will tolerate before it starts to lose its appeal. Quantifying this is far more difficult than physical congestion as individual perceptions of capacity will differ, not only according to the nature of the site itself but also the market attracted to it. A beach in, say, Fiji will be judged overcrowded much more quickly than, say, a beach in the UK at Bournemouth, while in a resort such as Blackpool a much higher level of crowding may be tolerated, even welcomed, as part of the 'fun experience'.

One attempt to measure the psychological capacity of a beach was carried out at Brittas Bay in Ireland in the early 1970s. Aerial photographs were taken of the number of tourists on the beach on a crowded Sunday afternoon and a questionnaire was circulated to those on the beach to receive their views about the congestion that day. It was found that most visitors would accept around 1000 people per hectare (10 square metres per person) without feeling that the beach was overcrowded.

Example

Koh Phi Phi Ley, Thailand

Koh Phi Phi Ley (Maya Bay) was, until the turn of the millennium, a rather isolated beach and natural beauty spot, one of the Phi Phi Island group near Phuket. That is until a popular film – *The Beach*, starring Leonardo di Caprio – romanticized for millions of young filmgoers the idea of 'lotus-eating' holidays in faraway places, resulting in hordes of backpackers descending on the area to search out the exact location of the film. The subsequent despoliation of the idyll was condemned by tourist officials in the country, although the resulting development of the nearby Ao Ton Sai resort on Koh Phi Phi Don has benefited locals economically. A five-fold increase in tourist fees was implemented in order to control visitor numbers to the site. The Phi Phi Island group were badly affected by the 2004 tsunami and authorities are keen to re establish the area as a popular venue for tourism.

In so-called *wilderness* areas, of course, the psychological capacity of the region may be very low, while areas sensitive to environmental damage may suffer physically even where there are comparatively few visitors. In the United States, Yellowstone and the Everglades National Parks are both physically under severe threat from tourism. Psychologically, too, they are so remote that any mass tourism will greatly reduce their attractiveness. In Britain, from the psychological viewpoint of the hiker, sites such as the Derbyshire Peak District should not support more than a handful of tourists per square kilometre, although the mass influx to its major centres such as Dovedale on an August Bank Holiday fails to act as a deterrent for the majority of day trippers. Indeed, it has been demonstrated in the case of Cannock Chase, the beauty spot near Birmingham, that this area draws tourists from the Midlands as much for its role as a social meeting place as for its scenic beauty.

The behaviour of tourists at wilderness sites will be another factor in deciding their psychological capacity. Many visitors to an isolated area will tend to stay close to their cars, so hikers who are prepared to walk a mile or so away from the car park will readily find the solitude they seek. This is obviously a key for tourism planners, as, by discouraging or forbidding car parking and access by vehicle to the more remote areas, they can then effectively restrict these areas to those seeking solitude.

Some authorities have tried to set standards for particular types of tourist activity as a guide to planners. Table 7.1 is based on one attempt, by the UN World Tourism Organization (then, WTO), to lay down guidelines in terms of visitors per day per hectare.

The *ecological* capacity to absorb tourists must also be taken into account. While too many tourists in a built-up area such as the narrow shopping lanes of York or Brighton can detract from tourism, the physical wear and tear on the environment is limited – at least, in the short term. Too many tourists in a rural or otherwise fragile environment, however, can destroy the balance of nature. This can be seen in the increase in tourists visiting African safari parks, where the number of vehicles hunting for the 'big five' at any one time can resemble a car rally in some areas of the parks (see Figure 7.2). An idea of the effect of

Table 7.1 Visitor capacity of selected sites.

Site/activity	Visitors per day/hectare
Forest park	15
Suburban nature park	15–70
High-density picnicking	300–600
Low-density picnicking	60–200
Golf	10–15
Fishing/sailing	5–30
Speedboating	5–10
Waterskiing	5–15
Skiing	100 (per hectare of trails)
Nature trail hiking	40 (per kilometre)
Nature trail horseriding	25–80 (per kilometre)

Source: E. Inskip, *Tourism Planning: An integrated and sustainable development*, van Nostrand Reinhold, 1991.

erosion can be gained from a report in *The Guardian*[2] that revealed 400 tons of sand are removed from the beach at Benidorm each year on the soles of holidaymakers' feet!

Some sites are particularly fragile. Many sand dunes have been destroyed or seriously eroded in the United States by the use of beach buggies and, as we noted earlier with respect to other sensitive ecological systems, by four-wheel drive vehicles. In the UK, similar problems are thrown up by motorcycle rallying, which can easily uproot the few clumps of dune grass on which an ecosystem depends. The UN Environment Programme has reported that three-quarters of all the sand dunes along the Mediterranean coastline between Spain and Sicily have disappeared as a direct result of the growth of tourism.

Figure 7.2 Congestion in the wildlife parks as safari vehicles hunt the 'big five' in Kenya. *(Photo by Chris Holloway.)*

Example

The Great Barrier Reef

The Great Barrier Reef off the coast of Queensland, Australia, is a World Heritage site, generating some A$1.5 billion per annum from tourism, but its 1450 miles of fragile coral reefs can be easily damaged by divers or snorkelers. Even touching or standing on live coral can be sufficient to kill it, yet some visitors go so far as to break off pieces for souvenirs. Coral can also be damaged by boats anchoring. Compounded by the effects of global warming, this is contributing to the death of large tracts of the Reef.

   In an effort to reduce its destruction, in 2004, the Australian government banned commercial fishing from 44,000 square miles of the Reef. Companies that thrive by running boat trips for tourists to visit the Reef are now aware of the threat to their livelihood and taking on the responsibility to educate their passengers. During the boat trips, tourists are given information on the fragility of the site and how it can be preserved by careful use.

Individual buildings attracting very high numbers of tourists have similar problems, requiring firm measures to manage and limit access. This can, of course, lead to disappointment for tourists. In recent years, crowds visiting the Uffizi Gallery and Galleria dell'Accademia (the site of Michelangelo's David) in Florence during peak holiday periods have become so great that the local authorities have had to take the unusual step of temporarily closing the buildings. Indeed, both Florence and Venice face exceptionally heavy demand from international tourists, the latter welcoming over seven million tourists each year, with 1.5 million seeking admission to the Doge's Palace and St Mark's Square alone, while on some days as many as 40,000 tourists have visited the Baptistry of San Giovanni and the adjoining Duomo in Florence. Such crowds produce high levels of condensation, which affect the thirteenth- and fourteenth-century mosaics. The authorities have responded by reducing coaches to the city from 500 to 150 a day, charging them high fees for the privilege and spot-checking arterial roads out of the city to enforce compliance. Numbers admitted to the Baptistry were reduced to 150 at a time and, for the first time, charges were applied for entry. In 2005, Italy's new culture minister proposed a big increase in prices charged at the most popular sites in Italy, in the hope that tourists could be diverted to lesser-known museums and attractions, but tourists and officials felt that the suggestion would be impractical.

   Another tourist site suffering from extreme popularity is the Taj Mahal in India. This building alone attracts some two million visitors a year and up to 6000 each day. Since 1995, a price differential was introduced, with higher entry charges for foreign visitors, and the Indian government periodically has attempted to impose further swingeing price increases (although these were reduced after tour operators complained). Such unique sites are highly price-inelastic, however, so only a rationing system is likely to limit demand.

Congestion in Britain's national parks

Many popular rural sites such as national parks are at risk from the numbers of visitors they receive and, in the case of Britain, their proximity to centres of high population. Well over 100 million visitors visit the UK's national parks each year. The Peak District is the

Example

Macchu Pichu

The long lost Inca city of Macchu Pichu, now a UNESCO World Heritage site, was rediscovered only in 1911. It is now the country's major tourist attraction, with 85 per cent of all visitors to Peru planning a visit there.

Public access was enhanced with the building of a railhead nearby and helicopter flights bring others from Cuzco. As a result, over 400,000 now visit the site annually and UNESCO has placed it on the danger list, recommending that daily admission should be limited to 2000 during the high season and 800 in the off season to avoid irreparable damage. The Peruvian government countered with a proposal to limit the number to 2500 daily and increased entry prices by 50 per cent. In 2000, it also announced plans to build a cable car to replace the buses transferring tourists from the railhead to the top of the mountain, but a public outcry from UNESCO and the environmental lobby forced a retraction of the plan (although the cable car would have eliminated growing concern about the environmental damage caused by buses climbing the present steep access road).

Initially, the site could only be reached via the Inca Trail, a hazardous narrow footpath that appeared to place a natural ceiling on visitor numbers, but the growth in trekking has matched that of visits via public transport. Just 7000 trekkers arrived by trail in 1988, but, a decade later, this had risen to 66,000.

The Peruvian government was forced to impose new controls to reduce erosion of the path. Walkers unaccompanied by guides or porters were banned in 2001, entry charges to the site itself were tripled and limits were introduced on the number of tour operators organizing the guided treks. No more than 500 trekkers daily (including porters) are now permitted to use the trail. The fees paid, however, go to central government and are not used to protect or restore the site.

Another Inca city has been discovered at Cerro Victoria and the government hopes that this can be developed to take some of the pressure off Macchu Pichu.

most popular – claimed to be the second most visited national park in the world after Mount Fuji in Japan, with over 22 million visitors annually and 3000 vehicles on peak days. As a result, footpaths are overused, leading to soil becoming compacted and grass and plants dying. Under some circumstances, the soil becomes loosened and is then lost through wind erosion. Derbyshire County Council has proposed barrier charges to reduce traffic entering the national park at weekends and on bank holidays in an attempt to reduce this congestion.

Another attempt was made, in the early 1990s, to counteract the erosion of the footpath across the moors near Haworth. Some 25,000 visitors had turned parts of the Brontë Way into a quagmire, making it necessary to set flagstones into the track. Other running repairs have had to be made to long-distance footpaths such as those on the Pennine Way and Cleveland Way. Such artificial landscaping, of course, creates a very different visual landscape from the wild moorland it replaces, but it is a solution that is being used more widely as such footpaths have to deal with greater numbers of visitors each year. In places, these popular paths in the national parks have widened to 45 yards.

Climbers, too, also damage the parks. With the increased interest in activity holidays, climbing is becoming a very popular pastime. Some 250,000 people climb Mam Tor in Derbyshire every year, for example, and this has so affected the mountain that the summit had to be restored with an importation of 300 tons of rock and soil.

There is, however, an inevitable trade-off between protection and economic well-being, as is demonstrated by the imposition of controls in the English Lake District.

Example

Lake District National Park

In 2005, the national park authorities in the Lake District introduced a
10 miles per hour speed limit around Windermere Lake, aiming to reduce
noise pollution and erosion and enhance the sense of peace for which the
district is renowned.

The decision has had a severe impact on the economy of the region.
The tourist information centre received 12,000 fewer enquiries in the first
six months of the year, boat registrations and launches fell sharply and the
waterskiers, jetskiers and powerboat drivers who are traditionally high spenders
withdrew, leaving local firms to face business losses that are believed to be costing the local economy over
£7 million annually. The local tourist board chairman accused the national park authority of 'ignoring its
duty to foster the economic and social well-being of local communities'.

Sustainability and winter sports tourism

One fragile ecosystem in Europe is under particular threat: the Alps. Because the system
is spread across no fewer than seven countries, collaboration to prevent the worst of the
environmental effects of tourism is made more difficult. The Alps receive over 50 million
international visitors a year and some 7 million passenger vehicles cross them each year,
as they lie at the heart of Europe. To accommodate the huge increase in winter sports
tourism that has occurred since World War II, some 41,000 ski runs have been built,
capable of handling 1.5 million skiers an hour (see Figure 7.3).

The region suffers in a number of ways. The proliferation of ski-lifts, chalets and concrete villages above 6000 feet and the substantial deforestation required to make way for
pistes, have led to soil erosion, while the high volumes of traffic crossing the Alps contribute to the acid rain caused largely otherwise by factory emissions. Those emissions are
having a serious impact on the remaining forests, 60 per cent of which have now been
affected. Artificial snowmaking machines have smothered alpine plants, reducing the
vegetation, while wildlife has also declined as the animals' territories have been reduced.
A new danger is posed by the introduction of roller skiing on grass and four-wheel drive
car racing in summer.

The potential damage, both ecological and economic, to the region is now so great that
an organization, Alp Action, has been set up, with the support of the Aga Khan, to help
preserve the Alps as a single ecosystem. It has to be added, however, that not all authorities
welcome further control in this fashion. Some Swiss cantons have expressed concern at the
potential slowdown in the economic development of their region that results from this
conservation movement.

Some local authorities have taken steps to control overuse. At Lech and Zuers in Austria,
skiers are counted by computer through turnstiles that give them access to the pistes. Once
14,000 – the deemed capacity – have been admitted, tourists are diverted to other sites.
Lillehammer in Norway, site of the 1994 Winter Olympic Games, took account of the
problems already occurring in the Alps when designing its new facilities. Apart from efforts
to minimize tree clearance, the authorities also took steps to avoid visual pollution in
an area where comparatively few buildings exist. Ski jump runs were moulded into the
mountainside to ensure that they did not project above the tree line and similar efforts
were made to conceal bobsleigh and luge runs in the forests. The speed-skating stadium
was built 20 yards away from the water's edge to protect waterfowl and leak-proof cooling

Figure 7.3 The ski runs at Bretaye, above the popular winter resort of Villars in Switzerland, suffer from congestion in the high season and increasingly uncertain snowfalls due to their comparatively low altitude.
(Photo by Chris Holloway.)

systems were embedded underground in concrete containers. Private cars were excluded from the town during the period of the Olympic Games.

Not only sports activities threaten snowscapes. Glaciers, the ecosystems of which are invariably fragile, attract large numbers of sightseers when located in accessible regions. At the Columbia Icefield in Banff National Park, Canada, giant snowmobiles are employed to bring tourists on to the glacier. The inevitable consequence will be damage to the surface of the site, unless strict control is exercised over the numbers of trips organized.

Erosion of constructed sites by tourists on foot

Although constructed sites are generally less fragile than natural ones, these too can be affected by erosion in the long term – externally by weather, internally by wear and tear from multiple visitors. Sites exposed to the elements may have to have access restricted, especially if they become so dilapidated that they pose a danger to visitors, as is the case with some historic castles.

The Acropolis in Athens has had to be partially closed to tourists to avoid wear and tear on the floors of the ancient buildings, while the wooden floors and staircases of popular attractions such as Shakespeare's birthplace in Stratford-upon-Avon or Beaulieu Palace in Hampshire also suffer from the countless footsteps to which they are subjected each year. Stratford, with a population of only 23,000, receives over 3.8 million visitors every year, a substantial proportion of whom will want to visit Shakespeare's birthplace or Anne Hathaway's cottage. The high numbers led major attractions to construct artificial walkways above the level of the floor to preserve the original flooring. Nearly a million people visit Bath's Pump Rooms and the Roman Baths complex each year and inevitably there are fears for the original stone flooring of the Baths. It may put the problem into context when it is revealed that Roman visitors, wearing hob-nailed boots, did even more damage to the original flooring than do contemporary visitors, though they were far fewer in number.

The danger of tourism to flora and fauna

Even souvenir hunting can affect the ecological balance of a region. The removal of plants has long given cause for concern (the Swiss were expressing anxiety about the tourists' habit of picking gentians and other alpine flowers even before the start of the mass tourism movement) and, in Arizona, visitors taking home cacti are affecting the ecology of the desert. Similarly, the removal, either as souvenirs or for commercial sale by tourist enterprises, of coral and rare shells from regions in the Pacific is also a cause for concern.

Perhaps of even greater concern is the threat posed to endangered animal species from the rise in tourism. There are many examples. While safari big game hunting is now limited largely to the use of cameras, animals hunted down by tourist vehicles in the game reserves have declined due to lack of privacy to mate. In the same way, loggerhead turtles in Greece and Turkey, and in the Caribbean, are distracted from laying their eggs by the bright lights of tourist resorts or the use of searchlights to observe their coming ashore to lay eggs on the beach.

Example

Saving the turtle

Widespread media publicity regarding the threat facing the turtles' survival has resulted in much greater general awareness of the problem and both operators and tourists have become more responsible when paying visits to egg-laying sites. The Travel Foundation made a financial award to Tobago, which has allowed beaches to be patrolled.

Tourists are now made aware of sustainability issues in a video shown at the airport on their arrival and both hotel staff and guests are informed about the need to protect nesting turtles. Tourists have restricted access to egg-laying turtles, although small groups are permitted to observe them from a suitable distance. The Foundation has also provided funding for demarcation buoys to be positioned near reefs in Tobago (and in Cancún, Mexico) to protect the turtles from anchor damage by tourist boats.

At Philip Island, near Melbourne in Australia, 500,000 people a year come to sit and watch the evening 'penguin parade' of fairy penguins coming ashore to their nests. This event has become highly commercialized and the large crowds are proving hard to control, even though ropes are in place to prevent people getting too close to the penguins. Flash photography is forbidden and wardens caution the audiences against noise or even standing up, all of which disturb and alarm the penguins. In practice, however, the public frequently ignore these strictures.

Animal behaviour can change as a result of prolonged exposure to tourists. In some countries, food lures are used to attract wildlife to a particular locality. For example, in Samburu National Park, Kenya, goats are slaughtered and hung up for crocodiles or leopards. This modifies hunting behaviour and may encourage dependency on being fed by humans (see Figure 7.4). In some wildlife parks, hyenas are known to watch for assemblies of four-wheel drive vehicles in order to take the prey from cheetahs' hunts. 'Bearjams' are created in Yellowstone National Park, USA, as bears trade photo opportunities for offerings of food.

Figure 7.4 Tourists welcome close encounters with wildlife, but is the taming of animals for this purpose to be welcomed? A cheetah is hand fed in Namibia.
(Photo by Chris Holloway.)

Example

Sustainable tourism in Botswana

An excellent example of sustainable tourism at a wildlife park is demonstrated at Xigera Camp, in Botswana's Okavango Delta. A sandpit between the river and camp is raked clean each night and, the following morning, the guide provides a short talk for the tourists, identifying the prints of nocturnal animals that have visited the site to drink.

Guests to the area are catered for at the 'chief's camp', situated on land leased by a specialist British tour operator from tribal authorities and employing well-paid locals, some of whom provide trips by mokoro (dugout canoe) through the delta. Furnishing is luxurious but ethnic and food is sophisticated yet locally grown.

The desire to bring back souvenirs of animals seen abroad poses another form of threat to endangered species. The Convention on International Trade in Endangered Species (CITES) imposes worldwide restrictions on the importation of certain animals and animal products from countries visited by tourists. Around 34,000 endangered species have been identified and the importation of many of these or their by-products is banned, including ivory, sea turtle products, spotted cat furs, coral, reptile skins and seashells, as well as certain rare plants. Concern is also expressed about the ill-treatment of animals that are kept in captivity for the amusement of tourists. While performing bears have largely been removed from the streets of some Eastern European countries following EU pressure, they are still a common sight in China. Even within the EU, one can still find chimpanzees and monkeys exploited for tourist photographs in countries such as Spain, and, of course, bullfighting remains not only legal but also a popular tourist attraction in that country and the South of France. A number of action groups in Britain have been set up to protect and free these animals.

Other environmental consequences of mass tourism

Many popular tourist towns have narrow roads, leading to not only problems with severe traffic congestion but also potential damage to buildings as coaches try to navigate through these streets. Increasingly, cars and particularly coaches are restricted in terms of access to the centres of such towns, with park and ride schemes or other strategies employed to reduce traffic. Impeding coaches from picking up and setting down passengers in the centre of towns such Bath or Oxford, however, can make it very difficult for coach companies to operate as many are on short stopover visits as part of a day trip.

Many developing countries face similar problems of congestion and erosion as the popularity of long-haul travel expands. Goa in India was hailed by many operators as an 'unspoilt paradise', but its wide appeal since the 1990s has caused environmental lobbyists such as Tourism Concern to draw attention to the dangers the region faces. Water shortages in the area are aggravated by tourists' consumption (one 5-star hotel uses as much water as five villages and locals face water shortages while swimming pools are filled) and sand dunes have been flattened. Apart from the environmental impacts, there are also social costs. The private beaches mean access by the locals is denied and 'Westernization' of the local carnival dilutes the traditional identity and culture of the region. The problems of Goa have been well publicized in recent years, but this has had little effect on reducing the numbers of visitors or ensuring that tourism in the area is sustainable.

Sometimes, well-meaning attempts by tourist officials to 'improve' an attraction can have the opposite effect. Historic rock carvings over 3000 years old in Scandinavia were painted to make them stand out for visitors. When the paint eventually flakes off, a process that has speeded up with the effect of acid rain, it takes part of the rock surface with it.

Any development of tourism will inevitably require the sacrifice of some natural landscape to make way for tourist facilities. An extreme example of this is to be found in the demand for golf courses. It has been estimated[3] that there are some 30,000 golf courses in the world, with a further 500 being built each year. Many of these are constructed in areas where water shortages would normally discourage their construction, such as in Dubai, Tunisia and the Egyptian desert, but the popularity of golfing tourism drives their development. Golf as a holiday activity, especially among Japanese tourists, has led to a huge increase in demand for courses in the Pacific region. For example, the island of Oahu in Hawaii, which had already constructed 27 courses by 1985, received a further 30 applications after the Hawaii legislature agreed to allow them to be built on agricultural land. Apart from the loss of natural scenery, golf courses also require huge amounts of fresh water, which, in some areas of low rainfall, imposes a severe burden on local resources.

Public-sector planning for control and conservation

We have now seen many examples of the environmental impact of tourism and a few illustrations of how the problems might be managed. Some argue that it is not enough for individual authorities to tackle the situation – it should be tackled on a global scale. Unfortunately, few governments so far have appeared willing to do so on this scale. International designation of an attraction as a World Heritage site by the United Nations Educational, Scientific and Cultural Organization (UNESCO) undoubtedly helps, but Stonehenge – arguably Britain's greatest heritage attraction – is so designated, yet the site has been called a 'national disgrace' by the Public Accounts Committee of the House of Commons, financial support from the Millennium Fund was refused and arguments continue about how best the site should be developed and protected. Estimated costs for burying the main road in a tunnel have doubled to around £470 million since the proposal was first made and possible alternative solutions have all been abandoned in the face of financial constraints. As a result, the site is threatened with being withdrawn from UNESCO's listing.

In Chapter 6, we looked at some of the moves that have been made since the early 1980s across the globe to embrace tourism sustainability. For the most part, the conferences and resulting papers have focused on making recommendations, leaving the question of mandatory control in the hands of national governments. Nonetheless, 150 countries signed up to the Agenda 21 proposals arising from the Rio Summit in 1992 and the EU has taken an active role in recent years in attempting to control the worst effects of environmental pollution, the Blue Flag scheme being typical of this. Costa Rica can be cited as an outstanding example of a sustainability aware developing country with a rapidly growing tourism market, issuing Certificates for Sustainable Tourism to tourist companies organizing holidays in the country.

The creation of national parks to preserve sites of scenic beauty is by no means of recent origin. As early as 1872, the United States established its first National Park at Yellowstone, while Europe's Abisco National Park in Sweden dates from 1909. The intention behind the creation of these parks was to ensure that visitors did not destroy the landscapes that they had come to see. Sustainability may be a word of recent origin in tourism, but the concept is much older. The World Conservation Union (IUCN) now recognizes more than 68,000 protected areas worldwide, covering an area of 5.7 million square miles, nearly 10 per cent of the globe. As sustainability becomes a more important issue each year, the volume swells.

Example

Gabon

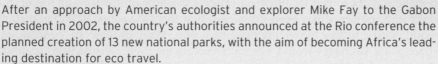
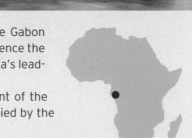

After an approach by American ecologist and explorer Mike Fay to the Gabon President in 2002, the country's authorities announced at the Rio conference the planned creation of 13 new national parks, with the aim of becoming Africa's leading destination for eco travel.

The new parks extend to over 11,000 square miles, around 11 per cent of the country's land mass, which is equivalent to the proportion of land occupied by the national parks created in eco-conscious Costa Rica.[4]

Of course, most countries and local authorities are generally well-intentioned, but they can also inadvertently become partners in despoliation when putting commercial advantage before aesthetic considerations. Spain, for example, experienced a sudden boom in tourism during the 1960s, but went on to allow massive overdevelopment along its east coast and in the Balearic and Canary Islands, which nearly destroyed its success.

Failure to maintain the quality of the environment in other directions can also lead to a massive loss of tourist business, as the popular Spanish resort of Salou found, following a drinking water scare in 1989. The widespread fall-off in Western European visitors to Spain in the 1980s and 1990s (mitigated to some extent by a rise in Eastern European and Russian visitors), however, caused a reversal of policy and much greater control being exercised over speculative tourism development. A good example of this can be found in the Balearics.

Parliament passed legislation in 1991 to nominate large tracts of land in Majorca, Ibiza and Formentera as zones restricted from further development. In Majorca, only four- and 5-star hotels were permitted to be constructed, with a minimum of 120 square metres of land per bed, in an effort to drive tourism upmarket. In order for planning permission to be granted for the construction of new hotels, developers have been required to purchase and knock down an existing and deteriorating hotel of inferior status. Badly run-down resorts such as Magaluf were given an injection of capital to widen pavements, introduce traffic-free zones, plant trees and shrubs and install new litter bins and graffiti-free seating. In all, Spain spent over £300 million in a five-year period (ending in the early 1990s) on improving facilities for tourists along its coasts.

In 2003, the Balearics took a further step in sustainability, by introducing an eco-tax that was designed to fund sustainable improvements to tourism in the islands. Unfortunately, insufficient thought went into its implementation. Hotels were expected to collect this from guests themselves and the resultant discontent led to the tax being scrapped by the new local government that was elected a year later.

Other countries notable for their failure to provide adequate controls as their tourism industry boomed (and failure to learn the lessons from Spain's experience) include both Greece and Turkey. Among developing countries, Goa in India and the Dominican Republic in the Caribbean were both unprepared for the scale of the mass tourism generated by tour operators in the 1990s and failed to control their development adequately.

Spain's experience is a cautionary one and the degree to which it has been successful in turning around its fortunes is notable. In general, however, the evidence suggests that, once a resort has gone downmarket, it can very hard to bring back higher quality tourists. Simply constructing new high-price hotels will not lead to success in attracting a new market.

Example

Governmental control on entry

Some countries have taken the view that, where tourism does not already have a strong hold, it is best to control entry to reduce the danger of environmental and cultural despoliation occurring.

The Government of Bhutan established a policy to limit the number of foreign visitors to just 15,000 per year. They introduced high charges to reduce demand ($200 per day, with reductions in the off season), but provided food, internal transport and lodging within these amounts.

Mustang, the kingdom on the border with China, which was absorbed into Nepal in 1951, was closed to all tourists until 1992. The Nepalese government has since introduced a limit of just 1000 foreign tourists to the region each year, charging $700 for a 10-day permit, of which only about 10 per cent goes back to the region.

At the local level, some form of public control is also essential to ensure that each new building is well designed and all existing buildings of quality are carefully preserved and restored. Heritage is also a sustainability issue, one that goes beyond the interests of tourism alone. It underpins the very fabric of a society and, in nations with a wealth of heritage buildings, each building lost through failure to protect it or enforce its restoration becomes an irreparable loss to the culture of those nations. Europe owes much of its tourism demand to the attractiveness of its traditional heritage and landscape, and destinations, whether rural, urban or seaside, that fail to concern themselves with the sustainability of their attractions cannot expect to retain their tourists.

melccnpote

Environmental protection in the UK

In Britain, sensitivity to the impact of tourism on the environment dates back at least as far as the nineteenth century. Concern over possible despoliation of the Lake District, then growing in popularity, led to the formation of a Defence Society in 1883 to protect the region from commercial exploitation. The National Trust was created in 1894 to safeguard places of 'historic interest and natural beauty' and promptly bought four and a half acres of coastal cliff-top in Cardigan Bay.

The National Parks and Access to the Countryside Act 1949 led to the formation of ten national parks in England and Wales, each administered by a National Park Authority. The Norfolk Broads achieved the equivalent national park status under the Norfolk and Suffolk Broads Act of 1988. The New Forest on the Hampshire/Dorset borders was raised to national park status in 2004 and the South Downs area is likely to follow shortly – the latter being formed from two existing Areas of Outstanding Natural Beauty. Scotland created its first two designated national parks – Loch Lomond and the Trossachs, then the Cairngorms – in 2002 and 2003 respectively (see Figure 7.5).

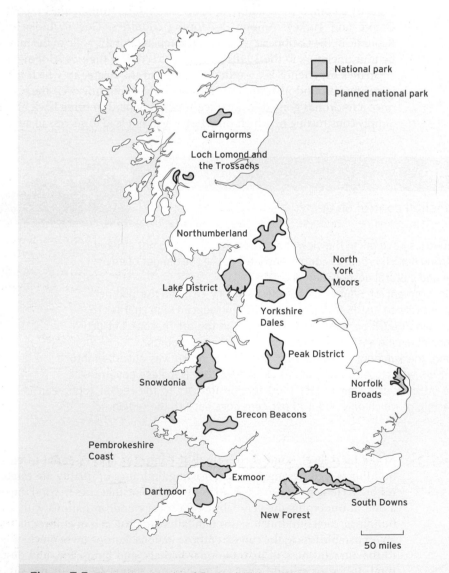

Figure 7.5 The national parks of England, Wales and Scotland.

Figure 7.6 Environmental concerns have led to protests against airport expansion – in this case, near Stansted Airport, UK.
(Photo by Claire Humphreys.)

The National Parks Act also led to the designation of 37 areas (nearly 8 per cent of the area of England and Wales) as Areas of Outstanding Natural Beauty, meriting protection against exploitation. The first of these, the Quantock Hills in Somerset, was so designated in 1957, while the last – the Tamar Valley in England's West Country – was designated as such in 1995. Since then, there have been numerous moves to protect features of historical or architectural interest or areas of scenic beauty from overdevelopment, whether from tourism or other commercial interests. Notable among these are some 150 designated nature reserves and a large number of Sites of Special Scientific Interest (SSSI), which contain rare flora or fauna. An EU Wildlife and Habitats Directive gives stronger protection to some of the most notable SSSIs, which were decreed special areas of conservation in 2000. The UK government recognizes the threat to these sensitive areas caused by growth in tourism and leisure generally and is attempting to control it, although the countryside remains under threat from the need for more land for the construction of roads, private housing, expansion of airports (see Figure 7.6) and so on.

The public/private-sector interface in the development of sustainable tourism

Planning controls, whether executed centrally or regionally, are essential if the inevitable conflicts of interest that arise between the public and private sectors are to be avoided. Private enterprise, unrestricted, will seek to maximize profits, often in the short term, and this can more easily be achieved by concentrating marketing effort on popular attractions and destinations, rather than investing in the development of new ones. Airlines will clearly find it more profitable to focus on the routes already generating the most traffic, while hotels in a boom resort will build large and relatively cheap properties if this produces the highest margins.

Tour operators and, to a lesser extent, travel agents exercise massive marketing power over destinations through their influence on the decisions of consumers about where to go and what to do. Operators can make or break destinations through their decisions to enter or withdraw from destinations – decisions that often border on the 'slash and burn' techniques outlined earlier. **Sustainability** means ensuring cooperation between carriers, hotel companies and operators so that any development is not for short-term gain but in the long-term interests of the locals.

This is by no means a condemnation of the industry as a whole. For every large company that seeks to exploit its market position, there are others that recognize their responsibility to their destinations, as well as numerous small companies, both airlines and operators, actively seeking market gaps – untapped markets, destinations where the opportunity to develop tourism would be welcomed by locals or a focus on superior facilities would be appropriate.

By contrast with the failures in development planning cited earlier, the planning of the Orlando Walt Disney World Resort site reveals a better approach to the protection of a fragile environment. The site chosen, in central Florida, was largely scrubland and a deprived area in need of economic support. Walt Disney Productions took due account of the potentially enormous impact that the theme park would have on the state, including new road networks and airport construction in its plans. Protected sites well away from the park itself and the emerging town were clearly designated and, arguably, the site itself stands as a model of good development. By contrast, the impact that development further south has had on the Everglades National Park, where the wetlands have been significantly affected by engineering to provide water for coastal expansion, including meeting the needs of tourists, has been far less positive.

The United Arab Emirates' coastline in the Middle East can be cited as further evidence of effective development planning for tourism. Dubai in particular has sunk vast resources, even constructing artificial islands offshore, into the area to attract tourists. It had seen little development previously and environmental protection is not a key issue. The airlines (including that of Dubai itself) are supporting this growth by massively expanding their services to the region.

The low-cost airlines have been widely criticized for the air pollution they generate, but, on the plus side, by exploiting opportunities at small regional airports and working in cooperation with specialist tour operators, they have brought prosperity to many regions that previously had only limited access to tourists. Clermont-Ferrand in France, Graz in Austria and Trieste in Italy all have reason to be grateful for their services in making these cities and regions more accessible to tourists. The budget airlines have also been responsible for generating substantial local employment for air crew and ground staff when concentrated at airports such as Stansted and Luton.

Example

Cox and Kings

Cox and Kings – the oldest British tour operator – has demonstrated a strong commitment to sustainable tourism, promising that, for every customer buying one of its 'environmental journey' holidays, it will buy an acre of rainforest in Belize, to be kept in its natural state in perpetuity. The relatively high cost of these package tours allows for some discretionary spending of this sort. The challenge will be to encourage downmarket operators to increase their prices to allow for a more sustainable product to be delivered.

The travel industry is continuing to take sustainability more seriously, with greater co-operation evidenced between the public and private sectors. Other notable examples include the Australian Nature and Ecotourism Accreditation Programme (NEAP) and Cooperative Research Centre (CRC) for Sustainable Tourism, South Africa's Fair Trade in Tourism (FTTSA) and the developing Sustainable Tourism Stewardship Council launched in Latin America in 2003 to explore opportunities for certification within the industry.

The World Travel and Tourism Council (WTTC) has worked with the industry since 1994 to develop the Green Globe awards for sustainability (albeit initially with limited success) and promote guidelines for travellers, disseminated in the form of leaflets. The WTTC has also taken on responsibility for the Tourism for Tomorrow awards, initiated by British Airways, which gain widespread publicity for sustainable tourism enterprises. Finally, in Britain the formation of the Travel Foundation, referred to in the previous chapter, signals cooperation between the public and private sectors, including some of the largest companies in the industry, reflecting for the first time a real commitment by the industry to the idea of sustainability.

American-owned companies operating globally have been notable for their commitment to sustainability, reflecting a strong environmental movement in that country. Walt Disney Enterprises, to take one example, recycles oils, paints and cleaning materials used on its sites. The Intercontinental Hotels chain undertook a worldwide environmental audit at the beginning of the 1990s, which led to a policy of recycling waste and introducing cruelty free (not tested on animals) toiletries in guests' rooms.

Other examples include German airline Lufthansa, which introduced snacks at departure gates to avoid wastage resulting from serving in-flight meals (as well as being sustainable, this reduces fuel consumption on flights and is highly cost-effective!) The UK company Center Parcs planned its resorts as car-free zones, offering visitors the use of bicycles during their stay.

The accommodation sector has led the way in introducing sustainable approaches, though initially through their desire to save on costs. The now well-established policy of reducing laundry bills by limiting the frequency of washing towels has extended to other cost-saving tactics that offer sustainable benefits. For example, some hotels in Hawaii have installed flow regulators on showers and taps to control water wastage. Even small businesses in the accommodation sector have taken initiatives. Bloomfield House, a bed-and-breakfast establishment in Bath, England, introduced a 10 per cent discount to guests arriving by public transport and similar discounts are offered by the Primrose Valley Hotel in St Ives, Cornwall (see Chapter 12, Figure 12.3).

The concept of the environmental audit is gaining acceptance among tourism companies, British Airways being one notable example of a firm having adopted it. While the publication of environmental reports, as an element of the annual report, has become a widespread policy among other industries in recent years, the travel industry is only gradually coming to terms with this innovation.

There is still scepticism among many commentators as to the extent to which sustainable activities can be viewed as a genuine response to the threat to our environment rather than a public relations exercise designed to win public favour. Many businesses chose to cut back on their sustainable investment when faced with difficult trading conditions in the post-2001 era and there is little doubt that a number will continue to pay no more than lip-service to the concept unless it can be shown to be in their financial interest to do so, based on demand from their customers. The fact that some 20 per cent of tourists are now believed to actively include some element of eco-tourism in their travelling[5] suggests that the point at which the demand will be significant enough may well be reached soon, although there is still doubt about the majority of the travelling public's willingness to pay more for their holidays if they are designed to be more sustainable.

Nonetheless, what will have started out for many companies as no more than a marketing ploy may later turn to a genuine commitment to improve the environment as lobbying by environmental interests takes effect and public awareness of the issues spreads.

Notes

1. See also 'Green tax looms for airlines', *The Times*, 12 June 2004, p. 4.
2. 'Everyone's a tourist now!', *The Guardian*, 27 January 1990.
3. O'Connor, J. (2003) 'Fairway to tourist hell', *The Observer*, 8 June.
4. Quamman, D. (2004) Saving Africa's Eden', *National Geographic*, September 2003, pp. 50–74.
5. *The Times*, 6 March 2004.

Further reading

Archer, L. (1994) *The Environmental Impact of Aircraft on the Atmosphere*, Oxford Institute for Energy Studies.

Eber, S. (1992) *Beyond the Green Horizon: Principles for sustainable tourism*, Tourism Concern/WWF.

Kalisch, A. (2002) *Corporate Futures: Social responsibility in the tourism industry*, Tourism Concern.

Websites

Blue Flag	**www.blueflag.org.uk**
Certification for Sustainable Tourism	**www.turismo-sostenible.co.cr**
Derbyshire County Council	**www.derbyshire.gov.uk**
Green Globe 21	**www.ec3global.com**
Institute for Sustainable Development in Business	**www.susdev.co.uk**
International Centre for Responsible Tourism	**www.icrtourism.org**
Journey Latin America	**www.journeylatinamerica.co.uk**
Keep Britain Tidy Campaign	**www.encams.org**
Marine Conservation Society (annual 'Good Beach Guide')	**www.goodbeachguide.co.uk**
Naturetrek (wildlife holidays and tours)	**www.naturetrek.co.uk**
Rainforest Alliance	**www.rainforest-alliance.org**
Responsible Tourism Partnership	**www.responsibletourismpartnership.org**
Tourism Concern	**www.tourismconcern.org.uk**

Questions and discussion topics

1. Some critics of tourism have argued that mass tourism is more environmentally friendly than individual tourism, on the grounds that budget airlines and charter airlines are carrying higher load factors and mass tourists do not intrude to the same extent on local environments. Is this a valid viewpoint? What are the counter-arguments?

2. What are the congestion problems in your area and what steps are local authorities taking to improve the situation? To what extent are these problems caused by tourism?

3. Is the age of tourists a determinant in attitudes towards sustainability? What other factors contribute to attitudes?

Tasks

1. Using the websites of AITO members, find out how much emphasis is placed on the issue of sustainability in the presentation of these tour operators' products.

2. Undertake a survey of visitors to a congested tourist site near you (a beach, tourist attraction, wilderness area and so on) to find out their attitudes to congested sites. What factors predominate – concern for the person (parking problems, queuing and so on) or concern for the environment? Can you identify any solutions that would reduce the effects of any of these problems?

Part 2

The travel and tourism product

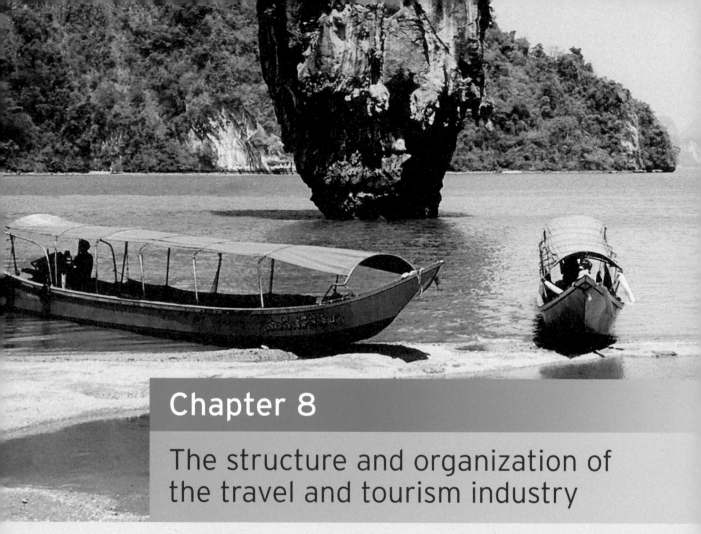

Chapter 8

The structure and organization of the travel and tourism industry

Learning outcomes

After studying this chapter, you should be able to:

- identify the integral and associated sectors of the travel and tourism industry

- explain the chain of distribution and how this applies within the industry

- understand the relationships, formal and informal, between each industry sector

- be aware of the extent of integration within the industry and the reasons for this

- identify the factors leading to change within the industry and predict likely directions it may take in the future.

Introduction

> Distribution channels in tourism create the link between the suppliers and consumers of tourism services, providing information and a mechanism enabling consumers to make and pay for reservations.

D. Pearce and R. Tan, (2004) 'Distribution channels for heritage and cultural tourism in New Zealand', *Asia Pacific Journal of Tourism Research*, 9 (3), pp. 225–37

The tourist product is a complex amalgam of different services, each of which must be brought together and presented to customers by the various sectors of the industry. The demand for tourism is first created, then satisfied by the concentrated marketing efforts of a wide variety of organizers who provide tourist products and services. These together form the world's largest and fastest-growing industry. Because some of these services are crucial to the generation and satisfaction of tourists' needs, while others play only a peripheral or supportive role, defining what is meant by a 'tourism industry' is fraught with difficulties.

Several services, such as catering and transport, obviously serve the needs of consumers other than tourists, too. Other services, such as banks, retail shops and taxis – or launderettes in a resort where a significant number of tourists are in self-catering facilities – may only serve tourists' needs incidentally along with local residents' needs, although at peak periods of the year the former may provide the bulk of their income. Inevitably, what one decides to include in a definition of the tourism industry must be, to some extent, arbitrary. Figure 8.1, however, provides a framework for analysis based on those sectors commonly seen as forming the core of the industry.

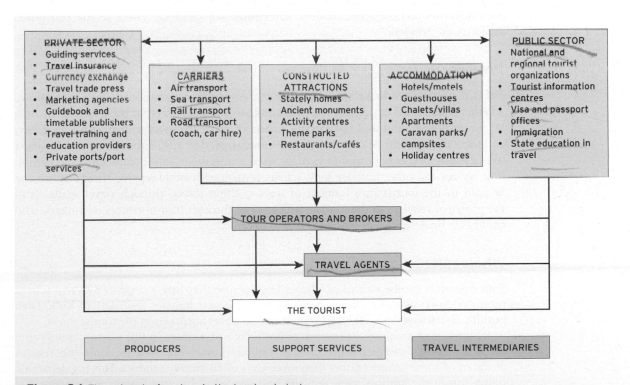

Figure 8.1 The network of sectors in the tourism industry.

The chain of distribution for tourism

Figure 8.1 is also an illustration of the **chain of distribution** in the travel and tourism business. This phrase is used to describe the system by which a product or service is distributed from its manufacturing/creative source to the eventual consumers. The alternative term **marketing channel** can also be used to describe this system. Traditionally, products are distributed through the intercession of a number of intermediaries who link producers or manufacturers with consumers. These intermediaries are either wholesalers (they buy in large quantities from suppliers and sell in smaller quantities to others further down the chain), or retailers (they form the final link in the chain and sell individual products or a bundled set of products to the consumer). The structure of the chain of distribution is shown in Figure 8.2.

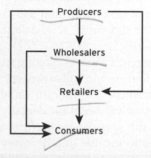

Figure 8.2 The chain of distribution or marketing channels.

Producers, of course, are not obliged to sell their products through this chain. They may instead choose to sell direct to consumers or retailers, thus avoiding some or all of the intermediaries. Wholesalers, in turn, sometimes sell products direct to the consumer, avoiding the retailer.

Producers

The core tourism product consists essentially of transport, accommodation and attractions, whether constructed or natural. The producers, or 'manufacturers', of these services include air, water-borne, road and rail carriers, hotels or other forms of tourist accommodation and the various forms of constructed facilities designed to attract the leisure and business tourist, such as stately homes or heritage sites, amusement parks, conference and exhibition venues and other purpose-built activity centres such as ski resorts. These services can be sold to the tourist in a number of ways – either direct, through travel agents (still the principal retailers in the tourism industry) or through tour operators or brokers, who could best be described as wholesalers of tourism.

Wholesalers

Tour operators can be viewed as wholesalers because they buy a range of different tourist products (such as airline seats, hotel rooms or coach transfer facilities) in bulk, then bundle or 'package' these for subsequent sale to travel agents or to the tourist direct.

By buying an amalgam of individual products and services in this way and presenting them as a single product – the package holiday – they are seen by some theorists as *producers* of a *new* product rather than *wholesalers* of an *existing* product. This is a debatable point, but in the authors' view they are best viewed as intermediaries, in the sense that their fundamental role is to bulk purchase products, organize them into bundles and sell those bundles off individually (this is discussed in more detail in Chapter 18). The current pattern of trading – in which both tour operators and agents are moving towards dynamic packaging, which involves bundling products to meet a consumer's needs at the point of sale (or 'unbundling the package tour' as some operators express it) – is muddying the distinction between the roles of operators and agents.

Example

Blurring the distinction between tour operators and travel agents

In the UK, the Federation of Tour Operators (FTO) suggests that 'tour operators are the organisers and providers of package holidays. They make contracts with hoteliers, airlines and ground transport companies, then print brochures advertising the holidays that they have assembled. Travel agents give advice and sell and administer the bookings for a number of tour operators'.[1]

These two roles are no longer distinguishable from one another, however. More tour operators are establishing operations that allow them the opportunity to sell direct to the customer, bypassing the travel agent. In response, travel agents are looking to tailor-make holidays for their clients, drawing on a range of travel elements from many different suppliers – a process know as dynamic packaging. For UK travel agents, this shift in business practices has been assisted by the development of technology systems such as Dolphin Travelscanner and Itour, developed by BlueSky Systems, that let agents find and book individual travel elements with ease.

As the linkage between the travel agents and the technology providers has developed, so the distinction between travel agent and tour operator has blurred.

Brokers – who bulk buy tourist products and sell in smaller quantities – are most frequently found in the distribution system within the air transport sector, although others involve themselves in the bulk purchase of hotel rooms or certain other services. As with tour operators, by purchasing aircraft seats in bulk, they are able to negotiate much lower prices, which can be sold on to tour operators or travel agents either individually or in quantity at net prices, allowing the other intermediaries to determine their own profit level and the selling price for the seats.

One of the commonest forms of brokering in the travel industry is found in the role of the **consolidator**. These are specialists working in airline brokerage who bulk purchase unsold charter aircraft seats to sell through intermediaries, thereby helping airlines to clear unsold 'stock'.

Retailers

Although retailing through the Internet is now becoming a significant threat to them, travel agents remain an important outlet for selling most travel products within the distribution chain, buying packages and travel services according to client demand. They carry no stock, simply acting as an intermediary between the consumer and the supplier – or **principal** – and their main role is to provide a convenient network of sales outlets for the travelling public.

Traditionally, agents did not charge for their services as they were remunerated in the form of a commission on each sale they negotiated. One of the most significant changes in distribution patterns in recent years, however, has been the tendency for suppliers to either reduce commission payments or, in some cases, scrap them altogether, often forcing agents to charge their clients for their services. Airlines were among the first principals to withdraw commissionable sales, mainly in the belief that they could reach the consumer more cheaply by direct contact via the Internet, than by depending on agents who, for the most part, retain no particular loyalty to any one supplier. This means that many agents are now obliged to add a fee when selling most airline tickets.

Some other transport companies and tour operators are beginning to follow suit, although the large operators are unlikely, at least for the foreseeable future, to adopt such a policy. There appears to be a global trend in travel retailing for agents to buy many of their principals' products at market price and add a service fee, but this presupposes there is an adequate level of agency sales expertise and product knowledge that adds value to the process when a customer books through an agent. In fact, the pressure on margins seldom allows retail agencies to provide the salaries and conditions that would enable them to recruit sales staff of the quality and skills needed to make this possible.

Ancillary providers

Apart from these core services – of producers, wholesalers and retailers – a wide variety of ancillary and support services interact within the distribution system. For convenience, these can be divided into public-sector organizations (those funded, controlled or organized through central or local governments) and those that are privately owned.

The former include national tourism organizations, such as tourist offices (see Figure 8.3), publicly owned airports or seaports, passport and visa documentation and other ancillary services such as public education and training institutions offering courses in tourism.

The private sector includes privately owned airports and seaports, services offered by freelance guides, travel insurance and financial services (including foreign exchange and credit card facilities), travel trade newspapers and journals, printers of travel literature, publishers of guides and timetables, as well as a number of specialist marketing services, such as travel consultants, advertising agents and brochure design agencies. In addition, there are

Figure 8.3 Maison de la Région Languedoc-Roussillon is the promotional body for this French region. It has opened a regional business centre in London to represent the interests of, inter alia, tourism, in partnership with the regional tourist board, alongside promoting food and wines of the region.
(Photo by Claire Humphreys.)

private visa agencies that will collect customers' documentation, check it and procure any necessary visas for a fee. This is becoming a more typical pattern for visa procurement as few embassies are willing to mail documents to clients and submission in person is often inconvenient, expensive and time-consuming. Most tour operators now use these inter-mediaries, too, as they have a good rapport with the embassies and consulates they use frequently and provide a dependable service.

The distinction between public and private bodies is not always straightforward. Some national and regional tourism organizations (the USA and the city of Berlin are two exam-ples) are run as private consortia, having been delegated the role by the public sector. Others, while nominally public, would collapse without the financial support they receive from the private sector.

Example

Public ownership of tourism attractions

The public sector can be involved in a number of ways in attracting tourists. In some cases, local or national government may have ownership of a building or destination (perhaps a national park for example) and will operate the facility as a tourist attraction in order to provide public access to the facility or to fund its upkeep and management.

In other cases, governments may provide grant funding to private-sector tourism businesses to support activities that are felt to be in keeping with government agendas. An example of this is the funding provided by the UK government to museums in order to encourage wider access to these cultural resources.

While some countries provide key elements of the travel industry through national or local government, other countries may choose to allow the private sector to provide these facilities. For example BAA, Britain's leading airport owner, is an example of a former public body (formerly the British Airports Authority), now a PLC, that exercises control over seven UK airports. The privatization of airports has proved lucrative for BAA, but there is concern that the current set-up is not in the best interests of the consumer (or the airlines that use BAA airports).

Example

Are there changes ahead for BAA?

Control of BAA passed into the hands of Spanish construction company Ferrovial in the summer of 2006 when it acquired over 80 per cent of BAA's shares. BAA operates seven UK airports, including three London airports – Gatwick, Heathrow and Stansted. The dominance of this company, especially its control of airports in the south of the country, has led to an investigation by the Competition Commission.

Following an initial review early in 2008, the Competition Commission announced that its initial thoughts tended towards the view that 'common ownership of the BAA airports is a feature of the market that adversely affects competition between airports.'[2] Its report suggests that BAA must sell off some of its airports, which is likely to bring other private-sector companies into this transport sector. Probably three of the airports will be sold off, including two of the London airports. Virgin Atlantic Airlines has expressed an interest in acquiring one of these.

For the most part, the tourism industry depends for its success on a close working relationship between the private and public sectors. Many tourist attractions, such as heritage sites, are publicly owned, either by the state or local authorities, while public authorities are also frequently responsible for the promotion and distribution of information about tourism (through, for instance, their tourist information centres). This interdependence between private and public sectors, which is an important element in the dynamics of the industry, will be explored in subsequent chapters.

Common interest organizations

A feature of the tourism industry is the extent of the association, voluntary or otherwise, that has taken place between businesses and/or public-sector bodies that share similar interests or complement one another's interests in some way. Such associations can take a number of forms, but typically fall into one of three categories:

- **sectoral organizations** based on the interests of a particular sector of industry (or link in the chain of distribution)
- **destination organizations** concerned with a specific tourist destination, whether country, region or resort
- **tourism organizations** based on a concern with travel or tourism activity as a whole.

Each of these can in turn be subdivided according to whether they are trade or professional bodies. The latter are normally composed of individuals whose common interest is likely to be based on objectives that include establishing educational or training qualifications for the industry or the sector, devising codes of conduct to guide members' behaviour and limiting or controlling entry to the industry or sector. Membership of such bodies is often associated with a personal drive to enhance status and prestige.

Trade bodies, by contrast, are groupings of independent firms, the common purpose of which will include such aims as the opportunity to exchange views, cooperation (especially in the functions of marketing), representation and negotiation with other organizations and the provision of identifiable services to their members. In some circumstances, the trade bodies may also take on activities more generally associated with professional bodies, such as restricting entry to the industry or sector and providing or recognizing appropriate qualifications.

Example

Professional bodies – the Tourism Society

Operating in the UK, the Tourism Society has over 1000 members, who are employed in the public, private and voluntary sectors of the tourism industry. The aim of the society is 'driving up standards of professionalism'.[3]

To work towards this aim, the Society holds a variety of conferences that help to develop the knowledge of its members and, in the past, they have provided communication and presentation skills workshops. Further, these conferences provide networking opportunities, which can open business opportunities for its members. In recent years, the Society has also worked to attract student members as they commence their careers in the tourism industry.

ОБРАТИМ: COMMERCIAL

Example

Trade bodies – Treasure Houses of England

Many sectoral organizations come together in order to benefit from opportunities to bulk buy at discount prices from their suppliers or sell themselves more effectively and at lower cost. Websites that offer a range of products rather than a single one, for example, will be more effective in reaching the public.

Treasure Houses of England is one such example in the attractions sector of the industry. Composed of nine of the leading stately homes in Britain, the consortium has its own website (**www.treasurehouses.co.uk**), produces a joint brochure and offers discounts at partner properties.

The structure of such bodies may vary considerably. In some cases – particularly in the larger organizations – there will be a paid administrative staff, while, in the case of smaller bodies (such as local marketing consortia), there may be no full-time staff and administration will often be carried out by volunteer staff seconded from member companies. A key characteristic of trade bodies, however, is that their membership is made up of autonomous companies or other organizations subscribing to the common purpose of the body concerned.

Sectoral organizations

Probably the most numerous organizations are those that reflect sectoral interests. As we saw in Figure 8.1, there is a wide range of sectors making up the tourism industry and each of these can be expected to have at least one common interest association. Professional bodies catering for sectoral interests include the Chartered Institute of Transport (CIT) and the Institute of Hospitality (formerly the Hotel, Catering and International Management Association). The Chartered Institute of Marketing (CIM) has a section devoted to travel industry members, known as the Chartered Institute of Marketing Travel Industry Group (CIMTIG), while tourism educationalists and consultants each have their own professional body – the Association of Tourism Teachers and Trainers and the Tourism Society Consultants' Group (both autonomous divisions of the Tourism Society).

Some bodies provide their own training for the industry (such as the CIT), while others rely on training organizations set up separately for this purpose (the UK-based TTC Training, for example). The UK has a sector skills council representing the hospitality, leisure, travel and tourism industries – People 1st – the role of which is to develop occupational standards for training and support qualification bodies to provide a streamlined and appropriate range of qualifications for the industry.

Sectoral trade bodies may be regional, national or international in scope. Some international bodies retain significant influence over the activities of their members. An example is the International Air Transport Association (IATA), which continues in its role of negotiating with international airlines worldwide even though some of its erstwhile power has diminished under the impetus to liberalize this sector of the industry. The International Federation of Tour Operators draws its members from European national tour operating bodies, including the British Federation of Tour Operators (FTO) – an influential consultative body made up of around ten leading UK operators.

Apart from the FTO, other examples of UK national bodies include the Association of British Travel Agents (ABTA), which represents both tour operators and travel agents, the

Example

The Association of British Travel Agents (ABTA)

ABTA, a sectoral trade body, has played a key role in the British travel industry. Due to legislation within the European Union that has had the effect of reducing the monopoly position enjoyed by ABTA in the past, however, it lost some of its influence in the latter half of the 1990s. ABTA nevertheless remains the principal trade body in the UK – the vast majority of package holidays sold in the UK being sold through its members, the financial safety net it provides remaining a key reason for this.

ABTA was founded in 1950, initially to represent the interests of travel agents, but later those of tour operators. It is consulted by government on issues and legislation affecting the industry. It is invaluable in helping smaller companies to keep abreast of changing legislation, advising and being advised by the Foreign and Commonwealth Office (in matters of safety, for instance), acting as a financial clearing house for members and interceding between customers and members where arbitration is required. ABTA also works closely with the Travel Training Company (TTC), which offers vocational qualifications for the industry. Furthermore, where travel issues of national importance arise, it is to ABTA that the media turn first for advice and consultation. The integration of the FTO with ABTA, announced in 2008, will further this influence.

One issue facing ABTA is that often the interests of its members have been in conflict, the interests of tour operators often being contradictory to those of travel agents. Furthermore, while ABTA claims to serve the interests of travel consumers, they may be in opposition to its role in serving the needs of its members. In one respect, however, ABTA has served the travelling public exceptionally well – the financial bonding it requires of members. This scheme remains a leading means of consumer protection in the industry and the organization's logo is widely recognized by members of the public – more so, for example, than the CAA's ATOL logo.

Meetings Industry Association (MIA), UKInbound, representing organizations that make ground handling arrangements for incoming visitors to the UK and the British Resorts Association (BRA). Similar bodies are to be found in all countries with a developed tourism industry. The American Society of Travel Agents (ASTA), for example, fulfils a similar role in the USA to that of ABTA in the UK, but also draws on members from other sectors of industry, as well as overseas members, due to the importance and influence of the USA as a tourist-generating country.

Regional bodies will comprise groups such as local hoteliers or tourist attractions. These will often act as pressure groups in their relations with local tourist authorities, but also provide arenas for discussion on issues of mutual interest to members.

Destination organizations

A destination organization is one that draws its membership from both public- and private-sector tourism bodies that share a common interest in the development or marketing of a specific tourist destination. That destination may be a resort, state or region, a country or even an area of the globe. Membership of such bodies is open to firms or public-sector organizations rather than individuals. These bodies generally share two common objectives:

- to foster cooperation and coordination between the various bodies that provide, or are responsible for, the facilities or amenities making up the tourism product
- to act in concert to promote the destination to the travel trade and tourists.

Consequently, they are trade, rather than professional, bodies. Examples range from such globally important regional marketing bodies as the Pacific Area Travel Association (PATA) and the European Travel Commission (ETC), to local marketing consortia made up of groups of hotels or tourist attractions within a particular region or resort.

A marketing consortium currently comprising public-sector (including national tourist organizations) and private-sector tourism interests (including airlines, care hire companies, attraction, tour operators and travel agents) represents combined interests in Germany, Austria, Hungary, the Czech Republic, Slovakia and Poland. This consortium was formed in 1999 as the Central European Countries Travel Association (CECTA) in order to market this large European region more effectively, stress its geographically central, rather than Eastern European, roots and take advantage of opportunities for growth following the advent of four of these nations into the European Union. At the other end of the scale, the Bournemouth Hotels and Restaurants Association, the Devon Association of Tourist Attractions and the Association of Bath and District Leisure Enterprises are all typical examples in England of localized groupings within a single country.

Example

Destination organizations supporting tourism in Victoria, Australia

There are numerous associations and alliances supporting tourism in the state of Victoria, Australia. They span many sectors and have a variety of goals and roles. One example is Tourism Alliance Victoria.

This membership group includes tourism organizations and individual businesses in the state. It includes accommodation providers, tour operators, regional and local tourism associations, attractions and local government tourism departments. The Alliance represents the issues of its members to national, regional and local government, as well as working to encourage tourism growth in the region. Furthermore, it works to provide professional development and has worked to establish benchmarks for professional services. In addition, research is compiled to evaluate the effectiveness of marketing activities, future product opportunities as well as visitor satisfaction.

The Australian Hotels Association – Victoria Chapter – provides support for hotelkeepers, as well as acting as a lobbying body for hotels and hospitality venues in the state. Membership spans both urban and rural hotels. It also provides information to members on how to enhance the operation of their daily business, such as details of staff training, industry codes of practice and regulations relating to alcohol licensing and gambling.

The Regional Victoria Conference Group (RVCG) is a group of conference venues, accommodation providers, tour operators and local government. By coordinating their marketing activities, they can promote the region as an attractive conference destination. The Group also lobbies to promote members' interests. Furthermore, it has worked to develop alliances with other tourism bodies, such as Tourism Alliance Victoria Tourism, Victoria's Melbourne Convention and Visitors Bureau (MCVB) and Meetings and Events Australia (Victoria) (MEA).

Other regional organizations include:

- Aboriginal Tourism Victoria (ATV)
- Accommodation Getaways Victoria (AGV)
- Australian Camps Association, Victoria (ACA)
- Backpacker Operators Association of Victoria (BOAV)
- Boating Industry Association of Victoria Inc (BIA)
- Victoria Food & Wine Tourism Council (VFWTC)
- Victorian Caravan Parks Association Inc (VCPA)

Tourism organizations

The activities of some bodies transcend sectoral boundaries within the industry. These organizations may have as their aim the compilation of national or international statistics on tourism or the furtherance of research into the tourism phenomenon.

The United Nations World Tourism Organization (UNWTO) plays a dominant role in collecting and collating statistical information on international tourism. This organization represents public-sector tourism bodies from most countries in the world. Also, the publication of its data enables comparisons of the flow and growth of tourism on a global scale.

Similarly, the Organization for Economic Cooperation and Development (OECD) also has a tourism committee, composed of tourism officials drawn from its member countries, that provides regular reports comprising comparative data on tourism developments to and within these countries. Other privately sponsored bodies have been set up to produce supporting statistics, such as the World Travel and Tourism Council (WTTC), the members of which are drawn from over 30 leading airlines and tourist organizations. This body also regularly commissions and publishes research data.

Within countries, bodies are set up to bring together public and private tourism interests as a means of influencing legislation, encouraging political action or sometimes to overcome crises affecting the industry. In the UK, the Tourism Industry Emergency Response Group was established to take action on problems facing the UK tourism industry and comprises representatives of the Department for Culture, Media and Sport (DCMS) and directors of principal tourism bodies. Wider aims are designed to be achieved by the Tourism Alliance.

Example

The Tourism Alliance

In 2001, the travel industry in Britain was severely affected by foot-and-mouth disease in cattle, which restricted travel to the countryside and inhibited visitors from abroad, especially North America. Travel organizations recognized that they needed a common mouthpiece to lobby government and handle future problems affecting the industry, feeling that the existing bodies were inadequate for this purpose. Thus, the Tourism Alliance was formed, bringing together a mix of public and private organizations, including ABTA, the Association of Leading Visitor Attractions, the British Hospitality Association, British Incoming Tour Operators' Association (BITOA, now UKInbound), the Association of Recognized English Language Services, the British Beer and Pub Association, the British Holiday and Home Parks Association, together with the Local Government Association and national and regional tourist boards (excluding Wales and Scotland, which have their own tourism forums). The organization has come to form a strong pressure group and debating forum.

Many countries with a strongly developed tourism industry establish professional bodies composed of individual members drawn from several or all sectors of the industry. The purpose of these bodies is to promote the cause of the tourism industry generally, while simultaneously encouraging the spread of knowledge and understanding of the industry among members. For example, in Britain there are two professional bodies devoted to the tourism industry generally, although they tend to draw their membership from different sectors of industry. The Institute of Travel and Tourism (ITT) originated as an institute designed to serve the needs of travel agents and tour operators and still draws its membership largely from these sectors, while the Tourism Society, a more recently formed professional body, attracts members particularly from the public sector, tourist attractions and the incoming tourism industry. As has been pointed out earlier, this body also draws members from the fields of tourism consultancy and education.

Occasionally, relevant organizations are set up by non-tourism interests, if tourism comes within their provenance. Such a body is the Confederation of British Industry (CBI)'s Tourism Action Group, established in 1993 to help advance the interests of tourism as one area of business. This body has concerned itself principally with improving the appeal of tourism as a career and the quality of training on offer to new recruits to the industry, improving the marketing of tourism overseas to the UK, ensuring tourist attractions come up to expectations regarding their quality and improving accessibility for tourism through an integrated transport system within the UK. In this work, the CBI complements many of the concerns of sectoral organizations within tourism.

Integration in the tourism industry

A notable feature of the industry over recent years has been the steady process of integration that has taken place between sectors of the tourism industry. If we refer to our earlier model of the chain of distribution (Figure 8.2) we can identify this integration as being either **horizontal** or **vertical** in character. Horizontal integration is that taking place at any one level in the chain, while vertical integration describes the process of linking together organizations at different levels of the chain (some writers also refer to **diagonal integration** – a term used to describe links between complementary businesses within each level in the chain).

All business is highly competitive and the tourism industry is no exception to this rule. Such competition, often encouraged by government policy, has been evident within the tourism industry, especially since the development of the mass market in travel that began in the 1960s. Following policies of deregulation, particularly those in the transport sector affecting air, rail and coach companies, competition became steadily fiercer throughout the latter part of the twentieth century and the early years of the new century. Competition forces companies to seek ways of becoming more efficient in order to cut costs. Integration makes this possible.

The benefits of scale

Horizontal integration enables companies to benefit from economies of scale by producing and selling more of a product. This reduces the unit cost of each product as the fixed costs incurred are spread over a larger number of units, whether these are hotel bedrooms, aircraft seats or package tours. Equally, buyers of these products, such as tour operators, can obtain lower net prices if they buy in larger quantities, just as airlines can negotiate lower prices if they order more aircraft from the manufacturers.

The savings achieved through both these economies of scale can be passed on to clients in the form of lower prices, making the product more attractive to the consumer. Vertical integration offers economies of scale through the integration of executive and administrative functions, as well as increasing leverage on the market through advertising and promotion.

The benefits of a changed distribution system

The World Wide Web is undermining some of the former purposes of integration by offering an alternative method of distribution and reducing the necessity of depending on so many links in the chain. Today, no hotelier need depend anymore on granting an allocation of beds to a local ground handler, who would sell them on to a tour operator, who in turn would make them available to customers via a travel agent. Beds can be sold direct via a website and in any number of foreign languages to meet the world market's needs. In so doing, distribution prices can be held down to a level where they may well undercut those possibly using traditional distribution techniques.

The benefits of size

Large companies offer benefits to both suppliers and tourists. Suppliers, knowing the reputations of the major companies in the field, are anxious to do business with them, in the belief that such firms are less likely to collapse in the face of competition than the small ones (a belief that is not always well founded, as shown by the collapse of the International Leisure Group – Britain's second-largest operator, at the beginning of the 1990s). The tour operator's operational risks are minimized because suppliers, faced with an overbooking situation, will be less likely to turn away clients from the tour operator who brings them so much business. Similarly, hotels uniting into larger groups will be able to negotiate better deals through their own suppliers for the bulk purchase of such items as food and drink, while larger airlines will bring greater bargaining strength to the negotiating table in their dealings with foreign governments for landing rights or new routes.

Most companies, if asked to identify their organizational goals, would cite market expansion as a major objective. Growth in a competitive environment is a means of survival and history testifies to the fact that few companies survive by standing still. Integration is a means of growth, enabling a company to increase its market share and simultaneously reduce the level of competition it faces by forcing less-efficient companies out of business.

Greater sales generally mean more revenue, so, potentially, there will be more funds to reinvest in the company to assist with the costs of expansion. This in turn enables the company to employ or expand its specialist personnel. Nowhere is this truer than in those companies the branches of which are individually quite small. A small chain of travel agents, for instance, or of hotels may for the first time be able to employ specialist sales or marketing staff or recruit its own training staff or financial advisers.

Higher levels of revenue also release more money for the marketing effort – a programme of national advertising in the mass media may become a real possibility for the first time. For example, in the UK it has traditionally been common for the multiple travel agents (such as Thomas Cook or First Choice) to undertake a post-Christmas TV advertising campaign, the success of which has enabled these dominant market leaders to extend their share of the travel market further at the expense of the independents.

In addition to these broad benefits offered by integration generally, there are other advantages specific to horizontal or vertical integration, which we will now examine in turn.

Horizontal integration

Horizontal integration can take several forms. One is the integration of two companies offering similar (that is, potentially competing) products. Two hotels at the same seaside resort may merge, for example, or two airlines operating on similar routes may unite. Such **mergers** may result from the takeover of one company by another or simply from a voluntary agreement between the two to merge and obtain the benefits, identified above, of a much larger organization. **Voluntary unions** can also be established, however, that allow the companies concerned to maintain their autonomy while still obtaining the benefits of an integrated organization. This is the case with a **consortium** – an affiliation of independent companies working together to achieve a common aim or benefit. One example of this affiliation is the marketing consortium, which allows independent companies to gain economies of scale in, for example, mass advertising or the publication of a joint brochure. The Best Western consortium, for instance, among other activities, produces a brochure listing all their member hotels. Alternatively, a consortium may have as its prime benefit the ability to purchase supplies at bulk prices for its members – a feature of groupings of independent travel agents such as the Advantage consortium, which, in this way, can negotiate higher commission levels from tour operators and other principals.

A second form of integration occurs between companies offering complementary rather than competing products. An example would be the linking of an airline with a hotel chain. As both of these are *principals* they are at the same stage of the chain of distribution and thus their integration is horizontal. Close links between the accommodation and transport sectors may develop as they are interdependent for their customers. Without hotel bedrooms available at their destinations, airline passengers may be unwilling to book seats, and vice versa. Recognition of this dual need has led many airlines to buy into or form their own hotel divisions, especially in regions of high tourist demand where bed shortages are common. This trend was common in the early years of the jumbo jet, when airlines woke up to the consequences of operating aircraft with 350 or more passengers aboard, each requiring accommodation over which the airline had little or no control. This led to the integration of several major airlines and hotel chains. Rising competition between airlines, which led to huge losses and massive investment in new aircraft, however, obliged many airlines to sell their hotel investments to raise capital in order to survive. Since those days, the commonest type of this relationship has been to have closely linked computer reservations systems (CRSs), which allow the airlines a measure of control over hotel bedrooms without having to make a major capital investment in the accommodation sector. The growth of dynamic packaging in the early 2000s reinforced the need for airlines to have access to accommodation, many developing their own websites to include hotel accommodation at prices competitive with specialist hotel websites.

Airlines are increasingly seeking to benefit from liaisons that do not involve competition on the same routes. **Interlining agreements** allow airlines to benefit from connections globally. These are commercial agreements between airlines to provide travel routes for passengers that require the use of multiple airlines. For example, a flight from Germany to the Cook Islands (in the Pacific) may use flights operated by both Lufthansa and Air New Zealand. Such agreements have been extended to code-sharing, which allows an airline to allocate its own flight number to a service operated by another airline. Close links have also been developed through the global airline alliances that have formed in recent years, such as Star Alliance and One World. Combined, these links can mean that, for example, transatlantic routes can provide 'feeder' opportunities into the US network of domestic routes, allowing foreign airlines to compete with US airlines to carry passengers between two US domestic airports. Such agreements also overcome the problems faced if these airlines were to try to merge – a move often seen as anticompetitive and likely to be challenged by monopolies commissions, which favour open competition.

The changing nature of tourist demand may also cause companies to diversify their interests horizontally. In the previous century, shipping companies woke up far too late to the realization that the future of long-haul travel lay in the air and, by the time they began investing in airlines, the sums involved were too great for the loss-making shipping companies to absorb.

At the retailing level, integration is also common, but because the traditional development of travel agencies has led in many cases to regional strengths, integration has tended to be regionally based, leading to the development of so-called 'miniples' – agencies with a significant number of branches within one region of the country only, which may well, within that region, outperform the multiple agents (more details of this are provided in Chapter 19). The massive growth in the number of branches of the big multiples has tapered off and has even been reversing in the opening years of the new century, while the performance of miniples such as Let's Go Travel and Global Independent Travel has actually improved. Initially, this had led to some large travel companies taking over a miniple as a means of building or strengthening its profile in a particular region, but, as competition increased and the profits of large companies were squeezed, the process has been reversing and miniples are regaining their autonomy.

Example

Travel House

Large chains are constantly rethinking their strategies. In the UK, the dominant idea within the multiple agencies was that expansion was vital in order to compete with rivals. More recently, the move to direct selling and the contraction in agency numbers has encouraged the dominant agencies (Thomson/First Choice and Thomas Cook/My Travel) to reduce the numbers of their branches, too.

In 2004, TUI, the world's leading travel agency chain, sold 21 of its Travel House branches (all located in Wales) back to the original owner, having purchased them only a year or two earlier. The sucess of this independent Welsh business is clear from its positive trading despite it being a difficult time for high street agencies. This can be seen from the announcement in 2007 that Travel House will continue to operate its branch in Camarthen, South Wales. This was important for the town as it followed an announcement by the two leading travel agents – Thomson and Going Places – that they were to close their outlets.[4]

Tour operating has also experienced growth through integration in the past decade – first that between large companies in Britain and later internationally (see Chapter 18 for more details). Two of Britain's leading companies – Thomas Cook and Thomson Holidays – are now both in German hands (the latter, part of world leader TUI). While integration in the principal travel sectors is likely to continue, it is unlikely to be as frenetic as it has been in recent years, given the instability of the industry and that most companies are keen to see a return to stable profits rather than chasing expansion. Some major ventures, such as expansion by European companies into North America, have in fact been reversed as the companies have consolidated their positions.

Vertical integration

As noted, vertical integration is said to take place when an organization at one level in the chain of distribution unites with one at another level. This integration can be **forward** (or downward in the direction of the chain), such as in the case where a tour operator buys its own chain of travel agents or it can be **backward** (or upward, against the direction of the chain), such as in the case where a tour operator buys its own airline.

Example

Libra Holidays Group

In 2004, tour operator Libra Holidays bought Helios Airways, a largely scheduled airline, in a move to expand its Cyprus tour operating programme. Formerly, the company had held a stake in Excel Airways, reducing this investment in order to invest in its own carrier.

Backward integration in the form of a takeover (such as in the Example above) is fairly uncommon. More frequently in the past, operators have set up their own airlines internally. Forward integration is more typical as organizations are more likely to have the necessary capital to buy businesses further down the chain of distribution as they require less capital investment than those above them in the chain. For example, even the largest independent travel agency chain might hesitate before embarking on an expansion to form its own airline. Even so, in rare cases, examples exist where even the smaller companies have successfully done so. Bath Travel, a miniple in England's south west, actually purchased its own aircraft to operate a limited programme of tours under the brand name Palmair, which it has successfully operated for a number of years. Strong brand loyalty in the region has undoubtedly helped to account for the success of this high-risk venture. It is true to say, however, that, generally speaking, the higher a company is in the chain of distribution, the greater the investment that will be required.

As with horizontal integration, organizations can achieve significant economies of scale by expanding vertically. Where total profits in individual sectors may be slight, a reasonable profit overall across the sectors may still be made by an integrated business that controls all levels in the chain. Even in a year of intense competition, tour operating companies owning their own airlines and retail sales outlets (neither of which may be committed to the exclusive sale of the operator's products) may still remain profitable.

As with the linking of complementary services in horizontal integration, many companies are concerned about ensuring the continuation of their supplies. A tour operator depending on a continuous supply of aircraft seats and hotel beds, and facing international competition for such supplies, can best ensure adequate and regular supplies by directly controlling them – that is, by integrating backwards, into the airline and hotel businesses.

Example

Integration at WA Shearings

An interesting example, combining vertical and horizontal integration, is that of leading British coach operator Shearings.

For some years, Shearings has been putting into practice an ambitious programme to own its hotels. The company employs its fleet substantially in its role as tour operator, running coach tours, and secures two benefits from its hotel ownership: control over the quality and availability of accommodation at any time of the year and an opportunity to maximize profits on its hotel *and* tour operating businesses.

Large multinational corporations are well equipped financially to diversify their interests into new products when they see opportunities arise. Many of the leading European tour operators have integrated airlines. These vertical links between airlines and tour operators are further examined in Chapter 18.

Integration leads to control

Several of the leading operators have, in recent years, sought to own and operate their own hotels in key resorts abroad to ensure both the availability of rooms and some control over their price. Integration here can be achieved either by direct purchase or setting up joint venture companies with partners in the hotel industry or other sectors of the industry. Such integration can offer the added advantage of improved control over the quality of the product. This is frequently difficult to achieve otherwise in the case of some international hotels and, indeed, ensuring that standards are uniform, consistent and of the required quality to suit the market is no easy matter. Although operators do own hotels, this has, up to now, been on a limited scale only, with many preferring to exercise control through a franchising scheme or branding, which allows control of standards while management remains in the hands of the hotel company.

Example

Joint venture

In November 2007, the Canadian tour operator Transat AT announced that it was going to enter into a joint venture with the Spanish-owned H10 Hotels chain through an agreement to operate five hotels, located in Mexico and the Dominican Republic. The agreement gave Transat a 35 per cent stake in this new venture, at a cost of US$55 million, allowing it some control over more than 1600 bedrooms.

President of Transat, Jean-Marc Eustache, stated that 'this joint venture is what we were looking for. It allows us to secure a number of quality hotel rooms and maximize the gains we derive from being vertically integrated.' President of H10 Hotels, Josep Espelt, stated, 'We are very pleased to partner with Transat, . . . this partnership is designed to be scaled up over time, and each partner will benefit from the strengths and leadership of the other.'[5]

Equally, the production sector will attempt to exercise control over the merchandising of its products. Airlines, shipping services and hotels are all multi-million pound investments, yet, curiously, in the recent past they had to rely to a considerable extent on a fragmented, independent and frequently inexpert retail sector to sell their products. Travel agents carry no stock and therefore have little brand loyalty to a particular travel company. It was a logical step for principals to try to influence distribution by buying into retail agencies. Many domestic US airlines' shops compete with agents for the sale of flight tickets, although those shops are being cut back as the airlines encourage sales through their websites and those of online distributors such as Expedia and Opodo. British Airways also sought to enter the retail sector and established 17 retail shops in the UK. Despite efforts to reduce operating costs, however, management forecast long-term losses and announced that all the shops were to close by the end of 2006.[6] The leading British tour operators have their own retail agency chains and engage in the practice of **directional selling**, in which counter staff are expected to give priority to the sale of the parent company's products. This is discussed in more detail in Chapter 18.

This forward integration is now becoming unnecessary with the growth of the World Wide Web. For *principals*, their distribution can be achieved directly to the customer rather than through retailing or wholesaling divisions further down the ladder. The no frills carriers have depended least on the chain of distribution. Thus, easyJet has never used retail agents and Ryanair has now abandoned them. Both depend to such an extent on the Web that they even penalize any direct bookings taken via telephone from their clients with a higher charge.

Within the European Union, vertical integration has drawn far less criticism from bodies such as the Competition Commission than has horizontal integration. In the UK, the Monopolies and Mergers Commission, as it then was, investigated the growing control of travel agency chains by tour operators and ruled that the links between operators and agents must be spelled out clearly at the point of sale (the travel agent). There are, however, some curious anomalies regarding the Commission's ruling, which exempts certain large operators and has failed to rule on sales via the Internet. Tourism organizations seeking to grow their operations may seek to expand across several sectors of the industry, both domestically and overseas, providing that this will not open them up to investigation by the monopolies bodies.

Vertical integration clearly poses a threat to independents in the retail sector. Airlines or tour operators opening their own retail outlets are likely to attract the market away from the independents by means of competitive pricing or other marketing tactics. Many independents have combated this threat by forming consortia, which allow them to negotiate better returns from their principals. This may in time lead to the creation of 'own brand' labels for tour operating (already tested on a limited scale), if this is judged the best means of competing with the multiples.

Conglomerates and international integration

No discussion about the changing structure of ownership within the tourism industry would be complete without an examination of the growing role of the conglomerates. These are organizations the interests of which extend across a variety of different industries in order to spread the risks incurred by operating within a specific industry such as tourism. Although tourism has the reputation of being a highly volatile industry, the long-term growth prospects for leisure generally have attracted many businesses from outside the industry itself. Breweries, for example, have expanded into hotels and holiday centres. In Europe, conglomeration is well established in numerous countries. Germany, for example, invested heavily in travel and tourism businesses through department stores and leading banks, although recently these have been divesting their interests as the German economy has faltered.

The travel industry is experiencing rapid internationalization in ownership. This is a process that has been hastened within Europe by the harmonization of member countries. Travel businesses have, as a result, been actively expanding their interests in each other's countries. While it is tempting to offer some examples of the current spate in such expansion, the pace of change is now so fast that any examples are likely to date very quickly. Readers are encouraged to keep in touch with the trade press in order to update their knowledge of this process. Suffice it to say that, increasingly, travel companies must look beyond their own national borders to understand the nature of the competition they face.

Notes

1. Federation of Tour Operators (2008) 'Tour operators and travel agents', FTO. Available online at: **www.fto.co.uk/operators-factfile/tour-operators**
2. Competition Commission (2008) 'BAA airports market investigation', Competition Commission News Release 12/08, 22 April.
3. Tourism Society (2007) 'Annual report and accounts 2006', Tourism Society. Available online to members at: **www.tourismsociety.org**
4. 'Travel firm here to stay', *Carmarthen Journal*, 16 May 2007.
5. 'H10 Hotels and Transat to establish JV', *Travel Business Review*, 29 November 2007.
6. 'British Airways axes 400 jobs', *Evening News*, Scotland, 15 March 2006.

Websites

Best Western (consortia information)	**www.whybestwestern.com**
Central European Countries Travel Association	**www.cecta.org**
Tourism Society	**www.tourismsociety.org**

Questions and discussion points

1. It has been suggested that high street travel agents will benefit from being able to dynamically package holidays. Do you think that this is really the case or will tour operators and principals instead capture the market for bespoke or tailor-made holidays?

2. Many students are now studying for qualifications such as honours degrees in tourism-related subjects. As a student or when they graduate, they may be asked to join a professional body such as the Tourism Society. What are the benefits of joining such an organization? How might it have an impact on their careers?

3. What are the benefits of a small business becoming a member of its local destination marketing organization? Are there drawbacks or limitations that should be considered?

4. What is meant by the term 'vertical integration'? Do you think there are benefits for a small hotel chain in forward integration?

Tasks

1. Tourist attractions may be owned by the public rather than the private or voluntary sectors. Investigate the tourist attractions in your local area to find examples of those owned by the public sector. Explain why governments may choose to own and operate tourist attractions.

2. The tourism industry has to respond to rapidly changing business environments. Identify the key changes affecting the industry in the last decade that have had an effect on the way in which tourism products and packages are distributed and prepare a set of notes to accompany a formal talk to members of the industry outlining those changes.

Chapter 9

Tourist destinations

Learning outcomes

After studying this chapter, you should be able to:

- understand the complexity of the destination as a tourism product

- recognize the importance of the image and the brand in destination marketing

- distinguish between different categories of destination

- understand the appeal of each form of destination

- explain why destinations are subject to changing fortunes.

Introduction: what defines a destination?

All consumers expect certain standards: cleanliness, accurate marketing, decipherable road signs, and so on. But they also want that 'special something' – be it a modern cultural icon or living heritage – that makes a destination unlike anywhere else. The Lyons Review of Local Government calls this 'place-shaping' and the future of tourism depends on its success.

Stuart Barrow, Public Affairs Manager, VisitBritain, 'Why globalization means "back to the future" for local identities', *Tourism Society Journal*, 134, Winter 2007, p. 11

In Chapter 1, we briefly outlined what is meant by a tourist destination. This chapter is be devoted to expanding on that definition, so that we can learn to understand the appeal that different types of destinations have for tourists.

Describing all the characteristics that go to make up a destination is one of the more difficult tasks in the study of tourism. It would be easy to say that the desire to visit a particular destination is the underlying reason for all tourism, but, in some instances, that is far from the case. The destination may be only one element in the appeal of the trip – sometimes a very minor one. When Concorde was flying, many tourists made it their lifetime ambition to travel on the world's only supersonic aircraft. Where it was flying *to* was of only minor interest to those enthusiasts. Equally, impressive cruise liners such as the *Queen Mary 2* (see Figures 14.1 a and b) may represent the actual destination for devotees of cruising and the ship's ports of call may be of only passing interest (some enthusiasts of cruising do not even disembark at ports of call en route). Anniversaries are often enjoyed on the Orient Express – the nostalgic rail journey offered by this distinguished train being the prime purpose for the trip – and the attraction of the long rail journey across Russia from Moscow to Vladivostok owes little to the brief stops that the train makes during its epic journey. Sometimes the ambition to drive along a historic route, such as the silk route across Asia or Route 66 across the United States, outweighs the places visited during the drive. Consequently, we should recognize that, very often, the *transport* selected by tourists can be as important as the destination to which they are travelling, making it not merely a means to an end, but an end in itself.

In other examples, the *attraction* has become the destination. This is true of many theme parks. Orlando in Florida did not exist as a tourist destination 40 years ago before Walt Disney Productions decided to make it the site of its second development, just as the location of Alton Towers in Northamptonshire in the UK had little to interest the visitor before the construction of this major theme park. Certain hotels, such as Raffles in Singapore, have become famous in their own right as destinations, not because of where they are, but *what* they are.

In discussing destinations, we must always bear in mind two important considerations:

- the physical and psychological elements of destinations
- the image and promotion of a destination.

Physical and psychological elements of destinations

The image of a destination relates to a number of physical attributes – attractions and amenities, buildings, landscapes and so on – together with perceptions allied to the destination, which include less tangible attributes, such as the hospitality of the local population, atmosphere generated by being there, sense of awe, alienation, *Gemütlichkeit* or other emotions stimulated by the place. The sense of awe one experiences standing on the rim of the Grand Canyon in Arizona can be contrasted with the sense of foreboding experienced when passing through Glencoe in Scotland, the sombre location of the massacre of the MacDonalds by the Campbells in 1692. Visiting the World War II concentration camp at Auschwitz-Birkenau in Poland, now a major tourist destination, generates feelings of shock and revulsion, but underlines the fact that our choice of destination is not dependent on seeking only pleasure or entertainment. At the other end of the scale, different emotions are engendered in a visit to the formal gardens at the Japanese Royal Palace in Tokyo, the Kirstenbosch Botanic Gardens near Cape Town in South Africa (see Figure 10.6), the picturesque English charm of villages such as Castle Combe in Wiltshire or the flower-bedecked balconies of buildings in Germany, Austria and Switzerland. All of these destinations could be, and often are, marketed to horticultural enthusiasts and all offer a psychologically satisfying visual appeal to the viewer.

The image and promotion of a destination

Destinations have very different appeals to different markets. Some people love crowds, others love isolation and find crowded beaches unbearable. Holidays in the mountains, for some, will awaken thoughts of majestic landscapes with few visitors apart from the occasional hiker, such as might be found in Tierra del Fuego National Park in Argentina. Others may immediately think of expensive resorts such as Gstaad in Switzerland or Courchevel in France, with their busy ski-slopes and lively social life in the bars and restaurants. It is fortunate that the appeals of destinations are so varied, allowing opportunities for tourism to be developed in almost any country and to almost any region, providing that they are aimed at the appropriate markets.

Destinations depend on their **image** for their success in attracting tourists, even if that image is frozen in time and no longer represents a true picture of the place. Most well-known tourist countries and destinations such as cities and beach resorts rely on the stereotypes that have been built up over the years and, as long as they remain positive, promotional bodies will seek to support such images in their advertising. Thus, the prevailing image of London for the foreigner is of guardsmen riding on horseback through the city, past Big Ben and the Houses of Parliament; Paris, on the other hand, remains forever the city of lovers, with couples embracing on the banks of the Seine with the Eiffel Tower or Notre Dame in the background. It matters little that these images are stale icons bearing little resemblance to real life in these modern cities. The power of an image is the branding iron that drives tourism and to jettison it in favour of a more modern, but less graphic, image is a far more difficult – and risky – task for marketing than keeping the original.

Example

Greece

Greece's image has traditionally rested on a mix of sun, sea, sand and a variety of classical historical sites. Following its hosting of the 2004 Olympic Games in Athens, however, its tourism industry experienced three consecutive years of growth and, by 2006, it was estimated to provide one in five jobs in the country, contributing about 18 per cent of GDP.[1] The Olympics had provided a positive uplift to the image of the country and, in 2005, the Greek government determined to widen the appeal of the country further, launching a ten-year plan that had as its main goal to differentiate and enrich the tourist product, while promoting and supporting the country's existing tourist industry by broadening the scope of its products. Activities that were to be developed were non-seasonal, available throughout the year, to include new options for alternative tourism (spas, thalassotherapy), cultural tourism, urban and conference tourism, marine diving, sailing and eco-tourism. The aim has been to reach a total of 20 million tourists per annum by 2015, representing roughly a 10 per cent increase, year-on-year. The advertising slogan 'Greece – explore your senses' was introduced to support the promotion.

Aware of the importance of image in selling destinations, many countries have embarked on a process of **image creation**, with advertisements incorporating quickly communicated slogans and/or readily identifiable logos, such as that of Greece in the above Example, often alongside the image of their iconic attraction, as a means of conveying the destination's properties to intending tourists. Slogans are generally emotive as much as informative. Recent examples include 'Chic Thailand', 'Sensational Brazil', 'Dynamic' or 'Sparkling Korea', 'Uniquely Singapore', New Zealand's '100% Pure', and 'Incredible India'. Croatia has opted for 'The Mediterranean as it once was', concisely conveying the experience of the destination, while at the same time drawing attention to the declining attractions of its competitors. By contrast, the pleasantly alliterative 'Enjoy England' says little about the product, while Scotland revised its own slogan, dropping 'The best small country in the world' in favour of the rather less inspiring 'Welcome to Scotland'. It has since been changed again to 'Live it. Visit Scotland.' Sri Lanka, on the other hand, settled for hyperbolic alliteration in its choice of 'Spectacular, spellbinding, sensuous Sri Lanka'.

Another approach is to couple famous faces with a destination. One highly successful example of this is New York, which, in its 'Ask the locals' campaign, has used its celebrities such as Robert de Niro to promote the city.

Example

The Australian tourism campaign

The Australian Tourist Board developed a controversial advertising slogan to market the country abroad: 'So where the bloody hell are you?' Playing on the country's image for blunt, down-to-earth talking, set against a backdrop of scenes revealing the wealth of attractions on offer, the campaign proved popular in the USA, but rather less so in Britain, where it was judged brash. As a consequence, however, the adverts received considerable publicity in the media, still helping to raise Australia's visibility.

Destination promotion is of limited benefit, unless it is accompanied by other supporting factors. It is important here to stress the role played by transport companies in this. Budget airlines, for example have expanded tourism to both existing and newly popular destinations by offering cheap fares and, in many cases, developing new provincial hubs. Many of these are sited in areas of which tourists had only limited knowledge previously. Among destinations to have benefited from the European no frills airlines in recent years are Turkey, Austria and regions of the former Yugoslavia, particularly Croatia and Slovenia, while, in 2007, Montenegro was identified by the World Travel and Tourism Council as the second-fastest-growing tourist destination in the world.

Categorizing destinations

It is convenient to divide destinations into five distinct groupings.

- The **centred** destination is the commonest – a traditional form of holiday arrangement in which the tourist travels to the destination, where they expect to spend the majority of their time, with perhaps occasional excursions to visit nearby attractions. The classic seaside holiday, winter sports resort or short city break represent the most common types in this grouping.

- Destinations that form a base from where the surrounding region can be explored. Some British seaside resorts have successfully reformulated their marketing strategy to sell themselves as bases for exploring the nearby countryside. Resorts in Devon and Cornwall, for instance, have drawn attention to their proximity to the national parks of Exmoor and Dartmoor, while Cirencester and Cheltenham have both promoted themselves as gateways to the nearby Cotswolds – one of the most popular tourist regions in England. Interlaken has successfully promoted itself for many years as the base for exploring the scenic Vierwaldstättersee region in Switzerland, while Gatlinburg in Tennessee promotes the town as a base for exploring the Great Smoky Mountains region.

- **Multicentre** holidays, where two or more destinations are of equal importance in the itinerary. A good example of such a holiday would be that of a tourist with an interest in exploring the new central European countries of the Baltic buying a package comprising stays in the three capitals of Tallinn, Riga and Vilnius.

- **Touring** destinations, which will be part of a linear itinerary, including stops at a number of points. A Caribbean cruise, for instance, will call at several ports en route, while a tour of the American Midwest or Far West or a rail journey across Canada will make stopovers a key element in the itinerary.

- **Transit** destinations, which merely provide an overnight stop en route to the final destination. Such stopovers may or may not be preplanned, but occur at convenient points, particularly for drivers contemplating long journeys by car. Typical examples are tourists driving by car from Britain, Scandinavia or Northern Germany to a Mediterranean destination who identify useful points at which to stop en route when they become tired. Such a destination may offers touristic opportunities also, but not necessarily – the principal aim is to break the journey. Location – in terms of driving distances from key generating markets – is therefore a key factor in developing stopover traffic, but an equally important consideration is the availability of suitable overnight accommodation.

Coastal tourism

When we think of coastal destinations, most of us conjure up an image of a typical **seaside resort** – this being the destination with most popular appeal along any coastline. The attractiveness of a seaside resort is the combination of sun, sand and sea, which still appeals to the largest segment of the tourist market, either as a form of passive recreation – lying in a deckchair or on the sand and watching the sea – or as a location for more active pastimes, including water sports and beach games.

This form of tourism remains popular. In 2003, 10 per cent of domestic trips in the USA involved going to the beach,[2] while 24 per cent of Australia's domestic trips in 2006, similarly, involved a trip to the beach.[3] In Britain, although numbers are declining, some 33 million Britons take trips to English seaside resorts every year and the country is fortunate in having 7720 miles of coast (of which, 1700 are owned by the Crown Estate and, hence, accessible to the public).

Many seaside resorts in Britain have moved on from their nineteenth-century image and now cater to a variety of different markets seeking very different benefits. The concept of a seaside resort can now embrace everything from the traditional workers' paradise to the village centred on a harbour catering to the yachting fraternity, to a cultural town with art galleries, museums and concert halls.

It is the traditional resort in the UK that has suffered the most decline, due to changing patterns in tourist demand. Above all, this is because these destinations have been slowest to invest in new facilities or renovate their heritage buildings. Many one-time popular resorts, such as Clacton, Cleethorpes, Llandudno, New Brighton, Skegness and Southport,

Figure 9.1 This kiosk is located at the seaside resort of Walton-on-the-Naze, Essex. It opens seasonally to sell food and beach products to holidaymakers.
(Photo by Claire Humphreys.)

have remained, to some extent, frozen in time, with their sweet shops selling candy floss and rock, their amusement arcades and funfairs, 'kiss me quick' hats, and fish and chip shop (see Figure 9.1). The market for these resorts has dwindled as older, loyal, regular visitors have died and their children choose to holiday overseas instead.

A handful of resorts accepted the challenge and invested. Blackpool remains popular simply due to its investment in funfair rides, nightlife amenities and its famous Illuminations – a light display. Modest investment by towns such as Scarborough have enabled the towns to survive, if not prosper, while some have striven to change their image by focusing on a single attraction. Bexhill-on-Sea, for example, has the de la Warr Pavilion – perhaps the greatest example of mid-twentieth-century architecture in the country – that was narrowly saved from destruction and has been restored to its former glory. Margate, trading on its earlier links with the painter J. M. W. Turner, is in the process of constructing an eponymous modern art gallery (see the Example) in the hope of attracting a new, more cultured market.

A few genteel resorts, such as Eastbourne, Worthing and Deal, have largely resigned themselves to the role of retirement resort, while some larger resorts have diversified sufficiently to be no longer entirely dependent on tourism. Bournemouth, for example, while retaining its tourist market through new investment in attractions and the restoration of its Victorian heritage buildings, is also large enough to have attracted industry (particularly banking and financial services) and education (with its language schools and new university) and these now boost its economy. The town is also close to the dense population centres of the South East. By constructing an artificial offshore reef, the town now plans to attract young surfers, too.

Brighton, while not sharing the same quality of beach (like much of the Sussex coastline, its beaches are pebbled), has built on its proximity to London and its cultural facilities to remain an important short-break destination. It has also developed a major new marina to attract yacht owners, while also expanding other non-leisure industries.

Example

The rise, decline and regeneration of English seaside resorts

Blackpool, Lancashire

The original spur to the development of Blackpool as a seaside resort was the introduction of the railway in 1846. It became firmly established as England's premier resort for northern workers when a promenade and two piers were constructed in the 1860s. The famous tower followed in 1894, modelled on the Eiffel Tower, and the pleasure beach theme park was completed before the turn of the century. The town attracted a peak of 17 million visitors in 1992 and continues to bring in around 10 million each year, drawn by the wide range of attractions and its Christmas Illuminations.

The town was disappointed not to be selected as site for Britain's first super-casino, which was seen as a key opportunity to grow tourism to the resort, but recently a new 15-year masterplan was announced to regenerate the seafront, at a cost approaching £174 million, which may yet see Blackpool return to its former glory.

Brighton, Sussex

Up until the 1780s, Brighton was a fishing village, but royal patronage and the construction of the Royal Pavilion in 1783 led to the town's development as a premier fashionable seaside resort. Two piers – the West Pier in 1866 and the Palace Pier in 1899 – boosted its popularity and encouraged coastal excursions. Its good railway connections and proximity to London led to its appellation as 'London by the Sea', popularizing day visits and short breaks.

Figure 9.2 Brighton's seafront and pier attract a variety of domestic and international tourists. *(Photo by Chris Holloway.)*

Margate, Kent

This South East resort grew in Victorian times and remained popular during the twentieth century, due to its famous Dreamland Amusement Park, attracting the C_2DE markets. These markets dried up with the growth of overseas holidays after World War II, however, and Dreamland closed.

Efforts have been made to revive the resort in this century, with the reopening of Dreamland in 2005 and plans for a new art gallery to commemorate the importance of this area for the paintings of J. M. W. Turner (1775–1851). With the aid of funding from the Arts Council, South East England Development Agency and Kent County Council, the gallery is expected to open in 2010 and the council is also encouraging artists' studios and galleries to open nearby. The eighteenth-century old town is being restored and streets pedestrianised, in the hope of emulating the success of other resorts like St Ives, Whitstable and Broadstairs, which boast attractive old town centres.

Figure 9.3 Seaside resorts in England.

Scarborough, North Yorkshire

This has been a popular resort in the North East of England since the late eighteenth century, when sea bathing was in fashion. Initially a fishing port, this gave way to its role as a prominent spa. Refurbishment of the prime buildings, including the Grand Hotel, the town's flagship property, and the Spa entertainment complex, is encouraging a stable domestic tourism market. Refurbishment of museums and art galleries, too, is helping to move the resort upmarket and the town has become one of the first in the country to offer free wi-fi access in the seafront areas.

Skegness, Lincolnshire

A popular holiday resort since the nineteenth century (with a pier constructed in 1881), the town received a boost in 1936 when it was chosen by Billy Butlin as the site for his first holiday camp.

After World War II, the resort's popularity dwindled and this coastal stretch became noted chiefly for its caravan parks.

Attempts are now being made to revive the resort, with repairs to the pier, and other investments.

Weston super Mare, Somerset

Another popular Victorian resort, it attracted visitors from Birmingham and the Midlands, but demand fell after World War II, and the town drifted downmarket due to a lack of investment.

Recently, investment and events tourism (such as the popular 'T4 on the Beach' pop concerts, attracting 70,000 visitors) have helped to turn the resort's fortunes around. The redevelopment of Knightstone Island, together with the promised full reconstruction of the pier after a disastrous fire in 2008, is leading to further improvements in the appearance of the seafront.

Littlehampton, West Sussex

Sea bathing became popular here around 1775 and, with the coming of the railway in 1863, the resort became an important South Coast holiday base up until the outbreak of World War II.

A noted effort to revive its fortunes has been the construction of Thomas Heathwerwick's East Beach Café (see Figure 9.4) in 2007, which is already an iconic architectural feature of the town. The riverbank has also seen regeneration, with the construction of a Look and Sea Centre with its viewing tower, bistro and exhibition centre.

Hastings, East Sussex

During the 1880s, this fishing village, coupled with its neighbour St Leonards, was transformed into an elegant resort for the Victorians. In the 1930s, it was modernized, with a lido, promenade and the country's first underground car park.

Badly run down in the post-war period, it received a £20 million regeneration in 2005, with a planned university campus and media centre.

Figure 9.4 East Beach Café, Littlehampton, West Sussex. This recent architectural masterpiece by Thomas Heatherwick is attracting more upmarket visitors to the seaside town.
(Photo by Chris Holloway.)

The major beneficiaries of changing tourist tastes have been the myriad small fishing ports and seaside villages in the UK, which have largely retained their character and resisted the temptation to expand due to strict planning controls. The scenic beauty of the many resorts in Devon and Cornwall (and notably those based around an estuary, such as Salcombe or Falmouth), for example, have made them highly desirable for second home owners and the self-catering market. Shops and restaurants have moved upmarket and some resorts in the South West, such as Padstow, have been able to build a successful tourist market based largely on the quality of their seafood restaurants. Where there is a strong cultural tradition, such as the colony of artists in St Ives, this has led to a focus on the arts, attracting many galleries, including a notable extension of London's Tate Gallery, which attracts over 200,000 visitors a year – three times the number envisaged when it was constructed. Those with the best marina facilities appeal to the wealthiest members of the yachting fraternity, ensuring that the markets attracted to such destinations remain high-spend. Being essentially rural as well as on the coast, such resorts provide a good base for exploring the surrounding countryside. The extent to which demand will inevitably continue to outstrip supply in destinations like these will ensure their long-term success, providing they can resist the temptation to expand to the point where they are no longer small, quaint resorts.

Many former UK tourist resorts, however, cannot expect to regain their lost markets, given the significant movement of popular seaside tourism, over the past five decades, away from the colder, Northern European beaches towards those of the Mediterranean as prices of flights fell and the tourists could be assured of sunshine and warm water – something that was never guaranteed for beach holidays in Northern Europe.

Similarly, the lower fares have enabled Americans to fly to their warmer beaches in Florida or California or even further afield to Mexico, the Bahamas and the Caribbean, abandoning the traditional northern beaches of resorts such as Atlantic City, New Jersey or the Long Island beaches of New York State.

Atlantic City fought back by renovating its beachfront and developing mega-casinos to attract the high-spend gamblers. This has restored the fortunes of the beachfront itself, but done little in terms of creating investment behind the foreshore. Miami has successfully rebuilt its market, however, by investing massively in the restoration of its art deco hotels and apartments along Miami Beach, resulting in a regeneration of tourism that has boosted the town economically.

The United States benefits from the exceptional climate and sandy beaches along many of its coasts and, in consequence, has many long-established resorts. Florida and Hawaii, in particular, are noted internationally for the quality of their seaside resorts, although their best beaches are by no means the best-known ones. Research by Florida University's Laboratory for Coastal Research identified the six best US beaches[4] (based on 50 criteria) as:

- Okracoke, North Carolina
- Caladesi Island State Park, Dunedin/Clearwater, Florida
- Cooper's Beach, Southampton, Long Island, New York
- Hanalei Bay, Kauai, Hawaii
- Coast Guard Beach, Cape Cod, Maine
- Hamoa Beach, Maui, Hawaii.

The fall in long-haul air fares has meant that European sun, sea and sand tourism has now extended to distant destinations such as Phuket and Pattaya Beach in Thailand, as well as medium-haul resorts such as Sharm el-Sheikh in Egypt and Monastir in Tunis. Both of the two latter resorts offer the opportunity to combine cultural visits with a traditional beach holiday. The monastery of St Catherine and the landscape around Mount Sinai have become major attractions in Egypt, while the Roman amphitheatre at el Djem and the opportunity to explore the fringes of the Sahara Desert have great appeal to tourists visiting the many resorts of the Tunisian coastline.

Example

Provincetown, Cape Cod

Provincetown is at the tip of Cape Cod, in Massachusetts, USA. A popular seaside resort, it experiences wide seasonal fluctuations in visitors – from as low as 4000 in winter to around 30,000 in summer.

Long a resort of choice for artists, the town is transforming itself into a destination for 'intellectual tourism', under the direction of Campus Provincetown – a public–private partnership offering educational courses leading to credits towards academic qualifications or certification. Art courses are proliferating and the Provincetown Theatre Company also runs a full-season programme for visitors. The result has been a significant improvement in the numbers of out-of-season visitors.

The new seaside tourism

In recent years, the Middle East has mounted strong campaigns to attract the North European markets to its seaside resorts and Arabian Gulf developments such as Sharm el-Sheikh, Hurghada and el Aqaba have been successful in penetrating those markets, largely through the medium of package tours. Since the turn of the century, however, new destinations have risen to prominence within the United Arab Emirates. Dubai has been at the forefront of this development.

Recognizing that supplies of oil – its major resource – are finite, the state has determined that its future lies in attracting international tourists and it is investing massively with this in view. Notably, this has involved the construction of a new shoreline, together with offshore artificial islands, offering opportunities for the sale of exclusive second homes alongside luxury hotel accommodation. Its combination of sun, sea and sand with outstanding shopping opportunities and planned museums and art galleries is already seducing many tourists away from their traditional European holiday resorts, although July and August temperatures of 40 and 50°C in the Gulf will deter visitors in the peak summer periods.

Dubai is building the world's largest airport in anticipation of receiving up to 15 million tourists annually by 2015 – a huge increase on the present figure of 6 million. The new airport is also intended to act as a key hub for long-haul flights between Europe, the Far East and Australasia. To reach these figures, however, Dubai is now seeking to attract lower-income markets, offering opportunities for other Gulf states, such as Abu Dhabi and Oman, to focus on wealthier holidaymakers by offering not only traditional seaside pursuits but also cultural visits to historic sites and adventure holidays using four-wheel drive vehicles in the nearby desert. Such packages are proving attractive to the new adventure-seeking middle-income tourists from Europe.

The future of the seaside

A question mark hangs over the long-term future of seaside resorts, in the face of the growing threat posed by **climate change**. Even in the relatively short term, sea levels are expected to rise two to three metres as a result of global warming. This would be enough to destroy popular resorts in countries such as the Maldives and many of the low-lying islands and atolls of the Pacific. Research on the rapid escalation in the speed of ice melting in Antarctica is even more worrying, suggesting rises in sea level over the present century exceeding even these figures – enough to destroy virtually all established resorts. Should such a catastrophe occur, holidays to these areas would be the least of our problems, but already such projections are threatening long-term investment in tourist facilities in such locations.

Example

The impact of global warming for coastal areas

In 2008, Deutsche Bank, which has made significant investments in tourism organizations, produced a report on the likely impact of global warming over the coming two decades.

Countries adversely affected were expected to be Southern Spain, Portugal, North Africa, Greece, India, South Africa, Thailand, Australasia and the Caribbean, while Turkey, Morocco and Australia itself would be the worst affected. Some parts of Spain would be less seriously affected, including the Balearics and the Atlantic Coast, while Southern France could benefit, as could Germany's northern coast.

Countries with most to gain from global warming – in terms of tourism demand – would be Scandinavia, Northern Europe, Russia, Canada and New Zealand.

In the shorter term, consideration must be given to the impact of the *sun* on our holiday habits and the growing fear of skin cancer (a key issue already discussed in Chapters 4 and 6) as research reveals the damage caused to the skin by more of the sun's rays penetrating a weakened ozone layer. Although many European and American tourists still tend to ignore the warnings being issued by scientists and the medical profession, the escalating figures for skin cancer among residents of the Northern hemisphere must inevitably start to influence demand for traditional seaside holidays. The challenge for the sunshine resorts will be to adjust both their facilities and their marketing to ensure that tourism can continue to survive without depending on the appeal of sun, sea and sand. One alternative is to provide facilities similar to those found at the beach but constructed indoors.

Example

Indoor beaches

One possible solution to the problem of exposure to the sun can be found in the development of 'indoor beaches', such as the Ocean Dome at Miyazaki in Japan. The world's largest indoor beach, complete with plastic palm trees, artificial breeze, a surf machine and opening roof, it initially proved immensely popular with Japanese visitors as an alternative to the traditional beach holiday. Unfortunately, however, the huge capital investment in this high-tech project proved too great to allow the company to break even and it went out of business in 2001.

Just south of Berlin, in Germany, a hangar has been modified to provide a similar dome covering 66,000 square metres, making it one of the largest buildings of its kind in the world. The Tropical Islands resort contains a lagoon swimming pool, beach with palm trees and waterfalls and can accommodate up to 7000 visitors at a time (**www.tropical-islands.de**).

The development of the indoor 'tropical' pools at the Center Parcs sites in Northern Europe, while less ambitious in scope, have proved highly profitable. In countries where the appeal of outdoor pools is restricted by poor weather, such domes offer an attractive alternative for swimming and recreation alike.

Apart from resorts themselves, coastlines have an obvious attraction for tourists, whether seen from the land – via coastal footpaths, cycleways or roadways (notable examples of the latter include the Pacific Coast Highway in California and the Amalfi Drive on Italy's west coast) – or from the sea (coastal excursions are still popular with tourists, even where no landing is included). England's longest coastal footpath – from Minehead to Poole in the South West – can take up to eight weeks to complete, tempting walkers who may not usually be attracted to the seaside to return time and again in order to undertake the walk in sections. In summer, excursion boats sail from Bristol and the Somerset and Devon coasts, circling the islands of Steep Holm, Flat Holm and Lundy. More ambitious visits are made by small cruise ships to islands in Arctic waters around Spitzbergen and Iceland, where conditions often do not favour landing, yet the bird and other wildlife along these coasts, coupled with the geological formations of the shoreline, still merit observation from sea-borne craft of all sizes. Some islands in the Pacific and Caribbean offer little beyond coral atolls or inhospitable beaches, but, even here, cruise ships have organized calls to allow passengers to bathe, snorkel or simply enjoy the unique experience of being on a 'desert island'.

Example

Thailand

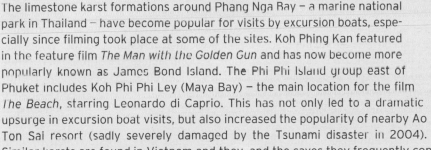

The limestone karst formations around Phang Nga Bay – a marine national park in Thailand – have become popular for visits by excursion boats, especially since filming took place at some of the sites. Koh Phing Kan featured in the feature film *The Man with the Golden Gun* and has now become more popularly known as James Bond Island. The Phi Phi Island group east of Phuket includes Koh Phi Phi Ley (Maya Bay) – the main location for the film *The Beach*, starring Leonardo di Caprio. This has not only led to a dramatic upsurge in excursion boat visits, but also increased the popularity of nearby Ao Ton Sai resort (sadly severely damaged by the Tsunami disaster in 2004). Similar karsts are found in Vietnam and they, and the caves they frequently contain, have become popular attractions for the growing numbers of tourists visiting the country.

The success that Dubai is enjoying with the development of artificial islands as tourist attractions is being emulated by other countries. Nearby Qatar has been slower to develop tourism, but, noting Dubai's success, has now embarked on a programme to build its own artificial island – the Pearl-Qatar at Doha, the capital, which is due to be completed in 2011. A similarly ambitious scheme to develop an island off the coast of Abu Dhabi is likely to become a huge draw for cultural tourism when completed. Four leading world architects have been retained to construct a series of cultural sites on Saadiyat Island:

- the Performing Arts Centre, designed by Zaha Hadid – an innovative building in organic form, with two concert halls, two theatres and an opera house, seating a total of 6300 people
- Guggenheim Museum, designed by Frank Gehry – this will be the world's largest Guggenheim art gallery
- Maritime Museum, designed by Japanese architect Tadao Ando
- Classical Museum, designed by France's Jean Nouvel – this will be an offshoot of the Louvre and will contain pictures on loan from France.

Construction will start in 2012 and is expected to be completed by 2018. The 670-acre site will include 5-star hotels, golf courses and marinas (**www.saadiyat.ae**).

Russian developers also have advanced plans for the construction of a 350-hectare artificial island in the shape of Russia. This island – to be known as Federation Island, near Sochi on the Black Sea coast – is due for completion in 2014. (Whether such constructions are prudent in the light of rising sea levels is entirely open to question.)

Example

Planning recovery from natural disaster: the case of Quintana Roo

On 21 October 2005, Hurricane Wilma struck the Eastern shores of Mexico. This was the first major hurricane in the area since 1988 (which delayed the development of tourism in the region for many years). The eye of the storm was 60 kilometres wide and it affected some 300 kilometres of coastline, hitting key tourist resorts in Quintana Roo, such as Cozumel Island, Playa del Carmen and Cancún. The slow-moving storm battered the coast for 63 hours before moving on.

Alerted in advance to the likely strength of the storm, however, and mindful of the previous year's tsunami, the Mexican government took precautions to protect the approximately 85,000 tourists in the area. Two days prior to the arrival of Wilma, an emergency evacuation was ordered and convoys of buses evacuated the most vulnerable 45,000 from the coastal region. As a result, no lives were lost.

The region of Quintana Roo occupies a sector of the Yucatán Peninsula, which is of great importance to tourism, accounting for about a third of Mexico's $11 billion annual tourist receipts and 8 per cent of GDP. The government therefore recognized the crucial importance of rebuilding facilities as quickly as possible.

An emergency fund of $5 million was already in place to tackle reconstruction, but further funds had to be found. Total damage in this instance was estimated at some $500 million (and lost tourism revenue following the storm accounted for another $400 million). The storm was viewed as an opportunity to refurbish facilities and renew the infrastructure of the resorts. One hotel in particular, le Meridien, had sustained virtually no damage, due to its unusual wave-like form and this provided an example for the rebuilding of other accommodation.

Rapid reaction by the Government ensured that flights to the region were re-established by mid-December and all 27,000 hotel rooms in the region were fully occupied by Christmas.

Attention then turned to the reconstruction of the beach itself. Even prior to Wilma, erosion was causing loss of sandy beaches around Cancún but the storm had compounded the problem. Research determined that three million cubic metres of sand would be needed to restore the beaches to their pre-1988 width of 60 metres. At a cost of $20 million of public-sector funds, the company then building Dubai's Palm Island was called in to restore the beaches. Moving some 40,000 cubic metres a day, restoration proceeded at a rate of 1 kilometre each week.

Apart from land-based tourism, Cozumel alone receives over 1300 cruise ship visits per annum and, in 2005, some 2.7 million passengers visited, spending on average $50 a day. Wilma severely damaged the docks. Reconstructing them cost $70 million. This work enabled the piers to be extended, however, allowing larger cruise vessels, such as the *Queen Mary 2*, to dock alongside. While construction proceeded, visiting cruise ships operated almost as normal, putting passengers ashore with tenders from anchorage.

Taking the longer-term view, the government plans to avoid overdependence on tourism in the region, seeking to develop agricultural activities such as horticulture and forestry. It also seeks to switch its tourism emphasis to eco-friendly programmes inland, closer to the Belize border (the Costa Maya). Here, the development of tourism is more carefully controlled: new hotels must be sited at least 50 metres back from the beach and surrounded by forest to retain a 'back to nature' feel; they must also be limited in height to the treeline. With an estimated 2000 Mayan settlements in the region currently awaiting excavation and exploitation for tourism, the area looks forward to a healthy economic future.

Source: 'Quintana Roo: rebuilding paradise', *National Geographic*, June 2006; a special report prepared by the Intelligent Investor, available on request by e-mailing info@theintelligentinvestor.co.uk

Urban tourism

Nobody knew what to make of the Pompidou Centre at first. Then they saw the visitor numbers. Then everybody started wanting something like that.

Hugh Pearman, 'How many stars can the skyline take?', *The Sunday Times*, 1 July 2007, p. 21

Another category of destination is the town or city. While seaside tourism has struggled to maintain its historic attraction for visitors in many parts of the world, urban tourism has prospered in recent years. This has been fuelled by a growing interest in cultural activities such as visits to theatres, museums and art galleries, as well as in historical – and modern – architecture and the appeal of shopping as a leisure activity.

Most countries have a plentiful stock of towns and cities of both architectural and historic importance. Capital cities have long held a particular draw for tourists (see Table 9.1), and the low fares on no frills airlines have attracted new markets to not just major cities but also smaller provincial towns throughout Europe, expanding the short-break holiday market of one to three nights. Formerly popular cities such as Amsterdam, London, Rome, Vienna and Paris have been joined by Lille, Copenhagen, Stockholm, Dublin and Prague, for example. Barcelona is now a leading city for short-break holidays as it has all the benefits required by the short stay visitor – good shops and restaurants, outstanding architecture (notably by Antoni Gaudí), quality hotels, fine museums and substantial investment in the local infrastructure. It also benefits from competitive prices compared with similar cities elsewhere in Europe.

Low transatlantic prices have made cities such as New York and Boston popular as short-break destinations for Europeans, especially for shopping trips (particularly when the value of the dollar is low against the pound and euro). Even Reykjavik, capital of Iceland, has become a popular short-break destination for Europeans for the past decade, in spite of its relatively high cost of living. Its attractions include its lively nightlife and the unusualness of its surrounding landscape, as well as the possibility of visiting a hot geyser nearby.

The UK is fortunate in that most incoming visitors have as their motivation the desire to see the country's heritage, much of which is found in the urban areas. Apart from

Table 9.1 The top ten city destinations (by arrival numbers).

City	Tourist arrivals
London	15,640,000
Bangkok	10,350,000
Paris	9,700,000
Singapore	9,502,000
Hong Kong	8,139,000
New York	6,219,000
Dubai	6,120,000
Rome	6,033,000
Seoul	4,920,000
Barcelona	4,695,000

Source: Caroline Bremner, 'Top 150 city destinations: London leads the way', Euromonitor International, 11 October 2007. Available online at: **www.euromonitor.com/Top_150_City_Destinations_London_Leads_the_way**

London and its myriad attractions, architecturally, historically and culturally, all the leading destinations in the UK are dependent on their heritage to attract the overseas tourist. The university towns of Oxford and Cambridge, the Shakespeare connection with Stratford-upon-Avon, Windsor with its royal castle, the cities of Bath, York, Edinburgh and Chester, all feature on the standard 'milk run' tours sold to the package tour market abroad. Apart from their beauty, all these cities benefit from having a very clear image in the public eye and strong associations, making them easy to market as products composed of a complex of benefits.

While large cities such as Paris, New York and London have the capacity to absorb substantial numbers of tourists, smaller, very popular cities such as Oxford and Cambridge in England, Bruges in Belgium and Sirmione on Lake Garda, Italy, suffer from severe congestion in summer, as thousands of foreign tourists visit by coach and car during the peak months, creating major problems of tourist management for the local authority. Marketing of these destinations has to focus on tight planning and control, coupled with efforts to extend the holiday season, so that tourists can be managed more easily. In Oxford and Cambridge, traffic pressures have become so intense that compulsory park and ride has become the norm. Both Sirmione and Bruges have ample parking facilities for cars and coaches on the outskirts of town, but these require visitors by car to either use bus transfers or walk some considerable distance to the heart of the city.

The urgent need for urban renewal in decaying cities coupled with rising interest in industrial heritage has led many governments to invest public funds in restoring previously dilapidated buildings as tourist attractions. Former warehouses, woollen mills in the north of England and other important centres of industry during the eighteenth and nineteenth centuries have been converted into museums or other buildings to attract tourists and the leisure market. In some cases, this has extended to entire areas of a city. An example is the jewellery quarter in Birmingham (now firmly on the tourist trail), where tourism has become an economic saviour, attracting residents back into the city centre. Other notable successes include the cities of Bradford and Glasgow, both of which suffered severe decline in the 1980s. They nevertheless contain some fine examples of Victorian and other architecture, which has become fashionable again after a long period of being out of favour. Bradford benefits from its location close to the Yorkshire Moors, and Haworth, home of the Brontës, now promotes itself as a base from which to tour, coupled with good shopping and entertainment.

As with all destinations, urban centres with an established reputation and image attract tourists more readily than those towns having no such clear image. Cities such as London, Paris, Rome, Venice and Amsterdam all have immediately recognizable, clearly differentiated images (although it is interesting to note that, in the 1990s, the London Tourist Board expressed concern that Japanese tourists were diverting to Paris rather than London. The explanation given was that, among Japanese visitors, female tourists are in the majority and they perceived Paris as being gentler and more feminine than London.).

Cityscapes are an important element in the appeal to tourists, not least because they have a clearly defined centre, well-established shopping and entertainment districts, attractive enclaves and parkland. English towns are noted for their many parks and floral displays; Milan for cutting-edge clothes and furnishing shops; Stockholm has its Gamla Stan, or Old Town, for historical appeal as well as an attractive waterfront. Some cities, however, suffer from a lack of such a clearly defined centre to provide the focus for a visit. Los Angeles, Moscow and Tokyo have this disadvantage, which reduces their appeal to the independent traveller. This said, the primary appeal of Los Angeles for the international market is Hollywood, while the Kremlin provides a focal point for visits to Moscow, as does the Royal Palace for Tokyo.

Stockholm is far from alone in benefiting from its waterfront location. Cities that had formerly been important seaports and had suffered from the decline in shipping in recent

Figure 9.5 The Victoria and Alfred waterfront in Cape Town, South Africa.
(Photo by Chris Holloway.)

years were slow at first to exploit the value of their waterfront sites for leisure purposes. Today, many cities have transformed what was formerly a decaying port into an area of recreation for residents and visitors alike. An outstandingly successful example is the Inner Harbour at Baltimore, USA, which, through a combination of private and public investment, was one of the first to become a magnet for tourists due to the wide variety of attractions it introduced along the restored harbourfront. In Australia, Sydney's Darling Harbour has similarly benefited from renewal as a leisure and marine site, as has the Victoria and Alfred waterfront in Cape Town, South Africa (see Figure 9.5). In the UK, more than a dozen waterfronts have been renovated, while retaining the many attractive warehouses and other features of their former port status. London's former Docklands, the Albert Dock area of Liverpool (the site of the Tate Gallery's first provincial art gallery) and docklands at Southampton, Bristol, Salford, Manchester, Swansea, Cardiff, Portsmouth, Plymouth, Newcastle, Gloucester, Glasgow and Dundee have all been developed to attract tourists as well as commercial activity. Other cities around the world that have landscaped their water frontages to attract tourists are Boston, San Francisco, Fremantle (the port for Perth, Western Australia) and Toronto.

Rivers and canals flowing through city centres can, likewise, add appeal when landscaped attractively. Major capitals, including Rome, London and Paris, have long traded on the appeal of their rivers, but, more recently, disused waterways have also been resurrected to appeal to tourists. A notable example is Birmingham's network of city centre canals, which have become a focal point for locals and visitors alike, with their outdoor canal-side cafés and pubs and narrowboat tours. Similarly, Bruges in Belgium successfully restored its canal network to make it a major feature of one of Europe's most attractive mediaeval cities.

Cities benefiting from a waterfront, but far from the coast, have the added option of creating an urban beach. This is what a growing number of cities have chosen to do, following the lead of Paris, which was the first inland city to create its own 'Paris Plage' in 2002 – a two-mile stretch of imported sand along the right bank of the Seine, incorporating potted plants, deckchairs, boardwalk hammocks and individual areas known by the names of famous Brazilian beaches – Ipanema, Copacabana and Maracaña. Although the original intention was to benefit the city's residents, tourists soon found this to be another key attraction of the city and, each year, the beach regularly attracts three million visitors. The idea was soon copied by other cities, including Berlin's Bundespressestrand, Amsterdam, Rome, Brussels, Vienna and London. Both Birmingham and Bristol have also tried this on a limited scale.

European capitals of culture

The EU boosts tourism to certain cities each year that can claim a strong cultural bias by awarding them the title **European Capital of Culture**. It has been offered to two cities each year since 2007 – exceptionally, three in 2010 – with each member country selected in turn for the honour. This award ensures that the chosen towns make substantial investments in infrastructure and superstructure in anticipation of the resulting increased tourist flows during the year of the award and for many years following. In 2008, Liverpool in England and Stavanger in Norway were awarded the title, followed by Linz in Austria and Vilnius in Lithuania in 2009. The nominees for 2009 to 2019 are shown in Table 9.2 and, while the countries have been identified, the specific towns or cities have not yet been selected beyond 2012.

Prior to Liverpool's designation in 2008, Britain last received the award in 1990, when Glasgow gained the title. The city enjoyed a substantial boost in tourism as a result of the designation and it was estimated that the award brought in some £2.5 billion in extra investment, a significant rise in hotel rooms and an increase in the number of tourism-related jobs to some 55,000. Above all, it changed the perception of Glasgow as a dirty, economically depressed city for all time.

Efforts to emulate the concept in the Americas, supported by the Organization of American States, have been frustrated by the financial basis for awards, in which regions are expected to put up funds in advance. The designation was last awarded to Cuzco, Peru, in 2007. UNESCO also sponsors the title of Arab Cultural Capital, with Damascus in Syria

Table 9.2 Nominees for European Capitals of Culture, 2009–2019

Year	Place
2009	Linz, Austria, and Vilnius, Lithuania
2010	Essen, Germany, Pecs, Hungary, and Istanbul, Turkey
2011	Turku, Finland, and Tallinn, Estonia
2012	Guimarães, Portugal, and Maribor, Slovenia
2013	France and Slovakia
2014	Sweden and Latvia
2015	Belgium and Czech Republic
2016	Spain and Poland
2017	Denmark and Cyprus
2018	Netherlands and Malta
2019	Italy and Bulgaria

enjoying this status in 2008, followed by Quds, Palestine, in 2009. To date, neither of these awards appears to enjoy the publicity or economic benefits so far achieved by the title European Capital of Culture.

Medical tourism

An increasingly important form of tourism, centred almost exclusively on urban areas, is that undertaken for medical reasons. While health tourism has a long history and is linked to spa tourism, about which more will be found towards the end of this chapter, the term **medical tourism** is now being used to refer to tourists who travel to another country specifically to consult specialists or undergo medical treatment.

British patients have sometimes been referred by the National Health Service for treatment in other EU countries, but others are seeking medical attention privately and often further afield. Private hospitals in Eastern Europe are now openly targeting patients in Britain who could not afford private treatment in their own country, but could be persuaded to pay the lower fees charged abroad. It has to be acknowledged that British patients are being driven by not only cost but also NHS waiting lists and by fear of MRSA, C. Difficile and other increasingly common diseases found in hospitals.

It has been estimated[5] that some 52,500 UK residents go abroad for medical treatment each year, spending in the region of £161 million in 2006. About half of them travel to have dental work undertaken and a large majority of the others do so either for cosmetic operations or hip and knee replacements.

Similarly, large numbers of Austrians now travel abroad for treatment, particularly to Sopron in Hungary for dental treatment and some towns on the Austro-Hungarian border now have economies based largely on dentistry. Many Danes travel to Szczecin in Poland for dental treatment, while the Finns visit Tallinn for eye tests and dental work.

Americans are responsible for some of the fastest growth in medical tourism. From just 150,000 tourists in 2004, there numbers grew to more than half a million travelling abroad for treatment in 2006, 40 per cent of them for dental work, according to the US Medical Tourism Association.

Good medical treatment delivered promptly, cheaply and efficiently is appealing in cases where lengthy waiting lists for operations exist, such as for hip replacements. Over 50 countries actively promote medical tourism and some 19 million medical tourists were estimated to have gone abroad for treatment in 2005,[6] at a total cost of some £10.5 billion (a figure that some have estimated as having risen five-fold by 2008 – see the Example). India alone received around 150,000 of these tourists in 2005 and expects to expand its provision for them to deliver revenue of over US$1 billion by 2012.

IVF treatment is promoted in medical centres in Kiev, Ukraine, cosmetic surgery in Venezuela, Brazil, Argentina and the UAE, while Budapest in Hungary and Cyprus promote dental treatment for visitors. Thailand, which, like Singapore, has a good record of Western medical training, offers private healthcare to medical tourists in Bangkok, Chiang Mai and Phuket, while South Africa attracts tourists for specialist cosmetic surgery. India has perhaps gone furthest, even taking a stand at the World Travel Market in London to promote its medical tourism. It offers specialist treatment at reasonable prices for dentistry, cosmetic surgery and alternative medicine such as Ayurveda. Organizations are now setting up package tours around such treatment, with accommodation at 4-star hotels included. Some forecasts put the total numbers travelling abroad for medical treatment at over 40 million by 2010.

There is some evidence that the medical traffic is not all one-way. Many wealthy visitors – reports place the number as high as 100,000 annually – are coming to Britain for medical treatment, some of them exploiting inadequate checks on NHS eligibility in order to receive treatment while on holiday in the UK. Exact figures on the numbers involved are hard to verify, but the government has taken steps to plug this loophole.

Example

The growth of medical tourism

Many countries across the globe are using their national medical provision to attract tourists. Costa Rica has been a popular destination for medical tourism since the 1980s, while India, Malaysia, South Africa and Cuba have also established reputations for both elective and cosmetic surgery.

Much of the attractiveness for the visitor is the lower cost of treatment. It is estimated that hip replacement surgery in Cuba is about one-quarter of the cost when compared to the USA.[7] Also important is convenience. The surgery can take place at a time suited to the patient, rather than relying on the lottery of extensive waiting lists.

In 2008, the medical tourism industry was estimated to be worth US$56 billion worldwide, with forecasts that this would almost double by 2012.[8] This includes the growing dental sector. There are concerns however, which may limit the popularity of medical tourism. Warnings that the lack of aftercare, especially if the patient experiences medical complications, can lead to the need for emergency treatment.

Rural tourism

The **countryside** offers a very different holiday experience from seaside and urban tourism. The widespread appeal of the countryside is of relatively recent origin, appreciation of nature dating back in Britain only as far as the nineteenth century, and even more recently in the case of other European countries. Initially limited to people in the higher socio-economic groups, led by those in aristocratic circles who enjoyed a 'seat in the country', its extension to the merchant, and later, labouring classes, emerged only as congestion and pollution made life unbearable in the big cities and escape to the countryside a necessity for health and tranquillity. Early appreciation of scenery, however, was somewhat artificial. Travellers to the countryside were accustomed to basing their expectations of the landscape on memories of the highly imaginative and frequently hyperbolic paintings by popular artists of the Romantic Movement. In some cases they even went so far as to observe the scenery by use of a 'Claude' glass – an elegantly framed mirror named after the eminent French landscape painter Claude Lorraine. Observers were encouraged to use these mirrors by standing with their backs to a scene and viewing its framed reflection.

Developing countries, even those with little appeal for the traditional tourist seeking attractive cities or beach resorts, are gaining from the increasing demand by more adventure-minded tourists for holidays 'off the beaten track'. In recent years, travellers have discovered such diverse rural gems as the Cameron Highlands in Malaysia, the northern hills of Thailand around Chiang Mai and the tropical heartland of Costa Rica, as well as attractive landscapes in more developed countries, such as the Cape York Peninsula in Australia and Canada's North West Territories. Regions such as Tuscany in Italy and the Ardèche in France are both now popular as second home locations for Northern Europeans.

The association of a particular rural area with literary or media connections can provide a powerful draw for tourism and regional tourist authorities have not been slow to take advantage of this. In England's West Country, Doone Country – set around the village of Oare and based on the North Devon setting of R. D. Blackmore's *Lorna Doone* – led the way for many other regions to promote their links with literature. It is possible to visit Catherine Cookson Country (the South Tyneside setting of many of her books) and the Tarka Trail in Devon, mythical home of Tarka the Otter, for example. Celebrities' places of birth often serve to promote the image of a town (see Figure 9.6) and their original birthplaces are frequently available for tourist visits. In some cases, this has led to annual

Figure 9.6 The birthplace of humorist author Jerome K. Jerome in Walsall, West Midlands. (Photo by Chris Holloway.)

festivals being held based on the celebrity's area of expertise, such as a literature festival. A Dylan Thomas Trail has been created in Wales that emphasizes the use of the Celtic Trail cycle route. Several sites in England have also promoted the association of their district with the mythical King Arthur, most notably the area around Tintagel in Cornwall.

Lakes and mountains

One of the principal draws of rural tourism is lakes and mountains – preferably a combination of the two. Areas offering both have been attracting visitors from the very beginnings of tourism. The Alps and Dolomites in central Europe – stretching through France, Switzerland, Germany and Italy – were catering to British and other holidaymakers as early as the nineteenth century, both for mountaineering and more leisurely pastimes such as walking. The attractiveness of the landscape in each of these countries is certainly heightened by the abundance of nearby lakes.

With a growing focus on activity holidays, mountaineering and high mountain trekking are gaining in popularity and may well help to offset any decline in winter sports resulting from inadequate snowfalls due to global warming. On a more modest scale, England's Lake District, with its combination of mountains and lakes, has special protection as a national park and ranks as one of the most popular tourist destinations in the British Isles.

The combination attracts distinct markets, with leisure visitors of all ages enjoying the scenery, either passively or on hikes, and younger, more active visitors mountaineering in summer, as well as participating in winter sports at other times, where circumstances allow. Demand for winter sports holidays is now putting huge pressures on the Alps, however, which have a fragile environment, easily damaged by overuse. Global warming is apparently affecting Alpine and other mountainous regions, with the snow line receding further up the mountainsides, leaving resorts at lower altitudes without snow for much of the season. This is causing Alpine regions to reinvest to focus their winter sports at higher

Figure 9.7 Mountain trekking in the High Tatras, Slovakia.
(Photo by Chris Holloway.)

altitudes. Snow lifts, gondolas and cable cars are under construction, with France alone investing more than one billion euros over a three-year period to retain their winter tourism markets. Resorts at lower levels, however, will have to focus on generating warm weather, and other, activities in lieu of winter sports.

Example

The impact of global warming on ski resorts in the Alps

Alpine resorts currently attract some 80 million skiers annually and are an important source of income to these regions in Switzerland, France, Germany, Austria and Italy. French ski lift revenue alone exceeded one billion euros in 2005/2006. Some lower-level resorts are already suffering from the impact of global warming, however, and the OECD has predicted that a third of all resorts will lose their snow cover if temperatures rise just two degrees centigrade. Abondance, at 930 metres and close to the Swiss border, was obliged to close as a resort in 2007 after sustaining a loss of 640,000 euros on ski lift operations. With lifts only up to 1,700 metres, the resort is now too low to guarantee snow for winter sports. The popular higher resorts, such as Val d'Isère, Tignes and Courchevel, are considerably more expensive and are investing heavily to protect their markets. In Austria and Switzerland, new, high-altitude resorts are being planned for the luxury winter sports market and, near Zermatt, there are plans to construct a 400-feet high glass and steel pyramid on the top of the Little Matterhorn by 2010. At 13,200 feet, this will become the highest hotel complex in the world: it will be complete with shopping centres, bars, restaurants, a conference hall and observation platforms. A similar scheme proposed for the Schatzalm, above Davos, is to include a 105-metre tall hotel. Needless to say, this is meeting strong resistance among locals and environmentalists, who have already blocked attempts at similar constructions on other mountaintops in the country.

The high cost of European ski resorts is making long-haul ski holidays more popular with Europeans. US resorts such as Aspen and Vail have long been popular, but other less familiar and more reasonably priced resorts such as Steamboat Springs in Colorado have been discovered by the European markets. Packages from the UK have also been launched to still more distant resorts such as Rusutsu and Niseko on Hokkaido Island, Japan, where snow is plentiful and skiing affordable. These two resorts are proving popular with the nearer markets of Canada and Australia, too.

The challenge of climbing major peaks in mountain ranges has moved on from the Alps to more adventurous locations like the Rockies, Andes and Himalayas. For those who do not want to climb, trekking to base camps along trails below the peaks has proved a challenge that is sought after by fit tourists of all ages. Specialist tour companies now organize both climbing and trekking expeditions even to Everest, forcing the Nepalese government to impose high charges for climbing rights in an effort to control numbers. Even though packages can cost in excess of £20,000, this seems to have little effect on stemming demand. For the less adventurous, simple rambling holidays are enjoyed by countless independent travellers to beauty spots all over the world and are also packaged for the inclusive tourist.

The scenic countryside

Although the British, and Irish, climate has proved a deterrent to those seeking to enjoy seaside holidays, it accounts for much of the demand for rural tourism. A temperate climate with frequent precipitation provides us with the richness of green fields and abundant woodlands that, coupled with rolling hills and stretches of water, make up the idyll that is the quintessential rural scenery of the British Isles. In spite of its small land mass, the countryside is incredibly diverse, from the meadows and tightly hedged fields in the South and West of England to the drystone walls and bleak moors of the north, from the flatlands and waterways of East Anglia and Lincolnshire to the lakes and mountains of Cumbria, from the wild beauty of the Welsh mountains and the Highlands and Islands of Scotland to the gentle Irish landscape surrounding the lakes of Killarney and the barren historic coastline of the adjacent Dingle Peninsula.

As modern living forces more and more of us to live in built-up areas, so the attraction of the countryside grows, many of us taking a day trip on the weekend or spending longer touring or perhaps holidaying on a farm. Rural tourism attracts international tourists, too, with a growing number of Continental visitors coming to tour Britain by car. In turn, many Britons take their cars to France or Germany to take touring holidays. The attraction of contrasts is important here: the Dutch, Danes and Swedes, who have flat scenery and waterways, find the undulating hills and mountains of their European neighbours very appealing.

To protect the vulnerable countryside from development and cater for the demand for rural recreation, Britain has created a network of national parks in England and Wales (see Figure 7.5), as discussed in Chapter 7. Following the passing of the National Parks and Access to the Countryside Act (1949), the Peak District National Park was the first to be created, in 1952, soon followed by nine others. The Norfolk and Suffolk Broads were given similar protected status in 1988 and the New Forest in 2006. There are currently 14 areas (including 3 in Wales and 2 in Scotland) with national park status or equivalent and another is expected to join them with the creation of the South Downs National Park in Sussex, which already receives more than 39 million visitors a year. The Cairngorms National Park became the largest in the UK when it was designated in 2003, totalling 1466 square miles, although the exclusion of the highland area of Perthshire adjoining the site was controversial.

Trail tourism

Hiking or rambling has become a popular pastime and Britain is fortunate to possess many country footpaths with public rights of way that the Ramblers' Association is anxious to protect as pressures on the countryside grow. In the UK, the Countryside and Rights of Way Act (2000), commonly known as the Right to Roam Act, opened up large areas of the country, giving ramblers the statutory right to ramble on 'access land' in England and Wales in 2005, extended in 2006 to beaches and coastlines. Natural England, the new national countryside agency, intends to open 2000 miles of coastline to walkers over time. The Land Reform (Scotland) Act 2003 offers similar rights in the North. The National Parks and Access to the Countryside Act also created a network of long-distance footpaths that are enjoying growing popularity with hikers. These national trails are illustrated in Figure 9.8. Among the most popular is the South West Coast Path, which extends for a total of 630 miles between Minehead in Somerset and Poole Harbour in Dorset.

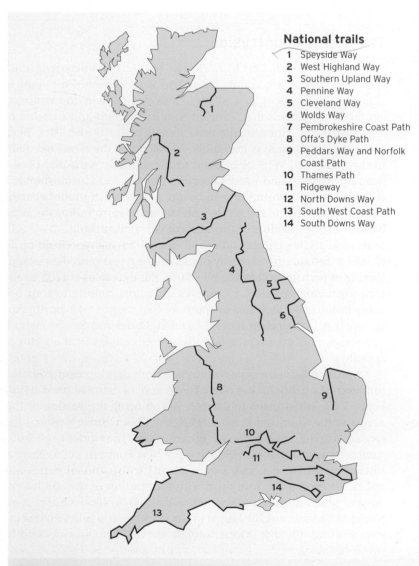

National trails

1 Speyside Way
2 West Highland Way
3 Southern Upland Way
4 Pennine Way
5 Cleveland Way
6 Wolds Way
7 Pembrokeshire Coast Path
8 Offa's Dyke Path
9 Peddars Way and Norfolk Coast Path
10 Thames Path
11 Ridgeway
12 North Downs Way
13 South West Coast Path
14 South Downs Way

Figure 9.8 Major national trails in the UK.

An ambitious plan to develop a trail to embrace six countries in Europe was completed in 2007. The North Sea Trail covers 2485 miles, running from Scarborough in England to Aberdeenshire in Scotland, then extending across to the Continent via the Netherlands, Germany, Denmark, Sweden and Norway. The aim is to develop cultural and trading links between the regions and will include the exchange of walkers on holiday.

Trails are also popular in the United States, where wilderness areas give maximum scope for challenging, long-distance footpaths, as well as a plethora of shorter trails in urban areas.

Example

Trails in the United States

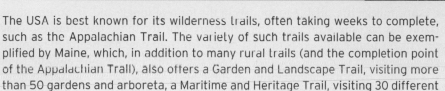

The USA is best known for its wilderness trails, often taking weeks to complete, such as the Appalachian Trail. The variety of such trails available can be exemplified by Maine, which, in addition to many rural trails (and the completion point of the Appalachian Trail), also offers a Garden and Landscape Trail, visiting more than 50 gardens and arboreta, a Maritime and Heritage Trail, visiting 30 different sites, and a Maine Art Museum Trail, taking in seven different museums.

In 2000, a new 4900-mile trail was opened between Delaware on the East Coast and Point Reyes in California, taking in a total of 13 states and 14 national parks.

Cycling, too, has experienced a regeneration of interest, as we will see in Chapter 15. This is a sport that is largely dependent on rural scenery (preferably flat land, although more active cyclists will also opt for hill touring or mountain bike holidays). Both independent and package tour cyclists are attracted to such holidays and operators offer inclusive tours by bike to a growing number of countries. Denmark and the Netherlands in particular offer ideal countryside for cycling, Denmark having woodland trails for cyclists that run alongside certain stretches of coastline, offering attractive glimpses of open sea through the trees. Most of these forms of tourism are also encouraged as examples of environmentally friendly tourism.

Waterscapes

Demand for leisure and recreation using boats has always been popular among the British and the rural waterways of Britain provide ideal opportunities for water-based tourist activities. The Norfolk and Suffolk Broads are a paradise for both yacht and motor boat enthusiasts. The Netherlands, France and Ireland are just three other European countries with canals and waterways and they attract growing numbers of tourists seeking the pleasure of 'messing about in boats', while the countless lakes of Finland and Sweden are also growing in popularity during the short Nordic summer, particularly with domestic tourists and second home owners. The appeal of water-dependent holidays will be fully explored in Chapter 14.

Sites that include major waterfalls are attractive to international tourists. Those that are readily accessible, such as Niagara Falls on the Canadian/USA border and Victoria Falls on the Zambia/Zimbabwe border, enjoy considerable popularity and have been built up as key destinations by their countries' tourism authorities. Zambian guides have more recently been escorting intrepid adventure tourists to the Devil's Pool at Victoria Falls, in which, at low water, it is possible (if slightly risky) to bathe on the very edge of the 360-foot drop – an experience promoted as 'swimming on the edge of the world'. More inaccessible falls – including the world's highest, Angel Falls in Venezuela – do not yet attract the numbers of tourists that could be anticipated at such unique scenic attractions if adequate transport and other infrastructure were in place.

Woodlands and forests

Areas of woodland and dense foliage provide yet another appeal for tourism. In the USA, the New England states of Vermont, New Hampshire and Maine and the Canadian eastern provinces attract large numbers of domestic and international tourists to witness the famous 'fall foliage' colours in the autumn. For those demanding more strenuous activities in woodlands, the USA has designated national trails, of which the best-known and most challenging is the Appalachian Trail, from Georgia to Maine, which takes several weeks to cover on foot.

More exotic foliage is available to tourists in the form of jungle and, in South America, the Amazon has become a popular supplementary tour for those travelling to Ecuador and Peru. Pristine jungle still exists in West Africa, which to date has been little exploited. Although small group tours are organized to see the gorillas in Rwanda and the Congo, tourism is limited by political instability in these areas of the world. Smaller but more accessible jungles still exist in developed countries, notably El Yunque Rainforest in Puerto Rico and rainforest in the Cape York area of Northern Queensland, Australia. Countries such as Borneo and Papua New Guinea also offer great potential for exploration of dense tropical forest, if political and potential health problems can be overcome.

In Britain, there are over 50 historic forests, as well as many further areas of woodland that attract day trippers or walking tourists. Burnham Beeches, near London, is noted for the superb foliage of its beech trees, while forests such as the New Forest (a royal forest and also a national park with a memorial commemorating the spot where King William Rufus met his death in a hunting accident) and Sherwood Forest (associated with Robin Hood) have close links with history, myth and literature.

Apart from its national parks, the UK has also introduced the concept of national forest parks – the Royal Forest of Dean becoming England's first national forest park in 1938. In the 1990s, the government announced the formation of a new National Forest, covering some 200 square miles, in the English Midlands. Some limited protection, at least in theory, is also afforded by designating sites as Areas of Outstanding Natural Beauty (AONB) or Sites of Special Scientific Interest (SSSI). There are 49 AONBs in England, Wales and Northern Ireland, and the North Pennines (covering 2000 square kilometres), in recognition of its world-class geological heritage, became the first European Geopark in 2003. This designation by UNESCO is expected to lead to greater interest in nature-based tourism and better protection for the environment. Scotland has another 44 sites paralleling the AONBs that are known as Natural Scenic Areas.

Agrotourism

> [Agrotourism] is a model for the development of mountainous and remote areas of the country. It also offers additional income to farmers and to various local communities, thus preventing them from abandoning their land.
>
> Brigitta Papastavrou, President of Agrotouristiki

Rural tourism as we have seen has long been popular with independent travellers and its importance to the economy of the countryside has been widely recognized in recent years. The concept of agrotourism (or agritourism) was developed in Italy and, from there, spread rapidly throughout the Mediterranean and beyond. Its aim is to develop sustainable tourism in agricultural areas of the countryside and it has become an important feature of rural tourism planning following the success of the development of gîte holidays in France. French government grants were awarded in the post-war years to help convert decaying farm buildings into rural cottages for tourist accommodation, and the gîte holiday became popular, particularly with independent British tourists. The Portuguese quintas, or rural estates, also attracted a strong following among tourists eager to experience something a little different from the standard forms of holiday accommodation.

There is now a programme of strong financial support from the EU, with grants that are allowing rural tourism provision to become increasingly luxurious. Recent developments also take account of the interest in adventure sports, many of which are best enjoyed in rural communities, and outdoor sports such as ballooning, horse riding and mountain biking are also now catered for.

Spain, Portugal, Cyprus, Greece and Italy have all invested heavily in agrotourism. Notable developments include those in the Epirus province in north-western Greece and at Sierra Aracena, a province of Seville, in Spain.

Example

The development of agrotourism on the Greek and Spanish islands

Amorgos, Greece

The Greek government has established a tourism authority – Agrotouristiki SA – to help rural communities set up and organize agrotourism. In particular, it offers help and advice on applying for government susidies to improve often inadequate facilities.

Amorgos, an island of 140 square kilometres in the Aegean, is one such island that is benefiting from this help. Relatively untapped by tourism, many sites on the island are accessible only on foot or by donkey ride. Accommodation is limited largely to pensions and private rooms, with two campsites for budget travellers. For those seeking peace and solitude, however, the island offers many attractions for walkers, including photography, birdwatching, wild flowers and archeological sites, some dating back to the fifth century BC.

Ibiza, Balearic Islands

The traditional Ibizan farmhouses – casaments – are simple, whitewashed buildings that lend themselves to the development of agrotourism. Starting initially with just two farms in the 1990s, Ibizan agrotourism has now grown to some 20 sites on the island.

The first were simple working farms, letting out rooms to supplement farming incomes, but, over time and building on initial success, later developments became more sophisticated. While all guarantee rural charm and fresh local food, some have become more luxurious. One such is Atzaro, opened in 2004. A 400-year-old farmhouse, it offers a swimming pool, 40-metre lap pool and private plunge pools for some of the accommodation. A spa with massage and treatment rooms, sauna and open-air restaurant all aim to attract the wealthier visitor. Also, an on-site cultural centre offers events such as art exhibitions and musical performances (**www.atzaro.com**).

While such facilities are designed to appeal to the top end of the market, the supporting infrastructure on the island remains weak. Inadequate public transport currently obliges visitors to use private car hire to reach sites.

Britain has also actively promoted its farming and rural holidays, which have become increasingly important to farmers as a source of revenue due to traditional revenues drying up.

Tourist boards and local authorities have helped the private sector to develop new ideas in rural tourism. One example is that of the West Midlands region, which piloted short breaks involving culinary trails – a cider trail in Herefordshire and a pork pie trail at Melton Mowbray, famous for its pies – designed to link farmers, food producers and the tourism industry under the banner 'farms, food and peaceful surroundings'. The Department for Environment, Food and Rural Affairs (DEFRA) reports that around half of Britain's farmers – mainly those in the South of England – have initiated some form of tourism enterprise, bringing in extra income averaging £5000 per annum. Activities range from B&Bs to holiday cottages and equestrian centres.

The growth of tourism in rural areas has encouraged an equivalent growth in other small-scale ventures dependent on tourism. Crafts are a notable example of this, with potters, glassmakers, woodworkers, basketweavers and countless other craftspeople opening up outlets in the country to make and sell their wares. The Countryside Agency reported in 2004 that some 300,000 people in Britain now earned their living from rural crafts, earning in excess of £1 billion, and the agency anticipated that crafts were likely to eclipse farming within 15 years.

Finally, mention should be made of summer camps for children – long popular in North America and likely to be adopted in the UK on a larger scale in the future. Over six million children attend summer camps each year in the USA, bringing prosperity to the areas in which they are sited (notably New England), and UK authorities have reckoned that up to 600,000 children would be attracted to similar facilities in Britain. These would

Example

Transfrontier conservation areas (TFCAs)

TFCAs represent a recent initiative to ensure intergovernmental cooperation between countries with common borders. The aim is to protect sensitive areas by improving their ecological management, to grow economic opportunities helping the economies of communities within the areas, to support cultural ties and traditions; and to aid peace in the regions. The formation of these parks helps to boost the tourism potential of the regions, too. Each country agrees to manage the areas as one integrated unit, removing all physical boundaries and allowing the free migration of animals and humans on the land (but not across boundaries outside the perimeters of the parks). The origin of this transborder cooperation can be traced back to the 1932 agreement between the Glacier National Park, in the USA, and Waterton Lakes National Park in Canada.

In 1997, the Peace Park Foundation was established by the World Wildlife Fund as a means of encouraging the development of transfrontier parks. The first of these creations was the Kalagadi Transfrontier Park, formed in 2000 between South Africa and Botswana by merging the Gemsbock national parks in both countries. The new park covers an area of 28,000 square kilometres, and is jointly managed by the two countries, gate receipts being shared equally. Once in the park, visitors can move freely, frontier formalities being restricted only to entering and leaving the park.

In 2003, a second park was established. The Great Limpopo Transfrontier Park occupies an area of 35,000 square kilometres and results from cooperation between Mozambique, South Africa and Zimbabwe (although fences remain between the latter two, due to political and economic problems). This new TFCP encompasses Kruger Park in South Africa, the Limpopo in Mozambique and Gonarezhou National Park in Zimbabwe and the result is the largest TFCP on the continent.

More than 20 TFCPs are currently in the planning stage in Africa, among them Namibia's Ai-Ais Hot Springs Game Park and South Africa's Richtersveld National Park. Namibia is also working with Angola to create the Iona Skeleton Coast TFCP, with the enticing possibility that this will eventually join with other Namibian parks to create a TCFP along the entire Namibian coastline. Other possibilities on the cards include cooperation between South Africa and Swaziland, South Africa and Lesotho, Malawi and Tanzania and a tripartite agreement between the governments of South Africa, Botswana and Zimbabwe, but these will all require better cooperation between the governments concerned to reach fulfilment.

not necessarily have to be sited within areas of highest tourist appeal, helping to spread the benefits of rural tourism and avoiding congestion at popular destinations.

Wilderness areas

As open countryside becomes rarer in the developed countries, measures are introduced to protect what remains, especially where this has been largely untouched until recent years. We have seen how Britain established its national parks, but this country was merely following the lead set by the United States (see Figure 9.9), which designated the world's first national park at Yellowstone in 1872. This huge park, containing the famed Old Faithful geyser, covers an area of some two and a quarter million acres on the borders between Wyoming, Montana and Idaho. Since then, numerous national parks have been created

1	North Cascades	16	Bryce Canyon	31	Voyageurs	46	Glacier Bay
2	Olympic	17	Zion	32	Isle Royale	47	Haleakala
3	Mount Rainier	18	Rocky Mountain	33	Hot Springs	48	Hawaii Volcanoes
4	Crater Lake	19	Arches	34	Mammoth Cave	49	Virgin Islands
5	Glacier	20	Canyonlands	35	Great Smoky Mountains	50	Biscayne
6	Redwood	21	Mesa Verde	36	Shenendoah	51	Black Canyon of the Gunnison
7	Lassen Volcanic	22	Grand Canyon	37	Acadia	52	Death Valley
8	Yosemite	23	Petrified Forest	38	Everglades	53	Dry Tortugas
9	Kings Canyon	24	Theodore Roosevelt (north unit)	39	Kobuk Valley	54	Joshua Tree
10	Sequoia	25	Theodore Roosevelt (south unit)	40	Gates of the Arctic	55	Saguaro
11	Channel Islands	26	Wind Cave	41	Denali		
12	Great Basin	27	Badlands	42	Lake Clark	**Not shown**	
13	Yellowstone	28	Carlsbad Caverns	43	Wrangell-St. Elias	56	National Park of American Samoa
14	Grand Teton	29	Guadalupe Mountains	44	Kenai Fjords		
15	Capitol Reef	30	Big Bend	45	Katmai		

Figure 9.9 National parks in the USA and territories.

in the USA and elsewhere throughout the world. The largest is North East Greenland National Park, covering an area of 373,300 square miles, but a recent significant move has been the formation in 2002 of 13 new parks, covering 11,294 square miles, created out of virgin forest in Gabon – a move described earlier in Chapter 7. This country currently has only a very small tourism industry, but hopes to attract a larger flow of tourists to replace the logging industry, which, in time, would threaten the destruction of the forest – the country's prime resource. Even these parks, representing 11 per cent of the country, are tiny when compared to the total protected territory in Africa, amounting to some 850,000 square miles. The future may lie in better cooperation between countries with contiguous borders, to enable still larger parks to be created.

Many wilderness areas contain spectacular scenery, drawing huge tourist crowds in their peak seasons who have to be monitored and managed. Examples include the Grand Canyon, Bryce and Zion Canyons and Monument Valley, where the appeal of solitude and communing with nature – the original concept of the USA's national parks – is soon lost in midsummer due to the sheer numbers of visitors.

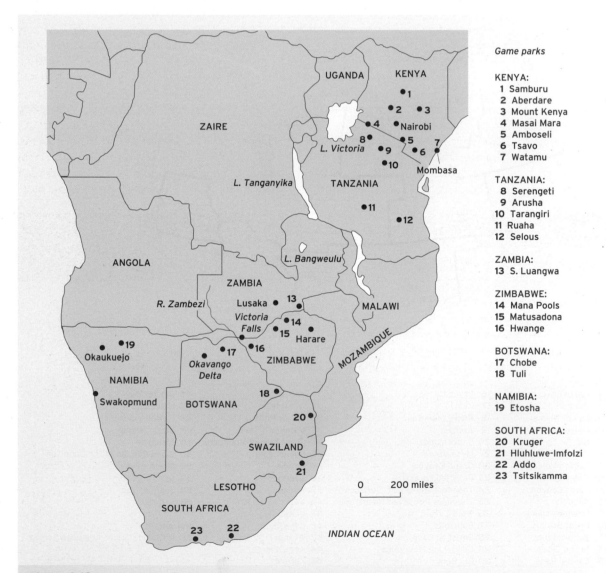

Figure 9.10 The major wildlife parks in South and East Africa.

Another way to designate land masses is the safari park, most commonly found in South and East Africa. The Sabi Sabi Game Reserve in South Africa was the world's first designated wildlife park, but, as other African nations started to become aware of the threat to their wildlife resources and the appeal wild animals hold for tourists, the number of parks quickly expanded and rangers were introduced to reduce poaching.

Island tourism

One form of destination lies somewhere between the rural and coastal in terms of its attractiveness and, because of its growing appeal, deserves a section of its own here.

Initially, offshore islands, easily accessible by boat or aircraft from the mainland, proved a draw. Helgoland, north of Germany, for example, was a popular destination for German tourists between the two World Wars (before it was saturation bombed by the Allies in World War II) and islands such as the Danish Bornholm and the Swedish Gotland attracted first the domestic tourist and then, more recently, international cruise passengers sailing around the Baltic.

In the Atlantic, the Canaries and Madeira have, of course, attracted tourists for many years, but, more recently, operators have developed tours to more remote destinations such as the Azores and Cape Verde Island. Often, their appeal is due to their isolation. They are predominantly rural in character and planning controls are often rigidly exercised to ensure that they remain unspoiled.

More recently, relatively inaccessible islands have become the challenge – especially those without air connections – the most isolated being sought out by specialist travellers. Examples include Pitcairn, St Helena, Tristan da Cunha, Easter Island and the Marquesas.

Lesser-known but less remote islands are also growing in appeal. Australia is a base for exploring many island paradises and they are now being actively promoted, to a greater or lesser extent, by the tourism authorities. Islands with which we are likely to become more

Example

Developing island tourism in the Mediterranean

The desire of many well-travelled tourists to seek out remote and less visited destinations has led to a rise in the appeal of islands. Many of them are underdeveloped, but can be located quite close to heavily populated regions. The Mediterranean offers one example of such islands.

While the French islands referred to overleaf are well known, at least to domestic tourists, there are many other islands in this part of the world that are little visited, either because they have been seen as having little to attract tourists or access has been restricted by the authorities in order to protect the environment.

The Tuscan Archipelago, off the coast of Italy, is an example of the latter. The seven islands that make up the Archipelago are managed by the Tuscan Archipelago Parks Commission. Uninhabited and a state-protected nature reserve and bird sanctuary, the islands have been off limits to all apart from researchers, but the Commission has now agreed to permit up to 1000 tourists each year to join guided visits to three of the islands: Pianosa, Giannutri and Montecristo. It is the last of these that is expected to attract the largest number of curious tourists, due to the famous book by Alexandre Dumas, *The Count of Monte Cristo*. Such an interest alone will not be enough to gain entry, however: tourists planning a visit are being required to undertake a day-long course on the environment, to ensure those visiting have sufficient awareness of ecological issues.

familiar include Norfolk Island, Whitsunday Island, King Island, Flinders Island, Three Hummock Island and Cato Island (promoted as the gay and lesbian kingdom of the Coral Sea Islands). Still less exploited, the formerly off-limits Lakshadweep Islands have recently received permits from the Indian government for visits by cruise ships from Goa and are likely to be popular with those who have 'been everywhere and seen everything'.

Closer to the principal populations generating tourism are islands in the Mediterranean. Many of them have enjoyed long-term popularity with domestic tourists, while others are relatively untouched. France, while boasting well-established beach resorts along its coasts, has also been able to build successfully on the appeal of its many offshore islands and, by carefully controlling development (in one case, by the creation of a national park), has enabled them to retain their natural landscape and seascape charm. On the west coast, the Île de Ré, Île d'Yeu and Belle-Île (near Quiberon) attract wealthy French visitors, as do the French islands off the Mediterranean coast, such as those near Hyères, the Île de Porquerolles, Île de Port-Cros and Île du Levant. By ensuring that supply never meets demand, these islands can select their markets on the basis of price alone. Other islands in the Mediterranean, such as Ischia and Capri, have long drawn tourists in their thousands, but others, far less well known, have tourism potential for more environmentally sensitive visitors.

Spa tourism

One important element of health tourism is treatment at spas. The term 'spa' is said to have originated from the town of that name in Belgium, although some claim that 'Sanitas Per Aqua' – health through water – is the true derivation of the term, which has been applied equally to resorts that provide healthy air (often mountain or seaside resorts) and others offering so-called 'healing' waters.

Although the original spa in Belgium and others like it at Vichy and Aix-les-Bains in France or Wildbad and Baden Baden in Germany have developed into urban areas, often becoming popular destinations in their own right (Bath, Cheltenham, Harrogate, Scarborough and Buxton being good examples in the UK), most spas are still small enough to be considered rural destinations. They form an important element in international tourism – one too readily overlooked by students of tourism in the UK, a country where spas have fallen out of favour to some extent.

Back in the seventeenth century, Britain itself could boast more than 250 active spas. Some were surprisingly urban. Streatham Vale, for example, now a London suburb, was a popular watering hole as early as 1659. By the twentieth century, though, their appeal had waned to a point where the final ten, then under the control of hospitals, were taken over on the formation of the National Health Service in 1948, but had their financial support withdrawn in 1976. The last publicly funded spa, Bath, closed in 1978. Following massive investment and prolonged delays, however, it was re-opened in 2007 and has enjoyed considerable commercial success. Droitwich Spa has also lingered on, providing medical treatment in a private hospital with a small indoor brine bath.

On the Continent, though, spa tourism (and its study as a subject in tourism courses) remains popular, with an estimated 1200 active spas, and the industry makes a valuable economic contribution to the GDP of several countries. In Germany, Hungary and the Czech and Slovak Republics, thermal treatment – in mud or mineral water baths – still plays an important part in health care. Italy's spas are also significant, with a large concentration around the Euganean Hills, south of Padua, notably at Albano Terme and Battaglia Terme, with some 200 hotels in the area being dedicated to the accommodation of spa visitors. North of Vicenza in the Dolomites, the spa town of Recoaro Terme has been noted since the eighteenth century for its mountain spring waters.

Typical treatments at all these resorts include mud baths, hydrotherapy, saunas, mineral baths, steam baths and beauty treatments. The popularity of spas in other areas of the globe is also well established. One in five American tourists visits spas each year, while in Japan, onsen (hot springs) such as Ikaho and Shirahone thrive on tourism (although scandals in the early 2000s, in which it was revealed that tap water was in some cases being provided in place of traditional water sources, severely undermined public confidence).

In the past, European spa treatments were often supported by the state health services, but escalating costs led to cutbacks. In 1996, for example, Germany reduced the amount of time state-funded health claimants were permitted to stay and reimbursement was limited essentially to treatment at domestic spas. Nevertheless, some 15 million Europeans daily continue to immerse themselves in thermal waters, in the belief that 'the cure' will alleviate their ailments, and the spas of Europe reap the benefits of this belief.

In Britain, which once attracted many domestic tourists to its spa towns, medical experts became more sceptical about the health benefits of spas in the twentieth century. Recent evidence concerning those with osteoarthritis and osteoporosis, and a growing interest in alternative medicine generally, is causing some medical experts to re-evaluate their former views, which is encouraging some former spas to reopen. National Lottery funding has been made available at Buxton, Malvern, Leamington Spa, Harrogate, Tunbridge Wells and Bath. Others may choose to follow suit if demand is evident, although not all funding will necessarily go towards recreating the medical facilities these famous spas once had.

Research by the English Tourism Council in 2002 estimated that some 13 million Britons had made visits to spas abroad, although not all necessarily stayed there to enjoy medical treatment as well. A number of tour operators in the UK are featuring spa treatment abroad in their promotions and over 300,000 British tourists continue to travel abroad specifically for treatment each year. The response to this demand is being met by the growth of purpose-built facilities supplied within the accommodation sector.

The successful destination

Three important points should be highlighted in relation to tourist destinations. First, the chances of their long-term success will be significantly enhanced if the benefits they offer are **unique**. There is only *one* Oberammergau Passion Play, there is only one Eiffel Tower, Grand Canyon or Big Ben, and these attractions can provide the focus for a destination's marketing campaign. Because of the singular properties of 'heritage' tourism, these types of destination retain their appeal even if their prices may become less competitive with those of other destinations, providing the increase is not exorbitant by comparison.

It is true to say, however, that the majority of the mass tourism movement is directed at sun, sea and sand destinations, which the Mediterranean and Caribbean countries provide so effectively. Such destinations are seldom unique and their customers do not require them to be so. They will be satisfied as long as the amenities are adequate, the resort remains accessible and prices are competitive. Indeed, the similarities in attractions and amenities, as well as the way these destinations are marketed, gives rise to the concept of the **identikit destination**, which results from the evidence produced by market research studies designed to find common denominators for the various international markets in order to develop a product with guaranteed mass demand. Such destinations have been developed through the activities of multinational tourism organizations. In the development of such destinations, the emphasis changes from an attempt to distinguish the product to one that concentrates on maintaining or improving its image by offering good standards that reflect value for money and ensuring that the destination remains competitive with other similar destinations.

The second point to stress is that the **more benefits** a destination can offer, the greater will be the attraction of the destination. Multiple attractions provide added value, so the concentration within a specific geographical area of a number of different products appealing to different markets (such as the City of Boston, Massachusetts, with the seaside attractions of Cape Cod and the rural appeal of New England fall foliage on its doorstep) will improve its chances of success.

Third, it should be clear that no destination can rest on its laurels. Most depend at least to some extent on visitors returning, so will need to update and augment their range of attractions continually to encourage repeat visits. This means constant investment. Destinations, like all products that depend on consumer demand, have lifecycles – that is, they experience periods of growth, expansion and, eventually, decline. If we examine the history of any well-known resort we can see the truth of this. Along the French Riviera, Nice, Cannes, Antibes, Juan les Pins and St Tropez have all in turn enjoyed their periods of being fashionable seaside resorts, but, ultimately, their visitors moved on to still more fashionable resorts, often to be replaced by less fashion-conscious, less free-spending tourists. A decline into decay can only be arrested through redevelopment and innovation. In some cases, resorts have been allowed to run down to an extent where the cost of renovation may be beyond the scope of the local authority and decay becomes inevitable.

Example

The case of Acapulco

Acapulco, on the Mexican Pacific coast and close to the US border, has been a hugely popular resort since the 1950s. Lack of investment in recent years, however, has allowed it to decline, to a point where the Mexican government recognized that a major scheme to upgrade the town was needed.

In spite of attracting some six million tourists every year, its beaches had become badly contaminated, with untreated effluent entering the water, and a population explosion in the surrounding suburbs had led to overcrowding and water shortages – water supplies being prioritized to serve the needs of the seafront hotel swimming pools. The fear was that the upper end of the market would be driven away and concern was also being expressed over rising crime rates resulting from turf wars between drug cartels in the district and the growth of child sex tourism.

In 2008, the government announced its intention to invest 440 million pesos (some £21 million) in improvements, notably to improving sanitation services.

Design of the built and natural environment

More recently, attention has focused on the importance of the **public realm** in satisfying tourists once they have been attracted to a destination.[9] The public realm may be commonly defined as the features of a destination that represent the environment in which the tourist stays and moves around, to include public amenities such as parks, squares, gardens, public toilets, litter collection, paved areas, street furniture, car parking and similar features of the built environment that are so important in creating the experience that tourists have and the image that they retain and later communicate to other potential travellers. These features complement the buildings – public and otherwise – that make up the physical characteristics of the tourist product.

Issues such as the size and scale of new buildings must be taken into consideration and, away from principal urban centres, buildings should be on a human scale that is not threatening to passers-by, but retains their interest. Most visitors to a town will explore it on foot, so good street-level design is vital. Use of local materials, whether in modernist or more traditional buildings, is important to create a sense of place. Local building materials are often more expensive to use than, say, concrete, but the additional costs are justified in the long run and may even bring in additional revenue from tourists anxious to see them in their own right. In Britain, examples may be found in the use of Bath stone in Bath, Cotswold stone in the Cotswolds, black-and-white half-timbering in the border country, thatch in the West Country and slate in the Lake District or Wales. Even for such mundane features such as public toilets, the use of local and natural building materials can greatly enhance the end result. Indeed, today it is sometimes insisted on by local authority planning departments. The benefit of using such materials is that they help to reinforce the characteristics of the brand image that the destination and tourist board is trying to create.

No building can be divorced from its setting and, just as thought must go into the design of the building itself, so the site itself must be landscaped attractively to maximize its appeal to visitors. Part of the attraction of an English village is the way in which the houses lie in the landscape, blending as if they were made for the setting. Where a development is on a slope, it becomes even more important to ensure that the buildings blend with the background. If the buildings are to be exposed to view – for example, a group of self-catering chalets high in the Alps – great care has to be taken to integrate them into the landscape. Buildings should not stand out on the skyline, but, if it is essential that they do, then their lines should be broken up with the use of trees and shrubs. On sloping sites, buildings can be 'stepped' or terraced up the hillside to keep their scale in harmony with the environment. Similarly, with waterside developments, buildings should be sited well clear of the waterfront itself, to allow for walkways along the banks that will attract both residents and visitors and ensure that those using the waterway are not intimidated by tall buildings.

The appeal of water is evident in the conversion for leisure use of so many redundant harbours and waterways in Britain. Here, the local authorities must determine whether the site is best retained as a dockland environment or themed as urban parkland. Enlightened authorities have come to recognize that the retention of traditional bollards, cranes and other paraphernalia of a dockside will provide a unique setting, making it even more attractive to visitors, together with the addition of a modest number of trees or shrubs.

Street furniture

Street furniture is something that we all take for granted, yet it plays an important part in reflecting the national landscape, too. One has only to think of the classic red telephone kiosks and letterboxes in Britain or the nineteenth-century 'pissoirs' (now sadly disappearing) and the traditional green boulevard chairs and tables still to be found on the streets of Paris to realize that such items play a part in formulating our picture of vernacular landscapes and townscapes. In Britain, a great deal of attention has been paid in recent years to the design of public seating and litter bins, but any item of street furniture, from letterboxes to telephone kiosks, from litter bins to bus shelters, from public toilets to refreshment stalls, from lamp posts to railings, needs to be carefully designed to be in harmony with the surroundings and reflect the image of the area in which it is sited. Increasingly, these sites must be designed to resist vandalism and, where possible, graffiti, too.

Local authorities must first determine whether to adopt a classic or modern design for their setting. Heritage sites such as York or Chester are more likely to opt for a traditional and classic design to blend with the architecture of the area. Unfortunately, this has led to the development of a ubiquitous design in cast iron with gold motifs, frequently bearing the crest of the city, that, while tasteful and elegant, does little to distinguish the city's streets from countless others in the same country. These designs are better, however, than some of the products they replace, such as the plastic litter bin (all too often cracked or misshapen), in a choice of battleship grey or garish yellow. Litter bins in particular need to be big enough to accommodate the huge amounts of litter created today by takeaway shops and the council must have a policy of emptying these frequently, otherwise the benefits of good design will be lost as rubbish piles up around the base of the bin.

Cities on the Continent, particularly those the centres of which were substantially rebuilt after the war or that wish to promote a modern, dynamic image, often adopt more modern designs. These can work equally well in the appropriate setting. Their cost may be substantially higher than more modest designs, but they not only improve the image of the city but also last much longer without repair or replacement.

Providing seating in towns and cities is a problem for the planners, as it tends to attract vagrants. The use of simple-to-maintain materials that will provide a brief respite for residents and tourists, but not encourage longer stays, can be the answer to the problem. Individual seats, rather than benches, also reduce their use by vagrants for sleeping.

Public amenities

Public toilets for tourists are often treated as a peripheral issue by planners, but their inadequacies are often picked on by tourist bodies such as UKInbound. Many tourist sites suffer from an inadequate supply of toilets, while others have had their toilets locked or shut down due to shortages of money for maintenance and supervision. Even Bath, one of Britain's principal tourist towns, has seen a sharp drop recently in the number of conveniences remaining open for tourists. While Britain is not unique in facing this problem, it is interesting to note that, in Japan, architectural competitions are promoted for public toilets, while the Chinese encourage architects to design toilets with the needs of American tourists in mind. The interest generated by the construction of the 'superloo' at Westbourne Grove in London, designed by architect Piers Gough in 1993 with an attached flower shop, reveals just how important good toilet design can be for tourism. This particular example not only won design awards but also was featured in English Heritage's advertisements in 1997. It should come as no surprise, therefore, that over 80 public toilets around Britain are actually listed buildings.

Car parks are a particular problem for designers as they occupy large areas of land and are often visually intrusive. In the countryside, efforts are now made to ensure that they appears as natural as possible. For example, logs can be used to separate the bays and the planting of substantial shrubs can help to conceal the cars themselves. Good, but not intrusive, lighting is important too, and the surface can be gravel rather than tarmac. In some small parking areas, it may be possible to use honeycomb concrete blocks that allow grass to grow through them, rendering the concrete surface almost invisible (see Figure 9.11).

Car parks must, of course, be situated well away from any high-grade heritage sites, which may mean that there will need to be special provision for the disabled. In cities, the urban setting will mean more man-made materials can be used in the car parks' construction, but this no longer means high-rise concrete. Designs have become more fanciful, including, in one case, mock medieval fortification. Car parks on open land have proved successful when they have been attractively furnished with decorative modern lamps and plenty of trees to break up the land mass. Given the high prices motorists are now resigned to paying for parking, underground car parks are often economically viable and, of course, have the least impact on the surrounding environment. In Salzburg, Austria – where public parking is at a premium – the local authority went so far as to blast a cavernous car park out of the adjacent cliff faces, underground parking being impractical.

Telephone and public utility lines can mar the appearance of even the most beautiful town or village. Fortunately, in Britain, local authorities have generally taken an enlightened

Figure 9.11 Good landscaping for a car park in Betws-y-Coed, North Wales. *(Photo by Chris Holloway.)*

view, hiding these unattractive necessities, but a visit to Spain or Greece will soon illustrate how much visual pollution is caused when overhead wires march along streets, linking into houses. Although the cost of burying wires is much higher, in the long run it is worth the investment if the site is much more attractive to visitors. The positioning of electricity pylons across the landscape in some of the most scenic parts of Britain – and the more recent intrusion of wind-powered electricity generators and mobile phone antennae – has also been strongly criticized by defenders of the traditional countryside.

Pedestrianization

Many towns popular with tourists have pedestrianized some of their principal thoroughfares. The result can greatly enhance the atmosphere of a street and encourage visitors to come shopping. Some of Britain's most attractive town centres, such as such as those of York, Brighton, Bath and Chester, and many Continental towns, feature narrow pedestrian walkways that have never been wide enough to support motor vehicles. In such towns, the narrowness of the lanes is their very attraction. Even in towns where such lanes do not exist, virtually all now have areas restricted to pedestrian use. In London, for instance, Convent Garden was redesigned on this basis after the fruit and vegetable market moved away.

Pedestrianizing will not in itself be enough to make the area a focal point for shoppers, however. The shops themselves must be appropriate for the setting and the street must be enhanced by well-designed street furniture, tree planting and the display of flowers or shrubs in tubs or other containers. When this is done tastefully, the end result can transform a street. The flipside, however, is that it will also attract much larger numbers of pedestrians, which can lead to congestion and a litter problem that the council must be prepared to tackle.

Horticultural displays

As mentioned above, the use of hanging baskets, floral beds in the centre of main access roads, extensive tree planting along the pavements and similar horticultural displays can make a pretty village outstanding and even an unattractive town bearable. Some of Britain's towns have made such a feature of their floral displays that they have become famous internationally. Bath's hanging basket displays are a highly attractive feature for summer visitors, while the massed floral beds that line the seafronts of towns such as Eastbourne and Worthing draw many older visitors to these resorts year after year. As many flowers bloom in spring, they can be used to attract visitors before the traditional peak summer season. Aberdeen is noted for its display of formal rose beds along its main roads, while, on the Continent, the sight of flower-bedecked chalets in Switzerland and Austria is indelibly associated with these countries' villages and highlighted in all tourist brochures.

The cost of transforming a town in this way is considerable, but, as a way to attract tourists, at the very least, councils need to consider investing funds to make the main approach roads more attractive – both those carrying car traffic to the centre and those providing the principal access for pedestrians to the centre from bus or train terminals. First impressions count for a lot when it comes to attracting tourists.

Art and tourism

There is a growing recognition today that art has a role to play in the tourism industry, not just through museums, galleries and arts events organized to attract the tourist, but in the everyday surroundings in which visitors find themselves. Ostensibly, 'street art' is designed to heighten the visual appeal of a town for its residents, but, once again, such embellishment will add to the attraction of the destination for the visitors, too. If the work displayed is by artists of international reputation, this will widen the appeal of the destination to international visitors. Sculptures by Henry Moore in Yorkshire or at the Serpentine in London, for example, attract dedicated groups of overseas and domestic visitors. Cities in the United States enforce local regulations requiring a small percentage of the total cost of any new development to be spent on public art at the site and the prestigious offices of major corporations will also judge it appropriate to enhance their forecourts with sculptures by leading artists of the day. In London, prominent British artists such as Eduardo Paolozzi were recruited to design the wall tiles during the renovation of the Central London Underground railway stations.

Towns can reinforce their images by the imaginative use of sculpture or art. In Germany, for example, Hamelin has its sculpture of the Pied Piper, while Bremen has greatly enhanced its pedestrian streets with scenes from Grimms' fairy tales. Brussels is famous for the Minneke Pis, the tiny bronze statue of a small boy urinating, copies of which are sold as tourist souvenirs and photos of him feature on many postcards. Copenhagen's major draw is its Little Mermaid statue, based on the Hans Christian Andersen fairy tale. More recently, the city of Berlin brought back into the town centre a statue of Frederick the Great that had been considered politically unacceptable in East Berlin before the fall of the Wall.

Britain is becoming more aware of the importance of art and the way in which it can serve the interests of the tourist industry. Notable features include two water fountain sculptures by William Pye, 'Slipstream' and 'Jetstream', commissioned by BAA at Gatwick Airport and a 130-foot long sculpture, 'Train' by David Mach, which is a monument to the record-breaking steam locomotive 'Mallard' and is comprised of 185,000 bricks and was unveiled in Darlington in 1997 (to considerable local criticism but widespread national publicity). Also, two sculptures, initially rebuffed by those in the locations where they were erected, achieved considerable publicity and, later, support from the local population when their benefits to tourism became clear. Artist Maggi Hambling's 12-foot high scallop shell memorial to composer Benjamin Britten on the beach near Aldeburgh, Suffolk, was initially vilified, too, as were Antony Gormley's series of Iron Men sculptures in his 'Another Place' setting on Crosby Beach, Merseyside. In the latter case, locals lobbied later, with the media, to defend the sculptures when the council proposed their removal, following their temporary display on the beach, and the council retracted. Both these artists' works have since become iconic symbols for the resorts in question.

Lighting

External street lighting can play an important role in enhancing a town, both with respect to the design of the lights themselves and to the effect they can create at night. Again, a choice must be made between traditional and modern lamps. Some towns have reinforced their quaintness by choosing authentic gas lighting, which has great popular appeal for tourists. In Norwegian villages in the weeks leading up to Christmas, the shopping streets are illuminated with real flares, giving visitors an impression of warmth and cosiness at a time when the long periods of darkness could otherwise lower the spirits of residents and visitors.

Floodlighting major attractions – a recognized practice for the great monuments in leading cities – has become much more widespread and its use can encourage tourists out on to the streets at night, thus extending the 'tourist day'. For example, the medieval town of Carcassonne in France operates son et lumière displays to narrate its history. European funding has also supported a joint initiative between Rouen and Amiens in France and Rochester and Canterbury in England that allows these cities to provide a series of free music and light events for visitors and the local population to enjoy.

White lights are normally recommended as the use of coloured lights – apart from settings where a fairground atmosphere is appropriate, such as at the Blackpool illuminations – is best avoided. The use of coloured lights to floodlight Niagara Falls, for example, many observers feel, turned a great spectacle into an example of downmarket kitsch. Limited use of coloured lighting can be helpful, though, in highlighting horticultural displays at night. Care must be taken not to overlight. Strong lights are particularly inappropriate in a village setting, for example.

Finally, mention might be due here of holding firework displays to highlight key events, such as national holidays or other days of commemoration. Independence Day, 4 July, in the USA, Bastille Day, 14 July, in France, and Guy Fawkes Day, 5 November, in Britain, are all days where fireworks commonly round off the day's events.

Signposting

All visitors look for signposts, so they become the most visible of all forms of street furniture. They serve three purposes:

- directional
- informative
- utility.

Let us look at each of these in turn.

Directional

Traffic signs point vehicles or pedestrians in particular directions and to specific sights. They must therefore be clearly legible, especially from a distance in the case of vehicle signs. They should be identified by use of a standard, immediately recognizable colour and their size and shape should also be uniform. Generally, standards for road signs are set by local authorities or government departments of transport.

Figure 9.12 An informative house plaque in Stellenbosch, South Africa. *(Photo by Chris Holloway.)*

Within towns, signposts directing tourists to specific attractions have received a lot of attention in Britain in recent years. Once again, a 'traditional' classic signpost has been devised, with modest variations in design, constructed of cast iron painted black with white lettering, though some towns have produced a variation on this. Bristol, for example, with its seafaring history, introduced royal blue as the standard colour.

The black-on-white finger posts – the signposts we find in many UK villages – are icons of national culture, some dating back to the seventeenth century. Sadly, they are now deteriorating and local authorities are being urged to repaint them every five years before they are lost for ever and have to be replaced.

Bristol has taken a lead in location signposting for visitors, producing a clear, well-designed signpost, incorporating a map of the city centre, as part of its award-winning 'legible city' initiative.

Informative

These are of two types. They may be used to alert tourists passing in vehicles to a particular attraction in the vicinity or be provided at a particular site, such as a viewpoint or monument, to give information about the site itself.

Signs outside a particular attraction will also be subject to local government regulations. For example, attractions in North America, which are generally very well signposted, often adopt a standard format for imparting information about national monuments. Such signs must be clearly legible, but may have more character in their design. In Britain, immediately recognizable blue plaques are widely in use to advise visitors of the fact that a property has been the home of some well-known person in the past. These are invariably of great interest to foreign visitors in particular, and the fact that they are often encountered accidentally when walking around the streets of a city gives them added appeal.

Example

Tourist signs in Britain

Following a long period where signposting was arbitrary and often banned from main roads in Britain, the Department of Transport introduced white-on-brown signs in 1986. There are 35 different pictographs representing every conceivable variety of tourist attraction. Regulations on the use of these and other signs are complex and quite restrictive. The use of white-on-brown signs, for example, is dependent on the numbers visiting the site (for example, historic houses must attract a minimum of 5000 visitors a year to warrant a road sign to it being approved). This, of course, introduces a catch-22 situation, where already well-established attractions are favoured over newly developed ones.

Utility

These signs are designed to direct visitors to public utilities such as toilets and telephone kiosks. They can be smaller in scale than the other forms of signs and will often make use of symbols, as do the white-on-brown signs – a particular boon for foreign visitors. They may have their own design and colour, but are also often incorporated into information signs in popular tourist towns.

Within specific tourist attractions, people's imagination has led to a great variety of signs and symbols being created. In medieval times, as few people could read, many shops

Figure 9.13 I can speak the language! This Welsh language sign at a garage in Machynlleth is a much-photographed subject of amusement for English-speaking tourists.
(Photo by Chris Holloway.)

hung signs outside with symbols of their trade. These have been retained, and sometimes resurrected, by shops in tourist centres and add visual appeal to the streets.

Politics and the need to cater for foreign visitors can often affect the layout and language of signs. In countries such as Belgium, in parts of Canada and in Wales, for example, bilingualism is the law, so every place name or instruction must be given in two languages. In the Baltic States, although there are many Russian speakers, the continuing resentment towards their former masters means that if any foreign language is to be used on signs, it is English. In China, Japan and Thailand, where many foreigners will drive cars but not understand the local scripts, signs in the large towns all have to be duplicated in English.

The media and their influence on tourist destinations

> We estimate around one in five of Britain's international visitors are [sic] inspired to come here by the images they see in movies or on TV.
>
> Tom Wright, Chief Executive, VisitBritain

One means by which destinations can regenerate their tourism economy or, in some cases, grow one where earlier it had scarcely existed is through the impact of programmes in the media, whether film, television or radio. The growing interplay between the media and tourism deserves special mention, given the extent to which the tourism industry is now exploiting for its own ends consumer interest in sites associated with 'celebrities'.

A noteworthy aspect of postmodern culture is the fascination that fame, however transient, holds for many people, as witnessed by the appeal of reality shows on television which guarantee minor celebrities instant fame. Tourist destinations have not been slow to exploit opportunities for publicity in the media, especially cinema and television, either by promoting the sites associated with these celebrities or offering inducements to film within their territory. In many cases, governments have colluded with local authorities and the private sector by directly subsidizing the media's production costs, well aware that the publicity engendered by global distribution of a film or television programme will generate tourists' interest. In Britain, the National Trust now actively solicits film companies for its sites, following the success of their heritage buildings when used as settings for costume dramas. Lyme Park, near Stockport, the setting for the popular BBC film of Jane Austen's

Example

The case of Borat

In 2007, the film satire *Borat: Cultural Learnings of America for Make Benefit Glorious Nation of Kazakhstan* appeared on global screens. Ruthlessly pillorying the Kazakh nation, the comic actor Sacha Baron Cohen, in his role as Borat, became an overnight sensation, receiving equal measures of admiration and vilification for his depiction of life in the former Soviet satellite country.

To the surprise of many, the film actually succeeded in putting Kazakhstan on the map for the first time, stimulating travel enquiries. In the weeks following the opening of the film in the UK, there was an increase of 300 per cent in searches for hotels in the country, while the Kazakh Embassy was receiving around 100 calls a week asking for information about tourist visas. Unknown to most of those who saw this movie, filming was actually done in the Romanian village of Glod, rather than Kazakhstan itself.

Pride and Prejudice, experienced a 178 per cent increase in visitors following the drama's showing on British TV. A report by the UK Film Council in 2007[10] estimated that some three million visitors were influenced to visit Britain by images seen in films or on TV, such an effect boosting tourism revenue by around £1.8 billion each year.

Tourist information offices all over the world are producing 'film maps' listing sites that appear in popular films. New York City has *Sex and the City* and *Seinfeld* tours, among numerous others, while Katz's Delicatessen, in the same city – site of the famous 'orgasm' scene in *When Harry met Sally* – has become a popular port of call for visitors from all over the world. In Britain, the enormous popularity of the book and film *The da Vinci Code* (the book alone sold over 50 million copies) enabled a popular 'trail' of sites associated with the film to be promoted by VisitBritain under the title 'Seek the truth', including Lincoln Cathedral (which quickly introduced a charge for visitors to see the actual locations used in the film), Rosslyn Chapel, Burghley House, Lincolnshire (standing in for the Chateau de Villette in Versailles), and Belvoir Castle, Leicestershire (Castel Gandolfo). The enormous popularity of the *Harry Potter* films, equally, has expanded travel to settings associated with the films in England – once again helped by a promotional trail entitled 'Discover the magic of Britain', which includes Gloucester Cathedral, Goathland Station (Hogsmeade) and Alnwick Castle (Hogwarts School of Witchcraft), which experienced a 120 per cent increase in visitors following the film, generating £9 million revenue for the area. More recently, VisitBritain launched a 'Comedy England' campaign, designed to attract visitors to sites famous for comedy in film or television. The six-month campaign in 2008 included reference to Torquay, setting for *Fawlty Towers*, Turville, site of *The Vicar of Dibley*, and Thetford, Norfolk, where *Dad's Army* was filmed.

Other parts of the world have also been quick to cash in on film and television settings as potential sources of revenue. The film *The Italian Job* has a cult following, to the extent that bespoke tours to the locations in Turin where it was filmed are now organized. A recent new version of the film boosted interest once more. In Australia, *Rogue* – a horror film in which day trippers in the Northern Territory are picked off one by one by a giant crocodile – was followed by another, *Wolf Creek* – in which backpackers (presumably the survivors) are again picked off in turn by a psychotic. Far from discouraging tourists, these two films led to a 10 per cent increase in backpackers to the area, helped by a supporting promotion from Tourism Top End (the board for the Northern Territory).

The popularity of domestic TV series helps to boost domestic tourism. Visitors to the North East of England still flock to the sites on the Yorkshire Moors where the television series *Last of the Summer Wine* and *Heartbeat* were filmed, with Sid's Café in Holmfirth – used in the former production – a popular venue with visitors. Turville in Bucks, the setting for the popular TV series *The Vicar of Dibley*, quickly became a featured destination on the tourist trail. More recently, the numerous Bollywood films now shot in the UK are helping to encourage visitors from the Indian subcontinent. *Nammanna*, for example, filmed in 2007, led to a substantial number of visitors from India to Lake Windermere.

The popularity of certain cult films guarantees a steady audience of aficionados to the locations where the films were shot. The enduring appeal of the 1945 film *Brief Encounter*, shot at Carnforth railway station in Lancashire, entices many tourists, particularly Japanese, to the now restored station with its replica of the famous refreshment room, which is open to the public for the sale of food and drink. This is a classic example of staged authenticity, being a reconstruction of the film set, which itself was modelled on the original. Such lack of true authenticity, however, fails to deter visitors. The long-standing popularity of the film *The Railway Children* (remade as a BBC TV film in 2000), which featured the Keighley and Worth Valley Steam Railway in West Yorkshire, led to the company promoting its *Railway Children* connections through leaflets, advertising and special events. In France, Provence tourist authorities have established a 'Marcel Pagnol route' to popularize the locations at which the French film *Manon des Sources* was filmed.

The power of Hollywood means that tourists, both domestic and foreign, flock to the locations of scenes in movies filmed in the United States. To cite recent examples of areas that formerly drew few tourists and now, as a result of popular films, attract many: the general store in Juliette, Georgia, which was the setting for the Whistlestop Café in *Fried Green Tomatoes* has now become a tourist attraction in its own right, and North Carolina, especially the area around Asheville, has been blessed by being the setting for numerous films in recent years, including *Cold Mountain*, *The Last of the Mohicans*, *Forrest Gump* and *Hannibal*. The state has actively promoted these settings in its marketing campaigns. The US tourism authorities ran a TV promotion in Britain during the winter of 2004/2005, and again in 2007/2008, with the strapline 'You've seen the films, now visit the sets', backed by scenes from famous films such as *Thelma and Louise*.

Entire regions and countries can be similarly boosted by media exposure. Notable in recent years has been the New Zealand government's exploitation of the *Lord of the Rings* cycle, with advertising directing tourists to film locations such as Matamata (Tolkien's Plains of Gorgoroth), Tongariro National Park and Nelson (the fact that Tolkien actually based Gorgoroth on the Ribble Valley area in England is conveniently overlooked!) Tunisia, where *Star Wars*, *Raiders of the Lost Ark* and *The English Patient* were filmed, has actively solicited film work and its tourism authority helped to develop an *English Patient* route for tourists. This phenomenon is not limited to Western settings and audiences. Bae Yong Joon, now known to fans as Prince Yong and the hero of the South Korean TV drama *Winter Sonata*, which has a huge following in Japan, made the country an acceptable destination for Japanese mass tourism, with a 10 per cent increase in visitors in 2003. Packages that included visits to locations in the star's films sold well.

This is just a handful of examples to demonstrate the power of the media in influencing tourism – a factor that is, for the most part, fully taken into account and built on by tourist information authorities today in their efforts to promote 'cultural tourism'. There are concerns, however, when these films are made in remote beauty spots that subsequently attract large numbers of tourists. Khao Phingkan in Thailand was the setting for the James Bond film *The Man with the Golden Gun*. This ideal setting was rapidly destroyed by unplanned development of tourism. As we have seen earlier, a similar fate befell Maya Bay on Phi Phi Ley Island, following the popularity of *The Beach*, which starred Leonardo di Caprio (arguably, as much damage is done by the film crew at these locations as by subsequent tourism).

Destinations of the future

What is clear is that consumers of tomorrow's holidays will be less content with the mundane: the search is on for more adventurous, original forms of holiday to exotic destinations. The search for 'something different' is already beginning to undermine traditional identikit destinations and hotels, which will need to position themselves more clearly and adapt their products to appeal to niche markets. Consumers have control over the transmission of information, too, with websites devoted to exchanging information about destinations and accommodation and making recommendations. Others are devoted to complaints about specific accommodation, resorts or carriers.

This drive for the novel, however, is likely to be tempered by cost. What is clear is that the volatility of fuel prices, which the world's economies experienced in extremis during 2008, is unlikely to be reversed, with serious ramifications for the industry's key destinations. Inevitably, the long-haul mass market to distant beach destinations will be affected as prices rise, with serious repercussions for developing countries. Even the current expansion in medium-haul Middle East resorts must be questioned. The days of budget travel by air may be limited, with many passengers switching to rail and coach travel and reducing their reliance on private cars. Decisions to curtail flights, or cease flying to some airports, are not easily reversed as oil prices fall back and volatility makes forward planning difficult. Less accessible destinations with poor public transport infrastructure will be the most seriously affected. While it is difficult to prophesy the exact shape of destination tourism over the next few years, what cannot be doubted is the huge upheaval faced by the industry, as it copes with worldwide recession, rapidly changing fuel bills and ever more threatening results of global warming.

Some futurists have prophesied that there will be little need to travel away from home in the twenty-first century. Holographs are capable of reproducing any environment artificially, so we will be able to recreate in the home any environment of our choosing to 'experience' foreign travel. This could include activity holidays, such as simulating white water canoe and raft rides, winter sports or the piloting of an aircraft. The UK telecommunications company BT announced in the late 1990s that it was working on the production of a machine that could reproduce some of the world's biggest attractions, not only on computer screens but also on wraparound screens or as holograms. Using the device, called 'Head', one could, in BT's words, 'visit Times Square or take a walk into a pyramid without leaving the room'. Whether this form of entertainment replaces travel or only serves to whet the appetite of most of those viewing such destinations remains to be seen. What is certain is that those who cannot now travel – the very poor, the severely disabled and so on – will, for the first time, be able to experience something akin to real world travel.

Example

Virtual tours

The Internet already provides opportunities for viewers to take virtual tours of key attractions around the world. Among websites currently available, one can view the Taj Mahal (**www.taj-mahal.net** – note that this requires the installation of Macromedia), Oxford (**www.chem.ox.ac.uk/oxfordtour** – also requires Macromedia) and UNESCO World Heritage sites (**www.world-heritage-tour.org**).

Some Disney World rides are already a halfway house to virtual travel, where sitting in a theatre gives the impression of a long and often frightening journey.

Other forecasters predict that underwater leisure cities will be built on the seabeds adjoining our coasts, where a controlled climate will make the annual exodus to the sun no longer necessary. Some of these predictions take us into the realms of science fiction, yet, as we have seen earlier, we are already on the fringe of underwater hospitality being a reality. The untapped resources of the ocean for tourism are gradually being examined. Some tour operators are already offering trips in a mini-submarine to the Amundsen Plain, 4400 metres below the sea at the North Pole, which are hailed as 'the ultimate adventure challenge'.

Space as a destination is very close as this book goes to print, with Japanese and American companies planning to build and launch hotels in space once the vehicles are available to get the tourists there. In 2004, SpaceShipOne won the US$10 million Ansari X prize, offered to encourage the development of space transport capable of taking people into space. To win the prize, the aircraft had to fly to the edge of space twice in a two-week period. Since this success, many companies have entered the market with plans to offer both edge-of-space flights and zero gravity flights. While announced timescales of 2015–2025 might be greeted with scepticism, the current acceleration in space exploration makes such developments feasible. It is no longer a question of if, but when.

Notes

1. Koutantou, A. (2006) 'Tourism industry sees growth in 2007, despite strong euro', Reuters, 15 December.

2. Travel Industry Association of America (2004) 'Domestic travel market report', Travel Industry Association of America.

3. Tourism Australia (2006) 'Activities – domestic tourism facts 2005/2006', Tourism Australia.

4. Clarlee, S. (2008) 'The best beach in America', *The Observer*, 26 August, p. 7.

5. Medical Tourism supplement, *The Times*, 22 March 2007. Statistics based on research carried out for TreatmentAbroad.net. See also 'Open wide for your next holiday', *The Observer, Cash*, 23 September 2007, and 'Open health market across Europe allows NHS patients to escape queues', *The Times*, 18 December 2007, p. 19. Evidence based on the IPS records suggests that the figure may have been as high as 70,000 in 2006.

6. Jeffrey, F. 'Put it on the plastic', *Travel Weekly*, 9 June 2006, p. 17.

7. McGinn, D. (2008) 'Sun, sand and surgery', *The Globe and Mail*, Canada, 23 January.

8. 'Medical tourism worth US$100 billion by 2012', *Al-Bawaba News*, 26 April 2008.

9. See, for example, V. T. C. Middleton (2008) 'Public realm: destination management', *The Journal of the Tourism Society*, 135, Spring.

10. UK Film Council et al. (2007), 'Stately attractions: how film and television programmes promote tourism in the UK', Olsberg/SPI.

Websites

Luxist blog about Federation Island, Black Sea
www.luxist.com/2007/09/23/russia-the-island

Travel Foundation   **www.thetravelfoundation.org.uk**

Tropical Islands (covered rainforest resort)   **www.tropical-islands.de**

Questions and discussion points

1. According to the World Travel and Tourism Council, in 2007 the three fastest-growing destinations for global tourism were Macao (a 24 per cent increase), Montenegro and the Seychelles. Advance possible reasons for each of these experiencing so much demand at this point.

2. Earlier in this chapter, it was revealed that Dubai has set out to attract 15 million tourists by 2015. At the same time, there are alarming reports in the international press of officials searching arrivals with undue zeal and arresting visitors carrying trace amounts of banned substances, which might in some cases have been picked up by footwear or bags en route. Fair Trials International, a legal charity, has declared that drug-related arrests have increased markedly since 2006, when the laws relating to banned substances were tightened, and now prohibited substances can include items such as antidepressants and cough mixtures. There are rumours that officials are paid a bounty for arrests and offenders face a four-year prison sentence.

   Iran also welcomes tourists, but these must conform to cultural norms, including the requirement that women cover their heads and follow the customs and mores of residents.

While the laws of a country are theirs to set, and must be obeyed by the visitor, are such laws appropriate for a country seeking expansion of its tourism trade? Will such restrictions deter international tourists? Are you yourself willing to travel under such conditions? What distinctions are to be made between regulations governing visitors to Dubai and Iran?

3. What examples can you think of where the transport or the accommodation itself would be the attraction for your trip, rather than the destination? Would your choice and reasons be shared by many other tourists? If not, why not?

4. Does the English seaside have a future? If so, will it depend on a throwback to nostalgia for the old image, or can it be resurrected to attract the domestic tourist in new ways? In your view, which resorts have the best prospects for successful regeneration?

5. Using the tourism categories identified at the beginning of this chapter, give examples of destinations known to you, both in your own country and abroad, that would exemplify each.

6. What is the trade-off between distance and cost for Europeans considering a skiing holiday in North America? Could these destinations be attractive for short breaks or only for longer holidays?

7. Should the floodlighting of buildings be discontinued, given the current emphasis on reducing energy usage and carbon emissions? Argue the case for and against.

Tasks

1. Investigate a tourist destination of your choice to evaluate the position of the destination in terms of its lifecycle. Discuss how this impacts upon the provision of facilities at the destination.

2. Select a city that has previously held the position of capital of culture and critically examine whether or not the hosting of the cultural year had a positive benefit on tourism in both the short and the longer term.

3. There are many cities that have developed film maps, using the popularity of a film to attract visitors to their destination. Discuss whether or not developing links with a popular film can be a long-term strategy for a destination.

Chapter 10

Tourist attractions

Learning outcomes

After studying this chapter, you should be able to:

- distinguish between a destination and an attraction and define each

- understand what it is that attracts tourists and which attractions appeal to each market

- appreciate the problem for attractions of changing tastes and fashions and propose solutions to overcome this

- recognize the potential for new attractions and how these can be developed.

Introduction: defining the attraction

> Tourism is also about activity and special interest — from fell walking to cathedrals, from international rugby to surfing, from golf to gardens, and from film locations to battlefields.
>
> Tessa Jowell, Secretary of State for Culture, Media and Sport, DCMS Prospectus, May 2004

What exactly do we mean by a **tourist attraction**? Trying to define it is no easy matter, but to understand the sector and how it operates we have to start with a definition. After all, it is generally the attraction that prompts the tourist to travel in the first place, but the concept of an 'attraction' is a very broad one, encompassing a great many different sights – and sites.

Sometimes we use the term synonymously with 'destination', the attraction in this case being the **benefits** inherent in the destination rather than any purpose-built facility specifically designed to appeal to tourists. The medieval town centre of Dinant, Southern Germany's Black Forest and Luquillo Beach in Puerto Rico are all 'attractions', but do not exist either primarily or necessarily to serve tourists' needs. Similarly, a trip to the seaside may be taken principally for the opportunity to enjoy a swim in the sea at a good beach in warm weather, while another trip may consist of a drive through the countryside to take in the scenery. For both trips, the attraction is the **destination** (in the first case, nodal, and, in the second case, linear), but in neither case is the attraction purpose-built to serve the interests of tourism, even if it may have been modified to do so. For example, the beach may have been cleaned up, deckchairs and windbreaks provided for hire and the appeal of the drive will be heightened if look-out points or picnic areas are provided by the local authority at which tourists are invited to stop off and enjoy their packed lunches. Equally, old buildings in town centres were not built with the purpose of bringing in tourists, but, over time, many have become architectural or historical sites that appeal to them.

All three of these 'destinations' – seaside resort, countryside and town – serve the needs of the local residents as well as tourists and, indeed, many residents may have chosen to live in that particular part of the world because of its attractiveness. German speakers have a useful term for this, *Freizeitswert*, implying the possession of enhanced leisure opportunities resulting from one's place of residence, which could usefully be incorporated into the English language.

There are other attractions, however, that *have* been constructed for the prime purpose of appealing to tourists, such as the Kröller-Müller Museum in the countryside near Otterloo in the Netherlands and, on a much larger scale, the Disney theme parks.

So, we must accept that no clear definition exists for the term. It is easiest just to accept that any site which appeals to people sufficiently to encourage them to travel there in order to visit it should be judged a 'tourist attraction'. It is helpful, however, to make some effort to categorize such attractions.

Swarbrooke,[1] who has considered a number of attempts at definition, splits attractions into four categories (modified here):

- features within the natural environment
- purpose-built structures and sites designed for purposes other than attracting visitors
- purpose-built structures and sites designed to attract visitors
- special events.

Fyall et al.,[2] similarly, distinguish between built and natural attractions and whether or not they are purpose-built. They also categorize on the basis of whether the attraction is paid for or free, privately or publicly owned, and a simple or complex product.

For simplicity's sake, we can conclude that attractions may be defined as natural or constructed (whether or not purpose-built for tourism) and, if not constructed, they may still be to a greater or lesser extent 'managed' to suit the purpose of tourism or, more rarely, left entirely in their natural state.

Some sites attract tourists because of events that occur there or have occurred there in the past. In either case, they will then be known as event attractions and these can be either temporary or permanent. Temporary events may be one-offs, at different sites on each occasion they occur (such as garden festivals in Europe that are arranged at intervals in different cities), while others (such as Ludlow Food Festival) are held at regular intervals at the same site. Some events are of very short duration – one day or even a matter of hours in the case of a concert.

Events, too, are also either artificial (constructed) or natural. The Changing of the Guard, for example, is a ceremony that attracts many overseas tourists visiting London, while the spring high tides that create the famous Severn Bore along the River Severn on the Wales–England border, the annual migration of wildebeest across the Serengeti Park in East Africa and the regular eruptions of Old Faithful, the geyser in Yellowstone National Park in the USA, are all examples of natural events that attract tourists.

Many sites owe their continuing attraction to some event in the past. Liverpool is an example of somewhere that has become a place of pilgrimage for many visitors, due, in this case, to its links with The Beatles in the 1960s – a connection strongly promoted during 2008, when the city became a capital of culture. Also, both John Lennon's home at 251 Menlove Avenue, Woolton, and Sir Paul McCartney's home at 20 Forthlin Road have been bought by the National Trust and are open to the public. Gettysburg, created a national military park in 1895, attracts millions of domestic tourists as it was the key battlefield site of the US Civil War in 1863, while Lourdes, a place of religious pilgrimage, owes its appeal entirely to events occurring in 1858, when a 14-year-old called Bernadette Soubirous was said to have experienced apparitions of the Virgin Mary.

One useful listing of different attractions was undertaken by the former English Tourism Council. While not totally comprehensive (its final category is something of a catch-all, while 'leisure attractions' might encompass anything from swimming pools and gymnasia to theme parks like the Walt Disney World Resorts), it does give us some direction for analysis of this sector of the industry:

- historic properties
- museums and art galleries
- wildlife parks
- gardens
- country parks
- workplaces
- steam railways
- leisure attractions
- other attractions.

In all, there are well over 6000 such attractions in the UK for which entrance figures are maintained, a quarter of them being historic properties and a similar number, museums. There were nearly 200 million visits to such attractions in England during 2006, indicating their importance for tourism. To this number must be added the numerous buildings open to the public for which no attendance records are kept. There are, for instance, nearly 3000 Grade I listed churches in England alone and 15,000 churches altogether in Britain – VisitBritain estimates that these receive more than 13 million visits a year.

The total number of attractions continues to increase every year, boosted by the granting of heritage and lottery funding (the Millennium Fund at the turn of the century accelerating the process). A few of them have proved almost instant successes. Our Dynamic Earth in Edinburgh estimated, and budgeted for, 430,000 visitors a year, but actually received

500,000 in the first four months. Many others, however, were hopelessly over-optimistic about their attendance figures and have either struggled to survive or collapsed – the notorious Millennium Dome perhaps being the outstanding example, running up debts in excess of £1 billion despite drawing the largest audiences in the country during the millennium year itself (it is noteworthy that, since being sold off to private enterprise, as the O_2 Arena it has now become one of the leading entertainment venues in the world). The National Centre for Popular Music in Sheffield, opened in 1999, was effectively bankrupt within seven months. It estimated 400,000 visitors a year but achieved only a quarter of that figure. The performance of the Earth Centre in Doncaster was even poorer. Forecasting 500,000 visitors when it opened in 1999, it attracted only 80,000 and collapsed financially in 2004. The following year, a 100,000 square feet community arts centre was proposed for West Bromwich, to be entitled 'The Public'. It was to be funded by the Arts Council and the ERDF and the forecast was that it would receive over half a million visitors each year, but, without clear focus or purpose, initial funding ran out and the project remains precarious.

It would appear that many large-scale attractions are overambitious in their visitor expectations. By contrast, most UK attractions do not anticipate hosting anything approaching these figures. Over 90 per cent are geared to receiving fewer than 200,000 visitors annually[3] and some of the smallest admit fewer than 10,000. These are not necessarily to be thought of as failing, however, if sponsored funding is available or costs are kept low and business plans carefully managed. This can be equally true of museums elsewhere in the world.

Example

The Memorial Museum, Caen

Le Mémorial de Caen museum opened in 1988, ostensibly to commemorate the Normandy D-Day landings in World War II. The decision was made to move the focus from warfare in order to develop the theme of peace, transforming the museum's mission by making the site a 'place of reflection on the contemporary world', covering various aspects of twentieth-century life.

As a result, there was a loss of focus and the museum's image became unclear – a problem compounded by exhibitions being mounted on unrelated themes, such as feminism, further confusing visitors. An extension was opened in 2002, with the aim of reviving the museum's fortunes, but, as attendances fell, further efforts were made to revive footfall by putting on more unrelated temporary exhibitions, such as Father Christmas, eco-responsibility and living without petrol.

By 2005, visitor numbers had fallen from a high of 560,000 to 400,000 and the museum was losing 400,000 euros annually.

Exhibitions in 2008 adopted a more focused approach, reflecting its overarching role as a peace museum, with programmes on the Righteous of France (French citizens who helped Jews in the war), the catastrophic attack on the World Trade Centre in New York and the issue of human rights.[4]

Table 10.1 identifies the top ten attractions in Europe. Note that the number one and two spots are both in Britain – one being a heritage site and the other of recent construction – while a further three are in Paris. Arguably, more than half of these could be considered iconic structures, according to the definition given shortly in this chapter. It is also noteworthy that two of them are art galleries – and an update of this list could well include the Tate Modern in London, which has been achieving astonishing success in terms of admissions (with an estimated 5.2 million visits in 2006), which will be further boosted

Table 10.1 The top ten leading attractions in Europe.

Attraction	Location
1. London Eye	London, England
2. Tower of London	London, England
3. Eiffel Tower	Paris, France
4. Musée du Louvre	Paris, France
5. Colosseum	Rome, Italy
6. Anne Frank House	Amsterdam, the Netherlands
7. Musée d'Orsay	Paris, France
8. State Hermitage Museum/Winter Palace	St Petersburg, Russia
9. Tivoli Gardens	Copenhagen, Denmark
10. The Alhambra	Granada, Spain

Source: TripAdvisor, in *The Times*, 6 July, 2007.

by the addition of an eye-catching 'ziggurat' extension, designed by Herzog and de Meuron, by 2012, at an estimated cost of £215 million.

It is important to recognize that many destinations owe their appeal to the fact that they offer a cluster of attractions within the immediate locality. Urban destinations are far less dependent on climate than are rural or coastal sites, and Britain (as in other temperate cities in Northern Europe, North America and Southern Australia) is fortunate in being able to attract year-round visitors to its cities' theatres, galleries and other indoor entertainments. The attraction of the seaside is also heightened, however – particularly in Britain, with its uncertain climate – by its being able to offer, either in the resort itself or within a short drive, a number of sites that are not weather-dependent, such as museums, amusement arcades, retail shopping malls, theatres and industrial heritage sites. In Britain, the need for a focal point, even in seaside resorts, had already been widely recognized by the nineteenth century – the great era for the construction of piers.

The focal point or icon

Contemporary tourism marketing implicitly or explicitly recognizes the importance of the focal point – or a synthesis of focal points – at a site, which acts as a magnet, attracting tourists. The focal point may be a historic building, such as a castle or monument, or it may be another type of construction owing its success to its architectural features, such as a tower, bridge or pier.

A supreme focal point is one that becomes a cultural icon and the more popular tourist destinations are those blessed with such an attraction. The fame of a cultural icon often extends far beyond the region itself, with the result that the images of the icon and destination are inseparable in the minds of prospective visitors. The power of such images has led to some locations setting out deliberately to create a cultural icon with which their region will be associated in the public mind – not always successfully. A few examples of the most successful will reveal the significance of the icon in tourism promotion (Table 10.2).

With the possible exception of the last in this list, none of these buildings was created with the deliberate intention of attracting tourists, yet, over time, their appeal has widened to a point where tourism flourishes because they exist. In the case of more recent projects (and no doubt boosted by the success of Bilbao, which, prior to the construction of the Guggenheim, had little to attract tourists), however, developers and architects have designed either with one eye on the potential for tourism or specifically with tourism in mind.

It is a postmodern irony that 80 per cent of visitors to the Guggenheim do not enter the building – its attraction for many is not the artistic contents, but the building itself. Frank

Table 10.2 Locations and their tourist icons.

Location	Cultural icons
London	Big Ben and the Houses of Parliament, Buckingham Palace
Paris	Eiffel Tower, Notre Dame
New York	Empire State Building, Statue of Liberty
San Francisco	Golden Gate Bridge
Sydney	Sydney Harbour Bridge, Opera House
Kuala Lumpur	Petronas Towers
Copenhagen	Little Mermaid statue
Bilbao	Guggenheim Museum

Gehry's innovative museum has influenced the design of countless more recent constructions straining for recognition as cultural icons within their communities, including the Kunsthaus in Graz, Austria, and the new Imperial War Museum in Manchester. Recruiting an architectural practice of international standing such as Foster and Partners (responsible, inter alia, for the renovated Reichstag in Berlin, the Millennium Footbridge in London and the Sage Concert Hall in Gateshead) is now seen as the first step in establishing a landmark building.

High towers used to be the icon-to-desire for tourist destinations. Today, it is more likely to be big wheels. Since the Prater fairground in Vienna built its 65-metre Riesenrad (big wheel) in 1897, engineers have sought to find ways to build still bigger ones. The London Eye – a 135-metre big wheel providing aerial views over the city – has proved both culturally and commercially successful, having rapidly become an integral component of Central London's cityscape. Following its success, other cities are striving to compete: Singapore has built a 165-metre big wheel, known as the Singapore Flyer, while Berlin and Dubai have even bigger wheels under construction at the time of writing. China aims to top all of these with its 208-metre Great Beijing Wheel, also due to be completed some time in 2009.

Example

The Grand Canyon, Arizona

Some people might judge the Grand Canyon to be sufficiently iconic in its own right, but a new feature has been added to this attraction to draw in even more tourists.

Opened in 2007, the Skywalk is a U-shaped walkway of glass and steel, with glass floor and sides, built to jut out 70 feet over the edge of the canyon, with a view of the sheer drop of 4000 feet to the bottom. While this 'bridge to nowhere' is built to accommodate several hundred people, numbers are restricted to 120 at a time. The feature lies within the Hualapai Indian Reservation, its people receiving the revenue generated by the attraction.

It is worth stressing that, while cultural icons such as these are crucial in attracting first-time visitors, all important tourist cities need to replenish and complement their stock of tourist attractions from time to time to encourage repeat business. The appeal of cities such as London and Paris is that they can attract so many visitors back again and again because of the wealth of attractions they offer – smaller, less well-known museums and newly constructed attractions alike.

Example

The Angel of the North

Officials in Gateshead, in the North East of England, sought the help of sculptor Antony Gormley to construct a landmark work of art to represent the Tyneside region. The intention was to create an image for an area that, up to that point, had had little sense of identity, either among the local population or throughout the country as a whole.

Gormley devised a 20-metre tall steel and copper sculpture – the largest in Britain – to surmount a hill outside the city, with its arms extending 54 metres (almost the width of a jumbo jet) in a sheltering embrace of the surrounding countryside (see Figure 10.1). The sculpture rapidly became an icon, gaining massive media publicity; its siting ensured that it would be seen by an average 90,000 motorists a day passing on the A1, as well as countless rail travellers approaching Newcastle on the East Coast main line. A survey in 2008 revealed four out of five people questioned could identify this sculpture, while only one in three recognised St Paul's Cathedral in London. Gateshead Council anticipated some 150,000 visitors a year would divert their trips to see it. Initially, there had been fear that the image would be seen as too modern for a traditionally minded local population and inappropriate to the site; but the overwhelming success and publicity which followed its erection soon won over the locals, who now take great pride in their new icon.

Figure 10.1 The Angel of the North.
(Photo by Colin Cuthbert, Courtesy of Gateshead Council.)

The 'B of the Bang' landmark, by sculptor Thomas Heatherwick, erected in Manchester, was commissioned with the clear aim of doing for that city what the Gormley sculpture has done for Tyneside, but faults in design and execution have attracted negative publicity since it was completed. Now plans have been announced to construct a similar landmark sculpture for the south of England, close to Ebbsfleet International Station and Ebbsfleet Valley, a region currently rebranding itself as the 'Gateway to England'. Visitors to Britain

Table 10.3 UNESCO World Heritage sites in the UK.

Giant's Causeway and Coast	Canterbury Cathedral, St Augustine's
Durham Cathedral and Castle	Abbey and St Martin's Church
Ironbridge Gorge	Old and New towns of Edinburgh
Studley Royal Park and ruins of Fountains	Maritime Greenwich
Abbey	Heart of Neolithic Orkney
Stonehenge, Avebury and associated sites	Blaenavon Industrial Landscape
King Edward I's castles and town walls in	Saltaire
Gwynedd	Dorset and East Devon Coast
St Kilda Island	Derwent Valley Mills
Blenheim Palace	New Lanark
Westminster Palace, Westminster Abbey and	Royal Botanic Gardens, Kew
St Margaret's Church	Liverpool Maritime Mercantile City
City of Bath	Cornwall and West Devon mining
Hadrian's Wall (frontier of the Roman Empire)	landscape
Tower of London	Antonine Wall, Scotland (designated 2008)

Note: The UK listing also includes the historic town of St George and related fortifications in Bermuda, as well as Henderson, Gough and Inaccessible Islands in the Pacific, which are dependent territories.

from the Continent travelling on Eurostar will pass this giant (at least 50 metres high, against the 20-metre tall Angel of the North) piece of artwork (expected to be a giant white horse) en route to London and, in all, some 40 million people are expected to pass it every year.

The truly outstanding sites of architectural, cultural or historic importance around the world are recognized as UNESCO World Heritage sites. In 2008, 851 such sites were listed in 141 countries. They include 660 cultural sites, 166 natural sites and 25 of mixed composition. Britain, with 25 sites, has almost 3 per cent of the total – for a small country, a favourable share – as Table 10.3 reveals, while the United States, by comparison, has just 20.

Historic buildings and architectural features

Probably what most of us think of first, when considering the appeal of an urban location to tourists, are its historical and architectural features. Often they are subsumed into a general 'feel' of the destination, rather than there being an appreciation of any individual building – the sense that the town is old and beautiful, its buildings having mellowed over time and their architecture quintessentially representative of the region or nation and its people. Thus, old cobbled streets lined with protected shopfronts, gabled roofs and ornamental features, such as those to be found in towns like York and Chester in Britain, Dinant and Tours in France, Rothenburg and Rüdesheim in Germany, Aarhus and Odense in Denmark, Bruges and Ghent in Belgium, all convey an overall impression of attractiveness and warmth, inviting us to shop there and enjoy the local food and lodgings (over 2500 hotels in Britain enjoy listed status, being of historic or architectural interest). These features are the supreme attraction of the 'old' countries of Europe, to which American, Arab and Japanese tourists alike are drawn when they first visit the country (and, where Britain is concerned, one should not underestimate the influence of Charles Dickens, whose nineteenth-century novels have had enormous impact in establishing the landscape and townscape images for which the country is known universally). In spite of an earlier disdain for older properties, the damage wrought by two world wars and the often poor quality of architectural construction in their aftermath, most nations in Europe have retained major elements of their old city centres, even, in some cases (as in Warsaw and

Dresden), building entire replicas of the pre-war city centre in an attempt to regain their original character and heighten their appeal to visitors and residents alike.

This type of attraction is not limited to the Old World. Quebec City is among a number of New World towns and cities marketing themselves as winter (and not purely winter sport) destinations to Europeans as well as North Americans, selling the charm of its old town under snow.

Britain has been more sensitive than some other European nations in retaining and restoring its buildings, having introduced a policy of listing historic buildings since 1950 (although the French had, in fact, introduced a similar, but less effective, policy at least 100 years earlier). Today, the nation boasts over 500,000 buildings listed as being of special historic or architectural interest.

In England and Wales, truly outstanding buildings fall into the Grade I category – of 'exceptional interest' – and make up about 2 per cent of the total. A further 4 per cent fall into the second category of Grade II* – of 'special interest'. Most others are listed as Grade II (in Scotland and Northern Ireland, similar buildings are categorized as A, B or C).

Today, all buildings in reasonable repair dating from before 1700 and most between 1700 and 1840 are listed, with strict controls over any cosmetic or structural changes to their exteriors. Among these, a handful (together with some of those scheduled as ancient monuments, but not necessarily all Grade I-listed buildings) stand out as icons, having sufficient power to draw visitors from all over the world. Castles and cathedrals, palaces and historic manor houses have such power, as do key sites of archaeological interest protected under the Ancient Monuments and Archaeological Areas Act (1979). The Tower of London alone receives over two million visitors annually, attracted not just by the building itself but also by the Crown jewels, which are on permanent display there.

At the other end of the scale, 'listed buildings' can include post-war prefabricated houses, garden sheds, army camps, pigsties, lamp-posts, even toilet blocks. The National Trust, with the aid of Heritage Lottery Funding, has even saved some of the last survivors of the back-to-back slums built in Birmingham between 1802 and 1831, some of which have been renovated and are now being rented out as visitor accommodation. The importance of all of these structures as key ingredients of our national heritage has been recognized by successive British governments.

Most such buildings in England are in the care of English Heritage, while those in Wales are cared for by the Welsh equivalent, Cadw, and those in Scotland by Historic Scotland. The Church Commissioners are responsible for most of the great cathedrals and historic churches, the focal points for tourism in so many cities in the UK, and they part-fund, with government help, the Churches Conservation Trust, which cares for more than 300 redundant churches earmarked as being of historic or architectural merit.

Apart from key sites, many other important buildings are open to visitors. There are believed to be well over 6000 historic houses, commonly referred to as 'stately homes', of which over 800 are open to the public. Others are under the care of the National Trust (National Trust for Scotland in Scotland), while still others are in private hands. The Historic Houses Association comprises around 1500 owners of private houses, of whom some 300 regularly open their houses to the public for at least 28 days a year (the minimum required to reduce inheritance tax). Some will only open by appointment and to small escorted groups, due to limitations of space. The particular value of all of these properties is their location, generally in the heart of the countryside, so they become a major support for rural tourism and the coach tour industry.

On the Continent, historic buildings play an equally important role in tourism for many countries. Notable among these are the châteaux of the Loire in France, Bavarian castles such as Neuschwanstein in Germany and medieval cities such as Florence and Venice in Italy. In Spain and Portugal, former stately homes – known respectively as paradores and pousadas and operated by the state – have been converted into luxury hotels, attracting upmarket touring visitors.

Sadly, many hundreds of buildings built by the British in their former colonies in India, Malaysia and the West Indies now lie in ruins due to the lack of resources to maintain them. Even Lutyens' famed government buildings in New Delhi are deteriorating rapidly in the harsh climate. Others needing urgent restoration, and with tourism potential, include Clive of India's house in Calcutta, the Georgetown trading post in Penang Island, Levuka in Fiji and Falmouth in Jamaica. English Heritage has made moves to contribute to their restoration before many such buildings are lost for ever.

Although the history of the new world is shorter, funding is more readily available and early buildings that have survived are treasured. Americans take great pride in their prominent historic buildings, such as Monticello in Virginia – home of Thomas Jefferson, third president of the United States – while the town of Williamsburg in the same state has been preserved as a living museum of the colonial period. Buildings from the Spanish colonial period are also well preserved, including the missions of San Luis Rey in California, dating from 1789, and what is believed to be the nation's oldest house in St Augustine, Florida.

Modernism and tourism

In the earlier discussion of people's search for a cultural icon, it will be readily apparent that modern buildings are becoming almost as important as historic ones in their ability to attract tourists. Commercial offices, private houses, bridges, monuments and memorials, towers and many other constructions that represent a fusion of artistic creativity and high technology are all becoming important, when sufficiently spectacular.

The more recent proliferation of Holocaust museums in Europe and North America were not specifically designed with the intention of boosting tourism, but the outstanding quality and originality of their designs (and the widespread media publicity that followed their construction) are ensuring that they become popular places to visit. This might be defined as one form of cultural tourism, were it not for the fact that the majority of sightseers are concerned less with aesthetics than with the appeal of a 'wow' factor – the adrenalin rush that accompanies viewing many new spectacles, such as the towering 'seven star' Burj al-Arab Hotel in Dubai or, on a more modest scale, the extraordinary 'art gallery' lobby of the renovated Cumberland Hotel in London.

Nothing defines a city better than a prominent landmark and the taller the landmark, the greater the impression on visitors – hence, the trend to build giant wheels in prominent cities around the world, discussed earlier in this chapter. They also offer striking vistas of the surroundings and bring in useful revenue.

Prior to the giant wheel, tourists have been – and still are – fascinated by the sight of tall towers or other buildings – the Eiffel Tower being an outstanding example and an immediately recognizable icon of Paris. Many destinations still strive to impress their visitors by building the tallest, most impressive towers in the world, with the result that towers of all descriptions are rising ever higher. That honour went, until recently, to Tower 101 in Taipei, which, at 1671 feet (509 metres), topped the former record holders – the 1614-foot (492-metre) tall Shanghai World Financial Centre and the 1483-foot (452-metre) tall Petronas Towers in Kuala Lumpur, Malaysia (the CN Tower, at 1815 metres, is essentially an observation mast, so is not considered a 'building' by all observers – or record-keepers). In any case, even this is soon to be overtaken by Tokyo's Sumide Tower, which, at 610 metres, will be taller than Tower 101 when it is completed in 2009. Moscow has plans for a city tower designed by the ubiquitous Foster architectural practice, which will rise to some 600 metres, making it the tallest building in Europe when completed in 2010.

Capping them all, though, is the Burj Dubai, in Dubai, due for completion in 2009. At around 2684 feet and 160 storeys, it is both the world's tallest building and the tallest structure. The building is linked to one of the world's largest shopping malls and, with other developments planned in Dubai, it puts the country firmly on the map as a market leader in tourism development. Dubai is expected to attract some 15 million tourists a year by 2010, at which point tourism to Dubai alone will contribute around 20 per cent of the UAE's entire GDP. How long the Burj Dubai will retain its crown is debateable. Saudi Arabia has already announced plans to build a mile-high (5250-foot) tower in the desert near Jeddah.

As was the case with the Guggenheim in Bilbao, the significance of modern architecture's appeal is that many of the great buildings are constructed on sites that are not traditionally visited by tourists. The following ten buildings have been cited as 'worth a visit from the international tourist':[5]

- Museum of Fantasy, Bernried, Germany
- Bao Canal Village, China
- concert hall at León, Spain
- Bodegas Ysios, Rioja, Spain (designed by leading architect Antonio Calatrava)
- Parliamentary Library at New Delhi, India
- UFA Cinema, Dresden, Germany
- 'Aluminium Forest' Visitor Centre, Utrecht
- Tango Ecological Housing, Malmö, Sweden
- Art Museum, Milwaukee, USA (also by Calatrava)
- Modern Art Museum, Forth Worth, USA.

These are hardly mainstream tourist destinations, but several could be described as actively striving to build their tourism markets and they are using contemporary architecture as one weapon in their arsenal to achieve this.

Example

The de la Warr Pavilion, Bexhill-on-Sea

In 1935, Earl de la Warr commissioned two leading modernist architects, Erich Mendelsohn and Serge Chermayeff, to construct Britain's first public building in the modernist style. The completed building, set on the shores of a very traditional seaside resort, did not receive universal approval – least of all from locals – and neglect and lack of investment after the war, together with a downturn in visitors to the resort, led to serious deterioration of its fabric.

At its nadir, the local authority considered leasing the building as a pub, which would have involved substantial modification, but architects and modernist enthusiasts mounted a successful campaign to save the building and restore it. Some £8 million was eventually found to restore the building to its pristine state and it reopened in 2005. It is now a Grade 1-listed building, which has put Bexhill-on-Sea firmly back on the visitor map. Over half a million visitors came to see it in the first year of its restoration and it is estimated that they boosted revenue in the South East region by £16 million.

The Pavilion now functions as an important centre for exhibitions of modern art, with the largest gallery space in the South East, and includes a concert hall, restaurants and other facilities for locals, who now recognize its importance and have come to take pride in it.

Source: *C20*, journal of The Twentieth Century Society, winter 2007/2008.

Figure 10.2 The de la Warr Pavilion at Bexhill-on-Sea, East Sussex – designed by Mendelssohn and Chermayeff in the 1930s and now considered the finest example of modernist architecture in Britain – draws tourists to an otherwise declining seaside resort.
(Photo by Chris Holloway.)

The growing influence of Bauhaus-style architecture in modern townscape development has generated interest in all forms of modern design, especially in housing. Cultural tours to the Frank Lloyd Wright and Richard Neutra houses in the United States and those designed by prominent Nordic architects such as Alvar Aalto in Denmark, Sweden and Finland, are now popular. Many of these properties are still in private hands, however, and can only be viewed externally, while others limit admissions due to demand and size.

The fickleness of public taste in modern buildings is problematic, both in terms of whether or not such buildings deserve to be listed and/or protected and if they are seen by tourists as worthwhile visiting. The numerous Art Deco period buildings in Miami Beach present us with a good example of this fickleness. For years they were spurned by the public and threatened with the prospect of being replaced by more modern hotels. Their value was not recognized until the 1990s, when there was a systematic campaign to restore them to their former glory.

Buildings in Britain must normally have been built at least 20 years before they can obtain listed status, but experience would suggest that attitudes towards Britain's modern buildings and decisions about whether or not they are of sufficient merit to attract sight-seers on historical or aesthetic grounds, may take much longer to mature. For example, Coventry Cathedral was severely damaged during World War II and replaced by an unashamedly modern building after the war by the architect Basil Spence. It was vilified for decades, but a poll conducted by English Heritage in 1999 found that it had become the country's favourite twentieth-century building. Other formerly despised modernist buildings now popular with the British public include Liverpool's Roman Catholic cathedral, the de la Warr Pavilion in Bexhill-on-Sea (see the Example above) and the 1951 Royal Festival Hall in London (also listed and recently the subject of a major restoration project).

The bridge is another type of structure that has always found favour with tourists. Indeed, American enthusiasts actually purchased and transported the former London

Figure 10.3 The Millau Viaduct in France. Half a million people came to view its construction from the specially built Cazalou viewing area before it opened and over a million visited the first year it was open.
(Photo by Chris Holloway.)

Bridge, re-erecting it on Lake Havasu in Arizona. Tower Bridge in London, the Pont du Gard in France, the Golden Gate in San Francisco and the Sydney Harbour Bridge are all well-established tourist attractions in their own right.

Advances in engineering are making the construction of modern bridges ever more awe-inspiring. The opening in 2004 of the world's highest bridge, the Millau Viaduct bridge (see Figure 10.3) across the Tarn Valley (another Foster design), is attracting many sightseers to the Massif Central region of France – apart from the 10,000–25,000 motorists who need to drive across it each day. The tallest of the bridge's seven piers is 343 metres – taller than the Eiffel Tower – while vehicles cross at a height of 270 metres. Again, local residents, who at first complained about it, are now relishing the inflow of tourists that the bridge has generated.

Seaside piers

I have come to appreciate the things that make England what it is are quite endearing and often admirable. The ability so gloriously evinced in the seaside pier – to be magnificent while having no evident purpose – is one of the qualities that set English icons apart and make them so memorable.

Bill Bryson, *Sunday Times Magazine*, 31 August 2008

The idea of a pier is a particularly British phenomenon. Very few are to be found in other countries, yet at one time Britain boasted more than 100. These soon proved to be attractions in their own right at many of Britain's most popular seaside resorts.

The first pier was constructed at Weymouth in 1812, soon followed by that at Ryde, Isle of Wight, in 1813. Their heyday, however, occurred between the mid-1800s and early 1900s, with 78 constructed between 1860 and 1910. They were first constructed to serve as walkways to reach the numerous paddle steamers moored offshore to provide excursions for holidaymakers, but were soon used for 'promenading' – a popular Victorian pastime. Margate Pier, built in 1853, was the first pier built purely for pleasure.

Piers have now become nostalgic accoutrements to seaside holidays at Victorian resorts and those that remain (some 55 in the UK in varying states of preservation) are currently enjoying something of a revival, with the formation of a National Piers Society to further public interest in their regeneration. Sadly it was too late to save the dilapidated West Pier in Brighton – a Grade I-listed pier – as it collapsed during a storm while efforts were still being made to raise funds for its restoration.

Archaeological sites

Archaeology is the study of human antiquities, usually through excavation, and is generally thought to be concerned with pre- or early history, although much recent research is concerned with industrial archaeology – that relating to study of the industrial relics of the eighteenth and later centuries.

Areas where early civilizations arose, such as the countries of the Middle East, are rich in archaeological sites. Egypt, in particular, attracts visitors from around the world to sites such as the Pyramids at Giza, the burial sites at the Valley of the Kings and the temples at Luxor.

Great Britain is also rich in early historical sites, such as those at Chysauster prehistoric village in Cornwall, the Roman remains at Fishbourne in Sussex, with some of the richest mosaic flooring in the country, and the Skara Brae Neolithic site in the Orkney Islands. Myth and history are closely interwoven in our heritage and the legend of King Arthur, which locates his castle of Camelot at Tintagel, and the association of this mythical king with the archaeological digs at Cadbury Camp in Wiltshire, exercise a fascination for young tourists in particular.

In the early 1990s, the world's largest collection of paleolithic art, embracing hundreds of ice age drawings of animals, was discovered in a remote area of northern Portugal. A fierce battle then developed between those seeking to dam the area as a reservoir and others wanting to conserve the site for tourism. The latter won the day and the Côa Valley Archaeological Park was opened to the public in 1996.

Industrial heritage

Britain became the seat of the industrial revolution in the eighteenth century and, over the past half century, interest has been awakened in the many redundant buildings and obsolete machinery dating back to this period. The fact that so many of the early factories and warehouses were also architectural gems has given impetus to the drive to preserve and restore them for tourism.

Other European countries as well as the USA and Australia have also recognized the tourism potential of such redundant buildings. Lowell, in Massachusetts, where a number of early mills survived intact, received massive federal government funding to be restored as an urban heritage park and, since the conversion of the buildings into museums, offices and shops, it has enjoyed considerable commercial success as an out-of-the-ordinary tourist destination. A similar success has been recorded in Britain for Ironbridge, where the industrial revolution is claimed to have originated in 1709. Now a UNESCO World Heritage site, it has enjoyed the benefit of substantial tourism investment on its seven sites spread over some 6 square miles.

The variety of industrial sites is astonishing. Early mining works in Britain, such as the coal and slate mines of South Wales or the copper mines of Cornwall, have been converted into tourist attractions, as have former docks and manufacturing buildings. Derelict textile mills in the north of England, driven out of existence by the importing of cheap textiles from developing countries following World War II, have taken on new life as museums or, in other cases, been converted into attractive new homes.

Open-air museums that are based on a combination of industrial archaeology and industrial heritage provide settings which, to be properly appreciated, require many hours, if not days, of viewing, so have helped to turn former areas of urban decay into profitable tourist attractions. Apart from Ironbridge, other significant developments in Britain include Beamish open-air museum in the north of England and the Black Country Museum near Dudley in the Midlands. The Big Pit Mining Museum at Blaenavon in South Wales and the Llechwedd Slate Caverns near Blaenau Ffestiniog in North Wales have both made important contributions to the local economy of the regions, with tourism helping to replace the former dependency on mining.

Other countries have emulated Britain in recognizing that their recent industrial heritage can play a part in attracting tourists. Countries with shorter histories, such as the United States and Australia, are fervent protectors of their earliest sites, both indigenous and of European origin. Former mining sites provide plenty of interest for tourists, not just in terms of their history but also sometimes for the opportunity they present for the tourists to do a spot of mining themselves. Bodie, California, was the site of early gold mining, and is now protected as Bodie State Historic Park. Tip Top, Arizona, was a silver mining area and is now attracting tourists, as is Macetown, New Zealand, an early gold mining area. Tourists in Australia are invited to pan for gold at former industrial sites (one of the authors struck lucky and still treasures the minute gold nugget he found!) Kolmanskop in Namibia, an abandoned diamond-mining town, is aiming to attract tourists to see not only its industrial heritage but also the lunar landscape that surrounds the site.

Example

European cooperation in industrial heritage

The European Union is encouraging cooperative ventures within its member states and the European Regional Development Fund has approved funding for a project designed to link industrial heritage sites in countries such as Britain, the Netherlands and Germany. The European Route of Industrial Heritage (ERIH) has been established to link two separate themes of such sites:

- *anchor points* national and international sites such as the Blaenavon Big Pit in Wales and the Völkinger Hütte in Saarland
- *key sites* the industrial heritage of a region and specific aspects of technology and innovation, which will apply to some 30 sites in the UK, including the Cornish tin mines and Strathisla Distillery in Scotland.

Sites will be linked by themed routes, such as the Saarland Route, which links the production of coal from Lorraine and labour from Luxembourg with the manufacture of steel in Germany.

Further information: **www.erih.net**

Modern industrial tourism

Interest in industrial heritage has now widened to include the desire to observe *modern* industry, too. A number of companies have recognized the possibilities of achieving good public relations by opening their doors to visitors to enable them to visit a workshop or museum of some kind and, in some cases, even permit a glimpse of work in progress at the factory.

American businesses were the first to recognize the public relations value of this sort of operation and car companies in particular were soon arranging visits to manufacturing plants where prospective purchasers could watch cars being built. Today, this practice is widespread in the USA and is particularly beneficial for tourism in the sense that most automobile plants are not sited in areas that would normally attract tourists. Those that have been opened to the public include General Motors' Chevrolet Corvette factory in Bowling Green, Kentucky (it is one of the state's major tourist attractions), the Toyota assembly plant in Georgetown, also in Kentucky, GM's Saturn plant at Spring Hill, Tennessee, the Nissan plant in the same state at Smyrna, BMW's Zentrum visitor centre at its plant in Spartanburg, South Carolina, and the Ford Rouge factory near Detroit, Michigan – the traditional home of car manufacture. Some visits to these plants are booked months in advance, such is their popularity. German-based car plants have also developed their own themed attractions, with Opel Live at Rüsselsheim and Volkswagen's Autostadt in Wolfsburg.

There are commercial benefits to doing this apart from creating good public relations. Watching the production processes of, for example, modern china and glass will stimulate an interest in purchasing it and people can be encouraged to do so from a factory shop. At Cadbury's, the confectioners located in Bourneville, England, chocolates have been made by hand and are sold to the public individually by members of staff in traditional costumes. Other museums based on publicizing internationally popular products include Guinness in Ireland, Swarovski Crystal in Austria, and Hershey Chocolate, Kelloggs and Coca-Cola in the USA.

China is probably the supreme example of a country where factory visits have been launched to encourage visitors to spend in their shops. What is often a minimal tour of the 'factory' itself is followed by an extended visit to the shop, fuelled by liquid refreshments to encourage visitors to linger and purchase. In other countries where high-value goods are for sale (for example, in precious gem shops in Namibia or South Africa), coffee or wine is served to visitors and they are encouraged to take their time in the shop while perusing the products to encourage sales.

In 1980, the Sellafield nuclear fuel plant in England was opened to visitors to help counteract much negative publicity about nuclear energy that had appeared in the media. This quickly became a major, and quite unexpected, draw for tourists in the area and, since, other nuclear processing plants have also opened their doors to give guided tours.

The variety of factories and workplaces now open to the public is considerable – from leading companies such as the car manufacturers to small individual workshops such as Langham Glass in Norfolk, which makes lead crystal glassware by hand and received an industrial award in 1993 for the numbers of tourists it was attracting.

Producers of alcoholic drinks have long tapped tourist markets. Sherry producers in Spain welcome visitors to their bodegas with demonstrations of sherry production (see

Example

Vineyard marketing to the elite

Vineyard owners have long recognized that their products attract upmarket visitors and prestige tours can be built around accommodating these valued clients. One notable enterprise operating at Margaret River in Western Australia is one-day chauffeur-driven tours, visiting vineyards in the region, with clients accommodated in classic Bentley cars.

Further information: **www.bridgeandwickers.co.uk**

Figure 12.8 and their success has been emulated by the Scotch whisky distilleries in Scotland. Of more than 100 distilleries, over 40 today admit members of the public and a distillery trail has been established for aficionados of single malt. French vineyards have been equally enterprising in opening their *caves* (cellars) for *dégustation* (tastings) of their fine wines – a tactic since copied by vineyards in South Africa, Chile and Australia.

Example
Open doors

In Britain, businesses and other public institutions open their doors to the public annually on a weekend in September, in order to encourage locals and tourists to visit. This has both a promotional and political purpose. Access to government departments, for example, acts as an opportunity to recruit, and – in the case of the Foreign Office particularly – to reassure the public that careers in government are open to all. At the same time, it offers to departments an opportunity to publicize a political issue through exhibitions on site. In Germany open government has encouraged many buildings to be opened to the public on a regular basis, most notably the Chancellery in Berlin which, with its cutting edge design, appeals to those with an architectural as well as political interest (see Figure 10.4).

Safety issues, following the bombing in London on 7 July 2005, are paramount, and an inevitable conflict emerges between the state's desire to give the public access to their democratic institutions and the need to ensure their security.

Figure 10.4 The Reichstag, Berlin – one of the most popular tourist attractions in the city – was designed specifically to allow visitors to watch the democratic process in action without compromising safety.
(Photo by Chris Holloway.)

Many craftspeople depend on tourists visiting their studios in order to sell their products and, as these studios are frequently set in the countryside, they stimulate tourism to the area. For this reason, public funding is sometimes made available to help companies willing to open to the public, as was the case with Langham Glass, mentioned above.

Transport-related attractions

Early forms of transport are another focus for tourists. In some cases, the equipment can be restored and brought back into service for pleasure trips, such as the many steam railways either in private hands or managed by trusts in Britain. Many of these railways run through very scenic countryside, especially those in Wales. The continuing role of classic modes of transport as tourist attractions will be examined more thoroughly in Chapters 14 and 15.

Transport museums are popular attractions in many countries. There are eight significant museums of transport and numerous smaller ones in Britain alone, encompassing a mix of aircraft, maritime vessels and public and private road transport.

Historic ships provide unique attractions for local museums. Some of the earliest are the Viking ships which have been found in Scandinavia, and some splendid museums have been created to display them, notably that at Roskilde in Denmark.

The only seventeenth-century warship to survive is the Swedish *Vasa*, which capsized and sank in Stockholm harbour soon after its launch in 1628. Raised in almost perfect condition, it is now a major museum attraction in Stockholm. Still in Scandinavia, Oslo in Norway provides the setting for the *Fram* – the vessel in which Roald Amundsen sailed in 1910, on his way to becoming the first person to reach the South Pole. Similarly, Captain Scott's vessel, the research ship *Discovery*, has now returned to Dundee, where it was built in 1901, and serves as a museum.

In Britain, the oldest surviving vessel built in Bristol's former shipping yards, the tug *Mayflower*, is still in working order and a key attraction on the floating harbour, offering regular trips for visitors in summer. Bristol is also the setting for Isambard Kingdom Brunel's *SS Great Britain* – the first iron-hulled screw-driven vessel, launched in 1843. Brought back from the Falklands as a rusting wreck in 1970, it is now being extensively restored with the aid of the Heritage Lottery fund. Together with the city's famous suspension bridge, also by Brunel, this early ship has helped to create a new identity for the city.

The sheer size and scale of more recent passenger vessels militates against their preservation. Perhaps the best-known of all twentieth-century ships, the *RMS Queen Mary*, was saved from the breaker's yard and is almost the only modern passenger ship to have been preserved, though, sadly, much of its original interior has been removed. It now serves as a dry-dock hotel near Long Beach, California, but the huge cost of its preservation has resulted over the years in big losses for its developers. Its sister ship, the *Queen Elizabeth 2*, completed its maritime career in 2008 and now serves as a floating hotel in Dubai.

Britain itself, formerly a leading maritime nation, has, sadly, no examples of its great passenger vessels of the last two centuries on display apart from the *SS Great Britain*, although there are numerous examples of fighting vessels from that and earlier centuries that have been preserved and are open to the public. *HMS Belfast*, a World War II cruiser, is moored near Tower Bridge in London and attracts some 200,000 visitors each year. Portsmouth is particularly lucky to have three great examples of historical maritime vessels, including Nelson's flagship, *HMS Victory*, the nineteenth-century *HMS Warrior* and the Tudor warship *Mary Rose*, raised from the sea in 1982 and still undergoing conservation. The combination of three vessels of historic value located close together in the same city acts as a powerful magnet for day trippers and helps to account for the large number of visitors who come to see them.

There are many vintage car museums throughout Britain, although Beaulieu is probably the best-known of these. Vintage aircraft are preserved at Yeovilton, among other sites, while, elsewhere, museums have been devoted to early carriages, bicycles and canal boats. Where artefacts are too large to house indoors, the costs of preservation are very high, adding to the difficulties faced by museums that wish to focus on such attractions. This was a factor in the collapse of the Exeter Maritime Museum in 1996.

Battlefields

Historic battlefield sites are also important tourist attractions, not least because many are situated in rural areas and encourage tourism to what otherwise may be unappealing countryside. A growing enthusiasm for knowledge of military encounters on the fields of battle has been encouraged by the popularity of historical documentaries on television, bringing awareness of these sites to a wider audience. In fact, many battlefield sites in the past have offered little for the tourist to see, the authorities feeling that the events taking place at the sites are best left to the visitors' imaginations. As a result, they have remained relatively undisturbed, but this also means that they are often under threat from development and may be compromised by the need for access roads. Local authorities are now making greater efforts to provide interpretation at these sites, using audio-visual displays and, in some cases, organizing associated events, such as staging mock battles at these sites on the anniversaries of the original engagements.

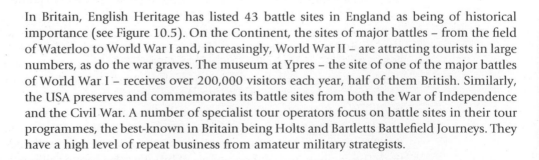

Example

Culloden Moor

Culloden Moor, near Inverness in Scotland, is the site of one of the key battles in Scottish history. It is where Bonnie Prince Charlie was defeated in 1746 by English troops, led by the Duke of Cumberland – ending efforts to restore the Stuart kings to the British throne. It was the last battle fought on British mainland soil. It has long been a popular site for visitors and a 20-foot tall commemorative cairn was built at the site in 1881.

Hospitality consultancy RGA was employed to conduct a feasibility study for a new visitor centre at the site and estimated that the project would draw more than 70,000 tourists each year. In 2008, the new £9 million centre was opened to the public, featuring an exhibition and interpretation space and a flexible arts and conference area, together with a shop and café. The Gaelic language is dominant in the interpretation and audio-visual material uses the contemporary Gaelic words, songs and music that the men and women of the area would have used at that time.

In Britain, English Heritage has listed 43 battle sites in England as being of historical importance (see Figure 10.5). On the Continent, the sites of major battles – from the field of Waterloo to World War I and, increasingly, World War II – are attracting tourists in large numbers, as do the war graves. The museum at Ypres – the site of one of the major battles of World War I – receives over 200,000 visitors each year, half of them British. Similarly, the USA preserves and commemorates its battle sites from both the War of Independence and the Civil War. A number of specialist tour operators focus on battle sites in their tour programmes, the best-known in Britain being Holts and Bartletts Battlefield Journeys. They have a high level of repeat business from amateur military strategists.

Gardens and arboreta

According to the National Botanic Garden of Wales, there are some 1846 botanic gardens in 148 countries around the world, which admit more than 150 million visitors every year. Key sites, such as Kirstenbosch Botanic Gardens near Cape Town, South Africa, attract visitors from all over the world (see Figure 10.6). The cultivation of gardens has an enthusiastic

LISTED SITES

English Heritage has listed 43 battle sites:

1 Maldon, Essex, 991; 2 Stamford Bridge, North Yorks, 1066; 3 Hastings, E. Sussex, 1066; 4 Northallerton, North Yorks, 1138; 5 Lewes, E. Sussex, 1264; 6 Evesham, Hereford & Worcester, 1265; 7 Myton, North Yorks, 1319; 8 Boroughbridge, North Yorks, 1322; 9 Halidon Hill, Northumberland, 1333; 10 Neville's Cross, Co. Durham, 1346; 11 Otterburn, Northumberland, 1388; 12 Homildon Hill, Northumberland, 1402; 13 Shrewsbury, Shropshire, 1403; 14 Blore Heath, Staffs, 1459; 15 Northampton, 1460; 16 Towton, North Yorks, 1461; 17 Barnet, N. London, 1471; 18 Tewkesbury, Glos, 1471; 19 Bosworth, Leics, 1485; 20 Stoke Field, Notts, 1487; 21 Flodden, Northumberland, 1513; 22 Solway Moss, Cumbria, 1542; 23 Newburn Ford, Tyne and Wear, 1640; 24 Edgehill, Warwicks, 1642; 25 Braddock Down, Cornwall, 1642; 26 Stratton, Cornwall, 1643; 27 Hopton Heath, Staffs, 1643; 28 Adwalton Moor, West Yorks, 1643; 29 Lansdown Hill, Avon, 1643; 30 Newbury, Berks, 1643; 31 Roundway Down, Wilts, 1643; 32 Winceby, Lincs, 1643; 33 Chalgrove, Oxon, 1643; 34 Cheriton, Hants, 1644; 35 Cropredy Bridge, Oxon, 1644; 36 Marston Moor, North Yorks, 1644; 37 Nantwich, Cheshire, 1644; 38 Naseby, Northants, 1645; 39 Langport, Somerset, 1645; 40 Rowton Heath, Cheshire, 1645; 41 Stow-on-the-Wold, Glos, 1646; 42 Worcester, 1651; 43 Sedgemoor, Somerset, 1685.

Figure 10.5 The English battle sites listed by English Heritage.

following in the UK, a fact not lost on those organizing visits; both private and public gardens, and arboreta, which are essentially museums for living trees and shrubs, are popular. The Royal Botanic Gardens at Kew attract in excess of two million visitors every year.

Many gardens popular with visitors are in the care of the National Trust, generally as adjuncts to stately homes. In some cases (as is the case with Stourhead in Wiltshire), the gardens may prove a stronger draw than the houses themselves and, in others, only the gardens are open to the public. Great landscape architects of the eighteenth century, such as Capability Brown and Humphrey Repton, built splendid parks to complement these buildings and, as recently as the twentieth century, famous gardens were still being constructed.

Figure 10.6 Kirstenbosch Botanic Gardens, South Africa.
(Photo by Chris Holloway.)

The great gardener designer Gertrude Jekyll is a notable example of this, her work often complementing that of the popular architect of great houses of the early part of the twentieth century, Sir Edwin Lutyens.

Apart from the gardens at Kew (a World Heritage site with well over a million visitors each year) and the Westonbirt Arboretum (see the Example), other popular attractions include Kew's off-shoot, a 500-acre site at Wakehurst Place, Haywards Heath (one of the National Trust's most popular attractions), the grounds of Hampton Court and the famous Wisley Gardens. The proximity of all these to London helps to ensure their success with day trippers.

Example

Westonbirt Arboretum

Westonbirt, in Gloucestershire, is one of the most important arboreta in Britain. English Heritage have designated it a Grade I-listed landscape in its Register of Parks and Gardens of Special Historical Interest.

Managed by the Forestry Commission, because it is on the fringe of the Cotswolds it is easily accessible by tourists. It receives more than 300,000 visitors a year – partly due to the pattern of regular events mounted year round at the Arboretum. In addition to summer concerts, it stages an annual Festival of Wood (in which dead trees are turned into sculptures), open-air plays, and, between June and September, a Festival of the Garden, featuring pieces of installation art that are then sold to raise money for Tree Aid, a charity planting trees in Africa. On midwinter evenings it offers an illuminated trail, the trees emblazoned tastefully with white lights, which attracts many tourists who might otherwise never visit the site.

Another highly successful attraction in Britain is the Eden Project in Cornwall, which received 1,285,000 visitors between April and September in its first year. Early research has indicated that 92 per cent of all visitors stayed in holiday accommodation nearby when they visited and so the Cornish economy has been forecast to benefit by some £1.8 billion over the site's first decade of operation, between 2001 and 2011. Its appeal is boosted by its proximity to another garden attraction, the Lost Gardens of Heligan, making it a popular coach trip for garden enthusiasts taking a short-break holiday.

Public and private sectors are now uniting to further this interest in all things horticultural. In Wales, a joint marketing initiative brought together seven leading gardens under the promotional theme Premier Gardens Wales. The bicentenary year of the Royal Horticultural Society, 2004, was declared the Year of Gardening in the UK, leading to the promotion of 200 prominent gardens around the country. Smaller private gardens are also regularly opened to the public throughout the summer each year under the National Gardens Scheme, to benefit charity. While primarily aiming to attract locals, in practice, enthusiasts will travel considerable distances to visit some of these gardens and must certainly be counted among day tripper figures for these regions. Indeed, a number of visitors will even have travelled from abroad to visit these gardens.

Example

The National Wildflower Centre

The National Wildflower Centre opened in Knowsley, Merseyside, in 2004. On a 35-acre site, the Centre's objectives are to promote the creation of new wildflower landscapes, encourage sustainability in the landscape and encourage visitors to learn informally about wildflowers.

The visitor centre has already received a RIBA award for its architectural design. Funding to establish the centre was raised through a number of sources:

	£
Millennium Commission	2,000,000
NWE Regional Development Agency	600,000
European Regional Development Fund (Objective 1 programme)	450,000
Other sources	1,300,000
Total:	4,350,000

Note: The initial visitor target was 25,000 visitors annually, at an entrance fee of £3.00.
Further information: **www.nwc.org.uk**

Indeed, because British garden enthusiasts are so willing to travel far to see unusual plants in beautiful settings, travel operators have developed specialist tours, and even cruises, to meet this demand. As early as the 1970s, the famed garden expert Percy Thrower had launched garden breaks at the Imperial Hotel in Torquay – a base from which a number of striking gardens in Devon and Cornwall can be visited. Today, garden tours are organized by a number of leading operators, including Gardeners' Delight Holidays, Saga Holidays and Page & Moy. Popular destinations include gardens in the Azores, the Indian Ocean, South Africa and New Zealand, while tours of Arab-influenced gardens in Andalucia, Spain, are also becoming popular. Growing awareness of Bonsai and Japanese landscape design is also leading to small groups travelling to visit the gardens of Japan.

Garden festivals (strictly speaking, these are event attractions) are also popular in Germany, France and the Netherlands. A national garden festival is held in Germany every two years and, in the Netherlands, every ten years. France, too, benefits significantly from garden tourism. The formal gardens attached to the châteaux in the Loire valley and Monet's garden at Giverny have become a major international tourist attractions – the latter especially so since its restoration. North America also has its share of notable garden attractions. Perhaps the most famous are the Butchart Gardens on Victoria Island, British Columbia in Canada, but popular and much-visited botanic gardens in the USA include the Denver Botanic Gardens in Colorado and Longwood Gardens, a 1000-acre site founded by the du Pont family at Kennett Square, Pennsylvania, which attracts over 900,000 visitors a year.

Example

Britain's garden festivals

In the declining years of the twentieth century, Britain mounted a number of garden festivals. They were seen as one means of resurrecting depressed urban areas. Organized over an eight-year cycle, they were held at:

- Liverpool in 1984
- Stoke on Trent in 1986
- Glasgow in 1988
- Gateshead in 1990
- Ebbw Vale in 1992.

Although highly successful, they offered little long-term benefit to their communities as, for the most part, they failed to attract visitors to the surrounding areas – most visits being restricted to the site of the festival itself. At the end of the year, all the sites were landscaped or developed, in contrast to the Dutch garden festivals, where the entire gardens are donated in perpetuity as regional parks to the communities in which they are constructed.

Theme and amusement parks

Purpose-built leisure parks are, not surprisingly, major attractions for tourists, and they receive the greatest number of visitors of all tourist attractions. It is estimated that global theme parks received over 328 million visitors in 2006, spending around $20 billion, which is expected to have increased to $24.7 billion in 2008.

The appetite for such parks to entertain the public seems never-ending and, in Europe, they have a very long history. Bakken, in Klampenborg near Copenhagen, lays claim to being the oldest amusement park in the world, having opened in 1583. London's Vauxhall Gardens opened in 1661, followed in the eighteenth century by Ranelagh Gardens and the Tivoli Gardens in Paris. By the nineteenth century, entertainment parks were firmly established, with the Tivoli Gardens in Copenhagen, which first opened in 1843, soon becoming one of the world's leading centres of entertainment. This park continues to attract over four million visitors annually. Blackpool Pleasure Beach – Britain's first seaside entertainment centre – opened in 1896 and is still one of the most visited tourist attractions in the country, with nearly six million visitors.

The world's biggest amusement park became established at around the same time at Coney Island, in Brooklyn, New York City. The world's first roller coaster was built there in 1884 and, by 1895, an indoor amusement park, Sea Lion Park, had been added.

Eventually, three separate parks – Luna Park, Steeplechase Park and Dreamland – opened on this seaside site between 1897 and 1904, with up to 250,000 visitors a day. A succession of fires destroyed two of the parks, but Luna Park remained popular until its decline after the Wall Street Crash in 1929, after which it struggled to survive until it finally closed in 1944. Plans have been put forward to regenerate the area with a $1 billion investment, after its steady decline in the 1950s and 1960s. Australia emulated the success of Coney Island in its early years with its own Luna Park in Melbourne in 1912, followed by a second in Sydney in 1935.

The 1920s were the heyday of these amusement parks. The Great Depression caused attendances to decline until a new generation of theme parks arrived in the 1950s. Although de Efteling was opened in Europe as early as 1951 with a fairy tales theme, and Bellewaerde Park followed in 1954, it was Walt Disney Enterprises that popularized the concept of the theme park with its development at Anaheim, California in 1955 and it reinvigorated the market. It was followed by a number of Disney developments around Orlando in Florida, the first of which opened in 1971, and now attracts tourists from all over the world.

Today's amusement parks fall into two distinct groups – theme parks and amusement parks – and can be classified, according to size, into three distinct categories:

- local parks, catering largely to the day tripper market
- flagship attractions, such as the Tivoli or Prater in Vienna, which draw on national markets and attract a significant number of foreign visitors, too
- icon, or destination, parks, such as those of the Disney empire, which have become destinations in their own right and attract a worldwide market.

The USA alone boasts over 750 leisure parks, but the large Disney parks account for by far the greatest number of visitors. They attracted 115 million people in 2007 (The Magic Kingdom at Orlando alone attracted 17 million) and the 10 other Disney parks are listed among the top 25 world attractions. The second-largest US operator, Six Flags, caters for nearly 30 million people. Disney operates on four site clusters in the USA, along with further sites near Tokyo and Paris and in Hong Kong. There are plans for another to be built on mainland China (probably Shanghai) in future years.

Example

Disneyland Resort, Paris

The initial problems the Walt Disney Company faced when expanding its concept into Europe make for an interesting case history in theme park management.

Disney decided to build a park at a site near Paris that is accessible to the largest European market – some 17 million people reside within 2 hours' drive – rather than near Barcelona in Spain, partly due to subsidies promised by the French government. In making this decision, however, Disney's management ignored the factor of the inclement weather of northern Europe, which makes it far more difficult to attract a market in the winter months than is the case in Florida. The management team also misjudged its market. The French resented the encroachment of American culture and initially proved more resistant to the park than the British and German markets, particularly as French tastes were not catered for (Disney failed to serve alcohol in its restaurants, for example, as it does not do so in the USA, although the French traditionally enjoy a glass of wine with their meals). By adding more all-weather attractions and applying for licences to serve alcoholic beverages, Disney was able to improve its appeal to the French, who now make up about half of all visitors. Additional investment in the site has not produced the turnover forecast, however, and the park is struggling to prove its long-term viability.

The clustering and scale of several of these attractions in one region of Florida, around Orlando, has given the European tourism industry the scope to develop package holidays focused on this region and, as a result, this destination has become one of the most popular in the world for long-haul package holidays. Visitors tend to spend several days visiting the parks, which has allowed a huge bed stock – approaching 100,000 rooms – to be constructed.

The Disney empire, with over 107 million visitors to its parks each year, has no direct competition. Its nearest global competitor, Merlin Entertainments Group, attracted 32.2 million in 2007, but it is expanding rapidly and has ambitious plans to expand by creating five new attractions each year. Its properties include Legoland and a majority holding in the Tussauds Group.

Another leading theme park operator in the USA, brewery giant Anheuser-Busch, was planning to put its ten properties on the market at the time of writing, with Merlin a possible bidder. The Walt Disney Company may also soon be challenged by another competitor, however, in the shape of Dubailand, scheduled to be built between 2010 and 2015, which will become the world's largest theme park. It expects to attract around 15 million tourists a year when it is completed in 2015 and will include a number of individual theme parks, among them Universal Studios, the Restless Planet, the Sahara Kingdom and the Falcon City of Wonders.

In Europe, there are in all some 300 parks represented by Europarks, the Federation of National Associations of Leisure Parks and Attractions in Europe. They attract around 180 million visitors each year – the 20 largest together attracted 59 million visitors in 2006. European parks tend to be smaller and have lower levels of investment in both development and marketing than do the Disney parks, but do not attempt to compete directly with them, drawing on mainly national markets instead. The handful of major parks do compete for international visitors, however.

Figure 10.7 identifies the major Continental sites and the larger UK sites. A number of the leading British theme parks attract over a million visitors every year, with Alton Towers in Staffordshire being by far the biggest crowd-puller. Other notable attractions include Chessington World of Adventures, Flamingoland in North Yorkshire, Lightwater Valley near Ripon, North Yorkshire, Thorpe Park in Surrey and Pleasurewood Hills, near Lowestoft in Suffolk. Entry numbers for several of these exceed a million people each year, but it is questionable how many more such major attractions can be built in the UK and still be viable. Several big planned projects in recent years – including the massive Wonderland theme park that was to be part of the redevelopment of the Corby steel mills site – have been abandoned or have not yet proceeded because of difficulty in raising capital and three other important theme parks have closed completely. Britain also suffers from a poor winter season for outside events, so many attractions do not attempt to remain open all year round.

The distinction between a **theme park** and an **amusement park** is not always a clear one, although the former is rather loosely based on some theme, whether geographical, historical or some other such concept. The future is a popular theme as it can allow the development to focus on advanced technology to attract the public. One of the most recent examples in Europe is that of Futuroscope, near Poitiers in France, where imaginative architecture of the future is combined with advanced technology. To cite one example, its theatre seats are fitted with hydraulic jacks that move them in sympathy with what is showing on the screen, so that sporting events such as white-water rafting can be experienced as well as observed. The park attracted over a million visitors in its first year, 95 per cent of whom were French.

European theme park operators are searching constantly for new themes that will draw the crowds. Germany, which has long enjoyed a love affair with America's Wild West (largely through the popular Western novels of Karl May), opened a new park, Silver Lake City, near Berlin in 2004. It is based on the images projected by Hollywood films over the past century.

Figure 10.7 The major theme parks in Europe.

The fascination with espionage guarantees attendance at museums dedicated to this theme. Berlin offers a museum detailing the counter-intelligence campaign against the Stasi (East German secret police), while, in France, plans have been drawn up for a new theme park to be opened south of Lyons that is to be called Spyland. It is expected to include a history of espionage, with accounts of the exploits of the intelligence services and a possible annual espionage film festival.

Before the development of such theming concepts, the predominant aim of the leisure park was to entertain by means of the traditional funfair, with stalls, helter-skelters, candy floss and other trappings that have been familiar for many decades. Later, parks began vying with one another to devise new rides and challenge younger visitors by incorporating ever more frightening 'white-knuckle' experiences in their major centrepieces. With the introduction of the new theme parks, while amusement rides remained an important element, the theme (such as associating the park with popular cartoon characters as in Parc Asterix and Disneyland) heightens the attraction for many. Building on the popularity of film and TV characters among younger visitors is important for a market that is composed chiefly of family groups.

'Crowd pullers' are now a principal ingredient in the promotion of all major parks today, which means ever greater capital investment (of the order of 5 to 10 per cent per annum) is required, particularly in gravity-defying rides. Some indication of their popularity will be seen from Table 10.4, which identifies some of the important rides in the major theme parks. This list is unlikely to be comprehensive for long as new rides are constantly being invented and introduced to better the 'tallest', 'longest' and 'fastest' that currently exist.

Mention should also be made of the success Lego has had in developing its own form of theme park in Europe. The global appeal of this children's building brick toy has enabled the company to expand the brand to its Legoland parks, first in its country of origin, at Billund in Denmark, and, later, to England, at Windsor, Günzburg in Germany,

Table 10.4 Some leading rides in Britain and the rest of the world.

Ride	Park
Apocalypse, Maelstrom and Shockwave	Drayton Manor, Staffordshire
Nemesis, Oblivion and Rita – Queen of Speed	Alton Towers, Staffordshire
Magnum Force	Flamingoland, Kirby Misperton, North Yorkshire
G Force and Jubilee Odyssey	Fantasyland, Skegness, Lincolnshire
MegaFobia	Oakwood Park, Pembrokeshire
Pepsi Max Big One and Grand National	Blackpool Pleasure Beach, Lancashire
Colossus, Tidal Wave, Vortex, Nemesis Inferno, Rush, Slammer, Stealth	Thorpe Park, Surrey
Space Shot	Pleasureland, Southport, Lancashire
Silver Star	Europark, near Rust, Germany
Dodonpa roller coaster	Fujikyu Highland Park, Fuji-Yoshida-shi, Japan
Steel Dragon 2000	Nagashima Spaland, Mie, Japan
Superman the Escape	Six Flags Magic Mountain, Valencia, California, USA
Top Thrill Dragster	Cedar Point Amusement Park, Sandusky, Ohio, USA
Big Shot Stratosphere Tower	Las Vegas, Nevada, USA
SheiKra	Busch Gardens, Florida, USA
Perilous Plunge	Knotts Berry Farm, Buena Park, Los Angeles, California, USA
Adventures of Spiderman	Islands of Adventure, Orlando, Florida, USA
Tonnerre de Zeus	Parc Asterix, near Paris, France
Thunder Coaster	Tusanfryd, Norway

Carlsbad in California and, in 2008, Chicago, Illinois. The sheer scale of these developments is on a level with the major theme parks and in terms of visitor numbers they count among the more important tourism attractions in their countries.

On a much smaller scale, there are innumerable other model village type attractions scattered around Britain, usually based in popular tourist destinations to appeal to visitors as impulse visits. These form just one group of small attractions that tourists enjoy but generally receive little attention from academics or support from public-sector bodies. Other such forms of tourist entertainment include amusement arcades, model railways, waxworks (including the increasingly popular dungeon settings) and similar small commercial exhibitions. They may be indoor or outdoor attractions and, together, make up the largest proportion of the attractions business. It would therefore be wrong to ignore their importance within the organizational structure of the industry, even though, for many, their income may be only a tiny fraction of that of the major amusement parks. Like all the smallest museums, their very existence is tenuous, often depending on the commitment of owner-managers and their families and a voluntary labour force.

Wildlife attractions

Wildlife is a growing attraction for tourists, and the industry has responded in different ways to meet this interest. At one time, the most common way for tourists to see wild animals was in the many zoos that exist in most countries around the world. The keeping of collections of animals goes back at least 2000 years, but the present-day concept of a zoo dates back only to the eighteenth century. In Britain, although zoos are known to predate the turn of the nineteenth century, the founding of the Zoological Society in London by Sir Stamford Raffles at the beginning of that century led to the interest that Victorian England took in caged animals.

Today, there are some 900 established zoos around the world, but attitudes to zoos have changed. People in Western countries have come to consider it cruel to keep animals in captivity. Nevertheless, zoos still enjoy high attendance figures, although not reaching the peaks of 30 years ago, and they are adapting to this change. Now, they stress their curatorial role, preserving rare species of wildlife, rather than displaying animals for the purpose of entertainment. There was a fear at the end of the 1980s, as attendances fell, that London's famous zoo in Regent's Park might be forced to close. Although that fear receded with a massive private investment of capital, this sharpened awareness of zoos as a whole in Britain, renewing interest in visiting them and encouraged the construction of better facilities to keep the animals in more natural settings so they are now less constrained.

With the growth of long-haul travel, more tourists are taking advantage of the opportunity to see these animals in the wild, usually in safari parks. The best-known of these are situated in South and East Africa, as we saw in Figure 9.10 in the previous chapter. Some of these big game parks have become world famous, including Kenya's Masai Mara, Tsavo, Amboseli and Samburu Parks, Tanzania's Serengeti National Park and South Africa's Kruger National Park. The attraction of these parks lies in the opportunity to see big game, such as lions, elephants, leopards, buffalo and rhino – the so-called 'big five' (although poaching is rapidly diminishing numbers of the last of these). All of these parks feature in tour operators' long-haul programmes, although political uncertainty in many African countries (notably Kenya in 2008) and the lack of tourism investment in some has hindered the expansion of tourism to the safari parks in recent years. This has, however, benefited some lesser-known parks in countries such as Botswana.

With the decline in zoo attendance, there have been some efforts to introduce the atmosphere of the safari park in Britain, notably at the Marquess of Bath's property at Longleat in Wiltshire. Running costs for such projects are high as they need to provide maximum security to protect visitors. Another safari park at Windsor was attracting close to a million visitors a year, but still proved a financial failure, closing in 1992.

Example

Seeking the rare animal

Many adventure travellers, having visited the leading wildlife parks around the world, set out to seek the unusual, rare animals in some of the most remote places of the world. An example is the Iriomote Wildcat, of which fewer than 100 are thought to survive. They live on Iriomote Island, Japan – a 35-minute ferry ride from Ishigaki Island. The island's population is just 2325, but tourist numbers have been increasing dramatically over the past 5 years, with more than 405,000 visiting in 2007. Needless to say, with these numbers, opportunities for seeing the wildcat are as remote as the island and some doubt its continued existence.

Source: 'Off Japan, rare wildcat lures tourists', *New York Times*, 17 February 2008.

Another form of wildlife park is the wildfowl reserve. Birdwatching is a popular pastime in Britain, and the Wildfowl Trust at Slimbridge in Gloucestershire has been a model for other sites around the country as birds can be viewed in their natural setting.

Birdwatching also attracts the specialist long-haul market, with tour operators such as Naturtrek and Birdquest among a number offering specialist holidays for the study of bird life, frequently accompanied by well-known ornithology experts who will lecture to clients en route. The appearance of rare birds attracts the enthusiasts. Thousands visit the Lizard in Cornwall every year in the hope of seeing the rare choughs, while it has been estimated that 290,000 annually visit osprey viewing sites in the UK, bringing around £3.5 million to the local economies.

Other attractions, for which tourism is a secondary consideration in some cases, include falconry centres and owl sanctuaries. Sanctuaries for other specific animals have been built in a number of places in Britain, such as the seal sanctuary at Gweek in Cornwall. Sanctuaries, of course, exist to protect and tend to wounded animals, but most are open to visitors, who make a useful contribution, through their admission fees, to the running costs of the project.

Finally, reference should be made in this section to the popularity of aquariums (now more commonly known as sealife centres), both in Britain and elsewhere. The popular revulsion to keeping animals in cages has not yet generally extended to fish (and although there are movements to close down entertainments incorporating captive seawater mammals such as porpoises and dolphins, they remain popular in the USA). Some notable sealife centres have been constructed in Britain, such as the London Aquarium, The Deep in Hull, the National Maritime Aquarium at Plymouth and the National Sealife Centre in Birmingham. Also, plans have been revealed by the National Institution for Research into Aquatic Habitats to build the world's largest aquarium near Stewartby, Bedfordshire. This 40-acre site will be eight times larger than the current world leader in Osaka, Japan.

On the Continent, the Sea Life Centre in Paris and Nausicaa, le Centre Nationale de la Mer, in Boulogne are two popular recent additions in this area. Many such centres have also been constructed in the USA – the one at Monterey in California being particularly notable for both the size of the tanks (one of which includes a full-scale kelp forest) and the fact that there is a unique pen with direct access to the Pacific Ocean, allowing sea otters to swim in to and out of the setting at will.

Cultural tourism

Cultural tourism – however it is defined – is one of the fastest-growing areas of tourism. In its widest definition it encompasses both 'high' and 'low' culture. The so-called 'fine arts' in all their forms – paintings and sculpture, decorative arts, architecture, classical forms of music, theatre and literature – are matched by 'popular culture' attractions, including sport and popular music, along with traditional forms of entertainment such as folk dancing, gastronomy and handicrafts. In postmodern societies, the former divisions between 'high' and 'low' culture have become increasingly artificial and certainly now have little relevance to the study of tourism as the industry has become adept at packaging and popularizing culture in *all* its forms.

France, noted for its dominance in the fine art field, has packaged art trails covering places Cézanne lived and frequented at Aix-en-Provence, Monet's garden at Giverny and areas associated with Gauguin, Manet, Renoir, Dégas, Pissarro and Sisley. Longer tours, too, such as the 'circuit Pissarro–Cézanne' and 'circuit Toulouse-Lautrec', have proved popular with cultural tourists.

Where a place is popularly identified with an author or artist, tourist interest follows automatically, but where such a link is less well established, it can still be built on. The poet Dylan Thomas' disparaging comments about the town and people of Laugharne have not stopped a steady flow of 25,000 visitors annually to the Boathouse where he lived between 1949 and 1953, despite the locals' preference for playing down this link. By contrast, the towns of Rochester and Broadstairs in Kent have both traded on their links with the Victorian author Charles Dickens (see Figure 10.8).

Elsewhere in Britain, numerous other associations exist between literary settings and tourist destinations, with clearly defined 'trails' having been set up, such as those between Thomas Hardy and Wessex, and Laurie Lee and Gloucestershire. Brontë country in Yorkshire offers 'Great British Literary Tours', while the popularity of Jane Austen's books,

Figure 10.8 Bleak House in Broadstairs, Kent, which trades on its association with the novel by Charles Dickens.
(Photo by Chris Holloway.)

fed by a seemingly endless hunger for costume dramas on UK television and in films, has led to high numbers of visitors flocking to locations associated with them. One regional tourist board, South West Tourism, promptly published a map covering no fewer than 89 film and TV locations in six counties.

A discussion of all the different forms of cultural attraction, ranging from 'high' to 'low' culture, would be far too extensive to be examined in any detail here, so you are directed to the many publications that focus on this sector to increase your knowledge of them and the issues arising from each.[6] This chapter serves as an introduction to the topic, highlighting some of the variety of cultural activities available that have become important for tourism.

Museums and art galleries

Both museums and art galleries are visited by huge numbers of tourists each year. In Britain alone, 54.6 million people visited museums and art galleries in 2006. Many are established primarily to serve the needs of the local inhabitants – at least initially – but others have quickly gained international reputations. Examples of the latter include the British Museum in London, the Ashmolean Museum in Oxford, the Louvre in Paris, the Smithsonian Museum in Washington DC and the Museum of Modern Art (MoMA) in New York. The significance of these for tourism is that they can act as a catalyst for visiting a destination and, in some cases, become the major reason for a visit to the destination, especially in cases where there are outstanding exhibitions.

Museums have a very long history and, in Britain, date back to at least the seventeenth century, when some private collectors opened their exhibitions for a fee. John Tradescant's Cabinet of Curiosities provided the foundation for the Ashmolean Museum at Oxford University in 1683. The equally famous Fitzwilliam Museum's art collection at Cambridge did not follow until 1816. In Britain now there are well over 3000 museums and, of the 1300 listed in the *Cambridge Guide to Museums,* there are 180 in London alone.

There are six main categories of museum in Britain.

- *National museums* usually funded directly by the Department for Culture, Media and Sport (DCMS), they include such famous museums as the British Museum, National Gallery, Tate Britain and Tate Modern art galleries, Victoria and Albert Museum, Imperial War Museum and Royal Armouries, Leeds. Certain national museums are funded by the Ministry of Defence, such as the RAF Museum in Hendon and the National Army Museum, both in London.
- *Independent (charitable trust) museums* financed by turnover – the National Motor Museum at Beaulieu being an example.
- *Independent non-charity museums* such as Flambards Museum in Helston, Cornwall. University collections are funded in a variety of ways, drawing on contributions from both public and private sources.
- *Regional museums* funded publicly or by a mix of public and private funding. The DCMS also funds museums such as the Geffrye and Horniman Museums in London and the Museum of Science and Industry in Manchester.
- *Local authority museums* such as the Cotswold Countryside Museum in Gloucester and the Georgian House and Red Lodge Museums owned by Bristol City Council.
- *Small, private museums* these depend entirely on private funding.

Museums have experienced two boom periods in recent history. The first of these was during the period between 1970 and the mid-1980s, when many of them were able to take advantage of government grants, coupled with charitable status, which meant that they avoided paying tax; and, later, especially in the lead up to the millennium celebrations, through Millennium Commission funding or Lottery grants. In the initial stage, a large number of redundant buildings, ideal for converting into museums, became available. The nostalgia boom and a generally positive view towards urban renewal and heritage all encouraged new museums to open. In the second stage, though, funding tended to favour larger projects.

The problem for those who manage museums is that the initial capital investment is not the only financial consideration. Many collections are donated or gifts of money are made in order to establish a museum, but steadily rising operating costs are seldom met by increases in revenue and, after the first two or three years, during which time the museum has novelty value, attendance figures slump. As new museums are opened, so the available market to visit them is more thinly spread. Museums have also been badly hit in recent years by the consequences of the Education Reform Act, which has made the financing of educational visits – the core business for many museums – more difficult.

Many museum curators argue in favour of subsidies, on the grounds that their museums help to bring tourists to an area and, once there, they can be encouraged to spend. Certainly, clusters of museums and other complementary attractions, such as shops, do give rise to greater numbers of tourists. The Castlefield site in Manchester is a good example of a 'critical mass' of attractions sited close together, making it an attractive day out. Conference and exhibition halls have long been underwritten by local authorities on just these grounds, but they are much more constrained financially than in the past and, in some cases, have been forced to reduce the support they formerly provided to the museums in their territory. This has led to winter closures in some cases or more restricted times of opening.

Example

The Leach Pottery

In more recent years, crafts have become recognized as valued forms of the arts, with leading crafts-people being hallowed nationally, notably in Japan.

The British potter Bernard Leach studied with some of the outstanding Japanese potters. He died in 1979 and is today recognized as one of the leading practitioners of this art.

He began working with ceramics at his cottage in St Ives, Cornwall, in the 1920s and, after his death, his home became a place of pilgrimage for many cultural tourists. In 2003, however, the cottage was put on the market. An outcry followed, with a public appeal for funds to save the building as a national heritage site. Numerous sources of funding were tapped, in addition to public donations, including:

- £450,000 from the European Regional Development Fund
- £100,000 from the Rural Cornwall and Isles of Scilly Partnership, which deliver funding on behalf of the South West Regional Development Agency
- £610,000 from the Heritage Lottery Fund
- £98,685 from the Arts Council, England South West.

As a result, the cottage has been restored as a national heritage museum, as well as an educational resource for postgraduate students. Leach's kiln, which helped to revolutionize the way UK potters fire their work, has been included in the restoration and a new museum exhibition space has been built. The organization also mentors business start-ups and provides studio space for talented potters.

The studio and museum opened in 2008 and complements the St Ives home of famed sculptor Barbara Hepworth, strengthening the cultural appeal of this seaside resort, which lies in the heart of one of England's most deprived regions – the sole region in the UK now qualifying for EU regional aid.

Further information: **www.leachproject.co.uk**

Museums have become increasingly self-sufficient and their curatorial role is now less significant than their marketing one. The national museums in London were briefly obliged to introduce charges – or at the very least they 'suggested contributions' – in the 1990s, resulting in a very sharp drop in attendance. Those that did not introduce charges benefited. Those that did decide to charge, however, were able to invest in refurbishing them, which, with government subsidies alone, would not have been possible. Since the obligation to charge has been removed, the galleries have experienced an upsurge in attendance and it is notable that seven of the top ten most visited attractions in Britain are museums or art galleries (see Table 10.5).

Table 10.5 ALVA attractions with over one million admissions in 2007.

Attraction	Total visits
Blackpool Pleasure Beach	5,500,000
British Museum	5,418,265 (pt c)*
Tate Modern	5,191,840
National Gallery	4,159,487
Natural History Museum	3,600,119
Science Museum	2,714,021
Victoria & Albert Museum	2,435,300
Tower of London	2,064,126 (c)
National Maritime Museum	1,695,739
St Paul's Cathedral	1,623,881 (pt c)
National Portrait Gallery	1,607,767
Tate Britain	1,593,277
Royal Botanical Gardens, Kew	1,427,096 (pt c)
British Library	1,355,423
Chester Zoo	1,335,773 (c)
Edinburgh Castle	1,229,703 (c)
London Zoo	1,132,366 (c)
Eden Project, Cornwall	1,068,244 (c)
Canterbury Cathedral	1,068,244 (pt c)
Westminster Abbey	1,058,362 (pt c)

Key: (c) charge for entry (pt c) charge for entry to some areas or exhibitions.
* The British Museum announced in mid-2008 that it had overtaken Blackpool Pleasure Beach, which had 6.04 million visitors in the preceding year. That was partly accounted for by the popularity of the Terracotta Warriors exhibition, which attracted 850,000 visitors.
Source: Association of Leading Visitor Attractions – see **www.alva.org.uk/visitor_statistics**

As a result of the reduction or withdrawal of public funding, museums have been obliged to become increasingly commercial in their approach. Buildings are redesigned to ensure that all visitors exit via the shop, and investigations are made into what sells or fails to sell, and into price-sensitivity. Galleries are hired for private functions, sponsorship is sought to finance exhibitions – and sometimes even whole galleries (such as the Annenberg and Hutong Galleries at the British Museum). Catering also has become an important money-raiser, with increasing emphasis placed on the location and design of cafés and restaurants. All principal museums in Britain are now expected to engage in fund-raising, both publicly and through their memberships and friends' associations.

Museums not sited close to major centres of population or with poor accessibility generally find it difficult to attract tourists in large numbers. One notable exception, to which several references have been made already, is the Guggenheim in Bilbao, which rapidly became an authentic cultural icon soon after its construction.

Example

The Guggenheim museums and their value to tourism

The Guggenheim museums have had particular success in attracting tourists, partly for their contents, but more notably for their architectural merit.

The construction of the Guggenheim in Bilbao was a deliberate move on the part of the local authorities to promote the city as an attractive place to visit. The proposed museum received very strong public-sector support and significant financial aid from the Guggenheim Foundation, which had the foresight to contract an outstanding architect, Frank Gehry, to design the unconventional building.

The result is that tourists beat a path to its door. There were over 1.3 million visitors in its first year, even though Bilbao had never been a traditional tourist destination and had, at least at that point, little else to attract tourists. Bilbao now enjoys success as a strong short-break destination.

There are currently Guggenheim museums in New York, Bilbao, Venice, Berlin and Las Vegas, and Frank Gehry has been retained to complete a sixth in Abu Dhabi. This is designed to put the UAE firmly on the cultural tourist map and will form part of a group of four world-class museums to be clustered on Saadiyat Island. Completion of the new Guggenheim is anticipated in 2011.

To attract new audiences and bring back previous visitors, many museums are moving away from the concept of 'objects in glass cases' in favour of better interpretation and more active participation by the visitors. New techniques include guides dressed in period costume, audio visual displays, self-guided trails using recordings, reconstructions of the past and interactive programmes that provide opportunities for hands-on experience.

In the kitchen of the oldest house in Toronto, to take one example, the guide demonstrates the making of soap, provides souvenirs of the finished product to the visitors and reveals that the soap can be eaten, too! Some museums are fully interactive, such as Explore at Bristol Museum, which is designed to explain science to those who do not know too much about it by giving them the opportunity to become involved in practical experiments. At the Big Pit Mining Museum in Blaenavon – a former colliery transformed into a mining museum in 1980 and now a World Heritage site – former miners act as guides, providing vividly illustrated tours that draw on their own former experiences in the mines. In a similar vein, former inmates interned on Robben Island under South African apartheid laws now address visitors to the island museum and show them the cell where Nelson Mandela was interned (see Figure 10.9).

An example of a 'living history' museum can be found at Llancaiach Fawr Manor, a sixteenth-century fortified house in the South Wales valleys. Here, actor/interpreters (more correctly referred to on the Continent as 'animateurs'), dressed in costumes of the period, act as 'below stairs' staff, guiding visitors around the site, using the language and speech patterns of the time and authentically recreating the year 1645.

It is important to distinguish a museum from other attractions. Many museums, for example, are the former homes of famous people and the trustees have a curatorial and research role in safeguarding and investigating documents of its famous owner, as well as encouraging tourist trade for commercial reasons. A good example of this is Graceland, the former home of Elvis Presley in Memphis, Tennessee. Long after the star's death, it continues to attract huge crowds of fans who come to see his house, his former possessions and his grave – especially in the year 2005, the seventieth anniversary of his birth. Graceland has become one of the major tourist attractions in the United States and is listed in the National Register of Historic Places. With over 700,000 visitors annually, it is now second only to the White House itself in terms of the number of visitors it receives each year.

Figure 10.9 A former political prisoner addresses visitors to the prison where Nelson Mandela was incarcerated, on Robben Island, South Africa.
(Photo by Chris Holloway.)

Religious tourism

Travel for religious purposes tends to be grouped among the 'miscellaneous' forms of tourism, falling outside the central purposes of leisure or business. It would be unfair to dismiss it lightly, however, as it represents a most important feature in the worldwide movement of tourists. The UNWTO estimates that there are around 330 million visits each year to key religious sites, with Our Lady of Guadalupe, in Mexico, the most visited shrine. All told, religious tourism is thought to contribute around £18 billion annually to these destinations.

Millions who follow the faith of Islam make the obligatory once-in-a-lifetime pilgrimage to Mecca, the birthplace of Mohammed in Saudi Arabia. If taken at the time of Ramadan, this is known as the Great Pilgrimage, or, Hadj. At other times, Umrah, or the Lesser Pilgrimage, attracts tourists for 11 months of the year. Some two million Muslims visit Mecca and Medina every year, of whom around 25,000 are from Britain; a further 100,000 British travel for the Umrah. While these trips are seen as an obligation arising out of the Islamic faith rather than a pleasure trip, they nevertheless bring substantial financial and commercial benefits to the country that caters to these tourists' needs. In Tongi, Bangladesh, the three-day Bishwa Ijtema gathering for blessings drew more than three million Muslim visitors from 80 countries in 2007.

Hindus are drawn to Amritsar and Varanasi in India, Buddhists to Shikoku in Japan, while Mount Kailas in China draws both Buddhists and Hindus to its peak to shed sins. Other multifaith sites include Jerusalem, which draws Christians, Jews and Muslims alike, due to its historical importance to all three religions. The political upheavals in that region, however, have discouraged the large numbers who would have been expected in earlier years. Bethlehem in particular, the claimed birthplace of Christ, being on the Palestinian side of the border, has suffered enormously from the slump in tourism to the region.

Prominent religious destinations for Christian pilgrims include the Vatican, St Katherine's monastery (often linked with visits to Petra in Jordan for package tours), Assisi and Lourdes (with one of the highest concentrations of hotels in Europe). The second most visited Christian site is thought currently to be the remains of Padre Pio of Pietrelcina in Italy, with around 7 million visiting his shrine at San Giovannia Rotondo each year. Indeed, religious visits have become so important in Italy that monasteries in that country are applying to either sell off their buildings to developers or take in high-paying guests as the numbers of monks and nuns decline. In Lazio alone, there were 257 applications to turn religious sites into tourism-related businesses in 2007.

Other countries also benefit from religious tourists. Millions also visit the site of a 1981 vision of the Virgin Mary at Medjugorje, in Bosnia and Herzegovina.

Example

The pilgrim trails

The Santiago Way – a pilgrim path that follows the 800-kilometre route to St James' shrine in Santiago de Compostela in Spain – was revived in the 1980s. It has since proved a popular pilgrimage for devout modern Christians, with some 180,000 making this journey of faith every year. As a result, the Via Francigena pilgrim trail from Canterbury to Rome, founded in the tenth century, is to be revived, along with the Via Carolingia, taking pilgrims from Aachen in Germany to Rome. The need for shelter and food en route and, perhaps, to take in some sights at the same time, ensures that there is a commercial interest in the routes for the tourism industry.

Many observers believe that popular culture gives expression to emotions formerly reserved for faith. So we see secular mass tourists visit the graves of their idols or sites with which they are associated or met their death.

Specialist operators exist to provide services for religious tourism. Tours are often accompanied by spiritual leaders and, in one sense, can be defined as educational tourism, but in other instances (such as pilgrimages to Lourdes, to seek intercession for a cure), the motive comes closer to that of health tourism.

It is open to debate as to which category the religious theme parks that are now appearing should be put in. First introduced in the United States, their appeal is now spreading and plans to construct a Christian theme park in Yorkshire – to be known as Ark Alive – were announced in 2005, subject to funds becoming available – the cost being estimated as around £144 million. Part educational, part missionary, part entertainment and quasi-history, these parks appear to be finding a new market for the curious and the committed alike.

Shopping

Shopping plays an important role in tourism. While retailing is not normally considered a sector of the industry, tourist purchases make up a considerable part of the revenue of many shops and in resorts shops may be entirely or very largely dependent on the tourist trade. Shops selling postcards, souvenirs or local crafts are often geared specifically to the needs of visitors and, out of season, may close down due to lack of demand.

Cross-border tourism is fuelled by shopping expeditions and, where large discrepancies in prices are noted on each side of the border, authorities often impose limits on purchases that can be transported back into the home country. For several years, the German and Austrian governments were concerned about cross-border shopping into Poland, the Czech and Slovak Republics and Hungary. Now that these countries have joined the EU, the concern has shifted, the governments in those countries now being concerned about shopping expeditions into the Ukraine and Russian Federation (although an obligation to obtain visas for entry into the Russian Federation acts as a hindrance). The EU's limit on importation of goods from non-EU countries, long limited to £145, increased to £340 in 2009. When there is a weak dollar, however, goods bought in the USA are still cheap, even after paying duty. With virtually no limit on the transfer of goods between EU countries, shopping expeditions from England to Calais across the Channel, from Helsinki to Tallinn across the Baltic and from Germany into Poland across the Oder are a major factor in the growth of tourism between these countries.

Tourist cities such as London, Paris, Rome and New York owe much of their popularity to the quality of their shops, greatly benefiting from the flood of visitors they receive from overseas, many of whom come to take advantage of sales periods or beneficial rates of exchange. To take one recent example, the relative value of the pound against the dollar was responsible for a substantial increase in shopping expeditions from Britain to New York in the run-up to Christmas in 2007. Similarly, many Britons make their way to the French supermarkets to stock up on alcohol and cigarettes, as well as cheaper food. Large department stores such as Saks Fifth Avenue and Bloomingdales in New York, Kaufhaus des Westens (KaDeWe) in Berlin (claiming to be the largest store in the world) and Harrods in London are heavily dependent on visitors spending their money with them and, of course, expenditure on shopping is an important feature in the tourism balance of payments.

The downside in small towns popular with tourists is that shops with products appealing to tourists can squeeze out those serving the more basic needs of their residents, simply because they can afford spiralling rates and rents.

Increasingly, shopping is being combined with other forms of leisure in the development of shopping malls, which have become virtual mini-towns in their own right, attracting huge numbers of visitors prepared to pass several hours enjoying themselves in an environment that encourages people to spend. Apart from shopping, amenities include restaurants, family entertainment and performance venues, all under cover (often underground) to allow year-round visits – which is important in northern cities during the winter. While China contains some of the world's largest shopping malls (the South China Mall in Dongguan, said to be the world's largest, is over 7.1 million square feet in area, while the Golden Resources Mall in Beijing, at 6 million square feet, offers a landscape embracing theme parks, bridges, giant windmills, pyramids, artificial rivers and a copy of Paris' Arc de Triomphe), those in the West are almost as impressive. For instance, the Mall of America, built in 1992 at Bloomington, Minneapolis, claims to be the second most visited site in the USA – some 40 million visitors a year. At 4.2 million square feet and offering 400 shops, 45 restaurants, 14 cinemas, a 7-acre amusement park and a miniature golf course, the site provides everything that the leisure shopper could hope for. It attracts a global market and, most notably, brings in shoppers from both European and Asian cities. The enormous West Edmonton Mall in Canada, covering an area of 48 city blocks in downtown Edmonton, vies with this mall to draw consumers from all over the world, boasting more than 800 shops, 110 eating establishments and 7 themed attractions. There are onsite hotels and events are mounted throughout the year.

These are merely examples of the largest in a huge variety of 'leisure malls' designed to attract visitors. In all, America boasts some 228 malls, attracting 55 million visitors annually, with a spend exceeding £8 billion. Some of these malls have more than 200 shops. Notably, eight of them have been built within easy reach of the theme parks at Orlando, Florida, and are clearly aimed to attract the tourist market. New York is constructing the first 'Green Mall'. DestiNY USA will cost in excess of £20 billion and cover an area of 800 acres. It will be the largest man-made structure in the world when it opens in 2009.

In Britain, some towns have copied the American concept and, in recent instances, have even gone as far as emulating the architecture of that continent, with New England-style themes, such as that found at the Bicester Village shopping centre near Oxford. Bicester, and similar malls in Swindon, Wiltshire and Ellesmere Port, South Wirral, have focused on the concept of 'designer outlets', which sell upmarket products, bringing high-spend shoppers from some distances away. Others focus on size and choice, although these are not comparable in size to those in North America or the Far East. Currently, the largest UK shopping malls are:

- Metro Centre, Gateshead   2,000,000 square feet
- Merry Hill, Dudley, near Birmingham   1,700,000 square feet
- Bluewater, Kent   1,650,000 square feet
- Meadowhall, Sheffield   1,420,000 square feet
- Lakeside, Thurrock   1,400,000 square feet

Bluewater in Kent and the Merry Hill Centre near Birmingham are examples of malls that serve large urban areas, attracting shoppers away from the town centres. Because of the range of leisure facilities they also offer, they attract large numbers of 'tourist shoppers' who travel considerable distances to enjoy a mix of shopping with a day out to the country.

'Factory outlet' malls such as those at Street in Somerset and Festival Park at Ebbw Vale in Wales offer direct sales to the public from manufacturers at discounts attractive enough to bring in tourists up to two hours' or more driving distance away. This is forcing local authorities to find ways to make their own shopping centres more attractive to visitors again. This requires substantial investment in reconstruction and, where appropriate, the provision of adequate parking. Covent Garden in London is a good example of where this has been successfully achieved. Some years ago, it was transformed from the site of a former fruit, flower and vegetable market and now combines the appeal of tastefully restored nineteenth-century buildings with a shopping mall in the heart of London. The added attraction of round-the-clock events, such as buskers, has made this shopping area an important addition to the visitor attractions in Britain's capital.

Some towns have established a reputation for their bookshops and, building on this, they have each marketed their town as a 'booktown' to avid book collectors and browsers. Hay-on-Wye was among the first to build on this kind of reputation, in 1961, but there are now around 20 such towns in existence in the USA, Japan, Malaysia, across the Continent and at Wigtown in Scotland. Two purpose-built booktowns are Fjaerland in Norway and Blaenavon in Wales – the latter already possessing World Heritage status for its Big Pit mine.

Example

Iconic shopping?

Shopping takes a new turn in Austria. Mpreis is a chain of 130 supermarkets that are fast becoming tourist attractions in their own right, due to the cutting-edge architecture employed in their design. Both the buildings and their interiors have been designed with an eye to attracting more than the usual local shoppers. Good media publicity has ensured that visitors are encouraged to travel considerable distances to observe these buildings close-up.

Source: **www.mpreis.at**

Souvenirs

No study of tourist shopping would be complete without a look at the role of souvenirs – essential items for most visitors. The collection of souvenirs as mementos of one's visit has a long history. Certainly, both Greek and Roman tourists were noted for their collections of memorabilia from their journeys and, later, during the period of the Grand Tours, prestigious souvenirs collected by aristocratic travellers would invariably include Italian landscape paintings and archaeological 'finds'. Historians have commented on how souvenirs were collected from the earliest days of travel in North America, when 'items cut from local rock or wood, beaded moccasins, baskets and . . . miniature canoes' featured prominently.[7]

Today, we can divide souvenirs into two groups – mementos picked up by tourists, (often of little value in themselves but representative of the sites visited) and those bought commercially from shops or local traders. The former will include items such as pebbes and shells collected on the beach, pressed flowers or leaves from jungles and parks, lava from volcanic eruptions or small shards of broken pottery that abound in places such as the area surrounding former Chinese emperors' tombs. For the most part, the collection of these items is harmless, although removing plants, flowers or seeds from parks and gardens is not an act to be encouraged – indeed, it is banned in areas where plants are under threat. Edelweiss in Switzerland and cacti in Arizona, for example, have been protected by laws in this way. Similar laws prevent the collection of rare stones or fossilized trees such as those found in the Petrified Forest in Arizona. It was not uncommon in earlier centuries for travellers to chisel off small chunks of stone from monuments such as Roman amphitheatres and the Egyptian Sphinx or, at very least, to deface them with graffiti. In our more enlightened times, however, this practice is frowned on and diminishing.

Commercial souvenirs are not only essential items of shopping for many tourists but also for some, such as the Japanese, gifts are culturally obligatory. Thus tourists buy mementos for themselves and for friends and relatives. This is one explanation for the relatively high spend of Japanese tourists abroad.

Some commercial souvenirs are bestowed on visitors without charge, such as the leis, garlands of flowers placed around the necks of visitors arriving in Hawaii. Visitors to China are often given small souvenirs of their visit, both while travelling within the country and when visiting sites such as the Great Wall in China.

Example

The Dala horse (*Dalahäst*)

Carving horses has been a traditional folk art in Sweden since at least 1624. The Dalecarlian horse in its present form has been hand-carved by the farmers of the Dalarna district in Sweden for over 200 years, painted in colours that are associated with traditional 'curbits' patterns.

In 1928, two brothers – Nils and Janne Olsson – began producing colourful copies of the horse in their shed at Hemslöjd on the edge of Lake Siljan, near the village of Nusn. A giant model displayed at the New York World's Fair in 1939 popularized the design abroad, leading to a strong export market. It was not long before the horses, which are now a symbol of Sweden, were by far the most popular souvenirs for tourists to bring home.

The horses' importance to the Swedish economy is such that their production and design are now carefully controlled by the authorities. The most popular colour is the red traditionally associated with the Falaröd red paint used on houses in the region. The horses are sold at prices ranging from SEK54 for a miniature just 3 centimetres high to as much as SEK8250 for the biggest model, at 75 centimetres high.

Further information: **www.nohemslojd.se**

The transmogrification of cheap baubles into indigenous craft items purchased by tourists as souvenirs is characteristic of recent tourism, exemplified by such items as straw donkeys and flamenco dolls from Spain, brass Eiffel Towers from Paris, straw hats from the Caribbean Islands or Bali and bamboo models of cormorant fishers from China. While widely derided, these mementos still have a place in many tourists' homes and, in the minds and emotions of their purchasers, they retain an association with the places from which they originated. The name 'airport art' is frequently used for such debased crafts, which are often on sale to tourists at airports, but the popularity of these items cannot be denied. They do also make a valuable contribution to the economies of the countries where they are purchased.

Finally, the significance of postcards as essential purchases while abroad should be noted. Since the advent of photography, the desire to send pictures of destinations visited home to family, friends and neighbours has become a well-established ritual, the motives for which have frequently been questioned. Whether for social contact, out of a sense of obligation to those less fortunate, to demonstrate one-upmanship or simply to inform, the drive to send cards is universal and, particularly among the developing countries, they are cherished by those receiving them, being pinned up on the walls of homes, offices and bars, signifying to others possession of a wide circle of well-travelled friends. Although modern technology now allows us to send home snaps taken on a mobile phone, there is something reassuring about the continuing popularity of the old-fashioned postcard. In Britain, 135 million postcards are sent each year, according to the Royal Mail in 2008 – an increase of 30 million in five years. The permanence of a postcard is also part of its attraction.

Gastronomic tourism

VisitBritain's research has shown that half of all visitors to the UK cite food and drink as being important to their holiday experience. Of course, eating and drinking have always been part of the enjoyment of a holiday, enhancing it where the food and drink in question are exceptional and/or exotic, as is often the case on holidays abroad. The extent to which Britons have become more adventurous in their eating and drinking habits in their own country can be directly attributed to their experiences as tourists abroad. There are instances, however, where the food and drink become the principal purpose of the trip, whether a short break or longer holiday. The reputation of French food and drink, to take one example, has led to this becoming a key attraction for many tourists of that country. The importance of good – or at least reliable – cuisine abroad anywhere is often a priority concern, not least as a measure of health and safety.

Countries with well-established reputations for their food or drink have ensured that these attractions are promoted prominently in their tourism campaigns, whether informally or in the form of package tours. A *dégustation* (tasting) in France is a widely recognized element in any tour of French vineyard regions, while distilleries in Scotland, breweries in Belgium, Germany and Denmark and bodegas in southern Spain have welcomed tourists by giving them opportunities to sample and purchase their products (see, for example, Figure 12.8). Enhanced awareness of good food has led to more flexibility in packages, allowing tourists to 'eat around', either in partner hotels or associated restaurants.

Stimulated by programmes on television, a much greater interest is taken today in preparing attractive and healthy meals. A number of leading chefs, particularly those having made their names on TV, have established cookery courses and these attract gastronomy tourists from afar. Examples include:

- Carla Tomasi, in Umbria and Sicily in Italy
- Alain Ducasse, a three Michelin star chef, in Paris, France
- Ferran Adrià, in Seville, Spain

- Rosemary Barron in Santorini, Greece
- Darina Allen in Cork, Ireland
- Rick Stein's Padstow Seafood School, England.

There is also a growing association between food and tourism within the UK and the days when sticks of rock, and fish and chips were the best-known food products and the quality of food served in hotels and restaurants was actually a disincentive to visit the country are long gone. Michelin starred restaurants, gastropubs, farmers' markets, even English wines, are now gaining a reputation among overseas visitors. Regional tourism bodies, in response, have not been slow to adopt food as an attraction in its own right. At various points in the recent history of tourism, authorities have promoted 'Taste of England/Wales/Scotland' campaigns, culminating in an 'Enjoy England, Taste England' promotion by VisitBritain that prominently features famous British chefs. Similarly, today, no museum or heritage attraction of any size is without its restaurant and shop, many of the latter selling food products grown or manufactured locally, such as Pontefract cakes, Kendal mint cake and local ice-creams.

Example

Ludlow, Shropshire

Ludlow in Shropshire has a population of just 10,000, but has succeeded in establishing an international reputation for the quality of its food. It has several outstanding restaurants (two with Michelin stars) and many fine local shops, including no fewer than six butchers selling organic locally produced meats.

In 1995, a three-day food and drink festival was launched, including an ale trail, festival loaves, cooking demonstrations and a popular regular feature, the 'sausage trail'. The event has since become an important annual event in the tourism calendar, attracting around 17,000 visitors. Food quality is monitored carefully to ensure consistency.

There is now some danger that it will become a victim of its own success, as it draws many thousands of visitors into an already popular country town that is within easy reach of the heavily populated Midlands. The introduction of park and ride schemes during the event have helped to reduce the worst of the transport problems, however.

Interest in gastronomic tourism has been boosted recently by the development of the 'slow food' movement. This was initiated by an Italian journalist in 1986 who, distressed by the invasion of fast food there, determined to reinstate a concern for good traditional regional food. The slow food movement has spread rapidly through Europe and now organizes tastings, themed dinners and visits, collecting and disseminating information about food and drink. Membership has risen to over 80,000, with *convivia* (branches) all over the world, including 40 in Britain.

Britain is just one of a number of countries now promoting food festivals as key events in the tourism calendar. Apart from Ludlow, there are food festivals in Nantwich and Abergavenny in the UK, while, in regions noted for particular food or drink products, events are mounted to celebrate their harvest – or simply to provide an excuse to widen their products' appeal. Examples include:

- Great British cheese festival, Cardiff, Wales
- Feria du Riz, Arles, France, celebrating rice dishes
- Galway Oyster Festival, Ireland

- I'Primi d'Italia, Foligno, Italy, celebrating first courses
- Truffle Festival, Alba, Italy
- Shrimp Festival, Honfleur, France
- Onion Festival, Weimar, Germany
- Chestnut Festival, Mourjou en Chataigneraie, France
- Baltic Herring Festival, Helsinki, Finland.

These are just a few examples of the autumn food festivals held in Europe, and it will be seen that the medium gives scope for an almost endless variety of activities centred on food and drink in some shape or form.

Other attractions

The scope for providing new attractions to feed the insatiable appetites of tourists is never-ending and it would be quite impossible to cover the subject fully in a single chapter. Sometimes attractions are unique to a destination, but share some common features with those in other areas or countries, thus offering scope for creating joint marketing schemes or twinning. An example of this is the Walled Towns Friendship Circle, established as a marketing association in 1992 by a group of European towns that benefit from one characteristic tourist attraction: an encircling fortification wall. Others depend on a unique feature of the district, coupled with an imaginative initiative in marketing it. For example, after the discovery of Cleopatra's sunken city adjacent to Alexandria Harbour, packages were organized to the site to allow tourists to dive and explore the ruins.

Diving, in fact, has immense appeal as an activity undertaken when on holiday. This is in line with the growth in activity holidays generally and some of the more extreme activities associated with it include ice-diving, iceberg wall dives, mine diving (exploring flooded mineshafts) and wreck diving. Examples of the latter include:

- Truk Lagoon, Micronesia, where over 60 shipwrecks from the 1944 Japanese fleet, including the Fujikawa Maru, a 7000-ton freighter, offer ideal opportunities for under-water exploring
- Bikini Atoll, in the Marshall Islands, which has over 40 World War II wrecks to explore
- Pensacola, Florida, where the USS Oriskany was deliberately sunk 23 metres off the coast to provide the largest artificial reef in the world
- Vanuatu, in the Pacific, where lies the SS President Coolidge, a former liner and troopship.

If all that underwater activity is too extreme, a more relaxing opportunity is provided in the form of undersea scootering, with Bob (breathing observation bubble) trips available to see fish close up, in a number of resorts, including Tenerife, in the Canary Islands, St Thomas, in the US Virgin Islands, and Cancún, Mexico. No diving experience is necessary!

In general, the attractions we have been examining in this chapter up to this point have been permanent sites, available to visitors at any time of the year. We will now turn to examine attractions of a more temporary nature, either arranged specifically to encourage tourism or sufficiently attractive to encourage tourists as well as locals to visit the site.

Events

Tourists will also visit a place in order to participate in, or observe, an event. In some cases, the events occur regularly and with some frequency (for example, the Changing of the Guard in London). In others, the events are intermittent, perhaps annually or even less frequently (such as arts festivals – the Venice Bienniale for example, held every two years, the four-yearly Olympic Games or the Floriade flower festival, which takes place in a different Dutch city every decade). In still other cases, there may be ad hoc arrangements to take advantage of a particular occasion. Such arrangements can last for as little as a few hours (a Christmas pageant or street festival, say) or many months (events associated with the cities of culture award or those organized around a historic anniversary, such as Maritime Britain, commemorating the bicentennial anniversary of the Battle of Trafalgar in 1805).

Anniversaries are a crucial catalyst, whether the anniversary is of a past event, as in Trafalgar, or the birth or death of famous figures from the past. Tourism authorities will invariably look towards the fiftieth, sixtieth anniversaries or beyond and plan suitable events up to five years in advance. The sixtieth anniversary of the ending of World War II in 2005 is a case in point and it was exploited to the full both commercially and politically.

If a centenary or even greater anniversary is involved, and the individual concerned was internationally famous, this provides an excuse for holding a major festival in their home town or country to attract foreign tourists. The 250th anniversary of Mozart's death in 2006, for example, offered scope for a worldwide celebration, not least in his home town of Salzburg.

Example

Kaliningrad, Russia

The Russian enclave of Kaliningrad provided a curious opportunity for joint festivities in 2005 when the Germans celebrated the seven hundred and fiftieth anniversary of the founding of 'their' town, Konigsberg (the former name for the town), while the Russians celebrated the sixtieth anniversary of its fall to the Soviet army. Political compromise allowed the two countries to mark the occasion separately with renovation work. The Germans paid for the renovation of the cathedral, while the Russians built a new Orthodox church and opened a space gallery to celebrate the number of cosmonauts who grew up in the area.

Events will draw people to an area that otherwise may have little to attract them. They may be mounted to increase the number of visitors to a destination or help spread tourism demand to the shoulder seasons. One interesting example of this is the costume events mounted by the Sealed Knot Society in England – a voluntary body with an interest in English history of the Civil War period, which, inter alia, recreates battle scenes on the original sites, drawing very large audiences (see Figure 10.10).

Certain forms of event will be likely to attract a market consisting of more older or wealthier people than young people. These groups are more likely to have the freedom to choose the time of their travel and, indeed, may even wish to avoid the crowds that are common in the peak seasons. Some off-peak events with these groups have been so successful that the destination has managed to turn a low winter season into a peak attraction. In Canada, the Quebec City Winter Carnival is a case in point.

There is, of course, a direct relationship between the degree of attractiveness of the event and the distances visitors are willing to travel to visit it. Some events, such as sports, will have global appeal, while the appearance of top pop singers and bands at stadiums holding many thousands of fans will be marketed internationally as a package to include travel and hotel accommodation.

The variety of festivals and events held around the world is enormous. Even sites as inhospitable as the Arctic in winter can attract visitors with appropriate events. In Kemi

Figure 10.10 A civil war re-enactment at the Piece Hall, Halifax, West Yorkshire.
(Photo by Chris Holloway.)

and Rovaniemi, Finland (both close to the Arctic Circle), an annual Snow Show includes art installations created by leading sculptors, as well as snowmobile and husky riding. Visitors can stay at the Snow Castle, an ice hotel. The staging of events in winter to bring in the off-season market is increasingly apparent. Throughout Europe, Christmas markets – a concept that originated in Germany and is still immensely popular there – have spread, to a point that numerous similar markets are now organized in British towns and cities. The market at Lincoln, the largest in the UK, draws 300,000 visitors annually.

This section has dealt with events aimed essentially at leisure travellers, but, of course, it must be remembered that events such as trade exhibitions and conferences are equally important for business travellers. This aspect of business travel is discussed in detail in Chapter 11, but it is worth mentioning here that many fairs, such as international expos – major but infrequent events – attract both business and leisure visitors. Often used as showcases to promote a country or its products, many of these are open to both trade and the general public and, if the appeal is strong enough, the destination can benefit from the fact that the markets it attracts are often high-spend international tourists willing to pay high gate fees, as well as inflated hotel prices for the duration of the fair. The success of many popular events can be jeopardized by greed, however, and overcharging by hotels, though widespread at events such as the Olympic Games, can both discourage some visitors and effect long-term damage on the reputation of the destination.

Smaller, but still significant, events capable of boosting the local economy are prominent features of many towns and villages around the world. Some have very long traditions. In Britain, ancient fairs continue to play a role in attracting visitors. Many trace their origins to the Middle Ages, often linked to the horse fairs organized by gypsies, and a strong element of Romany culture survives at these sites. Notable examples include the Ballymena Fair in Northern Ireland, the Appleby Fair in Cumbria, the Stow Fair in Gloucestershire and the Goose Fair in Nottingham.

In all countries where tourism is efficiently organized, events are mounted throughout the year to increase the flow of tourists. In France, festivals number in the thousands and, in 2007, included major sports events such as the Rugby World Cup, Tour de France and the French Formula 1 race, along with a variety of film festivals led by that in Cannes, an International Garden Festival and, of course, numerous cuisine festivals, including the Bocuse d'Or World Cuisine Contest and such exotica as the Festival of the Pig and the World Pastry Cup. To celebrate the arrival of the Beaujolais Nouveau, there were no fewer than 120 local festivals to choose from!

Arts festivals

Arts festivals, an important aspect of cultural tourism, have a long history in many countries, arising out of cultural and traditional festivals that often have local associations. In Britain alone, well over 500 arts festivals are held every year, lasting from two days to several weeks, and they attract some three million people, spending over £1 billion. More than half of these have been founded since 1980 and over 60 per cent are professionally managed. Most depend on sponsorship and financial support from the local authority. The leading events in the UK, in terms of revenue achieved, include the Edinburgh Festival and Fringe Festival and the BBC Promenade Concerts.

Major exhibitions draw an international audience of mass tourists. Thus, 1.1 million visitors attended the Barnes Foundation's exhibition 'A Century of Impressionism' held at the Musée d'Orsay in Paris in 1993, while a later showing of the Barnes Foundation's collection in Germany drew such crowds that the museum exhibiting the collection stayed open all night (a practice that has led to longer opening hours in Germany. Berlin has 'Die lange Nacht der Museen' twice a year, when all museums are open until at least midnight). Britain's Royal Academy has followed suit, on occasions opening for a full 24-hour period, thereby dramatically increasing their admission numbers. Blockbuster exhibitions, such as the Venice Biennale, frequently have as much to do with raising the social profile of the institution or city, and encouraging the public to perceive it as a leader in its field, as in directly raising revenue through entry tickets.

Several music festivals in Europe have achieved international recognition and visitors make significant contributions to the economies of the cities where they are held. In addition to these there are countless smaller festivals in the countries concerned, each of which makes an important contribution to local revenues because of tourists' visits to them. While the largest festivals tend to run during the high season, many smaller events are held outside the peak summer periods, especially in places that are subject to heavy congestion at such times.

In Britain, one UK festival guide by *The Times* listed over 100 different music festivals alone, with themes including jazz, classical, folk, opera, early music, rock, indie, 'cross-over', and festivals dedicated to a specific instrument (such as the cello) or composer (a number of anniversary concerts were organized for the music of Mozart and Elgar). Enthusiasts can be drawn even to remote areas of the country by the appeal of specific concerts, say, important music festivals held during the year in the Orkney and Shetland Islands, the Isle of Lewis and the Channel Islands. Glastonbury, WOMAD, Creamfields, the V Festivals and other outdoor events such as those held at Reading and the Isle of Wight draw entrance figures in the tens, even hundreds, of thousands (One Isle of Wight festival drew 600,000).

Ad hoc events can always be built around a commemorative date. Of course, if the festivals are capable of drawing people from greater distances and keeping them on site for longer periods of time, the average spend increases as visitors will need overnight accommodation and food and will be tempted to spend money on other activities during their stay.

Apart from music and the fine arts, crafts, drama, dance, literature and poetry festivals are popular. Some commemorate historical occasions and may be highlighted with parades, pageants and son et lumière events. Most provide an opportunity for hosts and guests to meet and get to know one another. As well as meeting a wide variety of tourists' needs,

Example

Folk festivals in the UK

Music festivals of all kinds have become a familiar way for local authorities, usually in partnership with private enterprise, to bring visitors into their towns. Classical, jazz, pop and folk festivals are all now common annual events in the UK, with major events such as the Glastonbury Festival in Somerset drawing crowds in their hundreds of thousands. Some idea of the range of events is shown in the following listing of the ten top folk festivals held in the UK during 2006:

- Celtic Connection, Glasgow — 2 weeks in June
- Shetland Folk Festival — 4 days in April
- The Big Session (Sesiwn Fawr), Dolgellau, Wales — 2 days in July
- Cambridge Folk Festival — 4 days in July
- Pontedawe International Music Festival, Wales — 3 days in August
- Whitby Folk Week — 1 week in August
- Towersey Village Festival, Oxfordshire — 5 days in August
- Shrewsbury Folk Festival — 4 days in August
- Blas, the Highlands (across the Scottish Highlands) — 9 days in September
- Open House Festival, Belfast — 11 days in September/October

Source: The Observer, 5 February 2006.

they also fulfil an essential requirement of contemporary tourism – that of sustainable development.

Sports tourism

The relationship between tourism and sports activities is now so well established that sports tourism is recognized as a field of study in its own right and there are several books devoted to the subject.[8]

At its most successful, sports tourism will draw the greatest number of tourists to any one site on the planet. Tickets to the Olympic Games, for example, are in such high demand that sports enthusiasts are attracted from all over the world. Similarly, football's World Cup, with matches staged throughout Europe, also draws huge crowds. World-class events in golf and tennis witness demand for tickets well beyond the available supply. The economic benefits of these events to the destinations where they are staged can be enormous.

Of course, sports activities are not limited to events where tourists are merely passive observers. On the contrary, they also seek to participate – in rounds of golf on famous courses such as St Andrews, in improving their tennis with the professionals at coaching schools in Florida and in competitive games around the world.

The Olympics effect

The enormous investment required to mount Olympics events in a country has drawn a lot of media criticism, particularly in the UK, which is to host the 2012 Games in London. Few believe the £9 billion (and rising) cost to be justified and certainly not in the

Example

The 2010 FIFA World Cup™

The FIFA World Cup,™ held every four years, is to be hosted in South Africa in 2010. South Africa's previous experience of hosting major sporting events includes the Rugby World Cup in 1995, the African Cup of Nations in 1996 and the Cricket World Cup in 2003. The FIFA World Cup™ is a true mega-event and is expected to attract at least 2.8 million spectators during the course of the tournament. Research shows that the event could boost tourism by R7.3 billion (U$1billion). It is the first time this mega-event will have been hosted on the African continent.

One of the underlying arguments for hosting the tournament in South Africa was to harness the project's potential to create new sustainable infrastructure. It is estimated that the event will create 12,000 new jobs as well as 5000 construction jobs, while accelerating major infrastructure projects, such as the Gautrain (an 80-kilometre mass rapid transit railway system under construction in Gauteng Province).

The event will be a major revenue boost for the country and the South African government is keen to see the various host cities transformed in advance of the event. The UNWTO is cooperating with FIFA to ensure that the economic benefits are shared by locals. Concern has been expressed, however, over the Cape Town stadium site being chosen (there will be a total of nine venues around the country). Originally, it was proposed that a stadium would be built in a deprived area of the Mother City. Following concern expressed by the FIFA delegation about the image of the surroundings (that is, the township shacks) and possible crime-risks to visitors, however, it was decided that the 68,000-seater stadium would be located in an affluent, predominantly white area of the city, adjacent to the sea, thus enhancing an already advantaged suburb. The decision is proving controversial among locals.[9]

expectation of making a profit from the event. Montreal, which mounted the Games in 1976, still had an outstanding debt of £1.2 billion to be paid off by 2008, while Barcelona, where the Games were held in 1992, invested £6.5 billion in mounting the events and the cost to Athens in 2004, estimated by the government not to exceed 4.5 billion euros, may actually have amounted to as much as 13 billion euros – one estimate suggesting that the event cost Greece 6 per cent of the country's GNP in that year. Atlanta did a little better – it spent only $2 billion in 1996 and claimed a profit equivalent to £525 million, but much of the infrastructure needed was already in place before the city won the Games. In 2000, Sydney overspent its £1 billion budget by £300 million, which was underwritten by the country's taxpayers.

In terms of boosting tourism, certainly the events attracted large numbers of visitors to the cities at the time, but even this did not necessarily benefit the cities outside of the venues themselves. The European Tour Operators Association claims that the Games attract only sports enthusiasts who do not spend money on leisure outside of the venues and both Los Angeles and Sydney actually experienced downturns in the numbers of people visiting their other usual attractions during the period that the Games were taking place. Even the belief that long-term tourism is boosted has been questioned. After 1992, Barcelona was shown to have slower growth in visitor numbers than either Prague or Dublin (all becoming popular short break destinations), while, in the aftermath of the Sydney event, New Zealand attracted more visitors than Australia (possibly accounted for by the popularity of *Lord of the Rings*, however). Seoul and Sydney both experienced a drop in tourist numbers in the year following the Games. In short, these events will certainly help to put a destination on the map, but may not necessarily ensure significantly large increases in the numbers of visitors thereafter than would be anticipated without the Games. Rather than measuring the impact of tourism as a justification, countries might be better advised to concentrate on the benefits achieved by reconstruction of impoverished areas. Athens in particular benefited from a vastly improved transport infrastructure. In both Athens and Sydney, however, the specially built venues have been severely under-utilized since the events were held there, and there must be concern that the same might happen to London after 2012. Nevertheless, Britain is putting great efforts into assuring the maximum success in driving tourism, both in-bound and domestic, in 2012 and VisitLondon has estimated that the Olympics will generate £2 billion in the period 2009–2016.

The growth and promotion of dark tourism

The beauty of tourism is that the number of products that can be devised to interest tourists is virtually unlimited. One reads regularly in the press of new ideas that have been promoted, of new – and frequently bizarre – reasons tourists advance for visiting a site. Perhaps our ideas of what it is appropriate to see have changed a little since the nineteenth century, when in England people would travel considerable distances to watch public hangings and, in the United States, Coney Island's amusement park displayed 300 dwarfs in 'Midget City' and publicly electrocuted Topsy, a performing elephant, as a tourist attraction.

Although such things would not be sanctioned today, there remains, nonetheless, a fascination – at times bordering on the macabre – with observing scenes, such as those exploiting sudden and violent death. The locations of these Chris Rojek[10] has termed 'black spots'. Rojek describes the flood of people who came to Scotland to see the scene of the Pan Am crash at Lockerbie in 1988. Similarly, following the earthquake that rocked the city of San Francisco at the end of 1989, visitors to the city were asking to be accommodated in hotels that 'overlooked the collapsed freeway', while Gray Line offered Hurricane Katrina tours in New Orleans following the disastrous flooding of the city. Ground Zero, the site of the 9/11 attack on New York's Twin Towers in 2001, is now firmly on the tourist circuit. The BBC reported in 1995[11] that visitors to Blackpool were clamouring to 'ride the Alan Bradley Death Tram' after a character of that name was killed in front of the tram in the popular soap opera *Coronation Street*.

The terms thanatourism[12] or dark tourism have been used to describe such tourists' fascination with death and the macabre. Motives for this may be thought questionable, although travel to 'dark' sites cannot necessarily be ascribed to gratuitous pleasure – visits to World War II concentration camps are popular, for instance (Auschwitz-Birkenau attracts more than 500,000 visitors every year – see Figure 10.11), but these, especially by Israeli parties, can often take the form of a pilgrimage, while for others the visit is tied in with an historical interest. Places associated with the deaths of major celebrities, however, do attract more than their fair share of curious observers. Jim Morrison's tomb at Père-Lachaise cemetery in Paris is said to be the most-visited grave in the cemetery, while those of Oscar Wilde, Edith Piaf, Marcel Proust and other representatives of 'high culture' draw far fewer visitors. The outbuilding in Seattle where Kurt Cobain, of the band Nirvana, committed suicide in 1994 was torn down, but the site is still visited by hundreds of admirers, just as hundreds still seek out the underground road tunnel in Paris where Diana, Princess of Wales, met her death in a car crash. Depressingly, it was revealed in 2008 that coachloads of tourists were descending on Praia da Luz in Portugal where little Madeleine McCann disappeared, to see the hotel and restaurant associated with the story that the media had headlined over many weeks.

Whatever the merits or otherwise of thanatourism, the quest for the bizarre features ever more prominently in the list of tourists' motivations. Sometimes this is a reflection of the desire for ever more dangerous activities, whether sporting or otherwise, particularly among younger tourists. A press listing of the most dangerous streets in the world led to a flurry of interest in visiting those at Snake Alley, Taipei, Khao San Road, Bangkok, Tverskaya Ulitsa, Moscow, and King's Cross, Sydney, while a book appeared in 2006 directing potential tourists to the worst places in the world to visit.[13] *The Sunday Times*[14] coined the term 'terror tourism' to describe the growing trend for tourists to plan visits to countries beset

Figure 10.11 The entrance to Auschwitz-Birkenau concentration camp in Poland.
(Photo by Chris Holloway.)

by political disturbances or even civil wars. Following the initial end to hostilities in Afghanistan and Iraq, specialist tour operators were quick to arrange visits to those countries for the more adventurous – or foolhardy – in spite of government warnings of the potential dangers, and difficulties faced by those booking in obtaining travel insurance. The problem for the industry is to judge whether such tourist attractions are educationally valuable or merely satisfy the prurient interests of the spectators. Indeed, the very term 'visitor attraction' when applied to sites such as these raises questions. Are visitors expecting to be entertained or does this desire arise from some deeper psychosis in modern society?

Example

Sustainable dark tourism

Visits to deprived urban areas in developing countries have been introduced by operators who ensure that local organizations and employees benefit from the revenue raised. In Delhi, India, visitors can join tours that have been organized to see the living conditions of slum children living on the streets. These tours, which also take in visits to overstretched medical centres and street schools, are led by guides who are themselves former street children. Tourists' fees go to charities that help to rehabilitate the children.

In Rio de Janeiro, Brazil, walking tours are available to visit favelas (slums) such as Dharavi, with its one million inhabitants. In all, 20 per cent of the population live in these areas. Visits are made to health centres and community projects. In Soweto, near Johannesburg, visits can include a stay at a B&B, shack tours and observation of the hospital, as well as the Nelson Mandela Museum. Similar tours are available in the townships around Cape Town, while slums in Mexico and Mumbai, India, are also attracting tourists.

Some have criticized these tours as voyeuristic, but they offer the potential for employment to locals and bring in valuable revenue to sustain the many community projects that enable locals to survive (see Figure 6.6(b) and Case Study 8).

Whether prurient or otherwise, there is no doubt that countries with a dark history are not slow to cash in now on its evident commercial value. In recent years, the world has seen the following:

- A museum of forensic medicine has opened in Bangkok, Thailand, displaying weapons used in murders, deformed babies and the hanged corpse of the serial child-killer and cannibal Si-Oui.

- A Lithuanian entrepreneur, Viliumas Malinauskas, has created a Stalin World theme park by preserving 65 bronze and granite statues of former Soviet leaders at Gruto Park, south west of Vilnius. Opened in 2001, the site includes reconstructed Gulag buildings, watchtowers and barbed wire fencing, with loudspeakers relaying marching music and Stalin's speeches. Plans to construct a railway between the theme park and the capital, along which visitors would be transported in cattle wagons, monitored by machine-gun-carrying guards in the observation towers, were greeted with outrage by Lithuanians who had suffered under the Soviet regime. Nevertheless, 200,000 visitors were admitted to the site in its first year. Vilnius itself also boasts a genocide and resistance centre, opened in 1992. Similarly, the former Nazi, and later KGB, prison camp at Liepaja, Latvia, now accommodates overnight visitors, who are treated as prisoners. The visits are popular with students, stag parties and corporate teambuilders.

- The Cambodian Government has turned Pol Pot's Khmer Rouge complex of huts and bunkers at Anlong Veng into a tourist resort.

- The construction of Ossi World, a theme park commemorating the former East German regime on the outskirts of Berlin, was aimed to appeal to *Ostalgie* – the nostalgia among East Germans for the old regime in the face of rising economic problems since unification. Plans for the park had the support of the Berlin Tourism Marketing Board. Stasi (former DDR security service) buildings in Leipzig, Halle and near Berlin are also popular venues for tourists. The Holocaust site at Dachau and Hitler's retreat at Berchtesgaden are among many 'dark tourism' sites in Germany dating from the Nazi period.

- Visitors to Rwanda can tour genocide sites where a million Tutsis were massacred in 1994. The war crimes tribunals in Kigali were also open to tourists, who could also visit the bunker hideouts of the Rwandan Patriotic Front Army.

- In 2004, Israel's tourism minister urged tour operators to include its 425-mile 'terror prevention fence', topped with razor wire and electronic sensors, which separates Israelis and Palestinians, in itineraries organized for foreign tourists.

Britain has not been slow to trade on the attraction of dark tourism sites, either. Among World War II sites currently open to tourists or being groomed as future sites, one can include the Eden Prisoner-of-War Camp at Malton, North Yorkshire, where some 30 World War II huts house displays commemorating events during the war; air raid shelters in Stockport; the former secret bunker at Kelvedon Hatch in Essex (which receives 60,000 visitors a year); Hack Green nuclear bunker near Nantwich; and the bunker built during the 1950s near St Andrews, Scotland, to house the regional government in the event of a nuclear war. Also, National Park rangers regularly lead guided walks to the sites of 60 crashed World War II planes in the Peak District and, in Belfast, tours are operated to former Northern Ireland troublespots, including the Falls Road, Shankill Road and the Peace Wall.

Certainly visits to sites of this nature can be illuminating and instructive, if not entertaining in the traditional sense of the word. Some sites, however, have been heavily restored – perhaps over-restored (as at the Auschwitz-Birkenau death camp, where the original gate and ovens have been replaced with replicas). The extent to which the interpretation at such sites is objective is also always open to question, depending as it does on the political colour and viewpoint of the day and those presenting the data. At another death camp, in Buchenwald, Bauhaus university students were recently recruited to design souvenirs and memorabilia to be sold at the site to raise money for its preservation. The intentions were doubtless good, but many critics described the move as 'disrespectful'.

The scope for innovative tourism

Dark tourism is not always macabre, but it can be bizarre and, in addition to the somewhat gruesome examples given above, others are of genuine educational interest or are designed to entertain. Some of the more curious tourist attractions, whether banal, bizarre or both, are listed below.

- Corpses displayed as tourist attractions. Perfectly preserved bodies retrieved from bogs in Denmark are on display in museums at Silkeborg and Moesgaard. Exhibiting corpses in this manner, however, raises serious ethical questions.

- Deep Ocean Expeditions operates three-seat submersibles to descend 4000 metres to the ocean floor off Newfoundland to see the Titanic, at a cost in excess of £20,000.

- China has opened the site of a hitherto secret armaments factory to allow tourists to practise on the firing range with rocket launchers and anti-aircraft guns. The tour is particularly popular with Americans and Japanese.

- The world's first dung museum opened at Machaba safari camp in Botswana. Necklaces of dried polished dung can be bought in the shop. In Sweden, moose droppings are sold as souvenirs to tourists visiting Lapland and have been given as gifts to conference delegates. The reactions of the delegates to these gifts was not recorded.

- Lignite pits near Hamburg attract tourists because of their resemblance to the lunar landscape.

- Two-hour guided tours are available around the municipal rubbish dump at Fresh Kills, Staten Island, New York. Visits to urban sewers have also proved popular in some cities.

- Special tours and cruises are arranged for visitors to approach active or recently active volcanoes. These include sites in Ecuador, Sicily, Crete, Nicaragua, Iceland and the Azores.

- In New York City, tours are offered to the Bowery, formerly the district for down-and-outs, and to East Harlem and the Bronx. In the latter tours, the former negative connotations associated with the areas have given way to an exploration of the districts' musical roots.

- Walking tours across the arches of Sydney Harbour Bridge have proved immensely popular. A jumpsuit and safety cable are obligatory accompaniments. So successful have these tours been that they have been emulated on bridges in Brisbane and Auckland. In the USA, the Purple People Bridge between Cincinnati, Ohio, and Newport, Kentucky – the longest pedestrian bridge in the USA, across the Ohio River – offers the more adventurous an opportunity to don harnesses and climb on to the upper trestles of the bridge, from where they walk out on to a glass floor above the river.

- Two-hour guided tours are on offer in Berlin's red light district, with off-duty prostitutes acting as tour guides. They will answer clients' questions on all aspects of the city, including their own activities.

- At Bovington Camp in Dorset, the Army's medical team puts on realistic displays of amputations for visitors.

- In Palermo, Sicily, tourists can be taken on tours to sites associated with the local Mafia, including a visit to a former Godfather's torture chamber.

- Many domestic tourists in the Philippines are attracted to the annual rite of Catholic fanaticism at San Pedro Cutud, where volunteers undergo crucifixion.

- Omanis visit Salalah, on the southern tip of Oman, between June and September each year because of the unusual rainfall in the monsoon season – this is the only area of the Arabian Gulf so affected. Perhaps the only example of rain *attracting* tourists?
- A Museum of Broken Relationships has opened in Berlin, where artefacts associated with break-ups are on display, including an axe used to smash an ex-girlfriend's furniture.
- A restaurateur opened a 'toilet diner' in Taipei, Taiwan, where diners are seated on toilets and given toilet paper for napkins. Its immediate success with the young market has led to a further 12 similarly themed restaurants being opened.
- On a lighter note, in June each year, the Festa do São João in Oporto, Portugal, encourages participants to hit each other over the head with plastic hammers. Overseas tourists are now making enquiries about joining in the fun.

Hoteliers are noted entrepreneurs and many have introduced special events to attract out-of-season tourists or fill rooms during the recession. 'Murder weekends' have been popular, while one hotel offered heavy discounts to people whose surname was Smith. Perhaps the prize for originality should be awarded to the group of hotels situated near the M25, London's notoriously crowded orbital motorway. These developed a series of 'M25 theme nights', with a 'motorway madness' banquet.

Other hotels attract tourists because of the bizarre form of their accommodation. In the USA, tourists can stay at a former research laboratory and the world's first underwater hotel, Jules' Undersea Lodge at John Pennecamp Coral Reef State Park in Key Largo, Florida, which accommodates swimmers only, as guests need to make a 21-foot dive to

Example

The Laboratory of Experimental Tourism

Joel Henry founded the Laboratory of Experimental Tourism (Latourex) in France in 1990. Its object is to find new ways to take original holidays for jaded tourists who have 'done everything'. His idea of experimental travel was initially centred on Ariadne's thread – the mythical ball of yarn leading Theseus through the labyrinth. From this, he dreamed up different ways to take trips, including getting a friend to pinpoint 20 places on a map that had some personal meaning and then going to visit them. Other ideas advanced have included the following.

- *Anachrotourism* using old-fashioned vehicles as transport or following an ancient guidebook.
- *Antipoddysey* visiting a point on the globe that is exactly opposite where you live.
- *Bi-tourism* taking alternate left and right turns on a trip until you encounter a dead end.
- *Countertourism* photographing sites that stand *opposite* a landmark.
- *Cuneitourism* visiting only sites recommended by locals.
- *Melanotourism* visiting sites connected to the word 'black', such as Blackpool, the Black Mountains, Montenegro.
- *Monopoly tourism* determining where to travel by throwing dice, using a local map, or visiting a randomly selected grid reference on a map.
- *Retourism* travelling to a distant destination as quickly as possible, then returning by the slowest possible route.
- *Retrotourism* using a century-old Baedeker guide to visit a destination and see the sights.

Some 40 ideas in all have been designed to give tourists a new perspective on towns they visit, introduce a process of serendipity and attempt to make people look at everyday sites and objects in a new light.

access the entrance! They can also bed down in railway cabooses at the Featherbed Railroad Company in Nice, California, spend a night in the cell block at the Jailhouse Inn in Preston, Minnesota, or sleep underground in the Honeycombs at the Inn at Honey Run, Millersburg, Ohio. Lower Saxony in Germany offers Hay Hotels, where sleeping bags in hay are provided for visitors. The hotels are said to be popular with cycling tourists and others have been opened in Poland, Denmark, Italy and the Czech Republic.

Effectively marketed, bizarre sites and events can draw tourists. One entrepreneur has gone further, however, by devising a totally new approach to tourism, as seen in the Example.

Henry's experiments are one of several new approaches to tourism. Others have suggested that couples split up and endeavour to find each other within a town without any guidelines or defined meeting places. An imaginative alternative was devised by the owner of the Blinde Kuh (blind cow) restaurant in Zürich, which is described in the next chapter.

Notes

1. Swarbrooke, J. (1995) *The Development and Management of Visitor Attractions*, Butterworth-Heinemann, pp. 1–3.

2. Fyall, A., Garrod, B. and Leask, A. (eds) (2003) *Managing Visitor Attractions: New directions*, Butterworth-Heinemann, pp. 6–9.

3. Fyall et al., 2003, p. 30.

4. See Sage, A. (2006) 'D-Day lost as peace breaks out in museum', *The Times*, 27 January, p. 40.

5. *Phaidon Atlas of Contemporary World Architecture*, cited by Binney, Marcus (2004) 'A guide to wonders of the modern world worth visiting', *The Times*, 10 May, p. 31.

6. A good starting point for an overview of cultural tourism is the series of four books produced following the 1996 International Tourism and Culture Conference organized by the Centre for Travel and Tourism at the University of Northumbria, edited by M. Robinson, N. Evans and P. Callaghan and published by the Centre and Business Education Publishers, Sunderland:

   • Volume I: *Culture as the Tourist Product*

   • Volume II: *Managing Cultural Resources for the Tourist*

   • Volume III: *Tourism and Cultural Change*

   • Volume IV: *Tourism and Culture: Image, identity and marketing*.

7. Löfgren, O. (1999) *On Holiday: A history of vacationing*, University of California Press.

8. See, for example, M. Weed and C. Bull (2004) *Sports Tourism: Participants, policy and providers*, Elsevier/Butterworth-Heinemann, and J. Higham (ed.) (2005) *Sports Tourism Destinations: Issues, opportunities and analysis*, Elsevier.

9. Adapted from George, R. (2008) *Marketing Tourism in South Africa* (3rd edn), Oxford University Press, p. 447.

10. Rojek, C. (1993) *Ways of Escape: Modern transformation in leisure and travel*, Macmillan.

11. *Technology Season*, BBC 2, 7 November 1995.

12. See, for example, M. Foley and J. Lennon (2000) *Dark Tourism*, Continuum, and A. V. Seaton (1996) 'Guided by the dark: from thanatopsis to thanatourism', *International Journal of Heritage Studies*, 2, pp. 234–44.

13. Cohen, M. (1997) *No Holiday: 80 places you don't want to visit*, The Disinformation Company.
14. Byrne, C. (1997) 'Terror tourists queue up for trips to war zones', *The Sunday Times*, 16 March.

Further reading

Anthony, R. and Henry, J. (2005) *The Lonely Planet Guide to Experimental Travel*, Lonely Planet Publications.

Jencks, C. (2005) *The Iconic Building: The power of enigma*, Frances Lincoln.

Stewart, S. (1984) *On Longing: Narratives of the miniature, the gigantic, the souvenir, the collection*, Johns Hopkins University Press, p. 86.

UK Film Council, *How Film and Television Programmes Promote Tourism in the UK*, UK Film Council, 2007.

Websites

The Dala Horse	**www.nohemslojd.se**
Eden Camp Prisoner of War Camp	**www.edencamp.co.uk**
EnjoyEngland (food and drink)	**www.enjoyngland.com/ideas/food-and-drink/eat**
Euro parks (European Federation of Leisure Parks)	**www.europarks.org**
Gruto theme park	**www.grutoparkas.lt**
Hinterland Travel (tours to Iraq, Afghanistan, etc.)	**www.hinterlandtravel.com**
Historic Houses Association	**www.hha.org.uk**
Regaldive	**www.regaldive.co.uk**
Slow food movement	**www.slowfood.com**
The National Wildflower Centre	**www.nwc.org.uk**

VisitBritain, British gardens
www.visitbritain.com/en/things-to-see-and-do/interests/british-gardens

Questions and discussion points

1. As explained in this chapter, the de la Warr Pavilion in Bexhill-on-Sea has undergone substantial renovation as a major icon of modernist architecture, with the hope that this will help to revive Bexhill's fortunes. Similarly, the great Art Deco Midland Hotel in Morecambe, Lancashire, was restored at considerable expense after being allowed to decay over several decades, reopening in 2008. With a declining infrastructure and without further investment in resurrecting these formerly popular resort towns, can it ever be possible to bring tourists back once they have gone? Are sightseers visiting Bexhill ever likely to stay for more than half a day? Can visitors be encouraged to stop over in a run-down resort, even if staying in a first-class property?

   Your answers to these questions have implications for other traditional resorts in England. Saltdean, also in Sussex, has a famous modernist lido, still in use, but its other iconic building, the Grand Ocean Hotel, is now an apartment block, and the place's popularity as a resort has dwindled. What other resorts can you identify with similar problems?

2. For the first time in 2008 the world famous Glastonbury Festival experienced difficulty in attracting bookings. Some viewed this as a criticism of the line-up, others put it down to the extremely bad weather that had tended to accompany the festival for the previous few years, turning the rural site into a sea of mud, but could the sheer proliferation of such festivals in the UK account in part for this? Is there a limit to the number of music festivals that can be economically successful each year?

3. How successful was Liverpool in 2008 – its year as City of Culture? With hindsight, did the city make the best use of its resources to attract domestic and incoming tourists? What criticisms can be made of the way in which the year-long event was managed?

4. Discuss whether or not souvenirs associated with well-established tourist destinations invariably tend to verge on the 'tacky' and, if so, are there opportunities to move this business upmarket? If so, suggest what form the souvenirs should take for any specific destinations with which you are familiar.

5. Will the Olympic Games in Britain in 2012, on balance, prove financially beneficial? Are quotes that the Games will generate about £2 billion for the economy realistic? Is it still a good thing to win the competition to host the Games? One effect of funding the Olympics in Britain is a reduction in funding for other cultural needs (for example, diverting the Big Lottery Fund from heritage projects to Olympic funding has reduced the money available for heritage by over £200 million). Consider the implications for tourism of such changes in funding.

6. This chapter has revealed that the sending of postcards has actually increased over the previous five years, by a large amount, in spite of modern technology offering alternative means of communicating with loved ones. What reasons could account for this?

Tasks

1. This chapter has featured a number of examples of gastronomic tourism. Undertake some research to find out how gastronomic tourism could be developed in the region where you live and/or work and, in a report, show how public/private cooperation with local industry might help to encourage the growth of this form of tourism.

2. Working in groups, develop some innovative approaches to new forms of tourism similar to the ideas suggested by Joel Henry. Select three of your best ideas and complete a report showing how they could be best implemented and disseminated to tourists.

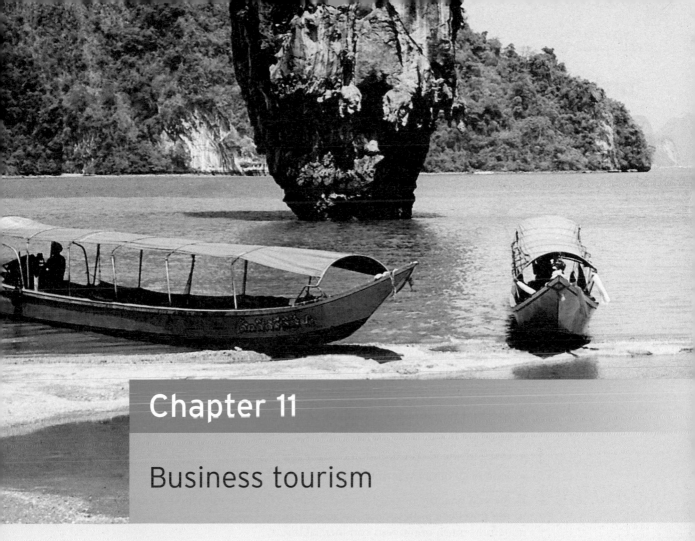

Chapter 11

Business tourism

Learning outcomes

After studying this chapter, you should be able to:

- understand the principal sectors of the business tourism industry and distinguish between them

- explain the objectives of the different types of meetings that may be organized, the various venues in which they take place and the roles of meeting planners

- define incentive travel, compare it with other forms of workplace rewards and demonstrate awareness of the challenges of organizing successful incentive travel programmes

- distinguish between trade fairs and exhibitions and understand the roles of those companies that supply services to this sector of business tourism

- understand the principal motivations behind individual business travel and appreciate the factors that companies take into account regarding the features of the business trips made by their employees

- understand the main trends that are having an impact on business tourism in the early twenty-first century.

Introduction

> No grand idea was ever born in a conference, but a lot of foolish ideas have died there.
>
> F. Scott Fitzgerald, *The Crack-up*, 1945

Travelling for the purpose of carrying out trade and engaging in commerce was one of the earliest types of tourist activity undertaken by enterprising members of ancient civilizations. Even at times in history when those undertaking any form of travel had to contend with the ever-present dangers of attack from bandits, pirates and highwaymen, as well as the severe discomfort of slowly progressing along poorly constructed roads or across perilous seas, the business motive was strong enough to drive intrepid merchants and other entrepreneurs to leave their native lands in search of distant markets in which to buy or sell goods and products not found locally.

Today, business tourism – principally, travel for commercial, professional and work-related purposes – represents the major non-leisure form of tourism and business tourists are widely recognized as the highest-spending category of travellers. This chapter examines the different characteristics of the various categories of business tourism and the trends affecting this industry.

Modern-day business tourism takes four principal forms:

- travel for the purpose of attending conferences and other types of meetings
- incentive travel
- travel to attend an exhibition or trade fair
- individual business travel.

In the vast majority of cases, each category of business tourism is in some way connected to the traveller's professional life or to their role in the buying and selling process that underpins much of modern commercial life.

Meetings

Travelling in order to attend a meeting of some kind is one of the most widespread forms of business tourism. Meetings take many forms and vary enormously in size and purpose, but the meetings that stimulate business tourism are primarily those organized with an objective linked to the attendees' professional activity.

This is most evident when the meeting's attendees all belong to the same profession or trade and are all members of the same professional or trade association. Many of the highest-profile meetings belong to this **association** category of meetings. They can attract many thousands of attendees (or **participants** or **delegates**, as they are also known) and their economic impacts on the destinations in which they are held can be considerable. For example, the conference of the European Society of Cardiology, the members of which are medical professionals specializing in cardiovascular diseases, now regularly attracts over 20,000 delegates. These five-day events provide the delegates from all over Europe and beyond with an invaluable opportunity to meet together and exchange ideas and information on new challenges and new techniques related to the field of cardiovascular medicine. It is clear that the collective spending of the delegates on items such as transport, accommodation and catering brings extensive economic benefits to the businesses operating in the cities in which this event takes place. The cities in which the conference has been held in recent years are shown in Table 11.1.

Not all meetings are of this magnitude, however. The vast majority are held with colleagues who work for the same company, and these are known as **corporate** meetings.

Table 11.1 Locations of the European Society of Cardiologists' conferences, 1993–2007.

Year and location	Number of participants
2007 Vienna, Austria	23,091
2006 Barcelona, Spain	25,501
2005 Stockholm, Sweden	18,242
2004 Munich, Germany	19,049
2003 Vienna, Austria	19,574
2002 Berlin, Germany	19,342
2001 Stockholm, Sweden	16,025
2000 Amsterdam, Netherlands	17,112
1999 Barcelona, Spain	17,074
1998 Vienna, Austria	16,709
1997 Stockholm, Sweden	14,101
1996 Birmingham, UK	11,686
1994 Berlin, Germany	16,436
1993 Nice, France	10,516

Companies large and small have a number of reasons for organizing meetings of their staff, but all are linked to the companies' need to operate effectively in the field of business. For example, many corporate meetings are held for the purpose of training staff in the skills and techniques that they need in order to perform well in the workplace – selling skills, customer relations skills, information technology skills and so on, depending on the nature of the company's business. Other types of corporate meetings may be arranged with the objective of giving managers the opportunity to discuss the company's future strategies – for marketing, expansion, crisis management and so on.

Most such meetings are comparatively small (ranging from a handful of employees to several dozen), so can be held in the type of small seminar rooms offered for hire by hotels. Indeed, a visit to most 4-star and 5-star hotels will provide information on exactly which corporate events are being held there that day as such meetings are usually prominently listed in the reception area, for the benefit of the delegates attending them.

All types of companies organize meetings for their staff, but some sectors tend to have more meetings than others. The finance (banking and insurance), medical and pharmaceutical, automotive and engineering sectors are the principal markets, in most countries, for the meetings industry.

While association and corporate meetings comprise the lion's share of this particular form of business tourism, they are not the only elements. **Governments and political organizations** at all levels (local, regional and national as well as international legislative bodies, such as the European Commission) also need to hold regular meetings to discuss strategies, choose candidates and announce new initiatives.

Among the most visible of these meetings are the annual conferences of political parties that are held in most countries. In the UK, for example, the 124th annual conference of the Conservative Party was held in Blackpool in 2007. It attracted around 10,000 attendees, including Conservative Members of Parliament and Members of the European Parliament, councillors and policy advisers, as well as representatives from the press and other media, business groups, charitable organizations, think tanks and campaigning organizations.

The other types of organizations that frequently hold meetings are neatly encapsulated in the American acronym **SMERF**, which stands for social, military, educational, religious and fraternal. The SMERF sector of demand for meetings is a useful catch-all category, covering most types of meeting that are not held by professional/trade associations, companies or government organizations.

- *Social meetings* This segment includes all groups meeting primarily for social interaction, such as collectors, hobbyists, special interest groups and non-military reunions. An example of such a meeting would be the Harley-Davidson Owners Group's 2008 annual rally and convention that was held in the city of Fredericksburg, Virginia, and which attracted 3500 attendees, generating 5000 room nights and resulting in approximately $2.6 million of spending for the local economy.

- *Military meetings* This segment largely comprises the reunions of people who served in the armed forces during periods of conflict. The intensity – and often the tragedy – that can characterize such conflicts means that those who lived through them often find comfort in reuniting with their fellow fighters at regular intervals to discuss their wartime experiences and commemorate their comrades who did not survive the hostilities. Many such meetings bring together veteran servicemen and women, such as the 600 ex-servicemen and women who attended the Battle for Malta Veterans Reunion that was held in Malta over a 7-day period in 2006.

- *Educational meetings* Those who attend such events are generally teachers, lecturers and academic researchers who meet in order to share their research in their particular subject area, as well as new challenges and other developments affecting the teaching of their specialist subject. A typical example of an educational meeting would be the annual conference of ATLAS (**www.atlas-euro.org**), an international association of lecturers specializing in the teaching of travel and tourism.

- *Religious meetings* Some of the largest gatherings organized in the world's major cities are for the purpose of bringing together, for one or more days, people who share the same faith. At such events, worship and prayer are often combined with debates and workshops during which topical issues relating to the attendees' particular religion are discussed. The 3000-person general assembly of the Presbyterian Church (USA) that was held in San José in 2008 is an example of such a major religious meeting.

- *Fraternal meetings* This segment includes primarily meetings of sororities, fraternities and other fraternal organizations. The attendees at fraternal meetings are often people who went to school or university together and wish to reunite from time to time, to relive the memories of their student days. University alumni reunions are a typical example of a fraternal meeting.

Association meetings and corporate meetings compared

While government and SMERF meetings display a wide and often colourful variety of themes, the vast majority of meetings fall into either the association or corporate segments, but they differ considerably from each other in a number of important respects. Consequently, it is important to understand the distinguishing characteristics of these two segments and be able to compare them accurately. Table 11.2 highlights some of the most important contrasts between the association and the corporate segments of the meetings sector of business tourism.

The meetings industry

As recently as 20 years ago, the expression 'meetings industry' was hardly ever used, in the sense of an umbrella term describing all of those businesses existing wholly or partly in order to provide the wide range of facilities and services that are required to make meetings possible and ensure that they are run professionally and effectively. Now, the use of this term is widespread and the meetings industry is firmly established as an expanding

Table 11.2 Association and business conferences contrasted.

Association conferences	Corporate conferences
Delegate numbers can be in the hundreds – even thousands.	Delegate numbers tend to be fewer – usually under 100 and often a few dozen.
The decision process for choosing the destination can be long and complex, often involving a committee.	The decision process for choosing the destination is shorter and simpler – it is often made by one person.
Spending per delegate per day can be moderate, as the delegates are usually paying out of their own pockets.	Spending per delegate per day can be higher, as the delegates' companies are usually paying.
These can last for several days, or even a week in the case of large international association conferences.	These are generally shorter and often last for only one day.
For associations, conferences represent an opportunity to make a profit, which can in turn be used to pay for the associations' running expenses.	For companies, conferences represent a cost that must be financed out of the profits made elsewhere by the companies.
Many association events are held in large, purpose-built conference centres.	Many corporate events are held in the seminar rooms of hotels.
The lead-time for an association conference can be several years.	The lead-time for a corporate conference is usually much shorter than for an association conference.
Association conferences are rarely cancelled as the by-laws of the association usually state that an annual conference must be held.	Corporate conferences can be cancelled more easily, particularly in times of financial hardship for the company.
Delegates' partners are usually welcome to attend association conferences, so parallel partners' programmes of events are often planned for them.	Delegates' partners are rarely encouraged to attend.

and vitally important profession in its own right. The principal elements of the meetings industry will now be reviewed.

Venues

All meetings require some form of venue in which the attendees can gather for the duration of the event. Derived from the Latin verb venire (to come), the word venue is used to denote the building in which delegates come together in order to attend the event. In its most basic form, a venue comprises four walls, a roof and a collection of chairs for the delegates' comfort, but the variety of venues is almost as great as the variety of meetings held within them.

Conference centres

Their city centre locations, sheer vastness and often iconic designs mean that these buildings are certainly the most visible indication that any city is active in hosting large meetings. Many conference centres, such as the harbour-front Hong Kong Conference and Exhibition Centre, have become important symbols of the cities in which they are located. These venues are most often used for meetings requiring large open spaces and are built on a scale that enables them to accommodate hundreds or even thousands of delegates. In addition, they generally offer space for the types of exhibitions that are often run in parallel with large conferences, as well as the high-quality audio-visual and other technical facilities that are essential to the success of such large-scale events.

In their construction, conference centres are either of the purpose-built or converted types. Most are purpose-built – that is, they were originally and solely planned to be venues for conferences (see Figure 11.1). Many of the most interesting and charming conference centres, however, particularly in Europe, were converted into meeting venues from their original, different, function (see Figure 11.2). Prisons, hospitals and factories are just

Figure 11.1 A purpose-built conference centre: the Queen Elizabeth II Conference Centre, London.
(Photo courtesy Queen Elizabeth II Conference Centre.)

Figure 11.2 A converted venue: le Palais Beaumont Pau, France.
(Photo courtesy Historic Conference Centres at Europe, www.hoce.com, and Le Palais Beaumont Pau, www.paucc.com.)

a few of the types of buildings that have been converted into conference centres to serve the meetings industry. For example, the Mediterranean Conference Centre in Valletta, Malta, was originally constructed as a military hospital, but was converted into an outstanding conference venue in 1990.

Their immense capacity makes conference centres, purpose-built or converted, particularly suitable for large meetings of associations. Because, as mentioned, attendees at international association conferences can number in their thousands, conference centres are usually the only type of venue capable of holding meetings on this scale, particularly when, as is often the case with medical events for example, space is required in which to situate a parallel exhibition of products relating to the theme of the conference.

Hotels

Long before the first conference centres were built, meetings were regularly taking place in rooms designed for the purpose in inns and hotels and, to this day, they remain the preferred type of venue for most of the world's meetings.

Whether hotels are situated in city centres, suburban locations, airports or rural areas, most depend to a significant extent on the income they earn from renting out their meetings rooms and the conference-related spending on catering and (for residential events) accommodation. Many hotel chains have branded their meetings facilities to ensure that customers using them are assured consistent standards of facilities and quality, wherever in the world a particular hotel may be located.

Example

Hilton Hotels

Hilton Hotels' Hilton Meetings brand is designed to provide personalized meeting services that enable clients to hold successful and hassle-free meetings for groups of 50 guests or fewer. Hilton Meetings was created in 2000 at Hilton hotels in the United Kingdom and Ireland and gradually expanded globally, finally being introduced to the majority of Hilton hotels in North America in 2008.

Hilton business clients can choose between a formal boardroom setting and flexible multipurpose room for their small meetings. These well-designed layouts are complemented by guaranteed standards of Hilton Meetings service and amenities that aim to minimize the environmental impact while offering time-saving technology and consistent personalized service.

Hilton Meetings guests have access to fresh and contemporary meeting spaces with high-quality furnishings, local artwork to help stimulate creativity and advanced technology to keep guests plugged in. All rooms include a 3M™ Digital Easel that instantly records flipchart content electronically into a variety of formats for Mac and PC computers and enables collaboration with participants in multiple locations via a shared meeting application. Radio-controlled clocks, keeping accurate local time, help keep guests on time, while high-speed Internet connectivity keeps guests connected.

Tables are designed with built-in table-top power and data points for easy connections and chairs offer extra comfort with their padded armrests and lumbar support. Meeting rooms also contain a refrigerator and safe that can hold at least four laptops, have doors that lock for added security and outside-in spyhole viewers to minimize disruption.

Dedicated meetings specialists are assigned to each Hilton Meetings room to assist with individual service needs. A 'Service Connect System' button links guests directly with their meeting specialist. Each meeting planner receives a welcome kit containing specific details about their event, the hotel and the meeting space and a welcome wallet holding lunch and break menus. Hilton also serves meeting participants food and beverage items specifically selected to help boost their energy and keep their minds sharp (such as peach smoothies or mini shish kebabs with lemon yogurt sauce) along with complimentary tea and coffee served all day.

Hilton's e-Events online group booking tool, Guest List Manager and Personalized Group Web Page features allow event planners to easily book their group event or meeting and promote their event to attendees.

The Hilton Meetings products reinforce Hilton's commitment to environmental sustainability. The hotelier has reduced the use of chrome in meeting room furniture and fixtures and is using sleek hard surfaces for tables to eliminate the need for linens and the chemicals used for cleaning them. To further support the brand's efforts to increase local sourcing, artwork featured in rooms is acquired from local artists.

Hilton Meetings is also fully supported by new online event management and meeting planning tools, which helps to reduce paper waste. In-room signage provides guests with tips on how to be an environmentally sensitive meeting participant, such as turning off the lights before leaving the room and recycling paper when it is an option. Also, rooms include eco-friendly meeting materials made from recycled paper and biodegradable ink. These materials are placed on self-service stands to eliminate full place settings of notepads and pens, which often create unnecessary waste. To further attempt to reduce waste, notepads contain lines on both sides of each page.

With the notable exception of the 'convention hotels' found in US cities such as Las Vegas, which offer meetings facilities capable of hosting conferences of several thousand attendees, most meeting spaces located in hotels are designed for smaller events of several dozen or several hundred attendees. Indeed, many hotel boardrooms are exclusive venues for fewer than 20 attendees. The average size of seminar rooms and other meeting facilities offered by hotel venues makes them eminently suitable for corporate events such as staff training sessions or senior management strategy meetings.

Academic venues

In many countries, universities and other educational institutions are active suppliers of meetings facilities, particularly during student holiday periods and weekends. With their lecture theatres, classrooms, audio-visual facilities and catering services, such venues offer everything that is required to host meetings, large and small. When such meetings are hosted outside the teaching period, student accommodation may also be used by those attending residential events.

In several countries, universities have created their own marketing consortia to promote themselves as meetings venues. For example, Venuemasters (**www.venuemasters.co.uk**) is a consortium that promotes the facilities available for hire to meeting planners at over 80 academic venues in the UK. Venuemasters' members are venues that are either owned by an educational establishment or have as their core business the provision of further, higher or professional education. The consortium offers a venue-finding service for organizations and companies in search of meeting rooms and, if needed, accommodation for their events.

While rarely offering the standards of luxury found in 5-star hotels, academic venues have the advantage of being able to offer their facilities at fairly competitive rates. For that reason, they are often used as the location for meetings where attendees are paying out of their own pockets and costs have to be kept at a moderate level. Certain association events as well as some types of SMERF meetings are therefore natural clients of the academic venue sector of the meetings industry.

Unusual venues

This category includes the meetings facilities offered by a wide range of properties such as museums, stately homes, castles, theatres and theme parks as well as other tourist attractions such as zoos and aquariums. For most of these, the provision of meeting facilities is an activity that is secondary to the property's principal function, but, nevertheless, an important source of revenue. For example, many sporting venues, such as football stadiums and horseracing tracks, supplement the income they earn from such events by hosting meetings when the facilities are not being used for their original and principal purpose. The world-famous Stade de France in Paris is a typical example of an unusual venue of this type, advertising itself as a meeting venue for events of up to 5000 attendees.

The main motivation for holding a meeting in an unusual venue is to make the event memorable and attractive to attendees. The organization holding the meeting can also benefit from the reflected glory of the great prestige associated with certain unusual venues. For example, any meeting held in the Victoria and Albert Museum in London will automatically benefit from the considerable cachet associated with such a venerable institution.

Other suppliers

It is clear that, in order to run a successful meeting, much more is required than simply a suitable venue. A wide range of facilities and services is necessary for the smooth running of any such event.

Attendees need to be fed and refreshed at regular intervals during the meeting, so the provision of food and beverages is vital, whether for a simple coffee break or lunch or the type of sumptuous gala that is often held on the final evening of a grand conference. On such occasions, the decoration of the tables and the dining room can be as important as the quality of the food and wines, particularly for prestigious events.

As well as professional catering, most meetings make extensive use of audio-visual resources to make their events look and sound as good as possible. This is one of the ways in which the production of meetings has changed most in the past few decades. The days of conference speakers making use of a flipchart or overhead projector to communicate with their audiences are long gone. In the twenty-first century, information and communications technology has revolutionized the meetings industry, as it has so many other sectors. Multiple screens, PowerPoint presentations and surround sound quality are now widespread, turning many large-scale conferences, such as those of political parties, into veritable 'shows', characterized by high-quality sound and near television production standards.

In an increasingly globalized world, the provision of interpreting services is of growing importance as meetings may well be attended by delegates who speak a variety of different languages. Conference interpreters are the people whose considerable skills make multilingual meetings possible and conference centres are generally designed to include interpreters' booths, where professional interpreters can listen to, translate and relay the conference speakers' words simultaneously and accurately – no easy feat.

Meeting planners

It is already evident from the above that the planning of meetings today can be a highly complex task. The destination and the venue must be chosen, the attendees' travel and, if necessary, visa requirements must be taken care of and their accommodation arranged, plus topics and speakers for the event must be selected. Some conferences, such as those of associations, must be marketed to prospective attendees and registration payments processed. At the actual event, someone must organize appropriate security measures, particularly if VIP attendees or speakers are involved, and someone must liaise with and manage the providers of audio-visual and catering services.

These tasks – and many more – are the responsibility of the **meeting planner**. In recent years, the role of the meeting planner has increasingly been recognized as a profession in its own right and its importance in the meetings industry cannot be overestimated. Many now bear the job title 'professional conference organizer' or PCO, although a range of other titles exist, such as events planner, conference coordinator and meetings executive. Many meeting planners are employed by a single organization – usually an association or a company – organizing, on a full-time basis, all of the meetings, seminars and conferences that their organization needs.

Others, often called **independent meeting planners**, are self-employed, offering their services to a variety of associations and companies on a consultancy basis, charging a fee for the meetings that they organize on behalf of their clients. This arrangement can be particularly beneficial to smaller organizations that do not hold sufficient events on a year-to-year basis to justify having such a person on their payroll as a full-time, permanent member of staff.

What we have termed the 'meetings industry', therefore, comprises those men and women who earn their living from the provision of facilities and services for the successful running of meetings large and small. Managing and marketing venues, supplying catering, interpreting and audio-visual services for meetings and taking responsibility for the coordination and planning of the actual meetings event – these are the principal functions of those who make successful events possible.

It is worthy of note, however, that, while some individuals and companies operate entirely and solely within the meetings industry, for many others, this sector of business tourism represents only a part of their activities. For example, many venues, in addition to providing space for meetings, also hire out their facilities for events such as concerts, weddings and graduation ceremonies. In many organizations, the planning of meetings is only *part* of the job the person who undertakes the task, does – a part that may not even be reflected in their job title, as in the case of a training manager or human resources executive who also organizes events from time to time. Many airlines and hotels, for example, are hardly aware of the role that they play in supplying vital services to the meetings industry by transporting and accommodating attendees and speakers.

Incentive travel

One particular type of meeting is usually regarded as being sufficiently distinct from all the others to justify it being given its own separate category. **Incentive travel** is the name given to the travel, usually in groups, of employees who have been awarded a luxury trip, entirely paid for by their company, as a prize for high achievement at work. The practice of using incentive travel to motivate employees to work harder was originally started by American companies in the 1950s and employers in the USA are still the major generators of this sector of business tourism. Since then, however, the use of incentive travel has spread throughout the industrialized world and is now widely recognized as being one of the most effective management tools for encouraging employees to be more productive and make a greater contribution to their employers' profitability.

The Society of Incentive Travel Executives (SITE), defines incentive travel as 'a global management tool that uses an exceptional travel experience to motivate and/or recognize participants for increased levels of performance in support of organizational goals.' Most incentive trips are won by individuals (or teams) who have sold, within a given period, the most units of whatever it is their companies make, whether this is tractors, insurance policies, pharmaceutical products or any other type of manufactured goods or services. For this reason, most of those who travel on incentive trips are members of their companies' salesforces.

Put simply, a company using incentive travel as a reward will announce a **competition** to their salesforce, informing them that their individual or team sales figures during a particular period (often 12 months) will be recorded for the purpose of determining who sold the most during that time. The prize for being one of the most successful salespeople during that period is the incentive trip, typically of three to five days' duration, which will be described in detail and in the most enticing terms, in order to encourage the sales staff to do their utmost in order to win the trip.

It would be no exaggeration to say that incentive travel is one of the most luxurious, highest-spending and therefore lucrative forms of tourism that exists. In order to motivate employees to work harder to achieve greater results in the workplace, the travel prize they are competing for must be an extremely attractive one. This is particularly the case when those competing to win the prize are managers who travel often, on business and for leisure, and are therefore not easily impressed by yet another flight and another hotel in a foreign destination. Exotic destinations, luxury accommodation and a dazzling variety of exciting and exclusive activities are classic features of incentive travel.

Incentive travel winners – those who get to go on these magnificent trips – must be given the impression that they are privileged and greatly valued by their employers, which is why incentive trips must delight and indulge those who are fortunate enough to receive this form of reward for their performance at work. The key word here is 'work' for, although incentive travel participants may look and behave like leisure tourists – dressing casually, relaxing, sightseeing and enjoying sporting and/or leisure activities – the motive underlying their trip is most definitely connected to the participant's working life, which is why this form of travel is firmly categorized within the business tourism sector.

Nevertheless, there are clearly alternative ways to motivate staff to work harder and reward them when they achieve outstanding results. The tool most commonly used by companies to 'incentivize' their employees is not incentive travel but *money* – usually cash bonuses for those who reach specific targets in their work. Gradually, however, more and more employers are beginning to realize that the use of incentive travel as a reward offers them a number of advantages that simply awarding staff the cash equivalent does not.

Example

The advantages of incentive travel and cash

Advantages of incentive travel over cash

- Employees spend time with each other, at leisure. This informal networking offers them the opportunity of getting to know each other better, which in turn can help create a stronger team spirit when they return to work, having shared a number of enjoyable and memorable experiences together.

- For the few days of the trip, the company has an opportunity to inculcate some of its most productive employees with 'company values'. Pep talks are a common feature of incentive trips – motivational speeches praising the incentive travel winners for their hard work and extolling the qualities of the company they work for. This is one of the management techniques employed by companies to reduce staff turnover and, in particular, retain those employees who make the most valuable contribution to their company's profitability.

- Incentive travel is more effective than money at encouraging non-winners to try harder to win the next competition run by their company. The incentive travel winners' absence from work and their subsequent return, full of stories of what they have seen and done on their trip make this a highly visible prize, as opposed to money, which is far less likely to be discussed with colleagues. Non-winners can be motivated to work harder to win next time when they hear their colleagues recount their incentive trip experiences.

- As incentive trips offer those who participate in them the opportunity to relax and/or engage in physical pursuits, it means that they tend to return to work refreshed and rested and this boost to their wellbeing can be beneficial to their performance in the workplace. At the same time, it is undeniable that the use of cash awards offers its own advantages, when compared with sending high-achieving staff on incentive trips.

Advantages of cash over incentive trips

- Low risk. Cash awards are attractive by the very nature of their simplicity. Money is always welcomed by the recipient, but the participant's response to an incentive trip is less predictable. Poor weather, the wrong choice of incentive destination or disappointing accommodation are among the factors that can turn what should be an enjoyable, motivating reward into its opposite.

- No loss of productivity. When some of the company's highest-performing members of staff are absent from work for several days, enjoying an incentive trip, the impact on the company's profitability can be considerable. With cash awards, the winners continue to work and there is no negative impact on the company's sales figures.

- Flexibility. The employee in receipt of a cash bonus for meeting a demanding sales target, for example, can spend the money on whatever he or she wishes or needs. This could be, of course, a holiday or short break, in which case the tourism industry benefits from the spending of this award, but it could equally be spent on home improvements, repairs to the family car or simply invested in a savings account.

- Finally, in an era when attention is increasingly being focused on employees' work–life balance – the balance between the time they spend working and the time they spend with friends and family – it is widely recognized that awarding an incentive trip, however luxurious, as a prize for high achievement at work does mean that the participants are automatically obliged to spend additional time away from home in order to take part in the trip. This may not always be welcomed by employees, particularly those who already find themselves spending evenings away from their friends and families, travelling on company business. Cash bonuses, therefore, can be a more motivating prize for such employees.

The incentive travel industry

In our review of the principal elements of the meetings industry, it was seen that a number of specialist suppliers are required in order to make the effective functioning of meetings possible – venues, audio-visual companies, interpreters and so on. By way of contrast, the incentive travel sector of business tourism largely makes use of the same services, facilities and resources that are used by leisure tourists – airlines and other forms of transport, hotel accommodation, tourist attractions, guides, shops, cultural and sports events and so on. Of course, the incentive travel sector does tend to make most use of that end of the tourism market spectrum characterized by 4- and 5-star hotels, exclusive restaurants and privileged, private access to tourist attractions and prestigious events.

The one type of specialist agency required in order to facilitate the functioning of the incentive travel industry is the **incentive travel house**. This is the term commonly used for an agency that designs incentive programmes for its clients – companies using this technique to motivate their staff. Agency staff are professionals who oversee the entire operation, from designing the rules of the competition for employees and the selection of winners, through the choice of the destination and activities for the incentive trip to the planning of the detailed logistics for the trip, including all transport, accommodation and catering arrangements.

While some companies entrust the planning of their staff incentive programmes to high-street generalist travel agencies, they are in a small, declining minority. Most companies understand that the planning and execution of incentive trips is so extremely technical and demanding in terms of the high expectations of the winners, that this process is best placed in the hands of specialist incentive travel houses.

One of the many pressures that those employed by incentive travel houses must contend with is the necessity of creating the essential 'wow' factor for every trip they organize. It is often claimed that 'wow' is the most important word in the entire lexicon of the incentive travel sector of business tourism as any trip that fails to surprise, delight and inspire the participants in this way can fairly be said to have failed in its objectives.

Supplying that 'wow' factor, as all incentive travel professionals understand, is not simply a case of spending vast amounts of the client's money on extravagant entertainments for its winning employees. Great creativity and imagination are the essential qualities required by anyone wishing to work in this aspect of the incentive travel industry. A vivid, but not particularly unique, example of these qualities at work in the design of an incentive travel programme is the group of incentive winners on a trip to Finnish Lapland, who were given fishing rods and instructed on how to cut a round hole in the Arctic ice so that they could spend the day fishing as Eskimos do. The cost of this simple activity was minimal, but the impact on the group was outstanding. It fired them with enthusiasm and enchantment – as all good incentive trips should.

Exhibitions and trade fairs

Some of the largest flows of business tourists are to be found when many thousands of people gather in a destination for one or more days to attend an exhibition. As the subject of this chapter is business tourism, the types of exhibition under consideration here are not of a cultural nature, such as exhibitions of paintings or sculptures found in art galleries and museums, but events where the exhibitors hire stands (or, in American English, booths) to present their companies' goods or services to those visiting the exhibition.

Although the word 'exhibition' is often used generically, it is common to distinguish between **exhibitions**, which attract the general public, and **trade fairs** (known as trade shows in the USA), which are mainly attended by business visitors. Thus, the Union des Foires Internationales (UFI), now known as the Global Association of the Exhibition Industry, gives the following definitions:

Exhibitions are market events of a specific duration, held at intervals, at which a large number of companies present a representative product range of one or more industry sectors and sell it or provide information about it for the purposes of sales promotion. Exhibitions predominantly attract the general public.

Trade fairs are market events of a specific duration, held at intervals, at which a large number of companies present the main product range of one or more industry sectors and mainly sell it on the basis of samples. Trade fairs predominantly attract trade and business visitors.

Those who travel in order to attend exhibitions are generally members of the public seeking to buy, or find information about, goods or services that they need for their own personal consumption. An example of this type of event could be the Stitch & Craft Show (**www.twistedthread.com**), which is held each year at the Olympia exhibition centre in London. It is open to anyone from the general public whose hobbies include stitching, knitting and handicrafts such as making greetings cards and jewellery. Visitors can purchase a wide range of materials and tools necessary for their hobby, as well as attend creative workshops and demonstrations at which they can learn new techniques.

Similarly, in each of the Polish cities of Warsaw, Krakow and Poznan, an annual exhibition, called the Education Fair, is held, organized by the World Educate Business Association (WEBA). The event is divided in two areas, one for universities and colleges and the other for boarding schools and high schools. Those who attend the exhibition are young people and their parents seeking information on study opportunities in Poland and other countries (**www.webafairs.com**).

Those who visit trade fairs are people who are in search of goods and services that are vital to the effective functioning of their businesses. For example, the biennial Forest Products Machinery & Equipment Exposition (**www.sfpaexpo.com**), held in New Orleans in 2009, showcases the latest products and services for the wood products industry, with manufacturers of industrial sawmill machinery, cranes, forklift trucks and other items essential to the forestry industry exhibiting their wares. Clearly, these are not intended to be purchased by members of the public for their own personal use, but by forestry and wood-processing professionals who attend this event, for business purposes.

An industry much more familiar to most people is the cinema sector of entertainment, which also has its own trade shows throughout the world. One such event is Cinema Expo International, held at the Amsterdam RAI venue (**www.cinemaexpo.com**). Those who travel to this event, from all over Europe and beyond, are mainly proprietors and managers of cinemas in search of information on, and the opportunity to purchase, the latest equipment and services required by their businesses, such as seating, staff uniforms, food and beverage kiosks, amplifiers and projection equipment.

Having made this distinction between exhibitions and trade fairs, it is certainly not the case that *all* events fall neatly into one or the other category. It is possible for the same event to be both an exhibition *and* a trade show. For example, an event primarily aimed at those running businesses in the construction industry may also be open to members of the general public who are interested in DIY as both categories of visitors to such an event will be keen to see the vast range of building materials and tools on show. It is common in such cases to have certain days that are reserved for trade visitors only and others where the general public may also attend.

It is clear that each one of all the hundreds of thousands of goods and services that we use in our personal and professional lives are bought and sold at their own exhibitions and trade shows, in destinations all over the world. From everyday objects such as shoes, books and mobile telephones, through much more expensive items such as cars, boats and holiday homes, to services such as educational courses, investment products and ski holidays, they all have their specific events, sometimes regional, sometimes national and sometimes international, to which potential customers can travel, in order to obtain information, negotiate and even possibly make a purchase.

Regarding patterns of travel to such events, it is often claimed that travel to exhibitions follows a different pattern from travel to trade shows. As most visitors to exhibitions are members of the public – people travelling with friends and/or family members – they tend

Example

Euro Attractions Show

A total of 7400 professionals from 69 nations attended the three-day Euro Attractions Show (**www.euroas.com**) held in Seville, Spain, in January 2007. As it was a trade show, it was closed to the general public, so visitors were primarily owners, general managers and operators of amusement and theme parks, family entertainment centres, waterparks and carnivals. Additional attendees represented fairs, exhibitions, zoos, aquariums, museums and science centres. Over 270 manufacturers exhibited their amusement park rides, inflatable attractions, high-tech automata, such as robots, theme park food and beverage products and costume characters.

Moreover, like many trade shows, the Euro Attractions Show offered a number of other valuable reasons for visitors to attend, in addition to the products on display. There was an educational programme, featuring presentations from industry experts on topics such as current trends in theme park attendance; there were tours of local attractions; there was a series of industry meetings featuring debates on issues affecting amusement and theme park businesses; and there were networking events for industry professionals, at which they were able to make new contacts and renew acquaintances with other owners and managers in this sector of the leisure industry.

on the whole to be making day-trips to such events. For example, a family may go to a local exhibition centre to visit a ski show with a view to buying new ski equipment or booking a ski holiday. For the family, this is a pleasant day out, the journey often made by car – much like a trip to their local shopping centre.

By way of contrast, many trade shows are of such a highly-specialized nature that they attract business visitors from other regions and, indeed, other countries – even continents. Such visitors, because of the distances they have travelled, tend to stay longer at their destination, creating valuable business for hotels and restaurants, as well as for the transport companies.

Not only do travel patterns for exhibitions and trade shows differ, but this sector of business tourism may also be distinguished from the other sectors covered in this chapter in the sense that both exhibitions *and* trade shows stimulate the travel of not one but two groups of people: the exhibitors and the visitors. So, whether the visitors are families on day trips or business owners who have travelled internationally to attend the event, the exhibitors inevitably remain in the destination for the duration of the trade fair or exhibition, bringing business to the local hospitality industry. At large events, the numbers of exhibitors can be substantial. For instance, the number of exhibiting personnel at the World Travel Market in London (**www.wtmlondon.com**) rose to over 20,000 in 2007, making it extremely challenging for anyone to find a vacant hotel room in the city during the four days in November when the event took place.

The exhibition and trade fair industry

The successful planning, marketing, hosting and execution of exhibitions and trade shows calls for the concerted efforts and expertise of a wide range of specialist professionals.

Exhibition halls and exhibition centres rent out their facilities to provide the basic shelter and security that are necessary when hosting these events. They also have to provide all necessary utilities such as electricity, water, gas and communication connections (telephone, ISDN, the Internet), as well as a clear signage system. Infrastructures, such as restaurants, parking areas (usually one for exhibitors and another for visitors), toilets and entrance areas, are other integral parts of these venues. Moreover, as conferences and seminars are often held as well as fairs and exhibitions, appropriate meeting room facilities are also included at these venues.

As exhibition halls and exhibition centres are often vast buildings, requiring many hectares of space, they are frequently situated in areas where land is cheaper, well away from city centres. Frequently, they are to be found between the city's centre and its airport, where there is ample space for parking and easy access for visitors arriving by air. Venues may be either owned by the local municipality, as is generally the case in countries such as Germany, Italy and France, for example; or privately owned and rented out with a view to making a profitable return for their owners.

While large venues such as the Geneva Palexpo are the places where by far the most exhibition and trade shows are held, it is important to remember that many smaller events may be held in hotels or other buildings such as arenas, concert halls or conference centres. Some events, due to the nature of the goods being exhibited, are, in fact, more suited to outdoor venues. For example, agricultural shows, where livestock and farm machinery are on show, or aviation trade shows, such as the annual EUR-AVIA event (**www.eur-avia.com**) held at Cannes Mandelieu International Airport on the French Riviera, are generally held in the open air.

Exhibition and trade fair organizers

The organizers of these events are the people and organizations who create the exhibition or trade show, rent the venue, then market the event to prospective exhibitors and visitors.

Example

Geneva Palexpo

Opened in January 1982, the Geneva Palexpo (palais des expositions, **www.geneva-palexpo.ch**) is situated at Geneva International Airport and 3.5 kilometres from the city centre. It has played host to 35 million visitors since its opening. To put that figure into perspective, it equates to approximately 80 times the current population of Geneva itself. The ensuing economic benefits for the canton of Geneva have amounted to many billions of Swiss francs. During the time it has been open, the available exhibition surface area has doubled to reach 102,000 square metres of continuous, covered exhibition space. The venue also offers the following services.

- *Event organization, marketing services* A team of multilingual professionals is available to help organize an event.
- *Press and public relations* For all communication and media activities.
- *Organizing the stand* Technical services to plan and build the stand.
- *Logistics and transportation* Help in handling and clearing customs.
- *Security, access, traffic, parking* Easy access, parking and security, designed by professionals.
- *Utilities (electric, plumbing)* Electrical and plumbing services will help in enabling stands to run power and water.
- *Telecommunications and audio-visual* A team of professionals to design turnkey solutions.
- *Onsite caterer* The official caterer provides a high-quality service for all types of catering throughout the Geneva Palexpo site
- *Catering partner* The selected catering partners provide a high-quality service, both within the exhibition halls and on the stands

In the second half of 2008, the events held at Palexpo included the following exhibitions and trade shows (those marked with an asterisk (*) indicate events open to professional visitors only):

03.10-05.10 APVO/UPSA	16th Exhibition of Secondhand Cars
03.10-05.10	Geneva Classics History transportation event. Exhibition devoted to vintage cars as well as other means of transport such as aircraft, boats and motorcycles.
04.10-05.10	Expo Dance 9e Salon de la Danse.
04.10-05.10	38th International Fair of Minerals, Fossils and Gems.
08.10-11.10	Utilexpo* 2nd regional exhibition for light and heavy goods vehicles.
08.10-09.10	Manageware* Exhibition for business intelligence, enterprise resource planning and business process management.
08.10-09.10	Salon RH* Exhibition for human resources.
11.10-31.12	Espace Junior A dream for all children aged 2 to 12!
12.10-12.10	Expat-Expo By, for and about the English-speaking community in Switzerland.
15.10-16.10	MEDC Expo 2008* Mobile equipment design and components expo 2008.
17.10-26.10	Voyance à Geneva Palexpo 22e Salon de la voyance.
21.10-24.10	20th EORTC − NCI − AACR* Symposium on 'Molecular targets and cancer therapeutics', with exhibition.
29.10-30.10	EMART Energy 2008* Meeting point for energy traders.
14.11-23.11	56th Geneva Fair Ideal home and art of living exhibition.
14.11-23.11	Floralies Internationales 2008.
29.11-29.11	Fair for International Studies and Careers To locate international training.

They earn a living from identifying opportunities for new exhibitions or trade shows and running these events, usually on a regular basis, for profit. A considerable amount of research must be carried out by them initially, to determine whether or not a particular theme for an exhibition or trade show is viable – in other words, are there sufficient numbers of exhibitors who are prepared to pay to have stands at an event dedicated to their industry? In turn, potential exhibitors will only agree to buy space at an event if they are satisfied that sufficient potential buyers will visit it, making their investment worthwhile. Therefore, one of the key tasks of organizers is to market it widely to potential visitors. The mark of a successful exhibition or trade show is when most exhibitors are satisfied with the numbers of visitors coming to their stands and most visitors are satisfied with the variety and range of products on display and, further, both groups consider it worthwhile returning to the event at a future date.

As stated earlier, visitors and exhibitors attend these events not only to buy and sell but also for the opportunity to attend educational sessions and networking events during the exhibition or trade show. It is another responsibility of the organizers to ensure that an interesting and topical series of seminars is programmed during the event and there are adequate opportunities for attendees to mix and mingle informally – for example at opening receptions or after-hours cocktail parties.

Stand/booth contractors

Most exhibitors rely on specialist contractors to design and build their stands. In recent years, this task has become an increasingly creative and technical one as stand design has become more imaginative and elaborate, using new materials and new technology to make exhibition stands ever more eye-catching and attractive to visitors.

High visibility is essential at such events where every exhibitor is vying with all others to entice visitors to approach their stand and engage with those who are there to sell or provide information on their companies' products. Colour, layout, lighting and prominent display of the company's logo all have a part to play in making a stand attractive and welcoming to visitors. Contractors may also be used to construct the stand before the event and dismantle it at the end.

Individual business travel

The final sector of the business tourism industry that was identified earlier is that of individual business travel, which may also be termed **corporate** travel. This sector comprises the trips of all men and women whose work obliges them to travel, either regularly or on an occasional basis. These employees are often known by the somewhat tongue-in-cheek title of 'road warriors', due to the time that they spend 'on the road' carrying out company business.

In the modern world, most organizations require some of their employees to travel from time to time in order to conduct some aspects of the company's business. Often, the objective of such trips is to find new customers, in which case a sales or marketing manager may be required to travel in order to present the company's products or services to prospective clients and negotiate prices with them.

As companies expand internationally, with branches in more than one country – and more and more often, as a result of globalization, in more than one continent – staff find themselves travelling to meet their colleagues in other branches and work with them for a few days to solve a problem or share their expertise. This type of transient movement of staff between different branches of a company is another driver of individual business travel.

Some people, whether they are company employees or self-employed, find themselves travelling regularly on business due to the nature of the job they do. For example, most investigative journalists, whether for the print media, radio or television, could not work effectively without frequently travelling in order to carry out their enquiries. Similarly, those who have highly specialized skills, such as hostage negotiators or opera singers, often find themselves travelling to where their skills are needed at any particular time.

Given, therefore, the number of reasons that exist for employees travelling on company business, it should come as no surprise that individual business travel is a major expense for many firms. Indeed, spending on business travel is second only to spending on staff pay. For this reason, most companies put into place a number of measures to control and limit their employees' spending on transport and accommodation while travelling on company business.

The main technique used for this purpose is the company's **travel policy**. It is rare these days for any company or organization (except, perhaps, for the smallest) *not* to have a written travel policy giving staff clear guidance on how they can – and, more crucially, cannot – spend their employer's money on individual business travel. Most such policies will state, for example, which class of air travel the employee is entitled to use when flying somewhere on behalf of the company. Typically, this will depend on a variety of factors, such as the length of the journey to be undertaken (short-, medium- or long-haul) and the employee's level of seniority within their company (junior, middle or senior management). Similar constrictions may be included in the travel policy for other elements of business trips, such as the class of hotel that may be used or the class of vehicle that may be hired. In this way, companies and organizations attempt to avoid the type of anarchic free-for-all that could arise if no controls were in place.

Many companies find it worthwhile employing a **business travel manager** to monitor the travel of employees and ensure that they comply with the travel policy. Business travel managers may also have the responsibility of negotiating with suppliers such as airlines, hotels and car hire companies on behalf of their employer. Large companies, in particular, are in a powerful negotiating position by virtue of the sheer volume of travel their employees undertake each year. So, while members of the general public using hotels only once or twice a year have very little leverage in terms of negotiating rates for overnight accommodation, a company with a salesforce of 50 people, spending between them several thousand nights per year in hotel rooms, is advantageously positioned to bargain with a hotel chain that has properties in the cities visited regularly by its salespeople.

A common task of the business travel manager, therefore, is to negotiate with a limited number of airlines, hotel chains and car hire companies, guaranteeing them a certain volume of business annually in return for preferential rates for the company's employees. When such agreements exist, the employees are generally instructed (in the travel policy) to use those suppliers rather than others with whom the employer has not negotiated preferential rates.

Nevertheless, although companies are constantly seeking the best value for money from travel companies and accommodation providers, it would be a mistake to believe that they always look for the very cheapest fares and hotel rates for their staff who are travelling on business. There are three main reasons for employers wanting to avoid cutting their business travel costs to the bare minimum:

- staff comfort
- staff safety
- staff loyalty and morale.

Staff comfort

Travelling in comfort can be an important consideration when it is vital that staff arrive at their destination fully refreshed and immediately ready to do the job that they have been sent to do.

Managers taking a long-haul overnight flight may save their company a considerable sum of money by travelling in economy class, but the probability that they will be able to sleep well and work at their seat – on their laptops, for example – is much less than if they were travelling in business class, with more personal space, more legroom and less likelihood of being kept awake all night by the crying baby from hell in the seat behind them. If they have not been able to rest and relax, they will hardly be in a fit state to attend an important business meeting in order to make a presentation or negotiate on behalf of their company. They may even need a day to recover from the flight, which means that an extra night in a hotel must be paid for, as well as meals and other expenses. Most importantly, a whole day's work may effectively be lost after both the outward and return journey, due to the business travellers' loss of sleep.

When all of these considerations are taken into account, the economy class ticket may seem less of a bargain than it appeared to be at the time of booking.

Staff safety

Employers have a legal duty of responsibility to do everything within reason to ensure the safety of those travelling on company business.

It is often claimed that business travellers face an even greater range of dangers than those travelling for leisure purposes. They are much more vulnerable, due to the fact that they are likely to be travelling alone, they make more attractive targets for criminals as they may be carrying information in their laptops that could be commercially valuable if it fell into certain hands and, in some countries, businesspeople may be targeted by kidnappers, who understand that their employers will be prepared to pay a substantial ransom for their safe return. Women travelling on business often feel the presence of these and other dangers more acutely than men and a great number of self-help organizations and websites (such as **www.womentraveltips.com**) exist to give advice on how to stay safe when travelling on business.

The safety of business travellers must therefore be of paramount concern to their employers. Accordingly, when a company's employee has to arrange to stay overnight in another city, in order to meet a client, for example, the company will usually authorize the booking of a room in a city centre hotel, although it may be much cheaper to book a room in a more distant, suburban hotel. This reduces the business traveller's need to travel around by taxi or public transport in an unfamiliar situation, thereby decreasing risk.

Staff loyalty and morale

Although many claim to enjoy it, individual business travel can be extremely trying at times. It temporarily separates people from their friends and families and can be a source of stress and frustration, in the same way that travel for leisure purposes can. Jet lag, gruelling security measures at airports and loss of opportunities for exercise are just a few of the common complaints of frequent business travellers. If, on top of these privations, business travellers also feel that their companies are cutting travel and accommodation costs to the bare minimum, they are hardly likely to feel positively about the firm they work for.

Resentful and unmotivated members of staff tend to feel very little loyalty to their employers. So, most companies, keen to retain their most valuable members of staff, will avoid adopting a penny-pinching approach to travel expenses and will resign themselves to paying for the occasional in-room movie or mini-bar item enjoyed by their intrepid road warriors.

The individual business travel industry

Most of the facilities and services used by individual business travellers are also used by leisure travellers. What they need from these suppliers have been discussed in detail elsewhere in this book, so, here, a few of the specific needs of business travellers will be considered and contrasted with the requirements of those travelling on holiday or for other leisure purposes.

Transport

A glance at the type of full-page advertisement paid for by airlines targeting business travellers, or at those who book their trips, shows that a major priority for those travelling on company business is punctuality. The expression 'time is money' certainly applies to the countless hours spent each year by business travellers waiting at airports or railway stations for delayed or cancelled flights or trains. Notwithstanding their personal stress levels and frustration, well-paid executives in this situation are (even in the age of wireless communications and laptops) generally far less productive than they would be if they were at their desks working. Punctuality and reliability of service are therefore much sought-after qualities for the individual business travel market.

Frequency of services is also a feature that is taken into account by business travellers choosing which carrier to use. Many individual business trips have to be flexibly timed, due to the uncertainty that can exist over when the work will be completed and the traveller is able to make the trip back home. Negotiations, for example, can run into unforeseen complications that delay the return trip or, conversely, they can go faster than expected, leaving the business traveller free to return to base earlier than planned. In either case, a frequent transport service allows for the flexibility that is required by the traveller faced with an unanticipated change of schedule (the ability to make last-minute changes to their itineraries is often given by business travellers as a further reason for avoiding the very cheapest fares, as these rarely offer the advantage of this type of flexibility).

An onboard environment conducive to work is key. As mentioned earlier as a justification for the use of business class seats, the ability to work while on the move is a pre-occupation of many business travellers – and their employers. Even before the ubiquitous laptop became an indispensable item in the carry-on luggage of anyone between the age of 16 and 60, those travelling on business tended to work for at least part of their journey – briefing themselves to prepare for their meeting, catching up on work-related reading, working through company accounts and so on. A tranquil environment, good lighting and, on trains, wi-fi connectivity and power sources for laptop computers and mobile telephones are examples of the types of facilities much sought after by those who wish to remain as productive as possible while travelling on business.

Accommodation

As with transport, accommodation that offers guests the ability to continue to work productively is at a premium for the business traveller. While leisure guests may be attracted to hotels that promise to be a 'home away from home', business guests tend to seek facilities that turn a hotel into an 'office away from the office', with Internet connections and the possibility of having documents faxed, photocopied and even (in some hotel business centres) translated. Lounges in business-orientated hotels are just as likely to be used for one-to-one business meetings as for drinks between leisure guests. There are also a number of other hotel services that are particularly appreciated by the business market, such as early check-in/late check-out, laundry services and the serving of meals in hotel bedrooms.

Business travel agencies

All but the very smallest companies and organizations tend to use some form of intermediary to book their business travel services. Some may use their high street travel agency, if their business travel needs are fairly simple and low-volume, but most medium- and large-scale companies make use of specialist business travel agencies – or travel management companies (TMCs) as they have come to call themselves – to make their travel arrangements, including the booking of transport and accommodation, providing advice on visa and vaccination issues and even, in some cases, issuing guidance on business etiquette for the destinations concerned.

In order to keep control of spending on business travel, most companies opt to employ a single TMC, usually chosen following a competitive tendering process and remunerated on a management fee basis. Some TMCs are small- to medium-sized businesses, but others, such as American Express Business Travel and Carlson Wagonlit, are vast companies with a global presence.

To a large extent, the recent evolution of business travel agencies mirrors that of the retail travel agencies discussed in Chapter 19 and the article given in the Example analyses some of the challenges facing these intermediaries in the age of information technology.

Example

Business travel agents

Business travel agents have spent a lot of time and effort during the past decade or so justifying their existence. To a large degree, the agents have been responding to the challenge of the Internet and the threat that customers would desert them in favour of online booking channels or simply do it themselves.

The erosion and, in many cases, wiping out of commissions paid by airlines changed the way travel agents were seen and how they perceived themselves. No longer simply agents of suppliers, they began to call themselves travel management companies (TMCs) and the commission was replaced by fees to clients.

A good thing, too, some said, because it would concentrate minds on the value of services being provided, but it also forced the agents to demonstrate that savings passed on to customers were significantly more than the fees they charged. This in turn spurred them to develop new services, such as providing companies with increasingly sophisticated information on the travel habits and expenses of their employees.

Have the TMCs succeeded in making the case? The answer is a qualified yes. Mike Platt, group industry affairs director of Hogg Robinson Group, claims the cost of using a TMC is 'no more than 5 per cent' of corporate travel expenditure but can reduce overall spending by as much as 30 per cent.

About 20 per cent comes in the form of air fare savings, partly by ensuring that travellers stick to company policy, flying whenever possible on airlines with which the company has negotiated ticket discounts – and sometimes added value – in return for providing those carriers with certain levels of business. Much of the other 10 per cent, says Mr Platt, is 'all the bits round the back', such as accounting and credit control. 'We have won the major battle in that companies have been over us with fine-tooth combs and we have persuaded them of the value we offer. The next battle is to persuade the travellers, who don't see those benefits. When they are asked to pay they don't see the bigger picture. They see a low fare they can book direct online and ask why they are paying us extra. The challenge for us and their employers is to get them to buy in – otherwise they will be more tempted to book outside travel policy.' He readily concedes that HRG needs to keep reinventing itself. It has been working towards providing analyses of total trip costs, so that travel managers would be able to review all the implications, say, of a traveller's decision to book a low-cost flight – from its impact on targets agreed with a preferred airline to the sometimes unconsidered cost of huge taxi fares from a secondary airport miles from town. 'We see ourselves more as a provider of various corporate services rather than purely making bookings. We are doing a lot of work helping clients to deal with anything from a flu pandemic to reducing the carbon emissions caused by travel.'

The attacks of September 11 2001 underlined the importance to companies of being able to locate their staff in emergency. TMCs have taken on this task. American Express Business Travel, for example, has launched TrackPoint, a Web-based tool which enables corporate travel managers to track down staff in the event of such disasters. It is already available to customers in North America and Europe, and is being piloted in the Asia-Pacific region.

Security delays at US airports have prompted efforts to spare frequent flyers the worst effects. BRD Travel, for example, is planning to offer US customers discounted access to the Transport Security Administration's registered traveller programme, which will be operated by the private sector.

With companies under increasing pressure to limit their contributions to global warming, TMCs are either already providing or planning to provide them with assessments of carbon emissions. The global distribution system (GDS) operator Sabre has developed a product that will help them do this. Each report is divided into four sections detailing the number of air segments (single flights) booked over a given period, distance flown, the amount of fuel burned expressed in kilograms and litres, the quantity of CO_2 produced as a result and a breakdown of the other greenhouse gases produced.

All this activity appears to be paying dividends. Figures from the UK's Guild of Travel Management Companies indicate an overall increase in trips organized by its members over the past two years. Total transactions with suppliers – airlines, rail operators, hotels and car rental companies – increased from about 10.2 million at the end of March 2004 to just over 11 million a year later and some 12.2 million by the same date this year. 'It seems', says the Guild's chief executive Philip Carlisle, 'that the business of business travel is quite healthy.'

A survey published by Carlson Wagonlit Travel painted a similarly optimistic picture in the short term. It showed that in North America and the Asia-Pacific, 63 per cent and 59 per cent of corporate travel managers expected their company's expenditure on trips to rise this year, while only 8 per cent and 11 per cent believed it would decrease. Europeans were a little less buoyant, with 49 per cent anticipating an increase and 15 per cent fearing a drop. In all cases, the remainder believed spending would match that in 2005.

In the longer term, however, TMCs may still have some defending to do. A significant majority of the managers questioned by CWT (87 per cent, 75 per cent and 76 per cent respectively) thought it 'very' or 'somewhat' likely that travel would be increasingly supplanted by video conferencing over the next five years. Self-booking tools, which can be primed to establish travel policy, may persuade some companies whose staff make predominantly straightforward bookings to eliminate the middleman.

Source: Roger Bray, 'Business travel agents', *Financial Times*, 4 September 2006.

Trends in business tourism

The rest of this chapter looks at some of the most important trends that will present opportunities and challenges to the global business tourism industry in the years ahead. Many of those trends are already emerging and others may be anticipated because of changes in the wider market environment.

The market for business tourism services and facilities is an extremely dynamic one – one that is highly sensitive to changes in the political, economic and social environment. This sector is also affected by the accelerating rate of innovation in information and communications technology. On the one hand it offers significant opportunities for the development of more attractive business tourism products, but, on the other, may also create certain threats to the long-term prosperity of this sector.

Economic trends

Emerging markets

The rise of new business tourism destinations in many developing economies of the world is a major – and ongoing – phenomenon in this sector. As recently as 60 years ago, North American cities and European capitals had a practical monopoly over the hosting of international association meetings, for example. They were virtually the only places equipped with the infrastructure required to host these large-scale events. The decades since then, however, have seen a burgeoning of destinations entering all sectors of the business tourism market: Australasia, South East Asia, South America and, more recently, Central and Eastern European countries and cities in the Middle East have entered the market as vibrant new destinations for the hosting of meetings, trade shows and incentive trips.

At the same time, developing economies create additional demand for business tourism events as their new businesses add to the need for corporate events, and members of the expanding professional classes increasingly have the means to travel to conferences and exhibitions in other countries.

This phenomenon is particularly seen in China and India, two of the world's fastest-growing economies, and countries widely believed to be major sources of international business tourism consumption in the years to come. These two countries represent the two economies that are set to generate the greatest expansion in outbound business travel for the short and medium-term. Citizens of these countries are already travelling to other destinations in their own regions, on business, but they will extend their scope to Europe and other long-haul destinations in rapidly increasing numbers in the years ahead. In China, growing levels of personal disposable income, Chinese companies' investment overseas and a fast-increasing number of international air connections with cities in major destinations, are factors that will ensure the rapid growth of Chinese outbound corporate meetings and incentive trips and Chinese delegates at international association meetings and exhibitions in the near future.

Growing corporate cost-consciousness

As competition between business tourism venues and destinations intensifies, buyers have become aware that they are purchasing services in a 'buyers' market'. Much of the corporate market in particular has lost no time in reaping the benefits of this situation and meeting planners have quickly learned how to negotiate to their best advantage. With no sign of imminent change in the relationship between supply and demand, corporate buyers are set to become even more cost-conscious in the years ahead.

Almost every survey of demand for business tourism events suggests that corporate buyers expect the number of events they organize to increase in the immediate and short-term future, but there is no corresponding indication that their budgets are going to increase at a proportional rate. On the contrary, most surveys reveal a general reduction of per-delegate expenses as the central issue for many companies becomes that of ensuring better overall value and a higher return on their investment. Therefore, all business tourism destinations, and the venues within them, must constantly look for ways to manage their tariffs and demonstrate the cost-effectiveness of these. Quality, but at an attractive price, will be a dominant requirement for the foreseeable future, as the majority of businesses now recognize the strengths of their considerable purchasing power.

Technology trends

Information and communications technology (ICT) has already transformed many aspects of the business tourism sector and there is no doubt that further advances in ICT will continue to have a profound impact on how such events are planned, promoted and experienced in years to come.

Young people now entering employment in this sector will never understand the extent to which the Internet alone has revolutionized the planning, marketing and execution of events such as conferences and exhibitions. It is rare indeed, nowadays, to find a major conference or exhibition without its own website, where potential participants can read, in advance, full details of the event, register to attend and plan their schedule for the event itself. Developments such as PowerPoint and hand-held devices that allow the audience to respond in real time to conference presentations have enhanced delegates' experience, while radio frequency identification (RFID) promises to make the tracking and identification of exhibition visitors more efficient. The rate of wi-fi deployment in conference and exhibition venues and in large hotels is expanding fast and is increasingly expected by people travelling on business.

Social trends

More female business tourists

Changes in the profile of the global working population have, in turn, had a very significant effect on the profile of participants in business tourism events. The most prominent of these is the ongoing increase in the proportion of women in professional employment. Women's share of professional jobs continued to increase in the first few years of the twenty-first century in the vast majority of countries, and this trend shows every sign of continuing. Women are already well represented in a number of professions, such as healthcare and finance, that are expanding rapidly in most countries. Women are also making inroads into traditionally male-dominated professions. For example, in some countries, the women's share of the ICT sector is already significant.

This continuing trend means that there are more women travelling on business, for all work-related purposes, including participation in conferences and exhibitions. The growing presence of female delegates at such events has had a number of impacts on business tourism services, from how conference and exhibition venues are designed (more toilet facilities for women), to the food served during breaks (lighter and generally healthier).

Another indication of the femininization of the market is the increase in popularity of spas as incentive travel products – and not only for women. Partly through the influence of female participants, the spa has become an amenity that a growing number of delegates expect in hotels and resorts.

More older business tourists

The European and North American working population is ageing significantly and will continue to do so for the foreseeable future, adding to the proportion of those in employment who are in the older age categories. Increasingly, people in their sixties and seventies are remaining in employment, either through choice (they find fulfilment through their work) or through necessity (they cannot afford to retire).

With a significant proportion of workers in the older age groups working in managerial and professional positions, it is highly likely that they will continue to travel on business and to business events, for a number of reasons.

- Because they can! As members of the baby boom generation start to enter their sixties, it is clear that they are considerably healthier, fitter and more socially involved than those of the previous generation were at that age. Travelling to business events and fully taking part in them presents them with none of the physical challenges that their parents would have faced in their sixties.

- Older workers understand that networking is particularly important to them as the type of upper-level management positions they are often seeking are not likely to be advertised. Attending conferences of their professional associations provides them with a valuable opportunity to network.

- There is a positive relationship between older workers staying in the workforce and their need for ongoing training opportunities. Particularly with so many older workers continuing to work in the fast-evolving 'knowledge industries', constant in-service training events are vital to them for keeping their skills up to date. This means that they will be increasingly present at corporate meetings that have a training objective.

- A growing number of retired people are choosing to continue being members of their professional associations – in many cases, for the mental stimulation that profession-based meetings provide, as well as for the opportunity to maintain contact with colleagues.

The challenge of attracting 'Generations X and Y'

Over the next few years, associations will face growing difficulties in attracting attendees to their events. This is partly due to the prevalent phenomenon of people being **time poor** – that is, a growing number of association members have extensive demands on their limited time. It appears, however, that the new and upcoming generation of association members – 'Generation X' (those born between 1964 and 1977) and Generation Y (born between 1978 and 1994) – may also take some convincing that there is value in attending conferences. Generation Xers, unlike their parents, do not so readily see the value of face-to-face events. As they have grown up with electronic media as a primary communication tool, face-to-face events are less attractive to them (this is even more the case with Generation Yers). If this contention proves to be accurate, it presents serious meeting attendance issues for associations, as these two generations, between them, account for a combined demographic of 120 million people in the USA alone.

What can be done to reach this vast and growing section of the workforce and interest them in attending MICE events? Understanding their profile, developing strategies and targeting each group with appropriate messages is the key to motivating Generations X and Y to join associations and attend their conferences. Both groups have a sophisticated understanding of technology and expect it to be well utilized; the Web wins over traditional media as a primary source of information; they often select personal fulfilment over monetary rewards, seeking a casual work environment, telecommuting options and time off to enjoy life.

As time moves on, the behaviour and preferences of Generations X and Y will come to shape corporate and association life. Therefore, time spent now in understanding their needs and convincing them of the rewards of attending face-to-face events will reap rewards in the future.

Corporate social responsibility

The field of corporate social responsibility (CSR) has grown exponentially in the last decade as companies increasingly seek to engage with their stakeholders and deal with potentially contentious issues proactively. Now, more companies than ever are engaged in integrating CSR into all aspects of their business, encouraged by a growing body of evidence that CSR has a positive impact on businesses' economic performance.

The US-based organization Business for Social Responsibility (BSR) defines corporate social responsibility as 'achieving commercial success in ways that honour ethical values and respect people, communities, and the natural environment.' This organization also says that CSR means addressing the legal, ethical, commercial and other expectations that society has for business and making decisions that fairly balance the claims of all key stakeholders.

The business tourism industry itself is beginning to show increasing awareness of the need to demonstrate its CSR and this will intensify in future years. As the drive for greater transparency grows, all industries and organizations, public as well as private, will be increasingly obliged to demonstrate their ethical, environmental and social credentials. All stakeholders in the business tourism industry, from airlines, hotels and venues to intermediaries and the delegates themselves, will need to examine their own commitment to CSR. This will mean that business tourism stakeholders will increasingly be obliged to demonstrate their concern for the natural environment as well as the host communities that live and work in the destinations where events take place. This is particularly the case when the standard of living of the host community is markedly below that of the business travellers themselves. The apparent luxury and extravagance that characterize certain events can stand out in very stark contrast to the abjectly poor and chronically disadvantaged conditions in which some of the local inhabitants live. For that reason, it is encouraging that a number of conference and incentive travel organizers have begun taking steps to invest in projects which have a positive impact on the communities residing in the destinations where their events are held. Conference delegates raising money for a local charity or incentive travel participants spending a day making environmental improvements to their destination are typical examples of this growing trend.

In the years ahead, more business tourism stakeholders will become aware of the benefits to themselves, and to host communities, of investing time and money in giving something back to underprivileged people living in some of the destinations where their events take place.

Conclusion

This chapter has reviewed the elements and characteristics of the business tourism sector, as well as some of the key trends and challenges that the sector is already dealing with and will continue to face in the future. There can be no doubt that the market environment for business tourism will continue to evolve and mutate in ways that are perhaps impossible to predict at the present time. It is in this very unpredictability, however, that the challenge and excitement of operating in this sector of the travel and tourism industry lies.

In the complex, volatile flux of market trends and forces, one element that will remain reassuringly constant is human nature itself. Men and women will continue to attend business tourism events, not only for the opportunity to obtain personal and professional development for themselves and business growth for their organizations but also for the simple pleasure of meeting those with whom they share a common interest or goal. Buyers and participants will be drawn to attractive destinations and venues that deliver efficiently run and memorable events, using state-of-the-art technology, as well as distinctive cultural experiences in a healthy and unique environment.

Questions and discussion points

1. Give as many differences as you can between leisure tourism (holidays, short breaks and day trips) and business tourism. Think in terms of who travels for leisure and who travels on business, who pays for the trips, when leisure trips and business trips take place, what types of destinations are used for business and leisure tourism, who decides on the destination and the lead time (the period of time leading up to the trip, planning it and so on) for business and for leisure tourism.

2. It is often claimed that videoconferencing (or teleconferencing) technology will largely obviate the need for delegates to travel to face-to-face meetings. Give as many reasons as possible in favour of, and against, replacing face-to-face meetings with videoconferences.

3. Put yourself in the position of someone wishing to buy a new laptop computer. You could find the ideal computer for you by visiting computer shops, computer websites and shopping online, ordering manufacturers' catalogues and browsing through them or you could travel to visit an exhibition of computer manufacturers' products. What, for you, would be the advantages of visiting an exhibition in order to find your perfect laptop?

4. Many people travelling frequently on business on behalf of their employer earn valuable airmiles when they fly to their destinations. Currently, the employees get to use those airmiles for themselves. Discuss the rights and wrongs of this situation. What arguments can be made in favour of the airmiles accruing to the business travellers' employers?

Tasks

1. More and more business travellers are female and there is a growing number of websites designed for women travelling alone on business. Visit as many of these websites as you can and write a report summarizing the advice that they offer. What innovations have hotels introduced in order better to serve this segment of their client market? Do all female business travellers want to be treated differently from their male counterparts?

2. Use the Internet to find the conference centre and the exhibition centre that are situated closest to where you live. Carry out the necessary research to identify three major conferences and three major trade shows being held in these venues during the month in which you undertake this assignment.

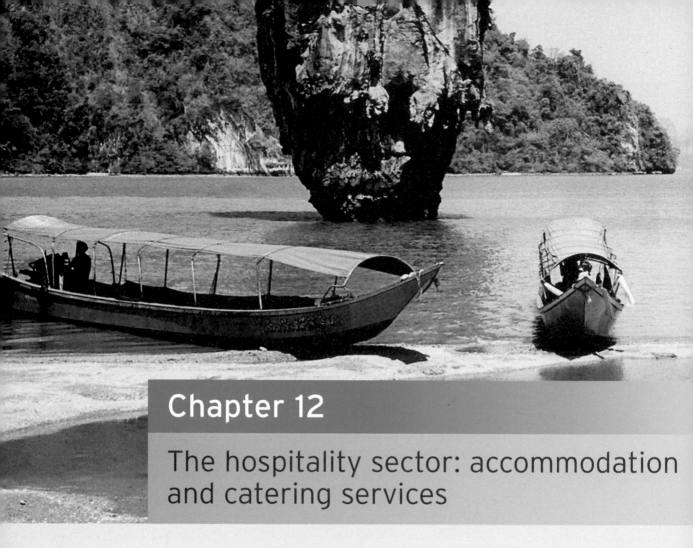

Chapter 12

The hospitality sector: accommodation and catering services

Learning outcomes

After studying this chapter, you should be able to:

- explain the structure and nature of the hospitality sector, distinguishing between the various categories of tourist accommodation and catering services

- describe how accommodation is classified and be aware of the problems involved in classification

- understand the nature of demand for accommodation and catering and how the sector has responded to changing patterns of demand over time

- understand the relationship between the hospitality sector and other sectors of the tourism industry.

Introduction

> In 1990, only one in five people stayed in a hotel – now that's one in three.
> It's no coincidence that that's the time in which branded budget has grown.
>
> Grant Hearn, Chief Executive of Travelodge, interviewed in *The Observer*,
> 27 January 2008

In this chapter, we are principally concerned with examining the commercial accommodation and catering sector. It must not be forgotten, however, that this sector represents just one element of the hospitality business and is often in competition with large non-commercial hospitality suppliers that are no less important to tourism. The VFR (visiting friends and relations) market is substantial and, in addition, there is a wide variety of other forms of accommodation used by tourists, including the tourists' own camping and caravanning equipment, privately owned boats and – of increasing significance for tourism in the twenty-first century – second homes, whether in the home country or abroad. There is also a growing market for home exchanges and the swapping of timeshare accommodation – a market that the industry has developed through the establishment of timeshare exchange companies.

It is, in fact, difficult to distinguish between the strictly commercial and non-commercial aspects of the hospitality business. Youth hostels and YMCAs, for example, are not necessarily attempting to make a profit, but merely to cover their operating costs, while it is increasingly common, as noted earlier, to find educational institutions such as universities and schools hiring out their student accommodation to tourists outside the academic terms, in order to make some contribution to the running costs of the institutions. One result of this has been a marked increase in the quality of student accommodation, with en suite bathrooms now the norm in new buildings.

Other forms of tourism that by their nature embrace accommodation would include privately hired yachts or bookings on a cruise ship. Operators in some countries provide coaches that include sleeping berths, while in others packages are available using specially chartered trains that serve as the travellers' hotel throughout the trip (see Figure 12.1). Independent travellers can also book sleeping accommodation on rail services in many popular tourist destinations. To what extent should all these services be counted as elements of the commercial accommodation available to tourists?

Certainly, any study of tourism must take account of these overnight alternatives and the expansion or contraction in demand for sleeping arrangements that compete with the traditional accommodation sector. The rapid rise in cruise holidays over the past few years, to take one instance, will have affected demand for more traditional forms of holiday in which travel and somewhere to stay are the norm.

Tourists staying in private accommodation away from their homes – whether with friends and relatives or in second homes owned by themselves or their friends – are still engaging in tourism and will almost certainly be contributing to tourist spend in the region as they will tend to use local commercial transport, restaurants and entertainment. Their spend must therefore be included in tourism statistics for the region.

Apart from the economic benefits of such tourists at the destination, there are frequently commercial transactions in the home country associated with their trips. Tour operators and budget airlines sell flights to airports near second homes (indeed, the expanding ownership of second homes among Britons in France, Italy and Spain has been a big contributing factor to the strength of the budget carriers) and many tourists will hire cars during the period of their stay, for which, in some cases, payment will be made through agents in the home country before departure.

Airlines, recognizing that home exchanges can also represent a healthy source of flight revenue, have developed and commercialized the home exchange business by establishing directories to assist people in arranging exchanges. Some national or regional tourist

Figure 12.1 On board the *Desert Express*, a luxury train offering comfortable sleeping and dining accommodation for passengers touring Namibia.
(Photo by Chris Holloway.)

offices also keep directories of homeowners who are prepared to make exchanges and others maintain lists of local householders willing to invite guests from overseas into their homes for a meal (a particular feature of US hospitality). More recently, commercial brokers have been set up to facilitate home exchanges around the world, for a modest fee (in the UK, **www.homelink.org.uk** and **www.homexchangevacation.com**; in the USA, **www.homeexchange.com**, for example).

The structure of the accommodation sector

The accommodation sector comprises widely differing forms of sleeping and hospitality facilities that can be conveniently categorized as either serviced (in which catering is included) or self-catering. These are not watertight categories as some forms of accommodation, such as holiday camps or educational institutions, may offer serviced, self-service or self-catering facilities, but they help in drawing distinctions between the characteristics of the two categories. Figure 12.2 provides an at-a-glance guide to the range of accommodation that tourists might occupy.

Hotels are the most significant and widely recognized form of overnight accommodation for tourists. They also form one of the key elements of most package holidays. What constitutes a hotel and distinguishes it from other forms of accommodation, however, is not always clear. The English Hotel Occupancy Survey defines it as an establishment having five or more bedrooms, not identified as a guesthouse or boarding house and not listed as providing bed-and-breakfast accommodation only.

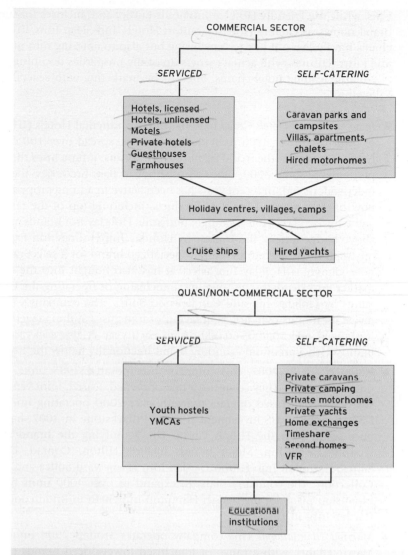

Figure 12.2 The structure of tourist accommodation.

The corporate chains

A feature of the industry is that, as mass tourism has developed, so have the large chains and corporations in the accommodation sector. The hotel and motel business has reached a stage of maturity in which a few major companies have come to dominate, if not the markets, then certainly the distribution chain. The policy of these groups is to create an international and uniform marketing image for each brand to assist sales around the world. Economies of scale have allowed the largest chains to increase their spend on international marketing, advertising and sales promotion in partnership with other sectors of the industry, such as transport companies and tour operators, while cutting costs and, in the case of the budget brands, reducing prices to consumers to well below those available through more traditional outlets. This expansion has also been aided by franchising, whereby hotels and motels are operated by individual franchisees paying royalties to the parent company for the privilege of operating under a brand name. This form of expansion has been used with great success around the world by companies such as Holiday

Inns, while the Friendly Hotel group holds European franchises for such well-established brand names as Quality Hotels, Comfort Hotels and Sleep Inns. To expand rapidly, the chains have taken not just to franchising but also to entering into management contracts and joint ventures, with actual ownership of the properties declining.

Notable leading hotel chains, often niche marketing with several brands, include the following.

- *InterContinental Hotels Group* In 2007, InterContinental Hotels (IHG) owned, managed or franchised over 3700 individual properties, spread over 100 countries. The largest hotel company in the world by number of rooms, it franchises the great majority of its properties – some 3200. Once an offshoot of Bass Breweries, the hotel group is now independent and, in recent years has been active in adding properties to its portfolio. It now offers a range of branded products, including top of the range InterContinental and Crowne Plaza Hotels, Indigo, mid-scale Holiday Inn brands and, coming in a little above budget prices, the Express by Holiday Inn/Holiday Inn Express chain. A recent innovation has been to develop a specialized brand for a select range of Holiday Inns, now known as Holiday Inn Select. It has also bought into the corporate hospitality market for extended stays, owning, franchising or operating the US brands Staybridge Suites by Holiday Inn and Candlewood Suites. The company's policy is currently to divest itself of its own hotels in favour of franchises and management contracts, where it plans to add 50,000–60,000 rooms each year. It also seeks to expand its range of brands with a premium economy brand fractionally below the Express level of hotel.

- *Hilton Hotels* In 2007, this company incorporated 2985 units, of which 380 were outside the USA. They comprise a mix of owned, leased, joint venture, managed, time-share and franchised operations, with over 2000 operating under franchise. Hilton USA, bought by US investment company Blackstone in 2007, has now amalgamated once again with the Hilton Group UK, reunifying the brand after many years of separate ownership. Major brands include Hilton, Conrad, Doubletree, Embassy Suites, Hampton Inn, Hilton Garden Inn, Homeward Suites and The Waldorf Astoria Collection. The company plans to expand to over 4000 units by 2012, with strong expansion plans for the budget Hampton Inn chain in Britain and mid-market Hilton Garden Inns in Turkey.

- *Marriott International* This company operates around 2900 units, mainly under the Marriott label, with a range of franchised lower-priced brands such as Fairfield Inn. Apart from the Marriott label, brands include Renaissance Hotels and Resorts, Ritz Carlton, Courtyard, Residence Inn, SpringHill Suites, TownPlace Suites, Fairfield Inn and a number of properties bearing the Bulgari brand name. Marriott has announced plans to launch a range of boutique hotels with Ian Schrager. It was Schrager Hotels that first launched the concept of the designer hotel. Some 200 stylish new units, to be branded 'Edition' are planned by 2012, targeting Starwood's W Hotels brand of highly successful boutique hotels (note that Richard Branson's Virgin Hotel division has also announced plans to launch an Urban Hotel brand emulating the W's success).

- *Starwood Hotels and Resorts* This company operates around 870 units, mainly managed, some owned and a number franchised. Major brands include Sheraton Hotels and Resorts, Westin Hotels and Resorts, le Meridien, St Regis, Luxury Collection, W Hotels, Four Points by Sheraton, Aloft and Element. Over 400 new projects were in the pipeline at the time of writing, with the first W Hotel in the UK now open in central London.

- *Accor* The first non-US-operated hotel chain in this list, this French company has expanded substantially in the past few years and operates around 3800 units in 90 countries, with a variety of brands ranging from luxury to budget. Brands include Sofitel Demeure, Novotel, Dorint, Suitehotel, Mercure, Coralia, Etap, Ibis and Formule 1. In North America, the brand operates under the Sofitel and Novotel brands alongside budget brands Motel 6 and Studio 6 (extended stay hotels). In a recent decision, the Sofitel brand has now been subdivided into three formats: Sofitel Luxury Hotels, Sofitel Legend (historic properties) and So by Sofitel (Boutique hotels aimed at the younger market). Current Sofitel units not fitting any of these categories adequately are being rebranded as Pullman Hotels. A new budget brand, All Seasons, was announced in 2007.

- *Envergure Hotels* The Envergure group is a second French-owned chain. Its brands include the 2-star Campanile Hotels along with Bleu Marine, Kyriad Prestige, Kyriad, Climat de France, Première Classe and Nuit d'Hotel.

As these chains market their products more aggressively, advertise extensively, work closely with large tour-operating organizations globally and, in addition to their own websites, provide an effective distribution network linked to the airline CRSs, they tend to have a more visible presence in the industry than their market share would suggest. In total bed terms, their total bed stock is small compared with the multitude of small, independently owned facilities, but these, until recently, have had less ready access to both the market and other sectors of the industry. With the growth of commercial websites, smaller units now have greater opportunities to reach their customers directly, even if not on the scale of the large corporations. Some independents have seen the value of coming together as members of a consortium in order to develop their website opportunities and compete more effectively with the large chains.

The expansion internationally of the two French groups is particularly interesting, given that generally the French have been slower to exploit the global market in other sectors than other countries, with the possible exception of the Club Méditerranée tour operation (in which Accor has a small stake). Again, the policy has been to satisfy a variety of market niches through brand imagery. Both companies have successfully sought in recent years to penetrate the UK market, too.

Further afield, other notable chains include the Mandarin group, concentrated in the Pacific Rim area, while Indian-owned Oberoi Hotels have expanded into Egypt, the Far East and Australia.

As with other sectors of the tourism industry, there is a growing belief that a handful of mega-chains such as these will in time come to dominate the global tourism market, with independents focusing on niche market opportunities.

A recent development has been the trend to initiate **brand extensions** across products – an example of which we have seen with the move by Bulgari into the hotel sector. The Versace brand has also moved into hospitality, with the opening in Australia of the Palazzo Versace. Several other fashion houses are developing plans to form partnerships with hotel chains that will bear the fashion brand's name, including Armani, Missoni and Moschino, which plan to focus on accommodation in or near prestigious shopping locations. Other examples of brand-stretching include *Maxim*, a men's magazine, which has opened a Las Vegas hotel and casino, while leading catering brands have also moved into accommodation, with McDonalds launching a chain of Golden Arch Hotels and the Hard Rock Café developing the Hard Rock Hotel brand.

Budget hotels

It is in the budget sector of the hotel industry that growth has been strongest in recent years, with a 50 per cent growth in the five years to 2007 and forecasts that this market will treble by 2027. Responding to this demand, the large chains have been concentrating on creating or developing their own budget-priced properties – a field formerly left largely to independent organizations or leisure conglomerates.

In Britain, well-established companies such as Granada or catering subsidiaries of the big brewers were leaders in the development of what is now termed 'limited service' hotels, to distinguish them from the type of accommodation sought by the backpacker market. Brands new to Britain, such as Days Inn and Sleep Inn, are joining more familiar brands to capture a share of this fast-growing market, especially in city centre properties, which attract growing numbers of short break tourists. The two leading chains, Travelodge and Premier Inn, have a strong hold on the market, however, and are developing strategies to ensure they stay in front.

- *Travelodge* Bought by Dubai Investment Capital in 2006 (and thus, in effect, a state-owned company), Travelodge is one of the leading budget brands, with 369 hotels in the UK in 2009 and 26,000 bedrooms. A number are in the pipeline and it has expectations of continuing this growth over coming years, with some 70,000 rooms by 2020, by which date it will control 10 per cent of the UK market. In 2008, the company already possessed around 30 coastal properties in Britain and has announced its intention to build a further 55 new hotels in similar locations. There are ambitious plans to expand abroad, too, with 100 units in Spain by 2020, to be held on 25-year leases. A recent innovation has been the introduction of the first 'recyclable' hotel. It consists of modules built in China comprising two rooms and a bathroom, with built-in beds, resembling shipping containers. These can be quickly assembled or disassembled on site, taking 25 per cent less time to construct than a standard unit, and are claimed to cut overall building costs by 10 per cent. The first such units, with 120 rooms, opened in London in 2008 and, if proved successful, up to half of all Travelodge hotels may take this form in the future.

- *Premier Inn* In 2004, the brewers Whitbread acquired the Premier Lodge and Scottish & Newcastle Hotel brands, merging these into their Travel Inn brand and renaming the group Premier Travel Inn, later simplified to the present brand name. The company expected to have control of around 570 hotels and 40,000 rooms in the UK by the end of 2008, making it the largest budget chain in the country. It, too, has ambitious expansion plans, with a forecast of 55,000 rooms by 2013. The group announced in 2008 that 60 per cent of its clientele were now business travellers – an indication of the degree to which businesses are downgrading accommodation in light of the depressed economy. It has further plans to expand into Dubai and India.

In 2008, merger talks were held between these two leading budget chains, which would have given them a 65 per cent share of the branded budget market in the UK. These merger proposals, however, have not advanced to date.

Recent trends are pointing towards a splintering of the budget hotel sector, with luxury budget accommodation at one end of the range, with brands such as City Inn and Big Sleep, while new super-budget brands, such as Purple Hotels, Yotel, Dakota, Base 2 Stay and easyHotels, are emerging at the other.

In mainland Europe, Accor Hotels has exploited the deficiency in this sector by introducing the super-budget chains Formule 1 and Etap, while others on the Continent have popularized low-budget brands such as B&B Hotels, Mister Bed, Villages Hotels, Unhotel and Fimotel. These very low-priced hotels have managed to reduce costs by developing a unitary design and automating many of the services provided – reception desks are only manned for short periods of the day and, at other times, entry is by the insertion of credit cards into a machine on the external wall. Similarly, breakfasts are self-service and highly automated.

The introduction of this style of hotel into the UK has not been simple. Land costs push up prices in Britain, while restricted furnishings and services appear too basic for the British market. For example, carpet soon replaced the linoleum that French hotel guests had seemed more willing to accept (undoubtedly, differing climates are a contributing factor to this choice).

The approach taken by Stelios Hadji-Ioannou, founder of easyJet, in developing the super-budget brand, is characteristic of current developments.

Example

easyHotels and the super-budget hotel

A new generation of super-budget hotels, easyHotels, was announced by Stelios Hadji-Ioannou in 2005. The first two opened in Kensington, London, and in Basel, Switzerland. Costs are ultra low, with a lead-in price of as little as £20 a night for advance booking, but rooms are basic – many are windowless and, while overall sizes vary, some are as small as just 60 square feet. Rooms do have TVs (at a premium) and minuscule shower and toilet cabinets, but are without wardrobes or even bedside lights. There are no communal areas or bars and housekeeping charges are extra. Sales are exclusively online, no advertising is undertaken and no discounts are offered to distributors such as travel agents.

Stelios believes firmly that these ultra low-priced micro-hotels will be the growth area of the future, in line with the growth in low-cost air travel, and points to budget chains such as Motel 6 adopting a similar strategy in North America.

The easyHotels may be judged roomy, however, when contrasted with Japan's 'pod' capsule hotels. Whether or not budget-conscious Western guests will eventually be reduced to, or be willing to accept, these coffin-like stacked bedroom boxes that have found favour in Japanese cities is another matter. The Travelodge 'shipping container' type room is perhaps the ideal answer for this end of the market, in terms of the acceptability of room size and value for money.

The character property

The competition between luxury hotels has led to new forms of market segmentation, based on product differentiation. Country house or townhouse hotels place emphasis on giving a personal service. Boutique and designer hotels – especially those taking advantage of the fashion for cutting-edge design – have attracted widespread publicity (a glance in any bookshop at the range of books devoted to cutting edge hotel design and 'hip' hotels will confirm this) and this has been given additional impetus by their tendency to attract celebrities and celebrity-hunters. Hotels in this category in London include The Halkin, Blakes, Great Eastern Metropolitan, One Aldwych, St Martin's Lane, the Sanderson and the Trafalgar Hilton, while in the USA there are the Hudson, Mercer, Morgans and Royalton Hotels in New York, the Avalon in Los Angeles and the Delano in Miami.

Ian Schrager was responsible for the ultra-chic Morgans Hotel in New York, but now believes that art, rather than designer, hotels, signify the way forward. The Hotel Vittoria in Florence (one of the Una Hotel chain) has staked a claim as being the most fashionable in the world, with mural portraits on each door and surrealistic decor. The Gramercy Park has original paintings by cutting-edge artist Jean-Michael Basquiat, and the Winston Hotel Amsterdam has walls lined with original modern art, while the Künstlerheim Luise, Berlin, goes one better – offering rooms that, in decor, resemble paintings by van Gogh, Magritte or Edward Hopper.

Other more recently constructed hotels have opted to go for the wow factor, either in relation to their architecture or sheer size. For example, the hotel Puerto America in Madrid, operated by Silken Hotels since 2005, has chosen to have each floor designed by a different famous architect. Size alone had little appeal in the past, as those mega-hotels in the former Soviet Union proved only too clearly, but if sold as luxury resorts in their own right, virtual cities within a city, they find a market as readily as the giant cruise ships carrying over 2000 passengers have done. Las Vegas boasts 10 such mega-hotels with over 3000 rooms.

Example

Size matters: the supersize hotel

In 2008, the world's largest inhabitable (and, incidentally, the world's second-largest) building opened in Macao, China. With a total area of 10.4 million square feet (large enough to accommodate a fleet of 90 Boeing 747s), the Venetian Macao Resort Hotel has 3000 all-suite rooms and 30 restaurants.

The property is themed as a pastiche of Renaissance Venice, with replicas of St Mark's and the Doge's Palace. With a million square feet devoted to meeting facilities alone and a 15,000 seat arena, the hotel is setting out to capture the MICE market and is gambling on the wow factor of its size attracting the business customer, in common with other large business-orientated hotels in China.

The Burj al-Arab Hotel in Dubai is famed not only as the tallest hotel in the world, but also for its self-claimed classification of 7-star status, defining ultra luxury. Within Europe, the Gran Hotel Benidorm, at 186 metres and 43 stories high, offers its own unique appeal. Central atriums with glass lifts, spectacular indoor and outdoor gardens or other eye-catching features all help to reinforce the hotel experience as being something more than just a room and a bed.

The Conrad chain, like many upmarket hotel operators, targets the corporate market, offering all-suite hotels as a principal feature in their luxury product, while hotels that have been converted from buildings formerly used for other purposes have deliberately retained their original character and have therefore appealed strongly to a business market of frequent users jaded by standardization and uniformity.

A good example of the latter is the small chain known as the Hotel du Vin & Bistro (part of the Malmaison Group), which purchases redundant properties in city centres, such as former warehouses and industrial buildings, redeveloping them as lodgings while retaining their original character. Emphasizing their catering strengths, they have succeeded in simultaneously creating some highly praised restaurants. On the Continent, similar aims are shared by Malmaison's Continental hotels and Germany's Sorat chain, Spain's Melia Boutique and Derby Hotels.

An interesting development is the effort now being made to 'brand stretch', linking well-known branded products with accommodation. As we saw earlier, the Bulgari brand is already employed, marketed by Marriott, Versace has also moved into the field and Baccarat has announced its intention to build a resort in Hawaii. The continuing appeal of high-status products for a celebrity-hungry market should ensure the success of this approach, with both Missoni and Armani lending their names in 2009.

Individual hotels have also succeeded in establishing unique personalities that attract niche markets. Examples in the UK include the Lace Market in Nottingham and the Scotsman in Edinburgh, housed in the former premises of *The Scotsman* newspaper. Such developments reveal alternative ways forward for hotel design – the days of the faceless and monolithic concrete block, favoured in the development of new resorts in the Mediterranean and elsewhere in order to permit rapid construction and cheap operation, are ending as the sophisticated travel market seeks better service and more character in its lodgings.

Hotels that can offer attributes unique to the country visited are always popular with tourists. The paradores in Spain or the pousadas of Portugal – national chains of state-operated inns located in historic properties – are proving highly successful despite their premium prices. Similarly, traditional haciendas in Mexico and the ryokans of Japan,

Figure 12.3 An independent boutique hotel – the Primrose Valley Hotel in St Ives, Cornwall. *(Photo by Chris Holloway.)*

Figure 12.4 A character hotel – the Compleat Angler, in Marlow, Buckinghamshire. *(Photo by Chris Holloway.)*

which offer an authentic flavour of the country's culture, greatly appeal to the independent travel market. In Britain, individual character properties owned by the National Trust, the Landmark Trust and similar organizations are in great demand. One of the National Trust's most popular properties is Peel Bothy – a tiny former shepherd's home at Steel Rigg, Northumberland, offering only very basic facilities, but seen as full of character.

Hotels of character appeal as strongly to leisure travellers as they do to business travellers. In recent years, the country cottage style of accommodation has been popular and has been dutifully incorporated into specialist groupings by the tour operators. An association between these properties and a former owner who happens to be well known enhances their appeal. Among cottages available for rent in the UK are those formerly owned by the poet Shelley, as well as writers R. L. Stevenson, D. H. Lawrence and Thomas Hardy, for example. The rise in popularity of cottage accommodation may have been triggered by the interest in French gîtes that developed in the 1980s.

At the other end of the scale, the Mansions and Manors brand consists of around 200 manor house owners who will offer bed-and-breakfast accommodation on a selective basis to the 'right kind of clients', but have no wish to commercialize their product or advertise directly to the public. This group of houses is therefore marketed directly through tour operators overseas. In the USA, the consortium Historic Hotels of America, established with the support of the US National Trust for Historic Preservations, recruits only hotels at least 50 years old. Among its members are the 1773 Red Lion Inn at Stockbridge, Massachusetts, and a former Carmelite convent in Puerto Rico, which dates from 1651.

Consortia

In an effort to counteract the distribution strengths of the large chains, independent hotels around the world have frequently banded together to form loosely knit consortia. While this allows the group to obtain some of the economies of scale achieved by the large chains, such as benefits of mass purchasing, more critically it reinforces their marketing strength, enabling them to improve distribution through a united website and the websites of other leading suppliers.

Many of the larger consortia, such as Best Western Hotels and Inter Hotels, operate on a global scale; others operate on a national scale, as does Flag Hotels of Australia, now established as a strong national brand in overseas marketing.

Similarly, some smaller, privately owned hotels have united within a themed consortium in order to market themselves more effectively at home and abroad. This is a highly appropriate strategy when developing a niche approach. For example, Small Luxury Hotels of the World, with nearly 300 hotels in 50 countries, focuses on building an image of hotels that are of a high standard but personal, while Grand Heritage Hotels – an American-owned consortium that is now drawing members from high-grade UK hotels – emphasizes luxury and status. Other specialist consortia operating in the UK include Pride of Britain Hotels, Scotland's Personal Hotels and Great Inns of Britain.

Classifying and grading accommodation

Classifying accommodation units of differing types and standards is no simple matter. The process of classification, either for the purpose of legislation or for the systematic examination of business activity, has been attempted on several occasions in Britain in the past (for example, under the Standard Industrial Classification System). These attempts were mainly designed to distinguish hotels and other residential establishments from sundry catering activities, however. Statistics seldom distinguish, for example, between guests staying at hotels and motels.

Within the small independent sector, the problem is even greater. There is a broad spectrum of private accommodation that ranges from the private hotel, through boarding house and guesthouse accommodation to bed-and-breakfast establishments and, in Britain, under law there is no clear distinction between the private hotel and the boarding house. The only distinction between these two and the guesthouse is that the latter will not have more than four bedrooms or more than eight guests. This distinction is important for legislative purposes, but need not concern us further here.

Tourists, however, are interested not only in what different grades of hotel offer in the way of facilities but also in the *quality* of the accommodation and catering they are being offered. To clarify these features, we need to distinguish between three terms: categorization, classification and grading. Although these terms are often used interchangeably, the following are their widely accepted definitions:

- *categorization* refers to the separation of accommodation into types – that is, distinguishing between hotels, motels, boarding houses, guesthouses and so on.
- *classification* distinguishes different examples of accommodation on the basis of certain physical features, such as the number of rooms with private bath or shower and so on.
- *grading* identifies accommodation according to certain verifiable objective features of the service offered, such as the number of courses served at meals, whether or not 24-hour service is provided and so on.

Readers will note, however, that none of these terms refers to assessments of quality, which call for subjective evaluation and are therefore far more difficult – and more costly – to validate, especially when standards, particularly in catering, can change so rapidly over time.

Provision was made under the Development of Tourism Act 1969 for the compulsory classification and grading of hotel accommodation in Britain, but this was widely resisted by the industry itself and the British Tourist Authority made no attempt to impose it at the time, instead relying on a system of voluntary registration first introduced in 1975. The separate National Tourist Boards of England, Scotland and Wales were left to devise their own individual schemes.

Urged on by the Scottish Tourist Board in particular, however, the three boards, in 1987, agreed a common scheme that graded hotels into six categories – 'listed', for the most basic property, or from one to five crowns, depending on the facilities offered. The system remained a voluntary one, but hotels taking part received regular checks from inspectors and could only display their blue and white signboard or advertise in Regional Tourist Board publications after they had been approved. The hotels were charged an annual fee.

While the system was clearly an improvement on the previous form of classification, in which the hotels themselves were responsible for advising the tourist boards of the facilities they provided. Because it remained voluntary only a very small proportion of the total accommodation sector in Britain registered.

Two years later, the boards agreed a unified system of grading quality, additionally designating accommodation 'Approved', 'Commended', 'Highly Commended' or 'Deluxe', in ascending order of quality. This was planned to take into account such subjective issues as hospitality, service, food and decor. These grades take no account of the facilities or status of the unit, so even a humble 'listed' unit can be rated 'Deluxe' if it meets the quality criterion. Other types of accommodation subsequently received symbols, too. Moons were awarded to lodges, keys to self-catering accommodation and 'Qs' to holiday centres.

Wales chose to develop its own scheme separately from that operating in England and Scotland. The self-catering scheme was applied to a range of different units, including cottages, flats, bungalows, houseboats and chalets, and quality was assessed in the same way as for hotels. Grading became based on such features as the appearance of the building, the decor and lighting, heating and furnishing, floor coverings and the crockery and utensils provided.

This system also proved far from satisfactory, given that the private sector had devised its own schemes for grading hotels – some national some international in scope – and, these were often more widely recognized by members of the public than were the public-sector designations. Of the private-sector schemes, the best known in Britain were those offered by the two motoring associations, the AA and RAC, both of which provided a star rating. In addition to these schemes, there were a number of guides on the market that provided subjective assessments of catering in hotels and other establishments, the best-known being the *Michelin Guide, Egon Ronay's Guide* and the *Good Food Guide*.

Over the years, further attempts were made to introduce legislation for a common grading scheme for hotels. The harmonization process within the EU gave an additional boost to these initiatives. Although some member countries do impose compulsory registration within their own borders, different grading schemes have been in use throughout the EU, each involving varying criteria, so the problems of standardizing within Europe remain. Clearly, however, no attempt to standardize throughout the EU could be considered unless the UK could itself put forward an agreed standard within its own boundaries. Consequently, talks were held in 1996 between the tourist board representatives and the two motoring organizations in order to try to achieve a commonly recognized system throughout the UK.

The outcome of these talks was only a partial success. The English Tourist Board and the two motoring organizations agreed to adopt a common scheme from the year 2000, based on hotel ratings of one to five stars. The Scottish Tourist Board rejected the scheme on the principle that it wished to lay greater emphasis on quality rather than facilities and therefore adopted a parallel scheme in 1997, while Wales introduced its own scheme in 1999. Agreement was reached between the three boards and the motoring organizations to adopt a common classification scheme for bed-and-breakfast establishments from the year 2000.

In 2004, the three mainland tourist boards and two motoring organizations met to attempt once again to thrash out an agreement on hotel classification that would be satisfactory to all parties. Agreement was reached on a common star rating (one to five stars) that was introduced gradually over an 18-month period, beginning in 2006. The committee took the view that it would not include budget hotels, as these were widely recognized as offering similar levels of quality and standards across all of their properties and tended to belong to well-established chains. Others, however, could, optionally, adopt the new scheme and request inspection. Similar star ratings apply to other forms of accommodation, such as inns and guesthouses, farmhouses, B&Bs and self-catering facilities.

As far as common systems across Europe are concerned, the British Hospitality Association feels that comparisons between hotels of similar status in different countries are virtually impossible to make. There are further complications, for example, in the fact that some countries impose higher rates of sales tax on their 5-star properties, making it unattractive for hotels in those nations to give their properties the higher rating even if standards are comparable with a 5-star property in Britain. In the meantime, tour operators have devised their own systems for assessing properties used for package tours abroad, to meet the needs of their own clients, leading to additional confusion among the travelling public. Thomson Holidays, for example, uses its 'T-rating', based in part on its own customers' assessments of accommodation.

Within the sector, concern is focusing on the provision of adequate training and achievement of professional service standards. The long hours, poor salaries at lower levels and generally unattractive conditions of work within the hospitality sector, coupled with an unusually high staff turnover rate, even by the standards of the tourism business, have made it difficult to raise standards of professional service to acceptable levels. Employers and associations are concerned to ensure that 'hospitality assured' standards, as laid down by the European Foundation for Quality Management's Business Excellence

Example

The UK official star ratings system

Sector and designators	*	**	***	****	*****
Hotels	All rooms en suite or private.	Dinner usually available every evening.	All rooms en suite, plus room service available.	24-hour room service, 50% have bath and shower.	Several permanent suites, enhanced services, e.g. concierge.
Guest accommodation	Simple, practical, no frills.	Well-presented and run.	All rooms with washbasin.	50% of rooms have en suite or private bathroom.	All rooms en suite or private bath, highest quality and service.
Campus	Simple, practical, no frills.	Well-presented and run.	Good quality and comfort.	Excellent standard throughout.	Exceptional with degree of luxury.
Hostels	Simple, practical, no frills.	Well-presented and run.	Single-sex dormitories, some family rooms.	En suite rooms may be available.	Choice of dormitories, family rooms or en suite rooms.
Self-catering	Microwave provided.	All beds full size.	Bedlinen available.	Linen provided, towels available. Access to freezer and washing machine.	Highest standards of quality and attention.
Narrowboat and cruiser	Acceptable quality, clean, adequate and quality furniture, fittings.	Good overall level of quality, good customer care, fitted radio.	Very good quality, well-maintained and decorated, more space and colour TV.	Excellent overall quality, highest comfort and attention to detail.	Exceptional overall quality, fixtures and fittings. Wider range of accessories, separate sleeping and living areas.
Hotel boat	Acceptable overall quality, clean and warm with adequate provision and quality of furniture and fittings.	Good overall quality and customer care, fitted radio.	Very good quality and comfort, well-maintained and decorated. Meals with wider choice of quality, freshly cooked.	Excellent overall quality and attention to detail, higher levels of comfort and service.	Exceptional overall quality, guest care and service, wide range of accessories, highest level of decor, fixtures and fittings.
Holiday parks	Simple, practical, no frills.	Well-presented and well-run.	Good level of quality and comfort.	Excellent standards throughout.	Exceptional with a degree of luxury.
Holiday villages	Simple, practical, no frills.	Well-presented and well-run.	Good level of quality and comfort.	Excellent standard throughout.	Exceptional with a degree of luxury.

model and based on a worldwide model of best practice, can be applied within their own establishments.

The nature of demand for accommodation facilities

The hotel product is made up of five characteristics:

- location
- mix of facilities (which will include bedrooms, restaurants, other public rooms, functions rooms and leisure facilities)
- image
- services it provides (including such indefinable features as the level of formality, personal attention, speed and efficiency of its staff)
- price it charges.

The location of a hotel will invariably be the first consideration when a tourist is selecting a hotel. Location implies both the destination (resort for the holidaymaker, convenient stopover point for the traveller, city for the business traveller) and the location within that destination. Thus, businesspeople will want to be accommodated in a city centre hotel close to the company they are visiting, while the seaside holidaymaker will seek a hotel as close as possible to the beach and transit travellers will want to be accommodated at a hotel convenient for the airport or a motel close to major roads.

In economic terms, a trade-off will occur between location and price. The leisure traveller will look for the hotel closest to the beach that still fits the budget, while the transit traveller may well opt for a more distant hotel that is prepared to offer a free transfer to the airport.

Location is, of course, fixed for all time. Thus, if the site itself loses its attraction for visitors, the hotel will suffer an equivalent decline in its fortunes (although the 'shipping container' approach of Travelodge, discussed earlier, may go some way to overcoming this problem).

The fact that high fixed costs are incurred in both building and operating hotels compounds the risks of running them. City centre sites are extremely expensive to purchase and operate, so the room prices have to be high. The market may resist such prices, but is nevertheless reluctant to be based at any distance from the centres of activity, even when good transport is available. This has been evidenced by the problems facing incoming tour operators accommodating American visitors on budget tours to central London at prices that are competitive with other city centres. The reluctance of many overseas tour operators to accept accommodation on the outskirts of the city for their clients has, in the past, led to loss of business in favour of other European capital cities.

Again, the demand for hotels centrally located in capital cities, leading to high capacity and profits, has caused those in the hotel business to maximize profits by upgrading their accommodation and appealing to business clients, rather than catering for leisure tourists demanding budget accommodation. Special services were introduced to attract niche customers. The London Hilton, for instance, was among several that introduced a women only floor, in deference to the increasing numbers of women travelling alone on business. This included a private check-in facility, increased security cameras and double locks on bedroom doors.

Meanwhile, the French Accor Group was among the first to identify the market gap for low-priced accommodation in big cities as the established hotel chains went upmarket and, as we have seen, launched its Formule 1 and Etap brands to tap into these markets. The two large budget chains in the UK have also invested heavily in London, with several sites in the city. Major cities also have frequent high profile events, such as conferences and

Example

Hotel niche marketing

The Novotel Hotel in Bagnolet, Paris Est, offers a good example of niche marketing aimed at attracting specific types of customer. It set out to appeal to Asian and, more specifically, Chinese customers. Offering relatively cheap, frugal rooms, the hotel provides two Chinese TV channels, a Chinese magazine in the room and menus translated into Chinese. A Mandarin-speaking receptionist is employed and the option of noodle soup is on the breakfast menu.

exhibitions, however, and, at such times, the demand for hotel rooms is reflected in every hotel, boosting its prices, so that the basic price advertised by the budget chains may, in practice, be seldom available.

Hotels will seek to maximize their revenue by offering a wide range of different tariffs to the different market segments they serve. By way of example, one city hotel provides, apart from the normal rack rate (published room rate), at least nine other rates, including special concessions for corporate bookings, conference rates, air crew, weekender traffic and tour bookings. In the climate of recession experienced by hotels in recent years, it has also been possible for clients to negotiate substantial discounts if they book late in the day. Hotel managers, recognizing that any sale is better than none, allow the desk clerks to come to an agreement regarding any realistic offer, which may be as much as 50 per cent lower than rack rate.

Hotel companies may be further constrained by the need to meet building regulations that apply to the location where they are building. Increasingly, concern about the environment and widespread recognition of the damage done to the architectural styles of resorts swamped by high-rise hotel buildings have led local authorities to impose stringent planning and other regulations on new buildings. This may mean using local (often more expensive) materials in place of concrete, using a vernacular style in the design of the building, limiting the height to four or five floors (some tropical destinations restrict hotel buildings to the height of the local palm trees) or restricting the total size of the building to ensure that it is in keeping with surrounding buildings.

Some characteristics of the hotel product

The demand for hotel bedrooms comes from a widely distributed market, nationally and internationally, whereas the market for other facilities that hotels offer will often be highly localized. In addition to providing food and drink for their own residents, hotels will be marketing these services (and sometimes additional services such as a leisure club with swimming pool) to other tourists or members of the local population. Clearly, hotels have to cater to at least two quite different market segments, which calls for different approaches to advertising, promotion and distribution.

Another characteristic of the hotel product is that demand is seldom uniform throughout the year or even throughout the week. Tourist hotels suffer from seasonality, involving high levels of demand during summer peaks and little or no demand during the winter troughs, while hotels catering chiefly to businesspeople may find that demand drops during the summer. Care has to be exercised in pricing leisure market hotels – while a differential is expected between peak and low seasons, if it is too extreme, competitive destinations will attract visitors away or they will simply not come.

Business hotels also suffer from periodicity, with demand centred on Monday to Thursday nights, while there is little demand for Friday to Sunday nights. The lack of flexibility in room supply, coupled with the 'perishable' nature of the product (if rooms are unsold there is no opportunity to 'store' them and sell them later), mean that greater efforts must be made to unload unsold accommodation by attracting off-peak customers to hotels in holiday destinations and leisure and family markets to business hotels at weekends. This also means that the atmosphere of these hotels will be very different depending on when customers stay there. Even the most upmarket hotels well located in big cities are often loath to lose the prospect of high room occupancy at weekends and will feel obliged to take reservations for groups from some operators, but, at the same time, will do their utmost to avoid disruption to their regular business clients. This can result in groups being forced to check in to and depart from hotels by back entrances. This, and other forms of distinctive handling – such as the allocation of separate dining areas in restaurants – can result in their being made to feel like second-class citizens if not managed properly.

Even with creative marketing and high discounting, many tourist hotels in highly seasonal resorts will find their occupancy levels falling alarmingly in the winter. They must then face the decision as to whether or not it is better to stay open in the winter in the hope that they will attract enough customers to make some contribution to overheads or close completely for several months of the year. The problem with the latter course of action is that a number of hotel costs, such as rates, depreciation and salaries for management staff, will continue whether or not the hotel remains open. Temporary closure may also result in difficulties in recruiting good staff, if jobs are known to be only seasonal.

In recent years, more hotels – especially the larger chain hotels – have opted to remain open and offer enhanced packages for those willing to travel out-of-season. The increase in second holidays and out-of-season short breaks in Britain have helped to make more hotels viable all year round, although room occupancy remains low out of season in many of the more traditional resorts.

Yield management becomes the criterion in this situation – the aim being to maximize revenue for the hotel, depending on the circumstances it faces and based on supply and demand at any given time. The hotel sector is also heavily dependent on the extent to which the public sector is willing to invest in order to make the resort attractive out of season. Popular tourist destinations such as Bournemouth, through a process of continuous investment and a deliberate attempt to attract the conference and non-seasonal markets, have been able to draw in high numbers of winter tourists, making it economic for many more hotels to remain open all year round. This, in turn, stimulates further business as local attractions and events are also encouraged to stay open throughout the year.

While we have talked chiefly in terms of the physical characteristics of the hotel, the psychological factors that attract visitors are no less important. Service, 'atmosphere', even the other guests with whom the customer will come into contact – all play a role when the choice of hotel is made. Only about 22 per cent of British holidaymakers choose to stay at hotels or guesthouses when holidaying in the UK, compared with some 47 per cent who do so when abroad. The difference is accounted for by the large VFR market in the UK, while demand for camping, caravanning and self-catering holidays and the rising ownership of second homes provide alternative opportunities, both at home and abroad.

According to an overseas visitor survey carried out in the UK, 59 per cent of overseas visitors stay in hotels at some point when visiting the UK, although the pattern varies, and many will choose a variety of different forms of accommodation during their tour. Some 20 per cent choose to stay in bed-and-breakfast accommodation, with 14 per cent staying in unlicensed hotels or guesthouses.

Factors such as class, age and lifestyle all have a bearing on the choice of sleeping accommodation. In particular, the nature of, and consequent demand for, large hotels will be quite different from that of the small guesthouse or bed-and-breakfast unit. A large hotel may well provide attractions of its own, distinct from the location in which it is situated. Indeed, in some cases the hotel may be a more significant influence on choice than the destination. This is often true of large hotel/leisure complexes providing a range of inhouse entertainment, as is the case with a number of North American and, increasingly, European hotels.

Similarly, some hotels are so closely linked with the destination that they serve that the combination of stay at hotel/destination becomes the established pattern. This is seen in Canada, where resorts such as Lake Louise and the Chateau Lake Louise Hotel are inextricably linked. This type of hotel and resort combination is rarer in Britain, although Gleneagles Hotel in Perthshire, Scotland, with its golfing links, provides one such example. It is, however, increasingly a characteristic of package holiday hotels and has been taken a stage further with the growth of the all inclusive package holiday, in which all food, drink and entertainment are included in the price. The Sandals Hotel chain, based in the Bahamas and Caribbean, was a major initiator of this development. By way of contrast, a noticeable trend in recent years has been the falling off in numbers of guests staying at non-licensed accommodation in the UK, to the benefit of the licensed hotels.

The provision of a good range of attractions, as well as a drinks licence, can help to offset the disadvantages that result from the unavoidable impersonality the large hotels. As the chains gain more of a hold on the total pool of hotel beds, an increase in the average number of rooms in each hotel tends to follow as larger hotels benefit from economies of scale. Hotels with more than 100 rooms remain the exception, however, and smaller properties emphasize the personal nature of their service as a feature in their marketing.

Refurbishment of the larger, less attractive hotels is seldom a viable option, the alternative being to pull them down and construct new ones more in keeping with popular taste. In Majorca, the local authorities introduced legislation requiring unattractive mid-twentieth-century hotels to be demolished before new, higher-quality buildings could be constructed, which led to the removal of many 1960s concrete eyesores in ageing resorts such as Magaluf, in favour of hotels with greater character.

In countries where change and novelty are features of market demand, hotel companies now 'theme' their properties to distinguish them from others, either in the style of their architecture or interior decoration. This, as was pointed out earlier in the chapter, is now becoming a common approach in expensive hotels around the world. Flamboyant architecture, often reminiscent of gothic fortresses, is springing up in the most unlikely places, such as Sun City in Southern Africa. There, a purpose-built resort complex has been designed to provide a simulacrum of 'African culture', while, in the Bahamas, there is the extravagant Royal Towers of Atlantis on Paradise Island where 'exotic' describes both the architecture and the prices.

Chain hotels provide in their budget for regular changes of decor to update their properties, while older hotels emphasize their traditional values and style. With the current boom in nostalgia, hotels that can retain the style of yesteryear, while nevertheless offering up-to-date features, such as modern bathrooms with good plumbing, can find a ready market for their product. A good example here is the restored Raffles Hotel in Singapore, which, after extensive refurbishment, has successfully blended modern comforts with the traditional architecture of the colonial era.

Increasingly, holidaymakers search for something different and unusual in the places they stay as part of their experience of travel. Specialist operators and independent hoteliers are catering to this need. Long-haul travellers can book into an authentic and traditional native long house in Skrang, Sarawak, while tourists to Canada are offered the choice of staying in a North American Indian tepee in Manitoba or an Inuit igloo in the Hudson Bay area.

Example

The quest for novelty

The refurbishment of former jails to serve the accommodation needs of tourists is now a well-established idea in the hotel business. The former Charles Street jail in Boston, USA, has become the Liberty Hotel and is a National Historic Landmark, while Preston, Minnesota, boasts another former jail that is now a hotel, as does Oxford, in England, where the former prison is now a Malmaison property.

Some former prisons have become *luxury* hotels – the former Sultanahmet Prison in Istanbul, Turkey, is now a Four Seasons Hotel. Alternatively, budget hotels have been established in jails in Canada, Switzerland, Slovenia, South Africa and Australia, and all find a ready market. At Oak Alley, Georgia, former slave quarters have been refurbished to accommodate tourists, while in Prague, the former secret police detention centre has become one of the most popular youth hostels in Europe.

If jails don't appeal, why not try ice hotels? Their number has expanded in line with popular demand and their appeal has helped to generate a winter tourism market in some most unusual locations, triggered by the construction of the world famous ice hotel at Jukkasjärvi in Swedish Lappland. Others can be found in Chena Hot Springs, near Fairbanks in Alaska, at Kangerlussuaq in Greenland, in Canada near Quebec City (where a nightclub accommodating 400 is a feature), in Norway and Switzerland, which boasts several, including those at Gstaad, Zermatt, Engelberg and Davos. All of these have to be freshly reconstructed after winter thaws each year and are generally open only between January and April, but they have proved a popular way to attract out-of-season tourists. For those seeking a similar experience in greater comfort, a heated glass igloo in Finland provides one alternative.

Other original approaches to accommodation include lighthouses along the Croatian coast, a windmill in Majorca, a police station in Lynton, Devon, a cider press in Abbeville, France, a signal box in County Kerry, Ireland, and converted pigsties in Garstang, Lancashire (The Piggeries) and Monteriggioni in Italy.

The impulse to do something different and sleep in something unique appears to be growing – the more far-fetched, the better. Treehouses have been constructed at several sites in Britain and the Orne District in France. The proprietor of the Dog Bark Inn at Cottonwood, Idaho, promotes his accommodation as the world's biggest beagle, and the sleeping accommodation is constructed within a giant carved sculpture of a dog. Another current fashion is underwater hotels. A modest and rather basic prototype, the Utter Inn on Lake Mälaren at Västerås in Sweden, appears to have started the trend, with others following at the Bahamanian island of Eleuthera and Key Largo, Florida. The Poseidon Mystery Island Hotel, expected to open in late 2009 in Fiji, will have 20 undersea rooms and a restaurant. Undersea dining is also in vogue in the Maldives and at Eilat, Israel, and more are planned in Dubai and other countries in the Middle East seeking to expand tourism.

These are all attempts at offering more than simply a room to sleep in. Today, adventurous tourists, whether travelling for business or pleasure, seek a package of physical and emotional experiences that, together, make up the total trip experience, and hoteliers are seeking to satisfy that need.

In some instances, tourists require no more than basic, but clean and comfortable, overnight accommodation. This is particularly true of adventure tourists, such as trekkers and other backpackers and a variety of simple accommodation is now being devised to meet this market's criteria. Micro-lodges provide one solution. To take one example, camping 'pods', accommodating up to four people, are available in some remote regions of the

UK. These provide little more than a simple shelter and are without beds, backpackers being expected to lay their bedrolls on the hard foam floors.

Among the most extreme example is that provided by Dasparkhotel, Ottensheim, Austria, where guests are accommodated in 2-metre wide authentic concrete drainpipes. Providing the very bare necessities, and situated conveniently close to public washing facilities, the site has proved popular with backpacking tourists, especially as no fixed tariff is enforced – guests pay what they think is a fair price for the accommodation.

The British holiday hotel

The traditional British domestic holiday of 14 nights in a small seaside guesthouse or un-licensed private hotel represents an experience that is all but dead. Many of these types of establishment have been forced out of business through an inability to respond to modern tourists' needs. This has come about largely due to the appeal of holidays abroad, with packages being no more expensive than those in the UK and budget flights costing less than domestic transport to the destination.

Overseas resorts have provided much better value for money and, of course, guaranteed sunshine. As a result of their experiences in hotels abroad, British holidaymakers now demand the same facilities in their home country, including improved standards of cuisine, choice of entertainment and en suite facilities. To survive, hotel proprietors have had to invest to meet these standards; not all were able to do so. The Section 4 grants available for hotel construction and improvement under the 1969 Development of Tourism Act were withdrawn in England in 1989 (and more recently in Scotland and Wales) and hotel rates were increasing even as recession reduced incomes.

The trend for domestic holidays to be of shorter duration posed both a threat and an opportunity. While short breaks help to extend the season, they also raise room costs, which cannot easily be recovered by higher prices, particularly during periods when the market is price-sensitive. On the other hand, such guests often provide a greater opportunity for profits than do long stay summer guests, who spend little time within the hotel itself. Short stay guests have less time or inclination to shop around and the shrewd hotelier can sell them tours, taxi rides, special meals or other extras, such as cards and souvenirs. Out of season, inclement weather will keep them in the hotel, where they are more likely to take their meals or spend money in the bars.

Traditional accommodation also faces the challenge of a shift to self-catering, both in Britain and abroad. This has come about partly as a way for tourists to hold down holiday prices, but of at least equal importance is the demand for more flexible types of accommodation and catering than have been available in the small hotels and boarding houses. The once popular fully inclusive holiday, comprising three meals a day, taken at fixed times of the day in the hotel, no longer meets the requirements of modern tourists, who may wish to tour the surrounding area by car during the day and will therefore want to eat irregularly or even forgo a midday meal. Self-catering accommodation meets these needs effectively and its popularity abroad with British tourists has led to the rapid expansion of similar facilities in the UK, at the expense of the boarding houses. Many smaller hotels have adapted their premises to provide self-catering units in order to survive. Motels have also expanded in number to meet the need for flexibility of those on touring holidays, but these units are really better suited to larger countries, where they serve the needs of long-distance motorists using motorway networks.

The B&B

The increasing desire of many tourists, particularly overseas visitors to Britain, to 'meet the people' and enjoy a more intimate relationship with the culture of the country they are visiting has benefited the smallest forms of accommodation unit, such as the guesthouse or bed-and-breakfast establishment. These are generally family run, catering to business tourists in the towns and leisure tourists in country towns, rural areas and the seaside.

B&Bs in particular provide a very valuable service to the industry, in that they can offer the informality and friendliness sought by many tourists (many have no more than three bedrooms), cater for the impulse demand that results from holidaymakers touring by car or bicycle and conveniently expand the supply of beds during peak periods of the year in areas that are highly seasonal and where hotels would not be viable.

There are estimated to be about 11,500 B&Bs in the UK, of which more than one-third have been certified using the tourist boards' grading systems. Most have six or fewer guests as this obviates payment of business rates and neither a fire certificate nor public liability insurance are required in order for them to operate.

This form of accommodation was virtually unknown in North America until relatively recently, but has boomed since the 1980s as the Americans and Canadians brought back with them the experiences they had gained in Europe. In general, however, these North American properties have moved upmarket, providing much more luxurious accommodation and facilities than would normally be found in their European equivalents.

A derivation of the B&B – home stays – offer a budget alternative that provides opportunities for international tourists to meet and interact more closely with locals in their own homes. Much more time is spent with the hosts, who may organize visits to local attractions or help their visitors to learn the host language. Examples include a stay with a Maori family in New Zealand (**www.amhnz.com**), a home stay in Santiago, Chile, which combines Spanish language lessons at a nearby college (**www.cactuslanguage.com**), a stay with a Masai or Samburu village family in Kenya (**www.boma-africa.com**) or the government-regulated home stays available in a Casa Particular in Cuba (**www. casaparticular.info**). Prices for stays in private homes often work out cheaper than those for a standard B&B and, in some cases, can be further reduced if visitors offer language lessons to the host, as in Beijing, China (**www.inthomestaychina.com**).

Farmhouse holiday accommodation

Farmhouse holidays have also enjoyed considerable success in recent years, both in the UK and on the Continent. European countries with strong agricultural traditions, such as Britain and Denmark, have catered for tourists in farmhouse accommodation for many years and, as farmers have found it harder to pay their way by farming alone, owing to the reduction in agricultural subsidies within the EU, they have turned increasingly to tourism as a means of boosting revenue, particularly in the low season. A study of farm tourism carried out in 1991 revealed that, at that time, 15 per cent of all farms in England (and 24 per cent in the West Country) had some form of tourism project on their land.

The trend towards healthier lifestyles and the appeal of natural food and the outdoor life have also helped to make farm tourism popular. Within rural areas, tourist boards have provided assistance and training for farmers interested in expanding their accommodation for tourism. Both Ireland and Denmark have been notably successful in packaging modestly priced farm holidays for the international market, in association with tour operators and the ferry companies. In the case of Denmark, this has been a logical development as it attracts tourists to what is generally recognized as an otherwise expensive country for holidays if based on hotel accommodation.

Camping and caravanning

The market for camping and caravanning holidays in the UK is substantial – around one in every five holidays in the UK is taken in caravans. Bourne Leisure, the leading firm in the leisure park business, attracts about four million holidaymakers a year to its 55 holiday parks, hotels and resorts in the UK, operating under the British Holidays, Haven, Butlins

Figure 12.5 Tarr Farm in Devon embodies the rural idyll.
(Photo by Chris Holloway.)

and Warner brands. While many holidays are, of course, taken in private touring caravans (of which there are around 480,000 in Britain), motor home holidays are also becoming ever more popular, with 112,000 privately owned vehicles in the UK. Static caravan and mobile home sites number 335,000, located in over 4000 UK holiday parks (of which almost half are star rated).

Holiday parks entered the tourist boards' grading schemes in 1987, with the introduction of agreed codes of practice for operators and a trade body, the British Holiday and Home Parks Association (BH&HPA), has been formed to represent the interests of operators.

Holiday centres

Although the Americans were running summer camps for children some years earlier, adult holiday camps as we know them today were very much a British innovation. They were introduced on a major scale in the 1930s and 1940s by three noted entrepreneurs – Billy Butlin, Fred Pontin and Harry Warner. Their aim was to provide all-in entertainment at a low price in chalet-style accommodation that would be largely unaffected by inclement weather.

The Butlin–Pontin–Warner style of holiday camp became enormously successful in the years prior to World War II and the early post-war era, but none is now family owned. Pontins still operates eight sites in the UK and Butlins and Warners are now part of Bourne Leisure, retaining their focus on family entertainment. Warner Holidays, however, has changed direction markedly and is now marketed to adults only. Haven's appeal is to three different markets, described as 'lively, all-action', 'leisurely' and 'relaxing'.

For the most part, the balance of the market is split between large numbers of independent companies, each operating a small number of sites. Some of these operate under franchise agreements to improve their marketing. Hoseasons, to take one example, is a leading holiday site franchisor and operates around 330 franchise sites. The market for holiday centres remains highly seasonal, falling almost entirely between May and September. It had been customary for centres to close during the winter months, but improved marketing, including mini-breaks and themed events, has helped to extend sales into the 'shoulder' months of spring and autumn. As a percentage of the total accommodation used in domestic tourism, though, the figure for holiday centres remains relatively small.

Holiday centres have been affected as much as any other accommodation facilities by changes in public taste. Before the war, they attracted a largely lower middle-class clientele, but, in the post-war period their market became significantly more working class and the canteen-style catering service and entertainment provided reflected the needs of this market segment. Bookings were made invariably from Saturday to Saturday and most clients booked direct with the companies. Each company had a quite distinct image for its clientele, who were strongly brand-loyal and booked regularly with their particular favourite.

More recently, these camps have attempted to move upmarket – a process heralded by a change in nomenclature from camps to holiday centres, villages or parks. The former predominantly working-class orientation has been modified to cater for wider social tastes. Large chalet blocks have given way to smaller units with self-catering facilities. A choice of catering styles has been introduced, ranging from fully serviced through self-service to self-catering – the latter enjoying the greatest rates of growth.

Butlins in particular has invested huge sums of money in redeveloping its remaining three centres to give them a more upmarket image. Additionally, the company has recently moved into the hotel business, constructing its first hotel adjacent to its Bognor Regis centre. Guests will enjoy superior accommodation, but must then purchase passes in order

Figure 12.6 Roughing it in the wilderness camps has given way to luxury lodges. Typical of these is the Vogelstrausskluft Lodge near Fish Canyon in Namibia.
(Photo by Chris Holloway.)

to enter the Butlins resort. These traditional centres now face strong competition from the new wave of holiday villages.

The new holiday villages

Holiday villages offer a new concept in resort marketing. In their present form, they owe their development to a Dutch innovator who opened the first of a chain of Center Parcs in the Netherlands in 1967, rapidly expanding into Belgium, France and the UK. These offered a very different holiday experience from that of traditional holiday centres, based on the recognition that North European resorts could not compete with sunnier climes and so facilities would have to take account of the inclement weather. This meant more indoor entertainment was provided as well as fully enclosed swimming pools.

First launched in Britain in 1987, these upmarket holiday villages have now grown to four: Sherwood Forest in Nottinghamshire, Longleat Forest in Wiltshire, Elveden Forest in Suffolk and Oasis Whinfell Forest in Cumbria. A fifth, on the Duke of Bedford's estate near Woburn, will be opened in 2009.

Offering a wide choice of all-weather facilities – most notably vast indoor pools with domed glass roofs and settings designed to resemble a tropical beach – the villages had an extraordinary measure of success in their early years, with an average 96 per cent occupancy all year round. Ownership is now split between those on the Continent and those in the UK. Another company with seven properties in the Netherlands, Gran Dorado, offers a similar product to that of Center Parcs.

Billy Butlin's early attempts to introduce his holiday camp concept to the Continent were unsuccessful, but more upmarket holiday villages have been highly successful. The market leader is Club Méditerranée, which is French owned and has a worldwide spread of holiday villages, from France to Tahiti. The success of this organization, which in 1950 was among the first to enter the package holiday business, has been attributed to its unique approach to its clients, who are referred to as gentils membres. It had been the practice for beads to be used instead of hard currency to purchase drinks on site, which heightened the feeling for the holidaymakers of being divorced from the commercial world while on holiday. Sadly, however, Club Méditerranée experienced a decline in profits after failing to keep pace with holiday centre developments at the end of the 1990s and has been forced into an expensive programme of renovation to restore its position in the market, with many of the old tactics giving way to a more commercial approach.

Second home and timeshare ownership

Second homes

Some words are also appropriate here about the growth of second home ownership and the effect that this is having on the tourism industry. Owning a second home in the country or by the sea is not a new phenomenon. Since the age of the Grand Tour, the British aristocracy and, later, wealthy merchants invariably had a country seat to retreat to at weekends and through the summer to escape the heat and dirt of the big cities. Similarly, wealthy Parisians owned a second property readily accessible from the French capital. Americans have been buying homes along the north-eastern shores of the United States since the nineteenth century, culminating in the ostentatious residences built as summer homes for the very wealthy along the shores of Newport, Rhode Island, in the 1890s (The Breakers at Newport being the most famous of these). Later, holiday homes were built on the West Coast and in Florida. Today, many wealthy Americans have two holiday homes: a summer home along the Cape and a winter home in Florida. In Europe, Nordic residents have a long tradition of owning second homes by the sea, even if many are of very simple cottage construction. Löfgren[1] claims that there were 500,000 such homes in Sweden by the 1970s, owned by a population totalling only some 8 million. A high proportion of these were built for Stockholm residents along the popular west coast of the country, some six hours' drive away. He estimates that 25 per cent of Swedes and a similar number of other Nordic residents owned second homes by the close of the twentieth century, in comparison with 16 per cent of the French and just 4 per cent of Americans.

These early second homes, however, were almost invariably constructed as summer homes for the owners and their friends. What has marked the big change in more recent times has been the commercialization of the second homes market. Owners now buy to let, frequently renting out their property when not for their own use through commercial rental agencies who manage the properties for a commission. The holiday homes rental market has soared in recent years as owners moved into property as a principal investment when the share market collapsed.

British residents were rather later in getting into property, but have more than made up for their tardiness in a frenzy of buying since the 1990s. At first this was confined mainly to Britain, but, as prices soared and restrictions began to be imposed on property construction in the more popular areas of the countryside such as the Lake District, South Devon and the Cotswolds, Britons began to turn to cheaper accommodation in Italy, France, Spain (especially the Canary and Balearic Islands) and Greece. More recently, homes in Florida and the newly admitted countries of the European Union, especially Malta, Cyprus and Slovenia, have been in demand. Investment in second homes has been fuelled by both an increase in disposable income among the better-off sections of British society and the fall in air transport prices. In the post 9/11 world, transatlantic fares dropped to an all-time low, while the growth of no frills airlines to smaller regional airports on the Continent has attracted investors to Romania, Bulgaria and Turkey (the last still intent on entering the EU eventually).

Example

Buy-to-let hotel rooms

The concept of buy to let has moved on to the hotel sector recently, with guest rooms available for purchase on 99-year leases in commercial hotels. In one such transaction in a London property, owners are permitted to spend up to 52 nights per year in their room, at a nominal charge, while on bookings for the rest of the year owners will receive 45–50 per cent of all the rental income. This, it is claimed, will produce a net income of up to 7 per cent per annum. Organized as a partnership between Guestinvest and Alias Hotels, the company plans to extend the scheme to 30 hotels in larger UK cities.

Further information: **www.guestinvest.com**

The exact number of second homes owned by British residents abroad is hard to establish and estimates vary wildly. A study by Saga Holidays in 2005[2] estimated that 324,000 second homes were owned in the UK, with another 178,000 abroad and these figures would rise to 405,000 and 249,000 respectively, by 2015. By contrast, research by Grant Thornton in 2006[3] suggested a figure of 300,000 people owning second homes abroad, rising to 2 million by 2025,[4] while one report from the Office of National Statistics (ONS) has put the figure as high as 2.6 million second homes owned by Britons abroad. A certain amount of under-reporting is inevitable, given the understandable desire to avoid releasing information on property ownership to the tax authorities. Certainly the number is sufficiently large to account for a fall in standard package holiday bookings, as owners (and renters) switch to the Net to buy their no frills flights.

The search for properties abroad has led to the use of the term **propotourism** – those taking holidays abroad to seek out their new properties.

What is of no less interest is the distribution of these second homes. The Saga research also reported that, of overseas properties, those in Spain headed the list, followed by France, Portugal and Italy, while in the UK, at least half – and some estimates suggest as much as three-quarters – of the housing stock in Salcombe, Devon, consists of second homes, as are around half of those in the popular seaside resort of Rock in Cornwall. Further, about one in three properties fell into this category in Newport, Pembrokeshire, and one in six in the Windermere area of the Lake District. A report on second home ownership in *The Times*[5] in the same year found 27.2 per cent of domestic property in the City of London to be second homes, 21.5 per cent in the Isles of Scilly and 10.9 per cent in the South Hams region of Devon (which includes Salcombe). Other areas of high second home ownership were listed as Central London, Cornwall, the Lake District and Cumbria.

Timeshare

Where an outright purchase is beyond people's means, the concept of timeshare properties offers an alternative means of enjoying a holiday in one's second home, whether in the UK or abroad. Statistics on timeshare ownership are notoriously inaccurate and out of date, although an American Resort Development Association report[6] estimated that, in 2002, around 6.7 million timeshares were owned around the world in 5425 locations. Nearly half of all owners are Americans. In Britain, the Timeshare Consumers Association estimated that there were 405,000 owners in 2001, of which about a quarter owned properties in the UK. At that point it was estimated that there were 131 timeshare resorts in the UK. Most of those owned abroad are in Spain (especially the Canaries) and Portugal. European ownership has triggered substantial demand for budget air tickets, undermining the traditional accommodation sector. Indeed, there are hotels in Britain that have responded to the challenge by converting some or all of their accommodation into timeshare ownership.

Timeshare is a scheme whereby an apartment or villa is sold to several co-owners, each of whom purchases the right to use the accommodation for a given period of the year, which may range from one week to several weeks. The initial cost of the accommodation will vary not only according to the length of time for which it is purchased but also depending on the period of the year chosen, so that a week in July or August, for example, may be three or four times the cost of the same accommodation in winter.

The scheme is reported to have been initiated at a ski resort in the French Alps in 1965, although at least one organization, the Ring Hotel chain in Switzerland, was developing along similar lines some years before this. By the early 1970s, timeshare had been introduced in the USA and the concept had also arrived in Britain by the mid-1970s. Since then, it has enjoyed enormous success, boosted by schemes allowing owners to exchange their properties for others around the world during their period of ownership. A number of timeshare exchange organizations have been established, of which the largest and best-known are Resort Condominiums International (RCI), with 2.4 million members registered worldwide in 2003, and Interval International (II). These companies keep a register of owners and, for a fee, will facilitate home exchanges around the world and organize flights.

Unfortunately, the sheer popularity of timeshare has led to high-pressure sales techniques being used by less reputable organizations using street touts to approach tourists visiting resorts abroad, which led initially to some poor publicity for the scheme in the press. The Timeshare Developers' Association was formed to give the industry credibility and draw up a code of conduct for members. Since 1991, the Timeshare Council has overseen the regulation of timeshare within the UK. The Office of Fair Trading keeps a watching brief on development within the UK, while the Organization for Timeshare in Europe (OTE) has developed a code of conduct for its members, oversees quality and offers a free conciliation service for consumers dealing with members.

Timeshare is not without its problems. It has been found that it is difficult to resell such properties due to the amount of new properties coming on to the market and, in some cases, management and maintenance fees have been high. There can be a problem in getting widely dispersed owners together to make decisions on the management of the property.

Notwithstanding these difficulties, timeshare remains popular and is likely to grow as an alternative to the traditional package holiday. A recent innovation has been the growth of timeshare operated by the leading hotel chains, such as Marriott, with its Vacation Club International brand. Hotel ownership has expanded the product by introducing spas and other activities along with the basic timeshare holidays.

Fractional ownership is also becoming a popular innovation in the hotel sector and a number of hotels have been constructed in London and elsewhere in which purchasers may take ownership of a room or rooms for 4 to 13 weeks, either for their own use or to rent out. Unlike timeshare, fractional ownership gives owners a stake in the property and, consequently, they may benefit from capital gains as well as income from hotel lets.

Educational accommodation

The significance of the educational accommodation sector must also be recognized. Universities and other institutions of higher education seeking to increase contributions to their revenue through the rental of student accommodation during the academic holidays have marketed their accommodation to tour operators and others for budget holidays. Often situated in greenfield sites near major tourist destinations, such as Stirling or York, the universities have experienced considerable success in this venture and have further expanded their involvement with the leisure market by providing other facilities, such as activity centres and public rooms for themed holidays.

The standards of university accommodation have greatly improved in recent years to meet the expectations of students themselves as their standards at home have risen. En suite facilities are now the norm, bringing the standards up to the levels that budget holidaymakers have come to expect and making them comparable to those of other accommodation for budget conferences and business meetings. This is proving to be a profitable source of revenue for the institutions during the academic holidays.

The distribution of accommodation

Large hotel chains have in the past enjoyed advantages in gaining access to their markets through their links with the airline sector. This close relationship dates back to the early 1970s when airlines, introducing their new jumbo jets, hastily set about establishing connections with hotels to accommodate their increasing passenger numbers. As a result, hotel chains gained access to the airlines' global distribution systems (GDS) – the computerized reservations networks that were a key factor in selling rooms to the international market.

While this link remains important, the development of the Internet has changed the nature of distribution, making the large hotel groups far more independent in their interface with customers. Apart from hotel representation on airline-owned (or formerly owned) websites such as Opodo and Orbitz, online agencies such as Expedia and Travelocity, which offer a range of travel products, feature hotels prominently and have become a powerful force in the distribution chain. Websites devoted to accommodation only are also springing up as alternatives to sites affiliated to carriers or other principals and intermediaries, with rooms at highly competitive prices. The larger hotel groups are increasingly relying on their own websites to reach their customers in an effort to cut costs by avoiding payment of commission to intermediaries.

Large hotels depend on group as well as individual business, so they must maintain contact with tour operators, conference organizers and others who bulk buy hotel bedrooms. The tourist boards can play a part in helping such negotiations by organizing workshops abroad to which the buyers of accommodation and other facilities will be invited.

All large hotel chains, and many smaller hotel companies, now have their own computer systems to cope with back-of-office and management information as well as providing access to their reservations system worldwide. Some chains maintain their own offices in key generating countries (and, of course, each hotel will recommend business and take reservations for others in the chain), while independent hotels reach the overseas markets through membership of marketing consortia. The former role of hotel representative agencies has dwindled as online booking agencies took over their role and the few that survive, such as Utell International, are now substantially electronic agencies. Even the smallest hoteliers today operate interactive CRSs via the Internet, although their prospects of reaching customers are enhanced when this is done in association with other accommodation units.

Some will think of travel agents as being the obvious distributive outlets, but few agents, apart from those dealing regularly with business travellers, are keen to handle hotel bookings as distinct from comprehensive travel services and, increasingly, travellers are prepared to search the World Wide Web themselves for their cheap airline seats and hotel rooms. Domestic bookings are traditionally made direct with hotels and, for reservations abroad, agents are unwilling to get involved unless they hold agreements with the hotels on the payment of commission. Some hotels will pay a standard 10 per cent, while others allow only a lesser rate or restrict commissions to room sales outside peak periods. Many agents are also unwilling to deal with overseas hotels without making a charge for the service. Where hotels package their product in the form of short breaks or longer holidays, however, they may be sold, like any other package, through an agent. Here, the agent is clear about the commission accruing, but may still be reluctant to stock brochures describing the product due to the limited rack space. The growth of dynamic packaging – essentially, tailor-made programmes put together by an intermediary such as an operator or agent by a search of websites – may provide agents with scope to retain their customers' loyalty as they can show that they are offering expertise beyond what travellers can find for themselves.

Traditionally, clients for UK holiday centres have also booked direct, but the centres are now more supportive of sales through travel agents. Leading companies such as Butlins now receive a substantial percentage of their sales in this way.

Finally, mention should be made of the sale of accommodation through public-sector tourism outlets. This is commonly found on the Continent. The Dutch tourist offices (VVVs) provide a reservation service for tourists and have done so for many years, for example. Today tourist information centres (TICs) in the UK also offer a booking service as one reflection of their increasingly commercial role. The 'Book a bed ahead' (BABA) system allows visitors to book either hotel or farmhouse accommodation through local TICs, for which a fee is charged and the TIC receives a commission from the principal. Increasingly, such bookings can be undertaken using a local computer reservations system, which improves the service that the TICs provide.

Environmental issues

All sectors of the tourism industry are becoming sensitized to the issue of eco-tourism – that is, ecologically sound tourism that can be sustained as tourist numbers continue to grow. Hotels are in a position to take a lead on this issue. They are also frequently the recipients of complaints by the eco-tourism lobby as a result of their practices. For example, hotels in Goa, in India, have been strongly criticized because of their profligate use of water for showers, swimming pools and so on in a region where the local inhabitants suffer from water shortages due to drought.

Where there are shortages of water – as there are, for example, in the Channel Islands in Britain – many hotels encourage their guests to use water sparingly – shower rather than bath, ensure taps are turned off and take other measures that reduce waste. Hotel proprietors elsewhere have recognized that there is unnecessary wastage and that, for instance, many guests would prefer not to have their towels and sheets replaced daily and savings can be effected by offering guests the choice of having fresh linen (which they may indicate by leaving towels on the floor in the morning) or reusing their linen (indicated by hanging towels up).

One example of an eco-friendly approach in the industry is the launch of the International Hotels Environment Initiative, referred to in Chapter 7, which now enjoys the support of many large chains. The initiative sets out to monitor the environmental performance of the participating hotels and offer practical advice, especially to small independent hoteliers, on how they can manage their hotels in a more environmentally sensitive manner. This includes encouraging them to reuse linen, use energy efficiently, consideration of methods of rubbish disposal and even replacing throwaway shampoo containers with shampoo dispensers in the bathroom. Such measures can provide substantial savings on costs for the hotels themselves, as well as helping to improve the environment as a whole and ensuring that, as far as possible, tourism in hotels is environmentally sustainable.

Example

The environmentally sensitive hotel

Bedruthan Steps Hotel in Mawgan Porth, Cornwall, ensures that staff are attuned to the environmental ethos. All receive regular training in green issues and volunteer to help in cleaning up the beach several times each year. Energy-saving boilers have been installed, low-energy light bulbs fitted and solar panels assist in heating the swimming pool. Customers who arrive by public transport are rewarded with a 10 per cent discount on their bill, while, for those coming by car, an optional charge is made, with funds raised going towards the cost of planting trees locally. Cleaning staff are obliged to use environmentally friendly cleaning products and all soaps used in the rooms are made locally. All toilets are fitted with dual flush mechanisms. The hotel also aims to source 70 per cent of its food locally. The hotel belongs to the Green Tourism Business Scheme (GTBS), members of which pledge to adopt sustainable practices.

Further information: **www.bedruthan.com**

Catering

In a Mombasa hotel, the exotic-sounding 'Chaguo la Mayai na viazi vya Kukaangwa ndani ya mafuta' turned out to be rather less exotic egg and chips.
Doug Jackson, in a letter to *The Times*, 28 November 2006

Distinguishing tourism catering

Catering, often seen along with hotels as distinct from other elements of the tourism product, is nevertheless a vital ingredient of the tourism experience and, as we saw earlier

Figure 12.7 A cheese stall at Montpellier market, France.
(Photo by Chris Holloway.)

in Chapter 10, it sometimes provides the prime motivation for a journey. A day trip to a famous restaurant or a drive to visit a popular inn at the weekend are both familiar forms of excursion that must be included in statistics estimating tourists' expenditure. Similarly, longer holidays to France are often taken primarily or mainly because of its strong tradition of outstanding food and drink.

One reason for this often being seen as distinct is that catering services are provided to both tourists and non-tourists alike and, as these two markets are seldom differentiated for statistical purposes, the exact contribution made by the hospitality sector to tourism is difficult to gauge. This is even more true of catering than accommodation as most guests staying at a hotel will be tourists, while many choosing to dine in a hotel restaurant or other eatery may well be locals simply enjoying a meal out. So, while it may be difficult to make the distinction, we should be aware that our interest here will not be on **institutional** catering, which is generally non-tourism orientated (although even here we cannot be categorical, given that many people travelling on business to visit another office will eat in that office's staff restaurant), but it does largely discount all catering in schools and other places of education, factories and so on.

Catering consists of food and beverages, while tourism catering takes place in a range of facilities, including hotels and motels, campsites and caravan parks, holiday camps and centres, restaurants, cafés, snack bars, pubs, nightclubs and even takeaway food shops. It will form an important element in many tourism-orientated facilities, including hotels, airports and catering outlets situated in popular tourist destinations, such as city centres and seaside resorts. In the latter, takeaways may provide a significant percentage of all food consumed by visitors, especially in the more downmarket resorts serving the needs of day trippers. The beauty of catering as a product is the variety of forms that it can take, ranging from a Michelin-starred restaurant to a humble takeaway, each offering a different experience and catering to very different markets.

Figure 12.8 Food and drink demonstrations are popular with gourmet tourists. Here, the making of sherry is demonstrated to visitors at a Bodega in Southern Spain.
(Photo by Chris Holloway.)

The meal experience

The **meal experience** can be said to comprise four elements:

- food and drink
- service
- decor, furnishing and fittings
- atmosphere.

By juggling these four elements, caterers can direct their efforts to reach a wide variety of niche markets, depending on the type of food served, its quality, level of service provided, the furnishings and price charged. A decision will be made as to whether the aim is to move customers through the eating place as quickly as possible, as in the case of many cafés in tourist destinations or hotels catering to tour operators' customers, or allow them to relax over a leisurely meal, as they do when dining in top-class restaurants – and, familiarly, in many more low-budget mainland European eating places, such as in Austria where racks with newspapers are often provided in cafés to encourage lingering over one's coffee or meal.

Eating out in resorts popular with tourists has always been relatively price-sensitive but excessive charges are not unusual, as we have seen in the case of Venice; and not only on the Continent – a recent report in the press drew attention to a charge of £9 for a bottle of mineral water in a central London restaurant! In line with rises in disposable income among tourists, the tendency has been to spend a great proportion of one's holiday money on food and beverages. Just as, at one end of the price range, fast food and drink outlets such as Starbucks, Costa, Burger King and the ubiquitous Irish pubs now proliferating all over Europe have benefited from this trend, so, at the other end of the market, the higher-priced eating outlets have moved to accommodate an increasing demand among tourists for exceptional meals, even if more budget accommodation is occupied.

Example

The mix and match approach to dining out

A number of tour operators in the UK now market their products through the mass media, in cooperation with national newspapers. These include short break destinations on the Continent, where a choice of accommodation is offered − budget or 4-star − on a bed-and-breakfast basis to enable customers to eat out in the restaurants of their choice. One such package offers stays in Annecy, France. While there are ample opportunities for fine dining in the town itself, it is by no means uncommon for those booking more moderate accommodation to choose to dine at least once at the Auberge du Père Bise in nearby Talloires, where the restaurant is noted as being among the finest in the country.

Tourists today are seeking new experiences when they eat out. No longer satisfied with full-board or half-board deals that lock them into eating in their hotel, they seek different meal experiences each day. Some tourist hotels have tried to accommodate to this need by allowing their guests to eat at other hotels in the area with which they have links, but the appeal of small, comfortable restaurants where they can eat well-cooked authentic local food is luring many tourists away from the all-inclusive package.

Hotels are keen to do what they can to ensure their customers eat on the premises, however, given that profits on food and beverage expenditure will often exceed those on the rooms. Thus, hotels cater for their customers in restaurants, cafés, bars and through room service and, in larger hotels, a range of different restaurants is provided, which might include ethnic food, a themed setting (such as a seafood restaurant), separate dining places to cater for business and leisure customers, group dining rooms for tour groups and one or more fast food outlets. We saw earlier a supreme example of this in the new Venetian Macao Resort Hotel, where customers are faced with the choice of no fewer than 30 restaurants. Because of a commonly held view that the food in hotel restaurants is inferior to those found in nearby restaurants (a view not entirely without justification, especially in budget hotels where contract caterers may be delivering frozen food for microwave reheating), hotels are now making a greater effort to improve their food and service, as well as offering greater choice to their customers.

Example

Are they eating in the hotel?

Some years ago, the CEO of a large chain of corporate hotels in the United States visited a number of the properties incognito, to judge the extent to which customers were using the dining facilities. Addressing the concierges, elevator staff and receptionists, he asked each if they could recommend a good place to eat in the neighbourhood. He received lots of recommendations, but none suggested the hotel! The need to promote its own products was subsequently stressed to staff in the hotel's training programmes.

The problem of providing value for money is increased where group catering in hotels is concerned. Functions are widely catered for in hotels of all sizes – from weddings to conferences – and the need to serve large groups quickly with a meal of an acceptable quality and give good service is a challenge. This is frequently best met, in the case of large group meetings, by offering buffet rather than table service.

The widespread desire of people to experiment with new taste sensations is leading to much more adventurous dining out and higher-priced restaurants are rising to the challenge. Heston Blumenthal, who has introduced highly unconventional food at his now world-famous restaurant The Fat Duck in Bray, Berkshire, has become renowned for such delicacies as snail porridge and mousse poached in liquid nitrogen. Sometimes, however, it is the bizarre that strikes a chord with customers, as exemplified by 'dining in the dark' – an idea initiated in 1999 by a restaurateur at Die Blinde Kuh in Zürich. His patrons, having selected their meals, are invited to eat in completely darkened rooms, served by blind waiters. The experience of such a key sense being removed allows diners to concentrate purely on the aroma of their food and its taste, which is said to enhance the experience. The restaurant has proved immensely popular and is fully booked at weekends for several months in advance. A Parisian restaurant, Dans le Noir, soon followed suit, but by blindfolding its patrons, and it has been so successful that a second was opened in London in 2005. Similar novelty meal experiences will undoubtedly follow.

Some restaurant chains have adopted a more conservative approach, but, by offering a unique dining experience, have shown that they can be hugely successful – one thinks of the Wagamama chain. Another interesting example can be found in southern France.

Example

Le Relais de Venise l'Entrecôte

The chain marketed under the brand l'Entrecôte opened in Paris in 1959 and has since spread throughout France (it opened in London also in 2005). The concept is simple: there is no menu, nor need for one. The restaurant offers a single course: green salad with walnuts, a trimmed sirloin steak with house recipe sauce (a closely guarded secret) and French fries, with a limited optional choice of desserts. The setting is a classic French brasserie (even in London) with mirrored walls and low lighting. No reservations can be made, but the success of the venture is evidenced by the long, passive queues that form outside every branch as opening time approaches. Tourists, both domestic and international, have discovered that it is excellent value for money and the quality of its ingredients is exceptional.

Another successful innovation has been introduced at a restaurant in Israel, were e-menus have been provided on tables, enabling diners to order their meals from touch screens on the computers. This idea has also been adopted by uWink, a restaurant in Los Angeles, California, that allows each order to be customized to meet US demand. This not only cuts down on labour (much of the normal waiter service is dispensed with), but has actually boosted sales – particularly for a busy restaurant where speed of service is a key ingredient.

In Britain, pubs have taken on a new lease of life as they have had to meet the challenges posed by drink driving laws and restrictions on smoking indoors (as well as threats that the EU will impose bans on outside heaters due to environmental considerations). Liberalization of the licensing laws, permitting alcohol to be served for more extended periods of the day was one of the few rays of sunshine in an otherwise difficult period for this sector of the industry. This has helped to boost sales in pubs and inns catering particularly to stopover travellers, enabling the industry to compete more equally with its European neighbours. Many pubs have also now chosen to focus on food at the expense of beverages, with a large growth in the number of gastropubs, offering high-quality food. The evidence is that the hospitality industry can rise to the challenge of changing circumstances, with the result being greater flexibility and choice in eating out. While the quality and service of food in hotels still has a long way to go in the UK, the food and beverage sector generally is fast losing its reputation among international tourist markets for execrable food and service.

Future developments in the hospitality sector

The recent history of the hospitality industry is dominated by the need for constant innovation to ward off competition by best meeting changing consumer demand for novelty and improved facilities. This pattern will surely continue, with markets broadly split between large chain hotels offering the wow factor, character properties marketed on the basis of architecture and history, fashion hotels, such as art hotels, filling niche markets and a rapidly growing budget sector selling not just on price but also on brand and image. The more extreme the design of the hotel, the less dependent it is on its location and, in a growing number of cases, the appeal will be the experience offered by the hotel rather than the location. A notable example of this is the Songjiang Hotel in China.

Example

The Songjiang Hotel

The Songjiang Hotel, on the outskirts of Shanghai in China, is to open in 2009. Built for the Shimoa group, its construction called for a quarry to be flooded to a depth of 10 metres. The hotel is sited on the cliff face of the quarry with the lower two floors below the waterline, from where customers will be able to watch marine life. On each side of the hotel, waterfalls will cascade down the side of the cliff face.

A range of watersports will be available for guests within the quarry. Environmental issues have been taken into consideration and, inter alia, ground heat will be used to provide for the hotel's energy requirements, in part.

The challenge for the catering industry over the next few years, particularly at the budget end of the business, will be to control costs at a time when food prices are rocketing throughout the world. Good service and quality can, to some extent, compensate if it can be shown that the customer is receiving value for money. While fast food chains will continue to provide an important proportion of tourist meals, notably for younger travellers, there is evidence among older, better-off travellers that quality of food and service is more important than price and that, if restaurants deliver value for money to tourists, in attractive settings, they can thrive.

Notes

1. Löfgren, O. (1999) *On Holiday: A history of vacationing*, University of California Press, p. 131.
2. Lewis, P. (2005) 'Second homes', Saga Holidays.
3. Cited in Judge, E. (2006) 'Britons claim a place in the sun', *The Times*, 18 November, p. 65.
4. Judge, 2006.
5. Elliott, V. (2006) 'Rescue plan may threaten sales of holiday homes', *The Times*, 18 May, p. 2.
6. American Resort Development Association (2004) 'Second homes and social trends', American Resort Development Association, 22 December.

Websites

Bizarre accommodation	**www.distinctlydifferent.co.uk**
Dasparkhotel, Ottensheim	**www.dasparkhotel.net**
Global Hotel Alliance	**www.globalhotelalliance.com**
Gran Hotel Bali, Benidorm	**www.grupobali.com**
Great Inns of Britain	**www.greatinns.co.uk**
Hotel buy-to-let	**www.guestinvest.com**
Ice hotels	**www.icehotel-canada.com**
	www.icepalacehotel.com
	www.ijssculptuur.com
Organization for Timeshare in Europe	**www.ote-info.com**
Pride of Britain Hotels	**www.prideofbritainhotels.com**
Scotland's Personal Hotels	**www.scotland-hotels.com**
Underwater hotel	**www.poseidonresorts.com**

Questions and discussion points

1. Some large hotel chains are developing upmarket hotels using fashion brands. To what extent do you think this will prove effective and is there a danger in linking what is, after all, a long-term proposition to the vagaries of the fashion world?

2. Can you see the e-menu idea, launched in Israel and the USA and mentioned in this chapter, as one way forward in modernizing the catering industry globally? While it has appeared to boost profits, can you see any downsides to the idea? Will it appeal to certain markets and be suitable for certain types of restaurant more than others?

3. Is flexible pricing an essential ingredient in hotel marketing or are there circumstances where fixed prices would be preferable?

4. In this chapter, we learned how Magaluf, among other Majorcan resorts, is removing its older mid-twentieth-century hotels in order to build modern ones that are more in keeping with public taste. To what extent do you feel that British hotel stock is failing to reflect modern taste and thereby failing to maximize sales opportunities?

5. Does the move to new premium budget hotels by the budget chains threaten the existing mid-budget chains? What factors in the economy are driving this demand?

Tasks

1. Undertake research to discover public attitudes to timeshare and views on the pros and cons of owning timeshare accommodation. Suggest how the information you have obtained could be useful to a timeshare developer in marketing its products.

2. Write a report giving your views on whether or not independent hotels have a future, given the greater marketing power of the chains and forecasts that these will dominate the future market for hotel accommodation. Explain how niche marketing might still be an effective weapon in the independent hotels' armoury.

Chapter 13

Tourist transport by air

Learning outcomes

After studying this chapter, you should be able to:

- understand the role that airlines and airports play in meeting the needs of tourism

- explain how air transport is organized and distinguish between different categories of airline operation

- understand the reasons for air regulation and the systems of regulation in force, both in the UK and internationally

- be aware of the dynamic nature of the airline business and the changes that have taken place in recent years

- analyse the reasons for success and failure of airlines' policies.

Introduction

> We are, in effect, subsidising an industry [aviation] that is poisoning our planet, in the name of another industry – tourism – that will, of course, be the first to suffer from the poisoning of our planet.

> Magnus Linklater, 'We're all heading for the fiery-furnace if we go on taking cheap flights', *The Times*, 26 July 2006

Tourism is the outcome of people travelling and staying and, as we have seen, the development of transport is a key factor in the growth and direction of the development of tourism. The provision of adequate, safe, comfortable, fast, convenient and cheap public transport is a prerequisite for mass market tourism. A tourist destination's accessibility is the outcome of, above all else, two factors: price (in absolute terms, as well as in comparison with competing destinations) and time (the actual or perceived time taken to travel between points of origin and destination).

Air travel (with a strong contribution from the no frills airlines in particular) has, over the past four decades, made short-, medium- and long-haul destinations accessible on both these counts, to an extent not previously imaginable. In doing so, it has substantially contributed to the phenomenon of mass market international tourism, with all the economic and social benefits and drawbacks that that has entailed. In Britain alone, the aviation industry was estimated to be worth some £13 billion to the economy in 2006 – around 2 per cent of GDP – directly employing over 200,000, with some 600,000 jobs indirectly dependent on the industry. The growing carbon footprint of the industry, however, is giving increasing cause for concern.

Public transport, while an integral sector of the tourism industry, must also provide services that are not solely dependent on tourist demand. Road, rail and air services all owe their origins to government mail contracts and the carriage of freight, whether separate from or together with passengers, makes a significant (and sometimes crucial) contribution to a carrier's revenue. It should also be recognized that many carriers provide a commercial or social service that owes little to the demands of tourists. Road and rail carriers, for example, provide essential commuter services for workers travelling between their places of residence and work. These carriers (and sometimes airlines, as in remoter districts of Scotland and the mid-West in the USA) provide an essential social and economic transport network linking outlying rural areas with centres of industry and commerce, thus ensuring a communications lifeline for residents. The extent to which carriers can or should be commercially orientated while simultaneously being required to provide a network of unprofitable social routes is a constantly recurring issue in government transport policy.

Most forms of transport are highly **capital-intensive**. The cost of building and maintaining lines in the case of railways and regularly re-equipping airlines with new aircraft that have the latest technical advances or upgrading airports requires massive investments of capital. Such levels of investment are available only to the largest corporations and, in some cases, subsidies from the public sector may be necessary for political or social reasons, such as those outlined above. At the same time, transport offers great opportunities for economies of scale, whereby unit prices can be dramatically reduced. For example, an airline operating out of a particular airport will have invested a huge amount of money upfront and will have to do so whether that airline operates flights four times a day or once a week. If those overheads can be distributed over a greater number of flights, however, the cost of an individual seat on a flight will fall.

The matter of economies of scale has to be attended by some caution, however. There comes a point where the further growth of organizations can result in diseconomies of scale, wiping out any benefits gained as a result of their size thus far. The difficulties now faced by larger traditional airlines attempting to compete with the leaner, more efficient budget airlines point up exactly this dilemma. Major airlines, for reasons of prestige, have in the past tended to opt for expensively furnished high-rent city centre offices, imposing added burdens on overheads; today, they have generally opted to move out to airport locations. It is the subsidized airlines of the developing nations that retain their high-rent offices in city centres.

The airline business

In Chapter 3, we explored the way in which the development of air transport in the second half of the twentieth century contributed to the growth of tourism, whether for business or pleasure. Travel by air has become safe, comfortable, rapid and, above all, cheap, for two reasons.

The first is the enormous progress in aviation **technology** that has occurred during this period, especially following the development of the jet airliner after World War II. The first commercial jet (the De Havilland Comet, operated by BOAC) came into service on the London–Johannesburg route in 1952. Problems with metal fatigue resulted in the early withdrawal from service of this aircraft, but the introduction of the hugely successful Boeing 707 – in service first with Pan American Airways in 1958 – and later the first jumbo jet – the Boeing 747, which went into service in 1970 – led to rapid falls in seat cost per passenger kilometre (a common measure of revenue yield). The costs fell in both absolute terms and relative to costs of other forms of transport, particularly passenger shipping, which up to the mid-1950s had dominated the long-haul travel business.

Both engine and aircraft design have since been continuously refined and improved. The wings, fuselage and engines have been designed to reduce drag and the engines have also become more efficient and less fuel-hungry. Increases in carrying capacity for passengers and freight have steadily reduced average seat costs, with jumbo jets accommodating up to 500 passengers.

The next phase in this development arrived in 2008, when the Airbus 'superjumbo' A380 – a double-decker aircraft seating between 550 and 800 passengers – entered service (initially with Singapore Airlines), promising further economies of scale (see Figure 13.1). Prices to passengers can only fall, however, if a high proportion of all those seats are filled. In the past, sudden jumps in capacity posed problems for airlines on some routes until seat demand caught up with supply.

Figure 13.1 The Airbus A380, in service with Singapore Airlines.
(Copyright, reproduced courtesy of Iain Masterton/Alamy.)

Of course, the introduction of these huge new aircraft posed other problems, too. They need longer runways and new methods of ground handling had to be devised. There is the requirement to load and unload up to 1600 passengers for one aircraft within a limited space of time, too, which is challenging and requires extensively redesigned terminals. There are precedents – in the loading and unloading of cruise ships, which are now being designed to take up to 5000 passengers, all of whom have to be disgorged in a short space of time for excursions at ports of call.

The motivation behind the development of such large aircraft is not simply efficiency – it also helps to overcome problems caused by growing congestion at airports throughout the world. This is becoming critical at leading hub airports, where there are already acute shortages of take-off and landing slots. It is also claimed that, with a reduced fuel burn per passenger, the carbon footprint of the airline will be reduced.

The supersonic Concorde was perhaps the only aircraft the design of which ran counter to this drive for economies of scale. Introduced into service in 1976, Concorde carried 100 passengers at speeds in excess of 1400 miles per hour. Quite apart from the technical problems that have to be overcome when designing an aircraft for supersonic flight, speeds above Mach 1 substantially increase fuel burn, so most current airliners fly at around Mach 0.85, just subsonic. On some key global routes, however, speed is more important than cost and business travellers, celebrities and other wealthy air travellers were prepared to pay highly for the privilege of cutting their travelling time. In spite of this, the high cost of operation, restriction in the numbers that could be carried, its comparatively short range and the excessive noise it made limited Concorde's use largely to routes over oceans rather than land. The initial high development costs were written off by the British and French governments and services were limited to flights between New York (and, initially, Washington) and London or Paris. The crash of a chartered Concorde in France in 2000 led to the grounding of all these aircraft and the termination of any form of supersonic travel for the foreseeable future.

Replacing the large commercial supersonic aircraft is a new breed of small executive jets currently under development. One such aircraft, the Cessna Citation X, is already capable of reaching Mach 0.92, very close to the speed of sound and, for the present, the industry is putting its faith in demand for just-subsonic aircraft satisfying the executive market for the next few years.

Periodically, crises have occurred in world oil supplies, resulting in escalating fuel costs. This had a huge impact on aircraft costs from 1973 to 1974 and, again, following the Gulf War, in 1991, the 9/11 crisis in 2001, the subsequent war in Iraq and its aftermath. Although in the past these crises have proved to be generally of short duration, the ongoing Middle East crisis and the rapid escalation in the cost of oil in the period beginning 2007 threatens to make aviation fuel far costlier over the next few years.

Some carriers will hedge by buying 20–50 per cent of their fuel forward, helping to mitigate the worst impacts of escalating prices. For example, British Airways hedged 75 per cent of its 2008 fuel costs at $90 a barrel and further hedged 35 per cent of its requirements for 2009, while budget carrier easyJet hedged 40 per cent of its fuel bill for summer 2008. Ryanair, however, neglected to do so, falling back on price increases for subsidiary items such as hold baggage to offset its losses on fuel. Thomas Cook, in a particularly astute move, not only hedged 92 per cent of the fuel requirements for its airline for 2009 but also drew up a contract that allowed them to benefit from any subsequent fall in oil prices, too.

Of greater concern, however, is the realization that oil supplies are not infinite. Demand is growing sharply and will outstrip supplies within 20 to 40 years, even after allowing for new finds. Moreover, oil prices are unstable and can fluctuate rapidly. Prices are expected to remain high in the future, given the demand from new economic powerhouses such as China and India and the world political climate. Consequently, the aircraft industry is searching in the short term for new ways to improve fuel economy, but, in the longer term, it will be imperative to discover new means of powering aircraft, unless the industry is willing to embrace a sharp drop in the overall number of passengers carried.

Example

Volatility in aviation fuel prices

The cost of fuel accelerated sharply between 2003 and 2007, but the world oil crisis that followed in 2008 forced up aviation fuel to unprecedented levels, with price rises of 60 per cent in a year, between mid-2007 and mid-2008. Forecasts at the time projected further rises, but, in the event, prices actually fell back. The damage had already been done to the industry, however, with US airlines experiencing one bankruptcy every week, including notable small carriers such as Aloha Airlines of Hawaii, SkyBus, Champion and Air Midwest. Shortly thereafter, IATA declared that a dollar rise accounted for a global increase for the aviation industry of $1.6 billion (*The Times*, 14 July 2008).

The three cost-cutting all-business-class operators across the Atlantic were particularly hard hit. Following the earlier collapse of Maxjet, Eos, which had launched services in 2005, disappeared, followed soon afterwards by Silverjet, which had launched only one year earlier but failed to raise additional finance in the heat of the oil crisis. It was reported at the time that Silverjet's fuel bill for the B767 transatlantic crossing had risen from £28,600 to £44,000 in a matter of weeks (*The Times*, 31 May 2008). Emirates Airline announced at the same time that its fuel costs had increased from 14 per cent of total costs in 2004 to 32 per cent in 2008, but many other airlines were reporting that fuel costs were representing half of their total operating costs at that point.

This problem was compounded by the agreement to liberalize air services between North America and Europe. Initially, it led to an increase in capacity on scheduled European airlines across the North Atlantic of 3.5 per cent between January and May 2008, while demand rose only 1.7 per cent. By July, the number of flights between the UK and USA had actually fallen by 3.3 per cent during the course of July of 2007 as airlines began downsizing their fleets to bring supply and demand into balance.

One effect of the increase in fuel prices was to bring smaller turboprop aircraft, with up to 70 passengers, back into favour for short-haul routes. Aircraft such as the Bombardier Q400 use 70 per cent less fuel on flights of up to 600 nautical miles (roughly 90 minutes' flying time) than on longer flights. Fuel price increases are also likely to favour the superjumbos on longer journeys as they are not only fuel-efficient but also reduce the figure for consumption of fuel per passenger. The larger scheduled carriers, meanwhile, took to loading fares with ever-increasing fuel surcharges and additional charges for 'extras' such as hold baggage.

The fall in oil prices in late 2008 failed to offset pressures arising from a simultaneous global recession and a sharp rise in the value of the US dollar (on the basis of which, oil prices are determined). Few aviation experts would be bold enough to predict where fuel prices will move over the next few years, let alone in the longer term, but the 2009 recession saw a rapid fall in price.

In the past, economies have been achieved through a combination of improvements to engine efficiency and reductions in weight. To achieve weight reductions, some airlines have reduced the number of beverages carried, withdrawn seat phones, replaced divisions between classes with curtains and even withdrawn or reduced the number of pages in their in-flight magazines.

Airlines are obliged to carry some reserves of fuel for emergencies, but on certain routes they will also carry excess fuel in order to avoid refuelling at airports where fuel costs are high. Airlines facing low profits from competition have to weigh up the advantages of introducing the latest fuel-efficient aircraft against the high capital costs of buying them – a problem that will be discussed later in this chapter.

Many experts believe that the jet engine has now reached a stage of evolutionary sophistication that will make it increasingly difficult to produce further economies, so cost-cutting exercises have replaced technological innovation as a means of reducing prices to the public. The search for more economy goes on all the same, however. There are promising

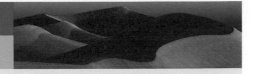

Example

Trimming fuel costs

On a typical long-haul flight, the weight of catering equipment and food alone exceeds 6 tonnes. Airlines are now making strenuous efforts to reduce weight. BA acted to reduce the weight of food carried, replacing the standard food trolleys with new lightweight versions. It also replaced onboard crew paperwork with an electronic version. Japan Airlines suspended beer sales and trimmed 625 grams by carrying fewer paper cups and even marginally reducing the weight of its cutlery. Virgin Airlines has pinpointed weight reduction as one of the keys to fuel reduction in the short term, setting out to find ways in which weight can be reduced on flights to cut costs, with a target of half a tonne off each payload. Changes made have included lightweight food packaging, as well as lighter seat fittings and cargo bins. Such measures, it is estimated, will reduce operating costs for each aircraft by $43,000 per annum.

Emirates Airlines announced its intention to remove much of the paper carried on board their new superjumbo A380s when these went into service. Withdrawal of in-flight magazines, entertainment guides and shopping catalogues are expected to have lightened these aircraft by as much as 1 tonne. The information usually provided by these magazines will instead be communicated through the medium of seatback television. Whether such caution was justified when, at the same time, the airline decided to incorporate two showers on board in the first class section, necessitating the carriage of additional water, is debateable.

developments in recent research that suggest the problems of carrying liquefied hydrogen rather than kerosene as fuel have been largely overcome. This would provide three times the energy per unit and allow aircraft to increase their range substantially.

During the 1980s, the technological focus changed to the development of quieter aircraft and aircraft capable of taking off from, and landing on, shorter runways. The emphasis on quieter engines originated in the USA, where controls on noise pollution have forced airlines to re-equip their fleets or fit expensive modifications to existing aircraft. In turn, the airlines press their governments to relax controls over night flying as if would enable them to operate around the clock, easing congestion and increasing their productivity. The British government – at one time reluctant to permit more than a token increase in night flying, especially from the London airports – is now under pressure to allow more flexibility, to reduce congestion.

Short take-off and landing (STOL) aircraft built by companies such as Fokker, Short and Saab for commuter services, seating 30–50 passengers, and slightly larger aircraft built for regional services, typically carrying 70–110 passengers, such as BAe Systems' RJX, Fairchild Dornier's 728 and 928JET and the Bombardier and Embraer CRJ and ERJ families, have all helped to revolutionize business travel, allowing airports to be sited much closer to city centres.

Another factor in the development of mass travel by air was the enterprise and creativity demonstrated by both air transport management and other entrepreneurs in the tourism industry. At a time of strictly regulated prices, the introduction of net inclusive tour-basing fares for tour operators, variable pricing techniques, such as advance purchase excursion (APEX) tickets and standby fares, helped to stimulate demand and fill aircraft seats. Later, innovative carriers introduced frequent flyer programmes, in which passengers are given additional free miles based on the mileage they accumulate with a carrier or one of its partners.

The budget airlines

By far the most important development in recent years has been the growth of **low-cost, no frills airlines**. Prompted by the deregulation of the airline industry in America, many

Example

London City Airport

London City Airport, situated in the Docklands area (see Figure 13.2), is
an example of such a development that has been partly dependent on
STOL technology for its success. The airport was initially hampered by
the lack of good connections to central London and a short-sighted marketing decision to promote the airport exclusively as a business airport,
with the expectation that passengers would arrive by taxi. The weakness of
this strategy quickly became evident and public transport connections were
encouraged. The airport now operates profitably and surface connections
have improved with the construction and opening of the Docklands Light Railway station within the
grounds, providing connections with the London Underground service. The result is that services and
routes have now expanded substantially.

Figure 13.2 The RJ-85, ideally equipped for short take-offs and landings, at London
City airport.
(Photo courtesy of London City Airport.)

small regional carriers came into being to fight for a share of the potentially lucrative
domestic airline market. Many, such as People's Express, faded quickly, but others, such
as Southwest Airlines (formed as the first low-cost airline in 1971) maximized new opportunities and went from strength to strength – Southwest is now the largest carrier in the
world (in terms of the number of passengers carried), with over 101 million passengers
in 2007.

With the liberalization of air transport in the EU a few years later, an explosion of no
frills carriers emerged, led by Ryanair, which, under Michael O'Leary, sought initially to

challenge the hold over the Irish market held by Aer Lingus and, later, undercut fares and develop new routes to regional airports throughout Europe. The entrepreneur Stelios Haji-Ioannou followed with the launch of easyJet.

These and other small carriers, together with rising seat-only sales on the charter carriers' aircraft, were soon impacting on the profitability of major airlines, forcing them to develop their own low-cost offshoots, initially with mixed success. Both British Airways' and KLM's early attempts to compete via their budget brands Go and Buzz met with failure and they were absorbed into the easyJet and Ryanair empires, respectively.

Inevitably, the leading 'heritage' airlines must decide whether to take the budget airlines on at their own game or distance themselves from this sector of the market by premium pricing. The budget airlines are here to stay and represent a growing proportion of the overall market for passenger services by air. At the time of writing, there were no fewer than 40 low-cost airlines operating in Western Europe, carrying over 100 million passengers annually to more than 400 destinations – coincidentally, transforming the economies of many of those places.

Budget carriers have also thrived in other parts of the world. In the USA, to take one example, more than a dozen budget airlines were trading profitably up to the point where fuel prices began to spiral. Apart from Southwest, they include Frontier Airlines, Spirit Airlines (the first ultra-low-cost airline in the USA), Air Tran Airways and Jetblue Airways (in which Lufthansa made a 19 per cent investment in 2006). Here, too, some of the established carriers made efforts to compete by forming their own budget brands, but Delta's Song was absorbed into the main carrier in 2006, leaving only United's Ted to continue the fight for a share of this market. These budget brands serve a wide network of routes throughout North America, including some routes into the Caribbean and Latin America.

More recently, specialist niche carriers have emerged to attract the top end of the market, creaming passengers from the business and first-class seats of the established carriers. On transatlantic services, ill-fated American operators MaxJet and Eos and British operator Silverjet introduced all-business-class configurations, with fares aimed at undercutting the lead carriers. With smaller fleets than the budget carriers, however, these premium services do not benefit from the economies of scale available to the lead carriers. MaxJet went into receivership in 2007, followed by Eos and Silverjet the following year (see the Example earlier in this chapter).

Example

Could Silverjet have become viable, given stable oil costs?

Getting an estimate of an airline's operating costs is never easy. One estimate,[1] made at the beginning of 2007, however, put Silverjet's total costs for a round trip transatlantic flight at £65,000, broken down as follows.

Fuel	£24,000
Staff	£ 8,000
Leasing charges	£ 6,000
Catering	£4,000
Maintenance, plus administrative overheads	£23,000

On this basis, and with seats selling at £999, the airline would break even with 66 seats sold. The airline's target was to sell, on average, 100 seats. As we have seen earlier, with price rises bringing the cost of fuel up to £44,000, substantial fare increases would be inevitable if the carrier were to remain viable, putting the carrier more directly in competition with the lead carriers for a share of the shrinking business market.

These independent carriers will soon find themselves competing against the heritage carriers. British Airways has launched a new direct, luxury-level service between Paris and the USA, using 82-seat Boeing 757s, under the brand OpenSkies. BA also absorbed the only remaining premium budget airline, l'Avion, which had been operating between Paris and New York, integrating it into the OpenSkies division.

The organization of air transport

It is convenient to think of the civil aviation business as being composed of a number of elements, namely:

- equipment manufacturers
- airports
- air navigation and traffic control services
- airlines.

As was mentioned earlier, each of these is not dependent only on tourists for its livelihood. Apart from non-tourist civilian passengers, they also serve the needs of the military, as well as those of freight and mail clientele, but the tourist market is important for each of these elements so they must be included as components of the tourism industry.

Equipment manufacturers

Equipment manufacturers are made up of companies manufacturing commercial airframes and engines. The demand for airframes (fuselages and wings) can be conveniently divided between those for large jet aircraft – typically carrying between 130 and 500 passengers, which provide the bulk of passenger services throughout the world – and those for smaller aircraft – seating as few as 18 passengers, which are employed chiefly on business routes or provide feeder services from rural airports. Separately classified are those companies manufacturing private jets, such as the Learjet – typically seating just four to nine passengers. This last category also has a role to play in business tourism, as these jets are extensively employed in air taxi services.

The world demand for airframes is dominated by just two manufacturers, each of which has a roughly equal share of the market: the US-owned Boeing Aircraft Company (which swallowed what was then the second-largest airframe manufacturer, McDonnell Douglas, in 1996) and Airbus Integrated Company (AIC), the consortium responsible for building the European Airbus, 80 per cent of which is built in mainland Europe and 20 per cent (the wings) by BAe Systems in the UK. The majority share in the Airbus consortium is held by the European Aeronautic Defence and Space Company (EADS), which comprises French-owned Aerospatiale Matra, German-owned DaimlerChrysler Aerospace AG (DASA), Spanish-owned Construcciones Aeronáuticas SA (CASA) and a small investment by the Russian Government through Vneshtorgbank (BAe sold its 20 per cent stake in Airbus to EADS in 2007). BAe also cooperates with other companies in the construction of smaller aircraft, to compete more effectively in the global market. The first challenge to the duopoly of these giant manufacturers (since the demise of McDonnell Douglas in 1997) appeared in 2008 when Canadian-owned Bombardier announced its intention to build a competitive aircraft for the short-haul market, to be known as the C-Series.

A handful of smaller companies build airframes, generally for smaller aircraft operating largely on regional routes. The two most important of these are Bombardier and Embraer of Brazil. Several others have failed in recent years, including Fairchild, Dornier, de Havilland, Fokker, Shorts and Saab, while even BAe ceased manufacturing regional jets in 2001. There are other potential challengers for the lucrative global markets in the shape of the Russians, who are marketing the Antonov 85-passenger 148 jet, and Sukhoi, who are partnering Boeing to develop the Superjet 100. Both are specifically designed for short-haul routes. China and Japan are also threatening to compete with the lead manufacturers in the longer term.

Aircraft engines are manufactured quite separately and three companies dominate this market: GE Aircraft Engines (USA), Pratt & Whitney (USA) and Rolls-Royce (UK). Due to the intense competition for contracts to supply engines to new airliners as they come onstream, these manufacturers, and other smaller companies, often cooperate in engine design and construction. One consortium set up for this purpose is International Aero Engines (IAE), comprising Pratt & Whitney, Rolls-Royce, MTU Aero Engines of Germany, Snecma Moteurs of France and Aero Engines Corporation of Japan. General Electric and Snecma also cooperate under the banner of CFM International Aero Engines and Europrop International comprises Rolls-Royce, Snecma, MTU Aeroengines and ITP (Industria de Turbo Propulsores). Pratt & Whitney and GE Aircraft Engines have worked together in the USA on the production of aero engines for the A380 superjumbo, in competition with Rolls-Royce.

As with airframes, we can see that this market, too, is effectively controlled by an oligopoly and the cost of aircraft development and production is now so high that international cooperation between the leading companies has become inevitable.

The world fleet of civil aircraft with 100 or more seats was estimated at some 13,300 aircraft in 2007 and an Airbus estimate in 2008 forecast that this would increase to 28,550 by 2026, so, in all, the company estimates that the total demand for new aircraft between 2008 and 2026 will be 24,300.[2] Airline growth has been estimated at 6 to 7 per cent per annum, but these figures must be thrown into doubt by the impact of fuel price increases. Forecasts in midsummer 2008 were for a fall of 20 to 30 per cent in the $530 billion of orders already placed with Airbus and Boeing.

The strength of the euro and weakness of the dollar may favour the US-built Boeing over the European-built Airbus when cuts become necessary for carriers. The average seat capacity is also rising sharply as economies of scale encourage the purchase of larger aircraft.

A single Airbus A340 costs $150–240 million, before discounts; an A380 around $300 million. From this, one can clearly see the importance of this industry to the countries where they are built and, particularly, the regions in which aircraft frames and engines are constructed. Indeed, aviation represents some 10 per cent of the US economy, with a million employees. The economic health of Seattle, headquarters of Boeing, is substantially dependent on the aviation industry. Toulouse in France and towns such as Broughton (North Wales, where Airbus A380 wings are built), Derby and Filton, near Bristol, are key centres of aircraft manufacture, and the economy of these cities and towns depends to a large extent on demand for new aircraft. Such demand is subject to global political and economic changes, however, so is extremely volatile.

Nevertheless, the potential long-term economic benefits of aircraft manufacture are such that other fast-developing low-cost countries are keen to enter the field, often with the backing of Western aircraft companies. The world's fourth-largest airframe manufacturer, Embraer, for example, is partly owned by a consortium of European aircraft manufacturers.

One further point to note is that aircraft, wherever they are manufactured in the world, are priced in US dollars, so currency shifts between the dollar and the euro are critical. Airbus costs are mainly in euros, so a hardening of this currency against the dollar – as occurred in 2007/2008 – is detrimental to Airbus profitability, making it harder to sell aircraft on the world market, while Boeing's task is made easier. Cheaper dollars, however, would make it attractive for Airbus to buy more parts from US sources.

The introduction of the new superjumbo in 2008 represents a significant gamble for the aircraft industry as to whether the future success of airlines will depend on high-frequency, low-volume routes or low-frequency, high-volume routes. The A380 normally accommodates

Example

The impact of 9/11

The destruction of the Twin Towers in New York on that day in 2001, was, inter alia, an economic disaster for the global airline industry.

In the immediate aftermath, 70,000 US and European jobs were lost and there was a 20 per cent reduction in capacity by November. Five leading US carriers sought bankruptcy protection under the Chapter 11 rules and, in Europe, both Swissair and Sabena – the national airlines of Switzerland and Belgium respectively – ceased flying.

Two years later, worldwide flights were still down by 5 per cent, but the US domestic market was hardest hit, declining steadily between 2002 and 2006. In all, IATA airlines lost $36 billion in 2002/2003, followed by large losses over the next two years. Not until 2007 were profits recorded once again, following a $3 billion loss in 2006 (sustained particularly by US carriers), but, by the end of the year, the overall level of debt of IATA airlines still amounted to £190 billion. The US airline industry remains in turmoil at the time of writing, with ongoing discussions between leading carriers to merge services. One major merger under consideration – between United and Continental Airlines – would, if approved, garner a 26 per cent share of the US market.

At a national level, it appears that British aviation is more resilient. The CAA reveals that passenger numbers in the UK actually increased from 181 million in 2001 to 189 million the following year, although charter traffic slumped. This could be attributable to the long decline of charter against budget carriers, however, as charter traffic has fallen continuously during the succeeding years, to a point where, in 2007, it was at the same level that it was in 1996/1997.

up to 550 passengers, although a possible stretched version, carrying up to 850–1000 passengers, may be marketed for high-density routes such as short domestic flights in Japan, where existing Boeing 747s are already operating with 569 seats.

Airbus Industrie is convinced that there is a market for these giant aircraft because the decreasing availability of take-off and landing slots at major airports and the growth of international air traffic favours large jets. It believes that around 35–40 city pairs have reached saturation point and expansion can only be achieved by increasing the passenger capacity of each aircraft.

To take one example, it is estimated that the advent of the A380 would allow London Heathrow to handle an additional 10 million passengers each year. In early 2008, the company upped its forecasted demand for superjumbos such as the A380 to 1700, then worth some £260 billion, and, by early 2008, it had taken firm orders amounting to 192. Airbus estimated its original breakeven point as being 250 aircraft, since adjusted to 370, but independent aviation experts have variously estimated it to be at between 420 and 515 aircraft, with escalating costs and disadvantageous exchange rates possibly driving this number up still further.

The manufacturer has also been hit by several serious delays due to technical problems in wiring up the aircraft, with repercussions on future orders. Only Singapore Airlines was able to get the aircraft into service by 2008, while major orders from carriers such as Emirates have been delayed.

Boeing, on the other hand, is convinced that future demand is for fewer trunk routes and more point-to-point services, which require small- to medium-sized jets. Its own forecast is for fewer than 500 superjumbos and it claims that only some 15 routes could support such giants. If proved correct, it will be touch and go whether Airbus can ever recoup the huge investment needed to build these aircraft. Boeing has cancelled proposals to build a competing superjumbo aircraft, the so-called Sonic Cruiser (there have been a number of possible 'rethinks' about this strategy as Boeing would be severely disadvantaged if the superjumbo were to prove a success). It is also known to have considered the feasibility of building a blended-wing delta-shaped aircraft with an 800-seat capacity that would require a fuel load less than three-quarters that of a traditional jumbo and be far quieter in operation.

In the meantime, its strategy is to develop the new 787 Dreamliner – a 200–300-seat passenger aircraft with a range of 7600 miles at an estimated cost of $160 million – as a replacement for the current generation of 757 and 767 aircraft. It claims this will be 20 per cent more fuel-efficient than the current 767 and, based on present industry estimates, it is also likely to be more fuel-efficient than the superjumbo, at 2.6 litres per passenger per 100 km, compared with estimates of 2.9 litres in the A380. This is largely due to lightweight materials used in the fuselage, which will be constructed of carbon fibre-reinforced plastic (CFRP), rather than aluminium, while the A380's fuselage is composed of a mix of CFRP and GLARE – a similarly lightweight laminate of aluminium and glass-fibre-reinforced glue.

The Boeing 787 Dreamliner was expected to be in service by the end of 2010 following several delays in construction and Boeing is predicting sales of 3100 aircraft (some 2000 757/767 aircraft are expected to be withdrawn from service over the next 20 years). It has proved to be one of the fastest-selling aircraft of all time, with 817 orders placed by the beginning of 2008. Meanwhile, Boeing will concentrate on extending sales of its 747-400ER (extended range) jumbo and the smaller, reliable and cost-efficient 737-900 'workhorse' for the cheaper end of the industry.

It has also announced plans to build two further aircraft. First, a stretched version of the 777 is to be introduced – to be called the 777-200LR with a range of 10,847 miles. This will provide airlines with by far the longest-range aircraft in the world, theoretically capable of non-stop flights between London and Australia (although the popular route to Sydney would be questionable, being against the prevailing winds). The longest flight in the world at present is the New York to Singapore route – an $18^1/_2$-hour flight using Airbus 340-500s and covering a distance of nearly 10,000 miles. Whether or not passengers would be willing to travel even further than this without a stopover is open to question.

A second proposal was announced in 2005, to construct a new version of the 747-400, to be called the 747 Advanced. This is to carry 450 passengers with a range of 15,000 kilometres (similar to the Airbus A380) and the company sees this as filling a gap (in passenger capacity) between the 777 and A380.

Not to be outdone, and to the chagrin of Boeing, Airbus has plans to compete with the Dreamliner, too. Its A350, which is similar to the existing A330 but with a longer range, will carry between 245 and 285 passengers, depending on range, and it was initially hoped that this could be in service two years after its rival's Dreamliner.

Two models are proposed: the A350-800 and the longer-range A350-900, which will carry 285 passengers. The design of this aircraft is believed to embrace materials that are fully composite in construction – that is, up to 70 per cent of components are to be built of reinforced or hardened plastics. This will substantially cut weight and, therefore, reduce the amount of fuel burned. If problems similar to those facing the current generation of new aircraft are encountered, however, it is unlikely that the A350 will appear much before 2014, which is thought to be near the time that the next generation of single-aisle aircraft will be developed to replace the current Boeing 737-200 and Airbus 320.

After the advent of deregulation in the USA and Europe, as noted earlier, there was a demand for smaller aircraft to provide feeder services from rural airports into hub airports, where people would then catch their long-haul or intercontinental flights. This demand was met by small aircraft, either twin turboprops or, seating 50 or more, pure jets. Since then, passengers have demonstrated a preference for direct flights between regional airports, even if at slightly higher fares, with a resultant increase in the passenger-carrying capacity of aircraft and the demise of several manufacturers of smaller aircraft.

Airports

Airport ownership varies from country to country. Sometimes they are state-owned (often by local authorities), but elsewhere they may be in private ownership or else ownership will be split between the public and private sectors. In many German airports, for example, local and state governments share responsibility for running the airport, while in Milan, control is exercised by a combination of local government and private enterprise. In Spain, all 47 airports (and some outside the country) are operated by the government-owned Aeropuertos Españoles y Navegacion Aerea (AENA) – the world's largest airport operator, which also runs all air traffic control in the country.

In Britain, it has been the practice in recent years for local authorities to divest themselves of their local airport ownership and return it to the private sector. Newcastle, Bristol, Leeds-Bradford and Exeter Airports have all been recently privatized, but Manchester Airport Group is a holding company comprising ten local authorities and operates not only Manchester Airport itself but also Bournemouth, Humberside and East Midlands Airports. A number of other local authorities retain a minority investment in Birmingham Airport. The significance of state ownership is that overheads and direct costs are more easily concealed, enhancing the airport's performance figures – on paper, at least. Under private ownership, however, it is easier to raise money to expand or develop new ventures.

Of the privatized airports, seven in the UK – including three in the London area (Heathrow, Gatwick and Stansted) – are owned and operated by BAA – a private company formed by the denationalization of the former state-run British Airports Authority, under the terms of the Airports Bill (1985). BAA also owns and operates some airports overseas. In 2007, BAA was bought by the Spanish company Ferrovial – a controversial move, given the monopoly this handed the private sector. Furthermore, these airports have been responsible for six of the world's fastest-growing long-haul routes since the turn of the century (closely followed by Singapore), with the key London–New York route attracting 2,658,000 in 2006.

Many of the airlines using these four airports would like to see BAA broken up to improve services, provide more competition and hold prices down – a move that now has the support of the Competition Commission. Its report, due in early 2009, will recommend the hiving off of three airports, Edinburgh, Stansted and Gatwick. This move is likely to be strongly resisted by BAA itself, but is almost inevitable following the contretemps regarding the launch of Heathrow Airport's Terminal 5.

Airports are experiencing geometric growth, with some 4.4 billion passengers worldwide in 2006, according to the Airports Council International. Within Britain alone, some 235 million passengers passed through airports that year and even conservative forecasts expect this to increase to at least 470 million by 2030 (more extreme forecasts offer a figure of 500 million by 2021). The UK's leading airport – London's Heathrow, which handled a total of 67 million passengers in 2006 – remains the busiest international airport in the world. Both Atlanta and Chicago Airports have greater throughputs when domestic passengers are taken into account, however – the former handling some 85 million in 2006. All these airports may lose their crowns when Dubai Airport completes its proposed development.

Airports require a good balance of passengers to freight to maximize their profitability, but also boost their revenue and profits through other commercial activities, such as shops, catering services and franchises for supplementary services, such as foreign exchange and car rental companies. The sale of duty-free goods to passengers booked to travel on international flights is particularly profitable. The abolition of duty-free sales within the European Union in 1999 impacted on airline and airport profitability, but, in the latter case, it was offset as the leading airports directed their marketing efforts into expanding shopping facilities generally, including duty-paid goods. BAA took over the largest company in the USA dealing with duty-free goods to protect profit margins.

Example

Dubai International Airport

Dubai is one of the fastest-growing destinations for tourists – not least due to the ambitious plans of that UAE to build up its tourism industry in the face of the long-term threat of declining oil reserves.

The present airport terminal, built to accommodate 25 million passengers a year, was handling around 36 million in 2007 and expects to handle as many as 75 million over the next few years. Meanwhile, plans are well advanced for a new airport – Al Maktoum International, at Jebel Ali, which will accommodate up to 120 million passengers a year, making it by far the busiest airport in the world.

An important hub at Dubai – conveniently placed for long-haul flights between Northern Europe, the Far East and Australia – will threaten present European hubs, siphoning off transit passengers and offering an attractive stopover destination for long-haul tourists.

Emirates – the major airline using Dubai as a hub – also has big expansion plans. It had 246 new aircraft on order in 2007, including 58 superjumbo A380s, and anticipates a total fleet of nearly 600 aircraft by 2019, which would make it the largest airline ever.

Evidence suggests that many travellers are willing to spend time and money on the purchase of goods at airports. One 1997 study found that airport profits rise by 20 per cent for every 10 minutes passengers are kept waiting by delayed aircraft, so it is hardly in an airport's interest to reduce congestion! In the mid-1990s, average 'dwell' time at European airports was 94 minutes – a figure that will have doubtless have increased as congestion has worsened, and check-in times have been extended to devote more time to screening passengers and baggage in a world beset by terrorist threats.

Earnings from the airlines using the airport are based on a complex set of landing charges, which are designed to cover parking charges, landing fees and a per capita fee for passengers carried, so a jumbo aircraft will be charged a considerably higher landing fee than will a small aircraft. In cases where civil aviation authorities pass on the cost of air traffic control to the airports or where the airport itself is responsible for it (as at Jersey Airport), a share of these costs will also be charged to landing aircraft.

Congestion at major international airports is becoming so acute that new technology is being pressed into service to improve ground handling. This is becoming even more urgent as the new generation of superjumbos is phased in. Increased automation is helping to speed up the throughput of passengers, and e-tickets (electronic tickets) issued at the airport against a confirmed reservation – first used widely by the no frills airlines – are rapidly being introduced by all the major airlines to reduce costs while simultaneously speeding up the check-in process.

This process is further speeded up for passengers who travel with airlines that allow them to undertake the check-in process themselves, using computers at the airport or, in some cases, in advance of arrival at the airport. The budget airlines are moving to a system where passengers can be checked in rapidly when travelling without hold baggage and, in some cases, those passengers travelling with baggage requiring to be checked are charged a supplement for the privilege. This is becoming more common and prices for the 'privilege' are increasing, as fuel costs spiral out of control.

Regardless of new technology, there are finite limits to the numbers of passengers that an airport can handle in a given time and those such as Heathrow are already close to their capacity. The addition of a further runway and new terminals may postpone the inevitable point where capacity is reached, but air corridors are already overcrowded in many parts of the world and, increasingly, aircraft are forced to 'stack' at busy periods, wasting fuel. This creates a knock-on effect, delaying later take-offs, and the combination of poor weather, lightning air traffic control strikes and the need for increased security in checking luggage at times of terrorist activity have all led to serious problems of congestion at busy airports all over the world.

In Britain, the pressures on London airports have encouraged the government to seek to disperse traffic to regional airports. The importance of major hubs for interline passengers making connections, however, means that delays in expanding Heathrow's capacity has inhibited economic growth. Protests against a fifth terminal at Heathrow, delayed for many years by consultation and lobbying until finally approved in 2001 and opened in 2008 (with disastrous consequences in the opening days, when both BAA and BA were ill-prepared for the change), is expected to allow a capacity increase of 50 per cent. Present runways, however, would be unable to cope with an increase of this magnitude and the pressure is now on for a third runway (as well as a sixth terminal) to be operational by 2020. This would be 2500 metres in length – sufficient for long-haul aircraft such as the Boeing 777 or Airbus 350 to operate – which would theoretically increase maximum flight capacity at the airport to around 702,000 per annum. In the meantime, aircraft will be permitted to use the existing two runways for both take-offs and landings from 2010.

Needless to say, there is strong opposition from the environmental lobby to any further expansion, but the UK government fears that refusal to develop will simply divert aircraft to Schiphol Airport, Amsterdam (with plans to expand to seven runways by 2020, effectively doubling flight capacity), which has already benefited from London's congestion by employing the hub-and-spoke system, picking up British regional passengers bound for intercontinental connections. Paris' Charles de Gaulle airport is another major competitor seeking to become a leading European hub, with expansion to 7 terminals and capacity for 80 million passengers.

The UK regional airports have shown their enthusiasm for expansion, but not always had the support promised by the British government, which, in the past, was slow to grant approval for American carriers to fly into regional airports, although, in today's more liberal climate of deregulation, we may now anticipate this development. Some airports also face difficulties due to local authorities' unwillingness to expand facilities in the face of opposition from local residents. By contrast, Continental airports have actively sought expansion, with the blessing of their central and local governments, and sometimes with financial incentives for the new carriers developing routes. Such subsidies were considered illegal by the EU, but it has since modified its stand, deciding to allow those that typically range between 30 and 40 per cent, depending on the economic circumstances of the region. Ryanair and easyJet are two of many no frills airlines that have taken advantage of the relatively low costs associated with regional airports to expand their services. However, Ryanair was obliged to pull out of Strasbourg and Charleroi (Brussels South) after the EU ruled that its high subsidies were illegal.

At popular and congested airports, gaining take-off and landing slots for new services is extremely difficult and, in consequence, they have been traded in recent years at between five and ten million pounds per pair. Slots are awarded to airlines through processes of negotiation, which usually take place in November each year, to cover flights in the following year. Scheduled services receive priority over charter and the so-called 'grandfather' rights of existing carriers (a concept challenged by the European Union) tend to take precedence over new carriers – so much so that, at airports such as Heathrow, a new airline seeking to gain slots may find it necessary to take over an existing airline in order to do so. This can give even financially troubled airlines high paper value if they control a large number of slots at significant airports. The Open Skies agreement, which came into force in 2008, liberalizing flights across the North Atlantic, will heighten demand for new services out of Heathrow.

Air Navigation and traffic control services

The technical services that are provided on the ground to assist and control aircraft while in the air and landing and taking off are not normally seen as part of the tourism industry, but their role is a key one in the operation of aviation services. Air traffic control (ATC) has the function of guiding aircraft in to and out of airports, giving pilots (usually in the form of continually updated automatic recordings) detailed information on ground conditions, windspeed, cloud conditions, runways in use and the state of navigation aids. ATC will instruct pilots on what height and direction to take and be responsible for all flights within a geographically defined area.

In Britain alone, it is estimated that, at any one time during daylight hours, there are some 200 aircraft in the skies. Aircraft movements (take-offs and landings) in Britain are expected to rise from around 2.5 million annually in 2007 to some 3 million by 2016, but older ATC systems would be incapable of handling this volume of traffic. ATC systems have therefore been updated throughout Continental Europe to allow many more aircraft movements to take place within a given period, but the introduction of new computers has been fraught with technical problems. The UK's NATS (formerly the National Air Traffic Service) controls take offs and landings at the 15 largest UK airports, as well as corridors in the skies over Britain and part of the North Atlantic. In 2007, this entailed handling over 2.5 million flights. Formerly a public service, this became a public–private partnership in 2001, with the government controlling 49 per cent and the balance largely in the hands of a number of UK airlines.

Improvement in altimeters on board newer aircraft has reduced the margin of error from 300 feet to 200 feet. This has allowed airlines to halve the vertical distance between aircraft at cruising speed from 2000 to 1000-foot intervals. Initially introduced on trans-atlantic routes, this ruling was controversially extended to the European mainland in 2002, virtually doubling the number of flights operating at between 29,000 and 41,000 feet. The present horizontal distance apart that aircraft must maintain, nose to tail, is 3 miles (at this same cruising height), with aircraft held at least 60 miles apart laterally. If these lateral gaps could also be halved, it would permit an eight-fold increase in the number of flights operating, although the problems of congestion at the airports themselves would still need to be solved. Landing intervals stand at 45 seconds. London's two major airports – Heathrow and Gatwick – are experimenting with cuts to allow intervals of 37 seconds – again, not without controversy.

Airlines

The services provided by airlines can be divided into three distinct categories:

- scheduled
- charter (in US parlance, supplementals)
- air taxi.

Scheduled services

Scheduled services are provided by some 650 airlines worldwide, of which around 240 are members of IATA, which represents 94 per cent of the major carriers. They operate on defined routes, domestic or international, for which licences have been granted by the government or governments concerned. The airlines are required to operate on the basis of their published timetables, regardless of passenger load factors (although flights and routes that are not commercially viable throughout the year may be operated during periods of high demand only).

These services may be publicly or privately owned, although there is now a global movement among the developed nations towards private ownership of airlines. Where fully state-owned airlines continue to operate – as in the case of Emirates and Singapore Airlines, as well as in many developing countries – the leading public airline is often recognized as the national flag-carrier. In the UK, all airlines are now in the private sector, although British Airways, privatized since 1987, is still seen by many as the national flag carrier. Privatization is not always seen as the best solution and, in one case, that of Air New Zealand, the government reversed earlier privatization by bringing back 80 per cent of the carrier into public ownership after the 9/11 disaster.

The importance of air transport within the national economy is such that even a government committed to private air transport, as the USA is, voted for public funds in the form of compensation and loans to be paid to aid the ailing US carriers in the wake of that crisis.

Airlines operating on major routes between hub airports within a country are known as **trunk route** airlines, while those operating from smaller, generally rural, airports into these hubs are referred to as **regional** or **feeder** airlines. In the case of the USA and certain other regions, these may also be termed **commuter** airlines, as their prime purpose is to serve the needs of commuting businesspeople, many of whom regularly use those routes. The growing development of hub-and-spoke routes will be discussed later in the chapter.

As was discussed earlier in this chapter, the growth of no frills, or budget, carriers – more correctly known as low cost low fare (LCLF) carriers – has been the major development in scheduled service operations in the past decade. These airlines have been successful due to a combination of efficient operations and low cost and have, as a result, sharply cut into markets formerly held by the traditional full-cost carriers, even where business traffic is concerned.

LCLFs will typically employ aircraft such as Boeing 737s on high-density short-haul routes with one class of seats. Virtually all bookings are taken direct, over the Internet. Tickets are inflexible and generally non-refundable. Passengers turning up late or failing to show lose the entire value of their tickets, often even including taxes – a highly profitable ploy by the airlines. Bookings are usually made and paid for well in advance to take advantage of lower prices, providing helpful cash flow to the companies. If routes prove unprofitable, the carriers pull out quickly – as demonstrated by Ryanair in the aftermath of fuel price increases and the gathering recession in the UK in mid-2008.

By operating out of secondary, less congested airports, low-cost carriers can reduce times on the ground and operate more flights per day. One study found that easyJet, for example, could employ its aircraft for 11 hours a day, while British Airways on comparable flights achieved only 8 hours.[3] Staff costs are also substantially lower than those of the traditional full-service carriers. One source[4] put British Airways' staff costs in 2001 at 27.85 per cent of their total, compared with those of Ryanair at 12.77 per cent. Similarly, the marketing costs of the two carriers were very different – 14.56 per cent for BA and 2.43 per cent for Ryanair.

The introduction of no frills flights has resulted in a very pared down service where not only meals and drinks are charged for but also the airlines do little to aid passengers in cases of delayed or missed flights. Extra charges are made for the carriage of items such as skis, golf clubs and surfboards and Ryanair was the first carrier to impose a charge even for normal baggage carried in the hold – a policy that is being taken up by the other budget carriers.[5]

The arrivals and departures of new low-cost carriers are now becoming so frequent that any attempt to list current operators would inevitably date this text before it came to print (two of the then popular budget airlines mentioned in the previous edition – Tango and Frontier – have, in fact, since ceased operating, while the Canadian/British Zoom Airlines collapsed just as this edition was going to the publishers). By way of example, some 20 global airlines collapsed just as the immediate result of the sharp rise in fuel prices in mid-2008. Suffice to say that, throughout the European Union, in North America, the Far East and Australasia, new low-cost airlines such as JetBlue in the USA, Virgin Blue in

Australia, Air Berlin in Germany, as well as Hungary and Poland's jointly owned Wizz Air (Eastern Europe's largest LCLF carrier) have appeared on the scene to challenge the longer-established carriers. By no means will all survive – many will merge or be taken over by competitors, as has been reported earlier in the case of Go and Buzz. Others will go under when faced with the cut-throat tactics of better-established and more efficient carriers. Still others will move from ultra-low fare niches to offering a service closer to those of the established airlines, as has been the case with some Air Berlin routes (while another low-cost carrier, Germania, has moved to all-charter operations). Budget carrier easyJet has set a new direction by developing its own holiday website in competition with tour operators and retail agents **http://holidays.easyjet.com.** It allows its customers to build their own inclusive tours by pairing budget flights with a bedstock of rooms in several thousand European hotels.

Example

MAXJet

MAXJet was a USA-based airline, initially founded as Skylink in 2003. Its intention was to operate a low-cost service across the Atlantic, code-sharing with US domestic carriers for connecting flights within the USA.

Concerned that budget services on a long-haul route would prove uneconomic, the company changed its name to MAXJet in 2005 and, instead, applied to operate an all business class service between New York (JFK) and London (Stansted). The aim was to appeal to the premium economy market, while also attracting the 'savvy' business market seeking to cut costs.

It operated 5 Boeing 767 aircraft, the average age of which was 18.2 years, seating between 92 and 102 in one class. Seat pitch was a comfortable 60 inches, with seats reclining 160 inches for sleeping.

Services commenced in November 2005, but, in 2007, the airline was in trouble and filed for Chapter 11 bankruptcy. Its failure was ascribed to rising fuel costs, increasing crew salaries and 'unforeseen' elements – notably the level of competition it faced not only from established carriers but also from other new competitors Silverjet and EOS.

With just five aircraft, it can be argued that the airline lacked the opportunity to benefit from economies of scale. The same can also be said of the other two new carriers serving this route, both of which failed shortly afterwards, due to a combination of inadequate finance, swingeing fuel price increases and a shrinking business travel market.

Another direction has been taken by new so-called boutique airlines, which focus on niche markets on routes where they can cherry-pick higher fare-paying passengers. A number of these operate in the USA and one or two, such as Lyddair, have followed suit in the UK. They appeal chiefly to business travellers, for whom superior service and speedier airport check-ins are important.

A slightly different approach has been taken by Club Airways, which is based in Geneva and is the world's first members only airline. Again, appealing to the business traveller, the airline operates scheduled flights for its members within Europe and includes a number of unusual benefits for executives, such as the use of private terminals to speed up check-ins. Lufthansa and Air France have also experimentally offered all business class flights.

Mention should be made of there being a move back to seaplane operations, after a gap of many decades. Although amphibious aircraft have been in use continuously for private charter work (particularly in wilderness areas such as exist in Canada, carrying leisure passengers on hunting and fishing holidays to isolated lakes), scheduled seaplane routes were abandoned soon after World War II (Pan American Airways had even operated regular transatlantic services in 1939). Now, both charter and scheduled services are being introduced in the Mediterranean, with Aqua Airlines offering charters between points in mainland Italy, Sicily and the Aeolian Islands. AirSea, a Greek/Canadian company, plans scheduled services between Corfu, Italy and the Greek mainland, with other possible routes later between Italy, Croatia and the Côte d'Azur. At the time of writing, talks were being held to consider possible services to and within the UK.

Charter services

Charter services, by contrast with scheduled services, do not operate according to published timetables, nor are they advertised or promoted by the airlines themselves. Instead, the aircraft are chartered to intermediaries (often tour operators) for a fixed charge and those intermediaries then become responsible for selling the aircraft's seats, leaving the airlines only with the responsibility for operating the aircraft. The intermediaries can change flight departures or even cancel flights, transferring passengers to other flights.

Major tour operators now invariably have their own charter airlines – a relationship that will be examined fully in Chapter 18 – and have opened their flights in many instances to bookings on a seat only basis to increase load factors. This is making the former distinction between scheduled and charter air services less clear-cut, with seat only sales on charter aircraft now commonplace, former charter airlines operating scheduled services and scheduled carriers operating their own charter subsidiaries. Monarch Airlines in Britain exemplifies this trend, being a former charter carrier, initially servicing the needs of its partner tour operator Cosmos Holidays, but gradually opening its flights to scheduled bookings, to the point where the company now operates a separate scheduled service under the brand Monarch Scheduled.

One result of the rapid increase in operating costs in 2008 was an urgent need among charter carriers to cut costs and establish partnerships. German-owned and leading tour

Figure 13.3 An aircraft from the German LTU fleet on the tarmac at Windhoek Airport, Namibia.
(Photo by Chris Holloway.)

operator TUI held talks with Lufthansa in 2008, planning to integrate the latter's German Wings division with its airline. In the same year, Thomas Cook discussed plans to merge its Condor division with Air Berlin. In the event, neither talks were fruitful.

Air taxi services

Air taxis are privately chartered aircraft accommodating between 4 and 18 people, used particularly by business travellers. They offer the advantages of convenience and flexibility as routings can be tailor-made for passengers (for example, a feasible itinerary for a business day using an air taxi might be London, Paris, Brussels, Amsterdam and London – a near-impossible programme for a scheduled service) and small airfields, close to a company's office or factory, can be used. There are some 350 airfields suitable for air taxis in Britain alone and a further 1300 in Western Europe (see Figure 13.4), compared with only about 200 airports receiving scheduled services. In the US, where there are over 5400 small local airports catering principally for private and business planes, 98 per cent of the population is said to live within 30 minutes' driving distance of an airport.

The attractiveness of air taxi services using these airports is that flights can be arranged or routings amended at short notice and, with a full flight, the cost for chartering can be commensurate with the combined business class fares of the number of staff travelling.

Aircraft in use range from helicopters such as the Bell Jet Ranger and the piston-engined Piper Twin Comanche (each seating three or four people, with a range of between 350 and 900 miles) up to aircraft such as Embraer's Bandeirante, which is capable of carrying 18 passengers up to 300 miles and up further still to top-of-the-range Gulfstream V aircraft, costing over $40 million. Larger aircraft can also be chartered as needed. The world's fastest private jet is currently the Hawker 400XP – a 7-seat aircraft capable of 538 mph, which has been a popular alternative for the super-rich since the demise of Concorde.

Most air taxi journeys are in the range of 500–600 miles, so these aircraft are ideal for many business trips within Europe. Around 885 business jets were sold around the world in 2006 and many find their way into the fleets of the air taxi companies. In the UK alone, some 150 such companies are available to meet the needs of the market.

A number of manufacturers are looking to develop a new breed of supersonic business jets to satisfy the needs of businesspeople and the very rich who mourn the demise of Concorde. Research by the Teal Group in 2007[6] estimated the immediate demand for supersonic business jets to exceed 400. These smaller aircraft do not cause the same level of disturbance at ground level as the much larger Concorde when travelling faster than sound as their aerodynamics create a ripple of small shockwaves instead of two explosive ones, so their impact has largely diffused before they reach the ground. Gulfstream is also currently experimenting with a 24-foot long spike on the nose of experimental aircraft, which would further reduce noise, producing a sonic boom up to 100 times quieter than that of Concorde. In addition to the Aerion, mentioned earlier in this chapter and due some time after 2011, other manufacturers planning SSBJs include Supersonic Aerospace International, which is working on the Quiet Supersonic Transport (QSST), which will have a range of 4000 miles and carry 12 passengers. Delivery is expected by 2013.

Of equal interest is the very light jet (VLJ), which is under development in around ten companies. These mini-jets, typically seating between four and eight passengers, while not capable of supersonic speeds (a typical example is Eclipse Aviation's E500, with a cruising speed of around 425 mph and a range of 1300 miles), are expected to sell at prices up to 30 times cheaper than current business jets, at around £1–2 million, and will carry far lower operating costs. Already, 200 operators have placed orders for the 6-seat Cessna Mustang.

Such low-cost aircraft could be marketed to business and leisure tourists as charter transport at a price competitive with commercial scheduled services. One can readily see the marketing opportunities for specialist holiday packages such as the honeymoon market.

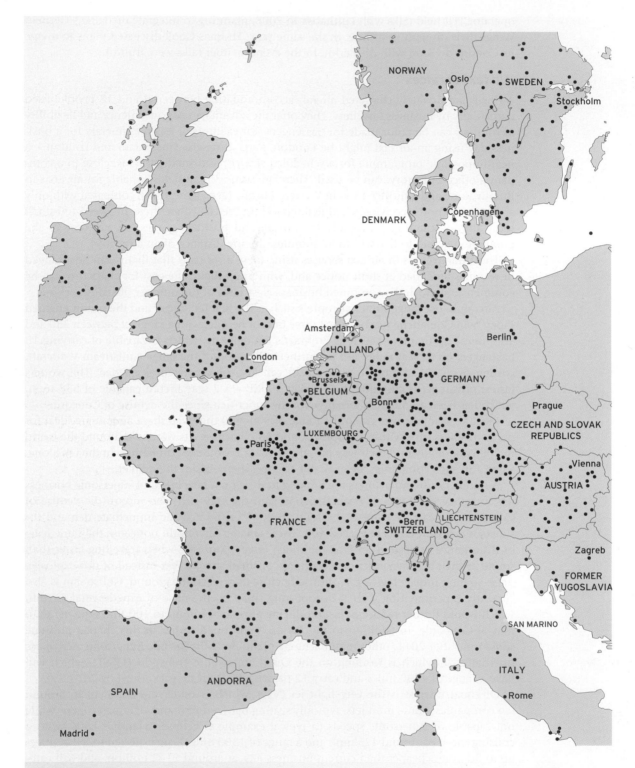

Figure 13.4 Airports and airfields in Europe.

One other development is enabling the savvy business customer to cut costs: where it might be difficult to justify the purchase or full-time lease of an aircraft for business purposes, part-ownership may well be worthwhile.

Example

Fractional ownership

Fractional ownership is a form of aircraft timeshare that gives a corporation access to a certain number of flight hours each year, dependent on the overall share of the aircraft purchased. This is proving a popular alternative to air taxis for many companies. One company – Netjets – operates a fleet of 550 aircraft and owners can buy amounts of flight time to suit their needs, the minimum being 25 hours each year. On this basis, costs come down to a level that is a justifiable expense for busy top executives.

Air transport regulation

The need for regulation

With the development and growth of the airline industry, regulation on both national and international scales soon became necessary. First and foremost, airlines had to be licensed and supervised to ensure passengers' safety. There are, for example, strict rules on the number of hours that air and cabin crew can work each day. Second, regulations are needed to control noise and pollution. Beyond these two requirements, the question of which airlines are permitted to operate to which airports and in what numbers becomes an issue of public concern, given the finite capacity of airports and air corridors.

As air transport has a profound impact on the economy of a region or country, governments will take steps to encourage the development of routes that appear to offer prospects of economic benefits and discourage those suffering from overcapacity. While the policy of one government may be to encourage competition or intervene where a route monopoly is forcing prices up, another government's policy may be directed at rationalizing excessive competition in order to avoid energy waste or even, in some cases, protecting the profitability of the national flag-carrier.

Some governments are tempted to provide subsidies in order to support inefficient publicly owned flag-carriers. Private airlines in Europe have long complained of this unfair protection against competition, which is contrary to EU regulations, but still survives in isolated cases within Europe. The EU Court of Justice, for example, ruled against Olympic Airlines (62 per cent owned by the Greek state) in 2005 for receiving illegal public aid.

Another characteristic of such protection is the **pooling** arrangements made between airlines operating on certain international routes, whereby all revenue accruing on that route is apportioned equally between the carriers serving it. This may appear to circumvent competition on a route, but is also one means of safeguarding the viability of the national carrier operating in a strong competitive environment. In developing countries, where governments are anxious to earn hard currency, the support of the national carrier as an earner of that currency through arrangements such as this may be justifiable.

Pooling arrangements are often entered into in cases where the airlines are not of comparable size in order to safeguard the smaller carrier's capacity and revenue. By rationalizing schedules, pressure is reduced on peak time take-off slots and costs reduced. Financial arrangements between the pooled carriers usually limit the amount of revenue transferred from one carrier to the other to a fixed maximum, to reduce what may be seen as unfair government support for an inefficient carrier. Increasingly, such pooling arrangements are no longer acceptable and may indeed be illegal, as is the case in the USA.

In some areas, air transport is an essential public utility that, even where commercially non-viable, is socially desirable in order to provide communications with a region where geographical terrain may make other forms of transport difficult or impossible (New Guinea, Alaska or the Hebrides in Scotland are cases in point). This can result in a government subsidizing one or more of its airlines in order to ensure that a service is maintained. Airlines themselves often argue that they provide vital channels of communication for business, trade and investment essential for the well-being of communities and, therefore, even profitable routes should be exempted from tax (aviation fuel, for example, is currently exempted).

Systems of regulation

Broadly speaking, air transport operations are regulated in three ways.

- Internationally, scheduled routes are assigned on the basis of agreements between governments of the countries concerned.
- Internationally, scheduled air fares are now subject to less and less control and, in both North America and Europe, airlines are free to set their own fares. Governments can still intervene, however, where predatory pricing is involved. Theoretically, governments protect carriers by permitting fares to fluctuate between acceptable maxima and minima, but such constraints have been largely abandoned in the developed countries as low-cost airlines attract passengers with rates that can fall so low only taxes and administration charges are paid for advance booked seats. In developing areas, however, the extent of regulation is often far greater, with airlines agreeing fares that may then be mediated through the traffic conferences of the International Air Transport Association. Agreed tariffs arrived at in this way are then subject to ratification by the governments of the countries concerned. Generally, less direct control is exercised over domestic fares.
- National governments approve and license the carriers that are to operate on scheduled routes, whether domestically or internationally. In the UK, the Civil Aviation Authority (CAA) has this responsibility and is also responsible for the licensing of charter airlines and of tour operators organizing package holidays abroad.

European countries that are members of the EU are now largely subject to its regulations and negotiations regarding the carriage of passengers by air. The EU, for example, has introduced legislation to protect passengers in the event of delays or denied boarding (in the case of an overbooking, for instance) with compensation payable to those affected, but, to date, the airlines have shown considerable skill in using force majeure rules to avoid payouts.

Example

British Airways

In 2005, BA was subjected to a strike by its contracted-out catering services, Gate Gourmet, during which some of its own staff came out in sympathy. Services were severely disrupted, but the airline claimed that strikes affecting the operation of an air carrier are 'extraordinary circumstances beyond the airline's control', limiting compensation. This remains a grey area in EU legislation, although the EU is attempting to tighten up enforcement of its compensatory laws. It can be argued however, that the process of contracting out services limits a principal's control over its own operations and weakens management, making it susceptible to such events.

The worldwide trend is to allow market forces to determine the shape and direction of the airline business, so regulation today is less concerned with routes, frequency, capacity and fares and more concerned with aspects of safety. Disagreements between governments over the regulation of routes or airlines can at times lead to major conflict, however, as is the case with the long-standing dispute between the British and US governments regarding traffic rights across the Atlantic, which is discussed below.

Air transport regulations are the result of a number of international agreements between countries dating back over many years. The Warsaw Convention of 1929 first established common agreement on the extent of liability of the airlines in the event of death or injury of passengers or loss of passengers' baggage, with a limit of $10,000 on loss of life and similarly derisory sums for loss of baggage (compensation is payable on weight rather than value). Inflation soon further reduced the value of claims and liability was reassessed by a number of participating airlines, first at the Hague Protocol in 1955, where the figure was increased to $20,000, and again at the Montreal Agreement in 1966, at which time the United States imposed a $75,000 ceiling on flights to and from the USA. It was also agreed that the maximum liability would be periodically reviewed.

In 1992, Japan waived all limits for Japanese carriers and, in the following year, the UK government unilaterally required British carriers to increase their liability to a limit of 100,000 SDRs (Special Drawing Rights – a reserve currency operated by the International Monetary Fund and equivalent to about $140,000).

Finally, in 1995, IATA negotiated an **Intercarrier Agreement on Passenger Liability**, which was designed to enforce blanket coverage for all member airlines, whereby any damages would be determined according to the laws of the country of the airline affected. Not all airlines agreed to implement this, however.

The five freedoms of the air

Further legislation concerning passenger aviation resulted from the Chicago Convention on Civil Aviation held in 1944, at which 80 governments were represented in discussions designed to promote world air services and reach agreement on standard operating procedures for air services between countries. There were two outcomes of this meeting: the founding of the International Civil Aviation Organization (ICAO), now a specialized agency of the United Nations, and the establishment of the so-called **five freedoms of the air**. These privileges are to:

1. fly across a country without landing
2. land in a country for purposes other than the carriage of passengers or freight – to refuel, for example
3. offload passengers, mail or freight from an airline of the country from which those passengers, mail or freight originated
4. load passengers, mail or freight on an airline of the country to which those passengers, mail or freight are destined
5. load passengers, mail or freight on an airline not belonging to the country to which those passengers, mail or freight are destined and offload passengers, mail or freight from an airline not of the country from which they originated.

These privileges were designed to provide the framework for bilateral agreements between countries and ensure that carriage of passengers, mail and freight between any two countries would normally be restricted to the carriers of those countries.

The move to greater freedom of the skies

Other freedoms not discussed by the Convention, but equally pertinent to the question of rights of operation, have been termed the 'sixth and seventh freedoms'. These would cover:

- carrying passengers, mail or freight between any two countries on an airline that is of neither country, but is operating via the airline's own country
- carrying passengers, mail or freight directly between two countries on an airline associated with neither of the two countries.

These various freedoms can best be illustrated using examples (see Figure 13.5).

While a handful of countries expressed a preference for an 'open skies' policy on regulation, most demanded controls. An International Air Services Agreement, to which more

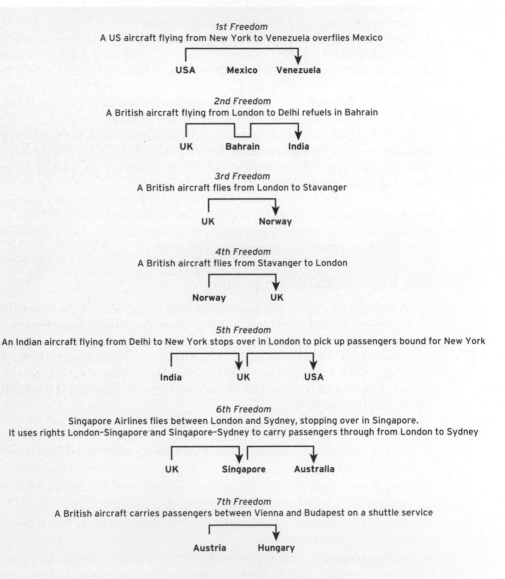

Figure 13.5 Some examples of freedoms of the air.

than 90 countries became signatories, provided for the mutual exchange of the first two freedoms of the air, while it was left to individual bilateral negotiations between countries to resolve other issues. The Convention agreed not to regulate charter services, allowing countries to impose whatever individual regulations they wished. Few countries, in fact, were willing to allow a total open skies policy for charters.

The Anglo-American agreement, which was reached in Bermuda in 1946, following the Convention, set the pattern for many of the bilateral agreements that followed. This so-called **Bermuda Agreement**, while restricting air carriage between the two countries to national carriers, did not impose restrictions on capacity for airlines concerned. This was modified at a second Bermuda Agreement reached in 1977 (and ratified in 1980), however, in line with the tendency of many countries in the intervening years to opt for an agreement that would ensure a percentage of total traffic on a route was guaranteed for the national carriers of the countries concerned. It was Britain's intention, in this re-negotiated agreement, to avoid overcapacity on the route by restricting it to two British and two American carriers.

A further agreement in 1986 extended the agreed capacities across the Atlantic, the tight control of capacity was relaxed and new routes were agreed, although the concept of **reciprocity** remained in force. The British government was only willing to concede new routes for American carriers if reciprocal routes would be granted to British carriers. US legislation also limited foreign ownership of American airlines to a minority shareholding, thus effectively restricting operational control to US ownership.

Negotiation on routes and carriers operated by member countries subsequently lay in the hands of the European Commission.

Carriage on routes within the national territory of a country (the so-called **cabotage** routes) is normally restricted to the national carriers of the country concerned. In some cases, however, this provides opportunities for a country's national carriers to operate exclusively on international routes in cases where these countries have overseas possessions. This is the case, for example, on routes out of the UK to destinations such as Gibraltar or on services between France and Réunion Island or the islands of Guadaloupe and Martinique in the Caribbean.

Under the EU's programme of liberalization of the air within member countries, the cabotage regulation – the final barrier to total freedom of operation – was dropped in 1997. Any airline of any member country can now file to operate services between cities within another member's borders. The British carrier Virgin Express currently operates flights between Brussels and Nice, while Air Berlin offers connections between the UK and Spain. While this liberalization should, in theory, have opened up competition and encouraged a wealth of new services throughout the EU, in practice, the difficulty of getting slots at congested airports, as well as delaying tactics by some governments attempting to support their own national carriers, have meant that it has taken time for the LCLFs to build up competition in some areas and very few are operating out of hub airports.

The role of the IATA

For many years, effective control over air fares on international routes was exercised by the International Air Transport Association (IATA) – a trade body with more than 240 airline members representing 94 per cent of all leading airlines. The aims of this organization – which was restructured in its present form in 1945, but traces its origins to the very beginning of air transport in 1919 – have been to promote safe, regular and economic air transport, to provide the means for collaboration between the air carriers themselves and cooperate with governments, the ICAO and other international bodies for the promotion of safety and effective communications.

In the past, IATA also had a role in setting tariffs – in effect, operating a legalized cartel. Fares were established at the annual tariff-fixing Traffic Conferences by a process of common agreement between the participating airlines, subject to ratification by the airlines' governments. In practice, most governments merely rubber-stamped the agreements. Critics argued that, as a result, fares became unnecessarily high on many routes and competition was stifled. Often, the agreed fares were the outcome of political considerations in which the less efficient national flag-carriers pushed for prices unrelated to competitive costs.

IATA also controlled many other aspects of airline operation, such as the pitch of passengers' seats, which dictated the amount of legroom they could enjoy, and even the kinds of meals that could be served on board. As a result, the airlines were forced to concentrate their marketing efforts on such ephemeral aspects of the product as service, punctuality or even the design of cabin crew uniforms, rather than providing a genuine measure of competition.

It was widely felt that this had led to inertia among the participating carriers, with agreements resulting from a desire to avoid controversy. Nor had the cartel ensured profitability for its members as they faced open competition from non-IATA carriers, which successfully competed on both price and added value.

Led by the USA and soon followed by other countries, airlines chose to withdraw from this tariff-setting mechanism and, as a result, IATA was restructured in 1979 to provide a two-tier organization: a tariff section to deal with fares, for those nations wishing to maintain this role, and a trade section to provide other benefits that an international airline association offered. IATA's role in tariff agreements has become steadily less important and airlines now largely determine their own service and catering arrangements. An interlining agreement also allowed passengers to switch flights to other member airlines freely – an advantage when they were paying full fares for their tickets, but in an age of low-price tickets for all air services, this no longer has the same appeal.

The principal benefit offered by IATA today is its central clearing house system, which makes possible financial settlements between members in the same manner as the British clearing banks. Tickets and other documents are standardized and interchangeable between IATA members while compatibility is established between members in air fare structures and currency exchange rates. Other procedures, too, such as the appointment, through licensing agreements, of IATA-recognized travel agents, are also standardized throughout the world. The computerized Bank Settlement Plan, introduced in the UK in 1984, permits monthly settlement of accounts with appointed agents through a single centre rather than with each individual airline and has enabled financial transactions to keep pace with the enormous growth in airline travel.

British regulation of air transport

In the UK, the Civil Aviation Act of 1971 led to the establishment of the Civil Aviation Authority, which has five regulatory functions.

- Responsibility for regulating air navigation services (jointly with the Ministry of Defence), through Britain's Air Traffic Control services.
- Responsibility for the regulation of all British civil aviation, including air transport licensing, the award of licences (ATOLs) to air travel organizers and approval of air fares.
- Responsibility for the airworthiness and operational safety of British carriers, including certification of airlines, airports, flight crew and engineers.
- Acting as adviser to the government in matters concerning domestic and international civil aviation.

- A number of subsidiary functions, including the research and publication of statistics, and the ownership and management of eight airports in the Highlands and Islands of Scotland.

Prior to the Civil Aviation Act, no clear long-term government policy had been discernible with respect to aviation in the UK. As governments changed, so did attitudes to the public or private ownership of carriers. With the aim of providing some longer-term direction and stability, a committee of enquiry into civil air transport, under the chairmanship of Sir Ronald Edwards, was established. The report, 'British air transport in the seventies', appeared in 1969.

The Edwards Report, as it became known, recommended that the government should periodically promulgate civil aviation policy and objectives; the long-term aim should be to satisfy air travellers at the lowest economically desirable price and a suitable mix should be agreed between public- and private-sector airlines. The state corporations (BOAC and BEA) were confirmed in their role as flag-carriers, but were recommended to merge and to start charter and inclusive tour operations. The idea of a major second-force airline in the private sector – to complement and compete with the new public airline – was proposed and the suggestion was made that a more liberal policy be adopted towards the licensing of other private airlines. Finally, the report proposed that the economic, safety and regulatory functions carried out by the previous Air Transport Licensing Board, the Board of Trade and the Air Registration Board should thereafter come under the control of a single Civil Aviation Authority.

The Civil Aviation Act, which followed the publication of this report in 1971, accepted most of these proposals. BOAC and BEA were merged into a single corporation – British Airways – while British Caledonian was confirmed as the new second-force airline – following the merger of Caledonian Airways and British United Airways – and the new Civil Aviation Authority was formed.

The CAA is financed by the users of its services, which are mainly the airlines themselves. Any excess profits are expected to be returned to the users through lower charges for its services. A subsidiary of the CAA is the Air Transport Users' Council (AUC), which acts as a watchdog for air transport customers. An international body with similar aims – the International Foundation of Airline Passenger Associations (IFAPA) – is headquartered in Geneva.

UK government policy, 1971–1987

In its proposal that a second-force airline be introduced in Britain, the Edwards Report clearly saw it as a mechanism to compete with the publicly owned flag-carrier across the North Atlantic routes. After the formation of British Caledonian, the government granted the carrier North Atlantic routes in 1973. Within two years, however, government policy had changed to 'spheres of influence', with the second-force airline licensed for complementary, rather than directly competitive, routes. Ignoring British Caledonian's claim that two British carriers on the North Atlantic routes would increase the British share of the total market by taking business away from American carriers, the CAA redistributed routes, giving British Caledonian South American routes, and restricted the North Atlantic largely to British Airways.

A White Paper in 1976, 'Future civil aviation policy', indicated the prevailing policy to end dual designation – a policy later overturned by the Conservative government during the 1980s as support for a totally deregulated air transport system gathered momentum.

An open skies policy being favoured by both the US and British governments in the 1980s led to effective deregulation of fares and capacity across the Atlantic, as well as on domestic routes in both countries. British Airways was privatized in 1987 and the subsequent redistribution and licensing of routes for smaller British carriers set the scene for liberalization throughout Europe.

The deregulation of air transport

Deregulation – or 'liberalization' as it has come to be known in Europe – is the deliberate policy of reducing state control over airline operations and allowing market forces to shape the airline industry. The US led the way with the Airline Deregulation Act of 1978, which abolished collusion in air pricing. The US regulatory body, the Civil Aeronautics Board (CAB), progressively relinquished control over route allocation and fares and was itself disbanded at the end of 1984. Market forces were then to take over, the government expecting that inefficient large carriers would be undercut by smaller airlines that had lower overheads and greater productivity.

In fact, the actual outcome was very different and caused advocates of deregulation in Europe to reconsider the case for total freedom of the air. The opening years of deregulation saw a rapid expansion of airline operations, with a three-fold increase in new airlines. Among the established airlines, those that expanded prudently, such as Delta, prospered, while others, such as Braniff, became overambitious and committed themselves to a programme of expansion that, as fares became more competitive, they could not support financially. While a few routes saw substantial early rises in fares, especially on long-haul domestic flights, on the whole fares fell sharply, attracting a big increase in passengers. This growth was achieved at the expense of profitability, forcing airlines to cut costs in order to survive. New conditions of work and lower pay agreements were negotiated, with some airlines abandoning union recognition altogether. Some airlines reverted to propeller aircraft on short-haul routes to cut costs and worries began to emerge about safety as it was believed that airlines were cutting corners to save on maintenance. Indeed, air safety violations doubled between 1984 and 1987.

Within a decade of deregulation, more than 100 airlines (including 2 out of 3 of the newly launched airlines) had been forced out of business or absorbed as profits changed to losses. Poor morale among airline crew, due to uncertainty about their future job security, led to indifferent service.

Supplementals, as the charter operators are known in the USA, were particularly badly hit as competing scheduled services dropped their fares. They had neither the public recognition nor the marketing skills to compete openly with the scheduled services and many simply ceased to operate. In the longer term, the 'mega-carriers' were the major beneficiaries. They comprised some ten leading airlines, of which the 'big three' – Delta, American and United – held the lion's share of the air travel market. Far from expanding opportunity, deregulation led to smaller airlines being squeezed out or restricted to less important routes by the marketing power of the big carriers. In 2001 (prior to the 9/11 catastrophe), American Airlines took over TWA, which had been operating under Chapter 11 bankruptcy rules.

A second consequence of deregulation was the development of **hub and spoke** systems of operation – feeder air services from smaller 'spoke' airports provide services in to the hubs to connect with the onward long-haul flights of the mega-carriers. This pattern initially enabled the airlines to keep prices down and New York, Chicago, Atlanta, Fort Worth/Dallas and St Louis became major hubs for domestic and international flights, some dominated by a single carrier.

With more liberal policies in force on both sides of the Atlantic, it became clear that renewed talks should take place to negotiate an open skies policy across the Atlantic, too. The Bermuda 2 Agreement having been ruled illegal under EU competition rules and with a further 16 of the 27 EU members having negotiated bilateral agreements directly with the USA, the EU initiated talks with US officials in 2004. The EU pressed for the limitation on foreign ownership of US carriers to be raised to 50 per cent and rights to be granted allowing European carriers to fly on domestic American routes in exchange for opening up inter-European routes to US carriers. US negotiators proved adamant in refusing to accept these terms, however.

Finally, in 2007, after extensive discussion, an **Open Skies Agreement** was reached, which came into force from April 2008. The agreement favoured the United States, in that American airlines are now permitted to operate on EU cabotage routes by extending their transatlantic operations (New York–London–Athens, for example) while America has sacrificed none of its closely guarded cabotage rights and foreign airlines are not permitted to secure more than 25 per cent of any American airline's voting rights. The agreement does allow any EU carrier to fly between any EU airport and any US city, however. With these rights, two things become apparent.

- Passengers originating in Africa and the Middle East and using London Heathrow (LHR) in transit to North America may in future use other carriers on the Continent, to the detriment of LHR transit revenue.

- Slots at LHR, already in short supply and estimated to be valued at £10 million per pair, immediately become more valuable. British Airways holds 42 per cent of slots, but BMI, Britain's second-largest carrier operating from this airport, with a 13 per cent share of slots, was then in a strong negotiating position.

Foreign EU airlines based at Heathrow with intra-European routes could now choose to drop them in favour of more lucrative long-haul transatlantic flights. Air France/KLM thus took the immediate decision to timetable direct flights between London Heathrow and Los Angeles, while British Airways countered by announcing the formation of its new carrier, OpenSkies, which would initiate flights direct between Paris and New York. Air France/KLM have also sought close cooperation with US carrier Delta to run a joint venture that will include common fares, schedules and capacity. This could include the use of Air France/KLM slots by Delta for transatlantic flights. The two airlines sought, and received, immunity from US antitrust laws in establishing this venture.

Lufthansa bought out Swiss carrier Swiss International in 2005, made a substantial investment in US budget carrier JetBlue in 2006 and has sought to join forces with Polish carrier LOT.

Early in 2008, British Airways was looking to form closer links with BMI to compete with the Air France/KLM-Delta link-up and, following abortive talks with Continental Airlines, renewed talks with American Airlines in 2008. BA's first attempt to link with the US carrier dates back to 1997 and further talks were held in 2002, but US anti-trust legislation had inhibited agreements up to that point. Prospects looked rather brighter for a closer partnership with the American carrier by 2008, against a backdrop of rising crisis in the aviation industry. At the time of writing, BA and American had applied to the regulators in the US and EU for antitrust immunity that would allow them to combine route networks, prices, purchasing and marketing, although fuller integration and joint ownership is impossible under present US rules on foreign ownership of domestic airlines. This followed the agreement between BA and Iberia to unite (BA at that point owned 13.15 per cent of Iberia and Iberia 2.99 per cent of BA; the companies were already jointly marketing some code-share flights).

A link between BA, AA and BMI would have led to two-thirds of all slots at Heathrow being controlled by this alliance – a ratio that would certainly meet with disapproval from the Competition Commission in the UK, whereas a BA/AA/Iberia working partnership can expect a greater chance of success. The BA–Iberia link-up has received approval and will make the new organization the largest airline in Europe and would lead to the newly merged airline holding almost half of all the slots at Heathrow. US operator Continental Airlines could be drawn into this agreement at a later stage.

An immediate outcome of the Open Skies Agreement was the rapid increase in capacity as airlines scrambled to introduce new services across the Atlantic. As we have seen earlier, this led to supply rapidly outstripping demand, which, coupled with an escalation in fuel costs, led to difficulties for the airlines on these routes and speeded up merger talks between the larger carriers. At the time of writing, it was anticipated that Delta and

Example

The scramble to merge

The combination of global recession, levelling-out of demand and high fuel prices is putting more pressure on airlines to merge. A study undertaken by Blue Oar Securities in 2008 suggests that no more than 6 big airlines will survive the current crisis in Europe, coupled with a few niche carriers, while up to 50 lower-division airlines will disappear. Survivors will be certain to include Air France/KLM, Lufthansa, the merged BA/Iberia and the two leading budget carriers, easyJet and Ryanair. The survival of any others is viewed as highly speculative.

Source: Blue Oar Investments, '*Into thin air*', Blue oar Investments, 2008, and Robertson, D. (2008) 'BA – Iberia merger would create biggest airline in Europe', *The Times*, 30 July, p. 5.

Northwest would merge to create the world's largest airline, Atlanta, although the services will continue to operate under the Delta brand.

With Open Skies successfully concluded across the Atlantic, talks were then held between the USA and Australia, to negotiate a similar liberalization. This led to a similar Open Skies agreement in 2008 for transpacific routes.

Developments in North American air traffic since 1990

Since the early 1990s, the North American airlines' struggle to survive has become more acute. Famous names like Pan American disappeared and, between 1991 and 1993, five airlines were forced to operate under America's Chapter 11 bankruptcy code, which permits an airline to continue to operate, although officially bankrupt, while restructuring its finances. The huge losses sustained by even the biggest airlines led to cancellations of new aircraft orders, the sale of assets and, finally, the formation of alliances with major international carriers – a trend that has become of major importance in the early years of the twenty-first century. Airline retrenchment led in turn to great difficulties for manufacturers of aircraft. They experienced widespread cancellations of orders in favour of leasing or the purchase of second-hand equipment, while the traditional leasing market in turn dried up.

The hub-and-spoke development, after its initial success in the United States, was challenged by new, low-cost regional carriers operating city-to-city on less significant routes. Some of these have been particularly successful – notably Southwest Airlines, a low-cost airline offering no frills flying at budget fares on some 60 routes and operating medium-size aircraft spoke-to-spoke in direct competition with the dominant hub-and-spoke operators. Southwest was the only US airline not to encounter losses after the 9/11 disaster.

By the start of the twenty-first century, some stability had returned, with a pattern emerging of powerful US mega-carriers (which have become known as the 'legacy carriers') on key domestic and international routes seeking alliances with leading foreign airlines in order to offer truly global air services. Most smaller airlines opted to concentrate on niche services, but the growth of no frills airlines in the US was initially limited, partly owing to effective marketing by the leading carriers, and partly owing to public concern over safety issues (the fatal 1996 crash of no frills carrier Valujet did nothing to reduce this concern). The big carriers established their own low-cost operations – Delta created Delta Express and, later, Song Air (since wound up); American Airlines, its Eagle division; United, Ted. The much-criticized practice of 'bracketing', in which larger carriers lay on cut-price flights shortly before and after those of rival cheap carriers, also threatened the survival of many of the new airlines. Only where the airline had sufficient resources to pack a route with flights (as was the case with Southwest Airlines) did this tactic prove impractical.

The 9/11 terrorist attack on New York's Twin Towers in 2001 quickly unseated the airlines' economic recovery. In the aftermath, virtually all the leading carriers sought Chapter 11 bankruptcy protection:

- Delta Airlines in 2004
- United Airlines between 2002 and 2006
- ATA Holdings between 2004 and 2006
- US Airways between 2002 and 2003 and again in 2004 and 2005 (when it was absorbed by America West)
- Northwest Airlines in 2005.

In the eight years that have followed the disaster, the legacy carriers have all struggled to survive, let alone return profits. With the consequent downturn in business generally following the crisis, the no frills carriers, led by Southwest Airlines, benefited at the expense of the mega-carriers. Attempts to meet this competition by forming their own budget airlines have not been wholly successful. Song, for example, has been reabsorbed into its parent airline. The big six cannot raise fares, owing to the competition they face from the no frills carriers, but, at the same time, they are faced with high staff pay (which is difficult to renegotiate with strong unions, although United successfully negotiated a five-year contract with its ground workers in 2005, slashing its pay costs), escalating oil prices, which are likely to remain highly volatile for the foreseeable future, and added costs for the extra security that has had to be put in place since 9/11. One result has been a cutting back in service levels, with economy passengers now paying for food and drink on board and refurbishment of aircraft interiors being undertaken less frequently.

In mid-2008, with oil prices at an all-time high, both legacy and budget carriers were facing unprecedented pressures on cost, causing American Airlines to introduce charges for hold baggage – the first legacy carrier to do so – while budget carrier JetBlue began charging a supplement for window seats. While oil prices later fell back, long-term trends anticipate high prices and the sheer volatility of the market for oil may force leading airlines to start laying up part of their fleets and reducing services.

The likely direction in the future will be for more integration and talks are ongoing between carriers at the time of writing. Discussions held between the legacy carriers proposing full mergers have tended in the past to be blocked by the competition authorities, but the crisis that faced the industry in 2008/09 is such that, inevitably, fewer airlines will survive and, should the authorities continue to oppose mergers, closer alliances in some shape or form will nevertheless be inevitable.

European liberalization

Elsewhere in the developed world, governments have also supported the steady erosion of state regulatory powers over the airline industry. In Australia, liberalized air policy led to the establishment of new airlines and, for the first time, a competitively priced domestic air service, with JetBlue filling the role formerly occupied by Ansett as Australia's second carrier. Europe's airlines were also moving slowly towards a 'market forces' policy, although in those countries where the state retained a financial investment in its airlines, the ethos of liberalization promoted by the European Commission was resisted. Iberia and Air France, for example, continued to receive public subsidies long after these became technically contrary to EU regulations. The path to liberalization had become irresistible, however, with the EU easing the transition by phasing it in three stages between 1987 and 1997, after which all EU carriers became free to fly anywhere within the EU, including cabotage routes, at fares they themselves determined, hindered only by the lack of slots at the major airports. Other European carriers outside the EU – notably Switzerland, Norway and Iceland – followed suit.

Airline deregulation in Britain had preceded that of other EU countries following a number of individual bilateral agreements with fellow EU members – notably Ireland and the Netherlands. This policy led to a substantial growth in the number of domestic carriers, as well as the numbers of passengers travelling.

No frills airlines were already springing up in Britain by the 1990s, operating chiefly out of regional and secondary airports, especially Luton and Stansted, which had slots available for expansion and charged lower fees. The less popular regional airports are often keen to subsidize start-up airlines or others developing new routes, with landing charges waived for an initial period and the promise of advertising support. High start-up costs for operators joining dense routes, the big expense of marketing to establish a new name in the public eye and the success of frequent flyer programmes among the large carriers constrained small carriers from directly competing with them. Also the low prices made levels of commission less attractive to agents, making distribution difficult. All this encouraged the budget carriers to sell their product direct, however, coinciding with the growth in online booking and easier direct distribution. Not all were successful, as we have seen, but the leaders – notably easyJet and Ryanair – were soon undermining even the largest carriers. The Irish carrier at first successfully competed head-on with Aer Lingus and then massively expanded its route network throughout Europe – to a point where, by 2008, it had overtaken all European legacy carriers to become the largest airline in Europe, carrying in excess of 49 million passengers (and, in late 2008, was seeking to take over Aer Lingus, of which it already controlled nearly 30 per cent). Inevitably the large carriers were forced to retaliate, first by launching their own low-cost carriers (BMI launched its offshoot BMIBaby, for example, which continues to trade) and subsequently by slashing the prices of economy tickets on their normal flights.

One side-effect of liberalization has been the virtual demise of the **bucket shops** – non-appointed travel agents, selling off illegally discounted airline tickets dumped on the market at short notice by airlines with spare capacity. Their place has been taken by brokers who may legally contract with the airlines for spare capacity and sell this cheaply through travel agents (who were formerly legally forbidden to deal with the bucket shop operators). Increasingly, however, airlines are selling off unsold seats cheaply through website providers. Indeed, the growth in numbers of Internet companies with programmes designed to handle these products is one of the leading characteristics of the airline business at the beginning of the new century. This will be examined later in the chapter.

The potential explosion of passenger traffic resulting from liberalization has been, as we have seen, severely curtailed by problems of congestion. Government statistics have projected flights from Britain to rise from 200 million in 2003 to, according to some estimates, over 470 million by 2030 – the bulk of this increase arising from demand out of South Eastern airports. Mainland Europe, too, is rapidly approaching saturation.

There are limits to the number of aircraft movements that can be handled at an airport within a given time and runways and terminals are already stretched to the maximum at peak times. Air corridors are also overcrowded in Europe and the 'stacking' of aircraft above airports prior to landing is costing airlines huge sums of money in wasted fuel.

Earlier, we explored ways in which the productivity of air corridors can be boosted by reducing height intervals between aircraft on some routes and it may be possible to reduce lateral and nose to tail intervals as technology improves and air traffic control systems in Europe are better coordinated. The easing of restrictions on night flights would be a further aid to growth, but local resistance, organized into powerful lobbies, has to be overcome first. Building larger aircraft may prove to be a solution in the short term, although, as we saw earlier in this chapter, Boeing is not convinced that there is a market for the super-jumbos, pointing to the trend for smaller aircraft to maximize yield. Such aircraft are likely to be introduced only on the most heavily travelled routes, such as high-density domestic routes in Japan, services across the North Atlantic and those between London and Far Eastern hubs such as Singapore or Tokyo. Airports, however, will have to resolve the problems of loading and unloading up to 800 passengers, as well as cleaning and refuelling, in a short space of time.

While the introduction of new fast rail services between the European capitals could theoretically offer some help by reducing demand for air travel on routes of up to about 500 miles, the overall growth in demand for air services poses severe problems for the industry in the long run. Worryingly, in Britain, the high cost of rail fares is tempting people away from rail and towards domestic air travel, with new budget-priced routes between towns as close as Southampton and Newquay, Bristol and Plymouth, and London and Manchester (even though fast trains operate every half hour on the latter route).

One further worry about the results of liberalization should receive a mention: the issue of air safety. Cost competition is driving some airlines to use older aircraft or that registered outside the UK. While the CAA has imposed restrictions on British scheduled airlines using foreign aircraft, there are no restrictions on UK tour operators chartering such aircraft to operate into and out of the UK, nor is any firm control exercised over the use of foreign aircraft registered in other EU countries. Pressures to meet targets on air traffic control, and the new compensation regulations introduced in 2005 by the EU against delayed flights have led to further concerns about passenger safety within the EU.

Example

The Joint Aviation Authority and Turkish airlines

In Europe, 39 countries belong to the JAA, which sets higher safety standards for civil aviation than those set by the ICAO in maintenance, operations and the training of pilots. In some cases, however, the JAA's control is more lax than that operating within the EU. Turkey joined the JAA in 2001. Turkey accepts the ascribed weight allowance per passenger on holiday charter flights as being 70 kilograms, while the European norm is 76 kilograms (children 32 kilograms). This, when multiplied by a typical payload of 200 passengers, allows the airline to carry an extra ton of fuel, giving it scope to fly direct and non-stop between the European capitals and the Anatolian coastal resorts. Two Turkish airlines used for charter flights, Fly Air and Onur Air, have been refused permission to use airports in certain European countries, owing to perceived inadequacy in safety standards on this point, even though they are abiding by JAA's standards.[7]

Further reading: The EU's banned list can be viewed at: **www.ec.europa.eu/transport/air-ban/list_en.htm**

The impact of 9/11 was as keenly felt on European carriers as it was by those in the US, coming as it did on top of an economic downturn that was already depressing airline profitability. Several airlines collapsed, only to return in a new, privatized form, including Sabena, the Belgian flag-carrier (replaced by SN Brussels) and Swissair (now simply Swiss and owned by Lufthansa). Air France and KLM merged their operations, becoming the largest non-US carrier in the world. It has been the no frills carriers, once again, however, that have gained most from the economic climate, undercutting their rivals, opening up new routes and finding new markets for air transport.

The economics of airline operation

The development of an airline route is something of a catch-22 situation. Airlines require some reassurance about traffic demand before they are willing to commit their aircraft to a new route, but air travellers look for regular and frequent flights to a destination before patronizing a route.

There is usually an element of risk involved in initiating any new route, especially as seat prices are likely to be high to compensate for low load factors (the number of seats sold as a percentage of total seats available) and high overheads (for both operating and marketing) before traffic builds up. When a route has proved its popularity, however, the pioneer airline is faced with increasing competition as other airlines are attracted by the increase in traffic – unless governments decide to control market entry. In an open-market economy, the original airline faces lower load factors, as the market is split between a number of carriers, requiring it to either increase the fares or reduce profit margins, although it may well have kept prices artificially low initially in order to build the market and recoup launch costs later.

Key routes, such as those across the North Atlantic, attract levels of competition that can make it difficult to operate any services profitably and many airlines that do operate on these routes have suffered losses and low load factors for many years.

The development of hub-and-spoke systems

Major airlines in the USA recognized that attempting to serve all airports with maximum frequency city-to-city flights was uneconomic, so developed the concept of the **hub-and-spoke system**. The hub airports provide transcontinental and intercontinental services, while the 'spokes' offer connecting flights from regional airports to meet these long-haul services. The latter services can be provided in aircraft that are smaller and cheaper to operate (often turboprops) by low-cost carriers, often working in strategic alliances with the major carriers. Flights are then banked into complexes and, in theory, greater efficiency is achieved. For example, a hub with 55 spokes can create 1500 'city pairs' in this way. Larger aircraft can be used between hubs and higher load factors and better utilization of aircraft are achieved.

Some 40 hubs were soon established in the USA alone, serving 25 of America's largest cities. Within a few years of their introduction, passengers taking advantage of hub-and-spoke systems accounted for three-quarters of the total at Atlanta airport and half at Chicago, Denver and Dallas/Fort Worth. Similarly, in Europe the hub-and-spoke system was brought into operation by leading airlines, notable among them KLM, which, with Schiphol Airport as its hub, had soon built up some ten waves of spoke flights a day to feed into its European and long-haul services. In this way, the airline was able to attract traffic from UK regional airports to connect with its major routes, in direct competition with long-haul flights from London's airports. Sabena and Air France, similarly, developed hub-and-spoke systems based on Brussels and Paris.

Such systems are generally best suited to feeding long-haul flights, as the additional stopover time called for by joining via a spoke is only a small proportion of the total journey. It later became apparent, however, that there are also diseconomies that accrue from operating these systems. The organization of hub-and-spoke flights requires frequent waves of closely spaced banks of arrivals and departures to be established, resulting in peaks and troughs at the hub airports, which puts further pressure on congested air and terminal space and leads to delays. It also requires larger numbers of handling staff on the ground during peaks and involves further peaking expenses. Obviously, on-time performance becomes even more significant under these circumstances and, if airlines are forced to delay departures while waiting for delayed inbound flights, costs rise.

Some airports are clearly better suited than others to coping with this way of working. Schiphol has benefited from hub-and-spoke flights being based in the same terminal, which means that delays in passengers making their connections are less catastrophic than at Brussels airport where they have to travel between terminals by airport bus.

There is now growing evidence that, in some circumstances, airlines remaining outside the hub-and-spoke system can be more profitable than those within it. They can do this by charging a higher fare for non-stop services, so even though the demand is not as great, it may still be equally profitable. This applies particularly to business flights, where non-stop services are seen as critical. We have noted elsewhere the success of Southwest Airlines, particularly in gaining market share by flying city-to-city within the USA. There are clear limits on the extent to which city-to-city services can be viable, however – it is dependent on passenger demand and the distances to be travelled.

The growth of strategic alliances

As the problems arising from open competition are obviously going to be long-term ones, the aviation industry has been caught up in a huge global restructuring exercise since the 1990s. This process is still evident in the first decade of the new century, as airlines jockey to be among the survivors in a war of attrition. We have noted that observers expect perhaps as few as a dozen global mega-carriers to survive beyond the early years of the twenty-first century, of which only three or four will be European.

European airlines had seen and taken account of developments in the North American market. They recognized that size, which provides economies of scale and scope, would be crucial to survival in the future. They also noted that US domestic carriers were expanding into transatlantic routes and are now benefiting from the five freedoms of the air in Europe, posing further threats to market share. The way forward for the European carriers is seen as lying in either mergers and takeovers or the development of strategic alliances with US carriers.

Alliances are easier to establish, but experience has shown that they can prove less durable. Political differences and differences of management style have frequently hindered effectiveness. The short-lived relationships between British Airways and United Airlines and between Lufthansa and Air France are cases in point, while the much-vaunted attempt in 1993 to form an alliance between Swissair, Austrian Airlines, SAS and KLM, known as Alcazar, also foundered before being implemented, owing to failure to agree on a US partner. The movement of airlines between the various alliances in order to gain competitive edge also demonstrates the highly fluid nature of these alliances.

Evidence now points to the success of strategic alliances as being dependent on expansion in three stages. First, there is a need to secure a dominant share in the home market. British Airways undertook expansion specifically through franchising, absorbing 100 per cent of Brymon Airways and soon held six franchises in the UK, as well as a further four overseas. Air France absorbed a number of domestic French carriers, as did KLM Dutch carriers. More recently, Air Berlin, initially an LCLF carrier, has expanded rapidly – first by buying DBA (a German domestic carrier first launched by British Airways) in 2006, followed in 2007 by its purchase of charter operator LTU, Europe's second-largest budget carrier, together with a 49 per cent share of Swiss carrier Belair.

The second step is to gain a strong foothold in the main European countries, especially the UK, France and Germany. This was achieved, for example, by SAS, which controlled 40 per cent of British Midland by the early 1990s, and KLM, which purchased Air UK.

The final stage is the globalization of the carrier, especially through investments in North America and the Asia/Pacific region. BA became a leader in this strategy, taking a minority investment in Australian carrier Qantas in 1992 and seeking similar investments in US carriers, although with little success to date, given the US antitrust laws and European Commission fears of monopoly power. The more recent Air France/KLM link-up with Delta is an indication of the achievement of this final step in the process.

Global alliances are now seen as the way forward. They embrace key airlines in Europe, North America and the Asia/Pacific region. While the specific membership of each of these changes quite frequently, the picture in 2008 was as follows.

- *One World* (formed 1998) with current members British Airways, American Airlines, Qantas, Cathay Pacific, Iberia, Finnair, Aer Lingus, Lan Chile, Japan Airlines, Malév, Royal Jordanian, together with affiliated regional carriers.

- *Star Alliance* (1997) with Air Canada, Air China, Air New Zealand, ANA, Asiana Airlines, Austrian Airlines, BMI, LOT Polish Airlines, Lufthansa, SAS, Shanghai Airlines, Singapore Airlines, South African Airways, Spanair, Swiss, TAP Portugal, Thai Airways International, United Airlines, US Airways and associated regional members.
- *Skyteam* (2000) with Aeroflot, Aeromexico, Air France/KLM, Alitalia, China Southern, Continental Airlines, Czech Airlines, Delta, Korean Air, NWA and associated regional airlines.

Two other former alliances – Wings and Qualiflyer – have become defunct as airlines merged or were driven out of service in the wake of the 9/11 disaster.

Globalization is an inevitable consequence of the growth of the international airline business. A strategic alliance offers opportunities for rapid global growth, coupled with marketing benefits that cannot be achieved as an individual airline. For example, it allows domestic spokes to be tacked on to international routes, as the long-standing alliance between the US carrier NWA (Northwest Airlines) and Dutch carrier KLM demonstrated. It increases the viability of marginal routes and allows carriers to compete on routes where, separately, they do not hold rights. Alliances enable companies to reduce costs by using larger aircraft to meet overall demand and sharing operational costs, such as counter space at airports and baggage handling. Marketing costs such as advertising may also be shared. Other operational benefits include control over air terminals. At Heathrow, terminal 5 has become the BA hub, terminal 3 is destined to become a One World hub, while the new terminal soon to replace terminals 1 and 2 will be assigned to Star Alliance carriers.

Alliances may range from the marginal – such as having an interline agreement to accept one another's documentation and transfer of passengers – to marketing agreements – such as joint frequent flyer programmes – and operational agreements – such as blocking space on one another's aircraft to sell their seats. The commonest advantage to be gained, though, is that of code-sharing.

Code-sharing

Domestic code-sharing was in practice within the United States as long ago as 1967, but was first introduced internationally in 1985, when American Airlines and Qantas agreed to share codes on routes across the Pacific.

Under a code-sharing agreement, two airlines agree to share their codes on through routes – for example, between New York and San Francisco and from San Francisco to Sydney. This has the marketing advantage of appearing to be a single through flight, but there are also very concrete advantages for passengers, in that flight timings are coordinated, transfer times between stopovers may be reduced (and carriers will often hold flights for up to 20 minutes for passengers connecting from flights that are code-shared) and baggage can be checked through to the final destination, reducing lost luggage. Carriers can sell each other's flights as if they were their own and will frequently block off space to do so. A further advantage is that code-shared flights are featured on computer reservations systems before other connections, as these offer passengers the best value. They may also benefit from multiple listing on the CRS as they will be listed under both carriers' services.

The establishment of code-sharing across the Atlantic has been crucial to the successful marketing of long-haul travel and has been extensively used by European carriers to gain access to US domestic destinations. European airlines recognize that US airlines will continue to dominate the global marketplace, partly owing, of course, to the huge demand for both domestic and international travel by American travellers. Success for the European carriers therefore depends on establishing close links with at least one of the leading US carriers.

An indication of the size of the world's leading carriers is given in Table 13.1, based on latest available IATA figures.

Table 13.1 Leading airlines of the world, 2007.

Airline	Passengers carried on all routes (000's)
Southwest Airlines	101,911
American Airlines	98,162
Delta Airlines	72,900
United Airlines	68,400
Lufthansa	62,900
Air France/KLM	57,600
China Southern	56,900
NorthWest Airlines	53,700
Japan Airlines	50,442
All Nippon	50,384

Note: When measuring passenger kilometres flown – a commoner method of judging carryings – a different picture would emerge, with the three US legacy carriers American Airlines, United Airlines and Delta Airlines in the forefront.
Source: Wikipedia, based on IATA statistics.

Airline costs

The selection of suitable aircraft for a route is the outcome of the assessment of relative costs involved (both capital and operating) and the characteristics of the aircraft themselves.

Capital costs

The global growth in demand for passenger services since the turn of the century has averaged between 5 and 7 per cent, and the ICAO has forecast that this pattern will continue up to 2016 at least, with highest growth in the Asia/Pacific region. This growth comes in spite of the impact of the 9/11 tragedy and the subsequent escalation in oil prices (although it has not taken account of the huge rise in oil prices occurring later in 2008 and subsequent forecasts have suggested a figure closer to 4 per cent). Airlines must therefore plan for continued expansion and regular renewal, with one eye on operating costs while also focusing on customer demand – for example, newer aircraft appeal to passengers in terms of both safety and aesthetics.

With the latest superjumbos costing in excess of $300 million, investment in new aircraft is a huge commitment (in 2007, Emirates Airlines alone ordered 58 A380s). Attractive loan terms are likely to be a key factor in closing sales and some manufacturers are willing to offer very favourable trade-ins on old aircraft in order to sell their new models. Orders for new aircraft are usually a package, embracing not only the aircraft themselves but also the subsequent provision of spares and possibly servicing. Additionally, there are periods when supply will exceed demand and, when there are many second-hand aircraft on the market, the competition between manufacturers for sales enables airlines to drive very hard bargains when purchasing new equipment.

Airlines also have the choice, of course, of leasing aircraft rather than purchasing them and, although they may incur penalties for doing so, if an airline is hit by recession and a sharp drop in demand, it may well cut back on orders already placed, choosing to lease rather than purchase to keep costs down. On occasion, this can result in an airline selling existing aircraft and leasing them back to release capital.

Operating costs

Mile for mile, short-haul routes (of up to 1500 miles) overall are more expensive to operate than are long-haul, although this is not simply due to the cost of the fuel used.

While the greater frequency of take-offs and landings on short-haul flights will mean high initial fuel consumption on each leg as aircraft gain height, research[8] has shown that an aircraft travelling long distances in a single hop can consume more fuel than one stopping three times on the same route. The example given was of a 9000-mile flight, which, flown non-stop, consumes 120 tonnes of fuel, while an aircraft taking three 3000-mile hops will need only 28 tonnes for each hop – a total of 84 tonnes. The explanation for this is that, ironically, long-haul aircraft use more fuel because they are carrying the weight of the extra fuel needed for the longer journey. When factoring in the additional costs of crewing and landing fees for both forms of travel, however, shorter-haul costs will rise higher than those of long-haul and force up ticket prices.

Example

The effect of oil price increases

An estimate in early 2008 (before the rapid escalation of oil prices in midsummer) put the typical fuel burn of flying a Boeing 767 or Airbus A330 between London and New York (3180 nautical miles) at 12,800 gallons, reducing to 10,800 gallons for the return flight, due to favourable tail winds. In 2000, with fuel costing just 87 cents a gallon, a return journey would have cost $20,532 in fuel alone. By 2008, aviation fuel had risen to $3.44 a gallon, putting the round trip fuel cost up to $81,152 – a four-fold increase. At the same time, intense competition was forcing airlines to keep ticket prices down.

Source: 'European airlines facing profit squeeze', *The Times*, 25 April 2008, p. 51.

Short-haul aircraft also spend a proportionately greater amount of time on the ground than long-haul aircraft. Aircraft are only earning money while they are in the air and depreciation of their capital cost can only be written off against their actual flying time. For this reason, it is important that they are scheduled for the maximum number of flying hours each day. According to the efficiency of the airline and the airports the airline uses, productivity can be increased without impairing the (legally determined) minimum service and maintenance time required (Boeing 747 servicing entails 35–60 work hours, with a complete overhaul, after 6000 hours of flying, involving 10,000 work hours). Here, the American carriers appear to be more successful than the European, with the big three US carriers flying at least ten hours per day on short- and medium-haul flights, against a European average of only seven hours (although there are marked differences between the productivity of the various airlines within Europe). In the USA, aircraft turnarounds (time spent on the ground between landing and take-off) can be as little as 30 minutes, while in Europe a minimum of 45 minutes is the norm. Budget airlines, however, perform significantly better than the traditional carriers, owing in part to their operating out of less congested airports.

Long-haul aircraft normally operate at a ceiling of 30,000–40,000 feet (supersonics were operating at 50,000–60,00 feet), while short- and medium-haul aircraft will operate at lower ceilings. While the cost of getting the long-haul aircraft to its ceiling will be greater than that of a short- and medium-haul aircraft, once at these heights, there is little wind resistance and the rate at which fuel is burned falls considerably.

Improving technology is constantly extending the distances that aircraft can fly non-stop. Singapore Airlines introduced the world's longest non-stop flights in 2003 when they started operating Airbus A345s between Singapore and Los Angeles (16 hours out, 18.5 hours back) and Singapore–New York (18 hours), while Virgin has announced its intention of operating the Boeing Dreamliner 787s direct from London to Perth (17 hours' flying time) and, after 2011, to Hawaii (16 hours). The customer appeal of travelling direct and reducing overall travel time is high, but may be offset by concern over very long, un-interrupted flights and growing awareness of the potential dangers of deep vein thrombosis (DVT). Recent research is pointing to a 12 per cent increase in the likelihood of developing DVT among long-haul passengers over other passengers.

Costs can be subdivided into the **direct** costs of operating and **indirect** costs. The former will include flight expenses (salaries of flight crew, fuel, in-flight catering), plus maintenance, depreciation, aircraft insurance and airport and navigation charges. Airport charges will include landing fees, parking charges, navigation charges (where these are passed on to the airline by the airport) and a per capita cost according to the number of passengers carried. Navigation charges vary according to the weight of the aircraft and the distance flown over a particular territory. Many of these charges are incorporated into the price of the ticket or are charged as a supplement to the passenger.

Example

Surcharges to passengers on a return flight from London to New York

The burden of surcharges is increasing sharply on airline travel. One estimate identified eleven different surcharges made in 2007 to the basic passenger fare on flights across the Atlantic:

Charge	£
Fuel surcharge	38.00 each way
Insurance/security	2.50 each way
Air passenger duty	20.00 each way
LHR passenger service charge	14.30
US international transportation tax	14.80
US Immigration and Naturalisation Service user fee	3.40
US Customs user fee	2.70
US animal and plant health inspection service fee	2.50
JFK passenger facility charge	2.20
US Civil Aviation security service fee	1.20
Total	162.10

The imposition of much higher fuel surcharges in 2008 would, of course, have significantly added to this burden.

Source: *Sunday Times*, 12 August 2007.

In the UK, current plans are for air passenger duty to end in November 2009, to be replaced by a 'per aircraft' charge, which is expected to be passed on to passengers. Airlines with newer fleets and higher load factors are expected to be able to pass on lower charges to their passengers than airlines without such advantages. This move may mean the elimination of low load factor destinations that operate as a public service, however, unless they can secure additional subsidies.

After 1998, the notional weight of passengers on EU services was increased, adding to costs. The previous 75 kilograms for males and 65 kilograms for females was replaced by a notional weight of 84 kilograms per capita for scheduled flights and 76 kilograms for holiday charters, in recognition of the trend for people to have increased in body weight internationally. This higher figure had already been adopted by US and some other carriers, but, in fact, the US opted for a still higher figure in 2005 – moving from 185 pounds (84 kilograms) to 200 pounds (nearly 91 kilograms) for males and a slightly lower figure for females. The US allows a further 5 pounds per passenger in winter, in recognition of the need for a higher fuel burn than in summer. These figures, however, include carry-on bags, unlike regulations in Europe. Japanese airlines operate on a notional body weight of 73 kilograms (regardless of the nationality of those carried), which enables Japanese carriers to gain advantage over others by providing more seats. The tendency towards obesity among the populations of the developed countries is causing concern for airlines anxious to control their costs as the average extra weight now carried increases fuel costs considerably.

Example

No frills airlines

The no frills airlines have taken steps to recover costs associated with the increasing weight of their passengers. Maersk Air have introduced three seat sizes: basic fares are paid for the smallest, with a pitch of 70 centimetres on their Boeing 737–700s. For a slightly higher fare, passengers can book a medium seat, with an 80-centimetre pitch, while an upgrade to an X-large seat can be made for an additional payment. Southwest Airlines, on the other hand, require obese passengers (discreetly referred to in the USA as COS – customers of size) to purchase two seats. It is a delicate matter for booking and check-in staff to determine how obese a passenger must be before they have to impose the extra charge! The test of obesity is whether or not the armrest between passengers can be dropped – something that would be debateable until the passenger was actually on board.

While the no frills carriers make efforts to improve their slim per capita profits as fuel prices increase, at the other end of the scale equal efforts are being made to reduce aircraft weight in other directions, as we saw earlier in this chapter.

Depreciation is the cost of writing off the original purchase price of the aircraft against the number of hours it flies (which may be as high as 4000 hours per year). Total depreciation periods vary. In the case of smaller, relatively inexpensive aircraft, it may be as short as 8 to 10 years, while wide-bodied jets may be depreciated over periods as long as 14 to 16 years. A residual value of, typically, 10 per cent of the original purchase price is normally allowed for. In some cases, it might be considered prudent to write off aircraft faster than this because obsolescence can overtake their operating life and airlines must keep up with their competitors by re-equipping at regular intervals. With falling profits, however, few airlines find it easy to re-equip and so the tendency is to extend depreciation time. On top of this, insurance costs will be around 3 per cent per annum of the aircraft's purchase price.

Indirect costs include all non-flight expenses, such as marketing, reservations, ground handling, administration and other insurances, such as passenger liability. These costs will vary very little however many flights are flown, so large airlines will clearly benefit from economies of scale here.

Fuel costs globally are quoted in US dollars and will therefore vary not only according to changing oil prices but also according to changing currency exchange rates. While oil prices fell back after their rapid rise in mid-2008, sterling's exchange rate against the dollar began to deteriorate at the same time, offsetting to some extent the benefits of cheaper oil for carriers operating out of the UK.

Fuel costs represented about 20 per cent of all operating expenses in 2007, but doubled the following year, so attempts to bring these costs under control are vital. As we saw earlier, airlines can contract to buy fuel in advance if they fear that prices will rise. Typically, it is the larger airlines with bigger financial reserves that are best placed to do this, but budget airlines, most concerned to control costs, have also hedged. In 2004, Ryanair bought forward its fuel needs until 2007, hedging against what were, at the time, wildly fluctuating prices, but then failed to extend its hedging when oil prices rocketed. In the USA, Southwest was the sole carrier to cap its fuel costs in 2005, at $26 a barrel, with a contract providing generous terms until 2009. With hindsight, this was an extremely shrewd move. Although hedging does not invariably save money (oil prices can go down as well as up), it does smooth out cash flow and reduce volatility.

Other ways to trim costs have included reducing the labour force, while renegotiating levels of pay and conditions of service (often at the expense of good staff–management relations), and moving activities to countries where costs are lower. Several companies have moved their accounts to India, while others have renegotiated contracts for maintenance or cleaning services with other low-cost countries. Savings can also be achieved by forming low-cost subsidiaries – a move taken by several traditionally high-cost European and American carriers. Above all, distribution costs can be trimmed, given the new means of reaching passengers direct. This will be discussed later on in this chapter.

Aircraft characteristics

These will include the aircraft's cruising speed and **block speed** – its average overall speed on a trip – its range and field length requirements, its carrying capacity and customer appeal. In terms of passenger capacities, airline development tends to occur in leaps. Thus, with the introduction of jumbo jets, the number of seats on an aircraft tripled, and with the new generation of superjumbos there has been a further sharp increase in capacity. While average seat costs fall sharply as seat numbers are increased, this can only be reflected in lower prices to passengers if sufficient seats are filled.

Carrying capacity is also influenced by the **payload** that the aircraft is to carry – that is, the balance between fuel, passengers and freight. An aircraft is authorized to 'take off at MTOW' (maximum take-off weight), which is its empty operating weight plus payload. At maximum payload, the aircraft will be limited to a certain range, but can increase this range by sacrificing part of the payload – that is, by carrying fewer passengers. Sacrificing both fuel *and* some passenger capacity may allow some aircraft to operate from smaller regional airports with short runways.

Cost savings can be made in a number of ways when using larger aircraft. It is a curious fact that the relative cost of pushing a large aircraft through the air is less, per unit of weight, than a small one (incidentally, this principle also holds true in shipping operations, in that large ships are relatively cheaper per unit of weight to push through the water than smaller ones). Larger aircraft experience proportionately lower drag per unit of weight; they are more aerodynamic. They can also use larger, more powerful engines. Equally, maintenance and cleaning costs per seat are lower.

Environmental concerns

Airline operations are facing a growing challenge, politically and economically, regarding the concern over aircraft emissions and their impact on the environment. Greenhouse gases – notably CO_2 (carbon dioxide) but also nitrogen oxide and vapour trails that trap heat in the atmosphere when aircraft are flying at height – are now widely acknowledged to add to the problems of global warming. The emissions created by global aircraft movements are estimated to account for around 3 per cent of these gases. As emissions are more damaging at higher altitudes, however, this figure can probably be doubled. Some estimates are far higher. The UK Department for Transport, for example, has placed the figure as high as 13 per cent and believes that, even allowing for a 50 per cent increase in fuel efficiency, emissions will still increase by 50 per cent by 2020, given the projected increase in flights. While these emissions are a relatively small percentage compared with those released in the process of generating electricity or deforestation,[9] their projected increase over the next decade gives cause for alarm. This has not been alleviated by the airlines' and aircraft manufacturers' efforts to reduce fuel burn (the average consumption in new aircraft such as the A380 and 787 will improve to around 3 litres per passenger kilometre, compared with consumption on earlier aircraft of around 5 litres). The British government is pledged to reduce CO_2 emissions by 20 per cent by 2020 and by 60 per cent by 2050, but there are doubts that these figures are achievable, especially given the same government's expansion plans for, inter alia, a third runway at London's Heathrow Airport.

Example

The impact of a third runway at Heathrow Airport

In 2006, some 67 million passengers used LHR Airport. As many as 122 million could use it, it is claimed, if a third runway is built. Environmentalists have lobbied hard to prevent its construction but it received government approval in 2009.

Some have argued that 95 million passengers could be accommodated on the present pair of runways if these were used more efficiently – such as ensuring higher load factors for each aircraft and using larger aircraft, such as the A380. British Airways has claimed that a third runway would actually *reduce* CO_2 emissions, as airlines would reduce the amount of taxiing before take-off and stacking before landing, although this takes no account of the increase in flights possible with a third runway in place.

Boeing and Virgin Airlines cooperated on research to judge whether or not towing aircraft to starting grids near the head of runways would help in reducing emissions, which it was thought might reduce ground emissions by some 50 per cent. In practice, however, it was found that wear and tear on the landing gear was too great to merit implementing this idea.

Individual airlines have made some rather half-hearted efforts to offset emissions. British Airways introduced a 'green fee', ranging from £5 on short-haul flights to £25 for the longest – the money going towards energy-saving projects in developing countries. The disadvantage of the scheme is that it is voluntary and fewer than 1 in 200 passengers volunteered to pay it when it was first introduced in 2005. Critics have argued in favour of taxation, pointing out that, were aviation fuel to be taxed at the same rate as petrol, a return flight from London to Sydney should attract taxes of £714.

The Conservative Party Policy Review Group made a number of proposals in 2007:

- the introduction of VAT on fuel for domestic flights
- a per-flight tax based on the amount of CO_2 generated by the flight
- a moratorium on all airport expansion
- oblige airlines to surrender short-haul slots to long-haul flights, forcing short-haul passengers to switch to rail transport.

The Chicago Convention precludes the unilateral imposition of fuel taxes by one country and there is little likelihood of obtaining a global agreement to tax aviation fuel. Given the high price of rail tickets in the UK, the final proposal would probably result in encouraging more car traffic on to already congested roads.

Many environmentalists are putting their faith in an emissions trading scheme, which would allow organizations, including airlines, to buy and sell carbon allowances at market prices – a proposal strongly condemned by the European Low Fares Airline Association. This could become law within the EU by 2011, but it is believed that the EU will grant permits to cover 96–97 per cent of present emission levels. There is some expectation that airlines will raise fares by the value of the free permits, while costs remain relatively unchanged, thereby standing to make billions in windfall profits.

The marketing of air services

Aside from economic considerations, the customer appeal of an aircraft depends on such factors as seat comfort and pitch, engine quietness and the interior design of cabins. In a product where, generally speaking, there is a great deal of homogeneity, minor differences such as these can greatly affect the marketing of the aircraft to the airlines and, in turn, the appeal the airline can make to its prospective passengers.

The recent introduction of flat beds in first and business class on long-haul aircraft is an important factor. Some airlines have configured their aircraft to allow only partial recline, such as up to 160°, while others recline a full 180° to make up into a flat bed. Some first-class flights now even provide double beds in enclosed suites to provide the ultimate in luxury travel. Such moves are important elements in capturing the key business and celebrity markets.

It is for the marketing division of an airline to determine the destinations to be served, although these decisions are often influenced by government policy and regulation. Marketing personnel must also determine levels of demand for a particular service, the markets to be served and the nature of the competition the airline will face.

Routes are, of course, dependent on freight as well as customer considerations and a decision will have to be reached on the appropriate mix of freight and passengers, as well as the mix of passengers themselves whom the airline is to serve – business, holiday, VFR and so on. An airline can be easily panicked into changing routes unless it recognizes that circumstances can provide opportunities as well as threats. A good example is seen in the collapse of the so-called tiger economies in Asia at the end of the 1990s. In spite of the economic depression experienced by many of these countries, air traffic to the region actually rose because Western travellers took advantage of the currency collapses to increase their leisure travel to the area.

Flight frequencies and timings will be subject to government controls. For example, it is common to find that the government will limit the number of flights it will allow to operate at night. Where long-haul flights and, hence, changing time zones are involved, this can seriously curtail the number of flights an airline can operate. Each individual aircraft is given a quota count (QC) according to the noise it dissipates. The QC of all aircraft flying from an airport at night is totalled and must not exceed the noise quota set by the government for that airport. Boeing 747-400s, for example, are rated at QC2, while the newer 777s and Airbus A340s are quieter, each rated at QC0.5, thus making more night flights possible. Congestion, of course, will have an additional 'rationing' effect.

It is particularly important for business travellers to be able to make satisfactory connections with other flights. To gain a strategic marketing advantage over competitors, an airline will want to coordinate its flights with complementary carriers, with which it must also have interline agreements (these allow the free interchange of documents and reservations). In planning long-haul flights, the airline must also weigh up whether to operate non-stop flights or provide stopovers to cater for passengers wanting to travel between different legs of the journey (known as 'stage' traffic). Stopovers will permit the airline to cater for, or organize, holiday traffic, which might be particularly attractive for passengers travelling across the Pacific, for instance, allowing additional duty-free shopping. Alternatively, it may dissuade business passengers from booking if their prime interest is to reach their destination as quickly as possible and another non-stop flight exists. Tahiti experienced a sharp downfall in visitors when the stretched 747-400 was introduced on the transpacific route and it first became possible to fly non-stop between Australia and North America.

Yield management

Following the planning stage, the airline must determine its pricing policy. Fixing the price of a seat is a complex process, involving consideration of:

- the size and type of aircraft operating
- the route traffic density and level of competition
- the regularity of demand flow and the extent to which this demand is balanced in both directions on the route
- the type of demand for air service on the route, taking into account demand for first or business class, economy class, inclusive tour-basing fares and other discounted ticket sales
- the estimated break-even load factor (the number of seats that must be sold to recover all costs) – typically, this will fall at between 50 and 60 per cent of the aircraft's capacity on scheduled routes and the airline must aim to achieve this level of seat occupancy on average throughout the year (budget airlines will set a much higher load factor as their norm).

The last two points are critical to the success of the airline's marketing. The marketing department is, above all, concerned with **yield management** – the overall revenue that is to be achieved on each route. **Yield** can be defined as the air transport revenue achieved per unit of traffic carried or the total passenger revenue per passenger mile. It is measured by comparing both the cost and revenue achieved per available seat mile (ASM). Balancing the proportion of discounted seats with those for which full fares can be charged, whether in economy or business class, is a highly skilled undertaking as there is a need to ensure that any reduction in full fare will lead to an overall increase in revenue. This is achieved by means of a combination of pricing and the imposition of conditions governing the fares.

Business class, for example, will achieve much higher levels of profit than economy or discounted tickets, so an airline with 10 per cent of its seats given over to business class may achieve 40 per cent of its income from the sale of those seats. The expected demand for the seats on a particular route will call for fine judgement, though. That is because discounted tickets must attract a new market, not draw higher-paying passengers to save money, so they must be hedged with conditions that make them unattractive to prospective business class passengers. Good yield management can, in some cases, even result in full-service airlines undercutting their budget rivals, as the former can charge much higher fares for reservations taken close to departure times, which helps them to offset the discounts given for early bookings.

One factor that will substantially help all airlines' yield is the introduction in 2008 of ticketless travel for all IATA carriers. Eliminating the cost of issuing tickets in favour of an e-ticket (with passengers simply being given a reference number for their flights) is expected to save carriers an estimated $3 billion every year.

The growth in bookings using the World Wide Web is a huge bonus for airlines' yield management as, quite apart from avoiding payment of commission, airlines receive payment directly from their passengers when they book, helping cash flow. Previously, payments would be made to travel agents and payment through the airlines' clearing houses could take up to two months.

Airlines have determined that, in many cases, they can increase yield by downsizing their aircraft and often at the same time increase flight frequency. This increased frequency can also build new passenger traffic, leading to still greater yield – especially where business traffic is concerned. Shuttle services for business travellers were pioneered at one time by Eastern Airlines in the USA, which operated at half-hour intervals between Boston, New York and Washington. These required no advance reservation and the airline guaranteed that a seat would be available. These services were later superseded by no frills carriers.

Boosting yield through frequent flyer programmes

In order to boost overall yield, many airlines have introduced the concept of **frequent flyer** programmes. The idea here is that passengers purchasing airline tickets are entitled to extra free travel, according to the mileage covered. This marketing campaign has been a victim of its own success: over 90 million members worldwide now collect these benefits. One estimate, made in *The Economist* at the end of 2004, claimed that the worldwide stock of airline loyalty schemes, or frequent flyer programmes, was above 14 trillion miles, worth over $700 billion, making them the second-largest convertible currency in the world after the US dollar.

American Airlines was the first to introduce such a scheme in 1981 with its AAdvantage scheme. It is now the biggest scheme in operation, with over 45 million members. Others quickly followed, such as British Airways' Executive Club, United's Mileage Plus, Virgin Atlantic's Flying Club. The programmes were later extended to allow miles to be accumulated on the value of products purchased at other outlets associated with the airline, such as shops, hotels and petrol stations, as well as partner airlines within the strategic alliances.

The popularity of these schemes has led to so many free seats being offered that airlines are now imposing limitations on their use. (United Airlines, for example, found that, at one point, almost all passengers on its Hawaii-bound flights were frequent flyers, virtually eradicating yield on that route). While frequent flyers can normally only make use of seats that would otherwise be vacant during the flight, each seat occupied costs the airline the price of the food and fuel consumed and, in total, this still adds up to a substantial cost for the airline.

There is some evidence that airline loyalty schemes are beginning to lose their appeal. Although two-thirds of regular travellers belong to the schemes, a study by Etihad Airways found that only 37 per cent had actually used their frequent flyer points and, by 2005, fewer than 1 in 5 were using them. This can be ascribed in part to the restrictions and conditions applied by the airlines to their use.

Deep discounting

All scheduled services operate on the basis of an advance reservations system, with the lowest (APEX) fares being available on routes where the booking can be confirmed some time in advance of departure. This allows the airline to judge its expected load factors with greater accuracy.

To fill up seats that have not been prebooked, the airline offers standby fares – available to passengers without reservations who are prepared to take their chances and turn up in the expectation of a seat being free. On many routes, particularly business routes, the chances of seats being available are good, because business passengers frequently book more than one flight to ensure that they can get back as quickly as possible after the completion of their meeting. Airlines will thus overbook to allow for the high number of no shows (up to 30 per cent on some routes), but must exercise caution in case they end up with more passengers than they can accommodate. If this occurs, they can upgrade them to a better class or compensate them financially and provide seats on another flight, but this may not be sufficient to satisfy an irate business passenger. The EU's insistence on high levels of compensation for these bumped passengers may cause some airlines to rethink their strategy in permitting business tickets to be refunded without question.

The airline distribution system

The distribution system consists of two elements: the reservation (or booking) and the issue and delivery of a ticket, where pertinent.

Traditionally, air tickets were sold and distributed through travel agents at an agreed rate of commission, with a proportion also sold direct by the airlines to their passengers. In the USA, the high volume of air travel allowed many more airlines to sell direct through branch offices in the larger cities than was possible in Britain. The development of the World Wide Web has now changed this pattern of distribution, with a far greater proportion of sales (and, in the case of some no frills airlines, all sales) being made through the Internet, either direct with the airlines or Internet intermediaries' own websites.

In the face of the crises impacting on the airline industry over the past few years, airlines have re-evaluated their distribution systems, seeking to cut costs wherever possible. The first to suffer in this process of re-evaluation has been the travel agent, with commissions first being trimmed, then cut savagely and now largely discontinued, requiring agents to charge their customers a fee for the service they provide. Such a move, however, may further deter customers from booking through intermediaries. As most leading airlines have tended to follow the no commission route, threats by agents to switch-sell air products have had little effect.

Example

British Airways

British Airways has been equivocal about agency sales for several years, gradually reducing and eventually eliminating commissions paid to agents. Agents then were obliged to impose a fee for bookings they made on behalf of their customers. In 2005, the airline announced its intention to charge a booking fee of £1 for all passengers booking online and a £15 fee to book long-haul flights over the telephone – in effect, ensuring that any passenger would be obliged to pay for the right to buy their own flight arrangements. BA declared that this was part of the airline's policy to charge customers the cost of their chosen method of booking.

Electronic ticketing (commonly referred to as **e-ticketing**) and so-called ticketless travel are now almost universal practices, greatly reducing an airline's costs. This further encourages airlines to push direct sales, with the consequent worrying (for travel agents) fall in the number of airline tickets being booked through intermediaries. Airlines are also moving to corporate self-booking for key business travellers, with carriers installing the necessary equipment in larger companies to allow customers to book direct via the Internet. There is little doubt that the challenge represented by these moves is requiring agents to rethink their whole rationale and means of operation. All electronic booking systems encourage passengers to book direct and their increasing ease of use, coupled with low fares, pose a major threat to agents.

The first step in the introduction of high technology to airline distribution systems was the computerized reservations system (CRS), which provided agents and their clients with a fast and accurate indication of flight availability and fare quotations, coupled with an online reservations service.

The next step was the introduction of the global distribution system (GDS), in which leading airlines themselves held major shareholdings. These rapidly spread to embrace worldwide hotel, car rental and other reservations facilities and the leading GDSs battled for market leadership in travel agents worldwide. The US systems – notably Sabre, Apollo and Worldspan – either competed against or integrated with the two leading European systems – Galileo and Amadeus.

The key to dominance in this field lies in the way in which agents make use of the information displayed. Access to a large number of major world airlines is possible using these systems and 75–80 per cent of all bookings are made using only the first page of information shown. Formerly, bias in the way information is displayed was declared illegal under US and EU law, but the US Department of Transportation ended restrictive regulations on the GDSs in 2004, as the airlines gradually reduced the stock they sold through this system in the wake of the 9/11 disaster, preferring to sell direct via their own websites.

In the following year, it became EU policy to allow airlines to have commercial agreements with the GDSs that resulted in their favouring certain carriers. While the US carriers no longer have a stake in the GDSs, European carriers do still hold interests in Amadeus. The GDSs are, in turn, having to face the challenge of new websites – either those of the airlines themselves or intermediaries such as expedia.com, ebookers.com and travelocity.com selling their services. These electronic retailers – the so-called **e-tailers** – have become a major force in the distribution system, particularly for the sale of late availability tickets.

The GDS companies argue that the establishment of websites by intermediaries is unnecessary, given that they themselves are coming to utilize the World Wide Web to provide the same range of travel products, but the intermediaries are successfully challenging these well-established and proven systems.

Apart from their own websites, airlines have also come together to organize joint websites for interactive reservations and information. The US website Orbitz was established in 2000 by five US carriers – American, Delta, United, Northwest and Continental – while the European Opodo network (initially launched by nine European airlines) followed in 2001. These offer access to hotels and car hire, in addition to airline flights.

The extent to which online bookings are replacing traditional channels of distribution may be judged when it is revealed that the leading no frills airlines are becoming almost totally dependent on sales via the Web and promote this medium prominently.

A feature of the current decade is the process of integration of the electronic booking agencies, which parallels both that of the airlines and other retailers of travel. Opodo bought a 74 per cent interest in Amadeus in 2004 (with the balance retained by the original air carriers) and has since moved into tour operating itself, having purchased five travel companies, including long-haul specialist Quest. The travel conglomerate Travelport – its holding company owning the Avis and Budget car rental firms – owns Galileo, cheaptickets.com and a large part of Orbitz.com and consolidated its hold on the GDS market with the purchase of Worldspan in 2006. The GDS company Sabre (now in private ownership), owns travelocity.com, which itself took over lastminute.com. This process of integration is likely to continue.

Future developments in the technological field are likely to involve the expansion of digital television, which will provide channels for consumers to communicate with the airlines direct and book their airline tickets in their own homes. This must inevitably lead to a further shrinking of sales through the more traditional distribution outlets.

The role of the air broker

One comparatively little-known role in the airline business is that of the **air brokers**. These are the people who act as intermediaries regarding the control of seats rather than merely their sale between aircraft owners and their customers. They provide a level of expertise to business clients, travel agents or tour operators who may have neither the time nor the knowledge to involve themselves in long negotiations for the best deals in chartering aircraft seats. They maintain close contact with both airlines and the charter market and can frequently offer better prices for charters than tour operators could themselves.

They play an important role in securing aircraft seats in times of shortage, and in disposing of spare capacity at times of oversupply. The broker takes charge of the entire operation, booking the aircraft and taking care of any technical requirements, including organizing the contract and arranging any special facilities.

In their role as so-called **consolidators** they purchase seats on scheduled airlines on demand, at discounted rates, and can sell these on to agents at the usual rates of commission. Leading companies in the UK include Gold Medal Travel, Travel 2 and Travel 4. Flight-only operators buy blocks of seats or a whole aircraft to sell wherever they can find a market. Avro is the leading UK company in this field, with over a million passengers every year. These roles are all ones that may be challenged by electronic direct booking systems.

What is the future like for air transport?

> The probability of $150–$200 per barrel seems increasingly likely over the next 6 to 24 months.

So wrote an analyst at Goldman Sachs in May 2008 when oil prices were skyrocketing to around the $140 mark. By September, oil prices were down to $108. Forecasting the future for oil and, equally, the future of air transport is fraught with difficulty, to the extent that even the experts frequently get it seriously wrong.

In looking to the future, one must take into account both the short and long term. The short term is dominated by the cost of oil and attempting to predict how this will influence both transport in general and air tourism movements in particular over the next five years is next to impossible, given the volatile swings this product experienced in 2008.

Many believe that the habit of going on holidays is so ingrained that it will be one of the last luxuries to be surrendered by consumers. Nevertheless, the short term has seen an increase in fuel surcharging that inevitably affected air transport, with even leading no frills carriers cutting back on services. While mass long-haul travel is likely to be hardest hit, there is already evidence of passengers becoming more prepared to transfer from short-haul air to rail, encouraged, too, by the belief that this is in the interests of the environment. Should oil prices recommence their upward movement – by no means an unlikely outcome given the parlous state of the world's economies – it does not take a great deal of imagination to forecast an increase in mergers, the collapse of smaller, underfinanced carriers and a continuing reduction in services, both in terms of destinations served and frequency on routes.

Aviation experts agree that the development of jet aircraft has reached a plateau – productivity and efficiency being unlikely to substantially improve. While costs per seat kilometre may fall as larger aircraft such as the Airbus A380, seating between 500 and 800 passengers, come onstream, any savings are certain to be outstripped by oil price increases.

As to the future of scheduled flights, at least three aircraft companies are looking to the possibility of regenerating supersonic flight in the long term, although few details are known. Aviation pundits believe that the future will depend on the ability to find environmentally acceptable vehicles to reduce present fuel burn and pollutants and both Boeing and Airbus are working towards this. The most probable solution is a batwing or delta-shaped body built largely of hardened plastics and accommodating up to 500 passengers sitting up to 40 abreast, with few or no windows and engines sited on top of the fuselage. Such aircraft could reduce fuel consumption by as much as two-thirds, but they are unlikely to be in production before 2025.

Perhaps it is desperation that is driving some air companies to look again at the dirigible as a means of developing low-cost air transport. A number of companies have experimented with dirigibles as a cheap, albeit slow, means of air travel in the future. Among these, new Zeppelin NTs were employed over London in 2008 on excursion flights, carrying up to 12 passengers at a height of 1000 feet, while others are currently in use for sightseeing trips in Southern Germany and California. Work goes on to test the viability of longer-range dirigible flights, with interest stimulated by the obvious sustainability of this form of travel. Virgin has shown an interest and work is under way to develop and test prototypes – one encouraging prospect being the 100-seat Skycat 200. The French are also working on a luxury airship, *Manned Cloud*, capable of carrying 40 passengers, which would travel at around 80 mph with a range of 3100 miles. They believe this could be in commercial use by 2020 and, as well as being entirely sustainable, the craft would serve as its own hotel, actually saving passengers money.

Perhaps for students, the most interesting area of speculation is the progress towards the development of hypersonic flight. The reality of space flight is almost on us as this book goes to press, with Virgin Galactic expecting to start scheduled suborbital flights from the Mojave Desert in 2009–2010, carrying 6 passengers 50,000 feet into space, where they will be detached from the mother ship and accelerate to Mach 3, giving them 5 to 10 minutes' experience of weightlessness. Even for a fare estimated at around $200,000, Virgin claim to have nearly 39,000 people registered to fly.

EADS offshoot Astrium is hoping to offer a competitive vehicle for four passengers a year or two later. Similarly, XCor is a US company planning to employ reusable rocket-powered Lynx 'space taxis' with just two seats, but at half the price of Virgin Galactic, and anticipates having these in operation by 2010.

An ambitious scheme by a former Concorde aeronautical engineer, David Ashford, is to launch an 'Ascender' aircraft. This consists of a combination of normal jet for take-off and landing, with rocket propulsion to escape the atmosphere, permitting suborbital tourist flights. His belief is that this would be feasible by 2010–2011. Designed to carry two passengers, the initial cost is expected to be in the range of £50,000–100,000 per passenger, but the scheme is limited by lack of funding.

Perhaps it is the Scramjet that offers the most exciting prospects for future high-speed air travel.

Example

The Scramjet

The Scramjet (the name has been coined from the concept – Supersonic Combustion Ramjet) is propelled by an engine that sucks in oxygen at high speeds, compresses it and feeds it into a chamber to mix with hydrogen. An early X43-a (unmanned) Scramjet achieved speeds of Mach 5 (Concorde's speed was a little above Mach 1), while research involving the cooperation of British, US and Australian scientists tested the aircraft to Mach 7–8 – in excess of 5000 mph – in 2004. Maximum speeds have been predicted of Mach 14, using available technologies and materials. In operation, this aircraft would allow people to travel between London and Sydney or London and Tokyo in just two hours.

NASA believes that passenger-carrying Scramjets could be in service by 2020, but others believe a 30- to 50-year time-span is more realistic.

Many aviation observers remain sceptical that these early deadlines are achievable. Similar plans by the Russians to offer five minutes in space for tourists by 2004, using their suborbital M-55 aircraft, were not achieved. Nevertheless, these are the first steps towards a realistic venture into space tourism – the ambition of many, so far achieved by no more than some half a dozen people.

Example

The first space tourists

There is some controversy about how many non-scientists/astronauts have actually travelled into space up to the time of writing.

The American Dennis Tito is unchallenged as the first *tourist* into space, in 2001, followed by Mark Shuttleworth, a South African-born Briton in 2002. The American Greg Olsen took the trip in 2005 and Daisuke Enomoto, who is Japanese, followed in 2006.

Those space travellers are thought to have paid between £11 million and £20 million for the privilege. Others to have taken the ride, however, include Toyoshiro Akiyama, a journalist for the Tokyo Broadcasting system, who did so in 1990 and Prince Sultan bin Salman, the head of the Supreme Commission for Tourism in Saudi Arabia, who became the first Arab in space. American politicians Senator Jake Garn and Congressman Bill Nelson are believed to have travelled there in the 1980s.

Few would be prepared to pay the huge sums involved to go on these trips, but research carried out by US aeronautical company Futron revealed that, while only 50 people a year would be willing to spend the equivalent of $20 million for a week in space, a further 15,000 a year would be prepared to invest $100,000 for a 20-minute suborbital ride, supporting the applications waitlisted for Branson's project. One American company, Space Adventures, is planning to offer space walks for £19 million, based on 190 hours of training at the Russian Cosmonaut School, 16 days on the space station and a 90-minute walk in space. The price would include round trip fares from the US to Kazakhstan.

The development of mass travel by air, faster intercontinental travel and travel into space is based on certain assumptions, however: that fuel costs will stabilize, no new means of propulsion or energy will replace those presently available within the next few decades and political and economic stability is assured, so that, in the future, people will have the means and time to travel around the globe much as they do today. Because none of these factors is certain any longer, research is focused on more down-to-earth projects aimed at reducing flight costs and cutting, or at least stabilizing, toxic emissions to ensure that mass air transport is sustainable. Less ambitious, perhaps, but more practical and realistic.

American aeronautical engineers are working on a blended wing-body aircraft that will reduce fuel burn so that it is half that of conventional jets, owing to reduced drag. This aircraft would fly at 45,000 feet, some 10,000 feet higher than present jet aircraft, and be windowless. The psychological consequences of this have not been researched as yet, although external views could be shown on a screen in the cabin.

A similar windowless aircraft is forecast to become operative within 20 years, but, as an aid to sustainability, it will be virtually silent from the ground. With engines mounted above the fuselage, this Silent Aircraft Initiative is a collaborative project between Cambridge University and the US's MIT. The plan is for a 250-seat aircraft with a range of 4000 miles and the potential to increase passenger capacity to 800.

Others are working on tilt-wing aircraft. A military aircraft with tilting rotors, the V-22 Osprey, was in service with the American military, but was withdrawn after it crashed. A civilian version, however – the BA609 – is undergoing tests by Bell Augusta in the USA. Tilt-wing aircraft would be able to take off and land in half the distance, at half the speed of conventional aircraft, a boon where airports have limited runway space.

A more conventional approach would be development of a new era of supersonic aircraft similar to the Concorde. Airbus is among a number of aircraft manufacturers considering whether or not to develop a new generation of supersonic aircraft. It believes that a 250-seat aircraft with a range of 5500 miles and speeds of up to 1500 mph could be in production as early as 2015. If this proves as fuel-hungry as the earlier Concorde, however, its economic viability would be in doubt, given the sustained high fuel costs.

A viable alternative may be the development of supersonic business jets. The Aerion Corporation is currently designing a 12-seat business jet that the company hopes to have in service by 2014. This aircraft will fly supersonic over oceans and, where permitted, over land, at speeds of Mach 1.6 and elsewhere at just subsonic speed (although it is claimed that the sonic boom of this aircraft would be barely noticeable on the ground). With a range of around 4000 miles, this would enable corporate travellers to reach London from New York in 4 hours and Tokyo in $9^{1}/_{2}$ hours, even allowing for a refuelling stopover.

Amphibious aircraft are still on the agenda for researchers. The Russian Beriev Be-200 is already in operation and could easily be adapted for civilian use. Carrying 72 passengers and with a range of 2250 miles, it would prove ideal for some European resorts, such as those on the Côte d'Azur and Lake Geneva. The particular advantage for the industry would be a reduction in airport costs as an amphibious aircraft requires nothing more than a jetty and a licence to use the waterways.

Another promising development is the Ground Effect Aircraft. Flying just 20 feet above the water to reduce drag and fuel burn, this vehicle could travel at speeds of up to 240 knots and would offer psychological reassurance for those who have a fear of flying at normal heights. The Russians have taken this a stage further, with the development of a surface-skimming hydrobus known as the Ekranoplan. Developed by Soviet researchers as a form of military transport in the 1980s and later used experimentally in air/sea rescue, the Model A90 Orlyonok can accommodate 150 passengers and has the capacity to be developed for civilian purposes to carry at least 250 passengers, with an anticipated cruising speed of over 300 mph and a range of up to 10,000 miles. This would make it possible to make transatlantic journeys overnight, at comparatively cheap fares and reach an entirely new market. German and American interests are still examining the feasibility of building such craft for commercial purposes.

Notes

1. d'Arcy S. (2007) 'Cut price club class', *The Sunday Times*, 4 February.

2. Based on Airbus company reports. Note that *Travel Weekly*, 20 July 2007, estimated the total world fleet of passenger aircraft as being 38,234 – presumably including much smaller aircraft. Forecasts should be treated with caution as they vary considerably from one year to another, given the changing economic climate and the inevitable optimism of the aircraft manufacturers that release them.

3. Tarry, Chris, (2002) Airline Analyst at Commerzbank, reported in 'Flights of fancy', *The Times*, 3 December, T2/7.

4. Estimates obtained from *The Observer*, 11 November 2001.

5. See, for example, Sandy, Matt (2007) 'How budget airlines boost profits with costly extras', *The Times*, 7 April. Other ancillary revenues are achieved through direct bookings for car hire, hotel rooms, insurance and even scratch cards.

6. Duun, J. (2007) 'Softening the supersonic boom', *The Sunday Times*, 11 March, pp. 14–15.

7. 'En Turquie, une tolérance risquée', *Le Figaro*, 29 July 2005, p. 7.

8. Based on study of airlines by BA, Airbus and Boeing, cited in Webster, Ben (2002) 'Long-haul flights on way back to Earth', *The Times*, 17 January.
9. 24 per cent and 18 per cent respectively, according to the 'Stern review on the economics of climate change', Economic Affairs Select Committee of the House of Lords, 2006.

Websites

a flight.to (includes charter and no frills flights)   **www.aflight.to**

Air Transport Users Council   **www.auc.org.uk**

ebookers   **www.ebookers.com**

EC Directorate-General for Energy and Transport (on rights and compensation)
http://ec.europa.eu/transport/air_portal/passenger_rights/information_en.htm

Questions and discussion points

1. In 2006, it was reported that 26 per cent of all passengers at London's Heathrow Airport were in transit. This figure is expected to rise to 31 per cent by 2010. Discuss the costs and benefits arising from transit passengers and whether or not it is right to encourage this traffic, given the environmental costs of air travel and the anticipated costs of expansion of Heathrow.
2. Is there a case for more, rather than fewer, airline regulations today?
3. Will ever-increasing security measures introduced at US airports choke off tourism growth to that country?
4. Examine the pros and cons of carbon offsetting as a means of reducing global warming by airlines.
5. What are the most promising markets for the A380? Which will win the battle for mass market travellers of the future – Airbus or Boeing?
6. In the aftermath of the escalation in aviation fuel costs, which sector of the airline industry will be hit hardest – the legacy carriers or the budget carriers?

Tasks

1. Undertake a programme of research among the public to find out their experiences of checking in at UK airports. Examine sensitivity to price increases for the privilege of flying from local regional airports rather than travelling to London Heathrow.
2. There are contradictory reports on the relative levels of pollution created by the aviation industry compared with other forms of industrial pollution. Collect data from the various bodies responsible for estimating this impact, identifying any discrepancies between their estimates. Compare your figures with those of the shipping industry and land-based transport. Produce a report that *either* makes a case for supporting the growth of the aviation industry *or* suggests means by which growth can be curtailed.

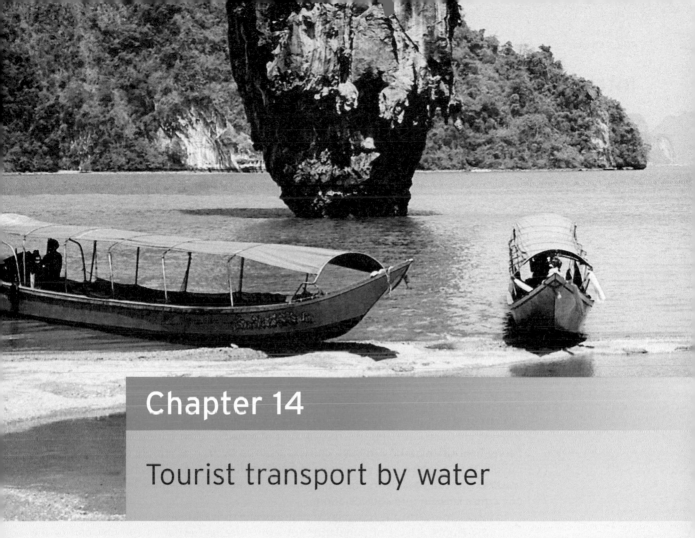

Chapter 14

Tourist transport by water

Learning outcomes

After studying this chapter, you should be able to:

- identify each category of water-borne transport and the role each plays in the tourism industry

- understand the economics of cruise and ferry operations

- identify the markets for cruising and how cruise companies appeal to each

- be aware of principal world cruise routes and the reasons for their popularity

- be familiar with other forms of water-borne leisure transport and their appeal to tourists.

Introduction

Cruise ships no longer are considered exclusively a mode of transportation from one port of call to another. They also have become deterritorialised vacation sites.

C. B. N. Chin, *Cruising in the Global Economy: Profits, pleasure and work at sea*, Ashgate, 2008, p. 66

Air travel has become by far the most popular means of travel for tourists, but very few of them treat it as anything other than the most convenient means of getting from A to B. Certainly the frustrations that accompany this form of travel, such as airport delays, queuing, congestion on the ground and in the air and the relative lack of comfort while airborne, tend to detract from the idea that flights are an enjoyable part of a holiday. Transport by water, on the other hand, *can* be enjoyable in its own right and for many it will be the dominant element in the holiday. When cruising, for example, the intention is not necessarily to arrive at a particular destination, but to enjoy getting there. Whether travelling by sea or inland on lakes, rivers and canals, water-borne holidays have never been more popular and shipping in all its forms plays an important part in the travel industry. According to one survey undertaken by the US Department of Transportation (in 2004), there were at the time 339 active ocean-going passenger ships, just 38 of which carried fewer than 100 passengers – a figure reflecting the importance of this sector to the travel industry in the early twenty-first century.

Travelling by water is inherently relaxing and cruising requires the luxury of free time, whereas air transport's appeal is largely that of speed – often critical when travelling to a long-haul destination. Although cruising tends to be seen as a more expensive form of holiday than air travel, the wide range of prices available today makes it attractive to most markets and comparable in price to many foreign holidays when the all-inclusive nature of a cruise is taken into consideration.

In recent years, cruising has staged an astonishing revival after several decades of decline and now enjoys a level of popularity not seen since its heyday in the first half of the twentieth century. The advantages of this form of travel are total relaxation and a price that includes all accommodation, food and entertainment (and some cruises now even include drinks and gratuities). Cruises allow the passenger to be carried from one destination to another in comfort and safety, in familiar surroundings and without the need constantly to pack and unpack. Short sea (ferry) vessels have also achieved high levels of comfort and speed on many routes, to a point where they now attract tourists not just as a means of transport, but as an enjoyable 'mini-cruise', with food and entertainment of a standard that a few years ago could be found only on a luxury cruise liner. Technological developments have helped to reduce high operating costs, while new forms of water-borne transport have been developed, such as the hovercraft, jetfoil and twin-hulled catamaran ferry. These have provided rapid communication over short sea routes and sometimes, as in the case of the hovercraft, across difficult terrain.

The pleasure that people find in simply being afloat has spawned many recent tourist developments, from yacht marinas and self-drive motor craft to dinghy sailing in the Mediterranean and narrow boat holidays in Britain and on the European mainland. The continuing fascination with older means of propulsion has led to the renovation and operation of lake steamers in England and on the Continent of Europe, purpose-built and often classic river boats operating on the Rhine and Danube in Europe, the Nile in Egypt and the Irrawaddy in Myanmar, excursion vessels operating out of seaports in many countries and even a paddle steamer plying the Mississipi River in the USA.

In this chapter, we will investigate the appeal and operation of these various forms of water transport. It is convenient to divide them into five distinct categories:

- line voyage shipping
- cruise shipping

- short sea shipping, more familiarly known as ferries
- inland waterway and excursion vessels
- privately chartered or owned pleasure craft.

These categories will be considered in turn.

The ocean liners

Line voyage services are those offering passenger transport on a port-to-port basis rather than as part of a cruise. Ships plying these routes are known as **liners**. This form of transport has declined to a point where very few such services exist any longer and those that do tend to be operated on a seasonal basis. The reasons for this decline are not hard to identify.

From the 1950s onwards, advances in air transport enabled fares to be reduced, especially on popular routes across the Atlantic, to a point where it became cheaper to travel by air than by ship. The shipping lines, which, until the advent of aircraft, had no competition from alternative forms of transport, could not compete: they faced rapidly rising costs for fuel and labour in a labour-intensive industry. The gradual decline in numbers of passengers as they switched to the airlines led to losses in revenue for the shipping companies that made it impossible to consider renovating ageing fleets or replacing them with new vessels.

By 1957, more passengers were crossing the Atlantic by air than by sea and the demise of the worldwide passenger shipping industry appeared imminent. Leading routes such as Cunard Line's transatlantic services, P&O's services to the Far East and Australia and Union-Castle and British India Lines' services to South and East Africa were either withdrawn or reduced to a skeleton service.

The resulting shake-up in management led to attempts to regenerate passenger demand, mainly by employing the same ships on cruises, but vessels built for fast line voyage services are not ideally suited to alternative uses (many still in service were built for the emigrant trade from Europe and offered four- or six-berth cabins without private facilities), while at the same time the appeal of cruising was beginning to decline. A small but loyal demand for sea transport remained among those, usually older, passengers who feared flying or enjoyed sea voyages and were willing to spend time getting to their destinations. Few lines were able to continue operations to serve such limited markets.

Today, only Cunard Line, among the major carriers, continues to provide a regular summer service across the Atlantic between Southampton and New York, currently with one liner, the *Queen Mary 2*, introduced in 2005 for this express purpose (see Figures 14.1 a and b). The company has also ordered a new vessel for delivery in 2010 – a new *Queen Elizabeth*, following the withdrawal of the old *Queen Elizabeth 2* in 2008. This will enable Cunard to reintroduce a two ship service across the Atlantic, reflecting a growing confidence in the long-term demand for line voyages. Outside of the summer months, these vessels will cruise, although their size limits the ports they can call at.

Example

Measuring the size of a ship

The size of all vessels is based on their gross registered tonnage, but it is inaccurate to refer to the 'weight' of a ship. That is because 'gross tonnage' refers to the internal volume of the vessel rather than its weight or displacement. One ton is equal to 100 cubic feet (a measure formally laid down in the Merchant Shipping Act, 1854). Net registered tonnage is the internal volume devoted to passenger and cargo space only, excluding any non-revenue-earning space, such as the engine room, crew accommodation and so on.

Figure 14.1a The *RMS Queen Mary 2*.
(Copyright, reproduced courtesy of Craig Ellenwood/Alamy.)

Figure 14.1b Interior of the *RMS Queen Mary 2*: the Queen's Grill.
(Photo by Chris Holloway.)

Apart from this transatlantic service, line voyages technically no longer exist. **Positioning voyages**, in which cruise ships are moved across the Atlantic in the spring and autumn to transfer cruise operations between the Caribbean and Mediterranean for the season, however, do allow these sailings to be sold as line voyages between Europe and Florida or Caribbean ports. Also, a handful of other passenger cargo liners exist around the world, such as the Mauritius Shipping Corporation's services between Mauritius, Réunion Island and South Africa, carrying around 268 passengers, and services from Tahiti carrying up to 60 passengers to the Marquesas islands and Tuamoto atolls in the South Pacific, as well as vessels, some carrying nearly 1200 passengers, operated and subsidized by the Indian government, which connect the mainland to the Andaman and Nicobar Islands. The RMS *St Helena* is the sole cargo passenger liner still operating in the Atlantic. At 7000 tons and carrying just 128 passengers, it was built with a British government subsidy to provide a lifeline to the island dependencies of St Helena and Ascension – the former presently has no airport – and the government continues to subsidize the company. The ship's base has alternated in recent years between Cape Town, South Africa and Portland, in Southern England, making calls at Lüderitz and Walvis Bay (Namibia) en route to the islands. This service has always been more important for its freight than its passenger capacity and is expected to be withdrawn when an airport, to be built on St Helena, is due to open around 2012 (although construction is yet to start and further delays have been announced).

Apart from these services, there are a number of cargo vessels operating around the world that also accommodate 12 passengers or fewer. This limitation is imposed because the International Maritime Organization requires a doctor to be carried as a member of crew if this number is exceeded. Some vessels take as few as two passengers, accommodated in the 'owner's suite', but all are clearly designed for lovers of sea travel for its own sake. Freight demand means that neither departure dates nor ports of call can be guaranteed, nor can it even be certain that passengers will be allowed to disembark at the destinations en route. Entertainment is limited – in some cases, non-existent – on board and passengers dine with the ships' officers. This is not a cheap alternative for long-distance travel – on the contrary, fares on cargo passenger vessels will be comparable to those on cruise ships – but they nevertheless attract an enthusiastic market and passengers frequently have to 'waitlist' their requirements (place their names on a waiting list) a year or more in advance.

Example

Innovative sea voyages

True lovers of sea voyages, frustrated by the decline in traditional ships and the limited opportunity for passenger cargo trips, are looking further afield. Almost every country offers some form of limited sea transport to adjacent islands or territories, especially among the Pacific Islands or the Indian subcontinent.

Nearer to home, an unusual and relatively little-known opportunity is to travel on *Patricia* – a working ship that tours UK lighthouses to carry out necessary maintenance. A small number of passengers is accommodated on each of these voyages, which have strong appeal for sea-going aficionados.

Further information: **www.trinityhouse.co.uk**

The decline of line voyages was not due solely to the rise of air transport. Enterprise was for many years restricted by the so-called 'conferences' – notably the Transatlantic and Transpacific Passenger Conferences – that governed the operation of fleets worldwide and restrained open competition. Shipping management must also bear much of the blame for its failure to adapt the product to meet changing needs. Ships were built without air conditioning or adequate numbers of cabins with en suite facilities – both essential requirements if ships were to attract the American market. The vessels' specifications and size made them inflexible and unsuitable for routes other than those for which they were built and little was done to adapt them for their new purposes. Shipping managers failed to recognize the extent of the threat posed by the airlines and were too slow to move into that sector themselves. Those that eventually attempted to do so then found that the capital investment required was beyond the resources they had.

Traffic conferences were not finally swept away until the 1970s, by which time the market was, to all intents, lost and the negative image of cruising, as appealing only to the old and infirm, had become firmly ingrained in the minds of the new generation of travellers. Whether the long-term decline of line voyages anywhere apart from the North Atlantic can ever be reversed is debateable, although tentative proposals have been put forward to build budget ships for transatlantic crossings, as a means of increasing that market, while research is also under way to test the feasibility of developing jet ships, capable of travelling at 40 knots or more. This would allow transatlantic crossings to be completed within 90 hours. One Danish prototype – the DK/A1500F – has been undergoing tests and has an expected speed of 45–50 knots, which would reduce the crossing time to around two and a half days. The reality is, however, nothing tangible has emerged that would be capable of sustaining such speeds over these periods of time in the years since jet ship technology was first mooted. Meantime, on the North Atlantic route, the *Queen Mary 2* continues the long tradition of line voyages for at least part of the year.

Cruising

While line voyages were also popularly used for leisure trips and P&O were marketing their ships for Mediterranean cruises by the mid-nineteenth century, the concept of the purpose-built cruise ship did not arrive until the beginning of the twentieth century. The first such ship, Hamburg-Amerika Line's 4400-ton *Prinzessin Victoria Luise*, went into service in 1900, but had a lifetime of only six years.

The cruise market emerged gradually, to a point where the ultimate cruise aspiration was a round the world voyage. The 42,300-ton *Empress of Britain* was launched in 1931 specifically to attract passengers to out-of-season round the world voyages, but the intervention of the Depression restricted its appeal. Shorter voyages from US ports became popular around this time, with the advent of Prohibition, as demand was created by the fact that alcohol could be consumed legally once the ship entered international waters. Later, these sailings were extended to Bermuda, Nassau and Havana.

The growth of cruising was delayed by World War II, but, in the immediate aftermath, cruising again became popular, with notable purpose-built ships such as Cunard's *Caronia* entering service in 1949. It went on to achieve enormous popularity, as the 'Green Goddess', for its annual round the world itineraries.

From the 1950s onwards, the passenger shipping industry shifted its emphasis from line voyages to cruising. Initially, this transformation proved difficult as vessels in service at the time were, for the most part, too large, too old and too expensive to operate for cruising purposes. Their size was a limiting factor, in terms of the number of ports they could call at, and they were built for speed rather than leisurely cruising. Fuel bills can be cut by operating vessels at slower speeds, but, ideally, cruise ships should be purpose-built to achieve their maximum operational efficiency.

During the 1960s and 1970s, ships of 18,000–22,000 tons, capable of carrying some 650–850 passengers, were built. Changes in demand and advances in marine technology however, have enabled recent cruise ships to be purpose-built in a variety of sizes. Providing there is sufficient demand, optimum profits can be achieved by employing larger vessels. These do not require any extra deck or engine crew and burn relatively little extra fuel, so adding extra passenger capacity lowers the cost per passenger. The trend since the 1980s has therefore been to build ships of steadily increasing tonnage, first in the range of 50,000–70,000 tons and later in excess of 100,000 tons, capable of carrying as many as 4000–5000 passengers. Since the 1970s, it has also become popular for companies to return older ships to the shipyards for 'stretching' – that is, cutting the vessel in half and inserting a new section to increase capacity.

There now appears to be a polarization of cruise ships between, on the one hand, very large vessels and, on the other, much smaller vessels operated by niche companies. This trend towards larger sizes is putting a strain on port facilities and requires significantly increased investment, especially in the Caribbean – the cruise market's most important destination.

It has been estimated that, currently, there are well over 340 cruise ships of one type or another operating worldwide, carrying more than 15 million passengers. At the beginning of 2009, a total of 39 new cruise ships were on order for delivery up to 2013 and there is some danger that supply will outstrip demand as new vessels come onstream. However, the phased withdrawal of older vessels will help to compensate for this, and the rate of new passenger shipbuilding will certainly decline after 2013 as fuel price increases will reduce demand. Carnival Cruises expects it to fall to around five vessels a year, halving the present rate of supply. The UK's share of this industry is shrinking, in spite of its being one of the great seafaring nations a few decades ago. Today, its ownership of the world cruise ship business is around 5 per cent, despite the British government's efforts to stimulate the industry by lowering the taxation rate on British shipping.

Cruise companies have enjoyed exceptional market growth in recent years, however, and, with passenger numbers forecast to increase to around 20 million by 2011 and to 25 million by 2015, (British passengers alone will reach 2 million by 2012), prospects remain generally healthy. Nevertheless, competition has kept prices down close to levels in the 1980s, putting pressure on profits.

More than half of all cruises operate out of US ports and Americans represent the majority of cruise passengers globally – at around 10.6 million passengers in 2007. According to the European Cruise Council, around 4 million European passengers booked a cruise in 2007 and that figure was expected to rise to around 4.6 million in 2008 and over 5 million by 2015. In terms of passenger demand, Britain takes second place after the USA, with 1.34 million passengers in 2007 (and an estimated 1.5 million the following year), followed by Germany with 763,000 in 2007 and rather fewer from Italy and Spain (see Table 14.1, later in this section). All the developed countries are experiencing a marked increase in demand for cruising, after a long period of decline, and growth in this market has averaged between 9 and 15 per cent per annum since the early 1990s. Even more encouraging, extrapolations by the Cruise Lines International Association (CLIA), which represents 19 of the world's major cruise lines, indicate that, given the small proportion of US residents to have cruised, the potential long-term market for cruising is around 35 million passengers – a forecast that presently drives the shipbuilding boom that began during the 1990s.

The majority of cruise ships are built today by just four West European yards, the leading three companies building nine out of ten of the new cruise ships. Fincantieri in Italy alone has an estimated 40 per cent of the passenger shipbuilding market, closely followed by Aker Yards' Chantiers d'Atlantique in France and Meyer Werft in Germany, while a fourth European yard, Kvaerner Masa-yards in Finland and other yards in South Korea and Japan are responsible for most of the rest of the world's fleet (passenger shipbuilding in Britain having gone into terminal decline in the 1970s). Most new-built vessels will be larger than 60,000 tons and with an average capacity close to 3000 passengers, but some of the largest ships will carry close to 4000 passengers. The largest ship at the time of writing is RCI's *Independence of the Seas*, at 160,000 tons and carrying 4375 passengers. It is one of several ships around this size.

The operating costs of even these giants are only marginally greater than conventional ships, while the addition of several hundred cabins leads to an increase in onboard spend and boosts overall profitability. With building costs that can go as high as $550 million

– more than twice that of a superjumbo aircraft – these ships represent a huge capital investment for their owners and are something of a gamble, given the volatility of fuel prices. RCI, however, is due to take delivery in 2009 of a still larger vessel, to be named *Oasis of the Sea*, which is expected to cost around $1.24 billion and its tonnage will be around 222,000. The ship is expected to have a total capacity of up to 6400, although the normal capacity will be around 5400 passengers. The ship is to be followed by the equally enormous *Allure of the Seas* in 2010. Even the largest passenger vessels, however, are still dwarfed by the supertankers (the *Jahre Viking*, by way of example, exceeds 260,000 tons). Even allowing for the anticipated withdrawal of older ships, the net increase in supply is still expected to exceed the growth in demand for cruising, posing questions over the future profitability of shipping companies. Trends point to further rationalization and integration for the largest companies.

The whole concept of a cruise holiday has changed from its traditional image. Cruise ships are coming to be seen as floating holiday resorts that conveniently move from one destination to another, offering new scenery every day and non-stop entertainment on board. The very large tonnage allows not only a vast range of public rooms, which on the newest ships include facilities for climbing walls and even ice-skating rinks, but also ensures that passengers have the widest conceivable choice of acquaintances to meet and make friends with on board.

In keeping with this desire to differentiate the product, shipping lines are focusing on novel forms of interior decor. The Norwegian Caribbean Line, to take one example, is restyling its Freestyle ships with cabins that more closely resemble rooms found in the modern art hotels, with curved walls and open bathrooms.

At the other end of the scale, a market has opened for vessels of typically 3000–10,000 tons, carrying around 60–250 passengers. Many of these are aimed at the luxury end of the market, including vessels such as *Le Levant* (90 passengers), the *Clipper Odyssey* (128 passengers) and, slightly larger at 8000 tons, *Le Diamant*, which carries 226 passengers. Many of the smaller ships provide a yachtlike form of cruising for those who are prepared to pay the higher prices these vessels are obliged to charge. They frequently attract wealthier over-55s who seek more adventurous destinations such as Greenland, Antarctica and the Amazon, and often do not accept young children. Many of these ships are able to enter harbours far smaller than would be possible for the traditional cruise ships, opening up new ports of call for cruising, such as Seville on the Guadalquivir River in Spain, Chicoutimi on the Saguenay River in Canada or the further reaches of the Amazon River and Iquitos in Peru. Small ships can also negotiate constricted canals, such as the Corinth Canal in Greece and the Panama Canal, neither of which is navigable by the larger cruise vessels. Small ships with ice-strengthened hulls can penetrate deeper into Antarctica, visiting the Ross ice shelf.

There is another important issue relating to the size of cruise vessels and that is the question of their **sustainability**. It is debatable whether building ever larger cruise ships is an appropriate strategy for the tourism business, even if they could be profitable. In purely practical terms, the effect on small island economies of vessels disgorging up to 4500 passengers simultaneously at port and within a strictly limited time period must be judged against any possible benefits of the visitor spend for the local economy there. Furthermore, the logistics and viability of putting such large numbers of people ashore and organizing shore excursions for them is another factor that will have to be weighed up carefully. Passengers are reluctant to queue up for two hours or more in order to go ashore or return to their vessels.

Cruise routes

Broadly, the world's major cruise routes are located in seven regions of the globe (see Figure 14.2). These are:

Fiji

Seychelles/
Mauritius

Bermuda

Madeira

Canary Islands

Hawaii

To Pacific Islands

4000 km

3000 miles

0

0

Figure 14.2 The major cruise routes of the world.

- Florida, the Caribbean, Bermuda and the Bahamas, including coastal towns of North, Central and South America
- the West Coast of Mexico, the USA (particularly Alaska) and Canada, plus Panama Canal transit
- the Mediterranean, divided between the western and eastern sectors
- the Pacific islands and Far East
- the Baltic Sea, northern European capitals and the west coast of Norway as far north as the North Cape. Extensions to Svalbard, Norwegian island territory north of the Arctic Circle, are rising in popularity, as are cruises to Arctic regions such as Iceland and Greenland, which are easily accessible from both Europe and North America
- West Africa and the Atlantic islands of the Canaries, Madeira and, increasingly, the Azores – occasionally, this is extended to the Cape Verde Islands
- round the world (usually permitting short-leg bookings).

Fly–cruises have enabled long-haul routes to become popular for those with more limited time to spare. It allows the development of routes from Europe and the East Coast of the United States to Central America, especially Costa Rica and the Mexican East Coast, the East Coast of the South American Continent and cruises around New Zealand (the latter being a popular route for the Australian market). Cruise vessels are also being drawn to the attractions of Indian Ocean islands such as Madagascar, the Seychelles, Réunion and Mauritius, with the principal port of embarkation being Mombasa in Kenya (small ports of call in this region, such as the island of Aldabra, are beginning to face the threat of a large influx of cruise passengers, as specialist cruise companies seek out ever more novel destinations for their discerning clients). Singapore is promoting itself as a major shipping hub for cruising, with interest rising in ports along the Indian coast, Hong Kong and the Indonesian 'spice islands'.

The Antarctic Peninsula is experiencing strong growth, too, often as an extension to South American ports of call and combined with calls at South Georgia and the Falkland Islands. Vessels bound for Antarctica are expected to meet the requirements of the extreme conditions they will encounter (although these cruises are limited to Southern hemisphere summer periods), with specially reinforced hulls. Ushuaia in Argentina has become the principal base for these vessels and is now of economic importance as a tourist destination, both as a port of departure for Antarctic-bound ships and as a gateway to the Tierra del Fuego National Park.

In the UK, round-Britain cruising has also achieved a measure of popularity in recent years. In addition to calls at the mainland and Ireland, these sailings often include visits to the Shetland, Orkney, Hebridean and Faroe Islands, with occasional forays to remote outposts such as St Kilda, a group of islands now without permanent residents.

Most cruising, however, continues to focus on either the Mediterranean or the Caribbean. These two regions account for over 60 per cent of all cruises, with the Scandinavian and Baltic regions accounting for a further 10 per cent. Most of these routes are seasonal, which means that shipping companies may be obliged to move their vessels from one region of the globe to another to take advantage of peak periods of cruising demand. These positioning voyages, as we have noted, are then sold as long cruises or even as line voyages where transatlantic sailings are involved, although they might include an en route call at a mid-Atlantic island such as Cape Verde, which is rapidly developing a tourism infrastructure in its own right. Baltic and North Cape cruises are operated during the northern hemisphere's summer period, with visits to the North Cape programmed to coincide with the high summer when passengers can experience the midnight sun. In the western hemisphere, Alaskan cruises are similarly programmed through the summer months, and are of particular appeal to Americans who wish to confine their travels closer to home, at times when political disturbances may be occurring anywhere within the Mediterranean region.

American cruise passengers are generally cautious about foreign travel and have always shown a preference for cruising in their own waters or those nearby. The onboard culture, and currency, are US-orientated and Americans, until recently, were not required to carry passports for cruises to the Caribbean – an important selling point when only a small minority of the population owned a passport anyway. The Caribbean also benefits from the proximity of the islands to the American mainland, as well as a climate that allows year-round cruising, although the winter's more temperate climate attracts the highest level of demand. Ports in Florida, such as Fort Lauderdale, Miami/Port Everglades and Port Canaveral, have become key bases for cruise ships – Port Canaveral alone embarking over two million passengers every year. Demand from Europe, too, is such that charter flights from Europe now provide connections with many of the vessels sailing from Florida's ports.

Fly–cruising has made a significant contribution to the growth of cruising from European countries. Passengers are carried by the cruise company on chartered aircraft to a warm-water base port from which they can directly embark on their cruise or spend a few days at a nearby resort before or after the cruise. This overcomes the problem of poor weather and rough seas (the Bay of Biscay, off northern Spain, can be a notoriously unpleasant stretch of water to cross at any time of the year) and ensures that passengers can be enjoying the sunshine and calm seas of the Mediterranean or Caribbean from day one of their cruise holiday. Cruise and stay – with a week ashore at a Caribbean hotel, followed or preceded by a week cruising – is another popular option for the European markets. Although many traditional, often older, cruise passengers still reveal a preference for embarking directly onto their cruise ship at a European port, it has proved a popular development among younger cruise passengers. In recent years, however, the demand for direct embarkation has remained strong enough within Europe for several companies to position their vessels at ports such as Southampton or Bremen, at least for the summer season. In 2007, 467,000 of all UK cruise passengers chose a cruise that sailed directly from a UK port against a total of 870,000 choosing a fly–cruise holiday.

The search for new destinations has led to the opening up of ever more adventurous cruise routes. Emulating American adventure cruises, companies such as Noble Caledonia and Jules Verne pioneered Pacific inter-island cruises and voyages in the Arctic and Antarctic regions, often using smaller, purpose-built vessels. They and other specialist operators also charter Russian vessels with specially strengthened hulls to penetrate further south along the Antarctic shores.

Such cruises are still largely aimed at the top end of the market, though, with prices starting as high as £500 or more a day. PSA, the British cruise association, categorizes the top cruise vessels as 'ultra luxury', with criteria that include passenger capacity (between 100 and 1000), a crew to passenger ratio of 1:2 and at least 40 square metres of space for every passenger.

While the US market dominates the global demand for cruising, with over ten million cruise passengers annually, more than four million Western Europeans cruise each year. Together, Britain, Germany and Italy account for 69 per cent of the European cruise market (see Table 14.1).

Among European passengers, the average length of a cruise was between 5 and 14 days in 2007, with nearly 60 per cent choosing routes in the Mediterranean or near-Atlantic (such as the Canary Islands and Madeira). The number of British passengers taking a cruise has grown particularly strongly in the past decade. While the Mediterranean remains popular, other more distant destinations are attracting the wealthier and more adventurous passengers (see Table 14.2).

Other strong growth areas are river cruising and cheaper cruises on ships chartered by tour operators. The demand for river cruising will be looked at in more detail a little later in this chapter.

Table 14.1 Leading sources of European cruise passengers, 2007.

Country of origin	Number of passengers (thousands)	Percentage of total
UK	1337	34
Germany	763	19
Italy	640	16
Spain	518	13
France	280	7
Total for Europe	4004	100
Total for USA (mainly embarking in the USA)	10,600	

Source: European Cruise Council, 2007, based on ECC/IRN research and CLIA figures.

Table 14.2 Major destinations of the European cruise market, 2007.

Destinations	Number of passengers (thousands)	Percentage from UK
Mediterranean/Atlantic Isles	2397	48
Northern Europe	651	18
Caribbean and other	957	35

Source: European Cruise Council/PSA-IRN Annual Cruise Statistics.

The nature of the cruise market

The thought of a cruise still carries, for many holidaymakers, two distinctly negative images. On the one hand, cruise ships are thought to be peopled by conservative, rather elderly passengers who choose to spend their days at sea playing bridge or sitting on steamer chairs covered with blankets, watching the horizon and drinking cups of bouillon, while, on the other hand, at the cheaper end of the market, the image is of ships as float-ing holiday camps, peopled by hyperactive, extrovert middle-aged passengers propping up the bars, looking for non-stop entertainment and enjoying five-times-a-day opportunities to eat, in between shipboard romances. While undoubtedly such stereotypes exist, and some shipping lines cater for each of these, such images are far from being an accurate general picture of cruising today.

The key factors that determine cruise demand can be identified as price, length of cruise and ports visited, but there are a number of other factors contributing to people choosing one cruise over another, not least the efforts made by the shipping companies to appeal to niche markets through their ships, onboard activities and destinations. Unlike other sectors of the travel industry, cruising is a product that enjoys strong brand loyalty, with well-established brands claiming a high proportion of repeat bookings, many of which are rewarded by deep discounts. With the rapid expansion of interest in cruising (which, in Britain, accounted for 6.3 per cent of all package holidays in 2006), the importance of niche marketing has never been so strong. Three distinct forms of cruise company have emerged to cater for this global demand.

- There are the major international cruise companies that draw on global markets and are tending to dominate the industry. The three leaders in this sector are the US-owned Carnival, by far the world's largest cruise company, which, over recent years, has absorbed many other leading cruise brands, including the former British companies

P&O and Cunard; its nearest competitor, RCI (Royal Caribbean International); and Star Cruise Line. These three carriers are estimated to control 80 per cent of the global cruise market. The first two focus largely on the North American and European markets, while Star cruises has a 70 per cent share of the Asian market. A fourth company, MSC, is expanding rapidly and, together, these four are forecast to control 87 per cent of the cruise market by 2010.

- There is a handful of long-established lines with few vessels, such as Hapag-Lloyd and Fred Olsen, that are strongly dependent on their home markets and to which cruise passengers demonstrate strong brand loyalty. Customer commitment may be to companies, but in some cases, it may be to individual ships. This category also includes the two Disney cruise ships, aimed particularly at the family market, and a cluster of companies operating super-luxury vessels that have a more international appeal, such as Regent SevenSeas, Yachts of Seabourn and Crystal Cruises. It also includes the ships run by Saga, which have been largely aimed at the senior citizens market, although the company is seeking to widen its appeal with its latest ship, *Spirit of Adventure*. These carriers operate large vessels, but they are not behemoths, so are unable to offer the range of activities and entertainment on board that are to be found on ships operated by the leading carriers. Their survival is due in part to the strong financial support they receive from their parent organizations. For example, the Disney Cruise Line is part of the Disney entertainment empire, Crystal Cruises has the backing of the leading Japanese shipping company NYK, Regent SevenSeas is part of Carlson, the American travel conglomerate, and Hapag-Lloyd belongs to the TUI travel empire (although, at the time of writing, it appeared likely that this cruise division would be hived off).

- There are niche cruise operators, generally operating much smaller vessels and with a narrower focus. Typically, they offer more adventurous destinations or activities designed to appeal to particular markets. These operators also have intensely loyal passengers. Examples include Swan Hellenic's *Minerva*, Voyages of Discovery's *Discovery*, Silversea Cruises' *HAS Prince Albert II* and Hebridean Island Cruises' *Hebridean Princess*. Sailings are aimed at the more sophisticated traveller and are frequently sold as cultural cruises, accompanied by experienced guides and lecturers. Smaller vessels are well suited to itineraries such as the summer cruises in the Baltic, with destinations that appeal to upmarket audiences with an interest in culture (see the itinerary and map shown in Figure 14.3). Expedition cruising, offering more adventurous destinations such as the Chilean fjords and Antarctica, in which landings are made by Zodiac tenders, calls for a more energetic (although not necessarily younger) market. These ships are often chartered or part-chartered to specialist tour operators that search out and organize ever more adventurous holiday destinations. In 2006, three times as many British passengers travelled on ships carrying fewer than 1100 passengers as had travelled in 1999.

Example

Marketing the Baltic

Due to the increasing popularity of the Baltic for cruising, an organization has been formed to market the region jointly. Cruise Baltic is a marketing body composed of 10 countries and 44 partners that, together, receive more than 2.34 million passengers each year. Copenhagen is the leading cruise port in the area, with 291 ships visiting in 2007, bringing more than half a million tourists to the city.

Further information: **www.cruisebaltic.com**

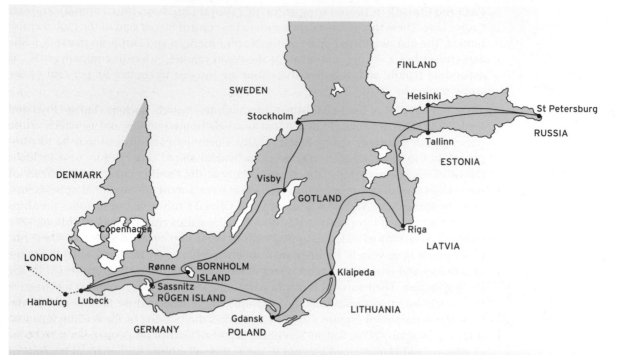

Figure 14.3 The Scandinavia and Baltic 'milk run'. The Baltic itinerary given as an example on this map is an ideal niche marketing route, allowing calls to be made at nine different countries within a two-week itinerary and only one day at sea without a port of call. The cruise can also be sold in segments, with connecting flights.

The economics of cruising

The present variations in the size of cruising vessels is a natural development, arising from the competition that emerged during the late 1980s as cruising once again became a popular form of travel. The losers in this competitive market were the higher-cost companies, particularly the US-owned ones. High labour costs and expenses incidental to flagging vessels in the developed countries led to the demise of a number of carriers, among them Regency, Dolphin, Premier, Commodore, Crown, Renaissance, Royal Olympic and American Classic Voyages. Through growth, mergers and acquisitions, the current three market leaders came to dominate the global cruise market, taking advantage of economies of scale (for example, Carnival provided identical meals on all brands of its ships operating in the Caribbean), typically flagging their vessels in countries offering substantial tax benefits, such as the Bahamas and Panama, and recruiting cheap labour from low-cost developing countries (the International Transport Workers' Federation estimates that more than half of all the world's cruise fleet now operate under flags of convenience (FOC), where taxation is either low or, in some cases, nil). Carnival has also diversified horizontally, with investments in hotels, lodges, luxury trains and motor coaches. The huge investments that these giant corporations can make in new vessels have led to a new form of cruising holiday – the ship itself becoming the destination, with an ever-widening range of activities and attractions on board, so that calls at ports en route become almost incidental to the shipboard experience.

Cruising appeals on a number of levels. The all-inclusive nature of a cruise, in which unlimited – and often excellent – food is on offer, the general ambience on board, the high levels of security that isolation on a ship can provide, the attraction of travelling with 'like-minded people' with whom it is easy to make friends, being thrown together within a confined space, the absence of constraint on the amount of baggage carried (other than on fly–cruises), all offer significant benefits. Indeed, for those with a real fear of flying, cruising directly from home ports provides the only means of travelling to far-flung places abroad.

While the concept of a floating hotel has become important as a way to sell cruises, many more traditional passengers still expect ships to look like ships. A great deal of care goes into the design of a modern cruise liner, in order to create the illusion of greater space, as well as include all the facilities that maximize the revenue-earning opportunities for the shipping company, in the form of shops, hairdressing facilities, casinos and bars. The design also takes account of the preferences of the nationalities of those travelling. Cruise ships aimed predominantly at the US market, for example, tend to make greater use of plastics, gilt stairways, mirrors, neon lights and bright colours, while the more traditional European, and particularly British, market will expect greater use of wood (although safety standards at sea encourage the use of more fire-retardant materials today) and quieter, more refined decoration.

The image of cruising as an older person's holiday is finally beginning to fade as companies such as Carnival and Island Cruises encroach on the traditional cruise market and reach a younger group of holidaymakers. According to the PSA, the average age of British cruise passengers in 2007 was 53 years, with around 8 per cent under the age of 26. Ocean Village, shortly to become integrated with P&O's ships, described its onboard regime as 'casual', claiming an average (of all nationalities on board) of only 43 years, while that of RCI is a little higher, at 48. Vessels appealing to the family market, such as those operated by the Walt Disney Company, are undoubtedly contributing to a lowering of these averages, while the more price-sensitive ships operated by the large tour operators will also attract a younger market. In the USA in particular, cruises are marketed as just another form of package holiday, comparable to an all-inclusive holiday on land. This has resulted in some 9 per cent of all Americans having taken a cruise, compared with only 2 per cent of the British.

Shipping companies have recognized the difficulty of appealing to varied markets and varied nationalities on the same vessel, however appealing this might be economically. Multinational passenger mixes call for multilingual announcements and entertainment on board, which will not be an attractive selling point. Passengers from different countries have differing habits and preferences in onboard food and entertainment. Those from Latin countries, for instance, prefer to take dinner later than those from the UK or USA. These differences lead cruise companies to niche market, whether by price, brand, market or type of cruise offered. Saga Holidays caters extensively for the upper end of the age market, P&O's vessel *Adonia* is reserved for adults only, while their *Oceania* was designed to appeal to passengers new to cruising, both in its style and routes. *Artemis*, introduced in 2005, is a smaller vessel of 45,000 tons with more traditional decor, designed to appeal to a conservative market.

Competition encourages shipping companies to emphasize product differentiation, while striving to build the newest ships, and offer the latest onboard facilities to meet the expectations of an increasingly sophisticated cruise market. Entertainment has become increasingly varied, with Cordon Bleu cookery courses, acting classes, wellness at sea programmes and a golf academy. On its North Atlantic crossings, Cunard's *Queen Mary 2* offers opportunities for intellectual stimulus, with lectures in association with Oxford University. One noted trend is to have greater variety in catering on board. P&O's *Oriana*, to take one example, has introduced a pizzeria on board, while Crystal Cruises offers a choice of Italian, Japanese and Chinese restaurants on its vessels. A notable feature of catering on board the most recent ships has been the appointment of celebrity chefs to oversee the restaurant menus.

In spite of the rise in popularity of cruising, it remains a highly volatile market and is quickly affected by adverse events, such as terrorist activities or upheavals in the Middle East. Americans in particular, as noted earlier, are cautious travellers and seek security abroad. The perception of danger in the Mediterranean will cause many to switch bookings to safer home waters in the Caribbean or Alaska – evidenced by there being something of a boom for those destinations whenever bookings to the Mediterranean decline. Cruise companies can also be forced, in these circumstances, to reposition their vessels to the already congested Caribbean, as a result of which, even with rising demand, oversupply leads to deep discounting for all cruise ships and so profits fall.

Cabotage rights extend to shipping operations as much as they do to airline operations (although these rights have been abandoned within the European Union, with cruise companies of member states being free to determine their own routes within the EU). In other parts of the world, vessels of foreign registry are not permitted to carry passengers between two ports within the same country, nor carry passengers from and back to the same port without an intermediate port of call in a foreign country.

American legislation is contained in the Merchant Marine Act (1920), better known as the Jones Act, which prohibits non-US-registered vessels from carrying passengers between two US ports without a call at a 'distant foreign port' (Canadian ports are close and therefore not counted as foreign for the purpose of the Act). The Act also requires ships travelling on cabotage routes to be US-flagged, US-crewed, US-built and subject to US domestic labour laws (although the Act has been amended to exempt certain routes and industries).

Example

Norwegian Caribbean Line

Following the collapse of American Classic Voyages in the wake of the 9/11 tragedy, Hawaii found itself with no major US-flagged cruise line.

NCL had been operating cruises from the Hawaiian Islands for a number of years, but was obliged to call at a foreign port under cabotage regulations. It programmed a call at Fanning Island (Tabuaeran) in Kiribati, the nearest non-US port, to satisfy the Jones Act, even though the call had little passenger appeal.

The company won exemption from the Act after reflagging its vessels, agreeing to build new vessels in US shipyards and abiding by US labour regulations. Subsequently, the company formed a new US-registered company, NCL America, and, since 2004, its vessels sailed under the American flag, allowing them to operate their Hawaiian cruises without the need to make an intermediate call at a foreign port.

More than 40 countries around the world continue to enforce cabotage rules, including Canada, Mexico and Japan.

Cruising is both capital-intensive and labour-intensive. A modern cruise liner can easily cost more than $250 million to build, with some, such as the *Queen Mary 2* costing in excess of $500 million (costs for a 222,000-ton vessel such as the new *Oasis of the Seas* exceeds $1 billion). The life expectancy of a cruise ship is fortunately far longer than that of an aircraft and, allowing for some rebuilding and complete interior renovation, a 50-year productive life would not be unusual. The *Queen Elizabeth 2* enjoyed a life of more than 40 years before her withdrawal from service in 2008.

Fuel burn is obviously an important consideration in overall operating costs, although perhaps not as critical as one might expect. Oil prices have typically represented only 4 per cent of overall costs,[1] although undoubtedly fuel price increases during the summer of 2008 will have inflated this figure. Steamships are generally less efficient than diesel-engined vessels, so most have been phased out over the past decade, as have other less fuel-efficient vessels. New, more efficient marine engines are making an appearance, burning liquefied natural gas, which emit much lower levels of carbon dioxide and nitrous oxide, although, so far, these engines are more suitable for ferry operations than cruising. Marine research is focused on improving the design of hulls and propellers, as well as developing new kinds of silicon paint to reduce drag in the water. At times of rapid escalation in fuel prices, as in recent years, the operating costs will rise sharply as a result, but competition and oversupply make a parallel rise in prices difficult to enforce, although some companies have taken to imposing an oil surcharge, in line with airline policy.

Vessels also need a substantial number of crew, both in passenger service and below deck – a 4- or 5-star cruise ship would carry as many as one member of crew for every two passengers, and a ratio of one to one is not unknown for the luxury top end of the market. With such labour costs, it is not difficult to see why luxury cruises are selling for up to $1000 a day. The decline in the fleets of the established maritime nations, such as Britain, can be partly accounted for by their uncompetitive operating costs compared with their cheaper competitors. Lower-cost nations, such as Greece and Russia, built up their own fleets, while, as we have seen, the more expensive nations were obliged to trim costs by registering their fleets in developing countries such as Panama, the Bahamas or Liberia and recruiting crews from countries where labour costs are low, such as the Philippines, Indonesia or India, to the chagrin of trade unions representing maritime crews in the developed nations. Virtually all leading cruise companies today recruit a substantial proportion of their deck staff from the Philippines. Some large companies also reduce the ratio of crew to passengers, aiming to deliver a 3-star, rather than 4- or 5-star, service.

Companies operating large fleets can also obtain some economies of scale by reducing the cost per unit of their marketing and administration. It has also become more economical to operate large ships rather than small ones and the trend is to build bigger and bigger vessels, to take advantage of this and maximize onboard spend. Five-star operators such as Silversea Cruises face a different problem, however. While high levels of profitability are hard to achieve for these vessels when capacity is low, any increase leads to difficulties in delivering the expected high standards of service. Optimum viability for the luxury end of the market is believed to be achieved, therefore, with vessels of around 25,000 tons, carrying a maximum of 400 passengers.

The largest ships are able to pare costs by providing smaller cabins with larger areas given over to public use. This provides space for shopping and other sales opportunities that, together with shore excursions, make up around one-third of a cruise line's revenue. Dining rooms accommodate large numbers within relatively confined spaces, either by having two sittings for meals or providing only large tables – tables for two are rare on board ships. Some companies have capitalized on this, however, by designing their ships to permit *all* passengers to be accommodated in the restaurant at a single sitting – an attractive marketing advantage.

The global political situation has not only led to higher fuel costs; ships and seaports also now need heightened security, just as do aircraft and airports. Passengers and their luggage have to be checked more carefully as they board and the vessels must be guarded around the clock while in port and under way.

Another feature of shipping that it shares with the airline industry is the highly fluid pricing structure that the industry now finds necessary to adopt. Deep discounting has become the norm for nearly all cruise lines, with discounts for early bookers, last-minute bookers, loyal clients, even for readers of certain newspapers and magazines. Identical cabins will be sold at different fares in Britain, on the Continent and in North America – the result, the shipping companies insist, of market conditions, although website searches by passengers are reducing this differential. Most cruises (82 per cent in the UK) are still sold through travel agents and they, in turn, offer discounts and incentives to secure the booking, on top of any discounts offered by the principal.

A useful rule of thumb in judging the relative luxury and spaciousness on board ship is to ascertain the size to passenger ratio (SPR), sometimes referred to as the passenger–space ratio (PSR). This is based on the vessel's gross registered tonnage divided by the number of passengers carried. If this amounts to 20 or fewer, the ship is likely to appear crowded, while a figure approaching 60 would be considered luxurious and command high daily rates (see Table 14.3). Tonnage alone is not a good guide as to the amount of space per passenger, however. *World of Cruising* magazine points out that the *Lirica*, at 60,000 tons,

Table 14.3 Comparing size and comfort of some leading cruise ships.

Ships	Tonnage	Star rating	Space ratio	Passenger to crew ratio
Grandeur of the Seas	74,137	****	38.00	2100/760
Oriana	69,000	****	37.80	1830/760
MSC Lirica	60,000	****	25.42	1600/760
Island Escape	40,132	***	26.50	1600/612
Black Watch	28,500	****	37.45	761/310
Emerald	26,431	***	26.60	1100/420
Marco Polo	21,000	****	24.10	800/356
Discovery	19,900	****	32.60	600/325
Braemar	19,900	****	26.10	727/320
Black Prince	11,000	***	26.69	412/200

Source: Modified from Voyages of Discovery brochure, 2005, based on September 2004 edition of *World of Cruising*.

has a PSR of 25.42, while the *Discovery* at 19,900 tons offers a PSR of 32.6, yet both are classed as 4-star ships.

Further economies are obtained by calling at a greater number of ports on any one itinerary and spending more time in port – both of which help to reduce fuel burn, while at the same time increasing the passengers' satisfaction. A reduction in speed also saves on fuel, but if vessels travel slowly and call at numerous ports, it is essential that the ports are grouped closely together. For this reason, the Caribbean, with its many islands of differing nationality, makes an ideal cruise destination.

Example

Cunard's transatlantic service

One example of effective cost-reduction in shipping operations was demonstrated by Cunard, which, in 1996, took the decision to extend the journey time for its *Queen Elizabeth 2* between the UK and New York from five to six days.

While this achieved significant savings in terms of fuel burn, reducing the average speed from 28.5 knots to 23 knots, it also offered other advantages, in marketing terms. A higher onboard spend was encouraged, while the passengers themselves saw an additional day's cruising as an added benefit. It also allowed the ship to arrive at a more convenient time of day for those with onward travel arrangements. This policy remains in force with the *Queen Mary 2*, passengers departing in the early evening and arriving at their destination on the morning of the seventh day. This pattern will no doubt be continued when the new *Queen Elizabeth* joins the fleet.

Further economies can be achieved by putting passengers ashore by tender (ship's launches), rather than tying up alongside. This may be a practical alternative when islands are pushing up mooring fees, but it does delay disembarkation and is a less attractive selling point.

Cruise lines have to ensure that their ships are used for the maximum amount of time during the year (just as airlines do), although this does not necessarily mean that they are used only for cruising. Some companies charter cruise ships to tour operators, while others have successfully chartered ships for use as floating hotels when accommodation pressures force tourist destinations to find alternative accommodation for special events.

Cunard was even successful in chartering its largest vessel, the *Queen Elizabeth 2*, for a period for Japan to use as a hotel. This represented a substantial saving to the company on operating costs as it required no use of fuel.

Competition has forced the leading companies to speed up their turnaround times at their home ports between cruises. Some turnarounds have been reduced to as little as 12 hours, although concern has been expressed that such tight scheduling does not allow for adequate cleaning between cruises, risking the spread of onboard diseases such as the Norovirus, which has plagued the shipping companies in recent years.

Example

New concepts in cruising

The World – a £182-million investment project by ResidenSea – represents a new departure for the cruise industry. This 43,500-ton ship (see Figure 14.4) was built in 2002 as a floating apartment block, with individual apartments – priced between £1.5 million and £5 million – sold off to wealthy investors as second homes. The original intention was that these were to be used mainly for their own pleasure, with the owners joining the ship at any point during its continuous round the world itinerary.

Initial sales were slow, so it was decided that some of the apartments would be sold for short legs only, while others would be made available for commercial rent to cruise passengers. Prices were set at the highest end of the scale, but resident owners were disappointed at the resultant mix of private ownership and commercial rental. The original financial backers were bought out by the owners, who now administer the ship's operations themselves, but many of the cabins remain on offer as rental flats.

Figure 14.4 *The World*, moored near the O$_2$ Arena, London.
(photo by Claire Humphreys.)

The Four Seasons Hotel group has announced its intention to build its own contribution to this type of venture and anticipate launching the Four Season Ocean Residences in 2010. Initially, a vessel of 48,600 tons is planned to accommodate 112 wholly residential private apartments, selling for between £2 million and £20 million. Management of the venture will be undertaken by the hotel division.

It took only a short leap of imagination to move from this concept to the launch of timeshare cruising. One company now offers the opportunity to buy timeshare points towards stays on one of its 27 ships. Apartments range in price from £100,000 to £800,000, depending on layout and the period of time chosen.

Further information: **www.privatsea.com**

Distribution is all important in this competitive sector and, although cruise operators have made full use of the World Wide Web to market their products, more than four-fifths of all cruise bookings in the UK are still made through travel agents. The complexity of cruising, however, makes it difficult for sales staff to acquire adequate knowledge of the variety of types of accommodation and ships available without gaining first-hand experience. In recent years, the PSA – the marketing arm of the passenger shipping business in the UK – has attempted to overcome this problem by mounting special campaigns to train agents through its training subsidiary Association of Cruise Experts (ACE) and has some 1200 agency members to date.

The larger shipping companies tend to receive greater support from travel agents, who find it easier to deal with companies owning a greater number and variety of ships and, therefore, a larger choice of both sailings and destinations. A growing number of agents, seeking ways to specialize as the commission received for other services has reduced, have switched their focus to the cruise sector, obtaining advantageous commission rates and developing their competence in selling in this sector. A Leading Cruise Agents' Alliance has been formed in the UK to bring these specialists together.

The cruising business

Although demand has been rising strongly for more than a decade, it has barely kept pace with the growth in supply, in terms of both the number of vessels and their overall size and capacity. An average of ten ships per annum joined the market in the years 1990–2004, with a further nine each year in 2007 and 2008 (at the time of writing). This has led to fierce competition in the industry, artificially high 'brochure prices' allowing the maximum price flexibility and deep discounting to clear unsold accommodation. Escalating costs, for both shipbuilding and operating (notably increases in oil price), have led to some retrenchment and slimmer profits have been followed by market concentration – a trend now familiar in many sectors of the tourism industry. Over-tonnage in American waters has forced cruise companies to turn to Europe to fill ships and several companies now offer free flights to the Caribbean to join their cruise ships based there.

As we have seen, there are currently two strong market leaders – Carnival Cruise Line and Royal Caribbean International, closely followed by Star Cruises, which targets Asian markets. In the UK cruise market, market shares in 2007 were:[2]

- Carnival UK – 42 per cent (based on 5 leading brands marketed in the UK – P&O, Cunard, Princess, Ocean Village and Yachts of Seabourn)
- Royal Caribbean Corporation Ltd (RCI) – 14 per cent
- TUI – 12 per cent
- Island Cruises – 6 per cent
- Fred Olsen – 5 per cent.

Table 14.4 Leading cruise operators and their ships, as at 2007.

Shipping line	Number of vessels
Carnival Cruises	20
RCI	20
Princess Cruises (Carnival)	17
Costa Crosiere (Carnival)	14
Hurtigruten	14
Holland America Line (Carnival)	14
Louis Cruise Line	12
NCL*	11
MSC (Mediterranean Shipping Co)	10
Celebrity Cruises (RCI)	9
P&O Cruises (Carnival)	6
Fred Olsen	5
Hapag-Lloyd	4
Silversea Cruises	4
Regent SevenSeas*	4
Thomson Cruises	4
Crystal	3
Star Cruises*	3
Windstar Cruises	3
Saga Cruises	3
Seabourn	3
Oceania*	2
Island Cruises**	2
Cunard Line	2
Ocean Village (Carnival) (due to be phased out)	2
Hebridean International	2
Disney Cruises	2
SeaDream Yacht Club	2
easyCruise	2

*Apollo Management, a private equity firm, owns Regent SevenSeas, Oceania and 50 per cent of NCL. Star Cruises owns the balance of NCL.
**Island Cruises was established as a joint RCI and First Choice venture. TUI Travel is to operate one of these two vessels, from 2009, the other being sold to Spain's Pullmantur.

A further 16 per cent is composed mainly of river cruising and niche cruising operators (see also Table 14.4).

Carnival Cruise Line deserves special mention here because of the way in which it has changed the face of cruising since the mid-1970s (see Figure 14.5). The company was formed in 1972 and has been noted for its string of acquisitions, which, since 1989, have included Holland America Line, Seabourn, Costa Line, Cunard Line, P&O and Princess Cruises, Windstar Cruises (since sold to Ambassadors International), Ocean Village, Swan Hellenic (now sold) and Aida. At the time of writing (in 2008), the company was operating under 12 different brands and, in its most recent annual report, it was operating 80 ships, with 15 on order for late 2009. The total capacity of these ships was 139,000 passengers at any one time.

Carnival, in particular, has been able to attract a much younger than average market for its major division, Carnival Cruises, which offers relatively cheap cruises of short duration, using large vessels of, typically, 70,000–100,000 tons or more. Its most recent vessels

		$ millions	
Six-month revenues:	Cruise	3930	77%
	On board/associated	1139	22%
	Other	56	1%
Operating costs:			
Cruise transportation, commissions		813	26%*
On board		198	
Payroll, etc.		560	18%*
Food		311	
Fuel		461	15%*
Other operating		740	
Other non-cruise		53	
	Total:	3136	
	Selling/administration	720	
	Depreciation/amortisation	472	
	Total:	4328	

*Percentage of cruise operating

Figure 14.5 Carnival Corporation & Carnival plc consolidated financial results, mid-2006.
Source: Carnival Corporation & Carnival plc consolidated annual report, 2006.

accommodate, usually, between 2000 and 3000 passengers. The fanciful names of the ships (*Paradise, Elation, Ecstasy, Sensation* and *Imagination*, for example) are pointers to the expectations their passengers will have of the kinds of experiences these cruise ships promise. They are sold as 'fun cruises', offering a wide range of onboard facilities, including shops and casinos (Carnival has claimed that some 14 per cent of its total revenue is onboard spend). A recent launch is the *Carnival Miracle*, a vessel of 88,500 tons with 16 themed lounges and bars, including a sports bar named after the cruise film *Jerry McGuire*, a nightclub in the shape of a gothic castle and another entitled Dr Frankenstein's Lab. Not perhaps to every cruise passenger's taste, but the market for which it is designed, overwhelmingly American, has responded favourably. The company has been particularly successful in attracting young, relatively high-spend passengers.

Carnival has also identified smaller niches. Its Fiesta Marina division of Hispanic-orientated tours was developed to tap into Spanish- and Portuguese-speaking markets in the USA and Latin America, based at a home port of San Juan, Puerto Rico – an island commonwealth of the US. Food, wine and entertainment on board were designed to suit Hispanic tastes, and dining hours are later than usual, in accordance with Hispanic preferences.

Niche markets are being tapped by both the shipping companies themselves and specialist operators around the world, often using chartered vessels. Even the largest vessels find their specialist markets. For example, in 2006, the *Ocean Majesty* was chartered by Just You, for single passengers only. In the USA, operators Atlantis and RSVP offer exclusively gay cruises, while Alternative Holidays caters to a similar market in the UK. Olivia, an operator in San Francisco, has chartered ships exclusively for lesbian passengers. The *Queen Mary 2* was sold as a gay transatlantic crossing for one sailing in 2007.

Health, safety and the environment

Health and safety issues are controlled by the International Maritime Organization (IMO), which requires ships and ports to conform to internationally set standards, and regulations pertaining to these issues are constantly being tightened up. The International Convention for the Safety of Life at Sea (SOLAS) (1974) is the principal regulation governing standards for ships and their crew and its directives are widely adhered to throughout the world, but the dominance of the Americans in the world cruise market and American concerns about both safety and hygiene have also resulted in strict standards being imposed on all foreign flag-carriers operating out of, or calling at, US ports. All such ships are subject to unannounced inspections by the US Vessel Sanitation Program. Vessels are rated for the quality of their water, food preparation, cleanliness, storage and repairs. An acceptable rating is 86 points out of 100, but it is not uncommon for even leading cruise ships of the world to be given grades considerably lower than this. Owners are then required to raise their standards. Adverse publicity in the press is a further incentive not to fail these tests. Over the past decade, there have been numerous outbreaks of contagious diseases on board cruise ships, ranging from viral gastroenteritis to the Norwalk virus (Norovirus) and such outbreaks get maximum publicity in the world's press.

New regulations governing environmental protection are also affecting the shipping industry. The IMO has recognized that global shipping emissions are much higher than had earlier been estimated and are now put at some 1.2 billion tonnes a year, against 650 million tonnes produced by the aviation industry (although this figure, of course, includes all maritime craft – container ships, tankers and so on). This represents around 4.5 per cent of all global CO_2 emissions. The environmental agency Climate Care estimates that larger cruise ships emit some 0.43 kilograms of CO_2 per passenger mile, compared with long-haul flights, even at high altitude, of 0.26 kilograms, although the PSA insists that passenger ships are globally responsible for only 1.4 per cent of greenhouse gases. Illegal cleaning of tanks at sea, discharge of oil and pumping of raw sewage into the oceans are of increasing concern in terms of their effect on the environment. One report[3] indicated that a single large cruise ship generates:

- 400–1200 cubic metres[4] of grey waste (waste water) daily, together with 70 litres of hazardous waste
- 800,000 litres of black waste (sewage) a week and 50 tons of solid waste.

The original International Convention for the Prevention of Pollution from Ships, adopted in 1973 and modified in 1978 (now known as MARPOL 73/78), laid down strict controls governing the disposal of waste at sea and was adopted by 136 maritime countries. Further rulings on environmental pollution came into force in 2004 and other measures are to follow in 2010. As a result, shipowners have either to invest substantially in upgrading their older vessels or will be obliged to scrap them in favour of newer ones.

The PSA claims that large cruise vessels now recycle 60–65 per cent of their waste and many ships (and all ships of Holland-America Line) have environmental officers on board to ensure compliance with rules and standards laid down by the US body CLIA. The Holland-America Line has gone further than most cruise companies, reducing speed to conserve fuel, harnessing waste heat and using silicon paint on the hulls of their ships to reduce drag. Newer vessels have the means to treat waste on board and hulls are painted externally with new non-toxic paints.

More recently constructed vessels, designed to achieve higher standards of safety, can attract lower insurance premiums. These vessels are also more technically advanced and have lower operating costs, resulting in older ships finding it difficult to compete. On top of this, owners are also required to be bonded against financial collapse, adding to costs. In this respect, the shipping and airline businesses face similar problems. Medium-sized operators are likely to be absorbed over the next few years by the three or four largest companies, leaving only the niche market cruise operators to remain as independents in the field.

The expansion of the cruise business has been welcomed for the benefits it can bring to holidaymakers, shipping companies and cruise destinations alike, but there can be less attractive consequences for some popular cruise ship destinations. Responsible cruising suggests not only environmental concern but also the need to ensure that destinations receive adequate financial rewards from ships' visits. The large shipping companies, however, are stressing onboard spend and the construction of ships that have become virtual leisure complexes in their own right has resulted in many port destinations experiencing a

Example

The impact of cruising on sensitive environments

The impact of mass cruising on island economies has already been remarked on earlier in this chapter, there being a growing threat to small islands such as Aldabra. Other sensitive locations have seen a huge surge in demand for cruising as frequent passengers seek out new, more isolated destinations to visit.

Notable among these are the islands of the Galapagos – the unique habitat of many species of animals and birds, which are now threatened by the enormous expansion in the numbers of visitors. The Ecuadorean Government, which formerly restricted visits to ships carrying a maximum of 100 passengers, now permits larger vessels to call and, today, in any one year, some dozen ships with up to 500 passengers are calling at the islands. The result has been an increase in visitors from around 20,000 to over 100,000 annually.

Similarly, Antarctica, seen by some as the last wilderness, is experiencing a marked increase in cruise ship visits and, by 2010, is expected to be receiving over 80,000 visitors a year, with potentially disastrous consequences for the environment.

decline in onshore spend, which parallels the problem faced by other destinations that have encouraged expansion by tour operators of the all-inclusive holiday concept. Bigger onboard spend equates to less being spent ashore – less money going into local shops, bars and transport companies. Some shipping companies have purchased their own, frequently deserted, islands on which they can land their passengers for barbecues and lazy beach days, ensuring, once again, that no revenue goes into the local economy. Private islands that are either owned or rented include:

- Great Stirrup Cay (NCL/Star Cruises)
- Coco Cay (RCI)
- Half Moon Cay (HAL/Carnival)
- Princess Cay (Princess Cruises/Carnival).

Larger ships also tend to attract passengers with lower incomes, resulting in a further reduction in the per person spend at ports of call, while the growth in size of cruise vessels, as we have seen, threatens massive congestion at small island ports. At the same time, the economic power exercised by the largest shipping companies can pressurize ports into reducing harbour costs, as the Example illustrates.

Example

The power of the large cruise operators

In 1991, the small port of Haines, Alaska, sought to impose a 4 per cent tax on tours operating from cruise vessels calling at the port, to help pay for local services. RCI resisted the move, removing Haines from its itineraries. This led to an economic downturn at the port. The drop in revenue resulting from the decline in visits by ships led to the closure of some shops and a rise in local unemployment. Haines rescinded the tax to get the port of call back on to RCI's route planning.

Source: L. Kroll (2004) 'Cruise control', *Forbes*, 174 (4), p. 96.

While aviation has drawn much of the fire for its contribution to global warming, passenger transport by sea is also now recognized as having environmental, sociocultural and economic consequences that need to be addressed.

Health and safety issues affect the carriage of disabled passengers, too. In 2006, the US Supreme Court ruled that the Americans with Disabilities Act applied equally to US and foreign cruise ships operating within US waters (contrary to British regulations, where the Disability Discrimination Act does not yet apply to shipping). As is the case with hotels, in order to comply with the Act, some cabins must be equipped to meet the needs of physically disabled passengers, including wider doorways for entry to the cabin and bathroom, while gangplanks have to accept wheelchairs. Currently, not all cruise lines accept guide dogs for the blind and some insist on disabled passengers being accompanied by fare-paying, fully able-bodied escorts to look after them. There are ample lifts on cruise ships, but this is not the case where river cruising is concerned, making these vessels far from ideal for disabled bookings, even though this is a form of travel likely to be favoured by both disabled and elderly tourists. Further complications arise in the case of cruise ships, where landings have to be made by tender or zodiac (the latter hazardous even for the able-bodied in swells and more so for elderly passengers). Encountering rough seas can pose a threat to the disabled, whether or not they are wheelchairbound. The question of compensation in the event of injuries then arises and whether or not exclusion clauses in contracts can overcome such threats.

The UK government is expected to legislate to do away with the current legal exemptions on disabilities applying to cruise ships and the lines are taking steps to keep ahead of the legislation. The Fred Olsen Line, to take one example, has purchased stair walkers to help disabled passengers when embarking and disembarking.

Budget cruising

While cruises are sold as package holidays in the USA and tour operators there have also played a part as intermediaries in bringing the product to the notice of the travelling public, British tour operators were in general slower to move into the cruise market. Some early attempts were made during the 1970s, when operators, including market leader Thomson Holidays, started to charter or part-charter cruise ships that they incorporated into their programme of inclusive tours, but efforts to bring down the overall prices of cruising led to dissatisfaction with standards of service and operation. Two decades later, Airtours, one of the leading operators, introduced its own ship, *Carousel*, with low lead-in prices and, for the first time, cruises were marketed as just another package holiday, with all meals and entertainment thrown in. Other leading operators soon entered the competition and, in 2000, Royal Caribbean International bought a 20 per cent stake in First Choice to form a joint cruise company, Island Cruises, with the clear intention of using the operator's retail outlets to push cruise sales in the UK.

The entrance of these tour operators into the mass market cruise business changed the face of British cruising. Not only did the average age of cruise passengers come down but also a whole new market was introduced to cruising. One major budget cruise company, Ocean Village, claimed that 60 per cent of its passengers were first-time cruisers. Undoubtedly, the budget cruise companies helped to account for the fact that 1 in 14 of all foreign package holidays booked in the UK in 2007 was a cruise. Tour operators also helped to popularize the short cruise in the British mass market, which brought down cruise prices, and the seven-day, or shorter, cruise has since enhanced the appeal of this form of holiday for both European and American passengers. A Cyprus-based company, Louis Cruises, further boosted the appeal of short cruises by offering two-night voyages from Limassol to Egypt and the Lebanon, mainly as excursions for holidaymakers staying on the island. Since then, the company has expanded its programme of short cruises to include sailings from Genoa, Piraeus and Marseilles, having taken over the MyTravel (formerly Airtours) vessels when it withdrew from the cruise business. With the merger between MyTravel and Thomas Cook, cruises are now marketed under the Cruise Thomas Cook label, but the operator neither owns nor charters vessels on its own account. Thomson, however, has expanded its cruise division and now operates four vessels.

Budget cruising has also been boosted by the arrival of super-budget company easyCruise.

Example

easyCruise

In 2005, easyJet owner Stelios Hadji-Ioannou announced the launch of his latest venture – easyCruise.

This is an entirely new concept in cruising. Customers can either make their own connecting flight arrangements or pay extra for flights to and from their departure points. Additional payment is made for all meals on board, which are taken cafeteria-style. The *easyCruise 1* is a small ship, at 2840 tons, and the product is typical of the easy group's approach to holidays. On its maiden voyage, it attracted passengers with an average age of just 35. Cabins can be booked for any variety of legs between ports around the Mediterranean, with a minimum of two nights on board. The cabins, which are very small, were initially sold at a rate of just £29 per double per night, with a supplement for housekeeping.

After the early success of the venture, a second vessel was introduced and the two ships now operate seasonally in the Mediterranean or Caribbean.

The future of the cruise business

For all the contributions made by the mass market tour operators and companies such as easyCruise, it is anticipated that most cruising will retain its upmarket image, at least within Europe. Both luxury and middle-priced cruising have been experiencing sharp rises in demand, in spite of deep discounting, and it is these that are seen as offering the best opportunity for long-term profitability. The market for this price bracket is very loyal – both P&O and Cunard have claimed that 60–70 per cent of their market is repeat bookings. The future of the cruise industry in general also looks healthy in terms of growth in demand, but perhaps less so in terms of profitability, especially given the expectation of rises in oil prices. One study by the PSA found that fewer than 1 in 60 British travellers has ever taken a cruise, far fewer than among the US population. That would suggest there is considerable scope for growth, but also points up the fact that cruise numbers, while growing fast, would have to rise substantially in order to match the levels achieved in the USA.

As we have noted, brand loyalty is strong among cruise passengers and great efforts are now made to differentiate individual ships as well, rather than depending on discounting to sell unsold cabins. Certainly Carnival, with its niche marketing to the younger holiday-makers in the USA, has led the way in this direction, while other companies have focused on theme cruising to survive. Indeed, cruise lines now offer a huge variety of special interest cruises, ranging from botanical cruises to classical civilizations cruising in the Mediterranean, accompanied by specialist, often well-known, guest lecturers, and from classical music cruises to jazz cruises, with onboard orchestras. Some shipping operators have experimented with new types of vessel. Radisson, for example, introduced twin-hull catamaran vessels, while both Windstar Cruises and Club Méditerranée offer luxury sail-assisted ships to widen the appeal of cruising. Small luxury ships are also in vogue. Society Expedition Cruises offer luxury cruising for around 100 passengers to exotic destinations such as the Amazon and Antarctic, while the similarly small (4260 gross tons) Sea Dream Yacht Club ships offer unparalleled luxury to more traditional destinations in the Caribbean and Mediterranean for just 110 passengers, with a crew of just 90 and a retractable platform at the stern from which passengers may swim, snorkel or sail while the ship lies at anchor. Diving holidays from even smaller ships are also growing in popularity, with vessels such as *SY Siren*, based in Thailand, *Four Seasons Explore* in the Maldives, *Komodo Dancer* in Bali and *Aqua Cat* in the Bahamas. These small vessels typically carry fewer than a dozen passengers in extreme luxury. Their popularity is likely to increase.

Looking to the longer term, research is continuing on designs for more fuel-efficient craft. Successful sea trials have taken place of vessels that complement the use of their engines with metal sails, increasing the overall speed while reducing costs – an important consideration at a time when fuel prices are rising sharply. Marine research in the short term is focusing on greater efficiency in engines to reduce pollution and improving designs and finishes to reduce drag.

The appeal of cruise ships that resemble floating hotels with a full range of leisure facilities has led to the construction of ever larger vessels, but whether *Oasis of the Seas* will see this trend taper off is debatable. One forecast (by Tillberg Design – the company responsible for designing the *Queen Elizabeth 2* and *Queen Mary 2*) expects to see even larger vessels, carrying between 5000 and 7000 passengers, who would be carried to shore in smaller vessels, as the mother ship would be too large to enter most existing ports. Such ships would indeed be veritable floating hotels, with gardens on the top deck and a range of environmentally friendly additions, including solar panels to generate hot water on board.

Proposals have also been advanced for much larger catamarans and trimarans (twin-hulled and triple-hulled vessels) than those currently in existence, capable of transporting large numbers of passengers at high speed and with far more comfort, without the customary problems of motion sickness experienced with single hull ships. Such vessels might be constructed that will be capable of crossing the Atlantic in under 48 hours.

The longer-term future of the shipping industry may be boosted by more advanced marine technology, now being researched. Japan is experimenting with the use of electro-magnetic thrusters for ships, which promise speeds in excess of 100 knots, and Toshiba has designed a prototype of one such vessel of 150 tons that is pushed through the water by the effect of counteracting magnets. This could, again, lead to the development of vessels that are much larger in size. Waterjet propulsion is also being tested for a new breed of container ship. The proposed 'Fastship', using a semi-planing monohull, is expected to be capable of speeds exceeding 40 knots and may be adaptable later for cruise vessels. Such developments could even encourage the reintroduction of line voyages between major ports in the world, although this is unlikely to occur in the near future. The pressure must also be on to develop new forms of energy to propel ships, given the continuing rise in oil prices. As we saw earlier, liquefied natural gas is already in use for ships on short sea routes, but, unlike the automobile industry, the development of hydrogen power for seagoing vessels does not appear to be imminent.

Ferry services

The term 'ferry' is one that embraces a variety of forms of short-distance water-borne transport. This includes urban transport in cities such as Stockholm, where people travel from the city centre to outlying suburbs and surrounding towns by water. Ferries of this type also attract tourists, who use it as either a convenient form of local transport or an original way to view the city. Some ferries, such as the Staten Island ferry, which links Manhattan with the borough of Staten Island in New York, and Hong Kong's Star Ferry, have become world famous and a 'must' for visiting tourists. Other notable ferry rides that serve the needs of both locals and tourists include the Bosporus ferries linking Europe and Asia in Istanbul, the many island ferries in Greece and Indonesia, the Manly ferry between Sydney and Manly in Australia, the Niteroi ferry crossing Guanabara Bay in Rio de Janeiro, the Mersey ferry in Liverpool (immortalized in various songs), the Bainbridge Island ferry in Seattle, the Alameda–Oakland ferry in San Francisco, the Devonport and Waiheke inland ferries in Auckland, New Zealand and the Barreiro and Cacilhas ferries crossing the River Tagus in Lisbon. Most of these, of course, have been designed primarily to provide essential links for local commuters, but, inevitably, they also provide important attractions for tourists either wishing to get a different view of a city or planning to visit more remote areas of a country, where convenient links by air may not be possible. Examples of the latter include the Greek islands, the Hebrides off the west coast of Scotland, the Isle of Wight off the south coast of England and crossing the Strait of Messina, between Italy and Sicily.

The key ferry routes for tourists, however, are those that are major links between countries separated by water, such as across the English Channel, between countries in the Baltic Sea, between Corsica and Sardinia and across the Adriatic between Italy, Greece and the Balkan countries. These routes may be vital for those wishing to take their car on holiday, but also provide an attractive alternative to flying for those with time to spare. Additionally, there are many places in the world where transport is dependent on good national ferry services, owing either to the number of islands belonging to the territory or the difficulty of reaching coastal destinations by air or sea. A notable example is the west coast of Norway, where small towns cut off from land routes and air connections depend on the Hurtigruten, or fast route, where daily ferries call at dozens of ports between Bergen and the North Cape. This itinerary has become so popular with tourists that full-size cruise vessels now ply the route. Other popular routes include the west coast of Canada and Alaska and the Hebridean islands off mainland Scotland's western coast.

The significance of the short sea ferry market can be appreciated when it is learned that, by the end of the last century, some 2150 ro–ro (roll-on–roll-off) ferries were estimated to be in operation worldwide and demand shows no signs of slackening. Some 43 million passenger journeys were taken from and to British ports alone in 2007. Of course, not all these passengers will be counted as tourists, which is an important point to remember. Typically, ferry services are designed to provide a communication network for local populations, while taking advantage of visitors to boost numbers and become profitable.

The growth of short sea voyages within Europe during the past two decades can be hailed as a major success story. The rise in demand for ferries over this period can be partly attributed to the general growth of tourism and trade in the region, especially between European Union countries, but the growth of private car ownership and independent travel have also played a significant part in raising demand. France, in particular, has always been a destination with a strong attraction for British holidaymakers travelling independently with their cars, although the relative strength of the pound to the euro is a key factor in influencing demand between the UK and the Continent. There has also been a steady rise in coach transport between Britain and the Continent, as coach companies introduced long-distance coach routes linking London with the capitals and cities of Continental Europe. Despite the challenge offered by the Channel Tunnel linking Britain and France since 1994, Dover remains by far the most important of the ports serving the Continent, with P&O and SeaFrance currently offering cross-Channel services from this port.

Good marketing by the ferry companies has played a part in stimulating traffic over the years. New routes have been developed to tap regional markets and provide greater choice, so passengers have been able to choose to travel to the Continent from a variety of ports along the south coast of England (see Figure 14.6). Not all new routes have proved viable, as price competition attracts tourists to the most popular routes even if they are not the most convenient. The generally high prices charged by ferries out of Kent to the Continent

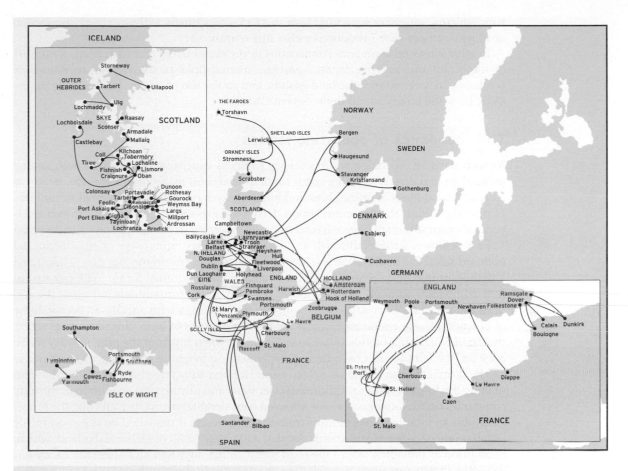

Figure 14.6 The major passenger car ferry services operating from ports in the British Isles. *(Courtesy of Travel Weekly.)*

(claimed to be the highest fares per mile anywhere in the world) were challenged by Danish company Speedferries, which undercut the prices of the established lines operating across the Channel but foundered in the current economic recession. Eurotunnel, too, has slashed prices to attract more passengers to the land link with the Continent.

From Britain, routes can be conveniently grouped into four geographical regions:

- English Channel (short sea crossing) routes, including services from ports such as Ramsgate, Dover, Folkestone and Newhaven
- Western Channel routes, including services from Portsmouth, Southampton, Poole, Weymouth and Plymouth
- North Sea routes, including services from Newcastle/North Shields, Hull, Felixstowe, Harwich and Sheerness
- Irish Sea routes, including services from Swansea, Pembroke, Fishguard, Holyhead, Liverpool, Stranraer, Cairnryan and the Isle of Man.

It should be stressed that, while these have been identified as key ports, services operating out of them do vary from time to time as competition forces out some companies and others attempt to operate new routes in their place. The expectation that a route, once announced, will continue to operate for many years is no longer true. Recent years have seen a number of companies' routes fail, while others have withdrawn services or reverted to alternative ports. Even one of the oldest ferry routes – between Newhaven and Dieppe, with a history of service stretching back to 1825 – was briefly without a ferry connection until new services were introduced earlier this century.

In addition to Britain's ferry connections to the Continental and Irish ports, a number of important smaller ferry services provide internal links to the Hebridean islands of Scotland, the Orkney and Shetland islands, and to the Isle of Wight, the Isle of Man, the Scilly Isles and Lundy Island in the Severn Channel.

The economics of operating ferries

As with cruising, operating short sea ferry routes is expensive, in terms of both capital investment and direct operating costs. Modern ferries on many routes are now nearly as large and sumptuous as cruise ships and building costs can run into hundreds of millions of pounds. Within the European Union, ferries are expected to be written off over a 27-year timespan, although Greece has traditionally operated its ferries for as long as 35 years.

Profitability is achieved through a combination of maximum usage of equipment and onboard sales. The termination in 1999 of duty-free sales within the European Union had a significant impact on cross-Channel revenue – it had accounted for up to 50 per cent of ferry companies' turnover, so ticket prices went up. Rapid turnarounds in port at the end of each journey are essential, as are round-the-clock sailings, with, ideally, an even volume of business all year round and a balanced flow of demand in both directions. In practice, this is, of course, impossible to achieve. In winter, when much of the pure holiday traffic dries up, the ferry services become very dependent on freight to contribute to their costs.

The shorter sailings to France, Belgium and Holland attract much better market demand than do the longer routes to Scandinavia, Germany and northern Spain, although the ferry companies on the latter routes have achieved considerable success in marketing the longer (24 hours or more) sailings as mini-cruises. Their success is modelled on the enormously popular service between Stockholm, Sweden and either Turku or Helsinki, Finland, which, in addition to providing one of the most scenic routes anywhere in Europe for a ferry service, also attracts customers through the sale of relatively cheap onboard drinks in a region where alcohol is prohibitively expensive. As a result, the ferry market between these two countries has grown to a point where the two major carriers, Silja Line and Viking Line, can support a string of superferries, the largest of which, at 60,000 tons, is capable of carrying in excess of 3000 passengers (see Figure 14.7). By including a stop at the Finnish-owned Åland Islands, which have special status within the European Community, duty-free goods can continue to be sold on board these vessels, which has maintained their popularity with the short-break market.

Off-peak sailings on shorter routes can be boosted by low fares, aiming a wide range of discounted prices at differing market segments. Quick round trips on the same vessel or short stopovers of one to three nights have expanded, while shopping expeditions to the French hypermarkets for food and alcohol prove popular, especially in the run-up to Christmas. While the termination of duty-free goods on these routes cut the market for short trips to France initially, the removal of customs barriers on duty-paid goods within the European Union and the relatively low cost of duty-paid alcoholic drinks in France compared with Britain has helped to boost sales on cross-Channel vessels.

At extreme off-peak periods and for night sailings, which attract fewer bookings, some ferry companies will price their sailings to make a contribution to fixed costs rather than cover all costs on every crossing. Low fares will stimulate onboard spend, making a useful contribution to total revenues. The ferry companies have increased their general shopping facilities in their newer ships in order to boost duty-paid sales. While this has not fully made up for the loss of the duty-free revenue, it has helped to reduce the impact of the withdrawal of this facility.

Leading ferry companies have made strenuous efforts to cut their operating costs in recent years, particularly their labour costs. New labour practices were introduced to

Figure 14.7 The superferry: Silja Line's *Silja Symphony* at Helsinki.
(Photo by Chris Holloway.)

increase the efficiency of crewing, but only after serious confrontations with the seamen's union. As with cruising, many staff from developing countries are now taken on. At the same time, the Safety of Life at Sea (SOLAS) regulations, which came into effect at the end of 2004 following the Stockholm Agreement signed in 1997 between Great Britain and six northern European countries, have substantially added to building costs.

The objective of these regulations was to increase the safety and stability of ro–ro ferries following the *Herald of Free Enterprise* disaster, when it sank at Zeebrugge in 1987 and nearly 200 people died, and the subsequent sinking of the ferry *Estonia* in the Baltic in 1994, with the loss of 850 lives. The Stockholm Agreement requires vessels operating in to and out of ports in the seven countries to be capable of remaining upright in waves up to 4 metres high and with 50 centimetres of floodwater on the car deck. It called for transverse bulkheads to be fitted on all ships to improve stability in rough seas, but these obligatory modifications can reduce car capacity and slow down the loading and unloading of vessels, leading to delays in turnarounds.

One study, by the DK Group, found that the global shipping industry wastes almost three million barrels of oil daily as a result of ageing vessels not having been upgraded with fuel-saving technology and, certainly, the global ferry market has made a contribution to this wastage. The research suggests that upgrading vessels by fitting new propellers and engines and installing new technology could reduce global marine fuel consumption by as much as 40 per cent.

The Channel Tunnel and ferry services

The Channel Tunnel was viewed initially as the single greatest threat to cross-Channel ferries since their inception. Opened to passenger traffic in 1994, the Tunnel has attracted the lion's share of the cross-Channel market, but has failed to drive the ferries out of business. In recent years it has even come close to financial collapse itself, due to the huge burden of capital debts it bears. The background to this problem is described more fully in Chapter 15, but here we will take account of the impact of this land link on ferry services.

Groupe Eurotunnel, which operates the Channel Tunnel, suffered a number of setbacks in building and operating the Tunnel, including repeated delays in opening, delays in obtaining equipment to run through the Tunnel and a disastrous and costly fire in a freight wagon at the end of 1996. Eurotunnel's original estimates of passenger numbers proved wildly optimistic, but, nonetheless, the company achieved a 51 per cent share of the Dover Straits traffic (Dover/Folkestone to Calais/Boulogne) within its first five years of operation. Eurostar, which offers rail connections between London, Lille, Paris and Brussels via the Tunnel, has also been successful in diverting a substantial number of air travellers back to rail between these destinations.

The ferries were quick to retaliate. P&O and Stena invested heavily in their short sea operations and merged their services on the route between Dover and Calais, following investigation by the Monopolies and Mergers Commission (now the Competition Commission). Improvements in passenger-handling facilities at Dover were introduced, allowing passengers to check in just 20 minutes before sailing. A 'turn up and go' service obviated the need for reservations, while, curiously, Eurotunnel itself withdrew this same benefit, obliging its passengers to hold a reservation before arrival at the terminal. New, faster ferries were introduced, with the travel time between Dover and Calais reduced from 90 minutes to 75 minutes. The emphasis of its marketing shifted, selling the crossing as part of a holiday, with time to relax and unwind on board. The Tunnel was disparaged as offering no more than 'a toilet and a light bulb'. Larger, more luxurious ships on the route helped reinforce the concept of a mini-cruise, with the result that the short sea routes have held up well, although the other longer routes suffered badly from the competition.

On the medium-distance crossings, a new generation of fast ships and catamarans came onstream. This resulted in the crossing time from Portsmouth to Cherbourg, for example, being reduced from 5 hours to 2 hours 45 minutes.

The problem for the ferry services is attracting sufficient trade during the winter months, when the Tunnel is seen by many passengers as preferable to a rough sea crossing, even if it is only 75 minutes long. By 2007, Eurotunnel appeared to be establishing itself more securely in the market, and, in that year, carried a total of 2,142,000 cars, representing 43 per cent of the market, with a further 65,000 coaches.

New modes of crossing

Alongside the introduction of the new fast ferries, alternative and still faster forms of water transport have become popular on many short- and medium-range routes. First hovercraft, then hydrofoils and, finally, catamarans, entered service, with the benefits of speed and a certain degree of novelty.

Hovercraft were used to initiate the first fast ferry crossings across the Channel as early as 1968. They offered several advantages over the traditional ferries. Riding on a cushion of air just above the surface of the water and able to travel over land as well as water, they avoided the usual capital costs associated with dock facilities, as the craft could simply be beached on any convenient and obstacle-free foreshore. Unfortunately, they also offered their passengers a somewhat bouncy and noisy ride by comparison with the more traditional ferries and could not operate in seas with waves greater than 2.5 metres. The vessels also suffered many technical problems in their development and throughout the years of their operation, so were finally withdrawn from service in 2000, being replaced by catamarans.

The hydrofoil offers better prospects for future development, even though it, too, suffered initial teething problems. This vessel operates with a conventional hull design, but, when travelling at speed, the hull is raised above the surface of the water on blades, or, 'foils'. This enables the vessel to travel at speeds of up to 60 knots. Recent models have been powered by jet engines (jetfoils), but their unreliability on open waters and inability to contend with high waves have hindered their adoption in British waters.

The most promising recent development in ferry operations has been the high-speed, wave-piercing catamaran (WPC). These have been operating on cross-Channel services since 1991 and have now replaced the hovercraft.

They are mainly twin-hulled vessels, large enough to accommodate cars, travelling at speeds of up to 40 knots. This type of vessel has now proved reliable in most weathers, operating successfully from Britain to Ireland and the Continent, as well as on key routes such as Dover–Calais and Harwich–Hook of Holland. Catamarans have also proved popular on routes across the Baltic Sea and other key European routes.

The popular Seacats (twin-hull) and Superseacats (monohull) offer a valuable service for passengers wanting the fastest possible crossing to the Continent but who might find the Channel Tunnel claustrophobic. The latest HSS (high-speed sea service) twin-hull ferries introduced by Stena have further stretched capacity, carrying up to 1500 passengers and 375 cars.

The downside, however, is the higher fuel burn of all these craft and some constraints still remain on their operation in rough weather – waves above 4 metres can lead to can cellations, which is a serious constraint in the winter months. What is becoming clear, however, is that, for a great many holidaymakers, the trend is to choose faster surface vessels that can compete with the Tunnel on time.

While the escalation in oil prices has had a major impact on all ferry operations since 2008, with many companies imposing a surcharge to meet rising fuel costs, the fast HSS catamarans have been hardest hit. They consume twice as much fuel as conventional ferries and their fuel, similar to aviation jet fuel, costs double that of standard marine fuel. As a result, Stena Line took the decision to extend its crossing times on some routes from the UK, reducing fuel consumption by 8 per cent. Whether these catamarans have a long-term future is questionable at this point, as long as oil prices remain high. Some HSSs are already being laid up and are to be replaced by more traditional vessels.

With growing concern over fuel prices, alternative forms of energy for marine vessels are receiving attention. One interesting development is that of the *Solar Sailor* – a 100-passenger catamaran ferry that went into service in Sydney Harbour in 2000. This vessel operates with solar and wind power, with a back-up electric motor running from batteries that store the energy the craft collects while running on the alternative energy sources. It is silent, smooth, creates no pollution whatsoever and its photocells are boosted 20 per cent by the sun's reflection in the water. A similar vessel equipped with solar panels, the *Helio*, is in operation as a ferry on Lake Constance between Germany and Switzerland, while other 12-passenger vessels operate excursion trips on Loch Lomond and the Norfolk Broads in Britain. Further developments in this form of vessel may well encourage its operation across the Channel.

The future of ferry operations

Work on still more advanced vessels is under way. In France, a quadrimaran, operating on four hulls, offering a much smoother ride, has been under development since the early 1990s and been tested successfully in the Caribbean, while a five-hulled pentamaran is also being tested at the time of writing. Capable of speeds in excess of 40 knots, these vessels are seen primarily as freight carriers, but they have the potential to be developed later as passenger carriers, particularly for short sea crossings.

Foil catamarans – a hybrid of the jetfoil and hovercraft – have also been tested to pro-totype stage. Capable of speeds of 30–40 knots, their low resistance in the water leads to 30 per cent greater fuel efficiency, so they would make a very useful contribution in the competitive UK ferry market – depending on their relative fuel burn and oil prices. Many existing fast ferries seem to be at a disadvantage in terms of fuel burn compared with more traditional ferries and some are being withdrawn as fuel prices escalate so such develop-ments are timely.

Yet another form of fast ferry, the Hoverplane, combines elements of catamaran, hovercraft and wing-in-surface-effect (WISE) in its design. 'Wingboats' built on the WISE principle operate by generating a stable cushion of air under the wing as the craft 'flies' close to ground or water. By travelling on this dense layer of air, the craft benefits from reduced drag and increased lift, thus achieving high levels of fuel economy. Exceptionally high speeds are anticipated at one-fifth of the normal fuel cost of a ferry, which should enable prices to be much lower than at present. It is expected that these craft, in their initial development, should be capable of carrying between 80 and 150 passengers over distances of up to 250 miles. An added advantage of such a vessel is that it requires neither runway nor port in the accepted sense of the words. The *Aéroptère* is one such vessel currently under development by the shipbuilding industry in France, with the support of the French government. This is a four-engine craft said to be capable of speeds up to 100 knots. Extremely fuel-efficient, it is thought to be ideal for short sea ferry routes. Prototypes could be tested as early as 2009.

More sustainable options are likely to be developed through solar-assisted power, but this form of energy is likely to be restricted to quite small ferries similar to that already operating in Sydney harbour.

Other European ferry operations

While the focus here has been primarily on connections between the UK and its Continental neighbours, the continuing importance of other routes, especially within Europe, must be recognized. In the Mediterranean, ferries provide not only vital connections to travellers on a port-to-port basis, but also the opportunity to package these routes as mini-cruises, calling at a variety of different countries. By way of example, services are available in the eastern Mediterranean between Venice, Dubrovnik, Piraeus, Iraklion and Alexandria or between Istanbul, Piraeus, Larnaca, Lattakia (Syria) and Alexandria. Other important routes include those between Patras (Greece) and Ascona (Italy) and between Nice and Corsica. Tourists who traditionally think only of travelling by air to Majorca may be unaware of the alternatives – travelling from Barcelona by catamaran with Trasmediterranea.

Figure 14.8 Trasmediterranea's *Juan Sister* operates between Cadiz and the Canary Islands.
(Photo by Chris Holloway.)

The Greek economy is heavily dependent on its shipping interests, with some 10 million passengers using ferries within the country each year. The significance of this area of the economy to Greece was such that EU cabotage restrictions were permitted to remain in place until 2004. The disastrous sinking of the poorly maintained and elderly ferry *Express Samina* in 2000, however, led the Greek government to withdraw the licences of some older vessels and bring deregulation forward by two years. Vessels from other countries are now allowed to operate freely in Greek waters (although few have taken up this challenge to date). This has spurred Greek shipowners to invest heavily in new equipment, as well as expanding their own activities outside the country. For example, the Greek Superfast Ferries – offering the first direct service between Scotland and the Continent – have been in operation between Rosyth and Zeebrugge since 2002.

Ferry operations in the Baltic call for special mention. Services here connect the Scandinavian countries and, in turn, provide vital connections for travellers between these countries and Germany. Independence for the three Baltic states of Latvia, Estonia and Lithuania, the entry of these countries into the European Union, the rebuilding of the historic port of Gdansk (formerly Danzig) in Poland and the reunification of Germany have all renewed interest in these destinations for tourists and both cruise ships and ferry crossings have achieved considerable growth in this area. The benefit of having St Petersburg in Russia as a major port in the Baltic has further stimulated interest in the region. With the enormous popularity of Tallinn as a tourist venue since EU accession and the short ferry journey between Helsinki and Tallinn – just 1 hour and 40 minutes by fast ferry – it has become a key route in the Baltic. It provides tourists with the opportunity for an attractive mini-cruise, coupled with bargain-priced shopping. Reference has already been made to the equally popular route between Stockholm and Helsinki. An overnight sailing can be treated as a mini-cruise, the 60,000-ton superferries carrying up to 2800 passengers at a time. The obvious success in this region of selling what were originally merely transport connections as luxury mini-cruises has established a trend that other ferry operators are keen to emulate.

Coastal and inland waterways tourism

The attraction of water offers many other opportunities for tourist activity, both independently and in forms that have been commoditized and packaged for visitors. Inland waterways – in particular, lakes, rivers and canals – provide exceptional opportunities for recreation and tourism and, in Britain, the renovation of former canals, derelict locks and similar watersites has added in recent years to the many opportunities for river and lake recreational travel.

The major waterways of the world have long attracted tourists. The Nile River in Egypt has provided inland waterway cruising for many decades and, in recent years, the popularity of this stretch of waterway led to an enormous expansion in the number and size of cruise ships operating as part of package holidays up to the early years of the 1990s. The volatility of the tourism business is well illustrated by the collapse of the Egyptian inland cruise market in the mid-1990s, when the country was hit first by terrorism in which tourists were targeted explicitly, and then drought, which caused navigational difficulties in the upper Nile region. In 2000, the Nile came back into favour briefly, until the advent of 9/11 and then the Iraqi war once again discouraged tourists from travelling to the Middle East.

Popular European river cruises include the Rhine/Danube (between Amsterdam, Holland and Passau in Germany, thence to Constanta in Romania), the Douro in Portugal and the French rivers Seine and Rhone. Elsewhere, rivers with strong tourist appeal include the Mississippi in the USA (where traditional paddle steamers offer a nostalgic cruise experience) and the Yangtze and Li Rivers in China, while the Volga and Russian waterways linking St Petersburg with Moscow, the Italian River Po and the German Elbe are all

Figure 14.9 The *Balmoral* operates excursions to ports along the coast in Western England during the summer.
(Photo by Chris Holloway.)

increasing in popularity. The Guadalquivir River in Spain allows small passenger craft to travel from the port of Cadiz as far inland as Seville and this has become one of the more recent innovations in river cruising. In South America, the Amazon River is sufficiently large to allow ocean-going ships to navigate as far inland as Iquitos in Peru. All of these river journeys have been packaged as tours and sold to tourists throughout the world.

Public craft are employed on coastal trips as well as on inland waterways. The popular excursion boats *Waverley* – one of the few remaining paddle steamers in the world – and *Balmoral* (see Figure 14.9) carry tourists on trips along the coast in Britain during the summer from ports in Scotland, South Wales and the West Country.

Others travel across the Scottish lochs and along the Caledonian Canal. The lakes steamer remains a familiar sight in many parts of the world, providing an important tourist attraction in the US and Canadian Great Lakes, the Swiss and south German lakes, the islands of southern Sweden around Stockholm and the Scottish lochs and English Lake District in Britain. Many of these are elderly craft that have been restored and are kept in tiptop condition because of their appeal to tourists. The Swiss, for instance, have recently restored their classic (1909 built) *Stadt Rapperswil* and *Stadt Zürich* operating on the Zürichsee (see Figure 14.10), while the Bodensee (Lake Constance) has 34 lakes steamers owned by five different companies operating between the ports of Germany, Switzerland and Austria. Both these lakes employ steamers essentially as regular transport for residents, but, because of their appeal as iconic tourist symbols, they are just as important to tourism as are the famous red double-decker buses of London.

It is the growing attraction of rivers and canals for the independent boating enthusiast that perhaps holds the greatest potential for development over the next few years. The networks of rivers and canals in countries such as Britain, Holland and France have been redeveloped and exploited for tourism and canals such as the Burgundy canals and the

Figure 14.10 A lakes steamer on the Zürichsee, Switzerland.
(Photo by Chris Holloway.)

Canal du Midi in the South of France, as well as the Gota Canal in Sweden, are being discovered by British tourists in growing numbers.

Example

Sea kayaking

Very small boats are often the only means of observing some stretches of coastline. In Greenland, for example, small boats can take visitors along virtually untouched stretches of coast and fishing vessels all over the world are often used as means by which passengers can be carried to isolated coves and bays for unique experiences in bathing or diving. Operators are recognizing the opportunities for niche water-based holidays, developing kayak holidays in such inaccessible regions as the Canadian Yukon, while, in Europe, kayaking holidays along the Catalonian coast in Spain (**www.funtastic-emporda.com**) provide adventurous holidaymakers with a chance to see coastlines accessible only by water.

Britain itself is particularly well endowed with canals and rivers suitable for navigation. In the mid-1800s, the nation could boast of some 4250 miles of navigable inland waterways, many of which had been developed for the movement of freight. As these became redundant with the advent of the railways, they fell into disrepair until many stretches became no longer navigable. In recent years, however, British Waterways (BW) has encouraged the development and use of these waterways for pleasure purposes and, in partnership with private enterprise, aided by voluntary bodies, it has helped to restore and reopen many formerly derelict canals.

Today, some 2200 miles of navigable British waterways are open and maintained by BW (see Figures 14.11 and 14.12) and the Board licenses 25,000 boats to use its network. In 2007, more than 450,000 canal boat holidays were taken in the UK and 31,000 narrowboats

Figure 14.11 A narrowboat enters a lock at Bingley, West Yorkshire.
(Photo by Chris Holloway.)

were in service on the canals. The Board revealed in the same year that more than 11 million tourists used the canal towpaths for recreational purposes, whether for angling, walking or cycling. Although it is a public body currently financed by annual grants from the Department for Environment, Food and Rural Affairs (DEFRA), the Board, at the time of writing, is seeking greater commercial freedom and may be sold off by the government.

Example

Will BW's UK canal network continue to prosper?

In 2005, British Waterways was awarded funding amounting to £575,000 by the South West RDA to conduct feasibility studies into the reopening of six miles of the Cotswolds Canal. Once completed, it was hoped that further funding from the RDA and the Heritage Lottery Fund would allow this important stretch of water to reopen, conserving 30 historic structures and creating multiuser trails. The total cost would amount to some £25 million, but the reopened canal was expected to generate 1200 new jobs and attract 215,000 extra visitors annually to the area around Stroud, acting as a catalyst for the redevelopment of the entire area. At the time of writing, however, the Board has decided to postpone further development in the Cotswolds that would have linked the Severn with the Thames, owing to pressures on funding and other priorities for the canal network. The local authorities are unwilling to consider further investment without partnership support, to the disappointment of many inland waterways enthusiasts. Nevertheless, in the previous decade, over 200 miles of new or restored canals have become available for water-borne transport in the UK.

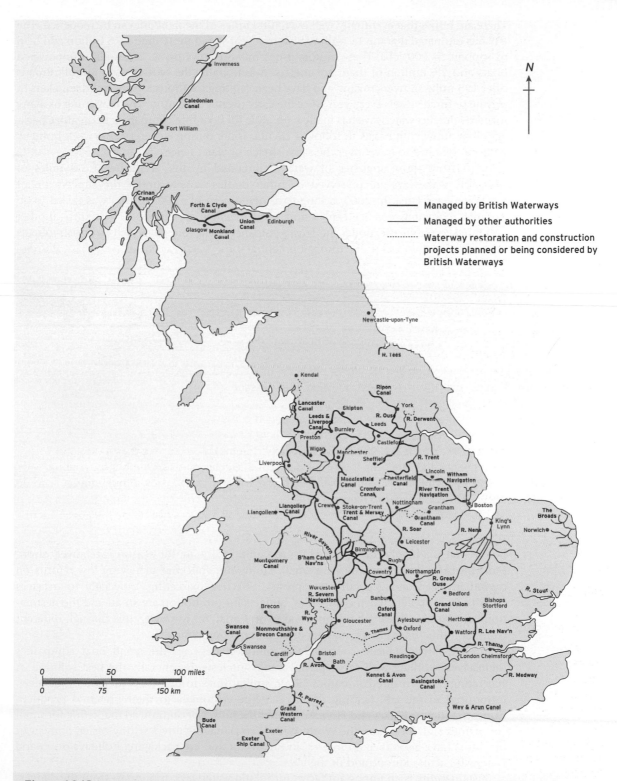

Figure 14.12 The inland waterways of Britain.
(Courtesy of British Waterways.)

There are hopes that eventually well over 4000 miles of the network can be reopened. The BW has estimated that the 11 million visitors a year spend more than £1.5 billion and help to support 54,000 jobs. These visitors use 2 million powerboats, 1.5 million unpowered boats and 2.6 million of them are anglers. Additionally, the Norfolk and Suffolk Broads offer 125 miles of river cruising and have been catering for thousands of holidaymakers in private or hired vessels every year since the early twentieth century. The reopening of many formerly derelict waterways has made it possible for boat hire companies to organize packages that allow enthusiasts to follow a circular route during a one- or two-week holiday, without the need to travel over the same stretch of water twice.

Apart from those stretches of water maintained by BW, a further 1250 miles of navigable waterways are preserved by other bodies, largely under the supervision of the Waterways Trust. In 2002, a long-term investment of £500 million was raised to go towards reopening derelict canals and nine schemes are in place to return another 300 miles to public use, under the Trust's guidance. Now foreign as well as British tourists are becoming attracted to the tourism potential these waterways offer.

Example

The Kennet and Avon Canal

The Kennet and Avon Canal stretches 87 miles between Bristol and Reading, where it joins the River Thames, allowing the passage of narrowboats and other small craft right across England.

After many years of voluntary labour, the canal was reopened in 1990 and further improvements were made in 2002 to the long flight of locks at Caen Hill, Devizes, to overcome leaks. The reopening supports employment for around 2600 people and produces a yearly income of £28 million. One estimate gives the investment in commercial development along this waterway between 1995 and 2003 as £350 million.

Boat rental is a highly competitive business and, in Britain, the season is relatively short. Most pleasure boat companies are small, family-run concerns, achieving low returns on capital invested and generally low profits. Effective marketing, especially to overseas tourists, is a problem when companies' budgets for promotion are small and the destination being sold is linear (the Kennet and Avon Canal, for instance, runs through different regional tourist board areas, making unified marketing difficult).

In such circumstances, cooperative promotion between the small boat companies themselves, working with other private-sector interests, is generally the best solution. A star rating for boat hire companies, along similar lines to that used for hotels, has been introduced in the UK, helping direct boat hire customers to their preferred products. Consortia such as Blakes and Hoseasons offer the power of centralized marketing for small companies and, for others, the World Wide Web is making direct selling easier. Some tour operators have also taken an interest in this sector and are packaging holidays on inland waterways across Europe and in the USA.

Sustainability is an important factor for inland waterways, too. Apart from the dangers of pollution from fuel and oil leaks in sensitive freshwater areas, the erosion of riverbanks caused by powerboats and sheer congestion on popular stretches of waterway create additional problems. The introduction of solar-assisted boats on the Norfolk Broads, mentioned above, may help, in time, to reduce the impact of private boats on this most environmentally sensitive region.

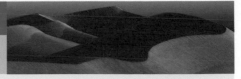

Example

Chemicals used in boat cleaning can harm sensitive water sites

The chemical tributyltin (TBT) is an anti-fouling composite that was commonly used by boatowners to prevent barnacles growing on the hulls of their boats. While this helped to reduce maintenance costs, it was found that, over time, it had a deleterious effect on plant life in the Norfolk Broads and has been responsible for destroying almost 90 per cent of the plants with which it comes into contact.

Although banned in 1987 in the UK, residues are still present in the sediment, leading to contamination when dredging takes place to provide adequate clearance for tourist boats. The chemical is still in use in many countries, including along the Ganges, Yangtse and Brahmaputra rivers.

Watersite development

In a similar fashion, the closure and subsequent dereliction of many of Britain's major docklands has offered another opportunity for redevelopment of these sites for recreation and tourism. Although primarily a consequence of urban redevelopment policy, the restoration of waterfront properties in sites such as the Cardiff and Brighton marinas, Bristol's Historic Floating Harbour, Salford Quays, Liverpool's Albert Docks, Southampton's Ocean Village and, of course, London's Docklands has, in turn, generated tourism to these sites, following the construction of their marinas and the subsequent introduction of attractions such as waterbuses and ferries, scenic cruises, floating restaurants and other leisure facilities. Lottery and millennium funding in Britain has spurred the redevelopment of previously derelict canals, notably in Birmingham and Manchester, where disused waterways edged by derelict warehouses have become smart residential communities, well supplied with restaurants and other leisure facilities. These sites are now linked by waterbuses and have become popular places for tourists to visit.

Similar developments have also taken place abroad, especially within the USA and Canada. The astonishing success of Baltimore's Inner Harbor development sparked off similar schemes in New York, San Francisco, Boston and Toronto, all of which now attract tourists in large numbers. In Europe, Stockholm and Oslo have both restored their decaying harbour sites. Sydney's Darling Harbour and the Victoria and Alfred waterfront in Cape Town, South Africa, have, likewise, been the subject of extensive renovation, making these areas honey pots for tourism (see Figure 9.5). While most of these sites have of course been planned for multiple use, including shops, offices and residential communities, the leisure use of the sites will inevitably attract tourists and generate additional income for the cities concerned.

Seagoing pleasure craft

This chapter would not be complete without some mention of the growing demand for holidays aboard seagoing pleasure craft – a demand that is now being met by the travel industry. It has been estimated that there are more than 400,000 boatowners in Britain and some 2 million people sail for pleasure. This is naturally leading to people wanting institutionalized boating holidays. Specialist operators and hire companies are now offering package holidays aboard small chartered sailing ships or steamboats, with facilities ranging from the luxurious, where the passengers are guests, to the more basic, where passengers play an active part in crewing the boat. Tour operators also cater for this growing demand for boating holidays with flotilla cruising holidays, especially in areas where there are many small islands where sheltered anchorage and fair weather conditions can be found. The Greek islands and certain Caribbean islands, such as the Windward and Leeward groups, offer ideal conditions for these types of packages, in which individually hired yachts sail together in flotilla formation from island to island. In this manner, tourists have the benefits of independent use of the yacht while also enjoying the social life of the group when together at anchor.

A phenomenon of the early twenty-first century has been the rapid expansion in ownership of superyachts around the world. These are categorized as vessels exceeding 30 metres in length and it has been estimated that 3706 such vessels were in service or on order in 2008 – 253 of them were delivered to their owners in 2007 alone.[5] There is a substantial economic benefit to ports harbouring these vessels, including mooring fees, labour, maintenance and leisure spend ashore by owners and their guests, although estimates have yet to be made of the contribution this business makes to the local economies.

As with much larger ships, fractional ownership is now emerging as a new means of owning leisure craft for holidays. Luxury yachts cost many millions and require expensive upkeep, but owning a *share* of one will cost only a fraction of the price and enable the owner to buy one or more weeks each year to enjoy holidays on board a luxury yacht with a full crew. One company, for example, offers a one-eighth stake in a £7 million yacht and owners may rent out some or all of their weeks to earn income.

What does the future hold for passenger ships?

Research is under way on more advanced forms of sea transport. This currently focuses on designs for more fuel-efficient craft. Successful sea trials have taken place with vessels that complement the use of their engines with metal sails, increasing the overall speed while reducing costs – an important consideration at a time when fuel costs are rising sharply. The appeal of cruise ships that resemble floating hotels with a full range of leisure facilities is leading to the construction of ever-larger vessels. Proposals have been advanced for much larger catamarans and trimarans (twin-hulled and triple-hulled vessels), capable of transporting large numbers of passengers at high speed and in far more comfort, without the customary problems of motion sickness experienced in single-hull ships. Such vessels might be constructed to cross the Atlantic in under 48 hours.

Japan is carrying out research on the use of electromagnetic thrusters for ships. Toshiba has designed a 150-ton vessel that is pushed through the water by the effect of counteracting magnets. This could lead to the development of vessels of much larger size. Sustainable transport development at sea is evident in the Solar Sailor ferry already in operation in Sydney, described earlier in this chapter.

The longer-term future of the shipping industry may be boosted by new marine technology now under development, such as the SES-200 Surface Effect Ship, which rides above the surface of the sea, or superconducting electromagnetic propulsion vessels that have been tested in Japan and offer potential speeds of above 100 knots. Waterjet propulsion is also being tested for a new breed of container ship. The proposed 'Fastship', using a semi-planing monohull, is expected to be capable of speeds exceeding 40 knots and may be adaptable later for cruise vessels. Such developments could further encourage the reintroduction of line voyages between major ports in the world, although this is unlikely to occur in the near future.

Sadly, none of these concepts appears to be likely to enter service in the immediate future, but over a 10 to 20-year cycle, the possibilities of this happening could rise dramatically.

Notes

1. Richardson, S. (2007) 'Cruise tourism: one of the fastest-growing sectors', *Tourism Society Journal*, 3 (133), Autumn, p. 14.
2. Kane, Frank (2005) 'On the good ship Carnival', *Observer Business*, 27 February, p. 16.
3. Malvern, J. (2008) 'Time to look elsewhere this year', *The Times*, travel section, 26 April.
4. 'The dirty truth', *Travel Weekly*, 8 September 2006.
5. Evans, M. (2008) 'Got the superyacht with swimming pool, helipad, minisub and missiles?', *The Times*, 1 March, p. 37.

Further reading

Chin, C. B. N. (2008) *Cruising in the Global Economy: Profits, pleasure and work at sea*, Ashgate.

Dickinson, B. and Vladimir, A. (1997) *Selling the Sea: An inside look at the cruise industry*, John Wiley and Sons.

Websites

Alternative Holidays	www.alternative-holidays.com
Atlantis Events	www.atlantisevents.com
British Waterways	www.britishwaterways.co.uk
Cruises	www.discover-cruises.co.uk
	www.cruise-network.com
	www.cruising.org
Department for Transport	www.dft.gov.uk
Inland Waterways Association	www.waterways.org.uk
Just You	www.justyou.co.uk
Olivia	www.olivia.com
Passenger Shipping Association (PSA) statistics	www.the-psa-co.uk
RMS St Helena	www.rms-st-helena.com
RSVP	www.rsvpvacations.com
Seatrade magazine	www.seatrade-global.com
Staten Island Ferry	www.siferry.com
Waterwayholidaysuk.com	www.waterwayholidaysuk.com
World Shipping Council	www.worldshipping.org

Questions and discussion points

1. What impact have the 2008 oil price rises had on the cruising business to date and how will they affect the long-term market for cruising?

2. This chapter explains the reasons for the death of line voyages in most parts of the world (apart from transatlantic services) in the mid-twentieth century. Some 40 years ago, however, similar views were being expressed about the future of the cruising industry, which has since bounced back. Could line voyages be revived? If so, where?

3. What markets are likely to be attracted to travel on cargo ships? What about river cruising? Explain the reasons for your opinions.

4. Examine the merits of travel in one of the new super-cruise vessels carrying 3000 or more passengers, versus cruises on small, yacht-like vessels with fewer than 100 passengers.

5. Dubai has recently become an important cruise base. Examine the appeal of the region for cruising.

6. Why do you think it is that no major airlines any longer invest in passenger shipping, neither do cruise companies invest in airlines?

Tasks

1. As marketing manager for a specialist upmarket cruise operator, you have been asked to determine your distribution strategy for the carrier. Examine alternative means of distributing your products, citing the pros and cons of direct marketing, selling through retail agents, wholesaling through operators or other intermediaries and determine how you will organize your distribution.

2. Review the websites of two contrasting companies marketing cruises – one an upmarket company, such as Seabourn, another aimed at the more budget end of the market, such as Island Cruises – and evaluate the effectiveness of the two sites in attracting bookings and promoting the products. How do the approaches differ in each case?

3. Some cruise companies include tips in their prices, while others prefer to leave it to passengers to determine the level of tips. An alternative approach is that of Norwegian Cruise Lines, which adds a fixed per diem charge to customers' bills for service, but also suggests that additional discretionary cash gratuities can be paid for exceptional service. Examine the pros and cons of each approach and select one for your own (midmarket) cruise company, giving reasons.

Chapter 15

Tourist transport on land

Learning outcomes

After studying this chapter, you should be able to:

- understand the role and scope of railways and their place in tourist travel

- be aware of the role and significance of the coach industry in tourism

- recognize the importance of the private car to tourist travel

- understand the role of car hire in domestic and foreign tourism

- be aware of the growing importance of tourist travel by bicycle and on foot.

The role of the railways in tourism

The train made modern Britain and the railways are carved into the national imagination just as they lattice the landscape.

Ben Macintyre, 'You were fast asleep at Crewe', *The Times*, 16 September 2005

Given the length of time that railways have been a part of the public transport system, it may be thought surprising that they have been so slow to take advantage of the growth of mass market tourism that followed World War II (1939–1945). It is all the more surprising when one considers the important role played by the railways in their 100 years of existence up to that point, at a time when rail transport was the principal means by which people took their annual holidays, travelling either to the coasts of their own countries or across the face of Europe to the Mediterranean. Rail transport's decline in popularity paralleled the rise in ownership of private cars, and rail companies appeared content to focus on what they saw as their prime markets – commuters and business travellers – and, of course, freight. Even before the outbreak of war, the decline in tourist travel by rail had been noticeable and the process only accelerated in Britain after 1947, when the railways were nationalized.

Improvements in coach transport, as public road vehicles become more comfortable, faster and more reliable, and the significant gap in price between road and rail encouraged those without private vehicles to switch to road transport for their holidays, while the better-off made increasing use of their private cars. A similar pattern occurred in the USA, where the switch was to domestic air travel alongside the growth in private car usage.

Instead of fighting back, the railways retrenched, cutting services and routes and concentrating on the main intercity routes. The US railway companies switched their focus to more remunerative freight, with passenger services largely restricted to a handful of well-established intercity routes – a strategy that continues to this day, despite the formation of Amtrak as a public service railroad system, with government subsidies to encourage regeneration of the rail services.

Unprofitable branch lines were closed, especially in Britain following the Beeching Report in the 1960s, and, as a result, many smaller UK coastal resorts and other rural destinations that attracted tourists became inaccessible by rail. The alternative of coach services linking with rail termini made tourist travel inconvenient and time-consuming and this, coupled with continuing disparities in fares and the relative decline in the cost of car travel, soon made the railways an unattractive choice for many destinations.

Privatization of the railways in Britain in the late twentieth century, which resulted in higher fares and inferior service, and the previous long-term lack of investment in track and signalling under public ownership, all made rail travel still less attractive for tourists. This was in contrast to developments on the Continent, where investment in high-speed rail over the past two decades has brought many tourists back on to the trains.

Rail travel cannot be dismissed as no longer important to tourism, and within Europe the rail companies themselves are now actively pursuing tourist markets over distances of up to 500 miles and in some instances further, in open competition with the airlines. Improvements in rail services within the UK are gradually enabling the railways to win back tourists from air and from other surface transport, aided by growing road congestion and crowded airports.

Some services in the UK remain popular, transporting domestic tourists from the major conurbations to key English resorts such as Brighton, Bournemouth and Torquay. Faster services combining Eurostar services from London with the high-speed network on the Continent are attracting British tourists not just to Paris and Brussels but also other popular tourist destinations such as Cologne, Lille and even the Côte d'Azur in the summer, while special through services are operated to the French ski resorts in winter.

Sharp fuel price increases, such as those that occurred in the 1970s and again since the beginning of the current century, have also helped to win back some domestic tourists from private car travel. Rail companies have become more marketing-orientated, often partnering specialist tour operators to target tourists. Rail and hotel packages in Britain have proved popular for the short break market, particularly to London and capital cities on the Continent. Efforts to entice rail travel enthusiasts have also met with some success, even though this is on a limited scale. Nostalgic day trips and excursions using old steam engines are popular, as are packages aimed at the over-fifty-fives. Recognizing that unsold off-peak seats represent substantial lost revenue, the railways have used variable pricing policies and promotions, sometimes in cooperation with well-known retail stores, to attract tourists and excursionists back to the railways.

Tickets offering unlimited travel by train, sold to inbound tourists only before their departure from their own countries, are yet another means of boosting rail travel. These include the Britrail pass within Britain and Eurailpass on the Continental mainland, while a Scanrail pass provides unlimited travel within the Nordic countries, coupled with a 50 per cent reduction on interconnecting ferry services. Such schemes are aimed at tourists, particularly those from America and Australia visiting Europe independently or on tailor-made itineraries, and appeal to the young backpacker market. Similar Railpass schemes are on offer on Amtrak services in the USA, and in Australia, although the distances involved, some less than adequate services and budget transcontinental air fares make rail travel in these countries less attractive to tourists.

The privatization of rail transport in the UK

Towards the end of the twentieth century, it became clear that action would have to be taken to improve the railway systems, both in Europe and North America. Heavily subsidized and lacking adequate investment over many years, railways were in a parlous state. Two alternatives presented themselves: either the state could move railways out of public ownership or it could agree to a programme of massive state investment to increase the appeal of the railways as a form of public transport.

In Britain, the Conservative government then in power took the decision to denationalize the railways. Private companies were to be allowed to bid to run parts of the British Rail system, while the maintenance and operation of all track, signalling and stations were to be hived off to a separate company called Railtrack. The government's belief was that a privatized railway system would become more efficient, ending the drain on government funds through subsidies, and competing more effectively with other forms of transport through new private investment that would attract travellers back to the railways. Privatization was initiated in 1993 and, by early 1997, 25 train-operating units in the UK had replaced the former monolithic rail system and a further three companies were formed to control rolling-stock.

While passenger traffic did increase on most services, partly as a result of better marketing, passengers became confused about the range of choice and fares facing them and journeys involving the services of more than one rail company became more complex. Competition between the rail companies led to passengers not being fully informed about the range of services available or the cheapest fares for their itineraries. Concern rose over the lack of promised investment by the rail companies and the impact of cost-cutting by some companies in order to boost profits, which, in some instances, led to safety violations and even accidents. Some disastrous mishaps arising from broken rails forced Railtrack into expensive investment in updating track and signals, severely disrupting mainline services. Distribution systems for rail tickets also suffered. Travel agents were already abandoning the sale of rail tickets as unprofitable before the advent of privatization and this was hastened by the additional complexities of dealing with a score of different rail companies.

The rail companies have been less innovative in seeking improvements in their distribution systems. A computerized reservations and ticketing system, ELGAR, was introduced – initially to handle bookings for the Channel Tunnel's Eurostar service and later extended to all members of the Association of Train Operating Companies (ATOC).

Eurostar's marketing and distribution was strongly criticized. Onward bookings beyond Paris and Brussels could no longer be made to any European destination, but were instead limited to major railway stations. Systems to sell tickets to the public via the Internet replaced the role of many travel agents, with companies such as thetrainline.com (owned by Virgin Rail and the National Express bus group) acting as electronic intermediaries for the sale of rail tickets. In 2008, agents' rail commission was cut from 9 to 5 per cent and, at the same time, Eurostar abandoned the ELGAR distribution system, further disincentivizing the retailing of rail tickets.

Continued criticism of rail services in Britain led eventually to changes in the structure of the organization. Network Rail replaced Railtrack as owners of track, signals and stations, with 27 rail companies gaining franchises to control the rolling-stock, usually under contracts of 5–8 years, although some were extended up to 20 years (curiously, these sometimes fell into public ownership once again – for example, Deutsche Bahn, owned by the German state, bought the franchise for Chiltern Railway in 2007).

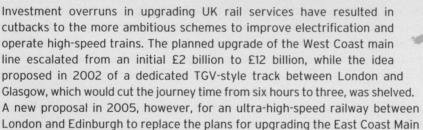

Example

Will Britain ever get domestic high-speed rail services?

Investment overruns in upgrading UK rail services have resulted in cutbacks to the more ambitious schemes to improve electrification and operate high-speed trains. The planned upgrade of the West Coast main line escalated from an initial £2 billion to £12 billion, while the idea proposed in 2002 of a dedicated TGV-style track between London and Glasgow, which would cut the journey time from six hours to three, was shelved. A new proposal in 2005, however, for an ultra-high-speed railway between London and Edinburgh to replace the plans for upgrading the East Coast Main Line, offered hope that the UK could have a service to match those on the Continent. Initially estimated to cost £33 billion, this would require depreciation over at least a 50-year period (as for TGV lines on the Continent), rather than the 30 years current in Britain. If it had gone ahead, it would have cut the journey time from four and a half to two and a half hours and be competitive with the no frills airlines.

In 2008, the Department for Transport decided to abandon any plans for high-speed domestic services, citing the increased pollution resulting from their operation as the reason. Also, in the view of the Rail Minister, Tom Harris, Britain's economic geography did not call for a high-speed network, the priority being to improve on congestion and reliability. This conflicts with government's stated intention to move people away from air travel to rail and ignores the much higher pollution levels of domestic air travel.

Furthermore, a study published in 2008 reveals that the cost of two high-speed lines between London and Scotland, then estimated at £31 billion, would provide £63 billion in economic benefits, particularly helping Northern cities. Inevitably, the lack of high-speed rail services in the UK will reduce its competitiveness regarding attracting visitors from abroad who wish to travel around the country during their stay.

Consequently, as matters stand, the only truly modern high-speed rail line in Britain to be recognized by the Union of International Railways is the Channel Tunnel rail link operated by Eurostar between London and the Channel Tunnel at Folkestone, now rebranded as HighSpeed One. Nevertheless, the faster rail services on the London–Manchester and London–Newcastle routes have attracted a significant share of the market back on to trains, reducing the demand for air services between these points.

Although the potential exists for a greatly expanded market for rail travel within the European Union, the full potential of this is only just beginning to be tapped in Britain with Eurostar's connections to the new high-speed train services onwards from Brussels and Paris. Marketing agreements between the European train operators and the interest in high-speed trains is changing attitudes to rail travel. An agreement between Eurostar and the Thalys international rail network helped boost rail travel between London and Amsterdam and this was followed by the establishment of a marketing alliance of the high-speed railways in the UK, France, Belgium, the Netherlands, Germany, Switzerland and Austria, under the brand name Rail Team. Train timetables throughout the region are now synchronized, a single timetable produced and common regulations (such as for children's fares) introduced. Most importantly, a single website, under development at the time of writing, will provide access to all these integrated services.

The Channel Tunnel and the railways

In Chapter 14, we examined the impact of the Channel Tunnel on ferry operations from the UK. Here, we must examine its impact on, and relationship to, land transport services elsewhere in Britain and in mainland Europe.

The Channel Tunnel is one of the great engineering feats of the twentieth century. With 37.8 kilometres of its 50 kilometre length under water, it takes pride of place as being the longest underwater rail tunnel in the world. While Japan's Seikan Tunnel between Tappisaki, Honshu Island, and Fukushima, Hokkaido Island, has the honour of being the longest rail tunnel at 53.8 kilometres, the section underwater is shorter, at 23.3 kilometres.

The first direct rail link between Britain and France was completed and opened to traffic in 1994, after frequent delays. It offers passengers the choice of two forms of transport: passenger travel on Eurostar from London to either Paris or Brussels, calling at Ebbsfleet (and, less frequently, Ashford in Kent) and Lille in northern France (with opportunities to transfer to high-speed trains for onward travel in Europe); and Groupe Eurotunnel's vehicle-carrying flat-bed rail service, operating between Cheriton (near Folkestone) and les Coquelles (near Calais). Cars are driven on to double-decker carriages (taller cars, those with trailers and coaches are accommodated in single deck carriages). These are then transported across the Channel and passengers can drive off to connect directly with the French motorway system in just a little over 30 minutes after leaving England.

Rail connections between London and the Continent have been firmly pitched at the business traveller. A fast line from the newly renovated St Pancras Station in London through Kent, which was fully opened in late 2007, allows Eurostar to operate at speeds up to 186 mph, cutting the overall journey time between London and Paris to 2 hours and 15 minutes (a little under 2 hours to Brussels). This compares with closer to 4 hours by air, when allowance is made for check-in times and the inevitable delayed departure, making journeys by rail a viable alternative for the business traveller as well as leisure tourists. This saving of 20 minutes led to a 25 per cent increase in income and a 21 per cent increase in traffic in the first quarter of its opening.

Eurostar (see Figure 15.1) carried 8.26 million passengers between London and Paris or Brussels in 2007, of which around 80 per cent were UK residents. According to Eurotunnel's Annual Report for that year, it now controls 72.8 per cent of the joint rail and air market to Paris. A two-hour trip from London St Pancras to Lille also enables the leisure tourist to connect with the French TGV (Train à Grande Vitesse) high-speed trains for onward travel to southern France or contiguous European countries, making Lille to Bordeaux a five-hour trip, while Calais to Marseille is of similar duration. This brings Marseille within seven hours of London, making the journey competitive with air travel (typically five hours as well as connections to and from local airports). Lille itself, heavily promoted as a destination in its own right, has become an important city-break market for

Figure 15.1 Loading a Eurotunnel train.
(Courtesy of Peter Titmuss/Alamy.)

British tourists to France. A fuller examination of the impact of Eurostar's transfer to its new London terminus at St Pancras is to be found in Case Study 4 at the end of this book.

At the insistence of the Conservative government, the Channel Tunnel was privately financed, with no public contribution. Its construction involved leading-edge technology and the project ran into delays and huge cost over-runs, leaving the parent company, Eurotunnel, with debts amounting to some £9 billion. Overambitious estimates of traffic and revenue were not realized, but this is not to say that the Tunnel has been a failure.

Within two years of operation, it had made sufficient inroads into the share of the short sea market to badly worry the ferry companies, which were obliged to slash their prices to compete. A fire in the Tunnel in 1996 was a serious setback, but despite this, Eurostar was carrying 66 per cent of all passenger traffic between London and Paris by 2003, while Eurotunnel itself has made similar inroads into the cross-Channel car market between Dover and Calais.

Eurostar's passenger rail services are now in the ownership of a consortium of rail, road and air transport businesses, with National Express coaches holding 40 per cent of the company. The minimum usage charge paid by Eurostar to Eurotunnel, agreed in the initial contract with the company, ended in 2006, but despite this loss, the newly restructured Groupe Eurotunnel has succeed in taking control of its finances, paying off some of its huge burden of debts and increasing load factors to a point where it became operationally profitable in 2007. The ferry operators must be drawing a communal sigh of relief as the prospect of a takeover of a bankrupt Eurotunnel would be their worst nightmare. That is because a mode of cross-Channel transport that would have the bulk of its capital costs erased and with far lower operating costs than those of any shipping company would make competition extremely difficult for the surface operators. If Eurotunnel continues its success in drawing the cross-Channel market away from both the airlines and ferry companies, long-term demand will rise substantially, to a point where capacity in the present tunnel could even be reached by 2025 and original projections start to become realistic forecasts again.

Example

The impact of the Channel Tunnel on England's South East

With a stop at Ashford in Kent, the high-speed line through South-East England threatens to add to the existing high levels of congestion in the region. Popular tourist destinations such as Canterbury and Leeds Castle, already overburdened with tourists, both domestic and travelling from the Continent, threaten to be overwhelmed by day excursionists and short-break visitors using the new services through the Tunnel. The prospect of large numbers of coaches meeting arrivals at Folkestone and Ashford to tour the Kent countryside is a nightmare scenario for the local authorities, whose task it is to manage congestion in the towns and on the rural roads in the county. To make matters worse, Kent (particularly its coastline) has been identified as one of the key areas of growth for housebuilding over the coming years.

The engineering firm Arup has proposed an extension of the Channel Tunnel route to Scotland via London's Heathrow Airport and Birmingham, with high-speed trains exceeding 200 mph. This is an exciting project on paper, but whether or not the necessary funding can ever be found or a government elected with the foresight and courage to commit to such a project is questionable. Similarly, a proposal to develop four new high-speed lines in Britain – to include a recommended tunnel linking Britain with Ireland via Dublin – seems a far-off dream at present.

Rail travel on the Continent

> When you invest in a high-speed train, it is for 100 years.
>
> Guillaume Pepy, Chief Executive, SNCF

Railway investment on the Continent is in marked contrast to investment in Britain's railways, whether they are under public or private administration. Continental rail companies and their governments recognized that investment in high-speed rail would encourage regional investment, giving rise to increased property prices and at the same time boosting tourism. In 1990, the EU approved the formation of a Trans-European Network for Transport (TEN-T) of high-speed road and rail links, the bulk of which were to be in place by 2005 (the full network to be completed by 2020). The initiative was supported by the European Commissioners in the expectation that rail would account for more than 23 per cent of all passenger kilometres travelled in Western Europe by 2010, alleviating the pressure on air and road services. Total investment in rail services will approach 225 billion euros, 80 per cent of which will be found from EU and national budgets, with the balance raised privately. By completion, nearly 94,000 kilometres of rail track will be in place throughout the EU.

In France alone, SNCF, the publicly operated rail service, and RFF, which is responsible for building and maintaining tracks, invested more than £22 billion of public money to build its 300-kph TGV service (see Figure 15.2). France now has over 1100 miles of high-speed track, while its latest TGV, in a test run in 2007, achieved a record speed of 357 mph (although such speeds are not sustainable with existing equipment). Payback on the investment is unlikely to be realized for up to 50 years (and local lines have been starved of funds while the new high-speed network was being established). There are savings to be achieved by improved connections and communications, however, and switching passengers and freight from road and air services to rail will help to meet the EU's target to reduce CO_2 emissions.

Figure 15.2 A TGV train.
(Courtesy of Directphoto.org/Alamy.)

Germany found £54 billion to build its own network of 280-kph ICE (Intercity Express) trains, with an even faster route between Cologne and Frankfurt, allowing the ICE3 330-kph train to halve the previous journey time. Italy introduced its Pendolino 250-kph tilt-body train on the Milan to Rome route, while Spain's AVE (Alta Velocidad Espagnola) offers a high-speed, 2 hours and 15-minute service between Madrid and Seville.

In 2008, RENFE, the Spanish railways operator, also brought into service a high-speed line for the Madrid to Barcelona service. The VelaroE travels at speeds up to 350 kph, cutting the 410-mile journey to just $2^1/_2$ hours. High-speed routes from Madrid to Málaga and Vallodolid are under construction. By 2012, the Spanish network should be linked with the TGV services at Perpignan and there are further ambitious plans for a total of 10,000 kilometres of high-speed track by 2020, with better signalling, which will allow speeds of up to 220 mph. The prospect of luxury trains running continuously between Northern Europe (including the UK) and the French Riviera or Spanish coastal resorts is a tantalizing one for the future of tourism.

Within Northern Europe, Thalys – a consortium of Belgian, French and Dutch rail interests – has enabled similar high-speed links to be developed between the member countries and Germany, with the popular Paris–Brussels route coming down to a mere 1 hour and 25 minutes. Sweden's hugely successful X2000 high-speed train has reduced the journey between Stockholm and Gothenburg to less than 3 hours, increasing rail's share on this route from 30 per cent to over 50 per cent and leading to the extension of the service to other Swedish cities as well as to Oslo, in Norway. In the latter country, the Signatur tilting train, introduced between Oslo and Kristiansand in 1999, gained sufficient popularity to ensure other routes were opened up throughout Norway. High-speed services of NS HiSpeed, the Netherlands rail company, joined the network in 2007. Greece, too, prompted by the Olympic Games held there in 2004, has introduced its own fast intercity services. The Pathé Line, designed to link Patras, Athens and Thessaloniki and expected to be in operation by 2009, reduces the travel time from Athens to Thessaloniki from $5^1/_2$ hours to just 2.

The advent of these high-speed networks is changing the face of European transport. Even allowing for the success of the budget airlines, rail services are finding that, if they can provide the reliability, comfort and speed at the right price, they can attract markets from other modes of transport. There is no uniform agreement that these new high-speed rail services can force airlines to withdraw from the routes, however.

Example

Can the airlines compete with high-speed rail?

The evidence appears mixed as to whether or not air can compete with rail on short-haul routes. Research carried out in France indicated that, for journeys up to 2 hours, rail could be expected to capture 90 per cent of traffic, while for those up to 3 hours, 75 per cent would still choose rail travel.

Air France did in fact withdraw its service between Paris and Brussels after the introduction of the Thalys high-speed route. On other routes, however, air services have either been reintroduced or, in some cases, even augmented. Aviation expert Tony Lucking pointed out that flights between Paris and Lyon actually increased in 2006, from 11 daily to 14, despite the availability of a train journey of less than 2 hours' duration. In Germany, the six daily flights between Stuttgart and Frankfurt were reinstated after an unsuccessful attempt to substitute rail for air on the 98-mile route. Even in Japan, where the Bullet train has attracted record numbers of travellers between Tokyo and Osaka, 56 daily flights have continued to operate on the route. He added that, of the 27 air services between Paris and the regions, 13 were protected by public service obligations.

Critically, he questions the green credentials of rail travel over air, claiming that the TGV and Eurostar use as much energy per passenger as an Airbus A321, while aircraft flying on short-haul routes fly lower than on long-haul, resulting in lower CO_2 emissions.[1]

It is likely that other factors are at work to determine modes of transport, including status, place of residence and attitudes within the business world – even habit. It is certainly the case, however, that demand from tourists, both business and leisure, for the new high-speed services from London to destinations on the Continent has increased, paralleling a rise in demand for new budget air routes. Minimum travel times by rail from London to key destinations on the Continent (sometimes entailing connections at Lille) are now given as:

- London to Brussels   1 hour 51 minutes
- London to Paris   2 hours 15 minutes
- London to Amsterdam   3 hours 30 minutes
- London to Cologne   3 hours 30 minutes
- London to Frankfurt   4 hours 40 minutes
- London to Geneva   5 hours 15 minutes
- London to Marseilles   6 hours 45 minutes.

Even popular Mediterranean resorts such as Cannes are now a comfortable day's journey away, at just over 8 hours. These timings ensure that, in many cases, both business and leisure travellers can be tempted back on to rail services – as can travellers from Paris, who can now reach Stuttgart in 3 hours 39 minutes, while the popular short-break city of Munich lies a little over 6 hours away.

Where formerly water acted as a barrier to fast surface transport, new bridges have helped to increase demand for the European rail networks, especially in Scandinavia. In Denmark, bridges across the Great Belt and the Øresund between Denmark and Sweden have now opened up continuous rail travel between London and either Stockholm or Copenhagen for the first time. The surface link that has brought Copenhagen and Malmö closer together has led to a partnership between the regions, encouraging international tourism to what was formerly a somewhat isolated and economically deprived region of Southern Sweden.

Where bridge construction is impracticable, tunnels are opening up other fast track routes through Europe, notably through the Alps. In 2006, work started on the world's longest tunnel, which will link Innsbruck in Austria with Fortezza in Italy, following the EU's plan to provide a continuous link between Munich and Palermo. The Brenner Base Tunnel will be 63 kilometres long (the length of the existing Gothard Base is just 57 kilometres) and is planned to cut the two million vehicles currently travelling every year from Germany and the North to the Mediterranean resorts – this flow of traffic is said to account for substantial levels of pollution as it makes its way through the mountains. The new twin tunnels through the Alps, due for completion in 2016, will be capable of carrying up to 400 trains a day.

Another major engineering project is the planned TAV rail link between Lisbon and Kiev, which will connect via Madrid, Barcelona, Lyon, Turin, Trieste and Budapest, but involves the construction of yet another 53-kilometre tunnel through the Alps, to carry up to 300 goods and passenger trains daily. Consequently, the programme has been delayed while environmentalists fight the noise, disruption and environmental damage that could potentially result from the line's construction.

Improved equipment and service, rapid connections between major cities and the avoidance of delays in congested airports are making European rail services appear increasingly attractive to the tourist market and there is little doubt that rail services will figure prominently in the future of European tourism. Moreover, under EU liberalization rules, present train companies within the member countries will be facing open competition from 2010, with non-EU companies being permitted to run international train services anywhere within the Community. With the writing on the wall, Air France was said to be in talks in 2008 with Veolia – one of Europe's largest rail freight operators – with a view to running passenger services under the Air France livery. By 2020, the amount of high-speed rail track is expected to further increase three-fold, to some 15,000 kilometres. Innovative marketing ploys, such as those given in the Example, will enhance demand for surface travel by younger travellers – or the young at heart.

Example

Innovation on the railways

In 2008, SNCF announced the withdrawal of its Train Bleu, with overnight wagons-lits sleeping cars between Paris and the French Riviera, disappointing many tourists who had elected to take the slow but comfortable route to the Mediterranean. SNCF claimed that the service was no longer economically viable, but it has replaced it with a very different concept that it expects will attract the youth market and enhance profitability. The iDnight services from Paris to Biarritz, Montpellier and Nice are designed as 'party trains', without sleeping accommodation, but offering all night bars and dancing.

Meanwhile, in Germany the Love Express was introduced on the run between Nuremberg and Munich. This service offers an opportunity en route for speed dating and promises a 64 per cent match rate. To no one's surprise, it has proved an unqualified success. 'I'm on the train, dear' may prove to be a call sufficient to strike terror into any number of German hearts.

With a very different appeal, the new Nordpark Funicular Railway running between Innsbruck and Hungerburg has already become a favourite with the tourists it was designed to carry up the mountains. Designed by cutting-edge architect Zaha Hadid, it lays claim to being the first 'designer railway', featuring architecturally impressive railway stations and termini, and has been planned to take account of changing patterns of tourist activity resulting from global warming.

Rapid transit services in the Far East

In Japan, the Shinkansen (popularly known as the Bullet train) has changed the face of high-speed transport and its reliability and high levels of service have proved immensely popular with tourists. The journey between Tokyo and Osaka, for example, takes three hours city centre to city centre by train, compared with an hour's flying time between airports, so 80 per cent of all passengers now use the train for this journey.

Japan takes immense pride in its Bullet trains – any delays are counted in seconds rather than minutes and the technical specifications of the trains are constantly improved. The most recently developed model is the Nozomi Series 800, introduced in 2004 and designed to travel at 260 kph – slightly slower than the earlier 500 series, which holds the record for normal operations at 300 kph.

Despite Japan's record, the award for fastest train service in the world now goes to the high-speed rail service built by the Chinese to link its two Olympic host cities, Beijing and Tianjin, in 2008. This service covers the 70 miles in just half an hour, at speeds up to 350 kph (217 mph), giving a taste of what can be anticipated in terms of global high-speed rail services later this century.

Classic rail journeys around the world

There remains a strong body of transport enthusiasts throughout the world for whom the 'romance of steam' remains a major attraction and they are willing to travel anywhere in the world for the privilege of taking a journey on one of the few remaining steam trains. Some of these have been reconditioned and lines relaid or reopened to cater to tourist demand, while others are sometimes mere shadows of their former selves, but appeal either through their exotic routing or due to nothing more than their romantic titles. Consequently, we now have two distinct forms of 'nostalgic rail' journey – on classic trains or on classic routes. In rare cases, the two coincide.

Classic train journeys are generally provided in reconditioned or reconstructed period coaches and are sometimes still drawn by steam engines. The *Venice Simplon-Orient-Express* is a leader in such nostalgic journeys, drawing on the appeal of its name and the image of ultimate luxury. The company now trades on that name, operating not only on the Continent, but also in the UK, the Far East and Australia.

At the top end of the market, such luxurious journeys in reconditioned trains or carriages are very attractive to tourists, who will build their itinerary around their rail journey. An example is the *El Andalus Express*, a vintage train comprising 12 carriages built in the 1920s and 1930s, operating between major tourist centres in southern Spain, such as Seville, Jerez and Granada, during spring and autumn. This itinerary, and others like it, are featured in upmarket programmes of specialist tour operators such as Great Rail Journeys of the World and Travelsphere. Hungary has introduced the *Royal Hungarian Express*, employing carriages built originally for the use of high-level party members under the communist regime, as a feature to attract tourists to destinations outside Budapest. The *Danube Express* is a recent introduction, operating between Berlin, Cracow, Prague and Istanbul.

Further afield, countries in which steam engines still operate, such as India and China (although, sadly, these have been largely phased out), attract both independent travellers and package tourists. Regular steam services in India may be mostly a memory, but *The Palace on Wheels* keeps that memory alive for those still anxious to experience the classic trains of imperial India.

In the Far East, a few steam-hauled trains still operate in Cambodia's highlands, while luxury trains designed to cater for the growing flood of tourists to Vietnam include the *Victoria Express* between Hanoi and Sapa and the *Reunification Express* from Hanoi to Saigon.

Figure 15.3 The *Desert Express* near Swakopmund, Namibia.
(Photo by Chris Holloway.)

In South Africa, the *Union Limited* is still steam-hauled and the famous *Blue Train* continues to cater to the top end of the market, while Rovos Rail's *Pride of Africa*, a train with 1930s' carriages, is chartered out to tour operators to provide an equally luxurious service between East and South Africa, via Victoria Falls. A popular and more modestly priced addition to the tourist trail, the *Outeniqua Choo-Tjoe* is a 1920s' steam-hauled train operating between George and Knysna, which travels through the scenic Wilderness National Park. Namibia, emulating the success of its neighbour, has introduced its own luxury train, the *Desert Express*, which operates out of the capital, Windhoek, to the coast and Etosha National Park (see Figure 15.3).

Australia has extensively promoted its famous trains – the *Indian Pacific* (a three-day service across the country between Perth and Melbourne) and *The Ghan* (from Adelaide across the red centre to Darwin via Alice Springs), while the Orient-Express company runs another luxury tourist train, the *Great South Pacific Express*, between Cairns and Sydney. The tilt train between Brisbane and Rockhampton is also proving popular, with tourists visiting the resorts of the East Coast and the Great Barrier Reef.

Longer rail journeys across the continents of Europe and Asia, while far from luxurious, fulfil the ambitions of true rail aficionados, who can choose between the *Trans-Mongolian Express*, *Trans-Manchurian Express* and *Rossiya*, or *Trans-Siberian Express*, and these too have been incorporated into programmes by specialist operators.

A recent introduction is the trans-Asia railway route, from Istanbul to Dhaka, linking in with European tracks. A tunnel across the Bosporus is planned to replace the ferry, which will form one of the final rail links in this 7000-mile journey, and the line, it is hoped, will eventually be extended to Singapore.

Finally, worthy of a mention is the service from Morocco via Western Sahara to Mauritania. Essentially a service to carry iron ore, it is supposedly the world's longest train – well over a mile in length. Tourist interest encouraged the authorities to put on

Example

The highest railway in the world

In 2006, the Chinese completed the highest railway in the world, between Beijing and Lhasa in Tibet. At its highest point, the Tangula Pass, the train reaches a height of 5070 metres (over 16,000 feet) and, at this height, the carriage compartments are pressurized, owing to the thin air. Also, oxygen cylinders are carried on board to cater for emergencies, which are not uncommon.

The construction of the rail track was in itself a major engineering feat as much of the route is across permafrost, requiring the track to be laid on causeways raised above the unstable ground. Curiously, to date no iconic name has been chosen for the train, but this has not stopped a surge of bookings from intrepid passengers from all over the world and the journey has been rapidly incorporated into specialist operators' rail itineraries.

a single passenger carriage and rail enthusiasts are now eager to book this very basic service between Nouadhibou and Zouerat – the one opportunity to experience the Sahara Desert by rail.

Rail services in North America

In North America, rail travel in the 1960s and 1970s declined in the face of lower air fares and poor marketing by the railway companies themselves, which chose to concentrate on freight revenue at the expense of their passenger services. The continuing losses suffered by most US rail companies, and the importance of the rail network in social communications, led the government to integrate rail services in the country into a centrally funded public corporation known as Amtrak. This organization has achieved some success in reversing the decline of passenger traffic and achieved some benefit after a rise in bookings by Americans nervous about flying, following the 9/11 disaster, although additional security measures, commensurate with those offered on airline flights, have added to the journey times.

While many of the famous names of the past, such as the Santa Fé *Superchief* and the *20th Century Ltd*, have gone for ever, the mystique of rail travel is maintained, at least in name, by others that *have* survived, including the *Lake Shore Ltd* on the Boston–New York–Chicago route, the *South West Chief* from Chicago to Los Angeles, the *Capitol Limited* from Washington to Chicago, the *California Zephyr* between Chicago and San Francisco, the *Empire Builder* between Seattle/Portland and Chicago and the *Coast Starlight* between San Francisco and Los Angeles. The only fully transcontinental service, the *Sunset Limited*, was severely disrupted by the flooding in Louisiana and, at the time of writing, was limited to the route between New York and New Orleans via Washington DC.

North American railways pass through some of the finest scenery in the world and both the United States and Canada exploit this in their rail journeys. Rail journeys to the Rockies already form an important element in excursions for those booking cruises out of North American ports on the west coast. The *Rocky Mountaineer* provides an opportunity to package scenic local transport when visitors travel to this region, while *The Canadian*, operating between Toronto and Vancouver via Jasper, has been restored to its original 1950s' style, with an observation dome on the rear carriage, giving tourists spectacular views of the passing scenery.

Tourists are also attracted to the restored or reconstructed nineteenth-century trains operating within the regions, notably in the Far West, such as the Silverton and Durango Railroad's steam train to Durango and the steam-hauled Grand Canyon Railway's trains. GrandLuxe Rail Journeys have introduced vintage Pullman carriages for their luxury scenic tours of the mainly western States.

By no means period or traditional, but nevertheless offering tourists memorable transport experiences, the *Talgo* tilting express travels from Seattle down the west coast, while, on the eastern seaboard, the *Acela* high-speed rail link between Boston, New York and Washington cuts the journey between Boston and New York from five hours to just over three (although even these services can be affected by the priority given to freight, which can lead to delays to passengers' schedules).

Even Mexico has entered the market for tourist passengers, the privately run *Maya Express* in Yucatán taking tourists between Cancún and other popular coastal resorts.

Rail nostalgia in the UK

In Britain, nostalgic rail enthusiasts are being given the opportunity to enjoy rail services that conjure up a period when travel by train was, in many cases, a luxury for the well-heeled. Among others on offer in recent times have been the:

- *Shakespeare Express*, between Birmingham and Stratford
- *British Pullman*, between London and Bath
- *Cathedrals Express*, between London and Salisbury (and other cathedral cities)
- *Jacobite*, operated by West Coast Railways between Fort William and Mallaig.

In Scotland, another successful venture has been the introduction of the *Royal Scotsman*. Although without the benefit of a genuine pedigree, the 1920s-style train, part-owned by Orient-Express, has been packaged with success in the American market, offering a very upmarket tour of the Scottish Highlands. These enterprises demonstrate that market niches exist for unusual rail programmes, which can undoubtedly be emulated in other tourist regions.

The continuing appeal of steam trains has led to a new steam train, built in 2008 by the A1 Steam Locomotive Trust, to operate classic rail excursion services on the national rail network in the UK.

The 'little railways' as tourist attractions

With the electrification of the railways in Britain, nostalgia for the steam trains of the pre-war period has led to the re-emergence of many small private railways. Using obsolete track and former British Rail rolling stock, enthusiasts have painstakingly restored a number of branch lines to provide an alternative system of transport for commuters and travellers and one more type of attraction for domestic and overseas tourists.

In Britain alone, there are over 250 railway preservation societies and more than 50 private lines in operation, with many other projects either in hand or under consideration. Some of these depend largely on tourist patronage, while others principally serve the needs of the local community. Their profitability, however, is often dependent on a great deal of voluntary labour, especially in the restoration of track, stations and rolling stock to serviceable condition. As these services are generally routed through some of the most scenic areas of Britain, they attract both railway enthusiasts and tourists of all kinds and undoubtedly enhance the attractiveness of a region for tourism generally. Notable examples include the Ffestiniog Railway and the Romney–Hythe service in Kent. A route now devoted exclusively to serving the needs of tourists is the Snowdonia Mountain Railway (see Figure 15.4), which has been in continuous service since the nineteenth century, transporting tourists to the highest point in England and Wales.

Figure 15.4 The Snowdonia Mountain Railway.
(Photo by Chris Holloway.)

The future of rail travel for tourists

The future holds the promise of trains travelling at much higher speeds than even the fastest in operation today. Magnetic levitation (Maglev) offers the prospect of rail journeys at speeds of up to 360 mph, but the cost of building these is prohibitive. This form of propulsion offers high speed coupled with exceptional quietness, the track consistsing of a metal trough generating a magnetic field that repels magnets on the train, causing the vehicle to ride 10 centimetres above the track. There is therefore little wear and tear and, in consequence, the cost of maintenance is much reduced.

The Germans and Japanese have led the research into developing Maglev propulsion and the first working line, constructed by the Germans, is the 270-mph route between Shanghai's Loyang Road Station and Pudong International Airport, covering the 19 miles in just 8 minutes. The company estimated that 20 per cent of its passengers in the initial years were coming aboard purely for the ride. It is intended that this line will be extended to Hangzhou, 105 miles to the south. Building costs will be high, but are estimated, per kilometre, to be less than half of those for building the Channel Tunnel. It has also approved construction of a high-speed traditional route between Beijing and Shanghai, which will reduce travel time for the 820-mile journey from 13 hours to 5.

In Japan, the Central Japan Railway's Maglev MLX-01, when it was tested, achieved a world record top speed of 361 mph (581 kph) in 2003. The country has firm plans to build a *Linear Express* Maglev railway between Tokyo and Nagoya – a distance of 180 miles, which the new train would cover in just 40 minutes. The target for completion of this line is 2025. There are also further proposals to build between Tokyo and Osaka, a distance of 300 miles. While building costs would be 30 per cent higher than for the Shinkansen, and electricity costs three times as much to run, maintenance costs would be extremely low and the speed would enable the line to compete even more effectively against air services.

Whether this project gets beyond the planning stage will again depend on the availability of public finance.

Although an earlier experimental route was built in England, linking Birmingham station with its airport in 1983, unreliability led to its closure in 1995 and, since then, Britain has been slower to research and develop Maglev or other advanced forms of surface propulsion. The British Government has, however, put forward proposals to consider the feasibility of establishing a public–private partnership with Ultraspeed (the private sector investing 70 per cent of the cost), the aim being to build a 300 mph 'Hovertrain', which would operate between London and Glasgow via Manchester. The cost was originally estimated at £30–£33 billion, with an anticipated construction period of 12 years. Both the cost estimate and construction period are probably optimistic, given the cost and time overruns on other ventures of this kind, and, in view of current government hesitancy over far less ambitious schemes for the West Coast line, the reality is that this scheme is likely to take decades rather than years to come to fruition.

In the USA, more prosaic schemes are being researched. Rail authorities have tested the Cybertran – a cross between a high-speed train and a light railway system – designed to provide fast, non-stop services at speeds of up to 150 mph between US cities.

One system even more advanced than the Maglev, however, is being explored in New Mexico. The Hypersonic Upgrade Programme (HUP) is supposedly capable of speeds up to an incredible 6500 mph (and has, in fact, achieved a speed of just 20 mph short of this in tests conducted during 2004), but the development and application of such a project for commercial use clearly lies some way in the future.

Russia and America have held talks to discuss the construction of a 50-mile tunnel under the Bering Strait and a 4600-mile rail track to provide a surface transport link between the two countries. While designed primarily as a means of competing with shipping across the Pacific for the carriage of freight, it would also enable the rail enthusiast to travel by rail between London and New York in 14 days. The costs of all these developments are substantial (the US–Russian project alone is estimated at £27 billion) however, so they are unlikely to materialize until much later this century.

Several of these initiatives will provide strong competition for short-haul air services, particularly on major business routes. In view of the existing congestion of many air routes and growing concern about aviation's pollution of the atmosphere, the development of alternative high-speed land routes is vital if trade – and tourism – are to prosper.

Coach travel

The term **coach** is used to describe any form of publicly or privately operated road service for passengers, other than local scheduled bus services (although Americans still use the term 'bus' to apply to their long-distance vehicles). It thus embraces a wide range of tourist services that are sold to the public, both directly and through other sectors of the travel industry, and these may be categorized under the following headings:

- express coach routes, both domestic and international
- private hire services
- tour and excursion operations
- transfer services.

Long-distance coach services provide a cheap alternative to rail and air travel and the extension of these services, both within the UK and from the UK to points in Europe and beyond, has drawn an increasing number of tourists at the cheaper end of the market, particularly those in the younger age groups. Younger passengers have also been attracted to adventurous transcontinental coach packages that provide, for a low all-in price, both

Figure 15.5 The Rotel sleeper coach.
(Photo by Chris Holloway.)

transport and minimal food and lodging en route (often under canvas). These services have been severely curtailed in recent years, however, due to political problems in transit countries such as Iran and Iraq.

Some services have been reintroduced, however, skirting major trouble spots, while others have been diverted to the African continent. Another form of cheap coach tourism is the Rotel sleeper coach, an innovation scarcely known in Britain, although, on the Continent, particularly in the German market, this is a popular form of budget long-distance coach holiday. In this form of transport, the coach either has built-in sleeping berths or pulls a sleeper trailer that, at night, can accommodate all the passengers in sleeping bunks (see Figure 15.5).

Apart from these exceptions, for the most part, coach travel obstinately remains the mode of transport of the older traveller, despite efforts by coach companies to widen their market. In the UK, most coach holidays are taken by those aged between fifty-five and sixty-four, with around two out of every three booked by the over-forty-fives. This is perhaps unsurprising, given the advantages that coach services offer to the older market – not just low prices (reflecting low operating costs vis-à-vis other forms of transport) but also the convenience of door-to-door travel when touring, overcoming baggage and transfer problems, and courier assistance, especially overseas where the elderly prefer to avoid problems of language and handling documentation. Additionally, coach operators frequently make arrangements to pick up and drop off passengers at points convenient to their homes. One result of this is that coach companies traditionally benefit from high levels of repeat business, often supported by loyalty rewards, such as discounts or special treatment like preferential hotel rooms.

Coach companies are now taking the view that their marketing efforts are best spent on raising the frequency of sales to the older market, rather than trying to attract a new younger market as the former market is expanding rapidly, as more people retire early. The most popular holiday destinations for British clients are Germany's Rhineland and Bavarian regions, the Austrian Tyrol and the Swiss Alps. While the long-distance coach market on the Continent is holding up reasonably well, the trend is towards short-break holidays by coach, in keeping with the growth of short-break holidays in general.

The operation of coach tours is a highly seasonal business, however, and companies are often forced to lay off drivers and staff out of season, unless they can obtain sufficient ad hoc charters or contract work (such as school bussing, useful for the coach companies as these commitments do not coincide with their busy holiday periods). Other out-of-season opportunities have been successfully marketed, however – notably Christmas market trips for British tourists to the Continent, pre-Christmas shopping trips to major cities and across the Channel, pantomime visits in the early part of the New Year and, of course, bank holiday trips.

Most coach companies specialize in certain spheres of activity. While some operate and market their tours nationally, others may concentrate on serving the needs of incoming tourists and tour operators by providing excursion programmes, transfers between airports and hotels or complete coach tours for overseas visitors. These coach companies must build up good relations and work closely with tour operators and other intermediaries abroad or in the home country.

Coach regulations in the UK

In Britain, under the terms of the Transport Act 1980, coach operators must apply to the Transport Commissioners for a licence, which will normally remain in force for five years and limit the operator to a specific number of vehicles. Applicants must have a good financial record and demonstrate adequate resources, including professional competence based on management experience and appropriate educational qualifications (for example, membership of the Chartered Institute of Transport). Members of the Confederation of Passenger Transport UK, which represents bus, coach and light rail companies, must also be bonded for 10 per cent of their touring turnover as insurance against financial collapse.

Coach operators are now governed by EU directives, which are designed to ensure adequate safety provisions for passengers. The concern with safety has been highlighted by recent incidents in the coaching industry, most notably a series of serious accidents on the Continent involving holiday coaches. The maximum number of hours' driving permitted for each driver per day are stipulated for all express journeys by coach, with stages over 50 kilometres. The controversial tachograph provides recorded evidence of the hours of operation and vehicle speeds of individual drivers.

While there can be little doubt that implementation of these regulations has led to higher safety standards in the industry, the effect has also been to increase the cost of long-haul coaching operations, making it more difficult for them to compete with rail or air services. To permit through journeys without expensive stopovers, two drivers must be carried or, more commonly, as rest periods must be taken off the coach, drivers are exchanged at various stages of the journey. With the constraint of a limited number of seats on each coach, this has the effect of pushing up costs per seat.

The 1980 Transport Act in Britain ended many of the restrictions on express coach services on routes of more than 30 miles. Prior to this, the licensing system favoured the development of national and regional oligopolies. The trunk routes in England and Wales were effectively controlled by the state-run National Bus Company (NBC), although a few smaller firms ran some regional and local routes. The Traffic Commissioners were generally prepared to consider granting new licences only where a new service was envisaged or a new market tapped, effectively ruling out competition. Restrictions also applied to coach tour operations (apart from tours operated by coach companies on behalf of overseas tour operators, in cases where all passengers had been prebooked abroad).

With the ending of regulation, a spate of new coach services of all types was introduced in 1981. A period of intense competition followed, in which the NBC emerged as the chief beneficiary, using the National Express brand name. Its dominant size offered it an advantage over its rivals as it was able to offer greater frequency of services and flexibility. With its huge fleet of coaches and a national network of routes, it was able to replace a defective vehicle at short notice with little inconvenience to its passengers – an advantage denied to its smaller rivals. Some new companies attempted to find niches by operating newer or unusual vehicles (such as luxurious foreign-built coaches). While this enabled them to compete in the short term, over time, most found that, given the prices they were forced to charge to recover their investments, they simply could not generate adequate demand for the luxury coaches and so they were forced out.

The 1985 Transport Act set the scene for almost total deregulation of Britain's bus industry the following year. This required the break-up and privatization of the NBC, providing small bus and coach operators with greater scope to compete and many new companies emerged. The newly privatized National Express, however, soon re-established its lead in the long-distance market as the National Express Group, establishing a partnership with Continental operators to create Eurolines (which it purchased in 1993), operating long-distance services between Britain and major cities in mainland Europe. The company also invested in the UK railways (including a share in Eurostar) and in North American and Spanish coach operations. A second beneficiary was Stagecoach, a small private company that, through aggressive acquisitions, became one of Britain's leading bus and coach companies, with interests in trams and ferries as well as the largest rail franchise in the UK, South West Trains. In 2003, the company also launched a popular low-budget coach service, Megabus, in the UK, later expanded to the USA. A third company, First Bus (later renamed FirstGroup) acquired prominent local bus companies and also successfully bid for train franchises, including the operator First Great Western, to become the third member of the triumvirate. All three have interests in overseas transport services.

In 2007, National Express – by then carrying over a billion passengers a year – made the decision to restructure its operations, forming new brands and a flagship east coast route in the UK. Forward management thinking led to the company hedging against fuel price increases before the oil crisis in 2008. In that year, 100 per cent of its fuel needs were hedged and it hedged a further 47 per cent in the following year. The company has also been the first to develop a 'supra' luxury coach service, designed to compete with rail services and aimed squarely at the business market. Seating just 40 passengers, these coaches are equipped with Internet access, videos, a hostess service and provide meals and drinks en route. This scheme is closely modelled on its successful Spanish four-hour VIP 'Gran Clase' service between Madrid and Bilbao.

With the arrival of two other medium-size operators, Go-Ahead and Arriva, five organizations now effectively control the scheduled bus and coach industry in the UK and all have made substantial investments in the UK rail services as well. This process of concentration in transport, both at home and abroad, is the direct outcome of the move to privatization – a move that has been watched with interest by companies and governments abroad, several of which have their own plans to move transport to the private sector. In common with the US airline industry a decade earlier, deregulation of the bus and coach industry appears to have had the opposite effect from that intended, with the growth of a handful of powerful oligopolistic scheduled carriers. Other coaching companies have found it easier to specialize in the inclusive tour markets, rather than compete openly with the leading carriers.

Coach tour-operating companies

Despite its rather archaic image, the coach tour remains popular among British travellers (see Figure 15.6). Operators best known for organizing package tours by coach have also tended to amalgamate since deregulation. Initially, two market leaders emerged from the string of takeovers – Wallace Arnold and Shearings – and these, in turn, merged in 2005, to form WA Shearings, which is now by far the largest coach tour operator in Britain, with

Figure 15.6 A typical modern touring coach on the Continent.
(Photo by Chris Holloway.)

well over a million passengers (principally the over-fifty-fives) each year. The company packages tours throughout Europe and in North America, Australia and New Zealand, acts as a travel agency for air and cruise holidays and has a string of shops. In addition to its fleet of coaches, it also owns over 40 hotels, is undertaking an aggressive campaign to secure more and is presently the sixth-largest hotel-owning company in the UK. This is typical of the movement towards horizontal integration among the coach companies and diagonal integration between the coach companies and the hotels they use. Smaller companies are finding it ever more difficult to compete and will have to find niche markets if they are to survive.

Example

Guide Friday

A good example of a niche operator, Guide Friday, set out to become the leading sightseeing bus operator in cities throughout Britain. Starting up in Stratford-upon-Avon, it now operates in 29 different locations.

Older open-top buses were purchased to keep costs down and reduce depreciation. As a result, the company can remain profitable even when operating for just the three busy months of the year.

Some specialists have chosen to move upmarket rather than attempt to compete directly with the market leaders. Coach charters are a popular means of achieving this. By purchasing luxury vehicles and fitting these out with videos, bar and catering facilities, more luxurious seating and accompanying hostesses, the coach companies can target niche markets for business routes, charters or long-distance luxury travel to compete with trains.

Example

Bakers Dolphin

Bakers Dolphin is a long-established West Country coach company offering a range of services, including domestic excursions, overseas coaching holidays and scheduled daily services from regional centres and London.

The decision was made to target upmarket holidaymakers more specifically by offering a Gold Service standard, so luxury coaches were purchased at a cost of £250,000 each to cater to this market. These are 36-passenger coaches, offering a 50 per cent increase in legroom. Rather than standard seats, leather-covered fully reclinable easy chairs offer unusual levels of comfort for a coach. Facilities include satellite navigation and DVD multi-track sound with earphones for each passenger, complimentary drinks en route and a rear lounge for further relaxation. The coaches are to be used principally for domestic and Continental tours.

Other operators have opted to provide coaches with sleeping accommodation. Unlike the Rotel coaches shown in Figure 15.5, these are used for charters, principally by the music and entertainment industry, for artists and crews touring to play gigs. Typically, they have sleeping facilities for between 8 and 16 passengers in comfortable, curtained-off bunkbeds, with seating areas at the rear and some also include full catering facilities, along with an accompanying hostess.

At the other end of the market, many small independent operators are engaged in small-scale enterprises that include transfers between airports and hotels, local excursions and city tours.

International long-distance scheduled operations form another sector of the budget coach market. The growth of shuttle services between Britain and the Continent, led by the Eurolines service, has been a prominent feature of budget travel for tourists within Europe (and the movement of labour between the EU member countries has fuelled demand for these services in recent years). These international stage journeys travel as far afield as Poland, Hungary, Greece, Finland and Turkey, their success varying according to the relative strength of sterling against other European currencies and the differential between air and coach fares.

The extreme scheduled coach route must be the OzBus, launched in 2007. It involves a 13-week journey between London and Sydney, with only the section between Bali and Darwin requiring a transfer to air services (the bus is shipped by sea). Its relatively high cost (close to £4000) has not appeared to discourage bookings (the price does include primitive accommodation and most food). This marks the first return to the hippy trail ventures popular in the mid-twentieth century and is proving popular with the backpacker market and returning Australians. Another long-haul service, the Buddhabus, or Butterfly Bus, has recently been launched, operating between London and Urumqi, in China – a distance of 5000 miles that is covered in just 16 days.

Coach operations in North America have become equally concentrated. For many years, two powerful coach companies – Greyhound Lines and Trailways – dominated the domestic coach market and their low fares enabled them to compete successfully against both the huge network of domestic air services and the private car. In 1982, however, road passenger transport was also deregulated in the USA, leading to a flood of small, low-priced coach companies, against which, in marked contrast to events in the UK, neither of the two giants seemed able to compete.

Trailways cut services in an effort to remain profitable, but, ultimately, merged, under new management, with Greyhound in 1987. Despite this move, the amalgamated company went into bankruptcy three years later. After further restructuring and the introduction of new vehicles, including minibuses, Greyhound emerged from bankruptcy to face new challengers from other small companies – notably US Bus, launched in 1998 with smaller, more comfortable vehicles.

Greyhound's problem was its dependence on low-budget travellers and the fact that many of its city termini were in run-down and depressed areas of the city. Although now out of bankruptcy and under the ownership of Britain's FirstGroup, the company has been forced to cut many of its services, having to compete not only with budget bus companies but also no frills budget airlines (notably SouthWest) and the Amtrak rail services, which are locally subsidized and have become more attractively priced. It has recently started to fight back with its own budget offshoot, BoltBus, offering cheap but relatively luxurious interiors.

The proliferation of small, low-priced bus companies over the past decade is a phenomenon of US travel. Stagecoach's Megabus, with its minimum $1 rides, has made an impact since its introduction to the USA, while other companies such as Chinatown Bus and Today's Bus have arrived on the scene to take on the national carrier on key routes. Also, online ticketing agency Gotobus has enabled passengers to book their tickets on the Web, so they can choose on the basis of price from a range of bus companies.

Finally, mention should be made at this point of the Gray Line organization – an American franchise offering coach excursions and tours not only within the USA and Canada but also in many other countries. Franchising globally on this scale is relatively uncommon within tourism, but offers a pointer to the possible direction the industry will take in the future, as large companies go multinational.

It must not be forgotten that, in many countries, vehicles in common use for local residents are attractions for visiting tourists, too. Just as some ferries across the world are must-see attractions, so famous local services will attract tourists just to sample the experience. Examples include London's double-decker buses and vintage buses in countries such as Malta and the Philippines, but this phenomenon is by no means limited to buses and coaches. The San Francisco cable cars, the tram and gondola rides to mountain tops in Hong Kong and Cape Town, black cabs in London, yellow cabs in New York, tuc tucs in Bangkok, tricycles and rickshaws in the Far East – these are all essential elements of the tourist experience of the destination and contribute to tourism revenue as well as forming the ideal way in which to see the sights of the city.

For every country with a well-developed tourism market, however, there are many others that make little effort to bring their local bus and coach services to the attention of visitors. Buying bus and tram tickets can be a daunting experience for ingénues visiting a foreign city for the first time, where tickets often have to be purchased in advance from kiosks, then punched in a machine on board the vehicle, yet all too often instructions are only available in the local language.

Promoting public transport encourages tourists to stay longer as they can be told how to visit attractions away from the town centre and transport costs are often very cheap so they need never fear being overcharged. In Finland, Helsinki has successfully marketed the internationally renowned Arabia ceramic factory, museum and showroom located out of town at the end of a tram route. By contrast, visitors to Tallinn in Estonia are offered no guidance in other languages on how to use public transport, despite the rapid growth in their numbers. Similarly, visitors to Beijing in China receive little guidance on the use of local buses, even though they are cheap and frequent.

Figure 15.7 Local transport in the developing world is often far from luxurious, but may tempt the intrepid backpacker. A scene in Jaisalmer, India.
(Photo by Chris Holloway.)

Example

The impact of free transport

An interesting problem has been thrown up by the introduction in Britain of free local scheduled bus services for the over-sixties in 2008. Concern has been expressed about the potentially unequal burden on the local economies of the increased demand in more popular tourist destinations.

Although government has provided grants to assist the regions in taking on this burden, it is believed that the costs in some cases will far exceed the subsidies provided, possibly requiring an increase in taxation for local residents, who themselves may find it difficult to obtain seats on local buses swamped by 'joy-riding pensioners'. This has already become a feature of local bus services in some coastal resorts. Alternatively, local authorities may choose to cut services in order to reduce costs.

It will take a year or two to know whether or not these fears are justified, but, more positively, the move can be expected to lead to increased travel and expenditure by senior citizens.

Before leaving the coach sector, we must look at a few examples where other road vehicles are pressed into service for tourists. Between the coach and the private hire car, a variety of sometimes unusual, if not bizarre, vehicles serve tourist needs. Specially constructed four-wheel vehicles are used by tourists in rough terrain or wilderness areas (see Figure 15.8).

Figure 15.8 Safari vehicles at Etosha National Park, Namibia.
(Photo by Chris Holloway.)

In some countries, the postbus fulfils the need for public transport where traffic is too limited to sustain a scheduled bus route. These are postal delivery vehicles that are also equipped to carry a limited number of passengers. They have long been popular in mountainous areas such as Switzerland and Austria, where they are operated by the Austrian Railways, but are also used extensively by adventure tourists and backpackers travelling independently.

Britain introduced these passenger-carrying vehicles for the first time in 1967, serving the community around Llanidloes in Wales, and, over time, some 200 postbus routes were established, principally in the less-populated communities in Scotland. Sadly, they are being phased out to a large extent, with only some 60 services still functioning at the time of writing. Such a service is vital in regions such as the Shetland Islands, and vehicles in use range from 4-passenger Land Rovers to 14-seat minibuses.

In Australia, similar services are provided by the mail planes. Tourists travelling on foot are finding these useful means of getting about where other forms of public transport are limited or non-existent and, in turn, these services are learning to attract visitors as well as locals. Indeed, the mail services in Australia have gone as far as packaging tours around their mail runs in the remote Flinders Range, including accommodation and meals.

Finally, mention must be made of the curious, not to say bizarre, use to which some vehicles are put to give rides to tourists. While they are too numerous to list extensively, one good example, from a nation for which bizarre tourism is the norm, will serve the purpose. In San Francisco, among other exotic transport modes such as duck boat trips in the harbour and antique car tours, visitors can take a 75-minute ride over the Golden Gate Bridge on an authentic antique fire engine, dressed in firefighter gear. More demure transport is on offer in Australia, where, as described in Chapter 10, wine lovers are offered an opportunity to tour the wine-growing area of Margaret River, Western Australia, in chauffeur-driven classic Bentley cars.

Example

Alternative transport – the new niche?

Chauffeur-driven Bentleys represent one end of the scale. At the other, some fairly bizarre methods of transport are now available to tourists to drive, rent or make use of in one way or another.

In France, the ever popular classic Citroën 2CV is being pressed into service to provide a uniquely French experience in car touring. The company responsible for hiring these cars in packages that include a wide choice of accommodation and meals, Les Belles Echappées, also provides a truly postmodern (as well as environmentally friendly) experience. It packages together the hire of an electric Solex moped with gourmet meals and accommodation at a 4-star Relais & Châteaux hotel, the Tilques Castle.

Further information: **www.les-belles-echappees.com**

The private car

Undoubtedly, the increase in private car ownership has done more to change travel habits than any other factor in tourism. It has provided families in particular with a new freedom of movement, increasing opportunities to take day excursions as well as longer trips. From the 1950s onwards, the costs of motoring have been falling in relative terms and car owners also tend to take into account only the direct costs of a motoring trip, rather than the full cost, which would include depreciation and wear and tear. Thus, car transport has long been favoured over public transport.

The effect of this preference on the travel industry has been considerable. Over the years, the hotel and catering industries responded by building motels, roadside cafés and restaurants, while formerly remote hotels and restaurants suddenly benefited from their new accessibility to these tourists. Car ferry services all over Europe flourished and countries linked by such services experienced a visitor boom. France remains, for the British, the leading holiday destination, being seen primarily as a destination for the independent and mobile tourist.

Camping holidays also boomed and tour operators reacted by creating flexible self-drive car packages, including packaged camping holidays in tents or mobile homes.

The rented cottage industry took off, the gîte holidays in France soon being followed by cottage and villa rentals in many other countries.

Fly–drive and rail–drive packages were introduced. The railways, too, adapted to meet the needs of motoring tourists, introducing motorail services that allowed people to take their cars with them on longer journeys, such as to the south of France and Spain.

In the twenty-first century, the desire for greater flexibility has to be weighed against the burden of a rapid escalation in the cost of motoring, particularly in terms of fuel. If those costs continue to rise, this may well curtail demand for motoring holidays, with serious implications for the types of holiday chosen. Many British-owned second homes, for instance, are in fairly isolated regions on the Continent, so access would be difficult without personal transport.

A decline in car usage may be beneficial for some aspects of tourism. New roads catering for mass travel include bypasses that encourage touring drivers to sideline small towns and villages. One example of this was the construction of the second Severn crossing into Wales, which sidelined Chepstow and led to a marked decline in visits to the town. Good roads cause environmental damage to the countryside (witness the devastation to an area of outstanding beauty caused by the construction of the M3 Winchester bypass) and have the effect of discouraging the impulse visitor from stopping and spending money in the towns. At the same time, the expansion of motoring and private car ownership in a small country such as Britain is leading to enormous problems of pollution and congestion. With car ownership in Britain standing at well over 30 million and rising, the country is rapidly approaching a standstill – literally the case on major motorways on bank holidays in the summer. Small resorts and scenic attractions cannot expand sufficiently to meet the demand for access and parking facilities without damaging the environment that the motorists have come to see.

The growing interest in our society in ecologically friendly tourism will inevitably discourage motorists from taking their cars to such destinations. Greater control can be expected in the future in the form of developments such as park and ride schemes, already provided at congested resorts such as Bath, Oxford and St Ives, as well as Polperro in Cornwall, where visitors are encouraged, and sometimes required, to park their cars at car parks on the outskirts and either walk or use public transport to travel in to the centre. Rationing by charging high prices for car parking (as has been introduced in Oxford) or limiting access or denying facilities for car parking (as occurs at the more popular US national parks and is now finding favour in some of the British National Parks) will inevitably become a characteristic of future tourist destinations when demand rises to a point where there is insufficient physical space to accommodate all who wish to arrive in their private cars. Many towns in the UK now adopt a variable pricing policy for parking, with comparatively low prices for parking up to two or three hours, to encourage shoppers and short-stay visitors, but rising sharply thereafter to discourage commuter parking. Prices then drop in the evening to encourage leisure visitors after the business traffic has left.

Example

Is congestion charging the solution to overcrowded cities?

Faced with massive congestion and resulting pollution from traffic fumes, the then mayor of London decided to introduce congestion charges in an effort to resolve the problem. These charges were ring-fenced, with the income earned being dedicated to improvements in public transport.

After an initial impact, the number of cars entering the city soon rose to earlier levels, despite an increase in the charge.

In 2007, the zone was expanded and plans announced to penalize so-called 'gas guzzlers' and other high-polluting vehicles by swingeing increases in the charge.

Other cities, both in the UK and abroad, are looking to follow suit, although there is considerable public resistance.

While congestion charges are predominantly aimed at encouraging commuters back on to public transport, the impact on tourism also has to be taken into account. To what extent is private car usage vital to either domestic or inbound tourist markets? Are tourist car rentals largely restricted to rural areas, limiting their impact on the economy? Would tourists visiting London actually prefer a vastly improved public transport system to the current chaos, even if it inhibited their ability to drive in the city? Do inbound tourists actually consider changing their holiday destinations on the strength of the congestion problems they might face?

These are highly relevant questions for the industry, but they have been inadequately researched. The next development to discourage car use is likely to be road pricing, with drivers paying a set fee per mile of the roadways they drive on. Tentatively, officials in

Britain have talked of figures of £1.30 per mile in the cities, with a nominal figure of perhaps 2 pence in rural areas. Again, little is known about the possible impact of such a move on tourism.

Caravan holidays

Caravanning has always been popular in Britain, since the manufacture of the first leisure caravan, the Bristol Carriage Company's 'Wanderer', in 1880. Today, there are some 3500 caravan parks in the UK and over 500,000 privately owned mobile caravans. The Caravan Club boasts 350,000 members and between 1 and 2 million people take caravan holidays every year. Caravan holidays have been falling relative to other forms of holidaymaking, however, largely as a result of the introduction of cheap air fares to the Continent.

In the USA, sales of trailers (the American term for caravans) have declined as motorhomes or campervans (motorized caravans) have found favour. These vehicles are widely known in the USA as recreational vehicles (RVs). Originating with the invention of the Curtiss Aerocar in the 1930s, they have steadily grown in popularity to a point where, today, more than 25 million Americans make use of them each year.

The industry responded by providing new and more luxurious camping facilities, with the franchise company Kampgrounds of America ensuring water and electricity were available at all its sites. RVs are widely available for rental, too, and are popular among European visitors touring the USA, especially in the far west. While not cheap to rent, they are luxurious by any standards, with amenities that compare well with many hotel rooms, including en suite showers. While some have been imported into the UK, their sheer size makes them unsuitable for use on most British roads. There are, however, specialist holiday companies that rent out motorhomes (see the website addresses at the end of this chapter) and they are becoming popular on the Continent where, in many countries, the roads are not too crowded and there are adequate facilities to park overnight.

The car rental business

It has been estimated that there are over 1000 car hire companies operating in Britain, with more than 130,000 cars available for hire (many being fleet cars on hire to private companies). The car rental business owes a substantial proportion of its revenue (and, in many resorts, virtually all its revenue) to tourists. While in total only 30–40 per cent of car hire is associated with leisure, small companies and local car hire operators get a disproportionate share of this, while the large corporations have the lion's share of the business travel market.

Car rental companies can be divided into two categories:

- large international companies or franchise operators
- small, generally locally based, independent hire companies.

Most of the larger companies charge broadly similar prices, but offer a choice of cars, hiring locations and flexibility (for example, the ability to pick up a car at one location and drop it off at another). This flexibility and convenience makes them attractive to business travellers, who are less sensitive to price, but insist on speed of service, reliability and a more luxurious standard of car. Contracts with suppliers generally tie them to favouring a particular make of car, on which they are given advantageous prices.

Hertz is the largest car rental agency in the world, with over 8000 outlets, while Avis, which also owns Budget Rent-a-car, is the largest car hire company in Europe. Ownership of these two companies has changed frequently over the years and their operation now appears secondary to the perceived value of the asset. Hertz was sold in 2005 to a group of private equity firms and Avis/Budget, at the time of writing owned by travel conglomerate Cendant, is expected to be on the market again in the near future.

As to the second category, there are literally hundreds of small, local car rental companies that generally offer limited choice but low price and the convenience of a local pick-up, although perhaps from only one or two locations. Because of their reliance on the leisure market, these companies work in a highly seasonal business, where they may be unable to maximize their opportunities for business in summer because they have insufficient vehicles. In addition, there are some specialist car hire operators that provide very luxurious vehicles, high-powered sports cars or even classic vehicles, for a small upmarket leisure or business clientele.

The competitive nature of the industry has once again resulted in good marketing playing a key role in the success of individual car rental companies. The expansion of outlets has been greatly aided by the introduction of franchising in the 1960s – a means of distribution now used by all the large companies. Three other factors have been critical.

- *Contracts with airports and railways* These allow car rental companies to maintain a desk at airport or rail terminals. The opportunities for business that are provided by having desk space in these locations make these contracts very lucrative and they are fought for by the major companies, occasionally changing as competitors offer higher bids at the termination of a contract agreement.

- *Links with airlines and hotels* This establishes good relations with – and, hence, referrals from – hotel chains and larger airlines, generates huge volumes of business and is critical for maximizing sales opportunities for business travel bookings. Large hotel chains may also offer desk space for the car rental company in reception areas.

- *Computer reservations systems (CRS)* The development of a good CRS (and, increasingly, global distribution systems, GDSs), together with accessibility via the websites of major airlines or intermediaries, plays an increasingly important role in the success of the larger car rental companies, which cannot afford not to be linked to such major systems. Equally, these information providers need car hire as an adjunct to their flight and accommodation sales via the Web. One company that has recognized this is online agency lastminute.com, which acquired the fast-growing leisure rental company Holiday Autos to complement its website operations.

Car rental companies also court travel agents, which provide a good proportion of advance sales for business and leisure travel. Attractive rates of commission of 15 per cent or more are still on offer to gain agency support. Car rental through the trade, however, is less common in the UK than in the USA. The growing 'seat only' airline reservations market helped to expand the demand for car hire overseas, as has the huge demand generated by second home owners travelling to their holiday homes across Europe.

Trading conditions for the car rental companies have been particularly difficult in the face of continuing high levels of competition in the trade and the terrorism threat since 9/11, which, coupled with adverse movements of European currencies against the dollar, have affected demand from Americans visiting Europe. While profits are thin for the leading franchises, others, including those associated with or owned by air carriers, have benefited from the introduction of low-cost air fares within Europe, which now make it cheaper for tourists to fly to their destination and hire a car there rather than drive all the way.

A recent development – and the direct outcome of website bookings – has been the introduction of companies organizing private transfers. With the growth of independent travel, more holidaymakers are putting together their own packages by searching the Web and this includes arranging transfers to their hotel abroad. Specialist companies are arranging transfers by taxi, mini-coach, private limousine – even helicopter – for customers on their arrival at airports abroad. These services can also be incorporated into dynamic packaging programmes by agents.

Cycling and tourism

Over the past three decades, holidaymakers have shown a much greater interest in cycling holidays than in the past, partly on the grounds of their ecological sustainability. The Cyclists' Touring Club boasts some 70,000 members in Britain and several specialist holiday firms have been established in recent years to cater for those seeking organized cycling holidays in Britain, on the Continent and even further afield. These include both leisure and sporting (off-road) pursuits, reflecting the growth in ownership of hi-tech equipment such as mountain bikes. Tour operators like Cycling for Softies, which specializes in cycling holidays in France, provide vehicles for the transfer of cyclists' baggage between accommodation stops, leaving their clients to travel light. This form of touring has proved very popular, falling into the 'Hilton hippies' category of demand, where roughing it by day is compensated by enjoying comfortable accommodation and gourmet food at night.

Rural destinations, particularly those in relatively flat but attractive landscapes, have recognized the growing popularity of cycling as an activity for visitors and encouraged cyclists by providing suitable trails and informative leaflets about the surrounding countryside. Small businesses, such as cycle hire companies, have sprung up to serve these visitors. An example is that of the village of Worpswede, north of Bremen in Germany, which is a popular venue for domestic cycling tourists. The village lies on the edge of the famed Teufelsmoor, a nature reserve, and the Worpswede Radtour offers five themed cycle rides through the region, ranging in length from 19 to 45 kilometres. France, too, has long popularized holidays by bicycle.

The interest in off-road biking has led to tour programmes catering for mountain bike tours in distant countries. Morocco, South Africa, New Zealand, the United States, Kyrgyzstan and Kazakhstan are just a few of the countries now offering mountain bike adventure tours.

Example

The Loire Valley

French enthusiasm for cycling is high. For years, local authorities in the Loire Valley region of France have closed off a 75-kilometre section of the River Loire levée between Angers and Saumur in June to allow a one-day celebration of cycling, the Fête de Vélo (see Figure 15.9). All other road traffic is banned and more than 20,000 cyclists are attracted from all over France for the occasion. Similar initiatives are now being taken by local authorities in Britain.

The success of this festival has been such that a regular cycle path extending 161 kilometres has now been established between Tours and Angers, via Chinon and Saumur. Known as the Loire à Vélo Trail, the route forms an initial part of what it is hoped will eventually become an 800-kilometre trail between Cuffy in the East and St Brévin-les-Pins on the west coast. Small companies serving the needs of cycling tourists have sprung up along the path, including bicycle rental companies and aquacycle rentals. Cycling for Softies is among the British cycle touring companies offering tailor-made itineraries along the trail. There are hopes that funding will eventually become available to extend the cycling trail all the way to Budapest.

Further information: **www.loire-a-velo.fr** and **www.cycling-for-softies.com**

Figure 15.9 Cyclists rest during the annual Fête de Vélo alongside the River Loire, France. *(Photo by Chris Holloway.)*

Example

Llanwrtyd Wells, Powys

In Wales, the town of Llanwrtyd Wells established the World Mountain Bike Bog Snorkelling Championships competition in 1985.

Contestants in wetsuits pedal mountain bikes underwater, using snorkels (tyres are weighted to keep contestants and their bicycles below the surface). Introduced as an amusing pastime, the game caught on and now attracts tourists in large numbers.

Further information: **www.green-events.co.uk**

There are fears that the rise in the numbers of cars on rural roads, resulting from drivers seeking relief from the growing congestion on trunk roads in Britain, will make cycling far more dangerous where there is no dedicated cycle path, discouraging people from taking cycling holidays.

Britain is now following the lead of other European countries like the Netherlands and Denmark, in providing dedicated paths for cyclists in and around towns, and new traffic-free long-distance cycle routes are also being established. Lottery funding of more than £90 million has been made available to the charity Sustrans to complete the National Cycle Network, consisting of 12,000 miles of dedicated cycleways (coupled with walkways) throughout Britain, emulating similar cycle routes across Europe. There is clearly high demand for this amenity as, according to Sustrans, over 338 million trips were made on the existing stretches of the National Cycle Network in 2006. Cycling still accounts for less than 2 per cent of all trips in Britain, compared with 18 per cent in Denmark and 11 per cent in Germany, but efforts are being made to increase cycle use, both as a means of local transport and for tourism.

In the interests of improving the environment, efforts are also being made to improve opportunities for cyclists in Britain to take their cycles on trains, which would encourage rural tourism by bike. While train services in Britain have offered this facility in the past, commercial concerns are making rail companies more reluctant to allow bicycles to be carried free and rules governing their carriage differ for each of the 27 railway companies and on every route, discouraging the practice. Integrated transport planning should include and facilitate this opportunity, but the privatization of the railways has made this difficult to enforce.

Tourists on foot

In examining the role of transport, one must not forget tourists who travel mainly on foot. The destinations that draw such tourists were touched on earlier in Chapter 9, but let us look at this area a little more here.

Walking holidays in the mountains have a long tradition and hiking and trekking have both grown in popularity in recent years. Ramblers associations represent the interests of these long-distance walkers, working to ensure that rights of way over both public and private land in Britain are protected. The European Ramblers Association was established in 1969 and, since that time, 11 European long-distance paths – the longest, from Norway to Turkey, stretching some 4500 miles – have been established, often refurbished long-existing routes. Some of these, such as the E2 Grande Traversée des Alpes or the five pathways through the Austrian Alps, are well maintained and extensively used, while others, such as those in southern Italy, Romania, the Ukraine and Turkey, have yet to be opened officially, although they are in use. Two of these European footpaths extend into England and Scotland – the route E2-GB stretching from Stranraer to Dover and eventually connecting with the Grande Traversée des Alpes. Such routes are particularly popular with German and Dutch hikers and are expected to attract growing numbers of British tourists.

Example

The Iron Curtain trail

In 2005, it was announced that a 4250-mile tourist trail would be developed to follow the route of the 'Iron Curtain' – a term denoting the border separating the West from the former Soviet Union. Stretching from the Arctic Ocean to the Black Sea, this former border snakes through scenic countryside that it is ideal to incorporate into cycling and walking holidays.

EU funding is being provided and each country along the route will make its own contribution to developing the infrastructure and superstructure needed to support the trail.

Tourism on foot is also important to towns and cities. In the most popular urban destinations, trails are often marked out by means of symbols on pavements or signposts (see Figure 15.10), just as markers on trees enable visitors to find their way along forest trails. Apart from the obvious attractions identified by these trails, promotional bodies are recognizing that walking tours provide the opportunity to introduce tourists to little-known

Figure 15.10 A signpost in London directs walkers.
(Photo by Chris Holloway.)

regions of the town, allowing poorer districts to benefit from the influx of visitors. Liège, in Belgium, offers a ten-day Festival de Promenade for tourists visiting the city in August, with more than 40 different walks of varying lengths, appealing to a variety of different tastes. British cities are increasingly recognizing the value of such initiatives.

Example

Walking tours of London

Regional tourist board VisitLondon has launched a collection of walking maps to draw tourists to the off-the-beaten-track parts of Bermondsey, Notting Hill, Belgravia and Soho, while the London Development Agency has identified districts of London that are in the early stages of becoming 'trendy' by attracting the arts crowd and their followers. Among districts identified are Deptford, Brixton, King's Cross and Wood Green – none of which would have been thought of interest to tourists in the past. Festivals and walking tours are planned to enhance this appeal.

An interesting development in urban tourism has been the concept of **sightjogging**, in which joggers accompany tour guides on a run while key attractions are pointed out to them. Berlin offers 90-minute tours, which have proved popular, while similar tours are on offer in the USA in New York, Washington DC, San Diego and Charleston. Purists might disparage this limited form of sightseeing, but, as an encouragement to exercise, the concept has its merits!

Future developments in land transport

In terms of future development, railways in particular are making substantial progress. Japan's Linear Express, capable of cruising at speeds up to 300 mph, has already reached the prototype stage. This train has the advantage of superspeed and being super quiet. The track consists of a metal trough generating a magnetic field that repels magnets in the train, causing it to ride 10 centimetres above the track. There is therefore little wear and tear and, consequently, the maintenance costs are much reduced. If the technology proves successful, rail services could certainly pose a major threat to air routes of distances over land up to 1000 miles.

We have seen the introduction of Maglev trains and even the possibility of these coming into service in the UK in the future. The government is examining the feasibility of establishing a public–private partnership (with the private sector investing 70 per cent of the cost) to build a 300-mph Ultraspeed 'Hovertrain' to operate between London and Glasgow via Manchester. The cost is estimated at £30 billion and construction, if undertaken, would (optimistically) be completed within 12 years. Such a service would be expected to largely erase air competition on these routes.

Finally, there has been much improvement in information about transport. There are now electronic noticeboards at bus stops that detail the arrival of the next bus. Moves are also afoot to ensure that all transport networks will eventually be linked by global positioning software, enabling travellers to track the current location of any form of transport.

Note

1. See Lucking, T. (2006 and 2007) letters to *The Times*, 20 December and 8 September.

Further reading

Penn, R. (2005) *A Place to Cycle: Amazing rides from around the world*, Conran Octopus.

Websites

Railways

Amtrak	**www.amtrak.com**
UKsteam Info	
(Steam train excursions in the UK)	**www.uksteam.info**
The trainline.com	**www.thetrainline.com**

Coaches

Coaches offering sleeper accommodation	**www.sleepercoaches.co.uk**
	www.jumbocruiser.com
	www.silvergray.co.uk
GotoBus	**www.gotobus.com**

Cars

Bridge & Wickers (chauffeured Bentley wine tour)	**www.bridgeandwickers.co.uk**
HolidayTaxis.com	**www.holidaytaxis.com**
Motorhome rentals	**www.hemmingways.co.uk**
	www.international-motorhome-hire.com
resorthoppa.com	**www.resorthoppa.com**
resorttaxis.com	**www.resorttaxis.com**

Cycling

Cycling for Softies	**www.cycling-for-softies.com**
Cycling holidays in the Loire Valley	**www.loire-a-velo.fr**
Mountain bike holidays	**www.exodus.co.uk**
	www.keadventure.com
	www.mountain-beach.co.uk
Sustrans (map of National Cycle Network)	**www.sustrans.org.uk**
World Mountain Bike Bog Snorkelling Championship	**www.green-events.co.uk**

On foot

City Running Tours	**www.cityrunningtours.com**
Sightjogging	**www.sightjogging-berlin.de**

Questions and discussion points

1. How far has Britain's failure to keep pace with railway developments influenced patterns of tourist traffic to and within the country?

2. Argue the case for and against public ownership of the railway system in your country, from the perspective of encouraging tourists.

3. Why are airlines still able to compete successfully with rail services in the UK on short-haul flights?

4. Motorail services throughout Europe have largely been abandoned in recent years due to falling demand and high costs. Can the market for this form of travel be resurrected and to what extent might high petrol prices encourage their reintroduction?

5. How can younger passengers be encouraged to use coach services?

6. Why are coach companies horizontally integrated with hotels, while airlines have largely divested themselves of investment in the sector?

7. How might congestion charges affect the self-drive tourist market in the UK?

Tasks

1. Imagine that your company is planning to purchase Rotel coaches to expand on its tour operating programmes and it has made you responsible for integrating these into the inclusive tour programme. Draw up a business plan, that, inter alia:

   - explains how you will use the vehicles
   - suggests where you will employ them
   - determines the markets at which your itineraries will be aimed.

   Justify your decisions in each case.

2. As a campsite operator at any seaside resort of your choice, undertake a SWOT analysis of the market for the coming five years and explain how you will tackle the threats posed by, for example, the oil crisis.

3. As a brand manager for a leading tour operator, make a case to your Managing Director for diversifying into cycling holidays, with supportive data.

Part 3

Intermediaries in the provision of travel and tourism services

Chapter 16

The management of visitors

Learning outcomes

After studying this chapter, you should be able to:

- explain the concept of visitor management

- identify different techniques employed to manage tourists

- understand the role of interpretation in visitor management

- be aware of the controls that can be implemented to protect the physical environment.

Introduction

> In the next millennium when everyone will have more leisure time, tourism will become the world's largest industry. No longer can it be regarded solely as a local, regional or even national issue, it is global. The implications of this for New Forest District are profound. On the one hand we need a prosperous tourism industry to sustain jobs and the local economy, on the other, environmental and social pressure from increased numbers of visitors could undermine the quality of life and the resources on which the industry itself depends.
>
> New Forest District Council, 'Our future together: a tourism and visitor management strategy for New Forest District', 1998

The global growth of the tourism industry has encouraged many destinations to consider the opportunities offered by attracting tourists to their area. As tourists seek new experiences, so the frequency of both short and long breaks has increased and the numbers of leisure tourists have increased. Destinations not traditionally seen as tourist resorts are becoming popular places to visit and, thus, pressure to respond to an influx of people lies at the heart of visitor management.

Visitor management involves finding ways to regulate visitors in order to minimize negative impacts and, where possible, maximize the benefits of tourism.[1] This chapter examines the range of techniques that can be employed by tourist businesses and destinations in order to control and manage visitors and, therefore, their impacts. These impacts extend beyond placing pressure on the physical environment – large numbers of tourists can also impact on the host community and its way of life. Furthermore, large tourist numbers can place pressure on infrastructure and superstructure, impacting on the economic balance of the destination.

Controlling the impacts of visitors

A great deal has been written over the past few decades, acknowledging the diverse impacts of tourism and, importantly, considering the ways in which negative impacts can be prevented. Visitor management can help to ensure that the expectations of tourists are balanced against the demands of the host environment, community and tourist businesses. Thus, successful visitor management requires a clear understanding of the demands of these groups and the extent to which they are prepared to compromise their positions in order to achieve a balanced outcome for all stakeholders.

A range of visitor management strategy models have been employed over the years, including the Recreation Opportunity Spectrum, Visitor Impact Management model, Visitor Experience and Resource Protection model and Visitor Activity Management program.[2] The approaches of these models are underpinned by an appreciation of the need to control negative impacts by establishing limits for tourism, embracing two key principles – carrying capacity and the limits of acceptable change.

Carrying capacity

This concept is that there is a finite capacity for a tourist facility or destination and what that is should be established in order to restrict any detrimental impacts. Specifically, this can be defined as 'the maximum use of any site without causing negative effects on the resources, reducing visitor satisfactions, or exerting adverse impacts upon the society, economy or culture of the area'.[3]

The origins of this concept derive from wildlife management, where it has been recognized that plants and animals require certain physical conditions to survive. Once an environment has been altered to a point where those conditions no longer exist, the wildlife populations cannot be sustained. This principle makes the assumption that impacts are likely to be relatively gradual, until a point is reached at which intense changes occur. For the principle of carrying capacity to be effective, clearly the limiting point should be set somewhere before such changes will happen. One critique of this approach proposes that intense impact on environments occurs when use of them first begins, with increased use only adding marginally to that impact. If that is the case, unless all tourists are banned, an increase in visitor numbers will cause little marginal distress to the landscape.

While both perspectives may have validity, it is achieving an understanding of the impacts of use that is the underlying principle here.

While the initial focus of carrying capacity may have been on damage to the physical environment, there is now greater awareness of other carrying capacities. Richardson and Fluker[4] identify five subtypes of carrying capacity, which include the:

- *physical* the number of visitors that the site was designed for or has the ability to accommodate
- *economic* the level at which the tourism business can operate before other industries are squeezed out by the competition for resources
- *perceptual* the level of use that can be accommodated before the psychological experience of visitors is negatively affected
- *social* the numbers of visitors that can be tolerated by the host community
- *ecological* the numbers of tourists that can use an area before damage is done to the natural or biological environment.

For some attractions, such as a staged Wild West show or a city bus tour, the maximum capacity may be fairly easy to determine, based perhaps on the numbers of seats in an auditorium or on the vehicle. For many other attractions, however, such a finite number is often difficult to establish.

Example

King's College Chapel

King's College Chapel, Cambridge, is an exceptionally popular tourist attraction, encouraging many visitors to travel to this university city each year.

When being used for services, the Chapel has a working capacity of around 1000 people. This figure, determined for health and safety reasons, ensures that worshipers can be seated in comfort. When open to tourists as an attraction, however, it is necessary to reconsider this figure. Tourists visiting the chapel are encouraged to walk around, exploring the many unique facets of this sixteenth-century building. As a consequence, the official carrying capacity is lowered, to around 600 people at any one time. The managers of the Chapel have elected to limit the capacity to 400, however, as they believe that having more visitors than this in the Chapel at any one time significantly diminishes the tourists' experience.

In order to avoid disappointment, tour groups are therefore required to prebook their visit and are allocated an entry time. Placing the visitors' experience ahead of profit from greater ticket sales suggests that the visitors' experience is deemed most important for the reputation of King's College.

It is worth commenting that it is difficult to establish one numerical capacity point as various stakeholders are likely to have different perspectives on where the limit lies. For the planners and managers of popular tourist destinations, objectives to protect animal and plant life will need to be balanced with objectives to maintain an environment acceptable to the host community, the tourists and the businesses seeking to profit from visitors. This may lead to conflicting pressures when considering maximum capacity.

Finally, even if an exact number is precisely established, it may then be difficult to control numbers so that they remain within that capacity limit. For example, attractions such as national parks may have several entry points, which makes restricting numbers difficult. Furthermore, fundamental principles such as the right to access national parks may make closure or restrictions unpopular or unenforceable in law. In such cases, a range of more subtle visitor management techniques, discussed in detail later in this chapter, may help to control demand.

As it may be difficult to establish and implement an exact carrying capacity, an alternative approach may be to determine the level of impact or alteration that is acceptable to these user groups, through compromise and negotiation, accepting that some change to the environment will occur.

The limits of acceptable change

This principle acknowledges that humans' use of the natural environment will ultimately lead to change. Therefore, the aim is to manage the destination or attraction through this change, acknowledging that impacts beyond a pre-established level will not be tolerated and responses will be implemented to ensure that the limits of acceptable change (LAC) are not exceeded. The management challenge 'is not one of how to prevent any human-induced change, but rather one of deciding how much change will be allowed to occur, where, and the actions needed to control it'.[5]

The LAC approach requires that the nature of different types of impacts are identified as well as noting where those impacts occur. Managers of the destination or site must then determine the levels of impacts that are acceptable and introduce initiatives to ensure that actual impacts remain within these boundaries or limits. Stankey et al.[6] propose that the LAC process consists of four major components:

1. the specification of acceptable and achievable resource and social conditions, defined by a series of measurable parameters
2. an analysis of the relationship between existing conditions and those judged acceptable
3. identification of management actions necessary to achieve these conditions and
4. a program of monitoring and evaluation of management effectiveness.

Over the years, this approach has been implemented at a variety of destinations and tourist sites, especially in wilderness areas in the USA.

Meeting the cost of visitor management

Both the strategic process of creating a visitor management plan and the implementation of operational methods to control visitors have an inherent cost. For example, there are likely to be significant costs involved in adapting the physical environment – such as constructing paths, a visitor management centre or signage – to control the behaviour of tourists. The costs may be passed on to the visitors, borne by the host community or met by local tourism businesses. In cases where the tourists are expected to meet (or pay a contribution towards) the cost of managing the impact of their activities, a direct charge

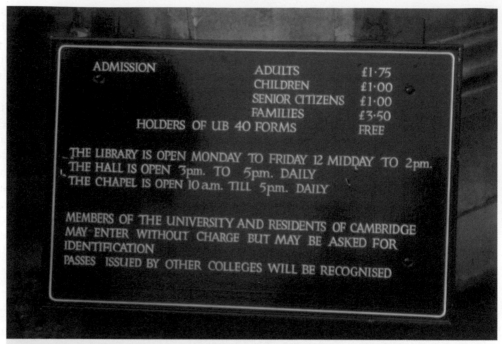

Figure 16.1 Variable pricing for tourists and locals is in operation in Cambridge. *(Photo by Claire Humphreys.)*

for access may be made, perhaps in the form of entry charges. Many popular heritage sites charge entry fees that contribute towards the costs of maintaining the site and making it accessible to visitors. In order to ensure that the local population is not excluded from accessing its local heritage site, a reduced charge or discounted annual fee may be offered (see Figure 16.1).

Example

Change in policy for entry charges to Indian heritage sites

In 2008, the Indian government announced that foreign tourists would no longer be charged entry fees to heritage attractions in US$ but would pay in local currency. In response to the weakening value of the dollar, foreign tourists were now to pay Rs250 for entry into Indian World Heritage sites, such as the Taj Mahal. In contrast to this, domestic tourists are charged an entry fee of Rs10.

Source: 'Now, Rs [rupee] appreciation reaches monuments', *Financial Express*, 14 March 2008.

As an alternative to entry fees, tourists may be required to purchase a licence to gain access to a destination. Limiting licences will further control the number of tourists accessing the protected area. An example of the requirement to obtain a licence is the trekking permit required to enter the Annapurna conservation area in Nepal. More than 25,000 trekkers visit this area annually and the fees collected for the permit to trek is estimated to improve the living standards of around 40,000 local people, as well as funding environmental protection and sustainable tourism initiatives.[7]

Trekking permits are also required for the popular route to Machu Picchu, Peru. A limit of around 500 permits per day are issued, although it is estimated that more than half of these are allocated to the guides, cooks and porters who support the tourists trekking the Inca Trail.

The host community may cover the costs of managing local resources, perhaps through the level of state or council taxes that they are required to pay, while businesses may be required to make a contribution through their business rates. Tourism companies may foot the bill for visitor management through demands to adapt their operations, perhaps by constructing supporting infrastructure, funding information provision, marketing campaigns or other similar activities.

While many tourist attractions are commercially operated businesses, some resources are under the control of governments. Natural environments, such as national parks and wilderness areas, as well as some built heritage sites, may be the responsibility of governments, who must provide the funding to protect, maintain and manage them. In such cases, governments may open such resources to the public and tourists as part of a remit to provide access. The costs of implementing effective visitor management are likely to be borne by the public purse.

Operational approaches to visitor management

The operational techniques employed to manage visitors and their impacts can be broadly separated into two categories: 'hard' and 'soft' management. The **hard management** techniques are those methods that restrict tourists' activities, perhaps through financial or physical controls. **Soft management** techniques focus on coercing a change in behaviour, through design or subtle persuasion.

Table 16.1 Examples of hard and soft visitor management techniques.

Hard techniques	Soft techniques
Closure of attraction or areas within an attraction.	Marketing.
Zoning.	Directional signage.
Permits and licences.	Limited infrastructure development.
Vehicle bans.	Codes of conduct.
Entrance fees.	Education and information provision.

While hard techniques have been a common approach employed to protect the environment and resources from the pressures of tourism, the use of soft techniques can help to balance the need to protect with the need to provide positive experiences for visitors. For example, educating visitors about the impacts they have and the ways in which these effects can be minimized can serve not only to encourage improved behaviour but also to provide a greater engagement with the activities undertaken to protect resources from demand pressures (see Figure 16.2).

More than 20 years ago, the Department of Employment and the English Tourist Board produced a report, 'Tourism and the environment: maintaining the balance',[8] designed to encourage improved management of tourism resources. This identified the following three key areas for managing visitors.

- *Controlling demand* may be achieved by attempting to spread the arrival of visitors throughout the year. Furthermore, it may be possible to control the areas that are accessed by visitors. This can ensure that tourism is more evenly spread across the area

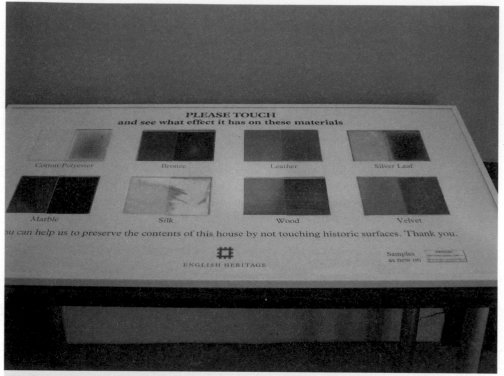

Figure 16.2 At Eltham Palace, near London, a display by English Heritage demonstrates wear and tear on the fabric of a building caused by visitors.
(Photo by Chris Holloway.)

(reducing the intensity of pressure). An alternative may be to contain visitors in one location that, while intensifying the pressure in one specific location, does allow protection of other areas left untouched by the tourists. Ultimately, control may be achieved by limiting total numbers, the amount of time that tourists can spend at a location or banning access altogether.

- *Altering visitors' behaviour* may be possible through increased awareness. Encouraging tourists to understand the impact of their presence and take responsibility for the effects that has may lead to improved behaviour, thus reducing the impact. Codes of conduct are often designed to encourage such responsibility.

- *Adapting supply* can ensure that the resources are better placed to cope with demand. This may include developing supporting infrastructure, such as roads and paths, toilets and information centres.

It should be appreciated that these areas are interlinked, and employing initiatives that seek to consider all three areas can provide greater benefits than just attempting to address one area alone. Therefore, the techniques identified in the following sections recognize the effects on all three realms.

Controlling demand and flows of visitors

All too often, discussion relating to visitor management at a destination only arises when problems start to emerge, yet it is vital that policies and the actions required to successfully manage the impacts of tourism should be introduced as soon as visitor flows begin. As demand levels change, so the strategies for managing visitors should be revisited. A variety of initiatives can be implemented to adjust the flows of visitors.

Pricing policies and strategies

Price mechanisms are often proposed as means of controlling tourist demand, with an increase in prices expected to reduce the number of visitors attracted. As prices are often relatively inelastic where major tourist attractions are concerned, however, this may not always have the desired limiting effect.

The benefit of employing a pricing policy is that it raises revenue that can help to finance the implementation of visitor management. Selective taxation on hotel accommodation or higher charges for parking can also be imposed, but some criticize this as a regressive tax, affecting the less well-off but having little effect on the wealthy.

For some attractions, the use of pricing as a means of controlling demand can be controversial. Several religious buildings (including St Paul's Cathedral in London and St Basil's Cathedral in Moscow) have introduced entry charges, often using the funds to assist with the costs of maintenance, but the charge does not sit easily with many, who feel that places designed for religious worship should not be limiting entry to those who can afford the charge.

Controlling access through ticketing and licensing

Limiting entry through some form of visa or licence is another practical alternative. Requiring prior application in order to gain access can allow destination managers or tourism businesses the chance to deter arrivals. The number of visas or licences can be restricted, both in total and across time periods – the latter helping to manage seasonality. An example is that implemented by the government of Bhutan, which limits tourists to a few thousand every year, each of whom is required to meet a minimum daily spend on their travel arrangements. Thus, control by licence simultaneously restricts tourists and provides the government with useful revenue, directly and indirectly.

Timed tickets, which allocate visitors to a particular time of day, help to spread demand for the resource, while providing tourists with an opportunity to participate in other activities in the meantime. This can significantly enhance the visitors' experience as well as benefiting the destination – visitors can see other attractions in the area as well as using the time to eat and shop, which can significantly increase their spend.

Restricting activities

In order to control the impacts of tourist demand, it may be necessary to set regulations or policies that restrict the use of tourist resources. There are various ways in which

Example

The Everglades ban all-terrain vehicles

The Florida Fish and Wildlife Conservation Commission (FWCC) announced a ban on these off-road vehicles that came into effect in July 2008. The extensive use of these cars in the Everglades area has led to substantial damage to plant and wildlife, as well as the widening of paths, creating 'virtual mud highways leading from the road into the marsh'.

Source: S. Cocking, 'New ATV ban scheduled to take effect July 1', *The Miami Herald*, 1 June 2008.

restrictions can be implemented. Failing to expand supporting infrastructure is an option sometimes chosen by local authorities in an attempt to discourage visitors. This can be effective, but, unfortunately, it can impact on local residents equally, whose frustrations with, say, inadequate road systems may lead to a political backlash.

Additionally, it may be considered appropriate to control the length of time tourists spend at the destination. This may be vitally important in popular locations, where keeping the visitors flowing is vital. Linked to this is a management approach that can restrict the use of sites at particular times.

In addition to restricting the time spent at an attraction, it may be helpful to restrict access by groups or the range of activities allowed at particular sites. For example, camping and camp fires may be banned in fragile forest areas of some national parks.

Marketing

Another form of control can be achieved through marketing, concentrating publicity on less popular attractions or geographical regions and promoting the low season. For example, the national tourist board VisitBritain might stress the appeal of the north-east of England in its marketing abroad, making little reference to the south west, which already attracts a high proportion of domestic tourists.

Attempts to do this may be frustrated by private-sector promotions, however. Airlines, for example, may prefer to concentrate on promoting those destinations for which they already have strong demand, although credit must be given to the no frills carriers, which have opened up new areas by flying to small provincial airports. There is always a danger that if the public-sector strategy is too successful and tourists are siphoned off to the new regions, the amenities and attractions at more popular sites could suffer a downturn in business. These popular sites may be better able to cope with large levels of tourism, while the diversion of visitors to other areas less able to cope with a large influx may cause new problems for both the established and the new destination.

Niche markets

To ensure a consistent demand for tourism all year round, it may be advisable for marketing efforts to try to attract specific niche sectors. For example, the conference market may be sought by a seaside resort destination as these events tend to take place outside the traditional summer holiday period. Thus, a large conference can fill bed spaces and use restaurants, transport and meetings venues at a time when other holiday markets are scarce.

Alternatively, marketing activities may focus on encouraging the traditional holiday-makers to visit at less popular times of the year. In some cases, external factors, such as school and public holidays, mean that some people cannot be encouraged to alter the time they travel, but other travellers may not be restricted by such factors. To take one example, retired or childless travellers may be encouraged to adjust when they travel to the shoulder season, spreading demand and reducing congestion.

Dispersal of tourists into less congested areas may be a valuable strategy in other ways, too. Changing the behaviour of the more flexible traveller may be achieved by offering lower prices, but importantly this can also be achieved through marketing and information provision, making the traveller aware of the benefits of travelling to the destination at a quieter time or to a less popular area of the destination. While the benefits for the traveller may include less congestion, fewer queues and improved service as staff are less pressured, it is also useful to highlight that such a shift in behaviour can help to protect resources, limiting pressure on the natural environment, reducing the likelihood of accidents and reducing other pressures that may affect the quality of life for the host community. In this way, tourists may be encouraged to adjust their travel patterns to protect the destination.

Demarketing

It may seem unimaginable to some businesses or destinations, but there are several examples where too many tourists wish to visit a place, leading to marketing activities being undertaken to deter visitors. Efforts may focus on trying to discourage visitors during peak times or dissuade those tourists who will be less profitable. Kotler and Levy defined the concept of demarketing as 'that aspect of marketing that deals with discouraging customers in general or a certain class of customers in particular on either a temporary or permanent basis.'[9]

A variety of adjustments to the marketing mix can be employed in demarketing, including increasing the price for some or all of the market, reducing promotional activities and limiting sales outlets offering access to the product. Such actions can be controversial, however. Restricting access to those who can afford the higher price may be perceived as elitist, while a reduction in promotional efforts by a destination management organization (DMO) may not be popular with local tourist businesses.

Altering visitors' behaviour

While acknowledging the benefits of reducing the impact of tourism through restrictions on demand, it is also helpful to appreciate that management of those tourists who do visit can also help to control the pressures caused. This will improve the tourists' experience, as it can reduce conflicts between different stakeholder groups

Interpretation, information and education

Information can be provided in a variety of ways, both prior to visiting and on reaching the attraction or destination.

One reason for providing information to visitors may be to meet obligations to educate – often an important remit for attractions funded by governments, such as galleries and museums. Providing an interpretation of exhibits or information about landscapes and buildings can help to fulfil this obligation.

Adequate information can also help to change the behaviour of visitors. For example, telling them about the pressures caused by tourism and the ways in which such pressures can be reduced can encourage visitors to develop an awareness of their responsibility and the impact of their activities, but it is important to stress that the majority of tourists do not set out to harm or damage the destination they visit. Cole[10] reports that, 'while some tourists may be open to learning, they are often unaware of appropriate behaviour and have little guidance on how to behave'.

It is often the combined activities of tourists en masse that cause significant pressures and problems for destinations. It is possible to adjust the behaviour of each tourist, however, through education and information, leading to significant adjustments to the overall impact for the destinations. There is a variety of ways in which visitors can be informed, including signage, guides and codes of conduct.

Signs and guides

There is an extensive diversity in the signs and guides available to inform and educate tourists. The reasons for their provision are also varied and they may be funded either by tourism businesses or governments at local or regional level.

Signposting can fall into two categories – informational or directional. Informational signs can provide interpretation of a particular point of interest or act as a marker, pointing it out. An example of this may be a blue plaque on a building identifying a location as the place of birth of a significant person in history (Figure 16.3). Informational signing is used to add to the knowledge of visitors, thus enhancing their experience.

Figure 16.3 Blue plaque marking the residence of philanthropist Quintin Hogg. *(Photo by Claire Humphreys.)*

Directional signposting is used to assist tourists to navigate, perhaps finding their way to a tourist attraction or locating particular amenities or facilities, such as toilets. Directional signage needs to be clear, consistent in style and suitably positioned.

Early warning is vital for car drivers navigating unknown routes, so signs must be positioned well in advance of junctions and repetition of signs may be needed. Directional signs may not necessarily take car drivers on the shortest or most direct route. Often routes are designed to encourage the use of bypass or ring roads, as well as keeping tourist traffic away from commonly congested areas. The growing popularity of satellite navigation systems, however, may lead to many of these diversionary tactics becoming ineffective.

Signs aimed at pedestrians must generally provide the most convenient and safest routes, taking into consideration the needs of those with pushchairs, in wheelchairs or those less stable on their feet.

Directional signs may also be provided for specific groups, such as walkers, cyclists or horse riders (see Figure 15.10, for example), each having their own specific requirements for convenient routes.

For a less well-known destination or visitor attraction it may be necessary to provide guides to help interpret the nature and importance of the place. Guides can play a very important visitor management role, however, so even well-known or established destinations use them to inform visitors, seeking to influence their behaviour.

Perhaps the commonest type of guide is the tour guide – a person who takes on an explanatory role, providing information about the heritage and history of a destination as well as describing the operation of machinery at an attraction or topics relating to the local population. An example may be seen in the case of the guide who takes a small group on a factory tour of the Ferrari car plant in Italy, explaining the equipment or processes en route. Alternatively an explanatory guide may be tasked with explaining the different stages of a religious service to observers witnessing it for the first time.

Guides may also take on the role of wardens, controlling the behaviour of tourists at the destination. In such cases, the guide may inform the visitor of expected modes of behaviour and remove or chastise tourists who do not conform. In that way the guide acts to protect the resources by reducing or removing threats caused by those tourists who may be ignorant of the effects of their actions. While the role of such a guide may sound severe, in reality it may only require him or her to ask and visitors will respond. For example, guides will commonly ask visitors to dress suitably when entering religious buildings, be quieter when walking through areas where rare animals may be spotted and avoid entering buildings if they are residences of the local population. In such cases, only when tourists ignore the advice is there a need for the guide to take more severe action.

A guide can also take the role of a director or leader, selecting routes that can take tourists to less congested areas or less well-known attractions, helping to relieve pressures on the destination. The guide can also determine the length of time spent at particular sites, which may be vital at popular sites as it ensures that a turnover of visitors is achieved. The guide who acts as a group leader may also be able to divert tourists to other attractions. There have been many examples of tour groups being taken to 'attractions' that offer little more than shopping opportunities (for which the tour guide may be provided with a financial reward for bringing the group there). While many tourists have negative reactions to such actions, the practice remains widespread.

Example

Rogue tour guides

In Australia, the New South Wales Office of Fair Trading was investigating several complaints of 'forced' shopping. The circumstances related to cases where the 'tour guide takes them to selected venues that have paid kickbacks' to gain the opportunity to hard-sell products and souvenirs to the visitors. More than 20 complaints had been received in the first three months of 2008. The Department of Fair Trading also reported that the problem was widespread in Surfers Paradise, Queensland.

In addition to the issue of forced shopping, complaints had also been received that tourists were being taken to Coolangatta, while being told it was Surfers Paradise, thus keeping the visitors away from the main tourist area and under the control of the tour guide.

Source: P. Gleeson, 'Tourists tell of rip-off rogues', *Gold Coast Bulletin*, 26 March 2008.

A final role for the tour guide may be that of public relations. Given that guides have the tourists in their company often for an hour or more, they have an extensive opportunity to provide positive information in order to enhance the image of the destination.

Travel guidebooks conveniently provide tourists with details about the destinations they are visiting. Books can include information on the history, attractions, facilities and amenities in the area, as well as some key phrases or words in the local language. The German publisher Baedeker set the standards when it started to print travel books over 150 years ago, providing accurate, detailed information in its travel guides, and, since then, companies such as Lonely Planet, Rough Guide, Frommer's, Fodor, Insights and numerous others have produced their own city and country guides covering the globe.

Information provided to visitors in the form of guides can have an impact on their behaviour at destinations. Written guides can be designed to highlight the range of facilities or attractions in an area, which can in turn encourage a longer dwell time. Guides can also be published to provide information about a specific attraction, detailing the history and enhancing the visitors' interpretation of exhibits. They can also act as a souvenir of a visit.

Difficulties faced when deciding to publish guides are extensive. If guides are to be sold to tourists, then the amount of information included must justify the price to be paid. Major attractions or destinations will need to consider several versions in different languages to serve their most popular markets. Adaptations for different markets may involve adjusting the content by identifying relevant areas of interest. If guides are to be provided free to visitors, then the costs of their production may need to be controlled, which may limit the size and quality of the guide. If free guides are to be offered, it may be necessary to consider how these complement any other guides available for purchase.

Technology has been successfully developed which means audio guides have become commonplace at tourist attractions. The use of human guides has been discussed above, but here we need to consider prerecorded commentaries available in places such as museums, tourist attractions and now, more commonly, on city bus tours.

Audio guides can provide an extensive range of information on specific topics, but, unlike a human guide, offer no opportunity for questions to be answered. They are often available in a variety of languages and can be programmed to provide specific segments of information at particular locations. In museums, signs close to exhibits can show codes that can be entered into an audio guide for the visitor to hear the relevant segment of explanation. Technology thus allows prerecorded guides to offer a level of control over the information provided to visitors.

The rapid growth in popularity of digital music players (including iPods and telephones that can play MP3 audio files) has also provided visitors with the opportunity to download files containing information designed to enhance their visit.

Example

Bring your own guide

As more and more travellers take their music players with them on holiday, so the online market for downloadable audio guides of city destinations has taken off. There are many different companies offering prerecorded information, often structured as a walking tour of the city with a charge being made for each download. Examples include Tourist Tracks (**www.tourist-tracks.com**), Audio Steps (**www.audiosteps.com**) and Tourcaster (**www.tourcaster.com**).

In the summer of 2007, the National Gallery in London decided to bring its art to the public, placing reproductions of its most popular paintings in locations across central London. To provide information to support this initiative, maps and free audio guides explaining the paintings were available to download, allowing the public to take a tour of these locations at their own convenience.

Codes of conduct

The creation of codes of conduct can place responsibility for the impact and problems caused by tourism on those who cause them or have a role to play in reducing them. The existence of such codes is more than just regulation of behaviour – it also plays a role in education, raising awareness of the problems and issues. While codes of conduct are often aimed at tourists, there are many cases where host communities and tourism businesses are encouraged to agree to codes of conduct to ensure that their actions and operations are responsible.

Example

Code of conduct against the sexual exploitation of children in tourism

In 2004, the United Nations World Tourism Organisation, together with End Child Prostitution, Child Pornography and the Trafficking of Children for Sexual Purposes (ECPAT) and UNICEF, introduced a code of conduct for the travel industry that is designed to protect children from commercial exploitation, especially in the sex tourism industry.

In agreeing to abide by the code of conduct to protect children, the tourist organization agrees to:

- establish an ethical corporate policy against commercial sexual exploitation of children
- train personnel in the country of origin and where children are sexually exploited
- introduce clauses in contracts with suppliers, stating a common repudiation of sexual exploitation of children
- provide information to travellers on the sexual exploitation of children
- provide information to local 'key persons' at destinations
- report annually.

This code of conduct has become a key instrument in the prevention of child sex tourism worldwide. The initiative is recognized by the travel industry, child protection organizations, several governments and international organizations. By March 2008, over 600 signatory companies in 23 countries on all continents had signed up to the code.[11]

Codes of conduct are suggested as being relatively easy to introduce as well as effective.[12] This is especially true in cases that include significant levels of restrictions, which, if implemented through local legislation, may take years to reach the statute books.[13]

The disadvantage of voluntary codes of conduct, however, is that they may have limitations, such as being unable to effectively penalise offenders when the regulations are breached or ignored. To be successful, such codes rely on a moral consensus being reached to abide by the principles in order to achieve the desired goals. As companies are being encouraged to consider their social responsibility roles, so greater pressure to abide by codes of conduct may be felt.

Adapting supply

In order to protect attractions such as natural and heritage areas, there is often a need to make changes or adaptations to the supporting infrastructure. This can help to ensure that the demands of tourists are best served, while reducing negative pressures on the resource itself.

Queuing

In many areas of life there is the need to queue – perhaps in a post office, a supermarket, to be served in a bar or café, waiting for a customer service assistant on the telephone. Unsurprisingly, queues are every bit as evident in the tourism business. While there are many initiatives aimed at reducing or dispensing with them, in some cases queues can be seen as a sign of popularity, attracting attention and, on occasion, they may even be encouraged.

Queues form when the arrival rate is higher than the time taken to service those arrivals. For example, passengers on a plane landing at an airport will disembark at the same time and reach customs together. As it takes time for the border security staff to process each of these passengers, the outcome will be the formation of a queue.

Having to queue can create a negative impression, affecting the visitors' experience. There has been extensive research into ways to shorten wait times as well as understanding attitudes towards waiting. Over 20 years ago, David Maister[14] explored the psychology of waiting and suggested eight propositions:

- occupied time feels shorter than unoccupied time
- an 'in process' wait feels shorter than waiting to get started
- stress and anxiety can make the wait feel longer
- uncertain waits feel longer than finite, known waits
- unexplained waits can appear longer than explained delays
- unfair waits appear longer than equitable waits
- waiting alone seems longer than waiting with a group
- the more valuable the service, the longer the customer will wait.

These propositions can give insight into strategies that can be introduced to manage the experience of waiting visitors. They can be commonly seen in the activities of those tourist operations where queues are prevalent – theme parks, airports, catering establishments and hotel receptions, for example. Here are some responses to managing queues.

- *Entertaining visitors while they wait* This can be achieved through a range of distractions, such as providing entertainers to amuse a queue waiting for a theme park ride. This does not necessarily have to be expensive or high-tech – for example, a wall of mirrors that distort the image can entertain visitors as they move slowly along the queue. A restaurant may ask customers to wait in the bar while their table is prepared or peruse the menu. While distracting customers from the wait, this can also provide the impression that they are in process, that their presence has been acknowledged and they will be seated in the restaurant in due course.

- *Start the process* It is useful to greet customers and assess their needs. This can ensure that customers have not waited only to discover later that they are in the wrong place or that they need not have joined the queue. This can help service providers identify VIP customers – the business may have a policy to service these customers in a different manner. For example, the airline easyJet has introduced a 'speedy boarding' ticket that customers can purchase when booking their tickets. The ticket allows travellers to use a dedicated check-in desk, generally with shorter queues, and board the plane first. While such tickets can be lucrative for the airline, they can help reduce perceived waiting times for passengers, which, in turn, may help to reduce anxiety and stress.

- *Use customers as a resource* Asking customers to complete paperwork while they are in the queue or even prior to arrival may reduce the time needed to service each customer, thus shortening the length of queues. Car hire company Avis offers frequent customers the opportunity to complete a hire agreement form in advance that can then be applied to all their rentals. This reduces the need for paperwork for each occasion and allows customers to bypass the hire desk, going straight to the parking lot to collect their prebooked car. This benefits both the frequent traveller as well as other customers as it reduces the queue at the service counter.

- *Informing customers of the length of time they can expect to wait* This is an important factor in enhancing customers' experience. While many flyers may be happy to wait an hour or more at an airport, often being entertained by the duty-free shopping or restaurants, once their expected departure time has passed, only short waits will be tolerated before their level of satisfaction is affected. Keeping customers informed of delays can allow each individual to make a choice about how the time is to be spent. For instance, advising that the plane will be delayed by an hour may allow the customer the chance to go to a bookshop to purchase reading matter, check e-mails or make business calls, have something to eat or grab a last-minute gift from a souvenir shop. While companies are encouraged to be honest about waiting times, there are occasions when expected delays are exaggerated so customers are pleasantly surprised when they experience a shorter delay than they had prepared themselves for. Restaurants, especially, may employ this tactic. Many theme parks, too, manage their queues by informing visitors of the time it will take to reach the front of the line.

- *Use equitable queuing systems* Confronting customers with several queues requiring them to make a decision can cause anxiety that other queues will move faster or the queue joined may be the wrong one. A common resolution to this problem is to create one long queue, with customers being allocated to a service agent only when they reach the front. This can encourage a sense of fairness. Signs are also important. Customers need to know that their particular need can be addressed by the service agents once they reach the front of the queue.

- *Introduce separate queues for those customers who can be serviced quickly* Cafés may create a separate counter for takeaway service, separating these customers from others who may need to wait for a table. Ski resorts and theme parks often employ a similar system for 'singles' or customers prepared to ride the ski-lift or rollercoaster without their friends alongside them. Such an initiative allows every seat to be filled, thus moving more passengers through the system, shortening the waiting time for all customers.

- *Consider the use of booking systems* Allocating fixed time slots can spread the arrivals of customers, but it is vital that the time between those slots is appropriate. If the slots are too far apart, then resources may be left idle, but if it is too short, then a backlog will build, frustrating later arrivals. Booking systems may also fail if customers do not show for their appointments, so it may be necessary to impose penalties on customers who fail to come at their allocated time. Applying penalties may be problematic, however. The causes of delays or missed appointments may be beyond the control of customers, who will have already suffered stress, so penalizing them still further can create antagonism towards the business. Flexibility regarding imposing penalties may be needed.

While businesses should evaluate *actual* waiting times, analysing what may cause congestion points within their operations, using a range of strategies to reduce the *perceived* time spent queuing to be served can be an important factor in enhancing customer satisfaction and effectively managing visitors.

Zoning

For popular destinations that receive large numbers of tourists, it may be beneficial to group together those who have similar expectations or patterns of behaviour. For example, those tourists who wish to relax and sunbathe on a beach may be separated from those who wish to play ball sports. This can be achieved by providing volleyball nets, goals and other such facilities in one area, making it attractive for those playing sports to move to that location. Similarly, at seashores or lakes, areas allocated to sailors, windsurfers and so on may be separated from those allocated to swimmers.

While zoning is an effective tool for managing a variety of demands for resources and reducing the potential for conflicts between users, it is also used to balance the demands of users with conservation ideals, protecting the natural environment. This has been seen in relation to the protection of marine parks as well as national parks.[15]

Zoning has also been used to balance conflicting demands of tourists and the host population. This may be achieved through planning policy and is used in urban as well as rural locations. Tourist zones are often prevalent in cities, where attractions, accommodation, amenities such as bars, restaurants, currency exchange facilities and so on, are clustered together, all benefiting from the large numbers of tourists drawn to these areas.

Example

Bateman's Marine Park, Australia

In 2006, the New South Wales state government announced plans to zone an area of the south coast as a marine park. The plans included an exclusion zone covering just under one-fifth of the total 85,000 hectares.

A local industry body, Coastal Rights, representing commercial fishermen, charter boat operators and tourist resort owners, suggested that this plan would have a major impact on their businesses.[16] Countering this, the Nature Coast Marine Group argued that the creation of the marine park would provide opportunities to grow eco-tourism in the region.[17]

Following months of consultation, protection of the area was introduced in June 2007, with the creation of four different zones:

- 19 per cent has been allocated to a sanctuary zone – the highest level of protection and where fishing and damage to plants and fish are prohibited

- 43 per cent was allocated to habitat zones – provide protection, but allow small levels of recreational and commercial fishing

- 37 per cent has been allocated for general recreational and commercial uses – although these activities must be environmentally sustainable

- 0.4 per cent of the area has been allocated for specific purposes – marinas, scientific research zones and so on.

While over AUS$10 million[18] was expected to be used to buy back the rights of commercial fishing businesses, as these activities were restricted in many areas, the introduction of the marine park did not hinder locals and tourists in pursuits such as swimming and diving. Although there were concerns voiced that zoning restrictions would deter tourists, initial reports suggest that these were unfounded, as 2008 actually saw increased numbers of visitors to the area.

Closure

While zoning areas for particular use can help to balance the conflicting demands of users, in some cases protection and visitor management can only be achieved by means of closure. One approach may be to close an area by erecting fences and security, refusing entry to the site. This can achieve a maximum reduction in access and ensure that an area is protected from the demands of tourists. Refusing entry to all visitors, including the local population, however, may be seen as extreme and a more moderate form of restriction may be desired.

Protection of some attractions or destinations may be achieved by restricting opening hours – perhaps only allowing afternoon visits or access just at weekends. This can significantly reduce the impact of visitors. If such an approach is to be employed, it is necessary to provide tourists and tour operators with information about the restricted hours. This ensures that tourists are not disappointed by arriving and finding that the attraction is closed. In such situations, marketing efforts should focus on explaining that the closure provides a means of protection.

The pressure caused by the excessive demands of tourism may also be managed by the use of selective closure. This may restrict access to particular parts of the destination or attraction, perhaps by means of a zoning policy, marketing efforts to divert attention or changes to the infrastructure. An example of limited closure to protect a site from the impact of visitors can be seen in the case of Stonehenge – a World Heritage site in the south west of England. The site introduced a rope fence around the stones, keeping tourists some distance from the historic stones. This has reduced the amount of erosion previously resulting from visitors touching and walking through the circle.

Pedestrianization

In recent years, it has become increasingly common to protect the central areas of towns and cities by restricting access by cars – in effect, pedestrianizing the area. Changing road systems is a complex and expensive task, but the rapid increase in car ownership has required cities – especially those with historic centres not designed to cope with modern-day traffic – to impose measures to control traffic flows. This has the added benefit of enhancing the experience of both locals and visitors, who no longer have to compete with the traffic for space. The absence of cars parked in historic city centres also enhances the visual experience of the site.

While it is common for pedestrianization to be a permanent feature, in some cases the closure may be for only short periods of time. For example, there are several provincial towns in France that close the central streets in order to allow street markets to take place. In Cambridge, England, closure of parts of the central area occur between 10 a.m. and 4 p.m., achieved by closing gates located at key entrance points to the central area.

When implementing pedestrianization, it is important to ensure that the improved environment also addresses health and safety demands. This may mean ensuring that emergency vehicles can gain access to the enclosed area if required. Areas must be made safe for all users, especially those who may have visual or mobility impairments. Pedestrianized areas can be used as social and event spaces for the local community, but, however used, it is vital that the area is perceived to be safe and free from crime.

Example

Limited pedestrianization of Oxford Street, London

Oxford Street is one of the busiest shopping streets in London, with more than 100 million shopping trips to the area ooccurring annually. It is also a major thoroughfare, carrying more than 220 buses an hour, but there has been government enthusiasm to improve the area, which is popular with both visitors and local shoppers.

In 2008, Westminster City Council announced plans for a £40 million improvement scheme that would see traffic reduction measures, including pedestrianization of the surrounding streets. Complete pedestrianization of this street has not been proposed, however, despite this being a manifesto pledge of the former mayor of London, Ken Livingstone. This will mean that the demands of foot traffic will be balanced with those of the traffic. Rosemarie MacQueen,[19] director of planning and city development, Westminster City Council, revealed that:

> plans include redesigning Oxford Street to reduce the volume of traffic, giving it wider pavements and part-pedestrianising some of the side streets for al fresco dining, street art and performances.

Improvements will also be made to ease pedestrian movement into neighbouring Regent Street and Bond Street. The goal is to achieve the changes in time for the 2012 Olympics.

Research into pedestrianization schemes in a selection of German and UK cities[20] revealed that, while pedestrianization of areas can lead, in the short term, to a downturn in trade for local shops, in the longer term it can lead to improvements in turnover. Thus, pedestrianization can gain great support from local enterprises, as well as being beneficial for locals and visitors who use the area.

Gateways

It is possible to manage the pressure caused by the influx of tourists by creating gateways. These are conveniently accessible routes providing access to popular areas, directing demand through those areas best able to cope with it and they are designed to manage the impacts of that demand. Encouraging tourists to use specific gateways to tourist

Example

The Glencoe Visitor Centre, Scotland

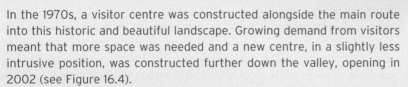

In the 1970s, a visitor centre was constructed alongside the main route into this historic and beautiful landscape. Growing demand from visitors meant that more space was needed and a new centre, in a slightly less intrusive position, was constructed further down the valley, opening in 2002 (see Figure 16.4).

The new centre includes an exhibition, which informs visitors about the area's historical past, relating to the seventeenth-century massacre, as well as providing information about the natural landscape. This uses multimedia, in a variety of languages to try to meet the needs of all visitors to the centre.

Alongside the exhibition is a café, shop, ranger outpost and lookout point. All of these facilities can help encourage informed behaviour by those choosing to walk or travel though the glen. In some cases visitors view the centre as the only stopping point necessary, thus this gateway resource helps to eliminate these visitors having any further impact on the natural environment. The lookout point with telescope may provide the closest view that some get to this mountainous area.

Figure 16.4 Glencoe Visitor Centre, Scotland.
(Photo by Chris Holloway.)

areas can be achieved by good signs, marketing, the location of convenient coach drop-off points and the creation of facilitating resources, such as visitor centres and parking spaces.

Visitor and tourist information centres (TICs)

Visitor and tourist information centres can play many roles: they can be used to educate visitors, perhaps affecting their behaviour, granting protection to the resource, and they can become an attraction in their own right.

In this way, visitor centres may provide convenient parking points for visitors, attracting tourists in a way that can then be conveniently managed. For example, in areas of natural beauty, they may act as a gateway or starting point for tourists' exploration of the area, perhaps on foot or by other transport. This role as a hub means that trails (walking, cycling and driving routes) can be constructed, influencing the behaviour of the visitors.

Trails and pathways

Trails may be used to disperse tourists, relieving pressure on an area and encouraging less well-known areas to be accessed. Alternatively, trails may be designed to cope with large numbers of visitors — perhaps by constructing surfaced paths, informative signs and toilet facilities. While such approaches may *increase* various impacts on these routes, they also serve to protect those areas that are less able to cope with such influxes of visitors. They can often be controversial, however, as the amount of construction necessary to hard surface paths to manage the footfall of the many visitors can mar the landscape, affecting its natural beauty. This has to be balanced with the fact that, in many cases, constructing such paths can control erosion of the land, as well as control the spread of damage. Furthermore, the surfacing of paths can create an environment that is better able to cope with increased numbers of tourists. The downside is that this ultimately makes access easier, further stimulating increases in demand.[21]

Transport links

Gateways can be linked with supporting transport services. This may include park and ride options, which can provide mass transport services to sensitive areas. These may exist in both urban and rural areas. Many historic cities have set up park and ride facilities to cope with the demand for access from the local population as well as visitors, while, in rural locations, including national parks, such schemes can limit the need for car journeys into wilderness or natural areas.

Example

Glacier Park, Montana

This national park, located in the northern part of the state, close to the Canadian border, operates a series of shuttle bus routes to provide the public with access to areas throughout the park. This especially focuses on servicing the popular 'Going-to-the-sun' route. Visitors are encouraged to use this service to help reduce congestion on the roads in the area and the level of emissions from private cars. It is also suggested that, as the cost of using the shuttle is included in the fee to enter the national park, it is cheaper for visitors than paying car parking costs.

Technology that can assist in visitor management

Many tourist businesses have employed a variety of technological methods to examine visitor behaviour in order to improve the experience for their customers. To take one example, Alton Towers, one of the largest theme parks in the UK, provided selected visitors with an electronic badge that used tracking technology to monitor the time they spent in particular areas of the park and the routes they took. This provided the park managers with information that could help them decide where to site new rides or catering facilities. Badge monitoring is often used at business events such as conferences and exhibitions, too, tracking the movements of visitors. Camera technology is also used to monitor visitor behaviour, identifying areas where queues might build up or tourists are reacting negatively to particular resources.

The Internet can provide a variety of opportunities to enhance visitor management, including the dissemination of information and the means to conveniently prebook tickets, thus allowing the flow of visitor arrivals to be managed. An example of this is the use of the Internet by airlines to manage visitors through the provision of online check-in. This can help to speed visitors through the airport system.

Future issues

As the number of tourist trips is predicted to grow, there is the need to manage the increasing pressure they put on resources. Coupled with this is an increased awareness of the need for environmental management, as well as protection of host communities. In addition, tourists are demanding new and unique experiences, as well as higher levels of quality and consistency from their holidays. On the supply side, new destinations, attractions and amenities are being established, creating greater levels of competition between businesses. Combined, these factors lead to increased demand to manage the visitors, enhance their experience and manage the problems and pressures that they cause.

Notes

1. Mason, P. (2005) 'Visitor management in protected areas: from hard to soft approaches', *Current Issues in Tourism*, 8 (2&3).
2. Richardson, J. I. and Fluker, M. (2004) *Understanding and Managing Tourism*, Pearson Education.
3. McIntyre, G. (1993) *Sustainable Tourism Development*, World Tourism Organization, cited in McCool, S. F. and Lime, D. W. (2001) 'Tourism carrying capacity: tempting fantasy or useful reality?' *Journal of Sustainable Tourism*, 9 (5), pp. 372–88.
4. Richardson and Fluker, 2004.
5. Stankey, G. H., Cole, D. N., Lucas, R. C., Petersen, M. E. and Frissell, S. S. (1985). 'The limits of acceptable change (LAC) system for wilderness planning', United States Department of Agriculture: Forest Service.
6. Stankey, et al., 1985.
7. Details of Annapurna Conservation Area Project (ACAP) are available online at: **www.visitnepal.com/acap**

8. Department of Employment and English Tourist Board (1991) 'Tourism and the environment: maintaining the balance', Department of Employment and English Tourist Board.

9. Kotler, P. and Levy, S. J. (1971) 'Demarketing? Yes, demarketing!', *Harvard Business Review*, 49 (6), pp. 74–80.

10. Cole, S. (2007) 'Implementing and evaluating a code of conduct for visitors', *Tourism Management*, 28, pp. 443–5.

11. *The Code Quarterly*, 15, January–March 2008. Available online at: **www.thecode.org**

12. Cole., 2007.

13. Garrod, B. and Fennell, D. A. (2004) 'An analysis of whalewatching codes of conduct', *Annals of Tourism Research*, 31 (2), pp. 334–52.

14. Maister, D. (1985) 'The psychology of waiting lines', *Harvard Business School*, Note 9, May, pp. 2–3.

15. Geneletti, D. and van Duren, I. (2008) 'Protected area zoning for conservation and use: a combination of spatial multicriteria and multiobjective evaluation', *Landscape and Urban Planning*, 85 (?), 10 April, pp. 97–110.

16. ABC (2006) 'Anglers angry over Batemans Bay marine park plan', *Australian Broadcasting Corporation News*, 15 July.

17. ABC (2006) 'Batemans Marine Park brings eco-tourism opportunities', *Australian Broadcasting Corporation News*, 16 April.

18. NSW government (2006) 'Batemans Marine Park Zoning Plan out today – news release', NSW government, 13 December.

19. MacQueen, R. and Dickinson, R. (2008) 'Response: Oxford Street's 100 million shoppers don't want a cloned mall: the West End is unique – let's keep it that way', *The Guardian*, 29 April.

20. Hass-Klau, C. (1993) 'Impact of pedestrianization and traffic calming on retailing', *Transport Policy*, 1 (1), pp. 21–31.

21. Mason, P. (2005) 'Visitor management in protected areas: from hard to soft approaches?', *Current Issues in Tourism*, 8 (2&3).

Further reading

Richardson, J. I. and Fluker, M. (2004) *Understanding and Managing Tourism*, Pearson Education.

Websites

Bath & North East Somerset Council, 'City of Bath World Heritage Site Management Plan', visitor management issues   **www.bathnes.gov.uk/worldheritage/3.6VisMgtIssues.htm**

'Wilderness.net, Visitor Use Management Toolbox'
www.wilderness.net/index.cfm?fuse=toolboxes&sec=vum

Questions and discussion points

1. Should visitors be responsible for funding initiatives implemented to manage their impacts?

2. Do you think that the use of closure to manage the impact of tourists should only be considered as a last resort?

3. Some visitor management techniques are designed to manage demand, while others are designed to adapt supply. Do you think that it is preferable to manage demand rather than supply?

Tasks

1. In the UK, a qualification for tour guiding (blue and green badges) is available. There is no national law requiring guides to be licensed, however. Select three other countries of your choice and investigate their policies for regulating and training guides. Report back on the different approaches used and evaluate the benefits and limitations of regulating this area of tourism provision.

2. Obtain three different codes of conduct from the tourism industry. Write a report that compares and contrasts these codes and provide an evaluation of their ability to effectively manage the impacts of visitors.

Chapter 17

The structure and role of the public sector in tourism

Learning outcomes

After studying this chapter, you should be able to:

- understand the part played by local, regional and central governments and their agencies in the planning and promotion of tourism in a country

- recognize the growing importance of the public sector in all aspects of tourism and its role in public–private partnerships

- define the term 'social tourism' and understand its significance for disadvantaged populations

- explain how governments and local authorities in Britain and elsewhere supervise and exercise control over tourism

- appreciate the organization of public-sector tourism in Britain.

Introduction

It's so crowded, nobody goes there any more.

Yogi Berra, US comedian, referring to the popular venue Toots Shor's

Tourism often plays an important part in a nation's economy by providing opportunities for regional employment, contributing to the balance of payments and stimulating economic growth. Countries that experience an influx of large numbers of tourists, however, also suffer the environmental and social consequences of mass tourism, unless care is taken to plan for and control the flow of tourists. Any economy that has become overly dependent on tourism can be massively weakened by a single political or natural disaster – as the chaos created in Bali following the terrorist strike there has shown. Tourists in the generating countries were 'strongly advised' against travelling to Indonesia for a whole year after the event and, as a result, tourism virtually came to a halt. Neither does it necessarily benefit a country to switch labour and other resources away from, say, agriculture towards tourism. For both economic and social reasons, therefore, governments cannot let market forces rule – they must take a direct interest in the ways tourism affects their country. The more dependent a nation becomes on tourism, whether domestic, inbound or outbound, the more likely it is that the government will intervene in the industry's activities.

The nature of government involvement

A country's system of government will, of course, be reflected in the mode and extent of public intervention. At one end of the scale, centrally planned economies may choose to exercise virtually complete control, from policymaking and planning to the building and operating of tourist facilities, the organization of tourist movements and the promotion of tourism at home and abroad. Since the collapse of the Soviet Union, such central control is now limited to a very few countries and even some of those nations still ostensibly operating centrally planned economies – China, Cuba and Vietnam, for example – recognize and accept the importance of private enterprise, and the benefits of private investment, in their tourism planning. China, ostensibly a centrally controlled economy, happily co-operates with privately owned American hotel interests to establish chains of hotels in popular tourist destinations throughout the country and accepts the independent movement of tourists on itineraries tailor-made by Western operators. Even Saudi Arabia, which for cultural and political reasons has long restricted the movement of independent Western tourists, is easing its constraints and allowing some freedom of movement for foreign tourists. Only North Korea and Turkmenistan still control tourism so rigidly that independent travel around either country is impossible.

Most other nations have mixed economies, in which public and private sectors coexist and collaborate in the development of tourism within their borders; only the balance of public versus private involvement will vary. Thus, the United States, with its belief in a free enterprise system and a federal constitution, delegates much of the responsibility for overseas promotion of the nation either to individual states or even to private organizations created for the purpose. Central government intervention in the USA is limited to measures designed to protect the health and safety of its citizens (such as aircraft safety and air traffic control). It even disbanded its public tourism body, the US Travel and Tourism Administration, in 1996, allowing private enterprise to fund overseas marketing. The public body has been replaced by the privately sponsored Travel Industry Association of America (TIA), which markets the USA abroad under a number of brands, including the Visit USA Association, Discover USA and Discover America, in some cases maintaining an office abroad to serve the trade's (but not the public's) needs.

Public ownership of transport is also generally declining, as rail and air services are denationalized, but, in some developed countries, there are still examples of widespread public ownership. The French government, to cite one example, owns 100 per cent of SNCF, the French rail network, 100 per cent of Aéroports de Paris, 44.6 per cent of Air France and has shares in SNECMA aero engines and aircraft manufacturer EADS. Public ownership of the railways undoubtedly made it easier to invest in the hugely expensive TGV network for which the country is now famous.

The system of government is not the only factor dictating the extent of state intervention. If a country is highly dependent on tourism for its economic survival, its government is likely to become far more involved in the industry than if it is not so important. The government department allocated the responsibility for tourism can highlight the perspective and importance placed on tourism by governments (see Table 17.1).

Table 17.1 Government departments responsible for tourism in a selection of countries.

Tourism	Industry/ economy	Environment	Art and culture	Other fields
India – Ministry of Tourism	France – Economy, Industry and Employment	South Africa – Environmental Affairs and Tourism	Ireland – Department of Arts, Sports and Culture	Australia – Department for Resources, Energy and Tourism
Malaysia – Ministry of Tourism	Germany – Economy and Technology	Tanzania – Minister for Natural Resources and Tourism	Korea (republic) – Ministry of Culture, Sports and Tourism	Greece – Ministry of Development
	Hong Kong – Commerce and Economic Development Bureau		UK – Department for Culture, Media and Sport	Jordan – Ministry of Tourism and Antiquities
				Luxembourg – Ministry of the Middle Class, Tourism and Housing

Source: C. Humphreys, author's own research based on ministry of tourism websites, 2008.

The relative importance attached by government to tourism in the UK can be judged by the amalgam of responsibilities assigned to the Department for Culture, Media and Sport. Not only does tourism not appear in the title of the department, the job title of the minister within the department, as of 2006, became Minister for Creative Industries and Tourism. This minister is now responsible for broadcasting, film, alcohol, entertainment licensing, the press, IT and science, in addition to tourism.

Countries where tourism has only relatively recently become a significant factor in the economy and that sudden growth has become problematic, are likely to exercise stronger control over the development of tourism than are those where tourism is either in its early stages of development or has developed slowly over a long period of time. Mauritius, for example, recognized that the wave of visitors it experienced in the early 1980s could soon lead to the country being swamped by tourists, destroying the very attractions that had brought the visitors to the islands in the first place, unless it took steps to control such key activities as hotel construction. Tunisia, too, learned that lesson and introduced control over hotel and other construction related to tourism early in the development of mass tourism to that destination.

Unfortunately, the potential for quick riches can exercise a greater influence than the long-term interests of the country and there are all too many examples of countries that have suffered from lack of sufficient control over building and development, leading eventually to a drop in visits as tourists turn to less exploited destinations. Overbuilding in Spain was held up as an example in the late 1960s and could have influenced subsequent development in other Mediterranean countries to which tourists turned en masse somewhat later. Nevertheless, the 1980s and 1990s witnessed overdevelopment in some key regions – first in Greece, then in the Portuguese Algarve and, later (despite initial efforts to control hotel-building), in Turkey. Corruption and nepotism – the significance of having influential 'connections' to overcome planning controls should never be underestimated – are very real enemies of sustainable tourism policies.

All countries require reliable supporting infrastructure in order to encourage tourism in the first place, which will inevitably involve local and central government. Adequate public services, roads, railways, harbours and airports must all be in place before the private sector will be interested in investing in the equally necessary superstructure of hotels, restaurants, entertainment, attractions and other facilities that will bring in the tourists.

Example

St Helena

St Helena is a British dependency in the Atlantic, 1200 miles west of Angola. One of only 13 remaining UK overseas territories, the island has a population of around 3900 and has suffered economic deprivation for many years, owing to its isolated setting and lack of an airport. Its sole regular link with the outside world is a government-subsidized cargo passenger ship operating out of Cape Town. With better communication links, its prospects of developing tourism would be good – with its rocky, semi-desert coastline, but an attractive tropical interior and two national parks. Its most notable feature is Longwood House – Napoleon's home during his final years of captivity.

The planned construction of an airport has been under consideration for a number of years and, in 2004, the Department for International Development invited proposals for a public–private partnership (PPP) to improve transport links and develop tourism for the island. Initial proposals were rejected on the grounds of 'unacceptable levels of financial and other risks and uncertainties' and the government's consultants eventually put forward plans entailing construction costs beyond what a PPP would accept as financially viable. More than four years later, there is still no firm decision regarding the awarding of a contract. The original plan was for the airport to be operational by 2010, but further delays followed in 2009 and no timescale can be currently envisaged for the development. Subsidies provided to the shipping company will cease once the airport is operational.

The cost of developing and operating the airport will be substantial, given that the planned runway is big enough to accommodate long-range Boeing 737-800s and Airbus A320s, which will call for a runway some 2250 metres in length, in a small country with very little flat land. The resultant improvement in communication, however, would allow the expansion of all kinds of trade, including tourism, which should result in a reduction in the need for subsidies from the UK that fund the island's budget.

St Helena's administration has welcomed the scheme, but it has not found universal acceptance among the islanders. Even the director of tourism has expressed concern that the development of an airport and upmarket resort could easily lead to the island being swamped by tourists, causing it to lose much of its present charm.

Developing nations may have a further incentive for involving government. Private developers may be reluctant to invest in speculative tourist ventures, preferring to concentrate their resources in countries where there is already proven demand. In this case, it may fall to the government to either aid private developers (in the form of grants or loans for hotel construction) or even to build and operate the hotels and other tourist amenities that will first attract tourists. Where the private sector can be persuaded to invest, it is often companies from the generating countries that first show interest, with the result that most of the profits are repatriated rather than benefiting the local economy. There is also the danger that private speculators will be more concerned with achieving a quick return on their investment rather than the slow but secure long-term development that will benefit the country most.

The state is called on to play a coordinating role in planning the provision of tourist amenities and attractions. Supply should match demand as closely as possible and the state can ensure that facilities are available when and where required and they are of the right standard.

As tourism grows in an economy, so its organization, if uncontrolled, can result in the domination of the market by a handful of large companies. Even in a capitalist system, the state has the duty to restrict the power of monopolies to protect consumers from mal-practice, such as unfair constraints on trade or exorbitant prices.

Apart from these economic reasons for governments becoming involved in tourism, there are also social and political reasons. In many countries, especially in developing nations, national airlines are state-owned and operated. While, of course, the income accruing from the operation of the airline is important to the state, there is also the political prestige of operating an airline, even if the national flag-carrier is not economically viable. In other situations, certain airline routes may be unprofitable, but, if they provide a vital economic lifeline to the communities they serve, they will need to be subsidized by the government.

Governments also have a duty to safeguard a nation's heritage. Buildings of historical or architectural interest (particularly UNESCO World Heritage sites and others of inter-national importance, such as Angkor Wat and its surrounding temples, a complex of magnificent twelfth-century ruins of Khmer culture in Cambodia) have to be protected and maintained, as must landscapes of exceptional merit. The state will therefore fund national heritage agencies (such as English Heritage, Historic Scotland and CADW in Wales) and establish national parks to protect sensitive sites and buildings.

Example

Protection versus development – the case of Pumphouse Point, Tasmania

Balancing the demands of developers seeking to provide tourist resources and encouraging the reuse of redundant buildings can often conflict with the desire to protect the natural environment.

After a decade of deliberation, the local council has finally given approval to develop at Pumphouse Point, Tasmania. The development of a former hydro-electric substation, located on the shore of Lake Clair, which sits within the Cradle Mountain Lake St Clair National Park, part of the Tasmanian Wilderness Area World Heritage site, has required exten-sive planning and consultation. Negotiations related to developing this site commenced in 1995, with controversial plans for a AUS$15 million wilderness lodge being given govern-ment approval. Alterations to the resort plans, as well as delays, however, led to the government reclaim-ing the site in 1999. In 2002, Doherty Hotels announced plans to develop a AUS$5 million resort, but withdrew in 2003. The latest plans aim to provide visitors with accommodation as well as an interpretation centre, designed to enhance visitors' appreciation and understanding of the physical and cultural locality.

Permission was granted in April 2008, although gaining the detailed construction approvals was expected to delay the start of construction until the end of the year. The decision to give approval for this development was controversial, with the National Parks Authority disappointed by the decision: 'We had hoped that the council would have regard for the Wilderness World Heritage Management Plan which basi-cally says developments shouldn't occur in parks, as a matter of course they should generally be outside.'[1]

The long search for a third London airport was extended by several years while the government weighed up the relative merits of the economic benefits of a particular site and the environmental damage that the development would cause. Still more recently, a long-running conflict emerged in the UK between conservation and economic development over the construction of a fifth terminal at London's Heathrow Airport. Economics won out, but not before the construction had been delayed for many years, undermining the strategic importance of the airport vis-à-vis its competitors on the Continent. Needless to say, the power of political lobbying may be the critical factor in any decision made by the public authorities.

We can sum up by saying that a national government's role in tourism can be manifested in the following ways:

- in the planning and facilitating of tourism, including the provision of financial and other aid
- in the supervision and control of the component sectors of the tourism industry
- in direct ownership and operation of components of the industry
- in the promotion of the nation and its tourist products to home and overseas markets
- in supporting key tourism interests in a time of financial crisis.

This clarification of the range of activities that need to be undertaken by national governments is helpful when they are considering their own responsibilities in relation to the provision and management of tourism.

Planning and facilitating tourism

Any country in which tourism plays a prominent role in national income and employment can expect its government to devise policies and plans for the development of tourism. This will include generating guidelines and objectives for the growth and management of tourism, both in the short and long term, and devising strategies designed to achieve those objectives.

It may be the case that the government feels the need to invest in the tourism industry in order to 'pump-prime' or stimulate investment, development and growth in a sector of the economy. For example, British government policy on tourism favoured investment in tourism to create employment opportunities, although the cost on the public purse was seen as a concern. While support for tourism was initially through grant aid, by the 1990s the government took the view that the industry was now 'mature' and further investment should be left to the private sector.

VisitBritain, as a quasi-autonomous national government organization with the responsibility to promote Britain abroad, had as its aims not just to increase the total number of tourists to Britain but also to spread visitors more evenly throughout the regions and across the months, to avoid the congestion of demand in the South and during the summer months. In Spain, as demand had already been created by the private sector for the popular east coast resorts and the Balearic and Canary Islands, its national tourist office policy has focused on promoting the less familiar north west coast and central regions of the country, while coastal development has become subject to increasing control.

Tourism planning calls for research – first, to assess the level of demand or potential demand to a particular region, second, to estimate the resources required in order to cater for that demand and, finally, to determine how those resources should best be distributed. As we have seen, demand is unlikely to be generated to any extent until an adequate infrastructure and superstructure are in place, but it is not sufficient simply to provide these amenities. Tourists also need staff to service the facilities – hotel workers, travel agents, guides – trained to an acceptable level of performance. Planning therefore implicitly

includes ensuring the availability of a pool of labour, as well as the provision of apprenticeship schemes or training through hotel, catering and tourism schools and colleges to
provide the skills and knowledge the industry requires.

In some cases, providing the facilities that tourists want can actually have a negative
impact on tourism to the region. To take one example, while the building of airports on
some of the smaller islands in Greece opened up these islands to larger flows of tourists,
it made the islands less attractive to the upmarket high-spending tourists, who preferred
the relative isolation that existed when accessibility was limited to ferry operations.

Government control over entry

Accessibility is a key factor in the development of tourism. It relies on both adequate
transport and the absence of any political barriers to travel. If visas are required for entry
to a country, this will discourage incoming tourism. At the beginning of the 1990s, the UK
imposed a visa requirement on citizens of Turkey seeking to enter Britain. The Turkish
retaliated by imposing a visa requirement on British visitors to their country. The flow of
tourists was almost entirely one way, however, so the Turkish emerged as the clear losers,
the visa requirement dissuading tourists from visiting their country.

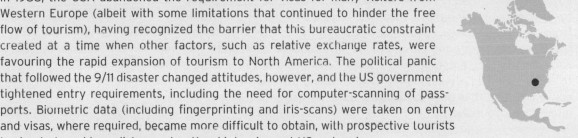

Example

Entry to the USA

In 1988, the USA abandoned the requirement for visas for many visitors from
Western Europe (albeit with some limitations that continued to hinder the free
flow of tourism), having recognized the barrier that this bureaucratic constraint
created at a time when other factors, such as relative exchange rates, were
favouring the rapid expansion of tourism to North America. The political panic
that followed the 9/11 disaster changed attitudes, however, and the US government
tightened entry requirements, including the need for computer-scanning of passports. Biometric data (including fingerprinting and iris-scans) were taken on entry
and visas, where required, became more difficult to obtain, with prospective tourists
having to travel long distances to attend interviews at US embassies.

Since October 2005, the Department of Homeland Security requires airlines and cruise ships to provide details of their passengers, prior to arrival. The information required includes each passenger's full
name, date of birth, gender, citizenship, passport details, country of residence, address while in the United
States and arrival and departure transport details. This has raised debate regarding the rights to privacy,
as well as concerns over protection and security of the data provided.

The difficulty in obtaining visas and concerns that the increased security will cause problems for arriving travellers has combined with other factors to influence arrival figures. Despite a weak dollar, arrival
figures in 2007 had yet to reach the levels that existed prior to the terrorist attacks of 2001.

The ending of visa requirements for trips to the Baltic states following the collapse of communism in Russia and the satellite countries led to a substantial increase in tourist visits.
Russia, by contrast, continued to insist on visas. The predictable result has been a drop in
the numbers of visitors to Russia while the Baltic states have enjoyed a significant rise,
which has accelerated since their entry into the European Union. Ukraine and Georgia
have also both since abandoned the need for visas for EU nationals, which will further
reduce demand for visits to Russia (and see Case study 10 for an example of how visas
hinder travel to the Russian exclave of Kaliningrad).

Maximizing revenue from inbound tourism flows is always a temptation for governments, but it is a practice that backfires if visitors can simply switch to alternative destinations offering similar attractions. Arguably, long-haul travellers will be more willing to accept reasonably high visa costs when travelling extensively in a country, but such costs are off-putting for short-break visits or calls by cruise liner (and St Petersburg has become an important port for cruises in the Baltic region).

China has restricted access to leisure travel for its citizens by granting visas only for selected destinations, with only six countries having approved destination status (ADS) by the end of the nineties. ADS allows Chinese visitors to participate in group tours for reasons other than business or education. The list of countries gaining ADS has rapidly expanded, however, and at the end of 2007 the USA became the ninety-fifth country to be added. With almost 41 million Chinese taking trips overseas in 2007, and up to 100 million forecast to do annually so by 2020, countries gaining ADS are hoping to gain a significant share of the massive market. Importantly, although ADS allows Chinese companies to offer tours to the overseas country, the travellers still require entry visas and these are not always easy to obtain.

Example

The benefits of expansion of the European Union's Schengen Agreement for non-EU visitors

In December 2007, the Schengen zone was expanded – 8 eastern European countries and Malta being added – so the Agreement now covers travel across 24 European countries. Border controls have eased for travellers between these countries. While EU travellers and visitors from the USA and Japan can travel without a visa in the EU zone, other travellers moving around Europe would have required a separate visa for each country they entered. Now, a single Schengen visa can provide access to all 24 countries, saving money as well making travel across Europe more convenient and thus making Europe a more attractive destination for some international tourists.[2]

The cost of obtaining visas as well as the complexity of applications can encourage travellers to choose to travel to countries that do *not* require visas.

Taxation policy

Government policies on taxation can impact on tourism, whether the taxes are applied directly to tourists (such as an entry or exit tax), the industry (such as on hotel accommodation) or indirectly (such as VAT or sales taxes, which can discourage shopping and benefit countries with lower taxes). It may even encourage day trips across borders to shop in areas where taxes are lower.

Transportation taxes, such as those introduced in 1997 both into and out of the state of Florida, increasing the cost of an airline journey for a family of four travelling to the Walt Disney World Resort by some £70 – a substantial percentage of their total flight costs – can have a significant impact on demand for a destination. Even within the European Union, variations in taxation can impact on tourism flows.

In 1993, Greece increased its airport departure tax threefold, to 5200 drachmas (roughly £15), sufficient to antagonize tour operators and persuade the 'marginal' tourists to switch to other Mediterranean destinations.

The British government's imposition in the 1993 Budget of an airport departure tax (Air Passenger Duty, or, APD) of £5 in the European Union and £10 elsewhere was widely criticized in the press and the decision to double this rate from November 1997 provoked fury in the trade. It was further increased in February 2007. If the revenue raised by such taxation were reinvested in the tourism industry, there would be less of a sense of outrage, but when it is introduced purely as a convenient means of raising taxation, travellers often feel that it is an injustice.

More recently the government has proposed removing the APD, replacing it with an aircraft tax (paid on each flight, rather than on the number of passengers), which is aimed at encouraging airlines to ensure flights operate close to full capacity. This is seen as a small step towards making the industry 'greener'. Overall, when one considers the level of taxes paid against the low-cost fares offered within Europe by carriers such as easyJet, it is apparent that taxes can regularly account for as much as 25 per cent of air transport costs.

Example

The Balearic Islands eco-tax

In 2002, the Balearic Islands' government, composed of a coalition of Socialist and Green parties, introduced an eco-tax as a means of discouraging low-spending visitors and funding enhancements of the islands' infrastructure to attract more upmarket visitors. The local government was concerned that the islands were attracting some seven million visitors a year, swamping the resident island population of 600,000.

The tax was imposed on hotel accommodation, ranging from €0.25 to €1.00 per night for hotels up to the 4-star category, €2.00 for the 5-star category.

There was an immediate negative reaction from the tourist trade abroad, which argued that sales for flights and package tours would drop and it had been introduced too quickly for tour operators to add to their brochures. There were also complaints that the tax was unfair as it applied only to hotels, not unlicensed accommodation, villas, B&Bs or privately owned second homes. As a direct result, it was eventually agreed that the tax be collected directly from travellers at their hotels.

A year later, the tax was scrapped, when a new centre-right government was voted into power. During the time in which it was in operation, however, it is estimated that the tax raised more than £25 million to help fund tourism projects. While the overall number of visitors to the Balearics did drop 7 per cent compared with the previous year, this could not be ascribed solely to the effect of the tax (visitors to the Canary Islands dropped a similar amount) and visitors from the UK actually increased by some 8 per cent.

Facilitating training

Another important factor determining tourism flow is the attitude of nationals in the host country towards visitors in general and those from specific countries in particular. Governments in countries heavily dependent on tourism must mould the social attitudes of their populations, as well as ensuring that those coming into contact with tourists have the necessary skills to deal with them. Customs officers, immigration officials, shopkeepers, hotel staff, bus and taxi drivers must not only be competent at their jobs but also trained to be polite and friendly as first impressions are important for the long-term image of a country.

The USA is one of several countries that have found it necessary to mount campaigns to improve the politeness and friendliness of officials dealing with incoming visitors, while some Caribbean governments have run training programmes to reduce xenophobia among the local populations and make residents aware that their economy depends on incoming tourism. In Britain, the government has supported industry moves to improve social and personal skills in handling foreign tourists, with training programmes such as Welcome Host, International Welcome Host and Welcome Management. Encouragement has also been given to learning foreign languages – a major weakness among personnel in the UK's tourism industry.

The responsibilities of central and local government

The very complexity of tourism makes its administration difficult as it does not sit easily in any one sector of government. For example, although responsibility for tourism in Britain lies with the Department for Culture, Media and Sport (DCMS), there are clearly other departments with a direct interest in the industry, including the Department for Environment, Food and Rural Affairs (DEFRA), the Department for Transport, the Department for Innovation, Universities and Skills and the Department for Business, Enterprise and Regulatory Reform (its responsibilities include the Regional Development Agencies, competition and consumer affairs). In practice, coordination between these various departments is difficult to achieve, hindering the effectiveness of the overall planning of tourism initiatives within the country. It is further hindered by the fact that the Scottish Parliament and Welsh Assembly each has responsibilities for tourism within its own region.

The responsibilities of central and local governments will also differ with respect to issues affecting tourism. Local government may be responsible for planning, policy and infrastructure and, as a consequence, have to address a number of issues that directly affect visiting tourists, including the provision of car and coach parking, litter control, maintenance of footpaths and promenades, public parks and gardens and, where appropriate, beach management and monitoring of sea water for bathing. These responsibilities are, to some extent, split between city and regional councils and conflicting views may surface between local authorities, as well as between local and central government. Local authorities are, of course, greatly influenced by the views of their local taxpayers, who are often unsympathetic to the expansion of tourism in their area, particularly if it is already popular with tourists. In countries where tourism is not a statutory obligation of local authorities (and Britain is such an example), they may not legally have to include tourism in their plans or provide funding for resources for tourists.

Financial aid for tourism

Governments contribute to the growth of tourism by financing the development of new projects. On a massive scale, tourist resorts have been constructed around Cancún on Mexico's eastern coast, while, in the 1970s, the Languedoc-Roussillon area in the south of France was the subject of development that included draining swampland and eradicating mosquitoes in order to build five new tourist resorts, including the now well-established Cap d'Agde and la Grande Motte. The success of these ventures demonstrates the effectiveness of large-scale private–public-sector cooperation in building new tourism resorts from scratch, with the public sector providing the huge funds necessary to acquire land and build the necessary infrastructure.

On a smaller scale, governments may also provide assistance to the private sector in the form of financial aid, offering loans at preferential rates of interest or outright grants for schemes that are in keeping with government policy. One example of the way in which such schemes operate in developing countries is for loans to be made on which interest only is paid during the first few years, with repayment of capital postponed until the later years of the project, by which time it should have become self-financing.

Other forms of government aid include subsidies such as tax rebates or tax relief on operating expenses.

Example

Are tourism subsidies just a cost?

On the island of Tasmania, Australia, the Minster for Tourism, Arts and the Environment stressed the importance of the grants the government offers to groups contemplating hosting events on the island. In 2007, more than 90 events were planned, with a total of AUS$360,000 being offered in grants to the organizers.

The value of these grants lies in their ability to attract visitors to the island, many of whom holiday on the island prior to or after the event. The estimated value of the spend from these events was declared to be more than AUS$24 million across the state – a return of more than AUS$66 for each dollar offered in subsidy.[3]

Government support is also necessary at a time of catastrophe. The recovery of popular Asiatic resorts following the disastrous Tsunami in 2004 has depended on a programme of massive international government aid, supported by direct contributions from millions of ordinary people around the world. Similarly, in Britain, after the devastating outbreak of foot and mouth disease in 2001, the government stepped in to offer financial aid to small tourism businesses in rural areas – they were granted 95 per cent tax relief and the Welsh Assembly extended 100 per cent rate relief to Welsh businesses with higher rateable values. Central government grants were also made available in the affected areas for marketing and investment in information technology.

Apart from financial aid from a country's own government, public-sector funds are also available from sources overseas. Within Europe, the European Investment Bank (EIB) provides loans at commercial rates of interest to small companies (normally those employing fewer than 500 staff). These loans have been provided for up to 50 per cent of fixed asset costs, with repayment terms of up to eight years, and the interest rates may be slightly lower in the EU's designated 'Assisted Areas'.

The European Regional Development Fund (ERDF) offers financial assistance for a range of initiatives, including many tourism projects. Between 2000 and 2006, funding was provided based on three objectives: focusing on promoting development in impoverished areas, supporting areas facing structural difficulties and supporting the modernization of training and education.[4]

The 2007–2013 plans focus on three new objectives: convergence, regional competitiveness and employment and territorial cooperation. Funds of €308 billion are to be allocated. Convergence (perhaps closest to 2000–2006's first objective) seeks to assist the least-developed regions and the bulk of the funding (over 80 per cent) is allocated to this goal. The funding to address these three objectives can be used not only as pump-priming for attractions directly aimed at tourists, such as museums, but also for infrastructure to support tourism, such as airports or car parking facilities.

To be eligible to receive ERDF convergence funding, regions must have incomes lower than 75 per cent of the EU average (although there is some funding available under the European Cohesion Fund for areas where income is below 90 per cent of European average). Areas that are eligible include the recent accession countries as well as:[5]

- Germany – Brandenburg-Nordost, Mecklenburg-Vorpommern, Chemnitz, Dresden, Dessau, Magdeburg, Thüringen
- France – Guadeloupe, Martinique, Guyane, Réunion
- Italy – Campania, Puglia, Calabria, Sicilia

- Spain – Galicia, Castilla-La Mancha, Extremadura, Andalucía
- UK – Cornwall and Isles of Scilly, West Wales and the Valleys.

Example

Rural and regional tourism in Romania receives EU funding

The Romanian National Authority of Tourism announced that its rural and regional tourism industry is set to receive €87 million of funding from the national government, along with €500 million from ERDF over a 7-year period commencing in 2007. The grants will be used to improve existing tourism resources as well as developing new attractions and facilities from existing cultural and natural resources. Development will also focus on the creation of new jobs and improving productivity (by increasing the revenues from existing operations).

One particular area of focus is on spa tourism, where funds would be available to improve accommodation facilities as well as acquire equipment to enhance the range of treatments available.[6]

EU funding is also available from the EU Structural and Cohesion Funds, which also fund initiatives in relation to the three new objectives. European tourism may also benefit, under some circumstances, from the European Social Fund or the European Agricultural Guidance and Guarantee Fund.

Developing countries can receive aid from the International Development Association, a subsidiary of the World Bank, which provides interest-free or low-rate loans. Another World Bank subsidiary, the International Bank for Reconstruction and Development, offers loans at commercial rates of interest to countries where alternative sources of funding may be difficult to find.

Social tourism

One little-known aspect of public-sector support for tourism is to be found in the encouragement offered by way of **social tourism** – little-known, at least in Britain, because it has been largely disregarded.

The concept of social tourism has been used in several contexts, so it is difficult to provide one specific definition. In some cases, this term is used to propose the idea that the opportunity to take a holiday is a human right and there should be provision by the welfare state for those unable to afford to take a holiday. From a supply side, the term is often used when considering circumstances where governments encourage tourism to specific areas in order to encourage economic development. To provide an encompassing definition, Minnaert et al.[7] suggest that 'social tourism is about encouraging those who can benefit from tourism to do so. This may represent a wide variety of groups, such as the host population of an exotic destination, tourists on a cultural holiday, persons with disabilities, their carers, the socially excluded and other disadvantaged groups.'

Economic support to encourage social tourism may be offered in the form of finance (grants, low-interest loans and the like) or direct support, such as the provision of free coach trips or holiday accommodation. One might use this generic term to also include the public funding of health tourism, which has been the practice of some countries' governments to subsidize as part of the general public health and well-being of its populations.

Social tourism is of course more likely to be supported by countries the governments of which have planned economies. Holidays are seen by those countries as necessary for maintaining the health and well-being of their working populations. In mixed economies such as those in Europe, several countries have been active in providing subsidized tourism for their deprived citizens, led by Belgium, France and the southern countries of the EU. Indeed, the Brussels-based International Bureau of Social Tourism (BITS) has been

Example

French social tourism

France promotes sponsored holidays for employees with its programme of 'chèques-vacances', a holiday voucher scheme operated through the Agence Nationale pour les Chèques-Vacances (ANCV). This public, industrial and commercial organization supervised by the Ministries of Tourism and the Economy, Industry and Finance, sells vouchers to some 23,000 organizations in France, the employees of which can spend them on a variety of holidays in France, its dependencies and the EU. They are accepted at more than 135,000 outlets, including transport, acommodation and restaurants.

The largest client group of ANCV are the comités d'entreprise (works councils), an employee/management committee set up to look after the welfare of employees. Companies are required by French law to operate these councils and there is a small allocation of company funds available to spend on workers' outings as well as those for providing the chèques-vacances that are then distributed to employees. More than 80 per cent of the ANCV's clients are works councils, which purchase around 54 per cent of all the cheques sold.

The ANCV earns income from both the sale of the cheques and their encashment once they are received by tourism businesses. They also earn interest on the money they hold over this time.

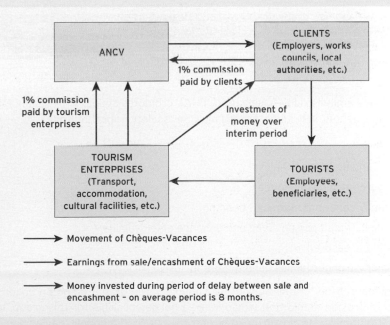

The income earned allows the ANCV to provide grant funding encouraging improvements and modernization of tourism enterprises, espcially encouraging facilities and equipment to be installed to enhance assessibility. In 2006, more than €5300 million was invested in assistance projects and more than 27,000 families were beneficiaries.

Source: ANCV, 'Annual report, 2006', ANCV, 2007. Available online at: **www.ancv.com**

active since 1963 as a base for the study and debate of social tourism issues and maintains a data bank, issues publications and conducts seminars on the subject.

There are well-established programmes of aid on the Continent for holidays for the mentally, physically and socially handicapped, although financial pressures are reducing these opportunities. The French government, for example, terminated its programme of welfare-funded spa holidays in 1999 – a severe blow to the spa tourism industry, which hosted over 600,000 French visitors who had been able to recover up to 70 per cent of their costs through their social security system. Other now well-established programmes of social tourism remain in place, however.

Little support of this kind is provided in Britain for the disadvantaged, although Britain has over 6 million registered disabled people. Responsibility for providing this service is delegated to local authorities (the Chronically Sick and Disabled Act 1970 imposed a statutory duty on local authorities to fund holidays for the disabled). Many authorities used to provide coach outings for the elderly and other disadvantaged groups, but, over the past 20 years, cutbacks in local authority funding have sharply reduced these services and the number of those receiving financial help from local councils has slumped. The result has been that social tourism has largely become the responsibility of the private sector.

Sponsored by the then English Tourist Board, and with the full support of the travel industry in the UK, the Holiday Care Service was set up in 1981. Essentially, it provided information about holiday opportunities for the disadvantaged. Later, this was expanded to include training programmes for members of the tourism industry. A number of specialist operators then turned to catering to the needs of these groups or providing discounted holidays for those with limited means. These responsibilities are now vested in Tourism for All, which is a national charity. The Travel Foundation also provides help for disadvantaged holidaymakers with the financial support of the industry.

Example

The Family Holiday Association

A national charity, the Family Holiday Association (FHA), promotes holidays for disadvantaged families. It suggests that holidays benefit individuals as well as wider society, reporting that:[8]

in general, holidays:

- improve well-being and reduce stress
- increase self-esteem and confidence
- strengthen family communication and bonding
- provide new skills, widen perspectives and enhance employability
- give long-lasting, treasured memories
- result in happier, stronger families and a more inclusive society.

Poverty is the principal reason for one out of three people in the UK not going on holiday at all. The FHA was set up in 1975 to provide grants that would make a holiday possible for this group. In 2007, the FHA enabled around 1400 families to go on holiday and over 100,000 people have been helped since its foundation.

The FHA has a high profile in the industry, with strong support from ABTA and AITO. It is funded largely by individual donations, but is also helped by trusts, corporate donations and income received from fundraising events.

Further information: **www.fhaonline.org.uk**

Holidays are also organized by the trade unions in Britain, which have established holiday homes and subsidize holidays for their members. Other bodies arranging holidays for the disadvantaged include Mencap, the Red Cross, Multiple Sclerosis Society and Winged Fellowship Trust. Both SCOPE (formerly the Spastics Society) and the Spina Bifida Association also own holiday homes where holidays can be provided for those suffering from these illnesses.

The UK government's involvement in helping the disadvantaged in this area is largely restricted to ensuring adequate access to tourism attractions, hotels and so on for the disabled. The Disability Discrimination Act (1995) has had a profound effect on tourist facilities in the UK, necessitating them to make substantial investments to meet the conditions of the Act. Services (including the provision of information for the blind and deaf, for example) have had to be accessible to the disabled since the final part of the Act came into effect towards the end of 2004, although there are exceptions granted in the case of heritage buildings that are impractical to convert.

Supervision and control of tourism

The state plays an important part in controlling and supervising tourism, as well as helping to facilitate it, where it is deemed necessary. It will, for example, intervene to restrain undesirable growth or unfair competition or, alternatively, help to generate demand by improving infrastructure or encouraging the building of hotels (as the Development of Tourism Act did in Britain in 1969). Governments also play a role in maintaining quality standards and protecting all consumers (in this case, tourists) from business malpractice or failure.

Local government may introduce visitor management policies (details of which were provided in Chapter 16) to control both the numbers visiting destinations and their actions and behaviour there. Visitor management may be enforced by local government, but it is often implemented by both government initiatives and the activities of private-sector tourism businesses.

A government can act to restrain tourism in a number of ways, whether through central directives or local authority control. Refusal of planning permission is an obvious example exercising control over the development of tourism. This is seldom totally effective as a mechanism, however, as when an area is a major attraction for tourists, the authorities will be unlikely to dissuade visitors simply by, say, refusing planning permission for new hotels. The result of such actions may simply be that overnight visitors are replaced by excursionists or private bed-and-breakfast accommodation moves in to fill the gap left by the lack of hotel beds. For example, Cornwall has had measures to control caravan sites since 1954, but the local authority has still found it difficult to prevent the growth of unlicensed sites.

Up to a point, planning for the more extensive use of existing facilities can delay the need to demarket certain attractions or destinations, but it is undoubtedly true that some tourist destinations are victims of their own success. Only in extreme cases are tourists totally denied access to destinations or attractions. In France, the prehistoric cave paintings at Lascaux have been so damaged by the effect of countless visitors' breath changing the climate in the caves that the French government has been obliged to introduce a total ban on entry to the site. An artificial replica has been built on an adjacent site, however, and it continues to attract many visitors.

In recent years, Britain has followed the example of some of its other European neighbours in attempting to stagger holidays by means of legislation, with some local authorities introducing a five-term school year with a shorter break in the summer. This is expected to aid the tourism industry and help avoid the worst peaking problems of the summer months. On the Continent, not only educational holidays but also industry holidays are staggered. In Germany, the *Länder* (individual states) are required to take their holidays on a rota basis over an 11-year cycle, thus avoiding the holiday rush that is common in Britain at the end of the school summer term. Factories, schools and businesses all plan their closures in keeping with the rota. France, too, divides the country into three zones, each of which takes the summer holiday at a different time. While this helps to avoid national peaking, it is not without drawbacks – for example, the mass exodus of German holidaymakers clogging the motorways from their particular *Land* when their turn arrives!

Sometimes governments exercise control over tourism flows for economic reasons. Governments may attempt to protect their balance of payments by imposing currency restrictions or banning the export of foreign currency in an attempt to reduce the numbers of its citizens travelling abroad. The last significant control of this kind in Britain occurred in 1966, when the government of the day imposed a £50 travel allowance and France also imposed restrictions on the amount of currency that could be exported in the early 1980s. There is little evidence to suggest such controls are particularly effective in preventing the outflow of foreign currency and, since the advent of the free movement of currency within the European Union, the right of its members to travel within the EU can no longer be restricted.

Whatever your view is of the euro, its introduction has benefited all tourists, including the British and others who remain outside the common currency agreement, but who no longer have to change their holiday money as they move from one euro country to another.

Concern over safety is a government responsibility and all governments will take measures to enforce standards of safety and prosecute breaches of safe practice. Transport companies are obliged to meet the necessary criteria to obtain licences to carry passengers, and tour operators are also subject to certain controls through the imposition of Air Travel Organizers' Licences (ATOLs). In many countries (although not yet in the UK), travel agencies are required to have a government licence to operate and, in others, tour guides are licensed by the government or a local authority. In France, motorboats must also be licensed, even in the case of visitors from abroad, following a spate of accidents caused by poor navigation.

EU legislation protects tourists in a variety of ways, taking precedence over national laws. Legislation introduced in 2005, for instance, requires airlines to pay compensation to passengers for delayed flights, with the extent of compensation varying according to the length of the flight. Prosecution is enforced through the CAA.

Example

EU legislation designed to protect and compensate airline passengers

Despite the efforts of the EU to protect airline passengers through legislation designed to ensure compensation from airlines, there have been many issues arising from this move. In many cases airlines cite a clause that allows them to avoid making compensation payments in cases of 'extraordinary circumstances'. So, for instance, if flights are cancelled due to inclement weather, security threats or strike action, then the airlines are not required to pay out.

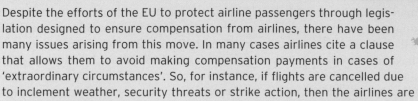

The compensation rules apply if a customer with a confirmed ticket is 'bumped' off a flight or the flight is cancelled, in which case, the airlines would have to pay up to €600. Exceptions apply, however, if more than 14 days' notice is given or if alternative flights are offered. As a consequence, the legislation is being reviewed to clarify the rights of the consumer to compensation.

Governments will intervene where it is thought that the takeover or merger of large companies could result in the emergence of a monopoly. In Britain, the Competition Commission exists to investigate such situations, but, in general, it has taken a relaxed attitude towards horizontal integration on the grounds that tourists have not been disadvantaged by the moves. The EU, however, has tended to take a stronger line on this issue and interceded in a number of cases in recent years, notably that of the proposed merger between British Airways and American Airlines.

Perhaps the commonest form of government supervision of the tourism industry in all countries is to be found in the hotel sector. Apart from safety and hygiene requirements, many governments also require hotels to be compulsorily registered and graded, display prices and the buildings are subject to regular inspection. Camping and caravan sites may also be subject to inspection to ensure consistent standards and acceptable operating conditions.

Finally, the government's concern with quality will lead to setting up systems of inspection, where safety is concerned, or training programmes and other means to enhance quality where it is seen as sub-standard. Again, Britain has recently promoted schemes leading to publicly recognized standards of quality, including the National Quality Assurance Schemes (NQAS) and Visitor Attraction Quality Assurance Scheme (VAQAS). The British government has recognized that tourism research statistics are inadequate and is encouraging improvements, notably through the collection and evaluation of data by the regional development agencies (RDAs). Local authorities are encouraged to support the collection of tourism data, but, again, without legal enforcement.

The organization of public-sector tourism

Having looked at the various ways in which public-sector bodies concern themselves with tourism, we can now usefully summarize their main activities below.

For the most part, government policies and objectives for tourism are defined and implemented through national tourist boards, although, as we have seen, in many cases other bodies directly concerned with recreation or environmental planning will also have a hand in the development of tourism. These boards are normally funded by government grants and their functional responsibilities are likely to include all or most of the following.

- *Planning and control functions*
    - product research and planning for tourism plant and facilities
    - protection or restoration of tourism assets
    - human resources planning and training
    - licensing and supervision of sectors of the industry
    - implementation of pricing or other regulations affecting tourism.
- *Marketing functions*
    - representing the nation as a tourist destination
    - undertaking market research, forecasting trends and collecting and publishing relevant statistics
    - producing and distributing tourism literature
    - providing and staffing tourist information centres
    - advertising, sales promotion and public relations activities directed at home and overseas markets.
- *Financial functions*
    - advising industry on capital investment and development
    - directing, approving and controlling programmes of government aid for tourism projects.

- *Coordinating functions*
  - linking with trade and professional bodies, government and regional or local tourist organizations
  - undertaking coordinated marketing activities with private tourist enterprises
  - organizing workshops or similar opportunities for buyers and sellers of travel and tourism to meet and do business.

National tourist boards will generally establish offices overseas in those countries from which they can attract the most tourists, while their head office in the home country will be organized along functional lines. This is demonstrated in Figure 17.1, taking the example of the Jordan Tourist Board. It has structured the responsibility for marketing tourism by generating regions, while other responsibilities are managed within specialist departments; for example, the interpretation of historic or cultural sites is overseen by the department responsible for Media and Communication, while attracting the MICE market is overseen by a department within the marketing function.

In some countries, some of these activities may be delegated to regional tourist offices, with the national board coordinating or overseeing their implementation.

This chapter provides a snapshot of public-sector tourism structure and operations by looking at the UK as an example, but it is important to note that the picture is not dissimilar in many other developed countries. It considers government involvement at national, regional and local levels.

UK government's involvement at national level

The illogical nature of the UK's tourism policy has been a feature of British governments for a number of years. The promises of support and a recognition of the contribution that tourism can and does make to the UK economy, coupled with simultaneous cuts in government funding, lack of development grants for tourism in depressed regions, the decline in support for an English national board vis-à-vis the other national boards and its eventual absorption into VisitBritain, all suggest a failure on the part of successive governments to think through rational policies that would give full support to tourism. Further damage is imposed on the industry by the unfavourable rate of VAT on restaurant and hotel accommodation in the UK in comparison with that in other countries, the imposition of passenger levies on air transport (now seen by governments as a comparatively painless means of raising extra revenue), an inadequate transport infrastructure (notably the railways and London Underground) and the continued failure to provide an integrated transport policy that would facilitate tourism.

Against these failures, however, one can point to one clear success achieved through a public–private partnership (PPP) – that of the awarding of the Olympic Games to London in 2012. Against what were seen as overwhelming odds favouring Paris, the PPP was able to make an effective case, based substantially on the benefits that would accrue to a deprived area of London, the new sports facilities that would become available to the population and the increase in permanent employment for locals resulting from the construction of the facilities. The long-term rejuvenation of one of the most impoverished regions of London is viewed by many as sufficient justification for the enormous expense that will be incurred to develop the facilities needed to host the games.

This one important success in encouraging and supporting tourism is unlikely to be emulated elsewhere. Government efforts to increase domestic tourism have been largely limited to exhortations rather than hard cash. While the government advocates a regeneration of seaside resorts, the costs involved are such that little is being done to halt their decline. In short, pressures on government spending make it unlikely that the policy of self-support will be reversed, notwithstanding a substantial and ever increasing deficit in the balance of payments on the UK tourism account.

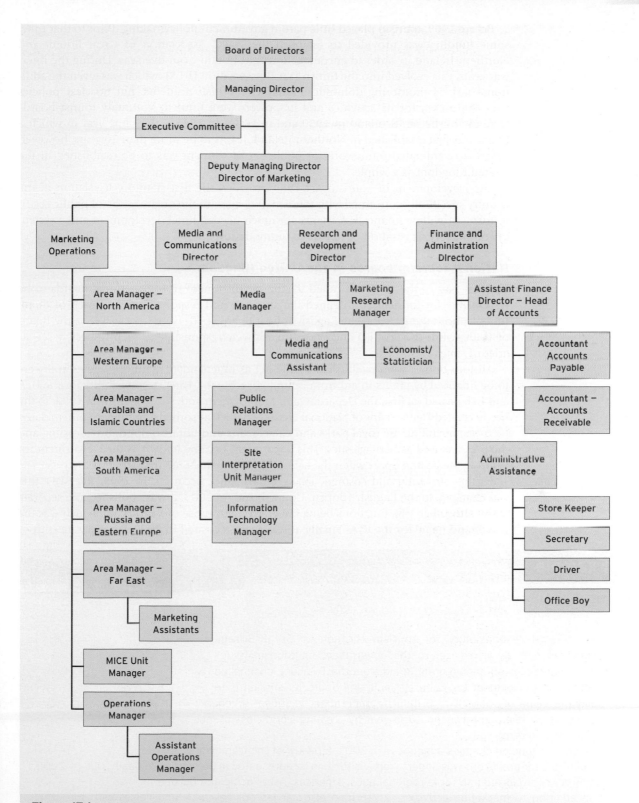

Figure 17.1 Organizational chart for the Jordan Tourist Board.
(Official website of the Jordanian government.)

Before 1969, tourism played little part in government policymaking. Prior to that time, some funding was provided to establish the Travel Association of Great Britain and Northern Ireland in order to encourage travel to Britain from overseas. During the inter-war years, this evolved into the British Travel Association (BTA), which was given the additional task of promoting domestic holidays for British residents, but no clear policies were laid down for its activities and its powers were limited. Voluntary tourist boards were established in Scotland in 1930 and in Wales in 1948 – the same year in which a board was first established in Northern Ireland. It was to be more than 20 years, however, before a coordinated framework for public-sector tourism was to be established in the United Kingdom as a whole.

The Development of Tourism Act 1969 provided the first statutory legislation in the country specifically concerned with tourism. It dealt with the organization of public-sector tourism, providing financial assistance for much-needed hotel development and a system of compulsory registration of tourist accommodation.

National tourism boards in the United Kingdom

The first part of the 1969 Act called for the establishment of four national boards to be responsible for tourism and defined the structure and responsibilities of each of them. Initially, both the BTA and the English Tourist Board (ETB) were responsible to the Board of Trade, while the Scottish and Wales Boards were responsible to their respective secretaries of state.

All four bodies were established by the Act as independent statutory bodies and were to be financed by grants-in-aid from central government. Later, responsibility for the BTA and ETB passed to, first, the Department of Employment and, subsequently, in 1992, to the newly created Department of National Heritage, which absorbed a number of other related interests, including the royal parks and palaces, arts and libraries, sport, broadcasting and the press, as well as heritage sites. This department became known as the Department for Culture, Media and Sport when the Labour government came to power in 1997.

Further structural and cosmetic changes have since occurred. In 1999, the ETB's title was changed, to the English Tourism Council, and, in 2003, it was abolished as a separate entity altogether – its functions being integrated with those of VisitBritain, which was the new brand name for the BTA. Finally, it was again recreated in 2009 as a separate entity.

Example

The role of VisitBritain

With general responsibility for tourism throughout Great Britain, VisitBritain acts as an adviser to the government on tourism issues and is financed by an annual grant-in-aid from the Treasury, channelled through the Department for Culture, Media and Sport. Its mission is to 'build the value of tourism to Britain by generating additional revenue throughout Britain and throughout the year by creating world-class brands and marketing campaigns'.[9]

In light of funding changes announced in 2007, a review of the framework of public-sector provisions was undertaken. VisitBritain is represented in 36 markets globally, but, by 2008, they were reorganized into three regional hubs: Americas, Asia-Pacific and Europe.

In addition to marketing activities, VisitBritain also carries out research and liaises with the other tourism bodies in the UK. Unfortunately, the funding cuts also led to plans to reduce UK staffing levels by 40 per cent, while overseas staffing was to be cut by 25 per cent,[10] leading to some concern among industry professionals, who suggested that it may now be difficult for the organization to fulfil its role.

Following the devolution of power to Scotland and Wales, responsibility for tourism for these parts of the UK was placed directly in the hands of the Scottish Parliamentary and Welsh Assembly governments. In Ireland, following the 1998 Good Friday Agreement, The Northern Ireland Tourist Board, which reports to the Northern Ireland Office, united in 2002 with its opposite number south of the border, the Irish Tourist Board, to form Tourism Ireland for marketing purposes.

UK government's involvement at regional level

The changes in structure outlined above heralded even greater upheavals that were to affect British public-sector tourism in the twenty-first century. One of the most significant changes has been the rerouting of DCMS funds for the English board direct to the regional development agencies (RDAs), which are responsible for all economic strategy in the regions and have, as a result, become all-powerful in directing policy and resources for tourism.

Regional development agencies (RDAs) and tourism

The nine RDAs were set up in 1998, funded directly by the Department for Trade and Industry. Theoretically, these bodies were to have been overseen by nine regional assemblies, consisting of nominated, rather than elected, councillors, but public opinion has swung strongly against the formation of these regional bodies after their firm rejection in the North East as yet another layer of public control and their future is still in doubt.

The RDA areas do not coincide with those of the regional tourist boards (RTBs), further complicating the administration of tourism, as the RTBs have not themselves been dissolved, although their funding has been sharply reduced.

The new RDAs are:

- South East of England RDA (SEEDA)
- South West of England RDA
- East Midlands Development Agency
- East of England Development Agency
- London Development Agency
- One North East
- North West RDA
- Advantage West Midlands
- Yorkshire Forward.

Tourism is only one of the new RDAs' remits – they are now responsible for developing economic strategies for their areas, including those for tourism, which the RTBs are then expected to follow. Sustainability has been emphasized in the government's plans for the RDAs' development and delivery of tourism strategies in the regions.

Regional tourist boards (RTBs)

Further changes are taking place, as the RDAs exercise their influence over the RTBs. RDAs work with RTBs covering their area. The North West RDA, for example, has five subdivisions, known as Destination Management Organizations. These have been entitled:

- Visit Chester and Cheshire
- Cumbria Tourism
- Lancashire and Blackpool Tourist Board
- Marketing Manchester
- Mersey Partnership.

They are designed to emphasize the importance of these destinations in marketing the region.

Example

The Cotswolds

The Cotswolds is one of the outstanding regions for tourists in England, yet its political, administrative and economic borders are differently defined. There is a Cotswold District Council (in Gloucestershire), its area falling within the remit of the SouthWest RDA, which funds Tourism SouthWest. At the same time, the most popular attractions within the Cotswolds are, in fact, located within the area covered by Tourism West Midlands, which is funded by Advantage West Midlands.

The RTBs support the RDAs to produce a coordinated strategy for tourism within their regions, market tourism in the region and encourage the development and improvement of tourist amenities and facilities that meet the changing needs of the market. These policies and activities should help to support the economic development plans of the RDAs.

RTBs have a particularly difficult role in their relations with local authorities. They must work with those authorities and cooperate with them in tourism planning, but their aims may conflict with those of the local authority. Geographically, RTB areas are often diverse and cannot logically be promoted as a single destination. Furthermore, political regions do not necessarily embrace what *tourists* understand as a 'tourist region' and the RTB's role will include the promotion of a brand image for a region that may readily cross county borders.

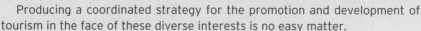

Example

The diversity of destinations for South West Tourism

South West Tourism represents counties ranging from Cornwall at its western extremity to Bristol on its northern boundary and parts of West Dorset on its eastern boundary. It is charged with the promotion of all these regions, although Bristol's Council makes no financial contribution to the board's funds, while the promotion of Dorset would arguably be better handled as an integral destination. One of its key stated aims focuses on 'ensuring a balanced representation of the region with regard to Coast v. Country, City v. Rural.'[11]

Producing a coordinated strategy for the promotion and development of tourism in the face of these diverse interests is no easy matter.

The Wales Tourist Board works with four regional tourism partnerships. These are:

- Tourism Partnership North Wales
- Tourism Partnership Mid Wales
- South West Wales Tourism Partnership
- Capital Region Tourism.

The principal role of these four organizations is to improve the competitive performance of tourism in Wales so that it better contributes to the economic and social prosperity of the area.[12]

In Scotland, 18 area tourism partnerships have been established to address local tourism priorities in an integrated manner. These are:

- Angus & Dundee Tourism Partnership
- Argyll, Loch Lomond and Forth Valley Area Tourism Partnership
- Ayrshire and Arran Area Tourism Partnership
- Borders Tourism Partnership
- Dumfries & Galloway Area Tourism Partnership
- East Dunbartonshire Area Tourism Partnership
- Edinburgh & Lothians Area Tourism Partnership
- Fife Tourism Alliance
- Glasgow Tourism Partnership
- Highlands Area Tourism Partnership
- Inverclyde Area Tourism Partnership
- Lanarkshire Area Tourism Partnership
- North East Scotland Tourism Partnership (NESTOUR)
- Orkney Area Tourism Partnership
- Outer Hebrides Area Tourism Partnership
- Perthshire Tourism Partnership
- Renfrewshire Area Tourism Partnership
- Shetland Area Tourism Partnership.

These partnerships aim to bring together representatives from across the private and public sectors, such as tourism operators, local tourism groups, chambers of commerce, local authorities, local enterprise companies and VisitScotland.[13]

Northern Ireland, in addition to its forming one region within the all-Ireland marketing consortium Tourism Ireland, has also established five new regional tourist boards. They are Causeway Coast and Glens, Kingdoms of Down, Fermanagh Lakeland Tourism, Belfast Visitor and Convention Bureau and Derry Visitor and Convention Bureau.

UK government's involvement at local level

We have now examined how tourism is structured at both national and regional levels. The third tier in this structure is the local authority level, where town, county and district councils also have statutory responsibilities and interests when it comes to providing tourist facilities – or at very least, encouraging inbound tourism where the potential for it exists, as part of the economic development plans for the area. This will generally include the provision of tourist information centres.

In Britain, the Local Government Act 1948 empowered local authorities to set up information and publicity services for tourism, which was reinforced by the Local Government Act of 1972, giving local authorities the power (but not the obligation) to encourage visitors to their area and provide suitable facilities for them.

The organization of tourism at local level is often curiously piecemeal. Counties and districts on the whole relegate responsibility for tourism to departments that are also concerned with a range of other activities, with the result that it is seldom given the significance that its economic impact on the area merits. Up until 20 years ago, fewer than half of the local authorities in England included any strategy relating to tourism in their planning, although Government Circular 13/79 had urged them particularly to consider providing for tourism in local structure plans and the then ETB had offered guidelines for local authorities to follow when drawing up such plans. The following key points were emphasized:

- assess the number and distribution of tourists in the area
- estimate future changes in tourism flows and implications of this for land use
- identify growth opportunities
- assess the impact of tourism on employment and income in the area
- assess the tourists' effect on traffic flows
- assess the tourists' demand for leisure and recreation
- identify the need for conservation and protection
- evaluate the contribution tourism could make to development, especially in the use of derelict land and obsolete buildings.

Local plans should take into account the impact of tourism and the resultant need for car and coach parks, toilets, information centres, tourist attractions and local accommodation. The inadequacy of parking and toilet facilities in resorts has been a frequent topic of criticism and cutbacks in local funding have magnified the problem recently.

By the beginning of the 1980s, tourists' needs were regularly addressed within many local authority structure plans, with local authorities coming to appreciate the economic contribution that tourism could make, even in traditionally non-tourist areas.

The principal responsibilities of county and district authorities that bear on tourism are as follows:

- provision of leisure facilities for tourists (such as conference centres) and residents (theatres, parks, sports centres, museums and so on)
- planning (under town and country planning policies) – note that district councils produce local plans to fit the broad strategy of the county councils structure plans and those plans are certified by the county councils
- powers to control development and land use
- provision of visitor services (usually in conjunction with tourist bodies)
- parking for coaches and cars
- provision of caravan sites (with licensing and management the responsibility of district councils)
- production of statistics on tourism, for use by the regional tourist boards
- marketing the area
- upkeep of historic buildings
- public health, including food hygiene and safety issues, as well as litter disposal and the provision of public toilet facilities.

Local authorities may also own and operate local airports, although in many cases they are now in private hands. The provision of visitor services will normally include helping to fund and manage tourist information centres, in cooperation with the regional tourist boards, which set and monitor standards. Local authorities will also fund tourist information points, information boards found at lay-bys, car parks and city centres.

Local authorities that have set out actively to encourage tourism have a number of objectives, some of which may conflict and each of which will compete for scarce resources. Local tourist officers will need to identify the resources they require to achieve their stated objectives and determine their priorities. Typical objectives might include:

- increasing the numbers of visitors
- extending their stay
- increasing their spend
- increasing and upgrading local attractions
- creating or improving the image of the area as a tourist destination
- stimulating private-sector involvement in tourism.

Local tourist officers act as catalysts between the public and private sectors and voluntary-aided bodies. As a focus for tourism in the area or resort, they become a point of reference, advising on development and grant-aided opportunities. Officers will help the local authority to determine and establish the necessary infrastructure that will allow tourism to develop, and carry out research and planning activities themselves. In some areas, they may become involved in the provision and training of tourist guides. In addition, they will undertake a range of promotional and publicity functions, including the preparation of publications such as guides to the district, accommodation guides, information on current events and entertainment and specialist brochures listing, for example, local walks, shopping, restaurants and pubs. The cost of most of these publications will be met in part by contributions from the private sector, either through advertising or, as in the case of the accommodation brochures, through a charge for being listed. Many resorts also now produce a trade manual, aimed at the travel trade and giving information on trade prices, conference facilities and coach parking.

Tourist officers may also organize familiarization trips for the travel trade and the media and, if the resort shows sufficient potential, may invite representatives of the overseas trade and media. They frequently play a part in setting up and operating the local tourist information centre (TIC), which may include a local accommodation-booking service. Some go as far as to actively package holidays for inbound visitors, including activity weekends or special interest short breaks. It should be noted that all of these functions are frequently the responsibility of a very small team, on occasion no greater than a single tourist officer and a secretary.

Unlike the regional tourist boards, where responsibilities are predominantly promotional, tourism planning and sustainable development form key elements of a local authority's functions. They may, consequently, be as concerned to reduce or stabilize tourism as to develop it, particularly when, as is so often the case in the popular tourist resorts, local residents are opposed to any increase in the numbers of tourists attracted. For this reason, in providing for leisure, the authorities must be as sensitive to local residents' needs as they are to those of incoming tourists. They must convince the residents of the merits of public investment in tourist projects. The development of conference centres in popular resorts such as Bournemouth and Harrogate was a controversial issue with local residents as very few private investors were willing to put money into centres such as these, but using public funds would have greatly increased the burden of debt on the councils initially. It is hard to convince local residents of the wisdom of investments that do not appear to provide a direct profit, but conferences do generate a healthy flow of indirect revenue as delegates spend money in local shops, hotels and restaurants. The added bonus is that much of this revenue will accrue outside the traditional holiday season. That was the thinking behind local authority investment in the ill-fated regeneration of Bath Spa, where cost over-runs spiralled to some £50 million as a result of mistakes in construction, leading to a massive debt burden for local taxpayers and delaying the opening years beyond the proposed completion date.

If local authorities contribute directly to RTB funds, they will clearly expect to play a role in their policymaking and serve on RTB committees. Where representatives of the private sector, such as local hoteliers, are also members of those committees, the latter's interests and objectives will often differ from those of the local authority, which can lead to conflicts in policymaking.

Tourist information centres (TICs)

TICs play a particularly important role in disseminating information about tourism, in the UK as elsewhere. There are well over 800 official TICs in Britain, with some 600 in England alone. Funding and staffing now come largely from the local authorities, assisted by the provision of support material and publications from the RTBs. The RTBs oversee the standards of each TIC and award them formal recognition. This has entailed, among other criteria, a requirement to employ salaried staff rather than rely on voluntary labour, as had been the practice in some TICs. Improved access, especially for the disabled and agreed minimum hours of opening have also become important benchmarks for recognition.

Many TICs have been forced to become more commercial due to government policy and the decline in funding by cash-strapped local authorities, which do not, in fact, have a statutory duty to provide these services. Apart from the now well-established Book a Bed Ahead scheme, TICs are increasingly introducing commercial products for sale within their shops, while seeking ways to cut costs to remain viable. Cafés and shops have been combined with exhibition and interpretation galleries in many TICs to attract tourists and get them to spend money in the centres.

A final point to make is the valuable contribution that TICs can make to tourism through the buildings they occupy. In many cases, TICs are housed in buildings of outstanding architectural or historic interest in a city and their careful preservation and adaptation for this purpose has ensured that the buildings are not only put to good use but also provide an additional point of focus for visiting tourists who are able to see the interior of a building that might otherwise be restricted. Increasingly, local authorities have come to recognize the important role that the TIC can play in drawing attention to modern design as well, whether in the traditional style and materials of local building or in a more modern concept where the new building can itself become a stimulus for tourist interest.

Information technology initiatives in the public sector

One means of providing tourist information cheaply is to have tourist information points (TIPs) – unattended stands providing information about local facilities. In many cases these will be located in TICs, but, in some cases, they are placed in popular tourist spots and can include sophisticated booking systems for local hotels, either using telephone connections or computer links.

The computer-linked accommodation reservation system was just the first step into IT taken by the public sector. The British boards have moved steadily towards developing and expanding their websites and now provide the public with a comprehensive package of information and booking services. The BTA devised its first VisitBritain website in 1997, incorporating details of tourist attractions, events and hotels, with accompanying advertisements. These have been complemented by national and regional boards' websites and, more recently, the development of an all-encompassing site known as EnglandNet.

EnglandNet has proved to be one of the most ambitious schemes undertaken by VisitBritain, in collaboration with the RDAs. Designed to provide the public with comprehensive information and booking facilities for virtually any tourist product in England, the website is open to operators and agents selling breaks, accommodation providers and the regional boards. The website is of particular value to SMEs, enabling them to reach their customers more effectively online. It allows companies to enter up-to-date information about their organizations on to the central database and that is used to provide website information for linked websites such as **www.enjoyengland.com** and **www.visitbritain.com**. The government has provided grants totalling more than £3 million through the DCMS and the site is still subject to further development at the time of writing. Products will be accepted on to the site, subject to their being quality assessed and graded.

Few can doubt that websites will become one of the most popular means of accessing accommodation bookings within the space of the next few years. Some local authorities are involved with plans to allocate rooms within their districts to tour operators for package tour arrangements. Such a centrally controlled allocation of hotel rooms would enable hoteliers to reduce their individual commitments to tour operators and therefore minimize wastage in the reservations process.

Plans are also under way for call centres to be set up within the TICs, which will allow the public to make bookings direct via the new website. This has given rise to concern that the public sector will be in competition with private-sector websites.

One other feature that deserves mention here is the emergence of electronic marketing units (EMUs) at TICs. These are databases accessible to passers-by outside the TICs, so their use is not limited to the opening times of the TICs themselves. Although the range of information available through these units is limited, it is expanding and already provides the basis for interactive communication between tourists and tourist facilities, which would allow visitors to make reservations for hotels, theatres and a host of other amenities.

The wider influences of the public sector on tourism in the UK

While departments with a specific responsibility for tourism play a major influential role in the development and management of the industry, the diverse nature of tourism and its impacts on so many different facets of the economy mean that there are often other government departments that have a vested interest in the way in which tourism is planned and managed. Furthermore, there are also public or quasi public bodies that, due to their roles, impinge in one way or another on tourism.

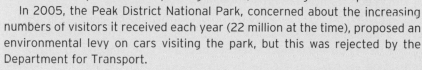

Example

Transport and tourism

The Department for Transport, quite apart from its public transport responsibilities, exercises control over certain types of signposting, and the signposting of attractions is of immense importance to the success of tourism. In January 1996, the relaxation of control over brown and white road signs for tourist sites led to information about these sites becoming far more readily available to passing tourists, enhancing tourist spend.

In 2005, the Peak District National Park, concerned about the increasing numbers of visitors it received each year (22 million at the time), proposed an environmental levy on cars visiting the park, but this was rejected by the Department for Transport.

The water authorities represent one example among non-government departmental interests that relate to tourism, as water-based recreation has come to play an important part in leisure and tourism planning. Local authorities and water authorities are now fully aware of the commercial leisure opportunities associated with open expanses of water. In this respect, it is interesting to note the extent to which tourism was taken into account in the planning and development of the Kielder Reservoir in Northumbria compared with earlier reservoir development.

Opened in 1982, Kielder is the largest man-made lake in Europe, with a shoreline 27 miles long, and is set within the largest man-made forest in Britain, Kielder Forest (which is managed by the Forestry Commission). Accordingly, the area has huge tourism potential and facilities to attract tourists were planned from the outset, including picnic areas, campsites, water sports, fishing and mountain bike hire.

Other quasi- or non-governmental bodies with interests that touch on tourism include Natural England (incorporating the former Countryside Agency and English Nature), the Forestry Commission, the Nature Conservancy Council, the Arts and Sports Councils, the National Trust and the Council for the Preservation of Rural England, yet there is no common coordinating body to bring these interests together.

National heritage bodies

Heritage plays a particularly important role in tourism – monuments, historic homes and cathedrals provide a wide variety of any area's tourist attractions. While many of these resources remain in private hands or are the responsibility of bodies such as the Church Commissioners, a number of quasi-public or voluntary organizations exist to protect and enhance these heritage sites. These bodies, therefore, fulfil an important role in the tourism industry. Even when heritage buildings are not open to the public, they still form an attractive backdrop to any townscape for passing tourists.

Internationally renowned UNESCO World Heritage sites draw people from all over the world and are carefully protected. UNESCO works to protect sites of international importance, encouraging management plans to be developed to ensure the protection and conservation of its recognized sites (more than 850 were recognized in 2008). It also provides around US$4 million annually in funding support.

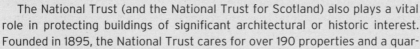

Example

Heritage protection in the UK

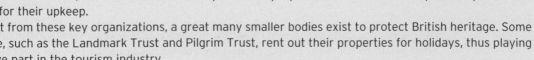

English Heritage has a dual conservation and promotion function as it now looks to industry and the public to raise the finances required to protect the buildings in its care, either through sponsorship of individual buildings or subscriptions to a national membership scheme. Cadw in Wales and Historic Scotland share a similar responsibility for historic properties in their territories.

The National Trust (and the National Trust for Scotland) also plays a vital role in protecting buildings of significant architectural or historic interest. Founded in 1895, the National Trust cares for over 190 properties and a quarter of a million hectares of land, acquiring properties for the most part through inheritance. Its properties include villages, nature reserves and woodland as well as individual buildings. It also operates a campaign under the title Enterprise Neptune to buy up and protect stretches of British coastline and, to date, it has acquired over 500 miles of coast. Operational costs are met by subscriptions from the very large number of members in Britain, but the Trust also anticipates that properties left will be accompanied by sufficient money for their upkeep.

Apart from these key organizations, a great many smaller bodies exist to protect British heritage. Some of these, such as the Landmark Trust and Pilgrim Trust, rent out their properties for holidays, thus playing an active part in the tourism industry.

Public private-sector cooperation

Due to the sheer complexity of tourism, there is frequently a lack of coordinated tourism policy at government level, while, at the same time, financial constraints are restricting public expenditure on tourism. Increasingly, the view is being taken that the public sector can best assist a country's prospects for tourism by reducing its role in development and promotion and entering into partnership with the private sector.

The desire to turn national tourism promotion over to the private sector or develop partnerships with the private sector has been led by developments in North America, where the USA abandoned its public-sector body in favour of the privately sponsored Travel Industry Association of America. Individual states have also gone down this road: Visit Florida is a public private-sector partnership that is funded in part by taxation on car hire within the state and sponsorship from some 3000 members of the industry.

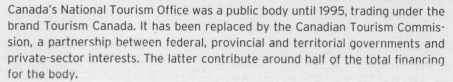

Example

Tourism Canada

Canada's National Tourism Office was a public body until 1995, trading under the brand Tourism Canada. It has been replaced by the Canadian Tourism Commission, a partnership between federal, provincial and territorial governments and private-sector interests. The latter contribute around half of the total financing for the body.

Regions, sometimes transnational, are also opting for a collaborative approach. An interesting example is that of the Øresund region, where Denmark is geographically separated from southern Sweden. The construction of a bridge linking the two countries has led to the formation of a joint marketing organization to promote Copenhagen, the surrounding region of Sjælland, Bornholm Island and southern Sweden, with privately funded support from SAS, the Scandinavian air carrier, and other regions. One notable effect of this marketing drive has been the economic improvement resulting from tourist flows into Malmø and southern Sweden – an economically depressed region. This exemplifies a general move to form destination management organizations, designed to form partnerships between the public and private sectors in order to promote tourism to a region more effectively.

Such moves towards a more commercial approach among the public bodies has paralleled public–private ventures. At local level, the formation of tourism marketing organizations, made up of representatives from both the public- and private-sector interests, is becoming a popular alternative to traditional public-sector tourism organizations.

In Britain, Plymouth was the first city to launch a partnership of this kind, back in 1977. The city's marketing bureau draws its members from those nominated by the city council and others elected by the private sector. The bureau is financed by a grant from the city's council, membership subscriptions and commercial activities. Other cities and districts to have followed suit include Merseyside, Birmingham, Greater Glasgow, Sheffield and Manchester, while bodies covering larger areas, such as the North Devon Marketing Bureau, are also following suit.

Not all these public–private partnerships or private initiatives have proved successful. Notable failures include the marketing bureaux of Chester and Bristol. There can be no denying, however, that the lack of collaboration between the sectors prior to the new partnerships was limiting their opportunities.

It should be stressed that public funds for private tourism projects have not ceased entirely. Many countries still offer subsidies in the form of grants, loans or other financial incentives that help to reduce costs for entrepreneurs in tourism. Where the state remains keen to see the development of private tourism, and funding for such development would not be forthcoming without direct public assistance, both central and local governments will still offer some measures of help.

Town twinning and tourism

No discussion of public-sector tourism can be complete without exploring the development of town twinning, even though the impact of this relationship between towns is seldom considered as an element of the tourism business.

The concept of town twinning emerged in the aftermath of World War II, as a means of overcoming hostilities between the warring nations and forging greater understanding between communities in different countries. Usually, the selection of a twin town is based on some common characteristics, such as population size, geographical features or commercial similarities. Local authorities and chambers of commerce arrange for the exchange of visits by residents of the twinned towns.

Although conceived as a gesture of friendship and goodwill, the outcome has commercial implications for tourism, as visitor flows increase between the twinned towns. While accommodation is normally provided in private homes, expenditure on transport, shopping and sightseeing can have a significant impact on the inflow of tourist revenue for the towns concerned – some of which may have little other tourist traffic. Friendships formed as a result of these links also lead to subsequent demand for travel. So far, no studies appear to have been made as to the financial contribution resulting from these links, but it is likely to be considerable overall.

The role of the European Union (EU)

By contrast with some EU nations where tourism makes an equally important contribution to the economy, Britain has chosen, largely, to allow the free-market economy to operate in the tourism field, with little attempt to centralize policymaking. As Britain becomes more closely integrated with the EU, however, British travel and tourism interests have become subjected to EU legislation. Most importantly, since harmonization came into force at the beginning of 1993, any constraints of trade have been largely abolished, allowing travel firms to compete within the EU on an equal footing and without legal hindrance.

Within the European Commission, at least 10 of the 23 directorates general (the Commission's departments) have some responsibilities that impact on the tourism industry, although the Tourism Unit itself is allocated to Directorate I within the Directorate General for Enterprise and Industry. As with government departments in Britain, there is no system for coordinating tourism interests across the directorates general.

The principal stated objectives of the EU as regards tourism include:

- the facilitation of tourist movements, through abolition of frontier controls, deregulation of transport, ease in transfer of foreign currencies, reciprocal health coverage and better information and protection for tourists themselves
- more effective promotion, through state aid and other means
- help in distributing the flow of tourists better, both geographically and seasonally, through emphasis on such features as rural tourism and by staggering school holidays
- other measures, to include better tourism training, easing taxation, etc.

Many of these ambitions had already been achieved to some extent before the introduction of harmonization. The scheduled airline industry has been fully deregulated and there have been no controls over charter flights within the EU. Shipping has also been fully deregulated.

The future role of the public sector in tourism

Governments across the globe are now recognizing the significant influence that tourism can have on a country's economy. The earnings that can be generated through taxation and foreign exchange are counterbalanced by the spending of their residents on overseas trips. There is also greater recognition of the important role that tourism can play in the regeneration of dilapidated areas of cities or the support it can provide to rural areas, supporting local amenities and businesses. The cost of supporting tourism (funding infrastructure development such as airports and marketing organizations such as VisitBritain), however, is a concern for many governments and this is encouraging the greater prevalence of public–private partnerships (PPP) to encourage private-sector tourism businesses to invest in the resources needed to support their operations. In cases where PPP is being encouraged, government is moving away from its role as 'financier' and towards that of 'coordinator'.

With border security an important issue for many nations, as immigration and anti-terrorism legislation heightens awareness of homeland threats, international travel is being inhibited by greater government demands to obtain personal information relating to visitors, either through detailed visa requirements or more complex border procedures. Governments therefore have to balance the demands of security with accessibility to ensure that tourists are not deterred from visiting. As the EU expands (and some internal border controls are removed), the movement of people across the region may be less easy to monitor. Furthermore, the nature and patterns of demand for tourism may shift as more of the European population can travel freely across the EU area.

Notes

1. Australian Broadcasting Corporation (2008) 'Disappointment over tourist approval in World Heritage Area', Australian Broadcasting Corporation, 16 April.
2. Rozhnov, K. (2007) 'Expanded Schengen attracts tourists', *BBC News*, 20 December.
3. Bingham, M. (2006) 'Wriedt outlines plan for tourist subsidy', *Hobart Mercury*, 12 October.
4. EC (2008) 'Provisions and instruments of regional policy', Summaries of Legislation, Structural Fund regulations, Objective 1, EC website. Available online at: **http://europa.eu/scadplus/leg/en/lvb/g24203.htm**
5. EU (2008) 'Legislation L243/44', *Official Journal of the European Union*.
6. 'Rural and regional tourism in Romania is to benefit', *Rompres*, 15 January 2007.
7. Minnaert, L., Maitland, R. and Miller, G. (2006) 'Social tourism and its ethical foundations', *Tourism, Culture and Communications*, 7, pp. 7–17.
8. Family Holiday Association (2007) 'Annual review', FHA.
9. VisitBritain's mission and other information are available online at: **www.tourismtrade.org.uk/aboutvisitbritain/default.asp**
10. Druce, C. (2008) 'UK tourism dismayed by cuts at VisitBritain', *Caterer and Hotelkeeper*, 7 August.
11. South West Tourism (2008) 'Promoting the region', South West Tourism. Available online at: **www.swtourism.co.uk/marketing/promoting-the-south-west/PromotingTheRegionIntroduction.ashx**

12. Visit Wales (2008) 'Regional tourism partnerships', Visit Wales. Available online at: **www.industry.visitwales.co.uk/server.php?show=nav.310**

13. VisitScotland (2008) 'Area tourism partnerships', VisitScotland. Available online at: **www.visitscotland.org/partnership_working/area_tourism_partnerships.htm**

Websites

EnglandNet   **www.tourismtrade.org.uk**

enjoyEngland   **www.enjoyengland.com**

Family Holiday Association   **www.fhaonline.org.uk**

Tourism For All   **www.tourismforall.org.uk**

VisitBritain   **www.visitbritain.com**

Questions and discussion points

1. Following a drop in worldwide visitor numbers over the past few years in the wake of stricter visa and border control issues, the US senate has drawn up a 'blueprint' to boost arrivals, based on training staff to be nicer at immigration booths.

   Charlotte Walshe, *Travel Trade Gazette*, 2 February 2007

   Discuss whether an improvement in the service and welcome provided by government custom and immigration officials will actually make a significant impact on the demand for a destination such as the USA.

2. Direct taxes on tourists (such as departure taxes or hotel bed taxes) are often unpopular with the tourist industry as they suggest that tourists will perceive the destination as more expensive. Discuss the reasons for a local or national government introducing a tourist tax. Do you think such taxes do actually affect the decisions tourists make over which destination to visit?

3. Social tourism includes the provision of holidays for socially or financially excluded families, people with disabilities and their carers. Discuss the many benefits that the chance to take a holiday can bring for the individual and also identify benefits that social tourism can bring to society more generally.

4. Sports and tourism have been separated within the ministries at the DCMS following London winning the 2012 Olympics bid. What are the long-term implications of having these two industries separated as the Olympic Games are planned and developed?

Tasks

1. As an employee in your local authority's tourism section, you have been asked to undertake some research investigating whether or not the department should establish a collaborative partnership with members of the local tourism trade to improve tourist visitor numbers and spend in your region. Write a report that identifies the benefits of such collaboration as well as commenting on the problems that may need to be addressed if it is to be a success.

2. Focusing on either the UK or a country of your choice, discuss how the role and activities undertaken by government to protect, manage and enhance tourism at national level differ from those undertaken by government at a local level.

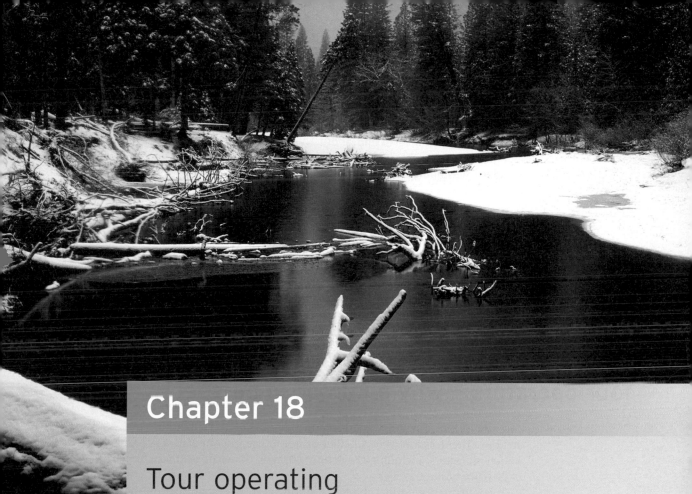

Chapter 18

Tour operating

Learning outcomes

After studying this chapter, you should be able to:

- define the role of a tour operator and distinguish between different types of operator

- explain the functions of each type of operator

- understand how operators interact with other sectors of industry

- understand how the activities of operators are constrained

- understand the basic principles behind the construction and marketing of a package tour

- understand the appeal of the package tour to its various markets

- evaluate alternative methods of tour distribution and recognize the importance of new forms of electronic reservations and sales systems for operators and their clients.

Introduction

> Seated beside me on the plane were a tired, elderly American and his wife. I asked him what was interesting about Hyderabad. He had not the slightest notion. He and his wife were going there because the place was 'in the package'. Their tour agent had guaranteed to include only places that were 'world famous' and so it must be.
>
> Daniel J. Boorstin, *The Image: A guide to pseudo-events in America*, Vintage, 1961, p. 91

The package holiday has made the process of organizing holidays much more straightforward than before. For many holidaymakers, the convenience of booking a package, which provides all the component parts of the holiday, has encouraged travel to locations that, otherwise, they would not have considered. This has overcome language barriers as well as concerns regarding the suitability of the products, such as accommodation, airport transfers or tours, all at a competitive price. Thus, the demand for packages has ensured that tour operators have continued to have a significant role in the tourism industry.

Tour operators – why a European perspective?

The use of tour operators as an intermediary in the travel booking process varies across nations. The decision as to whether or not to use intermediaries is influenced by a wide variety of factors, including the nature of travel (domestic or international) as well as the experience of the traveller.

It is often reported that the first tour operator was established in the UK, through the activities of Thomas Cook back in the nineteenth century. Many global players today, however, are European companies; for example, both Thomas Cook and TUI are German-owned, while Kuoni, a leading long-haul operator, is Swiss. Furthermore, the largest outbound travel market by far is the European region. In 2007, the UN World Tourism Organization (UNWTO) reported that over 56 per cent of global arrivals were from Europe (with the next largest markets being the Asia-Pacific region and the Americas, with 19 per cent and 17 per cent respectively).[1]

While it is acknowledged that the dominant Asia-Pacific markets of Japan, China and South Korea all now appear in the top ten of outbound markets (by spend), it should also be acknowledged that the total spend of these three markets combined is smaller than the spend of Germany alone.

Table 18.1 Tourism spend by key European and Asian countries.

Europe	$US billion	Asia-Pacific	$US billion
Germany	74.8	Japan	26.9
UK	63.1	China	24.3
France	32.2	South Korea	18.2

Source: UNWTO, 'Tourism highlight', ©UNTWO 9284400209, 2007.

For that reason, this chapter has focused largely on the European tour operator industry, acknowledging the traditional role of the tour operator as well as changing trends that are placing great pressure on tour operators to adapt in order to serve the rapidly changing markets:[2]

The decline of mass package tourism and subsequent rise of more individual forms of tourism, for some observers, is an inevitable tendency in contemporary tourism, reflecting more individuated, customized, and symbolic 'postmodern' consumption of goods and services.

The contemporary tourist markets, especially prevalent in Western Europe, have required many of the tour operators servicing this region to adapt their operations. Therefore, the experiences of European tour operators, explained within this chapter, can offer insight to other regions where similar changes in tourist demand are now being experienced.

The role of the tour operator

For many years, tour operators have formed the core of what we understand as the travel industry and, to a large extent, they can be said to have moulded the industry into the form familiar to us today. Traditionally, they formed an essential bridge between travel suppliers and customers, purchasing separately the elements of transport, accommodation and other services and combining them into a package that they then sold direct (or through travel agents) to consumers. Their position in the tourism distribution system is demonstrated by Figure 18.1.

Some take the view that tour operators are essentially wholesalers as they purchase services from the principals in large quantities and break these into individual units to sell to customers. Wholesalers, however, are not normally known to change the product they buy before distributing it, so for this reason, some argue that tour operators should be classed as principals in their own right, rather than simply intermediaries. Their argument is based on the premise that, by packaging a series of individual tourism elements into a single whole new product – the **inclusive tour** – the operator is actually changing the nature of those products. The service the tour operator provides is that of buying in bulk, thus, in theory, securing considerable discounts from the suppliers that could not normally be matched by customers buying direct. The operator is thus able to assemble and present to the customer a package – the inclusive tour – that is both convenient to purchase and competitively priced.

Recent years have witnessed a change to the ways in which travel products are bought and sold by operators. In the last quarter of the twentieth century, operators had begun to

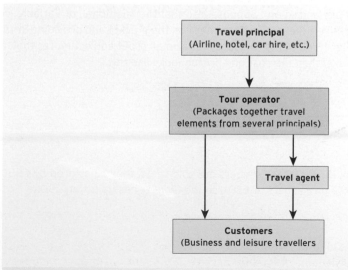

Figure 18.1 The tour operator's position in the chain of distribution.

sell unpackaged 'seat only' flights to agents and customers in order to fill seats on their charter flights and, with the advent of the World Wide Web, which encouraged principals to sell travel arrangements direct to customers, operators have become far more flexible in marketing their products. Many now offer each element of their packages separately or give their clients the opportunity to book their flights direct while helping them to organize the remaining elements of their holiday separately. While traditional 7- and 14-day packages will remain a popular feature in most operators' brochures, more flexible durations as well as tailor-made arrangements and individual elements of the package are now negotiable. The evidence in the UK is of a decline in the percentage of package overseas holidays – from 52 per cent in 2002 to 42 per cent by 2006.[3]

The packaging of travel elements by tour operators is also valuable to principals in the travel and tourism industry. The travel industry operates in a business environment where supply and demand are seldom in balance, nor can supply expand or contract quickly to take advantage of changes in demand. Both the airline and hotel businesses operate in circumstances that make it difficult to adjust their capacity in the short term.

The advantage of working with a tour operator – the case for airlines

Once a flight takes off, the airline has lost the opportunity to sell any empty seats on the plane and, thus, loses the potential to gain revenue on those seats. Maximizing the load factor (the percentage of available seats filled by passengers) is therefore key to maximizing revenue. Tour operators can help ensure that more seats are sold.

A charter airline with a single type of aircraft – say, a Boeing 757 with a maximum capacity of 239 passengers – cannot expand the number of seats to take advantage of peak opportunities, for example, nor reduce capacity if demand falls slightly. We say that supply is **lumpy** – that is, it cannot be expanded by a *single* seat, but must be expanded in

Example A

Costing a scheduled flight

Suppose that the fixed cost of flying a 140-seat plane from Paris to Athens and back is €43,540 (including capital costs, fuel, crew's pay and so on). Suppose also that the additional, or variable, cost per passenger is €30 (to cover administrative expenses such as check-in, the e-ticket and providing in-flight refreshments, extra fuel and so on). If the airline wants to budget for a small profit and estimates that, at a price of €425, it can expect to sell 112 seats, then the cost and pricing looks like this.

Fixed cost	€43,540
112 passengers x €30	€3,360
Cost of return flight	€46,900
Sell 112 tickets at €425 each	€47,600
Profit	€700

Of course, in the example, if only 110 passengers are sold seats, then sales drop by €850 (2 passengers at €425), costs by only €60 (2 passengers at €30), so the airline ends up losing €90.

Fixed cost	€43,540
110 passengers x €30	€3,300
Cost of return flight	€46,840
Sell 110 tickets at €425 each	€46,750
Profit/loss	–€90

blocks of seats – perhaps as many as 150 at a time in the case of aircraft. Carriers, therefore, seek ways to adjust demand to fill the available seats. It is important to do this to keep down costs per passenger and reduce the waste of resources as the aircraft costs a certain amount of money to run regardless of the number of passengers it carries and that fixed cost is likely to be the major element in any transport costs. Tour operators have played a very useful role in helping to achieve this for the scheduled airlines and, in return, the airlines can offer substantial discounts on seats that they know they themselves cannot fill. Example A demonstrates this.

The example shows a very simplified picture of pricing on a single route, but the complexity of pricing has substantially increased since the no frills airlines came into service, with the variations in prices becoming far wider (see Chapter 13 for a further illustration of this). Airlines also overbook in the expectation that a few passengers will not turn up in time for their flights, or will cancel without refund. Airlines retain the revenue (including tax, although this is only applied if passengers actually travel and, therefore, theoretically should be refundable), making a significant contribution to overall profit, especially if the seat can be resold.

Tour operators prove themselves useful to airlines by agreeing to purchase in bulk, say, 25 seats, which can virtually ensure that the airline will fly at a profit. The amount of discount that airlines give to tour operators must be considered, however. For example, if we continue with the Example above, as far as the airline is concerned, anything above €30 a head will be profitable, as the fixed costs are already paid for. Tour operators will want the lowest price possible to ensure that they can resell all 25 seats. Obviously, customers are unwilling to pay anything like the original €425 that was being asked or they would have already booked with the airline itself. Let's say that, after negotiating, the airline agrees to sell the seats to a tour operator at a net price of €225 each. The airline's budget for this case is shown in Example B.

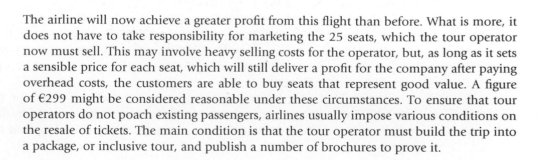

Example B

Costing a scheduled flight with a tour operator

Fixed cost	€43,540
137 passengers x €30*	€4,110
Cost of return flight	€47,650
Sell 112 tickets at €425 each	€47,600
Sell 25 tickets at €225 each	€5,625
Revenue	€53,225
Profit	€5,575

*Assumes all 25 seats are sold by the tour operator.

The airline will now achieve a greater profit from this flight than before. What is more, it does not have to take responsibility for marketing the 25 seats, which the tour operator now must sell. This may involve heavy selling costs for the operator, but, as long as it sets a sensible price for each seat, which will still deliver a profit for the company after paying overhead costs, the customers are able to buy seats that represent good value. A figure of €299 might be considered reasonable under these circumstances. To ensure that tour operators do not poach existing passengers, airlines usually impose various conditions on the resale of tickets. The main condition is that the tour operator must build the trip into a package, or inclusive tour, and publish a number of brochures to prove it.

As tour operators build their markets, they can eventually decide that they will have enough customers to fill an aircraft and consider either part-chartering a plane with other operators or even chartering a whole plane themselves. Eventually, they may be in a position to buy and operate their own airline to carry their customers, as do the leading tour operators in Europe.

Example

World of TUI Airlines

European tour operator TUI owns several airlines, which provide charter flights to service their package holiday operations. In recent years, rebranding has led to the renaming of some of these operations and now TUI has more than 100 aircraft serving destinations both within and outside Europe. The load factor reflects how close to full capacity the airlines operate on average (100 per cent would mean that every seat was sold on every journey). The data in the table is for the three-month period ending September 2007, so covers the peak holiday period for much of Europe.

Airline	Base	No. of aircraft	Load factor (%)
TUIfly (Hapag-Lloyd Flug and Hapag-Lloyd Express)	Germany	55	88.1
Thomson Airways (merging Thomsonfly and First Choice Airways) (ex-Britannia UK)	UK	48	90.7
TUIfly Nordic (Britannia Nordic)	Sweden, Denmark, Finland, Norway	5	95.5
TUIfly Nederland (Arkefly)	The Netherlands	4	89.9
TUIfly Belgium (Jetairfly)	Belgium	10	93.5
Corsair	France	8	82.2

Source: TUI, 'Interim financial reports', 2007.

The advantage of working with a tour operator – the case for hotels

In exactly the same way, hoteliers attempt to use tour operators to fill their unsold bedrooms. They, too, have substantial fixed costs in relation to operating their properties and so are willing to provide substantial discounts to operators and others willing to commit themselves to buying rooms in bulk. This is because, as with airlines, once the fixed costs of the property have been covered by revenue, any price that is greater than the variable cost will represent pure profit for the hotel, which will also then have the opportunity to sell extra services to its clients, such as drinks, entertainment and meals, those profits compensating for the low room rates that the operators have paid them. Furthermore, if the price is sufficiently attractive, the tour operator may even be able to provide the hotel with guests at times other than peak season. This will allow the hotel to operate all year round rather than have to consider closing during the off-peak period (closure means that no revenue is coming in at all, while the hotel will still attract costs for permanent staff, maintenance and so on).

Hotels in the Mediterranean have found it difficult to reach the North American market direct, so have been delighted for their hotels to be marketed by the tour operators in those countries. As a result, they came to depend largely, and in some cases entirely, on tour operators to sell their rooms.

Many of the larger tour operators started to own and run their own accommodation, but, in practice, this proved more difficult and most operators eventually divested themselves of their overseas properties, preferring to sign contracts with overseas proprietors, often for the entire capacity of the hotel and sometimes for several years in advance. The hoteliers' dependence on those contracts and their inability to reach the marketplace in any other way made them overly dependent on tour operators, which, in turn, used their dominant positions in the market to force down prices. Consequently the low profit levels achieved by the hoteliers led some to implement cost-cutting measures in the level of service they provided. The number of complaints rose as a result.

While parts of the package market appear to be unwilling to pay higher prices for better standards of service, there is some evidence that higher-quality accommodation is being demanded, with customers being prepared to pay slightly higher prices for the opportunity to upgrade. In light of this, some tour operators (such as Club Méditerranée) have elected to upgrade the quality of the accommodation they offer.[4]

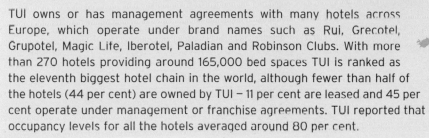

Example

TUI hotels and resorts

TUI owns or has management agreements with many hotels across Europe, which operate under brand names such as Rui, Grecotel, Grupotel, Magic Life, Iberotel, Paladian and Robinson Clubs. With more than 270 hotels providing around 165,000 bed spaces TUI is ranked as the eleventh biggest hotel chain in the world, although fewer than half of the hotels (44 per cent) are owned by TUI – 11 per cent are leased and 45 per cent operate under management or franchise agreements. TUI reported that occupancy levels for all the hotels averaged around 80 per cent.

Source: TUI, 'Interim financial report', TUI, 2007, and TUI, 'Annual report', TUI, 2006.

The growth of independent websites is beginning to change this picture. Not only can hoteliers now market their product direct to the public at prices that are competitive with those they offer tour operators but they also have access to other intermediaries, such as website accommodation providers. These include flight plus hotel and accommodation only online agencies and both provide important booking and information opportunities for the hotel sector, which is gradually relinquishing its sales dependence on tour operators.

The specialized roles of tour operators

The domestic operator

Tour operators fulfil a number of roles – they do not only carry traffic out of the country, although this is the role with which we most frequently associate them. Operators also exist to organize package holidays domestically – that is, to a destination within the country in which the tourists reside. For many countries, the numbers for domestic travel exceed those for international outbound travel (see Table 18.2).

Traditionally, tour operators that served the domestic market have formed just a small part of the travel and tourism industry, because it is relatively simple for tourists to make their own arrangements within their own country. In the past, it was uncommon to find a tour operator that simultaneously organized both domestic and foreign package holidays, although, of course, the originator of the package tour, Thomas Cook, started as a domestic

Table 18.2 Domestic tourism trips for European countries.

Countries	Overnight domestic holidays (%)
Spain	96.3
Greece	92.1
France	89.4
Portugal	88.7
Poland	87.1
Latvia	86.7
Finland	84.7
Italy	83.3
Czech Republic	81.0
Hungary	78.6
Estonia	77.2
Norway	71.6
Sweden	69.3
Lithuania	64.4
Slovakia	63.4
UK	60.6
Austria	52.1
Germany	50.4
Ireland	49.0
Netherlands	48.7
Denmark	48.0
Slovenia	45.6
Belgium	31.5
Luxembourg	1.4

Source: Eurostat, 'Inbound and outbound tourism in Europe', Eurostat 52/2007.

holiday organizer and only later expanded into foreign holidays. As concentration in the industry develops and competition becomes fiercer, however, the larger operators are tending to expand into the domestic market. Despite this, most companies in this sector are relatively small, often dealing directly with the public, and are therefore not involved in retailing through the trade.

The longest established domestic programmes are coach tours operated by companies such as Shearings and Wallace Arnold (which merged in 2005 to form WA Shearings), based in the UK, OAD Reizen, which operates in the Netherlands and Orbis Transport in Poland.

The incoming operator

Those countries such as Spain and Greece, which are predominantly destination rather than generating countries, will have an incoming travel sector that is as important as the outgoing sector. Organizations specializing in handling incoming foreign holidaymakers have a rather different role from that of outbound operators. Some are merely ground-handling agents, so their role may be limited to organizing hotel accommodation on behalf of an overseas tour operator or greeting incoming visitors and transferring them, often by coach, to their hotels. Other companies, however, will offer a comprehensive range of services, which may include negotiating with coach companies and hotels to secure the best quotations for contracts, organizing special interest holidays or study tours or providing dining or theatre arrangements. In some cases, companies specialize according to the markets they serve, catering for the inbound Japanese or Israeli markets, for example.

Example

Incoming operator – AlliedTPro

Swiss company Kuoni, a major tour operator, owns incoming agencies in Austria, Hungary, Italy and Spain, while its acquisition of Allied Tours in the USA allowed it to create AlliedTPro – a top tour operator for the US incoming market.

The origins of the company go as far back as the 1950s, but the recent growth of this company means that it now provides services to more than 600 tour operators across the globe. These services include providing airport transfers, sightseeing tours, tickets for entertainment events, such as theatre shows, and can also include arranging meals and activities for incentive travel or educational groups. The company also provides some ground-handling services for cruise companies. Annually it now serves almost half a million travellers visiting the USA.

Source: Kuoni, 'Corporate fact sheet – AlliedTPro', 2007. Available online at: **www.kuoni-dmc.com/profile/factsfigures**

In Britain there are more than 300 tour companies that derive a major part of their revenue from handling incoming business. As with domestic operators, most of them are small companies and more than a third are members of UKInbound, the aim of which is to provide a forum for the exchange of information and ideas among members, maintain standards of service and act as a pressure group in dealing with other bodies in the UK who have a role to play in the country's tourism industry.

Incoming tour operators' services are marketed largely through the trade and organizations work closely with public-sector bodies such as national tourist boards in order to promote their services.

Other specializations

Many operators recognize that their strengths lie in specializing in a particular niche. For example, some outbound operators choose to specialize according to the **mode of transport** used by their clients, such as coach tours, rail travel or self-drive holidays. Naturally, such tour operators are in competition with the transport companies that seek to boost their carryings by building inclusive tours around their own forms of transport.

Alternatively, specialization can be based on the markets they serve or the products they develop. The commonest distinction is between, on the one hand, the **mass market operators** that have as their products, typically, the sun, sea and sand holiday, designed to appeal to a very broad segment of the market, and, on the other hand, the **specialist operator**, which targets a particular niche market. By trying to distinguish their products from those of their competitors, these operators are not in such intense competition with each other and other operators and their market product is often less price-sensitive as a result.

Specialists have a number of advantages over mass market companies in the marketplace. Most carry small numbers of tourists and can therefore use smaller accommodation units, such as the small, family-run hotels in Greece, which are popular with many tourists, but too small to interest the larger operators. As the specialist companies generally use scheduled carriers and do not have the level of commitment to a particular destination that their larger colleagues have, they can be more flexible, switching to other destinations if market demand changes for any reason. Staff can generally be expected to have a good knowledge of the products and, as the market is less price-sensitive, the intense price competition found in the mass marketplace is absent, allowing companies to make reasonable profits. If they are successful, however, there is always the danger that one of the larger operators will be attracted to their market and either undercut them or attempt to buy the company. This has been a feature of the UK tour operating market in recent years, with the largest brands buying out medium-sized niche operators and fitting them into their own specialist products division (sometimes, later dropping the brand altogether or integrating it into their own mainstream brands).

Example

First Choice Holidays

One of the attractions of merging TUI with First Choice was the dominance of the latter in serving specialist niche markets. Prior to the merger, First Choice reportedly owned 96 specialist brands, but, following the merger, they have now been separated into three specialist sectors and three activity sectors. The specialist sectors focus on the following.

Sector	Area of focus	Brands include
Specialist – destination	These brands focus on providing a range of products and experiences at a few key destinations.	Marmara, Turchese, Signature Vacations.
Specialist – premium	This sector focuses on premium leisure travel experiences serving destinations across Asia, Europe and the Caribbean.	Hayes & Jarvis, Sovereign, Citalia, Meonvillas.
Specialist – life stages	These serve specific markets segmented by demographics, such as age.	Student City.com, Young Explorers, Jumpstreet.
Activity – marine	This division operates over 2400 yachts and motor boats.	Sunsail clubs, The Moorings, Crown Blue Line, Connoisseur, Emerald Star.
Activity – adventure	This sector focuses on providing a variety of adventure travel opportunities, including trekking and expeditions.	Exodus, Imaginative Traveller, Trek America, Waymark, Flexiski, Travelbound.
Activity – experiential	This division provides cultural and luxury escorted tours, primarily for the US market.	Travcoa, Brian Moore International Tours, Europe Express, Starquest Expeditions.

Source: E-mail correspondence with TUI corporate communications, 2008.

Many companies seek to specialize by geographic destination, but this can be a high-risk decision – as exemplified by the collapse of markets due to factors affecting one country or region. The SARS outbreak in 2003 caused some operators to withdraw their entire China programmes, while the unstable political situation in the Middle East has frequently affected operators specializing in holidays to Israel and neighbouring Arab countries. An extreme example is that of Yugotours. When civil war fractured the former Yugoslavia in the 1990s, Yugotours, which specialized almost exclusively in that destination, was forced to change not only its destinations but also even its brand name in order to build a new market. It failed to re-establish itself and the brand disappeared.

Specialization by market is common. Some companies choose to appeal to a particular age group, as does Saga Holidays, which has for many years been the UK's market leader in holidays for the over-fifties. The company now faces a challenge from Travelsphere's takeover in 2004 of Page and Moy, which, with four million customers, is targeting the over-forty-fives to widen the potential market. Others target the younger markets, such as Club 18–30 and 2wenties. The singles market – fast growing as social changes have increased the proportion of divorced people in our society – is served by specialists such as Solo Holidays. Other operators specialize by gender. WalkingWomen, for example, as the name implies, offers walking tours for females only. Targets are becoming increasingly tightly focused, with recent additions to the marketplace targeting one-parent families, such as Small Families or One Parent Family Holidays (a non-profit organization).

Obviously, there is ample opportunity to specialize according to the specific interests, activities or hobbies of clients and tour companies have been established to cater for such diverse needs as those of vegetarians, those with an interest in various cultural activities, golfing or angling enthusiasts – even such highly specialized activities as textile weaving. One company that has proved itself highly successful in its targeting is Cycling for Softies, which caters for tourists interested in using bicycles as a mode of transport but still seeking comfortable and well-equipped overnight accommodation (see Chapter 15). This company's main focus is on travel in France and it therefore specializes in both the destination and the market it serves.

Activity and adventure holidays together form one of the fastest-growing areas of specialization. Mintel[5] estimated that activity holidays will have grown by 13 per cent between 2005 and 2010, to around 18.2 million holidays per year.

Example

Adventure holidays by motorcycle

H-C Travel is an example of a company specializing by mode of transport.

Founded in 1994, the company claims to be the world's number one agency for holidays by motorcycle, offering trips on several continents, as well as tailor-made holidays. Examples include two-week biker treks on Royal Enfield bikes between Kathmandu and Lhasa across the Mongolian steppes, as well as journeys across the Moroccan Sahara Desert dunes or to the Yellowstone, Grand Canyon and Death Valley National Parks in the USA.

Further information: **www.hctravel.com**

The role of air brokers

One other role should be examined here – that of those who specialize in providing airline seats in bulk to other tour operators. These specialists are known as **air brokers** or, where their business is principally concerned with consolidating flights on behalf of operators that have not achieved good load factors for their charters, **consolidators**.

Air brokers negotiate directly with airlines, buying seats in bulk and arranging to sell them, either in smaller blocks or even individually to tour operators or travel agents. They provide the airlines, especially those companies that may find it difficult to obtain good load factors on some legs of their operations, with a good distribution service and, in return, the airlines are willing to offer very low net rates to fill their remaining seats. The brokers put their own mark-up on the seats and take on the responsibility of marketing them for whatever price they can get. Their operations led to the demise of the former bucket shop operators, who performed a similar function but often infringed IATA regulations by 'dumping' tickets at discounted prices on the market. Deregulation on an international scale has now virtually eradicated the former illegal operations and made ticket discounting 'respectable'. Many mark-ups are very low, with the broker making money on the huge turnover of seats they achieve.

Online intermediaries reflect the growth in modern air brokerage, with companies such as ebookers and Opodo becoming major players in the field.

Integration in the industry

Nothing spells out more clearly than this list of the rapid changes that have taken place and the competitive environment that exists within the industry. Mergers and takeovers became commonplace, coupled with an increasingly international perspective in the tour operating business, as operators have come to look abroad for opportunities to expand and dominate the market through purchasing power. The leading European tour operators' attempts to enter the difficult and highly competitive North American markets have tended to prove abortive, although the rationale behind the move was clear: a desire to spread the seasonal flow of traffic, thus obtaining better year-round usage of aircraft. The risk would also be reduced by ensuring a more even spread of revenue between markets in North America, the UK and mainland Europe.

The takeover or merger of businesses is termed **integration** and it can take place either at the same stage of the supply chain – horizontal integration – or at different stages of the supply chain – vertical integration.

Horizontal Integration

The amalgamation of two businesses which operate within the same part of the supply chain (such as a tour operator merging with or buying out another tour operator) is called **horizontal integration**.

The reasons for horizontal integration may include the ability to gain economies of scale in operations as well as increase purchasing power, the opportunity to gain greater market share, acquire or share a wider range of products and increase the market value of the company. It can also reduce competition as the merged businesses then work together.

Vertical integration

The amalgamation of companies at different stages of the distribution chain is termed **vertical integration**. In cases where control of suppliers is achieved, backward vertical

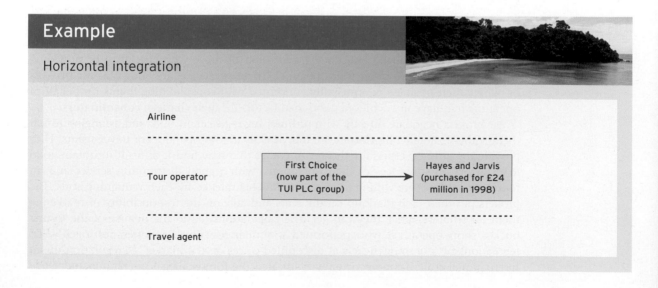

Example

Horizontal integration

Airline

Tour operator   First Choice (now part of the TUI PLC group) → Hayes and Jarvis (purchased for £24 million in 1998)

Travel agent

integration is said to have occurred; where control of the buyer of the product has been achieved this is termed forward vertical integration.

The benefits of vertical integration include the ability to control the suppliers (in the case of backward integration) or the retailers who sell the organization's product (in the case of forward integration). For tour operators, backward integration can help to control overall standards of the package and, at the same time, ensure that they maintain a ready supply of air seats and hotel rooms when demand is heavy. Forward integration into ownership of retail outlets can also help to avoid paying commission to external organizations, which can assist in enhancing the profitability of the group as well as expand the company's value. Furthermore, once a tour operator has control over its own retailing chain, it can move towards **directional selling**, where retail outlets direct customers to products provided by their parent companies, rather than those supplied by competitors.

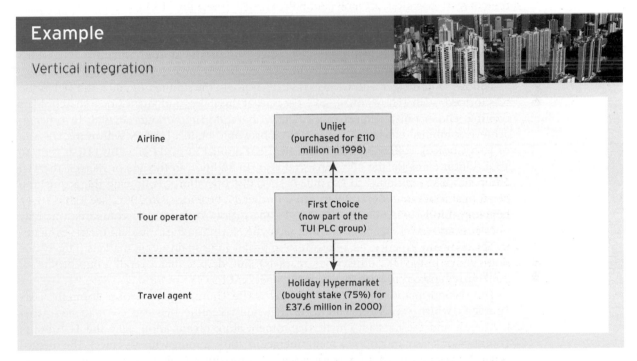

Example

Vertical integration

Even with the much greater levels of concentration in the industry found in the late twentieth century, the European Commission[6] has suggested that the growth of Internet travel providers as well as the existence of low-cost airlines has meant that the market remains competitive:

> The increased use of the internet and of online-distribution have opened up a direct route to market for smaller suppliers of package holidays and also allow travel agents and consumers to combine different travel components themselves.

Thus, it has been accepted that integration is not against the public interest, given that competition still ensures prices are kept down.

Tour operating within the European Union

The process of integration has been witnessed extensively across Europe, but some reports have suggested that it may be on the decline in some regions. For instance, established budget airline networks and high levels of Internet use in both the UK and Scandinavia have led business operations in these areas to provide strong challenges to the vertically integrated tour operator model.[7] The integration of travel companies across European borders remains prevalent, however.

Investment companies appear interested in many vertically integrated travel groups. For example, Spain's Orizonia was sold in 2007 to private equity groups Carlyle and Vista, while Blackstone purchased Travelport (which includes ebookers, Orbitz and Octopus Travel among its brands). Furthermore, businesses operating in other industry sectors are being attracted to large travel companies. For instance, the German department store and mail-order company Arcandor AG (formerly KarstadtQuelle AG) owns a majority stake in the Thomas Cook Group, while the large German tour operator Rewe Touristik is owned by a food retailer and Hotelplan is a subsidiary of Switzerland's largest supermarket chain, Migros.

The dominance of a few mega tour operators means that, for many European countries, their largest operators are not nationally owned (see Table 18.3). Some countries, for example Belgium, have no major locally owned tour operator.

The European tour operator market is dominated by a few mega-businesses that operate across multiple markets with multiple brands. Perhaps the most dominant is TUI, which is the leading tour brand in several European countries, including the UK and Germany.

Following its merger with UK-based First Choice in the summer of 2007, the TUI group was formed (with TUI AG owning 51 per cent of the shares and First Choice shareholders owning 49 per cent). Almost immediately, the company announced that, in order to achieve combined efficiencies, over 1000 jobs would be lost (mostly within the UK arm of First Choice). Following this, it revealed that annual turnover grew by 11 per cent, to 15.6 billion euros for the 2007 financial year. In addition to this major merger, the TUI group has also continued to expand its specialist operations. Following the acquisition of 16 businesses in 2006, it purchased a further 17 businesses in 2007 (see Table 18.4), targeting travel companies in the Asia-Pacific region, online travel companies, activity operators and travel organizations that serve the North American student travel segments.

The company experienced a downturn in profits in its mainstream markets (largely due to pressures in the UK and German markets), but, despite that, overall group profits for 2007 were reported to have increased by 5 per cent to £287 million.

The second major operator in Germany is the Thomas Cook Group, formerly C&N Touristik, which was formed in 1998 as a joint venture between German air carrier Lufthansa and the Karstadt/Quelle department store organization. Like the TUI group, Thomas Cook also undertook a major merger in 2007, joining with MyTravel. The merged company was expected to achieve sales of approximately €12 billion annually, with Thomas Cook a major operator in the UK, Germany and Scandinavia. In 2007 the Thomas Cook group served 19 million customers and, despite a decrease in revenue of 1.3 per cent overall, operating profit increased by 3.2 per cent to €375.3 million. The mainstream travel sector of its business is expected to remain dominant, although it has predicted that changes in customers' travel behaviour will mean that its independent travel sector will provide a larger proportion of revenue in future years.

A third major player is Rewe – a leading supermarket chain that controls tour operator LTU-Touristik, tour operator brands including ITS, Jahn Reisen, Tjaereborg, Dertour, Meier's Weltreisen and ADAC Reisen and over 2600 retail travel agencies. Rewe is ranked eighth in the global travel retail market, with a share of 1.3 per cent, but is ranked third in travel retail in Western Europe.[8]

The fourth major player in the European tour operator industry is Swiss-based Kuoni. A long-established brand, founded more than 100 years ago, it has sought to provide specialist products, allowing the company to achieve premium prices for its products. In recent years, the company has sold some non-core subsidiaries in an effort to streamline its operations, but has also purchased a 70 per cent shareholding in Norwegian-based Reisetorget AS, an Internet retail specialist for travel products, which was sought to enhance Kuoni's online sales.

Table 18.3 The top tour operators (and their brands) in selected European countries.

	TUI (Germany)	Thomas Cook (Germany)	Rewe (Germany)	Kuoni (Switzerland)	Locally owned tour operators	Other dominant tour operators
Austria	TUI Austria, 1-2-Fly, Magic Life, Terra Reisen, and Gulet Touristik.	Thomas Cook, Neckermann und Reisen.	Dertour, LTT Austria, Jahn, Meier's Weltreisen and ITS-Billa-Reisen.			
Belgium	Jet Tours, Jetair, Nouvelles Frontières, Sunjets.be, Voyages VTB, VIP Selection and Splash Travel.	Thomas Cook, Neckermann und Reisen and Pegase.				
Poland	TUI Poland (including Scan Holiday).	Thomas Cook Poland.			Orbis, Ving and Itaka.	
France	Nouvelles Frontières, Marmara.	Thomas Cook Voyages.			Club Med, Eurodisney Vacances SAS, Fram, Pierre & Vacances	
Germany	TUI Deutschland, 1-2-Fly and Airtours.	Thomas Cook Reisen, Neckermann und Reisen, Bucher Last Minute.	Dertour, LTU Touristik, Meier's Weltreisen, Jahn Reisen and Tjaereborg.		Alltours, FTI.	
Italy					Alpitour, Viaggi del Ventaglio (Ventaglio, Columbus, Caleidoscopio and Utat).	Costa Crociere (owned by Carnival Cruise Line, USA).
The Netherlands	TUI Nederland, Arke and Holland International.	Thomas Cook, Neckermann und Reisen and Vrij Uit.		Koning Aap, Shoestring and Kuoni Netherlands.	OAD (OAD Reizen, Bex Reizen, SRC-Cultuurvakanties), Vacansoleil.	

Table 18.3 (*continued*)

	TUI (Germany)	Thomas Cook (Germany)	Rewe (Germany)	Kuoni (Switzerland)	Locally owned tour operators	Other dominant tour operators
Nordic region	TUI Nordic, Fritidsresor and Star Tour.	Ving, Saga, Tjaereborg and Spies.		Kuoni Scandinavia, Alletider Resor and Apollo Rejser.		
Spain					Globalia (Viajes Halcón, Viajes Ecuador, TCI Cortes and Iberotours).	Iberostar (Iberojet, Viva Tours, Turavia and Solplan) (owned by a USA/Spanish investment group).
Switzerland	TUI Switzerland, Imholz, Vogele, Spinout and Flex Travel.			Kuoni Switzerland, Manta Reisen, Railtour Suisse and Kuoni World Class.	Hotelplan, TTS.	
UK	Thomson, Simply Travel, First Choice, Crystal Holidays, Thomson Ski and Snowboarding, Hayes & Jarvis, Sovereign and Exodus Travels.	Thomas Cook, Club 18–30, Neilson, Aspro, Direct Holidays, MyTravel, Panorama, Cresta and Tradewinds.		Kuoni and Kuoni World Class.	Cosmos (Tourama and Avro).	

Source: Edited from Mintel, 'European leisure travel industry', Mintel, September 2007.

Table 18.4 TUI's global acquisitions in 2007.

Company	Description	Date	Country	Value
Mainstream holidays sector				
Holidays Uncovered	Package holiday review website.	September	UK	£2.5m
MicronNexus	Online car broker.	September	Germany	£0.7m
Specialist holidays sector				
Young Explorers	Educational tours operator.	January	Canada	£0.8m
KSA Events	High school group sports tours.	April	USA	£3.0m
Splashline	Leisure holidays to Austrian student market.	May	Austria	£2.6m
New Horizons Tour & Travel	Student travel in group performance market.	September	USA	£2.5m
World Class Vacations	Student travel in group performance market.	September	USA	£4.5m
Activity holidays sector				
Western Xposure	Adventure travel operator.	February	Australia	£2.4m
i-to-i	Provider of meaningful travel experiences.	February	UK	£20.6m
iExplore	Premium adventure travel Internet portal.	February	USA	£4.6m
Quark Expeditions	Expedition cruising specialist.	April	USA	£9.8m
Hannibal Marco Polo	Danish adventure business.	May	Denmark	£10.0m
Australian Sports Tours	Group sports tours for the Australian market.	July	Australia	£10.5m
Ski Alpine	Schools skiing business.	August	UK	£1.3m
Starquest Expeditions	Round the world experiential business.	September	USA	£24.5m
Online destination services				
LateRooms.com	Seller of late availability hotel accommodation.	December	UK	£103.2m
Asiarooms.com	Online retailer of accommodation.	September	Singapore	£23.3m

Source: TUI, 'Pro forma financial information, TUI, December 2007.

All these operators have recognized the importance of gaining customer numbers to increase the scale of their operations and, thus, allow them to buy at the lowest price and control the markets. Transnational mergers will remain increasingly common, limited only by the anti-monopoly forces of the European Commission.

Example

The structure of the outbound tour-operating business in the UK

By the end of 2007, there were 781 tour operators in the UK that were members of ABTA – a decline from the peak level of 866 in 2004.[9]

The market is dominated by two main operators, TUI and Thomas Cook. Both companies have expanded their operations by purchasing smaller tour operating businesses and, between them, control hundreds of popular holiday brands including:

- TUI PLC – First Choice, Airtours, Crystal, Thomson, Hayes and Jarvis, Austravel, Exodus

- Thomas Cook Group – Airtours, Club 18–30, Cresta, Direct Holidays, Going Places, Neilson, Panorama, Sunset, Thomas Cook.

This horizontal integration has been a dominant feature of the UK tour operator sector for over 20 years.

The second characteristic in the industry has been a trend towards vertical integration, with the largest companies owning and/or controlling their own airlines, ground-handling agents at airports, electronic distribution channels and retail travel agencies.

The initial phases of sector concentration can be traced back to the rapid expansion that took place in the tour operating business after the 1960s in Britain (this occurred slightly later in other parts of Western Europe and North America). Driven by the belief that the holiday market was expected to see substantial growth, many new companies entered the tour operating sector, while those already established expanded quickly in order to maintain their dominance in the field. This led to a cycle in which many companies collapsed, owing to three main problems:

- growing too fast, borrowing too much to finance the expansion and, in some cases, lacking the management expertise to operate these larger companies

- making insufficient profit to survive in the face of intense competition, which drove down prices

- being hit by external problems, such as rises in the price of fuel, political unrest in some of the destination countries and economic recession in the UK economy.

Most UK operators are very small companies, with the top two operators dominating the market. Tour operator ATOL licensing data for the number of passengers carried shows that TUI and Thomas Cook dominated, with 6.9 million and 4.2 million respectively and only three other organizations carrying more than 0.5 million passengers (Expedia, Gold Medal Travel and Freedom Flights). The 25 next largest operators carried an average of 0.25 million passengers.[10]

Efforts have been made in recent years by the smaller operators to gain market share by impressing on the public their more personal levels of service and greater expertise, distancing themselves from the mass market operators. The Association of Independent Tour Operators (AITO), with a membership at the time of writing of some 150, works closely with the independent travel agents to sell distinctive products. The appearance of TIPTO (the Truly Independent Professional Travel Organization) in 1999, launched to offset directional selling by large agency chains of leading operators' products, reflects the concern felt among the smaller companies in the industry about the growing concentration of power in the hands of the leading companies.

Economic forces in tour operating

Three factors were at work in the second half of the twentieth century that encouraged the growth of the package holiday in Europe.

- The expansion of leisure time in the developed countries.
- This was accompanied by greater discretionary income in those countries.
- Package holiday costs were low, both in themselves and in comparison to similar holidays in the home country. This was due to the relatively low costs of accommodation and food in the Mediterranean countries, reductions in air transport costs due to advancing technology, liberalization of air transport regulations, the introduction of year-round operations, covering both summer and winter seasons, and bulk purchasing by tour operators.

The operators, recognizing the strong growth potential in the overseas holiday market, sought to expand their market shares and, at the same time, attempted to increase the total size of the market by encouraging those who traditionally took domestic holidays to travel abroad. To achieve this, they slashed prices. Large companies used their purchasing muscle to drive down suppliers' prices (at some cost to quality in a number of cases). They introduced cheap, 'no frills' holidays and, more recently, budget holidays that offered no transfers, no in-flight meals and no resort representatives. Arguably, this new offering can barely be considered a package, in the traditional sense of the word, but budget-conscious consumers have been attracted to it all the same.

Additionally, profit margins were trimmed. Leading tour operators, each determined not to be undersold, engaged in the periodic repricing of their holidays throughout the season, using the strategy of brochure reissues with cheaper prices to try to outpace their competitors, but operators always held to the hope that, given the right conditions, prices could be increased rather than decreased in the later editions.

In the past, overly optimistic forecasts of market growth led to surpluses in supply. Capacity generally exceeded demand each year and operators were then forced into offloading holidays at bargain basement prices. Not surprisingly, this led to a good deal of dissatisfaction among clients who had booked earlier when the prices were higher. This factor was key to the growth in late bookings.

Traditionally, bookings for package holidays had occurred in the weeks immediately following Christmas, allowing operators time to balance supply and demand and aiding their cash flow – deposits paid by clients in January would be invested and earn interest for the company until its bills had to be paid, which, in some cases, could be as late as September or October. Demanding full balances eight to ten weeks before departure proved similarly lucrative for operators.

Holidaymakers soon came to realize, however, that, if they refrained from booking holidays until much nearer to when they wanted to travel, they could snap up late booking bargains. The development of computerized reservations systems allowed operators to update their late availability opportunities quickly, putting cheap offers on the market at very short notice, which made late bookings convenient as well as attractively priced.

The early twenty-first century has seen the introduction of online booking, with websites accessible to both retail agents and the general public. This has further promoted the attraction of late booking, reducing the gap between deposits and final payments from months to a matter of weeks or even days. The uncertainty caused by these volumes of late booking also made tour operations management more difficult.

The year 2005 appears to have marked the first change of direction – the leading operators reduced their capacity compared with the previous year to reduce the likelihood of overcapacity. In addition, the new technology allowed operators to counteract late booking trends through the introduction of a policy of **fluid pricing**. First introduced by Thomson Holidays in 1996 and soon copied by the other leading operators, this entails offering holidays that are detailed in the brochures for different prices – large discounts being given for early bookings and lower or no discounts for booking nearer the time of the holiday. Some operators (and their agents) have even quoted prices above the standard brochure price where demand is sufficiently strong, although the legality of this move has been questioned.

Starting in the late 1990s, there was a tendency among operators to launch brochures for the upcoming year at ever earlier dates, resulting, at times, in agents having to find room for brochures covering three different periods – summer and winter of the current year, as well as summer of the following year. More recently, some sense has prevailed and a more rational approach has been apparent. There is evidence, however, that early launches of brochures did benefit operators, by boosting sales.

The cost to the tour operator of creating travel packages is affected by changes in the inflation rate, exchange rates or costs of supplies, particularly aviation fuel, which is priced in US dollars on the world market and is therefore affected by either increased costs or changes in the relative values of the local currency and the dollar.

Tour operators have to estimate their costs for all services up to a year ahead of time. They can anticipate higher costs by raising prices, but this may make them uncompetitive, or they can take an optimistic approach and price low, in the expectation of stable or declining costs. Originally, the latter was more attractive as moderate cost increases could be passed on to customers (within established limits) in the form of surcharges. Within Europe, however, such surcharges are now no longer acceptable. Legislation implemented by member states in response to the 1992 Directive on Package Travel states that 'a price revision is possible only for variations in transportation costs (including the costs of fuel), dues, taxes or fees chargeable for certain services (such as landing taxes or embarkation or disembarkation fees at ports) and the exchange rates applied to the particular package'.[11]

Stability in price can be obtained by 'buying forward' the fuel required for the following year, but this is only practical for the largest operators with sufficient financial reserves. While there is no formal 'futures' market in aviation fuel, negotiation is possible on future purchases of fuel on an ad hoc basis, but clearly at a premium, so purchasing forward will further affect the operators' cash flow.

The introduction of government taxes can also affect the total price paid by tourists. Such taxes might include hotel or bed taxes or departure taxes at ports. In 1996, the UK government introduced an 'exit tax', in the form of Air Passenger Duty, for all flights out of the UK, amounting initially to £5 within the EU and £10 outside the EU (a rate that doubled at the end of 1997). This resurrected the issue of hidden charges, with many tour operators not absorbing these taxes in their total price structures. Some claimed that to do so would make their prices unattractive against scheduled air rivals such as low-cost carriers, which have traditionally promoted their flight prices separate from taxes and charges. Nevertheless, greater pressure is now being placed on these airlines to promote the price inclusive of taxes rather than headline fares.

The long-haul market

The tendency for all mass-market operators to focus on low price rather than quality or value for money led to this type of tour moving downmarket. As it did so, tourists at the top end of the market, particularly those who had travelled frequently, began to travel independently more often and to more distant destinations.

The demand for long-haul packages has expanded much faster than that for short-haul. More than 20 per cent of all holidays are now taken to long-haul destinations annually and this is forecast to increase. The United States, with its particular appeal of the Walt Disney World resort in Florida, New Zealand and Australia have all witnessed mass market long-haul growth, while Thailand and Bali have successfully sold the idea of long-haul sun, sea and sand holidays. South Africa, India and the Middle East (notably Dubai), even Cuba in the Caribbean, have all seen substantial growth in visitors from Western Europe. All of those increases can be directly ascribed to the huge drop in air fares relative to other prices in the past decade.

The market leader for long-haul packages is Swiss-owned Kuoni Travel, with TUI and Thomas Cook also competing strongly for such destinations with their specialist divisions.

Seat only sales

The introduction of low-cost carriers into the aviation markets has encouraged travellers to consider booking travel components separately. In addition, as growing numbers of holidaymakers are either prepared to find their own accommodation abroad or are seeking flights to carry them to their second homes, timeshare apartments or friends' accommodation on the Continent, changes in the accommodation sector have further affected demand for traditional packages. As a consequence, some tour operators that own airlines providing charter flights to service their packages now offer seat only sales, in which passengers, although ostensibly buying a package, are, in fact, only using the air travel portion of the tour.

This type of 'package' was originally introduced by operators to fill surplus charter seats. Technically, to abide by international regulations, some form of basic accommodation had to be included in the package, although this was seldom used. After January 1993, EU legislation swept away the requirement to book accommodation within EU destinations and so seat only sales have now become an important feature of the travel industry.

Recent developments

There is little let-up in the volatility of the tour operating business. Political conflicts in the Balkans and Turkey at the end of the last century, wars in the Gulf and fears of terrorism that were heightened after the 9/11 tragedy, Bali and Madrid bombings and London and Sharm el-Sheikh bombings of July 2005, have all unsettled global travel and tour operations. Natural disasters such as the earthquake and subsequent Tsunami in the Far East at the end of 2004, similarly reduced long-haul travel to the affected regions severely. In spite of this catalogue of crises, the sector has shown itself in the past to be resilient and, while in the short term cancelled bookings and hotel reservations would impact severely on these destinations, recovery from even the worst disasters would normally be expected within a year of the event.

European operators have sought new locations to develop where hotel capacity is cheap and readily available, as traditional resorts began to price themselves out of the market. First, the more remote areas of Greece, then Turkey, became boom destinations for the Western Europeans seeking sun at rock-bottom prices. The evidence suggests that the inclusive tour market for the traditional sun, sea and sand destinations has probably peaked. For example, in the UK now, less than half of the population choose a package when buying an overseas holiday to Europe.[12]

Second home ownership has also had a marked effect on patterns of holiday-making. Many owners disappear from the inclusive tours (IT) market, tending to take most, if not all, of their overseas holidays in their own properties. This, however, has fuelled the growth of the no frills airlines and the benefits of travel are by no means lost to other sectors of the industry because second home owners purchase local products and services at their destinations, invite friends and others to their homes, rent out their properties either privately or through operators and participate in home exchange opportunities around the world.

In Europe, many in the population have now experienced a foreign holiday at some point in their lives. For example, over 70 per cent of the UK population has travelled overseas. Thus, it is reasonable to assume that the first-time market has been captured and the future growth of the IT market is likely to be concentrated on selling a greater *frequency* of holidays, with a focus on the variety of holidays offered:

The changing nature and demographics of European society is throwing up demand for new kinds of holiday. Growth areas include the following.

- Short breaks and city breaks, especially to more exotic destinations. Reykjavik, Barcelona and even New York have become popular destinations for short-stay tourism. The entry of the Baltic states into the EU has boosted short breaks to Tallinn and Riga, just as the earlier entry of the Czech Republic boosted Prague as the city break of choice.

- Expansion of the EU has led to an increased mobility of the residents of the new accession states. This has the potential to encourage greater VFR travel as some choose to work outside their home country, as well as offering wider travel opportunities due to the removal or reduction of visa restrictions, which allows convenient travel to countries across the Continent and further afield.

- Exotic long-haul, activity and adventure holidays. Elderly travellers are now far more active than formerly and packages catering to their needs and interests are now common. Early retirement packages at one end of the third age and longer life spans at the other contribute to this trend.

- Changing attitudes have meant that many tourists are seeking out experiences rather than just material products. A greater focus on self-development, culture and health is likely to see customers demanding specialist activities and experiential holidays.

Including more or less?

All-inclusive holidays have grown in popularity. Introduced in the Caribbean, the concept has now expanded to some European destinations, too – primarily Mediterranean coastal resorts. These are fully inclusive packages, even down to alcohol and all entertainment at the resort. Although popular, the sustainability of all-inclusive holidays is questionable, given that customers do not need to go out of their complex to buy anything while they are on holiday and local shops and services fail to obtain the benefits of the tourists' visit.

At the same time, some operators are electing to 'unpackage' elements of the package holiday that would have traditionally been included, such as airport transfers and in-flight catering. The operators are then able to increase their revenue by selling these as 'add-ons', especially common when customers buy no frills packages. Operators are also making additional charges for early check-in or late check-out of rooms, prebookable seats or upgraded seats (as charter airlines have introduced a premium economy cabin on their planes), the use of prestigious airport lounges and even to guarantee being seated next to a friend or relative.

Of course, traditional sales of excursions and car hire at the destination are also lucrative and resort representatives are actively encouraged to make such sales to the tourists. A further boost to operators' profits can come through the imposition of high cancellation charges as operators retain the revenue while remaining free to sell the same holiday subsequently to other holidaymakers.

Consumer complaints

One inevitable consequence of the process of 'trading down' to cheaper package travel has been an increase in customer complaints. Studies revealed that some 40 per cent of complaints arose from budget holidays – often based on late availability that came without prior identification of exactly what accommodation was to be provided (often only a guarantee of a level of star rating would be offered). While operators were responding to consumer pressure for low-cost packages, consumers were unwilling to accept the very rational argument that they got what they paid for – the minimum standards provided simply failed too often to meet consumers' expectations. Even more worrying to operators was the fact that only 40 per cent of those dissatisfied were prepared to make an official complaint – others simply refrained from booking with the company again.

One source of customer irritation was the practice of operators applying surcharges to their final invoices. Such surcharges are resented by travellers and are in any case not applied to scheduled fares (which can respond to market prices more quickly). It also became apparent that a handful of operators were misusing this facility and adding fuel surcharges in excess of actual increases in cost, or even when actual fuel costs had not increased at all, as a means of raising profits that had been slashed by open competition. The leading tour operators themselves helped to phase out surcharges by guaranteeing prices, while legislation also restricted the use of surcharges.

The nature of tour operating

An inclusive tour programme, as we have seen, is composed of a series of integrated travel services, each of which is purchased by a tour operator in bulk and resold as part of a package at an all-inclusive price. These integrated services usually consist of an aircraft seat, accommodation at the destination and transfers between the accommodation and the airport on arrival and departure. They may also include other services, such as excursions or car hire.

The inclusive tour is commonly referred to as a package tour and most are single destination, resort-based holidays. Tours comprising two or more destinations are by no means uncommon, however, and long-haul operators frequently build in optional extensions to another destination in their itineraries – a beach holiday in Kenya might offer an optional extension to one of the game parks, for example, or a visit to the Chilean fjords, flying to Santiago, might offer tourists the opportunity to extend the itinerary to Chilean-owned Easter Island.

In East Asia, multicentre holidays are very common, as many capital cities in the area are seen as meriting only relatively short stays of three to four nights. Increasingly, itineraries other than the most basic are tailor-made for clients, in terms of length of stay, accommodation, flights and activities at the resort. Dynamic packaging has become a more common booking approach and it permits either operators or their travel agents to put together tour programmes tailor-made especially to meet the demands of each individual client, using websites to contact suppliers.

Linear tours, such as those offered by coach companies that carry people to different destinations or even through several countries, were at one time the most popular form of trip and still retain a loyal following, but mainly among older clients. Even they lend themselves to tailor-made adaptation, with alternative flights to connect with the tours and short-stay extensions being arranged at the beginning or end of the holiday.

The success of the operator usually depends on an ability to buy a combination of products, put them together and sell them at an inclusive price that is lower than the customers could obtain themselves. The major international operators may book several million hotel beds for a season, thus negotiating very low prices from the hotel owners. Similarly, they bulk-buy seats on aircraft or charter whole aircraft at the best prices they can secure. The end result must be seen by the customers as offering value for money – either in terms of the final price paid or time saved shopping around. With package holidays becoming more and more a standardized product, not changing much for different destinations, the destination or country has come to play a lesser part in customers' decisionmaking. Destinations will be readily substituted if customers feel that their first choice is overpriced.

Tour operators can lower prices by either reducing their profit margins or cutting costs. Cost savings can be achieved initially by chartering whole aircraft instead of merely purchasing a block of seats on a scheduled flight. Further savings can be made by chartering the aircraft over a lengthy period of time, such as a whole season, rather than on an ad hoc basis – which is now the normal pattern of operating for the large companies. Ultimately, the largest operators reduce costs to the minimum by running their own airlines, which allows them to exercise better control over their operations and the standards of their products.

Owning your own aircraft ensures that, when the demand is there, you have the aircraft to meet it at a price you can afford. Emphasis then shifts to ensuring that the highest possible load factors – the percentage of seats sold to seats available – are achieved and the aircraft are kept flying for the maximum number of hours each day as they are not earning revenue while stationary on the ground, and parking fees can amount to hundreds of pounds every hour.

This requires careful planning to ensure that **turnarounds** (the time spent between arriving with one load of passengers and taking off with another) are as rapid as possible, commensurate with good standards of safety. Typically, this will result in up to three rotations in a single day, say, between a Northern European point of origin and a Mediterranean destination. These rotations may be made from a single point of origin (an airport) to a number of different destinations abroad or from several points of origin to a single destination abroad or from different points of origin to different foreign destinations. The latter flight plan is commonly known as a 'W' flight pattern (see Figure 18.2), which can be programmed to produce the maximum aircraft usage during a 24-hour period.

W-pattern flights are not necessarily carrying the customers of a single operator (even where the carrier is owned by one of the operators). Charters can be contracted to carry the passengers of a number of different operators between the same points of origin and destination, either sharing the flights or filling different flights. This can give rise to problems, one of which will occur when different operators contract for morning, afternoon and evening flights. If one operator decides to cancel, the airline concerned has to find alternative users for the aircraft, which may mean a longer flight commitment, causing delays or a change of flights to those passengers already booked on that flight. The knock-on effect of delays can become very apparent if there is a minor maintenance issue with the plane or air traffic controllers go on strike or mount go-slows. Tight flight scheduling, particularly into busy airports at the height of the season, can result in delays on one flight that can have repercussions on tour operator movements using the same aircraft over the next two or three days.

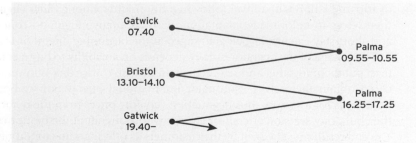

Figure 18.2 A typical 'W' flight pattern.

High load factors are achieved by setting the **break even** (the point at which the number of seats sold on each flight covers all its operating, administrative and marketing costs) at a point as close as possible to capacity. This brings down the average seat cost to a level that will encourage the greatest number of people to travel. On many well-marketed charter flights, the break even is set as high as 90 per cent or higher, while actual average load factors may be as high as 96–98 per cent. The company makes its profits on the difference between those two figures and, as, clearly, every extra person carried is almost pure profit (virtually all costs having been covered), then substantial reductions can be made for last minute bookings to fill those final seats. Conversely, if very few seats remain, the company may even choose to inflate the price, in the knowledge that there are always a few passengers who are willing to pay for a very specific flight at short notice. Of course, if the break even load factors have not been reached, the operator will not cover all costs, but it will still be better to attract as many people as possible for the flight, because they will at least make a contribution to the fixed costs of operating the flight, even if all costs are not recovered. Passengers may also buy duty-free goods on board (if travelling outside the EU countries) and an increasing number of short-haul airlines no longer serve food and drink free of charge, so the sale of these items on board becomes another important source of revenue, which makes a further contribution to profit for the airline – or, taking a broader view, for the parent company of the jointly owned airline/tour operator. Furthermore, if the operator has contracted for a set number of beds and is committed to pay for that number, it is better to carry passengers to fill those beds than for them to be empty.

Productivity in airline operations can be aided, as we have seen, by the procedure of **consolidating flights**. Charter flights with unacceptably low load factors can be cancelled and their passengers transferred to other flights or even departures from other airports. This helps to reduce the element of risk for the tour operator, otherwise break evens would have to be set at a lower level of capacity, so fares would be higher. Such consolidations are not available for groups carried on scheduled airline services and are, in any case, subject to considerable restrictions, such as adequate advance notice being given to the clients. Inevitably, they are unpopular with clients, so many companies now try to avoid them.

The problem of seasonality

A problem facing all sectors of tourism is the highly seasonal nature of most tourist traffic. Nowhere is this more apparent than in the demand for package holidays in Europe. This market, however, is also highly price-sensitive and longer periods of holiday entitlement over the past 20 years have helped to encourage many people to take their second holiday abroad, too – often outside of the peak periods. This has meant that operators can spread their fixed costs more evenly over the entire year, rather than concentrating them in the summer period, helping to reduce prices further. Most importantly, it has allowed the operators to contract for aircraft and hotels on a year-round basis.

If only a summer season is programmed, any tour operator that runs a charter airline to service its needs is left with a 'dead leg' twice in the year – an aircraft returning empty after the first flight of the season because it has no passengers to pick up and an empty outbound flight at the end of the season to pick up the last clients returning home. The costs of those empty flights have to be built into the overall pricing structure of the operation, but, if they can be avoided by offering year-round programmes, clearly the savings made can be passed on to customers.

Operators also use marginal costing techniques to attract clients out of season. This means that the holidays need to be priced to cover their variable costs and make some contribution to fixed costs. This recognizes that many costs, such as those encountered in operating hotels, continue whether the hotel is open or closed, so any guests that the hotel can attract will help to pay the bills. They will also enable the hotel to keep its staff all year round, thus making it easier to retain good staff. Some market segments – the retired, for example – can be attracted to the idea of spending the entire winter abroad if prices are low enough and hoteliers welcome these budget clients as they can still be expected to spend some additional money in the hotel bars or restaurants.

Operating scheduled programmes

Not all destinations allow charter flights to operate into their territory (often, in order to protect bookings on the scheduled flights of the country's airline). Nor will there be sufficient demand for flights to many destinations (such as those served by most long-haul programmes) to merit chartering an entire aircraft. For those forms of packaging, the tour operator can arrange the transport element through schedule airlines, using net inclusive tour-basing excursion fares (ITX) or group inclusive tour-basing (GIT) fares, either contracting individual seats based on client demand (around which a tailor-made holiday can be constructed) or contracting a block of seats on flights to satisfy the needs of a brochure programme.

Airlines will allow ITX fares to be applied subject to certain conditions attached to the programmes. A minimum number of brochures must be printed and/or the tours must be seriously promoted on a website and the programme must consist of a package of flight, accommodation and transfer or other feature. The tour programme can be organized using one or more carriers, but approval is usually sought through a particular carrier, which will validate the programme and provide a tour code number that will be printed on each ticket issued. Tour operators in the UK making a forward commitment on seats must also obtain an Air Travel Organizers' Licence (ATOL) through the CAA.

Control over tour operating

In order to protect both consumers and the wider tourism industry from rogue operators, a variety of regulations have been used. In some cases, these have come into force to protect consumers and their money, but, in other cases, they protect the commercial operations of scheduled airlines or the destinations and regions they serve. Many countries within the European Union require some form of licensing or qualification for tour operators (see Table 18.5).

Table 18.5 Examples of EU regulation of tour operators.

Countries	Type of documentation required
Czech Republic, France, Portugal, Slovakia	Trade Licence.
Hungary	Statutory Public Register – managed by the Hungarian Trade Licensing Office.
Italy	Licence – procedure managed by regional governments.
Malta	Licensed by the National Tourism Authority.
Poland	Register for organizers of tourism and tourism intermediaries.
Slovenia	Licensed by the Chamber of Commerce.
Spain	Qualify as travel agent according to administrative legislation.
UK	Air Travel Organizer Licence (ATOL) – managed by the CAA.

Source: H. Schulte-Nölke, C. Twigg-Flesner and Dr M. Ebers, *EC Consumer Law Compendium: Comparative analysis*, Bielefeld, 2006.

The EU and legal issues relating to package holiday operations

Concern was shared by the European Commissioners, which was also looking at the problems of protecting consumers in member states. As a result, the 1992 EC Directive on Package Travel was published, designed to clarify and extend responsibility to all sectors of the industry involved in providing and retailing package travel. Those regulations, which each member state was required to introduce into law, covered non-air-based holidays also. The measures included the following obligations.[13]

- *Information duties*
  - To provide a travel brochure, pre-contractual information and details of elements included in the contract, as well as information before the start of the journey. All information must be accurate as the directive specifically references the prohibition of misleading information.
- *Limitation of price revision*
  - To provide regulation of the situations when an increase in price (or, for some countries, also a decrease in price) may be possible while identifying the conditions for price revision.
- *Consumer rights*
  - To identify the right of the purchaser to transfer the booking as well as clarifying consumer rights in case of significant alterations to the package.
- *Additional duties of the organizer*
  - These include obligations to make alternative arrangements if the original package cannot be provided as planned, providing consumers with equivalent transport back to their point of origin and compensation when the product cannot be delivered as planned.
  - The operator also has a duty to provide assistance to consumers if they experience emergencies or difficulties while on holiday and, in the case of complaints, to undertake prompt efforts to resolve issues.
- *Liability*
  - To clarify the organizer's and/or retailers' limits of liability in cases where the package is not delivered according to plan or where the consumer has experienced a loss of enjoyment.
  - Schemes to provide security in case of insolvency of the tour operator are also considered.

Initially, the imposition of these regulations brought considerable problems for many tour operators and travel agents, not least because the interpretation of the regulations was unclear. In particular, it remained unclear what exactly constituted a 'package holiday' – was this to include business trips and tailor-made holidays? Would all organizers of packages, such as clubs or schoolteachers organizing educational trips, be included? 'Occasional' organizers were to be excluded, but the interpretation of what constituted 'occasional' posed further problems.

What does appear clear is that the additional burden of responsibility placed on tour operators led to some increases in cost for consumers, as operators attempted to cover themselves against any threat of legislation. The regulations imposed much greater responsibility on operators. For example, they directly penalize an operator if there is any dissemination of misleading information and provide for compensation to be paid for any loss suffered by consumers as a result of being misled. Furthermore, they make the tour operator directly responsible if hotels or other suppliers fail to provide the accommodation or services contracted for.

Example

The changing regulations for the UK-based tour operator

Regulating air travel packages

Regulations restricting tour operators were very limiting when the mass tour market developed in the 1960s. In particular, the regulation known as Provision 1 made it impossible to price package tours lower than the cheapest regular return air fare to a destination. The sole exceptions to this rule were in the case of affinity groups, which involved charters arranged for associations that exist for a purpose other than that of obtaining cheap travel. Travellers were obliged to have been members of the organization for at least six months before they became eligible for low-cost flights. The rule was designed to protect scheduled carriers and ensure adequate profit for tour operators, but it severely hindered the expansion of the package tour business. It was also widely abused by club secretaries, who backdated membership, and many spurious clubs were formed in order to provide the benefits of cheap travel.

When the CAA was established in 1971, restrictions were lifted, initially only during the winter months (leading to a huge increase in out-of-season travel), but, by 1973, this was extended to all seasons. At the same time, however, the CAA tightened up control on tour operators themselves, introducing in 1972 the requirement to hold ATOLs for charters and block-booked scheduled seats, and, at the same time, introducing a system for vetting operators on their financial viability. By 1995, all tour operators were required to hold ATOLs when selling any flights or air holidays abroad. Licences are not required, however, for domestic air tours or for travel abroad using sea or land transport.

Regulating to ensure financial protection of the industry

Following the collapse of an important tour operator, Fiesta Tours, in 1964, which left some 5000 tourists stranded abroad, the industry and its customers came to recognize the importance of introducing protection against financial failure.

On the whole, in the UK, successive governments have preferred to allow the industry to police itself rather than impose additional controls and so it was initially undertaken relatively effectively by ABTA on behalf of tour operators and travel agents.

In 1965, ABTA set up a Common Fund for this purpose, anticipating that there would be legislation for the compulsory registration of tour operators. When this did not materialize, ABTA introduced its stabilizer regulation, restricting ABTA tour operators to selling their package holidays exclusively through ABTA travel agents. In turn, ABTA agents were restricted to selling tours operated by ABTA tour operators. Many agents, however, resented having to contribute to a fund to insure operators and it also became clear that the provisions against collapse were inadequate.

In 1967, the Tour Operators' Study Group (TOSG – later to become the Federation of Tour Operators, FTO), established its own bonding scheme. A **bond** is a guarantee given by a third party (usually a bank or insurance company) to pay a sum of money, up to a specified maximum, in the event that the company becomes insolvent. That money would be used to meet the immediate financial obligations arising from the collapse, such as repatriating tourists stranded at overseas resorts and reimbursing clients booked to travel later with the company.

Later, ABTA itself introduced its own bonding scheme for all tour operating (and retail agency) members. The collapse in 1974, in the height of summer, of the Court Line group brought down Clarksons Holidays – then Britain's leading tour operator – and revealed, once again, that the level of protection was inadequate.

The government introduced an obligatory levy of 2 per cent of operators' turnover between 1975 and 1977, which established the Air Travel Trust Fund. These reserves were severely depleted, however, by collapses throughout the 1990s, particularly that of the International Leisure Group at the beginning of that decade, and the ATTF was obliged to call on the government for additional borrowing facilities when

▶

reserves ran dry. Since then, a number of alternative schemes have been introduced, in the form of either bonds or trustee accounts, including those schemes operated by the Association of Independent Tour Operators (AITO) Trust, the Travel Trust Association (TTA) and the Association of Bonded Travel Organizers Trust (ABTOT) for smaller operators. The Confederation of Passenger Transport (CPT), Passenger Shipping Association (PSA) and Yacht Charter Association operate their own schemes.

In July 2008, ABTA and FTO merged, thus providing combined expertise to better serve their tour operator members, while providing comprehensive protection schemes for their customers.

Regulating to manage complaints

ABTA operates its own arbitration scheme to resolve complaints by customers about its members. This is at a low cost to claimants, who are successful in about half of all cases brought. AITO provides a similar scheme. Alternatively, claims can be made through the courts under a new tracking system, which entails only moderate costs for plaintiffs.

Planning, marketing and operating package tours

Planning for the introduction of a new tour programme or destination is likely to take place over a lengthy span of time, sometimes as long as two years. A typical timescale for a programme of summer tours is shown in Figure 18.3.

In planning deadlines for the programme, it is necessary to work backwards from the planned launch dates. One critical problem is when to determine prices. These have to be established at the last minute before material goes to be printed, but inevitably this will be several months before the tour programme starts, so entails a good understanding (and some luck!) with regard to the movement of currency and the foreign exchange markets in the intervening period. Assessments must also be made of what the competition is likely to charge for similar products. The introduction of fluid pricing has eased the former inflexibility of brochure prices, although any changes made immediately after publication would be frowned on.

Market research

In practice, the decision to exploit a destination or region for package tours is as much an act of faith as it is the outcome of carefully considered research. Forecasting future developments in tourism, which, as a product, is affected by changing circumstances to a greater extent than most other consumer products, has proved to be notably inaccurate. As we have seen, tourism patterns change over time, shifting from one country to another and from one form of accommodation to another. With the emphasis on price, mass tour operators are principally concerned with providing the basic sun, sea and sand package in countries that provide the best value for money. Transport costs will depend on charter rights in to the country, distances flown and ground-handling costs.

Accommodation and other costs to be met overseas will be affected by exchange rates against the local currency and operators must consider these in comparison with other competitive countries' currency values when setting the price for the package. They should also anticipate how changing exchange rates may affect the number of clients likely to select any one destination, as it may appear expensive if the local currency is strong.

Operators also have to take into account such qualitative issues as the political stability of the destination, the support given for developing tourism to the destination by the carriers or tourist office of the country and the relationship between the host and destination countries. Increasingly, with an emphasis on sustainability, today operators are encouraged (if not yet forced by government legislation) to consider the impact on locals and the environment of any new development. Pressure groups and the media are slowly

RESEARCH/ PLANNING	YEAR 1	Summer	First stages of research. Look at economic factors influencing the future development of package tours. Identify likely selection of destinations.
		September/December	Second stages of research. In-depth comparison of alternative destinations.
	YEAR 2	January	Determine destinations, hotels and capacity, duration of tours, departure dates. Make policy decisions on size and design of brochure, number of brochures to print, date for completion of print.
NEGOTIATION		February/March	Tenders put out for design, production and printing of brochures. Negotiate with the airlines for charter flights. Negotiate with hotels, transfer services, optional excursion operators.
		April/May	Typesetting and printing space booked with printer, copy for text commissioned. Illustrations commissioned or borrowed. Early artwork and text under development at design studio, with layout suggestions. Contracts completed with hotels and airlines, transfer services, etc.
		June	Production of brochure starts.
ADMINISTRATION		July	Determine exchange rates. Estimate selling prices based on inflation, etc. Galley proofs from printer, corrections made. Any necessary reservations staff recruited and trained.
		August	Final tour prices to printer. Brochures printed and reservations system established.
MARKETING		September/October	Brochure on market, distribution to agents. Initial agency sales promotion, including launch. First public media advertising and trade publicity through press, etc.
	YEAR 3	January/March	Peak advertising and promotion to trade and public.
		February/April	Recruitment and training of resort representatives, etc.
		May	First tour departures.

Figure 18.3 Typical timescale for planning a summer tour programme.

persuading companies to take more seriously the pros and cons of new developments and how these can be effectively managed by the operators, the hotels they work with and the local authorities.

Once the tour operators have made their choice of potential destinations, they must produce a realistic appraisal of the likely demand for those destinations, based on factors such as the number of tourists the destinations presently attract, growth rates over recent years and present shares held by any existing travel companies. The mass market operators are unlikely to look at just a single year's programme – any commitment to a destination is likely to be for a substantial period of time. The specialist operator, however, may be more flexible about switching destinations according to changing demand. In contrast, mass market operators consider long-term contracts with their hoteliers abroad or even in some circumstances establish their own hotels.

Example

Thomas Cook – protecting against fuel and exchange rate volatility

In acknowledging that their business spans many countries and that they offer holidays to destinations globally, a key part of the risk-reduction activities of Thomas Cook is performed by the Group Treasury department. This department is responsible for reducing the risk of changing aviation fuel prices and changing exchange rates. Such a process is known as hedging, which was discussed earlier in relation to fuel.

To protect against fluctuations in exchange rates, the department uses financial instruments to fix the future prices for currency by agreeing contracts to buy (or in some cases sell) the overseas currencies at a fixed rate, for delivery on a specific date (often linked to the time suppliers' bills will be due). Thomas Cook requires that such hedging takes place as part of the budget process when it is establishing tour operating programmes or at the time the brochure is launched. Therefore, typically, currency is hedged for periods of 12 months to 18 months in advance.

To protect against the risk of fluctuations in the cost of aviation fuel, Thomas Cook uses either hedging contacts to agree prices for fuel at future dates or fuel commodity swaps. Such swaps effectively involve agreeing a set price for a set date with a commodity seller, then, if fuel prices on the open market are higher on the due date, the seller refunds the airline, but, if prices are lower on the open market, the airline agrees to pay the extra to the seller. Fuel price hedging may span a period covering three seasons and is usually denominated in US dollars.

The availability of suitable aircraft for the routes must be ascertained. This will, in part, dictate capacities for the programme as aircraft have different configurations and, on some routes, where aircraft are operating at the limits of their flight range, some passenger seats may need to be sacrificed in order to take on board sufficient fuel to cover the distance. In some instances, provincial airport runways may be insufficient for larger, fully laden aircraft and, again, fewer passengers may be carried to compensate.

All planning is, of course, also dependent on the company having the necessary finance available to operate and market the programme.

The process of negotiating

Once the decisions have been made as to destinations to be served, numbers of passengers to be carried during the season and dates of departure, the serious negotiations can get under way with airlines, hotels and other principals, leading to formal contracts. Those contracts will spell out payment due dates as well as the conditions for the release of unsold accommodation or the cancellation of chartered aircraft flights (or, in the case of block bookings on scheduled services, the aircraft seats), along with details of any penalties that the tour operator will incur for cancellation.

Airline negotiations

Normal terms for aircraft chartering are for a deposit to be paid on signing the contract (generally 10 per cent of the total cost), with the balance becoming due on each flight after it takes place. In negotiating for charter services, the reputation of the tour operator is of paramount importance. If they have worked with that airline or with similar charters in previous years, that will be taken into account when determining the terms and price for the contract. Relationships between the sectors of the industry are still based predominantly on trust as the threat of legal action, perhaps months after a dispute such as an overbooking problem has arisen, will do little to resolve problems at the time.

Part and parcel of the negotiations is the setting up of the tour operating flight plan, with decisions being made on the dates and frequency of operations, airports to be used and times of arrival and departure. All of this information will have to be consolidated into a form suitable for publication and easy to understand in the tour brochure.

A well-established operator does not wish to be at the mercy of market forces when dealing with charter airlines. In any given year, the demand for suitable aircraft may exceed the supply, which has encouraged the larger tour operators to form or buy their own airline, just to ensure that the capacity they need is available to them.

Hotel negotiations

Hotel negotiations – other than in the case of large tour operators, which may negotiate contracts for an entire hotel – are generally far more informal than are airline negotiations. Small and specialist tour operators selling independent inclusive tours may have no more than a **free sale** (or **sell and report**) agreement with hoteliers. These involve the hotel agreeing to guarantee accommodation for a specified maximum number of tourists (usually at least four, although it may be higher in large hotels with plenty of availability for certain days of the week) merely on receipt of the notification of a booking from the tour operator, whether by phone, fax or e-mail. This arrangement may be quite suitable for small tour programmes, but it suffers from the disadvantage that, at times, hoteliers will retain the right to close out certain dates. As these are likely to be the most popular dates in the calendar, the operator stands to lose both potential business and goodwill. The alternative is for the operator to contract for an allocation of rooms in the hotel, with dates agreed for the release of those unsold that are well in advance of the anticipated arrival dates.

Long-term contracts, either for a block of rooms or the entire hotel, have the attraction of providing the operator with the lowest possible prices, but they carry a higher element of risk. Some contracts have been drawn up by operators to cover periods as long as five years and, while at first glance such long fixed-term price contracts may seem attractive, they are seldom realistic and, in an inflationary period, may well have to be renegotiated to avoid bankrupting the hotelier (such an event would obviously not be in the operator's interest).

In addition to the operator spelling out exact requirements in terms of rooms – required numbers of singles, doubles, twins, with or without private facilities, whether with balconies or sea views and with what catering provision (room only, with breakfast, half or full board) – it must also clarify a number of other facts, including:

- reservations and registration procedures, including whether or not hotel vouchers are to be issued
- accommodation requirements for any representatives or couriers (usually provided free)
- handling procedures and fees charged for porterage
- special facilities available or needed, such as air-conditioned or non-smoking rooms, facilities for handicapped customers or special catering requirements, such as kosher or vegetarian food
- languages spoken by hotel staff
- systems of payment by guests for drinks or other extras
- reassurance on suitable fire and safety precautions (tour operators based in the EU have responsibility (and liability) for protecting their customers under the package travel directive, no matter where the hotel is situated)
- if appropriate, suitable space for a representative's desk and noticeboard (see Figure 18.4).

Figure 18.4 A typical representatives' hotel noticeboard.
(Photo by Chris Holloway.)

In negotiations consideration may also be given to the availability of alternative hotel accommodation of a comparable standard in the event of overbooking. Of course, a hotel with a reputation for overbooking is to be avoided, but over the course of time some errors are bound to occur and so guests will need to be transferred to other hotels. Tour operators must satisfy themselves that the arrangements made by the hotelier for taking care of clients in these circumstances are adequate. Any operator negotiating with a hotelier will be aware that they are likely to be sharing contracted space with other operators, not only within their own country but also from other countries. It is as well to be aware of one's own standing with the hotelier in relation to those other companies. For example, in Spain, it was not uncommon in the past to find that the German operators, which tended to pay higher prices for their rooms than did the British, would have their rooms protected in preference to British operators when overbookings occurred. With the decline in the German economy in recent years and the simultaneous strengthening of the British economy, the subsequent reductions in the numbers of German travelling to Spain may well result in the reverse now proving to be the case.

Independent companies can find themselves squeezed out of the market for European bed stock in popular resorts and, at times, even the mass market operators become aware that greater concentration in the industry can lead to more difficulty in tying up contracts with popular hotels. For this reason, as demand rises for key Mediterranean destinations – and also to ensure greater control over the major elements in the package – some operators turn to owning hotels at the destinations or at the very least having far more say in their management. First Choice announced in 2000 its intention to play a part in designing new hotels and influencing their layout, when long-term contracts are envisaged.

Example

TUI buys up an Italian village

In May 2007, TUI announced that it had purchased a Tuscan village –
Tenuta di Castelfalfi, located between the popular tourism destinations
of Florence, Pisa and Siena. The land, covering 11 square kilometres,
includes a mediaeval castle and golf course, as well as arable land.

Development of the area is to include renovation of the village, as well
as the addition of spa and shopping facilities alongside three new hotels (a
Robinson Club, a Dorfhotel and an Iberotel – all are TUI brands) and villas and
apartments.

Source: TUI, 'Press release – TUI plans biggest tourism project in company history', TUI, 16 May 2007.

Destination services negotiations

Similar negotiations will take place with locally based incoming operators and coach companies to provide transfers between airports and hotels and any optional excursions. Car
hire companies may also be approached so as to negotiate commission rates on sales to
the tour operator's clients and tailor-made transfers between airports and hotels.

The reliability and honesty of local operators is an important issue here. Some smaller
tour operators may not be in a position to employ their own resort representatives initially,
so their image will depend on the level of service provided by the local operators' staff.

If a local company is also operating optional sightseeing excursions, procedures for
booking these and handling the finances involved must be established. It should also be
clarified whether qualified guides with a sound knowledge of the clients' language are to
be employed on the excursions.

The role of the resort representative

Tour operators carrying large numbers of package tourists to a destination are in a position
to employ their own resort representatives. This has obvious advantages in that the company can count on the loyalty and total commitment of its own staff. A decision must be
made as to whether to employ a national of the host country or of the generating country
(although it should be acknowledged that, in some cases, the destination may receive
customers from several generating countries and the representative will need to be able to
serve all customers effectively). The advantage of hiring a representative from the local
community is that he or she will be fully acquainted with the local customs and geography, fluent in the language of the country and have good local contacts, which may
make it easier to take care of problems effectively (such as dealing with the police, local
shopkeepers or hoteliers). The flipside of this is that he or she is likely to be less familiar
with the culture, customs or language of the clients, which can act as a negative point for
tourists, especially for those on first visits abroad. Exceptional local representatives have been
able to overcome this problem and, if they themselves have some common background
with their clients, such as having lived for some years in the incoming tourists' country, they
can often function as effectively as would representatives from the generating country.

Furthermore, some countries impose restrictions on the employment of foreign nationals at resorts, which is a point that must be clarified before employing any representatives.
This used to be a problem at the popular Mediterranean resorts, but, with the development

of freedom of labour movement within the EU, tour operators are now free to decide for themselves what should be the background and nationality of their representatives.

The representatives' role is far more demanding than is commonly thought. During the high season, they can be expected to work a seven-day week and will need to be on call for 24 hours each day to cope with any emergencies. Resort representatives are usually given a desk in the hotel lobby from which to work, but, in cases where tour operators have their clients in two or more hotels in the resort, they may have to visit each of these hotels during some part of the day. Their principal functions include:

- handling general enquiries
- advising on currency exchange, shopping and so on
- organizing and supervising social activities at the hotels
- publicizing, selling and booking optional excursions
- handling special requirements and complaints and acting as an intermediary for clients, interceding with the hotel proprietor, the police or other local authorities as necessary.

These routine functions are supplemented by problems arising from lost baggage, ill health (needing to refer clients to local dentists or doctors) and even, occasionally, deaths, although serious problems such as these are often referred to area managers, who may oversee and manage representatives across several resorts in a region or country. The representatives must also relocate clients whose accommodation is for any reason inadequate or when overbookings have occurred and may also have to rebook flights for their clients whose plans change as a result of emergencies.

The representatives' busiest days are when groups are arriving or leaving the resort. They will accompany groups returning home on the coach to the airport, ensuring that departure formalities at the hotel have been complied with, arrange to pay any airport or departure taxes due and then wait to greet incoming clients and accompany them, in turn, to their hotels on the transfer coaches. In the not uncommon situation where flights are delayed, this can result in representatives having to spend very long hours at the airport, sometimes missing a night's sleep. On their return to the hotels, they must also ensure that check-in procedures operate smoothly, going over rooming lists with the hotel managers before the latter bill the company. Most operators also provide a welcome party for their clients on the first or second night of their holiday and it is the representatives' task to organize and host this. It also provides an important opportunity to sell excursions to the newly arrived guests. As profit margins are often tight for tour operators, there has been more emphasis placed on the sale of excursions in recent years. Many representatives have in the past been given sales targets to achieve and rewarded financially for good performance in this area.

The commercialization of the resort representative's role became steadily more marked, to a point where their duty to interact socially with the customers became less important to their managers. This led, eventually, to substantial reductions in the numbers of representatives employed and in some cases to their disappearance entirely. The explanation for this move comes partly from the increasing sophistication of the customers, many of whom are well travelled and no longer feel that they need a rep's help at the destination, as long as a company rep is available at the end of a phone.

Arguably, this development leads to two weaknesses in promoting a brand. First, it may reduce the opportunities for clients to engage in commercial transactions that will benefit the company and, second, it devalues the image of the company, in the sense that a representative is, in many cases, the only personal contact a tour operator has with its clients and, therefore, represents the brand. Smaller operators have not been slow to recognize that they now hold a significant advantage over the leaders if they simply employ personable individuals to represent them.

Where representatives continue to be favoured, they can expect to spend some time at their resort bases before the start of the season, not only to get to know the site but also report back to their companies on the standards of tourist facilities and pinpoint any discrepancies between descriptions in the brochures and reality. This has become increasingly important since the regulations imposed by the EU Directive on Package Holidays came into force. Representatives may also be expected to inform their companies if any changes occur during the season about which clients must be notified at the time of booking. In an effort to reduce complaints and handle them at source, some operators give representatives the authority to compensate their clients on the spot for minor claims and complaints.

Today some operators employ full-time staff who spend part of the year as representatives at their resorts, either in the summer or winter, while at other times they are brought back to head office to handle reservations or other administrative work. The job of a representative seldom offers genuine career opportunities, but, for some, there is the opportunity to progress, starting with positions as children's representatives and moving on to adult representative, senior representative, area supervisor and eventually area manager. Ultimately, the opportunity for progression lies back at head office, where the managers having overall responsibility for resort representatives recruit and train staff, organize holiday rosters, provide uniforms and handle the administration of the representatives' department. Nevertheless, for the large majority, opportunities for employment are limited to the high season.

Pricing the package tour

Key to the success of a tour operator's programme is getting the price right. It must be right for the market, right compared with the prices of competitors' package tours and right compared with the prices of other tours offered by the company.

Costing the package

A tour operator will normally purchase three main inputs to create inclusive tours: transport, accommodation and services. The latter will include transfers between airports and accommodation abroad and, possibly, the services of the company's resort representative at the site. The operator will also, of course, have to cover costs that arise within the company's headquarters, such as administration, reservations, marketing and advertising. Finally, the operator will have to cover the cost of commission paid to retailers and servicing those retailers. A typical inclusive tour from the UK might well have the kind of cost structure outlined in Table 18.6.

Table 18.6 The typical cost structure of an inclusive tour using charter air services.

Costs	Percentage of overall costs
Charter air seat	45
Hotel accommodation	37
Other services at destination	3
Head office overheads	5
Travel agencies' commission	10

As the profits achieved by most operators after allowing for agencies' commission are actually quite narrow – perhaps as little as 1–3 per cent of revenue, after covering all costs – operators will seek to top up their revenue in any other way possible. For mass market operators, the bulk of their revenue – in excess of 50 per cent, normally – is achieved through the sales of summer holidays. Perhaps another 15–20 per cent will be achieved through a winter tour programme and the balance through a mix of sales of excursions at the destination, the interest received on deposits and final payments invested, foreign currency speculation and sale of insurance policies.

One contribution to revenue is achieved by imposing cancellation charges. These charges will often substantially exceed any costs borne by the operator resulting from that cancellation and, indeed, the operator may well be able to sell the cancelled accommodation again, gaining twice. The EU Directive on Package Holidays now allows, in theory, the substitution of names by the clients to replace cancelled bookings, but this is impossible to enforce where many airlines do not accept name changes and countries require arriving passengers to hold visas.

Specialist operators that offer a unique product may have more flexibility and the freedom to determine their prices based on cost plus a mark-up that is sufficient to cover overheads and provide a satisfactory level of profit. The mass operators, however, must take greater account of their competitors' prices as demand for package tours is, as we have seen, extremely price-sensitive, especially for programmes offered in the shoulder or low season.

In the following section we will examine two alternative, but typical, examples of cost-determined tour pricing. The first will consider pricing for the mass market, the second, pricing for the specialist operator.

Mass market tour pricing

The first example is based on a German company providing time series charter travel and a two-week hotel stay at a Mediterranean beach resort destination, such as those found on the island of Majorca, Spain.

Example

Mass market operator pricing

	Flight costs	Package costs (including flight costs)
	€	€
Flight costs, based on 15 holiday departures (back to back) on Boeing 737-800		
189-seat aircraft at €20,725 per flight	621,750	
Plus one empty leg each way at beginning and end of the season		
out	20,725	
home	20,725	
Total flight costs	663,200	
Total cost per flight:		
(€663,200 ÷ 15 holiday departures)	44,213.33	
Cost per seat at 90% occupancy		260.08
(170 seats), i.e. €44,213.33 ÷ 170		
Plus passenger charges (e.g. airport fees at outbound and inbound airports, government taxes, security fees)		40.00
Net hotel cost per person, 14 nights half board		245.00
Resort agent's handling fees and transfers, per person		10.00
Gratuities, porterage		5.00
Total cost per person		560.08
Add mark-up of approx. 30% on cost price to cover agency commission, marketing costs (including brochure, ticket wallet, etc.), head office administrative costs and profit		168.02
Selling price (rounded up)		730.00

Many companies would add a small fee, say €15, in order to build in a no surcharge guarantee, especially in times of economic instability. Holidays that are cancelled are presently resold to the public – as mentioned, a source of considerable extra income as refunds do not have to be made to the original customer (who recovers these costs from insurance, if there is a valid claim).

In estimating the cost of a seat on the aircraft, operators must not only calculate the load factor on which this cost is to be based but must also aim to achieve this load factor on average throughout the series of tours they will be operating. This must depend on their estimates of the market demand for each destination and the current supply of aircraft seats available to their competitors. As the demand at high season will frequently exceed the supply of seats to the destinations, there is scope to increase the above price, and hence profits, for those months of the year, even if that results in the company being uncompetitive compared with other leading operators. As operators have in the past tended to overestimate demand, however, this is becoming a risky procedure. In the low season, meanwhile, supply is likely to exceed the demand for available packages, so companies may set their prices so low that only the variable costs are covered and only a very small contribution is made to the fixed costs (marketing, administration and so on), in order to fill the seats.

Each tour operator must carefully consider what proportion of its overheads is to be allocated to each tour and destination. As long as the expenses are recovered in full during the term of operation, the allocation of costs can be made on the basis of market forces and need not necessarily be apportioned equally to each programme and destination. In practice, most operators now recover their overheads by determining a per capita contribution, based on anticipated head office costs for the year and the total number of passengers the company expects to carry. Under this system, of course, each tour carries the same burden of office costs regardless of destination or price. There is a case for a more marketing-orientated approach to pricing, however, based on a consideration of market prices and the company's long-term objectives. In entering a new market, for instance, it may be that the principal objective is to penetrate and obtain a targeted share of that market in the first year of operating, which may be achieved by reducing or even forgoing profits during the first year and/or reducing the per capita contribution to corporate costs. Indeed, to some destinations the operator may introduce loss-leader pricing policies, other more profitable routes subsidizing the cost of this policy in order to get a footing in the market to a new destination.

Specialist tour pricing

The second example is of a specialist French long-haul operator that uses the services of scheduled carriers to Hong Kong, with a group inclusive tour-basing fare.

It will be noted that, in the case of this specialist operator, prices reflect market demand at different periods of the year and there is no equal distribution of office overheads as the profits and most overheads are recoverable in the high season prices charged to the market. The lead price gives very little profit for bookings made through the trade, but is strictly limited to one or two weeks of the year. Large profits can be obtained, however, over Christmas, Chinese New Year, during conferences and for other business committed to specific dates. There is a tendency to be cautious about milking excess profits from periods of increased demand. Several Gulf States carriers, for example, offer much lower prices to offset the need to change flights, so competition at all times of the year is quite high. If charges are set too high, operators may be left with availability during peak times.

The pricing policy shown here is common among the smaller specialist operators, which tend to use less sophisticated pricing techniques when fixing target profits. Many specialists operating in a climate where there is no exact competition for their product could be expected to charge a price that would give them an overall gross profit of 25 per cent or more, while most mass market operators, and some specialists, will be forced by market conditions to settle for much lower margins.

Example

Specialist operator pricing

	Package costs (including flight costs) €
Flight cost, based on net group air fares, per person	470
Plus air charges	70
Net hotel cost per person, 7 nights, twin room (HK$720 per room, = HK$360 per person per night; HK$12 = €1)	210
Transfers HK$90 each way (equating to €7.50 each way)	15
Subtotal	765
Add agent's commission	85
Total cost per person	850
Selling prices	
'Lead price' (offered on only one or two low season flights)	859
Shoulder season price	899
High season price (summer, Christmas and Easter holiday periods)	1049

In developing a pricing strategy for package tours, operators must take into account a number of other variables in addition to those shown above. Earlier, the point was made that the price had to be right compared with all competing products on the market. For example, when setting a price for a departure from a regional airport, the operator will look at how much more the client will be willing to pay to avoid a long trip to a major airport. In the example given above, for flights from France to Hong Kong, a traveller living near Strasbourg may prefer to fly from a regional airport to Hong Kong via Frankfurt with Lufthansa rather than make the journey to Paris in order to access an Air France flight. Equally, if a flight is to leave at two o'clock in the morning, the price must be sufficiently attractive compared with others leaving during the day to make people willing to suffer the inconvenience of travelling at that time. What special reductions are to be offered to children or for group bookings? As seat and other costs will be unaffected, whatever reductions the company makes for these bookings will have to be recovered in profits achieved through sales to other customers.

Discounting strategies

Discounts on published tour prices have become a widely accepted practice in the industry. Originally applied to late bookings in order to clear seats, the technique has more recently been used by the larger operators to persuade members of the public to book earlier, using a system of fluid pricing – the practice of prices for travel products altering as demand levels change, discussed earlier. Other operators prefer to offer guarantees to those who book early that there will be no increases in price prior to their departure.

Discounting is also influenced by travel retailers – they may elect to sell packages below the prices determined by the operators themselves by passing on to the clients a proportion of their commission. In practice, this has meant that the largest discounts can be allowed by the largest multiple travel agencies, as they can negotiate larger commissions, well above the 10 per cent norm, as they achieve higher sales levels and, in effect, can pass on to their clients almost all the 10 per cent basic commission. As this percentage represents the total commission that most independent agents receive from operators, the independents cannot match their prices and therefore find it impossible to compete on price alone.

Instead, many will offer alternative benefits, such as free insurance to secure a sale or an extra service, such as a free taxi transfer to the local airport.

Heavy discounting by the market leaders through their own retail chains has been a major factor in boosting their share of the mass market. Given the problems that have faced the industry over the past few years and the strong competition between operators to survive in a difficult marketplace, there is little likelihood of the industry moving away from deep discounting in the foreseeable future.

Cash flow

The normal booking season for summer holidays starts in the autumn of the preceding year, reaching its peak in the three months following Christmas, so a large proportion of deposits will have been paid by the end of March. Although the operators themselves will have had to make deposits for aircraft charters at the beginning of the season and may also have had to make some advances to hoteliers to ensure that the rooms they need are held, the final account for these services will not fall due until after the clients have completed their holiday. Operators will have the use of deposit payments for anything up to a year in advance and will have client's final payments at least eight weeks before they themselves have to settle their accounts. This money is invested to earn interest and, in some cases, that interest will actually exceed the net profits made by tour operating itself. Clearly, one effect of the tendency of holidaymakers to book their holidays later and pay by credit card will be a fall in interest earnings by the operators.

Yield management

The high levels of competition for summer holiday sales require operators to take a great deal of care to get the prices of their packages right, so that sufficient demand is generated to fill available seats. At the same time, they must not be so cheap as to threaten their profitability.

Yield management has been a key tool to this end for the airline industry, allowing each fare category to be allocated to a set number of seats, with the number of seats in each category being determined by the demand for any flight. Typically operating with a tiered pricing system for their fixed capacity, with early bookers able to purchase the cheaper seats, the price for seats moves up with the scarcity of seats (as the flight nears capacity). Such a technique is now being applied across the industry, including sectors such as hotels, car hire and tour operators.

For tour operators, the smooth running of yield management is frequently defeated by the excess capacity available in the market, forcing companies to 'dump' packages at whatever price they can achieve in order to help make a contribution to their overheads. There is some evidence that companies are improving their skills at yield management by improving their forecasting or a willingness to reduce capacity in order to achieve a better balance between supply and demand. While such actions have been taken largely in the form of implicit agreements between the major operators, there is always the risk that the smaller operators will see this as an opportunity to steal some market share from the brand leaders and increase their own capacity.

If prices are set too low initially and late demand in the season results in a sold out situation, the company will not have maximized its profit opportunities. At the same time, if the company finds itself involved in added expenditure in the course of the summer – for example, providing accommodation and meals for clients delayed by air traffic control strikes (which cannot be foreseen a year in advance but occur not infrequently in Europe) – what might have been a slim but acceptable profit can soon be turned into an overall loss.

Another aspect to consider is when to launch the new holiday programme. In the past, some operators have even launched programmes more than a year in advance. Companies launching their programmes ahead of their rivals will always hope to steal a larger proportion of the early booking market and, of course, have the consequent revenue that can be invested over a longer period. It is unclear, however, if the advantages of early sales achieved in this way are sufficient to offset the drawbacks, not least of confusing both agents and customers through the range of choice on offer at any given time. A further issue is that publishing this far in advance gives competitors full view of your prices, hotels and sales techniques, giving them an opportunity to adjust their marketing when they launch their own programmes.

The tour brochure

For many years, the tour operator's brochure was the critical marketing tool and the main influence on customers' decisions to buy. Tourism is an intangible product that customers are obliged to purchase without having the opportunity to inspect it and often from a base of very inadequate knowledge. In these circumstances – and given the often limited personal knowledge of products and destinations held by travel agents – the brochure became the principal means of both informing customers about the product and persuading them to purchase it.

For most companies, very large sums are still invested in the brochure itself, as well as advertising designed to persuade customers to visit travel agents to pick one up or order a copy to be delivered to their homes. In particular, the production of the brochure is likely to represent a very significant proportion of the total marketing budget for the year, with print runs, in the case of the largest operators, running into tens of millions, at a unit cost of well over £2 a copy.

Accordingly, it is essential for operators to ensure that this large expenditure achieves its intended results. Despite this, however, there is considerable wastage. In one study undertaken by the environmental lobby Green Flag International, it was estimated that of 120 million British travel brochures printed in one year, 48 million were never used. This wastage rate, coupled with the high cost of printing and distributing each copy, was estimated to add approximately £20 to the price of the average package holiday. More recently, tour operators have taken to providing brochures electronically, allowing customers to download copies directly from their websites or collect a CD-ROM from retail outlets. Such moves can help to reduce the high costs of distributing paper brochures, as well as reducing waste. Also, when a price update needs to be made, the online brochure can be quickly updated and made available to customers.

The brochure is no longer the critical tool it once was, as many operators now sell directly from their websites. Indeed, some small companies no longer print brochures at all, simply printing off relevant pages from their websites for those customers wanting a paper copy of their holiday arrangements. While this trend is likely to accelerate, for the present the brochure still remains an important tool, so must be considered here.

Brochure design and format

Larger companies will either have their brochures designed and prepared in their own advertising department or coordinate the production with a design studio, often associated with the advertising agency they use. The agency will help to negotiate with printers to obtain the best quotation for producing the brochure and ensure that print deadlines are met. In other cases tour operators will tackle the design of the brochure themselves – a process that is being increasingly aided by computer programs that allow desktop publishing, which means that the operator is able to produce the entire contents of the brochure, including all the illustrations, on an inhouse computer. The computer will organize the layout, selecting the best locations for text and illustrations to minimize use of space, thus helping to reduce the cost. Naturally, the financial investment in the technology necessary to undertake this work is considerable.

Smaller operators tackling the design of the brochure themselves are best advised to use the help of an independent design studio, which can provide the professional expertise required in relation to the brochure's layout, artwork and copy that are so important to ensuring that the result is a professional piece of publicity material. Most printers have their own design departments that can undertake this work for their clients, but, unless the company has had experience of the standards of work of a printer, they are probably better advised to approach an independent studio to do this work.

The purposes the brochure serves will dictate its design and format. A single ad hoc programme, for example, to a foreign trade exhibition, may require nothing more than a leaflet, while a limited programme of tours may be laid out in the form of a simple folder.

Folders can take a number of different forms, ranging from a **centrefold** to more complicated folds. Larger brochures (or, in printing terminology, **booklets**) consist of eight or more pages, printed in multiples of four sheets that need to be bound together in some manner. Smaller brochures are usually machine-bound by **saddle-stitching** (stapling through the spine), while larger brochures may be **side-stitched** with a glue-on cover or bound as a book. It is not the aim here to discuss printing methods in detail, so, for further reading in the subject, see the many excellent books on print publicity.

Purpose-designed brochures will usually include all of an operator's summer or winter tours within a single brochure. However, many larger operators have diversified into a great many different types of holiday – long-haul and short-haul, coach tours as well as air holidays, lake and mountain resorts as well as seaside resorts – and if all these were to be combined into a single brochure, it would run to hundreds of pages and be both clumsy to handle and very expensive to produce. There would also be high wastage, as clients who know the type of holiday they want will have to pick up the entire programme just to get details of the particular product they are interested in. Operators therefore produce individual brochures, even in some cases separating brochures by destination. This has the added advantage of filling more of the agents' rack space, leaving less available space for competitors. If the leading half-dozen operators produce as many as 70–80 different brochures – all top sellers for agents – this will require the agency to devote as much as half their rack space to these brands.

Example

New brochure format for Cosmos Holidays

Having launched a collection of four specialist destination brochures to provide travel agents with more in-depth information about each of the resorts featured in their product range, Cosmos Holidays has decided to revert to one brochure.

Cosmos acknowledged the difficulty of getting all four brochures rack space in travel agents and, as a consequence, customers were not getting to see its entire range of destinations. Furthermore this also limited the opportunity for travel agents to cross-sell similar holidays in different destinations. In order to fit all its destinations in one brochure, the traditional price panel for each holiday has been removed, with only indicative prices being listed instead.

Cosmos manager Ian Hailes also suggested that one brochure had the added advantage of being more environmentally friendly.

Source: 'Cosmos Holidays has reverted to producing one mainstream summer holiday brochure', *Travel Weekly*, 13 July 2007.

The first task of a brochure is to attract attention. Operators have often developed a **house style** for the covers of their brochures, which means that they have the same sorts of covers each time so that they are quickly recognized by customers when they are looking through the agents' racks. They usually have images of attractive models in beachwear combined with an eye-catching symbol and brand name across the top of the brochure. While some might contend that there is a disappointing sameness to the leading operators' brochures today, taken individually, the quality and professionalism of modern brochure design and printing is outstanding. As brochures must also reinforce an image of quality and reliability, the text and images contained in brochures must not only be attractive but also truthful, accurate and easily understood. Good layout, high-quality photography and suitable paper are all essential if a brochure is to do its job effectively.

Obligations affecting tour brochures

Tour operators are selling dreams and their brochures must allow consumers to fantasize a little about their holidays. It is also vitally important, however, that consumers are not misled about any aspect of their holiday. Care must be taken not to infringe the EU Directive on Package Holidays, which explicitly makes it an offence to make misleading or false statements concerning the provision of services. Legislation introduced in European countries to comply with the Directive clarified operators' responsibilities regarding misrepresentations of elements of the travel product, which has simplified proceedings for tourists, who can sue an operator for offences for which their suppliers abroad are responsible, requiring the operator, in turn, to sue suppliers in the destination country to recover their costs.

Information required in the brochure

To satisfy not only the inclusive tour excursion (ITX) fare for flights (which requires detailed brochures to be produced by the tour organizer) but also the need of clients for information on regular charter programmes, the operator should include the following details in the brochure:

- the name of the firm responsible for the IT
- the means of transport used, including, in the case of air transport, the name of the carrier(s), type and class of aircraft used and whether scheduled or charter aircraft are operated
- full details of destinations, itinerary and times of travel
- the duration of each tour (number of days'/nights' stay)
- full description of the location and type of accommodation provided, including any meals
- whether or not services of a representative are available abroad
- a clear indication of the price for each tour, including any taxes
- exact details of special arrangements – for example, if there is a games room in the hotel, whether or not it is available at all times and if any charges are made for the use of this equipment
- full conditions of booking, including details of cancellation conditions
- details of any insurance coverage (clients should have the right to choose their own insurance, providing it offers equivalent coverage)
- details of documentation, such as visas, required for travel to the destinations featured and any health hazards, or inoculations recommended
- in the case of activity holidays, the brochure must specify how fit clients are expected to be and what sort of experience they should have had.

A booking form is usually printed within the brochure to make a reservation. The terms and conditions of the booking should appear in full in the brochure, but should not be printed on the back of the booking form, as they need to be retained by the customer.

The e-brochure

Websites now frequently replace some elements of the traditional brochure, but the preparation of web pages has to be undertaken as carefully as that for brochures. While a website will share many characteristics with a brochure, there are important differences. Customers will read fewer words on a screen than on the printed page, so the visual elements take on greater significance. The particular advantage of a website is that it can be changed frequently and at short notice – in fact, it is critical that the site is always up to date, as this will be expected. Staff must be trained to undertake this and assess what changes have to be carried out. Sometimes whole programmes will need to be withdrawn or added. Many companies use their websites to personalize their approach to clients, giving portraits of staff and adding comments from tourists on the resort pages.

Example

The cost of websites

Despite the growing importance of websites as a way of interacting with customers, the operation of these 'online shop windows' appears to only cost marketing departments a small amount compared with more traditional activities. Research by design consultancy Emperor revealed that travel companies spend less than 10 per cent of their marketing budgets on their websites. This research also revealed that companies recognize it is vitally important that their sites do not carry outdated information, with 80 per cent of companies updating their sites at least weekly.

Source: 'Travel firms spend just 10% on websites', *Marketing Week*, 20 April 2006.

In many cases, tour operators will provide visitors to their website with the opportunity to download all or part of their brochure. In most cases, the format used is a PDF file (which can be read using widely available free software). In the past, it was common to allow the brochure to be downloaded through a hyperlink on the website. More and more, however, tour operators are realizing that they can make contact with those customers reading their brochures by sending the requested information as an attachment to an e-mail address. This provides the tour operator with the opportunity to follow up the brochure request with relevant e-mails to try to encourage the customer to book with them. This latter approach also allows customers to request only the parts of the brochure they are interested in.

Negotiating with printers

Printers do not expect their clients to be experts in printing methods, but those involved with the processing and production of a brochure should be reasonably familiar with current techniques in printing and common terms used. Printers need the following information:

Example

Accessing brochures online

Kuoni's 2008 Worldwide brochure is split by geographic region (Indian subcontinent – 70 pages; Far East and Pacific – 130 pages; Middle East and North Africa – 112 pages; Caribbean – 90 pages; the Americas – 36 pages) and its website (**www.kuoni.co.uk/brochures**) allows customers to select a region to download or even a country within that region. This is important as the entire brochure covers several hundred pages, many of which may not be of interest to customers. The information received by customers will always include booking information, giving details of the terms and conditions, too.

To download the brochure, customers select the regions that they are interested in and then they will be asked to enter an e-mail address. The selected pages are then compiled as a PDF document and sent to the e-mail adresss almost instantly.

- The number of brochures required.
- The number of colours to be used in the printing. Full-colour work normally involves four colours, but some cost savings should be possible if colour photography is not to be included.
- The paper to be used – size, format, quality and weight. The choice of paper will be influenced by several factors, including the printing process used. Size may be dictated by the industry's requirements. For example, a tour operator's brochure needs to fit a standard travel agents' rack. Paper quality varies according to the material from which it is made. It may be glossy or matt, but will be selected for its whiteness and opacity. Inevitably, there is an element of compromise here as very white paper tends to be less opaque and one must avoid print showing through on the other side of the sheet. The weight of paper chosen will of course depend on its effect on the overall weight of the brochure, if it is to be mailed in quantity. Operators may well cut the size of a brochure if it reduces postage costs to a lower band.
- The number and positions of illustrations (photos, artwork, maps and so on) used.
- Typesetting needs. There are over 6000 typefaces from which to choose and the style of type chosen should reflect the theme of the brochure, its subject and the image of the company.
- Completion and delivery dates.

When obtaining prices for printing, operators should approach several companies, as quotes can vary substantially from one printer to another. Many operators choose to have their brochures printed abroad. Good-quality work can be produced at very competitive prices for long print runs, but, obviously, the operator will want to see whether or not domestic printers can match the prices quoted by printers abroad as using a local printer will reduce transport costs. Most importantly, operators must avoid cutting corners to save money as an inferior print job can threaten the whole success of the tour programme.

The progress of the printing must be supervised throughout, either by the operator or its advertising agency. Proofs should be submitted at each stage of production to check on accuracy and a final corrected proof should be seen before the actual print run to ensure that there are no outstanding errors. As the brochure is such a crucial legal document, generally several members of staff will read it through before the final proof is passed for printing.

The printer should be asked to quote for not only the actual number of brochures that are expected to be required but also the run-on price for additional copies. Once a brochure is set up for printing, the cost of running off a few extra thousand is very small compared to the initial price and it may be better to do this rather than have to reorder copies at a later date.

Brochure distribution and control

Tour operators must make the decision to either use all of the retail agencies available to them or select those that they feel will be most productive for the company. Whatever decision is made, operators must also establish a policy for distributing their brochures to these agents. If equal numbers of brochures are distributed to every agent, many copies will be wasted.

Wastage can be reduced by establishing standards against which to monitor the performance of travel agents. A key ratio is that of brochures given out to bookings received. 'Average' figures tend to vary considerably for different operators, so, while one will expect to gain a booking for every 3–4 brochures given out (which may still mean that every booking carries the burden of some £10 in brochure production costs), specialist operators may have to give out as many as 25–30 brochures to obtain a single booking. The position is slightly better than this suggests as each booking will involve, typically, between two and four people.

If figures consistently poorer than these are achieved by any of its agents, the operator should look to them for an explanation. The problem could be accounted for by an agent's lack of control over their own brochure distribution – do they merely stock their display racks and leave clients to pick up whatever numbers of brochures they wish or do they make a serious attempt to sell to 'browsers'? Some agents retain all stocks of brochures except a display copy, so that customers have to ask for copies of the brochures they require. This is instrumental in cutting down waste and it increases the number of sales opportunities.

It is now the practice of most operators to categorize their agents in some way, in terms of their productivity. This could typically take the following form.

Agents	*Bookings per year*
Category A: top, most productive agents, multiples	100+
Category B: good agents	50–99
Category C: fair agents	20–49
Category D: below average agents	6–19
Category E: poor agents, producing little	0–5

Of course, for a specialist operator, the numbers of sales per category might be considerably smaller – a good agent may produce as few as ten bookings a year. The principle remains the same, however: the operator will determine, on the strengths of these categories, what level of support to give each of the agents. Those agents at the top of the scale can expect to receive as many brochures as they ask for, while at the other end, perhaps the operator will be willing to provide only a file copy or two to three brochures to work with. Many new or independent agents are finding it increasingly difficult to obtain any supplies of brochures from the major operators, which are tending to narrow the focus of their distribution policy.

The reservations system

In order to put a package tour programme into operation, a reservations system must be developed and implemented. The design of the system will depend on whether reservations are to be handled manually or by computer and on whether the operator plans to sell through agents or direct to the public.

Many tour operators still sell their tours principally through the high street travel agents, although direct sales through the leading operators' websites are increasing rapidly. In the

UK, the multiples – retail chains owned by the lead operators – are responsible for over 50 per cent of all package holidays sold by agents.

Manual systems are fast disappearing in favour of computer reservation systems (CRS), which offer a faster, more efficient service at a much cheaper price for the operator. A travel agent needs to contact the operator quickly when serving a client at the counter. If telephone lines are engaged, or not answered for long periods of time, the agent could become frustrated and decide to deal with a competitor who is easier to contact or the client will go home and then simply search for a holiday on a website.

Initially, the CRS operated only inhouse – that is, on the operator's own premises. Agents seeking to make a booking would telephone the operator, who tapped into the company's computer to check on availability. It was but a short step from this to link the agent directly to the CRS, providing a visual display unit (VDU) in the agent's office.

In the UK, Thomson – the market leader – was the first operator to decide that all bookings through agents should be handled by a specially developed system called TOPS, forcing agents to invest in the appropriate hardware if they wished to book holidays from this major player. Most other large companies rapidly followed suit.

These connections originally depended on the use of telephone lines to link the agent's VDU to the operator's CRS. This posed problems of cost and time-wasting for the agent if lines were busy and there was difficulty in accessing a CRS. Subsequently, agents were 'hard wired' directly into the operators' CRS, reducing the time taken to make bookings and allowing the agent to switch directly from one CRS to another without redialling.

Making a reservation

The computer will allow the agent to see whether or not the particular tour required by the client is available. If it is not, it will automatically display other dates or destinations that match the client's needs as closely as possible. Once the agent has established that a package is acceptable to the client, a booking is made (sometimes an option can be taken for 24 hours, but operators are now tending to accept only firm bookings). Any late changes to the holiday that are not in the brochure can be drawn to the attention of the client and agent on the screen at this time. The agent is provided with a code number to identify the booking and obtains a completed booking form from the client, together with a deposit.

The computer booking alone is sufficient to hold the reservation, so booking forms are now held in the agent's files rather than, as formerly, sent to the operator with the deposit. The operator will issue an interim invoice to confirm the booking, on receipt of the deposit, and a final invoice will be issued, normally about ten weeks before the client is due to leave, requesting that full payment will be due eight weeks before departure. Changes to the holiday cannot be made once the final invoice has been issued. After receipt of the final payment, the tour operator will issue all tickets, itineraries and, where necessary, vouchers and despatch them to the agent, who will forward them to the client. The advent of e-tickets and vouchers, however, is dramatically reducing the amount of paperwork sent by operators to their clients.

Prior to each departure, a flight manifest is prepared for the airline, with the names of all those booked on it. In the case of flights using US airspace, a considerable amount of personal information has to be supplied for every passenger – a security measure introduced after 9/11. Also, a rooming list is sent to the hotels concerned and resort representatives where appropriate. The latter should go over the rooming list with the hotelier to ensure that all is in order prior to the clients' arrival.

Larger tour operators will have a customer relations department. Its function is to monitor and handle passenger and agency complaints and administer quality control measures in the operation of the tour programme. It monitors the questionnaires that most operators give to their clients to complete at the end of the holiday. These provide regular statistical information that can be analysed to assess which hotels are meeting clients' expectations and which ones are failing to do so.

Late bookings

Tour operators are anxious to sell every one of their holidays. The ability to react quickly to deal with last minute demand for bookings plays a key role in fulfilling this objective. In the UK, around 40 per cent of summer holiday bookings are now booked after 1 April and a similar booking pattern has emerged for winter holidays. Coupled with the offer of last minute discounts, many operators have introduced procedures designed to pick up these late bookings, including the rapid updating of availability on computer reservations systems and a booking procedure that allows tickets to be collected at the airport on departure or, more commonly now, e-tickets to be used, which can be forwarded directly to the customer electronically. The new dot.com agents provide an excellent new medium for selling off unsold flights and accommodation at short notice.

The distribution network

Selecting retailers

Essentially, tour operators have to choose between two alternative methods for selling their holidays: retail travel agents or direct to the public (although websites can have a role in either of these approaches). Larger operators that have products with universal appeal and the market for which is national in scope have tended to sell the bulk of their holidays through the retail trade, but the development of websites has encouraged an increasing number of sales to be made direct – a development welcomed by the operators as they can thus save paying agents' commissions. Websites also aid retailers, in that agents now need to spend less time talking to their clients about the products or ordering brochures and can therefore stress their role as a personal link, which offers clients a sense of security. Companies with a policy of selling direct to the public will be examined in the next main section.

Few operators deal indiscriminately with all retail agents. The cost of servicing the less productive agents is often greater than the revenue they produce as they must not only be provided with expensive free brochures but also receive regular mailings to update their information and be supported by sales material and even, in some cases, visits from the operators' sales representatives. Even in the era of websites, many operators still find that the personal contacts established by good sales representatives leads to more sales than do mail-shots or phone calls. The operators must therefore decide whether to vary the support they offer to different agents, or even dispense with the services of some agents altogether.

We have already seen how brochure supplies are varied according to the productivity of agents. It has also been the practice of operators to support their best agents by offering them an overriding commission of between 1 and 5 per cent, in addition to the basic 10 per cent, for achieving target sales figures. The large multiples, due to the strength of their position in the retail trade, can negotiate the highest overrides, giving them the ability to discount substantially in order to attract yet more business.

Leading operators have reduced both support and commission to their agents in recent years and their process of directional selling has favoured sales through their own chains. This is proving a challenge for the independent agents, which will often work with independent tour operators and other small operators to make up for the shortfall in their sales of mass market tours.

The smaller operators – those strong in certain geographic regions or that cater for specific niche markets, often involving quite a small number of customers in total – are obviously not in a position to support a national network of retailers. Most of them will therefore choose to sell direct to their customers, although a handful may try to concentrate sales through a limited number of supportive agents.

Relationships with travel agents

It is customary for tour operators to draw up a formal agreement with the travel agents they appoint to sell their services. Those agreements specify the terms and conditions of trading, including such issues as the normal rates of commission paid and whether or not credit will be extended to the agent or settlement of accounts must be made in cash.

Under the terms of these agreements, the agents agree to support and promote the sale of their principals' services. In return, the operators agree to provide the support and cooperation necessary for the successful merchandising of the companies' products – that is, providing adequate supplies of brochures, sales promotion material and sometimes finance for cooperative regional advertising or promotion campaigns. Operators will also try to ensure that their retailers are knowledgeable about the products they sell. This will be achieved through the circulation of sales letters or mailshots, invitations to workshops or other presentations and inviting selected agents on educational study trips.

The educational study trip

The **educational study trip** (**familiarization trip**, or, 'fam' trip, as it is known in North America) is a trip organized by principals (whether tour operators, carriers or tourist offices of the regions involved) for a variety of purposes. For example, members of the media or travel writers will be taken to tourist destinations in order for the principals to gain free – and, hopefully, positive – media coverage. Travel agents are also offered opportunities to undertake trips in order to improve their knowledge of the destinations or encourage them to sell the region or product. Sometimes, these trips are used by tour operators as incentives to agents – that is, if certain targets are reached, trips will be provided as a reward.

Visits to a destination are known to be one of the most effective means of encouraging agents to sell a particular package. These organized trips also have a social function, enabling the operators to get to know their agents better and to obtain feedback from them. The cost of mounting educational trips, however, is high, even if a proportion of the costs is met by the hotels at the destination or the national tourist offices and carriers helping to organize the holidays, so principals will try to do everything they can to ensure that the trips give them value for money. This was not always the case in the past, where such visits abroad were often treated as purely social events, attractive as a travel perk rather than an educational experience.

The effectiveness of the trips has been improved by selecting the candidates more carefully, providing a more balanced mix of visits, working sessions and social activities and imposing a small charge for attendance, so that the managers of travel agencies will take care to ensure that the expense is justified in terms of an increased productivity and expertise of their staff.

The careful selection of candidates will ensure that all those attending share common objectives. Monitoring performance, by soliciting reports from those attending and checking the sales of staff from those agencies invited to participate, will help to ensure that the operators' money has been well spent.

The sales representative

Tour operators, like most larger travel principals, employ sales representatives to maintain and develop their business through travel agents and solicit new sources of business. The functions of the sales representatives are to call on travel agents (and others) to give advice about the products and services they offer and support their agents with suitable merchandising material.

These representatives act as one point of personal contact between the agent and operator when problems or complaints are raised and the often close relationships that develop between representatives and their contacts are valuable in helping to build brand loyalty for the company. They enable them to receive direct feedback from the marketplace about client and agency attitudes to the companies and their products. Representatives are also likely to play a valuable role in categorizing agents in terms of their potential and selecting sales staff for educational study trips.

Making sales calls in person is expensive, however, and most companies have now switched to using telephone sales calls to keep in touch with all but their most productive agents. As with the resort representatives abroad, however, the sales representative is another means by which the company can be distinguished from its competitors and the appropriateness of this trend towards less personal contact is questionable. It is true that many agents have mixed feelings about the merits of sales representatives, who are seen by some as time-wasting socializers. It goes without saying that if the representatives are to do their job effectively, they must be well trained; those who are not sufficiently knowledgeable about their companies' or competitors' products will relay a poor image of the company to the agent.

Example

The role the sales representative

'The time-honoured role of the travel trade representative is now dead', declared Richard Carrick of Hoseasons.[14] Not all principals agree.

Libra Holidays uses its overseas reps out of season to call on agents. Ten agents are visited each day and are given product training and helped with promotions and brochure racking, while the rep gets feedback on the company's pricing.

Superbreak Mini-Holidays has a seven-strong team of sales reps, backed by three Key Account Managers, who call on agents to offer product update information and help with training in the use of the Internet and Viewdata, problemsolving and brochure merchandising and racking.[15]

Operators selling direct

Apart from those operators that will inevitably sell direct to their clients, for the reasons outlined above, a handful of larger tour operators have chosen deliberately to market their products direct to the public. This movement was spearheaded by the Danish company Tjaereborg, which entered the UK market in the late 1970s with a promotional strategy that asserted if customers booked holidays direct, by cutting out the agents' commission, they would save money. While isolated bargains were certainly on offer, many holidays were no cheaper and sometimes more expensive than similar packages booked through an agent.

The reasons for this are not hard to understand. While travel agency commissions were indeed saved, huge budgets were required to inform and promote the holidays to the general public. The company had to invest millions in heavy advertising in the media and similar high costs were incurred by the need to have a large reservations staff and multiple telephone lines to answer queries from the public. Those costs were, of course, fixed, while commissions are only paid to agents when they achieve a sale.

Tjaereborg soon found that, after initial success, which was probably the outcome of curiosity, it was unable to achieve greater market penetration – especially as Thomson Holidays had rapidly joined the competition with a direct sell division, Portland Holidays. Tjaereborg, after turning in an indifferent performance for several years, was sold to First Choice (then called Owners Abroad), which eventually replaced the brand with another direct sell operation, Eclipse.

Whether holidaymakers choose to buy direct or use an intermediary is often dependent on cultural influences related to traditional buying habits for travel products. In the UK, evidence suggests that many British holidaymakers still seek the assurance of face-to-face contact with an agent, even if the product knowledge of that agent is limited. There are some interesting variations in the pattern of agency sales, however. For example, people in the London area demonstrate a higher propensity to buy their holidays direct than do those in other parts of Britain, and certain types of package tour, such as ski holidays and coach tours, also experience a higher proportion of direct bookings than others. The advent of interactive booking of travel arrangements using the Internet is now changing this pattern dramatically.

The German market is also experiencing changes in booking behaviour, with holiday-makers bypassing the agency channel to book direct (leading to a decline in the number of travel agencies in operation). The Internet has heavily influenced booking habits there, too, with consumers increasingly booking individual services directly with principals, but the news is not so good for *tour operators* hoping to sell directly to customers. Reports suggest that the package holiday – where the customer often requires quite a lot of advice – is still likely to be purchased through a travel agent, with forecasts suggesting that only around 25 per cent of package holidays will be purchased directly.[16]

In France, the high levels of Internet access, as well as changing consumer profiles, meant that, in 2006, more then £4 billion was spent on tourism products purchased on the Internet. More than 10 million French people arranged their travel and holidays online, benefiting both tour operators and principals directly. In reference to the changing French market, Euromonitor[17] reported that:

> International companies offering a wide range of services, such as transportation, accommodation, packages and last minute options, are likely to benefit from evolving market conditions. However, local operators that utilise the internet creatively have the opportunity to exploit demand for more individualised travel and sustainable tourism by targeting consumers directly without reference to intermediaries.

While every country has its own unique patterns, many follow similar patterns to those of the UK and Germany regarding package travel. In Belgium, package holidays make up about one-third of the travel products purchased, mostly through travel agents. In 2006, only 6 per cent of tour operator sales value was earned via the Internet. The Netherlands reports similar booking behaviour – most international trips for Dutch tourists are package holidays, the majority being booked through travel agents. Domestic travel for the Dutch, however, tends to be booked directly with the principals. The popularity of dynamic packaging is likely to lead to the decline of standardized package trips, which may further affect booking patterns.

The IT revolution and its impact on tour operating

No business is being transformed by information technology (IT) faster or more radically than the business of travel – and tour operating, of all the sectors of this business, is arguably the most affected by developments. Of course, the advent of modern technology is no longer a recent phenomenon – after all, computers were widely introduced into the trade as early as the 1960s, hastening the demise of the traditional manual booking system.

Table 18.7 Percentages of Internet sales for each travel sector for selected European countries.

	Denmark	Finland	France	Germany	Italy	The Netherlands	Poland	Spain	UK
Accommodation only	65.3	3.9	21.8	21.4	19.0	18.3	19.6	33.8	11.4
Flight only	13.0	67.3	39.6	41.4	38.7	64.8	33.0	30.0	21.8
Other transport only	7.3	1.4	4.5	2.0	8.9	1.0	1.5	NA	5.1
Car rental only	1.3	0.5	2.5	1.6	3.4	1.5	3.5	3.3	1.5
Dynamic packaging	1.7	2.7	8.1	12.4	6.7	5.4	6.1	2.6	19.9
Package holiday	11.0	24.1	22.6	19.9	22.4	4.1	36.3	26.5	39.4
Other travel retail online sales	0.3	0.0	0.9	1.4	1.0	4.9	0.0	3.9	1.0

Source: Edited from national travel retail reports provided by Euromonitor, 2007/2008.

It is the scale and pace of development, however, that is proving so disruptive for the industry, as new forms of booking and information facility become available to both the trade and customers. Even the telephone has become a tool for providing new ways to book holidays, with the growth of call centres and the development of Wireless Application Protocol (WAP), which allows customers to download material from various information sources on to their mobile phones.

The key question is not whether such new techniques will start to replace traditional methods of booking holidays, but rather how quickly the transition will occur and how completely it will come to dominate distribution. One can only speculate on what kind of future the traditional agency channels will have – or even traditional tour operators, given that suppliers can now reach their customers directly through websites and e-mail and customers are not slow to recognize they can put together their own packages as well as any operator. The number of holiday sales that are made online through the World Wide Web is growing rapidly each year, with both packages and travel components being purchased.

As can be seen from Table 18.7, the use of the Internet to book package holidays varies enormously across countries, with the UK and Poland both being high users of this approach, while the Dutch are more likely to use the Internet to book flights and accommodation separately.

The leading operators have responded to the growth in Internet booking of travel products, often with the introduction of their own booking sites. This is true not just for package holidays but also for their efforts to try to capture the growing numbers wishing to use dynamic packaging.

Some observers in the industry are adamant that the growth in online booking will neither lead to the closure of tour operators nor eradicate the travel agent and have pointed to the relatively slow take-up of this method of distribution among some parts of the European market. Some believe that the caution of some consumers, the lack of IT knowledge and skills among the older generation as well as uncertainty about the reliability of the many new dot.com companies will ensure that support for more traditional means of booking will continue. Others, aware of the rise in criminal activity associated with credit cards, are also reluctant to provide their card details over the Internet. Still others believe that independent agents will be more impartial in giving advice about travel products than will the suppliers' websites, as well as providing greater expertise in recommending holidays.

Undoubtedly, all of these views have some validity, discouraging sales through new channels. Operators and agents fight back by pointing out to the independent travel bookers that they will have no one to turn to when things go wrong (a message strongly reinforced when the Asian Tsunami struck in 2004) and accommodation and flights booked separately will not have the level of protection offered by a package in the event of the collapse of either of the suppliers or some other disaster.

Example

Clarification of Dutch laws leaves independent bookers unprotected

Following a complaint from a Dutch consumer who booked travel and accommodation using an online booking site, the law in the Netherlands defining packages and tour operators has been clarified.

The traveller experienced problems with the accommodation and sought to gain compensation from the online company. The arbitration court, however, decided that such arrangements did not constitute a package, so there was no obligation on the Web-based organization to be responsible for travel products provided by a third party, even if they were booked via its website.

The outcome of this decision means that travellers need to seek recourse from the supplier directly, if there is a problem.

Source: Euromonitor, 'Travel retail – Netherlands', Euromonitor, 17 October 2007.

The new IT systems of distribution can broadly be described as falling into one of the following three categories:

- information and reservations systems offered by the suppliers of travel products and available to travel agents or other retailers
- similar systems offered by intermediaries on behalf of travel suppliers
- similar systems offered by either suppliers or, through intermediaries, direct to consumers.

The principal means of delivering these new systems include Internet services on the World Wide Web via computers, interactive television channels and the increasingly sophisticated provisions of mobile telephones.

A feature of the rapid escalation of online providers was the subsequent and equally rapid collapse of many of these same companies – largely those acting as intermediaries for the travel suppliers. Inevitably, as suppliers set up their own communication networks to service the public directly, this threatens to undermine intermediaries. The intermediaries' role is assured, however, as long as they can continue to offer a wide range of products at competitive prices and are judged by the public to be at least as impartial as the more traditional outlets in providing these services. Whether or not major suppliers will be willing to continue to offer their products through intermediaries if they can satisfactorily sell a sufficient majority of them direct to the public is a matter that will determine the future of those intermediaries.

What we are seeing at this point is a gradual concentration of the intermediaries to a point where a bare handful will emerge as market leaders, just as occurred among traditional tour operators at an earlier stage. Companies such as Opodo, ebookers.com, lastminute.com, expedia.com and travelocity.com are reinforcing their strong positions in the market, but there has been consolidation within larger companies seeking to take control of those which have greater success (and regularly achieve high levels of hit rates from consumers).

The development of alternative channels is hindered by two factors. Operators have been slow to realize the potential of the new technology and, in general, marketing costs remain high for suppliers attempting to sell direct to the public. Nonetheless, more and more operators are becoming aware that selling via the Internet allows suppliers to trim, and possibly even eradicate, their two major sources of expenditure – commission and brochures. Already much information on destinations and facilities is available for public viewing on the Internet and, before long, all holiday information currently provided by operators through the medium of brochures will become accessible in this way.

Call centres, set up to take bookings over the phone, provide another convenient means of enabling operators to reach their customers cheaply while offering very competitive prices. Technology that allows tour operators to employ fluid pricing strategies means holidays can be more readily retailed through these call centres (or via the Internet) than through traditional channels. As a result, call centres have already led to reductions in the number of outlets operated by the retail chains, which cannot directly compete with this form of distribution.

Interactive television also has the potential to significantly alter the tour operator sector. TV shopping and travel channels, available through cable and satellite TV, attract the public to search for and book their holidays in this convenient manner. While this may act as a good medium for promoting holidays, it is still common for consumers to need specific details and advice about the products to be purchased. It is therefore unlikely to become the only communication link between tour operators and customers, many actually turning to the Internet or telephone to confirm their reservations.

The speed of development of the technology in this field is too rapid to allow a thorough treatment of the subject in a textbook. Students of tour operating must keep abreast of such developments through the trade press or other media. Suffice to say that, in addition to reservations systems, computers are now used widely to provide accounts and management information quickly and accurately to both operators and agents, while larger operators have also introduced accounting systems that allow the direct transfer of agency payments from agents' bank accounts to the operators'.

In any examination of the influence of new technology in industry, it would be facile to ignore the counter-argument that impersonal means of communication can only go so far in satisfying consumers' needs. It is helpful to look at parallels in other industries. In the world of print, for example, newspapers remain popular even though their data are available online and, despite the growth of online banking, customers still value direct contact with their bank. Operators would do well to look at developments in other fields and see what lessons can be learned to improve their own means of communication with their clients.

The future for tour operators

Consolidation within this sector is likely to continue. The merging of companies that has been experienced over the past two decades will also be seen with many online operators, as they seek to establish greater turnover as well as try to control a larger share of loyal customers. The growing popularity of dynamic packaging will give travel agents the opportunity to provide a tailored holiday product to their customers, drawing on travel elements from a range of suppliers. This may require a response from tour operators as demand for package holidays declines.

As tourists become more experienced and seek out more unusual or exotic experiences, specialist niche products are likely to become more popular. This may provide a distinct opportunity for smaller, independent tour operators, although already it is possible to see that the mega operators are trying to serve this market, giving attention to the specialist brands within their operations.

Notes

1. UNWTO (2007) 'Tourism highlights', UNWTO.

2. Yamamoto, D. and Gill, A. M. (1999) 'Emerging trends in Japanese package tourism', *Journal of Travel Research*, (2) 38, pp. 134–43.

3. Office of National Statistics (2007) 'Travel trends 2006', Office of National Statistics, p. 20.

4. Mintel (2007) 'European leisure travel industry', Mintel, September.

5. Mintel (2005) 'Activity holidays – UK', Mintel, September.

6. European Commission (2007) 'Press release IP/07/614', EC, 4 May.

7. Mintel (2007) 'European leisure travel industry', Mintel, September.

8. Euromonitor (2007) 'Rewe group – travel and tourism – world', Euromonitor, January.

9. Data from personal communication with ABTA's membership manager, 2007.

10. CAA (2007) *ATOL Business*, 29, summer 2006, p. 9.

11. Schulte-Nölke, H., Twigg-Flesner, C. and Ebers, Dr M. (2006) *EC Consumer Law Compendium: Comparative analysis*, Bielefeld.

12. Office of National Statistics (2007) 'Travel trends 2006', Office of National Statistics, p. 20.

13. Edited from information given in Schulte-Nölke et al., 2006.

14. *Travel Weekly*, 26 November 2004.

15. 'Death of salesmen?' *Travel Weekly*, 5 December 2004.

16. Euromonitor (2007) 'Travel and tourism – Germany', Euromonitor, 26 September.

17. Euromonitor (2008) 'Travel and tourism – France', Euromonitor, 9 January.

Websites

flexibletrips.com, Thomas Cook (accommodation only)   **www.flexibletrips.com**

H-C travel   **www.hctravel.com**

Hotelbeds, TUI (business to business accommodation only) **http://rz.hotelbeds.com**

Somewhere2stay.com, Cosmos (accommodation only)   **www.somewhere2stay.com**

Walking Women   **www.walkingwomen.com**

Questions and discussion points

1. There are many benefits for hotels in working with tour operators – a major factor being the guaranteed bookings for the rooms the tour operators contract for. The Internet has made it easier for customers to book with hotels direct, however. Discuss whether or not you think that the growing use of the Internet to book travel products will mean hotels will no longer need to work with tour operators to sell their rooms.

2. As the major European tour operators integrate vertically and horizontally through the merger or purchase of smaller (often specialist) travel companies, discuss the implications of this for consumers.

3. The mini case study in this chapter (TUI buys up an Italian village) identifies a major development in Italy by TUI that includes three hotels as well as a range of leisure activities. What are the benefits for TUI in having such control over the destination? Do you think this is also beneficial for tourists?

Task

1. Across the European Union, the Directive on Package Holidays has been implemented in local law, although each country has achieved it in different ways as their legal systems and travel industries are not standardized across Europe. For a country of your choice, evaluate the protection that this has given to consumers. Does the legislation also help to protect the tourism industry?

Chapter 19

Selling and distributing travel and tourism

Learning outcomes

After studying this chapter, you should be able to:

- explain the role of travel agents as a component of the tourism industry and their relationship with other sectors

- identify the functions performed by an agent

- be aware of the qualities necessary for effective agency management and service

- understand the considerations and the requirements for establishing and running a travel agency

- be aware of the constraints and threats to agents' operations and evaluate alternative solutions for their survival.

Introduction

> The traveller used to go about the world to encounter the natives. A function of travel agencies is now to prevent this encounter.
>
> Daniel J. Boorstin, *The Image: A guide to pseudo-events in America*, Vintage, 1961, p. 91

The European Commission has defined **travel agents** as retailers to leisure and business travellers, selling flights (charter or scheduled), accommodation, car hire, foreign currency, travel insurance and other travel services. They are generally paid a commission by the supplier of the service or, in the case of a package holiday, by the operator.[1] In some countries, the term 'travel agent' is used more generally, to refer to an organization operating in the travel industry (this may be as a retailer but also includes those acting as tour operators or tour providers). This chapter, however, specifically focuses on the travel agent as a retailer. The travel agent acts as an intermediary, conveniently linking customers with the providers of travel products. Providers of travel products are often termed **principals**, owning specific travel elements, such as hotels or airlines, as well as tour operators, which put together packages that combine several travel elements (see Figure 19.1).

Most travel principals continue to rely, to a greater or lesser extent, on travel agents as an important source of distribution and retailers continue to play a key role in the structure of the industry. Their share of business, however, is declining, even in the key area of inclusive tours, as customers turn to booking direct. The agent's role is changing, but there are grounds for trusting that it is far from collapsing, providing agents are willing to adapt.

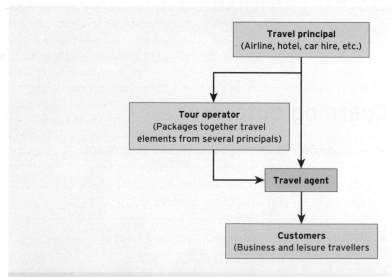

Figure 19.1 The position of travel agents in the chain of distribution.

Historical context

Agents selling travel arrangements have been in existence in the UK for well over 100 years. Indeed, the oldest – now the tour operator Cox and Kings – traces its origins back to the eighteenth century. The travel agent's principal role in earlier times was to sell shipping and rail services, but, with the coming of air transport and the development of the package tour business after World War II, their product range expanded.

Before World War II, shipping companies had been able to provide a good reservations and ticketing service direct to the public, with sales outlets in their city offices and at leading ports. Railways and coach operators had similarly established city centre terminals from which they could dispense tickets direct to the public. When the airlines arrived on the scene, however, their airport terminals were situated well away from centres of population and, as a convenient network of travel agents was in place by that time, they did not face the same pressure to establish their own sales offices. Although most leading airlines did establish a main selling office in capital cities and many also opened offices in other leading cities, the new demand for air tickets encouraged travel agents to expand their distribution outlets further. With the deregulation of air travel and a greater willingness on the part of passengers to book direct (first by phone or fax, later via the Internet), many airlines closed their town centre sales offices. Travel agents, too, have experienced a fall in air ticket sales in the past few years.

It was the travel agents themselves that developed the first air package tours. Retail entrepreneurs had the vision to see that, if they could buy seats on flights in bulk at discounted prices, they could reduce the cost of air fares and, thus, a huge mass market for foreign tours would develop. The packages they developed were, in turn, sold through other agents and, eventually, they became the retailers' principal source of revenue.

The scale of the retail sector

It is difficult to estimate the number of travel agents in existence globally. Many become members of their national association bodies, but, as such organizations often allow those tour operators who also provide retail services to join, their membership statistics can provide only limited detail regarding the numbers of business operating primarily as travel agents (see Table 19.1). While some countries require agents to be licensed, many have no compulsory registration scheme. Licensing schemes can vary in their format. For instance, in Ireland, the licensing of travel agents and tour operators is undertaken by the Commission for Aviation regulation (302 travel agents were licensed to trade during the last quarter of 2007). Alternatively, licensing may be through government bodies or linked to customer financial protection schemes. An example of both approaches is seen in Australia, where travel agents are licensed through their state governments but the state also requires them to be members of a travel compensation fund (which provides financial protection for

Table 19.1 Membership of travel agent associations.

Association	Membership
Association of Turkish Travel Agencies (TURSAB)	5426
Czech Republic – ACCKA	200
DRV German Travel Association	3252
Japan Association of Travel Agents	1266
National Association of Tourism Agencies – Romania	nearly 800
National Association of Travel Agents Singapore	318
Osterreichischer Reisebüroverband (ORV)	2300
Swiss Federation of Travel Agencies	830
Syndicat national des agences de voyages et des tours opérateurs (SNAV) – France	1392 agencies
Travel Agents Association of India	1200 IATA
Travel Agents Association of New Zealand (TAANZ)	459

Source: C. Humphreys, correspondence with membership managers of travel agents' associations, 2007.

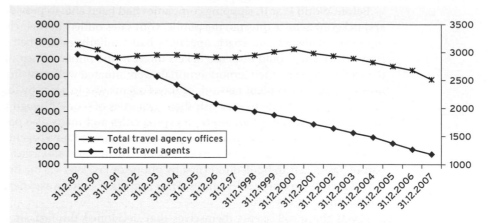

Figure 19.2 The decline in numbers of travel agents that are members of ABTA. *(ABTA private correspondence with membership manager, 2007.)*

customers should a travel agency collapse). In 2006, over 3200 head office and 1400 branch office travel agents were members of this scheme.

It should also be noted that customers' use of travel agents varies from country to country. Research[2] in 1990 found that, while 80 per cent of travel purchases in the UK were through travel agents, Belgium, the Netherlands and Switzerland recorded levels closer to 25 per cent. While the market has changed significantly since that time, it highlights the fact that different distribution channels are used in different nations.

The evidence further suggests that there has been a shift in the use of travel agents in the UK in recent years (see Figure 19.2). In mid-2007 there were about 1200 agents affiliated to the Association of British Travel Agents (ABTA), the leading trade body representing both tour operators and travel agents in the UK. These agents controlled 4340 outlets, and over 500 of these organisations were also listed as ABTA tour operators. This level is a significant decline since its high point, in the 1980s, when ABTA had more than 3000 members with almost 8000 offices.

The power of the travel agency chains

As the demand for travel services grew in the UK, travel agencies expanded their operation, opening new premises (or, in some cases, acquired smaller existing businesses) in order to service more customers. In addition, several tour operators sought to take control of the retailing element of their business so they also established large networks of outlets. For example, the purchase in the 1970s of the Lunn Poly travel agencies by Thomson Holidays (now part of the TUI group) ensured that the tour operator could provide an expanded network of retail outlets. These **multiples** could achieve business advantages through their centralized marketing activities, negotiating higher commission rates based on sales across the group and reduced costs through mass development and purchasing of key resources (such as computer systems).

The concern that the multiples would expand to a point where independents would be squeezed out of the market has receded to some extent in recent years. Indeed, the composition of the travel agency industry has changed dramatically over time. There was a fall in independent agencies (small privately owned businesses with only a few outlets) as the travel agency chains (with multiple outlets) expanded under the ownership of the major tour operators such as Thomas Cook and TUI, but, with the growth in call centres and electronic booking, the multiples are now starting to reduce the number of their own high street outlets. For example, in the UK, Thomas Cook reduced the number of outlets from 692 in 2001 to 612 by 2005.[3]

Competing with the multiples

Although the large number of branches owned by the leading chains appears to give them an insuperable advantage over the independents, that is not always the case. Medium-sized chains (often operating only in a limited geographic region) can provide strong competition. These chains, commonly known as **miniples**, typically control between 40 and 100 shops. They are, however, vulnerable to takeovers and some of the major players have been absorbed into leading operators' retailing organizations.

The independents have recognized that, on their own, they face an almost impossible task in competing with the multiples for the sale of mass market holidays. Since it became legal to discount the price of travel products at the point of sale, the independent agents have been under particular pressure from the discounting undertaken by the multiples. Such large chains, because of their substantial buying power, can negotiate commission overrides (an additional percentage of commission paid when higher sales targets are achieved), making it easier to undercut independent agents on price. The multiples can also invest more in the latest technology and programmes of national advertising than can the independents.

Independent travel agents have realized that, in order to compete on price, they need to collaborate with other travel agencies. This allows them to negotiate for higher commissions based on their joint buying power. As a result, there has been massive growth in alliances, particularly through the establishment of consortia. An example is the North American-based Vacation.com, which has a network of over 5000 agencies across the USA and Canada and combined sales of more than $18 billion.[4] An international consortium has also been formed – the Worldwide Independent Travel Agents' Network (WIN). Its membership spans 12 countries.

Example

Consortia

Travelsavers International

Formed in the USA in 1970, this marketing group has some 3000 branches in 14 countries worldwide. The travel agencies are not marketed under this brand name – all the agents retain their own identities. In the UK, they must hold ABTA or IATA membership to operate within this group.

Advantage

Established in 1978 and known initially as the National Association of Independent Travel Agents (NAITA), then as Advantage Travel Centres, this consortium supports around 750 branches. Agents may use their own trading names, but around half of the members have chosen to emphasize the Advantage brand in their names.

WorldChoice

Formed in 1976, this group operated initially as the Association of Retail Travel Agents' Consortia (ARTAC). This consortium comprises over 600 branches, including its own travel agencies. With so many branches, it is the largest high-street travel group in the UK. It is owned by the shareholders of its member travel agencies.

Global Travel Group

Formed 1993, this group has 800 members and operates its own bonding system.

Elite Travel Group

Established in 1977, this small consortium was formerly known as Midconsort Travel Group (reflecting its geographical focus on the Midlands region of England).

Freedom Travel Group

Formed in 2002, as the trading arm of the United Co-op Travel Group. With around 65 members, this group charges them a management fee based on the commission earned.

In 2005, three UK-based consortia – Advantage, WorldChoice and Global – reached an agreement to unite, creating the Triton Travel Group, which serves around 2300 branches. As a centralized purchasing organization, its combined purchasing power enhances its position in negotiations with suppliers. A full merger of these consortia is not planned, however. In May 2007, the Board of Advantage stated that such a merger would not be in the best interests of its own member agencies.[5]

The potential buying power of such groupings of independent agencies provides them with a very real chance of being able to compete with the large chains as they can share marketing costs as well as work with the smaller tour operators to ensure that they are represented in the high street. In addition, consortia membership can avoid the necessity for each agency to have separate licences when putting different components of a package together. Some believe that, in time, this could also lead to consortia establishing their own tour operations or even an airline (although the cost has proved too daunting up until now).

Franchising has generally been less successful as a strategy for competing with the multiples. The first chain in Britain to attempt to franchise on a wide scale, Exchange Travel, went into liquidation in 1990 and the Canadian-based Uniglobe chain has, similarly, found it difficult to establish itself in the UK, despite having a chain of offices exceeding 1400 worldwide. Interestingly, it has been reported[6] that one of the major multiples in the UK, First Choice, is offering franchises and two miniples, Just Go Travel and Bowen Travel Group, are among the first to sign up. So, although the future of franchising remains uncertain at this time, if multiples use it to provide further business growth, then the market will become even more competitive for independent agents.

The profitability of travel agents

Surprisingly few studies of travel agency productivity and profitability exist. One way to measure these is to examine their profit levels and turnover per employee. Earlier studies have generally found multiples to be more profitable than independents. Annual reports allow comparisons to be made between multiples and independent agents (see Table 19.2).

Occasional studies by national associations have been undertaken investigating the profitability of their members. Australia's Travel Compensation Fund analysed the finance reports of its members and reported average profitability for its leisure and business agents (see Table 19.3).

Some agencies have been successful in increasing profits through a supermarket approach to sales. For example, First Choice introduced the Holiday Hypermarket brand, with superstores primarily located at out-of-town retail parks. Thomas Cook has introduced Thomas Cook Direct, to sell its products direct to consumers, and many others have

Table 19.2 The profitability of UK travel agents, 2006/2007.

Company name	Turnover (£000)	Profit before taxation (£000)	Profit as % of turnover	Number of employees	Profit per employee (£)
Multiples					
Thomas Cook Retail Limited	284,588	17,702	6.2	6,800	2,603.24
Trailfinders Group Limited	550,086	15,554	2.8	1,129	13,776.79
Travelbag Limited	13,576	588	4.3	205	2,868.29
Consortia					
United Co-operatives Travel Management Limited	5,855	974	16.6	160	6,087.50
Independent					
Haslemere Travel Limited	3,440	21	0.6	12	1,750.00

Source: Company reports, 2007.

Table 19.3 Profitability of Australian travel agents, 2006

Average % of turnover not used to fund overheads	Turnover ($1m–$2m) %	Turnover ($2m–$3m) %	Turnover ($3m–$5m) %	Turnover ($5m–$10m) %
Leisure Agents	8	9	11	10
Business Agents	7	8	8	6
Conference Agents	10	16	7	14

Source: Travel Compensation Fund, 'Annual report', Travel Compensation Fund, 2006.

followed suit with a call centre approach, abandoning face-to-face contact with customers to keep down costs. All four of the UK's leading tour operator chains have tried selling their products through interactive TV, although only Thomas Cook and TUI Thomson currently operate their own channels. Despite more customers having access to interactive TV, however, it has not really seen success. In 2005, Expedia's TV travel shop failed, following losses of more than $46 million and, while Thomas Cook TV takes around 90,000 bookings each year (52 per cent of the total sales made via television), according to the company's Chief Executive,[7] 'the cost of each booking is too high at 14–15 per cent'.

The role of travel agents

The travel agent's role is dissimilar to that of most other retailers, in that agents do not purchase products for resale to their customers. Only when a customer has decided on buying a particular holiday do agents approach their principal on their customer's behalf to make a purchase. The travel agent does not, therefore, carry stock. This has three important implications for the business of travel distribution:

- the cost of setting up in business is relatively small compared to that of other retail businesses
- agents are only able to sell products made available by the tour operators or principals, so, in times of peak demand, they may be competing with other agencies to find the products that the customers wish to purchase

- agents are not seeking to dispose of products that they have already purchased, so may display less brand loyalty towards a particular product or company.

Arguably, the main role of a travel agent has always been to provide a convenient location for the purchase of travel. At those locations they act as booking agents for holidays and travel, as well as a source of information and advice on travel services. Their customers look to them for expert product knowledge and objectivity in the advice they offer. However, as agents choose to deal with an increasingly limited range of products on which they can maximize their revenue (the competitive nature of retail travel is such that profit margins are small and agents must find whatever means they can of surviving), objectivity in recommendations and travel advice may not be possible. Nor is it realistic to imagine that sales staff – who are often young and generally inexperienced in travel themselves – can have a thorough knowledge of every product available, and this limits their value as a source of information.

The range of products that an agent will choose to offer will vary not only on the basis of the commission each earns but also on the nature of demand within the catchment area, the degree of specialization of the agency and the preferences and marketing policies of the proprietor. An agency that is attempting to provide a full range of services to the public would sell air tickets, cruise and ferry tickets, rail and coach transport, car hire, hotel accommodation and package tours (which might include domestic travel). Additional services, such as travel insurance, traveller's cheques and foreign exchange may also be offered and some agents will also undertake to arrange travel documentation (such as arranging visas) for their clients. Some will even deal with theatre tickets.

Such all-round agents are rapidly disappearing in the face of commercial pressures, however. Owing to the small amount of revenue achieved on the sale of coach or rail tickets, many agents are now forgoing sales of these types, although some still believe that it is better to offer a full range of services, even if some offer little or no profit, on the grounds that customers may return to buy other travel arrangements later.

An alternative to providing a full range of products is for the agency to specialize in a niche product, such as cruising. Agents may specialize not only in the selection of products they offer, but also in the markets they serve. The clearest distinction is between those that focus on business travel (serving the travel needs of the local, and in some cases national, business community) and those that concentrate on leisure travel.

Distribution trends

It is becoming clear that the retail sector of the leisure tourism industry is now moving in two distinct directions: towards the fast turnover 'leisure sales shop' – a feature of the multiples' approach, which is essentially a booking service offering rock-bottom prices; or towards a more specialized advisory service for complex or expensive tailor-made travel arrangements, which allow the agency to charge fees for their services and avoid the usual pressure to discount.

The move towards charging fees for services has its precedent in the USA, where, for a number of years, travel experts holding the Certified Travel Counsellor (CTC) qualification have dealt with the more lucrative end of the package tour business. It is these operations that seem most likely to benefit if suppliers move to contracts with lower or zero commissions as their customers will be more disposed to pay fees for the services they are rendered.

Meanwhile, the traditional travel agent, attempting to provide a wide range of services with little discounting, faces a future that is increasingly uncertain as there are increasing opportunities for members of the public to book direct with the suppliers using the Internet. While the Internet has been seen as a major threat, research[8] in the USA has reported a decline in the use of the Internet to book travel.

The policy of mass market tour operators as well as airlines in recent years has been based on selective distribution – that is, favouring a smaller number of highly productive agents rather than dealing with all retail agencies. This policy has also been favoured by the multiple agents themselves, which choose to stock the products of a few key operators responsible for perhaps 80 per cent of the total revenue in the mass market. Thomas Cook, to take one example, introduced a policy to work with only about 400 companies, of which 30 were identified as 'premium selection'. If this tendency becomes widespread over the next few years, smaller tour operators will have to find other means of reaching their customers.

The tour operator-owned multiples also engage in **directional selling** – that is, they recommend their own companies' products to customers at the expense of those from other suppliers. This ensures that the majority of the sales of the larger tour operators' products are achieved through their own travel agencies. The UK's Foreign Package Holidays (Tour Operators and Travel Agents) Order (2000) requires that the links between operators and their agencies are made clear to customers. Publicizing such links will not necessarily work to the advantage of the independent agents, however – it may encourage the public to believe that the leading tour operators' programmes can *only* be purchased from the retail branches of those operators. While some independents are concerned that tour operators will eventually choose to retail their products exclusively through their own retail chains, currently this is thought unlikely.

Example

Agents involved in directional selling

In 2004, Amadeus, the travel technology provider, surveyed British holidaymakers and reported that more than two-thirds of travel agents had tried to encourage their customers to switch from the holiday company they originally requested to other providers.[9]

With over 70 per cent of travel agents admitting that they are likely to push companies paying them higher levels of commission, such directional selling was seen to be a strategic business decision by the management of those travel agents. As tour operators drive customers towards direct sell channels and lower commission levels, the fight for customer business has become competitive. Even independent agents are not immune from such behaviour. In many cases, encouraged by their management, they also make their selections from companies offering them the most favourable commissions.[10]

Changes to retail distribution

A number of other notable developments in travel retailing have taken place in the past few years in addition to those already described above.

Home-based sales agents

The field of home selling has expanded rapidly in recent years. Personal travel counsellors and online travel counsellors who work on a freelance basis sell on behalf of an agency and earn commission from that agency. That commission is then shared, with the travel counsellor receiving between 30 and 100 per cent of the total commission earned, depending on the level of support service provided by their host agency.

Tour operators encourage consumer loyalty

Tour operators have become more aggressive in boosting sales through their own outlets. To cite one example, merchandisers acting on behalf of a leading operator were recruited

Example

Travel Counsellors

Travel Counsellors is one company that has built up a major retailing base in travel, with home-based employees operating in the UK, Germany, the Netherlands, Ireland, Australia, South Africa and the USA. The summer of 2008 saw further expansion into Canada.

Turnover in 2007 was in excess of £212 million. It reported that over 40 per cent of its UK-based agents earned more than £300 per week in commission, but acknowleged that more than a third of their counsellors worked between 40 and 60 hours per week to gain such returns.[11]

The year 2007 saw their expansion into South Africa to compete with an existing home-based travel firm, eTravel. Worldwide, the company, by the end of 2007, had established more than a dozen agents in South Africa and now has more than 900 agents, supported by over 200 full-time employees.

to hand out leaflets at top resorts in Spain to holidaymakers (not necessarily their clients), offering discounts to those booking their holidays through their own retail chain for the following year. Thomas Cook was the first travel chain to introduce its own credit card to build customer loyalty, offering vouchers with the purchase of every travel product. As competition becomes fiercer, there can be little doubt that we will see an increase in such aggressive retailing and promotion.

Diversification into travel retailing by non-tourism businesses

The threat always remains of organizations outside the travel industry taking an interest in diversifying into travel retailing, especially where this is seen as a logical expansion of their existing activities and they have a retailing operation that can be easily adapted to take on these extra travel services. The highly competitive marketplace and legislation relating to financial and consumer protection, however, has added complexity to the business of selling travel, which may well be a factor in the decision of so many other retail organizations to avoid the travel business. Yet, in the Netherlands, the sale of holidays through banks is a long-established practice and, in Germany, large department stores have played a major role in travel retailing for many years.

Direct selling

Perhaps the greatest threat that travel agencies face in the short term is the move to direct selling which is now accelerating as use of the Internet expands. Can travel principals sell their products directly to the public at a lower cost? That is a vital question for both principals and tour operators.

On the one hand, selling direct to customers cuts out the high cost of servicing intermediaries as well as having to pay commission on each sale. On the other hand, it can involve substantial capital investment to set up sales offices and direct marketing costs can be high, especially if national advertising campaigns have to be mounted. Additional staff must be employed to operate call centres, too, and these must be adequately trained for the job.

Currently, many products available to customers direct on the principals' websites are offered at prices below those quoted to travel agents, leaving customers with little incentive to book through an agent. Companies that occasionally accept bookings from agents, even when selling most of their product direct (small hotels are a good example), however, usually recognize that to deliberately undermine the retail trade by, for instance, charging a lower price when accepting direct business from their customers, can jeopardize their relationship with travel agents, thus impacting on future business.

Example

Eurotunnel

When the Channel Tunnel first opened, the management of Eurotunnel largely ignored the strength of the retail travel trade, assuming that most clients would prefer to book their crossings direct. Thus it simultaneously antagonized the trade and reduced its own sales opportunities.

Later, the company realized its mistake and sought trade support when sales were poor, but this required Eurotunnel to make extensive efforts to build relationships with the travel trade to overcome its now negative perceptions of the company.

Some travel firms, however have little alternative other than to sell their products direct as their total capacity is too small for it to be considered by the retail distribution network. Consequently, such operators may adopt one of two distributive strategies: find a selection of key agents (likely to be independents rather than chains) that are willing to stock the product or sell all their holidays direct to the public. The AITO Special Agents Scheme is an example of the former. The small specialist operators that form the membership of the association have identified some 150 specialist agencies to handle their bookings.

Consumer access to reservation systems

Travel agents today have much more to fear from advances in technology that will allow access to operators' CRSs by the travelling public. This is a reality in the USA and France and it is already available for business travellers in the UK. Such access lets customers compare the availability and price of travel products in real time.

Changes in access to brochures

The proliferation of brochures and the policy of leading tour operators to produce a range of different, branded products, each in their own brochure, has forced travel agents to re-evaluate their policies on stocking brochures for customers. With the typical travel agency only having rack space for around 145 brochures, of which up to 20 per cent may be filled with the products of the leading operators, there is little opportunity for the smaller and specialist operators to get their brochures on those racks. While a few years ago that would have been disastrous for their trade, the introduction of the World Wide Web has led to companies becoming far more dependent instead on their websites to sell their products and many companies now make brochures available to download.

The product portfolio

The decision about which products to stock is taken not only on the basis of what it is thought will sell quickest or easiest. The introduction of tighter EU legislation over quality has forced many Europe-based agents to reconsider the companies with which they deal and, while override commissions undoubtedly play a role in the decision, equally the service the agent provides to the operator is taken into consideration. Agents that encounter difficulties in getting through to operators on the telephone or who find their e-mail communications or complaints are not answered quickly are less inclined to stock that operator's products. Companies insisting, for example, that agents use high cost phone numbers when telephoning, and then keep agents waiting on the line for extended periods, can antagonize the retailers.

While the apparently unbiased service provided by independent travel agents appears to be a marketing advantage, it is questionable whether or not clients themselves actually deal through an agent to gain this benefit, as the proportion of sales through travel agents is highest for the standard package holidays, which could, arguably, be booked direct with equal simplicity. This supports the view of many that travel agents only represent a *convenient* outlet for buying a holiday rather than an advisory service. One should also not dismiss the value of personal contact when making bookings. Many customers are still reluctant to make such a high-price purchase on the Web – there is a growing fear of fraud or identity theft when offering credit card details over the Web and so agents still offer some guarantee of financial security, which customers see as an advantage. Furthermore concerns that they may make mistakes or misunderstand booking conditions increase uncertainty and encourage customers to use the expertise of travel agents. Examples of such mistakes include the traveller who mistyped Sydney and, instead of ending up in Australia, flew to the small mining town of Sidney, in Montana, USA,[13] and the American customer who mistook the currency used in quotations and found the price quoted for a booked tour was not 789 euros, but, in fact, £789 sterling – at that time meaning that it cost about 40 per cent more than expected.[14]

The low proportion of bookings achieved by travel agents for domestic holidays owes much to the traditional pattern of booking holidays in the UK. Domestic holidaymakers have tended in the past to contact principals directly, often by writing to resort tourist offices for brochures and details of hotels. Holidays in Britain were neither conveniently packaged nor seen by travel agents as sufficiently remunerative to justify devoting precious rack space to brochures about them, or training staff in domestic product knowledge. Two factors have tended to increase sales through agencies more recently, however.

First, domestic holidays have risen in price in comparison with foreign holidays, so sales of holidays at home can equal or exceed the 'bargain basement' prices now offered overseas. Second, UK holidays are now better packaged by the tour operators, with the larger companies now including domestic holidays in their product portfolios. Combined, these factors provide travel agents with greater opportunity for earning higher returns on conveniently booked packages. As a result, the UK has experienced a small increase in the use of travel agents to book domestic holidays, from 17.6 per cent in 2001 to 19.2 per cent in 2005.[15]

Dynamic packaging

The boundaries between agent and operator are becoming blurred and are likely to become more so, helped by ever-improving technology.

Ian Mounser, Sales Director, Superbreak, 'All you need to know about dynamic packaging', *Travel Weekly* Special Supplement, March 2005, p. 34

There is an alternative, and it is being realized today – agents are using dynamic packaging to become tailor-made operators for their clients. The Web, which threatens their livelihoods, also offers the best prospect for their survival, if they adapt.

By accessing the websites of reliable suppliers, putting together a package of components that exactly meets a customers' needs and adding a mark-up allowing them a reasonable level of profit for the expertise they are delivering, agents are fulfilling a new role. Here, the consortia are often a step ahead. Worldchoice, for instance, has struck a deal with Thomas Cook that allows it to sell Thomas Cook's products under its own label. Members of the consortium are able to access its Cook's Flexible Trips dynamic packaging operation and are also protected under Cook's ATOL for the resultant package they create.

In the UK, ATOL regulations were amended in 2003 so that agents may no longer buy the separate components of an inclusive tour and package them without possession of an ATOL. Agents are faced with the choice of either buying the components from an existing ATOL holder (such as a tour operator's dynamic packaging website) or applying for a mini-ATOL to set themselves up as package operators. If flights are not included in the package, an ATOL is not obligatory, but if bundling other components, the agent must still comply with the conditions of the European Package Travel Regulations. This includes providing clear booking conditions, the service of a representative or 24-hour telephone assistance and accepting liability for damages, so business insurance is a must.

While dynamic packaging has been important in the UK and USA markets for some time, it is only just beginning to grow in the Australasian region. Research by consultants Phocus Wright is reported as revealing that dynamic packaging is expected to account for around 6 per cent of total Australasian bookings[16] by 2009, with Qantas, the national carrier, now offering dynamic packaging through its website. Travel agents in Australia that use dynamic packaging must be aware, however, of state regulations: 'Packaging a flight and accommodation effectively means agents are playing tour operator and must behave as such. Trading standards differ between the states, but often a wholesaler must provide guarantees on a whole range of matters.'[17]

Disintermediation and reintermediation

The growing use of the Internet to purchase travel products direct from the provider has meant that consumers have begun to bypass intermediaries. This removal of travel agents (as well as tour operators in some cases) from the chain of distribution is termed **disintermediation**.

This has caused obvious concern for travel agents and their response has been to reinforce their role in the chain of distribution by providing customers with an enhanced travel experience. The agents have reinforced awareness of their role in providing information, convenient booking and problem-solving in times of crisis.

Many specialist travel organizations (often online) have been established to support customers in purchasing various elements of their travel at their convenience. Such organizations allow different elements to be purchased through one site, often providing discounts when more than one element is purchased. The advantage of these websites to consumers is that they are independent of the suppliers and viewed as unbiased in terms of the range of products they offer. Airlines also value these outlets as a means of unloading surplus stock without degrading the brand. There have been a few great successes in such travel businesses, including expedia, lastminute.com, travelocity.com and ebookers, which sell, among other things, discounted and late availability travel – mainly airline seats, hotel accommodation and car rental – rather than focusing on package holidays.

The growing inclusion of such businesses within the chain of distribution has been termed **reintermediation**. This century has seen reintermediation grow, as specialist online providers offer customers improved price comparison opportunities as well as greater efficiencies in the time spent booking travel products.

Setting up and running a travel agency

The leisure travel agency

Traditionally, travel agents are located in major city centres, in the suburbs of large towns and, less frequently, in smaller towns. They are often termed 'bricks and mortar' or 'high street' agents, reflecting the locations of their buildings. To be successful, they tend be sited at street level and close to the centre of main shopping areas. They compete against the other agents drawing on the market within the local area. In the case of a large city, that area may extend only to the surrounding streets, but, in the case of an important market town, it may draw on residents living within a radius of 30 or 40 miles. There has also been noticeable growth in travel hypermarkets, located at the out-of-town retail parks. They attract high levels of trade as customers incorporate travel purchases into their other leisure shopping in these locations with convenient parking.

It is also worth noting that agents in city centres attract as their clients not only residents in the area but also workers employed in the area who may find it more convenient to make their travel arrangements close to their place of work than to do so nearer to their homes. It may also be the case, however, that a number of workers in the area will choose to pick up their brochures from the city branch, but make their reservations at an agency near their homes, where bookings can be arranged together with their spouse or partner. This may mean a high turnover of brochures with little return for the city agency – a problem particularly common in a major city like London.

As noted earlier, as holiday brochures can be downloaded by customers from the websites of tour operators there has been a reduction in the printing of brochures and these people will not be calling in to a travel agent's. In some cases, too, travel agencies themselves may hold only electronic copies of brochures, just printing the required pages for their customers. This has the benefit of reducing the need to stock all brochures and may mean that customers are not distracted by other products within the brochure but this places printing costs on the travel agent.

A recent development among specialized agencies is to focus on contacting their clients through websites or recommendation by word of mouth, thus making them less dependent on expensive street-level premises. These agents generally avoid the problem of timewasters – people who pop in to pick up brochures from which they will later book direct online or merely wish to get quotations to compare with those obtained from several other agencies in the area.

Example

Haslemere Travel

Haslemere Travel is an English agency that is moving away from the concept of just having a street-level shop serving purely as a convenient location for bookings and tickets. Much of its business is achieved through promotion via its website. It also claims to have doubled its sales in one year by closely monitoring every customer who contacts its shop. All enquiries, whether in person or over the phone or website are logged and traced for progress. Where a booking does not result, staff are encouraged to follow this up to find out why. This simple monitoring has resulted in an increase in bookings from 40 to 75 per cent.

Further information: **www.haslemeretravel.co.uk**

Setting up a travel agency requires little capital, although in some countries formal qualifications are a prerequisite. The International Air Transport Association (IATA)[18] also requires that a suitably qualified and experienced staff member is employed if the agency wishes to sell air tickets. As not every staff member has to be suitably qualified when the business is established, however, it is possible to operate with only one or two experienced employees. Consequently, the business appears extremely attractive to outsiders, who see it as a glamorous occupation with wonderful opportunities for cheap travel.

Establish a new business or purchase an existing agency?

Anyone contemplating opening a travel agency will have to consider the merits of buying an existing agency against those of establishing a new one.

There are considerable advantages to taking over an existing agency. To begin with, trading figures for recent years can be examined and the viability of the agency evaluated in relation to the purchase price. An agency that is operating successfully can be expected to retain its loyal clientele, if service remains comparable in the future. Against this, if there is a strong and loyal market already, the price for the agency may be high to include the goodwill. **Goodwill** embraces the reputation of the business and the expectation that existing customers will continue to buy from there.

Another advantage of buying an existing agency is that licences and **appointments** (agreements with tour operators to sell their products) are generally retained by the new management. Staff, too, can be retained and good, qualified and experienced staff are often not easy to find, especially for those seeking to set up a new agency.

The attraction of starting from scratch is mainly a financial one: the capital cost will be limited to office furnishings, fixtures, computers, phones and perhaps a new external fascia. Persuading principals to provide you with brochures, offer you appointments and pay commission on sales, however, may prove difficult, especially if the area concerned is already well served by existing agents.

Location, location, location

A popular phrase may be adapted here: 'There are only three things that are important when setting up an agency: location, location, location'. This drives home the fundamental point that, from your customers' point of view, the convenience of the location is the main criterion in their choice of a travel agent, especially if they require little more than a simple holiday booking service offering the best possible price.

Sites need to be researched carefully. Existing pedestrian flows should be noted, as should barriers, whether physical or psychological. For instance, shops on traffic 'islands' where pedestrians have to use subways to cross the road will find it difficult to attract passing trade. Parking is often difficult in town centres, so if there are too many restrictions and no nearby car parks, this can be a further important disincentive to your customers. The local planning office should be consulted to examine any plans for redevelopment in the area. Residential redevelopment in the immediate area could be an important plus for the site, while commercial redevelopment nearby may pose a threat.

Any agent expecting to attract casual passing trade who chooses a little-used side street away from the main shopping area merely because rents or rates are lower, will be at a major trading disadvantage. If, however, the agent aims to serve clients seeking a professional agency via the Internet or those seeking a specialist to advise on a complex travel itinerary, then that side street, or even an upper floor, may adequately serve the purpose.

Clients are attracted to roomy shops with plenty of rack space and a bright, cheerful, inviting atmosphere to tempt them in. Increasingly, windows are designed not as settings to display brochures or destination publicity, but as living advertisements for the shop's interior. Good lighting, warm colours, comfortable chairs, desks rather than impersonal counters, all affect clients' perceptions of the agency and their motivation to enter the shop. Once inside, the good agent takes advantage of the opportunity to make a sale, but enticing clients through the door is the first step in selling.

Example

TUI

Thomson Travel – the retail arm of TUI in Britain – announced two significant changes to the way that it would do business in 2005.

It planned to change the whole image of the travel agent, with far less clutter in its windows (allowing a fuller view of the interiors for passers-by) and a reduction in point-of-sale displays in favour of more discreet, comfortable and tasteful furnishings. This was its strategy in its battle for dominance in the multiples sector.

It also made the decision to expand its product range, most notably by the experimental sale of property abroad to second home buyers.

Operations

Sunday trading has become much more common in recent years, although it is often restricted to key booking periods of the year, such as the post-Christmas booking season. Longer opening hours are now deemed necessary to compete with the facility to make bookings on the Internet, which can still be made at any time of the day or night. An example of this is the Australasian-based travel agent Flight Centre, which announced Sunday opening in a bid to achieve business growth of 15 per cent.[19]

In the past, agents earned their revenue largely in the form of commissions on sales. Levels of commission have varied over time and according to the travel product sold, but, typically, have been highest for package tour sales (between 10 and 15 per cent), with transportation companies paying slightly lower rates and other services even less. This pattern has changed radically within the past few years, as principals have sought to remain profitable by cutting costs and finding cheaper means of distributing their products.

Many airlines have changed their payment structures to agents, often withdrawing commissions entirely, forcing the agents to charge a service fee to their customers for the sale of tickets. This has been a noted practice of the budget carriers, led by Ryanair, whose bookings are almost entirely via the Internet, but this soon became the practice of many international carriers, too. In September 2007, Qatar Airlines announced that they would be eliminating commission payments (they had been 9 per cent in 2004). This followed an announcement by its rival, Emirates, which chose to reduce its commission payments to 5 per cent.[20] Some airlines pay a fixed-level fee according to the class of ticket purchased (paying higher fees for business or first-class tickets). KLM moved from paying 7 per cent commission to a fixed fee in January 2001, while Lufthansa moved to a service fee in January 2002.[21] British Airways (now taking over half its bookings via the Internet) has moved in a similar direction, not only reducing commissions, but also withdrawing ticketing and GDS privileges for agents achieving less than £50,000 worth of sales.

The nature of the local market significantly affects such decisions, however. For example, in India, the use of travel agents is high, so the decision to reduce commissions in India was only announced in the summer of 2008, although neither SpiceJet nor GoAir, both low-cost airlines, have paid commission in recent years. In 2006, Kingfisher bucked the trend and announced that it would double the commission it paid (to 10 per cent), recognizing that it sold 60 per cent of its tickets through travel agents in India.[22] In the summer of 2008, however, it too announced a plan to bring in zero commission, after its competitor Air India implemented such a policy.

Among tour operators, Thomson led the way in reducing the basic rates of commission paid to its agents and introducing a complex reward system for greater sales effort, including directional selling. Recently, however there appears to be a general move towards increasing commission levels again to encourage loyalty. The Association of Independent Tour Operators (AITO) announced that it would provide a minimum of 10 per cent commission to its travel agents,[23] while Hays Travel (a large independent agency in the UK) has negotiated terms with the major tour operators and is refusing to accept less than 12 per cent commission on sales.[24]

Those principals that do pay commissions will generally offer higher levels to agents that are members of consortia – that is, they have banded together to achieve agreed sales targets in order to compete with the multiples. This can add 2.5 per cent or more to the earnings of the agent, particularly for the sale of package tours. It is still rare, though, to find an agent averaging earnings of more than 10–11 per cent on the total of the revenue achieved during the year. The likelihood is that, eventually, commissions will cease to be paid, with agents initiating fees to cover their expenses.

Agents at first resisted changes to the commission structure, arguing that their customers would be angered by attempts to charge a transaction fee and would therefore be more likely to book direct with the airlines. The introduction of ticketless travel by some airlines, which not only saves airlines and other travel suppliers the cost of issuing tickets, but also encourages direct bookings, has further reduced agency revenue.

Evidence from the USA tends to support the agents in their view that service charges have been difficult to impose. Commissions were capped by the airlines there in the mid-1990s, but the public initially resisted attempts to impose fees, turning to book on the Internet. In 1995, 70 per cent of all airline tickets issued in the USA were sold through agents, but this had dropped to just 30 per cent a decade later. Some 40 per cent of agents have left their jobs in the interim as a result, with many turning to working as travel counsellors from their homes. Virtually all US agents now charge transaction fees, while attempting to increase sales of package holidays and cruises to maintain revenues. Research by the American Society of Travel Agents (ASTA) suggests that fees are usually around $25 for arranging air travel[25] and that US customers now expect to pay such a service fee.[26]

Other regions of the world are following suit. In Brazil, negotiations between airlines and its national association of travel agents led to an agreed policy[27] that will mean the commission received for booking air tickets will move from being paid by the airlines to a standard service fee charged to customers. In Australia there has been a significant increase in earnings through service fees, with estimates that travel agents gain around 15 per cent of their earnings through fees.[28]

Example

Australian travel agents charge service fees

Research completed by the Travel Compensation Fund – a financial protection scheme for travel agents in Australia – reported on the use of service or transaction fees by its members. It found that, out of the 2900 businesses reviewed, almost one-third of agents were charging a fee to customers, with an average fee of around AUS$25 for domestic services and AUS$60 for making international travel arrangements (around 3 per cent of businesses were charging more than AUS$100).

Source: Travel Compensation Fund, 'Annual report', 2006.

In the UK, package tours represent by far the largest proportion of all agents' sales, although an increasing proportion of these involve some tailor-made elements. Typically, overseas holidays account for the majority of those sales, with air transport a declining element. Domestic holidays – a growing area of potential sales – have been estimated to take up to 4 per cent, while the remainder is divided between cruises, rail and coach bookings and miscellaneous services. Tailor-made packages, or dynamic packaging, are steadily eroding the traditional tour operator-based package tour product for many agencies.

The business travel agency

Those agents located close to city centres or other centres of business and industry, such as an industrial estate, may also try to capture the business travellers within their territory. This is a highly specialized market, however, for which staff must have greater skills and will be competing against the large business travel corporations that have contacts with suppliers, allowing them greater flexibility in negotiating prices.

Any commissions earned from suppliers may have to be split with business clients, as part of the contract to act as the travel agency for the company. It is increasingly common for business travel agents to negotiate discounted travel with the principal (receiving no commission), then pass on those improved rates to the company they serve, but charge a management fee for the service.

There are a number of approaches used in fee-based contracts, the most common being:

- a flat fee, usually payable per month, based on predicted levels of business
- rebate of any commission paid to the agency, the agency charging a fixed amount per transaction
- a simple fee per ticket set-up
- variable fees charged according to the complexity of the transaction
- a minimum fee charged per transaction with the guarantee of there being a minimum number of transactions per month.

It is also common to find contracts drawn up based on fees that depend on the agency achieving a certain level of cost savings for the company. Agreements will also generally include extended credit terms, whereby accounts do not have to be settled until 10 to 12 weeks after the receipt of tickets. One drawback of a system in which commission is fully rebated to the client is that the supplier, such as a hotel, gains no sales benefit from increasing its commission rates to its distributors, so must look for other strategies to gain the agency's support.

Management issues

Businesses are extremely demanding customers. The level of service that agencies must offer to retain their patronage is considerable. Focusing on the business community requires not only additional skills and knowledge but also a willingness to provide extended hours of service (for the convenience of the businesses) and a level of service far beyond what would be expected of counter staff in a leisure agency. Documentation such as visas may have to be arranged for clients, often at short notice, then delivered to their address, possibly out of normal business hours. Senior staff must be accessible at any time to arrange last minute travel. Professional business travel staff will expect to be paid well above the rates paid to counter staff in leisure agencies, yet the margins may be slimmer. The additional costs of handling these arrangements must be considered by the agent, particularly where credit is offered to businesses. It is not unusual for companies to delay payments until well beyond the dates they were due, while the agent is still obliged to make payments to principals on time. Thus the agency is helping to fund those companies' cash flow at its own expense.

All of this makes business travel a difficult field to enter as an independent, regardless of the level of personal service it is willing to offer. The financial attraction of the larger business accounts – often exceeding a million pounds a year – however, results in many agents competing for the business by offering extra levels of service, fares expertise to guarantee lowest prices and implant offices.

Implant offices are those based in the business client's own premises but staffed by the agency, specifically to handle the company's travel needs exclusively. To justify this, the company must be certain that the revenue generated will be sufficient to cover the high costs of setting up and operating such an additional branch.

As the highest discounts can be offered by agents negotiating the best deals with their principals, this has once again led to the multiple branch agencies dominating the business house market – American Express, Carlson Wagonlit, BCD, Hogg Robinson and FCm. Furthermore, some business travel agents are also members of international consortia (for example, Advantage Business Travel), which offer them even greater influence and purchasing power with the principals. With the global buying power of such groups, airline and other tickets can be purchased at the lowest possible price for business house clients.

Example

Changes to travel management companies (TMCs)

Changes occurred in the business travel agency sector during 2006 when the owners of the global agency BTI (Hogg Robinson Group and BCD Holdings NV) agreed to separate their interests in BTI and, although existing contracts with BTI customers were maintained, these two businesses have sought to establish their own networks.

While Hogg Robinson rebranded as HRG, BCD Holdings established BCD Travel following the purchase of TQ3 (from TUI AG) and combined Worldtravel BTI and the Travel Company. Their operations now span the globe with 1300 locations in 90 countries and estimated sales of around US$12 billion annually.[29]

FCm, owned by the Australian company Flight Centre, was launched to rebrand several business travel organizations that it had acquired, including Corporate Traveller (the business division of Flight Centre), Sydney Business Travel and Convention and Incentive Services (CIS). Since their launch, they have acquired additional travel businesses in India and the USA. They now have a worldwide network of partners and employ more than 5000 people.

Carlson Wagonlit completed the purchase of Navigant in August 2006, allowing it to double its operations in North America and strengthen its business in the Asia-Pacific region. With more than 20,000 employees on 150 countries, its operations are extensive.

The Guild of Travel Management Companies, established in 1967, is the professional body representing the leading business travel agents in the UK and accounts for some 75–80 per cent of all the airline tickets sold in the UK. The Guild's role is to represent the interests of business agents and their clients and improve the standards and quality of travel for its members through negotiation with suppliers such as airlines, airports and hotel chains. With its encouragement, associations have been established in Germany, Ireland, Italy, the Netherlands, Portugal and Spain and these groups work together as the Guild of European Business Travel Agents.

Large companies often employ specialist travel managers, who act as buyers of travel products for their employees and liaise between the employees and travel agency. Purchases arranged centrally allow the company to manage travel arrangements (perhaps to adhere to company travel policies) and use the specialist knowledge of the travel manager to gain better prices. These managers have their own professional body in the UK the Institute of Travel Management (ITM). It seeks to use its influence to obtain better deals for its members and acts as a mouthpiece and watchdog for this section of the industry.

There is an equivalent organization in the USA – the National Passenger Traffic Association (NPTA) – which has actually set up its own travel agency to make further cost savings for its members. Both the ITM and NPTA are represented in the International Business Travel Association (IBTA), which includes a number of Continental European organizations among its members.

Some large corporations have gone a stage further. Recognizing that they have the buying power to organize their own travel arrangements without the intercession of a travel agent, they will negotiate direct with airlines for their tickets and discount agreements, cutting out intermediaries entirely. Once again, the online suppliers and agencies are making it easier for the customer to benefit by going direct.

Travel agency skills and competences

Due to the extremely competitive nature of the retail travel business, two factors become important if the agency is to succeed: good management and good service. Good management will ensure that costs are kept under control, members of staff are motivated and the agency goes out actively to seek customers rather than wait for them to come through the door. Good service will ensure satisfied clients, help to build a loyal clientele and encourage word-of-mouth recommendation, which will increase the local share of the market for the agency.

Despite the expansion of the large multiples, most independent travel agents are still small businesses, in which the owner acts as manager and employs two or three members of staff. In such an agency there is little specialization in terms of the usual division of labour and staff will be expected to cope with all the activities normally associated with the booking of travel, which will include:

- advising potential travellers about resorts, carriers, travel companies and travel facilities worldwide
- making reservations for all travel requirements
- planning itineraries of all kinds, including complex, multi-stopover independent tours
- accessing relevant supplier and destination websites
- issuing documentation, including travel tickets and vouchers
- communicating by telephone, e-mail and letter with travel principals, tour operators and customers
- maintaining accurate files on reservations
- maintaining and displaying stocks of travel brochures
- mediating and negotiating with suppliers in the event of customer complaints.

It is ironic that the travel product requires perhaps greater knowledge on the part of retail staff than does virtually any other product, yet in many countries travel agents' salaries still lag behind those of others in the retail industry. This makes it particularly hard for agency managers to attract and retain skilled staff. Agents argue that competition and discounted prices make it impossible to pay higher salaries, although the opportunity for free or discounted travel does provide an additional employee benefit. Principals have come to accept that their retailers cannot be expected to have detailed knowledge of every product and concentrate instead on providing agents with easier access to information through websites, reservation systems and brochures.

In addition to product knowledge, therefore, the main skills that counter staff require include the ability to read timetables and other data sources, source 'best buy' airline fares, complete tickets and have sufficient knowledge of their customers to be able to match customers' needs with the products available. All staff today are also required to be familiar with the latest technology, including the use of e-mail, fax and accessing websites and computer reservations systems (CRSs) of all types.

The ticketing function is largely undertaken via computers and, arguably, fare quotations and ticketing skills are becoming less important for most agency staff, apart from those dealing with business travel. An understanding of the principles underlying the construction of fares, however, can be helpful – for example, so that staff can explain complex fares to customers – and, of course, there will be a continuing need for fares experts in the industry.

Constructing fares is a complex subject and entails a lengthy period of training, coupled with continuous exercise of these skills. A number of internationally recognized courses are available to provide these skills, including, in Britain, those offered by British Airways, which meet IATA requirements and can be taken up to the BA Fares and Ticketing Part II level, indicating full competence in meeting any requirement for fare construction and ticketing. In some cases, large travel agency chains have centralized the fare calculation role so that a handful of experts can quickly determine the lowest prices for a particular journey by air when requested by a member of their counter staff. For most air fares, however, agents are now dependent on quotations given by carriers or intermediaries via the CRS and websites.

In addition to the counter staff functions, agency managers (who frequently spend time at the counter themselves) are required to fulfil a number of administrative functions. On the financial side, these will include:

- maintenance and control of the agency's accounts
- invoicing clients
- effecting bank reconciliations (matching payments made and received on the bank statement with those in the customer and supplier accounts records)
- preparing and controlling budgets
- providing an estimate of the cash flow in the company on a month-by-month basis
- controlling expenditure.

Sales records must be kept and sales returns completed regularly for travel principals. All these back office jobs are often computerized, even in the case of smaller independent agencies.

Managers are also responsible for safeguarding their stock of tickets and other negotiable documents, promoting their business and recruiting, training and supervising office staff. Managers will try to ensure that staff are motivated – in general, to provide good customer service and, specifically, to achieve particular sales targets or goals. Managers will often use educational study or familiarization (fam) trips and training programmes as well as commission bonuses to enhance staff knowledge and motivation. Trips are usually provided by tour operators or destination marketing organizations in order to enhance the product awareness of travel agents and, thus, increase sales. There is now much greater emphasis on the educational element of such trips,[30] rather than these being free holidays, with little product knowledge being developed.

Finally, managers need to control and regularly update their websites and oversee the preparation and distribution of e-newsletters to clients. Regular contact with clients via the Internet or by post is now essential if business is to be retained and clients discouraged from booking direct on the Web.

Customer contact skills

The way in which staff communicate with clients is, together with the essential product knowledge they display, a key ingredient in an agency's success. These communication skills can be divided into three distinct categories:

- language skills
- personal and social skills
- sales skills.

Written communications with clients that demonstrate poor sentence construction, grammar or spelling reflect not just on the employee but also on the company itself. When such correspondence goes out under the signature of a senior member of staff, the image of the company suffers a still more serious blow.

Personal and social skills are also very important. Serving the public should not be confused with servility (being a servant). The key is ensuring that customers are served effectively and with respect. Customers expect to be received warmly, with a genuine smile of greeting. Staff are expected to be unfailingly calm and cheerful, whatever stress they may be experiencing during their working day. These qualities need to become second nature to counter staff.

First impressions weigh heavily and staff will be judged by their dress and appearance. Tourism employees must be prepared to adjust to the constraints that the job imposes if they wish to succeed in the industry. Employers will insist on neat hairstyles, suitably discreet make-up for female staff and high overall standards of grooming and appearance – often to the extent that counter staff in the agency chains will be required to wear a uniform. Personal hygiene is, of course, essential.

The way employees sit, stand or walk says a great deal about them and their attitude towards their customers. Staff who meet face-to-face with customers will be expected to look alert and interested, avoid slouching when they walk and sit upright rather than slump in their chairs. These non-verbal signals all say a lot about the attitude of the company to its customers. The scene of employees filing their nails or talking to their friends on the telephone while customers try to attract their attention is a common one in training videos and one that encourages us to think about how we present ourselves in public.

A warm, welcoming smile and friendly manner when greeting a customer approaching the desk will convey a positive view of the company and make the customer feel at home and in a buying frame of mind. Attentiveness to the customer is not only polite, it ensures that vital client needs are recognized, enabling the employee to match needs with products. When talking to customers and greeting them, the employee should maintain eye contact and a manner that will breed confidence in the agency and its staff's product knowledge. Even handshakes are important cues to confidence – they should be firm and offered willingly. Use of the client's name enhances the relationship.

Even the way in which staff answer the telephone can help to generate the right image of the company. Telephones should be answered quickly and competently. As there are no dress and appearance cues that enable the client to make a judgement, the voice becomes the sole factor. Trainers emphasize the need to smile, even when on the telephone, as an impression of friendliness can still be conveyed in the voice. If clients are asked to hold, they should be given the reason and regularly checked to ensure that they are still holding. If the person they are trying to reach is busy, an offer should be made to call them back and this should be followed up to ensure that they have been called back. Similarly, if employees cannot give an answer immediately to a problem, they should offer to call the client back with the answer in a short while and then ensure that they do so. Failure to call back is one of the commonest sources of frustration for clients and can easily lead to the loss of their business to a competitor.

The e-mail has become a significant mode of communication with customers. Research suggests that, as a booking tool, an e-mail takes 30 per cent less staff time than the telephone,[31] but it is vital that e-mails are dealt with promptly and accurately to ensure that customers feel they are receiving a high quality of service.

Good customer contact is deemed so important that many of the multiples use mystery shoppers to monitor the experience provided to customers. In such cases, mystery shoppers will telephone or visit the shop to make travel arrangements. After the visit, they will report back to management regarding the quality of the service they received. This technique can be used to identify weak points in service delivery and encourage staff to maintain or improve service levels by linking assessment to bonuses. It can also be used evaluate the services of competitors, too, and establish comparison benchmarks.

Travel trade magazines also employ mystery shoppers to compare shops in the same town, providing a regular article focusing on service levels. *Travel Trade Gazette* (TTG) and *Travel Weekly* both complete regular mystery shopper assessments, monitoring staff appearance, product knowledge, sales techniques (including whether holiday extras were offered), suitability of the product offered (in relation to the stated requirements of the shopper) and progression of the enquiry towards a booking.

The national tourist board for Australia has taken to using mystery shoppers to test agencies that specialize in selling holidays to their country in order to encourage accurate product knowledge.[32]

The sales sequence

Good social skills and high-quality customer service can build an atmosphere that encourages buying, but closing a sale requires an understanding of the techniques involved.

Effective selling is the outcome of four stages in the selling process, which together make up the sales sequence:

- establishing **rapport** with clients
- **investigating** clients' needs
- **presenting** the product to the clients
- getting clients to take action by **committing** themselves to the purchase.

Below, each of these stages is examined in more detail.

Rapport

To sell products successfully, one must first match them to the customers' needs. If the clients buy a product that they do not really want or which does not provide the satisfaction they were looking for, they simply will not come back again. As no travel agency can survive without a high level of repeat business, achieving one-time sales is clearly not enough; customers must be satisfied in the longer term.

To achieve this, the first step is to build **rapport** (a trusting relationship), by engaging clients in conversation, gaining their trust and learning about their needs. This process also allows the salesperson to judge how receptive clients are to new ideas and how willing they are to have products sold to them. Some customers prefer to self-select, so should not be badgered into a sale, while others need and seek advice more openly.

To generate a two-way conversation, the opening phrase 'Can I help you?' has to be avoided – it simply invites the reply, 'No thanks, I'm just looking'. A more useful way of opening a conversation would be to use a phrase such as, 'Do you have a particular type of holiday in mind?' or, to a customer who has just picked up a brochure, 'Were you just looking for sun, sea and sand holidays or had you something more adventurous in mind?' This forces a reply, and encourages the client to open a conversation.

Investigation

Once you have gained clients' trust, the next step is to **investigate** their needs more thoroughly. Once again, it is necessary to ask open questions that elicit full answers rather than a simple 'yes' or 'no'. The sort of information needed to draw out the client will include:

- who is travelling and the number in the group
- when they wish to travel and how long they want to stay at a destination
- their preferred mode of travel
- their choice of destination
- what they expect to pay.

The last is one of the hardest for junior staff. It requires good judgement to know whether the cost of the holiday is critical and, if so, what the limits might be. If customers mention a figure, one should not take it for granted that this is the maximum they are willing to pay. The industry has encouraged holidaymakers to believe that holidays are invariably cheap, but one is doing clients a disservice not to point out that cheapness is not necessarily value for money and, by paying a little more, one might have a better guarantee of satisfaction. The good salesperson is one who can encourage clients to consider products at a higher price while reassuring them that their best interests are being considered. It is generally better to wait for clients to give an indication of their budget than to question them directly on this point.

Clients may have only the vaguest idea about where they want to go, what they want to do, even what they expect to pay. Needs must never be assumed, even when there is a clear statement of intent. For example clients who say that they do not want to go on a package holiday may merely be revealing a deep-seated prejudice that such holidays are down-market. Alternatively, they may have had a bad experience of earlier such holidays. The salesperson's task is to tease out the real reason so that the appropriate product can be offered. For example, a tailor-made independent inclusive tour may offer the best solution, as the client would not be part of a crowd.

Sometimes it will be clear to the salesperson that the client has superior knowledge about the destination or is seeking information about a little-known destination. In these conditions, it is preferable to admit ignorance and either offer an introduction to another member of staff with better knowledge of the destination or offer to obtain more information for them.

Presentation

Once the salesperson is satisfied that they know exactly what the client needs, they may go on to the next stage – **presenting** the products that they feel will suit the client. The aim will be to present not only the features of the holiday being offered, but also their benefits:

'Travelling in the early spring, you have the advantage of lower prices *and* this can be the nicest time of the year in the Austrian valleys, as the blossom is out and it is before the mass of tourists arrive at the height of the season.'

Product knowledge is, of course, critical for success in gaining clients' confidence to the point where they will be willing to accept the salesperson's recommendations. Even if they feel that what they are offering is exactly suitable for their client, it is always a good idea to offer an alternative, so that the client has the opportunity to choose. If the salesperson then demonstrates just how one holiday is a better buy than the other, this will make it easier for the client to understand the options being recommended.

At this stage in the sales sequence, the salesperson will often have to handle objections. Sometimes objections are voiced only because the client needs reassurance or they have not yet fully understood the benefits being offered to them. At other times objections occur because not all the client's needs have yet been met and then a process of patient questioning may be needed once again to draw out the possibly hidden motives for the objections.

Commitment

This final stage closes the sale. This means getting clients to take action – ideally, to buy, but, of course, some clients will need more time to consider the offer. The aim of the salesperson is to get the best possible outcome from the sales sequence – taking an option (placing the required product on hold for the customer), getting the clients to call back later or getting them to agree that the salesperson may call them later to follow up the sale.

The good salesperson is always looking for the buying signals that reveal clients are ready to buy: 'Would you like me to see if I can get you a reservation for that date?' can prompt clients who are dithering about taking action. Care must be taken, however – never push clients into a sale before they are ready to buy or they may be lost forever.

After-sales service

Finally, having received the deposit for a firm booking, the salesperson must remember that the sales job is not yet finished. Different countries place various legal obligations on travel agents, so it may be necessary to provide customers with detailed information on visas or other terms and conditions of the booking (such as rights with regard to cancellation). Even after the booking has been confirmed, the tour operator or principal may make changes (such as altering flight times) and customers will need to be notified of these by the agent. In some cases flights may be cancelled and alternative arrangements will need to be discussed and agreed with the travellers. Clients may also want to make changes to bookings and will expect the salesperson to provide advice and make the arrangements accordingly.

Example

Travel agents benefit from US airline problems

The summer of 2007 saw the US airline industry struggling to minimize cancellations and desperately try to maintain punctuality levels – important when many passengers are connecting with other services. In the month of July, the Department of Transport reported that more than 30 per cent of flights arrived late, leading to a dramatic increase in customer complaints (which were more than double those for the previous year). Cancellations were running high, with poor weather and staffing issues adding to the usual pressures caused by mechanical problems. In fact, Northwest Airlines cancelled more than 12 per cent of its schedule during late June and July.

While the carriers do assist their passengers in getting rebooked when flights are delayed, this can often take time. Anecdotal evidence has suggested that US customers are returning to travel agents, who can help them when flights are delayed or cancelled. Small business owners in particular are recognizing that it takes time for them to rearrange travel, so they are passing this responsibility back to travel agents, who have the experience and contacts to deal with this efficiently.

Source: J. Roberts, 'Got your book – travel agents find business in airline problems', *The Commercial Appeal*, USA, Scripps Howard, 5 September 2007.

It is beneficial for agencies to try to gain the loyalty of customers, so the salesperson must continue to show interest and concern for clients, helping to reinforce the sale and their commitment to return to make future travel arrangements. Many agents now send a 'welcome home' card to their clients after their return from holiday, to invite them to come into the agency to talk about their experiences and ensure they will remember the agency in the future. The medium of e-mail is invaluable for keeping in touch with clients – communication is immediate and there is minimal cost involved.

Training and qualifications

Formal training qualifications for the industry are both diverse and confusing. Not all courses that have been introduced are universally welcomed or understood by the industry. Some national associations provide professional development training, which can help to maintain quality within the industry as well as enhancing the career opportunities of their members.

In the USA, the American Society of Travel Agents (ASTA) operates Model Agency courses, which encourage agency managers to evaluate their business operations and improve their services.

The Australian Federation of Travel Agents (AFTA) offers certificated courses to develop the knowledge and skills of those entering the industry, as well as continuous professional development through a skills accreditation initiative – the Australian Travel Professionals Program, which replaced their travel agents' qualification (ATAQ).

In the UK, ABTA has supported professional recognition for formal qualifications through its ABTA Gold awards for those in the industry and the awarding of Certified Travel Consultant and Certified Senior Travel Consultant status, according to qualifications achieved.

Example

UK qualifications in travel agency studies

After numerous changes to qualifications, both professional and academic, over the past few years, UK training provision is now overseen by People 1st, a government-sponsored skills body. The Certificate in Travel (for travel agents), formerly known as ABTAC, is among the most recently introduced programmes and runs in parallel with a similar Certificate in Travel for tour operators, both of which are generally supported by the trade. These are delivered through the trade's training body, TTC Training, which, although no longer owned by ABTA, retains close links with it.

National Vocational Qualifications (NVQs) are also available, supervised by City and Guilds, which, along with Edexcel, are the awarding bodies for travel services qualifications.

Students in full-time education can follow General National Vocational Qualifications (GNVQs), National Diplomas, or newly introduced GCSEs and A levels in travel and tourism, while a variety of programmes for business travel staff have been introduced by the Guild of Travel Management Companies.

Travel agency appointments

Most principals license the sale of their services through a process of contractual agreements with travel agencies, which, as noted earlier, are called **appointments**. In effect, these are a licence to trade and receive commission for sales achieved. Some principals dispense with this formality – hotels, for example, will normally pay commission on any sales made through a reputable travel agency without any formal agreement. In addition, agents may join trade associations to gain formal national recognition as travel agents.

Dealing with principals

Most contracts with principals are non-exclusive – that is, they do not prevent an agent from dealing with the principal's competitors. Occasionally, however, a contract may offer an agency the exclusive right to sell a product and may, further, restrict an agent's ability to deal with other directly competing companies.

Unless expressly stated in a contract, agents do not have the automatic right to deduct their commission from the monies due to principals. If bonus commissions are paid for targets achieved, it is generally the case that these sums of money are paid to agents at the end of the season, rather than immediately following the achievement of a target. These facts must be kept in mind by the agent when estimating their business cash flow.

A licence is required if commission is to be paid on the sale of services of members of IATA (apart from sales of purely domestic tickets). Although IATA carriers have been reducing or eliminating commissions for agents, some are continuing to pay them and it is important for travel agents that wish to offer a full range of services to either hold the necessary IATA appointment or have an arrangement with another agency that does so – that agent issuing tickets on their behalf. New agents are permitted to sell air tickets and earn income by sharing commission with an established IATA agent.

There were around 2800 IATA-accredited agencies in the UK in 2004. IATA's Agency Distribution Office deals with applications for licences, a process that can take up to 45 days.

A representative from IATA's Agency Investigation Panel visits the agent to judge whether or not the site is easily identified as a travel centre and suitable for the sale of tickets (while proof of turnover is no longer required of agents, IATA wishes to satisfy itself that the agency has the scope to generate business). The number and competence of staff will be judged, with at least one member of staff being expected to have two years' agency experience and, preferably, hold a Certificate of Travel Agency Competence, ABTAC and/or an equivalent qualification in fares and ticketing (holding an ABTAC qualification allows six months' remission in the experience required). The representative must also be satisfied that the agency premises are secure and any ticket stock held can be safeguarded, although this is becoming less of an issue with the growing use of e-tickets. These in turn are posing new security problems, as IATA must now take steps to reassure themselves that the agent will not issue hundreds of e-tickets and disappear with the clients' money.

If approved, a bond is taken out to cover the agency's anticipated monthly IATA turnover. An entrance fee is payable and there is a small annual subscription. This approval enables the agent to sell the services of all IATA members.

Approval is also required to make commissionable sales on the services of railways, coach tickets, domestic airline services and other principals, such as shipping and car hire firms. Obtaining approval for most of these has been largely a formality for agents holding ABTA and IATA appointments. Appointments to sell travel insurance, however, involve closer scrutiny as the agent will be acting as a broker for the insurance service concerned. Insurance companies have generally tightened up on standards for their brokers, including those retailers operating in the travel industry.

Membership of trade bodies

In the UK there are no legal requirements to meet when setting up as a travel agent, but, in some countries, including most of those within the European Union, governments do exercise licensing control over agencies. In some cases licensing is carried out at government level (such as in Australia and some parts of the USA). In addition to government licensing, many countries also have national associations, established to promote the interests of their members, which includes establishing standards of practice to protect customers and the industry, as well as lobbying government on policy affecting travel agents and their customers.

Example

The role of trade associations – the case of the Association of British Travel Agents (ABTA)

Until 1993, any travel agent wishing to sell the products of an ABTA tour operator had to be a member of ABTA. In turn, ABTA tour operators could only sell their services through ABTA retailers. This reciprocal agreement, known as Stabiliser, was technically a constraint on trade and, as such, was challenged by the Office of Fair Trading. The Restrictive Practices Court upheld the agreement in 1982, however, after an appeal by ABTA, on the grounds that it was in the public interest as ABTA's inhouse scheme of protection for consumers against the collapse of a member company was recognized as one of the best in the world. A Common Fund, provided out of membership subscriptions, allowed clients of a travel agency to continue with their holidays even if the travel agency they had booked with went into liquidation before the tour operator received payment for the tour. This complemented the protection offered by ABTA against the collapse of a tour operator. Many earlier conditions imposed on members by ABTA, however, such as a prohibition on discounting and the sale of non-travel products ('mixed selling'), were overturned by the Restrictive Practices Court.

In 2000, ABTA also removed the distinction between tour operator and retail agent membership, absorbing members into a single class. In July 2008, ABTA merged with the Federation of Tour Operators (FTO) to enhance its ability to support its members across the industry.

Membership of ABTA provided many advantages, but it also imposed various obligations. Premises were open to inspection and agents were obliged to abide by a strict Code of Conduct complementing that of the tour operator. Some key regulations remain. Members must satisfy ABTA about their financial standing and qualifications. ABTA also requires its members to have at least one member of its customer-facing staff with a minimum of two years' experience (reduced by six months for staff holding formal qualifications).

Some independent agents operate outside the ABTA framework. Regulations that previously constrained non-ABTA agents effectively limited them to selling fringe services, such as coach trips, or operating as so-called bucket shops (a term we met earlier, meaning outlets used by airlines to dump unsold tickets on the market at short notice and at heavily discounted prices). The abolition of the Stabiliser agreement and the introduction of the EU's Package Travel Directive led to much greater freedom for agents to operate outside of ABTA membership, however, and so it lost many of its controlling functions. Agents became free to trade with all ABTA and non-ABTA tour operators and are now subject only to legal requirements to carry satisfactory bonds against financial collapse. These changes did not lead to the wholesale withdrawal of members from ABTA.

ABTA represents the interests of both tour operators and travel agents. Given the potential conflict of interests between these two groups, and other conflicts that can arise between the multiples and independent agencies, the continuing support for ABTA within the trade may seem surprising, but the importance of having a strong body to represent trade interests in consultations with government and other industry bodies and the organization's role as a mouthpiece for the industry have ensured its survival. Retailers benefit from brand recognition, the clearing house that clears payments to tour operators and the financial protection offered by the ABTA bond, which is stressed in generic advertising.

Bonding

The introduction of the European Package Travel Directive meant that member states were required to incorporate financial protection within their legislation on travel operations. It should be noted that bonding is also often a requirement of operating as a travel agent in many non-European countries.

Bonding may be undertaken in one of three ways:

1. A sum of money equal to the value of the bond can be placed in a trust account. The agent can benefit from the interest accruing on the account, but cannot touch the capital itself. As this could involve putting up a substantial amount of money, it is rarely chosen except by the largest corporations.

2. The agent can obtain an insurance policy for the amount required, paying an annual premium.

3. The agent has the bank put up the bond, against either company assets or, more commonly, the personal guarantees of the directors. A fee is charged that is substantially less than the premium paid for an insurance policy, but the directors become personally liable for the amount of the bond in the event of the company's failure.

Following the introduction of the EU Directive that made bonding compulsory for any EU tour operator or agent, agents have made their own bonding arrangements, generally through banks or other organizations. In addition to this, any retail agent that operates tours will also be required to put up a tour operating bond.

Example

Australia's Travel Compensation Fund

To offer financial protection to customers, most Australian travel agents are required to participate in the Travel Compensation Fund (TCF), in addition to holding a licence from their state government (the Northern Territory does not yet participate in this national scheme for regulating travel agents).

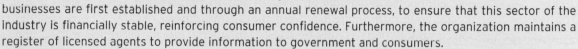

The TCF was established to provide financial compensation to consumers in the event of the collapse of a travel agent. The organization also monitors the financial viability of licensed travel agents, both when these businesses are first established and through an annual renewal process, to ensure that this sector of the industry is financially stable, reinforcing consumer confidence. Furthermore, the organization maintains a register of licensed agents to provide information to government and consumers.

In 2007, more than 4700 agency outlets were participants in the scheme, each being required to pay into the compensation fund. Recent changes to the regulations of the scheme mean that now the charge made is based on an assessment of the level of risk inherent in each organization. The renewal fee paid by members amounts to around AUS$350. The annual financial review submitted by the agents assists with assessment, as well as encouraging the financial monitoring of companies (in areas such as record keeping and managing client monies correctly).

In 2007, 18 companies collapsed, leading to more than 1600 claims affecting more than 6000 travellers. Almost AUS$4 million was paid in compensation for travel in that year – a significant increase in payments made the previous year, when 12 businesses folded, leading to claims of under AUS$1 million. In addition, claims from prior years brought the total settlements in 2007 to $4,060,490, with the average compensation amounting to $2923.

In order to recover some of the costs of this compensation, the Fund uses litigation and legal negotiation in relation to any collapsed business, though this can often take many years. Compensation for the customer, however, is provided swiftly – often within days of the claim being received – thus allowing customers the opportunity to book alternative travel.

Note though that compensation to customers is only for travel agency bookings; compensation is not paid where customers have booked direct with airlines or other principals which subsequently fail. Where the TCF has paid claims, State legislation also allows the TCF to recover the amount paid from the travel agent causing them - licensed or unlicensed (and directors), and any such recoveries are used to replenish TCF funds.

Source: Travel Compensation Fund, 'Annual report', 2007 and 2008. Available online at: **www.tcf.org.au**

The impact of computer technology

As we saw earlier, the industry has been profoundly affected by developments in technology over the past decade, particularly computers. As innovations in this field are constantly being launched or improved, information about this sphere of travel activity tends to date very quickly, so there will be little benefit to be gained from examining the detailed merits of any existing system here, and we shall take a general look at this area.

Today, computer systems in travel agencies are designed to offer three distinct facilities:

- front-office 'client relations' systems, enabling staff to access principals' CRS/GDS and websites, check availability and make reservations

- back-office systems, enabling documents such as invoices, vouchers, tickets and itineraries to be issued and accounts to be processed with principals
- management systems, producing updated figures on the company's performance to assist managers in guiding and controlling operations.

Systems have now been developed that will provide all three facilities for even the smallest independent agent, at prices that continue to fall. Alternatively, equipment can be leased to reduce capital investment and spread costs.

With regard to front-office sales and reservation activities, it is now mandatory to use computers rather than the telephone to make bookings with the leading tour operators and many principals. The retail travel sector is ideally suited to benefit from the use of computer technology. The products sold cannot be inspected directly before purchase, but may be viewed with the use of brochures or on screens; sales outlets require systems for determining the availability of transport and accommodation, often at short notice, and the ability to make immediate reservations, amendments or cancellations; complex fares and conditions of travel must be accessed in order to provide customers with accurate and current quotes.

Back-office functions can be greatly assisted by computer technology. It can produce travel documents such as tickets, invoices, vouchers and itineraries, all which can now be processed efficiently and, when needed, quite rapidly (many providers are moving towards computer-generated e-tickets, which can further enhance this process).

The travel agent also needs to process an ever increasing amount of accounting and management information quickly and computers are invaluable in this. Computers can also assist with processing customer payments, chasing customers for balances on their travel accounts, as well as managing supplier accounts. Storing customer details using database technology, they can be used to support marketing activities. More general office administration, such as personnel and payroll functions, can also be performed easily using dedicated software. In addition, business performance data can be retrieved to quickly assess areas such as sales levels and profit margins.

Global distribution systems (GDS)

In considering systems that are designed to access travel principals' reservations systems, one can distinguish between those developed by airlines and those developed by tour operators.

The airlines' travel reservation systems must be capable of booking seats on a large number of different airlines to allow maximum flexibility regarding route options (to allow a variety of origin and destination options to be available to customers). Agents currently achieve this principally by using one of the four major global distribution systems: Galileo, Amadeus, Sabre or Worldspan. In 2007, Galileo merged with Worldspan,[33] although this is not predicted to have negative effects on users as travel agents can move quite easily between GDS suppliers, thus encouraging competition between the now three providers. In recent years, there has been an effort to increase the range of products available through such systems,[34] possibly including low-cost airlines, and this may further increase the use of GDS by travel agents.

Tour operators' reservation systems

Systems to reserve products from the major tour operators are likewise accessed live on the computer. In the past this was done though a direct connection to the system using a specially designed terminal system known as Viewdata. More recently, however, many tour operators (as well as principals) have moved their operations to Internet-based systems, often incorporating specially designed reservations systems, such as the newly introduced 'I-tour', developed for Thomas Cook.[35]

Technology providing new retailing systems

While connections between suppliers and agents are being made simpler, there is still the need to provide travel agents with computer training to operate the many different systems used by suppliers (such training may be provided by the supplier). Many of those agents who have embraced technology wholeheartedly have also recognized the advantage of becoming electronic retailers, or, e-tailers (the term e-travel agent is beginning to be used to describe this function). Such agencies are adapting new technology to reach their clients online, through the Web or even through interactive digital television (IDTV). Sales via TV channels have captured a small share of the holiday market, but whether or not these will become a dominant force is yet to be seen. The move to relaunch the Sky Travel channel to focus instead on human interest programming does suggest that it may not become a major threat for travel agents.

Web-based travel retailers are also providing other Internet companies with the capability to sell travel products – by embedding their search and booking facilities within the host's website. In such cases, the design of the site is dictated by the host company, while the travel content is externally provided by the travel retailer. This allows the host the opportunity to offer its customers a range of travel products, while the Web retailer expands its sales opportunities. The host provider may also earn a small fee for each booking made through its portal.

Technology helps suppliers to serve customers directly

Suppliers, notably the airlines, are creating their own websites and it is against these that the e-tailers will have to compete. More widely, there is a rapid growth in business-to-consumer (B2C) sites, which are designed to cut out the intermediaries and sell direct to the public. In 2007, the UK tour operator Thomson reported that 60 per cent of its holidays were booked online (thus reducing its reliance on traditional travel agents). The airlines have formed their own intermediaries, as with Opodo and Orbitz, while their own websites attract consumers with competitive prices, both of which challenge sales through agents using the traditional GDSs.

The critical question is whether or not the high street agent can survive in the face of these new methods of distribution. There are claims that, while the World Wide Web offers more options to customers, it does not necessarily replace existing forms of distribution as answers to specific questions will need to be raised with agents. The question remains as to how agents can avoid clients coming to them to pick their brains and then going home to book their holidays on the Internet. In addition, the growth of sites such as tripadvisor.com, which allows travellers to post reports on travel products such as hotels, provides customers with extensive information to aid their decisions. Such sites are considered to be unbiased (although some unscrupulous hotels will post positive comments about their own properties) and are a growing source of information for Internet customers, reducing their need to speak directly to a travel agent.

Technology and generating markets for travel products

Not all markets are currently threatened by the changes in distribution network that have occurred though the development of technology and use of the Internet. While access to computers as well as connection to the Internet have occurred in many key markets, it has not penetrated all areas. For example, it has been reported that, in India, while online travel companies exist, low Internet usage, limited access to credit cards (with sufficiently high credit limits) and concern over payment security has restricted online sales.[36] To counter this, some online companies are considering opening high street outlets.

Opinion is divided on whether the majority of agents or only a handful of the most adaptable can survive the Internet explosion that has occurred in major travel-generating markets. Mandelbaum[37] proposed that a demand for good travel agents will continue to exist as they can assist clients when travel problems occur, are aware of the track records of products and can locate the latest special deals, often more quickly than a customer can find products though Internet searches. This suggests that those who are the most adaptable, offering a personal service, including expert advice, will be the ones who survive. The fact remains, however, that most agents have neither the knowledge nor the resources to undertake major change. Salaries are already low in the industry and the level of expertise among agents questionable when confronted with an increasingly sophisticated and well-travelled clientele. The move to cutting commissions and, in the case of the airlines, withdrawing commission entirely, must encourage many agents to charge fees. If agents are to become professionals, like solicitors, as many are arguing, how do they pay the salaries and obtain the staff with the qualifications that will be required to deliver this level of expertise?

The future of travel retailing

It is not just the travel agents, but also the entire travel industry that faces greater uncertainty than ever before. The introduction of B2C in travel – suppliers providing a direct interface with their clients – threatens both agents and tour operators. That is because, if customers are encouraged to book flights and hotels direct for less than is possible through intermediaries, how long will it be before it becomes customary for those same customers to put together their own packages?

To meet the demands of more experienced travellers who seek tailor-made trips, dynamic packaging has grown rapidly, the technology now allowing travel agents to conveniently create packages at cheaper overall prices than when separate products are purchased. This is an area that it is predicted will expand further.

New methods of retailing travel products are continually being launched. In an effort to achieve better profit margins in an increasingly competitive business environment, travel principals will be constantly evaluating new ways to distribute their products to the public. There may be further expansion of multiple or miniple agents buying tours from operators in bulk at net prices and selling these under their own brand names. Also, the squeeze on independents by the multiples is not expected to slow down. Common promotional tactics of the past few years – such as 5 per cent or no deposit bookings – are likely to become typical rather than exceptional marketing ploys. Deep discounting of holidays – a technique that favours the multiples and reduces agents' profitability – is no less popular today than when it was introduced in the previous decade. Other agents are likely to follow the example set by some that recruit home-based sales staff to visit customers in their homes, taking bookings using customized laptop computers linked to the operators' reservations systems. A freelance salesforce such as this, available at short notice 24 hours a day, may offer another solution to ensuring that travel agents have a future.

It is certain that the traditional corner-shop-type travel agent that we have known in the past is largely set to disappear. The agents of the future will be flexible, innovative and willing to move with the times and make use of the new tools of marketing that technology makes available. They can no longer be expected to share the range of product knowledge required by an increasingly sophisticated travelling public, but must find the means to access and make this information available to their clients more effectively, at a cost to customers that offers them value for money.

Meanwhile, a steadily increasing number of bookings will be made direct between principals and customers. The growth of broadband in the UK permits more consumers to surf the Net for information about travel and they will be encouraged to book direct. Digital

TV, which will replace all analogue TV in Britain by 2012 at the latest, will have hundreds of channels available for special interest programmes, including travel, making it an ideal marketing medium. At the same time, mobile phones will interact with the Internet and TV channels to enable travellers to call up information anywhere and at any time, check availability and make travel arrangements. The retail sector is the fastest-moving sector of the industry and is soon to be the subject of the greatest changes of all.

Notes

1. European Commission (1999) 'Commission decision – declaring a concentration to be incompatible with the common market and the EEA Agreement: Case No. IV/M.1524 – Airtours/First Choice', EC, C (1999) 3022 final – EN, 22 September

2. Dumazel, R. and Humphreys, I. (1999) 'Travel agent monitoring and management', *Journal of Air Transport Management*, 5, pp. 63–72.

3. Mintel (2006) 'Holiday booking process – UK', Mintel.

4. EMP Newswire (2007) 'Joystar joins Vacation.com', EMP Newswire, and Vacation.com (2007) 'Company history', Vacation.com, available online at: **www.joinvacation.com/cohistory.htm**

5. 'Triton conference merger proposal: "Deal not in best interest"', *Travel Trade Gazette UK*, 18 May 2007.

6. 'The small chains that have their eyes on the franchise', *Travel Trade Gazette UK*, 16 March 2007.

7. Mintel (2006) 'Holiday booking process – UK', Mintel.

8. 'Consumers using Internet to research travel continue to outnumber those booking online', *Enterprise*, 2007, 37, p. 5.

9. Skidmore, J. (2004) 'Agents accused of bias in selling', *The Daily Telegraph*, 6 November, p. 4.

10. ' "Carrot" approach to directional selling', *Travel Trade Gazette UK & Ireland*, 2006, 12 May, p. 7.

11. 'Homeworking firms reveal pay and hours', *Travel Trade Gazette UK & Ireland*, 2006, 24 November, p. 5.

12. Travel Counsellors (2008) media and press releases. Available online at: **www.travelcounsellors.co.za**

13. 'Oz trip spells trouble', *Scottish Daily Record*, 30 December 2006.

14. Marr, M. (2007) 'Online booking: one little, costly mistake: confusing euros and pounds added big bucks to the bill – big bucks I didn't have', *The Miami Herald*, 4 November.

15. Mintel (2006) 'Holiday booking process – UK', Mintel.

16. Adam, C. (2007) 'Package definitions get dynamic', *Travel Weekly Australia*, 7 July, p. 2.

17. Carroll, D. (2007) 'Solving the dynamic packaging puzzle', *Travel Weekly Australia*, 14 September, pp. 4–5.

18. Accreditation by the IATA is available at: **www.iata.org/training**

19. McMahon, I. (2004) 'Sunday trading move', *Travel Weekly Australia*, 10 November.

20. 'Qatar Air cuts rate to zero', *Travel Trade Gazette UK*, 10 August 2007.

21. Lubbe, B. (2005) 'A new revenue model for travel intermediaries in South Africa: the negotiated approach', *Journal of Retailing and Consumer Services*, 12(6), pp. 385–96.

22. 'Now Kingfisher hikes commission to agents (it sells 60 per cent of tickets through travel agents)', *Indian Business Insight*, 6 February 2006.

23. Noakes, G. (2006) 'AITO operators seal rate deal with retailers', *Travel Trade Gazette UK & Ireland*, 24 November, p. 12.

24. Hemmings, O. (2007) 'Hays stipulates 12% terms', *Travel Trade Gazette UK & Ireland*, 2 November, p. 1.

25. Pike, J. (2007) 'ASTA's findings on service fees', *Travel Agent*, 330, p. 12.

26. 'Charging fees', *Travel Agent*, 2006, 327, pp. 28–31.

27. Travel Weekly, (2007) 'TAM shifts agent fee to customers', *Travel Agent*, 66, p. 60.

28. Sweeney, C. (2006) 'Service fees "in full swing"', *Travel Weekly Australia*, 11 August, p. 4.

29. 'New business travel entity takes shape', *Travel Trade Gazette UK & Ireland*, 17 March, 2006, p. 2.

30. Wright, E. (2007) 'Fam academy', *Travel Trade Gazette UK & Ireland*, 2 November, pp. 56–7.

31. Beattie, D. (2004) 'Aussie technology use lags', *National Business Review*, 20 April.

32. Tourism Australia (2007) 'Italy – trade marketing activities'. Available online at: **www.tourism.australia.com/Markets.asp?lang=EN&sub=0342&al=495**

33. European Commission (2007) 'Mergers: Commission clears proposed acquisition of US provider of electronic travel distribution services Worldspan by Travelport', European Commission Press release, IP/07/1241, 21 August.

34. Talreja, V. (2007) 'GDS players to woo low-cost carriers', *The Economic Times*, 1 May.

35. Taylor, I. (2007) 'I-Tour tool could replace Viewdata', *Travel Weekly UK*, 20 July.

36. Ganesh, V. (2007) 'Online travel firms hit the ground, literally', *Hindustan Times*, 7 October.

37. Mandelbaum, R. (2004) 'Travel agents – it still pays to hire one, even in the Internet age', *Money*, April, p. 68.

Websites

ABTA	**www.abta.com**
IATA	**www.iata.org**
Travel Compensation Fund, Australia	**www.tcf.org.au**

Questions and discussion points

1. The mini case study in this chapter relating to Australia's Travel Compensation Fund examined the financial protection provided for products booked through travel agents. What advantages does the existence of this fund bring to both consumers and the travel industry?

2. Many travel agents in the USA now charge a fee for their services. Do you think that this will occur in all markets worldwide? Do you think that there are some customers who would prefer to pay a fee to have the assistance of a travel agent rather than make the booking themselves?

3. Dynamic packaging has allowed travel agents to offer flexible, tailor-made holidays for their customers. What are the benefits for the travel agent in being able to offer such products? What skills does the travel agent need if they choose to offer dynamic packaging extensively to their clients?

Tasks

1. Select a national travel agents' association (such as ABTA, DRV or SNAV) and investigate the role and activities of this association. Evaluate the many reasons for a travel agency deciding to join such an association, as well as highlighting any reservations or concerns that it may have about becoming a member.

2. You are planning a special trip and wish to visit an exotic location. Go to a travel agent in your local area and look at an online agency. Provide a report that compares and contrasts the ease with which you can do the following at the two agencies:

   • access brochures for an international holiday of your choice

   • gain information relating to a specific hotel in a holiday resort of your choice

   • find out about the visa requirements and healthcare risks of the destination of your choice.

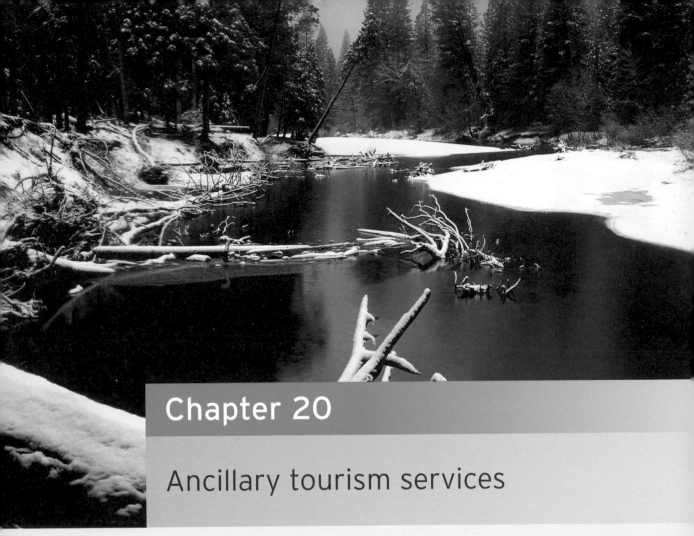

Chapter 20

Ancillary tourism services

Learning outcomes

After studying this chapter, you should be able to:

- understand the roles of guides, couriers and animateurs in meeting tourists' needs

- appreciate the use of insurance and financial services to assist the tourist

- identify the principal sources of information in use by travel agents

- be aware of marketing and consultancy services available to the tourism industry.

Introduction

> It was difficult to determine which was the hero's grave without the aid of an expert, but there was neither guide nor guardian on the spot.
>
> William Howard Russell, *My Diary North and South* Harper and Brothers, 1863, p. 29

Attempts to analyse the tourism industry can lead to the problem of defining the parameters of the industry. Some services depend largely or entirely on the movements of tourists, but are seldom considered to be part of the industry itself – customs services or visa issuing offices, for example. Other services that derive much of their revenue from tourism and yet are clearly not part of the industry include companies specializing in the design and construction of hotels, theatres, restaurants and other centres of entertainment.

There is a further category of miscellaneous tourism services that deserves to be examined more closely here. We will call these **ancillary services** – these are provided either to the tourist or to the suppliers of tourist services. Each of these will be dealt with in turn.

Services to the tourist

Guides and courier services

Unfortunately, there is as yet no term that conveniently embraces all the mediators whose function it is to shepherd, guide, inform and interpret for groups of tourists; nor can one conveniently link their functions to one particular sector of the industry. Some are employed by transport providers and tour operators; others work independently or provide their services freelance to companies in the industry.

In an industry that is becoming increasingly impersonal, as companies grow in size and tourism products themselves become more homogeneous, the role of those who interface with tourists becomes more and more important. Indeed, it may be the only feature of a package tour that distinguishes one product from another, yet, curiously, it is a role that has been progressively downgraded by the larger companies, often as a means of cutting costs. As experienced travellers see the provision of such support as less important, many tour operators have reduced the numbers of representatives in resorts, often providing any emergency assistance via telephone contacts instead. There are some areas where the use of support personnel is still popular, however, so we will examine these two similar roles – the courier and the guide. Couriers differ from guides in the sense that the latter lay stress on imparting information as the most important function of their job, while couriers may attach more importance to their social and people management functions.

Couriers

Couriers are employed by coach companies or tour operators to supervise and shepherd groups of tourists participating in tours (either on extended tours or day excursions). As well as being called couriers, they may be known as tour escorts, tour leaders, tour managers or tour directors (the latter terms imply greater levels of responsibility and status). One of their functions is to offer a sightseeing commentary on the country or region through which tourists are travelling and to act as a source of information.

Some companies dispense with the separate services of a courier in favour of a driver who is also a courier, taking on the responsibility of both driving the coach and looking after the passengers. Many drivers, however, have neither adequate general knowledge nor the necessary training to offer a truly professional guiding service and they should not, in any case, be diverted from their prime responsibility – that of driving the coach safely and expertly. Some countries frown on coach drivers who give commentaries while their coach is in motion and others forbid the practice.

Courier work is essentially freelance and offers little opportunity to develop a career. Apart from a handful of destinations that have truly year-round appeal (such as capital cities), most guiding work is temporary and seasonal, even though many professional guides choose to return to the job year after year. Some are able to find a combination of posts in summer and winter resorts, enabling them to take up paid employment for most of the year.

Prior experience is the principal criterion in gaining employment. While qualifications exist in many countries, they are not always essential to the role and, in Britain, professional training is available but by no means obligatory. The role attracts graduates with relevant qualifications such as languages or history, but many companies prefer to recruit couriers largely on the strength of their personality, ability to handle clients with sensitivity and tact and stamina – both physical and mental. In some posts, employers will lay emphasis on sales ability, as couriers may be required to sell supplementary services, such as optional excursions. Arguably, this is changing the nature of the role – commercial acumen replacing sociability.

Guides

Guides, or guide lecturers as they are frequently known, are retained by principals for their expertise in general or specialist subjects. Employment tends to be freelance and intermittent, with low-season jobs rare outside the large cities. Guides take pride in their professionalism and will often have well-established regional and national bodies to represent their interests.

In Britain, the Blue Badge is seen as the mark of attainment of professional status. It is awarded following formal periods of training and examinations, the wearer having passed national level 4 exams. The Green Badge is awarded for Associate status at level 3.

Example

The Blue Badge scheme

In the UK, there are approximately 2100 members of the Institute of Tourist Guiding (ITG) who hold the Blue Badge qualification, the majority of them based in London where guiding work is easiest to find.

The ITG was formed in 2002 and represents guides in England, Wales, Northern Ireland, the Isle of Man and the Channel Islands (the Scottish Tourist Guides Association fulfils a similar function in Scotland). While the ITG does not itself run training courses, it oversees those operated in colleges and by other training providers and sets the standard for Blue Badge and other guides.

The Guild of Registered Tour Guides is the sector's professional wing and campaigns for professional recognition and the implementation of Blue Badge standards throughout the industry.

This is a rather different picture from that in other European countries, where professional qualifications are often essential to secure a licence to operate. In France, for example, a local guide must be employed to guide in Paris, having demonstrated local knowledge in formally approved qualifications (although such qualifications can also be obtained by workers from other EU member countries, of course).

While qualified guides offer high levels of quality, many companies running coach sightseeing tours prefer to recruit amateur guides without qualifications to keep down costs. The 'added value' of a qualified guide is still seen by many employers as a luxury they cannot afford in a climate where cutting costs to achieve sales is imperative.

Example

Cracking down on illegal guides

In order to ensure that tourists have a good experience at the destination, many local authorities are introducing licensing systems to ensure the quality of the guides. This can also ensure that visitors are managed well at popular and often congested sites.

In New Zealand, the Department of Conservation (DoC) requires that companies providing guiding services must obtain a 'concession' that provides a five-year permit to guide across the popular tourist spots in the national parks. The DoC suggests that this system can maintain the safety of tourists – especially important when entering glacial areas in the mountains.

While many local operators obtain the necessary permits, the DoC is concerned at the number of foreign guides entering with their overseas tour parties, who are aware that they need a permit to guide but often operate regardless of this. As a consequence, the DoC has established a database of offenders across the area in order to track down and fine repeat offenders.[1]

A similar crackdown occurred in the Italian city of Rome. The introduction of a 'tour guide' unit as part of the city's traffic police led to the fining of many illegal guides. This move was supported by the 1200 licensed guides who feel that their income is being reduced by the illegal guides who operate across the city. In some cases, it is the licensed guides who are reporting cases of illegal guiding. There has been some criticism, however, of the exam that is taken to allow guides to obtain a licence, with suggestions that the focus does not match the needs of the tourists who visit Rome from across the globe. This has led to some businesses hiring local licensed guides to work alongside their own employees, in order to ensure that their customers are served properly.[2]

A separate category of guide is the *driver* who is also a *guide*. These are professional guides who operate on a freelance basis, taking up to four individuals on tour in their own vehicles. The close personal relationship that is built up on these tours between guide and clients is valued on both sides. This form of tailor-made package is popular with wealthier visitors to the UK.

The role of the animateur

The term **animateur** is now becoming more widely known within the tourism industry. It applies to those members of the industry who entertain tourists, either by acting out a role or providing entertainment or instruction. The English term 'entertainer' is not strictly comparable as this tends to be defined with either a stage role or **street entertainers**, who are typically jugglers, acrobats, fire-eaters or, increasingly popular in leading resorts, 'living sculptures' (see Figure 20.1).

The French term, however, relates to those whose task it is to interact with tourists in a broad range of roles that will enhance the destination or attraction where they work. It applies to the British role of the Butlin's holiday camp redcoat and to the US camp counsellor, as well as the compère on stage on a cruise ship. Other tasks include instructing tourists in sports or hobbies (ski instructors, surfing instructors), lecturing to cruise passengers or teaching them how to play bridge or other card games. Resort representatives are often expected to take on the role of animateurs when they form part of the evening's entertainment on stage at European camp sites. In Disney's theme parks there are a variety of animateur roles, the best-known of which is Mickey Mouse, but a host of other Disney characters are to be found on site, such as Alice in Wonderland, Snow White and even the Chipmunks. These workers normally have no speaking role and are there to make friends with younger visitors, posing for photographs and so on. Elsewhere, you might find animateurs dressed as historical figures at a heritage site. For example, at Williamsburg in

Figure 20.1 A living sculpture attracts tourists in Venice, Italy.
(Photo by Chris Holloway.)

Virginia, a number of staff are dressed in eighteenth-century costumes and will maintain their roles if questioned by visitors.

The job might be thought of as fairly basic, in terms of skills, but Continental Europeans take a different view – animation appears on the syllabus of French tourism and leisure qualifications, to cite just one example. This reflects the seriousness with which Continental tourism employees and employers view the role – it is one way to provide a professional service for the industry.

Financial services

This section will deal with financial services offered to tourists – insurance, foreign exchange and credit.

Insurance

Insurance is an important, very often obligatory, aspect of a tourist's travel arrangements, embracing coverage for one or more of the following contingencies:

- medical care and hospitalization (and, where necessary, repatriation – important where hospital services are of a low standard)
- personal accident
- cancellation or curtailment of holiday
- delayed departure
- baggage loss or delay
- money loss
- personal liability.

Some policies now also include coverage for the collapse of the travel agent or tour operator through which the tour was purchased – an increasingly important option in view of the growing instability in the industry, although bonded tours should be refundable in the event of a cancellation. The growth of budget airlines and their not infrequent demise point to the importance of adequate insurance, as scheduled air travel, apart from that in a package tour, is not currently protected by bonding. The inclusion of Airline Failure Insurance (AFI) is now commonly also offered to travellers when booking flights online.

Tourists may purchase insurance either in the form of a selective policy, covering one or more of the above items, or, more commonly, in the form of a standard 'package', which will include all or most of the above. The latter policy, although inflexible in its coverage, invariably offers the best value if comprehensive coverage is sought. Although most tour operators encourage their clients to buy their company's comprehensive policies, they are often more expensive than a comprehensive policy arranged by an independent insurance company. Travel agents may offer better-value insurance policies than those of an operator, but they, too, may be biased in favour of schemes paying them higher levels of commission. It is no longer legal to force clients to purchase a particular policy, although operators can demand evidence that customers are insured. Free insurance has become an attractive incentive in marketing package tours.

Other retailers are now competing with travel agents to sell travel insurance, including supermarkets, banks and high street shops, such as Marks & Spencer, while cut-price annual policies are marketed direct by insurance agents, so travel agents are faced with a very competitive environment in which to sell their products notwithstanding the attractive commissions paid.

Example

Travel Insurance in the USA

The travel insurance market in the USA has been changing over the past few years, with more travellers choosing to insure their travel arrangements. The United States Travel Insurance Association reported that around 10 per cent of travellers purchased travel insurance prior to the terrorist events of September 2001. Five years on, the number of Americans purchasing insurance packages had risen to 30 per cent of travellers.[3]

Different types of insurance cover are available, starting with cover for only trip cancellation and progressing to comprehensive insurance that includes medical cover and repatriation. One important factor influencing demand for travel insurance is that many Americans hold private health insurance, which can sometimes include cover for medical emergencies in foreign countries, so their need for cover is often focused on trip cancellation and baggage cover.

Key issues in choosing a policy are to ensure that medical coverage is sufficient to meet the needs (in the USA, bills in excess of $1 million are not uncommon for serious illnesses) and loss of any treasured individual items will be covered in full. The normal comprehensive coverage will limit compensation for total valuables and may restrict claims for any individual item lost or stolen to a figure that will be unlikely to cover the cost of an average tourist's camera, so it is important for holidaymakers to consider covering such valuables within their house contents insurance. Insurance at reasonable cost for older travellers is becoming harder to find as they are travelling more frequently but are also more likely to suffer medical difficulties than younger travellers. Doubling, or even tripling, the price of a policy is common for this group above the age of 65. Of equal concern are the high numbers of travellers who fail to insure themselves when travelling abroad. The availability of cheap flights through budget airlines and ownership of second homes abroad has encouraged people to take more short breaks but a study[4] for a UK insurance company revealed that a quarter of travellers fail to take out adequate travel insurance.

Insurance remains a lucrative business for both operators and agents, although claims have been rising in recent years. Some reports estimate that 10 per cent of holidaymakers make claims, often fraudulent, against their policies and this has led insurers to increase premiums to offset those losses.

Foreign transactions

Travellers today have an ever widening choice of ways in which they can pay for services and goods while abroad. These include:

- taking sterling or foreign banknotes with them – this can lead to loss or theft, though, and certain foreign countries have restrictions on the import or export of their currencies
- taking traveller's cheques, in sterling or currency, such as US dollars or euros
- arranging for the advance transfer of funds to a specified foreign bank or an open credit to be made available, through their own bank, at a foreign bank
- using travel vouchers
- using credit cards or charge cards
- travel money cards.

The introduction of the euro as common currency in many EU countries has made life easier for visitors touring a number of countries on the Continent. Purchasing foreign currency is relatively convenient, with many outlets offering exchange facilities. Leading travel agency chains operate their own foreign exchange desks, as do the high street banks, and the Post Office has also introduced a foreign exchange desk offering highly competitive rates. Some large department stores, for example Marks & Spencer, also provide currency exchange facilities in their major branches. Companies such as Travelex and TTT Moneycorp provide such facilities at airports and other transport hubs. The large number of foreign exchange facilities available provide people with a very wide choice, but charges fluctuate considerably and both rates of conversion and fixed charges need to be compared to judge what represents best value for money.

Traveller's cheques are also still widely used, being readily accepted throughout the world by banks and commercial institutions. They offer the holder guaranteed security, with rapid compensation for theft or loss – an advantage that outweighs the standard premium charged of 1 per cent of face value. The value of the system for suppliers is that there is generally a considerable lapse of time between the tourist purchasing traveller's cheques and encashing them. The money invested in the interim at market rates of interest provides the supplier with substantial profits. Market leaders in traveller's cheque sales in the UK are Thomas Cook (whose 'circular note', the predecessor of the traveller's cheque, originated in 1873) and American Express, which first introduced the concept in 1891. US$ traveller's cheques are useful almost anywhere in the world, and may be used as freely as cash itself within the USA.

Sending money abroad in advance of travel is useful when planning to spend some time in the same place, but it is expensive, unless electronic transfer is insisted on. It pays to shop around for the cheapest deal.

Travel vouchers such as Barclay's Visa and Citicorp provide for sterling prepayment for travel services such as car hire and hotel accommodation. Although prepaid vouchers of this kind have been in existence in the travel industry for many years, the credit organizations have greatly boosted their use in recent years.

Credit cards such as those of Visa and Mastercard (Eurocard on the Continent) are widely accepted throughout the world, but as transactions can take some time to filter through to one's bank account, users take a chance on the fluctuations of exchange rates. Some retailers, however, will now quote their prices either in local currency (such as Swiss francs) or pounds sterling and will debit accounts accordingly, so that British purchasers abroad will be aware of the actual cost for the item in their own currency. Bank charges for drawing cash abroad against both credit and debit cards can also be high. Charge cards such as American Express or Diners Club provide similar advantages and drawbacks (charge cards differ from credit cards in that accounts are due for settlement in full after receipt of an invoice from the company – credit is not extended – but the limit on charge card transactions is generally much higher than on credit cards – indeed, the company may impose no ceiling on the amount the holder may charge to their account).

As agents are required to pay a fee to the card companies when accepting credit cards in payment for travel, there has been some reluctance in the past to accept them, but credit card sales are increasing at such a rate that no agent can afford to turn this form of business away. For the most part, however, they do pass these costs on to their clients.

In the UK, payment by credit card offers the additional advantage to the traveller of the funds being protected by the card companies on amounts in excess of £100 in the event of the collapse of the agent, operator or airline with which they are dealing. The special free insurance coverage offered by some banks against the use of their cards has largely been withdrawn, however, due to the cost of servicing claims.

Another alternative recently introduced to the marketplace is travel money cards, provided by companies like Western Union, American Express, Mastercard and Fexco. These are prepaid cards loaded with a fixed sum of euros, dollars or sterling in the form of 'e-money' and a PIN code. Additional amounts may be loaded on to the card at any point, subject to an authorized maximum. The card can then be tendered for purchases or used to withdraw cash from ATMs abroad. They have already proved popular in the USA and are rapidly catching on in the UK. Their clear value is their relative protection against theft and fraudulent misuse as they cannot be used to clear a bank account and they also make it impossible for the holidaymaker to overspend. They are, however, rather expensive to use for withdrawing cash abroad and charges are made for encashing any unused balances after completing a journey.

Many countries now use chip and PIN cards, although, when used abroad, a signature is often required instead, which is felt to be less secure. Theft and the fraudulent use of cards is discouraging total reliance on plastic to make purchases and draw money when abroad. Tourists are now recommended to carry an assortment of small denomination notes, traveller's cheques and plastic cards when travelling.

Incentive travel vouchers

Incentive travel has shown considerable growth over the past few years, with companies providing their employees or dealers with attractive travel packages as rewards for achievement.

One option taken up by some companies is travel vouchers, issued in various denominations, that allow the recipient to choose their own travel arrangements. This is simply monetary reward for achievement in another form, but the appeal of travel has proved to be a stronger motivator than either cash or consumer durables. The vouchers offer greater flexibility and can be given in smaller denominations – to reward, for example, low absenteeism or the achievement of weekly targets. Some of these vouchers can only be exchanged against specific travel products or through certain travel agents, while others can be used to pay for any holiday arrangements purchased through any agent.

Duty-free shopping

Under the category of services to tourists, mention should also be made of duty-free shopping facilities, although the subject has been discussed elsewhere in this text. The purchase

Figure 20.2 An American Express office caters for foreign currency needs alongside travel arrangements. *(Photo by Claire Humphreys.)*

of duty-free goods at airports, on board ships and aircraft or at specially designated duty-free ports has been a strong attraction for tourists for a very long time.

Introduced during the first half of the twentieth century, mainly to satisfy the demands of travellers on the great ocean liners, it was extended to aircraft in 1944. The first airport duty-free shop arrived in 1947, when the Irish parliament passed the Custom-free Airport Act, giving Shannon this honour. Since those days, duty-free purchases of spirits and tobacco in particular have been effectively marketed by airports and carriers alike and the profits and sales of such items have always been substantial, accounting for large shares in the profits of many companies. Airports have achieved up to half their total operating profits through such sales, while some Scandinavian ferry companies obtain up to 70 per cent of their income in this manner.

This has led in some quarters to criticisms of profiteering, but airports reply to such criticisms by claiming that, without these profits, they would be forced to increase their landing charges, which would have a knock-on effect on carriers, which would then be forced to raise their fares. Without the benefit of duty-free shopping, transport fares do tend to rise appreciably – estimates typically point to increases ranging from 10 per cent to as high as 30 per cent. Rising congestion at airports, the requirement for earlier check-in times and flight delays all tend to enhance sales in airport shops. The high value of return in airport outlets can be seen in the announcement in 2008 that BAA would sell its duty-free shops for £546 million, providing the purchaser, Italian company Autogrill, with a 12-year concession to operate these outlets at its seven UK airports.

Tax harmonization in the European Union led to the withdrawal of duty-free privileges for travel between member states in July 1999 and many companies were badly hit by the move. To take one example, Eurotunnel alone saw a 72 per cent fall in its retail revenues in the months following the ending of duty-free sales across the Channel. Fares on cross-Channel services were raised sharply, although heightened competition succeeded in pushing them down again. In response to the decline in sales at UK ports, marketing efforts highlighted the opportunities to purchase duty-paid goods, often at French prices, which substantially undercut those in Britain. Countries such as Tunisia, Morocco and Turkey are close enough to provide alternatives for tourists for whom this benefit is important, but, with Malta and Cyprus both now drawn into the EU, the scope for duty-free visits to cheap holiday islands in the Mediterranean has dried up.

Services to the supplier

Education and training

Historically, the approach to training in the tourism industry has been a sectoral one. In the past, each sector of the industry was primarily concerned with training staff to become competent within its own sector, focusing on narrow job-specific abilities. In an industry comprising mainly small units with entrepreneurial styles of management, the benefits of formal education and training have seldom been acknowledged. Most employees of travel agencies, tour operators and hotels were trained on the job, often by observing supervisors at work. A handful of companies, such as Thomas Cook, however, were notable for their early recognition of the need for more formal, although still inhouse, training.

With the growing institutionalization of sectors, greater emphasis is placed on professionalism, the introduction of national standards and more formal modes of training. The difficulty of organizing day release for employees of smaller travel companies encouraged the development of distance learning packages. British Airways fares and ticketing courses, for example, which are offered either full-time or through self-study packs, have found national acceptance as a standard for those seeking to work in travel agencies and airlines, while Lufthansa provides similar nationally accepted courses in Germany, and the World Tourism Organization (UNWTO) and International Air Transport Association (IATA) organize internationally recognized distance learning packs for students of tourism throughout the world.

With vocational courses of this nature, the question of balance between job-specific skills and broader conceptual knowledge has long taxed employers and educationalists alike. Unlike most countries in Europe, many tourism employers in Britain still do not hold formal qualifications in high regard, still preferring to provide the job skills that are seen as essential to fulfil basic, sector-specific roles in the industry. Across the globe, however, universities and colleges now offer courses designed to provide not just essential skills but also a broader knowledge of the industry and the world of business. This includes undergraduate studies as well as postgraduate diplomas and Master's qualifications in tourism-related studies (including specialist areas, such as e-tourism, events and conference management).

The trade press

In addition to specialist academic journals, there is a large selection of weekly and monthly journals devoted to the travel and tourism industry. The weekly trade papers *Travel Trade Gazette* and *Travel Weekly* provide an invaluable service to the industry, covering news of both social and commercial activities, as well as providing the heaviest concentration of advertisements for jobs in the industry. Updates on the industry are also available to readers online.

In an industry as fast moving as tourism, employees can only update their knowledge of travel products by regularly reading the trade press, whether in hard copy or online. The newspapers complement the work of the training bodies, while, for untrained staff, they may well act as the principal source of new information.

Example

Tourism skills training in Britain

In Britain, the professional bodies in the industry introduced their own programmes of training and vocational education leading to membership, often carried out through full-time or part-time courses at local colleges of further or higher education. Examples of these early developments included courses offered by the Hotel and Catering International Management Association (HCIMA – now the Institute of Hospitality), the Chartered Institute of Transport (CIT) and the Institute of Travel and Tourism (ITT). However, with the rapid expansion of nationally validated travel and tourism courses in colleges of further and higher education which occurred from the 1970s onwards, there was a move to recognize formal qualifications, especially those offered by such bodies as the City and Guilds of London Institute (CGLI). In 2004, the government-funded Sector Skills Council licensed People 1st as the official body to develop training programmes for the hospitality, leisure and tourism industries. This body encourages the training organizations to provide what are perceived to be the right courses for the industry.

Within the school system itself, GCSEs at ordinary and advanced level specializing in leisure and tourism have also been introduced, with the support of key members of the industry, in order to interest school leavers in careers in travel. Attitudes among careers counsellors in schools, however, are slow to change and tourism continues to be seen by many as a career for the less academically able.

The trade press depends largely on advertising for its revenue, as the two weeklies are distributed free to members of industry. In return, they support the industry by sponsoring trade fairs, seminars and other events.

Within the general category of the press, one must also include those who are responsible for the publication of travel guides and timetables. The task of updating this information is obviously immense, especially in view of the worldwide scope of many of these publications. As their production becomes more complex each year, this is also a field that lends itself to computerization. Most guides now provide access for agents – and the public – electronically and it is questionable whether there will still be a demand for hard-copy guides of this nature for very much longer.

Example

OAG

The Official Airline Guide (OAG) was at one time virtually unchallenged as the world leader in airline time-tables, producing a three-volume guide listing 0.5 million flights, updated every month. Their listing includes budget airline flights as well as details of cargo schedules.

By the mid-1990s, technology was overtaking the hard-copy version and the business was further affected by the terrorist attacks in September 2001, which paralysed the airline industry, forcing airlines to cut their discretionary costs, including payment to OAG. The organization recognized that, to survive, it would have to invest heavily in new technology, so it has introduced an integrated fare search and booking function alongside its flight look-up service.

OAG has also announced a strategic alliance with FCm Travel Solutions – a corporate travel management company – to provide enhanced services for business travellers. Furthermore, OAG has introduced a flight-tracking service using SMS (text) messages that are sent to mobile phones.

Table 20.1 Examples of travel publications.

Publication	Details
Industry guides	
OAG flight guide	Printed guide providing information on airline schedules. This guide supports the online database of flight details.
World Travel Guide	Detailed country information, including details of passports and visas, health and climate, as well as resorts and excursions.
Travel magazines	
Business Traveller	A magazine aimed at the frequent business traveller, published worldwide.
Condé Nast Traveller	Aimed at the upmarket leisure sector, this magazine provides information on upcoming destinations and resorts as well as current issues for travellers.
National Geographic	An international magazine focusing on the environment and landscape across the globe.
In-flight magazines	
American Way	American Airlines
Discovery	Cathay Pacific
High Life	British Airways
Open Skies	Delta Airlines
The Australian Way	Qantas Airlines
Destination travel guides	
Lonely Planet	Country and destination travel guides, often used by budget and gap year travellers.
Fodor's	Country and city guides, aimed at a discerning travellers.
Michelin Red and Green guides	Guides to restaurants, travel and tourism businesses and sites of interest.

Note: Many agents now buy their guides and directories on CD-ROM or use the Internet to access directories instead of subscribing to hard copies.

Many travel guides are bought by both the trade and the travelling public (see Table 20.1). Corporate travel managers and frequent travellers on business are likely to want their own copies of guides, and agents may want hard copies to show to their customers when discussing alternatives.

Hotel guidebooks

Hotel guides, of course, have always served the needs of both the trade and the public, although many are produced commercially for purchase by the travelling public. They fall into three distinct categories:

- independent guides do not charge for entries and inspections are made anonymously – examples include the *Michelin Red Guide, Good Hotel Guide*
- paid-entry guides make a charge for listing – examples include Alastair Sawday's *Special Places to Stay*, Condé Nast Johansen's *Recommended Hotels*
- registration guides are funded by membership fees – examples include the AA and RAC handbooks.

Travel guidebooks

Travel guidebooks are enjoying huge popularity as more and more holidaymakers travel further afield each year and specialist book shops, such as Stanfords, have sprung up to cater for this growing demand. Such guidebooks must be updated frequently if they are to remain of any value, so many are produced on an annual basis. This, again, is an area that lends itself to computerization and much of the information held in guidebooks can be readily accessed using a computer. Travel guides for longer trips, such as Lonely Planet or Rough Guides, or cities, such as Dorling Kindersley's Eyewitness series, include accommodation and transport details alongside historical details of destinations, places to visit and restaurant recommendations for a variety of budgets.

Example

Podcasts

Some guidebooks can already be replaced by podcasts. Sound files can be downloaded over the Internet to a computer, then transferred automatically to an MP3 player, such as an iPod. This allows travellers to access spoken-word guides entirely for free. Virgin Atlantic was one of the first companies to offer podcast guides, launching a guide to New York, with others to follow. The key benefit of these is that they can be instantaneously updated, as well as being quick and easy to use.

Marketing services

A number of services exist to provide marketing support either wholly or in part to members of the travel industry. These include marketing consultants, representative agencies, advertising agencies, brochure design, printing and distribution services, suppliers of travel point-of-sale material and research and public relations organizations. To this list must be added the organizations that provide the hardware and software for the travel industry's computer systems.

This book does not propose to discuss in depth the marketing of tourism as the subject is comprehensively covered in a companion book.[5] Other books dealing with the topic can be found in the bibliography at the end of this book. The point to be made here is that both large and small companies in the industry can benefit from employing these specialist agencies and, in some instances, their services are, in fact, indispensable.

Tourism consultants

Management and marketing consultants offer advice to companies on the organization and operation of their businesses. They bring to the task two valuable attributes: expertise and objectivity.

Most tourism consultants will have had years of experience in the industry on which to draw, having been successful in their own fields before turning to consultancy, but, with the economic and political crises that have occurred over the past two decades and the resultant mergers and takeovers that have led to downsizing in the industry, it is inevitable that the pool of former executives in the industry have turned to consultancy work. The consultants' group affiliated to the Tourism Society alone lists over 300 individuals.

Consultants, not being directly involved in the day-to-day running of the companies they are employed to help, can approach their task without any preconceived ideas. They can therefore advise companies on either the general reorganization of the business or on some ad hoc issue, such as undertaking a feasibility study or the introduction of a new computer system.

Representative agencies

For a retainer or payment of royalties on sales, these organizations act as general sales agents for a company within a defined territory. This is a valuable service for smaller companies seeking representation abroad, for example. In the travel industry, it is most commonly found in the hotel sector, but carriers, excursion operators and public-sector tourist offices all make use of the facility in marketing their services in other countries. As with consultants, many of the employees of these agencies will have had prior work experience in the sector that they represent.

Advertising and promotional agencies

Many large travel companies – and an increasing number of smaller ones – retain an advertising agency. A number of these specialize in handling travel accounts.

Advertising agents do much more than design advertisements and place them in the media. They should be closely involved in the entire marketing strategy of the company and will be involved with the design and production of travel brochures. Many are equipped to carry out market research, the production of publicity material and merchandising or public relations activities. Some larger agencies also produce their own hotel/resort guides, using their own staff's extensive knowledge.

Travel companies may have their brochures designed by the design studio of their advertising agent, arrange for them to be produced by an independent design studio or, in some cases, their printer's studio may undertake the work. A growing number of brochures are now put together inhouse instead, however, with the aid of sophisticated computer software available to allow desktop publishing. Advertising agents can also help and advise in the selection of a printer for the production of brochures or other publicity material.

One recent innovation in publicity material for the trade is the use of technology to replace the hard-copy travel brochure. Initially, this took the form of video cassettes, but these have given way to CD-ROMs and, more recently, DVDs. They are designed to help customers reach a decision on holiday destinations, facilities and services. They are sometimes produced by tour operators, who make them available on loan to their customers through travel agents. The production costs are borne by the principals – operators, hotels, airlines – whose services are promoted. A number of companies now specialize in the production of these travel aids.

There was some initial concern that they might come to replace the brochure entirely, but, to date, there is little evidence to suggest that this is occurring – holidaymakers still like something tangible to flick through and refer to. With the development of direct communication between principals and consumers via the Internet and digital TV channels, if brochures are ever to be replaced, it is more likely that it will be by computer-accessed text and illustrations, which can be quickly updated and repriced.

Finally, mention should be made of direct mail and distribution services, some of which specialize in handling travel accounts. Some of these companies design and organize direct mail promotional literature aimed at specific target markets or travel retailers. They will also undertake distribution of a principal's brochures to travel agents.

Technical services

The rapid spread of the computer within all sectors of the travel industry has led to the establishment of specialist computer experts, who concentrate on designing and implementing purpose-made systems for their travel industry clients. Such systems include not only travel information and reservations functions but also accounting and management information.

Other computer organizations have been set up to provide networks that allow agents to access principals' computer reservations systems. With the pace of change that one has come to expect of this field, updating equipment and software is a regular function of the modern business and these organizations fulfil a vital role in ensuring that businesses are up to date and efficient in improving their service while keeping costs under control.

The future of ancillary services

For more than a decade, academics have been reporting that tourists are changing, seeking out travel opportunities that allow them to experience the unusual, rare or even provide for self-development and education. While the concept of a tourist guide may have often been seen as old-fashioned or outdated, as these tourists seek out such personal experiences, the role of the animateur or guide will remain important. The provision of human interaction to inform and entertain will provide opportunities for attractions, destinations and tourist resorts to enhance their offering.

Furthermore, as tourists gain greater access to information (with access to the Web expanding to all corners of the globe), the need to provide knowledge in a format that adds to the experience of visiting a place will become ever more important. Walking tours that can be downloaded on to MP3 players and virtual tours online will provide many visitors with a perception of the destination, but it will be the guides or animateurs who can bring the visit to life and make the experience memorable.

While modern film technology can provide stunts and scenes that are near impossible to achieve in real life (certainly not on a budget that most tourist attractions or destinations can afford), it is noticeable that many tourists still seek out 'low-tech' experiences where their interaction with humans (often perceived as 'locals') is a main attraction.

Notes

1. Booker, J. (2008) 'Crackdown on illegal guides', *New Zealand Herald*, 18 March.
2. Horowitz, J. (2005) 'At the Trevi Fountain: self-made guides in hot water', *New York Times*, 28 January.
3. Palmateer, P. (2007) 'Travel insurance gaining in popularity', *Central New York Business Journal*, 1 June.
4. Demetriou, D. (2007) 'One in four travellers uninsured', *The Daily Telegraph*, 26 May.
5. Holloway, J. C. (2004) *Marketing for Tourism* (4th edition), Prentice Hall.

Websites

Foreign and Commonwealth Office (travel insurance advice)
www.fco.gov.uk/en/travelling-and-living-overseas/staying-safe/travel-insurance

Institute of Tourist Guiding   **www.itg.org.uk**

People 1st   **www.people1st.co.uk**

Springboard UK   **www.springboarduk.org.uk**

Travel Trade Gazette   **www.ttglive.com**

Travel Weekly   **www.travelweekly.com**

Questions and discussion points

1. How can animateurs and guides enhance the experience that tourists have of a destination? Some destinations have elected to license their local guides. Discuss the ways in which licensing can ensure that the tourist experience is enhanced.

2. There is a concern that many travellers do not have adequate insurance cover when they travel. Why do you think so many travellers fail to take out cover? Is it apathy, cost-consciousness or simply a willingness to take risks? Annual travel policies are also becoming more popular. What reasons may be influencing travellers to opt to pay for an annual multi-trip policy?

3. Do you think that the method used to purchase foreign currency when travelling abroad is affected by the levels of travel experience of the visitor? Does the country being visited have an influence on the method selected?

4. Many tourism businesses are SMEs. How can tourism consultants and marketing agencies assist these small businesses? Are there any concerns that these businesses should consider when relying on external consultants?

Tasks

1. Undertake a search of the websites of *Travel Trade Gazette* and *Travel Weekly* (**www.ttglive.com** and **www.travelweekly.co.uk**) and compare their coverage of news with the hard copies of those papers. Write a report on the strengths and weaknesses of the websites and which you would prefer to use for updating your knowledge of the industry, giving reasons. Search the Web for other sources of travel trade information (such as **www.traveltrade.com**) and compare them with the two trade newspapers. While browsing the Web, you might encounter pop-up advertisements for related products. Assess the value of this form of advertising spend compared with other opportunities and include a section devoted to an analysis of the strengths and weaknesses of this medium in terms of reaching the travelling public.

2. Your local museum, which displays items that reflect the heritage of your home town or region, has consulted you as a tourism specialist. There is a proposal to use animateurs or guides to provide visitors with detailed interpretation of the exhibits. You must provide a comprehensive report to identify and discuss both the benefits and limitations of providing this form of interpretation.

Part 4

Case studies

Case study 1

The activities of a travel management company – HRG

Prepared by Claire Humphreys

Introduction

This case study focuses on a travel retailer that specifically operates to service the business tourism market. This case links with points and discussion in Chapter 11 as well as Chapter 19. The case looks at the services provided to support corporate travel, which will allow students to contrast its provision with that of leisure travel retailers. While the business travel sector is often perceived to be a lucrative one, this case study highlights the main issues facing a business operating in this demanding market.

HRG's background

Founded in 1845, the Hogg Robinson Group (HRG) has over 60 years of specific corporate travel expertise. Its corporate services interests today include owned or controlled corporate travel operations in 25 of the key driver and growth markets throughout Asia Pacific, Europe and North America. Supported by contracted partners, HRG's worldwide network extends to over 100 countries.

Totally committed to a value offering for clients, HRG offers a comprehensive range of corporate travel services, including corporate travel management, consulting, events and meetings management and sports, as well as expense management through its Spendvision operation.

Figure CS1.1 HRG logo.
(Courtesy of HRG.)

Although HRG previously had interests in the leisure travel business, it sold its 200+ UK street retail outlets to the tour operator Airtours (now part of the Thomas Cook group) in 1993, allowing it to focus on its corporate related business. This included its first international expansion with the acquisition of Bennett Travel Group AB (now HRG Nordic), operating in Scandinavia, and, within the last decade, it has also acquired Destination Services Russia (now HRG Russia), Rider Travel in Canada, ASL (now HRG Singapore), Kuoni's business travel activities in Italy, Austria, Germany, Hungary, Liechtenstein and Switzerland, USA-based Sea Gate Travel Group and Robustell (now HRG North America, after they merged with the company's existing Canadian operation) and Weinberg Travel in Belgium. In 2006, it further expanded operations in the Czech Republic, Slovakia and Poland,[1] bringing its worldwide network to over 100 countries.

A management buyout in 2000 led to the organization becoming a privately owned company, but October 2006 saw its relisting on the London Stock Exchange. HRG's turnover for the 12 months to March 2008 was £332.2 million, with a profit before tax of £24 million.

Company values

The organization sees the need to be focused on its staff, in order to ensure its long-term success. This includes training and personal development, which can ensure that employees are best positioned to service the clients' needs. HRG recognizes the vital role that its people play in delivering excellent customer service and it is 'committed to attracting, motivating and retaining the best talent and to being a company of choice with a waiting list of people to join'.[2]

HRG uses the acronym CHOICE to reflect the characteristics it wishes to instil in its employees, the letters standing for Committed, Honest, Outstanding, Innovative, Client-focused and Experts. It sees these characteristics as being vital skills that enable staff to best serve the demands of its many clients and set the company apart from its competition.

Services provided by this travel management company

HRG provides a comprehensive range of services for its clients, such as:

- corporate travel management – travel planning and booking, including ground transport, air, hotel and car hire
- expense management – assisting corporate clients with managing their travel budgets
- independent consulting – providing advice to companies on selecting their travel suppliers, as well as assisting with negotiating corporate rates with hotels, airlines and car hire companies
- travel management services for sports events and to sports teams
- meetings and events management, including sourcing venues, delegate and programme management.

HRG is often privileged to sensitive company information, which may include knowledge of business goals, financial data, future plans, personal details of employees and so on. Changes in travel policies, for instance, may be the direct result of changing business practices or financial policy. It is vital, therefore that HRG builds and maintains an open and trusting relationship with its clients. HRG may also be a part of an organization's crisis management and business continuity planning. The company provides a 24-hour service, as well as a people-tracking facility, ensuring that, in times of emergency, staff can be located swiftly and their travel arrangements can be adjusted in light of the crisis.

Several different structures of travel service provision may be used, largely determined by the needs of the client. For HRG, these generally fall into one of three main approaches.

- *Services provided from HRG offices* The client will contact the HRG employee who is their dedicated representative. The travel adviser will make the necessary travel arrangements, ensuring that these are in line with the travel policy of the client's organization.

- *Services provided through service centres* There are two models, either servicing a range of clients or servicing a client based in multiple countries. Multi-country service centres, normally dedicated to a single client, bring efficiencies of scale due to consolidation of services. Within national service centres, staff usually provide support to many different companies. The use of a travel adviser ensures that the client benefits from good rates (negotiated by HRG on behalf of all clients), as well as an efficient service (the client's staff do not have to spend excessive time seeking out, booking and updating their own travel arrangements).

- *Services provided through implant offices at the client's premises* In some cases, organizations elect to have HRG employees on site, to service their needs locally. In the past, this was a convenient way to access travel paperwork (tickets), but, as the industry moves more to paperless ticketing, there is less pressure to fulfil this need. Other services, however, such as arranging visas and offering advice to travellers, may mean that a face-to-face service is still desirable. The client must bear the cost of the implant, providing space on its premises as well as equipment and communications facilities. Often the decision to use an implant is made as part of wider business expectations, often for reasons of convenience, efficiency, costs savings and cost management, and the additional expense is seen as part of the many operational costs of doing business.

Commissions and fees

As with the leisure travel market, commission payments have been largely eliminated within the business tourism sector. Generally, travel providers (such as airlines, hotels, car hire companies and so on) will have negotiated discounted rates with HRG, which, in turn, will pass these deals on to its clients. In the case of clients with great demand for travel, corporate rates may be negotiated on frequently used services, allowing the company to gain better terms from these preferred suppliers. HRG provides an independent consultancy operation to assist clients in these direct negotiations with suppliers.

HRG earns its fees according to the contracted services selected by the client. For example, where the service centre is used, a fee may be charged based largely on the time spent serving the customer's needs. Alternatively a transaction fee may be charged, levied on specific transactions (this is not just on bookings but also on areas such as offering advice on visa requirements or travel safety).

In other cases, an organization may elect to pay a management fee (determined prior to the commencement of the contract) based on overall expected levels of business. These fees cover a defined level of service, staffing and business volumes and are designed to flex should servicing criteria change.

Acquiring clients – bidding for business

The lifecycles of TMC contracts are often quite short – on average, around four years, although some may be as short as two years. This will mean that the current TMC will have to renegotiate contracts regularly to retain its clients. There will also be occasions when it bids alongside other competitors to gain or retain business. While this may be beneficial for clients, helping them to gain preferential fee levels, this means that the TMC often operates in an intensely competitive market. In the long term, it is imperative for the TMC's travel advisers to develop a level of trust with the organization's travel manager. Such an understanding can ensure that the key business demands are fully appreciated and that the TMC can work with the client to help enhance their business efficiency and operations.

Pragmatically, the advisers focus their attention on maintaining contracts with existing clients or clients with whom there has been a previously positive relationship. The decision to bid for new business is largely dependent on relationships formed with the client and having an in-depth knowledge of the company's requirements.

Summary

For travel retailers reliant on commission, the business travel sector may seem to be a lucrative opportunity. The higher price paid for business class flights and quality accommodation may seem to offer great opportunities for increasing commission payments, but the cost of servicing this sector can be exceptionally high. It seems that any chance of success in this sector relies on the travel management company having the power to negotiate excellent terms with providers in the travel industry, such as airlines and hotels.

Notes

1. HRG (2008a) 'Company heritage', HRG. Available at: **www.hoggrobinsongroup.com/AboutUs/CompanyHeritage/tabid/1054/Default.aspx**
2. HRG (2008b) 'Vision and values', HRG. Available at: **www.hoggrobinsongroup.com/AboutUs/VisionandValues/tabid/1027/Default.aspx**

Questions and discussion points

1. Why might a corporate client choose to invest in an implant office rather than rely on a regional service centre?
2. What are the implications of the frequent pressure to bid for the travel service contract?
3. How important is the service-focused vision of HRG to making this business attractive to its corporate clients?

Case study 2

Brunel's *ss Great Britain*: conservation and interpretation – a potential conflict?

Prepared by Erika Neumann, Assistant Curator,
Brunel's *ss Great Britain*

Introduction

This case study offers an insight into some of the problems faced when presenting an unusual visitor attraction – here, a preserved passenger ship – to the public. In recognizing the need to maintain authenticity in conservation while both educating and entertaining visitors, this case study considers problems that are common to many other attractions and is informed by material to be found in Chapters 6, 10 and 16.

The high degree of success of the solutions chosen for the exhibit has been recognized by the attraction receiving a string of awards since its inception. It offers an excellent example of innovative and creative thinking in visitor management coupled with exceptional preservation techniques.

Background to the attraction

The *ss Great Britain* is the world's first iron-hulled, screw-propelled, ocean-going steamship. She was designed by Isambard Kingdom Brunel, built at the Great Western Dockyard in Bristol between 1839 and 1843 and launched there in 1843, with Prince Albert in attendance.

During her working life, the ss *Great Britain* underwent a series of changes – from being the world's first great ocean liner, to an emigrant clipper, a cargo ship and, finally, a floating warehouse in the Falkland Islands. When she became unsafe, she was towed to a remote bay and scuttled to the shallow seabed. In 1970, she was salvaged and returned to Bristol to the very dry dock in which she was built.

Since then, the ss Great Britain Trust (known as the ss Great Britain Project Ltd from 1971 to 2002) has been working towards her restoration and long-term preservation and making her accessible to the public. Brunel's ss Great Britain (the brand name of the Trust's visitor attraction and venue hire operations) is now one of the premier museums and heritage tourist attractions in the UK, having won 14 major awards across the areas of tourism, education, access and architecture. These include the Gulbenkian Prize for museums and galleries 2006 (now the Arts Fund Prize) and the EnjoyEngland Excellence Award for 'Large Visitor Attraction of the Year 2007', as well as the European Museum of the Year Award's Micheletti Prize for 'Best Industrial Museum in Europe 2007'. The ss Great Britain Trust has accredited museum status.

The Great Western Dockyard site encompasses the dry dock, the ship herself and the Trust's collection of original objects relating to the ss *Great Britain* and Brunel's other two ships as well as other maritime items, many of which are displayed in the Dockyard Museum. The site is open 7 days a week, 362 days a year.

Entry prices for 2008 were:

adult	£10.95
concession (senior citizens)	£8.25
student (with valid student card)	£5.65
child	£5.65
(children aged four, and under)	Free
family (two adults and three children)	£29.95

The tickets permit unlimited free return visits for 12 months and admission also includes many special events throughout the year. The highest total visitor figures, 200,000, were recorded in 2006, during Brunel 200, the celebrations of the bicentenary of the great man's birth. More than 154,000 people visited Brunel's ss *Great Britain* in 2007/2008, including 16,000 schoolchildren, and more than 16,900 guests were welcomed on board for events.

The organization

The ss Great Britain Trust is an independent museum and charitable company (Registered Charity number 262158) that receives no monetary subsidy from local or national government. It is a company limited by guarantee. The Trust's patron is HRH The Duke of York KCVO ADC.

The Trust's mission statement is:

> To preserve the ship, ss *Great Britain*, and her building dock for all time for the public benefit of all, and to place the same upon public display as a museum for the enhancement of the public understanding and appreciation of her social, commercial, scientific, and technological context and significance.

The ss Great Britain Trust is governed by a Board of Trustees, which has ultimate responsibility for the ship's conservation and the organization's work. The Board establishes the policies that shape all aspects of the Trust's work. Trustees are elected from among the general members of the Trust. The Trust's Director is responsible to the Board for pursuing strategic goals and for the day-to-day activities of the Trust, leading a team of 45 staff and more than 50 volunteers divided into five departments:

- curatorial and education services
- visitor services and events
- development and communications
- technical and conservation services
- finance and human resources.

The ss Great Britain Trading Ltd runs the Trust's visitor services, retail, catering and venue hire operations. It, too, is a company limited by guarantee and gift aids its profits on an annual basis to the ss Great Britain Trust.

The challenge

A key difficulty facing the management of the vessel is determining how best to present and interpret a large historic iron ship as authentically as possible without impacting on the remaining original structure, balancing high levels of access and an exciting visitor experience with conservation needs, which are paramount. This issue needs to be considered for two distinct areas – on board the ship and the exterior of the hull, plus the dry dock the ship sits in.

On board the ship

Restoration and reconstruction work on the ship started early on in the project, with, for instance, the decks being either replanked or rebuilt and staircases reconstructed. Over the years, access to and interpretation of the ship have evolved in several stages. In 1999, plans were finalized to 'relaunch' the ship in 2005 with an entirely new and more comprehensive, more accessible interpretation and create a new, exciting visitor experience. Three solutions were considered.

- On-board interpretation of one period from the ship's life, as is the case with many other historic ships, and as had been the case in earlier stages of the interpretation project. The ship has had many uses, however, each of which are significant in their own right, so this approach would prevent the visitor from experiencing most of these.

- To match the shipboard interpretation with the sequential steps taken in the adjacent museum. There, the display starts out in the 1970s and covers each period of the ship's working life in reverse chronological order, back to the original launch in 1843. Using this schema, the stern could represent the 1840s luxury passenger liner phase, the mid-section the emigrant steam clipper and so on. The historical data, however, does not suit this sequential layout as there are overlaps, with some periods being well represented through most of the ship, but others only sparsely. Often there is only data available for a particular area of the ship from one specific period.

- The disadvantages inherent in the first two approaches led the team to consider a third approach, which they adopted. It involves interpreting each cabin or deck based on the period for which the historical evidence relating to it is strongest. The visitor, before 'boarding' the ship, passes through the Dockyard Museum, travelling back in time, arriving on deck as though on launch day in 1843. This approach allows a close link to be made between aspects of the Museum's display and the material witnessed on board. Emphasis throughout is on the use of primary source evidence, such as passenger and crew diaries and letters, and contemporary images. In this way, visitors can be assured that each space is as authentic as possible. To take one example, Samuel Archer was

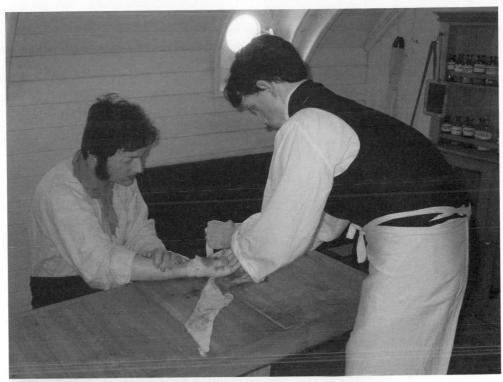

Figure CS2.1 The reconstructed surgeon's cabin.
(Photo by Chris Holloway.)

one of the surgeons serving on board. His diary contains considerable detail and has allowed an accurate representation of his cabin to be recreated (see Figure CS2.1).

Similarly, the weather deck, with its masts, funnel, wheelhouse and so on, has been recreated as it was on the day the ship was launched in 1843, based on a detailed painting by an eyewitness and a famous photograph. Most of the forward hold area of the ship remains untouched and enables visitors to view the internal structure of the ship as it was when the ship returned to Bristol in 1970.

In accordance with the Trust's conservation policy, the internal interpretations have been constructed without damaging the original structure of the ship. This, however, produces several inevitable anachronisms. For example, in the ceiling of the first class passenger dining saloon, reconstructed to represent the 1840s, there are cargo hatches from the ship's time as a cargo ship in the 1880s.

The on-board interpretations are made as realistic as possible by reconstructing the internal fabric with a high degree of authenticity, with well-researched set dressing and highly realistic mannequins that were cast from real people. Usually, these represent actual passengers or crew, such as Samuel Archer himself, while Isambard Kingdom Brunel sits reading a newspaper in the promenade saloon. Each figure is seemingly busy in his or her private shipboard world.

It was hoped that when first glimpsed, visitors would think the mannequins were real. The personal aspect of passengers' and crew's 'true stories' are an important factor that has also been the focus of a promotional campaign. Further sensory realism is provided by recreated smells, such as carbolic soap and vomit, and ambient sounds.

The Trust has taken the rare approach of letting visitors get up close to everything on board – they can walk into most of the cabins, lie on bunks and sit next to the mannequins. This greatly enhances their experience. The ship is also fully accessible to wheelchair users and a lift, hidden inside the funnel spaces, takes them from deck to deck (one of the few modern concessions that have been made).

A clear distinction is drawn between the intellectual learning processes available in the Dockyard Museum and the emotional responses engendered on board the ship. The Museum is full of original objects, each interpreted with illustrations and text. The ship, being full of sounds, smells and realistic reconstructions, creates an immersive experience of what it may have felt like to live on board. In keeping with this idea and to enhance it, there are no labels or any modern signs on board (other than those required for health and safety reasons, such as emergency exits) and no audio-visual screens. This helps to maintain the illusion of travelling back in time.

Audio tours

A fully automatic infra-red-triggered audio system further contributes to the immersive interpretation experience. Visitors can choose from four different tours: first class passenger, steerage passenger, maritime archaeologist or Sinbad the ship's cat (children's tour).

The tours encourage visitors to experience the ship as passengers and have been based on diary extracts and letters. Visitors hear about events that occurred during the ship's voyages and can 'listen in' on reconstructed conversations. Foreign language versions in German and French, for children and adults, are also available. As well as providing choice and satisfying visitors' individual interests, the opportunity to take a different tour helps to encourage repeat visits.

An audio tour for visually impaired visitors makes use of the audio system available to all visitors, but it has been specially written to include detailed information about the contents and interiors. Unlike the other audio tours, this tour also covers the dry dock and Museum.

The British Sign Language hand-held video tour for the hard of hearing provides a choice of two tours – one for adults and one for children. They are installed on touch screen video units, and guide users around the Museum and ship.

As well as these audio tours, volunteers are on hand to answer visitors' questions.

Ongoing interpretation on board the ship

In 2006, a project to construct a full-scale replica of the original 1843 steam engine was completed, using modern lightweight materials so that the fragile 165-year-old ship is not overloaded. It is powered by an electric motor that turns the moving parts (albeit at a much slower, but safer, speed than the original) and, accompanied by appropriate sounds and smells, it gives the visitor an authentic impression of how the massive original engine functioned.

In 2008, six horse stalls with mannequin horses were installed, as part of the ongoing programme of incremental enhancements to the historical interpretation. This setting includes soldiers from the ship's period of service as a troop transport during the Crimean War. Again, the interpretation is aided by busy mannequins, 'horsy' smells, very realistic 'fake' horse manure and a sound recording of real horses.

Hull and dry dock

Conservation goes hand in hand with interpretation

The *ss Great Britain* is now displayed in the dry dock in which she was built. All of the exterior of the hull shows the effect of salt corrosion, but prolonged exposure to sea water in the area below the waterline has accelerated this.

Relative humidity (RH) is a measure of the amount of water the air holds, compared with the maximum that it can hold at that temperature, expressed as a percentage. For a

Figure CS2.2 The underside of the ship, showing the glass plates sealing the hull from exposure to the elements.
(*Photo courtesy of Mandy Reynold.*)

fixed volume of air, increasing temperature causes a decrease in the RH, while decreasing temperature raises the RH level. New research commissioned from Cardiff University found that chloride-infested iron will virtually cease corroding if it is kept at relative humidity of 20 per cent or lower. A system was therefore sought that would keep the RH below 20 per cent and thus maintain a stable climate. The innovative solution that was found involved the installation of a glass plate, sealing off the dry dock at what would have been the waterline of the ship when she was afloat (see Figure CS2.2). Dehumidifiers keep the area under the glass plate at the required RH. The glass plate is covered by a thin layer of water, giving visitors on the dock side the illusion that the ship is floating, while visitors at hull level in the dry dock feel like they are underwater. The water layer also insulates and cools the system, saving approximately 20 per cent of the energy required to run it. Visitors are permitted to get close to the hull, but, due to its fragile state, they are asked not to touch it when walking around the dry dock.

The conservation plant was placed in the dry dock without intruding on the views down each side of the ship. The front face of the plant has been designed with windows, allowing visitors to see the internal components. Accompanying interpretation panels further explain the conservation programme (see Figure CS2.3) and dehumidification system (there is also a complementary dehumidification plant on board the ship that dehumidifies the inside of the hull, but this is located in an area of the ship that is not accessible to visitors).

The upper weather deck is protected from the elements by a hidden steel membrane beneath the wooden deck that serves as the 'roof' to the ship and keeps damaging rain-water out.

Figure CS2.3 An informative notice for visitors explains some of the difficulties involved in preserving the ship's hull.
(Photo by Chris Holloway.)

Conclusion

The conservation programme has succeeded in preserving the fabric of the ship, while the interpretation has achieved the aim of providing visitors with a better understanding of the ship's history and both intellectual and physical access have been improved. In addition, the project has had a significant impact on visitor numbers, bringing in increased revenue to help fund the ss Great Britain Trust's work.

Visitor research has been undertaken throughout the development and the organization's new website (**www.ssgreatbritain.org**), launched in 2008, includes an innovative visitor review page to further the gathering of visitors' feedback.

Before the 'relaunch' in July 2005, annual visitor numbers were approximately 70,000, and 'relaunch' budgeted estimates stood at between 110,000 and 120,000 visitors. Actual visitor numbers, including school groups and venue hire clients, peaked in 2006 with 200,000. This was partly due to the 'relaunch' and partly due to the Brunel 200 celebrations. Annual figures, including school groups and venue hire guests, now seem to be settling at the 170,000 level (these figures represent paid-for admissions). The free unlimited return visits for one year scheme is promoted heavily and well received by visitors. Return visits represent approximately 10 per cent of visitors.

Brunel's *ss Great Britain* particularly attracts families, retired couples, groups and school children. A breakdown of visitors by age (2007 data) is shown in Figure CS2.4.

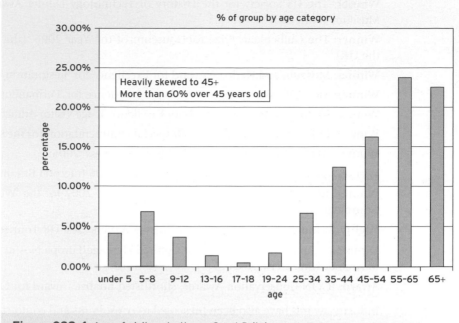

Figure CS2.4 Age of visitors to the *ss Great Britain*.

In research undertaken on site in 2007, visitors gave Brunel's *ss Great Britain* scores of 9 out of 10 or 10 out of 10 for value for money and enjoyment, and a significant proportion, 35 per cent, travel more than 2 hours to visit the ship (contrary to national trends and suggesting a high degree of motivation). In onsite market research undertaken in spring 2008, 38 per cent of respondents had received a personal recommendation.

Future plans

The next step in the ss Great Britain Trust's development plans is the construction of the Brunel Institute. Due to be completed by 2010, it will house the David MacGregor Library of nationally important maritime material, a state-of-the-art archive store and a lecture theatre and seminar room. The library will be open to all without an appointment and visitors will be able to request to see objects from the archive store. A series of innovative education programmes for both formal and informal learners will also be run from the Brunel Institute.

The success of the *ss Great Britain*

The Trust has won a succession of awards since the attraction's 'relaunch'. These cover tourism, heritage, education, conservation, interpretation, architectural merit and access, including the following:

Winner: Enjoy England's Awards for Excellence, Gold Winner: 'Best Large Visitor Attraction of the Year 2007'.

Winner: European Museum of the Year Award's Micheletti Prize for 'Best Industrial or Technology Museum 2007'.

Winner: RIBA/Crown Estate 'Special Award for Conservation 2007'.

Winner: The US Society for the History of Technology Dibner Award for 'Outstanding Museum Work 2007'.

Winner: The Gulbenkian Prize for 'Museum of the Year 2006' (the biggest arts prize in the UK).

Winner: Museum and Heritage Award for Excellence for 'Restoration/Conservation' 2006.

Winner: Museum and Heritage Awards for Excellence for 'Permanent Exhibition' 2006.

Winner: South West Tourism Awards for Excellence 'Large Visitor Attraction of the Year 2006'.

Winner: Civic Trust Award 2006, with special commendation for the ship's access systems.

Winner: ADAPT Trust Award for 'Excellence in Access' 2006.

Winner: Association for Heritage Interpretation '2006 Interpret Britain and Ireland Award'.

Winner: Royal Institute of British Architects Award 2007 for the 'Wessex' region, Special Commendation.

Highly Commended: British Guild of Travel Writers 'Best UK Tourism Project' 2006.

Diploma: European Union Prize for Cultural Heritage/Europa Nostra Award 'Conservation of Architectural Heritage' 2007.

Award: ICON Conservation Awards, shortlisted finalist, 'Award for Conservation' 2007.

Industry awards have also been presented to consultants and contractors for their work on the *ss Great Britain* project.

Questions and discussion points

1. The *ss Great Britain* is almost unique as a preserved passenger liner (the *RMS Queen Mary* at Long Beach, California, being another rare example). Self-evidently, no vessel of this size can be preserved fully under cover, so the superstructure will always be open to the elements, meaning that continuous maintenance of a relatively fragile object is required to an extent not usually found in a visitor attraction. Discuss the case for public funding for such attractions versus a privately operated visitor attraction such as *RMS Queen Mary* and consider ways, other than those described in the text, in which financial support can be raised for the ship's preservation.

2. Examine the three alternatives taken into consideration by the Trust when seeking solutions to the restoration and interpretation of this vessel and discuss the pros and cons of each.

3. The Trust has taken the unusual step of allowing visitors to 'get up close' to settings on board (although they are warned not to touch the delicate hull). Compare this approach with those at other attractions such as stately homes and consider the pros and cons of restricting visitor access and allowing them to wander freely around the attraction rather than in small escorted groups.

4. What issues of health and safety might be pertinent to an attraction such as this?

Case study 3

Marketing Belgrade as a conference destination

Prepared by Rob Davidson, with the help of Olivera Lazovic,
Director, Tourist Organization of Belgrade

Introduction

This case study, which draws principally on material in Chapter 11, as well as relating to the marketing of destinations discussed in Chapter 9, examines how Belgrade, the capital city of the Balkan country of Serbia, is marketed as a destination for business events, notably conferences.

Belgrade occupies a strategic place in Europe. Situated above the confluence of the Danube and Sava rivers, it has always been the meeting point and a major gateway between East and West. This characteristic of the city has, for centuries, made it a place that also generates a confluence of thought, philosophy, science and art, so it is a natural destination for conferences in the twenty-first century.

The case study reveals how tourism authorities in the region have pinpointed a particular niche market in business tourism and set about cultivating it. Following a turbulent period in its history, the city is now poised to become one of Europe's fastest-growing conference destinations.

Belgrade fact file

Population

Approximately 2 million, out of a total population for Serbia of 8 million.

International access

There are non-stop flights to Belgrade from a number of European cities and international airlines offer one-stop connecting flights from virtually anywhere in the world. Nikola Tesla Airport is only 18 kilometres from the city centre. Another airport nearby at Surčin is also used by many international carriers. Flights from most European capital cities can reach Belgrade in under $2\frac{1}{2}$ hours.

Belgrade is also accessible by rail and road. Indeed, the city lies at the crossroads of the E70 and E75 international routes, which provide the fastest connection between Western and Northern Europe on the one side and Southern and Eastern Europe on the other.

Belgrade's recent history

Having suffered from occupation by the Austrians in World War I and intensive bombardment and then occupation by German forces in World War II, Belgrade slowly began to recover from the devastating consequences of war as the capital of the Federal People's Republic of Yugoslavia. Due to the policies implemented by Josip Broz Tito's communist government, balancing Yugoslavia between East and West, Belgrade developed into an important political, cultural, economic and sporting centre. Important international meetings were held in Yugoslavia, including the First Conference of the Non-Aligned Countries in 1961 and the Conference on Security and Co-operation in Europe (CSCE), as well as many cultural and sporting events.

With the death of Josip Broz Tito on 4 May 1980, the Yugoslav disaster began, first economically and then politically. The disintegration of Yugoslavia began in 1991, as unresolved national and ethnic problems flared up and civil war broke out, bringing to an end the longest period of peace in the Balkans in the twentieth century. In June 1991, Slovenia and Croatia declared independence from Yugoslavia, closely followed by Bosnia and Herzegovina and Macedonia in 1992. Hence, in 1992, Belgrade became the capital of the Federal Republic of Yugoslavia, which consisted solely of the Republic of Serbia and the Republic of Montenegro. Reacting to the war in Bosnia and Herzegovina, the United Nations Security Council imposed economic sanctions against Yugoslavia in 1992.

A series of civil wars began in 1991, starting off with a short-lived conflict between the Yugoslav National Army and Slovenia. The war spread to Croatia (1991–1995) when Serbs started a rebellion and Croats sought to create a nationally homogeneous state. The Croatian war came to an end when the Croatian army took action against the Serbian population and expelled over 300,000 Serbs from the territory. The civil war in Bosnia and Herzegovina (1992–1995) was an ethnic and religious war between Serbs, Croats and Muslims, which was ended by the signing of the Dayton Agreement. Between 1996 and 1999, there was conflict in Kosovo and Metohija between the Kosovo Liberation Army and the Serbian military and police forces. After unsuccessful negotiations in Rambouillet, NATO began its bombing campaign against the Federal Republic of Yugoslavia, which began on 24 March and continued until 10 June 1999.

In February 2003, the state union of Serbia and Montenegro was formed. In May 2006, Montenegro declared independence from Belgrade, which then became the capital of a new, independent Serbian state. The new constitution of the Republic of Serbia was passed in November 2006.

That same year, in a competition to name the European cities and regions of the future organized by the *Financial Times* newspaper, Belgrade was named the 'City of the Future in Southern Europe'. The categories and criteria on which the expert jury based its decision were economic potential, cost of doing business, human resources, transport, information technology and telecommunications, quality of life for foreign investors and the best promotional campaign to attract direct foreign investment.

Belgrade as a conference and exhibition destination

Conference delegates constitute a significant segment of Belgrade's visitors and the city offers the essential resources for this type of business event: accommodation, conference centres, exhibition halls, experienced conference organizers and a rich supply of cultural activities for delegates (and those who accompany them) to enjoy. Seminars, symposia, congresses, fairs and scientific and professional gatherings are organized the whole year round in a large number of convention and trade fair buildings in Belgrade, of which the leading ones are the Sava Centre, Belgrade Fair, Belgrade Arena and Expo XXI. Moreover, the majority of Belgrade's hotels have their own facilities for conferences and trade fairs.

In the 1980s, Belgrade was ranked number five in a list of the best conference destinations in the world by the International Congress and Convention Association (ICCA) and the city is once again asserting itself as a centre for business events of all kinds.

Over the past decades, Belgrade has hosted many important international gatherings – the Conference on European Security and Cooperation, World Bank Assembly, Annual Meeting of the International Monetary Fund, Annual Meeting of UNESCO, Annual Meeting of the European Bank for Reconstruction and Development (EBRD) and world conventions of orthopaedic practitioners, dentists and surgeons, to name just a few.

Facilities for business tourism

The Sava Centre

Originally built to host the 1978 World Bank and International Monetary Fund assembly, the Sava Centre (**www.savacentar.com**) is the largest conference venue in South East Europe. This international convention, cultural and business centre is situated close by the confluence of the River Sava and the River Danube, only 5 minutes away from the city centre and 15 minutes from Belgrade's Nikola Tesla Airport. Close by are the hotels Hyatt Regency, Continental and IN.

The venue is a member of both international associations of congress centres – the AIPC and the ICCA. With its extensive space, technical facilities and highly qualified staff, the Sava Centre is able to organize the largest conferences and stage the most complex artistic performances. It has 69,720 square metres of effective space and a total area amounting to 100,000 square metres. It offers a large 4000-seat auditorium, 15 conference rooms, the services of an expert team of conference and artistic events organizers, exhibition space, modern audio-visual equipment, a press centre and a large number of offices equipped to the latest standards.

The Belgrade Fair

The Belgrade Fair (**www.sajam.co.rs**) has 14 pavilions covering 100,000 square metres of exhibition and commercial space, as well as outdoor exhibition space of 35,363 square metres with associated catering and other facilities. The central pavilion (Hall 1) is a huge, domed building, covering 21,280 square metres in total. Over 30 regular events are held every year at the Fair and many of the events are affiliated to prominent international organizations. The International Technical Fair, the International Fair of Clothing, the International Fair of Furniture, the Equipment and Interior Decoration and the International Building Trade Fair, for example, are all members of the Global Association of the Exhibition Industry (UFI). The International Motor Show is registered with the International

Figure CS3.1 The International Press Institute Congress, June 2008, at the Sava Centre, Belgrade.
(Courtesy of Serbia Convention Bureau.)

Organization of Motor Vehicle Manufacturers (OICA). The International Fair of Tourism is a member of the European Tourism Trade Fairs Association (ETTFA).

Belgrade Fair is a member of the Fairs Association of Central Europe (CEFA). The Belgrade World Trade Centre is a member of the World Trade Centre Association (WTCA). Apart from regular events, numerous exhibitions, concerts, and scientific and specialist gatherings are held under the domes of the Belgrade Fair.

The Belgrade Arena

The Belgrade Arena (**www.arenabeograd.com**) was opened in 2004 and, at that time, was the largest and most modern complex for all types of large-scale sport, entertainment and cultural events, as well as trade fairs and congresses. It is located in the central business area of New Belgrade, directly alongside the E70/E75 motorway and just 15 minutes from Nikola Tesla Airport. Nearby are the hotels Hyatt Regency, Continental and IN, and the city centre is only 10 minutes' drive away.

With a total area of 48,000 square metres and a total seating capacity of 23,000, the Arena still ranks among the top multi-purpose centres in Europe. Seating in the central hall is on six levels with 68 luxury boxes that can accommodate more than 768 guests.

On 24 May 2008, over 100 million Europeans saw the Belgrade Arena on their television screens as it was the venue for the 53rd Eurovision Song Contest, which was won the previous year by the Serbian singer Marija Seriforic. An additional 25,000 spectators were seated in the Arena itself to watch the event.

The EXPO XXI Convention Centre

Belgrade's EXPO XXI Convention Centre (**www.expoxxi.co.yu**) is part of Expomedia Group's Expo XXI International Expocentres chain. It is located in the central part of Novi Beograd, just 15 minutes from Nikola Tesla Airport and very close to the hotels Hyatt Regency, Continental and IN.

It comprises first-class multifunctional exhibition and conference space with the latest technology, capable of meeting the most stringent demands of events organizers. Its 2500 square metres of multifunctional space, with no supporting columns, can be adapted to the needs of larger and smaller conferences, congresses and seminars and can accommodate more than 3000 delegates. The flexibility of the space allows for plenary sessions to run alongside breakout sessions and independent workshops.

Belgrade hotels

There are about 20 hotels in Belgrade with conference and trade fair facilities. These include the Hyatt Regency Belgrade, Continental Hotel Beograd, Admiral Club, Balkan, Best Western Hotel M, Best Western Hotel Šumadija, IN, Majestic, Metropol Palace, Moskva, Palace, President, Park, Prag, Slavija Lux, Rex, Srbija and Union.

Unusual venues

A number of unusual venues in Belgrade are also available for the hosting of conferences. For example, there are the Belgrade Aviation Museum, Madlenianum Opera & Theatre and Belgrade Museum of Contemporary Arts.

Other facilities

As is the case for any successful business tourism destination, Belgrade offers a range of attractions that delegates can enjoy before, during or after the event that they travel to the city to attend. In the *Meetings and Conventions Planner's Guide 2007*, published by the Tourist Organization of Belgrade, the attractions of the city are summarized as follows:

We hope you will also come and discover the unique soul of the city, captured in its fascinating precincts which feature cafes and bars, fashionable shops, innovative cuisine, theatres, museums and galleries. Belgrade is also the beginning point for your exploration of some of Serbia's beautiful monasteries, wineries, farmhouse restaurants, ethno villages, spas, wildlife reserves, natural beauty and archeological sites.

Figure CS3.2 Delegates enjoying a VIP dinner at the Kalemegdan Restaurant, Belgrade. *(Courtesy of the Serbia Convention Bureau.)*

Marketing Belgrade as a business tourism destination

The Belgrade Convention Bureau

The Belgrade Convention Bureau (BCB) (**www.tob.co.yu**), which is a department of the Tourist Organization of Belgrade, markets Belgrade as an international meetings destination and provides assistance to organizations bidding for, or organizing, congresses, corporate meetings, incentive groups or exhibitions.

The staff at the BCB assist interested parties in planning meetings, seminars, conferences and conventions, from finding the right location to identifying the best agents. The BCB works through a partnership system.

All of Belgrade's leading hotels, venues and meetings supplier businesses are partners with the BCB. As a result, BCB provides meeting planners with direct access to a broad choice of the best meetings products and services available, such as those described below.

Bid assistance

Bidding for meetings or conventions requires a wide range of skills to be successful. These include strategic planning, organizational skills, leadership, creativity, lobbying and presentation skills. The ability to build strong partnerships with clients is also vital.

The BCB provides local and international hosts with a high level of knowledge and expertise in planning and compiling bid documents and packages, including:

- identifying and addressing bid criteria
- coordination and preparation of bid documents
- obtaining letters of support from government and industry leaders
- preparing preliminary budgets with professional conference organizers (PCOs)
- liaising between government and industry
- locating suitable venues in Belgrade and the surrounding area that meet bid criteria
- identifying accommodation packages that meet bid criteria
- tentative bookings of meeting venues, hotel rooms and social venues
- support and management of site inspections
- bid promotions, including distribution of promotional material and media assistance
- preparation of bid documents
- assistance with bid presentations.

Services to meeting planners

Once Belgrade has been selected as the destination for a meeting or convention, the BCB offers a range of services to meeting planners:

- meeting planners guide to Belgrade
- assistance with the selection of a PCO
- advice on destination issues – facility selection, pre- and post-touring, social events, etc.
- service referrals
- promotional materials/information kits
- government liaison.

The Serbia Convention Bureau

The BCB is assisted in its task of attracting international events to the city by the Serbia Convention Bureau (SCB, **www.serbiaconventionbureau.com**), which is the public body responsible for promoting the whole country of Serbia as a destination for conferences and other business events.

Officially opened in January 2006, the SCB markets not only the capital but also other Serbian cities, such as Novi Sad and Niš. In order to raise the profile of Serbia as a destination for conferences, the SCB exhibits at both EIBTM (**www.eibtm.com**) in Barcelona and at IMEX (**www.imex-frankfurt.com**) in Frankfurt, where meeting planners and incentive travel organizers have the opportunity to discuss Serbia as a potential destination for their future events.

The outcome of the BCB and SCB's work

The success of the BCB and the SCB in winning high-profile events for Belgrade can be seen in the variety of the organizations that have been persuaded to hold their conferences in the city. Some examples are:

- *2006*
  The 6th International Conference on the Environmental and Technical Implications of Construction with Alternative Materials
  The 18th Congress of Carpathian-Balkan Geological Association

- *2007*
  World Health Organization
  The 6th Ministerial Conferences held as part of the Environment for Europe

- *2008*
  City Break Conference
  The 57th IPI World Media Congress
  Danube Tourism Commission

- *2009*
  European Tourism Commission
  International Hotel and Restaurant Association Conference.

Figure CS3.3 Social event during an IPI Congress, hosted at the Royal Palace, Belgrade. *(Courtesy of the Serbia Convention Bureau.)*

Conclusion

Despite a turbulent recent past, Belgrade has been able to reinvent itself as a successful destination for not only leisure visitors but also the tens of thousands of international business tourists who come to the city each year as conference delegates.

Two factors have been crucial in establishing Belgrade as a fast-growing conference destination:

- a plentiful and varied supply of venues
- the professional marketing activities carried out by the Belgrade Convention Bureau, with the support of the Serbia Convention Bureau.

Questions and discussion points

1. Visit the websites of both the Belgrade Convention Bureau and the Serbia Convention Bureau. What differences are there in terms of the services offered by each?

2. Visit the websites for both the Belgrade Fair and EXPO XXI Convention Centre. What contrasts can you detect in terms of the different facilities and services provided for exhibitions/trade fairs?

Case study 4

Eurostar's move to St Pancras station and its impact on cross-Channel traffic

Prepared by Claire Humphreys, with help from Tracey Coleman, Eurostar Regional Manager, North America

Introduction

This case study examines the business of Eurostar – the train operating company that provides services through the Channel Tunnel, linking London with Brussels, Paris and beyond. While briefly acknowledging the financial issues faced by the company, the case study more specifically focuses on the changing business environment and the responses by Eurostar, particularly in terms of the opening of the new high-speed rail link and the move to St Pancras Station. The case study explores the market for train travel and especially considers the differing demands of the business and leisure segments. It also briefly looks at the introduction of Eurostar's carbon neutral status.

The case study links with material discussed in Chapter 11, dealing with the demands of the business tourism market, as well as Chapter 15, through its examination of the rail industry and the opportunities available to compete with the airline industry.

The Eurostar business

Launched in 1994, Eurostar has the exclusive rights to provide passenger rail transport through the Channel Tunnel. The service links London directly with Paris, Disneyland Paris and Brussels, as well as offering local interchange possibilities, currently through stations at Ebbsfleet and Ashford in Kent, and at Calais and Lille, both in the Nord-Pas-de-Calais region of France. There is also a direct weekly summer service to Avignon and a seasonal daily/nightly ski train service to the French Alps. Eurostar operates a fleet of 27 trains on the cross-Channel route (as well as using 4 additional trains to service domestic routes in France and Belgium).

On 14 November 2007, Eurostar moved from its terminus at Waterloo station in London to a new international station, located at St Pancras, near King's Cross. This move tied in with the opening of the new high-speed rail link, which provided Eurostar with its own track network rather than using the existing domestic network. This new track allows Eurostar trains to travel faster, uninterrupted by the slower domestic services, shortening journey times to the Continent.

When the business was launched in 1994, ownership was in the hands of the national train operators in the UK (British Rail (BR)), Belgium (SNCB) and France (SNCF). These three bodies held the shares of the Eurostar Group. At that time, however, massive changes were occurring in the structure, ownership and operation of the rail network in the UK. Privatization had led to the creation of a subsidiary company, European Passenger Services, which was created to retain British Rail's interest in the company. That subsidiary was subsequently sold to London and Continental Railways (LCR) as a further part of the privatization process. In October 1996, the organization was renamed Eurostar (UK) Ltd, as a private limited company.

Figure CS4.1 Eurostar train at the refurbished St Pancras terminal, London.
(Photo by Claire Humphreys.)

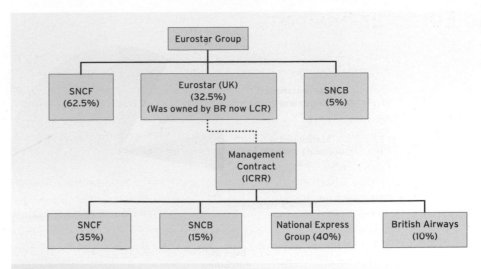

Figure CS4.2 The ownership and operation of Eurostar.

The management of the UK operations has been contracted out to an organisation called Inter Capital and Regional Rail (ICRR). It won the bid to manage the UK operations until 2010.[1]

The business of Eurostar is run by a joint Board, comprising directors of Eurostar (UK), Eurostar Group and representatives of SNCF and SNCB.[2] There is considered to be great public interest (by the state, financial bodies and general population) in Eurostar, largely due to the involvement of state bodies SNCF and SNCB, as well as the close links that exist between LCR and the UK government. The Office of National Statistics suggested that the UK government's underwriting of debts for LCR, which also owns stakes in the Channel Tunnel rail link, gives it power over the business and therefore has effectively made this a 'public sector non-financial corporation – similar in status to the Royal Mail or London Underground.'[3]

Financial position

For all of its operational life, Eurostar has battled against the debts incurred as a result of high start-up costs, lower than forecast passenger numbers and, consequently, yearly operating losses. While reported turnover has almost doubled since its launch, its high operating costs leave it firmly in the red (see Table CS4.1). Significant proportions of the high operating costs for Eurostar are due to payments for track access (31 per cent) and to travel through the Channel Tunnel (23 per cent) (see Figure CS4.3).

Table CS4.1 Turnover and profit levels since the launch of Eurostar.

(£millions)	1996	1997	1998	1999	2000	2001	2002	2003	2004	2005	2006
Turnover	88	130	163	168	187	193	191	189	211	221	234
Operating profit	−141	−173	−135	−109	−84	−121	−63	−94	−345	−126	−129

Source: Annual reports available through Orbis, see Orbis, 'Eurostar (UK) Ltd 2007', Bureau van Dijk, 2007.

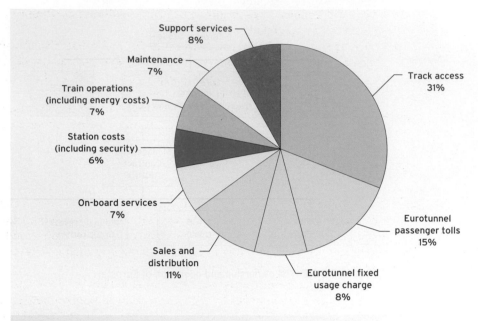

Figure CS4.3 Breakdown of operating costs.
(Eurostar's Chairman, Guillaume Pepy, Sir Robert Reid Lecture, 2007, Chartered Institute of Logistics and Transport.)

Demand

The numbers of passengers using Eurostar has grown steadily since it started operating but, since the turn of the century, has seen many fluctuations (see Figure CS4.4).

The fluctuations in demand may be attributed to many issues, including the foot and mouth epidemic in the UK in the spring of 2001 and the far-reaching impacts of the 9/11 terrorist attack in the USA, also in 2001, which significantly reduced global travel. The

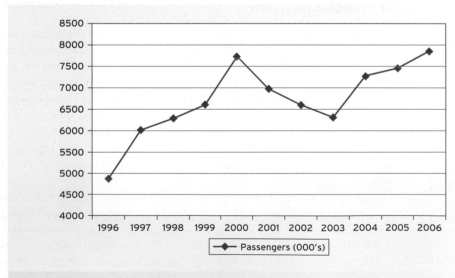

Figure CS4.4 Passenger numbers.

UN World Tourism Organization reported a significant downturn in international travel in both 2001 and 2003.[4,5]

The terrorist attacks on London in July 2005 also had a significant initial impact on tourism in the city. VisitBritain reported a drop in domestic traveller bookings to London of 30 per cent for the two months following the attack (although an increase in other regions was noted and international tourism remained robust).[6]

More recently, poor weather in the run-up to Christmas 2006 meant that many airlines were unable to run their planned services and, in their efforts to get home, travellers switched to Eurostar.[7,8]

Serving different markets

The key markets for Eurostar have traditionally focused on two realms. The first is those businesspeople for whom travel is a necessary part of their work and who are considered to be professional, educated, middle-aged and conservative. The second group are the 'urban intelligent' who live and work in London, perhaps in their late twenties up to early forties and for whom a lifestyle of leisure travel is key.[9]

The move to St Pancras and the new station at Ebbsfleet have opened up the possibility of new markets geographically, with areas north of London now coming into consideration. In May 2008, Eurostar and the Association of Train Operating Companies (ATOC) announced the introduction of a 'through-ticket', which provides 130 British towns and cities with tickets that include domestic *and* Continental rail travel to Brussels and Paris.[10] This initiative sought to encourage markets from outside London to consider Eurostar as an option for Continental travel.

Furthermore, Eurostar differentiates between its offline and online markets, where 'online' refers to those markets in the immediate catchment areas (those in the vicinity of London, Paris and Brussels), while 'offline' refers to those who have to travel significant distances before they become part of the catchment areas (such as American and Australian tourists visiting London). Marketing initiatives differ for those offline, while pricing policies and booking channels are adapted to encourage these markets to consider using the train rather than air routes around Europe.

Eurostar has also recognized the importance of its trade partners in helping to sell its product. In its overseas (offline) markets, Eurostar works with Rail Europe to provide international customers with knowledge of the routes and services offered. Other trade partners sell Eurostar tickets and/or can point customers at the Eurostar website to enhance sales levels.

A focus on business travel

The introduction in November 1996 of a business traveller loyalty scheme was an important addition to the product offered by Eurostar. The scheme was recently reworked, to reward passengers based on the actual price paid for their tickets. A further change has been made to the company's premium sector, too, with the 'reclassification of Eurostar's first-class service into Business Premier and Leisure Select. Standard class remains unaffected.'[11] Eurostar also offers a business lounge at its terminus, to service the needs of its Business Premier passengers.

This move to segregate premium-class business passengers from premium-class leisure travellers both recognized the demands of business professionals, who wish to work while travelling, and who expect a business class experience similar to that found in travelling business class on airlines. As a consequence, Business Premier passengers have a separate priority check-in desk and fast track service through security, use of the business lounge and the option for their breakfast meal to be served as 'express' (thus allowing them more time to work afterwards).

The carriages for Leisure Select passengers have larger seats than standard class and travellers are served a meal while onboard, but they must check in along with the standard-class leisure passengers.

Each train has 16 passenger carriages and 2 buffet cars, with approximately 6 carriages being allocated to either Business Premier or Leisure Select (each of these two groups having their own carriage). Allocation is altered depending on the demand for the service at particular times of day, determined by the Eurostar yield and revenue management team.[12]

Market issues

There are many challenges in the marketplace for Eurostar. The travel business in which it operates is dynamic and very competitive. The establishment and growth of the low-cost airlines has reshaped the short break market and influenced price competition. The company easyJet was founded in 1995 and now operates out of three of London's five airports, while the longer-running Ryanair also operates from airports in London and the south of England. These two airlines together carried over 75 million passengers in 2006, serving many routes across Continental Europe. The growth of the low-cost carriers and the poor reputation of the UK rail industry served to encourage markets away from train travel.[13]

Following changes to regulations regarding carry-on luggage for flights in 2006, 2007 saw further increases in security measures introduced at UK airports, causing significant chaos and queues. A fun (but rather unscientific) survey by *The Sun* in 2007 reported a 51-minute wait to check in at Heathrow and a further 22 minutes to get through security control.[14] Security changes also meant that the drop-off and pick-up locations were moved from outside the terminal to the short stay car parks, resulting in additional congestion, as well as requiring passengers to arrive earlier in order to walk to the terminal from these car parks.[15]

The low-cost airlines influenced the shape of the travel business in another way, with the development of strong online distribution channels. The requirement to book air travel online in order to use the low-cost carriers enhanced consumers' awareness of the possibilities of booking other elements of the travel product online. Many other factors have created changes in demand by consumers, too. The introduction of the low-cost carriers has meant that short-haul travel has become a commodity for many people, increasing the demand for short breaks to Europe and beyond.

Initially, travelling on Eurostar offered a sense of novelty – in terms of experiencing the trains and travelling through the Channel Tunnel – but as more travellers have taken this option, its curiosity value has declined. The image of the rail industry in the UK may also weigh against it somewhat when people are deciding between train travel and flying. Furthermore, the destinations offered directly by Eurostar are often perceived as limited. Services are provided to Paris and Brussels frequently, with stops at Ebbsfleet or Ashford, Lille and occasionally Calais. A limited service to Disneyland Paris (launched in June 1996), a weekly service in summer to Avignon (launched in July 2002) and the Ski Train, serving alpine resorts during the winter season (launched in December 1997), also provide additional route options. Many people are not aware of the opportunity to connect on to other high-speed trains, providing indirect services, which does extend this list much more widely to include destinations throughout Europe. Eurostar has reported, however, that ticket sales using connecting TGV services were up more than 10 per cent in the first half of 2007, so it is becoming more widely known.[16]

Travelling by Eurostar

The introduction in the UK of the first part of the high-speed railway line in 2003 allowed the journey time to be cut by 20 minutes. Almost 50 miles of purpose-built track ran from the Channel Tunnel into Kent, before trains moved to the domestic rail network, travelling more slowly into London's Waterloo Station. Completion of the final part of the high-speed link and the move to St Pancras has reduced the journey time by a further 20 minutes (see Table CS4.2).

Table CS4.2 Eurostar journey times in minutes.

Route	Opening (1994)	2003	2007
London–Paris	180	155	135
London–Brussels	195	135	111

Note: The Brussels route time dropped to 150 minutes in 1997, following the opening of the Belgian high-speed track.
Source: 'Rail', *Travel Trade Gazette*, 2006, 15 December, pp. 10–11 and R. Collis (1997) 'For short haul, take a high-speed train', *International Herald Tribune*, 19 December.

The punctuality of services is also seen as a key factor in trying to encourage travellers to select Eurostar over airlines. The opening of the first part of the high-speed link in 2003 allowed Eurostar to compete with airlines on punctuality (89 per cent for Eurostar and 70 per cent for competitor airlines)[17] and Eurostar have since reported punctuality levels of over 91 per cent for 2007.[18]

The speed of check-in and the city centre to city centre links are seen as important factors in encouraging travellers to opt for rail on the London to Paris and Brussels routes. With a check-in time of 30 minutes as standard (and only 10 minutes for business class travellers), few airports can match this speed (only London City airport offers a 30-minute check-in time). The central location of the stations in the cities is also considered important as passengers can quickly disembark from the train, do not have to wait to collect luggage and are in the heart of the city so do not need to take a long bus or taxi ride as is often the case for an airport.

Coinciding with the opening of the high-speed track, several journalists reported attempts to contrast air and rail journey times between central London and central Paris. Eurostar's claims that it is faster were often upheld as, despite the longer rail journey, the shorter check-in times and central locations allow rail passengers to reach their destinations more quickly than travellers who fly.

Eurostar generally operates 15 train services to Paris and 8 trains serve the Brussels route daily. This extensive schedule ensures that business passengers can benefit from the choice of departure times, enabling them to fit their travel more conveniently into their working schedule than is possible using other means of transport.

The routes served by Eurostar are incredibly competitive. In consequence, some players are electing to close their services. In February 2007, BMI announced that it would terminate its services between Heathrow and Charles de Gaulle, Paris. Its chief executive, Nigel Turner, said that 'there are now eight airlines operating 72 flights a day between London and Paris, and with a 37% reduction in the overall air market in the past four years there simply aren't enough passengers to fill them'.[19] Each Eurostar train is capable of carrying 750 passengers (including more than 200 premium class seats). This is similar to the capacity of two Boeing 747 jets. It is important to note that, as Eurostar trains cannot be reduced or extended much in response to demand fluctuations, capacity management opportunities are limited to adjustments to the frequency of service.[20]

A rail alliance

In 2007, Eurostar launched an alliance with other European rail operators to try and enhance its rail product. This alliance is called Rail Team and is a cooperation between Deutsche Bahn (Germany), SNCF (France), Eurostar (UK, France and Belgium), NS Hispeed (Netherlands), ÖBB (Austria), SBB (Switzerland), SNCB (Belgium) and their subsidiaries Thalys and Lyria. It seeks to operate coordinated rail links that will stretch from London to Hamburg in the north, Vienna in the east and Marseille in the south. The requirement that the operator utilizes a high-speed rail network has meant that no UK domestic train operators are currently part of this alliance.[21]

This alliance aims to ensure a smooth journey when using connecting rail networks, the booking and ticketing covering the entire journey (if one part of the service is delayed, then tickets will still remain valid on connecting journeys).[22] It is planned that the high-speed networks will expand across Europe over the next decade, allowing for even greater rail possibilities (see Figure CS4.5). It is recognized, however, that European competition rules restrict the setting of common fares, so when the tickets for all elements of the journey are combined, fares may not be competitive with the direct services offered by airlines.[23]

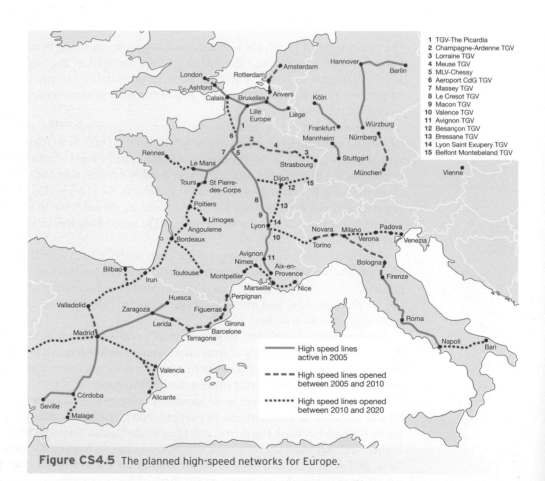

Figure CS4.5 The planned high-speed networks for Europe.

New stations

The move to the St Pancras International terminal was followed by the opening of a new station in Kent. Previously, Eurostar trains stopped at Ashford, but the new rail link takes a different route, stopping at a newly built station at Ebbsfleet in Kent (near the M25 and Bluewater shopping centre). A second station is planned at Stratford (East London), but, as it is currently located in the heart of the 2012 Olympic site, it will not be available until development has progressed to the point at which travellers can access the station.[24]

The predicted journey time from St Pancras to Ebbsfleet is about 10 minutes. A reduced frequency of service will continue to serve Ashford International station, although this change has caused some consternation for those planning development and regeneration initiatives in the area.[25]

The St Pancras terminal has been designed to have six Eurostar platforms, as well as platforms for some domestic services. It includes upmarket arcade shopping, a farmers market[26] and a champagne bar said to be the world's longest,[27] as well as becoming home to the Renaissance St Pancras Hotel (the Renaissance brand is part of the Marriott hotel chain). The 58-acre site around King's Cross and St Pancras stations also represents one of the largest inner-city redevelopment opportunities in Europe, with plans for 1800 new homes, a wide mix of shops, cafés, bars and restaurants and an education and cultural centre. The scheme includes the refurbishment of over 20 historic buildings and structures.[28]

Environmental awareness

Increased media attention regarding the environmental damage and pollution caused by travel has started to encourage travellers to consider the impact of the decisions they make about where to go and how to get there. The Chairman of Eurostar, Guillaume Pepy, commented that greater environmental sensitivity has helped to increase Eurostar's sales: 'An increasing number of big companies are advising their personnel to use the train for short distances.'[29] Eurostar also produced a report that suggests, per passenger, a Eurostar train emits ten times less carbon dioxide than an aircraft flying between London and Paris.[30,31] The anti-Heathrow pressure group Hacan Clearskies reported that more than 60 flights a day head to Paris and 30 to Brussels. The use of trains on short-haul destinations served by rail links instead of planes would allow more than 100,000 flights to be cut annually.[32]

The 'Tread Lightly' initiative

The commitment to become a carbon neutral train operator, coinciding with its move to St Pancras in November 2007, led Eurostar to introduce its '10 commitments'. These include reducing paper usage (moving to e-ticketing and barcode ticketing), recycling and greater use of biodegradable materials, replacing train air-conditioning systems with less damaging systems, sourcing locally produced food where possible for train services, reducing energy wastage and encouraging travellers to use public transport to reach the Eurostar terminals.[33] The planned installation of energy efficient devices on its trains, to improve driving efficiency, is also under way.[34] While much of their carbon neutral status will be achieved through investment in offsetting programmes, a further goal has been set – to reduce CO_2 emissions by 25 per cent before 2012.

The media have been drawing attention to companies seeking to 'greenwash' their organizations (promoting their green credentials), but several reports have noted the environmental advantage of trains over planes.[35,36] This has been a concern for some airlines – easyJet complaining to the Advertising Standards Authority about a Virgin Trains' advert suggesting that trains emit 75 per cent less carbon dioxide than an equivalent air journey, ironically just weeks after it was criticized for inaccurately portraying its own green credentials.[37]

Pricing

The complex range of fares had meant that potential travellers perceived Eurostar as expensive. This also gave the impression that complex rules had to be considered if the best prices were to be accessed by customers. The same pricing structure had been in place since the launch of business in 1994, but the yield management approach used by airlines encouraged Eurostar to revisit its strategy and this ultimately led to a simplification of the pricing system.

Consumer research showed that customers were prepared to pay a small brand premium for travelling Eurostar, but the headline fare needed to be dropped from £79 to £59 to achieve greater success. At the same time, many of the complex restrictions were removed from tickets.[38]

The move to St Pancras also saw the launch of special fares from Glasgow to Paris, with a combined ticket for the Virgin GNER service to Euston and Eurostar across to France.[39] Eurostar has also offered cheaper fares for travellers departing from Ebbsfleet, in order to promote the station and encourage families to consider this option for their holiday travel.[40]

Summary

The changing business environment has provided a range of opportunities for Eurostar, as well as introducing many factors that will impact on the long-term growth in passenger numbers and the overall profitability of the organization. The move to St Pancras station, the completion of the high-speed line and the Continental rail alliance have all helped to enhance the rail product provided by Eurostar.

Notes

1. Eurostar (2008) 'Ownership & structure', Eurostar. Available online at: **www.eurostar. com/UK/uk/leisure/about_eurostar/company_information/ownership_structure.jsp**.
2. Nugent, G., Gittings, J. and Dawson, N. (2004) *Learning to Fly: The difference an idea made to the relaunch of Eurostar in 2003*, Institute of Practitioners in Advertising.
3. Clark, A. and Seager, A. (2006) 'Debt-laden Channel tunnel rail link is "nationalised"', *The Guardian*, 21 February.
4. WTO (2006) *Tourism Highlights 2006*, WTO, p. 12.
5. WTO (2005) *Tourism Highlights 2005*, WTO, p. 12.
6. 'London calling', *Travel Weekly*, 25 November, 2005.
7. Milmo, D. (2006) Stranded passengers turn to rail as flight chaos continues: train companies report brisk business as airports hit by another day of bad weather', *The Guardian*, 23 December.
8. 'Airlines lose out to Eurostar', *Airline Business*, February 2007, p. 18.

9. Coleman, T. (2007) Interview with Regional Manager, Eurostar.

10. Eurostar (2008) 'Press release: Eurostar and ATOC announce through fares to Continental Europe are now from over 130 towns and cities', Eurostar, 6 May. Available online at: **www.eurostar.com/UK/uk/leisure/about_eurostar/press_release/ eurostar_atoc_announce_through_fares_continental_europe_now_from_over_130_ towns_and_cities.jsp**.

11. 'Eurostar rejigs loyalty scheme', *Marketing*, 2005 9 July.

12. Coleman, 2007.

13. Marketing Society, 'Fly Eurostar' campaign entered for Marketing Society Awards 2004.

14. Phillips, M. and Francis, N. (2007) 'Queue's who: we rate British airports for crowds, cafés and check-in', *The Sun*, 2 August.

15. 'Heading for the airport? Here's how to cope with new security measures', *The Observer*, 8 July, 2007.

16. 'Eurostar H1 sales up 13.6 pct; to increase train runs in 2008', *AFX International Focus*, 18 July, 2007.

17. *Eurostar: How Mr JetSet made Eurostar mean business*, Institute of Practitioners in Advertising, IPA Effectiveness Awards 2006.

18. Eurostar (2008) 'High Speed 1 delivers a record year for Eurostar', Eurostar, 9 January. Available online at: **www.eurostar.com/UK/uk/leisure/about_eurostar/press_ release/high_speed_1_record_year_eurostar.jsp**.

19. *Airline Business*, February 2007.

20. Eurostar, 'Fleet & safety' Eurostar, 13 June 2007. Available online at: **www.eurostar.com/ UK/uk/leisure/about_eurostar/company_information/fleet_safety.jsp**

21. Taylor, I. (2007) 'Eurostar to join rail alliance', *Travel Weekly*, 30 March, p. 24.

22. 'Eurostar in joint rail-travel push', *Marketing*, 4 July 2007.

23. Wright, R. (2007) 'High-speed train operators link up to take on airline alliances', *Financial Times*, 3 July.

24. Eurostar (2007) 'The countdown has begun . . .', Eurostar 10 July. Available online at: **www.eurostar.com/media/pdf/WEB_2966_UK_Blue_Moon_map_flyers.pdf**

25. 'Changes in train', *Regeneration and Renewal*, 12 October 2007.

26. Glancey, J. (2007) 'The miracle of St Pancras', *The Guardian*, 11 October.

27. Coleman, 2007.

28. Department for Transport, 'The regeneration benefits of the CTRL', Department for transport, 12 August. Available online at: **www.dft.gov.uk/pgr/rail/pi/ctrl/ theregenerationbenefitsofthect1**

29. OD, 'Eurostar reports sales gain, cites passenger ecology concerns', *Agence France-Presse*, 18 July 2007.

30. Webster, B. (2006) 'Eurostar's Continental stitch-up', *The Times online*, 15 November.

31. Beattie, J. (2007) 'Eurostar good for business: green travel', *Evening Standard*, 11 October.

32. Beattie, 2007.

33. Eurostar (2007) '10 commitments', Eurostar, 21 August. Available online at: **www.eurostar.com/UK/uk/leisure/about_eurostar/environment/commitments.jsp**

34. 'Energy meters and power-saving devices added to Eurostar trains', *Professional Engineering*, 25 April 2007.

35. Martin, A. (2006) 'Paint the train green', *The Guardian*, 11 October.

36. 'New UK railway line High Speed 1 to be inaugurated on November 14', *Asian News International*, 11 October 2007.

37. 'Greenwash brands risk reputation', *Marketing*, 10 October 2007.

38. Marketing Society, 2004.

39. Miller, W. (2007) 'Scots rush for £89 Eurostar tickets to Paris', *Evening Times*, 19 September.

40. 'Eurostar cuts prices to lure regular flyers', *Travel Trade Gazette*, 28 September 2007.

Questions and discussion points

1. As pressure to consider our carbon footprint increases, Eurostar announced that the move to the new station at St Pancras would also herald the start of carbon neutral journeys – its Tread Lightly initiative. Do you think that such a move will encourage more travellers to make journeys by train rather than by private car or air?

2. How will the expansion of the high-speed rail network affect tourist travel around the Continent? How is Eurostar working to encourage UK visitors to take advantage of these developments?

3. What are the implications of having three different classes of service on each train? Are there drawbacks to this?

Case study 5

The pressure of visitors to Cambridge

Prepared by Claire Humphreys
(With thanks for the assistance of Derek Buxton, Tourism Office,
Kings College; Frankie McGhee, Tourism Services Manager,
Visit Cambridge; and Nick Milne, Conference Manager,
Robinson College)

Introduction

This case study focuses on the city of Cambridge, specifically concentrating on two themes – that of visitor management (to complement points discussed in Chapter 16) and on the accommodation sector (linking with themes developed in Chapter 12).

Several case studies and academic articles have focused on tourism in this, one of England's busiest tourist cities, often noting evidence of good practice in its planning for tourism. Throughout the 1980s and 1990s, efforts were made to implement tourism strategies and policies designed to manage rather than promote tourism.

This case study provides a picture of Cambridge as we come to the close of the noughties. The city has experienced greater pressure than in the past to reduce tourism funding by local government, although visitor management – along with the wider remit of city centre management – is still firmly on the agenda.

The city of Cambridge

The city of Cambridge is located in East Anglia, about 1 hour north of London by road, connected to the UK motorway network by the M11, which passes its western suburbs. Each year, over 4 million visitors are estimated to come to this small historic city and, with the 2001 census recording a population of just under 109,000, this means that, annually, tourists outnumber residents by a ratio of about 40:1. Thus, visitor management has become an important factor in maintaining the residents' quality of life as well as ensuring that the infrastructure can withstand the tourist onslaught.

The value of tourism to the city is estimated to be in the region of £355 million, with over 9000 people employed in the industry. Many of these jobs are part-time, however. Estimates suggest that only 6778 full-time equivalent jobs are supported by the tourism industry.[1]

The majority of visitors to the city are from the UK (over 70 per cent)[2] and the market is dominated by day trippers. A 2004 survey reported that only 20 per cent of the visitors to the city stayed overnight. The council has recognized this low level of overnight visitors and has announced initiatives to encourage longer stays, which, in turn, should increase tourism earnings. While in principle this seems to be a great opportunity, it is vital that consideration be given to the accommodation sector, which would need to service this increased demand.

The accommodation sector

In 2007, an estimated 2883 serviced bed spaces were available in the city, in hotels, guest houses and bed-and-breakfast accommodation. For visitors looking for non-serviced accommodation, the city also has available 60 caravan pitches and 55 self-catering units. Additionally, around 7000 bed spaces are available in college accommodation, many of which only become available out of term time.[3]

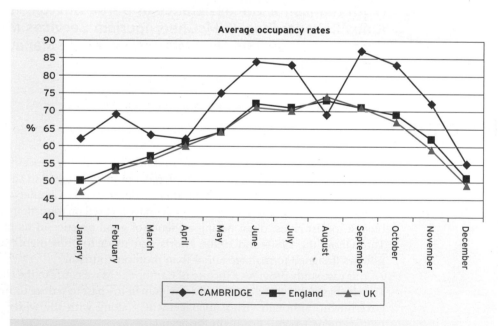

Figure CS5.1 Average room occupancy in Cambridge, 2007.
(Courtesy of EET.)

There is significant pressure on serviced accommodation. Although the number of bed spaces has almost tripled since 1975, occupancy levels remain high – significantly above the regional average. In 2007, the average occupancy levels were 72 per cent, compared with 62 per cent for Cambridgeshire as a whole and 52 per cent for the East of England region.[4] The peak months of June, July, September and October all had average occupancy levels in excess of 80 per cent. The quietest month was December, when average occupancy levels dropped to 55 per cent. All other months experienced average occupancy levels ranging between 62 and 75 per cent. These figures are also significantly higher than the national average (see Figure CS5.1).

The colleges significantly add to the accommodation stock during the summer months (and during other academic holiday periods, such as Christmas and Easter) by making student accommodation available to visitors. Of the 31 colleges in Cambridge, the vast majority (28) offer visitor accommodation, providing around 6727 bedrooms. In most cases, they are only available to groups, rather than individuals. Only 7 colleges offer bed-and-breakfast facilities for groups of fewer than ten people. Furthermore, over 60 per cent of the bedrooms provided by the colleges do not have en suite facilities – often an important requirement for conference delegates or groups of leisure visitors.[5]

Local government policy for tourism

Cambridge City Council (CCC) introduced its first tourism strategy over 30 years ago, as part of a coordinated effort to manage the pressures that tourism was placing on the city, especially its historic centre. The tourism strategy for the city has been revised and updated regularly, with the latest strategy being published in 2001. The city is reviewing the position, as the action plans linked to the 2001 strategy covered the period to 2006.

Since the 1980s, CCC has recognized the need to implement a policy that focused on managing rather than promoting tourism.[6,7] Importantly, the strategy recognized the need to concentrate on the value of tourism rather than just attracting greater visitors numbers. Broadly, the five strategies implemented since 1978 have sought to address a range of strategic aims, which are to:

- increase the benefits
- manage the problems caused, especially for the environment
- enhance the visitors' experiences
- assist different sectors of the tourism industry
- primarily in the 2001 strategy, to consider sustainability.

Specifically, the 2001 strategy incorporated four aims, which were to:[8]

- provide a high-quality visitor experience
- market Cambridge as an all-round quality destination
- ensure tourism is more sustainable
- reduce barriers and widen access for all kinds of visitors.

Underlying this strategy was an expectation that partnership – working with other key stakeholders in the city – would be vital for the successful implementation of these goals. With this in mind, the City Council appointed a Head of Tourism and City Centre Management team (CCM), in the belief that bringing together these two key areas should help to ensure that many of the resources used by tourists are managed in line with the demands of the residents.

There is a close affinity between the goals desired by CCC and those stated in the tourism policy of East of England Tourism, the regional tourist board. In 2005, the Regional

Development Agency for the area (EEDA) announced that direct tourism funding to the regional tourist board would be doubled, to £1 million.[9] A new agenda was set for the regional tourist board – it now focuses on:[10]

- attracting new visitors from within and outside the region
- encouraging partnerships with and between local business and local governments within the region
- developing marketing and PR campaigns, as well as gathering market intelligence
- encouraging sustainable quality to improve visitors' experience.

The local and regional policies for tourism link in with national policy on tourism. The strategy 'Tomorrow's Tourism', was introduced in 1999 and, more recently, the action plan for the Department for Culture, Media and Sport suggested a focus on four priorities for tourism:

- marketing and e-tourism
- product quality
- workforce skills
- improved data.

Overlapping links between areas of priority for national, regional and local government have ensured that the strategic planning for tourism in the city has been coherent. Over the past few years, however, greater pressure has been placed on controlling public spending and, as a consequence, there has been a shift towards greater commercialism, encouraging the private sector to work in partnership with government to support tourism projects. This has impacted on some visitor management initiatives across the city.

Visitor management

As mentioned above, the management of tourism is combined with CCM. This has the valuable advantage of ensuring that the demands from both residents and visitors for access to, and use of, the city's resources can be balanced. Furthermore, a key role of CCM is to encourage and develop partnerships between the different organizations involved in providing resources in the central core area. These include shops, tourist attractions, colleges, government services, such as street cleaning, property developers, market stall holders and many others. By coordinating initiatives supported by these groups, a range of projects have been implemented, including the production of shopping guides and introduction of a crime reduction scheme.

An example of negotiating with stakeholders to enhance the visitor experience can be seen in the case of punting. This is a popular attraction specific to the city – punts being long flat-bottomed boats, propelled along the river by means of a long pole pushed against the bed of the river.

Many thousands of tourists take organized punting trips, including a guided tour of the backs of the colleges, while others elect to hire boats to punt along the river themselves. In recent years, however, the punting industry has been under scrutiny.

The largest punt provider, Scudamores, operates from several central riverside locations, but competes with many smaller punt hire businesses. Competition for customers had become so fierce that many punt companies hired touts to encourage customers to use their services. The hard sell from these touts was said to be overwhelming, creating a negative experience for visitors.

To address this problem, negotiations with the punting companies has led to the licensing of touts, restricting the number of touts allowed for each operator. This has been seen as a positive move to improve visitors' experiences of the city, but whether it has significantly reduced the pressure felt by tourists remains to be seen.

At the same time as the issue of touting came to people's attention, some independent punting companies were in conflict with college managers.

The navigation authority for the stretch of river running through the centre of the city is the Conservators of the River Cam, which issues licences to punting companies. This licence does not, however, give punting companies the right to pick up or drop off tourists along the riverbanks by the colleges (as these areas are private land), so, even though the independent punting companies had been able to obtain river licences, there were few places for them to legally embark passengers, restricting their ability to operate.

Many chose to attract customers at popular tourist spots, often by the colleges, which meant that some riverbanks became heavily eroded. This created hostility between the colleges, the punting companies and, indirectly, the Conservators of the River Cam. Increased monitoring on the river has been organized in an attempt to manage this issue.

Operational techniques

One of the major problems faced by Cambridge is the issue of congestion. Pressure around the city comes from the high level of commuter traffic, but this is compounded by incoming tourists. The city council has undertaken a range of initiatives to reduce the congestion caused by residents, commuters and tourists.

Transport system

Technology has allowed the historic centre to be closed to private cars, while still allowing access for local buses and taxis. This is achieved through a system of bollards, which can be lowered by drivers of authorized vehicles using an electronic sensor. This allows the central area to become virtually traffic free, providing more space for shoppers, visitors and locals to walk freely around the streets (see Figure CS5.2). One particularly congested area, Silver Street, which is very narrow, now operates a 'tidal flow' system, using the bollards to allow only one-way traffic. The system permits traffic entry towards the city between 6 a.m. and 10 a.m. and away from the city (4 p.m.–midnight) to assist departing traffic during the evening rush hour. In addition, other roads are closed between 10 a.m. and 4 p.m., which ensures that some streets are pedestrianized during that time.

More directly impacting on tourism has been the change in the location of the drop-off points for tour buses. In the past, coaches would head into the centre of the city to offload their passengers. The closure of the central area, however, has been combined with the allocation of a new coach drop-off location on Queen's Road. While this has removed traffic from the central area, one concern raised was that this leaves tourists with a five- to ten-minute walk into the historic centre. In addition, few facilities are available at the new coach stop – there is no shelter for tourists waiting for their coaches to return, and toilet and catering facilities are some distance away. Furthermore, while space for several coaches is available, there had been no accurate data on the number of coaches that visit during the peak season. Popular arrival and departure times have led to coaches waiting outside of this drop zone or having to queue to access the official spaces. Those on foreign coaches face an added hazard. As their doors are on the right side of the vehicle, passengers are obliged to disembark directly on to the busy road, parking spaces being available only on one side of it.

To encourage commuters and visitors to avoid driving into the city centre, a park and ride system has been introduced. Five sites around the city have been developed, with a capacity for almost 5000 cars. These sites are conveniently located on the key arterial routes into the city. An estimated 3.4 million passenger journeys are made annually on the park and ride system.

Figure CS5.2 Bollard system, restricting access to the city centre.
(Photo by Claire Humphreys.)

To further discourage private cars in the central area, the price of car parking is kept quite high. The charge for using the park and ride system (£2.20 in 2008) remains cheaper than parking for 2 hours or longer in the central area. An additional incentive is that up to three children can travel free with each paying adult.

Research of current users reveals that almost half (46 per cent) chose to use park and ride because it was cheaper than parking in town, while 21 per cent stated that they used the system because it was easier than driving into the city centre.[11] One issue discouraging tourists from using the park and ride system, however, is its limited hours of operation. The sites generally close at 8 p.m., which means that day trippers cannot use them if they plan to spend the evening in the city. Furthermore, no overnight parking is allowed, making it impossible for staying visitors to use the system.

Cycling is especially popular in Cambridge. A key factor driving this is a regulation made by the university, which states that undergraduate students are restricted from owning motor vehicles within the neighbourhood of Cambridge. The relatively flat terrain and the compact city centre have also encouraged many local residents to use cycles to get around.

Estimates suggest that cycling accounts for 25 per cent of journeys to work – one of the highest levels in Europe.[12] A high level of use is also reported by those tourists staying in the city while studying at the local language schools during the summer holiday. These groups may have limited knowledge of UK road rules or local cycle laws – a factor that may cause problems for local drivers.

One difficulty of such high levels of cycle use is finding space for cycle parking. In order to lock cycles to prevent theft, railings and fences are often used as convenient fixed points, often leading to congestion on pavements and footpaths. With this in mind, the council's local plan specifically requires that new developments must provide space for cycles (see Figure CS5.3), while council funding has led to the introduction of one of the largest undercover cycle parks anywhere, with space for over 200 bicycles.

Figure CS5.3 Cycle parking outside Cambridge train station.
(Photo by Claire Humphreys.)

Cycle hire is also widely available in the city, providing a convenient way for visitors to get around the city. The city council has produced a cycle route map, available online and from the tourist information centre, to raise awareness of the routes available.

In recent years, there has been talk of implementing a congestion zone for the city. CCC acknowledged this in its annual report for 2008/2009, suggesting that a zone should only be implemented if further improvements to public transport facilities are made and providing that the funds raised by the scheme are used on local projects. Introducing a congestion zone remains a hotly contested issue in the city.[13]

Information provision

Providing information to tourists can ensure that the experience of visitors is enhanced and it can also help to increase **dwell time** – the amount of time spent in the area.

CCC has funded a tourist information centre (TIC), located inside the Guildhall, the council's main building. In recent years, funding has been reduced and the TIC has been under pressure to become more commercial in its activities. This has led to the introduction of a premium-rate phone service to provide visitor information. The TIC provides information leaflets, a bed reservation service and a conference venue-finding service, as well as overseeing the blue badge and green badge guided tours.

Guiding

The blue and green badge guides provide an important visitor management function for the city. In order to control the impact of visitors, the colleges now require groups visiting their premises to be accompanied by a guide. The advantage of this is that guides can ensure the behaviour of tourists does not contravene the rules and regulations of the colleges. The guides perform a similar function for the wider historic area.

The TIC offers several tours daily to visitors who have not arrived in groups. Guides operating these organized tours can ensure that the movement of tourists around the city is controlled and can encourage dispersal to less well-known areas, as well as managing the time spent at the popular attractions. Guides also ensure visitor safety, by avoiding areas where tourist demands (for example, to stop and take photographs) are likely to be problematic.

Marketing

While the attractions in the area undertake their own marketing, the TIC also undertakes coordinated marketing campaigns. Often this means working in partnership with local tourism enterprises to promote the area to business and leisure visitors. This includes producing brochures, many of which focus on amenities such as accommodation, restaurants and bars, as well as attractions.

The TIC also provides information via its website (**www.visitcambridge.org**). This has become an important source of information for visitors, used primarily prior to arriving in the city. In 2007, over half a million people visited the website to search for information or book accommodation.[14] Providing information can influence visitors' behaviour, encouraging longer stays, as well as dispersing tourists into other areas of the city as they explore a wider variety of attractions.

Signs

Signs at the outskirts of the city have been used to encourage drivers to use the park and ride facilities. Signs show real-time availability of parking, helping drivers to select areas that are likely to be less congested. Of greater concern, however, are the signs in the historic centre.

In 2008, the city council announced plans to improve street signs in the central area and, in partnership with the City Centre Management group, have implemented trials of different types of signs.[15] One motivation for this initiative has been the acknowledgement that, over the years, many different styles of signs have been introduced into the area, cluttering the streetscape. At the same time, navigation for new visitors has been unclear. One added advantage of rationalizing and improving signs is that shops and attractions in the area can benefit from improved levels of footfall past their doors. The design and materials used in the construction of the new signs will be in keeping with the existing streetscape. The improved signs are expected to enhance the experience for visitors.

The colleges

The city's landscape is dominated by the college and university buildings. Many of the colleges are popular visitor attractions, but it must not be forgotten that their primary purpose is education. Many of the colleges, therefore, have needed to manage the conflicting demands of the visitors and the academic environment.

Excessive visitor numbers led King's College to charge a fee for access to the chapel. A trial charge in 1993 required adults to pay £2 to enter the college, which noticeably reduced numbers from an estimated one million to a more manageable level of around 300,000. The outcome was seen to be a much improved experience for the tourists.

King's College was not the first to introduce entry charges, though. St John's started charging in 1992 and, as most of the centrally located colleges now charge, it has now become expected by many tourists.

Charging has ensured that tourists with a low level of interest in the attraction are effectively deterred from entering. Groups of visitors are required to prebook their visit, allowing the college to manage demand through timed ticketing of these groups.

The demands of being an academic institution also mean that, at certain times of the year, such as during exams, the colleges must close their doors to tourists. While this may be disappointing for visitors, these dates are generally well-publicized, both by the colleges and the TIC.

For King's College, the chapel must also be closed to tourists when it is being used for services, concerts and during filming of the 'Nine lessons and carols' Christmas service (which is televised around the world).

The dominance of the colleges in city centre management

Ownership of much of the land in the city centre is in the hands of the colleges. This is not true just for the academic buildings but also for many of the shopping streets in the historic centre. Located above many of the shops is rental accommodation for students and, therefore the colleges have an interest in maintaining the central areas.

A higher footfall attracts shops and businesses to locate in the area, which, in turn, can increase the property rental values.

Many of the colleges are relatively wealthy as they are major landowners in the city, provide employment, have a strong reputation for academic excellence, attract visitors and thus are an integral part of city life. This power and dominance has often meant that city council management plans for the historic area must also be negotiated with these institutions.

The provision of visitor accommodation

It will now be apparent that the colleges are an important component of the tourism industry, not just as attractions but also as accommodation providers. In most cases, they are for organized groups rather than individual visitors. Many colleges now employ a conference organizer to maximize the use of their accommodation and meeting spaces outside of term time. The newest college, Robinson, which was opened in 1981, specifically included in the design of the building facilities aimed at attracting the conference market. They included providing a large, theatre-style meeting space, breakout rooms, en suite bedrooms and an additional dining space, so both students and conference visitors could be accommodated simultaneously.

In 1998, Conference Cambridge was established to represent 28 colleges as well as 7 venues, including university sites, faculty buildings, Cambridge University Press and the Møller Centre. Funded by the venues it represents, the remit of the organization is to attract conference business to the city generally, especially to locations run by its members. This includes acting as a venue-finding service for professional conference organizers (PCOs).

This organization effectively competes with the local TIC's conference booking service, Destination Cambridge, which offers a venue finding service for over 100 venues in the area. The existence of the two entities may be confusing and inconvenient for PCOs and some of the venues must question the cost inherent in the duplication of services provided to sell their conference space and accommodation.

The accommodation provided by the colleges is a key factor in supporting tourism in the city. High occupancy levels exist despite the provision from colleges and, as their policies are set to encourage more overnight visitors, this pressure may continue to ensure high rack rates for accommodation. Care needs to be taken as such high rates can themselves deter visitors from staying overnight in the city.

Summary

A wide range of initiatives have helped to manage the pressure from tourists in the city. Several of them address pressures created both by visitors and local residents who desire to access this compact historic city. Proactive planning, controls and restrictions, diversionary tactics and information provision all help to adjust visitors' behaviour and manage the impacts resulting from tourism.

Notes

1. East of England Tourism (2004) 'Compendium of tourism statistics – volume and value of tourism', East of England Tourism.

2. East of England Tourism, 2004.

3. Cambridge City Council (2008) 'Tourism: facts and figures', Cambridge City Council.

4. East of England Tourism (2008) 'Serviced accommodation occupancy annual report 2007', East of England Tourism.

5. Conference Cambridge (2008) 'Facilities overview', Conference Cambridge. Available online at: **www.conferencecambridge.com/home/index.php?m=venues&a=facilities**

6. Cambridge City Council (2001) 'Cambridge tourism strategy 2001–2006', Cambridge City Council, p. 5.

7. Maitland, R. (2006) 'How can we manage the tourist historic city? Tourism strategy in Cambridge, UK, 1978–2003', *Tourism Management*, 27, pp. 1262–73.

8. Cambridge City Council, 2001.

9. East of England Development Agency (2008) 'Tourism, leisure and heritage', East of England Development Agency.

10. East of England Tourism (2008) 'Business plan and budget 2008/9, January', East of England Tourism.

11. Ross-Bain, C. (2008) Personal correspondence with the park and ride manager, March.

12. Cambridge City Council (2008) 'Cambridgeshire's policy on cycling', Cambridge City Council. Available online at: **www.cambridgeshire.gov.uk/transport/around/cycling/cambridgeshires_policy_on_cycling.htm**

13. 'Majority oppose congestion charge', *Cambridge News*, 6 May 2008.

14. Cambridge City Council, 2008.

15. Cambridge City Council (2008) 'Street signage consultation', Cambridge City Council. Available online at: **www.cambridge.gov.uk/ccm/content/arts-and-entertainment/finding-your-way.en**

Questions and discussion points

1. Some of the visitor management techniques employed by the city of Cambridge are funded through tourists' contributions. There are several other approaches, however, that are funded by local government, through local business and resident taxes. What is the justification local government gives for using local taxes to fund such initiatives?

2. Are some of the visitor management techniques employed likely to deter tourists from coming to the city?

3. Many hotels within the Cambridge area achieve high occupancy levels. What are the implications of this for the local council's tourism strategy, which is trying to encourage overnight visitors rather than day trippers?

4. Many of the colleges provide accommodation in the student halls of residence out of term time. In most cases, this is limited to groups only and often attracts small conferences, language school visits to the city and, occasionally, wedding parties. Discuss the importance of the amenities (accommodation, catering and so on) provided by the colleges.

Case study 6

Business tourism in Tanzania

Prepared by Rob Davidson

Introduction

This case study examines the African country of Tanzania as an emerging destination for conferences and incentives, with an emphasis on the country's infrastructure for this market. This is a country best-known for leisure tourism, notably wildlife safaris, but in recent years it has increasingly been the destination for international conferences and incentive trips. It draws on material to be found in Chapters 9 and 11.

Tanzania fact file[1]

Location

Tanzania, comprising the mainland and the Zanzibar archipelago, is the largest country in East Africa, bordering Kenya to the north, Rwanda, Burundi and the Democratic Republic of Congo to the west and Zambia, Malawi and Mozambique to the south. Tanzania is located between 29 and 41 degrees east and between 1 and 12 degrees south.

Capital city

Dodoma is the administrative capital and Dar es Salaam is the business capital.

Population

Approximately 35 million.

Area

It is 945,000 square kilometres.

Ethnic groups

On the mainland, the people are mainly native African, 99 per cent (of whom 95 per cent are Bantu, consisting of more than 130 tribes) and the remaining 1 per cent others (Asian, European and Arab). On Zanzibar, the people are a mixture of Swahili, native African, Arab, Indian and Chinese.

Religions

On the mainland the proportions are Christian 45 per cent, Muslim 35 per cent and indigenous beliefs 20 per cent. On Zanzibar, over 99 per cent are Muslim and the remainder are a mix of Hindu, Christian and Zoroastrian.

Languages

Swahili, with English being widely spoken, plus many tribal languages.

Climate

Tanzania's climate is predominantly tropical, the average daily temperature being 30°C. Coastal areas are usually hot and humid, with cooling sea breezes. Tanzania has two rainy seasons and the hottest time of the year is from December to March. In high-altitude areas, such as Kilimanjaro and the Ngorongoro Highlands, temperatures can fall to below freezing.

Access

There are three international airports – Dar es Salaam, Kilimanjaro and Zanzibar. At the time of writing, international air carriers Air India, British Airways, Ethiopian Airlines, Egypt Air, Emirates, Gulf Air, Oman Air, Kenya Airways, South African Airways, Swiss and KLM fly into Tanzania. Charter flights operate throughout the country. Train travel is possible throughout Tanzania.

Visa requirements

Visas are required by visitors from many countries coming to Tanzania, so tourists are advised to check this with their Tanzanian embassy or consulate prior to departure and purchase visas before arriving in Tanzania. While it is possible to purchase a visa on arrival in Tanzania, it can mean standing in a long, slow-moving queue after an international flight and finding that only US dollars are accepted.

Departure tax

A departure tax of US $30 must be paid by all passengers departing Tanzania on international flights. This tax is generally included in the price of the ticket, if departing from the mainland. When departing from Zanzibar, payment must be made in cash at the airport.

Tourism in Tanzania

In 2008, Tanzania's tourism industry was reported as having been growing at a steady rate for the preceding seven years, according to an article by Thomas Steinmetz published in eTurboNews (**www.eturbonews.com**). According to the Governor of the Bank of Tanzania, tourism earnings in 2008 were expected to generate US$1 billion – approximately three times the annual income gained from the Tanzanian agriculture industry. The Minister for Natural Resources and Tourism said that over 750,000 tourists were expected to arrive in Tanzania in 2008, declaring, 'We attribute this growth to several factors, not the least of which is that Tanzania has a stable and peaceful environment with a democratically elected government'. According to the Minister, increased air access, with many carriers now flying directly into Tanzania, new luxury hotels on the mainland, improved infrastructure and tarmac roads on safari circuits were also major factors contributing to the development of tourism in Tanzania.

The manager of the Tanzania Tourist Board was cited as saying that the improvements in tourism were the outcomes of the diversity of the tourist attractions and the existing allure of Tanzania's wildlife, its having seven World Heritage sites, the cultural richness and friendliness of the Tanzanian people, miles of beautiful Indian Ocean coastline and the exotic Spice Islands of Zanzibar. He continued, 'Over the last ten years, Tanzania has become a standalone destination. In the past, many tour operators to East Africa offered Tanzania as an add-on or extension to other countries. Now, there is such a great demand by clients to spend their entire time in Tanzania that the same tour operators offer more than one Tanzania-only itinerary'.

Tanzania's main international markets are Britain, Germany, the United States, Italy, France, Spain and the Scandinavian countries. Tanzania also receives a sizeable number of tourists from South Africa and Kenya. In 2007, the United States surpassed Britain as the leading source of tourists, with 59,000 visitors, slightly more than Britain's 55,000.

Tanzania as a conference destination

Tanzania attracts predominantly two sectors of the business tourism industry: conferences and incentive trips. Let us consider first the country's infrastructure for the meetings sector.

In the 2008 *Tanzania Conference Directory*, the country is described in the following terms, as a destination eminently suitable for conferences:

> Tanzania is a politically stable and welcoming country, a nation where modern convenience and ancient tradition co-exist in harmony. The range of facilities available throughout Tanzania meets the needs of any event planning team. Modern hotels in all the major cities offer a variety of conference rooms and can supply all the technical equipment necessary to ensure a professional, successful conference. Many Tanzanian hotels employ conference coordinators who specialize in the running of conventions and work tirelessly to ensure a smooth delivery of the conference agenda.

One example of a hotel that is well-equipped to host conferences is the 230-room Mövenpick Royal Palm Hotel in Dar es Salaam, which offers meeting rooms with a capacity of up to 600 delegates. A great number of high-profile events are held in this hotel each year. For example, in April 2008, the hotel was the venue for the high-profile launch of the Tanzanian advocacy campaign to accelerate efforts in reducing maternal, newborn and child mortality. The event took place under the auspices of the World Health Organization's Partnership for Maternal, Newborn and Child Health and was attended by Tanzanian President Jakaya M. Kikwete and Norwegian Prime Minister Jens Stoltenberg, with approximately 200 guests and local media.

Some of the largest meeting events held in Tanzania are held in the country's principal purpose-built conference centre, which is not to be found in either its administrative or business capital, but in Arusha, one of the country's fastest-growing cities.

Arusha is the former headquarters of the East African Community, an economic and customs union between Kenya, Tanzania and Uganda. One legacy of this status is the

Figure CS6.1 Arusha International Conference Centre.
(Photo by Rob Davidson.)

Arusha International Conference Centre (AICC) (see Figure CS6.1). Established under the Public Corporations Act, 1969, by a presidential order, AICC is 100 per cent government-owned, but operates as a fully fledged commercial entity without any subsidies from the Tanzanian government.

It is situated exactly halfway between Cape Town and Cairo and offers a number of conference halls and rooms that cater for meetings for between 10 and 1000 delegates. Most of the rooms are equipped with simultaneous interpretation systems for up to four different languages. Additionally, the AICC provides exhibition areas, conference secretarial offices, audio-visual equipment (including PowerPoint, overhead slide projectors, flip-charts, video recording), document reproduction services and conference assistance staff. There are also inhouse catering facilities for tea and coffee breaks, luncheons and cocktail parties.

According to its website (**www.aicc.co.tz**), the Centre hosts an average of 100 meetings each year, with an annual average of 11,000 conference delegates, thus contributing immensely to the socio-economic development of Arusha and the country at large. The AICC has been the location for many prominent deliberations, including the Rwandan War Crimes Tribunal and the Burundi Peace Negotiations, during which Nelson Mandela, former president of South Africa, addressed the delegates.

Many of the events hosted by the AICC are association conferences and Table CS6.1 shows details of some past meetings.

The AICC is a member of two international associations – the International Congress & Convention Association (**www.iccaworld.com**) and the International Association of Congress Centres (**www.aipc.org**), both of which aim to increase the level of professionalism concerning how conference centres are managed and marketed and to promote the conference industry as a whole.

Table CS6.1 Association conferences hosted by the AICC.

Dates	Events	Numbers of delegates
8–13 July 2007	19th INTERPOL Africa Regional Conference	200
27–29 November 2007	26th Tanzania Veterinary Association and TSAP Joint Meeting	250
3–5 December 2007	22nd NBMM Professional Conference	450
10–14 December 2007	5th African Population Conference	1200
10–14 March 2008	47th International Federation of Air Traffic Controllers Association Meeting	800

Tanzania as an incentive travel destination

The 2008 *Tanzania Conference Directory* gives details of ideas for incentive travel experiences in Tanzania:

> From a luxury safari in the Serengeti to dining under the stars in Zanzibar's atmospheric Stone Town, there is something to suit everyone's taste and budget. For the energetic, there's Africa's highest point, Mount Kilimanjaro, to be climbed, and a host of watersports including snorkeling, diving and sailing.

An outstanding example of an incentive trip to Tanzania was the Motaquip Annual Award that took place in Zanzibar between 26 February and 4 March 2007, organized by the BI agency, for 29 employees of Motaquip. The trip was described by James Thornton in the 8 June 2007 issue of the magazine *Conference & Incentive Travel* (**www.citmagazine.com**) as follows:

Figure CS6.2 Arusha welcomes delegates to the 2008 Leon H Sullivan Summit. *(Photo by Rob Davidson.)*

Case study: Motaquip inspires with Zanzibar trip

The automotive company had a lot to live up to and required a destination that would impress well-travelled delegates. Stunning Zanzibar delivered on all fronts.

THE BRIEF: Peugeot-owned Motaquip, the UK's largest automotive parts company, runs an ongoing incentive scheme for its top-performing distributors and their partners, culminating in an overseas trip. In 2006, they performed particularly well, so the focus for the trip was to be on rest and recuperation.

This, however, was an audience well used to being incentivised by high-end trips, so getting the destination right was vital. 'Our people have been to a variety of locations in recent years such as Cape Town, Mauritius and New York, so the challenge is always to take it to a new level with an aspirational destination,' explains Peugeot's then advertising and sales promotion manager Helen Main (now direct marketing manager). 'Zanzibar was an ideal choice – a great place for rest and recuperation and certainly not on most people's "been there" list. It inspired them to work hard to secure a place.'

CHALLENGES: Of course, taking a group somewhere exotic, remote and chilled out creates its own hurdles. 'The flights were a challenge,' admits BI senior project manager (events) Anouk Kreek. 'We flew the group from London to Dar es Salaam on British Airways and then used a smaller Kenya Airways aircraft to Zanzibar. Everything went well, but dealing with local carriers was a challenge in terms of getting commitment in advance for group bookings.' Also, schedule limitations meant that on the way back the group had to go first to Nairobi, then Dar es Salaam to London.

BI found that suppliers on the ground also had quite a laid-back attitude. 'We had to work hard to make sure suppliers understood everything we wanted, but it all worked out in the end', says Kreek.

Although the focus was firmly on relaxation, Main also knew that a strong programme of activities, albeit leisurely ones, would have to be lined up. 'The island is beautiful but there is not a lot of infrastructure, so you are mainly limited to using the hotels,' she says. 'We had to think carefully about what we would do on the four evenings and off-site during the day.'

SOLUTION: Between Main and BI, an itinerary was created with enough of the right activities in place to keep the group occupied.

If the evening entertainment was going to be limited to hotels, Main wanted to stay at the 5-star Zamani Zanzibar Kempinski, where the group was based. The solution was to devise four evening dining options in different locations around the beachfront hotel. A welcome dinner and drinks by the pool were arranged for the first night, while on the second a beach barbecue with a traditional dance show was laid on. The third evening came hard on the heels of a fairly busy day, so an evening of drinks and a finger buffet was arranged out on the hotel's jetty overlooking a coral reef, followed by a film show under the stars on sun loungers. On the final night, there was a gala dinner, followed by a DJ and dancing overlooking the Indian Ocean.

The slightly convoluted flight home was unavoidable but it threw up positives, according to BI client services director Michele Cain: 'The flight to Nairobi was later and meant the group could leave the hotel after lunch and connect with an overnight flight to London.' Peugeot's Main agrees: 'Everyone had firmly bonded by then, so the journey home was fine. The gala dinner had gone on until 4 am the previous night for some people, so leaving at 3 pm was ideal.'

EXECUTION: As the group arrived after an eight-hour flight from Heathrow to Dar es Salaam and the transfer to Zanzibar, the rest of the day was given over to free time, before the poolside welcome dinner in the evening. On the second day, activities included a visit to a spice farm. The tour took delegates through the tropical forest of the farm, followed by a tasting session. At the end, each delegate received a special presentation basket of island spices.

Day three started with a guided tour of Zanzibar's capital Stone Town, where delegates bought souvenirs before heading off for the day's main event – an exclusive cruise aboard a traditional dhow. Three boats took the group to a private sand bank in the ocean for a barbecue lunch. As well as relaxing in the idyllic location, options included snorkelling on the coral reef.

The centrepiece of the final day was a visit to a local primary school, where the group interacted with the pupils and teachers. It was a moving experience, according to BI's Kreek. 'The group was genuinely touched – seeing the limited facilities the children had made them appreciate their own education', she says.

Delegates presented the children with educational gifts such as pens, but the Motaquip staff wanted to do more. The traditional souvenirs purchased in Stone Town were auctioned off during the evening's gala dinner, raising £1,300 to pay for desks, books and uniforms. The school's annual budget is £500.

VERDICT: According to Cain, the experience was a success. As well as the school visit, delegates were particularly taken with the dhow cruise. 'Motaquip has taken groups to some stunning places over the years, but delegates said it was the best incentive they had seen. Sometimes it can be hard to truly incentivise people, but Zanzibar delivered in every sense,' she says. 'Things such as journey time became irrelevant once the group arrived and saw how spectacular it was.'

As part of the agency running the event, she may be bound to say that, but her client agrees. 'We did questionnaires after the trip and everyone said it was the best event they had been on with the company,' says Main. 'It achieved all the things I wanted it to and, in terms of re-incentivising staff, has got everyone working hard to be on next year's trip.'

It is important to note that the participants in many of the incentive trips to Tanzania do not use luxury hotels for their accommodation as the Motaquip group did, but instead sleep under canvas in exclusive camps and lodges, situated in locations far from the urban centres. In its 2007 review of ten of the best such lodges in Africa, *Conference & Incentive Travel* magazine included the following three from Tanzania.

- *Mnemba Island Lodge, Zanzibar* (**www.andbeyond.com**)
  The Mnemba Island Lodge is strictly a destination for high-end small group incentive trips only. Situated on an exclusive island just off the north-eastern tip of Zanzibar in the azure Indian Ocean, it is surrounded by an atoll of coral reefs, which have been declared a marine conservation area and boasts some of Africa's best dive sites. The lodge has just ten beachside bandas, or cottages, built of indigenous materials. Each *banda* also has a private beach *sala* (pavilion) with sunbeds. There is also a dining room and bar in the main area. Water-based activities on offer include windsurfing, kayaking and fly-fishing, and Zanzibar itself is just 20 minutes away by boat.

- *Ngorongoro Crater Lodge, Tanzania* (**www.andbeyond.com**)
  This deluxe property perches on the edge of a three million year-old volcanic crater in the heart of Maasai country. Inspired in design by the tribe's *manyattas* (homestead), it lies in the Ngorongoro Conservation Area, 3000 square miles of wilderness that is home to more than 25,000 animals. The lodge is a favourite with the Royal Geographic Society. Visitors can take safaris and sundowners overlooking the Lake Eyasi and there are also meeting spaces for up to 60, while marquees can hold more than 100. Service is top of the agenda here, with a ratio of three staff to each guest.

- *Kirawira Camp, Western Serengeti, Tanzania* (**www.slh.com**)
  Kirawira takes the luxury camping ethos on with its Victorian-style canvas lodges. There are touches here that evoke the past, with tents furnished with chintzy chaises longues, Persian rugs, antique escritoires, wind-up phonograms, leather-bound travelling cases, brass shooting sticks, carved rocking chairs and stud-backed smoking chairs – and all in the heart of the Serengeti with its bountiful wildlife. The camp staff can arrange off-site corporate teambuilding exercises, such as excursions up Kilimanjaro, ballooning over the Serengeti or testing trading skills at Zanzibar's spice markets. Tents can also be rearranged into conference configurations or boardrooms.

Conclusion

Tanzania, like many other destinations, has sought to diversify its tourism product by providing facilities for business tourism in addition to those for leisure. The vast majority of the investment has been made by the private sector – notably, operators of 4-star and 5-star hotels and luxury lodges. The country's dependence on its income from tourism of all kinds is evident, so the types of high-spending visitors who come to the country to participate in conferences and incentive trips are undoubtably welcomed. Tanzania faces strong competition from other, longer-established African destinations, however, such as South Africa and Kenya. Time will tell whether or not Tanzania can successfully secure a place for itself on the map of major business tourism destinations.

Note

1. Tourism Confederation of Tanzania and the Tanzania Tourism Board (2008) *Tanzania Conference Directory*, ZG Design.

Questions and discussion points

1. From reading this case study, what do you think are the assets of Tanzania specifically as a business tourism destination? Can you identify any real disadvantages of this country as a place for the hosting of international conferences and incentive trips?
2. Undertake research to find out how Tanzania markets itself as a destination for conferences and incentive trips. Investigate, for example, whether or not this country is covered in the trade press (magazines such as *Conference & Incentive Travel*) and whether Tanzania exhibits at international trade shows for this sector, such as EIBTM (**www.eibtm.com**) and IMEX (**www.imex-frankfurt.com**).
3. Reading the details of the Motaquip incentive trip to Zanzibar, what current trends in the business tourism sector does this example illustrate?

Case study 7

Women managers in UK travel and tourism – a case of a 'glass ceiling'?

Prepared by Brandon Crimes, Senior Lecturer, Tourism Group, Business School, University of Hertfordshire, and Paul E. Smith, Principal Lecturer, HR Group, Business School, University of Hertfordshire

Introduction

This case study examines the situation of women managers in travel and tourism in the UK. It is based on joint research carried out in 2007 with an industry partner, Shine People and Places, that specifically focused on possible explanations for the relative lack of women in senior management positions in the sector. The research was based in the UK, but Hemmati[1] suggests that this gender pyramid is evident in the sector worldwide. This case study has relevance for elements of Chapter 5, since failure to recruit the best talent for tourism jobs, regardless of gender, will have an impact on the economic benefits achieved by a destination. There are also practical applications, particularly for visitor management (Chapter 16), as well as issues regarding employment in other sectors of industry.

Travel and tourism is one of the largest industries in the UK, accounting for 2.9 per cent of the UK's gross value added, and worth approximately £85.6 billion with over 2 million jobs being generated directly and indirectly (**www.tourismtrade.org.uk**). The World Travel and

Tourism Council (WTTC) has reported that the future forecast for employment needs for this global industry will reflect the demand the industry creates for labour, from 198 million in 2002 to 249 million by 2012.[2]

Where these employees will be drawn from will obviously vary from country to country and, given the vulnerable and seasonal nature of the travel and tourism industry, some caution should be exercised when predicting future labour trends. Nonetheless, what can be identified as a key strategy for destinations is to improve the quality of the tourist experience so that not only can they compete with other destinations but also ensure that the delivery of that tourist experience meets the ever more demanding critera of increasingly well-travelled and informed consumers, thus creating a memorable visit.

The increasing importance placed on the delivery of the tourism experience is clearly going to be dependent on the skills and education of those employed to actually plan, promote and provide not just a memorable experience but also one that actually surpasses tourists' expectations. As Page and Connell note, 'The performance of a business in tourism will be based on the quality of its human talent.'[3]

As someone studying tourism, you will be aware of the gender balance on your course. Indeed, the number of students enrolled on all tourism courses in the United Kingdom in 2004/2005 records a high number of females – of the 11,800 enrolled, some 68 per cent were female.[4] Indeed, the subject has proven to be attractive to females over the past decade and it is interesting to note that the situation in education is no different from the proportions in the industry as a whole. For many females joining the industry in the UK, however, there is a possibility that they may not achieve their full potential and perceived barriers to career progression are not only evident, but have remained, despite legislation on equal opportunities and sex discrimination. Furthermore, according to a survey carried out by the Department for Education and Skills in 2005, the difference in levels of pay between males and females is also evident among those undertaking training apprenticeships, which is reported as being as much as 26 per cent: 'the statistics revealed a general rule: the more female trainees an industry had, the less they were paid.'[5] Those statistics, from the survey, were:

- average weekly pay of male apprentices – £153
- average weekly pay of their female counterparts – £113

Travel and tourism as an industry has an image of being very exciting, with few problems in attracting new entrants for frontline and first employment experiences. The opportunity for women to develop their career potential further up the line, however, may be hindered by not only a number of internal factors but also the fact that the management environment in which they seek to do so is often dominated by males.

Despite this sector having a majority of female employees, using figures from Purcell's work[6] demonstrates the extent to which the sector is 'gendered', with accommodation and catering being characterized by a numerically female-dominated workforce, nearly three-quarters of whom were employed part-time, but with the travel organizations and carriers sector being predominantly a male preserve. Data provided by the Office of National Statistics for December 2005 highlight the significance of the numbers of females employed in the tourism and hospitality industry (see Table CS7.1).

As with other sectors, this phenomenon has been referred to as the 'glass ceiling', whereby promotional opportunities are advertised within an organization, but are not achieved by women, and women are absent from senior roles within the organization.

The glass ceiling is given this name as it is an invisible yet very real barrier that women experience when they apply for promotion for top jobs.[7] A variety of explanations have been offered for this and various possible determinants proposed.[8] It has been suggested that attitudinal, behavioural and structural barriers exist that hinder career advancement for many women.[9]

Table CS7.1 Numbers employed in the tourism and hospitality industry by gender, 2005.

Occupations	Males	Females
Hotels	97,600	140,800
Restaurants	255,300	258,400
Pubs, bars and nightclubs	141,200	192,700
Food and service management	56,600	121,800
Gambling	33,600	44,000
Travel and tourist services	30,900	79,400
Visitor attractions	5,300	3,300
Holiday parks and self-catering	14,300	30,600
Hospitality services	93,500	268,500
Total	**729,500**	**1,115,580**

Source: ONS, 'Labour force survey, 2006', ONS.
Note: Data may not add up to give totals due to rounding.

While much research has been carried out into the role of women in management and a range of theoretical explanations exist to account for why women may be under-represented in organizations, the following are frequently given:

- having and looking after children
- characteristics of management jobs
- lack of provision for flexible working (crèche facilities etc.)
- organizational policies and practices
- overt discrimination
- perceptions of gender and stereotyping
- male culture and 'old boys' network'
- women's self-perceptions and aspirations
- gender-related traits
- lack of training and mentoring

One theoretical perspective, the gender-centred, suggests that intrinsic biological differences between men and women account for the preponderance of men in senior management – that is, men are more likely to have the required traits and behaviours for such posts.

Further evidence regarding differences in pay between senior directors in organizations, based on research by the UK Institute of Directors, has found that female directors earn up to 26 per cent less than male ones and a gender pay gap is evident in many service and voluntary sectors.

The research

The research described below was undertaken in conjunction with Shine People and Places, a company that specializes in people management and, in particular, the mentoring of executives in management, particularly females in the travel and tourism industry. The aim of Shine is to help companies design and deliver management and mentoring programmes to train, develop and support junior managers. It has devised programmes to encourage and support specific employee groups, such as young graduates, women and ethnic minorities.

Previous research by the company had identified the challenges that senior women in the travel industry faced. One of Shine's initiatives has been the introduction of the annual Shine Awards. These are seen as important events, designed to not only recognize the achievements of female managers in the travel and tourism industry, but also profile role models of women in management within this industry (**www.shinepeopleandplaces.co.uk**).

The aims of the research were to solicit the views of senior managers in the travel industry regarding their perceptions of the reasons for the relative under-representation of women in senior management positions. It was felt important to capture the views of both male and female managers in the sector so as to ensure issues of equality and attempt to measure any differences in responses.

A list of questions was designed and distributed online to ensure response rates were satisfactory. The research sought the views of middle and senior managers, both male and female, regarding women in management in travel and tourism. There were 182 responses, of which 122 were female and 60 were male. Some 61 per cent of the sample occupy senior management positions.

Policies and procedures

It was found that 60 per cent of respondents stated their organizations had a formal policy on equal opportunity or managing diversity, while 40 per cent did not. The lack of formal procedures indicated by the latter is probably a reflection of the large number of small firms in the sector, small firms being less likely to have formal procedures. The majority (82 per cent) felt that their organizations valued diversity. Few respondents (11 per cent) felt that a glass ceiling existed in their own organizations, although 30 per cent felt it was evident in the sector as a whole.

Perceptions

Managers were asked for their perceptions regarding women in management and the possible reasons for the relatively small proportion of women in senior management positions. A list of their statements appears in Table CS7.2, together with the percentages of those strongly agreeing or agreeing with each of those statements (males' and females' combined), plus the Kendall's tau-c value. Where there was a significant difference between the responses by gender (significance <0.05), that is also indicated, with significantly more women than men strongly agreeing or agreeing to those statements. The results are summarized in Figure CS7.1, which subdivides the responses by gender.

So, what do these results show? Reviewing the results in aggregate (that is, responses of males and females combined), 93 per cent of respondents (the highest percentage obtained) either strongly agreed or agreed that both men and women have the required traits and abilities to be successful in senior management, though 72 per cent strongly agreed or agreed that males are more likely to hold top positions in the sector, 59 per cent strongly agreed or agreed that female aspirations to reach top management positions are broadly the same as men, with 23 per cent being unsure, and 80 per cent strongly agreed or agreed that women's career progress relative to men's in the sector was hampered by breaks in their career due to childbirth and childcare.

Respondents were then asked to rate the importance of the statements giving reasons for the under-representation of women. Combining the numbers for the first, second and third most important, career breaks due to childbirth and childcare came out as the top reason and combining work with family responsibilities second, as shown in Figure CS7.2. This was true of the aggregate figures, as the table shows, but also for the totals for females and males. A higher proportion of males to females rated these two options, however. This situation was reversed for 'male culture and the old boys' network' and 'preconceptions of

Table CS7.2 Perceptions of possible reasons for lack of women in senior management.

Statement	% strongly agree/agree (male and female combined)	Kendall's tau-c value	Significance (<0.05)
1. The characteristics of senior management posts discourage women from applying.	22	.056	
2. Women's career progress in the sector is hampered by the attitudes and behaviours of male managers.	36	.325	Yes
3. Women's career progress in the sector is hampered by the existence of male culture and 'old boys' network'.	42	.382	Yes
4. Women's career progress in the sector is hampered by organizational practices on selection and promotion.	20	.352	Yes
5. Men are more likely to hold top positions in the sector because, in general, men are more likely than women to have the particular traits and abilities required for such positions.	9	.035	
6. In today's world, women have particular traits and abilities that make them more suited to top management positions than men.	35	.350	Yes
7. In general, both men and women have the required traits and abilities to be successful in senior management positions	93	.053	
8. Males are more likely than females to hold top positions in the TTL&H sector.	72	.285	Yes
9. When it comes to promotion to top posts in the TTL&H sector, women are discriminated against.	23	.266	Yes
10. Women are less ambitious to reach the top management positions in the sector.	26	−.055	
11. Women's career progress in TTL&H is hindered by the dominance of male executives within the sector.	38	.335	Yes
12. Women's career progress in TTL&H is hindered by a lack of self-confidence in their own ability.	37	.228	Yes
13. Women's career progress relative to men in TTL&H is hindered by breaks in their career due to childbirth and childcare.	80	.090	
14. Female aspirations to reach senior positions in the sector are broadly the same as those of their male colleagues.	59	−.092	
15. Ambitious women often choose to develop their careers in sectors that enjoy a greater profile than TTL&H.	29	.016	
16. The TTL&H sector is worse than others in allowing for personal commitments to be reconciled with work pressures.	31	.114	
17. Women's career progress in the sector is hindered by a lack of obvious mentors, male or female.	41	.345	Yes
18. Women's career progress in the sector is hindered by a lack of female role models.	38	.356	Yes
19. Women's career progress in the sector is hindered by preconceptions of women's abilities.	29	.356	Yes
20. More than in other industries, women's career progress in TTL&H is hindered by family/personal commitments.	38	.191	Yes
21. Women's career progress in the sector is hampered by a lack of relevant training and development opportunities.	27	.283	Yes

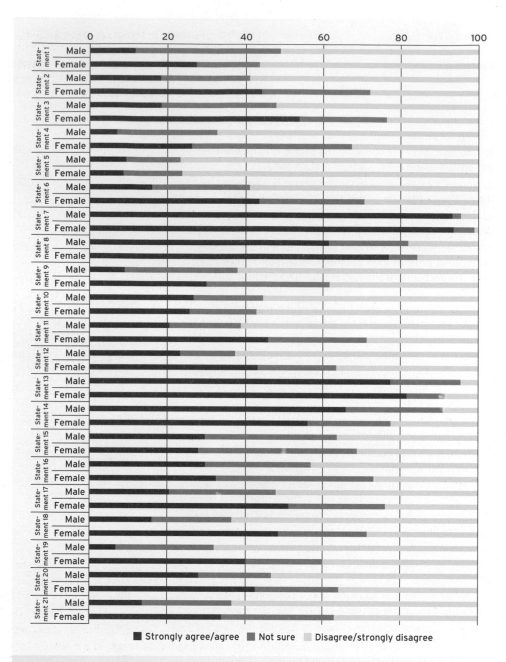

Figure CS7.1 Analysis of results in Table CS7.2, by gender.

women's abilities', which were rated as important explanatory factors by a greater proportion of females.

The results therefore showed the reasons for the under-representation of women in senior management positions in travel and tourism as perceived by the managers surveyed. Although there was agreement as to the top two reasons, which related to childcare and family responsibilities, there were significant gender differences for a number of the other explanations.

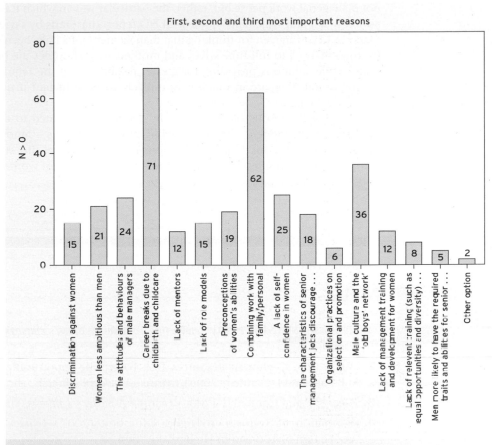

Figure CS7.2 Leading explanations offered.

Suggested strategies

Respondents were asked to rate the usefulness of different possible strategies to increase the proportion of women in senior management positions in the sector. The strategy that received the highest rating was 'achieving equal pay in the sector'. Other useful strategies identified (in order of importance) were: childcare and crèche facilities, training and development for women, flexible working, opportunities for peer networking and providing mentoring and coaching for female managers. There were few gender differences in these responses.

Conclusion

The results of the research point to career breaks due to having children and looking after them, plus the difficulties of combining work with family and other responsibilities as being perceived by those in management roles as the most important determinants for the under-representation of women in senior management. The fact that childcare and family responsibilities still fall primarily on women is salutary yet inescapable.

At one level, therefore, suggested solutions would be couched in practical and structural terms – greater provision of flexible working, career breaks and the provision of crèche facilities. Liff and Ward,[10] though, put forward the possibility that women may be rejecting not managerial work per se but, rather, the particular way in which it is currently organized. Similarly Liff and Wajcman[11] quote a NEDO report that starts by saying that a visitor from Mars could be forgiven for thinking that management jobs have been specifically designed for men married to full-time wives and mothers who shoulder the burden of family life. Thus, while solutions providing for greater flexibility and the requirements of childcare are important, they are in themselves unlikely to be sufficient if underlying aspects are left untouched.

Analysing the results of this survey by gender also pointed to the need for mentors and female role models, as well as highlighting perceptions – among women managers in particular – of more deep-seated aspects of organizational life, such as a male culture and prejudicial attitudes. While these remain, the numbers of women in boardrooms are unlikely to achieve much more than token status.

Notes

1. Hemmati, M. (ed.) (1999) *Gender and Tourism: Women's employment and participation*, UNED-UK.

2. WTTC (2001) 'Human Resources Task Force: HR opportunities and challenges', in S. J. Page and J. Connell (2006) *Tourism: A modern synthesis*, Thomson, p. 242.

3. Page, S. J. and Connell, J. (2006) *Tourism: A modern synthesis*, Thomson, p. 242.

4. Association of Tourism in Higher Education (2007) *Tourism Intelligence Monitor*, Association of Tourism in Higher Education.

5. Abrams F. (2007) 'Bad hair pay', *The Guardian*, 18 September.

6. Purcell, K. (1997) 'Women's employment in UK tourism: gender roles and labour markets', in M. T. Sinclair (ed.), *Issues and Theories of Gender and Work in Tourism*, Routledge.

7. Davidson, J. D. and Burke, R. J. (2004) *Women in Management Worldwide: Facts, figures and analysis*, Ashgate.

8. van Vianen, A. E. M. and Fischer, A. H. (2002) 'Illuminating the glass ceiling: the role of organizational culture preferences', *Journal of Occupational and Organizational Behaviour*, 75, pp. 315–37.

9. Wood, G. L. and Lindorff, M. (2001) 'Sex differences in explanations for career progress', *Women in Management Review*, 16 (4), pp. 152–62.

10. Liff, S. and Ward, K. (2001) 'Distorted views through the glass ceiling: the construction of women's understandings of promotion and senior management positions', *Gender, Work and Organization*, 8 (1), pp. 19–36.

11. Liff, S. and Wajcman, J. (1996) ' "Sameness" and "difference" revisited: which way forward for equal opportunity initiatives?', *Journal of Management Studies*, 33 (1), pp. 79–94.

Further reading

Baker, V. (2007) 'Why men can't manage women', *The Guardian*, 14 April.

Baum, T. (2007) 'Human resources in tourism: still waiting for change', *Tourism Management*, 28 (6), pp. 1383–99.

British Hospitality Association (2006) 'Trends and statistics', British Hospitality Association. Available online from: **www.bha.org.uk**

Clark, A. (2007) ' "New technology, old sexism" says ousted HP executive', *The Guardian*, 10 October.

DCMS (2004) 'Tomorrow's tourism today', DCMS. Available online at: **www.culture.gov.uk/ reference_library/publications/4618.aspx**

Dennis, J. (2006) 'In it for the people', *Travel Weekly*, 17 November.

Dennis, J. (2006) 'Travel "still a man's world" ', *Travel Weekly*, 12 October.

Dennis, J. and James, L. (2006) 'We want our equal share', *Travel Weekly*, 3 March.

EU (2001) 'Working together for the future of European Tourism', EU, COM (2001) 665 final, 13 November.

Fitzpatrick, M. (2007) 'Flights of fancy', *The Guardian*, 7 July.

Henery, M. (2007) 'Portrait of a generation: thirtysomething women in their stories', *The Times2*, 19 June.

Hilpern, K. (2007) 'Authorities expected to close the pay gaps at work', *The Guardian*, 28 March.

Longbottom, S. (2007) 'Female role models needed', *Travel Weekly*, 29 June.

Mayling, S. (2006) 'Women urged not to be shy', *Travel Weekly*, 25 November.

Page, S. J. and Connell, J. (2006) *Tourism: A modern synthesis*, Thomson.

Robb, N. (2007) 'Are women bored of the boardroom?', *Travel Trade Gazette*, 16 March.

Taylor, I. and Dennis, J. (2007) 'Why keeping mum sounds just perfect', *Travel Weekly*, 15 June.

Tickle, L. (2007) 'Is the glass ceiling a thing of the past?', *The Guardian*, 24 October.

'The battle for brainpower: a survey of talent', *The Economist*, 5 October 2006.

Treanor, J. (2007) 'Women quit before hitting glass ceiling', *The Guardian*, 8 March.

Ward, L. (2007) 'Successful women pay tribute to guides', *The Guardian*, 30 October.

Ward, L. (2007) 'Women bosses lose out as gender pay gap widens in the boardroom', *The Guardian*, 8 November.

Ward, L. (2008) 'The baby blues: study finds a third of mothers slip down career ladder', *The Guardian*, 27 February.

Wittenberg-Cox, A. and Maitland, A. (2008) *Why Women Mean Business: Understanding the emergence of our next economic revolution*, John Wiley.

Woolcock, N. (2008) 'Top employers hire fewer women graduates', *The Times*, 31 January.

Websites

Shine People and Places   **www.shinepeopleandplaces.co.uk**
VisitBritain   **www.tourismtrade.org.uk**

Questions and discussion points

1. What do you consider are the factors that attract female students to study travel and tourism courses and what female role models can you identify from the industry?
2. Suggest why a pay gap may exist in the sector and whether or not this is appropriate in terms of recruiting talent.

3. What will be the nature of jobs in travel and tourism in the twenty-first century and what will be the prospects for women in management?

4. What do you understand by the term 'glass ceiling' and how can organizations in travel and tourism tackle the perception of its existence within the industry?

5. Certain jobs in the travel industry call for 'emotional labour'. Are women better suited to such jobs and does this restrict their access to higher-level jobs where emotional labour may be less of an issue?

Case study 8

Sustainable tourism in the townships of South Africa

Prepared by Richard George, Senior Lecturer, School of
Management, University of Cape Town, South Africa

Introduction

This case study provides an invaluable example of sustainable tourism, and relates particularly to the material in Chapter 6, as well as having important implications for Chapter 5.

The conditions for residents of slums throughout the world are appalling, but tourism
does provide them with opportunities. It can offer a means of helping locals to help themselves, as well as ensuring – as in this case described here – that tourist funds are generated
within the district and go to support those in that district. At the same time, the tours
offered enable visitors to interact authentically with residents of the host country in unstaged
surroundings, giving the former a better understanding of the problems faced by the host
country and its residents.

Background to the growth of the townships

Brazil has its favelas, Argentina its *villas miseria* and South Africa its townships. Universally,
they are known as 'shanty towns' or, quite starkly, 'slums'. These residential areas, which
are very much symbols of social inequality in their respective countries, have now become

popular attractions on the international tourist trail. Guided drive-through tours provide tourists with a glimpse of slum life and an insight into the history, culture and spirit of the people who live in these communities.

Within South Africa, the townships that were created during the oppressive times of apartheid are a major form of tourism revenue. The first township tours began operating in the early 1990s, when they were offered to Soweto (South-Western Township) in Johannesburg. Soweto is the largest township in South Africa with a population of more than 4 million people, a university, schools, churches, hospitals and the biggest shopping mall in South Africa.

As mentioned, the origins and development of the townships are very closely associated with apartheid. Indeed, they are a direct result of the apartheid regime and the black African people's struggle for democracy.

'Apartheid' (apartness, segregation) is the one Afrikaans word that is known the world over. Although the practice of segregation in urban areas is centuries old, it was written into South African law only in 1923, with the passing of the Native Urban Areas Act. This law divided urban land into residential areas for blacks and for others. The acquisition of land for residence for black people was allowed only in those areas assigned to people of colour – the townships. Apartheid was made state policy in 1948, its principal aim being the segregation of the races. This was further entrenched in 1950 when the Group Areas Act was passed, making specific zones available to certain races for living and business purposes.

During the 1980s, the townships became centres of opposition to the ruling National Party government. Although apartheid and several restricting laws were abolished in the early 1990s and a democratic government elected in 1994, the townships in South Africa have continued to sprawl as people from rural areas have relocated to the cities and large towns in search of employment and access to education, health, water and electricity services. Squatter camps, informal settlements, low-cost housing and economic semi-detached houses have proliferated. Today, each township is beset with its own social problems, including the development of illegal squatter camps, poverty and high rates of unemployment (estimated to be as high as 50 to 70 per cent in some areas), HIV/Aids and crime.

The development of township tours

Cape Town is situated in the south-west of the country, nestled in between the Atlantic Ocean and the 1-kilometre-high iconic Table Mountain. Besides the 'Mountain of the Sea', Cape Town boasts visitor attractions such as Robben Island – the former prison colony that once housed political prisoners – a cosmopolitan nightlife, world-class restaurants, idyllic wine farms and blue-flag-status beaches. In recent years, however, one of the fastest-growing tourism markets in Cape Town has been township tours. This growth has been fuelled by, first, an increasing demand from, mainly overseas, tourists who have the desire to learn about and experience life in these communities and, second, the major increase in the numbers of tour brokers who have realized the benefits and growth potential of this niche market, so organize bus and coach tours to the townships.

The majority of township tours in the Mother City begin with a visit to the District Six Museum, located in the east precinct of the city centre. District Six was once home to a mixed community of 60,000 people, who were forcibly removed following the 1950 Group Areas Act and rehoused in the townships on the outskirts of Cape Town. Their former homes were demolished and the heart was ripped out of the city. Today, all that remains of the neighbourhood is the museum, a handful of buildings, a mosque and a church.

At the museum, tourists hear about the atrocity of apartheid, the planning of the townships and the effect that forced removal had on the social, cultural and economic lives of the people. The District Six Museum keeps both the memory alive and showcases a number of exhibits, including a park bench that bears the notice 'Europeans Only, Sleg Blankes'.

TABLE CS8.1 Township sites and their attractions.

Primary township tourist sites			
Langa	**Gugulethu**	**Nyanga**	**Khayelitsha**
Tsoga Environmental Resource Centre, Guga Sthebe Cultural and Arts Centre, Chris Hani School, Walking Tours – including old and new hostels, Tigers Place (shebeen experience), Dompass Court (old book of life office), Baptist Church – famous for gospel tours.	'Gugulethu Seven' Memorial (in memory of the political activists shot dead by police in 1968), Market, Sivuyile ('we are happy/glad') Tourism Centre, Mzoli's Place (famous public braai and networking area), Amy Biehl Memorial.	Nyanga market, Maphindi's Place (pub and grill).	Vicky's B&B, Waterfront tavern, Lookout Hill, Khayelitsha Craft Market, Community Projects (Abalimi, Golden Flowers).

Source: Rainbow Tours.

Most of the tours include visits to the black townships of Langa, Gugulethu, Nyanga and Khayelitsha (see Table CS8.1). Langa (a Xhosa word meaning 'sun') is the oldest existing township in South Africa, dating back to 1927. Khayelitsha is Cape Town's biggest township, with approximately 1 million residents, and is also its newest. This sprawling township, which was established in 1983, has one of the highest unemployment rates in South Africa. Tours to the coloured townships of Mannenberg and Mitchells Plain are considered dangerous, however, and so they are not on the township tour itinerary.

Irrespective of the township being visited, the tours usually include the following

- A visit to a shebeen (an illegal pub or tavern). Traditional shebeens are usually small wooden huts where old crates are used as seats. Tourists get to taste traditional Xhosa beer (*umgqombothi*) made from mielie meal (maize) and sorghum malt. Taverns or bars are more modern and offer entertainment such as pool tables, TV and music.

- A walk around and a visit to a migrant hostel (where 9 migrant workers lived in each room and 54 shared a tap and toilet during the apartheid era). The buildings now house people and families who cannot afford to pay any rent.

- A visit to a *sangoma* (a witchdoctor or traditional healer) and a fortune teller, including the possibility of consultation.

- A visit to a preschool/nursery, which often includes the children singing and dancing.

In all of the Cape Town townships *spaza* shops (informal, small shops, often based in a private house), restaurants (offering either Xhosa, Cape Malay or township dishes), arts and craft centres, markets, hairdressing salons, small businesses (such as car mechanics, furniture makers, shoemakers, crafters and sweet traders) and schools can be found. Traditional cultural events, such as gumboot dancing (a dance originally developed by mine workers, performed wearing Wellington boots), entertain the tourists.

The economic benefits of township tours

During the course of a township tour, visitors have the opportunity to purchase souvenirs and locally made curios and artwork. Often the content of each tour is at the discretion of the driver guide, who may well be a resident of the township. Tourists are encouraged to purchase services such as food and refreshments and craft work rather than make donations. The tour brokers donate a percentage of their revenue to township projects, working in conjunction with not-for-profit organizations such as the Red Cross.

Enver Mally, founder of the Tourism Community Development Trust and pioneer of one of the first township tour operators in Cape Town – Grassroute Tours – emphasizes that exponential growth within the township tourism sector can best be attributed to improved perceptions of safety and security: 'Tourists began realizing that they were in a "protective bubble" and that their lives were not in any immediate danger and, therefore, through word of mouth, the market grew.'

One of the main benefits of the township tours is that they encourage and allow tourists to spend money in these areas, as well as spread information about the local citizens. This naturally stimulates many township inhabitants to start entrepreneurial enterprises, including B&Bs, restaurants, crafts stalls/shops and organizing tours. It also increases the residents' standard of living in the medium to long term. The Tourism Community Development Trust is just one such initiative. It stipulates that all its operators pledge a contribution (approximately 10 per cent) of their tour profits to development.

The problems of operating township tours

Mally is aware that that there are numerous negative aspects that have sprung up alongside the benefits of the significant growth in township tourism: 'There are many tour operators that exploit the community for their own financial gain. New companies offering township tours do not attempt to find new routes or new areas to visit. Therefore, there is no initiative to increase the distribution of wealth.' Also, in order to stop the exploitation of the township's community, widespread levels of involvement need to be achieved.

An additional negative issue is that many visitors do not know how to interact with the locals and often inadvertently insult many of them. This has the potential to cause friction between the tourists and the local community.

Figure CS8.1 Visitors meet township locals.
(*Courtesy of Rainbow Tours.*)

Last, the growth in township tourism presents a growing incentive for criminal behaviour. Although there have been few reports of crimes against tourists, such as pickpocketing and mugging, as Mally points out, 'Crime [is] an ever present threat to the future success of my business'. Indeed, the safety and security threat to township tourism was made evident during May 2008 when a series of xenophobic attacks made worldwide news. Over 50 foreigners (from other African countries) living in the townships were killed during a spate of violent outbreaks that occurred in townships throughout the country. Although no tourists were harmed (the attacks targeted mainly African foreign nationals), subsequent media exposure resulted in a number of township tours being cancelled.

The market for township tours

There are more than 55 registered companies offering tours to Cape Town's townships. Operators range from the independent (residents-turned-entrepreneurs) to large companies, such as Hyton Ross, Ikapa Tours and Welcome Tours. Reportedly, however, large-scale impersonal approaches have breached the unwritten contracts of respect between resident and visitor.

Are township tours merely 'urban safaris', in which locked minibuses full of camera-clicking tourists whizz past bemused residents? Not so, according to one township resident: 'People don't come here and gape. They like talking to the residents and we like talking to them. It's good for us, it shows us that people are interested in us and that we haven't been forgotten.'

Although no research data currently exists on township tourism, it is apparent that township tours are especially popular with overseas tourists rather than regional (SADC) or domestic tourists. Estimates suggest that less than 5 per cent of township tourists are South Africans.

South Africa has the FIFA 2010 World Cup to look forward to. This mega event will be held in all of the major cities around the country and promises to bring jobs and a sense of hope to many South Africans. Several township tourism businesses, such as B&Bs and tour operators, are already targeting their marketing activities at 'soccer tourists'.

Websites

Tourism Community Development Trust

http://tcdtrust.org.za

http://daytours.drivesouthafrica.co.za/cape-town

Questions and discussion points

1. How could tour operators encourage domestic tourists to participate in township tours? Why do you think more locals do not go on tours of the townships?

2. Discuss the negative sociocultural impacts of townships tours on the local communities.

3. What problems are faced by small-scale operators such as Grassroute Tours and how can they effectively market their tours abroad?

4. What issues of safety and security are raised in this case study and how can they be managed effectively?

Case study 9

Bournemouth's artificial surfing reef

Prepared by Chris Holloway, with the help of Jon Weaver,
Marketing and Events Manager, and Jo Mountain, Resort PR
Development Manager, Bournemouth Tourism

Introduction

This case study, which supports material to be found in both Chapters 9 and 10, reveals
a highly unusual and innovative way to help the growth of tourism that has been implemented in a popular resort on Britain's South Coast. It has built on a specific strength to
stimulate a niche market and attract more youthful visitors to a destination that has long
been associated with older, more traditional visitors. It provides a good example of one
way in which private capital can help to fund public-sector tourism developments.

Background to tourism at Boscombe

Bournemouth is one of Britain's premier seaside resorts on the South Coast and one that
has seen considerable investment and redevelopment in recent years. This investment
has ensured that visitor numbers remain high (currently 5.2 million per annum) and are
spread more evenly throughout the year than in the past. These improvements have focused
predominantly around the centre, however, where Bournemouth Pier and the principal

Figure CS9.1 Surf's up in Boscombe.
(Courtesy of Bournemouth Tourism.)

hotels are located, while outlying suburbs, such as Boscombe, a mile and a half from the centre, have received less attention; yet it is well-supplied with hotels and enjoys an equally attractive stretch of coastline and fine beaches.

Plans to revitalize the Boscombe district have been mooted for a number of years. Although the town benefits from its own pier, it had been allowed to degenerate in recent years. The Mermaid Hall building at the end of the pier was closed in 1989 and the remainder of the pier was closed to the public in 2005. Since then, the structure had deteriorated to the point of becoming dangerous. The beach hut complex, which formed the first and second floors of the Boscombe Overstrand to the east of the pier, was also in poor condition and largely out of use. While Boscombe continued to attract visitors during the summer, the market was composed largely of less well-off families, although surfers provided a small market for the district during the winter months.

Redevelopment proposals

The council had discussed plans for redeveloping the Boscombe seafront for a number of years, but financial pressures and the potentially high costs involved had deterred action being taken. Investment was now seen as essential, however, to move the area upmarket and lengthen the town's season.

The key to achieving this was seen to lie in finding the means to expand the surfing market. An initial proposal to construct an artificial surf reef had been made as far back as 1998, but plans were firmed up to assess the cost–benefit and viability of such a scheme.

Research revealed that surfers are high-spend visitors. A survey in Cornwall disclosed that surfers spend on average 8 per cent more than other holidaymakers. Surfing is a fast-growing sport, with over 300,000 adherents of both sexes, some 8000 being members of the British Surfing Association. In addition to accommodation, food and entertainment, surfers invest in tuition costs, and in many cases can be expected to purchase surfing equipment locally, typically spending £500 or more on kitting themselves out. Estimates put the British surfing industry as worth some £200 million per annum – a figure that is growing rapidly.

The economic assessment, therefore, suggested that investment in this field would be cost-effective, boosting the economy for small businesses in the area that could support surfers and their spectators.

At the time of the review, surfing was taking place in Boscombe on around 153 days each year, with good surfing available on 77 of those. Over 5000 visits were made to the beach each year for the purposes of surfing. It was estimated that, with an artificial reef in place, the number of good surfing days could be doubled, ensuring more than 10,000 visits per annum. An artificial surf reef was therefore viewed as the key economic factor for the entire regeneration scheme – it would give Boscombe its own identity, raise the profile of the district and, in particular, attract a large volume of visitors during the off-peak winter season, turning the area into a year-round destination.

Surveys were carried out on local residents to assess support for the reef project and its accompanying improvements. Residents indicated a high level of support, especially for restoration of the Boscombe Pier (89 per cent), while nearly two-thirds gave explicit support to the concept of an artificial surfing reef. Younger residents were even more anxious to see the development carried out, with three-quarters of those under 25 surveyed supporting the surf reef.

Impact analysis

The ideal site for the planned reef, it was determined, was between the first two groynes to the east of Boscombe Pier and in front of the Overstrand complex. The reef would occupy approximately 1 hectare and be sited roughly 225 metres offshore. The reef itself would be composed of 55 large sand-filled geo-textile bags, some up to 70 metres in length.

A feasibility study had been conducted and reviewed in the period 1999/2000. Overall, the environmental impact of the reef had been judged to be, at worst, neutral. Marine life would be expected to thrive on the reef and there would be no damaging effects to the beach itself. Additionally, experts judged that the reef could, in some measure, benefit

Figure CS9.2 The artificial reef as it appears in situ.
(Courtesy of Bournemouth Tourism.)

coastal defences. The bags themselves are extremely strong and the dangers of any damage arising from their placement were assessed to be minimal (although long-term guarantees would be in place to cover for this contingency).

The economic impact assessment conducted by the council suggested that the reef would generate direct income of some £3 million per annum and create an image value of some £10 million per annum, resulting from a variety of publications and media interest on a national scale. All told, the reef would create an estimated 60 full-time and 34 part-time jobs. The reef, together with other regeneration in the area, would also impact on property and business values in the area, benefiting locals.

The expected design and construction costs of the surf reef were approximately £2.68 million. Financing the scheme, and the balance of the £10 million Boscombe Spa Regeneration Project, was to be achieved by selling a section of the Honeycombe Chine car park to property developers for the construction of housing. To minimize the loss of the car parking spaces, further provision for car parking was planned to the west of the pier, roughly halving the number of parking spaces lost.

Implementing the final scheme

The go-ahead for the surfing scheme was given early in 2005. Formal planning permission was not required for this development, but the consent of the Crown Estate had to be agreed before proceeding. Later in the same year, approval was given for the parallel transformation of the Boscombe seafront, to include:

- refurbishing Boscombe Pier, with space for catering and retail, removal of the Mermaid Hall and its replacement with a new, shorter viewing platform and a featured heritage display along the central walkway

Figure CS9.3 The artificial reef is hoisted prior to its positioning offshore.
(Courtesy of Bournemouth Tourism.)

- a landscaped piazza, with public artwork, in front of the pier, linking recently renovated gardens and parkland with the seafront
- a revitalized Boscombe Overstrand complex, incorporating surf-themed shopping and tuition facilities, a ground and first-floor glass-fronted restaurant with panoramic sea views and an RNLI beach lifeguard station, together with facilities directly aimed at surfers, including changing rooms, showers and 59 beach huts, or 'surf pods', available for daytime hire and lease
- new associated toilet facilities and land train garaging.

The project – to be known as Boscombe Spa Village – is costing around £10 million, funded, as noted above, by the sale of land for property development. The reef and redeveloped spa are planned to be fully operational by autumn, 2009.

Early indications of revitalization

The regenerated area is already attracting new, upmarket facilities, including new boutique hotels such as Urban Beach (**www.urbanbeachhotel.co.uk**), boutique clothing shops, upmarket cafés such as Boscanova and the Whole Food Co-op. In the 18-month period during 2006/2007, and even before the contract for the reef had been signed, property prices in the district increased by 30 per cent. The reef – the first of its kind in the northern hemisphere – is expected to attract a variety of new water sports fans for kite surfing, windsurfing, wakeboarding, kayaking, scuba-diving, sailing and skimboarding.

Questions and discussion points

1. To what extent might climate change help or hinder this project?
2. What level of risk is entailed in such an original approach to developing tourism?
3. Given the adverse publicity other destinations that attract young surfers have suffered, such as Newquay or Rock in England, is there a danger in encouraging large groups of visitors from this sector of the market? What steps should the local authority take to ensure that the destination neither moves downmarket nor creates too many problems for local residents and businesses or other more conservative visitors?
4. Is Bournemouth's approach one that could be emulated at other seaside venues, whether in England or elsewhere? What factors would a local authority need to take into consideration in examining this opportunity?

Case study 10

A new Russian window to the West: the Province of Kaliningrad

Prepared by Dr Elena Kropinova, Immanuel Kant State University of Russia, Kaliningrad, and David Bruce, Principal Lecturer, Bristol Business School, University of the West of England, Bristol

Introduction

This case study examines the development and marketing of a relatively little-known region, but one with ample attractions to offer the more adventurous tourist. It identifies some of the barriers to tourist development, especially those of transport networks, border controls and documentation. In this regard, it draws on material in Chapters 5 and 17, as well as Chapter 9, while the issues of environmental sensitivity discussed relate to Chapter 7.

Anyone researching the impact of gambling tourism on the nearby nation of Estonia may wish to consider the merits and drawbacks of plans to generate gambling in the region.

Location, background and economic context

Kaliningrad, the Russian exclave on the Baltic, is the westernmost territory of the Russian Federation, bordered on the landward side by Poland and Lithuania. The administrative

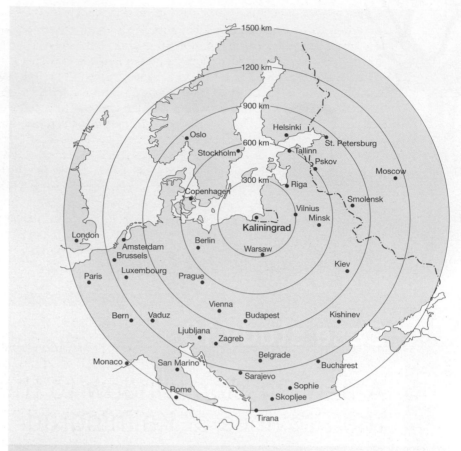

Figure CS10.1 Where is Kaliningrad?
(Courtesy of Professor G. Fedorov.)

land border of the territory is therefore also part of the frontier of the Russian Federation with the European Union. Kaliningrad can refer to both the province, or Oblast, and the city, which was formerly the East Prussian city of Königsberg. To avoid confusion, in this case study we will refer to the whole territory as Kaliningrad Oblast and to the city simply as Kaliningrad.

Kaliningrad Oblast (closer to Amsterdam than to Moscow – see Figure CS10.1) extends about 200 kilometres east to west and 100 kilometres north to south. Including the Russian parts of the Kaliningrad and Curonian Gulfs, the area totals some 18,000 square kilometres. The resident population is 937,000 (2007 figures), making it one of the highest-density regions of Russia, higher than the neighbouring country of Lithuania. 77.8 per cent of the population is urbanized and nearly half live in greater Kaliningrad itself.

The economic crisis of 1992–1998, associated with the disintegration of the Soviet Union and complexity of the transition towards a market economy, was intensified for the Kaliningrad Oblast because it had at the same time become an exclave, separated from the mainland of Russia by foreign states. As a result, there were sharp reductions in the production of goods and services in all the economic sectors represented in the Oblast. Many enterprises in mechanical engineering, pulp and paper, food and other light industries closed. Even with 90 per cent of world amber resources concentrated in the area, extraction of amber also declined.

After 1996, with the creation of the custom-free zone for the whole Oblast, a great number of new joint venture and foreign enterprises were set up, mostly converting imported raw materials and half-ready products into finished goods for the whole Russian market. Small businesses developed rapidly. Since 1999, when the revitalization of the Russian economy became evident, the growth in engineering has been dramatic. The assembly of cars, TV sets, refrigerators, vacuum cleaners and other consumer goods, as well as meat processing, canning and furniture and carpet businesses, have created about 300 new enterprises supplying other Russian regions. Oil extraction from the shelf of the Baltic Sea has started, doubling the total extraction in the Oblast. The first stage of the Kaliningrad Power Station-2 (TEZ-2) (400 megawatt) has made the energy resource base of the region very strong. By 2007, industrial production in the region was nearly twice what it had been in 1990 and the role of the region in servicing Russian export–import trade had greatly increased. Construction, trade and tourism began to develop, but the region did not overcome its agricultural decline, with production still below 1990 levels in 2007.

With 422,000 people, the most industrialized and economic centre in the Oblast is Kaliningrad itself. All the other 20 urban settlements are much smaller and less economically significant – the largest being Sovietsk (43,000), Chernyakhovsk (41,000) and Gusev, Svetly and Baltiysk (20,000–30,000 each). There are three futher small towns and over a thousand rural settlements.

Nature-based recreational resources

The key natural factor that attracts visitors to the Kaliningrad Oblast is the sea coast. It enjoys a relatively benign climate compared with other resort districts in Russia and the Baltic States. The mean temperature in July is 17–18°C, total sunshine hours are over 1800 a year, sometimes reaching as high as 2200, which is more than at the resorts of the Leningrad Oblast (around St Petersburg), Estonia or Latvia. Water temperature in summer ranges from 17 to 19°C and, in the warmest years, can reach 20–21°C.

The variety of the landscape, from below sea level polder lands to hills up to 240 metres, as well as bodies of inland water – Curonian and Vistula lagoons, Lake Vyshtenetskoe and the rivers Pregolya, Neman and Krasnaya – are all important. Rivers, lakes and lagoons provide good recreational opportunities for tourists and fishing fans, even in the winter (on the iced lagoons). There are also attractive stretches of canal.

Vegetation also plays an important role. Almost all of it is man-made. In the forest areas, coniferous and broad-leaved species prevail, while in coastal towns and settlements rare and decorative plants brought from various parts of the world and acclimatized to local conditions can be seen. Natural therapeutic resources of mineral waters, bromine brines of sodium chloride composition and therapeutic cure muds are used extensively. Proven reserves of these resources are capable of satisfying the requirements of spas for hundreds of years.

Kaliningrad Oblast is characterized, on the one hand, by inimitable natural complexes such as the Curonian and Vistula spits, with their unique dune landscapes and the 50-metre deep Lake Vyshtenetskoe and, on the other, man-made or altered cultural landscapes. As a consequence of economic activities, the natural vegetation of the land has been changed and forests are predominantly secondary or cultivated. Meadows are also artificial. Forests, meadows and natural wetlands account for only a quarter of the total land area. At 17 per cent, the percentage of forest land is very small compared to neighbouring Lithuania, with over 30 per cent, Finland with 52 per cent and Sweden with 56 per cent. A well-developed road network makes all the territory easily accessible, but there is high recreational pressure on small areas of undisturbed natural landscape.

In short, sandy beaches, a mild marine climate, an abundance of sunny days, coniferous and broad-leaved forests along the coastline, the unique landscapes of the Curonian and Vistula spits, rivers and lagoons, mineral waters and therapeutic muds combine to create good opportunities for the development of tourism, recreation and therapies.

Historical and cultural heritage

The unique history of the Kaliningrad Oblast means that heritage tourism is the main reason for tourists to come to the area. It is possible to distinguish the following types of cultural and heritage tourism:

- famous architectural monuments and architectural styles representing different epochs, reflecting the civil and military history of the area
- the works of famous representatives of science, culture and art representing the development of cultural exchange in the area – at an average density of over 100 things to see per square kilometre, Kaliningrad Oblast is one of the most fascinating regions in all Russia (See Table CS10.1).

Table CS10.1 The items of history and culture in Kaliningrad Oblast.

The historical phase	The items
Pre-German (Prussian or Western Baltic)	Burial grounds, ancient settlements (mainly on the Sambian peninsula).
German period (thirteenth to mid-twentieth century), Teutonic period; Napoleonic wars; World Wars I and II	Castles (Balga, Tapiau, Neuhausen, Labiau, Insterburg), churches, fortifications, battlefields, monuments, other historical buildings and places.
Soviet period 1945–1990	Ports and maritime history; enterprises (amber extraction and processing plants).

	Relative significance			
	Federal	Regional	Local	Total
Architectural	15	328	812	1155
Archaeological	3	144	183	330
Historical	9	220	66	295
Art	1	49	6	66
Landscape architecture	–	17	–	17
Total	28	758	1067	1853

Source: Cultural policy of Kaliningrad region, 2001, p. 52.

Cultural and historical establishments

15 museums and galleries – World Ocean Museum and Historical Museum, Amber Museum, Art Gallery and so on.
5 theatres – 3 drama theatres, 1 music theatre and 1 puppet theatre.
5 cultural and amusement parks, including 1 sculpture park in Kaliningrad.

Stages in the development of the area as a tourism region

Three major periods in the development of Kaliningrad Oblast as a tourism region can be identified:

1. the East Prussian period, up to the time of World War II
2. the Soviet period from about 1950 to 1990
3. the Russian 'exclave' period, from 1990 to the present time.

In the first, or East Prussian, period the coastal resorts were discovered, explored, developed and matured. This process transformed the fishing villages on the Baltic Sea coast and the Curonian Gulf into the resorts Europeans knew – Rauschen, Kranz, Pillau and so on – by the beginning of the twentieth century. Between World Wars I and II, they continued as part of Germany, in the exclave of East Prussia. The whole of the remaining German population of East Prussia was expelled in the late 1940s and a different, though smaller, Russian population was moved into the newly named Kaliningrad Oblast from the rest of the Soviet Union.

The second period is the Soviet period, from about 1950. The resorts were barred to international tourists, but some of the seaside towns developed for trade union-based tourism and local recreation, while other areas were zoned for agriculture, construction, food processing and other industries. Some, such as Pillau/Baltijsk, were completely closed off as part of a special border area and developed as the largest base for the Soviet Baltic fleet. Only two resort towns with a wider significance remained – Svetlogorsk (formerly Rauschen) and Zelenogradsk (formerly Kranz), both specializing in health and cure tourism. Priority was given to developing large year-round sanatoria designed to cure and protect from disease citizens of the other parts of the Soviet Union. There were also some tourist bases and hostels. Operating mostly in the summer, these were aimed at local people from the Kaliningrad Oblast. There was also a large expansion in the number of children's summer camps, but health-cure or spa-type recreation services dominated the supply. The average number of tourists per year at that time was about 400,000.

The third Russian exclave period of Kaliningrad Oblast, since 1990, itself falls into three phases. First, there was the decline phase (1989–1994), which saw the closure of a number of the health-cure recreation accommodation facilities (especially those belonging to factories or institutions), the beginnings of privatization and the establishment of the first non-state accommodation facilities. While there was a sharp decrease in the numbers of Russian health-cure tourists and a similar decrease in recreation for the local population (especially children), this period saw the first influx of foreign excursion tourists. This development was, however, limited by the number of beds available, quality of services and small range of tourist products – it was dominated by nostalgia tourism from Germany.

The second phase was the transformation period (1995–1999). Those years saw mass privatization of accommodation, reconstruction of the older units and the development of small-scale private hotels. As the market spread, there was also an increase in the quality and variety of tourism services, as 'best practice' was absorbed from foreign resorts.

Since 2000, there has been a period of growth, based on the spread of demand for tourist services from Russian tourists, combined with the construction of new hotels and hostels. Existing and new hotels have earned 'stars' and have strengthened their competitive advantages in the Russian and foreign markets. New tourism products have been created, tourism information centres opened and the international market has been targeted with new foreign representation offices, participation in international tourism exhibitions, Internet presence, sales and so on.

The image of and facilities in the Kaliningrad region

For most Western (especially German) people, Kaliningrad is always associated with Königsberg – formerly the beautiful capital city of East Prussia, with its Royal Castle, and home to the eighteenth-century philosopher Immanuel Kant. Literally nothing above ground remains of the castle, however, as it was comprehensively destroyed at the end of World War II. During the Soviet period, it could not even be mentioned because of its association with Hitler's Germany. In contrast, the summer of 2008 saw the opening of an exhibition featuring a model of Königsberg by the famous German artist Forst Durring in the Business Centre Europe – the largest and most modern Commercial Centre in Kaliningrad. One of the guests was Wilhelm von Boddien – the architect who had been chosen for the reconstruction of Berlin Castle.

As for the famous philosopher Immanuel Kant, his memorial and last resting place are in the outer wall of the Lutheran cathedral, which survived the destruction of the old inner city and is now being fully restored, the atmosphere of his spirit emanating into the surrounding park. Kaliningrad's University – heir to its Prussian predecessor – has strong traditions relating to the great philosopher and, in 2006, it was renamed the Immanuel Kant State University of Russia.

For Russian citizens, Kaliningrad is a port city, home of amber and a Baltic resort. Now, more and more of them associate Kaliningrad with the Western world and consider it to be some kind of 'abroad'. This can be explained partly by the need for Russians travelling from the mainland to the exclave overland to have foreign passports (and apply for transit Schengen visas to pass through Lithuania). At the same time, there are some signs of the West here, such as red roofs with chimneys, narrow streets, old and new Lutheran and Catholic churches, medieval city gates and strong fortresses.

The market

Tourism is now one of the most rapidly developing sectors of the local economy. In 2006, 356,000 tourists visited the Kaliningrad region, while in 2007 the number rose to 456,000 – an increase of 28 per cent. By comparison with 1997 (164,000 visitors), the number of tourists has increased nearly three-fold. For the first time, tourist numbers have overtaken those of the last years of the Soviet Union in the 1980s.

Russian tourists in 2007 accounted for 314,000, or 69 per cent, of all visitors (compared with 77 per cent in 2005). One half of these were tourists from within the Kaliningrad Oblast, while the other half were from other regions of Russia.

In 2007, international tourist numbers reached 142,000, with 50 per cent from Germany, 15 per cent from the Baltic States, mainly Lithuania, 9 per cent from the Scandinavian states, 4 per cent from Belarus and 4 per cent from other countries. The average length of stay was three days. This is up on the 1990s' figure of one to one and a half days, but the target for the authorities in the Oblast is seven days.

The services

Tourism services include accommodation (state-organized and in the private sector), transport (air, railway, car and sea), intermediaries (travel agents and tour operators), entertainment and sightseeing (natural and man-made) and other services (private and public).

Outbound tourism services have developed simultaneously with (or sometimes following) the growth in needs of the Kaliningrad Oblast population. Initially, tourism companies focused on meeting the demands of the local population to visit markets in neighbouring countries in order to purchase goods for personal use, as well as for small-scale wholesale trade. Thus, cross-border, primarily trade tourism, development (shop tours) was fostered.

The geographical spread of this type of tourism gradually extended to Lithuania, Poland, Belarus and Germany. After first developing bus tours, Moscow-based companies and their Kaliningrad offices offered charter air package tours to destinations like Turkey, Egypt and the United Arab Emirates. This internationalization of the market required development and the extension of the competence of organizations offering tourist services. This, in turn, resulted in a growth in demand for information and educational services. For domestic and inbound tourism, however, the intensive development of tourism led to the emergence of new institutions, such as the Department of Tourism of the Kaliningrad Oblast Administration (formerly the Committee for Tourism and Interregional Relations) and the Committee for Tourism Development of the Regional Duma (or Assembly). Similar structures have emerged at the municipal level.

Tourist companies

The key players in the Oblast's development turned out to be companies. According to the state statistical data, 114 tourism companies operate in the Oblast. Most of them are situated in the centre of Kaliningrad or within 15–20 minutes' walk. These include tour operators specializing in receiving international tourists coming to the region by their own motor transport, which operate under various brand names. A second (and the most sizeable) group deals with both receiving and despatching tourists. Finally, there are those offering primarily outbound package tours.

The year 2007 was, in many respects, difficult for tourism companies. Hardening of visa regulations (long-term free of charge 'cross-border' visas for Kaliningrad Oblast residents were abolished) weakened the small enterprises specializing in tours to the nearby aqua-parks of Poland, as well as those offering short culinary shopping and cultural tours to Lithuania. Hardening of visa regulations for journeys to European Union countries, too (for example, some countries require personal visits to distant Moscow or St Petersburg for fingerprinting and other procedures before considering an application), have resulted in a reduction in the demand for outbound tours (educational tours to the United Kingdom, for example). Similarly, visas for more than 72 hours to visit Kaliningrad Oblast as part of Russia require substantial fees and advance planning.

Nevertheless, in spite of the hardening of visa regulations for residents of the region visiting Poland and Lithuania in 2007, the dynamics of inbound tourism remain positive. It is a good point that there are a number of consulates of European countries (Poland, Lithuania, Germany, Latvia, Sweden) in Kaliningrad where Kaliningrad citizens could apply for visas.

Promotion and tourist information services

The development of tourism in the Kaliningrad Oblast, and particularly the growth of inbound tourism, have generated a need for tourist information centres. Initially, due to the lack of funds, the functions of information centres were fulfilled by existing tourism companies. The first eco-information centre, doubling as a tourist information centre, was established in the early 1990s in the natural park on the Curonian Spit. Since 1999, publicity material has included the 'Tourism passport of the region' containing information about the tourist infrastructure of the Kaliningrad Oblast in two languages (Russian and English) and, since 2003, 'Tourism of the Amber Land' has been available on the Administration of the Kaliningrad region's website (**www.tourism-kaliningrad.ru**). A 30-minute film, 'The Treasures of the Amber Land', is also available, in three languages. Videos about the tourist attractions in the Kaliningrad region are produced and released for sale – 'Travelling for health: The Amber Land', 'Tourism of the Amber Land – sightseeing and recreation' and 'Fortifications of Königsberg'.

Only in 2007 was the first official tourism information centre opened in Kaliningrad City, joining those in Svetlogorsk and Zelenogradsk, which operate successfully. Now there are 5 in the whole Oblast, which would seem inadequate when compared with the neighbouring Warmino-Mazurian region in Poland, which has 38. Kaliningrad tourist companies still play significant roles in this sphere, working professionally on international specialist exhibitions and promoting both their establishments and the Oblast as whole. Exhibition activities by tourist companies alone pay out about RUR10 million (nearly 300,000 euros) annually and, in addition, hotels, recreation centres and sanatoria participate in exhibitions.

The measures taken are insufficient for the active promotion of the Kaliningrad region in the international market, however. Considerable state funding is required for private exhibition space, publication of booklets, guidebooks, posters and maps in both Russian and the main European languages. Moscow-based tourism institutions, often well represented at international tourism exhibitions such as the ITB in Berlin and the World Travel Market in London, need to recognize Kaliningrad Oblast more as being part of Russia. For example, mainstream Intourist brochures show a map of Russia that misses out the exclave altogether.

Accommodation infrastructure

Tourism enterprises are very unevenly spread over the territory of the Oblast. This situation goes back to the time of the Soviet Union, when the major attraction for USSR tourists was the sea coast and the major type of activity was beach and sanatorium resort recreation. As a result, most tourism organizations were located along the coastline (90 per cent). When the Oblast was opened up to foreigners, the situation changed significantly. Historic and cultural buildings and the like, from the point of view of international tourism, were the main reason to travel to the area. This has triggered infrastructure development in other districts of the region.

The inclusion of the Kaliningrad region in the Baltic tourist routes, as well as the development of business tourism, has seen a growth in the demand for comfortable accommodation. This has been met by a jump in the number of hotels – from 5 in 1990 to 83 in 2003 – and in the number of rooms.

The Kaliningrad region now has 123 accommodation units, including 83 hotels (with rooms for 3140 guests), 19 sanatoria (3838 places), 21 health improvement and relaxation centres (1266 places), 30 tourist hostels (1765 places) and 25 children's camps (4240 places), which are available for seasonal accommodation. Guesthouse and country estate accommodation has also become popular (there are more than 100 units spread throughout the region). In total, there is accommodation for approximately 15,000 guests at any one time.

The quality of the accommodation has changed considerably. Most of the sanatoria have been renovated and supplied with modern equipment. In addition to refurbished hotels, new ones have been built, to European Union standards. Development has mostly been in Kaliningrad, the border towns (Sovetsk, Bagrationovsk) and the resort towns (Svetlogorsk, Zelenogradsk), but there are still a lot of half-completed construction sites, where work started in the early or mid-1990s, but was not completed due to the subsequent economic crises.

Occupation levels of hotels reach 30–40 per cent during the low season (October–April) and effectively 100 per cent during high season (May–September). At the same time, there are few hotels that offer high-quality service and would be suitable for international events, with conference halls, equipment for simultaneous translation and so on. Therefore, the issues of both quantity and quality of tourist accommodation must be addressed by the Oblast.

Outside the city of Kaliningrad, accommodation has been developed, first, within the coastal resort towns – Svetlogorsk and Zelenogradsk – second, on the Curonian Spit, which is the least-developed area in terms of accommodating demanding tourists and is currently focused on day trips to the national park, the Curonian Spit and, third, in the inland districts, where special tourism attractions exist, so individual hotels prevail. For instance, the hotel Kochar in Chernyakhovsk is known as an expensive, luxurious hotel, but is filled only during international horse racing competitions (no more than five times a year).

With the changes in the circumstances of the Oblast, the business of tourism has changed in parallel and the Oblast Tourism Programme, 'Development of the Kaliningrad region as a tourism centre in 2007–2011', sees all districts as having some tourism potential. Among the areas that are being focused on are, first, the construction of hotel complexes offering additional services (spa centres, conference centres and so on) and, second, to include historic or 'heritage' features (such as gothic, castle-style hotels, hunting estates and so on).

Catering

The Kaliningrad region has over 120 bars and restaurants and a great number of cafés (including seasonal ones) with more than 7300 seats. According to the statistics, they serve around 846,000 guests annually, but the actual number is at least twice as large.

The substantial development of this part of the service sector can be explained by the fact that catering enterprises require relatively low capital investment and comparatively simple refurbishment and modernization, which, again, do not call for substantial investment. Another important factor is that this kind of service is used by both tourists and the local population.

It is, however, difficult to find catering outlets with living Russian folklore themes. While there are restaurants and café bars trying to reflect traditions of Eastern Prussian culture in their exteriors and interiors (or, at least, in their names), there is a need to develop restaurants that reflect the Russian tradition. Where such places exist, as with the tavern Razguljaj, they are very popular. The brand Razguljaj is developing, with two establishments already open along the lines of the chain of taverns Elki-palki in Moscow – Ёлки-палки – styled in the best of Russian traditions and offering high-class Russian cuisine. The prices are high for a fast food restaurant but are designed for customers with above-average incomes.

The revival of the Königsberg brewing tradition has resulted in the opening of several beer restaurants. Such places are complementary to hotel catering facilities.

Leisure time entertainment

During recent years, leisure time entertainment has changed dramatically. In addition to casinos, gaming machine centres, billiard clubs and bowling centres, popular in the mid-90s, further active leisure facilities have developed. In 2003, two ice rinks were opened (one of them available all year round). The entertainment centre 'City-park' offers roller skating and that together with the opening of the aqua-park has been a significant factor in the increased attractiveness of Kaliningrad as a tourism and recreation centre. A disadvantage of club life in Kaliningrad is the low level of activity of local music groups, although this is partially compensated by regular visits from Russian and international performers.

During the year, several open-air festivals are organized in the city for various celebrations or promotion campaigns by some companies. The most interesting of these takes place in midsummer, during the celebrations dedicated to the Day of the City. Then theatrical shows are performed, concerts and discos are held, followed, of course, by great fireworks displays. These can also be promoted to tourists.

Smaller towns of the region are insufficiently served with leisure time and entertainment complexes – even children's playgrounds are limited in the resort and recreational areas. The importance of such complexes to ensuring an enjoyable stay has been noted by a great number of tourists participating in various surveys. Well-developed leisure and entertainment centres could help to extend the tourist season. Such properly developed centres could even become the purpose for visiting the Oblast, particularly Kaliningrad itself.

Gift and other tourist shops

The market for tourist souvenirs, goods produced in Kaliningrad and, particularly, unique goods such as amber, has considerable scope for expansion. Rental points for equipment that tourists need still require development. They should be located close to where they will be used – boat and catamaran rentals at the lakesides in Kaliningrad city and the Blue Lakes, motor-boat rentals on the Pregol riverfront locations, yacht and sailing-boat rentals at the Pribrezhnyj settlement on the Kaliningrad gulf and bicycle and roller-skate rentals in the city parks and, as cycle paths are developed in the city, bicycle rental outlets could be opened in hotels. This, however, remains a prospect for the future.

Transport as a factor in tourism development

Kaliningrad is a very important transport interchange, connecting Russian regions with many foreign countries. It is the crossroads for a number of road and air routes and is the changeover point for Russian- and European- (standard) gauge railways. There are also good prospects for passenger sea and river/canal transport, but they have not yet been sufficiently developed. Visa problems, however, as discussed above, do reduce this potential.

The following positive developments can be noted: the Polish airline LOT opened the Kaliningrad to Warsaw route in the summer of 2002 and Baltic Air opened up the Kaliningrad to Copenhagen and Kaliningrad to Riga routes. In 2007, KD-Avia (Kaliningrad Airlines) opened Kaliningrad as a hub, with routes connecting Kaliningrad, on one side, to a number of European airports in Germany, France, Italy, Spain and the United Kingdom and, on the other side, to a number of Russian and CIS airports. The network of airports belonging to this hub will be widened as several dozen more planes are leased.

The reopening of the railway route from Kaliningrad to Berlin has been a particularly popular attraction, due to the availability of both Russian and European rail gauges, which makes it possible for trains from the Polish side and those from the Lithuanian side (Russia, Belarus, and Latvia) to arrive and their passengers to interchange at Kaliningrad station.

With a new ferry berth in Baltijsk, a Sassnitz (Germany) link has been opened up, as has a sea route to St Petersburg, creating additional possibilities for cruise tourism development in the south-east Baltic and for the Oblast region in general. A catamaran from and to Gdynia (Poland) also comes in, but at present without landing its passengers – they come just for the voyage and duty-free shopping onboard.

Until recently, Kaliningrad was not included in the list of ports with developed yacht tourism, but the region has extensive natural resources – the Curonian and Vistula Gulfs – and there is the possibility of opening a marine border crossing in the Rybachij settlement, which would allow international yachts to enter the Russian sector of the Curonian Bay, thus stimulating development of Rybachij. The marine route of Kaliningrad to Elblong is currently functioning. The opening of the port at Pionerskij for passenger ships (including international) is a significant addition to the regional transport infrastructure.

Both rail and water are generally efficient modes of transport in terms of minimizing the global warming impact of tourism and, clearly, Kaliningrad could be well placed to develop them, although, as an exclave, it also shares the attributes of an island in terms of its dependency on air links.

A sensitive environment

Kaliningrad Oblast is one of the most attractive and significant areas on the map of Europe in terms of its local ecology and, hence, it has huge potential for the development of eco-tourism. Several indicators point to the Oblast's suitability – wild nature, ethno-cultural heritage, scientific and educational facilities and an existing information centre for ecology in tourism. Bio-resources are of special value for this type of tourism and the area is very rich in both unique and rare categories of animals and plants, some of which are included in the Red Book of endangered species. It is also rich in whole ecosystems, such as bogs, marshes, littoral meadows and so on. It is therefore important to follow the principles peculiar to eco-tourism in general to develop this appropriately.

The national park Curonian Spit within the Kaliningrad Oblast is a major part of the World Heritage site designated by UNESCO in 2000 (the rest is in Lithuania) and is the most developed area for ecology-based tourism in the region. There are currently very popular nature tours, including the Dune Efa (the highest dune in Europe), the Dancing Forest (a unique area of weirdly twisted and curved living tree trunks), as well as the landscape of the Curonian Spit itself. There are important seasonal migrations of birds passing over the Spit and birdwatchers can visit the swan lake (in Rybachiy settlement). Most of the 140,000 yearly visitors to the national park visit the ornithological station by the Russian Academy of Science, where ringing of the hundreds of thousands of migrating birds is carried out. European Commission-funded projects have supported the development of the Curonian Ecological Information Centre, which organizes ecological educational tours. In summer, over 2000 visitors enter the park each day.

Prospects for development

The Kaliningrad Oblast seems to have all the necessy prerequisites for dynamic sustainable tourism development in terms of a favourable geographical location, excellent natural resources and a rich historical heritage. As yet, however, the infrastructure for tourism is underdeveloped and is seen as being less competitive when compared to the neighbouring regions. They have similar development potential, as have other subregions of the Baltic.

There are certain discrete areas of growth in tourism in the Kaliningrad region, but they are not linked to a unified, joint system, so they are developing in uncoordinated ways. There is an almost complete absence of networking and no significant large players that might provide leadership in developing the Oblast as a single tourism complex with more active integration into both the Russian and wider European tourism markets.

To improve the efficiency of the tourism sector services and increase their competitiveness, measures are needed to develop a networked tourism system with enhanced service delivery technologies. These would, in turn, create a favourable institutional environment for attracting Russian and foreign investment (see Table CS10.2).

In the absence of large players in tourism in this area, programmes and projects initiated by state authorities to create the basic infrastructure and coordinate development play an important role. Tourism is mentioned as a priority for development in the strategy for regional development in the 'Programme of socio-economic development of the Kaliningrad Oblast to 2016', as well as in the strategies of a number of the municipalities (Kaliningrad, Zelenogradsk, Svetlogorsk, Pionersk, Jantarny and so on).

The 'Programme for the development of the Kaliningrad Oblast as a tourism centre in 2007–2011' has also been developed by the Oblast authorities and approved by Decree of the Government of the Kaliningrad Oblast on 22 February 2007. The programme is aimed at ensuring a favourable environment for the development of a competitive tourist recreational complex on the territory of the Kaliningrad Oblast that makes effective use of the regional tourism potential and available resources. The programme for its implementation is focused on the following areas:

- enhancing the legal framework for the creation of favourable legal and organizational conditions for the development of tourism and recreational faciles
- information and advertising policy and promotion of the regional tourist product to develop a positive image of the region as a tourism centre and increase tourist flows into the Oblast

Table CS10.2 Measures to stimulate the development of the service sector to meet the needs of tourism.

Measures	Specific actions
Development of a networked tourism system.	Establishment of complementary accommodation, catering and entertainment units. Construction of basic infrastructure facilities (water, gas, heat, and electricity supply). Construction of sufficient transport infrastructure facilities.
Organizational measures to enhance service delivery technologies for tourism and recreation.	Adoption of modern service technologies (membership of chains of hostels, hotels, motels and other recreational establishments guaranteeing proper service quality, for example). Development of thematic routes. Improvement of the Oblast-wide system for staff training and retraining.
Ensuring favourable institutional environment for investment.	Administrative measures: • support of organizations working in tourism and recreation, including small business enterprises • elimination of administrative barriers while retaining government control over service standards • consideration of tourist routes during preparation of town and country plans. Regulatory measures: • creation of favourable legal conditions for economic agents operating in tourism and recreation while retaining/enhancing sufficient protection for wilderness, rural and urban environment to protect the natural and heritage resource base.
Financial support measures.	Ensuring finance from various sources (budgets of all levels, extra-budgetary funds, foreign investment). Active employment of market instruments, as well as tendering procedures, for the fair allocation of budgetary funds.

- development of the infrastructure for tourism and recreation and thus increase attractiveness of the region to investors
- support and development of special interest tourism as well as the diversification of the tourist service mix
- extension of international and inter-regional cooperation in tourism – integration into Russian and international tourism markets and inclusion on international (European) tourist routes
- improvement of the regional system of staff training, retraining and advanced training.

It is planned that RUR31.8 million from the regional budget will be spent on implementing this programme. Funds will also be garnered from the Russian Federal budget, including RUR533.4 million within the framework of the Federal Target Programme for the Development of the Kaliningrad Oblast up to 2010. Substantial amounts of private investment are expected, too – RUR8 billion for the development of the infrastructure for tourism, RUR846.6 million for the construction of a multifunctional exhibition complex, RUR53.7 million for promoting the region through tour operators and other tourism organizations, while a further RUR25.2 million will be generated from the European Commission Structure Fund within the framework of transnational projects (development of a network of bicycle paths and elaborating new tourist thematic routes).

The programme seeks to develop a competitive tourist and recreational industry, which will become one of the leading industrial sectors in the Oblast. It is planned to transform the Kaliningrad Oblast into one of the most attractive tourism and recreation destinations in the entire Baltic region and Europe at large. It is planned that tourist numbers will increase to 1.2 million a year by 2011, each staying, on average, seven days. This would represent a remarkable seven-fold increase in about five years.

There are two large-scale projects being initiated by the Russian Federal Authorities. One of them is the development of a special economic zone for tourism and recreation for the Curonian Spit. Within this project, RUR1.5 billion will be invested by the Russian Federal Authorities to develop infrastructure for tourism. Also, RUR5.8 billion of private investment is expected in order to realize projects within the framework of the programme. The feasibility study for the special economic zone, however, requires that the status of the Curonian Spit as a national park and UNESCO World Heritage site needs to be taken into acount, which is why none of the projects proposed so far has been approved for development.

There is even more uncertainty about a project for the creation of a gambling zone in the Kaliningrad Oblast. It is planned for an area near the Jantarny settlement, on the south-western coast of the Oblast on former agricultural land and without any kind of infrastructure. If this project is realized, however, Jantarny and the neighbouring area will become the centre of a large tourism complex. All the coastal sites will be connected together by a new sea coast highway, which will also connect to Kaliningrad and an airport, construction of which began in 2008.

A number of new important projects are being developed by large Moscow investors: for instance, a complex development of the coastal area to the north of Jantarny and a yacht marina in the northern part of the Oblast at Pionesky. The Fishing Village on the river frontage of Kaliningrad (see Figures CS10.2 and CS10.3) demonstrates how derelict land is being transformed.

Figure CS10.2 The Fishing Village before development.
(Courtesy of Archive of the Fishing Village.)

Figure CS10.3 The Fishing Village after redevelopment.
(Courtesy of Dina Sheliak.)

Up to the present, important avenues for developing tourism in the Oblast, such as international cooperation, have not been fully exploited, but could significantly increase the competitiveness of all participants. It is especially important to reinforce the participation of the Oblast and municipal authorities in the Euroregion cooperation structure, of which five Kaliningrad Oblast districts are members (Baltica, Lyna-Lava, Neman, Saule and Sheshupe), and the European Commission-supported Interreg projects where tourism is one of the priorities.

With all these plans, projects and prospects, Kaliningrad Oblast seems set to be one of the fastest-growing tourism regions in all of Europe. As we have seen, however, the current restrictions and increasing visa complications between Russia and the EU countries are Kaliningrad Oblast's single most acute problem, yet it has the most to gain from fruitful cooperation between Russia and the EU.

Questions and disscussion points

1. What is the current extent of knowledge about this region among your group? Among the local population in your country? Procure a good scale map of Kaliningrad Oblast and identify the regions and towns referred to in this case study.

2. Contrast the maritime transport links available in the Baltic region to Kaliningrad and compare these with routes to other countries in the region, including mainland Russia. What short sea routes would be viable to ports in the Oblast?

3. What markets do you think could be attracted to this region and with what purpose? What products in the exclave do you think offer the widest appeal for the international tourist market?

4. Given the limited resources available to the tourism authorities in the region, consider the strategies outlined in Table CS10.2 and determine which should receive priority, to benefit the region most effectively.

5. Analyse the difficulties and potential benefits of attempting to form promotional partnerships for the purposes of tourism with contiguous countries within the region, similar to those found in other areas of the Baltic.

Further reading

Note

The flow of books on tourism now appearing on the market is such that any attempt to offer a comprehensive listing of available and appropriate textbooks to aid the reader would be unnecessarily long and less than helpful. Instead, in this new edition, the list given here will, for the first time, include those books that will allow students to read around the topics covered in this book at a level appropriate for their courses. The books have been chosen for their suitability for those studying tourism at post-A level up to under-graduate level and are identified according to their principal topics, apart from those that, in the view of the authors, offer useful supplementary reading about the nature of tourism in general – these are included in the section for Chapter 1. Books earlier than 1980 are included only where they are classic and seminal books or throw light on some particular aspect of tourism that cannot be readily found in more recent books. Publications other than books are largely excluded – again, except where they are deemed vital to the con-temporary study of the subject.

General reference

Beaver, A. (2005) *A Dictionary of Travel and Tourism Terminology* (2nd edn), CABI.

Burles, D. and Quinn, B. (2006) *World Travel Atlas* (10th edn), Columbus Travel Publishing. *Insight Deluxe World Travel Atlas and CD-ROM*, GeoGraphic Publishers GmbH, Munich, 2007.

Jafari, J. (ed.) (2000) *Encyclopedia of Tourism*, Routledge.

Jones, I. and Mason, P. (2007) *Routledge Dictionary of Leisure and Tourism*, Routledge.

Medlik, S. (1996) *Dictionary of Travel, Tourism and Hospitality* (2nd edn), Butterworth-Heinemann.

Weaver, D. (ed.) (2003) *The Encyclopaedia of Ecotourism*, CABI.

Chapter 1 An introduction to tourism

Alford, P. (2000) *E-Business in the Travel Industry*, Travel and Tourism Intelligence.

Allcock, J. B., Bruner, E. M. and Lanfant, M.-F. (eds) (1993) *International Tourism: Identity and change*, Sage.

Biederman, P., Lai, J., Laitamaki, J., Messerli, H., Nyheni, P. and Plog, S. (2008) *Travel and Tourism: An industry primer*, Prentice Hall.

Boniface, B. and Cooper, C. (2005) *Worldwide Destinations: The geography of travel and tourism* (4th edn), Elsevier Butterworth-Heinemann.

Boniface, P. (2001) Dynamic *Tourism: Journeying with change*, Channel View.

Boorstin, D. J. (1962) *The Image: A guide to pseudo-events in America*, Penguin.

Brown, F. (1998) *Tourism Reassessed: Blight or blessing?*, Butterworth Heinemann.

Burkart, A. J. and Medlik, S. (1981) *Tourism: Past, present and future*, Heinemann.

Burns, P. and Holden, A. (1995) *Tourism: A new perspective*, Prentice Hall.

Butcher, J. (2002) *The Moralisation of Tourism: Sun, sand and saving the world*, Routledge.

Callaghan, P. (ed.) (1989) *Travel and Tourism*, Business Education Publishers.

Cochrane, J. (2008) *Asian Tourism: Growth and change*, Elsevier.

Cohen, E. (2004) *Contemporary Tourism: Diversity and change*, Elsevier.

Cooper, C., Fletcher, J., Fyall, A., Gilbert, D. and Wanhill, S. (2008) *Tourism Principles and Practice* (4th edn), Pitman.

Cooper, C. and Hall, M. (2008) *Contemporary Tourism: An international approach*, Butterworth-Heinemann.

Davidson, R. (1993) *Tourism* (2nd edn), Pitman.

Davidson, R. (1998) *Travel and Tourism in Europe* (2nd edn), Longman.

Davidson, R. and Cope, B. (2003) *Business Travel: Conferences, incentive travel, exhibitions, corporate hospitality and corporate travel*, Prentice Hall.

Faulkner, B., Laws, E. and Moscardo, G. (eds) (2001) *Tourism in the 21st Century*, Continuum.

Goeldner, J. R. and Ritchie, J. R. Brent (2006) *Tourism: Principles, Practices, Philosophies* (10th edn), Wiley.

Lavery, P. and Van Doren, C. (1990) *Travel and Tourism: A North American–European perspective*, Elm Publications.

Lickorish, L. J. and Jenkins, C. (1995) *An Introduction to Tourism*, Butterworth-Heinemann.

Lockwood, A. and Medlik, S. (2002) *Tourism and Hospitality in the 21st Century*, Elsevier Butterworth-Heinemann.

Lumsdon, L. and Swift, J. (2001) *Tourism in Latin America*, Continuum.

Lundberg, D. and C. (1993) *International Travel and Tourism* (2nd edn), Wiley.

Medlik, S. (1999) *Understanding Tourism*, Butterworth-Heinemann.

Mill, R. C. and Morrison, A. (1992) *The Tourism System: An introductory text* (2nd edn), Prentice Hall.

Page, S. and Connell, J. (2006) *Tourism: A modern synthesis* (2nd edn), Thomson.

Pape, R. (1964) 'Touristry: a type of occupational mobility', *Social Problems*, 2/4 Spring.

Pompl, W. and Lavery, P. (1993) *Tourism in Europe: Structures and development*, CABI.

Rogers, T. (2003) *Conferences and Conventions: A global industry*, Elsevier.

Ryan, C. (1991) *Tourism, Terrorism and Violence*, Research Institute for the Study of Conflict and Terrorism.

Seaton, A. V., Jenkins, C. L., Wood, R. C., Dieke, P. U. C., Bennett, M. M., MacLellan, L. R. and Smith, R. (eds) (1994) *Tourism: The state of the art*, Wiley.

Sharpley, R. (ed.) (2002) *The Tourism Business: An introduction*, Business Education Publishers.

Sharpley, R. and Telfer, D. (2007) *Tourism and Development*, Routledge.

Shone, A. (1998) *The Business of Conferences*, Butterworth-Heinemann.

Swarbrooke, J. and Horner, S. (2001) *Business Travel and Tourism*, Butterworth-Heinemann.

Theobald, W. (ed.) (2005) *Global Tourism: the Next Decade* (3rd edn), Butterworth-Heinemann.

Toffler, A. (1970) *Future Shock*, Bodley Head.

Vellas, F. and Bécherel, L. (1995) *International Tourism*, Macmillan.

Vukonic, B. (1997) *Tourism and Religion*, Elsevier Science.

Wall, G. and Mathieson, A. (1997) *Tourism: Change, impacts and opportunities* (2nd edn), Longman.

Weiler, B. and Hall, C. M. (eds) (1992) *Special Interest Tourism*, Belhaven Press.

Youell, R. (1998) *Tourism: An introduction*, Addison-Wesley Longman.

Chapter 2 The development and growth of tourism up to the mid-twentieth century

Adams, C. (2003) *Transport and Travel in the Roman World*, Sutton.

Adamson, S. H. (1977) *Seaside Piers*, Batsford.

Addison, W. (1951) *English Spas*, Batsford.

Alderson, F. (1973) *The Inland Resorts and Spas of Britain*, David & Charles.

Bennett, T. (1995) *The Birth of the Museum: History, Theory, Politics*, Routledge.

Braggs, S. and Harris, D. (2000) *Sun, Fun and Crowds: Seaside holidays between the wars*, Tempus.

Brendon, P. (2005) *Thomas Cook: 150 years of popular tourism*, Secker.

Brodie, A., Sargent, A. and Winterby, G. (2005) *Seaside Holidays in the Past*, English Heritage.

Burton, A. and P. (1978) *The Green Bag Travellers: Britain's first tourists*, Deutsch.

Buzzard, J. (1993) *The Beaten Track: European tourism, literature and the ways to culture, 1800–1918*, Clarendon Press.

CABI (1993) *Fashionable Resort Regions: Their evolution and transformation*, CABI.

Casson, L. (1974) *Travel in the Ancient World*, George Allen and Unwin.

Chaney, E. (1998) *The Evolution of the Grand Tour*, Frank Cass.

Corbin, A. (1994) *The Lure of the Sea: The discovery of the seaside in the Western world, 1750–1840*, Polity Press.

Cormack, B. (1998) *A History of Holidays, 1812–1990*, Routledge/Thoemmes Press.

Delgado, A. (1977) *The Annual Outing and Other Excursions*, George Allen & Unwin.

Drower, J. (1982) *Good Clean Fun: The story of Britain's first holiday camp*, Arcadia.

Feifer, M. (1985) *Going Places: The ways of the tourist from imperial Rome to the present day*, Macmillan.

Gordon, S. (1972) *Holidays*, Batsford.

Havins, P. J. N. (1976) *The Spas of England*, Robert Hale.

Hembry, P. (1990) *The English Spa, 1560–1815: A social history*, Athlone Press.

Hern, A. (1967) *The Seaside Holiday: The history of the English seaside resort*, Cresset Press.

Hibbert, C. (1969) *The Grand Tour*, Weidenfeld & Nicolson.

Hindley, G. (1983) *Tourists, Travellers and Pilgrims*, Hutchinson.

Jakle, J. A. (1985) *The Tourist: Travel in 20th-century North America*, University of Nebraska Press.

Kapuscinski, R. (2008) *Travels with Herodotus*, Penguin.

Löfgren, O. (1999) *On Holiday: A history of vacationing*, University of California Press.

Lloyd, M. (2003) *The Passport: The history of man's most travelled document*, Sutton.

Maillet, A. (2004) *The Claude Glass: Use and meaning of the black mirror in Western art*, Zone Books.

Mighall, R. (2008) *Sunshine: One Man's Search for Happiness*, John Murray.

Moir, E. (1964) *The Discovery of Britain: The English tourists, 1540–1840*, Routledge & Kegan Paul.

North, R. (1962) *The Butlin Story*, Jarrolds.

Ousby, I. (1990) *The Englishman's England: Taste, travel and the rise of tourism*, CUP.

Perrottet, T. (2003) *Route 66AD: Pagan holiday on the trail of ancient Roman tourists*, Random House.

Pimlott, J. A. R. (1976) *The Englishman's Holiday*, Harvester Press.

Sillitoe, A. (1995) *Leading the Blind: A century of guide book travel, 1815–1914*, Macmillan.

Smith, P. (ed.) (1998) *The History of Tourism: Thomas Cook and the origins of leisure travel*, Routledge/Thoemmes Press.

Somerville, C. (1990) *Britain Beside the Sea*, Grafton.

Stokes, H. G. (1947) *The Very First History of the English Seaside*, Sylvan Press.

Studd, R. G. (1948) *The Holiday Story*, Percival Marshall.

Swinglehurst, E. (1974) *The Romantic Journey: The Story of Thomas Cook and Victorian Travel*, Pica.

Swinglehurst, E. (1982) *Cook's Tours: The story of popular travel*, Blandford Press.

Walton, J. K. (1983) *The English Seaside Resort: A social history 1750–1914*, University of Leicester Press.

Walton, J. K. (2000) *The British Seaside: Holidays and resorts in the twentieth century*, Manchester University Press.

Walton, J. K. and Walvin, J. (1983) *Leisure in Britain, 1780–1939*, Manchester University Press.

Walvin, J. (1978) *Beside the Seaside: A social history of the popular seaside holiday*, Allen Lane.

Ward, C. and Hardy, D. (1986) *Goodnight Campers! The history of the British holiday camps*, Mansell.

Weaver, D. and Lawton, L. (2006) *Tourism Management* (3rd edn), Wiley.

Chapter 3 The era of popular tourism: 1950 to the twenty-first century

Akhtar, M. and Humphries, S. (2000) *Some Liked it Hot: The British on holiday at home and abroad*, Virgin Publishing

Apostolopoulos, Y., Leontidou, L. and Loukissas, P. (eds) (2000) *Mediterranean Tourism*, Routledge.

Bray, R. and Raitz, V. (2000) *Flight to the Sun: The story of the holiday revolution*, Continuum.

Cohen, E. (2004) *Contemporary Tourism: Diversity and change*, Elsevier.

Hodgson, G. (1995) *A New Grand Tour*, Viking.

Lencek, L. and Bosker, G. (1998) *The Beach: The history of paradise on Earth*, Secker & Warburg.

Middleton, V. and Lickorish, L. (2005) *British Tourism: The remarkable story of growth*, Elsevier Butterworth-Heinemann.

Richardson, D. and Richards, B. (2000) *ABTA: The first 50 years*, ABTA.

Chapter 4 The demand for tourism

Apostolopoulos, Y., Leivadi, S. and Yiannakis, A. (eds) (1996) *The Sociology of Tourism*, Routledge.

Clift, S. and Grabowski, P. (eds) (1997) *Tourism and Health: Risks, research and responses*, Cassell.

Clift, S. and Page, S. (1995) *Health and the International Tourist*, Routledge.

Clift, S., Luongo, M. and Callister, C. (2002) *Gay Tourism: Culture, identity and sex*, Continuum.

Cohen, E. (2005) *Contemporary Tourism: Diversity and change*, Elsevier.

Davidson, R. and Cope, B. (2003) *Business Travel: Conferences, incentive travel, exhibitions, corporate hospitality and corporate travel*, Pearson Education.

Decrop, A. (2006) *Vacation Decision-making*, CABI.

Gullahorn, J. E. and Gullahorn, J. T. (1963) 'An extension of the U-curve hypothesis', *Journal of Social Sciences* 19, pp. 33–47.

Hall, C. M. and Ryan, C. (2001) *Sex Tourism: Marginal people and liminalities*, Routledge.

Hall, C. M., Timothy, D. J. and Duval, D. T. (eds) (2004) *Safety and Security in Tourism: Relationships, management and marketing*, Haworth Press.

Hughes, H. (2006) *Pink Tourism: Holidays of gay men and lesbians*, CABI.

Johnson, P. and Thomas, B. (eds) (1992) *Choice and Demand in Tourism*, Mansell.

Krippendorf, J. (1991) *The Holiday Makers: Understanding the impact of leisure and travel* (2nd edn), Heinemann.

MacCannell, D. (1992) *Empty Meeting Grounds: The tourist papers*, Routledge.

March, R. and Woodside, A. (2005) *Tourism Behaviour*, CABI.

Mayo, E. J. and Jarvis, L. P. (1981) *The Psychology of Leisure Travel: Effective marketing and selling of travel services*, CBI.

Novelli, M. (ed.) (2005) *Niche Tourism: Contemporary issues, trends and cases*, Elsevier.

Page, S. J. and Connell, J. (2006) *Tourism: A modern synthesis* (2nd edn), Thomson.

Patterson, I. (2006) *Growing Older: Tourism and leisure behaviour of older adults*, CABI.

Pizam, A. and Mansfield, Y. (eds) (2005) *Consumer Behaviour in Travel and Tourism*, Jaico Publishing.

Plog, S. (1991) *Leisure Travel: Making it a growth market again!*, Wiley.

Rapoport, R. and R. N. (1974) 'Four themes in the sociology of leisure', *British Journal of Sociology*, 15, pp. 215–29.

Rath, J. (ed.) (2006) *Tourism, Ethnic Diversity and the City*, Routledge.

Reader, I. and Walter, T. (eds) (1993) *Pilgrimage in Popular Culture*, Macmillan.

Richards, G. (ed.) (2007) *Cultural Tourism: Global and local perspectives*, Haworth Hospitality and Tourism Press.

Robinson, M. and Boniface, P. (eds) (1998) *Tourism and Cultural Conflicts*, CABI.

Robinson, M., Evans, N. and Callaghan, P. (eds) (1996) *Culture as the Tourist Product*, Business Education Publishers.

Rogers, T. (1998) *Conferences: A twenty-first century industry*, Addison-Wesley Longman.

Ross, G. F. (1994) *The Psychology of Tourism: Australian studies in tourism No. 1*, Hospitality Press.

Rutherford, D. (1990) *Introduction to the Conventions, Expositions and Meetings Industry*, Van Nostrand Reinhold.

Ryan, C. (1995) *Researching Tourist Satisfaction: Issues, concepts, problems*, Routledge.

Ryan, C. (ed.) (2002) *The Tourist Experience* (2nd edn), Continuum.

Sheller, M. and Urry, J. (eds) (2004) *Tourism Mobilities: Places to play, places in play*, Routledge.

Swarbrooke, J. and Horner, S. (1999) *Consumer Behaviour in Tourism*, Butterworth-Heinemann.

Swarbrooke, J. and Horner, S. (2001) *Business Travel and Tourism*, Butterworth-Heinemann.

Swarbrooke, J., Beard, C., Leckie, S. and Pomfret, G. (2003) *Adventure Tourism: The new frontier*, Butterworth-Heinemann.

Timothy, D. and Olsen, D. (eds) (2006) *Tourism, Religion and Spiritual Journeys*, Routledge.

Urry, J. (1995) *Consuming Places*, Routledge.

Urry, J. (2002) *The Tourist Gaze: Leisure and travel in contemporary societies* (2nd edn), Sage.

Uysal, M. (ed.) (1994) *Global Tourist Behaviour*, International Business Press.

Voase, R. (1995) *Tourism: The human perspective*, Hodder & Stoughton.

Waitt, G. and Markwell, K. (2006) *Gay Tourism: Culture and context*, Haworth Hospitality and Tourism Press.

Woodside, A., Crouch, G., Mazanek, J., Oppermann, M. and Sakai, M. (eds) (1999) *Consumer Psychology of Tourism, Hospitality and Leisure*, CABI.

Zurick, D. (1995) *Errant Journeys: Adventure travel in a modern age*, University of Texas Press.

Chapter 5 The economic impacts of tourism

Ateljevic, I., Pritchard, A. and Morgan, N. (eds) (2007) *The Critical Turn in Tourism Studies: Innovative research methodologies*, Elsevier.

Badger, A. (1996) *Trading Places: Tourism as trade*, Tourism Concern.

Buglear, J. (2000) *Stats to Go: A guide to statistics for hospitality, leisure and tourism studies*, Butterworth-Heinemann.

Bull, A. (1995) *The Economics of Travel and Tourism* (2nd edn), Longman.

Clarke, M., Riley, M. and Wood, R. C. (1997) *Research Methods in Hospitality and Tourism*, International Thomson Business Press.

Coles, T. and Hall, C. M. (2008) *International Business and Tourism: Global issues, contemporary interactions*, Routledge.

Dwyer, L. and Forsyth, P. (eds) (2006) *International Handbook on the Economics of Tourism*, Edward Elgar.

Fennell, D. (2007) *Ecotourism* (3rd edn), Routledge.

Frechtling, D. (2001) *Forecasting Tourism Demand: Methods and strategies*, Butterworth-Heinemann.

Go, F. and Jenkins, C. (eds) (1998) *Tourism and Economic Development in Asia and Australia*, Pinter.

Goodson, L. and Phillimore, J. (eds) (2004) *Qualitative Research in Tourism: Ontologies, epistemologies and methodologies*, Routledge.

Harrison, D. (1995) *Tourism and the Less Developed Countries* (2nd edn), Wiley.

Ioannides, D. and Debbage, K. G. (eds) (1998) *The Economic Geography of the Tourist Industry: A supply-side analysis*, Routledge.

Jennings, G. (2001) *Tourism Research*, Wiley.

de Kadt, E. (1979) *Tourism: Passport to Development?*, OUP.

Knowles, T., Diamantis, D. and Bey El-Mourhabi, J. (2001) *The Globalisation of Tourism and Hospitality: A strategic perspective*, Continuum.

Kozak, M. and Decrop, A. (eds) (2008) *Handbook of Consumer Research in Tourism: Theory and research*, Routledge.

Ladkin, A., Szivas, E. and Riley, M. (2002) *Tourism Employment: Analysis and planning*, Channel View.

Lennon, J. (ed.) (2003) *Tourism Statistics: International perspectives and current issues*, Continuum.

Lundberg, D., Stavenga, M. H. and Krishnamoorthy, M. (1995) *Tourism Economics*, Wiley.

Page, S. J. and Connell, J. (2006) *Tourism: A modern synthesis* (2nd edn), Thomson.

Pearce, D. (1989) *Tourist Development* (2nd edn), Longman.

Pearce, D. G. and Butler, R. W. (eds) (1992) *Tourism Research: Critiques and challenges*, Routledge.

Pearce, D. G. and Butler, R. W. (eds) (1999) *Contemporary Issues in Tourism Development*, Routledge.

Preuss, H. (2007) *The Economics of Staging the Olympics*, Edward Elgar.

Ritchie, B. W., Burns, P. and Palmer, C. (eds) (2005) *Tourism Research Methods: Integrating theory with practice*, CABI.

Ritchie, J. R. Brent and Goeldner, C. (eds) (1994) *Travel, Tourism and Hospitality Research: A handbook for managers and researchers* (2nd edn), Wiley.

Sharpley, R. and Telfer, D. (eds) (2002) *Tourism and Development: Concepts and issues*, Channel View.

Sinclair, M. T. and Stabler, M. (1997) *The Economics of Tourism*, Routledge.

Smith, M. and Duffy, R. (2003) *The Ethics of Tourism Development*, Routledge.

Tribe, J. (1999) *The Economics of Leisure and Tourism* (2nd edn), Butterworth-Heinemann.

Veal, A. J. (1997) *Research Methods for Leisure and Tourism: A practical guide* (2nd edn), Longman.

Wall, G. and Mathieson, A. (2006) *Tourism: Changes, impacts and opportunities*, Prentice Hall.

Williams, A. and Shaw, G. (eds) (1991) *Tourism and Economic Development: Western European experiences* (2nd edn), Wiley.

Wong, K. and Song, H. (eds) (2002) *Tourism Forecasting and Marketing*, Haworth Hospitality Press.

Chapter 6 The sociocultural impacts of tourism

Ashworth, G. J. and Larkham, P. J. (1994) *Building a New Heritage: Tourism, culture and identity in the new Europe*, Routledge.

Bauer, T. and McKercher, B. (eds) (2003) *Sex and Tourism: Journeys of romance, love and lust*, The Haworth Hospitality Press.

Beech, J. and Chadwick, S. (2006) *The Business of Tourism Management*, Prentice Hall.

Boissevain, J. (ed.) (1992) *Revitalising European rituals*, Routledge.

Boissevain, J. (ed.) (1997) *Coping with Tourists: European reactions to mass tourism*, Berghan.

Boniface, P. (1995) *Managing Quality Cultural Tourism*, Routledge.

Boniface, P. and Fowler, P. (1993) *Heritage and Tourism in the 'Global Village'*, Routledge.

Briguglio, L., Archer, B., Jafari, J. and Wall, G. (eds) (1996) *Sustainable Tourism in Islands and Small States: Issues and policies*, Pinter.

Bushell, R. and Eagles, P. F. (eds) (2006) *Tourism and Protected Areas: Benefits beyond boundaries*, CABI.

Butcher, J. (2007) *Ecotourism, NGOs and Development: A critical analysis*, Routledge.

Butcher, S. (2003) *The Moralisation of Tourism: Sun, sand . . . and saving the world?* Routledge.

Butler, R. W. and Hinch, T. (eds) (1996) *Tourism and Indigenous Peoples*, International Thomson Business Press.

Clift, S. and Carter, S. (eds) (2000) *Tourism and Sex: Culture, Commerce and Coercion*, Cassell.

Cooper, C. and Wanhill, S. R. (1997) *Tourism Development: Environmental and community issues*, Wiley.

Dahles, H. and Keune, L. (eds) (2003) *Tourism Development and Local Participation in Latin America*, Cognizant Communication.

Doxey, G. V. (1975) 'A causation theory of visitor–resident irritants: methodology and research inferences, *Proceedings of the Travel Research Association Sixth Annual Conference*, San Diego.

Graburn, N. H. H. (ed.) (1976) *Ethnic and Tourist Arts: Cultural expressions from the Fourth World*, University of California Press.

Gullahorn, J. E. and Gullahorn, J. T. (1963) 'An extension of the U-curve hypothesis', *Journal of Social Sciences*, 19, pp. 33–47.

Hall, C. Michael and Lew, A. (2008) *Understanding and Managing Tourism Impacts: An integrated approach*, Routledge.

Harris, R., Griffin, T. and Williams, P. (eds) (2002) *Sustainable Tourism: A global perspective* (2nd edn), Elsevier.

Harrison, L. and Husbands, W. (1996) *Practising Responsible Tourism: International case studies in tourism planning, policy and development*, Wiley.

Hickman, L. (2007) *The Final Call: In search of the true cost of our holidays*, Eden Project Books.

Holden, A. (2007) *Environment and Tourism* (2nd edn), Routledge.

Kockel, U. (ed.) (1994) *Culture, Tourism and Development: The case of Ireland*, Liverpool University Press.

Lane, B. and Bramwell, B. (1997) *Sustainable Tourism: Principles and practice*, Wiley.

Lino, B. (ed.) (1996) *Sustainable Tourism in Islands: Vol. 1: Issues and Policies; Vol. 2: Case Studies*, Mansell.

MacCannell, D. (1989) *The Tourist: A new theory of the leisure class* (2nd edn), Schocken Books.

Middleton, V. with Hawkins, R. (1998) *Sustainable Tourism: A marketing perspective*, Butterworth-Heinemann.

Mowforth, M. and Munt, I. (2008) *Tourism and Sustainability: Development, globalization and new tourism in the Third World* (3rd edn), Routledge.

Pattullo, P. (1996) *Last Resorts: The cost of tourism in the Caribbean*, Cassell.

Pearce, P. L., Moscardo, G. M. and Ross, G. F. (1997) *Tourism Community Relationships*, Elsevier Science.

Price, M. (ed.) (1996) *People and Tourism in Fragile Environments*, Wiley.

Priestley, G. K., Edwards, J. A. and Coccossis, H. (eds) (1996) *Sustainable Tourism?: European experiences*, CABI.

Reisinger, Y. and Turner, L. (2003) *Cross-Cultural Behaviour in Tourism: Concepts and analysis*, Butterworth-Heinemann.

Richards, G. (ed.) (1996) *Cultural Tourism in Europe*, CABI.

Richards, G. and Hall, D. (eds) (2000) *Tourism and Sustainable Community Development*, Routledge.

Scheyvens, R. (2002) *Tourism for Development: Empowering communities*, Prentice Hall.

Smith, V. (ed.) (1992) *Hosts and Guests: An anthropology of tourism*, Blackwell.

Smith, V. and Brent, M. (eds) (2001) *Hosts and Guests Revisited: Tourism issues in the 21st century*, Cognizant Communication.

Stabler, M. J. (ed.) (1997) *Tourism and Sustainability: Principles to practice*, CABI.

Sutton, W. A. (1967) 'Travel and understanding: notes on the social structure of touring', *International Journal of Comparative Sociology*, 8 (2), pp. 218–23.

Swarbrooke, J. (1999) *Sustainable Tourism Management*, CABI.

Wall, G. and Mathieson, A. (2006) *Tourism: Changes, impacts and opportunities*, Prentice Hall.

Wood, K. and House, S. (1991) *The Good Tourist*, Mandarin.

Young, G. (1973) *Tourism: Blessing or blight?* Pelican.

Chapter 7 The environmental impacts of tourism

Aronsson, L. (2000) *The Development of Sustainable Tourism*, Continuum.

Boo, E. (1990) *Eco-tourism: The potentials and the pitfalls*, World Wildlife Fund.

Bramwell, B. and Lane, B. (eds) (1993) *Rural Tourism and Sustainable Rural Development*, Channel View.

Bramwell, H., Henry, I., Jackson, G., Goytia Prat, A., Richards, G. and van der Straaten, J. (eds) (1996) *Sustainable Tourism Management: Principles and practice*, Tilburg University Press.

Buckley, R. (ed.) (2004) *Environmental Impacts of Ecotourism*, CABI.

Cater, E. and Lowman, G. (1994) *Ecotourism: A sustainable option?* Wiley.

Croall, J. (1995) *Preserve or Destroy: Tourism and the environment*, Calouste Gulbenkian Foundation.

Eagles, P. F. and McCool, S. F. (2004) *Tourism in National Parks and Protected Areas: Planning and management*, CABI.

Eber, S. (ed.) (1992) *Beyond the Green Horizon: A discussion paper on principles for sustainable tourism*, Tourism Concern/World Wildlife Fund.

Elkington, J. and Hailes, J. (1992) *Holidays that Don't Cost the Earth*, Victor Gollancz.

Fennell, D. A. (2007) *Ecotourism* (3rd edn), Routledge.

Font, X. and Tribe, J. (eds) (1999) *Forest Tourism and Recreation: Case studies in environmental management*, CABI.

Forsyth, T. (1996) *Sustainable Tourism: Moving from theory to practice*, Tourism Concern/Worldwide Fund for Nature.

France, L. (ed.) (1997) *The Earthscan Reader in Sustainable Tourism*, Earthscan/Kogan Page.

Hall, C. M. (ed.) (1998) *Sustainable Tourism: A geographical perspective*, Longman.

Honey, M. (1999) *Ecotourism and Sustainable Development: Who owns paradise?*, Island Press.

Hunter, C. and Green, H. (1995) *Tourism and the Environment: A sustainable relationship?*, Routledge.

Inskip, E. (1991) *Tourism Planning: An integrated and sustainable development*, van Nostland Reinhold.

Ioannides, D., Apostolopoulos, Y. and Sonmez, S. (eds) (2001) *Mediterranean Islands and Sustainable Tourism Development: Practices, management and policies*, Continuum.

Neale, G. (ed.) (1997) *The Green Travel Guide*, Kogan Page.

Newsome, D., Moore, S. and Dowling, R. (2002) *Natural Area Tourism: Ecology, impacts and management*, Channel View.

Page, S. J. and Connell, J. (2006) *Tourism: A modern synthesis* (2nd edn), Thomson.

Tribe, J., Font, X., Griffiths, N., Vickery, R. and Yale, K. (2000) *Environmental Management for Rural Tourism and Recreation*, Continuum.

Wahab, S. and Pigram, J. (eds) (1997) *Tourism Development and Growth: The challenge of sustainability*, Routledge.

Wall, G. and Mathieson, A. (2006) *Tourism: Changes, impacts and opportunities*, Prentice Hall.

Wearing, S. and Neil, J. (1999) *Ecotourism: Impacts, potentials and possibilities*, Butterworth-Heinemann.

Weaver, D. B. (1998) *Ecotourism in the Less Developed World*, CABI.

Chapter 8 The structure and organization of the travel and tourism industry

Buhalis, D. and Laws, E. (eds) (2001) *Tourism Distribution Channels: Practices, issues and transformations*, Continuum.

Gee, C., Makens, J. and Choy, D. (1997) *The Travel Industry* (3rd edn), Wiley.

Hodgson, A. (ed.) (1987) *The Travel and Tourism Industry: Strategies for the future*, Pergamon Press.

Horner, P. (1991) *The Travel Industry in Britain*, Stanley Thornes.

Pearce, D. (1992) *Tourism Organisations*, Longman.

Pender, L. (2001) *Travel Trade and Transport: An introduction*, Continuum.

Sinclair, M. T. and Stabler, M. (eds) (1991) *The Tourism Industry: An international analysis*, CABI.

Uysal, M. and Fesenmaier, D. (eds) (1993) *Communication and Channel Systems in Tourism Marketing*, Haworth Press.

Weiermair, K. and Mathies, C. (eds) (2004) *The Tourism and Leisure Industry: Shaping the future*, Haworth Hospitality Press.

Chapter 9 Tourist destinations

Ashworth, G. J. and Goodall, B. (1990) *Marketing Tourism Places*, Routledge.

Ashworth, G. and Hartmann, R. (eds) (2004) *Horror and Human Tragedy Revisited: The management of sites of atrocities for tourism*, Cognizant Communications.

Ashworth, G. and Tunbridge, J. (1990) *The Tourist-Historic City*, Belhaven Press.

Ashworth, G. J. and Voogd, H. (1990) *Selling the City: The use of publicity and public relations to sell cities and regions*, Belhaven Press.

Bachmann, P. (1988) *Tourism in Kenya: A basic need for whom?* Peter Lang.

Barke, M., Towner, J. and Newton, M. (1995) *Tourism in Spain*, CABI.

Brodie, A. and Winter, G. (2007) *England's Seaside Resorts*, English Heritage.

Brown, F. and Hall, D. (eds) (2000) *Tourism in Peripheral Areas*, Channel View.

Burton, R. (1994) *Travel Geography* (2nd edn), Pitman.

Butler, R., Hall, C. M. and Jenkins, J. (1998) *Tourism and Recreation in Rural Areas*, Wiley.

Cohen, M. (2006) *No Holiday: 80 places you don't want to visit*, The Disinformation Company.

Cohen, M. and Bodeker, G. (2008) *Understanding the Global Spa Industry*, Butterworth-Heinemann.

Conlin, M. V. and Baum, T. (1995) *Island Tourism: Management principles and practice*, Wiley.

Davidson, R. and Maitland, R. (1997) *Tourism Destinations*, Hodder & Stoughton.

Frost, W. and Hall, C. M. (eds) (2008) *Tourism and National Parks: International perspectives on development, histories and change*, Routledge.

Gabler, K., Maier, G., Mazenac, J. and Wober, K. (1997) *International City Tourism: Analysis and strategy*, Pinter Cassell.

Getz, D. and Page, S. (1997) *Business of Rural Tourism*, International Thomson Business Press.

Goodall, B. and Ashworth, G. (1987) *Marketing in the Tourism Industry: The promotion of destination regions*, Routledge.

Hall, C. M. and Johnston, M. (1995) *Polar Tourism: Tourism in the Arctic and Antarctic regions*, Wiley.

Hall, C. M. and Page, S. J. (eds) (1996) *Tourism in the Pacific: Issues and challenges*, International Thomson Business Press.

Hall, C. M. and Page, S. J. (2005) *The Geography of Tourism and Recreation* (3rd edn), Routledge.

Hall, D., Marciszewska, B. and Smith, M. (eds) (2006) *Tourism in the New Europe: The challenges and opportunities of EU enlargement*, CABI.

Hancock, D. (2006) *The Complete Medical Tourist*, John Blake Publishing.

Higham, J. (ed.) (2005) *Sports Tourism Destinations: Issues, opportunities and analysis*, Elsevier.

Howie, F. (2001) *Managing the Tourist Destination: A practical interactive guide*, Continuum.

Huybers, T. (ed.) (2007) *Tourism in Developing Countries*, Edward Elgar.

Judd, D. R. and Fainstein, S. (eds) (1999) *The Tourist City*, Yale University Press.

Kearns, G. and Philo, C. (1993) *Selling Places: The city as cultural capital, past and present*, Pergamon Press.

King, B. (1997) *Creating Island Resorts*, Routledge.

Kozak, M. (2004) *Destination Benchmarking: Concepts, practices and operations*, CABI.

Law, C. M. (ed.) (1996) *Tourism in Major Cities*, International Thomson Business Press.

Law, C. M. (2002) *Urban Tourism: The visitor economy and the growth of large cities* (2nd edn), Continuum.

Laws, E. (1995) *Tourism Destination Management: Issues, analysis and policies*, International Thomson Business Press.

Lickorish, L. J., Bodlender, J., Jefferson, A. and Jenkins, C. L. (1991) *Developing Tourism Destinations: Policies and perspectives*, Longman.

Lockhart, D. and Smith, D. (eds) (1996) *Island Tourism: Trends and prospects*, Cassell.

Morgan, N., Pritchard, A. and Pride, R. (eds) (2001) *Destination Branding: Developing a destination proposition*, Butterworth-Heinemann.

Müller, D. K. and Jansson, B. (2006) *Tourism in the Peripheries*, CABI.

Oppermann, M. and Chon, K.-S. (1997) *Tourism in Developing Countries*, International Thomson Business Press.

Page, S. J. (1995) *Urban Tourism*, Routledge.

Page, S. J. and Getz, D. (1997) *The Business of Rural Tourism: International perspectives*, International Thomson Business Press.

Papatheodorou, A. (ed.) (2006) *Managing Tourism Destinations*, Edward Elgar.

Ringer, G. (ed.) (1998) *Destinations: Cultural landscapes of tourism*, Routledge.

Selby, M. (2004) *Understanding Urban Tourism: Image, culture, experience*, I. B. Talaris.

Shackley, M. (1996) *Wildlife Tourism*, International Thomson Business Press.

Sharpley, R. (1996) *Tourism and Leisure in the Countryside* (2nd edn), Elm Publications.

Sharpley, R. and J. (1997) *Rural Tourism: An introduction*, International Thomson Business Press.

Shaw, G. and Williams, A. M. (eds) (1996) *The Rise and Fall of British Coastal Tourism: Cultural and economic perspectives*, Mansell.

Shaw, G. and Williams, A. M. (2004) *Tourism and Tourism Spaces*, Sage.

Singh, S., Timothy, D. and Dowling, R. (eds) (2003) *Tourism in Destination Communities*, CABI.

Smith, M. K. (2006) *Tourism, Culture and Regeneration*, CABI.

Soane, J. V. N. (1993) *Fashionable Resort Regions: Their evolution and transformation*, CABI.

Tyler, D., Guerrier, Y. and Robertson, M. (eds) (1998) *Managing Tourism in Cities: Policy, process and practice*, Wiley.

Tzanelli, R. (ed.) (2007) *The Cinematic Tourist: Explorations in globalization, culture and resistance*, Routledge.

Weaver, D. and Lawton, L. (2006) *Tourism Management* (3rd edn), Wiley.

Williams, S. (2009) *Tourism Geography: A new synthesis* (2nd edn), Routledge.

Chapter 10 Tourist attractions

Ashworth, G. and Hartmann, R. (eds) (2004) *Horror and Human Tragedy Revisited: The management of sites of atrocities for tourism*, Cognizant Communications.

Beech, J. and Chadwick, S. (2006) *The Business of Tourism Management*, Prentice Hall.

Bowdin, G., McDonnell, I., Allen, J. and O'Toole, W. (2006) *Events Management*, Elsevier.

Buckley, R. (2006) *Adventure Tourism*, CABI.

Crouch, D., Jackson, R. and Thomson, F. (eds) (2005) *The Media and the Tourist Imagination: Converging cultures*, Routledge.

Dann, G. and Seaton, A. (eds) (2002) *Slavery, Contested Heritage and Thanatourism*, Haworth Hospitality Press.

Drummond, S. and Yeoman, I. (2000) *Quality Issues in Heritage Visitor Attractions*, Butterworth-Heinemann.

Fjellman, S. (1992) *Vinyl Leaves: Walt Disney World and America*, Westview Press.

Fyall, A., Garrod, B. and Leask, A. (eds) (2003) *Managing Visitor Attractions: New directions*, Butterworth-Heinemann.

Gammon, S. and Jones, I. (2001) *Sports Tourism: An introduction*, Continuum.

Getz, D. (1990) *Festivals, Special Events and Tourism*, Van Nostrand Reinhold.

Getz, D. (1997) *Event Management and Event Tourism*, Cognizant Communications.

Getz, D. (2001) *Explore Wine Tourism: Management, development and destinations*, Cognizant Communications.

Gibson, H. J. (ed.) (2006) *Sport Tourism*, Routledge.

Goldblatt, J. J. (1990) *Special Events: The art and science of celebration*, Van Nostrand Reinhold.

Goodey, B. (ed.) (1997) *The Handbook of Interpretive Practice at Heritage Sites*, Wiley.

Hall, C. M. (1992) *Hallmark Tourist Events: Impacts, management and planning*, Wiley.

Hall, C. M., Sharples, L., Cambourne, B. and Macionis, N. (2002) *Wine Tourism around the World: Development, management and markets*, Butterworth-Heinemann.

Hall, C. M., Sharples, L., Mitchell, F., Macionis, N. and Camborne, B. (2003) *Food Tourism around the World*, Butterworth-Heinemann.

Harrison, R. (1994) *Manual of Heritage Management*, Butterworth-Heinemann.

Hewison, R. (1987) *The Heritage Industry: Britain in a climate of decline*, Methuen.

Hinch, T. and Higham, J. (2003) *Sport Tourism Development*, Channel View.

Hinch, T. and Higham, J. (2007) *Sport Tourism Development*, Channel View.

Hjalager, A.-M. and Richards, G. (eds) (2002) *Tourism and Gastronomy*, Routledge.

Hudson, S. (2000) *Snow Business: A study of the international ski industry*, Cassell.

Hudson, S. (ed.) (2003) *Sport and Adventure Tourism*, Haworth Press.

Hughes, H. (2000) *Arts, Entertainment and Tourism*, Butterworth-Heinemann.

Jencks, C. (2005) *The Iconic Building: The power of enigma*, Frances Lincoln.

Johnson, P. and Thomas, B. (1992) *Tourism, Museums and the Local Economy*, Edward Elgar.

Klugman, K., Kuenz, J., Waldrep, S. and Willis, S. (1995) *Inside the Mouse: Work and play at Disneyworld*, Duke University Press.

Kozak, M. (2008) *Managing and Marketing Tourist Destinations: Strategies to gain a competitive edge*, Routledge.

Leask, A. and Yeoman, I. (eds) (1999) *Heritage Visitor Attractions: An operations management perspective*, Cassell.

Lennon, J. and Foley, M. (2000) *Dark Tourism: The Attraction of death and disaster*, Continuum.

Lovelock, B. (ed.) (2007) *Tourism and the Consumption of Wildlife: Hunting, shooting and sport fishing*, Routledge.

Murphy, L., Benckendorff, P., Moscardo, G. and Pearce, P. (2009) *Tourist Shopping Villages: Forms and functions*, Routledge.

Prentice, R. (1993) *Tourism and Heritage Attractions*, Routledge.

Preuss, H. (2006) *The Economics of Staging the Olympics*, Edward Elgar.
Richards, B. (1992) *How to Market Tourism Attractions, Festivals and Special Events*, Longman.
Richards, G. (ed.) (2001) *Cultural Attractions and European Tourism*, CABI.
Richards, G. and Wilson, J. (eds) (2007) *Tourism, Creativity and Development*, Routledge.
Ritchie, B. and Adair, D. (eds) (2004) *Sport Tourism: Interrelationships, impacts and issues*, Channel View.
Robertson, M. and Frew, E. (eds) (2008) *Events and Festivals: Current trends and issues*, Routledge.
Robinson, M., Evans, N. and Callaghan, P. (eds) (1996) *Tourism and Culture: Image, identity and marketing*, Business Education Publishers.
Robinson, T., Gammon, S. and Jones, I. (2000) *Sports Tourism: An introduction*, Continuum.
Rogers, T. (2003) *Conferences and Conventions: A global industry*, Elsevier.
Rojek, C. (1993) *Ways of Escape: Modern transformations in leisure and travel*, Macmillan.
Shone, A. with Parry, B. (2001) *Successful Event Management: A practical handbook*, Continuum.
Swarbrooke, J. (2002) *The Development and Management of Visitor Attractions* (2nd edn), Butterworth-Heinemann.
Syme, G. J. (1989) *The Planning and Evaluation of Hallmark Events*, Gower.
Timothy, D. and Boyd, S. (2003) *Heritage Tourism*, Prentice Hall.
Timothy, D. and Olsen, D. (eds) (2006) *Tourism, Religion and Spiritual Journeys*, Routledge.
Toohey, K. and Veal, A. J. (2007) *The Olympic Games: A social science perspective* (2nd edn), CABI.
Uzzell, D. (ed.) (1989) *Heritage Interpretation: Vol. 1: The Natural and Built Environment, Vol. 2: The Visitor Experience*, Belhaven Press.
Walsh-Heron, J. and Stevens, T. (1990) *The Management of Visitor Attractions and Events*, National Publishers.
Watt, D. (1998) *Event Management in Leisure and Tourism*, Addison Wesley Longman.
Weed, M. (ed.) (2007) *Sport and Tourism: A reader*, Routledge.
Weed, M. and Bull, C. (2004) *Sports Tourism: Participants, policy and providers*, Elsevier Butterworth-Heinemann.
Yale, P. (1991) *From Tourist Attractions to Heritage Tourism*, Elm Publications.
Yeoman, I., Robertson, M., Ali-Knioght, J., Drummond, S. and McMahon-Beattie, U. (2004) *Festival and Events Management: An international arts and culture perspective*, Elsevier.

Chapter 11 Business tourism

Allen, J. (2000) *The Ultimate Guide to Successful Meetings, Corporate Events, Fundraising Galas, Conferences, Conventions, Incentives and Other Special Events*, John Wiley & Sons.
Allen, J. (2002) *The Business of Event Planning, Behind-the-scenes Secrets of Successful Special Events*, John Wiley & Sons.
Astroff, M. and Abbey, J. (2006) *Convention Sales and Services*, Waterbury Press.
Campbell, F., Robinson, A., Brown, S. and Race, P. (2003) *Essential Tips for Organising Conferences and Events*, Kogan Page.
Davidson, R. and Cope, B. (2003) *Business Travel: Conferences, incentive travel, exhibitions, corporate hospitality and corporate travel*, Pearson Education.
Davidson, R. and Rogers, T. (2006) *Marketing Destinations and Venues for Conferences, Conventions and Business Events*, Butterworth-Heinemann.
Harrill, R. (ed.) (2005) *Fundamentals of Destination Management and Marketing*, IACVB
Krugman, C. and Wright, R. (2007) *Global Meetings and Exhibitions*, John Wiley & Sons.
McCabe, V., Poole, B. and Leiper, N. (2000) *The Business and Management of Conventions*, John Wiley & Sons.
Rogers, T. (2008) *Conferences and Conventions: A global industry*, Butterworth-Heinemann.
Silvers, J. R. (2004) *Professional Event Coordination*, John Wiley & Sons.

Swarbrooke, J. and Horner, S. (2001) *Business Travel and Tourism*, Butterworth-Heinemann.

Weber, K. and Chon, K. (eds) (2002) *Convention Tourism: International research and industry perspectives*, Haworth Press.

Chapter 12 The hospitality sector: accommodation and catering services

Cunill, O. (2006) *The Growth Strategies of Hotel Chains: Best business practices by leading companies*, Haworth Press.

Go, F. and Pine, R. (1995) *Globalization Strategy in the Hotel Industry*, International Thomson Business Press.

Lawson, F. (1995) *Hotels and Resorts: Planning, design and refurbishment*, Butterworth-Heinemann.

Lockwood, A. and Medlik, S. (eds) (2002) *Tourism and Hospitality in the 21st Century*, Elsevier.

Medlik, S. and Ingram, H. (2000) *The Business of Hotels* (4th edn), Elsevier.

Chapter 13 Tourist transport by air

Ashford, N., Martin Stanton, H. P. and Moore, C. A. (1991) *Airport Operations*, Pitman.

Barlay, S. (1994) *Cleared for Take-off: Behind the scenes of air travel*, Kyle Cathie.

Bell, G., Bowen, P. and Fawcett, P. (1984) *The Business of Transport*, M&E.

Benson, D. and Whitehead, G. (1985) *Transport and Distribution*, Longman.

Blackshaw, C. (1991) *Aviation Law and Regulation*, Pitman.

Button, K. (ed.) (1990) *Airline Deregulation*, David Fulton.

Calder, S. (2003) *No Frills: The truth behind the low-cost revolution in the skies*, Virgin Books.

Committee of Inquiry into Civil Air Transport (1969) *British Air Transport in the Seventies*, HMSO.

Dandel, S. and Vialle, G. (1994) *Yield Management: Applications to air transport and other service industries*, Institute de Transport Aerien.

Dobson, A. (1994) *Flying in the Face of Competition*, Avebury Aviation/Ashgate Publishing.

Doganis, R. (1991) *Flying off Course: The economics of international airlines* (2nd edn), George Allen & Unwin.

Doganis, R. (1992) *The Airport Business*, Routledge.

Eaton, A. J. (1995) *The International Airline Business: Globalisation in action*, Avebury Aviation/Ashgate Publishing.

Graham, A. (2003) *Managing Airports: An international perspective* (2nd edn), Butterworth-Heinemann.

Graham, B. (1995) *Geography and Air Transport*, Wiley.

Hanlon, J. P. (1999) *Global Airlines: Competition in a transnational industry* (2nd edn), Butterworth-Heinemann.

Lumsdon, L. and Page, S. J. (2004) *Tourism and Transport: Issues and agenda for the new millennium*, Elsevier Butterworth-Heinemann.

Page, S. J. (1999) *Transport and Tourism*, Longman.

Pender, L. (2001) *Travel Trade and Transport: An introduction*, Continuum.

Phipps, D. (1991) *The Management of Aviation Security*, Pitman.

Shaw, S. (1990) *Airline Marketing and Management* (3rd edn), Pitman.

Wells, A. T. (1994) *Air Transportation: A management perspective* (3rd edn), Wadsworth.

Wheatcroft, S. (1994) *Aviation and Tourism Policies*, Routledge.

Williams, G. (1994) *The Airline Industry and the Impact of Deregulation*, Avebury Aviation/Ashgate Publishing.

Chapter 14 Tourist transport by water

Berger, A. (2004) *Review of Ocean Travel and Cruising: A cultural analysis*, Haworth Press.

Cartwright, R. and Barid, C. (1999) *The Development and Growth of the Cruise Industry*, Butterworth-Heinemann.

Chin, C. (2008) *Cruising in the Global Economy: Profits, pleasure and work at sea*, Ashgate.

Dickinson, R. H. and Vladimir, A. N. (1997) *Selling the Sea: An inside look at the cruise industry*, Wiley.

Douglas, N. and Douglas, B. (2004) *The Cruise Ship Experience*, Pearson.

Dowling, R. K. (ed.) (2006) *Cruise Ship Tourism*, CABI.

Jennings, G. (2007) *Water-based Tourism, Sport, Leisure and Recreation Experiences*, Elsevier.

Peisley, T. (2003) *Global Changes in the Cruise Industry 2003–2010*, Seatrade Communications.

Chapter 15 Tourist transport on land

Beech, J. and Chadwick, S. (2006) *The Business of Tourism Management*, Prentice Hall.

Chapter 16 The management of visitors

Beech, J. and Chadwick, S. (eds) (2006) *The Business of Tourism Management*, Prentice Hall

Evans, N., Campbell, D. and Stonehouse, G. (2003) *Strategic Management for Travel and Tourism*, Elsevier.

Fyall, A., Garrod, B. and Leask, A. (eds) (2003) *Managing Visitor Attractions: New directions*, Butterworth-Heinemann.

Glaesser, D. (2003) *Crisis Management in the Tourism Industry*, Butterworth-Heinemann.

Gunn, C., with Var, T. (2002) *Tourism Planning: Basics, concepts, cases* (4th edn), Routledge.

Hall, C. and Page, S. J. (2006) *The Geography of Tourism and Recreation* (3rd edn), Routledge.

Holloway, J. C. (2004) *Marketing for Tourism* (4th edn), Prentice Hall.

Horner, S. and Swarbrooke, J. (2004) *International Cases in Tourism Management*, Elsevier Butterworth-Heinemann.

Inskip, E. (1991) *Tourism Planning: An integrated and sustainable development*, Van Nostrand Reinhold.

Inskip, E. (1994) *National and Regional Tourism Planning: Methodologies and case studies*, Routledge.

Leask, A. and Yeoman, I. (eds) (1999) *Heritage Visitor Attractions: An operations management perspective*, Cassell.

Leiper, N. (2004) *Tourism Management*, Pearson.

Page, S. (2007) *Tourism Management* (2nd edn), Butterworth-Heinemann.

Pender, L. and Sharpley, R. (2005) *The Management of Tourism*, Sage.

Richardson, J. I. and Fluker, M. (2004) *Understanding and Managing Tourism*, Pearson.

Swarbrooke, J. (2002) *The Development and Management of Visitor Attractions* (2nd edn), Butterworth-Heinemann.

Chapter 17 The structure and role of the public sector in tourism

Allcock, J. B. (1990) *Tourism in Centrally Planned Economies*, Pergamon.

Ashworth, G. J. (1991) *Heritage Planning*, Geo Pers.

Ashworth, G. J. and Dietvorst, A. G. J. (1995) *Tourism and Spatial Transformations: Implications for policy and planning*, CABI.

Bosselman, F., Peterson, C. and McCarthy, C. (1999) *Managing Tourism Growth: Issues and applications*, Island Press.

Bramwell, B. and Lane, B. (eds) (2000) *Tourism Collaboration and Partnership: Politics, practice and sustainability*, Channel View.

CABI (1993) *Tourism in Europe: Structures and development*, CABI.

Deegan, J. and Dineen, D. (1997) *Tourism Policy and Performance*, International Thomson Business Press.

Edgell, D. (1990) *International Tourism Policy*, Van Nostrand Reinhold.

Edgell, D. (1999) *Tourism Policy: The next millennium*, Sagamore.

Elliott, J. (1997) *Tourism: Politics and public sector management*, Routledge.

Godde, P. M., Price, M. and Zimmermann, F. (2000) *Tourism Development in Mountain Regions*, CABI.

Godfrey, K. and Clarke, J. (2000) *The Tourism Development Handbook: A practical approach to planning and marketing*, Cassell.

Gunn, C. (1997) *Vacationscape: Designing Tourist Regions* (4th edn), Van Nostrand Reinhold.

Gunn, C. and Var, T. (2002) *Tourism Planning: Basics, concepts and cases* (4th edn), Routledge.

Hall, C. M. (1994) *Tourism and Politics: Policy, power and place*, Wiley.

Hall, C. M. (1994) *Tourism in the Pacific: Development, impacts and markets*, Pitman.

Hall, C. M. (2008) *Tourism Planning: Policies, processes and relationships* (2nd edn), Prentice Hall.

Hall, C. M. and Jenkins, J. M. (1995) *Tourism and Public Policy*, Routledge.

Heath, E. and Wall, G. (1992) *Marketing Tourism Destinations: A strategic planning approach*, Wiley.

Jeffries, D. (2001) *Governments and Tourism*, Butterworth-Heinemann.

Johnson, P. and Thomas, B. (eds) (1992) *Perspectives on Tourism Policy*, Mansell.

Leslie, D. and Muir, F. (1997) *Local Agenda 21, Local Authorities and Tourism: A UK perspective*, Glasgow Caledonian University.

Montarani, A. and Williams, A. (eds) (1995) *European Tourism: Regions, spaces and restructuring*, Wiley.

Morgan, N. and Pritchard, A. (1998) *Tourism Promotion and Power: Creating images, creating identities*, Wiley.

Owen, E. and Owen, L. (2007) *From Candy Floss to Mountain Bikes: A view of the Wales Tourist Board*, UWIC.

Reid, D. (2003) *Tourism Globalization and Development: Responsible tourism planning*, Pluto Press.

Singh, T. V. and Singh, S. (eds) (1999) *Tourism Development in Critical Environments*, Cognizant.

Timothy, D. J. and Wall, G. (2000) *Tourism and Political Boundaries*, Routledge.

Tolley, R. S. and Turton, B. J. (1995) *Transport Systems, Policy and Planning*, Longman.

Chapter 18 Tour operating

Beech, J. and Chadwick, S. (2006) *The Business of Tourism Management*, Prentice Hall.

Grant, D. and Mason, S. (1993) *The EC Directive on Package Travel, Package Holidays and Package Tours*, University of Northumbria.

Kächer, K. (1997) *Reinventing the Package Holiday Business*, Deutscher Universitas Verlag.

Laws, E. (1997) *Managing Packaged Tourism*, International Thomson Business Press.

Page, S. J. and Connell, J. (2006) *Tourism: A modern synthesis* (2nd edn), Thomson.

Poustie, M., Ross, J., Geddes, N. and Stewart, W. (1999) *Hospitality and Tourism Law*, International Thomson Business Press.

Poynter, J. (1989) *Foreign Independent Tours: Planning, pricing and processing*, Delmar.

Poynter, J. (1993) *Tour Design, Marketing and Management*, Prentice Hall.

Yale, P. (1995) *The Business of Tour Operations*, Longman.

Chapter 19 Selling and distributing travel and tourism

Beech, S. J. and Chadwick, S. (2006) *The Business of Tourism Management*, Prentice Hall.
Bottomley Renshaw, M. (1997) *The Travel Agent* (2nd edn), Business Education Publishers.
Burton, J. and L. (1994) *Interpersonal Skills for Travel and Tourism*, Longman.
Coopers & Lybrand (1997) 'Travel Agents' Benchmarking Survey', Coopers & Lybrand.
Horner, P. (1996) *Travel Agency Practice*, Longman.
Page, S. J. and Connell, J. (2006) *Tourism: A modern synthesis*, Thomson.
Syratt, G. (1995) *Manual of Travel Agency Practice* (2nd edn), Butterworth-Heinemann.

Chapter 20 Ancillary tourism services

Holloway, J. C. (2004) *Marketing for Tourism* (4th edn), Prentice Hall.
Pond, K. L. (1993) *The Professional Guide: Dynamics of tour guiding*, Van Nostrand Reinhold.
Reily Collins, V. (2000) *Becoming a Tour Guide: Principles of guiding and site interpretation*, Continuum.

Key trade, professional and academic magazines and journals

In addition to the growing number of international academic and professional publications listed below, readers are also directed to the many magazines and journals aimed at the general public, many of which are valuable sources of material for students and practitioners of travel and tourism. They include such periodicals as *Airline World*, *Flight International*, *Buses*, *In Britain* and so on.

ABTA News	monthly
Annals of Tourism Research	quarterly
ASEAN Journal on Hospitality and Tourism	bi-annually
Asia Pacific Journal of Tourism Research	quarterly
ASTA Travel News	monthly
British Travel Brief	quarterly
British Traveller	monthly
Business Traveller	10 per annum
Business Travel World	monthly
Coaching Journal and Bus Review	monthly
Countryside Commission News	monthly
Current Issues in Tourism	bi-monthly
Event Management	quarterly
Executive Travel	monthly
Executive World (British Airways)	monthly
Flight International	weekly
Holiday Which? (Consumers Association)	quarterly
ICAO Bulletin	monthly
Information Technology and Tourism	quarterly
Information Technology in Hospitality	quarterly
Insights	monthly
International Journal of Hospitality and Tourism Administration	quarterly
International Journal of Tourism and Hospitality Research	quarterly
International Journal of Tourism Research	bi-monthly
International Tourism Quarterly (EIU)	quarterly

Journal of Air Transport Management	quarterly
Journal of Convention and Event Management	quarterly
Journal of Ecotourism	quarterly
Journal of Hospitality and Tourism Research	quarterly
Journal of Hospitality Marketing and Management	8 per annum
Journal of Human Resources in Hospitality and Tourism	quarterly
Journal of the ITT	quarterly
Journal of Leisure Research	quarterly
Journal of Quality Assurance in Hospitality and Tourism	quarterly
Journal of Sport and Tourism	quarterly
Journal of Sustainable Tourism	bi-monthly
Journal of Tourism and Cultural Change	3 per annum
Journal of Tourism Studies	bi-annual
Journal of Transport Economics and Policy	Jan/May/Sept
Journal of Travel and Tourism Marketing	8 per annum
Journal of Travel Research	quarterly
Journal of Vacation Marketing	quarterly
Leisure, Recreation and Tourism Abstracts (CABI)	quarterly
Leisure Studies (Leisure Studies Association)	quarterly
Motor Transport Weekly	weekly
Scandinavian Journal of Hospitality and Tourism	3 per annum
Service Industries Journal	Mar/Jul/Nov
Tourism (Bulletin of the Tourism Society)	quarterly
Tourism Analysis	quarterly
Tourism and Hospitality Planning and Development	**3 per annum**
Tourism and Hospitality Research	quarterly
Tourism, Culture and Communication	3 per annum
Tourism Economics	quarterly
Tourism Geographies	quarterly
Tourism Geography	quarterly
Tourism in Focus	quarterly
Tourism in Marine Environments	biannually
Tourism Intelligence Quarterly	quarterly
Tourism Management	bi-monthly
Tourism Recreation Research	3 per annum
The Tourism Review (AIEST)	quarterly
Tourism Review International	quarterly
Tourism Trendspotter	bi-monthly
Tourist Studies	3 per annum
Transport (CIT)	bi-monthly
Transport Management	quarterly
Transport Reviews	quarterly
Travel Agency	bi-monthly
Travel and Tourism Analyst (EIU)	bi-monthly
Travel Business Analyst	10 per annum
Travel GBI	monthly
Travel Industry Monitor (EIU)	quarterly
Travel Research Journal	quarterly
Travel Trade Gazette	weekly
Travel Trade Gazette Europa (Continental edition)	weekly
Travel Weekly	weekly
World Leisure Journal	quarterly
World Travel (Tourisme Mondiale) (WTO)	bi-monthly

Many of the articles from these journals are available online and some journals are now produced exclusively to access on the Internet. The following are useful sources of such information.

Articles in Hospitality and Tourism, monthly abstracting service, Universities of Bournemouth, Oxford Brookes and Surrey, available at: **http://libweb.surrey.ac.uk/aht2**

e-*Review of Tourism Research*, an electronic bulletin for tourism research, available at: **http://ertr.tamu.edu**

International Tourism and Hospitality Database, CD-ROM, Wiley.

Journal of Hospitality, Leisure, Sport and Tourism, bi-annual e-journal, available at: **www.heacademy.ac.uk/johlste**.

TourCD (Leisure, Recreation and Tourism Abstracts), CD-ROM database, CABI.

Index